A
DICTIONARY
OF
NEW ENGLISH

Clarence L. Barnhart
Sol Steinmetz
Robert K. Barnhart

Longman

Longman Group Limited
London

Associated companies, branches and
representatives throughout the world.

First published 1973
Reprinted 1974
ISBN 0 582 55504 3

Printed in the United States of America

To FRANCES K. BARNHART,
without whose support this and all my
other books could not have been written.

C.L.B.

TABLE OF CONTENTS

PREFACE

This dictionary is a lexical index of the new words of the past decade, a record of the most recent terms required and created by our scientific investigations, our technical and cultural activities, and our social and personal lives. Each entry has one or more quotations of a length sufficient to help convey the meaning and flavor of the term; and pronunciations, etymologies, and usage notes are added in many cases to assist the understanding of a word and its use.

By "New English" we mean those terms and meanings which have come into the common or working vocabulary of the English-speaking world during the period from 1963 to 1972. We chose 1963 as the beginning date since this date marks the termination of the record of new English, except for sporadic examples, in most general dictionaries now available to the general public. The new words and phrases were collected from the reading of over half a billion running words from United States, British, and Canadian sources — newspapers, magazines, and books published from 1963 to 1972. The 5,000 or so new entries and meanings have been selected from over one million quotations in our files. The names of the readers for quotations are given on p. 11; without the work of the readers it would have been impossible to produce this dictionary. Two senior readers, Barbara M. Collins and Andrea B. Olsen, have been especially diligent and expert over a long period of years; we are especially grateful to them for helping us obtain a balanced sampling of words from the vast number of writers and speakers of English.

We have introduced a new type of illustrative reference in this book. Even the best of dictionaries, those that are not satisfied with contriving illustrative sentences and phrases but seek to show usage with authentic material, have long been content to give "citations" showing that a certain word or meaning exists. We have extended our "citations" so that they become "quotations" with enough of the surrounding context to show the way in which the word or meaning is used. It is the environment, as it were, of the word or meaning, that provides an explanation of a word rather than a mere definition. Moreover, by giving a greater amount of context we make this book more useful to the social scientist, the linguist, and the student of literature, and more readable to the average user.

In order that the reader may know the source of a quotation without consulting a bibliography we provide each quotation with a full bibliographical reference.

The editors have benefited greatly from the advice of an international advisory committee of distinguished linguistic scholars, librarians, and teachers. For indication of pronunciation the Committee recommended use of the symbols of a broad transcription of the International Phonetic Association (IPA); we have therefore adapted an IPA pronunciation system under their supervision. Such an international system should facilitate the use of this dictionary throughout the world. Special efforts were made to include words and meanings from both sides of the Atlantic. Two members of the Committee assisted in the labeling of

British and American meanings—Brian Foster and I. Willis Russell. In addition, one of our consulting editors, Anthony Wharton, checked all labels of Briticisms. We hope that we have been reasonably accurate in distinguishing British, American, and Canadian English for the international market. The labeling of regions of use is based on the evidence of current use in our files and is not always evidence of the place of origin of a term. Another member of the Committee, Reason A. Goodwin, has checked each pronunciation and etymology and the grammatical facts given about each entry. The plan of the entire book was submitted to the Committee and all features of it have been considered by them.

We could not have produced this book without the aid of the editorial staff. This is not an individual effort but the work of the same staff that produced the Thorndike-Barnhart dictionaries and the *World Book Dictionary* (to accompany the *World Book Encyclopedia*). We have used here the same professional techniques as for the books we produce for the textbook and general market.

All three editors have read critically every line of this dictionary. In spite of our joint efforts, we may have slipped from time to time—sometimes from lack of complete evidence. We will welcome any corrections or comments on any item; and of course we welcome the submission of new terms for inclusion in future editions. If you should write to us, please give the date, the publication, the title, and the page reference of the quotation or quotations you extract to support your comment. We will welcome information from you and acknowledge it.

In a way this book goes back to Sir William Craigie. Years ago Sir William taught the senior editor, who was then a graduate student at the University of Chicago, the art of collecting citations. Sir William was teaching a course in lexicography, which involved collecting citations for *A Dictionary of American English*. The same methods that Sir William applied to historical dictionaries, have been applied here to show how the vocabulary of English, as used in America and Britain, is currently evolving. We hope that *The Barnhart Dictionary of New English* will be especially useful to all non-native speakers of English reading English newspapers, magazines, and books and encountering neologisms. For native speakers, we hope that it will be a supplement to standard dictionaries and an aid to people interested in or dealing with words: style editors, English scholars, writers, and word enthusiasts.

CLARENCE L. BARNHART

SOL STEINMETZ

ROBERT K. BARNHART

EDITORIAL ADVISORY COMMITTEE

LADISLAS ORSZÁGH

Chairman of the Lexicographical Committee of the Hungarian Academy of Sciences; formerly Professor of English at the University of Debrecen, Hungary.
General Editor of *Angol-Magyar Szótár: Magyar-Angol Szótár* [English-Hungarian and Hungarian-English Dictionary].

I. WILLIS RUSSELL

Professor Emeritus of English, University of Alabama.
Chairman of the Research Committee on New Words and vice-president of the American Dialect Society.
Editor of "Among the New Words" department in *American Speech*.

EDITORIAL STAFF

Consulting Editors

Brian Foster (British English)

Reason A. Goodwin (Linguistics, Pronunciation, and Etymology)

I. Willis Russell (American English)

Anthony Wharton (British English)

General Editors

David K. Barnhart

Ruth Gardner McClare

Frances Murlin Halsey

Associate Editor

Anne-Luise Bartling

Editorial Assistants

Maria Bastone

Jane A. Boland

Julia Galas

Helen V. Graus

Office Assistants

Leroy J. Brightman

Albert S. Crocco

Elizabeth E. Fristrom

Dolores L. Hannigan

Rosemary E. Keppel

Gloria Dorothy Linden

Virginia L. Spellman

Marion A. Towne

READING STAFF

Senior Readers

R. A. Auty

Barbara M. Collins

Richard L. Wright

Dannydelle W. Dandridge

Andrea B. Olsen

Readers

Dawn Louise Borgeson

Ruth B. Cavin

Sonja H. Coryat

Valerie Dean

Marie A. Ferenga

Sylvian Hamilton

Jane Knight

Janet Shreck McKeel

Robin Smith

Theresa P. Strelec

11

EXPLANATORY NOTES

Contents of the Dictionary

This is a dictionary of new terms and meanings which have become a part of the English common or working vocabulary between 1963 and 1972. It is an informal and necessarily incomplete record of the most important terms of the last ten years. Many new terms have not been included: highly technical or scientific terms used largely in professional work, dialect and slang expressions of limited currency, and nonce or figurative terms created for ephemeral use. Such terms of limited usefulness have not yet become a part of the common vocabulary.

"Common vocabulary" is aptly defined in the *Oxford English Dictionary* in the section labeled "General Explanations":

> So the English Vocabulary contains a nucleus or central mass of many thousand words whose 'Anglicity' is unquestioned; some of them only literary, some of them only colloquial, the great majority at once literary and colloquial,— they are the *Common Words* of the language. But they are linked on every side with other words which are less and less entitled to this appellation, and which pertain ever more and more distinctly to the domain of local dialect, of the slang and cant of 'sets' and classes, of the peculiar technicalities of trades and processes, of the scientific terminology common to all civilized nations, of the actual languages of other lands and peoples. And there is absolutely no defining line in any direction: the circle of the English language has a well-defined centre but no discernible circumference. Yet practical utility has some bounds, and a Dictionary has definite limits: the lexicographer must, like the naturalist, 'draw the line somewhere', in each diverging direction. He must include all the 'Common Words' of literature and conversation, and such of the scientific, technical, slang, dialectal, and foreign words as are passing into common use, and approach the position or standing of 'common words', well knowing that the line which he draws will not satisfy all his critics. For to every man the domain of 'common words' widens out in the direction of his own reading, research, business, provincial or foreign residence, and contracts in the direction with which he has no practical connexion: no one man's English is *all* English. The lexicographer must be satisfied to exhibit the greater part of the vocabulary of *each* one, which will be immensely more than the whole vocabulary of any one.
>
> In addition to, and behind, the common vocabulary, in all its diverging lines, lies an infinite number of *Proper* or merely denotative names, outside the province of lexicography, yet touching in thousands of points, at which the names, and still more the adjectives and verbs formed upon them, acquire more or less of connotative value. Here also limits more or less arbitrary must be assumed.[1]

---

[1] by permission of The Clarendon Press, Oxford.

We cannot hope to include every new term on the circumference of our language, but we hope we have included the majority of new terms that are approaching the center of the language. As one well-known lexicographer has said, "A new word is a word that has not yet been recorded in the dictionaries."

The newness of the new English recorded here applies primarily to content, for the meanings of old words in new applications, such as *cage* and *cameo*, or idiomatic phrases, such as *can of worms* and *carry the can*, and the figurative and transferred meanings of names, such as *Camelot* and *Carey Street*, are things that need noting as features of the growth of the language. Old elements combine: in compounds *(carborne, card-carrying, cardioactive)*, in chemical nomenclature *(carborane)*, in acronyms *(Capcom)*, in blends *(carbecue)*, and in many technical phrases *(calligraphic display, Capri pants, caravan park,* and *carbon date)*. Forms and elements entirely new in English appear principally in words quoted or borrowed from other languages *(cachaça, café filtre,* and *caporegime)*.

General Principles of Selection

Any record of a living language is at best a haphazard affair. It must be only a sampling, but if it is a broad sampling it is a mirror of current cultural modes and fancies, of technical achievements and social growth or squalor, and in the end a crucial test of the financial resources of the compiler.

Within those limitations, we made an examination of the quotations in our file and evaluated the collection of only the past ten years, from 1963 to 1972.

Before 1963 we had been sending quotations to an English dictionary of record, and the Merriam Unabridged has reflected the record of English up to the early 1960's also. So by checking the largest and most reliable standard English dictionaries to ascertain that none of the entries in the selection had appeared in them before, we were able to substantiate the judgment that these words and meanings were "new."

These quotations were examined for their lexicality, frequency, topical interest, and similar properties. Items that did not meet the tests of interest and importance, and those which appeared in the files showing substantial currency before 1963 have been reluctantly excluded, though a number of terms are still considered "new" by many *(autobahn, Black Muslim,* and *cryogenics)*. Such terms are to be found in the Merriam Unabridged and the more important of them are usually in the latest editions of the college dictionaries.

On the other hand, words that have suddenly emerged from obscurity — of the scientific laboratory or other restricted and narrow usage — are included in spite of their existence before 1963. Generally they are technical terms of the sciences which have come to influence our technologically based modern society. And no check was made of technical dictionaries, as one of our objects was to record technical terms as they come into the common vocabulary; we wish primarily to be a companion to standard English dictionaries and to bring them up to date.

The editors were compelled by limitations of space to omit various types of words that may reasonably be called "new" but that nevertheless could not be regarded as lexical or "dictionary material" in the strict sense of the word: these included proper names of undeniable currency such as *Al-Fatah* and *Bangladesh*, and acronyms and abbreviations of well-known organizations, political parties, and the like, such as *DOT* (for Department of Transportation) and *SANE* (National Committee for a Sane Nuclear Policy). Yet there is no rule without exceptions, and in a few instances the editors felt that certain terms of an admittedly "encyclo-pedic" nature should still be included in the dictionary because of their extra-ordinary importance or currency; an entry such as *SALT* falls in this category.

Prefixes, Suffixes, and Combining Forms

Following the style of standard dictionaries, the main entries in this book appear in boldface type and are listed in alphabetical order, whether the entry is written as one word, as a hyphenated compound or derivative, or as a non-hyphenated compound or derivative.

Derivatives and compounds are given separate entry whenever they cannot be satisfactorily explained by a combination of the prefix, suffix, or combining form with the root word. Any effort to evaluate the productivity of word elements must be somewhat frustrating but we feel that some attempt must be made. New affixes (as *acousto-*) and new meanings of affixes and combining forms (as **anti** or **a-**) are recorded under the affix or combining form. Unusually active affixes and combining forms are hard to measure. Some are so active and productive (*re-*, *un-*, *-er*, etc.) as to make even a representative sampling beyond our resources. Such affixes and combining forms as **astro-, bio-, cosmo-, immuno-, -ian, -in, -manship,** and **-ville** are entered and examples of their use and productivity are given. The user should look first under the affix or combining form. If the word is not given there, it may have a specialized meaning of the affix or be unusually frequent or there may be some interesting information about the word containing the affix that warrants separate entry. Thus, **anticodon** is difficult to explain as a combination of *anti-* + *codon*. We therefore give it separate entry:

> **anticodon,** *n.* a group of three chemical bases that form a unit in transfer RNA and serve to bind a specific amino acid to a corresponding group (called a codon) in messenger RNA.

Most terms involving the suffix *-nik* are given under **-nik: cinenik, citynik, computernik, no-goodnik,** etc.:

> **-nik,** a slang suffix used to form nouns. *Sputnik*, whose successful launch in 1957 heralded the birth of the Space Age, was the model for *beatnik*, which became widely current in the late 1950's. *Beatnik* inspired the coinage of a number of nouns ending with the Russian personal suffix *-nik*, meaning "one who does or is connected with some-thing." Most of the new *-nik* words closely followed the meaning of *beatnik* in denoting a person who rejects stan-dard social values and becomes a devotee of some fad or idea or takes part in some mode of life. This class of words included *folknik* (folk-song devotee), *peacenik*, *protestnik*, *jazznik*, *filmnik* or *cinenik* (movie fan), and *Vietnik* (one who opposes U.S. involvement in Vietnam). Many words in *-nik* are in some degree derogatory, inviting disparagement or ridicule.
> **cinenik:** Secter chose the 1965 Commonwealth Film Festival in Wales for the movie's ["Winter Kept Us Warm"] world premiere

and it enchanted the cine-niks there. *John Bernard, Maclean's, Nov. 19, 1966, p 23*

citynik: A kibbutz is a collective settlement, where all are equal, each giving according to his abilities and receiving according to his needs. . . . The day starts at dawn—in mid-summer this means four o'clock. It is surprising how quickly a reasonably healthy citynik adjusts to the hours and graft. *Denis Herbstein, "Working Holiday: Kibbutzim," The Sunday Times (London), Jan. 4, 1970, p 67*

computernik: Despite the alarums of the computerniks and the current promulgation of the notion (from over the Canadian border) that bound volumes are doomed to obsolescence, the book would appear to be here to stay. *William Tarz, Review of "Rare Books and Royal Collectors" by M. L. Ettinghausen and "A Primer of Book Collecting" by J. T. Winterich and D. A. Randall, Saturday Review, Oct. 22, 1966, p 59*

filmnik: Another favorite is urbane, eccentric Woody Allen, who is currently flipping the filmniks by writing a Japanese movie in which the dubbed-in sound track is totally different from what is occurring on-screen. *Time, March 4, 1966, p 27*

goodwillnik: This editor didn't once ask me if I knew anything about music or had any right to write about it. Or, for that matter, whether I could write about anything. He wanted a goodwillnik, and whatever my feelings about this man's regulations, I think it was most admirable of him to spell them out. *Robert Evett, "Music: The Critics and the Public," The Atlantic, Sept. 1970, p 117*

jobnik: For any serviceman, the proudest insigne is the unit crest with a red background designating a battle unit. The "jobnik" —a soldier with a desk job—is looked down on. *Time, June 22, 1970, p 30*

no-goodnik: Lew Archer's job is to find a 17-year-old girl who has run off with a 19-year-old nogoodnik. *Anthony Boucher, The New York Times, March 3, 1968, p 37*

protestnik: . . . Tom Lehrer [a satiric singer] plinks away at targets ranging from air pollution to nuclear proliferation. Among his bull's eyes: those guitar-plunking protestniks *(The Folk Song Army)* whose St. Joan is Baez as they "strum their frustrations away." *"Records," Time, Nov. 12, 1965, p 4*

See also the main entries PEACENIK, VIETNIK.

Some, however, as **peacenik,** on the ground of frequency alone deserve separate entry:

> **peacenik,** *n. U.S. Slang.* a person who engages in peace demonstrations; an active opponent of war. Compare VIETNIK.
>
> What is the real offense of a long-haired peacenik who holds his fingers in a V as the hardhats come marching by? *Peter Schrag, "America's Other Radicals," Harper's, Aug. 1970, p 45*
>
> When Barbara Howar was asked on the CBS special how somebody with her peacenik views could keep going out with Kissinger, she said, in a reply cut from the show, "Politics make strange bedfellows." *Joseph Kraft, Harper's, Jan. 1971, p 61*
>
> [see -NIK]

A derivative new word can be found either under the affix or combining form or as a separate entry. The safe rule to follow is to look first under the affix or combining form; there important main entries are often listed.

16

These three types of entries are related in that they are replacements of longer words or phrases. But whereas abbreviations are not spoken or treated as words but pronounced letter by letter, acronyms and clipped words are spoken and treated as regular words. The three types are illustrated by the following entries:

> **ASP,** abbreviation of AMERICAN SELLING PRICE.
>
> **ASP** (æsp), *n.* acronym for *Anglo-Saxon Protestant.* Compare WASP.
>
> **del·i** ('del i:), *n. U.S.* short for *delicatessen.*
>
> **div·i** ('div i:), *n. British.* short for *dividend.*

Symbols, which are neither shortenings nor replacements of longer words but letters chosen arbitrarily or by some system to represent or designate something, are also indicated where they occur. For example:

> **BZ,** a symbol for an incapacitating gas whose effects include disorientation, drowsiness, and hallucination. Compare CS, GB, VX.

Variants

Because of the great variation found in the spelling of new words, the editors tried, wherever possible, to give only one spelling to each entry, usually the one they considered most frequent or most likely to occur. In cases where usage seems to be evenly divided between two spellings, both are given as the entry words. We do not, however, list as head words all forms that occur in the various quotations. Thus, the form *Art Déco,* given in the first quotation under **art deco** or **Art Deco,** is not included as a head word. Since we have not attempted to do more than provide a finding word as the main entry, forms given in the quotations may be at variance with those in the head word.

Pronunciation

The pronunciation of a hard or unfamiliar word is given immediately after the entry word; well-known words are not pronounced in this dictionary.

The pronunciation key (given in full on p. 27, 28) is composed of symbols with values within the range of their use in a broad transcription of the International Phonetic Association. The sole exception is the letter *y,* which we use to represent what in English is spelled with *y* in *yes* and *you* and *yarn* (for IPA y, a non-English vowel sound, we use Y).

In indicating the pronunciation of *vowels and diphthongs* we have chosen, at points of difference, to represent "American" rather than "British" speech. Thus although the key contains (ɔ) to represent an "aw"-type of "British" pronunciation of the *o* in *hot,* we use the (ɑ) which represents an "ah"-type vowel that is preponderant in America.

17

Attributive Nouns

Nouns that are frequently found to be used in attributive position are labeled·
after the definition as either *Also used attributively* or *Often used attributively:*

> **docking,** *n.* the joining of orbiting spacecraft. *Also used attributively.*
>
>> Rendezvous and docking in orbit is a difficult operation; even with men in charge. The first Gemini attempt nearly ended in disaster. *Science Journal, Jan. 1968, p 10*
>> The simple task of clamping Agena's tether to Gemini's docking bar is an exhausting struggle. *Time, Sept. 30, 1966, p 54*

However, we have used quotations freely with the noun in attributive position without feeling that it is necessary always to specify this use after the definition. Note, for instance, *C-and-W repertoire* in the quotation under **C&W** or **C-and-W.**

Speech Area Labels

The labels *U.S.* and *British* are used to signal that the labeled term is associated primarily with the indicated region and that the terms so labeled are most likely to be heard and used within an area without being spotted as out of place. Wherever possible, equivalent or corresponding British and American terms are contrasted in definitions, as under **postcode** and **zip code.**

Foreign-language Labels

This book notes the occurrence in English contexts of a fair number of words and phrases from other languages. They may be used freely in English contexts as travelers' local color ("close by is a *hamam* or bath") or may name institutions or events of other lands. Such foreign words and phrases reflect contact with speakers of other languages. A certain amount of French or of other languages may be used with literary swank or flourish or to fill some niche where a native word seems to be lacking (such a word is *aficionado*, which has become so far Englished as sometimes to be respelled with two *ff*'s like *affection*). For all such words we use language labels, such as *French, German,* or *Russian,* as indicators that the writer or speaker is deliberately or consciously using a word which he knows to be foreign instead of using an English equivalent (e.g. *crise de confiance* instead of *crisis of confidence*), as distinguished especially from a foreign word that has no English equivalent and is therefore a genuine loanword, as unavoidable from the user's standpoint as a native word (e.g. *aikido*). To be sure, this distinction cannot be made with absolute certainty or maintained with iron-clad consistency, and the reader will find borderline cases in this book where a "foreign" word could have been treated either with or without a label.

Usage Labels

With the single exception of the label *Slang*, usage labels such as *Colloquial,*

Formal, Rare, Nonce, and the like are not used. One of the striking things about the creations of slang is their range over practically all segments of the vocabulary, even some tampering with grammatical relations: *a together person, tell it like it is.* This is in large measure a result of the drive for novelty, freshness of expression, even a defiance of what is established. A dictionary of new English is bound to include a great deal of it unless the editors stick arbitrarily to the more or less technical vocabulary that names new things and ideas.

The label *Transferred sense* is given in cases where the basic or concrete sense of a new term has been transferred to figurative or analogical uses. For example:

> **body count, 1** a count of the enemy killed in a military operation. Compare KILL RATIO. **2** *Transferred sense.* **a** a count of those killed in a particular way. **b** any count or tally of individuals.
>
> **equal time,** *U.S.* **1** an equal amount of free air time given, usually at the same hour of another day, to an opposing political candidate, party, group, or citizen, to broadcast their views over radio or television. Compare FAIRNESS DOCTRINE. **2** *Transferred sense.* an equal opportunity to reply to any charge or opposing view.
>
> **flip side, 1** the back or second side of a phonograph record, especially the one with the recording of lesser importance. **2** *Transferred sense.* opposite number; counterpart.

If a label applies to an entire entry, it is placed immediately after the entry word; otherwise it is limited to its definition:

> **hit,** *Slang.* —*n.* an injection of a narcotic drug, especially heroin. —*v.i., v.t.* to give oneself or another person an injection of narcotics; to shoot up.
>
> **as-told-to,** *adj. U.S.* written by a professional writer. . . .

Definitions

The editors have tried to keep the definitions simple, generally relying on carefully selected quotations to supply details and complex explanations that in standard dictionaries would be covered in the definition. Wherever a quotation supplies the actual meaning, no definition is given and the reader is instructed to "See the quotation for the meaning":

> **hairtician,** *n. U.S.* See the quotation for the meaning.
>   Competition among barbers is surely more intense today than ever before. It has driven barbers to call themselves "hair stylists to men" and "hairticians". . . . *William Whitworth, "Profiles: Just A Little Off The Top," The New Yorker, Oct. 21, 1967, p 63*
>   [from *hair* + *-tician,* as in *beautician*]

Occasionally the reader is directed to read the quotation for additional facts that he may need in order to round out his understanding of the term's meaning:

> **flake²,** *n. U.S. Slang.* an arrest to meet a quota or to satisfy

pressure for police action. See the quotation for details.

"An accommodation collar," he [Patrolman William R. Phillips] said, is an arrest, to satisfy superior officers, that is presented in court with such weak evidence that acquittal is assured. "A flake," however, is the arrest, on known false evidence, of a person for something he did not do. *James F. Clarity, "Members of Panel Find Language is Corrupted," The New York Times, Oct. 20, 1971, p 36*

[probably so called from the flimsiness of the evidence submitted]

The use of these devices was prompted by the desire to shift the emphasis from the traditional dictionary definition to the quotation, which is of course the basis of the definition:

Murphy's Law, any of various humorous rules of thumb. See the quotations for examples.

Your reference to Murphy's Law touches on only part of that ancient Irish potentate's laws. . . . His set of the laws of life refer with circularity to nothing, everything and anything. They are: 1) nothing is as easy as it looks; 2) everything takes longer than you think it will; and 3) if anything can go wrong, it will. *Daniel C. McCarthy, Manhattan, in a Letter to the Editor, Time, April 13, 1970, p 6*

Murphy's Law states that if it is possible to connect two things together the wrong way round, then someone will do it that way. *Marcus Langley, "The Profit Motive and Practical Realities," New Scientist, Sept. 21, 1967, p 601*

"Recently," [Roger] Baker writes, "I learned of a governing principle known as Murphy's first law of biology. It states: 'Under any given set of environmental conditions an experimental animal behaves as it damn well pleases.' " *C. L. Stong, "The Amateur Scientist," Scientific American, June 1970, p 143*

Definitions of entries having several meanings are listed in the order of their greatest frequency in our judgment:

man, *n.* **the Man,** *U.S. Slang.* **1** the white man; white society personified.

The Man systematically killed your language, killed your culture, tried to kill your soul, tried to blot you out. . . . *Calvin Marshall, "The Black Church: Three Views," Time, April 6, 1970, p 71*

"In fact," she [Miss Ruth Eisenbraun] was saying, "the society as a whole is loosening up. If I were black, the South is where I'd prefer to be. Nobody in the North believes now in integration because they've never had it, but here, in an economic and social way, they've had integration all along, though of course entirely on the Man's terms. . . ." *John Updike, Bech: A Book, 1970, p 122*

2 the Establishment in general; the system.

"Kent and Cambodia were made to order for radicals. Something like Dowdell's death was made for them: 'The pigs got Tiger. You can't trust the Man. Come on with us.' I can hear them now." *Bill Moyers, "Listening to America," Harper's, Dec. 1970, p 59*

3 the police.

". . . I catches up with one fella in an alley after he put my TV in a truck. He keeps denyin' what I seen him do with my own eyes, so I blasts him and takes him bleedin' down to the Man." *Nathaniel Folmar, quoted in "The Beautiful People of Detroit," Maclean's, Dec. 1967, p 27*

To the bombers and kidnappers the Man is Authority. He is every policeman. *"The Politics of Gelignite," The Manchester Guardian Weekly, Nov. 7, 1970, p 1*

[originally used by Southern blacks to counteract the whites' use of "boy" in addressing or referring to black men]

Where the frequency of the various meanings appears to be evenly divided, however, the earliest meaning or the one closest to the earliest is given first:

max·i ('mæk si:), *n.* **1** a skirt, dress, coat, etc., reaching to the ankle or just above it; a maxiskirt, maxidress, maxicoat, etc. Compare MICRO, MIDI, MINI.

When you have seen one maxi, you have seen them all, though Saint Laurent makes his droopier than ever with mufflers and downdragged crochet berets, but pants-suits have infinite variations. *Ernestine Carter, The Sunday Times (London), Feb. 2, 1969, p 58*

2 the ankle-length style of fashion.

In their desperation to whet consumer demand by the good, old American economic device of forced obsolescence, the industry's merchants, manufacturers and editors have been touting the midi, the maxi and other varieties of lowered hemlines. *Marylin Bender, The New York Times, July 5, 1968, p 50*

—*adj.* **1** reaching to the ankle or just above it; ankle-length.

Teen-agers and college girls rushed for maxi coats and shops reported good sales in the style. *Ruth Mary Dubois, "Fashion," The Americana Annual 1970, p 287*

2 larger or longer than usual.

As fashions grow minier, accessories are waxing maxier. Witness the popularity of superwatches—huge, outsize timekeepers that measure 3 in. across and come with round, square and octagonal faces. *Time, Nov. 10, 1967, p 47*

In the Dublin suburbs there is a mini-car in nearly every garage, and downtown the traffic jams are becoming very maxi. *John F. Henahan, "Still Life in the Ould Turf," Saturday Review, Sept. 23, 1967, p 4*

[from *maxi-*]

This is also done in some cases where starting with the earliest meaning will show an interesting semantic development:

parameter, *n.* **1** a measurable factor which helps with other such factors to define a system.

Various individual experiments have climbed past various obstacles to reach positions close to the break-even level. In fact, in some instances two of the three essential parameters (density, temperature and confinement time) have already been achieved. *William C. Gough and Bernard J. Eastlund, "The Prospects of Fusion Power," Scientific American, Feb. 1971, p 63*

2 any defining or characteristic factor.

. . . the President should "use the moral influence of his office in new ways designed to reduce racial tensions and help develop a climate of racial understanding." None of those things can be done overnight, but the fact that Nixon was willing to make his chastisement public suggests—as Finch put it in bureaucratese—that the President at least understands "the parameters of the problem." *Time, Aug. 3, 1970, p 9*

The mind with all its parameters and limits ingrained through years of constant failure to aim beyond the "feasible" and "allowable," the "probable." I read Timon of Athens today. . . . *Ward Just, "Soldiers," The Atlantic, Nov. 1970, p 65*

Function of the Quotations

Every definition is followed by one or more quotations selected to perform several functions:

1) to show the word's use in an actual context and a natural environment:

> **main,** *v.t. Slang.* to inject (heroin or a similar drug) into a vein.
>
> . . . all my friends were on heroin. I snorted a couple of times, skinned a lot, and after that I mained it. *"Kids and Heroin: The Adolescent Epidemic," Time, March 16, 1970, p 17*
>
> [shortened from *mainline, v.*]

2) to furnish additional details about the meaning or connotation of the word that the definition cannot properly supply:

> **lunar rover,** a vehicle for exploratory travel on the lunar surface. Also called MOON CAR, MOON CRAWLER, MOON ROVER. Compare LUNOKHOD.
>
> Scott and Irwin will take three field trips (one a day) in the lunar rover to numerous craters, the mountain and the rille. *Everly Driscoll, "Mission Into The Moon's Past," Science News, July 10, 1971, p 30*
>
> Apollo 15 was first of three missions to transport heavier payloads than the earlier flights and to carry an electric-powered vehicle resembling a golf cart, called Lunar Rover. With the added mobility afforded by the Rover, crews of these missions can make extensive trips away from the lunar module—up to a theoretical maximum of 35 miles. *William Hines, "Space Exploration," The World Book Science Annual 1972 (1971), p 367*

3) to call attention to the range of use through several quotations from different sources, times, and places:

> **lon·geur** (lɔŋˈgər), *n.* a variant spelling of *longueur*, meaning a long or tedious passage in a book, play, etc. The original spelling was taken directly from French, and was apparently first used by Lord Byron in his epic poem *Don Juan* (1821). However, evidence showing the use of the simplified English spelling has been accumulating since the late 1950's, as the following sampling of quotations indicates:

In our contemporary life we had the battle of Passchendaele and the Russian Revolution, but taking things by and large, and month by month, one was aware of extensive stretches in which nothing historically worth while seemed to be going on — longeurs which the Director of History (with a capital H) would not have tolerated in his scenario. *Claud Cockburn, The Guardian (London), Nov. 2, 1959, p 7*

All of the Irish critics welcomed the play as a fine piece of historical drama. . . . Sean White wrote The Irish Press that "it has strength despite its central longeurs." *The New York Times, May 24, 1963, p 16*

The last part of the book (and the first written) is much less interesting and has many longeurs. . . . *Bernard Bergonzi, "Bouillabaisse," Review of "A True Story" by Stephen Hudson, The New York Review of Books, March 17, 1966, p 22*

The piece [*Grande pièce symphonique* by César Franck] is loose in construction and, as so often with Franck, one feels that its *longeurs* could do with a little pruning. *Stanley Webb, The Gramophone, April 1968, p 540*

However, despite the show's contradictions and longeurs, it does at least attempt something audacious and original and for that I respect it. *Michael Billington, "Media Satire," The Times (London), May 29, 1970, p 7*

4) to indicate the type of writing in which the word appears by the title and often the name of the author of the article, letter, poem, etc.:

luminal art, a form of art that uses the arrangement or projection of colored electric lights to create images, moving patterns, flashing designs, etc. Also called LUMINIST ART.

Along with everything else, art has gone electric. . . . The new luminal art has suddenly emerged as both international and popular. A record 42,000 visitors showed up when Kansas City's Nelson Gallery staged a month-long "Sound Light Silence" show last November. *"Art: Techniques," Time, April 28, 1967, p 36*

Kinetic art deals with movement, with which a great deal of contemporary work — including most luminal art — is concerned, directly or indirectly. *Benjamin de Brie Taylor, "Art: Kinetic and Luminal Art," 1968 Collier's Encyclopedia Year Book, p 129*

Order of the Quotations

Since it would be fruitless to give a historical account of words whose available attestation in publications spans a mere ten years, the order of the quotations is not necessarily chronological and no attempt is made to give the earliest quotation available. The emphasis is placed instead on the utility of the quotations. A quotation from 1970 may precede a quotation from 1967; a quotation from a British or Canadian source may precede one from a U.S. source; quotations from U.S. and British sources are often given to show usage in both areas:

acidhead, *n. Slang.* a user or addict of the hallucinogenic drug LSD.

Reality was to be fled; Peter [Fonda] became the acidhead of the house. "In those days, it wasn't an illegal drug," he says. "It was pure, non-chromosome-breaking, non-habit-forming, non-dangerous. So I dropped 500 micrograms and never came back." *Time, Feb. 16, 1970, p 60*

I asked a constable . . . if he could tell me where to go to watch the acid-heads taking a trip. . . . *Patrick Ryan, "The Swinging City," Punch, Sept. 6, 1967, p 339*

[from *acid*, a slang term for LSD + *head*, a slang term for drug addict. See HEAD.]

Sources

The source of each quotation is in italic type after the quotation: *The Times (London), April 29, 1968, p 2*
Whenever it is helpful in understanding the context we give also the author's name and the title of the article:

> *Bonnie Buxton, "The Unchaperoned Girl's Guide to Europe," Maclean's, June 1967, p 56*

To make the sources readily identifiable the names of the publications are spelled out and the dates are given in full so that the reader does not have to refer to a bibliography.

Etymologies

Etymologies, giving the source or history of words, are added in brackets at the end of entries. Only those words whose forms or meanings call for some explanation are given etymologies. The usual type of etymology, such as is found in standard dictionaries, needs no explanation here; it is common practice to etymologize such terms as *aikido* (a Japanese loanword), *Cold Duck* (a German loan translation), *cloxacillin* (a technical term made up of Latin elements), *glasphalt* (a blend of *glass* and *asphalt*), *eutrophicate* (a back formation of *eutrophication*), and the like. For the special purposes of this book, however, the editors availed themselves of the etymological brackets to insert in them information that concerns changes in the meaning and use of words that are already part of the language. Thus, shifts in the function of words are noted in the etymologies. Examples are:

(1) verb use of the noun:

> **litterbug,** *v.i.* . . . . [verb use of *litterbug*, n.]

(2) noun use of the adjective:

> **nasty,** *n.* . . . . [noun use of the adjective]

Likewise, extensions of meanings are sometimes noted in the etymological notes whenever restrictive labels before definitions are not applicable. Examples are:

(1) a figurative sense of _____:

> **launching pad,** a place from which something starts; springboard. . . .
> [figurative sense of the term for a rocket- or missile-launching platform]

(2) a transferred sense of _____:

> **track record,** the performance record of a person, business, etc., in a particular field or endeavor. . . .
> [transferred sense from the racing term for the record of speed set by a contestant at a particular distance and track]

(3) an extended sense of _____:

> **lifer,** *n. U.S. Military Slang.* a career officer or soldier. . . .
> [extended from the original meaning of *lifer* a person sentenced to prison for life (attested since the early 1800's)]

This use of the etymological brackets has enabled the editors to indicate, in brief, formulaic fashion, numerous changes in the function and meaning of older words that otherwise might go unnoticed.

Footnotes

In order to separate editorial comment from definitions or to give ancillary information of interest about usage or other matters, we sometimes give footnotes or usage notes at the end of an entry. Footnotes are indicated by an arrow (▶). The notes under **paramedic** and **intermedia** deal with usage; those under **camp** and **kiss of life** with derivation; those under **establishment, gunboat diplomacy,** and **dark comedy** with cultural or historical facts. Here are two examples:

> **à la page** (a la 'paʒ), *French.* up-to-date; keeping up with the latest fashion.
> His became a name — not famous, but one of those names that people mention to show they are à la page. . . . *Shirley Hazzard, The Bay of Noon, 1970, p 79*
> ▶ In French this phrase is virtually obsolete among the younger half of the population, who now use *dans le vent* (literally, in the wind) for this sense.

> **alm,** *n.* a charitable gift.
> He was a squire to the last second of his life. He never gave anything that wasn't an alm — even his love. *Isaac Bashevis Singer, "The Egotist," The New Yorker, Jan. 16, 1971, p 35*
> ▶ The new singular *alm* is a back formation of the singular and plural *alms*, whose final -s has been long taken as a

plural inflection in such constructions as "For alms are but the vehicles of prayer" (John Dryden, *The Hind and the Panther*, 1687). This formation parallels the classic instance of *pea*, which evolved from the earlier singular and plural *pease*.

Cross References

In addition to the usual cross references given in dictionaries from one variant spelling or form to another, or from a derived form to the root form, or from an entry giving information that supplements the first entry, we relate one scientific or technical term to correlative terms where possible. Thus, under **abscisic acid** we call attention to **brassin** and **cytokinin**:

> **ab·scis·ic acid** (æb'sis ik), an organic substance that inhibits plant growth. *Abbreviation:* ABA Also called DORMIN. Compare BRASSIN, CYTOKININ.
>
> **bras·sin** ('bræs ən), *n.* a plant hormone that stimulates the division, elongation, and lateral enlargement of plant cells. Compare ABSCISIC ACID, CYTOKININ, KINETIN.
>
> **cy·to·ki·nin** (ˌsɑi touˈkɑi nən), *n.* a plant hormone that directs the differentiation of cells into the roots and shoots of young plants. Compare ABSCISIC ACID, BRASSIN, KINETIN.

Under **alap** we refer to other terms that are part of a particular pattern of terms:

> **a·lap** (ɑːˈlɑːp), *n.* the first movement in the performance of a typical raga, the traditional Hindu musical form. Compare JOR, GAT.
>
> **jor** (dʒɔr), *n.* the rhythmic second movement of a typical raga, the traditional Hindu musical form. Compare ALAP, GAT.
>
> **gat** (gɑːt) or **gath** (gɑːθ), *n.* a complex rhythmic passage that usually marks the final movement or section of a raga, the traditional Hindu musical form. Compare ALAP, JOR.

PRONUNCIATION KEY

A. Vowels and Diphthongs

æ   a in *hat* (hæt)

ɑ   o in American *hot* (hɑt)
ɑ: a in *father* ('fɑ: ðər)
ai i in *nice* (nais)
au ou in *out* (aut)

e   e in *set* (set)
ei a in *gate* (geit)

i   i in *hit* (hit)
i: ee in *feet* (fi:t)

ɔ   o in British *hot* (hɔt)
ɔ: aw in *raw* (rɔ:)
ɔi oi in *oil* (ɔil)

ou o in *go* (gou)
u   oo in *book* (buk)
u: oo in *boot* (bu:t)

ə   u in *cup* (kəp), a in *ago* (ə'gou)

B. Accented Vowels with R

ar ar in *part* (part)
er ar in *care* (ker)
ir ear in *hear* (hir)

ɔr or in *lord* (lɔrd)
ur oor in *poor* (pur)
ər ir in *bird* (bərd)

C. Syllabic Consonants

əl le in *little* ('lit əl)
əm m in *prism* ('priz əm)

ən on in *prison* ('priz ən)
ər ar in *altar* ('ɔ:l tər)

D. Consonants

(1) Ordinary Letter Values

b in *bed*
d in *did*
f in *fat*
g in *go*
h in *had*
k in *kit*
l in *leg*
m in *man*

n in *not*
p in *pig*
r in *run*
s in *sad*
t in *tan*
v in *vat*
w in *wet*
y in *yes*

z in *zoo*

ʃ	sh in *she* (ʃiː)		ð	th in *then* (ðen)
tʃ	ch in *chin* (tʃin)		ʒ	s in *measure* ('meʒ ər)
ŋ	ng in *sing* (siŋ)		dʒ	j in *join* (dʒɔin)
θ	th in *thin* (θin)			

E. Foreign Sounds

Foreign words are for the most part pronounced with the nearest equivalents in English sounds. For example, the close *e* of a French word such as *né* is represented by *ei* as in English *nay* (nei). The following symbols, however, are used for some specifically foreign sounds:

a	a in French *patte* (pat)
œ	eu in French *heure* (œr)
x	ch in German *ach* (ɑːx)

Y u in French *du* (dY)

~ over a vowel letter, nasal vowel, as in French *sans* (sɑ̃), *vin* (væ̃), *bon* (bɔ̃), *un* (æ̃), Portuguese *são* (sɑ̃u)

F. Accents

ˈ primary stress, as in bəˈluːn *(balloon)*

ˌ secondary stress, as in ˈel əˌvei tər *(elevator)*

A

a-, *prefix.* now freely added to verbs to yield predicate adjectives with rather more vivid effect than the participle in *-ing*, and especially to verbs that denote some picturable activity, motion, or sensation. Examples collected from recent sources include the following:

asquish, *adj.* squishing.

Within a few hours, the corridor outside the Congressman's office was asquish with trod-upon fruit. *Time, July 4, 1969, p 12*

aswivel, *adj.* swiveling.

Most of her sisters, from Judy O'Grady to the Colonel's lady, would be more concerned about the sad inevitability of the day when they promenade out to the dustbin with the spud-peelings, full steam ahead and all hips aswivel like Monroe, and the wolf-whistling comes to a stop. *Patrick Ryan, New Scientist and Science Journal, April 29, 1971, p 246*

awhir, *adj.* whirring.

. . . the sapphire skies are astir and awhir with rising warplanes. *Sylvia Ashton-Warner, The New York Times, May 16, 1970, p 24*

In addition, this usage has been extended to make a vivid replacement for the past participial form in *-ed* in the predicate (or following the noun to which it applies), as in:

aclutter, *adj.* cluttered.

New York City, already aclutter with candidates for mayor, got one with a difference last week. *Time, July 2, 1965, p 18*

aglaze, *adj.* glazed.

When Bud Morgan knelt to pull them away Bett whirled and bit him between thumb and forefinger, drawing blood. She coiled back as he leashed her. Her lips drew back in a snarl, her eyes were dark and aglaze. She had no seeming sense of what she had done. *Jessie Ford, "The Savage Sound," The Atlantic, July 1967, p 44*

A. & R. man, one who supervises artists and repertory, especially for a phonograph-record company.

Man comes out onstage (can't see who it is, owing to glare from lights, but must be Rudolf Bing, Met's A. & R. man). . . . *"The Talk of the Town," The New Yorker, Oct. 9, 1965, p 47*

"Just a few friends—artistes, A. & R. men, managers, agents, writers like yourself—people, you know, who feel deeply about the future of beat music." *Alan Coren, "Once I Built a Pop Group," Punch, Sept. 30, 1964, p 485*

[*A. & R.,* abbreviation of *Artists and Repertory*]

ABC art, another term for MINIMAL ART.

. . . its [minimal art's] use of simple "primary" shapes, as in the critic Barbara Rose's term "ABC art", with its implication of going back to the basic alphabet. *Guy Brett, "Simply Vertical," The Times (London), March 18, 1970, p 15*

ab·scis·ic acid (æb'sis ik), an organic substance that inhibits plant growth. *Abbreviation:* ABA Also called DORMIN. Compare BRASSIN, CYTOKININ.

The first of the new approaches makes use of a natural plant hormone, abscisic acid or ABA, normally involved in the processes of leaf fall and plant dormancy. *New Scientist, Dec. 10, 1970, p 427*

[from the *abscission* or separation of parts of a plant from the stem]

ab·scis·in (æb'sis ən), *n.* any of a group of organic substances that regulate plant growth.

Abscisins . . . have the ability to accelerate abscission, senescence, and the onset of dormancy; they also retard the growth of plants and inhibit germination. Two abscisins, now known as abscisin I and abscisic acid, have been isolated. *Fredrick T. Addicott, "A-Z Abscisins," McGraw-Hill Yearbook of Science and Technology 1968, p 93*

absolute address, the specific location where information is stored in a digital computer.

At most installations yet another translation must be performed: from the assembly language output of the compiler into the machine language codes, often entirely numeric, that activate a particular machine. At this stage, for example, all symbols used for problem variables will be converted into specific memory location numbers, or "absolute addresses." *Van Court Hare, Jr., Introduction to Programming, A BASIC Approach, 1970, p 100*

absurd, *n.* **the absurd** or **the Absurd,** a literary and philosophical term descriptive of the absurdity or pointlessness of the human condition from an existential point of view and associated with the works of Albert Camus, Jean Paul Sartre, Eugene Ionesco, Samuel Beckett, and Edward Albee.

. . . Mr. Esslin defines his own influential catchphrase in four long essays on Beckett, Adamov, Ionesco and Genet; then spreads into an informative and international catalogue of related playwrights (Pinter, Frisch, Grass, etc.); and settles into a solid discussion of the tradition and significance of the Absurd. *The Times (London), April 20, 1968, p 23*

—*adj.* of or relating to the absurd.

The "absurd" theatre of Ionesco and Beckett, the so-called "new novel" of French authors like Alain Robbe-

Grillet, and a good deal of the choreography done by young modern-dance groups in New York and elsewhere can also be seen as part of a general revolt against self-expressive, meaningful art in the Renaissance tradition. *Calvin Tomkins, The New Yorker, Nov. 28, 1964, p 65*

absurdism, *n.* concern with the absurd in literature and drama.

The three parts into which his novel [*The Artificial Traveler* by Warren Fine] is divided are marked off by distinct shifts in style—from straight, clean narrative, which he is good at, to earthy mysticism, and finally to absurdism, black comedy, and parody, leading to an obscure climax. *The New Yorker, March 9, 1968, p 154*

absurdist, *n.* a playwright or other writer who stresses the absurd in his work. See also THEATER OF THE ABSURD.

Like the Absurdists (the avant-garde of the late 1950s and early 1960s), Artaud rejected the theatre of realism.... *Julius Novick, "Theater," Britannica Book of the Year 1969, p 728*

—*adj.* characteristic of absurdists or of the theater of the absurd.

There is a lot of witty, high elegant and absurdist dialogue and some terrible puns. *Renata Adler, The New York Times, April 12, 1968, p 50*

ac·an·thas·ter (ˌæk ən'θæs tər), *n.* the crown-of-thorns starfish, a large predator of coral islands throughout the Pacific.

... the starfish also engorges the living polyps that give coral its bright colors; where a herd of acanthasters has grazed, the devastated coral left behind is dead white.... They can stay alive for six months without eating, but when they eat they eat heartily: a big acanthaster can kill fifty years of coral growth in a night. A female can lay twenty-four million eggs at a clip. *E. J. Kahn, Jr., "A Reporter At Large: Micronesia Revisited," The New Yorker, Dec. 18, 1971, p 112*

[from New Latin *Acanthaster planci*, the name of the species, from Greek *ákantha* spine or thorn + *astér* star]

accommodation collar, *U.S. Slang.* an arrest to meet a quota or to satisfy pressure for police action.

"An accommodation collar," he [Patrolman William R. Phillips] said, is an arrest, to satisfy superior officers, that is presented in court with such weak evidence that acquittal is assured. A flake, however, is the arrest, on known false evidence, of a person for something he did not do. *James F. Clarity, "Members of Panel Find Language is Corrupted," The New York Times, Oct. 20, 1971, p 36*

acid, *n. Slang.* the hallucinogenic drug LSD (lysergic *acid* diethylamide).

I really felt I was through with drugs, at least acid and speed for sure. I am not going to get into that kind of thing again. *Jonathan Strong, "Patients," The Atlantic, March 1969, p 44*

According to the newest scientific work on the pure marijuana chemical, the size of the dose means the difference between a pleasurable experience and a psychological blow-out. In very rough terms, marijuana is perhaps one-hundredth as strong as LSD, but with enough of it, the smoker might just as well be flying on acid—headed straight down. *Patricia McBroom, Science News, Nov. 18, 1967, p 500*

acidhead, *n. Slang.* a user or addict of the hallucinogenic drug LSD.

Reality was to be fled; Peter [Fonda] became the acid-head of the house. "In those days, it wasn't an illegal drug," he says. "It was pure, non-chromosome-breaking, non-habit-forming, non-dangerous. So I dropped 500 micrograms and never came back." *Time, Feb. 16, 1970, p 60*

I asked a constable . . . if he could tell me where to go to watch the acid-heads taking a trip. . . . *Patrick Ryan, "The Swinging City," Punch, Sept. 6, 1967, p 339*

[from *acid*, a slang term for LSD + *head*, a slang term for drug addict. See HEAD.]

acidless trip, *U.S.* a slang term for SENSITIVITY TRAINING. Compare ACID TRIP.

The supporters of sensitivity training call it a new frontier in social psychology, a means of making people more innovative, honest, trusting, and free. It is not a form of psychoanalysis, they say, but a significant outgrowth of adult education rooted in emotions rather than intellect. Numerous organizations—corporations, universities, churches, government agencies—view it as a method of helping people break the communication barrier. Skeptics term it "the acidless trip" or "instant intimacy." *Ted J. Rakstis, "Sensitivity Training: Fad, Fraud or New Frontier?" Encyclopedia Science Supplement (Grolier) 1970, p 79*

acid rock, a type of rock 'n' roll music with sound and lyrics suggestive of drug-taking or psychedelic experiences.

Significantly, The Band's [a rock group's] music is quiet . . . . But for those who take to them—musicians, college kids who have grown tired of the predictable blast-furnace intensity of acid rock, and an ever-growing segment of the young—The Band stirs amazement and glee. *Time, Jan. 12, 1970, p 38*

acid trip, *Slang.* a hallucinatory experience resulting from taking LSD. Compare ACIDLESS TRIP, BAD TRIP.

Like Western-lovers grooving on scalping scenes . . . this audience was digging the Youngun equivalents: acid trips, nude body paintings, pot smoking, . . . the works, man. *Dan Wakefield, "Movies: Action on the Generation Gap," The Atlantic, Dec. 1968, p 146*

. . . only the tinted glasses he wore matched the best-selling pop poster that made Peter a symbol to and of the NOW generation—so powerful a symbol that he sometimes receives telephone calls from kids on bad acid trips thinking of suicide. *Lee Israel, The New York Times, Sept. 8, 1968, Sec. 2, p 3*

acoustical hologram, the pattern formed in acoustical holography.

By "illuminating" an object with pure tones of sound instead of with a beam of coherent light one can create acoustical holograms that become three-dimensional pictures when viewed by laser light. *Alexander F. Metherell, "Acoustical Holography," Scientific American, Oct. 1969, p 36*

acoustical holography, a method of holography in which high-frequency sound waves instead of light waves are used to make a pattern or picture of an object. See also HOLOGRAPHY.

. . . acoustical holography could explore for oil and

mineral deposits at depths of several miles. *"Making 3-D Pictures with Sound," Time, Nov. 10, 1967, p 41*

From the beginning of holography studies it was realized that one can record a hologram at one wavelength and reconstruct it at another. Hence, a hologram can be recorded with sound waves and then reconstructed with light. This technique is called acoustical holography. *A. F. Metherell, "Holography with Sound," Science Journal, Nov. 1968, p 57*

acoustic coupler or **acoustic data coupler,** a device for transmitting data over telephone circuits without making an electrical connection.

In addition there are attaché-case size typewriter units which can be connected to a computer from any location boasting a telephone. This has become possible with production of an acoustic coupler, which is about the size of one of the more expensive battery operated transistor radios. *Pearce Wright, "Patients of the 'Polite' Computer," The Times (London), Aug. 5, 1970, p 8*

Each client will get a portable teletype and a thing called an "acoustic data coupler" that allows the teletype to send messages to a computer over any old telephone. *The New York Times, June 26, 1968, p 70*

acoustic perfume or **acoustical perfume,** another term for WHITE NOISE.

When the noises to be overcome are only mildly offensive or not too great in volume, they can sometimes be masked by an overlay of pleasant sound, which thus has a function similar to that so gallantly fulfilled by perfume through the ages—hence the name, "acoustic perfume." *Eugene Raskin, "Noise," 1968 Collier's Encyclopedia Year Book, p 25*

a·cous·to- (ə'ku:s tou-), a new combining form, now used chiefly in technical writing, meaning "of or involving sound or acoustic waves" or "acoustic and _____."

acousto-electric, *adj.:* Acousto-electric oscillators may also be useful for measuring changes in applied stress. *New Scientist, May 23, 1968, p 402*

acousto-electronic, *adj.:* Compression and expansion filters could be laid down on a single acousto-electronic strip. *W. T. Gunston, Science Journal, May 1970, p 44*

acousto-optic, *adj.:* . . . an acousto-optic modulator which switches the beam on and off. *Advertisement by Bell Labs, Scientific American, Sept. 1970, p 199*

acousto-optical, *adj.:* The acousto-optical unit serves the same purpose as the electronic interface which joins measuring equipment to a computer. . . . *Ian M. Firth, New Scientist, May 21, 1970, p 376*

acoustoelectronics, *n.* a branch of electronics dealing with the conversion of electrical signals into a flow of acoustic waves traveling along a solid surface.

. . . the 1970s will herald a new era of electronics—namely, "acoustoelectronics," based on surface acoustic-wave technology. *Jeffrey H. Collins, New Scientist, July 30, 1970, p 245*

ac·qua al·ta ('a:k kwa: 'a:l ta:), *Italian.* high water, especially in reference to the recurring floods that submerge the historic central part of Venice.

It was about four in the morning when the sirens began their rising and fading wail as for an air raid. . . . it took the night clerk some minutes to answer. It was, he said re-

assuringly, "just another warning for *acqua alta." Irving R. Levine, "Venice," The Atlantic, Jan. 1971, p 16*

acrophobe, *n.* a person who has an abnormal fear of heights.

The height itself worries few tenants: no acrophobe would ever think of moving in. *Time, Jan. 4, 1971, p 48*

▶ See the note under AGORAPHOBIC.

ac·ro·sin ('æk rə sən), *n.* a spermatic enzyme.

On the cap, or acrosome, of a spermatozoon, there is an enzyme called acrosin, which chews through the protective layers around an ovum with an action rather like the protein-digesting enzyme trypsin. *New Scientist, Jan. 14, 1971, p 54*

action, *n.* in various slang expressions:

a piece of the action, a part or share in something.

And last year mink breeders from Scandinavia to California were falling over themselves to buy a piece of the action. . . . *Maclean's, June 4, 1966, p 1*

In a confrontation at Harlem Hospital Center, the Council of Community Voices on Narcotics, a coalition of organizations formed to fight addiction in the Negro communities, asked the officials to give them "a piece of the action." *The New York Times, July 25, 1968, p 34*

where the action is, the place of greatest activity, development, etc. Compare WHERE IT'S AT under WHERE, *adv.*

. . . it is clear today that the early years of a child's life are critically important in the development of learning processes and capacity. "In many ways," he observed, "that's where the action is." *The New York Times, Dec. 24, 1967, Sec. 1, p 40*

action painter, an artist who produces action paintings.

When the French Dadaist painter Hans Arp tossed colored paper squares in the air and glued them where they fell, he linked the rectangles of cubism to the gobs of paint slung by the later "action" painters. *Martin Gardner, "Mathematical Games: The Eerie Mathematical Art of Maurits C. Escher," Scientific American, April 1966, p 110*

. . . a well-known "action" painter was living on the top floor of his Ridge Street tenement, and Manny had to take forty canvases in lieu of back rent. *Richard M. Elman, "Manny Gelder: Slumlord," The Atlantic, Nov. 1966, p 130*

action painting, a style of painting emphasizing spontaneous expression by splashing or dripping paint on the canvas or by using broad, vigorous brush strokes. Compare DRIP PAINTING.

American Action painting at its inception was a method of creation—not a style or look that pictures strove to achieve. *Harold Rosenberg, "The Art World," The New Yorker, May 25, 1968, p 116*

activation analysis, the identification and measurement of chemical elements in a substance by analyzing the radiations emitted by the elements present after the substance is bombarded with nuclear particles, especially neutrons. Compare NEUTRON ACTIVATION ANALYSIS.

Living-body activation analysis involves the radiation of a patient, or part of a patient, with thermal neutrons or other radiation to induce radioisotopes which can be measured to determine the elemental composition. *Gordon*

L. Brownell, "Radiation Biology," *McGraw-Hill Yearbook of Science and Technology 1971*, p 369

Using proton activation analysis, he [Dr. George Lutz] bombards the sodium sample with high-energy protons. This produces radioactive isotopes of carbon and oxygen .... *Science News*, June 6, 1970, p 554

ac·tu·a·li·té (ak tY a li:'tei), *n. French.* **1** topical interest.

Rattling around in the back of the mind of Tussaud's are thoughts for new "entertainments" with movement, sound, smell, and actualité, like their magnificent Battle of Trafalgar. *Philip Howard, The Times (London), April 22, 1970, p 4*

2 actualités, *pl.* current topics; news.

There are certain things—interviews, documentaries, discussions, what the French call *actualités*—that television can do superbly well. ... *Francis King, The Listener, Sept. 5, 1968, p 316*

ACV, abbreviation of AIR CUSHION VEHICLE.

The ACV ... derives support from an entrapped bubble of air between the vehicle and the ground or water surface .... *James P. Romualdi, "Transportation," The World Book Science Annual 1968, p 379*

added-value tax, another name for VALUE-ADDED TAX.

On September 10 the [Belgian] government announced its decision to postpone until January 1971 the introduction of the added-value tax, which all EEC [European Economic Community] countries had agreed to institute by January 1970. In view of the economic boom and labor shortages, the government feared the new tax would cause an upsurge in prices. ... *Amry Vandenbosch, "Belgium," The Americana Annual 1970, p 127*

ad·e·nyl cyc·lase ('æd ə,nil 'sai,kleis), an enzyme that manufactures CYCLIC AMP.

Sutherland and his co-workers had established that cyclic AMP is produced from adenosine triphosphate (ATP) by an enzyme, adenyl cyclase, located at the surface of cells. *Scientific American, Oct. 1970, p 48*

ad hoc·er·y (æd 'hak ər i:), Also spelled **ad hoccery** and **ad hockery.** *Slang.* decisions, policy, rules, etc., made ad hoc.

That deficiency of "ad hocery"—former Bureau of the Budget Director Charles Schulze's term—may be seen quite clearly in the lawyers' desire to judicialize human affairs. *Arthur Selwyn Miller, Saturday Review, Aug. 3, 1968, p 40*

Apart from the network of swap agreements ("ad hoccery" as Mr Callaghan called it when he was Chancellor) it is the only concrete result of the years of wrangling over monetary reform. ... *William Davis, The Manchester Guardian Weekly, Jan. 16, 1969, p 22*

So, in what one BP operational researcher has called "a mixture of machines and ad-hockery", the company arrived at an essentially circum-African solution, relying heavily on Iran. ... *New Scientist, June 13, 1968, p 558*

ad-hocracy, *n. Slang.* rule by ad hoc committees.

[Alvin] Toffler's consistent theme is transience. He describes the death of permanence in society, the quickening pace of life, the shortening time-span of human relationships due to growing mobility, the erosion of bureaucracy through organizational change: he even visualises the disposable institution or new "ad-hocracy" replacing permanent hierarchies. *Anthony Wedgwood Benn, "Ad-hocracy," The Listener, Oct. 29, 1970, p 588*

[blend of *ad hoc* and *-cracy* rule of or by]

admass, *adj. British.* of or relating to high-pressure advertising and publicity over the mass media to stimulate sales, with detrimental influence on the culture of society.

. . . Mr. Platter never takes precise aim before firing his satirical peashooter and also offers no well-defined, radical alternative to the admass society he dislikes. *Michael Billington, The Times (London), Sept. 18, 1970, p 6*

. . . Hancock makes the most of limited opportunities in scripts designed apparently to hit the widest admass audience of benevolent credulity. ... *Bernard Hollowood, Punch, Feb. 13, 1963, p 246*

There were enormous difficulties facing the affluent teenager in an "admass" society, largely because of adults' uncertainty about moral standards. *The Times (London), Jan. 3, 1964, p 6*

[coined by J. B. Priestley from *ad*vertisement + *mass*: "Economics I do not pretend to understand, and sometimes I suspect that nobody does. But I understand people, and I know that the system I christened *Admass*, which we borrowed from America and did not improve, and constant inflation have made people unhappy." *J. B. Priestley, Punch, July 18, 1962, p 77*]

advance, *U.S.* —*n.* the making of arrangements ahead of time for the reception of a visiting political candidate; the work of an advance man.

In political campaigning, "bad advance" means that a Presidential candidate flies into a key city, lands at the wrong airport, and rides in a closed car down back streets to a huge stadium, where he addresses a lonely handful of party workers over a broken mike while the press is still looking for him at the other airport. "Good advance" means that the candidate is mobbed at the airport by fervent, unmanageable crowds, leads the press in a triumphant motorcade through a blizzard of confetti, fights his way into a jammed rally as brass bands blare, ascends a platform on which all the right people are seated in the right seats, speaks to the cheering, sign-waving multitude over a p.-a. system that works beautifully, and, that evening, sees the whole visit prominently featured by Walter Cronkite. *"The Talk of the Town: Advance Man," The New Yorker, June 12, 1971, p 30*

—*v.i.* to prepare for a candidate's visit; do the work of an advance man.

Campaigning does not often go as smoothly as this, but when an extraordinary man named Jerry Bruno was "advancing" for John Kennedy, Robert Kennedy, Lyndon Johnson, and others, it sometimes came close. *"The Talk of the Town: Advance Man," The New Yorker, June 12, 1971, p 30*

—*v.t.* to prepare for a candidate's reception in (a place); do the work of an advance man in.

He became a volunteer in Proxmire's 1954 campaign for governor (Proxmire lost), and when Proxmire became a senator, in 1957, Bruno joined his staff full time. In 1957, Bruno went to work for John Kennedy—"organizing Wisconsin"—and during the 1960 Presidential campaign and the Kennedy Administration he "advanced" thirty-four cities. *"The Talk of the Town: Advance Man," The New Yorker, June 12, 1971, p 30*

advance man, *U.S.* an assistant to a political candidate who makes arrangements ahead of time at scheduled stops for meetings and demonstrations of support for the candidate. See also ADVANCE.

In a recent New Jersey appearance, police tried to bar a handful of demonstrators. Ron Walker, Nixon's chief advance man, told the police to let the protesters in. *Time, Nov. 2, 1970, p 7*

"A good advance man should be able to judge people," he [Jerry Bruno] told us. "Weed out the doers from the talkers and sidestep the phonies. Be able to walk between disputes, be available all the time, and know when to blow up." *"The Talk of the Town: Advance Man," The New Yorker, June 12, 1971, p 30*

▶ The earlier sense of this term was that of an agent who goes ahead of a circus, theatrical troupe, etc., to make arrangements for performances and advertise the show.

adventure playground, *British.* a children's playground with materials for spontaneous play.

In an adventure playground there is space to let off steam, materials for building, painting, carpentry and dressing up. *The Listener, April 16, 1970, p 57*

Sir John Nelson, general secretary, said that an adventure playground was needed every half mile in each big city. *The Times (London), Sept. 26, 1970, p 2*

ae·quor·in (i'kwɔr ən), *n.* a luminescent substance secreted by the jellyfish *Aequorea aequorea,* used in the optical examination of events occurring within cells.

The protein, which they named aequorin, emits a beautiful bluish light, and the agent that causes it to do so is the calcium ion. *Graham Hoyle, "How Is Muscle Turned On and Off?" Scientific American, April 1970, p 90*

. . . techniques have been developed which allow the injection in sufficient quantities of aequorin into large muscle fibres from barnacles and giant nerve axons from squid. *New Scientist, July 16, 1970, p 121*

aeroallergen, *n.* a substance in the air that causes or induces an allergy; an airborne allergen.

Advances in Environmental Sciences, Vol. I. . . . Deals with the application of science and technology to the control and improvement of environmental quality, in specific areas such as oxides of nitrogen, biodegradable detergents, and aeroallergens and public health. *"Books of the Week," Science News, March 14, 1970, p 279*

aerobics, *n.* a system of building up the body by means of exercises which develop the use of oxygen by the body. *Also used attributively.*

. . . I had in the meantime switched to Aerobics, and my lungs and heart were correspondingly mightier. *Harold Broadkey, The New Yorker, Jan. 25, 1969, p 28*

An aerobics fan must attain a weekly score of at least 30 points on Cooper's scale [Kenneth Hardy Cooper, inventor of the system]. *Time, March 8, 1971, p 30*

[from the adjective *aerobic,* applied to organisms that thrive only in the presence of oxygen; ultimately from Greek *āér* air + *bíos* life]

aer·on·o·my (er'ɑn ə mi:), *n.* a science dealing with the upper atmosphere of the earth or other body in space.

The "Eltanin" . . . had traveled in some of the coldest weather and roughest waters in the world, providing . . . observations on physical and chemical oceanography, aeronomy, meteorology, marine geology, geophysics, and ornithology. *Laurence M. Gould, "Antarctica," Britannica Book of the Year 1968, p 95*

[from *aero-* atmosphere + *-nomy,* as in *astronomy*]

aeroplankton, *n.* the microorganisms of the air.

At considerable altitudes above the earth's surface the spores of bacteria and fungi can be obtained by passing air through filters. In general, however, such "aeroplankton" do not appear to be engaged in active metabolism. *G. Evelyn Hutchinson, Scientific American, Sept. 1970, p 45*

aerotrain, *n.* a train that is an air cushion vehicle running on a concrete track.

Only one out of four and a half Parisians will commute in the year 2000, compared with one in three at present, but even in that advanced space age 12,500 solid citizens will commute by foot rather than be packed into aerotrains or the like. *Joseph Carroll, The Manchester Guardian Weekly, Sept. 8, 1966, p 7*

France's new wheelless "aerotrain" broke the world record for track vehicles, its builders claimed, by doing 215 mph. *Tom Wicker, "Roundup of 1967," 1968 Collier's Encyclopedia Year Book, p xix*

[from French *Aérotrain,* the name of the prototype]

aflatoxin, *n.* a poisonous substance secreted by some strains of a common mold, *Aspergillus flavus,* found especially on peanuts, cottonseed, and corn. Aflatoxin is thought to cause certain cancers in animals as well as abnormalities in human chromosomes.

The discovery of the toxicity of peanuts contaminated with aflatoxin led food technologists throughout the world to give careful consideration to the occurrence of other toxicants in foods. . . . *Henry B. Hawley, "Natural Toxic Agents in Foods," Britannica Book of the Year 1969, p 346*

[from *A*spergillus *fl*avus + *toxin*]

Afro, *n.* a bushy way of arranging the hair, originally fashioned on an African style. Also shortened to 'FRO.

Michael, with the loveliest, fullest, twelve-year-old Afro you'll hope to see, has the history of the group down pat . . . . *"Music—the Jackson Five at Home," Time, June 14, 1971, p 48*

—adj.

It [a shop] has posters of Rap, Stokely, Eldridge, and Malcolm along with the dashikis, clenched fists and afro combs. *The New York Times, June 11, 1971, p 35*

The girl was rather light-skinned, with an Afro hair-do cut like a loaf of bread; she spoke to Bech in a voice from which all traces of Dixie had been clipped. *John Updike, Bech: A Book, 1970, p 113*

—adv. or predicate adj.

Since last June, Laura has been wearing her hair Afro. "My God, yes, black is beautiful," says Laura. *"Getting It Together: The Young Blacks," Time, April 6, 1970, p 46*

Afro-Americanese, *n.* another name for BLACK ENGLISH.

33

The language is Afro-Americanese, and the point is a plague o' both your houses — although Mr. Killens understandably hopes Whitey's plague will be a bit worse. *Phoebe Adams, "Short Reviews: Books," Review of "The Cotillion or One Good Bull is Half the Herd" by John Oliver Killens, The Atlantic, Feb. 1971, p 129*

Afro-Americanism, *n.* American Negro culture.

The rush is on. Come and get it: Afro-Americanism, black studies, the Negro heritage. From Harvard to Ocean Hill, from Duke to Madison Avenue, they are trying, as they say, to restore the Negro to his rightful place in American history and culture. . . . *Peter Schrag, "The New Black Myths," Harper's, May 1969, p 37*

Afro-American studies, a program of courses, especially in a college or university, dealing with African and American Negro history, culture, and contemporary affairs. Also called BLACK STUDIES.

Black students argue that the goal of Harvard's Afro-American studies should be to build up the black liberationist mentality and teach specific skills that can aid its cause. *Time, Jan. 26, 1970, p 44*

Af·roed ('æf roud), *adj.* wearing an Afro.

In Manhattan, . . . Afroed young blacks and a scattering of long-haired whites demonstrated in Angela's [Angela Davis's] support. . . . *Time, Oct. 26, 1970, p 28*

Afroism, *n.* interest in and devotion to black African culture and the expansion of black African power. Compare NEGRITUDE.

Afroism is still alive. Stokely Carmichael lives in Dar-es-Salaam, dashikis still sell, and the Afro hair style is ever more popular. But this cultural nostalgia is rather like long hair on white students — a matter of fashion and radical chic. Of much greater importance is the organisation muscle in African affairs developed over the past three years by several groups of young professional blacks. *Martin Walker, The Manchester Guardian Weekly, May 22, 1971, p 16*

Afro-Saxon, *n.* a black man who is part of the white establishment or is in favor of working within the white establishment.

Many West Indians maintain that black power against black governments makes little sense. But militants dismiss their present leaders as "Afro-Saxons" and press for revolutionary change. *Time, May 4, 1970, p 48*

—*adj.* consisting of Afro-Saxons; having the outlook or attitude of Afro-Saxons.

As in Bermuda, Jamaica, and elsewhere in the English-speaking West Indies, dissident black citizens continued to rally round extremist banners to oppose their own elected, so-called "Afro-Saxon" governments. *Philip Kopper, "Biography," Britannica Book of the Year 1971, p 162*

afterheat, *n.* the residual heat produced by a nuclear reactor. *Often used attributively.*

Mr. Jacobs chose to ignore the editor's note preceding my article in which he said, "The failures analyzed in this article occurred in the afterheat system of the Oak Ridge Research Reactor and therefore it is worthwhile to note that it has been determined that at its present operating power of 30 MW, the ORR requires no forced convection afterheat removal." In other words, the failure is of academic interest only. *Elbert P. Epler, Oak Ridge, Tenn., in a Letter to the Editor, The Atlantic, June 1971, p 36*

age-ism, *n.* discriminatory practices against the aged.

It is as though the aged were an alien race to which the young will never belong. Indeed, there is a distinct discrimination against the old that has been called age-ism. In its simplest form, says Psychiatrist Robert Butler of Washington, D.C., age-ism is just "not wanting to have all these ugly old people around." Butler believes that in 25 or 30 years, age-ism will be a problem equal to racism. *Time, Aug. 3, 1970, p 49*

[patterned after *racism.* Compare SEXISM.]

Age of Aquarius, an epoch of the world described by astrologers as marking the advent of freedom in all areas of life, the rule of brotherhood on earth, and the conquest of outer space. The notion of astrological epochs developed during the Renaissance, when it was widely believed that the conjunction of certain planets . . . gave rise to new religions. See also AQUARIAN.

. . . the Senate's minority leader . . . warned his colleagues that "Clearly the temper of this Age of Aquarius calls for less bureaucratic omphaloskepsis [meditation while contemplating one's navel]." *Robert Bendiner, The New York Times, Jan. 19, 1970, p 46*

Evangelist Billy Graham, in New York City for a crusade at Shea Stadium, fingered his collar-length silver-blond curls and gave his blessing to the Age of Aquarius. "I don't object to long hair in any way," he insists. "I have nothing but love for those who wear it." Today Billy Graham, tomorrow the world. *Time, July 6, 1970, p 6*

ag·gior·na·men·to (ə,dʒɔr nə'men tou), *n.* the policy of updating or modernizing Roman Catholic doctrines and institutions, adopted as one of the goals of the Second Vatican Council 1962-1965.

Without mentioning any of these activities, the Pontiff made it clear that the idea of aggiornamento, or updating, projected by the late Pope John in calling the Council could not be distorted to cover change. *Robert C. Doty, The New York Times, April 26, 1968, p 38*

[from Italian *aggiornamento,* literally, a bringing up to date, from *aggiornare* to bring up to date, from *a-* to + *giorno* day]

aggro, *n. British Slang.* **1** aggressiveness.

The styling for all mannequins, black or white, is more sophisticated, more gentle, both in England and in Europe. Afro with no aggro, you could say. *Prudence Glynn, The Times (London), May 5, 1970, p 9*

He [John Kenneth Galbraith] enjoyed the status and glamour of high duty . . . yet is enraged by the crude aggro, the administration's most frequent posture. . . . *Kenneth Allsop, "America Abroad," Punch, Nov. 12, 1969, p 801*

2 aggression. Also spelled AGRO.

Ardrey enters the debate quite specifically when dealing with violence and aggression. The latter, he implies, is a term which includes the striving of plants and animals to grow. . . . Thus to Ardrey life itself is no more than one long aggro. . . . *Robin Clarke, "New Books," Review of "The Social Contract" by Robert Ardrey, Science Journal, Jan. 1971, p 94*

Agnewism, *n.* **1** the ideas and views of U.S. Vice-President Spiro T. Agnew, especially his emphasis on law and order.

Does not New York wish to stand out against Agnewism, the Southern strategy, the debauching of the Supreme Court, the attack on dissent and the fake issues and false choices the administration seeks to make the pivots of our politics? *Arthur Schlesinger, Jr., The New York Times, Oct. 30, 1970, p 40*

2 a word, phrase, or statement expressing such views.

Whenever President Nixon has been confronted with an Agnewism and asked if it was the Administration's view, the President has always said that Mr Agnew "speaks for himself." *Alistair Cooke, The Manchester Guardian Weekly, July 11, 1970, p 3*

ag·o·ra·pho·bic (ˌæg ər əˈfou bik), *n.* a person who has an abnormal fear of open spaces. Compare CLAUSTROPHOBIC.

She [Freda Wenham] has seven children but that is not her problem. [She] is an agoraphobic. She suffers from a morbid fear of public places and for seven years has been a virtual prisoner in her Brighton home. *Helen Davis, "Freda Wenham's Phobia," The Sunday Times (London), April 25, 1971, p 37*

► This is a noun use of the adjective *agoraphobic*. The usual noun ending for one suffering from a specific phobia is *-phobe*, as in *acrophobe, Anglophobe, heliophobe*; we would therefore expect *agoraphobe*.

agro, *n. British Slang.* another spelling of AGGRO.

The skinheads live for "agro" (causing "aggravation") and "bovver" (street fighting). While they favor the boot as a primary weapon, they also use their heads to "nut" or butt a victim, and whatever other weapons come to hand: bricks, rocks, bottles, knives, and razors. *Time, June 8, 1970, p 37*

Agro-boy, *n. British Slang.* another name for SKINHEAD.

In the lower depths the Agro-boys have already emerged to present a caricature of working-class conservatism and prejudice. Anti-intellectual, anti-layabout, anti-foreign (the exception they have made in favour of West Indians more than compensated by their hatred and persecution of Pakistanis). *George Melly, Revolt Into Style, 1970, p 251*

agrochemicals, *n.pl.* agricultural chemicals.

In agrochemicals, Fisons depends heavily on licenses from other companies. *The Times (London), Feb. 19, 1970, p 27*

agro-industry, *n.* an agricultural industry.

Barbara Ward recommends creating rural agricultural centers that would provide the "agro-industries" necessary to employ the peasants left jobless by the Green Revolution — warehouses, fertilizer plants, facilities to manufacture silos and other storage units, work forces for loading and shipping. *Time, July 13, 1970, p 27*

a·hem·er·al (eiˈhem ər əl), *adj.* not constituting a full day.

In the process Wolfson employed unnatural ahemeral cycles of light and dark; that is, cycles not totalling 24 hours. *Ronald Murton, "Behind the Face of the Biological Clock," New Scientist and Science Journal, July 29, 1971, p 254*

[from *a-* not + Greek *hēméra* day + English *-al*]

ai·ki·do (aiˈki: dou), *n.* a Japanese method of self-defense consisting of a series of holds and throws that involve strong powers of concentration and a harmonious coordination of body movements.

To avoid the danger of developing a fighting mental attitude, there are no competitive matches in the art of aikido and kyudo. *Jonathan R. Eley and Martin Patrick Myrieckes, "Special Report: The Art of Self-Defense," The 1970 Compton Yearbook, p 445*

[from Japanese *aikidō*]

airbag, *n.* a sturdy plastic bag stored in an automobile dashboard and designed to inflate immediately upon collision to form a protective cushion.

Safety features — especially the controversial safety air bags — captured wide attention. . . . Ford hinted that the air bags would appear on one of its models as early as 1971. *Jim Dunne, "Automobiles," The 1970 Compton Yearbook, p 139*

Both these cars also have air-bags instead of safety belts. *The Sunday Times (London), April 25, 1971, p 1*

. . . Volvo engineers are a little worried that the airbag, for instance, will be imposed on them before their own very detailed examination of its value and feasibility has been completed. *Ian Breach, The Manchester Guardian Weekly, Sept. 5, 1970, p 16*

air bearing, a bearing in which a shaft or other moving part is supported by the pressure of thin jets of air.

Or you can take the sort of work that is going on in the National Engineering Laboratory on air bearings. If air bearings were to be widely used in industry, this would make a tremendous difference to the noise level in factories. *Anthony Wedgwood Benn, The Times (London), March 29, 1968, p 25*

Air bearings can be connected to any convenient source of compressed air and usually require little pressure. *Time, Nov. 22, 1968, p 63*

air bridge, a link or passage formed between two or more places by aircraft.

An air bridge formed by 159 chartered flights linked Rotterdam and Glasgow with Milan yesterday. *The Times (London), May 8, 1970, p 4*

. . . with an air-bridge to the "revolutionary airport" before or shortly after the fighting was over, they quickly replenished his [King Hussein's] rapidly depleted armoury. *David Hirst, "Hard Winter for Guerrillas," The Manchester Guardian Weekly, Jan. 2, 1971, p 5*

airbus, *n.* a jet aircraft designed to carry passengers on short to medium-range flights.

As air traffic grows thicker, collisions become more likely. The advent of very large passenger-carrying aircraft — the Boeing 747 and later the "airbus" types brings with it the frightening possibility of almost a thousand people dying in a single collision. *Victor Attwooll, New Scientist, Dec. 10, 1970, p 144*

Mr. Sheinin [a Soviet aircraft designer], who has been writing widely on the general concept of the airbus . . . expects subsonic airbuses and supersonic liners to complement each other in the civil-aviation systems of the late nineteen-seventies and through the nineteen-eighties. *Theodore Shabad, "Soviet Shows Model of Airbus, A 350-Seater Due in 3 Years," The New York Times, May 6, 1972, p 5*

Aircav, *n.* a unit of the U.S. armed forces conveyed by aircraft to combat areas.

By now the Aircav, too, has realigned its forces after the first days of hectic seizing of opportunity. *Fred Emery, The Times (London), May 18, 1970, p 6*

air cushion vehicle, *U.S. and Canada.* a vehicle that travels above the ground or water on a cushion of air produced by propellers or fans. The equivalent term in Great Britain is HOVERCRAFT. The abbreviation, *ACV*, is probably more frequently used in the United States than *air cushion vehicle.* Also called GROUND EFFECT MACHINE.

A flexible rubber "skirt" around the edge of an air cushion vehicle (ACV) traps air pulled down between the water's surface and the bottom of the ACV by two huge fans. *Science News, June 4, 1966, p 445*

Quicker exploitation of the mineral riches of Canada's polar continental shelf is in prospect as a result of the development . . . of a new highspeed method for hydrographic survey in ice-infested waters. The new method was born from the marriage of an air cushion vehicle (ACV) to a towed body hydrographic sounding system. *"ACV Makes Soundings Through Ice," Science Journal, May 1969, p 17*

airhouse, *n.* an inflated plastic structure used especially to shelter building operations.

For the desired outdoor memorial purpose, the heavier, self-sealing fabric used for inflatable air-houses might provide the puncture-proofing needed to deflect the penknives of schoolboys and the bullets of symbolic assassins. *Patrick Ryan, "And the Last Word . . . on Statues," New Scientist and Science Journal, April 8, 1971, p 71*

air miss, *British.* an official designation for a narrow escape from collision by two aircraft flying too close to each other.

Yesterday's incident, with at least half a mile separating the two aircraft, falls into the category of an "air miss" rather than a "near miss," one of the dozen or so reported by pilots over Britain every month. *John Chartres, The Times (London), Feb. 6, 1970, p 4*

airmobile, *adj. U.S.* consisting of or relating to troops moved to combat zones by helicopters.

In an effort to bolster its mobility and firepower in Vietnam, the Army has decided to convert a paratroop division into an airmobile division. *The New York Times, May 10, 1968, p 12*

More pilots were necessary because the Army was making greater use of airmobile tactics in Vietnam. Since the beginning of the Vietnam buildup, more than 1,000 Army units have been activated. *"Army, United States," The 1967 Compton Yearbook, p 124*

air piracy, the hijacking of an aircraft. Also called SKYJACKING.

Aircraft and passengers in this new air piracy are kidnapped and held to ransom under threat of death, and aircraft wantonly destroyed as acts of nihilistic revenge. *John F. Thompson, The Manchester Guardian Weekly, Sept. 19, 1970, p 2*

Americans have been hit hardest by air piracy. Yet the United States Government does nothing against air pirates and proposes additional taxes on American travelers to finance new security measures. *Harry J. Lipkin, Rehovoth, Israel, in a Letter to the Editor, The New York Times, Nov. 12, 1970, p 42*

air pirate, a person who hijacks an aircraft. Also called SKYJACKER. See also the quotations for AIR PIRACY.

They [terrorists] include all air pirates and all who attack and murder the occupants of school buses and all unarmed civilians. *Terence Prittie, The Times (London), Sept. 11, 1970, p 11*

airspace, *n.* radio frequency channels; airways.

But the black reality is that the Marine Offences Act forbids British firms to use pirate airspace. *Michael Bateman, The Sunday Times (London), June 20, 1971, p 15*

▶ The older meanings are (1) a space filled with air, and (2) the space above an area or country.

air-taxi, *n.* a small passenger airplane making local flights in or between cities and towns not serviced by regular airlines. *Also used attributively.*

Anguilla is in the sterling area, and an air-taxi to St. Martin costs only two guineas. *Graham Norton, The Sunday Times (London), Dec. 29, 1968, p 30*

A flying buff, he owns a small air-taxi service with a fleet of three STOL (for short takeoff and landing) airplanes in the San Francisco area. *Time, Nov. 8, 1968, p 69*

—*v.i.* to make local flights; fly short runs.

"Our strategy," he [Mayor John Lindsay, of New York] said, "is to encourage the transfer of private air traffic to other than the major airports. That's why we are working so hard on STOL-port facilities attached to Manhattan.

"The private planes then could use other airports and air-taxi into Manhattan." *Richard Witkin, The New York Times, July 27, 1968, p 53*

a·lap (ɑːˈlɑːp), *n.* the first movement in the performance of a typical raga, the traditional Hindu musical form. Compare JOR, GAT.

. . . he [Ravi Shankar] broke off his *alap* (or rhythmless introductory section) in order to bow to applause before beginning the *gath* proper, which is something that would not happen in India. *Winthrop Sargeant, "Musical Events," The New Yorker, Sept. 21, 1968, p 138*

Its *alap* (the uncadenced statement of a *raga's* emotive and melodic potential with which its elaboration is always preceded) was played with apt indifference to gushing phraseology. *The Times (London), May 27, 1968, p 14*

[from Sanskrit *alāp*]

à la page (a la ˈpaʒ), *French.* up-to-date; keeping up with the latest fashion.

His became a name—not famous, but one of those names that people mention to show they are à la page. . . . *Shirley Hazzard, The Bay of Noon, 1970, p 79*

▶ In French this phrase is virtually obsolete among the younger half of the population, who now use *dans le vent* (literally, in the wind) for this sense.

alarm bells, a signal of danger or warning that causes apprehension.

Upon my departure a few months later I thought it right—for a variety of reasons—to sound the alarm bells ringing and this I attempted to do within the columns of your paper. *Robert Lusty, Hampstead, England, in a Letter to the Editor, The Times (London), Feb. 18, 1970, p 9*

To be sure, everybody connected with the scheme avoids with horror this kind of language, and some of my informants will be provoked with me for using terms which could touch off alarm bells on Capitol Hill. *John Fischer, "The Easy Chair," Harper's, Nov. 1970, p 22*

► *Alarm bell* or *alarum bell* was the term used from at least the time of Shakespeare (cf. Henry IV, Part II; III, i,17) to Poe's day (cf. *The Bells*) to designate "the tocsin of burghs in olden times" (*Oxford English Dictionary*).

al den·te (ɑːl 'den tei), *Italian.* cooked so as to be firm or not too soft.

It [rice] was too hastily cooked, a little too much *al dente*, and there was too much saffron in it. . . . *M. F. K. Fisher, The New Yorker, Nov. 16, 1968, p 178*

Put linguine in boiling water and cook according to direction on the package or until test strands come up al dente or firm "to the tooth." *Raymond A. Sokolov, The New York Times, June 24, 1971, p 44*

a·le·a·tor·ic (ˌei liː ə'tɔr ik), *adj.* (of a musical composition) performed so that the outcome is dependent on chance. Also, ALEATORY.

There is a certain amount of aleatoric, or chance, music here and there, but the structure of the work is entirely tonal, or perhaps one should say "modal," because of the frequent use of Oriental scales. *Winthrop Sargeant, "Musical Events," The New Yorker, Nov. 9, 1968, p 178*

. . . Mr. Kay's partly aleatoric score, which he himself conducted, has a brightness yet power that is just right. *The New York Times, Feb. 29, 1968, p 28*

[from Latin *āleātōrius* dependent on chance (from *āleātor* gambler, player with dice) + English *-ic*]

a·le·a·tor·ism (ˌei liː'æt əˌriz əm), *n.* dependence on chance in the performance of music.

Although the overall forms of the three settings are fixed, the score makes use of a device known as controlled aleatorism. *Tim Souster, "Music: Last Week's Broadcast Music," The Listener, April 18, 1968, p 513*

Its characteristically controlled aleatorism produced a broadly conceived structure, in which the musical tension and weight of the simple block sections were so judged as to produce a most satisfying formal direction. *The Times (London), March 2, 1968, p 19*

a·le·a·tor·y ('ei liː əˌtɔr iː), *adj.* another word for ALEATORIC.

Mr. Joachim's "Contrastes" is not music at all. It is a collection of sound effects, and it has aleatory passages. (All aleatory — or "anything goes" — music is a bore.) *Winthrop Sargeant, "Musical Events," The New Yorker, Feb. 10, 1968, p 109*

ALGOL or **Algol** ('ælˌgɑl), *n.* acronym for *Algorithmic Language*, a computer language using algebraic notation. Compare BASIC, COBOL, FORTRAN.

The school-children were helped by three circumstances; they were young, they were using Algol — a powerful programming language — and they had a clear understanding of the problems they were solving. *R. E. Giles, "Starting Young With Computers" New Scientist, Jan. 5, 1967, p 36*

Alice-in-Wonderland, *adj.* existing in fantasy; unreal or illogical; self-contradictory. Compare LOOKING-GLASS.

The recent United States Supreme Court decision (North Carolina v. Alford) which permitted a defendant to plead guilty to a crime while simultaneously expressly contending his innocence makes me wonder in what kind of Alice-in-Wonderland world our criminal court system operates. *David Blackstone, New York, in a Letter to the Editor. The New York Times, Dec. 8, 1970, p 46*

a·li·yah (ɑː liː'yɑː), *n. Hebrew.* Jewish immigration into Israel. Compare OLIM.

Israel has not exactly discouraged the nationalistic upsurge, since it looks to Russia, with its 3.5 million mostly skilled and educated Jews, as one of the last remaining sources of a sorely needed aliyah — literally ascent — or wave of immigrants. *Time, May 31, 1971, p 26*

all-at-once-ness, *n.* the condition in which many things happen or are experienced at the same time.

Central to his [Marshall McLuhan's] theories — or "probes," as he calls them — is the insight that technology is profoundly reshaping modern man: Instead of "the alphabet and print technology," which fostered fragmentation, mechanization, specialization, detachment and privacy, we now have an "electric technology," which fosters unification, involvement, "all-at-once-ness" and a lack of goals. *John Leo, The New York Times, May 26, 1968, p 72*

The all-at-onceness of the "field approach" to problems is rapidly replacing the fixed, visual approach of applied or "resolute" knowledge. *Robert Lewis Shayon, Saturday Review, April 15, 1967, p 46*

all-nighter, *n.* something that lasts all night.

And there, in the midst of the latest creations for war, there is a Pan American 707 of all things, ludicrously out of place, like a dowager at a hippie all-nighter. *Bernard Kalb, Saturday Review, Nov. 30, 1968, p 27*

Time on the machine [a generator] needs to be booked in advance and due to high demand it often entails an all-night stand. Callaghan is trying to circumvent these enforced all-nighters by building a set-up which uses a superconducting magnetic for the adiabatic demagnetisation. *Gerald Wick, New Scientist and Science Journal, Feb. 18, 1971, p 382*

allograft, *n.* a graft of tissue taken from another individual's body. Compare XENOGRAFT.

Skin loss from burns and extensive traumatic avulsions were treated in 41 infants and children (New Orleans, La.) by temporary cutaneous allografts of adult cadaver or fetal origin. *"Surgery," Britannica Book of the Year 1970, p 520*

. . . earthworms *(Eisenia foetida typica)* from one geographical region rejected first-set allografts from worms of other regions. *New Scientist, Nov. 20, 1969, p 391*

[from Greek *állos* other + English *graft*]

al·lo·pu·rin·ol (ˌæl ou'pyur əˌnɔːl), *n.* a drug that prevents the formation of uric acid in the blood.

Allopurinol, originally regarded as a drug that specifically inhibits the enzyme xanthine oxidase, inhibits other liver enzymes as well, Dr. Vesell reports. The drug is taken by thousands of patients with gout. *Science News, July 11, 1970, p 37*

[from Greek *állos* other + English *purine* + *-ol* (chemical suffix)]

al·lo·ster·ic (ˌæl ə'ster ik), *adj.* involving a change in the shape of an enzyme at a site other than the catalytic site.

. . . allosteric effects can make big differences to enzyme activity in the direction both of stimulation and inhibition. *John C. Marsden, New Scientist, Jan. 22, 1970, p 155*

[from Greek *állos* other + *stereós* solid + English *-ic*]

al·lo·ster·y (ə'lɑs tər i:), *n.* allosteric condition or effect.

The enzymes that make up the metabolism of the living cell change their shape as they work. . . . Though the theory was propounded some time ago, this is the first direct evidence of the phenomenon, known as allostery. *Barbara Ford, "Biology: Enzyme Changes Shape,", Collier's Encyclopedia Year Book 1970, p 138*

all-terrain vehicle, a light-weight, rugged motor vehicle for travel over rough terrain. *Abbreviation:* ATV

Proliferating from Maine to California, they [off-road vehicles] now include 200,000 dune buggies, 2,000,000 trail bikes, 1,100,000 snowmobiles and, newest of all, 25,000 all-terrain vehicles (ATV's). *Time, Nov. 23, 1970, p 41*

alm, *n.* a charitable gift.

He was a squire to the last second of his life. He never gave anything that wasn't an alm — even his love. *Isaac Bashevis Singer, "The Egotist," The New Yorker, Jan. 16, 1971, p 35*

► The new singular *alm* is a back formation of the singular and plural *alms*, whose final *-s* has been long taken as a plural inflection in such constructions as "For alms are but the vehicles of prayer" (John Dryden, *The Hind and the Panther*, 1687). This formation parallels the classic instance of *pea*, which evolved from the earlier singular and plural *pease*.

Al·ma·nach de Go·tha ('ɔ:l mə,næk də 'gou θə), the royalty of Europe.

This week, with half the Almanach de Gotha joined by Neil Armstrong, sacrificial lamb of modern capitalism, and Bob Hope, the US Army's court jester, ECY [European Conservation Year] in Britain has come officially to an end. *Jon Tinker, New Scientist, Dec. 10, 1970, p 463*

[generic use of the name of a statistical publication which lists in detail the genealogies of the European royal families, published since the 1700's, originally in Gotha, Germany]

alpha-helical, *adj.* consisting of a single spiral or coil.

Myoglobin is made up of straight runs of alpha-helix from one side of the molecule to the other, so that about three quarters of the whole chain is in the alpha-helical form. *David Blow, New Scientist, Oct. 26, 1967, p 219*

alpha helix, the single spiral or coil structure of certain protein molecules. Compare DOUBLE HELIX.

It seemed almost unbelievable that the RNA structure was solved, that the answer was incredibly exciting, and that our names would be associated with the double helix as [Linus] Pauling's was with the alpha-helix. *James D. Watson, "The Double Helix," The Atlantic, Feb. 1968, p 112*

A line of hydrogen bonds forms the backbone of the alpha helix of a protein; the base pairs of the famed double helix of DNA are joined by hydrogen bonds. . . . *Amos de-Shalit, "Books," Review of "Hydrogen Bonding in Solids: Methods of Molecular Structure Determination" by Walter C. Hamilton and James A. Ibers, Scientific American, Nov. 1968, p 166*

al·pha·met·ic (,æl fə'met ik), *n.* a type of mathematical puzzle in which an arithmetical problem is presented with letters instead of numerals, each letter standing for a particular but different digit.

This cryptarithm (or alphametic, as many puzzlists prefer to call them) is an old one of unknown origin. . . . *Martin Gardner, "Mathematical Games," Scientific American, Feb. 1970, p 112*

[from *alpha*bet + arith*metic*]

alphascope, *n.* a device on a computer which displays words and symbols on a screen.

An alphascope is basically a keyboard, on which the operator types to communicate with the computer, and a CRT [cathode-ray tube] screen on which the computer replies. *R. Elliot Green, "Interactive Computer Graphics," Science Journal, Oct. 1970, p 67*

The simplest use of the CRT is a device called the alphascope, which replaces the teletype printer by presenting the words and symbols on a screen instead of on paper. *Robert Parslow, "Thinking with the Machine," New Scientist, June 4, 1970, p 7*

A higher resolution cathode-ray tube to write alphanumeric characters is used as a visual display unit or "alphascope", thus providing a silent method of fast information retrieval. *Bob Parslow, "Time Sharing — New Computer Revolution," New Scientist, Jan. 2, 1969, p 17*

[from *alpha*numeric (using both letters and numbers) + *-scope* instrument for viewing]

alternative society, a society representing cultural values other than those of the present social order.

In late 1969, Theodore Roszak published his book "The Making of a Counter-Culture" which talked of the youth movement as an alternative society and as a valid culture with its own art, its own music, and its own vocabulary. . . . And as long as marijuana is smoked, that sacrament of the youth culture, something of the alternative society will remain. And in the last resort America is rich enough to support a parasite group or an alternative society. . . . *Martin Walker, "Economics of Dropping Out," The Manchester Guardian Weekly, April 3, 1971, p 6*

a·man·ta·dine (ə'mæn tə,di:n), *n.* Full name, **amantadine hydrochloride.** a synthetic chemical that inhibits the penetration of viruses into cells. Amantadine is used against Asian influenza and is reported to be effective against Parkinson's disease, though it is not a vaccine nor an antibiotic.

From experiments with dogs, Drs. R. P. Grelak, R. Clark, J. M. Stump and V. G. Vernier conclude that amantadine releases catecholamines, neurohormones, from storage sites in peripheral nerve tissue. "We think that amantadine may have the same action within the central nervous system," they report. These hormones, particularly dopamine, play an intimate role in the tremors experienced by patients with Parkinson's disease. *Science News, July 25, 1970, p 63*

The drug is amantadine hydrochloride. It was tried out on 37 patients and one of the points emphasized is that for all practical purposes side or toxic effects were absent. *The Times (London), Feb. 6, 1970, p 4*

[formed by alteration (influenced by *amine*) of *adamantane*, an organic compound]

ambisextrous, *adj.* sexually attracted to or involved with both sexes; bisexual.

In 1736 she [Lady Mary Wortley Montague] ran off to

Venice with a dreamily beautiful but coldly ambisextrous adventurer, to whom she wrote 26 stormy love letters that appear for the first time in these volumes. *Time, March 11, 1966, p 67*

[from *ambi-* both + *-sextrous*, by analogy with or as a pun on *ambidextrous*]

ambivalent, *n.* a bisexual person.

In any case, as a broad generalisation, provided that there is no "early" conditioning which makes homosexuality or heterosexuality the accepted norm, either or, indeed, both states can well be regarded as normal. End-product transvestists or ambivalents would continue to be the exception. In a word such people may be and often are homosexuals but homosexuals are rarely the transvestists or ambivalents. *Rowland Bowen, Cornwall, England, in a Letter to the Editor, New Scientist, Dec. 17, 1970, p 522*

[noun use of the adjective *ambivalent*]

Amerasian, *adj.* of mixed American and Asian descent.

. . . this book [*For Spacious Skies* by Pearl S. Buck] deals with the author's concern and efforts to help the Amerasian children of U.S. servicemen in Korea, Japan, Okinawa and Vietnam. *Science News, Aug. 27, 1966, p 140*

—n. a person of mixed American and Asian descent.

Among the Thais, they are referred to as red-haired babies. Among the sociologists concerned with the problem, they are called Amerasians. *Terence Smith, The New York Times, April 30, 1968, p 6*

[from *American* + *Asian*, patterned after *Eurasian* of mixed European and Asian descent]

American Dream, 1 a widely used catchphrase for the ideals of democracy, equality, and freedom upon which the United States was founded.

The Hornell Farm that Hicks painted about 1848 is nothing less than the American dream made tangible. Human beings are there in the background. Portraits of cattle and horses fill the foreground. *Michael McNay, "The Artless Americans," The Manchester Guardian Weekly, Sept. 19, 1968, p 21*

Unlike Consciousness I, Consciousness II [terms coined by Charles Reich in *The Greening of America*, 1970] people are aware of the erosion of the American Dream. But they are equally out of date. *Time, Nov. 2, 1970, p 13*

2 the American way of life; American culture or society.

The American Dream—even if some of us see it as a nightmare—has become the common property, and fare, of the entire world. *Kenneth Allsop, "Utopia Inc.," Punch, March 5, 1969, p 361*

. . . black people have all too often found the American dream a nightmare. *DeVere E. Pentony, "The Case For Black Studies," The Atlantic, April 1969, p 81*

▶ The term may have been popularized by its use as the title of various literary works, notably *The American Dream* (1961), a play by Edward Albee, and *An American Dream* (1965) by Norman Mailer.

Americanologist, *n.* an expert on the American government and its policies. Compare KREMLINOLOGIST.

The most important one, titled "Questions calling for a Practical Answer," was written by Georgy Arbatov, director of Moscow's U.S.A. Research Institute and widely regarded as the Kremlin's foremost Americanologist. *Time, Aug. 23, 1971, p 10*

Anatoly Gromyko, the 37-year-old son of the Soviet Foreign Minister, who resigned from the diplomatic service after rising to the rank of First Secretary at the London Embassy is now one of Russia's leading "Americanologists." *Victor Zorza, The Manchester Guardian Weekly, Dec. 6, 1969, p 6*

Americanophobe, *n.* a person who hates the United States.

. . . neither hippies nor militant students, neither war resisters nor Americanophobes, whatever view one may take of their acts or goals, resemble the old intelligentsia in its heyday. . . . *Isaiah Berlin, "The Role of the Intelligentsia," The Listener, May 2, 1968, p 565*

American Selling Price, the price charged by American manufacturers for a product, used to determine the amount of duty to be paid on a similar product imported into the United States, instead of basing the duty on the actual cost of the product to an importer.

The Administration, ignoring chemical industry pleas that it be retained, urged the repeal of the American Selling Price (ASP), a method of customs valuation that has protected U.S. dyestuff producers since the 1920s. *Arthur R. Kavaler, "Chemical Industry," The 1970 World Book Year Book, p 267*

Americologue, *n.* a student of American society.

Some months ago, one of our leading Americologues— Sir Denis Brogan, I think—complained of a callow cult of Los Angeles among the young. *Reyner Banham, "Encounter with Sunset Boulevard [Los Angeles]," The Listener, Aug. 22, 1968, p 235*

[from *Americo-* American + *-logue* student, as in *Sinologue*]

am·ni·o·cen·te·sis (ˌæm ni: ou sen'ti: sis), *n.* the insertion of a hypodermic needle into the amniotic sac to withdraw fluid for analysis of the embryo's cells.

Averting the birth of children with sexlinked disorders demands the identification of female carriers. At present the technique known as amniocentesis is used to withdraw a small number of cells from the amniotic fluid in order to type the embryo, and an abortion is induced if necessary. *R. G. Edwards and Ruth E. Fowler, "Human Embryos in the Laboratory," Scientific American, Dec. 1970, p 53*

[from *amnion* the membrane enveloping the fetus + *centesis* surgical puncture (from Greek *kéntēsis* a pricking)]

amniography, *n.* the process of taking an X-ray photograph of the amnion to locate defects in a fetus.

. . . amniography . . . entailed X-raying a pregnant woman to procure pictures of the amniotic fluid in the womb and of the condition of the placenta. . . . *Alexander Paton, Oglesby Paul, et al., "Medicine: Concern for the Unborn," The 1970 Compton Yearbook, p 339*

[from *amnion* the membrane enveloping the fetus + *-graphy* process of recording]

amnioscope, *n.* an instrument for examining the fetus within the amnion.

Several researchers . . . are trying to develop a "fetal amnioscope" that . . . would enable the doctor to view the fetus directly and take a sample of fetal blood and fetal skin, permitting a faster and more accurate diagnosis of more disorders than can now be diagnosed from amniotic fluid cells. *Jane E. Brody, The New York Times, June 3, 1971, p 53*

[from *amnion* the membrane enveloping the fetus + *-scope* instrument for viewing]

amnioscopy, *n.* examination with an amnioscope.

In some clinical centres, amnioscopy is performed on patients at high risk in the latter weeks of pregnancy. *Geoffrey Chamberlain, New Scientist, April 9, 1970, p 66*

amp, *n. U.S. Slang.* an electrically amplified guitar.

That year I got my very first really good guitar. . . . I got a $150 Les Paul, the one I cut my first record with. A friend of mine had an amplifier, and he lent that to me. When I paid Mr. Towater, that was his name, for the guitar, I got me a Gibson amp and then paid for that the next year. *Carl Perkins, "The Top Beats the Bottom," The Atlantic, Dec. 1970, p 98*

[shortened from *amplifier* or *amplified guitar*]

AMPase (‚ei‚em'pi:‚eis), *n.* an enzyme thought to be involved in the transport of ions across cell membranes.

In a very neat experiment James Gurd, also of NIMR [National Institute of Medical Research], London, has shown the enzyme AMPase to be present on some walls of liver cells and absent from others. "*New Evidence for Membrane Asymmetry," New Scientist and Science Journal, March 4, 1971, p 467*

[from *AMP* (abbreviation of *adenosine monophosphate,* a compound of adenosine, a constituent of nucleic acid, and one phosphate group) + *-ase* enzyme]

ampicillin, *n.* a type of penicillin that is more active against various bacteria and more resistant to the enzyme which destroys penicillin (penicillinase) than ordinary penicillin. Compare CLOXACILLIN, OXACILLIN.

. . . Dr. J. A. Clarke and Drs. A. J. Salisbury, O'Grady and Greenwood have photographed the effects of the synthetic penicillin ampicillin upon a staphylococcus and a streptococcus. *New Scientist, March 27, 1969, p 699*

One of these drugs is ampicillin, . . . which acts against *P. aeruginosa, S. aureus* and other micro-organisms that, in one of the great epics of self-defense in the natural world, came to dominate as mutant strains producing the enzyme penicillinase. *Science News, Aug. 22, 1970, p 164*

[from its chemical name *amino* benzyl *penicillin*]

Amtrak, *n. U.S.* a government-controlled public corporation, officially known as the National Railroad Passenger Corporation, created in 1970 to run the essential rail passenger service linking major cities which private enterprise is unable to provide.

Amtrak announces two kinds of savings for New York train travelers. . . . We're making the trains worth traveling again. For reservations or information, call your Amtrak Travel Agent. . . . *Advertisement by Amtrak, The New York Times, May 31, 1972, p 19*

A new system of rail passenger service is now being launched, called Amtrak, but on the principle that, being partly public and thus a form of socialism and thus wicked, it should be so bad as to discourage people from using it. *John Kenneth Galbraith, "North America," The Sunday Times (London), Nov. 7, 1971, p 92*

[irregular shortening of *American Track*]

analogue, *n.* a person's counterpart; one's opposite number.

The precise request transmitted to British Foreign Minister Douglas-Home July 8 by his Irish analogue, Patrick Hillery, is that London order its North Ireland satellite, the Stormont regime of Belfast, to cancel certain Protestant parades. . . . *C. L. Sulzberger, "Foreign Affairs: Again the Wild Irish," The New York Times, July 10, 1970, p 32*

an·ar·cho- (æn'ɑr kou-). This is a chiefly British combining form used in noun and adjective compounds and meaning "anarchist" or "anarchist and." Recently formed compounds include:

anarcho-authoritarianism, *n.:* What Berlin does not ask himself, however, is whether the rigid totalitarianism of a few decades ago—and we might raise the same question about the fluid anarcho-authoritarianism of today—is a phase in a prolonged crisis of Western civilization. . . . *Irving Howe, "Books," Review of "Four Essays on Liberty" by Isaiah Berlin, Harper's, Aug. 1970, p 94*

anarcho-liberal, *n.:* Tito himself said recently that "both dogmatists and anarcho-liberals" have been acting against the basic principles of the party. . . . *Sam Cohen, "Yugoslav Economy in Turmoil," The Manchester Guardian Weekly, Feb. 7, 1970, p 7*

anarcho-pacifist, *n.:* Anarcho-pacifists with strong lunatic leanings, their anti-imperialist non-violent protesting has, over the years, grown gradually more militant. *Punch, Dec. 17, 1969, p 996*

anarcho-revolutionary, *adj.:* The Greek Foreign Minister, Mr. Pipinelis, claimed in Athens yesterday that "an international anarcho-revolutionary movement," which had infiltrated Western parliamentary, political and intellectual circles, was instigating the world-wide campaign against Greece. *The Sunday Times (London), Dec. 21, 1969, p 6*

anarcho-situationist, *n.:* Nanterre has thrown up a new "extreme-extremist" group which has achieved the near-miracle of getting well left of the Maoists. . . . While the National Assembly in Paris was debating education policy last week, Nanterre was trying to elect a council. The anarcho-situationists stopped the voting by rampaging through the polling station. *The Times (London), April 20, 1970, p 9*

anarcho-socialist, *adj.:* The traditional centres of anarcho-socialist revolt in Barcelona and the coalmines of Asturias have now given way to the industrial workers in the Basque provinces. *The Manchester Guardian Weekly, Dec. 5, 1970, p 13*

Anglophone or **anglophone,** *n.* an English-speaking native or inhabitant of a country in which English is only one of two or more official languages. *Often used attributively.* Compare FRANCOPHONE.

It is because our fizzy Canadian cocktail has intoxicating qualities, because a dazzling future lies in wait for francophones and anglophones (or as international expert John Holmes said wittily, anglo-saxophones)—it is precisely for these reasons that we should hold together, along with the valuable New Canadians. *Alan Harvey, "St. Malo Letter," Saturday Night (Canada), Oct. 1967, p 19*

The second fact is that "the Westminister model", so assiduously bequeathed by Britain to the now independent Anglophone states in Africa, has proved to be neither suitable for African conditions nor acceptable to Africans. *John Fletcher-Cooke, Oxford, England, in a Letter to the Editor, The Times (London), Jan. 25, 1972, p 15*

[from French *anglophone*, from *anglo-* English + *-phone* speech (from Greek *phōné* voice, speech)]

Anglophonic, *adj.* of an Anglophone; attuned to English. Compare FRANCOPHONIC.

Humorous as Michael Bentine occasionally is, you need an Anglophonic ear and a history book to understand much of what is going on. *Douglas Marshall, "Television," Maclean's, Aug. 1968, p 58*

angries, *n.pl.* angry opponents or protesters against some social or political condition.

To demonstrate their disgust and alienation from sexist society, the angries picket the Miss America contest, burn brassières, and dump into "freedom trashcans" such symbols of female "oppression" as lingerie, false eyelashes and steno pads. *Time, Nov. 21, 1969, p 56*

Expectations are wrongly aroused by the conventional form of his [David Mercer's] plays and by the fact that his young angries do, as it happens, talk like real-life students. *D. A. N. Jones, The Listener, Aug. 8, 1968, p 162*

[originally *Angries*, shortened from *Angry Young Men*, name of a group of young British writers of the 1950's, including John Osborne, Kingsley Amis, John Braine, and Alan Sillitoe, whose works were marked by anger at social inequities. The group mentioned was not a real group in the sense of a school of writers banding together. The name *Angry Young Men* was coined by the British press.]

annihilate, *v.t.* to cause (a nuclear particle and an antiparticle) to unite and thereby change to another form of energy.

When a proton-antiproton pair is annihilated, mesons are emitted. These mesons rapidly decay to electrons, massless neutrinos and X rays. *Clifford E. Swartz, "Antimatter," Encyclopedia Science Supplement (Grolier) 1967, p 281*

Such anti-worlds, if they exist, would not be detectable by normal astronomical observation, while any collision of ordinary matter with anti-matter would annihilate both, converting their substance into pure energy. *George Schwartz, "Soviet Accelerator Triumph," The Times (London), Feb. 23, 1970, p 5*

—*v.i.* to be annihilated.

When an electron and a positron meet they annihilate to form a photon, which is as near to being a pure bundle of energy as there is. *Dietrick E. Thomsen, Science News, July 13, 1968, p 44*

anomalous water, a type of water that behaves like a noncrystalline material (such as glass) rather than like a crystalline solid (such as ice) at subfreezing temperatures. Its discovery was announced in 1966 by Professor Boris V. Deryagin, a Soviet physical chemist. Also called POLYWATER, ORTHOWATER, SUPERWATER, WATER II.

Anomalous water, or polywater as some people call it, is an apparent form of water with strange properties that lead some scientists to believe it is a polymer, or macro-molecule, built of ordinary water molecules. *Science News, Oct. 3, 1970, p 286*

Anomalous water (or polywater), which attracted much attention in recent months, was shown to be not an unusual form of water but ordinary water containing ionic impurities that cause it to have unusual chemical and physical properties. *William J. Bailey, "Chemistry," 1972 Britannica Yearbook of Science and the Future, 1971, p 216*

anti-, *prefix.* **1** of or belonging to the hypothetical world consisting of antimatter (the counterpart of ordinary matter).

antiman, *n.:* Since we define protons and positive pi-mesons as particles, the more energetic pi-meson would be a particle. However, anti-world inhabitants would define anti-protons and negative pi-mesons as particles. In their experiment, the more energetic pi-meson would be an anti-particle. On this basis, we could identify anti-man. *Gerry Wick, in a Letter to the Editor, New Scientist, July 23, 1970, p 205*

antinucleus, *n.:* The laws of nature as presently understood predict antinuclei of arbitrary complexity. Nevertheless, because antimatter annihilates rapidly with matter, its creation in the matter environment of Earth is something of a feat, possible only with particle accelerators. *W. Lee, "Antideuteron," McGraw-Hill Yearbook of Science and Technology 1967, p 106*

antiquark, *n.:* In theory, there are three quarks and three antiquarks, and all the so-called elementary particles, of which there are a hundred or more, consist of pairs or trios drawn from among the basic six. *"Particle Physics," Science News Yearbook 1970, p 242*

See also the main entries ANTIDEUTERIUM, ANTI-ELECTRON, ANTIHELIUM, ANTIHYDROGEN, and ANTI-WORLD.

2 that which rejects or reverses the traditional characteristics of _____, a use chiefly abstracted from the terms *antihero* and *antinovel.*

anticommunity, *n.:* America is one vast, terrifying anti-community. The great organizations to which most people give their working day and the apartments and suburbs to which they return at night are equally places of loneliness and alienation. Modern living has obliterated place, locality, and neighborhood, and given us an anonymous separateness of existence. *Charles A. Reich, "The Greening of America," The New Yorker, Sept, 26, 1970, p 42*

antientertainment, *n.:* There have been some pretty unsparing anti-entertainments just lately. *Maurice Wiggin, The Sunday Times (London), March 23, 1969, p 59*

antiheroine, *n.:* A voyeuse and a bore, [James T.] Farrell's anti-heroine, Beatrice Burns, flits from group to group at her party, revealing a compulsive need for one meaningful moment in a life of disappointment. *Maclean's, March 1968, p 80*

antimemoir, *n.:* If antimemoirs are written to tell "what survives," what puts a thumb to the shaping of a man's destiny, a hateful childhood would seem to be one of those influences. *Lewis Galantiere, "The Last Enemy Overcome," Saturday Review, Nov. 16, 1968, p 45*

antimusic, *n.:* Their occasionally inspired flashes of innovation and experimentalism were dragged down too often, however, with repetition, painful dissonance and screaming antimusic. *Robert Shelton, The New York Times, July 12, 1968, p 16*

antinovelist, *n.:* . . . Latin-American novelists . . . have succeeded the French antinovelists at the top of that duty-reading list, fiction department, which we never quite get around to. *Melvin Maddocks, "Hardbound Vaudeville," The Atlantic, June 1969, p 101*

antiplay, *n.:* The antihero, the antiplay and the antitheatre production . . . seems to set up an antiaudience. . . . *Philip Hope-Wallace, The Manchester Guardian Weekly, Dec. 5, 1968, p 19*

antipoet, *n.:* Basically, however, he [Thomas Merton] is a modern antipoet. *Time, Jan. 24, 1969, p 72*

antitheater, *n.:* The greatest strength of surreal "antitheater" is, in point of fact, intensely theatrical: visual images that slice faster than pain can follow to the deepest resources of the imagination. *Time, Feb. 16, 1970, p 64*

anti-art, *n.* the rejection of traditional art forms or theories in contemporary art. Also called NEO-DADA.

. . . he [Oswald Spengler] allowed for the death of art but was not prescient enough to foresee the rise of anti-art — all those forms of organized aesthetic violence, achieved with the latest mechanical and electronic devices, that are hastening the whole process. *Lewis Mumford, "Reflections: European Diary," The New Yorker, July 6, 1968, p 40*

— *adj.* relating to or characteristic of anti-art.

In another object at the Rowan [Gallery], three blotchy and tattered but brightly coloured rags have been thrown over three upright poles. . . . This little ensemble, explicitly anti-art, is also reminiscent of some forms of religious shrine, which give an intense significance to ordinary pieces of material. *Guy Brett, The Times (London), April 22, 1970, p 9*

Of late, this gifted sculptor [Robert Smithson] (when he sculpts) has been preoccupied with "sites and non-sites," an anti-art idea that has inspired him to seek out various rocks . . . and place them in painted metal bins. *Time, Feb. 21, 1969, p 10*

anticodon, *n.* a group of three chemical bases that form a unit in transfer RNA and serve to bind a specific amino acid to a corresponding group (called a codon) in messenger RNA.

Each type of amino acid is transported to the ribosome by a particular form of "transfer" RNA (tRNA), which carries an anticodon that can form a temporary bond with one of the codons in messenger RNA. *Francis H. C. Crick, "The Genetic Code," Scientific American, Oct. 1966, p 55*

Moreover the anticodon, the bit of the chain of bases that "sockets" into the codon carried by the messenger-RNA, appears to lie in both cases in the same place on the central "petal" of the clover leaf. *New Scientist, Aug. 11, 1966, p 322*

antideuterium, *n.* the counterpart of deuterium in antimatter.

The first real antinucleus to be found was antideuterium, or antihydrogen 2, in 1966. *Science News, Feb. 28, 1970, p 218*

antideuteron, *n.* the counterpart of the nucleus of deuterium in antimatter.

Soviet nuclear physicists . . . extended their experiments to study the interactions of protons with antideuterons and of deuterons with antiprotons. *Graham Chedd, Peter Stubbs, and Gerald Wick, "Delving Deeper Into Antimatter," New Scientist, June 18, 1970, p 567*

antidumping, *adj.* imposed to discourage the practice of selling goods in large quantities below market price in foreign countries.

Nor have they particularly bright recovery prospects, although a respite for fertilizers may have been won with the anti-dumping duty. *Margaret Stone, The Times (London), Feb. 21, 1970, p 15*

antielectron, *n.* the counterpart of an electron in antimatter; an electron with a positive charge.

Dirac postulated the existence of the antielectron or positron with the same mass as an electron but with an opposite charge. *W. Lee, "Antideuteron," McGraw-Hill Yearbook of Science and Technology 1967, p 106*

See also the quotation under ANTIWORLD.

anti-European, *adj.* **1** opposed to the social, cultural, or economic unification of western Europe.

M. Pflimlin, who was the last Prime Minister of the Fourth Republic, left the Government in 1962 in protest against an anti-European speech by de Gaulle. *Edward Mortimer, The Times (London), April 13, 1970, p 4*

2 opposed to Great Britain's entry into the European Common Market.

The formidable leader of anti-European feeling in the Conservative Party and in the country will clearly be Mr. Enoch Powell. *Mollie Panter-Downes, "Letter from London," The New Yorker, July 4, 1970, p 62*

— *n.* a person who is anti-European. Compare PRO-EUROPEAN. See also EUROPEANIST.

If Mr. Aitken is right, the anti-Europeans are in for a nasty shock one of these days, when they suddenly realize they have got it all wrong, and have left it too late to concoct a different argument. *Patrick Brogan, "European Opinion," The Times (London), Feb. 24, 1970, p 4*

antifertility, *adj.* capable of destroying fertility; contraceptive.

Anti-fertility agents are as vital for bringing pigs into oestrus simultaneously for breeding purposes, as for containing the human population explosion. *New Scientist, Feb. 1, 1968, p 232*

antiform, *adj.* rejecting the traditional or prepared materials used in making works of art. See also CONCEPTUAL ART.

. . . the decade . . . wound up in a conscious rejection of both new and old art materials in preference for the earth, rocks, animal matter, and raw substances (strips of felt, rubber, and copper sheets, lead pellets) of the anti-form movement. *Harold Rosenberg, "Keeping Up," The New Yorker, Feb. 21, 1970, p 84*

antihelium, *n.* the counterpart of helium in antimatter.

Soviet physicists have reported the creation and detection of nuclei of anti-helium, thus strengthening the hypothesis that the universe is composed symmetrically of ordinary matter and anti-matter. *George Schwartz, The Times (London), Feb. 23, 1970, p 5*

antihero, *n.* a hero whose unconventional characteristics are opposite to those of a traditional hero.

He [Joe Namath] is something special: a long-haired hard-hat, the anti-hero of the sports world. *James Reston, "Joe Namath, the New Anti-Hero," The New York Times, Aug. 21, 1970, p 32*

► Originally a literary term, referring to the protagonist of a novel, play, or story.

antihydrogen, *n.* the counterpart of hydrogen in antimatter.

The combination of antiproton with a positron would form an antihydrogen atom, and quantum mechanics predicts that it would have almost exactly the same properties as the atom of ordinary hydrogen; for instance, it would emit light at the same wavelengths. *Hannes Alfvén, "Antimatter And Cosmology," Scientific American, April 1967, p 106*

anti-Marketeer, *n.* an opponent of Great Britain's entry into the European Common Market. See also ANTI-EUROPEAN.

. . . the two speeches clearly reflect the growing self-confidence of the anti-Marketeers in the Government since the publication of the White Paper giving revised estimates of the cost of entry. *Ian Aitken, "Anti-Marketeers More Confident," The Manchester Guardian Weekly, April 4, 1970, p 8*

[from *anti-* + Common *Marketeer*]

antineoplastic, *adj.* preventing the growth of tumors, especially cancerous ones.

The enzyme L-asparaginase was known to be a potent antineoplastic (tumor-preventing) agent in animals, and it was said to have given complete remission in some human leukemias. *Robert G. Eagon, "Microbiology," 1970 Britannica Yearbook of Science and the Future, 1969, p 291*

[from *anti-* + *neoplastic* (from New Latin *neoplasia* new tumor)]

antipollution, *adj.* counteracting or directed against environmental pollution, especially air pollution. Compare ANTISMOG.

Pumping out any more ground water in the city's vicinity is forbidden, and industries must attach antipollution filters to factory smokestacks. *Time, July 25, 1969, p 27*

Nearly all anti-pollution devices appear to be costly, and while it is unlikely that anyone is actually for pollution, few are willing to assume the costly burden of eliminating it. *Alberta Rogers, New York, in a Letter to the Editor, The New York Times, Jan. 20, 1970, p 36*

antipollutionist, *n.* a person who advocates strong measures to prevent or reduce environmental pollution. Compare ENVIRONMENTALIST.

Anti-pollutionists and conservationists should surely be as much concerned with prevention as with cure. *M. L. F. Smith, London, in a Letter to the Editor, The Times (London), April 8, 1970, p 26*

antipoverty, *n.* *U.S.* a program to combat poverty, especially such a program sponsored by the government.

At a time when the Federal budget is being drastically cut in every area from antipoverty to crime control, the House of Representatives has passed an expanded highway construction bill. . . . *Edward I. Koch, City Councilman, The New York Times, July 21, 1968, Sec. 4, p 13*

anti-roll bar, a bar installed in an automobile suspension system to prevent rolling and provide greater stability on curves.

The handling and suspension have been modified by the addition of an anti-roll bar and the interior trim has also been improved. *The Sunday Times (London), Jan. 19, 1969, p 21*

an·ti·ro·man (ä ti: rɔ'mä), *n.* another name for

NOUVEAU ROMAN (a type of experimental novel developed chiefly in France in the 1960's).

. . . if there is a new avant-garde and a new aesthetic —based on, say, John Cage, William Burroughs, Samuel Beckett, the concrete poets, the novelists of the *anti-roman*, and for that matter drugs and negritude—isn't that simply a continuation of all that has been happening in art in our century, and in that sense a problem for art? *Malcolm Bradbury, "Books: Antennae," Review of "Innovations," edited by Bernard Bergonzi, The Listener, Sept. 19, 1968, p 374*

[from French]

antiscience, *adj.* of or relating to those who oppose scientific research pursued at the expense of humanitarian interests and values. Compare ANTITECHNOLOGY.

. . . Dr. Philip Handler, president of the National Academy of Sciences, sees a real threat in an antiscience and antitechnology bias he says is developing. *Science News, May 2, 1970, p 432*

Science and technology are needed to solve our problems, argues Dr. Jonas Salk, who developed the vaccine for the prevention of poliomyelitis, warning against those who recommend anti-science and anti-technology remedies. *James Reston, "Aspen, Colo.: The Philosophers at Bay," The New York Times, Sept. 2, 1970, p 36*

Science, then, requires a new spokesman—one who is not content to hand out the traditional arrogant rhetoric which is at best irrelevant to the issues at stake and at worst an irrational and deceitful pack of lies which can only add fuel to the already fiercely burning fires in the antiscience camp. *"Wanted: New Science Spokesmen," Science Journal, Sept. 1970, p 3*

antisex, *adj.* another word for ANTISEXUAL.

In the new developments, Dr. Fiedeldy Dop found that the parents of young children were often in a rattled state, which he attributed partly to the fact that "there's no privacy—the apartments are anti-sex." *Anthony Bailey, "The Little Room," The New Yorker, Aug. 8, 1970, p 44*

antisexist, *adj.* opposed to sexism or sexual discrimination.

The National Organization for Women (NOW) and other feminist groups have called on women to stage a Strike for Equality on Aug. 26. Last week, in a preliminary demonstration, feminists brandished anti-sexist placards beneath the Statue of Liberty. *Time, Aug. 24, 1970, p 12*

antisexual, *adj.* hostile to sexual expression or activity. Also, ANTISEX.

Only someone riddled with guilt could take these basically erotic elements and turn them into such a leering, antisexual and, finally, soporiferous farce. *Vincent Canby, The New York Times, May 4, 1968, p 46*

Says Harvard Theologian Harvey Cox: "*Playboy* is basically antisexual." *Time, March 3, 1967, p 37*

There are occasional gleams of poetry, but the combination of rhetoric and religiosity, the supersexual and antisexual idealism that seems so effortful and not quite sincere, was rejected by my literary stomach. *Edmund Wilson, "Paris," The New Yorker, May 21, 1966, p 61*

antisexuality, *n.* the quality of being antisexual; antagonism toward sex.

Worse still, the social and ethical attitudes embodied in the *fallas* [painted effigies burned during the spring fair in Valencia, Spain] are ferociously conservative—a ghastly fate to befall a popular art. They are, in general, xenophobic, anti-youth, anti-sexuality, and anti-revolution. *Kenneth Tynan, "The Judicious Observer Will Be Disgusted," The New Yorker, July 25, 1970, p 51*

antismog, *adj.* designed to prevent, reduce, or eliminate smog. Compare ANTIPOLLUTION.

Anti-smog equipment fitted to cars in the United States has reduced hydrocarbon emissions by 80 per cent. *Geoffrey Charles, "Clean Petrol Will Raise Costs," The Times (London), March 10, 1970, p 5*

antitechnology, *adj.* opposed to technological research and development pursued at the expense of humanitarian interests and values. Compare ANTISCIENCE.

The antitechnology chorus, which includes many accredited scientists, is voicing concern in behalf of the "common man." *"Review of the Year—Technology," Encyclopedia Science Supplement (Grolier) 1970, p 332*

antiviral, *n.* a substance that destroys or inhibits the action of viruses.

At present, the list of known antivirals is short, though potential agents are under study. *Hadassah Gillon, Science News, Nov. 1, 1969, p 414*

[noun use of the adjective *antiviral*]

antiworld, *n.* a hypothetical world consisting of antimatter.

Theorists have speculated that the universe contains "anti-worlds" containing anti-matter made up of anti-electrons, usually called positrons, anti-protons and anti-neutrons.

Such anti-worlds, if they exist, would not be detectable by normal astronomical observation, while any collision of ordinary matter with anti-matter would annihilate both, converting their substance into pure energy. *George Schwartz, "Soviet Accelerator Triumph," The Times (London), Feb. 23, 1970, p 5*

ao dai ('ɑ: ou 'dɑi), the traditional women's dress in Vietnam, consisting of a long, high-necked tunic split to the waist on either side and worn over wide pajamalike trousers.

Sut On looks around her and knows what she will never be: a lithe Annamese girl, pretty in an *ao dai*. Her bones are too broad, her legs are too heavy, and even if she ever put on an *ao dai* and got accustomed to the material, just above it her face would be a dead giveaway—she will always look Chinese. *Johanna Kaplan, "Dragon Lady," Harper's, July 1970, p 81*

Pretty Saigon girls in ao dais posed for their boy friends' cameras before the city's monuments. *Time, Feb. 16, 1970, p 19*

a·part·heid (ə'pɑrt‚heit), *n.* separateness; exclusiveness.

Instead of celebrating the multiplicity of things that movies can do better or more easily than the other arts, and in new ways and combinations, they [those who loved movies] looked for the true nature of cinema in what cinema can do that the other arts can't—in artistic apartheid. *Pauline Kael, "The Current Cinema: Movies as Opera," The New Yorker, Jan. 13, 1968, p 90*

Their [children with high IQ's] very brightness sets them apart from their fellows; that measure of apartheid can inflict lasting psychological damage, even turn them into delinquents instead of dons. *Elspeth Huxley, "Growing Up in Britain," Punch, March 22, 1967, p 409*

[extended sense of the term for racial segregation]

ape, *n.* **go ape,** *Chiefly U.S. Slang.* to lose self-control; go wild with enthusiasm, excitement, etc.

. . . how simple it was to get past these M.P.'s. They looked petrified. Stricken faces as he went by. They did not know what to do. It was his dark pinstripe suit, his vest, . . . the barrel chest, the early paunch—he must have looked like a banker himself, a banker gone ape. *Norman Mailer, "The Steps of the Pentagon," Harper's, March 1968, p 102*

Then when the guys found out it was true, they just went ape. *Time, Aug. 9, 1968, p 42*

When they get away from their customary urban environment, many of "The Summer People," as the locals call their clientele, tend to go ape. *Patrick Skene Catling, Punch, Jan. 24, 1968, p 118*

ape hanger, *U.S. Slang.* a tall bicycle or motorcycle handlebar.

Tyke bike, which is $3.98 at Gimbel's, among other places, has a solid wood frame and seat. four rubber-tired wheels, and the swooping handlebars known among the motorcycle avant-garde as ape hangers. *"On and Off the Avenue," The New Yorker, Dec. 11, 1965, p 164*

ap·o·ap·sis (‚æp ou'æp sis), *n.* the point in the orbit around a heavenly body farthest from the center of the body.

. . . its [faster-orbiting vehicle's] companion, in a 50° orbit with apoapsis 20,500 miles and periapsis 530 miles, undertakes the scrutiny of selected areas of Mars to gain a better idea of surface and atmospheric changes, seasonal variations, and the still enigmatic dust storms and Martian clouds. *"Off to Have a Longer Look at Mars," New Scientist and Science Journal, May 6, 1971, p 305*

[from *apo-* off, away + *apsis* orbit]

ap·o·cyn·thi·on (‚æp ə'sin θi: ən), *n.* another name for APOLUNE.

The terms "pericynthion" and "apocynthion" were selected about ten years ago by some people at MSC [Manned Spacecraft Center, Houston] who did not want to mix Latin and Greek terms; however, even today only about 20% of MSC uses the term "pericynthion" and the majority of the Aerospace industries use the terms "perilune" and "apolune." *Memorandum from the Mission Planning and Analysis Division, Manned Spacecraft Center, Houston, excerpted in The New Yorker, Oct. 11, 1969, p 91*

[from *apo-* off + Latin *Cynthia* goddess of the moon]

apolune, *n.* the point in a lunar orbit farthest from the center of the moon. Also called APOCYNTHION. Compare PERILUNE.

Within minutes, Intrepid was successfully inserted into a low lunar orbit with an apolune (high point) of about 50 miles. *Time, Nov. 28, 1969, p 35*

[from *apo-* off + French *lune* moon]

Ap star ('ei'pi:), a star of spectral type A having a peculiarity in its spectrum.

Readers will recall that Ap stars have spectra revealing a bewildering array of rare elements not present on other stars and huge excesses of certain more common elements. *New Scientist and Science Journal, April 8, 1971, p 73*

[*Ap*, from *A* (the spectral type) + *p* (for *peculiar*)]

APT, abbreviation for:
1 advanced passenger train (a train capable of speeds up to 150 miles per hour).

The APT, now under construction, will be powered by British Layland gas turbine engines and will cruise at over 240 km/h on today's track. *Noël Penny, "Gas Turbines For Land Transport," Science Journal, April 1970, p 59*

2 automatic picture transmission (by weather satellites equipped with television cameras).

More than 150 stations in 45 countries have been receiving and using APT pictures since ESSA II was launched. *Louis J. Battan, "Weather Prediction: A World Plan," The World Book Science Annual 1967, p 157*

3 automatically programmed tool (a means of operating or controlling machinery by computers). Compare NC.

APT is a generic name for what is actually a family of programming systems with varying capabilities which run on various types and sizes of computers. *John E. Ward, "Numerical Control of Machine Tools," McGraw-Hill Yearbook of Science and Technology 1968, p 63*

aquafarm, *n.* an artificial pond, lake, stream, etc., used for raising fish, oysters, and other aquatic animals.

The Lummi [Indian] tribe of Washington State, a sea-oriented people along Puget Sound, are using federal funds and considerable hard labor to develop the most advanced aquafarm in the U.S. *Time, Feb. 9, 1970, p 19*

aquanaut, *n.* a skin diver or other person who engages in underwater exploration and research, often living for extended periods of time inside a habitat, submarine, or other underwater vessel. Also called OCEANAUT. Compare HYDRONAUT.

Five teams of aquanauts will work 12 days each on the sea floor off the coast of California in Sealab III, breathing an atmosphere that is 92.4% helium. *Picture legend, The Americana Annual 1969, p 512*

It is not so widely appreciated, however, that his colleague the diver or aquanaut, who attempts to explore, work and today even live in 'inner space' under the sea, is exposed to many similar hazards. *Science Journal, Jan. 1968, p 53*

[from *aqua* water + *-naut*, as in *astronaut*]

Aquarian, *adj.* of, relating to, or characteristic of the AGE OF AQUARIUS.

The pretext for this mass gathering [the Woodstock Music and Art Fair at Bethel, N.Y.] was an outdoor music festival advertised as "three days of peace and music" and subtitled "An Aquarian Exposition," in reference to the newly dawning Age of Aquarius on the astrology charts. *Abigail Kuflik, "Woodstock," The Americana Annual 1970, p 482*

'If only we can find ourselves, seek out our own deeper human personality, we may usher in the Aquarian Age in a world of living nature instead of empty destruction.' *The Sunday Times (London), March 26, 1972, p 10*

—*n.* a person born under the sign of Aquarius, January 20-February 18.

Presumably a Taurian heaving erasers at an Aquarian may have his cosmic reasons. *"Teaching by Horoscope," Time, Oct. 18, 1971, p 41*

aq·ua·tel (ˈæk wəˌtel), *n. British.* See the quotation for the meaning.

An aquatel consists of a fleet of houseboats moored at a marina which provides restaurants, shops, car parking, a laundry and similar amenities. *John Carter, "Sights Set High for Tourism," The Times (London), April 14, 1970, p 19*

[blend of *aquatic* and *hotel*, patterned after *motel* (blend of *motor* and *hotel*), and perhaps *boatel* (blend of *boat* and *motel*)]

arbo, *adj.* (of diseases) transmitted by arthropods, such as mosquitoes.

While cautious, Dr. Prince suggested that the material that had been found in the blood may be part of a member of the arbo family of viruses, some of whose members are known to cause several forms of encephalitis, a type of inflammation of the brain. *Richard D. Lyons, The New York Times, July 28, 1968, p 34*

[contraction of *arthropod-borne*]

arbovirus, *n.* an arthropod-borne virus that causes encephalitis.

Arthropods, especially mosquitoes and ticks, are of vast importance for the transmission of the members of a large family of viruses, the arboviruses. *Christopher Andrewes, New Scientist, March 18, 1965, p 729*

archmonetarist, *n.* an extreme monetarist; an ardent supporter of monetarism.

The archmonetarists, led by Professor Milton Friedman . . ., believe that changes in growth of money supply operate on the economy with such a long time lag that it is quite impossible for the authorities to know at any one moment what their policy should be. *Anthony Harris, "Money Isn't Everything," The Manchester Guardian Weekly, May 9, 1970, p 22*

[from *arch-* extreme, preeminent + *monetarist*]

arcology, *n.* a completely integrated planned city or environment within a single structure.

There are arcologies for sea, shore or plain, for populations the size of Sarasota (30,000), Atlanta (400,000) or Dallas (1,000,000). . . . Because the diameter of an arcology is short, walking, bicycling, escalator, elevator, moving sidewalk, pneumatic or electric vehicle transport make automobiles unnecessary except for travel outside the arcology—eliminating another prime source of pollution. *Estie Stoll, "Arcology," Encyclopedia Science Supplement (Grolier) 1971, p 287*

[coined by the American architect Paolo Soleri from *arch*itectural *ec*ology to designate the concept of creating a balance between architecture and the environment, especially in his book *Arcology: The City in the Image of Man,* 1969]

area code, *U.S. and Canada.* a three-digit number used to telephone long distance directly by dialing this number plus the local telephone number. Compare *British* STD.

The area code for the whole state of Montana is 406. If you use the area code when you call Long Distance, your call goes through faster and easier. *Advertisement by AT&T (Bell System) in The New Yorker, March 18, 1967, p 197*

area navigation, a system of aircraft navigation that uses airborne computers to receive and process the signals from ground radio beacons to calculate the position of the aircraft in flight.

Area navigation means that a pilot knows where he is at any time in the course of a flight, and is thus able to take whatever route to his destination is the most direct, least congested, or safest, according to instructions from control. It is an alternative to the approved system of beacons, which tell the pilot his distance and bearing from each as he comes within its sphere. *"A New Air Freedom," New Scientist, May 28, 1970, p 412*

ar·gi·nae·mi·a (ˌɑr dʒəˈniː miː ə), *n.* an inherited metabolic disorder in which a person lacking the necessary enzyme (arginase) is unable to metabolize the amino acid arginine.

. . . arginaemia . . . manifests itself as very high blood levels of arginine and presumably results from a deficiency in cellular mechanisms for breaking down the amino acid. *Stanfield Rogers, "Skills for Genetic Engineers," New Scientist, Jan. 29, 1970, p 194*

[from *argin*ine + *-aemia* disorder of the blood (from Greek *haima* blood)]

ar·gi·nase (ˈɑr dʒəˌneis), *n.* an enzyme that breaks down arginine (an amino acid present in plant and animal proteins).

There is a virus causing tumours in rabbits which also increases the concentration of an enzyme called arginase in the animals' blood. *Bryan Silcock, The Sunday Times (London), Nov. 30, 1969, p 9*

[from *argin*ine + *-ase* enzyme]

a·ri·ga·to (ɑː riːˈgɑː tou), *interj. Japanese.* thank you.

The show's many dance numbers are mesmeric revels. The cast is totally winning, and so are the demon drummer and his galvanizing group up behind the scrim [thin curtain]. In midsummer New York, *Golden Bat* is a surprising tonic for whom one can only say *arigato. T. E. Kalem, "The Theater," Time, Aug. 3, 1970, p 69*

aright, *v.t.* to make right; correct.

One way the Russians are trying to aright this imbalance . . . is by slyly inserting into medium-range missile sites (now aimed only at European targets) new intercontinental long-range missiles. *C. L. Sulzberger, "Foreign Affairs: The Strategy of Meaning," The New York Times, April 17, 1970, p 36*

► *Aright* is commonly used only as an adverb. The *OED* shows that *aright* existed as a verb in the 1400's but it has been thought obsolete for the past five hundred years.

arm-twisting, *n., adj.* strong pressure.

Arm-twisting by the Governor and legislative leaders to pass a controversial bill is common in Albany. *Sydney H. Schanberg, The New York Times, April 11, 1968, p 41*

. . . the President . . . has put into operation his famous arm-twisting technique in support of a strong Bill. *Richard Scott, The Manchester Guardian Weekly, June 20, 1968, p 2*

array, *n.* any arrangement or assemblage of elements forming a complete unit. Compare PACKAGE.

. . . millions watched on television as Aldrin removed the unit from the bay of the *Eagle*, carried it out about 60 feet from the craft and set the array on the lunar surface. *James E. Faller and E. Joseph Wampler, "The Lunar Laser Reflector," Scientific American, March 1970, p 43*

The array consists of two lines of seismic detectors, each nearly nine km long, and each having 11 equally spaced instruments, with a common time base. *New Scientist, Feb. 6, 1964, p 362*

arrogance of power, a catchphrase used to attack or impugn the policies of a country, etc., as being due to the arrogance that comes from having too much power.

It is high time, I suggest, that we Americans quit deluding ourselves that we are not as other men, that our nation, the most powerful in history, possesses some unique immunity to the corruption and arrogance of power. *Robert Claiborne, New York, in a Letter to the Editor, The New York Times, Sept. 26, 1970, p 28*

Is it too much to insist that Israel should discontinue displaying its arrogance of power and should stop bombing civilian centers—irrigation projects, churches, mosques, schools? *Muhammad H. El-Farra, Ambassador, Permanent Representative of Jordan to the United Nations, New York, in a Letter to the Editor, The New York Times, Feb. 14, 1970, p 26*

[coined by U.S. Senator William Fulbright in the 1960's and used by him as the title of a book, 1967, in which he questions the validity of American intervention in the affairs of foreign countries]

art, *v.t.* **art up,** to give artistic pretensions to: make arty.

But in the event everything is so obsessively arted-up with bits and pieces remembered from Bergman, Fellini, Resnais, Lelouche and practically anyone you care to name, that it makes little or no independent sense. . . . *John Russell Taylor, "San Francisco Film Festival: a Thrilling Cassavetes," The Times (London), Nov. 3, 1970, p 15*

[verb use of the noun *art*, possibly on the analogy of *tart up* dress or fit out brightly and gaudily]

art de·co or **Art De·co** (ˈɑr ˈdeiˌkou), a style of decorative design characterized by ornateness, asymmetry, geometrical forms, and bold colors. The style was popular in the 1910's and 1920's and was successfully revived in the late 1960's. *Also used attributively.*

. . . the great Exposition Internationale des Arts Décoratifs, held in Paris in 1925, . . . celebrated and wrote finis to, the style known in retrospect as Art Déco, which had supplanted the Art Nouveau of the nineties and the early Edwardian years. . . . *"Briefly Noted: The Decorative Twenties," The New Yorker, Jan. 3, 1970, p 68*

. . . for Mr. Battersby Art Deco started before 1914 and died in 1925 with the Paris exhibition. *Norbert Lynton, The Manchester Guardian Weekly, Jan. 3, 1970, p 18*

Bentley-Farrell-Burnett Designs . . . produced the vivid Art Deco-style placards you see in the windows of Achille Serre shops. . . . *Bevis Hillier, "A Case for Book Jackets," The Manchester Guardian Weekly, Jan. 31, 1970, p 17*

He [Henry Geldzahler, curator of contemporary arts at the Metropolitan Museum in New York City] collects art deco objects as well as modern paintings, secretly yearns to go to Hollywood. *Time, Oct 24, 1969, p 62*

[from French *Art Déco*, shortened from *Arts Décoratifs* Decorative Arts]

artmobile, *n. U.S.* a trailer truck fitted out to exhibit paintings and sculptures as it travels from place to place.

It [The Virginia Museum of Fine Arts] was the first museum to establish an artmobile. . . . Now there are four artmobiles. . . . *Howard Taubman, The New York Times, Dec. 4, 1967, p 65*

[patterned after *bookmobile* a traveling library]

artsy, *adj.* **1** having a dilettante interest in art.

But the school I went to was not artsy. Mostly it taught kids to be commercial artists and I was told that a good poster was one that would get the motorist when he was driving past at 25 miles an hour. *Sidney Newman, The Listener, Dec. 14, 1967, p 784*

2 overly decorated; too elaborate in design.

Forty years ago these [sections of Toronto] were stolidly working-class; now they've been colonized by anti-suburbanites who have renovated entire streets into neo-Edwardian artsy elegance. *Alexander Ross, "A Status Guide to Toronto," Maclean's, Nov. 1968, p 75*

Book adaptations and artsy photographic portfolios are mixed with nonfiction articles that seem to have a very limited audience indeed. *Time, April 26, 1971, p 36*

[variant of *arty;* form influenced by *arts* (and *crafts*)]

art trou·ve ('ar tru:'vei), *French.* found art (art not fashioned by the artist but taken as found and adapted for its artistic value or effect).

(What it is in fact producing is *art trouvé.*) In this idiom one looks within a certain subject area (for instance driftwood on a beach) and picks out those shapes which are evocative. In the same way one looks at the output of the computer (restricted to a certain subject area) and again picks out patterns which are evocative. The dilemma with *art trouvé* is that the ordinary eye may see nothing unless it looks long enough and it is unlikely to look long enough unless it sees something. *Edward de Bono, Science Journal, March 1970, p 81*

Arvin or **ARVN** ('ar vən), *n.* **1** acronym for *Army of the Republic of (South) Vietnam.*

The operation seems to have greatly boosted the morale of the South Vietnamese army (Arvin), which now has a total strength of more than 1.1 million men, the fourth largest army in the world. *Frank Barnaby, "Chasing the Vietnamese Will-o'the-wisp," New Scientist, Dec. 17, 1970, p 501*

2 a member of the Arvin.

I was watching, in microcosm, the sort of war the Americans wage in Vietnam, and the kind of fighting for which they have generally helped to train the Arvins (regular soldiers, as opposed to regional and popular forces, in the Army of the Republic of Vietnam). *David Fairhall, The Manchester Guardian Weekly, May 29, 1969, p 5*

ash·ram ('a:ʃ rəm), *n. U.S.* a hippie retreat or commune.

"So like it would be really groovy to see a meeting going on between people like you two . . . or a guy named Mike Bowen, who's going to start an indigenous psychedelic ashram. It could be like allied seekers getting together." *Allen Ginsberg, quoted by Jane Kramer, "Profiles: Paterfamilias," The New Yorker, Aug. 24, 1968, p 40*

Whether he was selling snake oil to farmers in the Southwest . . . or living it up in those all-purpose ashrams known as "studios" in Greenwich Village, [Kenneth] Rexroth was on top of the left-wing game. *Time, Feb. 25, 1966, p 76*

[extended sense of the Hindu term for a hermitage, monastery, or religious retreat]

ask, *v.i.* **ask out,** *U.S.* to retire, withdraw, or resign; bow out.

Apprised of his [Headmaster Wilfred O'Leary's] tough

ways as principal of Roslindale High, six teachers asked out even before he arrived. *Time, Jan. 8, 1968, p 33*

as-maintained, *adj. U.S.* according to the standard weights and measures maintained by the National Bureau of Standards or a similar organization.

Currents and voltages are almost always measured in terms of as-maintained units and converted to absolute units based on the measured value of the conversion factor. *Barry N. Taylor, Donald N. Langenberg, and William H. Parker, "The Fundamental Physical Constants," Scientific American, Oct. 1970, p 68*

ASP, abbreviation of AMERICAN SELLING PRICE.

Abolition of the ASP was one of the conditions agreed during the Kennedy Round trade negotiations. . . . *The Manchester Guardian Weekly, July 25, 1970, p 23*

ASP (æsp), *n.* acronym for *Anglo-Saxon Protestant.* Compare WASP.

"What makes you think she's different from any other ASP (Anglo-Saxon Protestant)?" *Nadine Asante, "A Mixed Marriage," The Manchester Guardian Weekly, March 19, 1964, p 13*

John Lindsay's parents were descended from pure-blooded WASPs (White Anglo-Saxon Protestants)—though, as Lindsay is fond of pointing out, "If you are really hip, the correct term is ASP; all Anglo-Saxons are white, so why be redundant?" *Time, Nov. 12, 1965, p 21*

asphalt cloud, a mass of asphalt particles ejected by an antiballistic missile to consume the heat shields of enemy missiles.

In the asphalt-cloud technique, the ABM disperses millions of particles in the path of enemy missiles. When the rockets plunge into the atmosphere, the highly combustible bits of asphalt that they have picked up ignite from frictional heat; the asphalt burns so rapidly and creates such great temperatures that the heat shields on the ICBMs are all but consumed. Then the missiles either burn up or are so deformed that they veer off course. *Time, Oct. 12, 1970, p 33*

assemblage, *n.* **1** an artistic work made from bits and pieces of cloth, wood, metal, scraps, and other fragmentary objects.

As colored images, the canvases of Frankenthaler, Louis, and Olitski are arresting, especially as one comes upon them after two or three roomfuls of assemblages. *Harold Rosenberg, "The Art World," The New Yorker, July 29, 1967, p 78*

2 the technique or art of making assemblages.

Dada has contributed to every new technique employed in this century that it did not actually invent—collage, which is everywhere; its extension, assemblage, which includes junk sculpture, "found" objects and a hundred cousins; the "environment" as well as the Happening; kinetic sculpture, whether motorized or not, and on and on. *John Canaday, The New York Times Magazine, March 24, 1968, p 30*

assemblagist, *n.* a person who makes assemblages.

One of the first artists to look appreciatively at these molds was Alfonso Ossorio, an obsessive assemblagist who produces gaudy conglomerations out of the found objects that he squirrels away against the day when he may need them. *Time, Dec. 19, 1969, p 36*

assembler language or **assembly language,** another name for COMPILER LANGUAGE.

The makers offer a library of programs to go with it [a desk computer], including . . . an assembler language, and a general mathematics library. *New Scientist, Jan. 11, 1968, p 79*

Manufacturers today are expected to supply . . . a fairly simple assembly language which makes it possible to instruct the machine without recourse to its own confusing language of zeros and ones. . . . *The Times (London), Jan. 7, 1965, p 14*

as-told-to, *adj.* U.S. written by a professional writer in collaboration with the subject of the book or article.

. . . Dewi [Ratni Sari Dewi, wife of Indonesia's former president Sukarno] has packed up six-month old Kartika Sari and flown off to New York City and the hospitality of Cindy Adams, wife of a nightclub comedian and author of an as-told-to autobiography of Sukarno. *Time, Sept. 22, 1967, p 25*

. . . he wrote an as-told-to account of the visit, but the book won immediate and widespread denunciation as a fake, because "Adams's description of Timbuctoo was of a dull, filthy and exceedingly unattractive town." *Charles Miller, Saturday Review, Nov. 30, 1968, p 52*

as·tro- ('æs trou-). A new meaning of this combining form, abstracted from or fashioned on *astronaut*, is "of or having to do with outer space, space travel, etc." Compare COSMO-. The following are some examples of compounds formed with *astro-* in this sense:

astrobug, *n.:* A spacecraft with a crew of 10 million tiny "astrobugs" was launched from Cape Kennedy today in America's second biosatellite experiment. *The Times (London), Sept. 8, 1967, p 1*

astrodog, *n.:* The astrodog stands up on its house, levels an indignant paw at the boy's retreating figure and barks, "Report that man to mission control!" *Barnaby Conrad, "Good Ol' Charlie Schulz," The 1970 World Book Year Book, p 147*

astromonk, *n.:* Honolulu (AP)—Astromonk Bonny died suddenly at midnight Monday 12 hours after the monkey put down in the Pacific Ocean following 130 orbits around earth in a space capsule, the U.S. space agency reported. *The Tuscaloosa News, July 8, 1969, p 3*

astromouse, *n.:* "You've heard of astrobugs—this is astromouse," Dr. Reynolds said. "He is a desert mouse of the Southwest, a pocket mouse, and has a lot of capabilities for space research." *The New York Times, Jan. 7, 1967, p 8*

astrophotographer, *n.:* The *Apollo 12* team of Charles Conrad and Alan Bean took similar pictures at their landing site. In spite of the excellence of modern color film, however, the true color of the moonscape still eluded the astrophotographers. *Donald Stebbing, "Photography," The 1970 World Book Year Book, p 460*

as·tro·bleme ('æs trou,bli:m), *n.* a scar left on the earth's surface by a meteorite.

Most shatter-coned astroblemes are of moderate size, a few miles across, but two of Precambrian age attain diameters of a few tens of miles across—the Sudbury structure in Canada and the Vredefort Ring of South Africa. *Robert Dietz, "Shatter Cones and Star Wounds," New Scientist, Nov. 28, 1968, p 502*

[from *astro-* star + Greek *blêma* a shot of a missile, or a wound from such a shot]

astrochronologist, *n.* a student of the history and evolution of stars and galaxies.

The new breed of astrochronologists use techniques similar to the familiar potassium-argon radioactive dating method employed by geophysicists. *New Scientist and Science Journal, June 17, 1971, p 668*

astrodynamics, *n.* the study of the action of force on bodies in outer space.

. . . there are not many books which deal with this particular subject matter (aside, that is, from the astrodynamics content), and despite these reservations, it should prove particularly useful to students. *Terence Nonweiler, "Books," Review of "Space Vehicle Dynamics" by K. J. Ball and G. F. Osborne, New Scientist, Jan. 2, 1969, p 37*

astrogeology, *n.* the study of the physical features and composition of heavenly bodies.

Progress in the field of astrogeology continued with information recorded from unmanned space vehicles. Surveyor 3, after its landing on April 19 in the Ocean of Storms, provided new information about the lunar surface. *Kenneth F. Clark, "Astrogeology," 1968 Collier's Encyclopedia Year Book, p 263*

astronautess, *n.* a female astronaut.

. . . said NASA's administrator, Dr. Thomas O. Paine . . . "I would hope to see the first British astronautess fly before the end of the decade." *Angela Croome, "NASA Appeals for International Co-operation," Science Journal, May 1970, p 11*

astrospace, *n.* the space beyond the nearby planets; space among the stars.

. . . there exists. . . . a variety of mobile machines with arms which can either move limited distances or are completely free moving. A variety of these crawling anthropoids emerged from the experimental applications in nuclear power to astrospace and aerospace propulsion. But. for the planned exploratory of planetary surfaces—a sphere which is the first to generate in the public visions of roving anthropomorphic robots—there has been but limited development to date. *H. A. Ballinger, "Machines with Arms," Science Journal, Oct. 1968, p 59*

Atlanticism, *n.* a policy of close political cooperation between the countries of western Europe and North America.

. . . "M Pompidou increasingly abandons the positive aspects of General de Gaulle's policy in order to draw closer to the United States and slide towards Atlanticism—something which is contrary to the interest and independence of France." *Charles Hargrove, "Elysee Scoffs at Gibe About Nato," The Times (London), Jan. 13, 1972, p 6*

[from the *Atlantic* Pact, which formed the basis of NATO (North *Atlantic* Treaty Organization)]

Atlanticist, *n.* a supporter of close cooperation between western Europe and North America.

Jean Lecanuet, the conservative candidate who entered the political scene as an "Atlanticist" a little over a year ago, has found that he cannot rouse any audiences by promising to save the Atlantic alliance and restore U.S.-French friendship. *Henry Tanner, The New York Times, March 5, 1967, p 3*

atmospherium, *n.* a room or building like a planetarium for simulating atmospheric or meteorological phenomena.

... capped with a hyperbolic paraboloid roof, the Atmospherium creates thunderstorms from tiny clouds in a matter of minutes. *Horace Sutton, "Gamesmanship in Nevada," Saturday Review, Nov. 4, 1967, p 54*

[from *atmosphere* + *-ium*, as in *planetarium*]

atomarium, *n.* a room or building in which devices showing the structure and use of atoms are exhibited.

Following the pattern of the atomarium in Stockholm, Sweden, this booklet [*The Cranbrook Atomarium*] describes the demonstrations of the new museum displays at Cranbrook which explain some of the phenomena of atomic and nuclear physics. *Science News Letter, Dec. 26, 1964, p 407*

[from *atom* + *-arium*, as in *planetarium*]

atom probe, a device for observing the behavior of a single atom.

A remarkable mass spectrometer of single atom sensitivity, invented in 1967 by Professor Erwin Müller, of Pennsylvania State University, has begun to show its powers in the study of corrosion and gas adsorption effects. The instrument, the so-called "atom probe," consists of a field-ion microscope with a small hole in its fluroescent screen; beyond the hole is a flight tube, at the end of which is a detector having single-particle sensitivity. *"The 'Atom Probe' Shows Off Its Paces," New Scientist, July 2, 1970, p 6*

at·ra·zin ('æt rə zən) or **at·ra·zine** ('æt rə‚zi:n), *n.* a moderately toxic chemical widely used as a weed killer.

Some species might even become resistant to sprays, although the only example so far appears to be a United States groundsel reported to be undeterred by simazin and atrazin. *Leonard Amey, "Weed-free Crops a Pipe Dream," The Times (London), Nov. 23, 1970, p 13*

[from *amino* + *triazine* (chemical compound with a ring of three carbon atoms)]

atto-, a prefix meaning one quintillionth of any standard unit in the international meter-kilogram-second system of measurements (SI UNIT).

The General Conference [on Weights and Measures] has approved 14 such prefixes, ranging from "atto" (10^{-18}) to "tera" (10^{12}). *Lord Ritchie-Calder, "Conversion to the Metric System," Scientific American, July 1970, p 23*

[from Danish *atten* eighteen]

attrit, *v.t.* *U.S. Military use.* to wear down by attrition; weaken by harassment or abuse.

Wear him down. Wear the Cong down, and he'll quit. Put him through the meat grinder. Attrit him. He is hurting, said the American commander in mid-1967. *Ward S. Just, "Notes on Losing a War," The Atlantic, Jan. 1969, p 40*

[back formation from *attrition*]

ATV, abbreviation of ALL-TERRAIN VEHICLE.

Such rudimentary rules are virtually unenforceable, and marauders on ATVs or snowmobiles occasionally strip hunters' shacks or loot vacation homes. *Time, Nov. 23, 1970, p 41*

A₂, *n.* the virus responsible for Asian flu. See also HONG KONG FLU.

A severe bout of A_2 years earlier left some persons' systems ready to react instantly and forcibly against any related virus. *Time, Jan. 31, 1969, p 36*

audiolingual, *adj.* involving the use of hearing and speech instead of written or printed material.

... the new thrust has been on conversational skills and on the method of oral rather than written communication initially. Electronic language laboratories have been widely installed to facilitate this audiolingual approach. *William M. Alexander, "Education," The Americana Annual 1970, p 264*

audiotactile, *adj.* of or relating to both hearing and touch.

The hospital was partly audio-tactile, the patient being obliged to address his pleas to wall-tubes sieve-ended like the speaking grills in confessional boxes, and then wait for the answers to boom back at him from the ceiling like flight announcements. *"On Manners, Music, and Mortality," an interview with Igor Stravinsky, Harper's, Feb. 1968, p 41*

[patterned after *audiovisual*]

audiotape, *n.* a sound tape recording as distinguished from a videotape.

Consider the technological possibilities we now possess. We have television, audiotapes, records, newspapers, magazines, encyclopedias, movie films — and computers to run them all. *Harvey Wheeler, Saturday Review, May 11, 1968, p 51*

audiotyping, *n.* typing which is done from tape recordings as distinguished from written material.

In the area of audiotyping, the work recently done by I.B.M. in establishing certain comparable output norms, which grapple with the many variables involved, may be of interest to people who want to make a low cost measurement of the productivity of their typing services, present and potential. *B. W. Rowe, The Times (London), June 26, 1968, p 27*

augmentor, *n.* a type of robot that serves as an extension or replacement of a person in performing excessively hard or dangerous work. Compare MAN AMPLIFIER, TELEOPERATOR.

The augmentors are designed to take over or aid in actual labor, such as handling objects that are too big, too small, too far away, too heavy or too dangerous for men. ... General Electric has a family of other augmentor robots, including O-man, which hangs from a crane and can lift two and a half tons. ... *Jonathan Eberhart, "Robots: Sim, Sam and the Beast," Science News, March 9, 1968, p 238*

Aunt Jane, *U.S. Slang.* See the quotation for the meaning.

... black Christians must relearn the whole-hearted involvement with religion that typifies the churches' "Aunt Janes" [1]. ...
[1] Affectionate black-church term for the amen-saying, clapping, lustily singing black-church "sister." Women make up a strong majority of most black congregations. *Time, April 6, 1970, p 71*

aunt sally, *British Slang.* an easy target of criticism or attack.

So OK, it's easy to be rude about South Africa. Of all the aunt sallies ... available there is none on which there is such general agreement, and small chance that she will hit back in any way which hurts. *Monica Furlong, "Television," Punch, July 6, 1966, p 28*

[from the game *Aunt Sally*, in which sticks or balls are thrown at a woman's figure called *Aunt Sally* to knock it down]

Aunt Tabby, *U.S. Slang, used disparagingly.* a woman who does not support the cause of Women's Liberation. Also called AUNT THOMASINA.

The new feminism parallels the black movement in many ways. Both are encumbered for example, by a huge fifth column—for blacks, the Uncle Toms; for women, Aunt Tabbies, also known as Doris Days. *Time, Nov. 21, 1969, p 58*

Aunt Thomasina, *U.S. Slang, used disparagingly.* another name for AUNT TABBY.

Accommodators and temporizers within the Women's Lib movement were spoken of as Aunt Thomasinas. *Benjamin DeMott, "In and Out of Women's Lib," The Atlantic, March 1970, p 112*

[patterned after *Uncle Tom*]

au pair (ˌou 'per), *British.* **1** a foreign girl who does housework, tutoring, etc., for a family without pay in exchange for food and board. *Often used attributively.*

Don't worry, it's probably the au pair registering her annoyance at the lack of food in the refrigerator. *Cartoon legend, "Life and Times in NW1: Objets Trouvés," The Listener, Feb. 1, 1968, p 139*

The original idea of the *au pair* girl was German: a 'house-daughter' she was to be, living as one of the family, morally protected and not asked to do much more than arrange the flowers and take the children to the park. *Katherine Whitehorn, Observer Supplement (London), Nov. 22, 1964, page not recorded*

2 to be an au pair.

Mr. Letica's subjects were three Yugoslav girls who are brushing up their English, au pairing or toiling among our bureaucrats.... *Bernard Hollowood, Punch, Aug. 13, 1969, p 278*

[noun and verb use of the earlier adjective (recorded in the *OED Supplement* with a 1928 citation from the *Sunday Express*), from French *au pair*, literally, on equal terms]

Australia antigen, a substance found in the blood of persons infected with serum hepatitis (an acute virus inflammation of the liver).

Serum hepatitis is frequently transmitted to patients receiving transfusions of blood from individuals who may be unknowing carriers of the so-called Australia antigen associated with the hepatitis virus. *"New York to Screen Blood Donors," Science News, Dec. 19, 1970, p 456*

au·teur (ou'tœr), *n.* a motion-picture director whose films bear the stamp of his personality or style.

Familiar though we are with the axiom that European *auteurs* produce unmistakably personal visions, we have seen Hollywood movies, even the movies of our most "distinctive" directors, as committee efforts. *Jacob Brackman, The New Yorker, July 27, 1968, p 41*

Joseph McGrath is undoubtedly, in the cult phraseology of the moment, an auteur. *The Times (London), Nov. 21, 1968, p 16*

[from French *auteur*, literally, author]

au·teur·ism (ou'tœrˌiz əm), *n.* personal style in directing films; movie direction by auteurs.

The rising popularity of foreign movies, in which directors exert more of a personal influence, at times, than in Hollywood films, gave *auteurism* a mighty shot in the arm.

A. D. Murphy, "The Now Movie: New Room at the Top," Saturday Review, Dec. 28, 1968, p 22

autoaggressive disease, another name for AUTO-IMMUNE DISEASE.

. . . the "autoimmune" diseases (which we now call *autoaggressive*) result from a breakdown in the central system that, in health, regulates normal growth beyond an early stage of embryogenesis. *Philip Burch, New Scientist, Feb. 12, 1970, p 9*

autoanalyzer, *n.* any of various devices or systems for the automatic analysis of the chemical constituents in a substance, process, etc. *Also used attributively.*

Mr. P. D. Faint and Mr. G. H. King, of Technicon Instruments Ltd., in a paper on the results of an autoanalyser study of between 30 and 40 tablets from each of seven pills made by six manufacturers, say they show the need for a single tablet assay. *John Roper, The Times (London), April 24, 1970, p 4*

Dr. Ralph E. Thiers of the Duke University Medical Center... demonstrated a 12-channel blood-testing instrument called an Autoanalyzer.... *Faye Marley, Science News, Oct. 1, 1966, p 245*

Automatic methods of estimating the activity of asparaginase [an enzyme that acts on the plant amino acid asparagine] in whole bacterial cells were developed using an Autoanalyser; this made it possible to screen a wide variety of different strains of bacteria. *H. E. Wade and D. A. Rutter, "Asparaginase Treatment for Leukaemia," Science Journal, March 1970, p 65*

[from *AutoAnalyzer*, a trade name for a device invented in 1950 by Dr. Leonard T. Skeggs of Cleveland]

autochanger, *n.* an automatic record changer.

Whether you choose a single-record player or an autochanger, which will play a stack of six or eight records one after another, depends on your listening habits. *John Borwick, "Let Your Ear Choose HiFi Set," The Times (London), Nov. 14, 1970, p II*

autocide[1], *n.* self-destruction.

The surest method of eradicating a species is to destroy its ability to reproduce.... The relatively small amount of information already available has suggested a number of approaches to preventing the reproduction of the insect and bringing about the autocide of disease-carrying species. *Jack Colvard Jones, Scientific American, April 1968, p 108*

[from *auto-* self + *-cide* killing, as in *homicide*]

autocide[2], *n.* suicide committed by crashing one's car.

No one can know for sure, but more and more police and traffic experts suspect that "autocide," as one expert calls it, is an important cause of traffic deaths. *Time, March 10, 1967, p 19*

[contraction of *auto*mobile sui*cide*]

► This term is not entirely new. It was coined forty years ago with another but similar meaning and apparently had a very short-lived existence:

The National Safety Council of the United States of America, which is said to have been searching for a suitable term to cover "motor-vehicle fatalities," may think that it has found a very nice one in the selected word "autocide," but the choice is not one that will please the purists.... it sins against the rule that two languages should not be mixed up in the same word—the first two syllables are of Greek extraction and the last one comes from Latin. *Baltimore Sun, Oct. 21, 1931, p 14*

autocue, *n. British.* an electronic prompting device which automatically displays, line by line and in large lettering, the text of a speech or lines to be used by a performer on a television show. The equivalent U.S. term is *TelePrompter,* a trade name.

... his monologue was all the more impressive for being given without the aid of an autocue (a sort of electronic prompt machine) and with a minimum of note-glancing. *Chris Dunkley, The Times (London), June 4, 1970, p 10*

Under normal studio conditions Autocue can be read easily from distances of 25 ft., the typeface being half-inch block lettering for clarity, on a master unit with up to four slave viewers sited for members of a production. *W. H. Kennett, The Times (London), July 2, 1968, p VIII*

auto-destruction art or **auto-destructive art,** a form of art in which the art object, usually a mechanical device, destroys or obliterates itself. See also MACHINE ART.

Happenings, "impossible art," auto-destruction art, milti-media events are alternative pursuits that can engage an artist's inventive powers.... *The Manchester Guardian Weekly, Jan. 10, 1970, p 20*

A manifesto by Gustav Metzger relates auto-destructive sculptures to auto-destructive tendencies in contemporary society: "Auto-destructive art is the transformation of technology into public art." *Harold Rosenberg, The New Yorker, Oct. 21, 1967, p 197*

autodrome, *n.* an automobile race track.

The Jarama, circuit some 20 miles north of Madrid, is an artificial track.... It has no local topographical features and is really an autodrome which could be located almost anywhere in the world. *Maxwell Boyd, The Times (London), April 17, 1970, p 15*

[from *auto-* + hippo*drome*]

autogestion, *n.* the management of factories, farms, etc., by committees of workers.

In certain cases, they even go so far as to discuss autogestion, that is to say, the pure and simple confiscation of the firm by its workers. *Marc Ullmann, The Times (London), May 29, 1968, p 11*

[from French, literally, self-management]

autoimmune disease, any of a class of diseases caused when the body forms antibodies against some of its own cells and tissues. See also the quotation under AUTOAGGRESSIVE DISEASE.

There is even the possibility that under certain abnormal conditions the body may form antibodies against some of its own components. It forms an immunity against itself, so to speak, producing a variety of disorders that are classified as autoimmune diseases. *Isaac Asimov, Encyclopedia Science Supplement (Grolier) 1967, p 185*

Lupus erythematosus [a disease of the skin and connective tissues] is the most perfect example of an autoimmune disease. *Science News, March 7, 1970, p 257*

autopia, *n.* a place completely given over to motor vehicles, with no provision for pedestrians or other modes of transportation.

The whole area having been turned into one huge autopia, virtually devoid of public transportation, the majority of potential playgoers and concertgoers choose TV and hi-fi over the hazards of driving, compounded by the desperate search for a parking lot that does not have the "FULL sign" out. *Henri Temianka, Saturday Review, Sept. 23, 1967, p 33*

The notion that downtown should be for people, not automobiles, seems at last to be catching on in America. It may be that 1970 will mark the beginning of the end of "Autopia," as city planner Victor Gruen has called our surrender to the automobile. *Wolf Von Eckhardt, Saturday Review, Oct. 3, 1970, p 62*

[blend of *auto* and *utopia*]

au·to·pis·ta (ˌɑu touˈpiːs tɑː), *n.* an automobile expressway in Spanish-speaking countries.

The Mediterranean autopista, longest at 522 miles, will stretch from the French frontier through Barcelona, Valencia and Alicante to end inland at Granada. *The Sunday Times (London), July 30, 1967, p 22*

[from Spanish]

au·to·put (ˈɑu touˌput), *n.* an automobile expressway in Yugoslavia.

At Dugo Selo, a short cut brings the tourist to the autoput avoiding Zagreb. *Methodi Kusseff, "Balkan Excitement," The Times (London), Jan. 2, 1971, p 21*

[from Serbo-Croatian]

au·to·route (ˈɔː touˌruːt), *n.* an automobile expressway in French-speaking countries.

...a deluxe model powered by an engine of Maserati design and able to burn up the autostradas, autoroutes and autobahns of the Common Market at 150 miles an hour. *John L. Hess, The New York Times, Jan. 12, 1968, p 36*

[from French]

▶ The quotation above mentions the terms *autobahn* and *autostrada.* The former applies to the German expressways and the latter to the Italian ones (although both terms have been occasionally used in the broad sense of "any expressway"). Both terms have been used in English since the early 1950's and therefore are not "new"; all dictionaries now include *autobahn. Autopista* is the term in Spanish-speaking countries; *autoput* is the term in Yugoslavia. *Motorway* is the term used in Great Britain.

auto-timer, *n.* a device that turns on a stove burner or an oven at a preset time, making it possible to cook food while one is away.

For instance you can now buy auto-timers which make it possible to come home to a hot supper... hot plates which have a pan-sensing device to prevent liquid boiling over....*Hilary Gelson, "Gas Versus Electricity," The Times (London), March 12, 1970, p 8*

avalanchologist, *n.* an expert in the study of avalanches.

...Avalanchologist André Roche and other institute scientists now classify avalanches in two basic groups. *Time, March 9, 1970, p 34*

a·vale·ment (əˈvæl mənt), *n.* a skiing technique for accelerating on downhill turns.

Nobody else has quite mastered his [Jean-Claude Killy's] *avalement* technique of accelerating on the downhill turns —rocking back on his haunches and thrusting his skis so far forward that he seems certain to fall. *Time, Feb. 9, 1968, p 34*

Avalement is now accepted as the key to faster skiing, providing one has the strength of thigh.... *John Hennessy, "Another Killy Emerges from France," The Times (London), Dec. 23, 1970, p 11*

[from French, literally, a lowering, from *avaler* to go downhill]

avaluative, *adj.* not ready for evaluation.

Evasion-responsive academics call facts "supportive," techniques "innovative" and theories "avaluative." If proof is less than total, it may be said to have the "ring of authenticity." *Israel Schenker, The New York Times, Jan. 10, 1970, p 33*

[from *a-* not + *valuative*]

aversion therapy, a therapy against a harmful habit or addiction by inducing an aversion to it. Compare BEHAVIOR THERAPY.

Russell's experiment is another application of what psychologists call aversion therapy.... A heroin addict, for instance, is given a drug (Scoline) that seriously impairs his ability to breathe. Just before the drug takes effect, he gets his usual dose of heroin. After several such harrowing experiences, he presumably kicks his habit. *Time, March 2, 1970, p 58*

The medicine was aversion therapy—a highly controversial method of punishing the patient to change his behaviour. *Peter Pringle, The Sunday Times (London), May 9, 1971, p 8*

London (AP)—Two British psychiatrists say they have cured a husband of infidelity by giving him a 70-volt shock every time he looked at a photo of his paramour. Dr. John Barker and Dr. Mabel Miller of Sheldon Hospital, Shrewsbury, said the husband is now totally indifferent to the other woman, a neighbor. Describing the treatment— "aversion therapy"—in the medical magazine Pulse Friday, the doctors said it had been used successfully in experiments with gamblers and homosexuals, but they believed this was the first instance of it being tried on the old familiar triangle, *The Tuscaloosa News, Dec. 4, 1966, p 49*

awash, *adj.* drunk.

Presently, a woman entered, a brown gamine with a certain look of money about her, like a faint shimmer along her limbs. She was already a trifle awash, on the arm of a pretty, perfumed, fluorescent youth whom she introduced to Fawzi by his first name and sang, "Isn't he beautiful?" *Marshall Frady, "An American Innocent in the Middle East," Harper's, Oct. 1970, p 72*

axe, *n. U.S. Slang.* any musical instrument.

The language, the argot of rock is grounded in sexuality. The instrument is your "axe." What you play on it are "licks" and "chops." *Sara Davidson, "Rock Style," Harper's, July 1969, p 60*

The fogeys didn't know an "axe" (a guitar) from a hole in the ground. *Time, Feb. 14, 1969, p 43*

... musicians occasionally refer to their instruments as "axes".... *Whitney Balliett, "Musical Events," The New Yorker, June 28, 1969, p 76*

Remember that Tiny Tim, despite his success, is the kind of entertainer who used to bring his axe to parties and hope people would ask him to play. *Alexander Ross, "Tiny Tim—God Bless Him," Maclean's, Nov. 1968, p 67*

[perhaps originally applied to a saxophone, whose short form, *sax*, rhymes with *axe*, and whose shape may have suggested that of an axe. Later it was chiefly applied to a guitar or other stringed instrument, and eventually extended to any instrument used by rock 'n' roll bands.]

A-Z, *adj.* all-inclusive.

Each of its ["The Encyclopedia of Ireland," edited by Victor Meally] sections (Wild Life, Archeology, Government, Education, Language, Tourism, and The Arts, among others) gives a lively and expert A-Z account of itself, with the aid of 573 black-and-white illustrations. *David M. Glixon, "Let's Look It Up," Saturday Review, Nov. 16, 1968, p 62*

[from the idiom *from A to Z*]

a·zu·le·jo (ˌɑː θuːˈle hou), *n. Spanish and Portugues.* colored tile, usually blue. *Also used attributively.*

It [Santa Cruz in Seville] is a place of miniature plazas like stage sets, planted with orange trees, of Moorish gateways and *azulejo* tiles, of hidden courtyards and jasmine-covered walls. *Edwin Cox, "Murder and Jasmine," Saturday Review, Nov. 18, 1967, p 63*

► The phonetic respelling indicated above reflects the Spanish pronunciation. In Portuguese the word is approximately (ˌə zuːˈlei ʒuː).

B

backgrounder, *n. U.S.* a meeting or a memorandum for journalists in which a government official explains the background of a government action or policy.

... Henry A. Kissinger, has reported in numerous "backgrounders": "If we had done in our first year what our loudest critics called on us to do, the 13 per cent that voted for Wallace would have grown to 35 or 40 per cent; the first thing the President set out to do was to neutralize that faction." *Daniel Ellsberg, "The Quagmire Myth," The New York Times, June 26, 1971, p 29*

Immediately after the White House briefing, Congressman Ford called in some reporters for a "backgrounder," in other words, a report to them as to what has happened for background purposes. A "backgrounder" permits newspapermen to publish information given them though without attribution to the source. *Drew Pearson, The Tuscaloosa News, Aug. 5, 1965, p 4*

backlash, *n.* **1** *U.S.* a reaction of antagonism by whites to the pressure for racial integration exerted by the black civil-rights movement. *Often used attributively.* Also called WHITE BACKLASH.

Reaction had set in, of course, call it backlash or frontlash. *C. Vann Woodward, "What Happened to the Civil Rights Movement?" Harper's, Jan. 1967, p 33*

If the potential backlash voter is a mixture, so are his motives. Some simply resent growing violence in the streets.... Some feel threatened by Negroes moving into their neighborhoods, and their response is visceral. *The New York Times, Oct. 23, 1966, Sec. 4, p 2*

2 any antagonistic reaction.

The law required the use of the French language in addition to English.... It aroused a sensational, though temporary, backlash of English-speaking opinion, concentrated in Westmorland county, where the Canadian Loyalist Association has its headquarters. *W. S. MacNutt. "New Brunswick," The Americana Annual 1970, p 494*

—*v.i.* to produce an antagonistic reaction.

What evidence is there that the public want to be matey with the famous instead of awestruck? The Wilson-Heath image of the clever Little Man is backlashing. *R. G. G. Price, "Criticism," Punch, Sept. 3, 1969, p 392*

back·pro·ject ('bæk prəˌdʒekt), *v.t.* to project (an image) on the back of a translucent screen for viewing from the front.

... A projector, the first designed specifically for shipboard installation,... backprojects a full-scale 42- × 36-inch colored image of a chart onto the underside of its transparent top. *Science News, Oct. 22, 1966, p 335*

—*n.* a backprojected image.

Eva Schwartz's sets —light, ground-row [low, flat scenery]

pieces against street back-projects encased in a vast gilt picture-frame — are witty and practical. . . . *The Times (London), April 28, 1970, p 7*

backscatter, *v.t. Physics.* to scatter (rays or particles) backward by deflection.

Researchers ... worked out a simple, non-destructive technique for measuring the strength of egg shells. They measure the number of beta-particles from a ruthenium-rhodium radioactive source, back-scattered by the egg shell. *New Scientist, May 21, 1970, p 382*

However, because of the large angle at which the reconstructing beam will be reflected from the silver planes, interference will occur between waves that are back-scattered by the planes. *Illustration legend, "Advances in Holography" by Keith S. Pennington, Scientific American, Feb. 1968, p 48*

[verb use of *backscatter, n.,* the scattering of rays or particles by an obstacle]

back-street, *adj.* furtive; clandestine.

By limiting the number of doctors available to perform legal abortions it could produce an increase in illegal back-street abortions. *The Times (London), Feb. 14, 1970, p 4*

backup, *n.* one kept in reserve as a substitute or for assistance.

Except for what Attridge called a minor computer glitch ("glitch" is space talk for "hitch"), which caused a premature shutdown of a rocket, LM-1 passed its tests so successfully that its backup, LM-2, did not have to go up. *Henry S. F. Cooper, Jr., "A Reporter At Large: LM (Lunar Module)," The New Yorker, Jan. 11, 1969, p 38*

bad-mouth, *v.t. U.S. Slang.* to malign; slander.

Black American expressions like "be with it," "do your thing" and "bad-mouth" (to talk badly about someone) are word for word translations from phrases used widely in West African languages, including Mandingo. *David Dalby, "Jazz, Jitter, and Jam," The New York Times, Nov. 10, 1970, p 47*

Then the spurned client goes around bad-mouthing Lawyer Burnett: 'Don't hire Burnett because the son-of-a-bitch won't sue. He's bought off.' *Larry L. King, "Warren Burnett: Texas Lawyer," Harper's, July 1969, p 72*

Whether his remarks will hurt or not will not be known until campaign time. If he continues to "bad mouth" the legislature, it might win some public praise but it will cost him a lot of support among a group of men who could help him or hurt him come election time. *The Tuscaloosa News, Sept. 16, 1969, p 4*

bad news, *U.S.* something or someone disturbing, troublesome, or undesirable.

"... Some of them [the larvae of the linden moth] are black and some are brown.... And they're there, twisting.

But they're bad news. They eat the hardwood leaves. The government's trying to figure some way to get rid of 'em." *James Dickey, Deliverance, 1970, p 54*

...."I knew the kid was bad news first morning I met him, sipping Angie's coffee." *Norman Fruchter, "Single File" (a novel), quoted by John Updike, "Books," The New Yorker, April 10, 1971, p 148*

bad trip, *Slang.* a frightening experience involving hallucinations, pain, etc., caused by taking a psychedelic drug, especially LSD. Compare ACID TRIP. Also called BUMMER.

Kids on bad trips were treated by volunteer physicians, and were urged over a makeshift public-address system to "bring a few joints [marijuana cigarettes] for the doctors." *Time, Aug. 10, 1970, p 11*

bag, *n. U.S. Slang.* **1** one's principal interest or habit.

Black Studies is not my bag. But doesn't it approach the ridiculous to say or imply that black students are "proposing to study black history in isolation from the mainstream of American history?" *Kenneth S. Tollett, Houston, Texas, in a Letter to the Editor, Harper's, April 1970, p 6*

2 a situation, matter, or problem.

"Let's take his pants down," I said to Bobby. He looked at me.

"God damn phraseology," I said. "We're in another bag now, baby. Get his pants off him, and see if you can tell how bad he's hurt...." *James Dickey, "Two Days in September," The Atlantic, Feb. 1970, p 98*

3 a portion of a narcotic drug or the envelope containing it.

In the argot of the drug world, it is "paraphernalia": the necessary accouterments to merchandising heroin. The small glassine envelopes or "bags," used to package heroin, are paraphernalia. So, too, are the legal, harmless powders used to dilute the drug, usually quinine, dextrose, lactose or mannite. *Time, July 20, 1970, p 15*

A typical bag of heroin purchased on the street ordinarily contains only from 0% to 5% heroin. *Sidney Cohen, "Narcotics and Hallucinogens," The Americana Annual 1970, p 486*

baggys, *n.pl. U.S.* baggy shorts, such as boxers wear, used by male surfers. Compare JAMS (def. 2).

... among their boyfriends "baggys" (loose-fitting swim trunks) were de rigueur. *Peter Bart, The New York Times, Aug. 10, 1965, p 31*

bag job, *U.S. Slang.* an illegal search for evidence of espionage.

He [J. Edgar Hoover] also banned what intelligence called "surreptitious entry" — meaning burglary — and a companion tactic, the "bag job," in which agents enter a home or office and examine or copy documents, personal papers or notebooks. In the past, numerous spies — notably Rudolf Abel — have been exposed by bag jobs. *"The File On J. Edgar Hoover," Time, Oct. 25, 1971, p 31*

bailout, *n.* an emergency rescue or relief, especially through financial aid.

Very soon we may have the Securities Investor Protection Corporation, but a bailout with government funds does not supply a satisfactory long-term solution. A tighter pattern of rules and enforcement is sorely needed. *The New York Times, Dec. 21, 1970, p 35*

[from the verb phrase *bail out* to help out or rescue]

▶ *Bailout* is recorded only in the sense of bailing

out or parachuting from an aircraft in an emergency.

bait-and-switch, *adj. U.S.* designed to induce customers to purchase a more expensive item than the one advertised at a much lower price.

The commission found that "bait-and-switch" advertising was among the "numerous techniques" used to deceive purchasers. This involves the advertising of a low-priced product to lure the customer into the store, where he is urged to buy a higher-priced article. *John D. Morris, The New York Times, July 9, 1968, p 19*

The Competition Act also makes it a criminal offence to engage in misleading advertising, unfair pyramid selling, bait-and-switch selling (plain switch selling in Britain).... *Harlow Unger, The Sunday Times (London), July 11, 1971, p 40*

Baker-Nunn camera, a large telescopic camera for photographing orbiting satellites as part of an optical network for tracking satellites.

Anderle's paper, in particular, discusses the reduction of observations of satellites by worldwide networks of Baker-Nunn cameras. *Ralph B. Baldwin, "Geology of the Solar System," Science, April 12, 1968, p 177*

[named after James Gilbert *Baker* and Joseph *Nunn*, American inventors of optical instruments who designed the camera, first used in 1957]

ball, *v.i. U.S. Slang.* to have a good time, especially in a wild, uninhibited way; have a spree.

"What's different now," said a Haight [Haight-Ashbury section of San Francisco] dope peddler, "is that speed's better than it used to be. There's not so much amphetamine poisoning and you can ball on it, which you could never do before...." *The Manchester Guardian Weekly, May 2, 1970, p 16*

[verb use of *ball*, *n.*, slang term meaning a good time, especially in the phrase *to have a ball*]

ball game, *U.S. Slang.* **1** a center or field of action.

"Most of the news in the papers we [television news broadcasters] cannot cover and we will never be able to. When it comes to covering the news in any kind of detailed way, we are just almost not in the ball game." *David Brinkley, quoted by Herbert Brucker, in "Can Printed News Save A Free Society?" Saturday Review, Oct. 10, 1970, p 55*

2 a state of affairs; situation.

... if an invasion took place the Chinese might enter the war. If this were to happen, some official of our government would no doubt announce that we were in a "whole new ballgame," which would mean that none of the policies or promises made in the past were binding any longer, including the prohibition against the use of nuclear weapons. *"The Talk of the Town," The New Yorker, March 13, 1971, p 30*

balloon, *n.* **like a lead balloon,** without the slightest effect.

So Nixon said it. And then went on to say, what nobody has ever quarrelled with, that the time had come 'to move mankind from an era of confrontation into an era of negotiation'. A short pause for loud and prolonged cheers. I don't know whether they came, but even this magnificent cliché fell on the ears of Marshal Tito like a lead balloon. *Alistair Cooke, "Acts of God," The Listener, Oct. 8, 1970, p 475*

balloon astronomy, the collection of astronomical data from photographs, etc., taken at high altitude through a telescope attached to a balloon.

Martin Schwarzschild, "father of balloon astronomy," was awarded the 1967 Albert A. Michelson Award by Case Institute of Technology of Case-Western Reserve University, Cleveland, O. . . . He was cited for "leadership in the theory of stellar evolution, and for pioneering application of balloon-borne telescopes for observations of the sun, stars, and planets." *"Awards and Prizes: Astronomy," 1969 Britannica Yearbook of Science and the Future, 1968, p 257*

bal·lute (bə'lu:t), *n.* a combination balloon and parachute used for deceleration.

The attraction of the Woomera range is that recovery can be made on land. After being decelerated by 'ballute', a type of drag balloon, the test model would be soft-landed either by parachute or an extensible rotor. *Science Journal, Dec. 1970, p 10*

[from *ball*oon + parach*ute*]

banalize, *v.t.* to make banal; reduce to something commonplace or ordinary.

The great and good traditional virtues have been eroded: love, generosity, self-denial, truthfulness, honesty, loyalty, friendship, kindness to children. That many of these traits have been banalized by advertising seems incidental. *Marshall D. Sahlins, Review of "Culture Against Man" by Jules Henry, Scientific American, May 1964, p 140*

banana, *n. U.S. Slang.* a derogatory name for an Oriental who is part of the white establishment or is in favor of working within the white establishment.

In the San Francisco Bay area, with a large population of Japanese-Americans and many militants, young protesters have picketed S. I. Hayakawa, the president of San Francisco State College who is a steadfast believer in assimilation, calling him a "banana" — yellow on the outside, white inside — the equivalent of the blacks' epithet "Oreo." *Norman Pearlstine, "The 'Quiet Minority': Militancy Up Among Wary Japanese-Americans," The Wall Street Journal, Aug. 8, 1972, p 9*

bananas, *adj.* **go bananas,** *U.S. Slang.* to go crazy.

. . . Liza [Liza Minnelli] moved into the sheltered regimented Barbizon Hotel for Women. Liza says: "I went bananas!" *Time, March 9, 1970, p 43*

band-aid, *adj. U.S.* patched up or put together hastily; serving as a stop-gap; temporary.

The American feeling is probably that quick "fire brigade" action is not enough and better and better economic coordination might prevent the need for such heavy reliance on financial "band-aid" solutions. *Clyde H. Farnsworth, "New US Monetary Initiative," The Times (London), April 20, 1970, p 19*

[generic use of *Band-Aid*, trade name for a prepared adhesive bandage]

bandh (ba:nd), *n.* (in India) a general suspension of work and business as an act of protest. Compare GHERAO.

Life was at a standstill in West Bengal today as people stayed away from work in response to a call by leftist parties for a 24-hour bandh. . . . *The Times (London), July 15, 1970, p 6*

[from Hindi *bāndh* a stop]

bandh·nu ('ba:nd nu:), *n.* tie-dyeing (in which parts of the fabric are tied off so that they will not be colored).

The art is almost as old as India — where it is called *bandhnu*. It is as new as the boutiques that blossom along Sunset Strip and Madison Avenue — where it is called tie-dyeing. *Time, Jan. 26, 1970, p 40*

[from Hindi *bāndhnū,* from *bāndhnā* to tie]

bandmoll, *n. U.S.* a girl who associates with a rock 'n' roll band; a groupie.

. . . "Groupies" [a film] reveals a way of life that has shock and curiosity value for the audience. The subject of baby bandmolls is such a good one that it holds one's speculative interest. . . . *Pauline Kael, "The Current Cinema," The New Yorker, Dec. 5, 1970, p 167*

[patterned after *gun moll* a gangster's girl friend]

banger, *n. Slang* a noisy, old vehicle.

The Illustrated One, at ease astride his ancient Harley two-stroke banger. . . . *Roger Angell, "Sad Arthur," The New Yorker, March 14, 1970, p 33*

A system that allows him to pass his test one day in a 10-year-old "banger" and climb straight into a 150 mph Jaguar the next is the height of dangerous folly. *Maxwell Boyd, The Sunday Times (London), Feb. 5, 1967, p 17*

bang-zone, *n. U.S.* the area affected by a sonic boom.

The Handbook contends that a single SST [supersonic transport], flying from New York to California, would leave a "bang-zone" 50 miles wide by 2,000 miles long. *Time, June 1, 1970, p 64*

bank card, a credit card issued by a bank.

Development of existing bank cards — including both cheque guarantee cards and credit cards as we know them today — will play a major role in the advance towards a "cashless and chequeless society." *James Robertson, "Paying by Computer," New Scientist, July 23, 1970, p 181*

banque d'af·faires ('bāk da'fer), (in France) a commercial bank that engages in industrial and commercial investment and management of securities.

The merchant banks (banques d'affaires), on the other hand, whose role was to invest in industrial and commercial companies and to manage such holdings, were not allowed to take deposits for less than 12 months. . . . *Gilbert Géas, "Paris," The Times (London), July 6, 1970, p I*

These men head investment-banking houses in New York City, merchant-banking ventures in London, banques d'affaires in Paris, and similar institutions in Belgium, the Netherlands, Italy, Germany, Sweden, and Australia. *T. A. Wise, The Times (London), Aug. 19, 1968, p 17*

barf (barf), *v.i. U.S. Slang.* to vomit.

One of the guards hooted above the noise of the plane engines, "Hang on, sweethearts!" Then he leaned over to me and said, "Hope none of 'em barfs." I asked if they would be allowed to remove their sacks if they became sick. *Orville Schell, "Cage for the Innocents," The Atlantic, Jan. 1968, p 30*

[probably imitative of the sound of retching]

bariatrician, *n.* a specialist in bariatrics.

One East Coast bariatrician orders his pills in batches of between 500,000 and 1,000,000. . . . *Peter Dickinson, "In Praise of Plump Women," Punch, Feb. 1, 1967, p 153*

bariatrics

bar·i·at·rics (ˌbær iːˈæt riks), *n.* the medical treatment of overweight people.

...the booming business of weight-doctoring (called bariatrics by its practitioners) is endangering the health of the country because the drugs used may have nasty side-effects.... My own objections to bariatrics are equally scientific, but different. Man is a peculiar animal in many ways.... And one of man's chief peculiarities is that every specimen is wholly different from every other specimen to a degree unparalleled elsewhere in creation.... Appetite, height, girth and weight.... They all have their own natural size. *Peter Dickinson, "In Praise of Plump Women," Punch, Feb. 1, 1967, p 153*

[from *bar-* weight (from Greek *báros*) + *-iatrics*, as in *geriatrics*]

bar mitz·vah (bɑr ˈmits və), to confirm (a 13-year-old Jewish boy) in the Synagogue.

"...I'd just been bar mitzvahed when I went off with my brother to pitch snake oil on the Pennsylvania carnival circuit." *Irvin Feld, quoted in Time, May 4, 1970, p 74*

[verb use of the noun phrase. The verb exists only in English; the original Hebrew (or Yiddish) term does not function as a verb.]

ba·ro·co·co (bəˌrou kəˈkou), *adj.* combining the baroque and rococo styles; grotesquely elaborate.

He [Hal Prince, a producer] discovered what came to be the show's essential conception in Eliot Elisofon's picture of Gloria Swanson amid the ruins of Manhattan's Roxy Theater, a barococo movie palace that was demolished in 1960. *Time, May 3, 1971, p 33*

[blend of *baroque* and *rococo*]

baroquerie, *n.* **1** baroque quality or character.

...complaints about his [the violinist Ricci's] almost total lack of fashionable baroquerie (no trills, no double-dotting) become mere quibbles. *The Sunday Times (London), Jan. 12, 1969, p 56*

2 something baroque.

In an altogether different vein is what Mr. Gordon calls a "beautiful and nutty" country Chippendale chair, which is full of serpentine curves and baroqueries and still has its original coat of paint—a flamboyant turquoise. *"On and Off the Avenue," The New Yorker, Dec. 2, 1967, p 182*

[from French]

baroreceptor, *n.* a nerve cell or group of cells that are sensitive to pressure.

The pressure is sensed by the baroreceptors located in the aortic arch at left and right carotid sinuses. *John E. Jacobs, "Biomedical Engineering: Cardiovascular System," McGraw-Hill Yearbook of Science and Technology 1967, p 120*

[from *baro-* pressure (from Greek *báros* weight) + *receptor*]

bar·ri·a·da (ˌbɑr riˈɑː ðɑː), *n. Spanish.* a city quarter, especially a slum inhabited by poor migrants from the country.

From there, as the city [Lima] thins, the road widens to four lanes, cutting through occasional barriadas—fields of houses huddled around dirt streets and open sewage.... *Richard N. Goodwin, "Letter From Peru," The New Yorker, May 17, 1969, p 52*

But I do regret deeply the real victims in this situation [the Peruvian government's nationalization of foreign businesses], the masses of Latin Americans whose tomorrows are hopeless without increasing foreign investments to industrialize and modernize their societies. If no one protects these investments, the man in the *barriada* and the *favela* is the one most to suffer. *Val Clear, Lima, Peru, in a Letter to the Editor, Time, April 25, 1969, p 12*

bar·y·on (ˈbær iˌɑn), *n.* any elementary particle which can be transformed into a neutron, proton, or meson.

The term "baryon" designates the nucleon [neutron or proton] in all its different states of excitation. Baryons are known by many special names depending on their particular mass energy. *Victor F. Weisskopf, "The Three Spectroscopies," Scientific American, May 1968, p 16*

[from Greek *barýs* heavy + English *-on*, as in *electron*]

base pair, a combination of two of the four compounds (adenine, cytosine, guanine, and thymine) which make up the molecules of DNA (deoxyribonucleic acid, the main carrier of genetic information in living cells).

A mutation can affect the chemistry of the hereditary material—the DNA and RNA [ribonucleic acid, which expresses genetic information by the synthesis of specific proteins]—in various ways. For example, it can alter the sequence of the base pairs that constitute the triplet code alphabet of the hereditary language. It can also entail the loss of a base pair, resulting in a "misreading" of an entire "line" of the hereditary text. *Björn Sigurbjörnsson, "Induced Mutations in Plants," Scientific American, Jan. 1971, p 87*

bash, *n. British and Canadian Slang.* a try.

"Let's have a bash at electronics," decided James Findlay of Findlay Irvine. *The Sunday Times (London), March 30, 1969, p 32*

"Now," my friend said, "we'll just take a bash at the lower slope." *Kildare Dobbs, Saturday Night (Canada), April 1968, p 57*

BASIC or Basic (ˈbei sik), *n.* acronym for *Beginners All-purpose Symbolic Instruction Code*, a computer language using common English terms in program construction. Compare ALGOL, COBOL, FORTRAN.

BASIC for Beginners is a readable self-instruction for the beginning student of the computer language BASIC, widely used at time-sharing teletypewriter terminals, particularly in schools and colleges. *Philip and Phylis Morrison, "Books," Review of "BASIC for Beginners" by Wilson Y. Gateley and Gary G. Bitter, Scientific American, Dec. 1970, p 126*

batch processing, a form of data processing in which all related operations are grouped in a batch before any of them is executed.

In batch processing, a series of jobs, often a whole day's work, is prepared in advance on some input medium. For example, with punch-card input, the job-card decks representing the different jobs to be done are accumulated in large trays. *R. Clay Sprowls, "Computer," Encyclopedia Science Supplement (Grolier) 1971, p 145*

Batch processing exhibits significant importance when applied to the lengthy complex mathematical calculations required for many theoretical problems. *Max Tochner, "Computer-Assisted Analytical Chemistry," McGraw-Hill Yearbook of Science and Technology 1971, p 60*

baton gun, a gun that fires large hard-rubber

bullets, used in riot control. Compare STUN GUN.

The weekend saw the introduction of two weapons by the Army, water cannon and the rubber baton gun. *David Wilsworth, "Mob Gets First Taste of Rubber Bullets," The Times (London), Aug. 3, 1970, p 1*

baton round, the hard-rubber bullet used in a baton gun.

Baton rounds (as the rubber bullets are called) with the pistol which fires them. *Picture legend in New Scientist and Science Journal, Aug. 12, 1971, p 375*

battered child syndrome or **battered baby syndrome,** a condition of severe bruises or other injuries exhibited by a small child, usually under four years of age. Allegedly caused by accident, they actually result from beatings or other extreme punishment administered usually by parents.

One of my correspondents ... is working with a psychiatric clinic charged with investigating families in which "the battered child syndrome" has produced a beaten child. *Elizabeth Janeway, "Happiness and the Right to Choose," The Atlantic, March 1970, p 124*

The battered baby syndrome ... what no one formerly realised was that the battering had been done on purpose by loving parents. *Elspeth Huxley, "Growing Up in Britain," Punch, April 5, 1967, p 489*

baud (bɔːd), *n.* a unit of speed in data processing equal to one binary digit per second.

The new machine at Shell Centre will provide a considerable increase in capacity, and the leased lines forming the communication links will handle 4,800 bauds (bits per second) in the near future compared with 1,200 and 2,400 at present. *The Times (London), July 19, 1968, p 19*

[originally a unit in telegraphy (one dot per second), named after J. M. E. *Baudo*t, 1845-1903, a French inventor]

beamwidth, *n.* the angular width of a radio or radar beam.

The aerial provides modest resolution, particularly in the 1.3 to 9 MHz band, and has a mid-band beamwidth of about 40°. *R. G. Stone, "Radioastronomy from Space," Science Journal, March 1970, p 71*

beard, *n. U.S. Slang.* a person who wears a beard, especially a college student, teacher, or other intellectual.

The only beards to be found upstate are on the 45-odd huge State University campuses that gradually are pushing the Adirondack Mountains back into Canada. ... *Tom Cawley, "The Art of Red Barn Campaigning," The New York Times, June 6, 1970, p 30*

In the San Francisco area, where last year almost 60,000 housewives, hippies, businessmen and beards marched, only 15,000 zealots turned out. ... *Time, May 3, 1968, p 21*

beautiful people or **Beautiful People,** the wealthy, fashionable people of high society and the arts who set the trend in beauty and elegance. *Abbreviation:* BP

"The establishment yearns for the days of the Kennedys. ... The shuttle society—artists, nobles, the beautiful people—used to make a pilgrimage down here [Washington, D.C.] to do its bit nightly." *Maxine Cheshire, quoted by Adam Raphael, in "Come Back Jackie, All is Forgiven," The Manchester Guardian Weekly, July 18, 1970, p 24*

Though the columns of *WWD* [Women's Wear Daily] are filled with the social doings of what he [John Burr Fairchild] calls the "Beautiful People," he resolutely shuns their company and their entertainments. *Time, Sept. 14, 1970, p 76*

"... we don't like all these Beautiful People who think they're so great because they got an invitation [to an exhibition of John Lennon's lithographs]. They're the ones who are exploiting our culture." *"The Talk of the Town," The New Yorker, Feb. 21, 1970, p 29*

beaver, *v.i. British.* to work like a beaver; work hard.

Between 1952 and 1963 Mr [Anthony] Barber was beavering around in the lower reaches of Government office. He was successively Parliamentary Private Secretary to the Air Ministry, a Government Whip, Lord Commissioner of the Treasury ... and later Financial Secretary to the Treasury. *Dennis Johnson, "The New Men," The Manchester Guardian Weekly, Oct. 17, 1970, p 11*

They may look like clerks beavering away, but emphatically aren't. They remind you theirs is an occupation of quality and calibre. *"Midwives to Brain-children," The Sunday Times (London), Aug. 8, 1971, p 33*

[verb use of the noun]

beddo, *n.* any of various beds designed in Japan that may be raised, rotated, rocked, etc., by electronic means.

Going to bed in Japan these days often requires a good night's sleep in advance. No more can the weary traveler anticipate curling up on the traditional straw mat, bundled between layers of silken spreads—or even on a regular bed, which is rare in Japan. Instead he is likely to find himself a helpless passenger aboard a vehicle that sways from side to side, swoops abruptly to the ceiling, or flips up and down in three-quarter time. For a *beddo* only sounds like a bed. In fact it is an electronic adventure. *Time, Dec. 12, 1969, p 52*

Beddos are play beds which bring all the fun of the fair [Expo '70]—and possibly more—into the boudoir. *New Scientist, May 7, 1970, p 269*

[from Japanese *beddo* bed, from English *bed*. The traditional Japanese sleeping mat or mattress is called *tatami*.]

bedsit, *British. —v.i.* to occupy a bed-sitter (a room serving both as bedroom and sitting room).

A year ago Kensington Council bought the house in the West Cromwell Road where she bedsat, in order to pull it down. All the other tenants moved out, leaving her and an old lady as the only tenants in a place full of creaking floorboards, darkness, decay, and a feeling of Boris Karloff making strange noises behind the wainscotting. *Philip Howard, The Times (London), June 18, 1970, p 9*

—n. a bed-sitter.

... Rose was a bundle of insecure apprehensions, afraid to move from her tatty bed-sit lest the menacing forces outside should take over to deprive her of the small comforts that buttressed her loveless life. *Kenneth Pearson, The Sunday Times (London), Jan. 7, 1968, p 27*

[back formation from *bed-sitter*]

bedspace, *n.* the space for beds or the number of beds in a hotel, hospital, dormitory, etc.

Christian Action has established an emergency accommodation bureau for foreigners in a borrowed builders' hut in the courtyard of St. Martin-in-the-Fields, Trafalgar Square. It is finding bedspace for a steady stream of stranded visitors. *Garry Lloyd, "Bureau to Help Young Tourists Find Beds," The Times (London), Aug. 11, 1970, p 3*

A computer lists available bedspace at the hospital nearest the patient's home. *Martin Tolchin, The New York Times, March 13, 1968, p 35*

beehive, *n.* a woman's hair style in which the hair is shaped like a conical, coiled beehive.

The beehives and butch cuts [crew cuts] were bobbing in merriment now, David Rabie's being perhaps the only grim face in the room, but then he was counting empty tables. *Larry L. King, "Whatever Happened to Brother Dave?" Harper's, Sept. 1970, p 55*

"--- I am also one of the top hairdressers in the world. Seventy-five dollars an hour! I created the beehive hairdo." *Zorro David, quoted in "The Talk of the Town," The New Yorker, Aug. 22, 1970, p 31*

beehived, *adj.* wearing the hair in the beehive style.

The door swung and a little beehived girl ducked under my arm into the cold air. *James Dickey, Deliverance, 1970, p 16*

beer bust, *U.S. Slang.* a party at which beer is the main beverage.

Later in the month, 500 members frolicked as guests of the bank at a barbecue and beer bust. *Time, Aug. 22, 1969, p 53*

Not that you can trot down to Woolworth's and pick one [continuous-wave helium-neon laser] up for your next beer bust. *Morton Grosser, "A Little Light On The Subject," The Atlantic, June 1971, p 93*

before-tax, *adj.* gained or received before taxes are paid. Also called PRETAX.

Before-tax book profits of U.S. corporations declined in the fourth quarter of 1969 to a seasonally adjusted annual rate of $91,500 m. [thousand] (£38,100m.). . . . *The Times (London), March 19, 1970, p 23*

"When I pay talent or buy feature film," said an executive of a competing TV station, "I've got to use after-tax dollars. They use before-tax dollars." *Alfred Balk, "God is Rich," Harper's, Oct. 1967, p 71*

beggar-my-neighbor or **beggar-thy-neighbor,** *adj.* based on or involving a gain of advantage by the losses of another.

It would not be an exaggeration to say that we stand on the brink of the first major outbreak of trade war since the beggar-my-neighbor catastrophes of the inter-war period. *Hugh Stephenson, "Suspended Animation in Common Market Talks," The Times (London), April 29, 1970, p 13*

The last time such beggar-thy-neighbor policies became common, during the 1930s, they contributed mightily to the century's worst economic depression. *Time, May 16, 1969, p 74*

[from the card game *beggar-my-neighbor*, which is won by capturing all of one's opponent's cards]

behavior therapy, a form of psychological therapy in which a patient is conditioned to replace old habits or patterns of behavior with new ones. Compare AVERSION THERAPY.

The scientists, convinced of the errors of Freud, maintain that therapies based on conditioning and learning theory—grouped under the umbrella term "behaviour therapy"—are much more effective and practical than in-depth, "arty" therapy which lays bare the patient's soul. *New Scientist, Dec. 24, 1970, p 541*

Unlike psycho-analysis, which may go on for years, behavior therapy is often completed in fewer than 30 sessions—and it claims success in 85% of its cases. *Time, Aug. 2, 1971, p 50*

be-in, *n.* an informal gathering, usually in a park or other public place, for the purpose of being together and doing whatever one likes.

What, the Judge wanted to know, was a "be-in." With great sweetness and delicacy, Ginsberg explained it was "a gathering of young people imbued with a new planetary life-style." *Alistair Cooke, "My Lai: Grim Alternatives," The Manchester Guardian Weekly, Dec. 20, 1969, p 4*

[see -IN]

be·ke (bei'kei), *n. French Creole.* a white settler.

Martinique still has its white aristocracy, the *békés*. *The Times (London), Sept. 7, 1970, p III*

She was a child in Jamaica. . . . Her old nurse, Christophine, is an obeah [practicing a kind of witchcraft] woman, and warns her that this kind of thing is not for the *béké* to play with. *Gerald Kersh, "The Second Time Around," Review of "Wide Sargasso Sea" by Jean Rhys, Saturday Review, July 1, 1967, p 23*

"There are many rich families here [in Guadeloupe], very rich. They are the *békés*, the white planters." *James Egan, "Le High-Life in Guadeloupe," The Atlantic, Dec. 1965, p 120*

belle é·poque (bel ei'pɔːk), **1** typical of the turn of the century.

In the U.S., the style is called either *Belle Époque* (after turn-of-the-century coiffures), or "Oscar's hairdo" (after Designer Oscar de la Renta, who put topknots on all the models at his spring collections last month). *Time, Dec. 5, 1969, p 56*

Mr. Glazebrooke has turned the area into a "belle epoque" pavilion with a sunny, airy effect achieved by lighting, cream-colored walls broken up by painted art nouveau arches, and deep gold carpeting. *Bernadette Carey, The New York Times, Oct. 1, 1966, p 20*

2 the era of the turn of the century.

Though his collection is not all of motoring, here we find a record of that *belle époque*, with goggled, face-masked and windswept drivers, snapshots of mud-caked, thundering races in French villages, Jenatzy in the last Gordon Bennett Cup race, strange pedal-carts and adventures awheel in a 35 h.p. Peugeot. . . . *The Times (London), Sept. 27, 1967, p 13*

[from French *la Belle Époque*, name given to the period 1880-1905, literally, the Beautiful Era]

bellicism, *n.* warlike tendency; belligerence.

American imperialism is under attack on every flank by the world's forces of progress. In order to stand up to this powerful movement and in order to camouflage his bellicism President Nixon proclaimed his doctrine of a new peace strategy. *Prince Souphanouvong, leader of the Pathet Lao, the Communist-affiliated Lao Patriotic National Front, in "A Call for Peace in Laos," The New York Times, Nov. 9, 1970, p 41*

[from Latin *bellicus* of war, warlike; patterned after *pacifism*]

bells, *n.pl.* bell-bottom trousers.

Having purchased a pair of red velvet bells for thirty dollars and finding them not to his liking after wearing them for a day (wrong size, wrong color), he returned to Sekhmet, on St. Marks Place, to make an exchange. *Eli Waldron,*

"Three Likely Lads of Limbo," The New Yorker, March 21, 1970, p 39

belly board, a small surfboard for riding the waves on one's belly.

Up and down the coast, towns have roped off prime sections of beach for the "belly boards," not only to protect swimmers but also to encourage the trade the surfers bring. *Time, June 25, 1965, p 52*

bellyhold, *n.* the hold for cargo beneath the passenger cabin in the fuselage of an aircraft.

A further problem will be that in spite of increase of cargo in pure freighter aircraft, the bulk will continue to be flown in the bellyholds of passenger aircraft. *Arthur Reed, "Airlines Have to Think Big." The Times (London), June 2, 1970, p III*

belted-bias tire, an automobile tire with a belt of cord fabric or metal around its circumference beneath the tread. Also called BIAS-BELTED TIRE. Compare RADIAL-PLY TIRE.

In the United States, sales of the belted bias tire both to motorists and to automobile manufacturers began to rise rapidly in 1968. The tire, composed of the body of a conventional tire with a belt around the circumference of the carcass—was introduced in 1966. *Edwin B. Newton, The 1969 Compton Yearbook, p 400*

. . . this tyre would be in the form known as belted-bias. In it the polyester plies or cords which criss-cross diagonally over the road surface of the tyre are covered by a belt of fibreglass. *Judith Jackson, The Sunday Times (London), June 16, 1968, p 16*

Be·nin (bə'ni:n), *n.* a Bantu tribe of western Africa noted for its art work, especially in jewelry and sculpture. *Often used attributively.*

At Sotheby's sale of primitive art and eastern sculpture, K. J. Hewett paid £5,000 for an important Benin ivory sceptre, the finial decorated with a human figure carrying a gong and a beater. *The Times (London), Dec. 1, 1970, p 12*

Bennett, *n.* Also called **Bennett's Comet.** a comet first sighted in Pretoria, South Africa in December 1969, characterized by a surrounding cloud of hydrogen ten times larger than the sun. Compare TAGO-SATO-OSAKA.

Comet Bennett, discovered on Dec. 28, 1969, by John C. Bennett at Pretoria, S.Af., became one of the most spectacular comets in many years. It revolves around the sun once every 17 centuries in an extremely elongated ellipse whose plane is practically perpendicular to that of the earth's orbit. *Joseph Ashbrook, "Astronomy," 1971 Britannica Yearbook of Science and the Future, 1970, p 137*

Bennett's Comet . . . was seen from many parts of Britain at daybreak yesterday. *The Times (London), March 28, 1970, p 1*

bent, *adj. British Slang.* dishonest; crooked.

The Basement Theatre . . . offers a sympathetically deadpan account of the farce with a pair of smoothly criminal performances by Patrick Carter and John Bott as the two bent priests. *Irving Wardle, "Funeral Games, Basement Theatre," The Times (London), Dec. 1, 1970, p 14*

What are the motives of his [the film director Kenneth Loach's] delinquents? In what way are they representative of their class? How seriously are we to take the husband's whine that 'everybody's bent' but only the working class gets caught? *Eric Rhode, "Poor Cow" (title of a film by Kenneth Loach), The Listener, Dec. 14, 1967, p 770*

The vision of the policeman as Dixon of Dock Green is offset by another depicting him as a bent sadist. *Christopher Serpell, "Next Year in Europe," The Listener, Nov. 4, 1971, p 605*

bester, *n.* a hybrid sturgeon developed in the Soviet Union for its ability to spawn in its home grounds instead of migrating upstream.

Nikolyutin then went for a marriage of opposites—the large and vicious beluga with the small peaceful sterlet. The resulting bester has done the trick. . . . Soviet news sources mention that the bester tastes good too, though they do not compare its roe with the original caviar. *New Scientist and Science Journal, May 13, 1971, p 388*

[from *beluga* + *sterlet*]

bi (bai), *adj. Slang.* sexually attracted to or involved with both sexes; bisexual.

He looked at Mick Jagger and shouted to a henchman: "Hey, Dave, this guy is bi." *Derek Malcolm, "What A Performance," The Manchester Guardian Weekly, Jan. 23, 1971, p 21*

bia·ly ('byɑ: li:), *n.; pl.* **bialys** or **bialy.** *U.S.* an onion roll.

[Allen] Ginsberg's stepmother, Edith, was in the kitchen fixing a big breakfast of bagels, bialy, lox, cream cheese, and scrambled eggs. . . . *Jane Kramer, "Profiles: Paterfamilias," The New Yorker, Aug. 24, 1968, p 63*

[shortened from Yiddish *bialestoker*, named after *Białystok*, the Polish city where the type of roll originated]

bias-belted tire, another term for BELTED-BIAS TIRE.

The addition of bias belted tires to GM cars cost the buyer approximately $29. *Jim Dunne, "Automobiles," The 1970 Compton Yearbook, p 139*

biathlete, *n.* an athlete who competes in a biathlon.

. . . Denver looked a dead duck, threatening us, as had Grenoble four years ago, with long journeys into the mountains in pursuit of skier, bobber, tobogganist and biathlete. *John Hennessy, "Winter Olympics," The Times (London), Jan. 29, 1972, p 16*

[blend of *biathlon* and *athlete*]

biathlon, *n.* a sports event combining a contest in cross-country skiing and rifle shooting.

The world biathlon championships (skiing and shooting), still held annually although the other Nordic events were biennial, took place at Altenberg, E. Ger., on February 19. *Howard Bass, Britannica Book of the Year 1968, p 692*

[from *bi-* two + Greek *áthlon* contest]

bi·don·ville (bi: dɔ̃'vi:l), *n.* a shantytown, or settlement of makeshift houses, often built from tin cans cut and hammered flat.

The Ministry of the Interior has estimated that there are 75,346 people living in bidonvilles throughout France. *Stephen Castles, The Manchester Guardian Weekly, Jan. 24, 1970, p 7*

[from French *bidonville*, from *bidon* a fairly large tin can for liquids + *ville* town]

bien vu (byæ 'vʏ), *French.* well thought of; highly regarded.

It must have been on May 5 or 6 that General Maurice apparently called to discuss his future prospects with Hankey, and the latter told him that he was *bien vu* by

bierkeller

Lloyd George [British prime minister, 1916-22], and suggested several appointments he might get. *Stephen Roskill, "A Challenge to Lloyd George," The Times (London), April 4, 1970, p 19*

bier·kel·ler ('bir‚kel ər), *n.* a German-style beer hall.

The opening of Bierkellers in London and elsewhere, where litres of strong German draught beers can be obtained at around 10s. a time (one litre is usually enough), has helped. *Iain Mackenzie, "Foreign Rivals to the Pint," The Times (London), March 12, 1970, p VIII*

[formed in English from German *Bier* beer + *Keller* cellar]

Big Bang, a cosmic explosion of densely packed gaseous matter which may have occurred from 10 to 15 billion years ago and constituted the origin of the universe. *Also used attributively.* Compare STEADY-STATE.

According to existing ideas, after the Big Bang took place the galaxies were flung outward like shrapnel moving away from each other in straight lines. *Nicholas Valery, "Sussex University Plays Host to World's Astronomers," Science Journal, Oct. 1970, p 10*

. . . Schmidt's statistical study . . . suggests that quasars were born in the greatest number no more than one or two billion years after the "big bang" that created the universe. *"Science and the Citizen: The Antiquity of Quasars," Scientific American, Jan. 1971, p 47*

Big Banger, a supporter of the theory that the universe originated with the Big Bang. Compare STEADY-STATER.

Galaxies take something like 10 billion years to evolve, he [Professor Fred Hoyle] says, which is comparable to the age Big Bangers give to the universe. *Peter Stubbs, "A King of Infinite Space," New Scientist, June 20, 1968, p 621*

big beat, *U.S. Slang.* rock 'n' roll. *Also used attributively.*

You can blow your mind to the big beat uptown. Cool it in a candlelit cavern downtown. *Advertisement by the Australian Tourist Commission, Harper's, May 1968, p 22*

In two hours of leggy displays, big-beat tunes, psychedelic lights and slapstick chases, the production [*The Last Stop*, a Czech musical satire] fearlessly dissects the incompetence and corruption of the old set of Communist leaders and even lampoons the new set a bit. *Time, July 19, 1968, p 25*

Big Science, scientific research involving large capital investment.

"Big Science" is coming to a turning point, to some sort of stabilization in terms of the national products, after having grown many times faster. *Dennis Gabor, "Science of Civilization," New Scientist, July 24, 1969, p 184*

As an alternative to annexation or satellization, there is the choice of *competition.* This demands that European businesses, particularly those in the area of "Big Science," become fully competitive on the global market. *J.-J. Servan-Schreiber, "The American Challenge," Harper's, July 1968, p 39*

biker, *n. U.S.* a motorcyclist, especially one belonging to a motorcycle gang.

So the Hippies collided with the slums, and were beaten and robbed, fleeced and lashed and buried and imprisoned, and here and there murdered, and here and there successful, for there was a scattered liaison with bikers and

Panthers and Puerto Ricans on the East Coast and Mexicans on the West. There came a point when, like most tribes, they divided. . . . So the Yippies came out of the Hippies, ex-Hippies, diggers, bikers, drop-outs from college, hipsters up from the South. *Norman Mailer, "Miami Beach and Chicago," Harper's, Nov. 1968, p 96*

The image of the biker as delinquent will take a long time to eradicate. "You meet the nicest people on a Honda," proclaims the Japanese firm that has cornered nearly 50% of the bike market in the U.S.; but the general belief is that you still meet the nastiest ones on a chopper [motorcycle]. *Robert Hughes, "Myth of the Motorcycle Hog," Time, Feb. 8, 1971, p 35*

bikeway, *n. U.S.* a road on which only bicycles are permitted.

Just as highway building spurred the auto industry, construction of bikeways is expected to boost cycling. *Time, June 14, 1971, p 60*

Bolck has suggested that ramps and bikeways be built to keep pedaling students from running down their pedestrian counterparts. *The Tuscaloosa News, Oct. 27, 1970, p 11*

bilateral, *n.* a conference or discussion involving only two sides.

. . . the so-called "Bonn bilaterals," meaning West Germany's talks with East Germany, Russia and Poland. *C. L. Sulzberger, The New York Times, April 3, 1970, p 36*

[noun use of *bilateral, adj.*]

bin, *n.* **the bin,** the insane asylum.

"What was that about hospital?" Maximilian asked. "Edward could tell you."

"They put me in the bin because I suddenly had a talking jag," Edward said. "I couldn't stop chatting. I talked non-stop one day for twenty-three hours." *Penelope Gilliatt, "Nobody's Business," The New Yorker, July 3, 1971, p 25*

Moving house is to most women a step toward the bin, but Mrs Axelrod counted up that her London house is the thirty-third that she has moved into and done up. *Ernestine Carter, "Funny Man's Wife," The Sunday Times (London), Oct. 10, 1971, p 45*

[shortened from *loony bin*]

bi·nocs (bə'naks), *n.pl.* short for *binoculars.*

No binocs, no bird book.

Asher had forgotten his binoculars. . . . *Gilbert Rogin, "The Regulars," The New Yorker, Nov. 7, 1970, p 42*

► Clipped words such as *binocs, sec* for second of time (as in: *Wait a sec while I tie my shoe*), *deli* for delicatessen, or *pres* for president, are frequent in informal usage. Clipped forms are especially common in student jargon: *psych* for psychology, *eco* for economics, *bio* for biology, *phys ed* for physical education.

bio-, a prefix with the sense "biological; relating to living things," *bio-* has been used in the past chiefly to form terms in the natural sciences, but recent usage has extended its application to less scientific and more socially oriented contexts, as in *biodestructible, bio-parent, biopolitics, biohazard.*

bio-acoustics, *n.pl.:* Using a cassette tape deck, a 12-watt amplifier, and a plastic horn loudspeaker run from a 12-volt car battery, he [Dr. T. Brough, a scientist studying the cries of starlings] reproduced this cry as the flocks were coming in to roost.

When he first aimed it at a flock the birds moved on. . . .

These "bio-acoustics" thus provide a cheap and effective means of moving on starling flocks. . . . *New Scientist, March 5, 1970, p 449*

bio-contamination, *n.:* . . . NASA takes seriously its responsibilities with regard to bio-contamination of the planet! *New Scientist and Science Journal, May 6, 1971, p 305*

biocybernetics, *n.:* Perhaps the most extraordinary paper at the AAAS meeting came from Manfred Clynes, head of the Biocybernetics Laboratories at Rockland State Hospital, New York State. Clynes, over the last few years, has developed a way of fitting differential equations to emotions such as love and anger. *New Scientist, Dec. 31, 1970, p 580*

biodestructible, *adj.:* "Mr. Merton, is this biodestructible or residually permanently inert?" *Cartoon legend, The New Yorker, Aug. 1, 1970, p 32*

biodeterioration, *n.:* Some recent work by two researchers, John Mills and Dr Howard Eggins, at the Biodeterioration Information Centre of the University of Aston, shows that some common fungi will thrive on polythene [a plastic] that has been oxidized beforehand. *New Scientist, Aug. 20, 1970, p 379*

bioexperiment, *n.:* The next project of any kind with bioexperiments aboard will be Skylab in 1972, and those will involve only pocket mice and drosophila flies. *Science News, July 4, 1970, p 7*

biogeology, *n.:* Preston Cloud and Aharon Gibor ("The Oxygen Cycle") are respectively professor of biogeology and professor of biology at the University of California at Santa Barbara. *Scientific American, Sept. 1970, p 33*

biohazard, *n.:* . . . two flags drooped from a pole: a yellow quarantine flag and, above it, a red-white-and-blue banner — an international biohazard flag. *Henry S. F. Cooper, Jr., "Letter from the Space Center," The New Yorker, Jan. 3, 1970, p 46*

bio-parent, *n.:* Bio-parents permitted frequent visits. Telephone contact allowed. Child may spend summer vacation with bio-parents. *Alvin Toffler, "The Fractured Family," The Times (London), Sept. 26, 1970, p 15*

biopolitical, *adj.:* There may be a biogeographical significance in its [blossoming blackthorn's] breaking earlier in this location, but I would not attribute a "biopolitical" one to it! *A. E. Pennifold, Brighton, Sussex, England, in a Letter to the Editor, The Times (London), April 25, 1970, p 9*

bioproductivity, *n.:* And their influence—the inflow of the rivers with a mean annual discharge of 1900m³/sec alone accounts for almost 1/3 of the fresh-water entering the Mediterranean—has become one of the major factors governing bioproductivity of the North Adriatic. *Tony Loftas, "Mediterranean Pollution—Another Year of Neglect," New Scientist and Science Journal, July 15, 1971, p 145*

See also the entries below.

biocidal, *adj.* destroying life or living things.

Of the approximately 800 biocidal compounds used as pesticides, many . . . are degraded to elementary materials that can be recycled. *Robert W. Risebrough, "Pesticide," McGraw-Hill Yearbook of Science and Technology 1971, p 319*

biocide, *n.* destruction of life. Compare ECOCIDE.

We are gradually committing biocide—killing every living thing on the earth including ourselves. . . . *Los Angeles Times, quoted in advertisement of a book, "Arcology," by Paolo Soleri, Scientific American, Sept. 1970, p 262*

[from *bio- + -cide* killing, as in *genocide*]

biocrat, *n.* a scientist or technician who represents the interests of the biological sciences or their allied professions.

Unfortunately, between the two [private citizens and lawmakers] there is a bureaucratic monolith of biocrats and administrators, and the channels of communication, though theoretically present, are tortuous and fraught with obstacles. *Peter Beaconsfield, "Internal Pollution—Our First Priority," New Scientist and Science Journal, March 18, 1971, p 602*

[from *bio- + -crat,* as in *bureaucrat*]

biodegradability, *n.* susceptibility to biodegradation; proneness to decomposition by biological agents, especially bacteria.

Starch is another substance tried and found wanting by industry because, when modified to perform the functions of phosphates, it loses its biodegradability and so could build up in the environment. *Science News, Dec. 27, 1969, p 592*

"Ten years ago we mainly did acute toxic work on a new product", says Dahlström. "Now we start with a close look at its biodegradability". *Jon Tinker, New Scientist, April 1, 1971, p 18*

biodegradable, *adj.* that can be decomposed by biological agents, especially bacteria. Compare SOFT.

Oxygen-demanding wastes are biodegradable by using oxygen that is naturally present in the water or artificially supplied in treatment processes. *Robert E. De La Rue, Jr., "Water Pollution," McGraw-Hill Yearbook of Science and Technology 1968, p 23*

As the effluent moves through the soil, the biodegradable material is metabolized by the soil microorganisms. *Herman Bouwer, "Water Purification," McGraw-Hill Yearbook of Science and Technology 1971, p 435*

biodegradation, *n.* the decomposition of a substance through the action of biological agents, especially bacteria.

Recent advances in biodegradation of plastics . . . offer startling contrast to the previous general belief in the immutability of plastics exposed to possible bacterial attack . . . . *P. J. Fowler, "Biodegradability in Plastics," New Scientist, Sept. 24, 1970, p 648*

biodegrade, *v.i.* to undergo biodegradation.

Some petroleum compounds that do biodegrade do so over "a much longer time than anticipated," says [R. E.] Kallio, citing recent work at the University of Illinois. *"Man and Marine Ecology: Crisis in the Estuaries," Science News, Oct. 30, 1971, p 293*

bioengineer, *n.* an expert in bioengineering.

Professor Andrew A. Frank, a University of Wisconsin bioengineer, who has completed a four-legged walking machine, is now working on a two-legged version which will simulate normal leg action. *New Scientist, Sept. 3, 1970, p 473*

In industry, bioengineers generally develop and build improved instrumentation to assist in the medical diagnosis and treatment of patients. *Morris F. Collen, "Medicine," 1972 Britannica Yearbook of Science and the Future, 1971, p 277*

bioengineering, *n.* the application of the technology of engineering to problems of medicine, especially in the creation of more responsive artificial limbs.

The Boston arm is just one of many remarkable devices being developed by a partnership between technology and medicine in a new field called biomedical engineering or bioengineering. *Judith Randal, "The Promising New Science of Engineering," The World Book Science Annual 1969, p 99*

bioethics, *n.* the study of the ethical problems involved in biological research with organ transplantation, genetic engineering, artificial insemination, etc.

Andre Helligers, professor of obstetrics and gynecology and director of the newly established Kennedy Institute for Human Reproduction and Bioethics at Georgetown University in Washington, said his guess is that "operations like the one at Georgetown will become institutionalized and more wide spread." *"Ethics in Biomedicine: A Call for Action," Science News, Oct. 30, 1971, p 294*

Cancer Researcher Van Rensselaer Potter of the University of Wisconsin has suggested in a new book, *Bioethics*, that the U.S. create a fourth branch of Government, a Council for the Future, to consider scientific developments and recommend appropriate legislation. *Time, April 19, 1971, p 34*

biofeedback, *n.* control of one's brain waves, especially the alpha waves, in order to maintain a particular mental state. This is usually achieved with the help of a portable electroencephalograph that emits an audible signal when sufficient alpha waves are produced. *Often used attributively.*

In industry, major companies like Xerox and Martin Marietta are investigating biofeedback training to spur creative thinking and reduce executive tension.... *"Alpha Wave of the Future," Time, July 19, 1971, p 32*

biological clock, a biological mechanism that governs the rhythmic or cyclic activities of organisms. Compare BODY CLOCK.

The daily activity cycle is just one of many rhythms in man that are regulated by biological clocks. *Picture legend, "The Rhythm of Life" by Arthur J. Snider, The World Book Science Annual 1968, p 113*

biological engineering, the artificial selection of different strains of a plant or animal species to improve the structure, function, or yield of an organism, especially a plant or animal of agricultural importance.

Early agricultural man, in his development of crops like Indian corn and wheat, accomplished technical miracles that have still to be surpassed by contemporary plant science. This kind of "biological engineering"—to produce reliable food crops from wild grasses—achieved a phenomenal result without the benefit of profound insight into the mechanism of heredity or the chemistry of DNA [deoxyribonucleic acid, the carrier of genetic information]. *Joshua Lederberg, "Humanics and Genetic Engineering," 1970 Britannica Yearbook of Science and the Future, 1969, p 82*

biomathematician, *n.* a specialist in the mathematical study of biological processes, especially the simulation of such processes by means of computers or mathematical models.

...biomathematicians have made computer models of systems in the human body, including the respiratory, nervous and circulatory systems. *Morley R. Kare, "Bionics," Encyclopedia Science Supplement (Grolier) 1970, p 115*

biomedical engineering, another name for BIO-ENGINEERING.

To these two principal pursuits, the modern biomedical engineer would also add a third: an application of the management techniques developed largely within the engineering industry. Thus, in its complete form, biomedical engineering is seen as involving a break with the traditional organization of medicine so that the new technology can be exploited unhampered by a system based upon the methodology of a previous era of medicine. *Tony Loftas, "Biomedical Technology," Science Journal, June 1969, p 48*

biomedicine, *n.* the biological and medical study of man's tolerance to environmental stresses, especially in space travel.

The role of science—particularly biomedicine—[should] be upgraded as a mission objective to help justify the substantial cost of space exploration. *Science News, Jan. 10, 1970, p 37*

biomorphism, *n.* representation of living forms in art.

As Mr. Rubin points out, the biomorphism of Hans Arp, André Masson, Max Ernst and Joan Miró introduced a much-needed note of lyricism into the austerity of experimental painting. It softened the shape of things to come, prepared the way for Arshile Gorky, William de Kooning and Matta Echaurren. *Anatole Broyard, Review of "Dada and Surrealist Art" by William S. Rubin, The New York Times, June 29, 1971, p 35*

bi·on·ic (baɪˈɑn ɪk), *adj.* of or relating to bionics.

In building a submarine, designers wish to determine the most efficient shape for the hull. The bionic approach to this problem consists of studying organisms that exhibit the desired characteristic of moving through water with the least amount of resistance. *Morley R. Kare, "Bionics," Encyclopedia Science Supplement (Grolier) 1970, p 115*

[from *bio-* + *-onic*, as in *electronic*]

bi·on·i·cist (baɪˈɑn ə sist), *n.* an expert in bionics.

Bionicists attempt to solve technical problems by the application of mechanical and electrical mechanisms comparable to those found in nature. *Morley R. Kare, "Bionics," Encyclopedia Science Supplement (Grolier) 1970, p 114*

bi·on·ics (baɪˈɑn ɪks), *n.* the science of applying the formations of various biological structures to problems of engineering in electronics, computer programming, construction, etc.

We have said that bionics is a relatively new science. After all the very word "bionics" did not exist before 1959. It was derived from the Greek word "bion" meaning living and "ics" meaning like. In other words the goal of the programme is to make...self-organizing machines, intelligent machines or learning machines. *D. R. Moore and A. C. Speake, "New Learning Machines for Future Aerospace Systems," New Scientist, March 10, 1966, p 626*

biorhythm, *n.* rhythmical or cyclic changes occurring in the functions or activities of organs or organisms. Compare CIRCADIAN RHYTHM.

Several universities are currently completing studies validating three long-term cyclical patterns called "biorhythms": a 23-day physical cycle, a 28-day emotional cycle (unrelated to the menstrual cycle). *The New York Times, April 24, 1966, Sec. 6, p 12*

biorhythm upset, upset of the body clock.

Symptoms of biorhythm upset, known popularly as the

jet syndrome, are experienced by jet airplane travelers who fly through several time zones in 12 hours or less. The local time between their place of departure and their destination may differ by 5, 6, or even as much as 10 hours. *Arthur J. Snider, "The Rhythm of Life," The World Book Science Annual 1968, p 115*

biosatellite, *n.* an artificial satellite carrying living plants or animals for space-environment research.

... the first three American biosatellites are already full and the money for further launchings has not yet been granted. *New Scientist, Sept. 12, 1968, p 531*

The subject was a pigtail macaque monkey named Bonnie, launched from Cape Kennedy in a 1,550-pound capsule, Biosatellite 3.... *"Survival in Space: Bonnie," Science News Yearbook 1970, p 60*

Fourteen biological specimens have been chosen for the first flight, in 1965, of National Aeronautics and Space Administration's biosatellite. Its purpose is to study the effects of radiation, weightlessness and the absence of earth's rotation, combined, on living things. The announcement last week from the space agency said the initial experiments will include pepper plants, wheat seedlings, amoebae, frog and sea urchin eggs, bread mold, fruit flies and embryonic beetles. Total weight of the experimental package will be about 50 pounds. *The New York Times, Feb. 23, 1964, p 7*

bioscience, *n.* the branch or body of science dealing with biological phenomena outside the earth's atmosphere, including biomedicine, exobiology, etc.

In addition to biomedical studies of man in space, NASA is also looking at biological experiments. Although there are four such experiments on Skylab—pocket mice, human tissue, vinegar flies and potatoes—and much ground-based research, the new bioscience program has not yet been formalized. The first era of bioscience ended with the death of the monkey Bonnie after its eight-day space voyage and the remaining biosatellites were canceled. *Science News, Aug. 1, 1970, p 93*

bioscientific, *adj.* of or relating to bioscience.

While not specifying the cost of expanded bioscientific research, the ... panel compared it to the cost of aborting a single Apollo mission for medical reasons and judged it to be worth the cost. *Barbara J. Culliton, "The Weightless Burden of Space," Science News, Dec. 13, 1969, p 561*

bioscientist, *n.* an expert in bioscience.

Bioscientists studying the effect of the space environment, or more properly the absence of the Earth's environment, on living systems usually need to recover the organisms for examination in the laboratory. *John E. Naugle, "Space Probes," McGraw-Hill Yearbook of Science and Technology 1968, p 363*

biotelemetric, *adj.* of or used in biotelemetry.

At the present time, the weight of a practical biotelemetric transmitter is approximately 9-15 g [grams] per channel of information, and the transmitting distances range up to 20 mi. *O. Z. Roy, "Biotelemetry," McGraw-Hill Yearbook of Science and Technology 1969, p 115*

biotelemetry, *n.* the monitoring of vital functions of a person or animal and the transmission of the data to a distant point for readings by electronic instruments. Also called ECOTELEMETRY.

The data is recorded on a series of graphs.... The only requirement for the patient is that he be seated comfortably in the chair, with his hands resting on conductive armrests. No paste electrodes or other biotelemetry linkage are needed. *Science News Letter, June 4, 1966, p 450*

Biotelemetry is being used to monitor human response to environmental stress (exercise, heat, cold, space flight), critical illness (myocardial infarction, postsurgery), birth (fetal heart sounds), during surgery and its associated anesthesia, and any situation in which the elimination of encumbering wires or the direct connection of the subject to a recorder is desirable. *Harold Sandler, "Biotelemetry," McGraw-Hill Yearbook of Science and Technology 1971, p 130*

Bircher, *n.* *U.S.* a member of the John Birch Society, an extreme conservative and anticommunist group formed in 1958. Also called BIRCHITE, JOHN BIRCHER.

George Thayer here [in *The Farther Shores of Politics*] presents a Baedeker of the outer marches of politics in the United States today—the neo-Nazis, the Klansmen and other racists; the Birchers, the Black Nationalists, the Communists, the pacifists and many more. *The New York Times Book Review, March 10, 1968, p 12*

"I would say to those who are known in this hour in our country as Birchers." he [Carl Sandburg] said.... "I would say that those who propose to impeach a Chief Justice of the Supreme Court of the United States, without saying what evidence they have—they are hoping that they blow out moral lights around us." *Herbert Mitgang, Saturday Review, Aug. 12, 1967, p 19*

[from the John *Birch* Society (named after John *Birch*, a U.S. Air Force captain killed by the Chinese Communists in 1945)]

Birchism, *n.* *U.S.* extreme conservatism in politics.

... the Dallas [Texas] environment ... is so accepting of rightist politics that Birchism can become a simple habit. *Alan C. Elms, "Normal Extremists," Science News, Feb. 21, 1970, p 197*

Birchite, *U.S.* — *n.* another name for BIRCHER.

As long as [Governor George] Wallace's percentages were down around 5 percent, his strength in the North was for the most part limited to Birchites.... *Michael Janeway, "Campaign 1968," The Atlantic, Nov. 1968, p 12*

— *adj.* characteristic of Birchers; extremely conservative.

The Intermountain Observer, a weekly with a statewide circulation, ... provides an urgently needed contrast to the generally conservative (and often Birchite) tone of the Idaho press. *John Fischer, "The Easy Chair," Harper's, Dec. 1968, p 25*

bird, *n.* **1** any flying craft, such as an airplane, rocket, or space vehicle.

The fuselage is 280 feet long, compared with the 318 feet to which its predecessor grew as engineers drew in more seats and bigger fuel tanks to try and keep the increasingly expensive bird profitable. *Science News, Nov. 2, 1968, p 440*

Much the biggest bird ever, as rocket men said, flew for the first time, the US rocket Saturn V. *The Annual Register of World Events in 1967 (1968), p 403*

2 *U.S. Slang.* the eagle as an insigne of military rank.

Every few months there is a new colonel's list ... and over morning coffee, the man and his wife read down it to see who won: *my God, that bastard made it.* And checking over the career to see what it was that had gotten bird for him. *Ward Just, "Soldiers," The Atlantic, Oct. 1970, p 93*

3 *British Slang.* an attractive girl or woman. Compare DOLLY BIRD.

The realistic and rather weary stage setting before which Cassill tries his tricks is postwar Britain, and involves a Minister of War and an assortment of more or less ravishing birds more or less for hire. *Review of "Doctor Cobb's Game" (a novel) by R. V. Cassill, Time, Nov. 16, 1970, p 107*

4 *British Slang.* a prison sentence; time served in the "cage" (prison).

Tough cynical men, they [the prisoners] had long passed the novitiate stage in the life of crime and were doing their 'bird' with reasonable grace. *Arthur Barton, "Without Conviction," The Listener, June 1, 1967, p 718*

bird strike, a collision between an aircraft and a flock of birds.

"Bird strikes" are a problem to jets all over the world. Last month in Sydney a Boeing 707 with 136 passengers had to make a crash landing after colliding with a flock of gulls at take-off. *Timothy Brown, "A Bird in the Hand Is Worth 100 in the Engine," The Sunday Times (London), Jan. 4, 1970, p 5*

...of the 430 bird strikes reported to the Air Transport Association between January 1961 and April 1963, damage was done either to the airframes or to the engines in 202 of these strikes. *Philip Wagner, "The War with the Birds," Harper's, April 1967, p 82*

bistable, *adj.* capable of assuming either one of two states or conditions at one time, but not both at the same time. Electronic components such as switches, which are either on or off, or computer parts which require only two states, 0 and 1, are bistable.

Automatic lung ventilators, which augment or replace a patient's own respiration, are a natural application for fluidics since the respiration cycle is very similar to the basic action of bistable wall-reattachment devices. *Kenneth Owen, "The Industrial Logic of Fluidic Circuits," The Times (London), March 20, 1970, p 33*

bit, *n. Slang.* a typical or standard practice, procedure, or way of acting; a familiar set of actions or things.

So I did the Palm Springs bit, I did the Las Vegas bit, I did the golfing bit. *Steven V. Roberts, "Coast 'Boaters' Find Serenity Amid Throngs," The New York Times, June 30, 1971, p 24*

I'm wearing the uniform: the button-down shirt, the V-neck, the stay-presseds, the penny-loafers, the whole bit. *Calvin Trillin, "U.S. Journal: Iowa," The New Yorker, April 20, 1968, p 178*

[originally the theater sense of an act, routine, or other piece of stage business]

biz·zazz or **bi·zazz** (bə'zæz), *n.* variant spellings of PIZZAZZ.

...I knew that we absolutely had to have something with more bizzazz going for the young people. *Daniel Berrigan, quoted by Francine du Plessix Gray, in "Profiles: Acts of Witness," The New Yorker, March 14, 1970, p 66*

black, *v.t., v.i. British.* to boycott in protest against the employment of nonunion workmen or in a demonstration of sympathy with striking union workers.

The strike of Hull trawlermen gained support yesterday when oil crews who supply the fishing vessels with fuel "blacked" the St. Andrews' Dock from which the Hull trawlers sail. *Ronald Kershaw, "Oil Crews Support Hull Strikers," The Times (London), Feb. 17, 1970, p 19*

black belt, 1 the highest degree of proficiency in judo or karate.

Morris—stocky, balding and 45, with a black belt in judo—is similarly inclined to realize Walter Mitty fantasies. *Jon Ruddy, Maclean's, April 1968, p 1*

2 a person awarded this degree. Compare BROWN BELT.

A new series of Karate Classes will begin on Monday, July 20th, under the direction of Patti-Lee Ivens, a Black Belt. *Donald Barthelme, "Newsletter," The New Yorker, July 11, 1970, p 23*

blackboard jungle, 1 a school in which a condition of disorder and lawlessness exists.

New schools may be built, new curricula devised, and the teacher-pupil ratio cut in half, but if the children who attend these schools come from lower-class homes, the schools will be turned into blackboard jungles and those who graduate from them, or drop out of them, will in most cases be functionally illiterate. *The New York Times, Oct. 12, 1970, p 37*

2 a condition of disorder and lawlessness in schools.

There should be welfare officers in the schools to deal with the "blackboard jungle." *The Times (London), April 2, 1970, p 4*

[from *The Blackboard Jungle*, title of a novel, 1954, about juvenile delinquents in a New York City vocational school, by the American writer Evan Hunter, born 1926; released as a motion picture with the same title in 1955]

black box, 1 any unknown system, especially one considered solely in terms of input and output without an understanding of its workings.

"To some programmers it [an electronic computer] might as well be a hamster on a treadmill generating the output. The computer—for many purposes—may be thought of as a black box." *Rudolf Loeser, quoted by Richard Todd, "You are an Interfacer of Black Boxes," The Atlantic, March 1970, p 66*

2 any electronic device for automatic control that can be installed or removed as a unit.

Black boxes are devices, usually a resistor in series, which, when attached to home phones, allow all incoming calls to be made without charge to one's caller. *Daily Telegraph Magazine (London), March 17, 1972, p 18*

[originally an electronic unit, often housed in a black-colored box, which was put into an aircraft for use in radar detection, monitoring of flight conditions, etc.]

black capitalism, *U.S.* the ownership and management of private businesses by black entrepreneurs.

Still, black capitalism has had its disappointments for both sides. Several ambitious, white-supported projects have failed. Black leaders acknowledge that Negroes who want to be their own bosses should be given more aid, but some doubt that black-owned business will employ enough people or generate enough wealth to help significantly in lifting the ghetto masses toward economic equality. *Time, July 20, 1970, p 65*

black comedy, a form of comedy whose humor derives from absurd, grotesque, or morbid situations. Also called DARK COMEDY.

Hal Prince's "Something for Everyone" [is] a Bavarian black comedy about a handsome young man (Michael York)

who transforms the lives of a family of down-at-heel aristo-
crats by seducing them all. *Richard Roud, The Manchester
Guardian Weekly, Nov. 14, 1970, p 20*

'Both should provide a good base for black comedy,
which thrives on the unpleasant'. *Daily Telegraph (London),
March 24, 1972, p 15*

[translation of French *comédie noire*]

Black English, a dialect of English spoken by many
American blacks. Black English originated in the
South but is now also used in northern cities. It is
distinguished by special pronunciation, intonations,
vocabulary, and also grammatical or syntactic structure (as by the use of additional present-tense
forms: I work, I am working, I be working, I a-working, I be a-working). Also called AFRO-AMERI-
CANESE.

"Black English" is not an illiterate language, as many
think, but remarkably rich in nuances. *Time, April 6, 1970,
p 98*

Present research by linguists has focused on Black
English both as a system in itself and as a variety of Eng-
lish which systematically differs from Standard English.
Some of the differences between Standard English and
Black English, though seemingly small, have important
consequences for the communication of a message. *Walter
A. Wolfram and Ralph W. Fasold, "Toward Reading Mate-
rials for Speakers of Black English: Three Linguistically
Appropriate Passages," Teaching Black Children to Read,
1969, p 139*

black hole, a hypothetical hole in space into which
massive stars and other heavenly objects that have
condensed to a certain radius collapse under the influence of gravity. Also called COLLAPSAR. See also
ERGOSPHERE, SCHWARTZSCHILD RADIUS.

If theory can be believed, the final outcome of this
process in nature is a "black hole" in space into which
matter can be said to have vanished, leaving, however, all
its gravitational effects behind. The black hole would act
as a kind of hungry vortex into which other objects — and
even other energies, such as light — would be drawn, and
all their properties ironed away into additional curvature of
space. *Tom Alexander, "Science Rediscovers Gravity,"
Encyclopedia Science Supplement (Grolier) 1970, p 63*

... supernova cores may have too much mass to form a
gravitationally stable object like a neutron star; they may
form continually collapsing objects, so-called black holes,
instead. *Science News, Dec. 26, 1970, p 472*

It [a dying star] may contract forever, approaching but
never reaching a radius of a few kilometers and a density
exceeding 10^{16} grams per cubic centimeter. It is then one
of the "black holes" predicted by the general theory of
relativity: objects so compact that even light cannot escape
their gravitational pull. The black hole is the destiny of all
stars whose terminal mass considerably exceeds the mass
of the sun. No black hole has ever been observed, but then
it is not clear by which of its properties an astronomer
might observe it. *Malvin A. Ruderman, "Solid Stars," Scientific American, Feb. 1971, p 24*

black humor, a form of humor in literature based
on absurd, grotesque, or morbid situations. Also
called DARK COMEDY or BLACKNESS.

A prince of black humor, he has long represented antic
gloom; now his eminence symbolizes the coming of commercial age of that genre. *The New York Times, Jan. 14,
1968, Sec. 6, p 30*

... as fictionalised reportage it has a compelling quality

because Ford's revulsion and black humour come through
so strongly. *David Williams, Review of "Incident at Muc
Wa" (a novel) by Daniel Ford, Punch, Jan. 3, 1968, p 32*

black humorist, a writer of black humor.

Kurt Vonnegut was mourning the follies of the world with
laughter long before the term "black humorist" had been
coined. *Time, April 11, 1969, p 68*

black lung, 1 a disease that afflicts coal miners.
See the first quotation for details. Compare BROWN
LUNG DISEASE.

Black lung is a form of pneumoconiosis, a chronic lung
inflammation caused by inhaling coal dust over long periods
of time. *Peter J. Taylor, "Occupational Medicine," Britannica Book of the Year 1970, p 509*

To combat black lung disease, which now afflicts about
100,000 miners, he [Charles C. Johnson, Jr.] established
interim limits on the amount of airborne coal dust permitted in a mine shaft.... *Time, March 16, 1970, p 62*

A Bureau of Mines spokesman says conditions for miners
have improved to some extent but the fatality rates and
black lung incidence shows that the problem is not under
control. *"The Miners' Plight," Science News, Sept. 4, 1971,
p 141*

2 *Used figuratively.*

"That city room is an outhouse," Jimmy Breslin says.
"You can get black lung just by working on the rewrite desk
for a week." *Jack Newfield, Harper's, Sept. 1969, p 95*

black money, *U.S. Slang.* income not reported to
the government for tax purposes because of its
illegal source.

The way this works is beautifully simple. Lansky's
couriers take the Mafia's "black money" — profits from
illegal activities — to secret bank accounts in Switzerland,
where the money is "washed clean in the snow of the Alps,"
as the joke goes. What happens is that middlemen in
Europe take the money out of the accounts and route it
back to the states through various devices such as mortgages and loans. *Nicholas Gage, "The Little Big Man Who
Laughs at the Law," The Atlantic, July 1970, p 65*

black nationalism, *U.S.* the movement for identifying all black people as a nation or a group separate
from the influence of white people.

Nor does the theme [change in Harlem]. In one form or
another, it has nearly always been black nationalism — from
the West Indian brand of Marcus Garvey and his followers
to the more militant brand of Charles (Morriss) 37X
Kenyatta.... *"The Talk of the Town," The New Yorker,
Jan. 7, 1967, p 20*

black nationalist, *U.S.* a supporter or advocate of
black nationalism.

George Thayer here [in *The Farther Shores of Politics*]
presents a Baedeker of the outer marches of politics in the
United States today — the neo-Nazis, the Klansmen and
other racists; the Birchers, the Black Nationalists, the
Communists, the pacifists and many more. *The New York
Times Book Review, March 10, 1968, p 12*

blackness, *n.* **1** another term for NEGRITUDE or
NEGRONESS.

"Talking Black" was essentially an exploration of the
new consciousness of blackness as a positive concept
among Negroes. *George Gent, The New York Times, June 27,
1968, p 87*

2 another term for BLACK HUMOR.

Nonetheless, the strongest critics of blackness are found

among humorists, many of whom believe that humor that does not make people laugh is not humor at all. *"American Humor: Hardly A Laughing Matter," Time, March 4, 1966, p 26*

Black Panther, a member of the *Black Panther Party,* an organization of black Americans seeking to establish black power in the United States by extreme militancy. *Abbreviation:* BP Also shortened to PANTHER.

Six Black Panthers — including Eldrige Cleaver — pleaded not guilty Tuesday to attempted murder and assault charges stemming from a gun battle with policemen in West Oakland.... *The New York Times, Sept. 19, 1968, p 48*

Yet he [Bobby Seale] is frank in consigning his white supporters to second-class citizenship, and insists that they obey without question the decisions which are made by the Black Panther leadership alone. *John Fischer, "The Easy Chair," Harper's, Aug. 1970, p 18*

For by midmorning Harvard Square would be packed by hairy wrecks and bra-less butterballs hawking their wares — Fem Libs, Black Panthers, SDS-ers, Weathermen, nihilists, hedonists, devilworshipers, and unspecified crazies all proclaiming The Only True Salvation.... *Larry L. King, "Blowing My Mind at Harvard," Harper's, Oct. 1970, p 98*

Black Paper, *British.* an authoritative document that criticizes or censures an existing policy, practice, institution, etc. Compare GREEN PAPER.

Yet, as spending on education rises, so, too, does public concern or bafflement about its aims and method, as shown in the acrimonious debate initiated by the Black Papers on education. *Colin Brock, "How Should Parents Assess a School?" The Times (London), Dec. 30, 1970, p 7*

[patterned after *White Paper,* an official policy report by the British government]

black power, *U.S.* power of black Americans to establish their rights by collective action. It is a slogan used by the black civil-rights movement, and was especially popular in the 1960's. Compare BROWN POWER, RED POWER, FLOWER POWER.

The researchers report in the June AMERICAN POLITICAL SCIENCE REVIEW that blacks who favor black power do not see the political world as one where blacks can gain only at the expense of whites. Nor do blacks interpret the concept as racism, general black takeover or violence. Yet many whites implicitly fear this.

Blacks were divided in their attitude toward the concept: 42 percent were favorable while 50 percent were unfavorable. Those who favored black power saw it as a "fair share for black people" or "black unity." Blacks who were unfavorable to the concept saw it as empty and meaningless. *Science News, July 25, 1970, p 68*

During the early 1960's,. [Stokely] Carmichael studied Marxism in Guinea, which is considered the most procommunist country in West Africa. He picked up many of his ideas on black power from Guinea's President Sekou Toure, who presented him with a long, flowing African robe. This has always been one of Carmichael's prize possessions. *The Tuscaloosa News, Dec. 1, 1968, p 2*

The term "Black Power" has meant different things to different people since it was chanted by Negroes during the Mississippi march of last June. To some it has meant only that Negroes should organize themselves politically as other minorities have in the past. To others it has had disturbing connotations of black racism — even black violence against whites. Last week a definition of what Black Power means to those who coined the term — Stokely Carmichael, 25, the new head of the Student Nonviolent Coordinating Committee, and the young Negroes around him — became available in the form of a "position paper" written by them last winter. Although much of the document appears obscure, it may ease the fears of those whites who have thought of Black Power in terms of Negroes breaking out of their ghettos to pillage and burn. *"Black Power: Myth and Reality," The New York Times, Aug. 7, 1966, p 2*

If you are a Negro, "Black Power" can mean anything from "kill Whitey" to the peaceful election of a Negro sheriff. *The Wall Street Journal, July 22, 1966, p 1*

A more serious issue is posed by the slogan "Black Power." No matter how often it is defined, this slogan means anti-white power. In a racially pluralistic society, "Black Power" has to mean that every other ethnic group is the antagonist. It has to mean "going it alone." It has to mean separatism. *Roy Wilkins, in a Circular Letter from the National Association for the Advancement of Colored People, Nov. 25, 1966*

Black Radio, (in psychological warfare) radio broadcasts by one side that are disguised as broadcasts by the other.

Black Radio daily 30-minute programs repeated once, purports to be the voice of dissident elements in North Vietnam. *Memorandum from Maj. Gen. Rollen H. Anthis, an Air Force aide, Aug. 27, 1964, quoted in The New York Times, June 13, 1971, Sec. 4, p 37*

black studies, another name for AFRO-AMERICAN STUDIES.

In this city, Negro high school students in an integrated high school struck, demonstrated and caused various difficulties because there were no "black studies" offered in the curriculum. *John W. Hillton, New Orleans, in a Letter to the Editor, Time, March 30, 1970, p 2*

If a 1965 graduate were to return today to Harvard — or Berkeley or Kent State — he would have no trouble in recognizing the old place.... Close scrutiny might reveal a few changes around the edges: ... ROTC courses abolished, government research curtailed, black studies added, and probably a new president. But underneath the cosmetics, the bone structure of the university, the traditional departments, remain much as they were fifty years ago.... *John Fischer, "The Easy Chair," Harper's, Feb. 1971, p 20*

blahs, *n.pl.* Usually in the phrase **the blahs.** *U.S. Slang.* a fit of ill humor or vague bodily discomfort or uneasiness; the sulks or, sometimes, the blues.

Have trouble sleeping? Suffer from the predawn blahs — wakefulness and worries at 4 a.m.? *Champ Clark, "Mystique of Pro Football," Time, Nov. 9, 1970, p 36*

The *Columbia News,* a rural Georgia weekly, observed: "As long as there have been sweaty, hot summers, there have been cases of the blahs. We all get them, but somehow they seem worse this year." *"The Idea is to Cool it a Little," Time, July 27, 1970, p 9*

blast, *n. U.S. Slang.* a party.

The girls were looking for campus clothes and the first item on their list was pants to wear to "beer blasts and dances." *Bernadine Morris, The New York Times, Sept. 6, 1968, p 46*

blip, *v.t.* to replace (a censored word, expression, or remark on a videotape) with one or more sounds like "blip."

... Johnny Carson with Judy Brown, a model on whose

back he wrote a check to see if it would be cashed. Some of his nightly quips are "blipped" from tape before air time. *The New York Times, April 29, 1968, p 86*

— *n.* a brief expression; a note.

That a consulting firm had been called in — no matter one of the best — also registered a blip of concern. *Warren G. Bennis, "Searching For the 'Perfect' University President," The Atlantic, April 1971, p 42*

blitzer, *n. U.S. Football.* a player who moves in quickly to block a ball passer.

"He's done it all," said Sherman. "He's blocked well, picked up blitzers, caught the ball and has been a very quick runner with a good cut." *William N. Wallace, The New York Times, Sept. 6, 1968, p 51*

[from *blitz, v.,* to charge a ball passer + *-er*]

blockbust, *v.t.* to cause white property owners to sell (their houses, etc.) hastily and usually at a loss by making them fear that black people are about to move into the neighborhood.

... speculators ... have just begun to appear on the Concourse [Grand Concourse, an avenue in the Bronx, New York]. "They've started to blockbust some buildings here," said an aide to Representative James H. Scheuer, who represents the area. *The New York Times, July 21, 1966, p 29*

[back formation from *blockbusting*]

blockbuster, *n.* a speculator who engages in block-busting.

The block-buster induces panic selling to himself and then resells to incoming Negroes who are driven by the severe housing need to pay exorbitant prices. *Norman Fowler, The Times (London), Nov. 2, 1967, p 4*

blockbusting, *n.* the act or practice of causing residents of a white neighborhood to sell their property hastily and usually at a loss, from fear that undesirable people, especially black people, are about to move into the neighborhood and that property value will decline. *Often used attributively.*

An American estate agency technique known as "block-busting" — which takes place when Negroes move into white residential areas — was described at a teach-in on immigration and integration at the Borough Polytechnic in London yesterday by Mr. Hunt, Conservative M.P. for Bromley, Kent, who has visited America and studied integration problems there. *The Times (London), Jan. 27, 1966, p 6*

Several communities initiated "we-will-not-sell" campaigns to maintain "racial stability" by keeping white families from "panic selling" their houses because of "fear-tactics" by "block-busting" landlords. *Thomas A. Johnson, The New York Times, June 1, 1971, p 28*

During and right after the war, the Hough area, farther eastward, with its bigger and better homes and many apartment buildings, opened to blacks through a combination of block busting and white flight. It immediately felt the tremendous impact of larger families as blacks from the South poured into the city to work in its steel mills and heavy industry. *Paul Delaney, The New York Times, June 1, 1971, p 28*

[from *block* a city area + *busting* breaking up]

block club, *U.S.* a group of city dwellers organized to protect the block or area in which they live.

"Block clubs" have been organized in some white areas adjoining Chicago's South Side ghetto. Suspicious of interlopers, the clubs keep track of autos passing through the streets. They also follow up on arrests and prosecution of offenders. *Time, Oct. 4, 1968, p 21*

Reverend Hubert Locke ... comments: "All the things that police departments are supposed to do — precinct councils, encouragement of block clubs, storefront offices — were pioneered in Detroit, and they just haven't done the job." *William Serrin, "God Help Our City," The Atlantic, March 1969, p 116*

block release, (in Great Britain and on the Continent) a system of temporarily releasing industrial personnel from their jobs to enable them to attend a more advanced course of study.

The School of Management Studies at the St. Helen's College of Technology, is recognized as one of the major non-university schools of management sciences in the country, and provides specifically for block-release students.... *R. W. Cooley, "Operational Research," The Times (London), Feb. 11, 1970, p VII*

blow, *v.t. Slang.* to smoke or inhale (a narcotic drug).

For the whole of the voyage they were "popping pills and blowing marijuana." *Ian McDonald, "Cambodia Granting Asylum to Hijackers of Ship," The Times (London), March 17, 1970, p 1*

It was common knowledge that Jimi [Hendrix] blew every kind of dope invented.... *Jacob Brackman, "Overdosing for Life," The New York Times, Oct. 27, 1970. p 45*

bluegrass, *n. U.S.* traditional country music, especially of the southern U.S. Compare COUNTRY-AND-WESTERN.

The biggest impact is being made on folk [music] fans by a special kind of country music — bluegrass. Bluegrass occupies the intellectual wing of country music. *Jack Batten, Maclean's, June 6, 1964, p 26*

After two hours someone suggests it is time for a musical interlude. A bluegrass trio appears from nowhere. *Richard Gilbert, "Foreign News: New York," The Listener, Oct. 3, 1968, p 428*

[named after the *Bluegrass* Boys, a band that specialized in this type of music in the 1940's and 1950's, from the *Bluegrass* State, a nickname of the state of Kentucky]

blue helmet, a member of the international military peacekeeping force of the United Nations, whose uniform includes a blue helmet.

The proposal to contribute Swiss contingents of "blue helmets" to peacekeeping actions as an alternative to full UN membership was supported and opposed, the most reserved position being that the country should retain its neutrality but prove its willingness to cooperate with other nations through its traditional Red Cross activities and diplomatic "good offices." *Melanie F. Staerk, "Switzerland," Britannica Book of the Year 1967, p 714*

"However, the United Nations Secretary General, on the advice of a high official of the organization, of American nationality, decided to recall the Blue Helmets...." *Gamal Abdel Nasser, quoted in The Times (London), Feb. 19, 1970, p 10*

blue movie, a pornographic motion picture.

Since there is absolutely no censorship for the Festival, the bluest of blue movies can be seen in Cannes during the first half of May. *Irwin Shaw, "Performing Arts," Harper's, Sept. 1970, p 33*

blusher, *n.* a cosmetic to give the skin a rosy color.

Some wore pancake or foundation and ... islands of makeup holding up smaller islands of blusher or gleamer. *Kathrin Perutz, "Teenage America," Harper's, March 1970, p 98*

Blushers were used liberally to give the face a shining quality. Generally more makeup was used to achieve a less made-up look. *Kenneth E. Batelle, "Hairstyles," 1971 Collier's Encyclopedia Year Book, p 234*

BMEWS ('bi: myu:z), *n.* acronym for *Ballistic Missile Early Warning System* (which provides warning against a surprise attack by ICBM's, or intercontinental ballistic missiles).

FOBS would therefore not be detected by the West's ballistic missile early warning system (BMEWS) as soon as would ICBM's. *Robert E. Hunter and Geoffrey Kemp, "Defense: Soviet Union," Britannica Book of the Year 1968, p 272*

boa·tel (bou'tel), *n.* a hotel at a small-boat basin or marina for use by boat owners or passengers. Compare AQUATEL.

Another major enterprise being promoted in France was a 100-mile wall of resorts, towns, motels, and boatels along the Mediterranean coast, roughly from Nimes to Perpignan. *T. M. P. Bendixson, "Architecture: Western Europe," Britannica Book of the Year 1966, p 103*

[blend of *boat* and *motel*]

bo·cors (bou'kɔr), *n.pl.* *French Creole.* voodoo sorcerers or medicine men.

Duvalier was a city intellectual, not a "country doctor." He never had a practice and indeed country doctors are virtually non-existent in Haiti, apart from the *bocors*, the voodoo witch doctors. *G. T. Corley Smith, "The Grim Chronicle of Papa Doc's Rule in Haiti," The Times (London), March 26, 1970, p 11*

bod biz, *U.S. Slang.* a slang term for SENSITIVITY TRAINING.

To many Americans, these activities typify a leaderless, formless and wildly eclectic movement that is variously called sensitivity training, encounter, "therapy for normals," the bod biz, or the acidless trip. Such terms merely describe the more sensational parts of a whole that is coming to be known as the human potentials movement — a quest conducted in hundreds of ways and places, to redefine and enrich the spirit of social man. *Time, Nov. 9, 1970, p 54*

[from *body* + *biz*, for *business* (as in *show biz*)]

body-builder, *n.* a person who develops and strengthens the body by systematic exercise and diet.

In *Heads*, a girl torn between a brainy weed and a moronic body-builder solves their problem by exchanging their heads with the help of an axe.... *Irving Wardle, "Midday Monsters," The Times (London), March 4, 1970, p 13*

body burden, radioactive or other toxic material absorbed in the body.

Lead, too, is under close scrutiny. It has always been one of the "body burdens" — a favorite scientific phrase — that all of us carry around with us, because it settles in our bones. *Edith Iglauer, "A Reporter at Large," The New Yorker, April 13, 1968, p 107*

When an organism ingests food containing a radionuclide [radioactive particle], a certain portion of the latter is absorbed into the body. This "body burden" is then ex-

creted at a rate dependent on a number of variables.... *R. G. Wiegert, "Radioecology," McGraw-Hill Yearbook of Science and Technology 1968, p 329*

body clock, an internal mechanism of the body supposed to regulate physical and mental functions in rhythm with normal daily activities. Swift transition through several time zones during jet flight disturbs the body clock. Compare BIOLOGICAL CLOCK. See also CIRCADIAN RHYTHM.

Dr. Underwood and Dr. Menaker can offer no explanation of how light reaches the clock, but they believe that other animals may possess similar systems for keeping the body clock on time without the use of their eyes. *"Ornithology: Pill Tests on Pigeons," The Times (London), Oct. 21, 1970, p 13*

body count, 1 a count of the enemy killed in a military operation. Compare KILL RATIO.

... American policy at the highest staff levels was to seek to inflate the actual numbers of indigenous guerrilla forces as compared with the numbers of "main line" North Vietnamese units to look better, or "gain face," with higher and higher body counts as the war dragged on in the delta. *William J. Simon, Woodhaven, N.Y., in a Letter to the Editor, The New York Times, June 3, 1971, p 38*

2 *Transferred sense.* **a** a count of those killed in a particular way.

... Dr. Richard H. Seiden, associate professor of behavioral sciences at Berkeley, qualifies the bridge [Golden Gate] as "the No. 1 location for death by suicide in the entire Western World" — a fitting distinction for San Francisco, whose suicide rate of 38.2 per 100,000 is about twice that of the state of California, and more than three times the national rate. The claim may be accurate, but the Golden Gate is one of the few major U.S. spans that keeps a body count. *Time, Aug. 24, 1970, p 40*

b any count or tally of individuals.

State and Federal aid programs that are based on live body counts will provide less support to the cities and increase their support to the suburbs, unless such programs are changed. *Raymond Vernon, Cambridge, Mass., in a Letter to the Editor, The New York Times, Sept. 11, 1970, p 40*

body-jewel, *n.* an ornament worn on the body instead of on clothing.

Accessories were often called body-jewels and were chain-mail type networks of linked metals, chainbelts, ... snake rings, snake bracelets and arm bracelets, and slave footstraps. *Kathryn Zahony Livingston, "Fashion," The 1970 World Book Year Book, p 342*

body language, the unconscious gestures and postures of the body as a form of communication.

The basic movements of body language — Dr. [Ray] Birdwhistell calls it "kinesics" from the Greek "kine," to move — are still being described, a task that may take another generation or two.... This doesn't mean students of body language can't read body movements, to a limited extent, even at this stage of research. *Barbara Ford, "Body Language," Encyclopedia Science Supplement (Grolier) 1971, p 99*

I went to a sensitivity-training center and I learned body language, but it didn't help my marriage, because I was a tool of male imperialism and that was what I was really resenting all the time. *Penelope Gilliatt, "Nobody's Business" (a short story), The New Yorker, July 3, 1971, p 27*

What happens is the building's [Guggenheim Museum's]

scale overwhelms Rodin's small, spontaneous sketches made not as precise and deliberate studies for major sculptures but, for the most part, as limbering-up exercises in which he could explore what might be called "body language," expressing torment, agitation, intimacy, tenderness. *Emily Genauer, "Art and the Artist," New York Post, March 25, 1972, p 34*

body mike, *U.S.* a microphone worn on the body, usually around the neck.

Mr. Cryer and Miss Towers appear to sing well, although, with the now ubiquitous and damnable amplification of sound with stage-apron and body mikes, we hear not their real voices but their canned ones. *Brendan Gill, The New Yorker, Jan. 23, 1971, p 66*

body paint, a paint or cosmetic preparation for coloring, decorating, or painting designs or figures on parts of the body.

But lately we have it on the delphic word of Mary Quant that, in the seventies, "we shall move towards exposure and body cosmetics" in everyday dolly fashions. To match this prophecy an enterprising firm has brought to the market a range of 12 brilliant body paints which are quick-drying, harmless to the pelt, and removable with soap and water. *New Scientist, Jan. 1, 1970, p 5*

... who is that woman draped along the banister rail wearing nothing but body paint? *Russell Baker, "Sensuous Goings-On and On," The New York Times, Dec. 6, 1970, Sec. 4, p 11*

body stocking, a woman's tight-fitting, one-piece undergarment of stockinglike material, that usually covers most of the body.

... quite diaphanous and quite long dresses of black silk-and-nylon with a faint floral silk-screen print are just $95, and in this instance the only requisite is a body stocking beneath. *"This And That," The New Yorker, April 25, 1970, p 106*

All-in-one Body stocking with 30 denier stretch body and legs in 20 denier stretch Nylon to give a sleek line. *Chorlton's 1970 catalog [British], Spring/Summer, p 293*

bodysuit, *n.* a woman's tight-fitting, one-piece garment covering the torso, used informally for outer wear or in combination with skirts or slacks.

Warner's, the "granddaddy of the bodysuit family," brought out "You-Curve," a bodysuit in stretch tricot net with three matching panties in different leg lengths, all with stocking locks. *Phyllis W. Heathcotte, "Fashion and Dress," Britannica Book of the Year 1970. p 344*

body-surf, *v.i.* to ride on the crest of a wave without using a surfboard.

Surfers usually train for surfboard riding by body surfing. *Sam J. Greller, "Surfing," The 1968 World Book Year Book, p 590*

Holt fished from the rocks, body-surfed in the great Pacific waves that pound southern Australia's Mornington Peninsula.... *Time, Dec. 29, 1967, p 14*

boiloff, *n.* a loss of liquid rocket fuel by vaporizing when the temperature reaches the boiling point. *Often used attributively.*

The idea is simple but in practice the cost is not low, boiloff rate of about 0.2 per cent per day is several times as high as for most above ground insulated tanks, and some frozen earth tanks have failed as a result of excessive heat inleak. *J. M. Stephenson, "LNG—Fuel for the Future?" Science Journal, March 1970, p 40*

bolt-on, *adj.* designed to be bolted on.

Here, it was found, there is little difference in repair costs. This is because the labour content of a Continental car repair bill usually is lower, due to the common use of bolt-on outer panels. *John Drummond, "The Premium You Pay For Not Buying British," The Times (London), Feb. 14, 1970, p 18*

But, decked out with bolt-on guns and rocket launchers, the shaking, rattling and rolling choppers are less than perfect for close-in fire support. *Time, May 12, 1967, p 28*

bomb[1], *n.* **the Bomb,** nuclear weapons and the potential threat they impose.

From the somber afternoon of the nuclear age, two physicists, father and son, look back at its dawn. The elder had helped to build the Bomb. The younger has been blighted by it. *Time, Aug. 24, 1970, p 64*

bomb[2], *v.t.* *U.S.* to hit (a baseball) a long distance.

... Hal McRae ... bombed the first pitch thrown to him to left field for a two-run homer. *Joseph Durso, The New York Times, March 19, 1968, p 57*

... Gary Gentry ... threw a pitch to Rico Carty that the Atlanta outfielder bombed off the left-field wall on a line but about two feet foul. *Roger Angell, "The Sporting Scene," The New Yorker, Nov. 1, 1969, p 155*

[probably from *bomb, n.,* U.S. term for a long pass in football]

bomb[3], *v.i.* *U.S. Slang.* to flop; fail.

Yet big-name stage shows and acts (*Camelot, My Fair Lady,* Jack Benny) almost consistently bomb at the box office wherever they play in Edmonton. *Hal Tennant, "Montreal? Wrong. It's Edmonton," Maclean's, March 1968, p 19*

It is Big Brother's second album. The first was a record company named Mainstream and it bombed. *The New York Times, Sept. 1, 1968, Sec. 2, p 18*

bomb[4], *n. British Slang.* a fortune.

Let's say I'd put my granny's savings in it, not to make a bomb, but as a secure blue chip for a steady income and long-term capital growth. *Michael Baily, "Inter-city—British Rail's Blue Chip," The Times (London), Sept. 14, 1970, p 8*

bombed, *adj. Slang.* intoxicated, especially by alcohol or drugs.

"I've come into work bombed on sleepers a couple of times (they make you go round like you're drunk); the boss warned me." *Quoted by Victoria Brittain, "How the Drug Clinics Work," The Times (London), Aug. 18, 1970, p 6*

Usually, when an editor says he got bombed last night, he means he had too much to drink. *Time, Dec. 5, 1969, p 62*

bomblet, *n.* a small bomb.

Instead, the Romans chose to celebrate the advent of 1971 in the Chinese fashion. Beginning last night at dusk, and reaching its pinnacle at midnight, the city was shaken by the explosion of thousands of petards or homemade bomblets.... *George Armstrong, "In With a Bang," The Manchester Guardian Weekly, Jan. 9, 1971, p 4*

There's no wasteful overkill to bomblets—just a nice, uniform distribution of energy. *Daniel Lang, "A Reporter at Large," The New Yorker, Jan. 9, 1971, p 55*

bo·moh ('bou mou), *n.* a Malayan medicine man.

Thus when the latest frog fight broke out at Sungei Siput in November, local astrologers and bomohs (witch doctors) predicted another major calamity for Malaysia. *Time, Jan. 18, 1971, p 21*

bonkers, *adj. Slang.* crazy.

. . . she has a choice of feeling guilty and sane or civic-minded and bonkers. *Mavis Gallant, "Reflections: The Events in May: A Paris Notebook," The New Yorker, Sept. 14, 1968, p 105*

I'd had a bad mental time. I wasn't going bonkers, but I'd had a lot of overstrain and overwork, and I was sick of being under the London critical eye. *Harry Corbett, "Four Actors in Search of a Character," The Listener, Aug. 31, 1967, p 272*

[originally British slang, meaning tipsy, slightly drunk]

▶ *Bonkers* was popularized in Great Britain during the 1964 General Election when Quintin Hogg (now Lord Hailsham) said that anyone voting for the Labour Party must be bonkers. See also the note under PREGGERS.

boo, *n. U.S. Slang.* marijuana. *Also used attributively.*

The story, sounding as if it originated with somebody full of Mexican boo smoke, came to prominence in *The Independent American*—a Louisiana-based fright-sheet published by a former New Orleans public-relations flak so far-out he once accused Barry Goldwater of being "tinged with socialism." *Larry L. King, Harper's, Aug. 1965, p 49*

Is the traditional boola-boola of Yale being replaced by plain boo, which, translated from the underground argot, means marijuana? *The New York Times, Feb. 28, 1967, p 39*

boob tube, Usually in the phrase **the boob tube.** *U.S. Slang.* television. Compare TUBE. See also THE BOX.

. . . they [the silent majority] watch forty-eight consecutive hours of football on the boob tube. . . . *Roger Angell, The New Yorker, Jan. 3, 1970, p 27*

What chance does a child have to develop a taste for books if he never has a minute to himself when the boob-tube isn't blaring forth or he himself is not being whisked off to Scouts or dancing lessons? *Mrs. Roy W. Meyer, Mankato, Minn., in a Letter to the Editor, Saturday Review, Oct. 10, 1970, p 21*

boo·ga·loo (ˌbuː gəˈluː), *n.* a dance in two-beat rhythm in which dancers move with shuffling feet, swiveling from side to side and rotating their shoulders and hips.

"I thought Roger was going to bed."

"Maybe but I think he just wanted to get rid of the civilians. You cain't tell—we might go out and do the Boogaloo." *William Whitworth, "Profiles (on Roger Miller, the songwriter): Why Don't We Just Hum For A While?" The New Yorker, March 1, 1969, p 39*

—*v.i.* to dance the boogaloo.

Today, however, a ballerina may have to arch on point in one sequence, boogaloo in another, then writhe on the floor like a snake. . . . *Time, March 15, 1968, p 30*

[probably influenced by *boogie-woogie*]

bootstrap, *v.t.* **bootstrap oneself,** to get into or out of something by one's own effort.

Implying that the court's previous decisions on the subject were shaky at best, [Chief Justice] Burger said: "I will not join in employing recent cases rather than the Constitution to bootstrap ourselves into a result." *Time, July 6, 1970, p 43*

Somehow we have to bootstrap ourselves to a thriving

export trade and the consequent favourable balance of payments. *New Scientist, Nov. 30, 1967, p 525*

But Democrat Bradley is no insular ghetto politician. A lawyer and retired police lieutenant who had bootstrapped himself out of poverty, Bradley organized what he called a "coalition of conscience." *Time, June 6, 1969, p 20*

▶ *Bootstrap* in a figurative sense appears in dictionaries only as a noun, chiefly in the idiom *pull, raise, or lift oneself by one's bootstraps,* or as an adjective, as in the phrase *a bootstrap operation.* The verb idiom to *bootstrap oneself* has not been recorded so far.

booze-up, *n. British Slang.* a drunken revel or spree.

To run, not like Gauguin to Tahiti and the brown-skinned girls, but to Margate and the bawdy simplicity of coach-party booze-ups. . . . *Stanley Reynolds, Review of "I Can't See My Little Willie" (a play) by Douglas Livingstone, The Times (London), Nov. 20, 1970, p 15*

Vac is an account of a broken marriage—as what modern novel isn't? The narrator gives his wife love but not fidelity and tells her so. Most of it is a rapid flow of booze-ups and copulations. *R. G. G. Price, "New Novels," Review of "Vac" by Paul Ableman, Punch, April 17, 1968, p 584*

Boston arm, a type of artificial arm developed in Boston, Massachusetts.

Doctors and engineers unveiled today what they called the "Boston arm," an electronically operated artificial limb that an amputee flexes simply by willing it to flex, as is done with a natural arm. *The New York Times, Sept. 13, 1968, p 1*

The developers believe that the "Boston arms," now ready for mass-production, may be adapted for use by more than 7,000 thalidomide children. *"Transplants: The Surgical Revolution," Science News Yearbook 1969, p 16*

bou·bou (ˈbuː buː), *n.* a long, shapeless garment worn by men and women in Mali, Senegal, and some other parts of Africa. Also spelled BUBU.

. . . the Moslem from the north swishing along in the bou-bou sells plastic bags to the tall Mauretanian who wears the turban and has the look of Arabia etched on his face. *Horace Sutton, "Booked for Travel," Saturday Review, Oct. 31, 1970, p 45*

[from a native name in Africa]

Boul·war·ism (ˈbuːl wəˌriz əm), *n.* a method of collective bargaining.

. . . "Boulwarism," named after Lemuel Boulware, G.E.'s [General Electric's] labor relations chief in the 1950s . . . calls for management to make and stick to an initial "firm, fair" offer to employees and to attempt to convince workers of the offer's merits by conducting vigorous "employee marketing" campaigns. *"Inflationary End to a Class War," Time, Feb. 9, 1970, p 71*

bourgeoisification, *n.* the act or process of becoming bourgeois; assuming the characteristics considered typical of the middle class. Compare EMBOURGEOISEMENT.

I find that many comrades stress the possibility of a military coup in Chile. I am more inclined to think that at present the greatest danger would be a bourgeoisification from within. . . . *Regis Debray, quoted in The Manchester Guardian Weekly, Feb. 6, 1971, p 4*

[from *bourgeois* + *-ification,* as in *magnification*]

bourgeoisified, *adj.* characterized by bourgeois ideas or practices.

On the other hand, the *fidelistas* [supporters of Cuban premier Fidel Castro] may also well be right in fearing that, as Communist parties enter into the parliamentary game, make coalitions, join cabinets, they will develop a stake in the system, become bourgeoisified, and forget to make the revolution. *Arthur Schlesinger, Jr., "The Lowering Hemisphere," The Atlantic, Jan. 1970, p 84*

[from *bourgeois* + -*ified*, as in *magnified, certified*, etc.]

bou·ti·quier (bu: ti:'kyei), *n.* the owner of a boutique.

Adolfo ... was an important boutiquier when other custom milliners ventured no farther hors d'oeuvre [outside the (chief) work] than an occasional scarf or handbag. *Lois Long, "On and Off the Avenue: Feminine Fashions," The New Yorker, Oct. 18, 1969, p 158*

[from French]

bov·ver ('bɒv ər), *British Slang.* —*n.* street fighting, especially by gangs of rowdies.

During the 1870s his [Lionel Jeffries'. character actor] grandfather, Charles Jeffries, ran an East End gang called the Skeleton Army whose specialty was bovver at Salvation Army meetings. *The Times (London), April 29, 1970, p 12*

—*v.i.* to engage in street fighting.

Skinheads don't bovver with the West Indians, probably because they are tough. *Time, June 8, 1970, p 38*

[probably from the Cockney pronunciation of *bother* meaning "disturbance"]

bovver boot, *British Slang.* a type of heavy hobnailed and steel-toed shoe designed for kicking and causing injury, typically worn by rowdies in street fighting. Police in England often "request" fans to remove their bovver boots before they enter a soccer field. Also called CHERRY RED.

... the skinhead had kicked Miss Singer in the shins with his bovver boots. *M. C. Kerigan, Essex, England, in a Letter to the Editor, New Scientist, Sept. 17, 1970, p 600*

His [William McIlvanney, poet] language is often as clumsy and ugly as his material; his metaphors can be used with the indiscriminateness of bovver boots. *Richard Holmes, The Times (London), May 2, 1970, p IV*

bow thruster (bau), a propeller in a ship's bow, operated by remote control.

The liner was manoeuvred by use of a bow thruster, which forces jets of water through tubes underwater to turn the nose of the ship. *The Times (London), Feb. 6, 1970, p 1*

"What is the thing called the bow thruster?" Mr. Christy asked....

"It is the forward propeller, operating in a tunnel in the bow, which can push the ship and make it possible to dock easily in any port," the Captain said. *"The Talk of the Town," The New Yorker, June 26, 1971, p 33*

box, *n.* Usually in the phrase **the box,** *Slang.* television. Compare TUBE. See also BOOB TUBE.

Last week I saw Dr [Billy] Graham on the box, stating his firm belief in the actual and the physical return ... of his Lord Jesus Christ.... *Donald Gould, "A Groundling's Notebook," New Scientist, Dec. 10, 1970, p 457*

Unfortunately, the producers of these films were unwilling to let it rest at that, and the result can make the next few weeks of moviegoing almost as dispiriting as staying at home with the "box." *Arthur Knight, "Movies Are Better Than Ever?" Saturday Review, Dec. 2, 1967, p 53*

BP, 1 abbreviation of BEAUTIFUL PEOPLE.

Papers were regularly filled with features and with candid-camera shots of BPs going in and out of smart restaurants. *Time, Sept. 14, 1970, p 79*

2 abbreviation of BLACK PANTHER.

Gregory gave her the number of Black Panther HQ., and the BPs sent over a bodyguard. *William F. Buckley Jr., "A Week's Journal," The New Yorker, Aug. 28, 1971, p 37*

brad·y·ki·nin (,bræd i'kai nən), *n.* a protein substance that causes dilation of small blood vessels and is believed to produce some of the signs of inflammation, such as swelling and pain. Compare NEUROKININ.

The work which led to this concept may also provide an increased understanding of pain mechanisms (*Medical World News*, Vol. 6, No. 18). The tool for this research was a substance called bradykinin. It is a peptide—a short chain made up of nine amino acids which is produced when proteins in the blood plasma are broken down by certain enzymes. Bradykinin was first discovered in snake venom in 1949. *New Scientist, June 10, 1965, p 698*

[from *brady-* slow (from Greek *bradýs*) + *kinin* any of various proteins involved in dilation and contraction of tissue, from Greek *kínein* to move]

brain death, death of the cerebral cortex, shown by flat tracings on an electroencephalograph. Also called CEREBRAL DEATH.

... a special Harvard University committee has recommended that brain death, or irreversible coma, be considered a definition of death and has drawn up a set of guidelines for determining when there is no discernible activity of the central nervous system. *Scientific American, Sept. 1968, p 85*

A flat electroencephalogram for at least five hours is considered to be evidence of brain death. *J. E. Tesar, "Organ Transplants," Encyclopedia Science Supplement (Grolier) 1969, p 157*

brain drain, the emigration of scientists, scholars, etc., to countries that offer better job opportunities.

Eleven foreign-born American scholars—sociologists, physicians, literary critics—assess the brain drain, its causes and its effect upon American learning. *Science News, Sept. 21, 1968, p 296*

The study concludes that only a heavy "brain drain" of skilled technicians from the rest of the nation has prevented serious shortages in the state.... *Fred M. Hechinger, The New York Times, April 21, 1968, p 54*

brain-drain, *v.i.* to emigrate to a country where better jobs are offered to scientists, scholars, etc.

Twice a year he [William Cooper] goes to the US and Canada, seeing scientists who have brain-drained westwards and want to come back. *Hugh Hebert, The Manchester Guardian Weekly, April 10, 1971, p 21*

—*v.t.* to cause to brain-drain.

... his intensive style of research is well suited to the atmosphere of the Johnson Research Foundation in Philadelphia, to which he is a frequent visitor. He hasn't been brain-drained yet, though.... *New Scientist, April 2, 1970, p 31*

The institute has recruited a large portion of its faculty from the growing reservoir of "brain-drained" Indian scientists in the West, even paying the cost of resettling them and their families. *The New York Times, Jan. 12, 1968, p 69*

brain drainer, a scientist, scholar, etc., who emigrates to another country for a better job.

...the general attitude towards the brain drainers is more one of supplying them with information about jobs available than following up Mintech's [Ministry of Technology's] programme to "go out and get the people Britain needs." *Jean Phillips, Science Journal, Jan. 1969, p 13*

bra·less ('brɑ: lis), *adj.* favoring the discard of brassieres as a symbol of women's liberation. Compare TOPLESS.

"Miss Loren [Sophia Loren], what are your views on the braless movement?" *"The Talk of the Town: Questions at Radio City," The New Yorker, Oct. 3, 1970, p 31*

Brans-Dick·e theory ('brænz'dik i:), a theory of gravitation according to which light and other electromagnetic waves passing through a strong gravitational field should have a lesser degree of curvature and of velocity than that predicted by the gravitational equations of Einstein's general theory of relativity. It was formulated by the American physicists Carl H. Brans and Robert H. Dicke in 1961. Also called SCALAR-TENSOR THEORY.

Both theories predict that when a light ray passes near a massive body like the sun, it will be bent and slowed. But the Brans-Dicke theory predicts about 10 percent less bending than Einstein's does. The bending produces an apparent shift in the star's location. *Science News, June 13, 1970, p 574*

bras·sin ('bræs ən), *n.* a plant hormone that stimulates the division, elongation, and lateral enlargement of plant cells. Compare ABSCISIC ACID, CYTOKININ, KINETIN.

Isolated recently by investigators at the Department of Agriculture research establishment in Beltsville, Md., the brassins...take their name from the genus *Brassica*, a group of plants that includes the oilseed producer rape, whose abundant pollen is the source of the new hormones. *"Messenger No. 5," Scientific American, Sept. 1970, p 91*

brawn drain, the emigration of laborers, athletes, etc., to countries that offer better jobs or opportunities.

The survey offers only one ray of encouragement for Mr. Wilson: so far there is no sign of a brawn drain. *The Sunday Times (London), Oct. 23, 1966, p 6*

[patterned after *brain drain*]

bread, *n. Slang.* money.

"Anyway, she could get to New York on five hundred, couldn't she?" "Sure," shrugged Gary....This chick wasn't running away, he flashed, not with that kind of bread. *Don Mitchell, "Thelma," The Atlantic, June 1970, p 74*

breadboarding, *n.* the construction of an experimental system, such as an electronic circuit, on a flat surface specially equipped to lay out experimental models of circuitry.

More and more, engineers use digital computers to simulate new electronic systems. It's often faster and cheaper than breadboarding....*Advertisement by Bell Telephone Laboratories in Scientific American, May 1968, p 11*

The components were interconnected with metal or plastic tubing to form a fluidic device. This approach is suitable for constructing experimental circuits, breadboarding, and developing new fluidic concepts. *Alonzo R. Parsons, "Fluidics," McGraw-Hill Yearbook of Science and Technology 1968, p 14*

break-bulk, *adj.* of or relating to the breaking down of carload shipments into smaller shipments for various destinations.

Many shippers have expressed concern over the rapid trend to container shipping and the ousting of ordinary tonnage for break-bulk consignments. *The New York Times, June 24, 1968, p 74*

breathalyse, *v.t., v.i. British.* to subject or submit to a test of intoxication, usually by means of a breathalyser.

Constable Hitchen had said: "In all fairness to Mr. Holmes he should be breathalysed." *The Times (London), Oct. 20, 1970, p 6*

Would it not be sensible to amend the Bill so that the police power to stop and "breathalyse" people should be limited to when the police believe people are affected by alcohol, or suspect an offence is being committed? *The Times (London), Dec. 1, 1967, p 8*

[back formation from *breathalyser*]

breathalyser or **breathalyzer,** *n.* a device that measures the concentration of alcohol in a person's blood by analyzing the breath in a chemical test. When a person breathes into a breathalyser his breath is passed through a chemical substance which changes color in proportion to the alcoholic concentration in his breath.

...the breathalyser test...meant blowing into a plastic bag; if the crystals in a connected tube turned green it was *prima facie* evidence of too much alcohol in the system, and the driver was then required to submit to a blood or urine test to establish the precise degree. *The Annual Register of World Events in 1967 (1968), p 46*

The breathalyser (dreadful word) did seem to be cutting the Hogarthian swill fractionally. *Philip Hope-Wallace, The Manchester Guardian Weekly, Jan. 4, 1968, p 13*

[from *Breathalyser*, a trade name]

breath test, *British.* a test of intoxication, usually by means of a breathalyser.

Its opponents argue that the breath test cannot be accurate because of the distortion of alcohol in the mouth. *The Manchester Guardian Weekly, Nov. 22, 1969, p 12*

breath-test, *v.t. British.* to breathalyse.

In Britain last year, of 73,455 motorists breath-tested by police, 29,586 were found to be negative, many of whom would almost certainly have been found to have had a blood-alcohol intake above the 80 mgs limit if a more accurate breath-testing appliance had been used. *Adam Raphael, "US Criticises Breath Tests," The Manchester Guardian Weekly, June 19, 1971, p 5*

Brezhnev Doctrine, the doctrine that the USSR has the right to intervene in the affairs of other Communist countries in defense of Communism.

In May, Leonid I. Brezhnev, general secretary of the Soviet Communist Party, himself went to Prague to sign the treaty, which legitimized the presence of Soviet troops in Czechoslovakia. The treaty also incorporated the essence of the so-called Brezhnev doctrine, stating that the "support, the strengthening and the protection of socialist acquisitions, which were achieved through heroic efforts and sacrifice-filled toil by the people of the two countries, are the joint international duty of the socialist countries." *Otto Pick, "Czechoslovakia," Britannica Book of the Year 1971, p 239*

bridgebuilder, *n.* a person who strives to resolve differences between opposing persons, parties, systems, etc.

Initially he [Halvard Lange] followed [Trygve] Lie's line, that of bridgebuilder between East and West, but the deterioration in the international climate made this an attitude difficult to sustain. *The Times (London), May 21, 1970, p 10*

broad-brush, *adj.* not detailed; incomplete or imperfect; rough.

Government economists . . . have taken several routes to arrive at admittedly broad-brush estimates that air pollution costs U.S. citizens between $14,000,000,000 and $18,000,000,000 a year in direct economic loss. *Tom Alexander, "Some Burning Questions About Combustion," Encyclopedia Science Supplement (Grolier) 1970, p 181*

As a "broad brush" indication of the state of health of a project, the Confidence Profile may be used. *Ralph Benjamin, "Putting the Manager in the Picture," New Scientist, Sept. 28, 1967, p 665*

brother, *n. Afro-American use.* **1** a fellow black; soul brother.

"I'm now at the position Booker T. Washington was about sixty or seventy years ago," [Hosea] Williams said. "I say to my brothers, 'Cast down your buckets where you are' — and that means there in the slums and ghettos." *Bayard Rustin, "The Failure of Black Separatism," Harper's, Jan. 1970, p 29*

2 any black man.

With his sudden visibility on the battlefield, the Negro has achieved the most genuine integration and the fullest participation in policies that America has yet granted. "And," it was pointed out during the soul session, "the brother is dying in order to participate — again." *The New York Times, May 1, 1968, p 1*

brown-bag, *v.t., v.i. U.S. Slang.* to bring one's own (liquor or food) to a restaurant, club, etc., usually in a brown paper bag. Originally the term was applied to the practice of providing one's own liquor in states prohibiting its sale in public establishments.

The Big-Four ambassadors meeting in Berlin to negotiate . . . developed a ritual of retiring after each session for a long and lavish luncheon . . . it was decided that the Americans would cater the meal during one meeting. The arrangement did little to promote *détente*, however. The mistrustful Russians brown-bagged their own caviar and vodka. The Americans . . . served hamburgers. No agreement on Berlin is in sight. *"The U.S.: American Notes: Hold the Onions," Time, Feb. 8, 1971, p 6*

Brown-bagging is the genteel disguise adopted by a patron to furnish his own liquor when he dines at the local restaurant. *Harry Golden, "How to Live with a Chair You Hate," Saturday Review, June 17, 1967, p 14*

brown belt, **1** a degree of proficiency in judo or karate next below the black belt.

Mr. Trudeau, when he officially takes the post after Mr.

Pearson retires later this month, will be the first Prime Minister in Canada to hold a brown belt in karate. *The New York Times, April 8, 1968, p 8*

Brown belt holder dies in judo match. *Headline in The Times (London), Sept. 29, 1970, p 3*

2 a person awarded this degree. Compare BLACK BELT.

Winners in the form divisions were Toyotaro Miyazaki of Jackson Heights, Queens, black belt; Larry Pomilio of North Miami Beach, Fla., brown belt. . . . *The New York Times, April 1, 1968, p 66*

Brown Berets, **1** an organization of Mexican Americans seeking political power and greater economic opportunity in the United States.

They have formed the Brown Berets, modeled on the Black Panthers, and set up a $2,200,000 Mexican-American Legal Defense and Educational Fund, financed by the Ford Foundation. *Time, July 4, 1969, p 16*

2 the berets worn by its members.

The slogan "Red Power" is a copy of "Black Power", just as the "Brown Berets", the headgear of the extremist wing of the Mexican-Americans, is a copy of the emblem of the Black Panthers — and the police are already familiar with it. *The Times (London), March 11, 1970, p 11*

[name patterned after the *Green Berets*, a guerrilla-fighting unit of the U.S. Army in Indochina]

brown fat, a tissue containing deposits of fat whose oxidation is a major source of heat in animals, and especially in man.

The human baby has brown fat tissue between the shoulder blades, around the neck, behind the breast-bone and around the kidneys — all positions duplicated by the rabbit. *G. S. Dawes, "Hazards of Birth," Science Journal, June 1970, p 90*

brown lung disease, a disease that affects workers in cotton mills. Compare BLACK LUNG.

Byssinosis, a chronic and disabling lung disease of cotton workers, has been known for two centuries but, although recognized as a serious problem in England, it was not considered to be of importance in the U.S. A careful survey in two cotton mills by E. Zuskin and her colleagues from Yale, however, revealed that 25% of cardroom workers and 12% of spinners had the disease. . . . Meanwhile, pressure was being exerted in Washington to make the condition ("brown lung disease") compensable under the workmen's compensation acts. *Peter John Taylor, "Medicine: Occupational Medicine," Britannica Book of the Year 1971, p 492*

Brown Power, a slogan used by Mexican Americans, modeled on the term BLACK POWER. Compare RED POWER.

Being a member of the Mexican-American minority group, which lately talks of "Brown Power," I have one question to ask of Harvey Wheeler. Would he also advocate having a brown Congress for my particular minority group and eventually perhaps a red Congress for the American Indians? *Alma G. Vasquez, Harlingen, Texas, in a Letter to the Editor, Saturday Review, June 8, 1968, p 35*

brutalist, *adj.* of a style of architecture that emphasizes massiveness and the suggestion of brute strength by exposing concrete in large, chunky masses.

The rebuilding is partly new brutalist, as in the flats

along the waterfront, where the concrete, happily, has already weathered out of its early crudity.... *Nesta Roberts, "Survivor in the Warm South," The Manchester Guardian Weekly, July 3, 1971, p 14*

Breuer, whose recent work included New York City's almost windowless, brutalist Whitney Museum of American Art, was involved with plans for a monumental new wing for the Cleveland (O.) Museum of Art. *Sandra Blutman, "Architecture," Britannica Book of the Year 1969, p 105*

—*n.* an architect of the brutalist school.

The Brutalists also have done much to advocate new forms of mass housing (see Park Hill Estate). *The Sunday Times (London), May 7, 1967, p 54*

bubble, *n.* a woman's hair style in which the hair is arranged in a round, bubblelike shape.

A few days later I visited a local Black shop.... I was startled to see a not-young white woman, spike heels, a jumper and blouse, platinum hair piled high in a bubble hairdo.... Again and again my eye was drawn to the scene of platinum bubble and afro and the cartridge belts separating them.... I realized that either the woman or her teenaged daughter was a pacesetter and wanted to be first with a new trend.... *Mary E. Mebane, "Headlong Into the 19th Century," The New York Times, June 11, 1971, p 35*

bubbletop, *n.* **1** a dome-shaped transparent umbrella.

The biggest news in umbrellas since Mary Poppins sailed away with hers is the bubble-top. Made of transparent vinyl that bottles the wearer in his own waterproof demi-jar, the new models have taken the country by storm .... The body may not be fully sheltered, but head and shoulders stay totally dry. People can see where they are going, or who is coming at them. *"Under the Bubble-Top," Time, May 24, 1971, p 37*

2 a transparent, dome-shaped cover or roof of an automobile, especially one that is bulletproof and used on cars of public officials for parades and the like.

But the late President [John F. Kennedy] would in all probability be alive today if the people on the Dallas streets had seen him through a bubbletop.... *Richard H. Rovere, "Letter From Washington," The New Yorker, June 15, 1968, p 92*

bu-bu ('bu: bu:), *n.* another spelling of BOU-BOU.

Inside the Centennial Ballroom, a babel of people in long white Moslem robes and colored bubus (tribal gowns) mingled with those in formal tie and tails wearing rows of medals. *Time, Jan. 17, 1969, p 28*

bugger, *v.t.* **bugger up,** *Slang.* to bungle or botch.

Size apart, is there a recognisably Willis sound? ... "You can tell which Willis made, at which period of his life, and who buggered it up afterwards. My great-grandfather wouldn't put his name on organs. He said if people couldn't tell who made them they couldn't read anyway." *Christopher Ford, "Father Willis's Masterwork," The Manchester Guardian Weekly, July 10, 1971, p 16*

▶ Professor Brian Foster reports: "*Bugger* in the sense of 'to spoil, ruin, check or change drastically' is noted by Partridge, *Dictionary of Slang,* but without the preposition. Even in 1972 this is an indecent term in England, particularly in the South, where there is still an awareness of the basic meaning (to commit sodomy) totally lost in the North. Some

years ago I watched a B.B.C. television programme showing car-racing. One of the cars was known as 'The Little Bug' and when it won the excited commentator unfortunately cried 'The Little Bug 'as done it'. This was understood as 'The little bugger's done it' by many listeners, who telephoned their protests."

Buggins's turn, *British.* promotion based on length of service or seniority rather than on merit.

In an age of union bureaucrats and Buggins's turn at the helm, Cannon was a fighter. *John Torode, "Cannon's Road from Wigan Pier," The Manchester Guardian Weekly, Dec. 19, 1970, p 15*

Our system is hierarchic. It was always possible to maintain this as long as those at the top of the pyramid could keep the rest down, and work has always been a good way of doing that. ... When the headman's axe was no longer seriously accepted as a solution, we invented the law of "Buggin's turn." *Rex Malik, "Wages of Automation," New Scientist, Aug. 28, 1969, p 424*

▶ Though not a new expression, this phrase has been gaining considerable currency in recent years. R. W. Burchfield, the present editor of the *OED Supplement,* writing in the *Sunday Times* (London) issue of March 20, 1966, cites a 1901 source in which the term was used. The source is a letter, dated January 13, 1901, in which Admiral of the Fleet Lord Fisher wrote to the Earl of Selbourne the following observation: "Favouritism was the secret of our efficiency in the old days.... 'Buggins' turn' has been our ruin and will be disastrous hereafter."

bulldagger, *n.* *U.S. Slang.* a female homosexual who acts as a male. Compare BUTCH.

She was extra ugly. There was a rumor that Saralee was a bulldagger. I don't know if that was true or not but she was certainly rough enough to be a man. *Louise Meriwether, Daddy was a Number Runner, 1970, p 25*

[alteration (probably influenced by *dagger*) of *bulldyke* a "male" dyke or lesbian]

bullet, *n.* **bite the bullet,** to submit or resign to a painful course without further protest or delay (in allusion to the alleged practice of having a soldier bite a bullet for lack of anesthesia while undergoing a painful operation in the field).

"He [Senator Robert P. Griffin of Michigan] was within a hair of turning around. But the White House had him locked in, and finally he bit the bullet and said he would stay where he was." *Richard Harris, "Annals of Politics," The New Yorker, Dec. 12, 1970, p 93*

The former film star added that college administrators should be willing to "bite the bullet" and stand up to demonstrators. *The Times (London), April 9, 1970, p 8*

He [President Richard M. Nixon] decreed that it was "time to bite the bullet" and end political appointment of postmasters and rural mail carriers, urging their selection by competitive exams. *Time, Feb. 14, 1969, p 18*

After asking Congress to "bite the bullet" and pass his proposed 10 per cent income tax surcharge, the President himself bit the bullet by agreeing to a much larger accompanying spending reduction than he believed was in the national interest. *The New York Times, Aug. 2, 1968, Sec. 4, p 4*

bullet train, a high-speed passenger train of Japan.

Japan's 125 m.p.h. "bullet train" between Tokyo and Osaka is the technological wonder of the Eastern world. *Time, July 6, 1970, p 59*

The famous "bullet" trains cover the 309 miles to Tokyo in 3 hours 10 minutes of luxury travel, and you see Mount Fuji from the train. *Penelope Turing, The Times (London), March 14, 1970, p IX*

bull point, *British.* a point scored against an opponent; an advantage.

England beat an unconvincing South Africa with a second half rally; Wales drew with South Africa as injury time had almost ticked itself out. On the strength of that, it looks like a bull point for England. *U. A. Titley, "England Three-Quarters Look Stronger," The Times (London), Feb. 28, 1970, p 10*

bummer, *n. U.S. Slang.* **1** a disappointment.

"Atlanta is a bummer. My old lady and I split after we got busted by the pigs." *Ed Wilcox, "Bridge the Gap—Learn to Rap," Sunday News (New York), March 28, 1971, p 127*

But, except for the big hits, the newer kinds of movies don't satisfy *anybody.* . . . all the films released this summer have been box-office bummers. *Pauline Kael, "The Current Cinema," The New Yorker, Oct. 3, 1970, p 76*

2 another term for BAD TRIP.

"Hey, Rodge, man, are you on a bummer?" Allison asked. "No," Miller said. "Maybe I'm just tired. *"William Whitworth, "Profiles: Why Don't We Just Hum for a While?" The New Yorker, March 1, 1969, p 41*

The culture has its own in-group argot: "bummers" (bad trips) and "straights" (everyone else), "heat" (the police) and "narks" (narcotics agents) and being "spaced out" (in a drug daze). *Time, Sept. 26, 1969, p 41*

The worst bummer of all time was recorded by Robert Louis Stevenson. It seems that the good Dr. Jekyll tripped out on a mysterious powder and ended up as the nefarious Mr. Hyde. *"The Drug Scene: Dr. Jekyll and Mr. Cocaine," Science News, April 17, 1971, p 264*

bump, *v.t.* to cancel plans for travel to (a place).

An October, 1970, entry, set down more than a year in advance, called for Plimpton's presence at a Hong Kong meeting of the Commission for the Advancement of Christian Higher Education in Asia, of which he is one of fifteen members (eight Asians, seven Westerners), but as the time for this drew near, the annual New Members' Dinner of the Century Club also approached. At this fixture, the neophytes are traditionally welcomed by their president. The club Plimpton won out over the do-good Plimpton; Miss Ruby was instructed to bump Hong Kong. *Geoffrey T. Hellman, "Profiles: Period-Piece Fellow (Francis T. P. Plimpton)," The New Yorker, Dec. 4, 1971, p 80*

bumper sticker, a sticker bearing a printed slogan for display on an automobile bumper.

. . . the two political bumper stickers available at the bookstore of the Ernest L. Wilkinson student center say "I'm Proud to Be an American" and "I'm a Member of the Silent Majority." *Calvin Trillin, "U.S. Journal: Provo, Utah," The New Yorker, March 21, 1970, p 122*

In the bumper-sticker dialogue of the freeways, they answered MAKE LOVE NOT WAR with HONOR AMERICA or SPIRO IS MY HERO. *Time, Jan. 5, 1970, p 8*

bunny, *n. Slang.* a pretty girl who appeals to men as a pet or plaything.

Tired of being used only as secretaries and bed bunnies, the female members of Germany's student S.D.S. [Students for a Democratic Society] staged a walkout—but not before hurling invective and rotten tomatoes at the organization's male chauvinists. *Time, Aug. 17, 1970, p 25*

[from the *Bunnies,* young pretty nightclub waitresses at Playboy Clubs, dressed in scanty uniforms with fluffy tails and long ears to suggest a bunny (rabbit)]

Bun·ra·ku (buːnˈrɑːkuː), *n.* the traditional Japanese puppet theater.

In its own country a dying art, the Bunraku has had an extensive influence on the west—as on such diverse figures as Claudel and Gordon Craig: and for anyone with serious theatrical interests it is not an experience to be missed. *The Times (London), June 11, 1968, p 15*

Today the Bunraku tradition is fresh and overwhelming in its power. *Charles Lewsen, "Time Out with Puppets," The Times (London), Jan. 3, 1972, p 8*

Burkitt's lymphoma, a cancer of the lymphatic system especially prevalent among children in central Africa, and associated with the Epstein-Barr virus.

Burkitt's lymphoma is the most likely human cancer to be virus-induced. *New Scientist, Nov. 12, 1970, p 313*

The story of a series of medical discoveries, of a safari tracking down a form of cancer that afflicts African children, a cancer known as Burkitt's lymphoma for the doctor who found both the virus and a cure. *Science News, Aug. 15, 1970, p 138*

[named after Dennis *Burkitt,* a British surgeon at Mulago Hospital in Kampala, Uganda, who first identified the disease in 1957]

burn, *n.* the firing of a rocket engine or a retrorocket to produce thrust.

During the second or third earth orbit, if all is well, the third stage will fire again, to accelerate the spacecraft to more than 24,000 miles per hour, pushing it out of earth orbit toward the moon. If the burn is successful, the spent third stage will be separated from the spacecraft shortly after injection onto the path to the moon. *Science News, Dec. 21, 1968, p 614*

A "perfect burn" pulled them out of lunar orbit and towards a splashdown in the Pacific. *The Manchester Guardian Weekly, July 24, 1969, p 3*

—*v.t.* **1** to fire (a rocket engine or retrorocket).

Armstrong had to burn the engines for another 70 seconds to reach a smoother landing site about 4 miles away. *Wernher von Braun and Frederick I. Ordway, "One Giant Leap for Mankind," The Americana Annual 1970, p 22*

2 *U.S. Slang.* to sell fake or inferior narcotics. See also BURN ARTIST.

Another hippie, a tall gaunt young man, complained that East Village hippies were always being "burned," cheated. "You buy heroin or grass and find it's powder, not what you paid for at all." *Martin Arnold, The New York Times, Oct. 15, 1967, Sec. 1, p 77*

—*v.i.* to undergo a burn; be fired.

The engine had to burn for more than seven minutes in order to produce a final velocity of 4,128 miles . . . per hour. *Wernher von Braun and Frederick I. Ordway, "One Giant Leap for Mankind," The Americana Annual 1970, p 26*

burn artist, *U.S. Slang.* a person who sells fake or inferior narcotics.

"Who do you have on Haight Street today?" he [a San Francisco dope peddler] said disgustedly. . . . "You have burn artists (fraudulent dope peddlers), rip-offs (thieves), and snitchers (police spies)." *Adam Raphael, The Manchester Guardian Weekly, May 2, 1970, p 16*

burns, *n.pl. U.S. Slang.* sideburns.

Sandy [a male character in the movie "Carnal Knowledge"] is a superannuated swinger, complete with stash, burns and a 17-year-old hippie on his arm. *Stefan Kanfer, "Cinema," Time, July 5, 1971, p 55*

burton, *n.* **go** or **knock for a burton,** *British Slang.* to cease to be; pass completely out of existence; disappear.

. . . the old British horsey class nonsense seemed to have gone for a burton. Nobody had any manners any more. *René Cutforth, "René Cutforth Gets Demobbed," The Listener, Dec. 19, 1968, p 810*

. . . There is no competition to keep advertising rates down because each company has monopoly rights in its region—so the first principle of "capitalist efficiency" goes for a burton, down the drain. *Bernard Hollowood, "Money for Jam," Punch, June 28, 1967, p 929*

The chairman, Cyril Stein, said: "It knocked our profits for a burton." *The Times (London), Sept. 11, 1967, p 21*

[originally applied to persons absent, missing, or presumed dead, from the expression *gone for a Burton* (listed in Eric Partridge's *Dictionary of Slang,* 1950), literally, gone for some *Burton* ale or beer, which was brewed at Burton on Trent. This original meaning may have been an RAF expression.]

bus, *n.* one of the stages of a rocket or missile.

Alternatively, MIRVs are carried on a low-thrust final stage called a bus which has a single guidance system. *Frank Barnaby, "The March to Oblivion," New Scientist and Science Journal, Feb. 11, 1971, p 292*

bust, *Slang.* —*v.t.* **1** to arrest.

I have never been busted for pot, my hair doesn't brush my shoulders, and you won't catch me nude in the park. I am so straight, in fact, that I actually have a job. *Henry Muller, "Some Tips on Coping with Parents," Time, Aug. 17, 1970, p 38*

2 to make a raid on.

Galahad . . . says they [the police] have "busted" or raided his apartment "about 30 times" in the last two and one-half months. *Stephen A. O. Golden, The New York Times, June 1, 1967, p 39*

—*n.* **1** an arrest.

They [people at the Woodstock Music Festival] asked for volunteers to pick up garbage, and they made announcements warning those leaving to be careful on the way out—not to take grass [marijuana] with them, because of busts on the highway, and so on. *"The Talk of the Town," The New Yorker, Aug. 30, 1969, p 21*

2 a raid, especially by the police.

The bust at the end of the movie, with police gassing, kicking, and clubbing students until we can't stand it anymore, is finally an effective piece of film-making. *David Denby, "Commercials for Revolution," The Atlantic, Oct. 1970, p 143*

butch, *Slang.* —*adj.* **1** (of a female homosexual) assuming a masculine role.

She was never interested in boys sexually and perhaps one of the secrets of the success in our relationship is that she is completely butch and I am completely feminine. *Molly Parkin, "Me and My Mate," The Sunday Times (London), Jan. 25, 1970, p 60*

2 (of a female) having a masculine appearance.

The rather butch nun holding the baby is actually a boy Picasso knew who was dressed up to add to the picture a religious note; and the doctor is Picasso's father. *Sheldon Williams, "Father of the Man," The Manchester Guardian Weekly, Jan. 9, 1971, p 21*

—*n.* a female homosexual who acts as a male.

In the 1960's he [a male homosexual] may be the catty hair-dresser or the lisping, limp-wristed interior decorator. His lesbian counterpart is the "butch," the girl who is aggressively masculine to the point of trying to look like a man. *Time, Oct. 31, 1969, p 39*

[probably from *butch*, U.S. slang term for a tough-looking youth, from *Butch*, a common nickname for a boy]

Buts·kell ('bəts kəl), *adj.* of or characterized by Butskellism.

Some years ago, British politicians used the term "Butskellism" to define a large area of common ground on Government policy between reform-minded Tories such as R. A. Butler and the late Hugh Gaitskell, leader of the Labor Party. Although he was a protégé of Mr. Butler in the work of modernizing the Tory party after its 1945 defeat, Mr. Heath now seems bent on a sharp break with the "Butskell" approach to problems. *The New York Times, Nov. 2, 1970, p 46*

Buts·kel·lism ('bəts kəl,iz əm), *n.* a condition in which political opponents support similar policies. See also the quotation under BUTSKELL, above.

. . . the increase in the number of floating voters began in the era of Butskellism, when R. A. Butler, Hugh Gaitskell and others effectively reduced the distance between the Conservative and Labour parties on domestic issues. *Richard Rose, "Six Years of Shifting Viewpoints in a Volatile Electorate," The Times (London), May 15, 1970, p 10*

[blend of Richard Austin *But*ler, born 1902, English Tory politician, and Hugh Gait*skell*, 1906-1963, English Labour politician + *-ism*]

butterfly, *v.i., v.t.* to fly from one thing to the next much as a butterfly seems to fly aimlessly from one resting spot to the next; flutter or flit.

Every year sees the appearance of fictional contrivances that pause briefly as larvae in book form before butterflying their way onto the screen. *Time, April 27, 1970, p 98*

If you are not committed to your job, you can take all this lightly and butterfly away to the next one. *Penny Radford, "Surviving in the Office," The Times (London), Dec. 29, 1970, p 15*

[verb use of the noun]

buttlegging, *n. U.S.* the illegal transportation and sale of cigarettes on which no cigarette tax has been paid.

U.S. Attorney Whitney North Seymour Jr. discusses lucrative buttlegging business at recent press conference.

Picture legend, "Bonanza For Buttleggers" by Richard Mathieu, Sunday News (New York), March 19, 1972, p 146

[from *butt* (U.S. slang term for a cigarette) + *-legging*, as in *bootlegging*]

button-down, *adj. U.S.* urbane; suave; sophisticated.

The dominant mood at 57th Street and Park Avenue is, on the contrary, one of low-key, button-down professionalism, an atmosphere that permits the languid inquisitiveness of a college seminar, yet requires also the relentless intensity of a Madison Avenue firm with a big client to merchandise and only a few months in which to do it. *The New York Times, June 24, 1968, p 16*

Last week the National Urban League, long attacked by militants as the button-down, archconservative wing of the civil rights movement, embraced Black Power—in its achievable definition. *Time, Aug. 9, 1968, p 17*

[from the *button-down* shirt collars thought of as worn by conservative professionals and businessmen]

button man, *U.S. Underworld Slang.* a low-ranking member of the Mafia who does the dirty work. Also called SOLDIER.

Mafia bosses, who had built careful layers of insulation around themselves—never dealing directly with button men, trusting only a few close lieutenants—found their protective covering being stripped away. *Time, July 12, 1971, p 18*

In fact, he was a juvenile delinquent from New York City who killed a number of men for hire. Today he probably would be a button man for the Mafia. *John Fischer, "The Easy Chair," Harper's, April 1971, p 12*

buy-in, *n. U.S.* a procedure on the stock exchange in which a broker who does not receive a purchased security by a specified date may buy it elsewhere.

A buy-in occurs when a broker fails to receive from another broker securities he has purchased for a customer and he enters another order in the open market for the shares so that he can deliver them. Any resulting loss is charged to the nondelivering broker and his customer. *Robert D. Hershey Jr., The New York Times, Aug. 3, 1968, p 29*

buy-out, *n.* the purchase of the entire stock of a product.

About 80 per cent of the machine's [370/135 computer's] components are of British manufacture—in a typical year IBM says it places orders for about £25 million worth of buy-outs in the UK. *New Scientist and Science Journal, March 18, 1971, p 614*

[from the verb phrase *buy out*]

buzz word, any well-established or familiar term in the jargon of business, government, technology, etc.

"Guideline" has become something of a Democratic economists' buzz word, and the Nixon White House prefers "yardstick." *"From Freeze to Controlled Thaw," Time, Nov. 22, 1971, p 36*

A last word on metaphors. Today the swing is towards buzz-words from business rather than technology, as witness the anonymous author of the preface to *Catalyst*

Handbook. He calls catalysts "these chemical entrepreneurs". *Arthur Conway, New Scientist, Sept. 10, 1970, p 545*

byō·bu ('byou bu:), *n. sing.* or *pl. Japanese.* a painted folding screen, usually with six panels.

From the 7th century, when the first *byōbu* were introduced from China, the art of screen painting absorbed the best talents in Japan. *Time, March 15, 1971, p 35*

byte (bait), *n.* a unit of information consisting of a group of usually eight bits or binary digits, used especially as a measure of the size of the memory unit in a digital computer.

The B3500 system, which utilizes a combination of tape and disk storage, will provide a data memory bank of some 100m. [million] bytes as well as a 40m. byte disk file, and 2m. bytes of system memory. *"£550,000 Order for Burroughs," The Times (London), Feb. 3, 1970, p 23*

The model 195's fast main core storage—with a capacity of up to four million bytes (a byte is eight binary digits, or bits)—provides approximately the storage needed to handle all the computer instructions for a space mission, from launch to recovery. *David Hamilton and Michael Kenward, "A Giant Machine From IBM," New Scientist, Sept. 4, 1969, p 478*

In some machines, memory is organized into six- or eight-bit arrays called bytes. *M. V. Mathews, "Choosing a Scientific Computer for Service," Science, July 5, 1968, p 24*

Memory uses 32-bit words, is addressable and alterable by 8-bit bytes, halfwords, words, and doublewords. *Advertisement by SDS, in Scientific American, Feb. 1967, p 11*

[probably from *bi*nary dig*it* *e*ight]

Byzantine, *adj.* characterized by much scheming and intrigue; Machiavellian.

In spite of the protests of Aleksandr Solzhenitsyn, the celebrated Russian novelist, the often Byzantine struggle to publish his works in America and Europe continues unabated. *The Times (London), Oct. 3, 1968, p 10*

Was French party politics, with its Byzantine maneuvers and its feuding factions, really en route to a transformation? *Peter Braestrup, The New York Times, Jan. 2, 1966, Sec. 4, p 3*

William Randolph Hearst, like Stalin, was known to be fairly Byzantine in his punishments. *Pauline Kael, "Onward and Upward With the Arts," The New Yorker, Feb. 27, 1971, p 44*

[in allusion to the political scheming of the Byzantine emperors after Justinian]

BZ, a symbol for an incapacitating gas whose effects include disorientation, drowsiness, and hallucination. Compare CS, GB, VX.

BZ... is a psycho-chemical, the chemical identity of which is still secret, although the WHO [World Health Organization] report speculates that it belongs to the family known as benzilates. *Matthew Meselson, "Chemical and Biological Weapons," Scientific American, May 1970, p 21*

"Can you imagine the public outcry if you used something like BZ [an Army-developed hallucinogen] to put down a prison riot and some of that gas drifted over the walls and into a nearby town?" asks an Army chemical-warfare expert. *"Science and Space: Weapons That Don't Kill," Newsweek, Oct. 18, 1971, p 39*

C

CA, abbreviation of CHLORMADINONE ACETATE.

The minipill relies on a single hormone—chlormadinone acetate, known as CA—to inhibit pregnancy. *Peter Durisch and Tony Geraghty, The Sunday Times (London), Jan. 25, 1970, p 1*

cable TV or **cable television,** a system for transmitting television programs by coaxial cable to individual subscribers. *Abbreviation:* CATV

Cable television was originally introduced in the area in 1962 to provide better reception because Shooters Hill to the south consistently interfered with Television pictures. *Penny Hunter Symon, The Times (London), Jan. 21, 1972, p 2*

...cable TV offers, technologically, a chance for great variety in programming. *The New Yorker, April 25, 1970, p 138*

Suddenly the media are full of the wonders of cable television. *Timothy Johnson, "Science and the Paymasters: Truth About Cable TV," New Scientist and Science Journal, Aug. 5, 1971, p 312*

ca·cha·ca or **ca·cha·ça** (kə'ʃɑ: sə), *n.* Brazilian rum.

Fumes of *cachaça* knock me over, like gas fumes from an auto-crash. *Elizabeth Bishop, "Going to the Bakery" (a poem), The New Yorker, March 23, 1968, p 40*

...one drifts away into the dreamy unreality of a Brazilian *favelado* who drank too much *cachaca*. *Richard Bourne, "The Cruel Continent," Review of "Summer at High Altitude" by Gordon Meyer, The Manchester Guardian Weekly, May 2, 1968, p 10*

[from Portuguese *cachaça* rum]

ca·fé fil·tre (ka'fei 'fi:l trə), *French.* coffee prepared from hot water passed through ground coffee with a filter under it.

In a café, covering a held close-up of a cup of swirling *café filtre*, there is a long voice-over monologue about the subjectivity that suffocates and the objectivity that alienates.... *Penelope Gilliatt, "The Current Cinema: Godard," The New Yorker, May 2, 1970, p 104*

cage, *n.* a sheer or lacy outer dress worn over a slip or a dress.

The trade, which invents words and meanings faster than *Variety* does, now calls many of these dresses "cages"—that is to say, there is a fairly close-fitting slip underneath the yards and yards of floating fabric. *Lois Long, "On and Off the Avenue: Feminine Fashions," The New Yorker, March 19, 1966, p 184*

cake, *n.* a whole with reference to the parts into which it may be divided, especially parts to be shared, spent, or the like. See the note below.

...President Julius Nyerere of Tanzania...called for a new kind of African Socialism, acknowledging its beginnings in poverty, intended to raise the life of those at the bottom a little and hold down those at the top, giving all a more equal share of the cake. *Anthony Lewis, "Brook Farm Below the Equator," The New York Times, Jan. 5, 1970, p 36*

But when is the consuming public going to have a share in the larger cake, (to whose creation they too have contributed), in the form of a decrease in prices? *E. M. Hughes-Jones, The Manchester Guardian Weekly, Nov. 29, 1969, p 2*

Research permeates all aspects of governmental action, some more, some less thoroughly. There is no single 'science cake' to be cut up and parcelled out. *C. H. Waddington, "Assessing the Priorities," Science Journal, Oct. 1969, p 106*

▶ An older synonym of this word is *pie. Pie* refers to the familiar graph known as a *pie chart,* which is a circle divided into sectors resembling the slices of a pie.

cal·ci·to·nin (ˌkæl sə'tou nən), *n.* a hormone that regulates the amount of calcium in the blood. Also called THYROCALCITONIN.

It is thus essential that calcium levels are rigorously controlled—a job which is primarily the responsibility of two hormones, calcitonin and parathyroid hormone. The major "reservoir" of calcium is the skeleton, calcitonin inhibiting the release of calcium ions and parathyroid hormone mobilizing the element from the bones. *"Parathyroid Hormone Surrenders Its Secrets," New Scientist, Dec. 3, 1970, p 362*

Peter Sanderson and his associates at the Peter Bent Brigham Hospital in Boston and D. Harold Copp at the University of British Columbia began to look into the possibility that there was also some mechanism that exerted a positive control on the accumulation of calcium in the blood. They soon found evidence that such a mechanism was indeed at work.... Copp, on the basis of experiments similar to Sanderson's, concluded that the agent must be a hormone that he named calcitonin, signifying that it participated in regulating the tone, or concentration, of calcium in the blood. *Howard Rasmussen and Maurice M. Pechet, "Calcitonin," Scientific American, Oct. 1970, p 42*

[from *calci*um + *tone* + *-in* (chemical suffix)]

calefaction, *n.* another name for THERMAL POLLUTION.

The release of waste heat into the environment is called thermal pollution or calefaction. *Paul Bienfang, "Taking the Pollution Out of Waste Heat," New Scientist and Science Journal, Aug. 26, 1971, p 456*

call-back, *n.* the recall of a product by its manufacturer for the purpose of correcting previously undetected defects.

...Pontiac announced to the press last November that it was calling in 16,000 Tempest, GTO and Le Mans cars to correct a suspected steering-shaft misalignment. By February both Chrysler and Ford had adopted G.M.'s policy. Last month alone, automakers announced at least six call-backs involving more than 180,000 cars and trucks. *Time, June 2, 1967, p 50*

cal·li·gramme or **cal·li·gram** ('kæl ə,græm), *n.* a poem whose lines are arranged to form a picture appropriate to the poem's subject. Compare CONCRETE POEM.

There will also be photocopies of illustrations to Apollinaire's books by Dufy, Derain, Picasso, Chirico, Matisse, Marcoussis, and calligrammes, both typographical and handwritten,...and catalogues containing prefaces by Apollinaire. *The Times (London), Aug. 19, 1968, p 5*

"A leading French graphic designer" has put together more than 1,000 diverse and fascinating illustrations around the theme of the symbol turned real, and has given us as well an informed and particularly well-documented text. There are two large divisions: the letters of the alphabet drawn to have meaning beyond the symbolic, and "calligrams" (as Apollinaire named his "lyrical ideograms," the written word given visual form). *Philip Morrison, "Books," Scientific American, July 1971, p 121*

[from French *calligramme*, from *calli-* beautiful + *-gramme* writing]

calligraphic display, a type of graphic display of a computer's output. See the quotation for details.

Two broad classes of computer-display systems are now in common use: calligraphic displays and raster displays. Calligraphic displays "paint" the parts of a picture on the cathode ray tube in any sequence given by the computer. The electron beam in a calligraphic display is moved from place to place in a pattern that traces out the individual lines and characters that make up the picture. Raster displays make pictures in the same way that television sets do: the image is painted in a fixed sequence, usually from left to right and from top to bottom. *Ivan E. Sutherland, "Computer Displays," Scientific American, June 1970, p 57*

call-in, *n.* *U.S.* a radio or television program which broadcasts telephone calls, comments, or questions made by listeners to the studio. *Often used attributively.* Also called PHONE-IN. Compare HOT LINE (def. 3).

...since then a marathon seven-thirty-in-the-morning-to-midnight call-in has been going on, which McCarthy supporters have dubbed the "Telephone Revolution." *"The Talk of the Town: Telephone Revolution," The New Yorker, July 20, 1968, p 28*

On the other, the complaints in some cities were encouraged by newspaper editorials and call-in radio shows. *Evert Clark, "Up in the Clouds with the SST," Saturday Review, Jan 6, 1968, p 85*

[see -IN]

Cambodianize, *v.t.* to put conduct of (the Indochina war in Cambodia) under Cambodian control.

We can well imagine the Vietnamese telling the United States that they will leave Cambodia just as soon as they have "Cambodianized" the war there. *"The Talk of the Town," The New Yorker, May 30, 1970, p 21*

[patterned after *Vietnamize*]

Camelot, *n.* a time or place of glamorous doings, in allusion to King Arthur's court and applied especially to the Kennedy administration and Washington, 1961-1963.

Here is a very thoughtful lady talking about Camelot: "There was an *aura* of romance about it, but it wasn't real. And at the parties, there was always that high frenetic male laughter, *all* of the men competing with one another, and the music blasting, just *blasting.*" *John Corry, "Washington, Sex, and Power," Harper's, July 1970, p 65*

At several Cambridge dinner parties one heard faculty-types discuss...institutional politics, their glory days in Washington when Camelot reigned, their books or research or career frustrations. *Larry L. King, "Blowing My Mind at Harvard," Harper's, Oct. 1970, p 102*

cameo, *adj.* miniature; on a small scale.

They were gathered in a spacious downstairs den, along a massive table of food—a cameo panorama of the whole Arab world: sober Lebanese businessmen, a dour Palestinian with a moist handshake who introduced himself somberly by his "underground name," a silent Syrian with the fierce profile of a scimitar.... *Marshall Frady, "An American Innocent in the Middle East," Harper's, Oct. 1970, p 60*

...there are several bright cameo performances, notably a precise and uproarious impersonation of an epicene hotel clerk by Anthony Holland. *"Cinema: Manhattan on the Rocks," Time, June 8, 1970, p 74*

—*n.* a cameo role or performance in a film, play, etc.

Marvellous cameo of elderly mayor from Frederic March, goodish small-town atmospherics but very simplistic moralising from Ralph Nelson, the director. *Derek Malcolm, "London Cinema: In Search of Flesh and Fortune," The Manchester Guardian Weekly, Oct. 10, 1970, p 21*

Certainly the most deeply insulting cameo known to women is that worked to death by Barry Appleby's Daily Express family, the Gambols, in which that inane woman is constantly buying a frivolous new hat. *The Sunday Times (London), April 23, 1972, p 42*

camp, *n.* anything so exaggerated, banal, mediocre, or outmoded that it is considered clever or amusing because of its unsophisticated artistic quality. Compare HIGH CAMP, LOW CAMP.

..."the essence of Camp is its love of the unnatural: of artifice and exaggeration. And Camp is esoteric—something of a private code, a badge of identity even, among small urban cliques." *Susan Sontag, quoted by Richard Schickel, "Marshall McLuhan: Canada's Intellectual Comet," Harper's, Nov. 1965, p 64*

The Moiseyev [ballet company from the U.S.S.R.] comes to us as if from another era; it knows nothing of camp, absolutely nothing (as it proved almost a decade ago in *Back to the Apes*) of the concept of cool. *Arlene Croce, "The Moiseyev and Us," The Atlantic, Nov. 1970, p 133*

—*adj.* amusing or clever for its exaggerated, banal, outmoded, or mediocre artistic quality; campy.

Everyone is supposed to murmur respectfully how brilliant Oscar Wilde's comedies still are, but personally they seem to me horribly dated; camp art carried beyond the boundaries of triviality into oblivion. *Clive Barnes, The New York Times, July 6, 1968, p 9*

Winchester Cathedral: The new "old" sound of flapper music blares sweet and Camp on Fontana Records' easy-speaking album of the New Vaudeville Band....His

[Geoff Stephens's] tenor falsetto is electronically processed to give it that 1920s sound. *"Checklistings: Records," Maclean's, Feb. 1967, p 84*

It is significant, I think, that the first piece of writing, so far as I know, in Medieval literature which can be called vulgar and camp in a pejorative sense is the *Stabat Mater*. W. H. Auden, *"The Martyr as Dramatic Hero," The Listener, Jan. 4, 1968, p 2*

—*v.i., v.t.* to act in a campy manner.

camp around, The man who steals the show, if not the bank's money, is David Warner of England's Royal Shakespeare Company, who swoops and camps around in the perfect comic caricature of the decadent nobleman. *Jay Cocks, "Cinema: A Surplus of Capers," Time, Nov. 23, 1970, p 105*

camp it up, Mr. [Richard] Burton has the edge; Mr. [Rex] Harrison camps it up rather too much. *Richard Mallett, "Criticism: At the Cinema," Punch, Oct. 29, 1969, p 719*

[Ross] Hunter stressed that "Thoroughly Modern Millie," which is budgeted at over $7-million, will not be a satire on the period but will "play it straight. We're not going to camp it up," he said as he unenthusiastically attacked his fruit salad. *Peter Bart, The New York Times, July 17, 1966, Sec. 2, p 9*

▶ The term *camp*, used since at least the 1940's as a private code word in sophisticated theatrical and literary circles, was popularized by the American writer Susan Sontag in the 1960's, chiefly through her essay *Notes on 'Camp,'* which appeared in the fall 1964 issue of *Partisan Review*. The exact source of the word is uncertain, though it is known that it was originally a purely homosexual term. In the May 1965 issue of *Saturday Night*, the Canadian critic Nathan Cohen writes: "For years I have been using the word 'camp' as a convenient euphemism to describe the elements in a play or ballet which expresses a homosexual viewpoint or sensibility." Lester V. Berrey and Melvin Van Den Bark's *The American Thesaurus of Slang* (1942) lists as one meaning of *camp* "a male homosexual brothel or gathering place." Eric Partridge, in *A Dictionary of the Underworld* (1950), suggests an Australian origin; apparently *camp*, adj., was an Australian slang synonym for "homosexual" in the 1930's (Sidney J. Baker, *Australian Slang*, 1942). Earlier sources cited by Partridge (Leverage 1925, Hargan 1935) give *camp* as underworld slang for "a low saloon" and "brothel" respectively.

camper, *n.* a vehicle equipped with a stove, bunks, and often bathroom facilities for travel and camping out. Many campers are separate boxlike units placed on the bed of a pickup truck.

On each ferry from the mainland there is usually a Jeep or a Land Rover with six or so ten-foot surfing rods standing tall from the front bumper. Or sometimes it is a car called a camper, a pickup truck with bunks over the driver's cab and living space in the rear. *Ralph Maloney, "Places: No Man on Ocracoke," The Atlantic, March 1967, p 124*

Though Mrs. Savoie has been tenting for years, she now takes to the road with her husband, seven children and 69-year-old mother-in-law in their converted bus. "With our camper," she explains happily, "everything is built right in. We just add food and clothes and take off." *"The Outdoors: Pampered Campers," Time, June 9, 1967, p 43*

campy, *adj.* characteristic of camp; amusing or clever because of exaggerated, banal, old-fashioned, unsophisticated, or mediocre quality.

It seemed to me that Lawrence Kornfield's staging overemphasized the campy elements and at the same time underplayed the very special verbal stylishness of the piece. *Clive Barnes, The New York Times, March 25, 1968, p 53*

...Disney contributed *The Happiest Millionaire* and *The Family Band*, and Universal came through with *Thoroughly Modern Millie*, a "campy" reincarnation of the 1920's. *Arthur Knight, "Motion Pictures," 1968 Collier's Encyclopedia Year Book, p 375*

The Ti-Popistes celebrated their birth by issuing a little catechism of *Ti-Popisms* and 500 buttons at fifty cents apiece. The first group of buttons read simply *Ti-Pop*, but the latest model shows a picture of Duplessis with a halo. These buttons are for fun, like all those campy buttons from New York, but they are also intended as a send-up of clerical jewellery....*Wendy Michener, "The Very Irreverent Crusade of Ti-Pop," Saturday Night (Canada), Feb. 1968, p 29*

can, *n.* **carry the can,** *Slang.* to take the blame or responsibility.

It was he [Kenneth Robinson] who "carried the can" for increasing prescription charges as Minister of Health, the post he held until 1968....*The Times (London), Feb. 12, 1970, p 25*

Now, in 1970, senior military men want to lay down new rules, a new definition of the role of the Army. No more Vietnams, where the armed forces carry the can for civilian stupidities. *Ward Just, "Soldiers," The Atlantic, Nov. 1970, p 71*

can-carrier, *n.* *Slang.* one who carries the responsibility for an undertaking.

As secretary of MCC [Marylebone Cricket Club] for the past nine years, and of the Cricket Council, Griffith has been cast as spokesman, can-carrier, and in some quarters as chief villain. *Christopher Ford, "People and Places: Straight Bat and Sticky Wicket," The Manchester Guardian Weekly, May 22, 1971, p 14*

cancer stick, *Slang.* a cigarette.

First of all we spend about £30 million each year on importing the stinking weed. Admittedly, we recover a useful chunk of this money by exporting manufactured cancer sticks, principally to the natives of Kuwait, Aden and Hong Kong, who have been brought up to appreciate English blends. *Donald Gould, "A Groundling's Notebook," New Scientist, April 2, 1970, p 23*

can-do, *adj.* *U.S.* eager to get things done; diligent and enthusiastic.

Any war always claims the best men the army has, the colonel said, because they are the studs, the changers, the can-do boys.... The others, the one-year tourists, they tend to get back OK. *Ward Just, "Soldiers," The Atlantic, Nov. 1970, p 89*

She [Liz Carpenter] applied the same forthright approach to selling a first family. Nothing was too good for the client. LBJ [Lyndon B. Johnson] obviously thought of her as a "can-do" lady in the jargon of that administration, and once told a friend: "Liz would charge hell with a bucket of water." *Catherine Stott, "Selling the First Family," The Manchester Guardian Weekly, Dec. 12, 1970, p 16*

C & W or **C-and-W,** abbreviation of COUNTRY-AND-WESTERN.

Tommy Common Sings Country Classics: . . . Common has a C-and-W repertoire that can't miss, a pleasant twang-free voice, and enough steel-guitar accompaniment to make the whole thing authentic. *"Records," Maclean's, Sept. 1968, p 88*

candyfloss, *n. British.* flimsy or insubstantial ideas, proposals, projects, etc.

We must look more closely at what the Tories will do in the longer run. The cuts in themselves do not perhaps tell us very much. Some clearing up of the candyfloss of the Wilsonian Government is perfectly sensible. *Jo Grimond, "The Economy: Hollow Package," The Manchester Guardian Weekly, Nov. 14, 1970, p 10*

[figurative sense of the British term for cotton candy]

canoe slalom, a white-water sport in which a canoeist must maneuver his craft through gates similar to a slalom course in skiing.

"They mess around with canoe slalom," says Kynoch, with a canny glint in his voice, "which as you know, is another new event in the Olympics." *"Hunter's Meat," The Sunday Times (London), Nov. 7, 1971, p 30*

can of worms, *U.S. Slang.* a complicated and unsolved problem.

The whole area of screen acting is probably going to be a big can of worms in the next few years. *Pauline Kael, "The Current Cinema: Waiting for Orgy," The New Yorker, Oct. 4, 1969, p 148*

The variations seem infinite, but the New Hampshire primary is, in the local patois, a can of worms. *Louis Heren, The Times (London), March 8, 1968, p 9*

cap¹, *n. British.* a contraceptive diaphragm.

I threw away the prescription and the remaining pills and had myself fitted with a cap. *Barbara Blake, The Sunday Times (London), Sept. 7, 1969, p 47*

The sincerity of the Pope's trenchwork is unquestioned. Nor were his alternative options easy: if the cap, the pill, and the loop had suddenly been legitimised, numerous sacrificially obedient Catholics in many countries would have been distressed. *"The Catholic Dilemma," The Manchester Guardian Weekly, Aug. 1, 1968, p 1*

cap², *n. Slang.* a capsule of heroin, LSD, or other drug.

". . . I shoot all the dope I can get, though." "You high now?" "No. I had two caps this morning. That's all." *Bruce Jackson, "Exiles from the American Dream," The Atlantic, Jan. 1967, p 47*

capacitate, *v.t.* to induce capacitation in (sperm).

Dr Bob Edwards, who was at the symposium, employed a test-tube method of capacitating sperm in his recent *in vitro* human fertilization experiments. *"Trends and Discoveries," New Scientist, March 27, 1969, p 698*

capacitation, *n.* a series of physical changes that sperms undergo before attaining the capacity to penetrate and fertilize an egg.

Recent studies have called into question the role of uterine changes in spermatozoa during capacitation. Hamster eggs have been fertilized in vitro with spermatozoa taken directly from the male seminal tract. *R. G. Edwards and Ruth E. Fowler, "Human Embryos in the Laboratory," Scientific American, Dec. 1970, p 48*

Capcom ('kæp,kʌm), *n.* acronym for *Capsule Communicator* (the person at a space flight center who communicates with the astronauts during a space flight).

What we needed, if not a poet in space, was an imaginative writer on the ground, able to provide some unique understanding of the real significance of those metallised dialogues between Capcom and LEM [lunar excursion module] pilot. *J. G. Ballard, "Lost in Space," Review of "A Fire on the Moon" by Norman Mailer, The Manchester Guardian Weekly, Dec. 5, 1970, p 19*

Their pulse rates rose to around a hundred and fifty (anywhere from sixty to ninety is normal), and Dr. Hawkins urged the Capsule Communicator, or CapCom, who was talking to the astronauts by radio, to get them to take things easier. *Henry S. F. Cooper, Jr., "Letter From the Space Center," The New Yorker, April 17, 1971, p 136*

capital-intensive, *adj.* requiring great expenditure of capital to increase productivity or earnings. Compare LABOR-INTENSIVE.

The [Cuban] authorities complain of being desperately short of manpower, and where possible capital-intensive techniques are being introduced. *Richard Gott, "Castro's Crop of Trouble," The Manchester Guardian Weekly, Oct. 31, 1970, p 7*

As it is capital-intensive, the Queensland sugar industry has higher costs than the labour-intensive sugar industries it has to compete with on the crowded world market. . . . *Anne E. Rasmussen, "Barrier Reef for Sale?" New Scientist, March 26, 1970, p 622*

Between now and 1980 the capital-intensive international oil industry will need to invest as much as $255,000m. [million] to satisfy the non-communist world's needs for oil and natural gas, according to a report published by the Chase Manhattan Bank. *Clive Callow, "Outside Help for Costly Ventures," The Times (London), March 10, 1970, p II*

The service sectors have in common the fact that they are disproportionately labor-intensive rather than capital-intensive, even though some sectors (particularly transportation and communication) have extremely high ratios of capital to output. *W. Halder Fisher, "The Anatomy of Inflation: 1953-1975," Scientific American, Nov. 1971, p 20*

cap·o ('kæp ou), *n. U.S. Underworld Slang.* the head of one of the units or branches of the Mafia.

To accomplish his goal, Colombo tapped deep-seated, legitimate grievances among Italian Americans and—shocking editorial writers and Mob *capos* alike—jumped into press conferences and picket lines. *Time, July 12, 1971, p 15*

Subpoenas have been served in the last few days upon Carlo Gambino, head of one of the major Mafia "families," several of his "capos" (captains) and officers of one or more locals. . . . *Charles Grutzner, The New York Times, May 7, 1968, p 18*

[from Italian *capo* head, from Latin *caput*]

cap·o·re·gime (,kæp ou ri'ʒi:m), *n. U.S. Underworld Slang.* a member of the Mafia next below a capo in rank and serving as his lieutenant.

Inside the hospital, *caporegimes* and "button men," or soldiers, the lowest-ranking Mafia family members, prowled the corridors near Colombo's room. *Time, July 12, 1971, p 14*

[from Italian *caporegime* head of regime]

capper, *n. U.S. Slang.* end; ending; climax.

Another friend, who knows Hollywood well, thought it was the end of an era. "It's the capper to drugs. People were at the point where they were taking anything. It was insane. But they won't go back now. Booze and pot, but no more of the big brutal stuff." *Frank Conroy, "Manson Wins!" Harper's, Nov. 1970, p 55*

Stop, You're Killing Me is an apt title for a bloodstained package of three one-act plays by James Leo Herlihy.... The first is a monologue in which ... Gloria (Sasha von Sherler), tells about the delicious party she just gave — serving up her guests in bite-sized morsels ... she delightedly pounces on a waifish little girl somebody brought.... The fact that the waif died of drug withdrawal the next day is merely the perfect capper for Gloria's account of the evening. *Time, March 28, 1969, p 31*

[from *cap, v.*, to crown, climax + the suffix *-er*]

Ca·pri pants (kə'pri:), *U.S.* tight-fitting women's trousers, worn informally. Also shortened to CAPRIS.

This imaginative state [California] that popularized freeways, supermarkets, swimming pools, drive-ins, backyard barbecues, the bare midriff, house trailers, Capri pants, hot rods, sports shirts, split-level houses and tract living has a former B-movie actor in the Governor's chair at Sacramento.... *Charlotte Curtis, The New York Times, June 2, 1968, Sec. 1, p 1*

[named for the island of *Capri*, in the Bay of Naples, Italy, where the fashion of wearing such pants may have originated]

Ca·pris (kə'pri:z), *n.pl. U.S.* short for CAPRI PANTS.

"They [granny dresses] are a good change from Capris and a top for parties," says 20-year-old Gail Eckles. *Time, Oct. 8, 1965, p 44*

caravan park, *British.* an area where holidayers may park their caravans or house trailers. The equivalent U.S. term is *trailer park.*

Between the hotels and a group of chalets there is accommodation for 580 visitors. Plans for further expansion, including ... a caravan park, will increase this capacity to 1,080 by 1971. *John Kerr, "Good Housekeeping at Aviemore," The Manchester Guardian Weekly, Nov. 29, 1969, p 10*

carbecue, *n.* a device for disposing of a junked car by rotating it over fire.

Another is the "carbecue," a machine that turns an old automobile body into a solid lump of metal by pressure and heat. *Robert Trumbull, The New York Times, Jan. 2, 1968, p 39*

[from *car* + bar*becue*]

carbon-copy, *v.t.* to make an exact copy of; to duplicate.

But what Ariane Mnouchkine and her collaborators have achieved can't be carbon-copied any more than what Jean Vilar was doing at Avignon and Suresnes around 1950. *Bertrand Poirot-Delpech, "French Theatre: Politics and Aesthetics," The Manchester Guardian Weekly, Sept. 4, 1971, p 14*

[verb use of *carbon copy* a copy made with carbon paper; an exact copy]

carbon date, the age of a fossil, artifact, etc., measured by the amount of radioactive carbon in it.

Weapon points were found — of the same type as the Plainview and Eden Valley points discovered in Texas and Wyoming — where they had lain in conjunction with the skeletons of animals, and could therefore be dated by the carbon 14 test: most of the animals were long since extinct, and the approximate carbon date was between six and seven thousand years ago. *Sheila Burnford, "Time Out of Mind," The Atlantic, July 1964, p 38*

carbon-date, *v.t.* to date the age of (a fossil, artifact, etc.) by measuring its content of radioactive carbon.

... an impressive team of co-workers from the Oxford University Museum and elsewhere drilled out about 25 g of bone powder from each of three of the Lady's [Red Lady — remains of a woman unearthed from cave of Paviland, farm on cliffs of Gower Peninsula in Wales, in 1822] bones and carbon-dated it to within a geological inch of its life. The age is 18,460 years plus or minus 340 BP (before the present). *John Hillaby, "The Red Lady of Paviland," New Scientist, Dec. 19, 1968, p 679*

Since 1962 archaeologists Cynthia Irwin-Williams, representing Harvard, and Juan Armenta Camacho of the University of Puebla in Mexico have been turning up the artifacts — hide scrapers, leather-working instruments and projectile points — from an ancient geological deposit known as the Valsequillo Gravels, near the town of Puebla. The tools are unsophisticated and generally unlike any other known New World artifacts. ... The tools themselves, being stone, could not be carbon-dated. Therefore, dates had to come from analysis of volcanic ash that overlies some of the sites, and from the shells. *Science News, May 13, 1967, p 447*

carbon fiber, a synthetic fiber of great strength and lightness, made by carbonizing acrylic fiber at very high temperatures. See also HYFIL.

Development of carbon fibres, first produced in the U.K. and subsequently used for a revolutionary plastic material for aircraft and precision engineering, began to evolve on an international scale. *Philip M. Rowe, "Man-Made Fibres," Britannica Book of the Year 1970, p 426*

car·bo·rane ('kɑr bə,rein), *n.* a compound of carbon, boron, and hydrogen having unusual thermal properties. *Also used attributively.*

The existence of complete series of polyhedral borane anions and carboranes was not apparent at the beginning of the present decade. *M. F. Hawthorne, "Boron Compounds," Review of "Polyhedral Boranes" by Earl L. Muetterties and Walter H. Knoth, Science, July 12, 1968, p 153*

One of the most promising of recent approaches has been the inclusion of carborane clusters in polymer chains. *Malcolm Frazer and Brian Currell, "Polymers Without Carbon," New Scientist, April 10, 1969, p 64*

[blend of *carbon* and *boron* + *-ane* (chemical suffix)]

carborne, *adj.* carried in or traveling by motor car.

The shopping public is ... increasingly car-borne. *The Times (London), March 16, 1970, p 13*

The car locator systems now being considered by the [police] department have two essential segments: a small carborne radio transmitter and a permanently based sensing device. *The New York Times, Nov. 5, 1967, Sec. 1, p 129*

car·cin·o·ge·nic·i·ty (,kɑr sin ə dʒə'nis ə ti:), *n.* the quality of being carcinogenic; the property or tendency of a substance to produce cancer.

The presumption that the carcinogenicity of mineral oil

is attributable almost solely to its content of polycyclic aromatic hydrocarbons was seriously questioned by new evidence of the importance of co-carcinogenic straight-chain aliphatic constituents of the oil. *Francis J. C. Roe, "Medicine: Cancer," Britannica Book of the Year 1971, p 479*

card-carrying, *adj.* having the characteristics of a type of person; typical.

In this book [*A Sort of Life* by Graham Greene] which is really a gentle, painful odyssey between centuries, the first hint of Greene as a new man, as a card-carrying representative of the modern condition, comes when, in 1920, he is sent, astonishingly and at the age of sixteen, to an analyst in Kensington after an abortive attempt to run away from home. *L. E. Sissman, "Books," The New Yorker, Oct. 2, 1971, p 129*

... Miss [Joan] Rivers, a card-carrying yenta, displays gravelly authority in "Just Like a Man," a song from "Two's Company" for which Ogden Nash has furnished an extra pair of closing lines.... *Douglas Watt, "Popular Records," The New Yorker, Oct. 24, 1970, p 169*

[an extended sense of the term used in politics to describe a member of the Communist Party (that is, one who carries a membership card) as distinguished from Communist sympathizers, and later applied to anyone devoted or strongly attached to a particular party, doctrine, etc., as "a card-carrying capitalist" or "a card-carrying Democrat"]

car·di·nal·i·ty (ˌkɑr dəˈnæl ə ti:), *n.* the size of a mathematical set, without regard to the kinds of elements contained in the set. See also CARDINAL NUMBER.

All finite sets with the same number of elements have the same cardinality, and all infinite sequences have the same cardinality as the set of integers. *Lynn Arthur Steen, "New Models of the Real-Number Line," Scientific American, Aug. 1971, p 97*

cardinal number, a number that expresses the size of a mathematical set, or how many elements it contains, without regard to the kinds of elements it contains.

[Georg] Cantor developed his theory of cardinal numbers by defining two sets as being of equal size (or of the same "cardinality") if there is some function, or rule, that establishes a one-to-one correspondence between them.... Cantor's great achievement was to assign sizes (cardinal numbers) even to the uncountable sets. *Lynn Arthur Steen, "New Models of the Real-Number Line," Scientific American, Aug. 1971, p 97*

▶ The original and still commonest use of this term is that of a number used in counting, such as one, two, three, as distinguished from *ordinal numbers* (first, second, third). Modern mathematics has extended the meaning of *cardinal number,* but not of *ordinal number.*

cardioactive, *adj.* stimulating the heart's activity.

Wildenthal developed a method for maintaining these [fetal mice] hearts in organ culture in the contractile state for 3-4 weeks and found that they responded normally to a number of cardioactive drugs, such as acetylcholine and ouabain. *Honor B. Fell, "Organ Culture," McGraw-Hill Yearbook of Science and Technology 1971, p 53*

[from *cardio-* heart + *active*]

car·di·o·my·op·a·thy (ˌkɑr di: ou maiˈɑp ə θi:), *n.* progressive weakness, enlargement, etc., of the heart muscle.

Six to 20 or more months of complete bed rest is apparently saving people with ... diseases of the heart muscle itself—disorders generally called cardiomyopathies. ... *The New York Times, Nov. 24, 1966, p 58*

[from *cardio-* heart + *myopathy* disease of the muscles]

cardioversion, *n.* restoration of normal heartbeat by using electric shock.

The preferred treatment for sustained ventricular tachycardia [abnormally fast heart action] is an intravenous injection of lidocaine [a local anesthetic]. If that fails, normal rhythm can usually be restored by delivering a mild and carefully timed electric shock through the chest wall, a procedure called cardioversion. *"Science and The Citizen: Home Remedy," Scientific American, Feb. 1971, p 47*

[from *cardio-* heart + *version* a turning]

Carey Street, *British.* bankruptcy.

The thorny path that leads down Carey Street. ... *Title of an article by Ronald Irving in The Times (London), Oct. 10, 1970, p 9*

Boys may ... be content with casements ... divided into economical panes that a chap can risk putting a missile through without bringing his parents into Carey Street. *New Scientist, Dec. 14, 1967, p 641*

[after the name of the street in London where the Bankruptcy Court was formerly located]

carnapper or **carnaper,** *n.* a car thief.

The seats have massage units to reduce driving fatigue (or jiggle you to sleep), the tires light up at night, and if a carnapper tries to break into all this luxury, the doors give him an electric shock. *Nan Robertson, The New York Times, Sept. 9, 1968, p 48*

Carnapers stole here early this morning a Volkswagen car owned by former Rep. Florante C. Roque. *The Manila Chronicle, Philippines, July 6, 1965, p 1*

[from *car* + kid*napper* or kid*naper*]

carrier bag, *British.* a bag with handles for carrying miscellaneous packages obtained while shopping. The U.S. equivalent is *shopping bag.*

It's a small shop. If people don't get out of your way you can tread on hamsters. The woman, at last making for the door, dropped her carrier-bag negotiating me. She thanked me for picking up the tins, but gave me a funny look all the same. *Basil Boothroyd, "A Time for Protest," Punch, March 27, 1968, p 451*

There are [in Israel] books on the war, long-playing records recounting its highlights, even carrier bags with the occupied territories neatly shaded in on coloured maps. *Gerald Kaufman, "Views," The Listener, Feb. 1, 1968, p 133*

carry-on, *adj.* small enough to be carried aboard an airplane by a passenger.

And in the luggage shop, on the street floor, there's three-to-a-set Lark baggage for plane riding, all of it carry-on. ... *Mollie Panter-Downes, "On and Off the Avenue: This and That," The New Yorker, July 4, 1970, p 59*

Coats and carry-on baggage are stowed in large overhead storage compartments. *Time, Jan. 19, 1970, p 41*

ca·se·id·in (keiˈsi: ə dən), *n.* one of a group of substances produced in the milk of mammals that provide immunity against certain infectious diseases.

A group of new immunizing substances which foster the protective mechanisms of the mammalian body against severe infectious diseases has been developed. . . . The caseidins are not a single substance but a family of compounds which differ from each other according to the mammalian milk used. The researchers employed milk from cows, sheep and gazelles. The substances were obtained by applying a suitable enzyme to the main protein of milk—casein, from which the name of the substances caseidins, is derived. *"Science and Technology News: Israelis Make Immunizing Substances," Science Journal, June 1969, p 19*

cash and carry, a store that sells goods, usually at a discount, on the basis of cash payments and no services.

The number of cash and carries has grown from 398 in 1967 to 610 at the end of last year. Retailers of all sorts have turned to the cash and carry to help them compete against the cut prices in supermarkets. This has had an influence on other sectors of the retail trade. *Sally White, The Times (London), March 16, 1970, p 15*

cashomat, n. *U.S.* a machine that releases cash when an identification card is inserted and the amount of cash needed is punched on a keyboard.

First developed in Europe, the cashomats are also in use at banks in Massachusetts, Pennsylvania and New York. . . . The machines are obviously convenient for after-hours withdrawals. *Time, Oct. 10, 1969, p 59*

[*cash* + *-omat*, as in *automat, laundromat,* etc.]

cassette, n. a small cartridge of magnetic-tape reels that can be inserted into a tape player for automatic playback and recording.

"Where do I put these?" he asked Mr. Edele, holding up a fistful of cassettes. "It's the Now music for the barbershop." *"The Talk of the Town," The New Yorker, Dec. 5, 1970, p 50*

In addition to more two-year community colleges, which this obviously requires, the commission urges a big expansion in off-campus education—correspondence courses, TV lectures, home teaching cassettes. *Time, Dec. 7, 1970, p 60*

cassette TV or **cassette television,** any of various systems in which videotapes in cassettes are used in special television receivers so that the viewer can select and watch any of the taped programs at any time.

The cinema industry has shown interest in the cassette TV systems which will probably appear on the market in the next few years. *Glen Lawes and Michael Kenward, "Technology Review," New Scientist, Aug. 27, 1970, p 420*

'Cassette television' is the generic name for the new systems, which enable the viewer to select his visual entertainment or instruction from an almost unlimited stock, comparable to the stock of audio (disc or tape) records. There exist, or are about to be developed, three such systems. *Dennis Gabor, Innovations: Scientific, Technological, and Social, 1970, p 57*

Castroism, n. another word for FIDELISMO or FIDELISM.

I am certainly not in favor of *Castroism* or Maoism making headway in Latin America. . . . *Max Nomad, New York, in a Letter to the Editor, Saturday Review, July 2, 1966, p 22*

Castroist or **Castroite,** *n., adj.* other words for FIDELISTA or FIDELIST.

He [Che Guevara] claimed that South America would be Castroist within five years. *Robin Chapman, "Cuba," Britannica Book of the Year 1967, p 249*

Public figures made a series of statements that the government had been compromised not only by Castroites but by other foreign agents. . . . *Malcolm W. Browne, The New York Times, Aug. 4, 1968, Sec. 4, p 3*

The exact role of Communists and Castroists in the April uprising has not yet been fully clarified. *Bruce B. Solnick, 1966 Collier's Encyclopedia Year Book, p 194*

But the Castroite Venezuelan guerrillas, fighting a representative, popular, and rich government, are not about to take Caracas. *The Atlantic, Nov. 1966, p 36*

CAT, abbreviation of CLEAR AIR TURBULENCE.

CAT . . . the meteorologists think, develops near the crest of a standing wave [of air]. *New Scientist, March 19, 1970, p 544*

catalytic converter, an antipollution device in automobiles which contains a chemical catalyst for oxidizing the pollutant exhaust gases (carbon monoxide, nitrogen oxides, and hydrocarbons), thereby converting them to harmless products (carbon dioxide, nitrogen, and water vapor).

Specifically, they [Detroit car manufacturers] want to remove the lead from petrol for the laudable technical reason that it clogs up the catalyst in the catalytic converter, Detroit's best answer to the growing pressures for cleaner cars. The converter, a small box rather like a silencer, is designed to remove most of the carbon monoxide and unburned hydrocarbons that currently make their way into the air, via the exhaust pipe, by catalytic odixation. *Peter Gwynne, Science Journal, Dec. 1970, p 6*

. . . 400 city-owned automobiles will be equipped with catalytic converters designed drastically to reduce pollution from noxious exhaust gases. *Julius Raskin, Brooklyn, N.Y., in a Letter to the Editor, The New York Times, June 14, 1970, p 40*

cat·e·chol·a·mine (ˌkæt əˈtʃou ləˌmiːn *or* ˌkæt əˈkou ləˌmiːn), *n.* any of a class of hormones, such as adrenalin, that act upon the nerve cells.

[Lithium] may act by interfering with the metabolism of the catecholamines, which are involved in all brain activity. *Science News, April 18, 1970, p 390*

It appears then that through α-adrenergic receptors catecholamines cause lightening of the skin, whereas through β-adrenergic receptors they cause darkening. *Milton Fingerman, "Chromatophore," McGraw-Hill Yearbook of Science and Technology 1971, p 144*

[from the chemical substances *catechol* + *amine*]

catsuit, n. *British.* a one-piece pantsuit.

As he was being led to his first display case of the day, a seminar in the postwar American novel, a *zoftig* woman in a purple catsuit accosted him by the chapel. *John Updike, Bech: A Book, 1970, p 121*

His [the designer's] suits are either one-piece worsted cat-suits, or trousers and jerkin-type top. *The Times (London), May 31, 1968, p 10*

CATV, originally the abbreviation of *Community Antenna Television* (an early system of cable TV), now used as an abbreviation for CABLE TV.

Conventional TV broadcasters do have very real grievances, for CATV could be piratical unless properly regulated. It was started to bring television to isolated or poor reception areas. CATV entrepreneurs raised hilltop antennas, plucked the signals of distant channels from the air and then relayed them, generally by coaxial cable, direct to subscribers' TV sets. *Time, June 1, 1970, p 66*

CB, abbreviation of *chemical and biological*. Compare CBW.

They [U Thant's consultant experts] called clearly for the accession of all states to the 1925 Geneva Protocol, . . . and an agreement to halt the development, production and stockpiling of CB agents. *"Conflict on CBW," New Scientist, July 17, 1969, p 107*

From the military point of view, one of the major problems in the development of CB weapons is that of finding adequate delivery systems. *David Pavett, "Making a Desolation," The Listener, May 16, 1968, p 624*

CBW, abbreviation of: **1** chemical and biological warfare.

Several years ago the Campaign for Nuclear Disarmament claimed there was a highly secret chemical warfare establishment in Cornwall. Those who thought they knew their British CBW scene were politely sceptical. *Robin Clarke, "Nancekuke: Britain's Backyard Nerve Gas Station," Science Journal, Dec. 1970, p 8*

2 chemical and biological weapons.

Which countries are, in the future, most likely to use CBW on an extensive scale? Would these be the smaller powers? . . . "From that point of view, interest in CBW would be centred in the Third World, in non-nuclear powers." *Frank Barnaby, "SIPRI's [Stockholm International Peace Research Institute's] Loss, Sussex's Gain," New Scientist and Science Journal, July 15, 1971, p 139*

ce·di ('sei di:), *n.* the basic unit of money in Ghana. 1.02 cedi equals $1.

Ghana's economic crisis, represented by the recent 44 per cent devaluation of the cedi, is on a scale that would threaten the existence of the government in many African countries. *Michael Wolfers, The Times (London), Jan. 10, 1972, p 5*

cell therapy or **cellular therapy,** a method of rejuvenation or physical restoration by the injection of suspensions of cells prepared from the organs of embryonic sheep. *Abbreviation:* CT

Last week, for instance, there was this fellow I was confronting who believes that almost any sickness (except infections) can be cured by injecting suspensions of appropriate cells from foetal sheep. It's called cell therapy. *Donald Gould, "A Groundling's Notebook," New Scientist and Science Journal, Aug. 19, 1971, p 424*

Many famous persons claim to have been benefited by cellular therapy. . . . On theoretical grounds, the treatment is not without hazard, and no controlled laboratory experiments have demonstrated a lengthening of life-span or improvement in vigor of animals subjected to it. Cellular therapy is not generally accepted by the medical profession in Europe and it is not officially permitted in the United States. *"Prolonging Your Life," 1972 Britannica Year Book of Science and the Future, 1971, p 84*

cellularized, *adj.* divided into cells or small compartments.

The directors also tell shareholders that the *Manchester Miller* will be converted this summer into a fully cellularized container vessel which will help meet the demands for space on the company's Montreal container services. *The Times (London), April 21, 1970, p 22*

When Richard Nixon's entourage visited the White House, one campaign aide expressed surprise at how "cellularized" Lyndon Johnson's staff is. *Time, Nov. 22, 1968, p 19*

centerfold, *n.* an illustrated center spread that is extra long and has to be folded into a magazine or book, and unfolded to be seen in full.

On one such occasion, a Phantom pilot was surprised to see his Soviet counterpart hold up a centerfold from, of all things, *Playboy* magazine. *Time, June 28, 1971, p 20*

centimillionaire, *n.* a millionaire who has a hundred million or more dollars. *Also used attributively.*

Ordinarily, David Rockefeller, chairman of the Chase Manhattan Bank and a centimillionaire in his own right, would expect to have no trouble at all negotiating a loan from his friendly neighborhood banker. *Time, Jan. 12, 1970, p 47*

In the decade since, the "centimillionaire" population has more than tripled, and those with $150 m. [million] or more have grown to 66. *The Times (London), April 29, 1968, p 17*

[from *centi-* a hundred + *millionaire*]

central casting, *U.S.* the casting department of a film studio. Often used figuratively, as in **straight from central casting,** stereotyped, typical, or conventional.

Pine Bluff (pop. 57,000) is Mid-America right out of Central Casting. There is a Main Street, an Elm Street, a kindly doctor and a lot of gossip. *Time, Nov. 30, 1970, p 32*

. . . almost everyone in the Italian theatre seems to be noisily auditioning for a part in a rather dated play about the Italian theatre. And most of the applicants are straight from central casting. *Kenneth Tynan, "The Theatre Abroad: Italy," The New Yorker, Oct. 21, 1967, p 92*

central city, *U.S.* a city that is the center of a metropolitan area. Also called CORE CITY. Compare INNER CITY.

The Times has expressly concerned itself with the problems of the central cities despite the fact that these views may not jibe with those of many of its suburban readers. *Henry W. Maier, Mayor of Milwaukee, Wisconsin, in a Letter to the Editor, The New York Times, March 17, 1970, p 42*

The Negro ghettos of the central cities became increasingly crowded in 1969, and the conditions of ghetto life showed no dramatic change. *Richard Harwood, "United States," The Americana Annual 1970, p 720*

. . . the Advisory Commission on Inter-Governmental Relations noted that "the schools serving low-income central city children are receiving less per pupil as well as per capita than those serving the most affluent suburbs." *Michael Harrington, "The Urgent Case for Social Investment," Saturday Review, Nov. 23, 1968, p 33*

central dogma, 1 the theory that the transmission of genetic information is an irreversible process always determined by the nucleic acid DNA (deoxyribonucleic acid, the carrier of genetic material in the cells). See the first quotation. Compare TEMINISM.

For more than a decade, most scientists have accepted the "central dogma" of molecular biology without question. Stated simply, that dogma holds that the heredity information in living cells is always passed along in the same direction: from the "double helix" DNA molecule to the single-stranded messenger RNA molecule, which in turn directs the synthesis of protein—which is essential to all life. *Time, July 20, 1970, p 57*

. . . Dr. H. M. Temin, now at Wisconsin University, claimed to have found in a cell invaded by an RNA virus a stretch of DNA that matched with the viral RNA. The RNA seemed to be acting as a template for DNA synthesis —in direct contravention of the central dogma. *"Ariadne's Record of the Year," New Scientist, Dec. 31, 1970, p 607*

2 any idea which is accepted unquestioningly.

But in America for the last century, the image of the clinician-researcher has been increasingly the model, and it is now central dogma for medical educators, who accept it unquestioningly. *Michael Crichton, "The Miseducation of Doctors," The New York Times, Oct. 16, 1970, p 41*

centrism, *n.* a moderate or middle-of-the-road position in politics.

He [Willi Stoph, Prime Minister of East Germany] has acted as a mediator between people of differing opinions, always supporting the principle of "centrism," which would seem to explain why his position has never been challenged. *Gretel Spitzer, "Loyal Path to the Summit for Willi Stoph," The Times (London), March 14, 1970, p 6*

cerebral death, another name for BRAIN DEATH.

Death of the brain, called cerebral death, is currently used by Cooley and many other heart surgeons as the yardstick for selecting [heart transplant] donors. *Johnson McGuire and Arnold Iglauer, "Heart Disease," The Americana Annual 1969, p 335*

cesium clock, a type of atomic clock which measures time by the vibration frequency of atoms of the element cesium.

The Navy men borrowed several cesium clocks from the United States Naval Observatory. These are among the most precise clocks in existence. *Walter Sullivan, The New York Times, Aug. 10, 1968, p 27*

chainbelt, *n.* a belt made with interlinked metal rings.

The Age of Accessories continued to flower in wild fantasy and individualism, particularly among the young . . . . Accessories were often called body-jewels and were chain-mail type networks of linked metals, chainbelts, . . . snake bracelets and arm bracelets, and slave footstraps. *Kathryn Zahony Livingston, "Fashion," The 1970 World Book Year Book, p 342*

chairperson, *n.* *U.S.* a person who presides at a meeting; a chairman or chairwoman.

And a group of women psychologists thanked the board for using the word "chairperson" rather than "chairman," but argued that too much sexual discrimination still exists within the APA [American Psychological Association] and in the academic world. *"APA Annual Meeting; The Psychologist As Social Engineer," Science News, Sept. 11, 1971, p 166*

Chandler wobble or **Chandler's wobble,** a variation of the earth's rotation upon its axis.

The Earth's pole undergoes a nutation [oscillation], the Chandler wobble, with a predominant 14-monthly period whose motion is somehow kept going despite the sub-

stantial effects of viscous damping forces. *"Monitor: Earthquakes May Parallel, not Cause, Polar Wobble," New Scientist and Science Journal, Jan. 21, 1971, p 105*

Others thought that the quake might be connected with the slight eccentric movements of the spinning earth known as Chandler's Wobble. *Time, Feb. 22, 1971, p 37*

[named after Seth Carlo *Chandler,* 1846-1913, American astronomer, noted for his determination of the laws of variations of the earth's pole]

charbroil, *v.t.* to broil with charcoal.

Highway 101 ribboning down the coast . . . the smell of charbroiled hamburgers cooking, motels with artificial gas-flame fireplaces. *Sara Davidson, "Open Land," Harper's, June 1970, p 96*

Since nobody charbroiled steak for us or handed round copies of *McCall's,* our diversions were few. *Philip Norman, "America Notebook," The Sunday Times Magazine (London), May 16, 1971, p 66*

charge nurse, a nurse charged with the supervision of a ward.

The gradings referred to by Mr. Newman are used only to determine spheres of authority and therefore salary and in no way has the Sister/Charge Nurse been degraded or redesignated. *P. A. I. Vick, The Times (London), Aug. 27, 1970, p 7*

I was eager and anxious to go to work; I couldn't imagine any hospital that would offer more of a challenge than Bellevue. Besides, strange as it may seem, I had been favorably impressed by Dr. Stevens, the chief of surgery, by Jerry Baker, the resident, and by Sharon Avery, the charge nurse. *William A. Nolen, M.D., The Making of a Surgeon, 1970, p 23*

cha·ris·ma (kə'riz mə), *n.* strong personal appeal or magnetism, especially in politics.

"After George Papandreou, I have the widest popular base in Greece. I do not need George Papandreou. . . . I am the only other man in the party with such charisma." *Andreas Papandreou, quoted by C. L. Sulzberger, The New York Times, Oct. 26, 1966, p 42*

. . . even in a democracy, high intelligence and courage can bring leaders to the fore without the aid of charisma or demagoguery. *Dean Acheson, Washington, D.C., in a Letter to the Editor, The New York Times, June 28, 1971, p 30*

► Originally a theological term for a supernatural grace or gift bestowed by God on select individuals (from Greek *chárisma*), the word began to be widely applied in the 1960's to various celebrated figures and personalities, especially political candidates. It is often roughly equated with "sex appeal" and "glamour."

Charlie or **Charley,** *n.* *U.S. Military Slang.* **1** a Vietcong guerrilla.

. . . as one American official has put it, "everything that moves in Zones C and D is considered Charlie." *Thomas Whiteside, "A Reporter at Large: Defoliation," The New Yorker, Feb. 7, 1970, p 36*

2 the Vietcong.

. . . Colonel Braim issued a final order to his battalion commanders: "You've got 18 hours left. Go out and kill some Charley." *Time, April 13, 1970, p 29*

[shortened from *Victor Charlie* or *Victor Charley,* the communications code name for *V.C.,* abbreviation of *Vietcong*]

char·rette (ʃə'ret), *n.* a meeting of a group assisted by experts in various fields to discuss problems.

. . . the charrette depends on the constant interplay of ideas. Its most important aspect is the participation of people normally outside the decision-making process. *Time, May 11, 1970, p 40*

[from French, cart (in the phrase *en charrette* in a cart), perhaps originally so called in allusion to the practice of French architecture students of working hastily on their design drawings in carts which took them to their school]

chat show, *British.* another name for TALK SHOW.

Genuinely spontaneous *good* talk is the rarest thing, even in real life, and almost unknown in the chat show. *Maurice Wiggin, "August for the People," The Sunday Times (London), Aug. 29, 1971, p 22*

Finally to that ill-starred Sunday-morning chat-show *It's something else,* which ended its run with an edition which was—for the first time—compulsive listening. *Mollie Lee, "Radio Uz," The Listener, Dec. 9, 1971, p 819*

check trading, the practice of selling bank checks to a customer, who then repays the amount of the check plus interest in installments.

But so ill-defined is check trading's status that a recent court case indicated that it could possibly be a form of money lending. *Sally White, "The Friday Column: Controlling the Consumers' Credit," The Times (London), April 3, 1970, p 25*

chemical laser, a laser that uses the energy of chemical reaction rather than electrical energy.

Chemical lasers differ from ordinary lasers in that molecules with abnormally large amounts of energy are produced by particular chemical reactions, not by some external source of radiation. *The Times (London), Feb. 26, 1970, p 63*

Chemical Mace, another name for MACE.

A Chicago policeman wields a pressure can of Chemical Mace in an attempt to subdue antiwar demonstrators. . . . *Picture legend, 1969 Collier's Encyclopedia Year Book, p 181*

The Surgeon General of the United States warned today that the antiriot Chemical Mace might be more harmful than anybody once thought. *The New York Times, May 3, 1968, p 17*

chemosensory, *adj.* of or relating to the stimulation of sensory organs by chemical substances.

The chances are strong that the behavioral cues provided by the chemicals act through the chemosensory systems of the animals involved (that is, olfactory and gustatory systems). . . . *Richard H. Gilluly, "Taste, Smell and Ecology," Science News, Aug. 7, 1971, p 98*

Some fishes have been found to possess almost incredible chemosensory acuity. Harold Teichmann of the University of Giessen was able to condition eels to respond to concentrations of alcohol so dilute that he estimated the animals' olfactory receptors could not have received more than a few molecules. *John H. Todd, "The Chemical Languages of Fishes," Scientific American, May 1971, p 99*

chemosterilant, *n.* a chemical substance used in chemosterilization.

The use of chemosterilants—compounds which sterilise insects and make them unable to breed—has been a promising recent development in man's war against insect pests. *New Scientist, Oct. 22, 1964, p 210*

chemosterilization, *n.* sterilization of insects, rodents, and other pests by chemicals that affect the reproductive organs or drive, especially of males.

Chemosterilization—a weapon used successfully to control insect population—is now pointed at rats. *Science News, Oct. 11, 1969, p 329*

cheong·sam ('tʃɔːŋ'saːm), *n.* a dress with a high collar and slit skirt, worn especially by Chinese women.

Tell her you've always thought she'd look beautiful in a cheongsam. And you'd like to take her to a little shop where she can buy one. The shop is in Hong Kong . . . and the cheongsam is that devastating slit-skirted dress women wear in the Orient. *Advertisement by Pacific Area Travel Association, The New Yorker, Oct. 24, 1964, p 73*

In Malaya an army of 1,000 amahs donned Sunday-best sarongs, *cheongsams* and saris, piled into a fleet of busses and drove into Kuala Lumpur, the capital, where they minced prettily through the winding streets waving placards inscribed: WE WANT JUSTICE AND WE ARE NOT ANIMALS. *Time, Sept. 6, 1963, p 29*

[from Cantonese *cheuhng sāam* long dress]

cherry red, *British Slang.* another name for BOVVER BOOT.

Their [the skinheads'] hair is shaved within an eighth of an inch from the scalp, and they are dressed in oversized workpants, thin red suspenders and hobnailed, steel-toed boots costing about $10 and known as "cherry reds." *Time, June 8, 1970, p 37*

Chi·ca·no (tʃi'kɑː nou), *n.* a Mexican American; a person of Mexican birth or descent living in the United States. *Often used attributively.*

Denied to blacks, assimilation for years robbed the Chicano community of a nucleus of leadership. Today the forfeiture of this newly acquired cultural awareness seems to the young Chicano a prohibitive price to pay. The new courses in social bribery are taught by the blacks. *John Gregory Dunne, "To Die Standing," The Atlantic, June, 1971, p 45*

At Crystal City High School, Anglos and Chicanos lead separate lives. The Anglos say the division is a result of Gutiérrez' racism; the Chicanos say it's merely that the division that always existed is now acknowledged by both sides. *Calvin Trillin, "U.S. Journal: Crystal City, Texas," The New Yorker, April 17, 1971, p 107*

He is deeply devoted to the Roman Catholic Church and is a member of the Cursilistas, a group trying to revive religion among Chicanos. *Time, June 14, 1971, p 19*

[from Mexican Spanish *Chicano,* from the Chihuahua dialect pronunciation of *Mexicano* Mexican as (me tʃi:'kɑː nou) with loss of initial unaccented syllable]

chick·let or **chick·lette** ('tʃik lit), *n.* *U.S. Slang.* a young woman; a girl.

There is some show-stopping (if irrelevant) footwork by a trio of pretty chicklets billed as Extraordinary Spooks. *Time, Dec. 27, 1968, p 47*

When Michelangelo Antonioni made his first American public appearance, late in 1968, at the San Francisco Film Festival, Variety's Rick Setlowe reported that before

Antonioni arrived "a chicklette with lank, flowing hair turned to her bearded companion and pronounced with wide-eyed awe, 'He's flying in from Death Valley'." *Pauline Kael, "The Current Cinema: The Beauty of Destruction," The New Yorker, Feb. 21, 1970, p 95*

[diminutive of *chick*, slang term for a girl, originally a shortening of *chicken*, also slang for a girl]

Chi·com ('tʃai'kɑm), *n. U.S.* a Chinese communist. *Also used attributively.*

Also to be heard from are the ChiCom dreaders with their dire forebodings about the mighty Red Chinese nation, a dedicated monolith poised to crush all Asia at any provocation. *John Nichols, Time, Jan. 27, 1967, p 7*

The Communist troops moved through Thanh My hurling various sorts of explosives—grenades, satchel charges and homemade devices called "Chicom grenades," which are fashioned from Coca-Cola cans filled with plastique or TNT, rocks and nails. *Time, June 22, 1970, p 34*

▶ *Chicom* has been used as a derogatory term since the '950's but has been generally overlooked by dictionaries, probably because it did not seem likely to remain in the language, though our files show its use to persist. One of the earliest uses known to us was by President Eisenhower, as shown in this quotation:

"I believe it is perfectly legitimate for us to talk to the Chicoms about stopping firing," declared President Eisenhower at a recent press conference—thereby puzzling a lot of Americans who don't know what "Chicoms" are. *The New York Times, June 5, 1955, p 17*

childproof, *adj.* that a child cannot open or otherwise tamper with to endanger himself; safe for children.

It [a car] has all the usual features including childproof locks, a big boot [luggage compartment], wide doors and decent seats. *Judith Jackson, "Friend of the Fleets," The Sunday Times (London), May 2, 1971, p 13*

Legislation is now in preparation to . . . require producers of household poisons to render their containers "childproof" by making bottles and packages harder to open. . . . *Time, Dec. 12, 1969, p 64*

childrenese, *n. U.S.* a language for communicating effectively with one's children.

. . . in a slightly less de-humanized mood, parents have been offered lessons in how to speak "childrenese." *Eda and Lawrence LeShan, The New York Times, April 7, 1968, p 97*

"It's much harder than learning French," commented one suburban American mother recently, while trying desperately to master "childrenese," the new language parents in the United States are using to speak to their children. *Andree Brooks, The Times (London), May 13, 1968, p 9*

Children of God, a sect of the Jesus Movement whose members hold the world to be near destruction.

The Children of God eschew tobacco, liquor and premarital or extramarital sex, devoting themselves within their nearly self-sustaining communes to chanted prayers, hymns sung ecstatically, an almost constant study of the Bible, meditation and conversing in languages that they say come to them through prayer on the spur of the moment. *James T. Wooten, "Ill Winds Buffet Communal Sect," The New York Times, Nov. 29, 1971, p 41*

Chileanize, *v.t.* to put under control or authority of the Chilean government.

Besides Chileanizing the copper industry, he [former President Eduardo Frei] expropriated 1,224 private estates and distributed the land to 30,000 families. *Time, Oct. 19, 1970, p 30*

China watcher, an expert student or observer of Communist China and its government. Also called PEKINGOLOGIST.

China watchers in Hong Kong deduce that similar problems of disobedience probably exist elsewhere in China as well. *Time, Feb. 21, 1969, p 29*

The official New China News Agency spends a lot of money each day spreading the propaganda throughout the world. The great bulk of it is ignored by all but the most dedicated China Watchers. *"The Amazing Powers of the Thoughts of Mao," The Manchester Guardian Weekly, April 3, 1969, p 10*

Chinese restaurant syndrome, a group of symptoms which appear in some people after eating Chinese food. See the first quotation for details.

Reports appeared in the U.S. press of a so-called Chinese restaurant syndrome (headache, dizziness, flushing), which was attributed by some authorities to the excessive use of monosodium glutamate (MSG). *Henry B. Hawley, "Food Processing and Technology," Britannica Book of the Year 1970, p 350*

Monosodium glutamate (MSG), the flavor-enhancing food additive that causes Chinese Restaurant Syndrome in some individuals . . . came under more fire late last year when a St. Louis investigator reported that it damaged newborn mice and called for its removal from all baby foods. . . . *Science News, Aug. 22 and 29, 1970, p 172*

chin turret, a turret for a gun located immediately below the nose of a bomber or gunship.

The man in the rear flies the helicopter and fires the rockets and Gatling-type six-barreled machine guns fixed on stubby wings on each side. The forward man fires a six-barreled minigun in a movable chin turret under the nose.

"This is what we call a professional gunship," said Col. J. Elmore Swenson of Columbus, Ga. *The New York Times, Jan. 7, 1968, p 5*

chip, *n.* a very small piece of silicon on which integrated circuits can be printed. Compare WAFER.

Over the last decade, for example, the number of components that a designer can pack on a single silicon chip has increased a thousandfold. This means that the entire electronic system for a desk calculator is contained on three silicon chips, each no more than one eighth of an inch square. *Michael Kenward, "Technology Review: Big Advances in Small Circuits," New Scientist, Dec. 10, 1970, p 441*

Medium scale integration with 50 to 100 or more gates per integrated circuit component, chip or module is generally assumed to be the hardware technology of the fourth generation. *Earl Joseph, "Towards a Fifth Generation," Science Journal, Oct. 1970, p 102*

chlorinated hydrocarbon, any of a class of synthetic pesticides, formed by a chlorine-carbon bond, that are among the most persistent of environmental poisons.

The most troublesome pollutants among pesticides are the so-called hard pesticides, principally the chlorinated hydrocarbons—DDT, dieldrin, aldrin, endrin, lindane, chlordane, heptachlor, and some of their relatives. *Science News Yearbook 1970, p 306*

chlor·mad·i·none (klɔr'mæd ə,noun), *n.* Also called **chlormadinone acetate.** a drug used to prevent pregnancy. *Abbreviation:* CA

Like the other man-made hormones that constitute the pill, chlormadinone is built up from chemicals extracted from the root of the Barbasco plant, a species of wild Mexican yam. *Alfred Byrne, The Sunday Times (London), July 9, 1967, p 3*

Chlormadinone, the "one-every-day" birth control pill, was on general-prescription sale in Britain, France and Mexico and was being widely tested in the U.S. *Time, Feb. 9, 1970, p 39*

J. Martinez-Manautou and co-workers gave chlormadinone acetate, an anti-estrogenic progestogen [a synthetic hormone] in a continuous daily dose of 0.5 mg. to 1,045 women in Mexico for a combined total of 8,652 months. Pregnancy was successfully prevented without inhibiting ovulation. *Thomas L. T. Lewis, "Gynecology and Obstetrics," Britannica Book of the Year 1969, p 496*

cho·le·sta·sis (,kou lə'stei sis), *n.* a stoppage in the flow of bile.

Cholestasis (failure to secrete bile into the intestines) was studied by S. Sherlock. The condition has multiple causes. Jaundice develops slowly and is accompanied by itching of the skin. The feces are pale for lack of bile pigment and fatty for lack of bile salts. Secondary events include deficiency of the fat-soluble vitamins A, D, and K and of calcium. *Joseph B. Kirsner, M.D., "Medicine," Britannica Book of the Year 1968, p 508*

[from Greek *cholḗ* bile + *stásis* stoppage]

chopper, *Slang.* —*v.i.* to fly by helicopter.

Whenever he [General Creighton W. Abrams] can, he choppers to the field and once a month flies to Bangkok to visit his wife. *Time, Feb. 15, 1971, p 19*

... he [Sir Michael Le Fanu] broke away for a moment from chatting about helicopter flights, "choppering around" as he calls it.... *Terry Coleman, "Dry Ginger," The Manchester Guardian Weekly, April 4, 1970, p 13*

—*v.t.* to transport by helicopter.

A four-ship British task force anchored in the bay and began choppering food, clothing, medicine and water purification pills to the remote coastal areas. *Time, Dec. 7, 1970, p 28*

[verb use of *chopper, n.,* helicopter]

chuff, *v.t.* **chuff up,** *British Slang.* to cheer up; encourage; please.

"This other guy started ahead of me by about 20 yards," Brown said, "so I sprinted up beside him and said 'I'm clapped out.' It chuffed him up a bit and I ran along in his slip stream...." *Dudley Doust, "Eric the Brown Looking Over ...," The Sunday Times (London), Aug. 22, 1971, p 17*

[of uncertain origin]

chuffed, *adj. British Slang.* pleased; happy.

The sight of Irish Favour winning his second race in a week and his fourth in all delighted Breasley. But with next year's handicaps in mind, he admitted to being not nearly so chuffed at seeing him win by as much as eight lengths and with a 5 lb. penalty into the bargain. *Michael Phillips, "Racing: Sassafras Retiring to Stud in Ireland," The Times (London), Oct. 30, 1970, p 15*

I gather, Nessie, that you are very shy, but if you could at least show yourself for a few minutes this summer the

Colonel and lots of other people would be frightfully chuffed. *William Davis, "A Monstrous Tale," Punch, June 18, 1969, p 897*

chunnel, *n.* a tunnel for railroad trains built under a channel of water.

In recent years the idea of a channel tunnel—popularly known as the "chunnel"—has been revived. *Walter Sullivan, The New York Times, July 17, 1966, Sec. 4, p 12*

Chunnel Gets Axe. *Title of article by Michael Moynihan, The Sunday Times (London), Jan. 7, 1968, p 1*

[blend of *channel* and *tunnel*]

churn, *v.t.* **churn out,** to produce in a regular flow without much thought or expression, usually with some abundance.

... I settled to the role of hack, of churning out bits and pieces about absolutely everything. *Michael Parkinson, "Pleasure: The Truth about Sports Reporting," Punch, Dec. 31, 1969, p 1098*

... a bit of care can make stamp collecting even more profitable and enjoyable. Issues to steer clear of are the ones churned out by countries which are out to make money from the collector, produced simply for the album and not for use. *Donald Wintersgill, "Paper Money," The Manchester Guardian Weekly, Nov. 8, 1969, p 20*

How, after churning out all this bunk, Frady can have produced a book worth reading I don't know, but he has. *Ronnie Dugger, "For a White House Lily-White?" Saturday Review, Oct. 5, 1968, p 26*

chutz·pah or **chutz·pa** ('xuts pə), *n. U.S. Slang.* brazen audacity; shameless impudence; nerve; gall.

Takara was so adept at copying that it set some kind of Japanese record for chutzpah. Its first models were almost exact duplicates of the chairs produced by the leading U.S. manufacturer, Chicago's Emil J. Paidar Co. *Time, Aug. 10, 1970, p 61*

"Kennedy has plenty of chutzpah talking about liberalism," a McCarthy worker said.... *The New York Times, May 7, 1968, p 26*

[from Yiddish *khutspe,* from Hebrew *ḥutspāh*]

ciao (tʃau), *interj. Italian.* **1** greetings.

Crowds of children were swimming off the rocks along the Posillipo,... they sometimes looked up to us and waved, and she waved back or called out "Ciao," while I set out a jug and glasses on a table between us. *Shirley Hazzard, The Bay of Noon, 1970, p 152*

2 good-by.

Vocabularies, on the other hand, are far more fickle and subject to alien seduction. In Mexico City, for example, the Italian *ciao* has virtually replaced adiós among college students, and even the least traveled bootblack will say OK instead of its Spanish equivalent. *Enrique Hank Lopez, "The Late Late Lovers," The Atlantic, July 1967, p 100*

cin·e- ('sin ə-), combining form meaning "motion picture," "film," "cinema," very productive during the 1960's. Some recent examples of its use:

cinecult, *n.attributive:* Langlois showed the films, and for a short time Van Peebles was a cinecult celebrity. *Time, Aug. 15, 1971, p 43*

cine-holography, *n.:* Research workers have been talking about cine-holography ever since the laser turned Dennis Gabor's idea of holography into a useful tool rather than a curiosity. *Glen Lawes and Michael Kenward, "Technology*

Review: Holographic Films Come Closer?" New Scientist, Aug. 27, 1970, p 420

cineménage, *n.:* Like Polonsky's Willie Boy, Andy Warhol is here, and as I feared when I wrote about "Flesh" last week it must have been his temporary absence from his cineménage which made that film likeable. *Dilys Powell, "Journey to the Underworld: Films," The Sunday Times (London), Jan. 25, 1970, p 54*

cine-record, *v.t.:* The child was left to 'play' in the room for 10 minutes while the experimenter cine-recorded the behaviour from an adjoining cubicle. *Corinne Hutt, "Curiosity in Young Children," Science Journal, Feb. 1970, p 69*

cinestrip, *n.:* ... 15 to 45 seconds ... is ample time to obtain long cinestrips at various speeds. *Jeanne Bockel, "Looking into Swallowing Problems," Science News, June 20, 1970, p 601*

cin·e·ma·theque (ˌsin ə məˈtek), *n.* a movie theater showing experimental and unconventional films.

Spearheaded by [Andy] Warhol, the underground has begun to emerge from the cellars of the cliquish film societies that provided their original audiences. Today, almost every major American city boasts at least one "cinematheque" where these pictures, shot on 16mm film, are constantly on display. *Arthur Knight, "Look What's Happening to the Movies," The 1969 World Book Year Book, p 120*

Underground film-makers have known this for years; seeing their work snapped up from the cinematheque library and regurgitated into television commercials. *The Times (London), Jan. 31, 1968, p 7*

[from French *cinémathèque* a motion-picture film library]

ci·né·ma vé·ri·té (si: neiˈma vei ri:ˈtei), a type of documentary film or film-making that attempts to capture the sense of documentary realism by spontaneous interviews, the use of a hand-held camera, and a minimum of editing of the footage. Also shortened to CINÉVÉRITÉ.

Shot in *cinéma vérité* format over a period of four months last summer, *Carry It On* revolves around Harris' arrest in July for noncooperation with the draft. *Time, Aug. 24, 1970, p 61*

The reception desk at Leacock-Pennebaker is unmanned, but the wall-size bulletin board facing the elevator bombards her with the stares from famous/beautiful people photographed in company films—Bob Dylan, Janis Joplin, Norman Mailer, Jack Kennedy, Bob Kennedy, Godard. The pictures are part of cinema-verité filmmaking's Hall of Fame. *Barbara H. Kevles, "In Search of Nan Page," The Atlantic, July 1970, p 75*

[from French *cinéma-vérité*, literally, cinema-truth, cinema-realism]

cin·e·phile (ˈsin əˌfail), *n. British.* a lover of motion pictures; a movie fan.

August is always a lean month for cinephiles in search of new French films. *"Paris Guide: Cinema," The Manchester Guardian Weekly, Aug. 21, 1971, p 14*

The director is Don Siegal, a master of action (but not here) and something of a cult hero—a season of his movies is on at present at the National Film Theater. Not exactly to my taste, but I think I can see why some of the shrewder cinephiles find his style attractive. *Eric Rhode, "Films," Review of "Madigan," The Listener, March 21, 1968, p 389*

ci·né·vé·ri·té (ˌsi: nei vei ri:ˈtei), *n.* short for CINÉMA VÉRITÉ.

Nevertheless in that moment a scene was rigged for the camera. Not even the most stringent piece of cinévérité has ever been completely free of that kind of thing. *Christopher Ralling, "The Truth About Documentaries—or Documentaries About the Truth," The Listener, Dec. 19, 1968, p 826*

cinq-à-sept (sæk aˈset), *n. French.* an evening visit (literally, five-to-seven) with one's mistress or lover.

... the motivated men of Government cannot afford to take three-hour lunches, and the traditional *cinq-à-sept* is out of the question for a 12- to 15-hour-day man. *Time, Nov. 30, 1970, p 34*

cir·ca·di·an (sərˈkei di: ən), *adj.* functioning or recurring in 24-hour cycles.

Regulation and Control in Living Systems . . . Attempts to bridge terminological and conceptual differences in communicating between control engineer and biologist in presenting physiological control systems, circadian regulation, control in the endocrine system, and regulation in animal societies and populations. *Science News, April 8, 1967, p 340*

If man does indeed possess a circannual clock and its nature becomes accessible to investigation, the implications may be as important as those of the circadian clock, to which we are all biologically bound. *Eric T. Pengelley and Sally J. Asmundson, "Annual Biological Clocks," Scientific American, April 1971, p 79*

[from Latin *circā diēm* around the day + English *-an*]

circadianly, *adv.* in 24-hour cycles.

Temperature and urine flow are but two among many physiological functions which fluctuate circadianly, and they could be influenced by the great variety of circadian fluctuations in our environment.... *J. N. Mills, "Keeping in Step—Away From it All," New Scientist, Feb. 9, 1967, p 350*

circadian rhythm, the 24-hour cycle of physiological activity in living organisms governed by the biological clock. See also BODY CLOCK. Compare BIORHYTHM.

Biologically, however, the scientists expressed great interest in the phenomenon called circadian rhythm—man's biological clock that regulates his normal body cycles. *Everly Driscoll, "Testing Man's Value in Space," Science News, Oct. 10, 1970, p 304*

cir·can·ni·an (sərˈkæn i: ən) or **cir·can·nu·al** (sərˈkæn yu əl), *adj.* functioning or recurring in annual cycles.

Following investigations of hibernation in five species of ground squirrel *(Citellus),* E. T. Pengelley and K. H. Kelly, from the University of California, Riverside, have suggested that these animals have a similar internal rhythm of approximately a year. They have named this faculty a "circannian" rhythm.... *New Scientist, Dec. 22, 1966, p 688*

The discovery of a circannual clock in hibernators has of course been followed up with investigations of other animals marked by conspicuous annual changes in behavior or physiology. *Eric T. Pengelley and Sally J. Asmundson, "Annual Biological Clocks," Scientific American, April 1971, p 75*

[from Latin *circā annum* around the year + English *-ian* or *-al*]

circular polarization, a phenomenon in which magnetically induced polarization of light rotates clockwise or counterclockwise.

Dr. [James C.] Kemp has developed a theory of another magnetic effect on light: circular polarization. In any light beam the waves vibrate in directions perpendicular to the direction the beam is going.... In a circularly polarized beam, the changes in the direction of vibration are not arbitrary, but proceed in an orderly rotation around the axis of propagation. *Dietrick E. Thomsen, Science News, Oct. 3, 1970, p 290*

circumstellar, *adj.* surrounding or revolving about a star.

What is this cool object?... Harold L. Johnson and V. C. Reddish of the University of Arizona have argued that it may be an extremely bright supergiant star that has been reddened by either interstellar dust or a circumstellar envelope of some kind. *G. Neugebauer and Robert B. Leighton, "The Infrared Sky: The Coolest Objects Observed," Scientific American, Aug. 1968, p 59*

The new infrared data may clear up; circumstellar dust clouds are implicated, and stable shells can only be formed towards the end of the star's life. *"Monitor: Monitoring Infrared from the Night-sky," New Scientist, Dec. 10, 1970, p 428*

[from *circum-* around + *stellar* of a star]

cislunar, *adj.* of or referring to space between earth and moon.

This indicated a low concentration of dust of interplanetary space, perhaps 1/10,000 of that found near the earth and 1/100 of that in cislunar (earth-moon) space. *Kurt R. Stehling, "Space Exploration: Space Science," The Americana Annual 1964, p 606*

[from *cis-* on this side + *lunar* of the moon]

cla·dis·tic (klə'dis tik), *adj.* based on hereditary factors and relationships. Compare PHENETIC.

... systematists ... developed methods of classifying animals for other purposes: numerical (phenetic) classifications, based on relative degrees of similarity and ignoring evolutionary history and, at the other extreme, the cladistic classifications, based on assumed lines of descent while ignoring similarity. *Ronald R. Novales, "Zoology," Britannica Book of the Year 1970, p 169*

[from *clad-* (from Greek *kládos* sprout, branch) + *-istic,* as in *statistic*]

clanger, *n. British Slang.* a resounding blunder (especially in the phrase **drop a clanger**).

He has good reason for embarrassment for the Americans seemed to have dropped a fair sized clanger. *Stephen Aris, The Sunday Times (London), April 28, 1968, p 34*

It looks as if we are proposing to make a meal of Zambian High Commissioner designate Simbule. Whitehall has got all hoity-toity about his speech in Dar-es-Salaam in which he referred to Britain as a toothless bulldog. The wires between here and Lusaka have been getting steadily hotter and Katilungu, the man about to go home, has been leaned on by the Commonwealth Office. Nobody disputes, of course, that it was a crashing clanger but the deep breathing now going on seems a bit more than is warranted. *The Manchester Guardian Weekly, May 11, 1967, p 6*

clapped-out, *adj. British Slang.* ruined by decay, neglect, or waste; dilapidated.

One notorious coward, who ran as if his laces were tied together ... could command any position on the field, simply because he owned a huge, clapped-out Chrysler which carried eight people, or a clear majority of the side. *Derek Robinson, "Love That Try!" Punch, Oct. 23, 1968, p 569*

Effluent and over-fishing have also made dangerous inroads into the beds.... "Now look at the beds. Bloody clapped out they are: It takes a tide to pick what I used to in an hour." *Tom Davies, "Cockles and Muscles — But Should the Oyster Catchers Stay Alive-oh?" The Sunday Times (London), June 6, 1971, p 24*

clappers, *n.* **like the clappers,** *British Slang.* very fast.

"He's about eighty miles up now," whispered Futter, "and going like the clappers. Peak of physical condition, these chaps. Have to be." *"When the Roll is Called up Yonder," Punch, July 16, 1969, p 102*

... Benson ... sets out for London. He drives like the clappers, and arrives in some disorder at a quarter to six. *Michael Frayn, "In Motion," The Listener, Nov. 28, 1968, p 704*

class action, a legal action brought on behalf of all to whom the case applies.

The legislative program described by [former Congressman] Ottinger would amend: Federal law to broaden the right of citizens to bring "class actions" against polluters and to provide a fund to help defray legal expenses in such actions. *Danbury (Conn.) News-Times, quoted in The New Yorker, May 9, 1970, p 116*

Today in the United States District Court, in Hartford, two imprisoned brothers and Roman Catholic priests, Philip and Daniel Berrigan, are bringing a class action on behalf of themselves and other federally held prisoners. *The New York Times, Dec. 14, 1970, p 43*

claus·tro·pho·bic (ˌklɔːs trə'fou bik), *n.* a person who has an abnormal fear of enclosed spaces. Compare AGORAPHOBIC.

Thomas H. Budzynski, at the University of Colorado Medical Center, has been applying EEG [electroencephalograph] biofeedback procedures to anxiety problems and psychosomatic disorders. Stutterers and claustrophobics can be taught to relax without the use of tranquilizers. *Robert J. Trotter, "Listen to Your Head," Science News, Nov. 6, 1971, p 316*

[noun use of the adjective]

▶ See the note under AGORAPHOBIC.

claw, *v.i.* **claw back,** *British.* to retrieve (money spent on increased government benefits and allowances) in the form of additional taxes.

Above that level, the 15 per cent proposed surcharge evens things out, but not enough to claw back the big concessions on the first £2,000 of income. *The Guardian (London), April 22, 1972, p 15*

claw-back, *n. British.* **1** retrieval by the government of money spent on increased benefits and allowances by a corresponding increase in taxes.

His [Mr. Ian Macleod's] alternative Budget proposals, given the money available, would have been a 10s. family allowance increase with claw-back which would cost £30m. [million]. *Hugh Noyes, "No Division by Tories on Budget," The Times (London), April 16, 1970, p 2*

2 a drawback.

The pleasure [in the *Diaries of Samuel Pepys*] is various and pervasive — even with its occasional claw-backs. It is in drink and food, in drinking wine with anchovies; in travel on the river, in walking by moonlight; in his singing and music; in company, theatre-going, sights, sounds, ceaseless curiosity.... *Geoffrey Grigson, "English Epicurean," The Manchester Guardian Weekly, Dec. 5, 1970, p 18*

[from CLAW BACK]

claymore mine, Also shortened to **claymore.** an electrically detonated mine that sprays small metal pellets.

...the constant going off of claymore mines, rockets, and other forms of ammo would get on his nerves.... *Thomas Parker, "Troop Withdrawal—The Initial Step," Harper's, Aug. 1969, p 63*

The homemade Claymore is a wooden box a foot long, four inches wide, six inches deep. *Brian Moynahan, "Battle of the Ulster Bombs," The Sunday Times (London), Oct. 31, 1971, p 10*

[probably named after the *claymore* sword of the Scottish Highlanders]

clean, *adj.* free from the use of narcotic drugs. Compare DIRTY.

...only one-tenth of heroin addicts are ever completely "clean again". In Washington, where the quality of drugs is poor and withdrawal less dramatic than in say, New York or Chicago, Dr. Dupont and several ex-addicts claim that 10 per cent is far too pessimistic a figure. *Victoria Brittain, "Teenage Heroin Epidemic That Has Alarmed US," The Times (London), March 13, 1970, p 11*

clean room, a thoroughly sterilized room used for laboratory work, the manufacture of critical space-craft parts, etc.

Soldering iron handle for use in clean rooms helps eliminate potential dust and solder contamination while insulating fingers against high temperature. *Science News Letter, Sept. 18, 1965, p 191*

clear air turbulence, a violent disturbance in air currents, caused by rapid changes of temperature associated with the jet stream. Clear air turbulence is characterized by severe updrafts and downdrafts that affect jet aircraft flying at high altitudes. *Abbreviation:* CAT

Intensive studies ... may well solve some of the thornier weather problems connected with such phenomena as hurricanes, air-sea interchange, electrical storms or clear air turbulence. *"Standing Waves and CAT above the Rockies," New Scientist, March 19, 1970, p 544*

To the airline pilot, the wave means "clear-air turbulence." This sounds strange, since for the glider it is so smooth. But the glider stands still in the wave. The jet flies through it at 550 mph, with maybe a 70 mph tailwind added, and then the wave is like a thank-you-ma'am in the road, taken too fast: it can lift the passenger right out of his seat and put the coffee on the ceiling. *Wolfgang Langewiesche, "The Upward Miracle: The Arts and Joys of Gliding," Harper's, Nov. 1971, p 129*

client, *n.* short for **client state.**

The so-called Rogers [Secretary of State William Rogers] initiative, which would never have been launched if Washington had not felt it had Moscow's tacit agreement, was based on this understanding: each super-power would induce its own Middle Eastern client to subscribe to a compromise settlement. As a first stage Arabs and Israelis were persuaded by their respective patrons to consent to a cease-fire with an accompanying stand-still on military movements. *Christopher Serpell, "Foreign News: Salami Tactics," The Listener, Oct. 8, 1970, p 474*

...Washington and Moscow must bring their clients to heel in order to avoid involvement in another armed confrontation. *C. L. Sulzberger, "Before Chaos Takes Over," The New York Times, Nov. 1, 1970, Sec. 4, p 15*

client state, a dependent state or government. Also shortened to CLIENT.

...the peace movement had not taken Nixon's politics serious until November 3rd. Now we know that his true intention is to continue a pro-West client state in Vietnam.... *David Hawk, quoted by Francine du Plessix Gray, "A Reporter At Large: The Moratorium and the New Mobe [New Mobilization Committee to End the War in Vietnam]," The New Yorker, Jan. 3, 1970, p 42*

...the US flies "armed reconnaissance flights" and in the east of Laos "interdicts men and supplies" travelling down the Ho Chi Minh trail towards South Vietnam. In fact, this country is more utterly a client state than any other in South-east Asia. *Ian Wright, The Manchester Guardian Weekly, Feb. 28, 1970, p 4*

Still another group, the former French colonies, had in some cases to be virtually forced into independence, an independence that made mockery of the term. "France's client states," the *Economist* was to call them in 1965. *Scott Thompson, "Second Round for Africa: Independence on Trial," The Atlantic, Oct. 1966, p 80*

cliffhang, *v.i.* to hang in suspense.

On the problems of language and their solution he [George Steiner in his book *Extraterritorial*] rather melodramatically makes man's future cliffhang.... *Melvin Maddocks, "Babel Revisited," Time, July 26, 1971, p 52*

With last year's 17-1/2 per cent dividend thinly covered by earnings of 19-1/2 per cent including overspill relief, Guthrie will be cliffhanging again this year—barring a real turnup from Lintafoam. *The Sunday Times (London), July 23, 1967, p 19*

[an extended meaning of *cliffhang, v.,* to be in suspense over the outcome of a *cliffhanger* or melodramatic serial]

climbout, *n.* the immediate, steep climb of an aircraft during takeoff.

Noise on takeoff will be less offensive than the 747 because the SST [supersonic transport] climbout will be steeper and faster. *James J. Harford, "Up the SST," The New York Times, Dec. 1, 1970, p 47*

...the BR 941 can cruise at 220 knots and stalls at only 45 knots. It can take off in less than 700 ft, land in 345 ft, with steep climb-out and approach paths. *James Hay Stevens, "Build-up of the VTOL Challenge," New Scientist, April 23, 1970, p 174*

Cli·o ('klai ou), *n.* a statuette presented annually as an award for the best production, acting, etc., in commercial advertisements during the year on American television.

In honor of such memorable performances, this year, for the first time, the American TV Commercials Festival is awarding a Clio, the industry's equivalent of an Oscar, to the best actor in a commercial. *Time, April 28, 1967, p 57*

clo·fi·brate (klou'fai,breit), *n.* a drug that lowers cholesterol levels in human beings and removes fats from tissues.

Particular attention is being focused on clofibrate, a

substance that sharply reduces the levels of cholesterol and other fatty substances in the blood. *The New York Times, Nov. 24, 1968, Sec. 4, p 10*

clom·i·phene ('klɑm ə,fiːn), *n.* Also called **clomiphene citrate.** a fertility-inducing drug.

This substance, clomiphene, makes a false biological signal to the hypothalamus and causes it to set in train the sequence of events which leads to ovulation. *Arnold Klopper, "The Reproductive Hormones," Science Journal, June 1970, p 46*

Clomiphene, in addition to making it possible for childless couples to have children, has inadvertently resulted in a notable number of multiple births. *Betty Jo Tricou, "Drugs," The World Book Science Annual 1967, p 285*

[shortened from *chloramiphene*]

clone, *v.t., v.i.* to reproduce or propagate asexually.

Cauliflowers have been cloned at the National Vegetable Research Station.... Simply by cutting slices of cauliflowers, at their market-ready stage, and putting them in nutrient solution a single plant can be made to yield many more plants. *Glen Lawes and Michael Kenward, "Technology Review: Cloned Cauliflowers for Greater Productivity," New Scientist, June 18, 1970, p 581*

Cloning, or duplication of identical organisms, as has been achieved with frogs, is not genetic engineering in the real sense, he [Dr. James Danielli] asserts, nor are efforts to create test-tube babies, although cloning and creating life in a test tube are often canopied under the heading of genetic engineering. *Joan Lynn Arehart, "Genetic Engineering: Myth or Reality?" Science News, Sept. 4, 1971, p 152*

[from *clone, n.,* a group of organisms produced asexually by a single progenitor, from Greek *klón* twig]

closed-loop, *adj.* of or relating to an automatic control process or unit that adjusts or corrects itself by a feedback mechanism. Compare OPEN-LOOP.

Closed-loop systems, where the experiment is directly controlled by computer, are currently being developed. Their prototypes can be seen in industrial control systems, where ... devices, ranging from elevators to oil refineries, are controlled automatically. *Anthony G. Oettinger, "The Uses of Computers in Science," Scientific American, Sept. 1966, p 163*

Oddly enough, a circulating water channel, which is rather like a controlled closed-loop river, is a difficult experiment facility to design and operate well. *"New Aid for the Shipbuilders," New Scientist, March 30, 1967, p 654*

The Schenk "Hydropuls" closed-loop, servo-hydraulic loading system, incorporating a loading actuator and programming system, is at the heart of the installation. *Kenneth Owen, The Times (London), Feb. 27, 1970, p 27*

The word system as used here means feedback system or closed-loop system. The closed-loop configuration is the structure within which all decisions take place and all growth and control processes occur. *Jay W. Forrester, "Social-System Dynamics," McGraw-Hill Yearbook of Science and Technology 1971, p 26*

closet homosexual, a person who hides his homosexuality; a covert homosexual.

I know men in high and low places in society, in government, at work, who would shrivel in shame if people suspected that they were even closet homosexuals. Just the other day, one young, liberated homosexual burst out, "Homosexuality is so horrible in this life, you've *got* to find

someone to be homosexual with." And the most successful sexual athlete I've encountered, in the sense of "making" handsome men with Olympian frequency, was undoubtedly the unhappiest human I have ever been near. *Faubion Bowers, "Homosex: Living The Life," Saturday Review, Feb. 12, 1972, p 28*

closet queen, a slang term for CLOSET HOMOSEXUAL.

The whole first part of the movie nags us with the author's exposure of his characters; the actively "normal" parents, for instance, have created a hyperaggressive daughter who wants to "mold" men, and a son who wants to be a girl and who winds up, literally, as a closet queen. *David Denby, "Movies, On Fracturing The Funny Bone," Review of the movie version of Jules Feiffer's play "Little Murders," The Atlantic, April 1971, p 99*

closet queer, *U.S.* another slang term for CLOSET HOMOSEXUAL.

"Hell, he's one of those tough fags," would be the answer. But he's married and has three children, I would point out about someone else. "A closet-queer, obviously," the answer would shoot back. *Joseph Epstein, "Homo/Hetero: The Struggle For Sexual Identity," Harper's, Sept. 1970, p 39*

clothback, *n.* a clothbound book.

The appearance in print of the first of the Nuffield Advanced Science courses will be enthusiastically welcomed by many. First, perhaps, by those already using the trial materials, who can discard 5 lb of duplicated loose leaves for a pair of large pocket-sized clothbacks. *John Blatchly, "For Student and Specialist," New Scientist, Oct. 1, 1970, p 44*

cloth-cap, *adj. British.* of or belonging to the laboring or working class, particularly in opposition to other classes.

So-called top hat pension schemes are spreading in popularity and, even if they are not yet in vogue among cloth cap workers, their use is no longer confined to the very highly paid executives for whom they were first designed. *The Times (London), June 11, 1966, p 17*

... from within the Labour Party there have been those — ever since the leadership of Hugh Gaitskell — who see the cloth-cap associations of trade unionism, with overtones of the class struggle, as out of date and an electoral liability. *"Trade Unions and the Labour Party," The Manchester Guardian Weekly, Sept. 12, 1968, p 1*

[from the *cloth caps* commonly worn by workers in Great Britain]

cloth-eared, *adj.* having cloth ears.

The public world is dominated today by the cloth-eared and insensitive noisemongers. *"Probe: And the Last Word ... On Silence," New Scientist, April 16, 1970, p 101*

cloth ears, defective or tone-deaf hearing.

"They've got cloth ears. Sometimes you get someone left behind who swears you didn't even call the flight...." *Jeremy Bugler, The Sunday Times (London), Oct. 9, 1966, p 5*

... imagine Mr. Balanchine's generation hearing Webern for the first time; it must have thought it was wearing cloth ears. ... *Clive Barnes, The New York Times, March 30, 1967, p 54*

clout, *n. U.S.* power, influence, or prestige, especially in politics.

Now, in the waning months of his Administration, he [President Johnson] no longer had enough clout left to force through a scheme which was bound to infuriate virtually every member of Congress. *John Fischer, "The Easy Chair: Open Letter to the Next President," Harper's, Sept. 1968, p 16*

At the same time, Israel was exercising all the diplomatic clout she could muster to bring outside pressure on the Algerian Government. *Terence Smith, The New York Times, July 28, 1968, Sec. 4, p 2*

clox·a·cil·lin (ˌklɑk səˈsil ən), *n.* a synthetic form of penicillin effective against germs that have developed resistance to natural penicillin. Compare AMPICILLIN, OXACILLIN.

The antibiotic was cloxacillin, as this is effective against the staphylococcus that causes about half the infections found both at the end of lactation and at calving. *The Times (London), Jan. 8, 1968, p 11*

[from its chemical name *chl*orophenyl-methyliso-*oxa*zolyl peni*cillin*]

cloze (klouz), *adj.* of or based on the cloze procedure.

[J. Wesley] Schneyer (1965) explored the effects of the cloze procedure upon the reading comprehension of sixth grade pupils. Two types of cloze exercises were used; one built on every-tenth word deletions and the other on noun-verb deletions. Schneyer based his two deletion systems on the lexical-structural dichotomy. . . . *Eugene Jongsma, The Cloze Procedure as a Teaching Technique, 1971, p 9*

[alteration of *close, v.,* as used originally in Gestalt psychology and later in communication theory in the sense of "to complete a pattern parts of which are missing or have been deleted"]

cloze procedure, a testing procedure for comprehension in reading which measures the ability of a reader to supply words which have been systematically deleted from a reading selection.

The "cloze procedure" has been developed to enable teachers to determine the ability of the child to handle materials; it will also indicate the ability to handle concepts as well as word and sentence structures. *Robert M. Wilson, Diagnostic and Remedial Reading for Classroom and Clinic, 1972, p 247*

cluster college, one of a group of small autonomous liberal-arts colleges within a university, modeled on those of Oxford and Cambridge.

. . . some forty American universities already have taken steps toward the development of smaller units or "cluster colleges," each enrolling no more than 200 to 1,000 students and each with its own basic faculty which is selected on the basis of talent for teaching undergraduates. *Paul Woodring, "A View from the Campus," Saturday Review, Aug. 17, 1968, p 53*

CM, abbreviation of COMMAND MODULE.

And so, on July 16, Apollo 11 lifted from its launch pad at Cape Kennedy. Approximately 108 hours later, Neil Armstrong and Edwin E. Aldrin, Jr., were leaving man's first footprints in the lunar "soil." . . . Meanwhile, the third Apollo 11 crew member, Michael Collins, circled the moon in the CM, one of the few Americans unable to watch Armstrong and Aldrin. *"Review of the Year—Space Exploration," Encyclopedia Science Supplement (Grolier) 1970, p 304*

Co·an·da effect (kouˈæn də), the property or tendency of any fluid passing a curved surface to attach itself to the surface. It is also called the WALL-ATTACHMENT EFFECT, and is an important principle of fluidics.

A common demonstration of the Coanda effect is seen when a falling jet of water from a tap defies gravity and runs along a spoon or jar just brought into contact with it. *B. J. Cooper, "Fluidics Grows Up," Science Journal, Dec. 1968, p 53*

[named after Henri *Coanda,* a French engineer who described the effect in 1932]

coattail, *adj. U.S. Politics.* based on the ability of a strong candidate to carry weaker ones along to victory with him. See also COATTAILS.

On Capitol Hill, Rockefeller promoted "coattail power" —meaning that he can get more Republican Congressmen elected in November than Nixon. *Time, June 28, 1968, p 13*

The Republican showing was much weaker than had been expected and gave little coattail prestige to Callaway. *Geoffrey Y. Cornog, "Georgia," 1967 Collier's Encyclopedia Year Book, p 229*

coattails, *n.pl. U.S. Politics.* the ability of a strong candidate to carry weaker ones along to victory with him.

. . . Paul O'Dwyer, an anti-war McCarthy supporter, upset strong Kennedy and Humphrey men in the Senatorial primary, suggesting that McCarthy had coattails. *Jeremy Larner, "Nobody Knows . . . Reflections on the McCarthy Campaign," Harper's, May 1969, p 83*

He [Governor Nelson Rockefeller] also said he [Governor George Romney] was "a politician with broad coattails that can sweep in the rest of us as they coast along . . . the man the Republican party needs in this Presidential election this fall." *The New York Times, Feb. 6, 1968, p 16*

[from the idiom *ride on someone's coattails* to get ahead by sticking closely to someone who is advancing or successful]

coat-trailing, *British.* —*n.* incitement to quarrel or controversy; provocation.

In Molière, the beggar is specified simply as *un pauvre.* Here he is characterized as an evangelist figure, and the deal is struck in front of a cross. . . . Even with Jouyet's authority, this Christian coat-trailing strikes me as dubious. *"The Arts: Satanic Libertine, Dom Juan," The Times (London), March 20, 1970, p 10*

. . . criticism of Cromwell . . . and an enjoyable piece of coat-trailing on the debt of the Enlightenment to the Reformation fill out some of the themes suggested in two more general studies. . . . *R. G. G. Price, "A Landscape New Lit," Review of "Religion, the Reformation and Social Change" by H. R. Trevor-Roper, Punch, Aug. 23, 1967, p 292*

—*adj.* provoking; provocative.

This consensus—the conventional wisdom of parliamentary liberalism—is expressed with force and charm in Humphrey Berkeley's new book and in spite of his engagingly coat-trailing title, most of his attention is devoted to it. *David Marquand, "Down to Size," Review of "The Power of the Prime Minister" by Humphrey Berkeley, The Listener, April 11, 1968, p 476*

[from the British idiom *trail one's coat* (for someone to tread on), meaning to provoke an attack or quarrel; the original idiom was *drag* (or *trail*) *one's coattails*]

COBOL or **Cobol** ('kou,bɑl), *n.* acronym for *Common Business Oriented Language*, a computer language widely used in industry and government. Compare ALGOL, BASIC, FORTRAN.

COBOL has also passed through several stages of improvement and by 1968 also had been adopted as an American Standard. *Van Court Hare, Jr., Introduction to Programming: A BASIC Approach, 1970, p 27*

Compiler writers learnt their trade and eventually standard languages emerged: Algol and Fortran for scientific purposes and Cobol for business applications. *A. d'Agapayeff, "Software Engineering," Science Journal, Oct. 1970, p 96*

cock·a·ma·mie or **cock·a·ma·my** ('kɑk ə,mei mi:), *U.S. Slang. —adj.* foolish, absurd, or nonsensical.

If there are some confining or irritating or cockamamy rules of the house . . . these should be explained in advance. *Robert Evett, "The Critics and the Public," The Atlantic, Sept. 1970, p 118*

—n. something foolish, absurd, or nonsensical.

. . . Arlen characterized the drama as "a ninety-minute uninterrupted cliché . . . the most asinine and inept piece of cockamamie that I'd seen all year." *Richard Burgheim, "Performing Arts: Television Reviewing," Review of 1967 CBS Playhouse show "The Final War of Olly Winter," Harper's, Aug. 1969, p 100*

[probably an altered form of *decalcomania* the fad or mania for using decals]

cocktail belt, a suburban area thought of as typically inhabited by cocktail drinkers. Compare COMMUTER BELT.

Consider, for example, two large primary schools of almost identical design and suburban location, one of which serves a neighbouring industrial zone while the other stretches out to the lower cocktail belt. *Colin Brock, "A Guide to Modern Education: How Should Parents Assess a School?" The Times (London), Dec. 30, 1970, p 7*

cock-up, *n. British Slang.* a clumsy muddle or mess; confusion.

This is why Marx still towers above his whole field, and why William James does, too, since he, with Freud, adds up to a sort of American Marx. The Russians have made a proper cock-up of Marx, and the Americans of James-Freud. *Wayland Kennet, "Read-all-about-it," Review of "Revolution" by William Braden, The Sunday Times (London), June 6, 1971, p 31*

Peter Jenkins believes in the "cock-up" theory of history. There are no conspiracies, no villains, and very few heroes; everything can be explained by reference to an endless series of confusions, mistakes, and misjudgments. *W. E. J. McCarthy, "Too Late A Hero," Review of "The Battle of Downing Street" by Peter Jenkins, The Manchester Guardian Weekly, Sept. 12, 1970, p 19*

cod, *adj. British.* of the nature of a parody or take-off; mock; burlesque; farcical.

And why are these trendy mirthmen falling back on such traditional devices as cod advertisements and cod answers-to-correspondents, the staple of joke factories elsewhere? *E. S. Turner, "Busty Substances," The Listener, Nov. 25, 1971, p 730*

He and Miss Black repeated the cod opera sketch they did in their stage revue last year and which contains a treasurable moment when Mr. Howard looks at an embroidered silk purse hanging about his waist and forestalls our derision by explaining: "Well, I wasn't going to leave *this* in the dressing room." *Michael Billington, The Times (London), March 20, 1968, p 8*

[adjective use of *cod, n.,* a slang or dialect word for a hoax, a humbug, of unknown origin]

code, *v.i.* **code for,** to specify the genetic code for synthesizing (a particular protein, etc.).

. . . they contain more than enough RNA—about 3300 nucleotides—whereas only 3000 or so are needed to code for the three proteins. *Peter Stubbs and Gerald Wick, New Scientist, Dec. 18, 1969, p 590*

. . . the structural genes that code for this enzyme [phosphorylase kinase] were identified from research with inbred mouse strains in which the parent consistently has a higher level of muscle glycogen than the offspring. *Barbara J. Culliton, Science News, Aug. 9, 1969, p 119*

co·don ('kou,dɑn), *n.* a group of three chemical bases in a certain order, forming the genetic code for producing a particular amino acid.

A sequence of three nucleotides—known as a codon —is required to specify one amino acid. . . . The codon which consists of three uracil residues, for example, specifies the amino acid phenylalanine; other codons act as punctuation marks, coding for the beginning and end of a protein. *Robert Cox, "The Ribosome—Decoder of Genetic Information," Science Journal, Nov. 1970, p 57*

Since there are 64 different triplets, but only 20 amino acids, most amino acids are coded by more than one codon. The amino acid leucine, for example, has six codons, proline has four, and tyrosine has two. Only methionine and tryptophan have one each. *Francis H. C. Crick, "The Language of Life: The Genetic Code," 1969 Britannica Yearbook of Science and the Future, 1968, p 134*

[from *code* + *-on,* as in *ion, nucleon,* etc.]

cods·wal·lop ('kɑdz,wɑl əp), *n. British Slang.* nonsense; rubbish.

The farmers have begun to voice their passionate objections to the loss of their homes and livelihood. . . . Up stands a farmer. "Codswallop, sir," he says as only a Devon farmer can. *Peter Pringle, "Spectrum: Environment, The Human Cost of Saving Beauty," The Sunday Times (London), July 11, 1971, p 7*

"That what they teach you up college?" sneered Hidius Bulbus. . . . "Filling your head with a lot of radical Christian codswallop about equal rights." *Alan Coren, "Defence Axe to Save £MMD a Day by LXIX?" Punch, Jan. 17, 1968, p 74*

[originally a phrase *cod's wallop*]

coffee-table, *adj.* of or relating to coffee-table books; characterized by unusually large size and lavish illustration.

Yet the welter of data implies that it is scarcely bedtime reading for the common man with a purely cultural interest in science. So who is its target? The relatively small group of amateur astronomers? Most, I feel, would rather outlay the cash on improving their observing equipment since it is always this rather than literature that is inadequate. Presumably, therefore, its buyers will be mostly schools and libraries with a smattering of coffee-table enthusiasts. *Peter Stubbs, "Books: Out of This World," Review of "The Atlas of the Universe" by Patrick Moore, New Scientist, Nov. 12, 1970, p 339*

coffee-table book, an oversized, expensive, and richly illustrated book, usually dealing with a specialized subject and designed for display on a coffee table or the like.

Like many coffee-table books, this one is very scholarly, and I suppose that the accuracy and intelligence of presentation is intended to make up for the book's physical unwieldiness. *Martin Dodsworth, "For Bard-lovers," Review of "The Complete Pelican Shakespeare," edited by Alfred Harbage, The Manchester Guardian Weekly, Sept. 6, 1969, p 19*

Though it offers a lot more, "Art and the Seafarer" seems like a well-appointed coffeetable book. It would have no trouble qualifying for one. It is large (10 by 12) and because of the heavy, glossy paper used, weighty enough. *The New York Times, July 20, 1968, p 25*

cofigurative, *adj.* of or designating a form of society in which each generation or peer group evolves its own values.

Margaret Mead [American anthropologist] establishes models of three kinds of societies and their methods of transition from one generation to the other. The oldest she calls "postfigurative," in which grandchildren, parents, and children exist together. Wisdom resides in the old, who have lived through it all, and change is slow. The "cofigurative," like the United States before 1940, where often the grandparents' languages and traditions were meaningless to their children and to their children's children, was a society in which adults and children alike learned from their peers, a society of mobility and improvisation. This society we are now still trying to perpetuate after its day is past.

What we now require and what Margaret Mead . . . believes is coming is the "prefigurative" society, worldwide, in which the role of parents, to oversimplify her argument, perhaps, is only to nurture the child, to be custodians of the world and the child until he is old enough to teach us. *John Thompson, "Books: Flaming Youth," Review of "Culture and Commitment" by Margaret Mead, Harper's, Jan. 1970, p 95*

cold, *n.* **come in from the cold,** to come out of a condition of isolation or neglect.

Main interest of the moment is centred on Cambridge. Taking advantage of the blizzard conditions they have spent a period of "splendid isolation" . . . at the bleakest of training waters, even in normal conditions at Ely. . . . So it is with great interest that we await for an enigmatic Cambridge [boating crew] to "come in from the cold". *Jim Railton, "Cambridge Come in from the Cold," The Times (London), March 10, 1970, p 12*

[popularized by the title *The Spy Who Came in From the Cold*, a best-selling novel (1964) of espionage by John Le Carré (pseudonym of David Cornwell, former British diplomat)]

Cold Duck, *U.S.* an inexpensive mixture of sparkling burgundy and champagne.

There were posters on the walls from old musical-comedy films, and, in celebration, coffee and Cold Duck were served. *"The Talk Of The Town," The New Yorker, Sept. 11, 1971, p 32*

The Nation's thirst for Cold Duck began to rise last August. . . . Whether they were moved by the fad or frugality, New Year's revelers decided that Cold Duck was just the tipple with which to see out the inflationary old year and toast in the uncertain new one. *Time, Jan. 12, 1970, p 47*

[translation of German *Kalte Ente*, alteration of *kalte Ende* cold ends, a phrase used to describe leftover wines mixed and served at the close of a party]

cold mooner, a person who believes that there is no thermal or volcanic activity in the moon's core and that the craters on the moon were formed by the impact of meteorites rather than by volcanic activity. Compare HOT MOONER.

. . . probably most of the moon's craters were formed by meteorite impact and not by volcanic activity. The cold mooners, led by Dr. Harold Urey, are definitely in the ascendant. *Adam Raphael, "Moon Shock Waves Shake Scientists," The Manchester Guardian Weekly, Nov. 29, 1969, p 3*

There are two main theories about the nature of the moon, namely the Hot Moon theory and the Cold Moon theory, and the rivalry between the hot-mooners and the cold-mooners (referring to the temperature of the core) is the center of this story. *Jean M. Halloran, "Books in Brief," Review of "Moon Rocks" by Henry S. F. Cooper, Harper's, Sept. 1970, p 106*

Cold Warrior, a politician or statesman who plays an active part in the power struggle between the Soviet Union and the western nations known as the Cold War.

The selection of Robert McNamara and Roswell Gilpatric for the Department of Defense (although neither was an enthusiastic Cold Warrior) affirmed further the continuing delegation of foreign policy to businessmen and the New York Establishment. *John Kenneth Galbraith, "Who Needs The Democrats?" Harper's, July 1970, p 50*

Such veteran cold warriors as Henry Cabot Lodge and Dean Acheson, arguing that the only riskless settlement is victory on the battlefield, contend that the U.S. should not seek negotiations but do more to win the war. *Time, Dec. 22, 1967, p 16*

[blend of *Cold War* and *warrior*]

col·lage (kə'lɑːʒ), *v.t.* to compose in the form of a collage; assemble, combine, or paste (a collection of odd parts or pieces) on a surface to form an artistic composition.

At the Lisson gallery Peter Schmidt is showing a series of "Monoprints", made by collaging together the most varied material from his own past. . . . *Guy Brett, "The Arts: Kitaj's Spectres," The Times (London), April 28, 1970, p 7*

The platform is painted and collaged in Rauschenberg's customary manner, with such random objects as a tennis ball, a rubber heel, a shirt sleeve, and numerous action photographs from magazines and newspapers. *Calvin Tomkins, "Profiles: Moving Out," The New Yorker, Feb. 29, 1964, p 84*

[verb use of the noun]

col·lap·sar (kə'læp‚sɑr), *n.* another name for BLACK HOLE.

Cameron agrees that a large particulate disc is present but calculates that the binary system is in a high state of evolution and that the secondary component is a collapsar. *"Monitor: First Glimpse of the Dusty Rim of a Cosmic Black Hole?" New Scientist and Science Journal, Jan. 21, 1971, p 104*

These dimouts could not be due simply to a black hole passing in front of Epsilon Aurigae; the collapsar would have to be improbably large to cause that effect. *Time, April 5, 1971, p 32*

[from *collapse* + *-ar*, as in *quasar* and *pulsar*]

collectivism, *n.* the tendency to act or think as a group instead of individually.

The entrapments of collectivism are overwhelming: TV and radio, which permeate our privacy and destroy the aloneness out of which it becomes possible to learn to build a self; drugs, which smash the mirror of personal identity; ... the debilitation of the arts; the great gray educational machine; the devaluing and disparaging of the imagination. ... *Jerzy Kosinski, "Dead Souls on Campus," The New York Times, Oct. 13, 1970, p 45*

▶ The usual sense of *collectivism* is that of collective economic control by the state, as in a socialist country.

collegiality, *n.* the doctrine of the Roman Catholic Church that the bishops, as spiritual descendants of the Apostles, collectively share ruling power over the Church with the Pope.

Thus the theological concept of "collegiality," endorsed at the [Vatican] council, means that bishops are not to be regarded as agents of the home office in Rome, but as co-governors of the church along with the Pope. *The New York Times, March 9, 1968, p 15*

collide, *v.t.* to strike together; bring into collision.

At Cambridge, a bypass that allows beams of electrons and positrons to be stored in the accelerator's ring so that they may be collided has recently been completed, and beams of both positrons and electrons successfully held in it for a sufficient amount of time. The next steps are to store the two kinds of particles simultaneously, collide them and increase the beam intensities. ... *Dietrick E. Thomsen, "High-Energy Physics Suffers a Setback," Science News, March 21, 1970, p 299*

▶ The transitive verb has been regarded as archaic or obsolete since the 1800's.

color-blind, *adj.* not discriminating between blacks and whites; unbiased as to a person's color.

... the Governor of South Carolina called for a state government that would be color blind. *Mary E. Mebane, "Headlong Into the 19th Century," The New York Times, June 11, 1971, p 35*

Dr. Donald Meeks, PhD, assistant professor of psychiatric social work at the University of Toronto, had for five years been lost in the relatively color-blind university worlds of Boston and Toronto, where he [a Negro] had been permitted for days at a time "to regard myself as just another human being." *Alan Edmonds, "The Beautiful People of Detroit, A Report on How It Feels to Be Black," Maclean's, Dec. 1967, p 49*

color-code, *v.t.* to code or key by the use of different colors to denote different items or categories.

... return envelopes have been color-coded with orange trim for Ontario, green for Quebec. *The New York Times, March 19, 1967, p 22*

... by the time full-scale defoliation operations got under way in Vietnam the U.S. military had settled on the use of four herbicidal spray materials there. These went under the names Agent Orange, Agent Purple, Agent White, and Agent Blue — designations derived from color-coded stripes girdling the shipping drums of each type of material. *Thomas Whiteside, "A Reporter At Large: Defoliation," The New Yorker, Feb. 7, 1970, p 34*

color-key, *v.t.* another word for COLOR-CODE.

The Forum's color theme invades the 25-acre parking lot. Season ticket holders get three color-keyed tickets, one for parking in the right colored area, the second for entry to the reserved seats (follow the coppertone or gold pathway), and the third for admission to the Forum Club. *Eric Hutton, "This is the Team That Jack Built," Maclean's, Dec. 1967, p 58*

colourway, *n. British.* a color scheme.

Patterns and plain colours blend happily together, within fairly loosely defined colourways and sizing is standardized. *"Counterpoint," The Times (London), Dec. 4, 1970, p 16*

combination drug, an antibacterial drug made up of two or more active ingredients.

First to go from the drugstores, and already decertified by the FDA [Food and Drug Administration] are many of the "combination drugs," so called because they contain two antibiotics, or an antibiotic and one of the sulfa drugs. ... Some contain streptomycin, which may cause deafness, especially in children, and so should never be used unless it is the only drug that will kill the particular microbes involved. *Time, July 25, 1969, p 38*

combinatorics, *n.* a branch of mathematics that deals with the permutations and combinations of elements in finite sets.

Niven writes an informal, clear algebra of combinatorics for high school students and mathematical amateurs. *Philip and Phylis Morrison, "Books," Review of "Mathematics of Choice, or How to Count Without Counting" by Ivan Niven, Scientific American, Dec. 1966, p 145*

combine, *n.* an artistic work made up of a combination of painting, collage, and construction.

His [Merce Cunningham's] feeling that any movement can be part of a dance has its echo in the assemblages and combines of Robert Rauschenberg, among others. *Calvin Tomkins, "An Appetite for Motion," The New Yorker, May 4, 1968, p 78*

comb-out, *n.* a combing and arranging of the hair to form a hair style or keep it in place.

Vanessa [Redgrave] washed her own hair in midafternoon, then summoned Beverly Hills *Coiffeur* Carrie White for a comb-out and had her add a cascading fall for greater thickness. *Time, April 21, 1967, p 58*

come, *v.i. Especially U.S.* **1 come on,** to make a strong impression; have a strong effect (shortened from the phrase *come on strong*). In the phrase *come on like gangbusters*, the reference is to the name of an old radio program that came on the air with a crescendo of loud sounds.

[Senator] Muskie is not coming on like gangbusters. He is coming on the way Ohio State plays football, slowly and methodically, doing one thing at a time with just enough momentum to keep going forward. *Joseph Kraft, "Reports and Comment: Washington, The Muskie Problem," The Atlantic, June 1971, p 6*

... he [Robert Finch, then Secretary of the Department of Health, Education, and Welfare] is the youngest of the Secretaries, and he comes on as the can-do guy, a style that is very popular around here. *Elizabeth B. Drew, "Washington," The Atlantic, April 1969, p 14*

2 come out, to become openly homosexual.

Today's homosexual can be open ("come out") or covert ("closet"), practicing or inhibited, voluntary or compulsive, conscious or unaware, active or passive, manly ("stud") or womanly ("fem"). The difference between unconscious willingness and conscious unwillingness has thinned. Now the homosexual's variations are seen as such that he may act homosexually and not *be* homosexual, or be gay only off and on. *Faubion Bowers, "Homosex: Living The Life," Saturday Review, Feb. 12, 1972, p 24*

co·mé·die de moeurs (kɔ: mei'di: də 'mœrs), *French.* comedy of manners; comedy characterized by wit and social satire.

Certain themes were followed up over a period of years, like the "Scherzi" (jokes) series improvised between 1735 and 1740, and present a vivid comedie de moeurs very much paralleled by the caustic ironies of Goldoni. *Caroline Tisdall, "Golden Age and Youth," The Manchester Guardian Weekly, Sept. 4, 1971, p 20*

Fishes, Birds and Sons of Men, as its name might suggest, has variety within these general patterns. There are several *comédies de moeurs*, sharp in detail and in dialogue.... *Kenneth Graham, "Books: Dreams of the Southland," Review of "Fishes, Birds and Sons of Men" by Jesse Hill Ford, The Listener, April 18, 1968, p 511*

► Note the French plural form in the quotation from *The Listener*, which also includes the French diacritical mark and italicizes the term to show that it is foreign. *The Manchester Guardian Weekly* treats the term as if it were English. The use of a French instead of an equivalent English term is more fashionable in Great Britain than in the United States; an American writer would almost always use *comedy of manners* instead of the French term.

co·mé·die lar·mo·yante (kɔ: mei'di: lar mwa'yãt), *French.* sentimental or romantic type of comedy; (literally) tearful comedy.

They [Nicholas and Alexandra of Russia] arrived in a historic bundle of ideas and tastes and works—genre painting, *comédie larmoyante*, "Pamela," "Emile." *Naomi Bliven, "Babes in the Wood," Review of "Nicholas and Alexandra" by Robert K. Massie, The New Yorker, March 23, 1968, p 154*

co·mé·die noire (kɔ: mei'di: 'nwar), *French.* black comedy (comedy based on absurd, grotesque, or morbid situations).

...in *Schicchi* [Puccini's comedy *Gianni Schicchi*], while amused at Schicchi's guile, we feel vaguely uncomfortable at the *comédie noire* being enacted before us. *Alan Blyth, The Listener, Oct. 13, 1966, p 549*

comedywright, *n.* a writer of comedies.

She [Bech's mother]...pointed out to him, with that ardor for navigational detail that had delayed their arrival here,... the massive Jason Honeygale, Tennessee's fabled word-torrent; hawk-eyed Torquemada Langguth, lover and singer of California's sheer cliffs and sere unpopulated places; and Manhattan's own Josh Glazer, Broadway wit, comedywright, lyricist, and Romeo. *John Updike, Bech: A Book, 1970, p 178*

command module, the unit or section of a spacecraft which contains the control center and living quarters. *Abbreviation:* CM Compare SERVICE MODULE, LUNAR MODULE.

The crew of Apollo 13 returned safely to the earth on April 17, 1970. The astronauts remained in the lunar mod-

ule until just before reentry into the earth's atmosphere; they then moved into the command module,... and jettisoned the lunar module. *Richard S. Johnston, "Astronautics and Space Exploration: Apollo 13," 1971 Britannica Yearbook of Science and the Future, 1970, p 126*

Common Marketeer, one who favors joining the Common Market, especially in Great Britain.

Blackpool has as big and variegated a fringe this week as Edinburgh at festival time. Thirty-six meetings:... Friends of Israel, enemies of Israel, Common Marketeers and anti-Marketeers. *"Miscellany: Blackpool's Fringe Benefits," The Manchester Guardian Weekly, Oct. 3, 1970, p 11*

communard, *n.* a member or inhabitant of a commune.

To live in a commune...undermines the property ethic.... When a dozen people share the bills, they can afford to carry a couple of communards who want to take a week off, or who want to try to survive by selling newspapers, or selling marijuana, or pan-handling. *Martin Walker, "Looking for a New Utopia," The Manchester Guardian Weekly, March 27, 1971, p 6*

commune, *n.* a place where anyone can stay for a night, a week, or as long as he likes, living with others like himself and usually sharing work or expenses with other members.

A major purpose of today's communes—organized by such varied movements as hippies, political radicals, religious groups and humanistic psychologists—is to seek a sense of family warmth and intimacy, Dr. Rosabeth Kanter, a sociologist at Brandeis, reports in the July PSYCHOLOGY TODAY. Two major forms of the commune are emerging: the anarchistic and the growth center. *Science News, July 25, 1970, p 68*

communications gap, a failure of understanding, usually because of a lack of information, especially between different age groups, economic classes, political factions, or cultural groups.

...our modern Technological society is now so complex that its problems can only be managed by innumerable cadres of specialists. As a result there is a growing gulf—a widening "communications gap"—between the governors and the governed. *"The Gipsy's Warning" (an editorial), New Scientist, May 30, 1968, p 445*

The communications gap can also have a serious effect on the refugee relief and rehabilitation programme. *Michael Wolfers, The Times (London), Feb. 2, 1970, p 5*

► The model for *communications gap* and several other popular "gap" phrases was the political catchphrase *missile gap*, coined during the 1960 U.S. presidential election to describe the alleged Soviet superiority over the United States in rocket weapons. Subsequently many phrases such as *news gap, production gap, culture gap,* and *development gap* began appearing. Among the latest and best known of these phrases are CREDIBILITY GAP and GENERATION GAP.

commute, *n.* a trip to and from work by a commuter.

...a liberal-minded chap in a New York suburb put his house on the market and got ready to move to one where there was more room for his family and which was an easier commute. *Jerome Beaty, Jr., "Trade Winds," Saturday Review, Oct. 12, 1968, p 16*

When he [Donald T. Regan, president of Merrill Lynch, Pierce, Fenner & Smith] returned to Pine Street [in New York City] he continued living in Bryn Mawr [near Philadelphia] to let his four children grow up in accustomed surroundings. That decision has meant a two-hour commute twice a day ever since. *Time, April 19, 1968, p 53A*

[noun use of *commute, v.i.*]

commuter belt, a suburban area typically inhabited by commuters. Compare COCKTAIL BELT.

"An empty country church," says the Rev. Philip Goodrich, vicar of a commuter-belt church near London, reflecting the sentiments of many Britons, "is somehow a much sadder phenomenon than an empty urban church." *Time, March 28, 1969, p 46*

...a marked contrast emerges between the industrial and rural counties on the one hand, and the middle-class commuter belt on the other. *The Times (London), April 27, 1966, p 6*

commuterland or **commuterdom,** *n.* the suburbs where commuters live.

The brightly lit hurly-burly of Times Square inspired Greek-born Chryssa to build stainless steel, neon and Plexiglas in a work called "The Gates." It now stands at the gates to commuterland, in Grand Central Station, in hot competition with surrounding commercial neon. *Picture legend, "Sculpture: The New Shapes," Time, Oct. 13, 1967, p 38*

...the past sixty years have seen the growth of commuterdom, with all its attendant frustrations, health hazards, and crazy economics. The existing bus and train services simply are not good enough for many commuters who find it easier to take their car to work. *"Comment: Commuterland," The Manchester Guardian Weekly, Sept. 5, 1968, p 13*

The canal crosses the expanding commuterdom around Farnborough, Fleet and Aldershot. *Brian Jackman, "Canals, Living and Dying," the Sunday Times (London), Aug. 1, 1971, p 20*

commuter tax, an income tax levied by a city on people who commute to work there.

Let me state unequivocally that I will be proud to continue these same payments in the form of a commuter tax to insure such fine departments as the New York City Fire Department and Police Department. *Charles G. Bennett, The New York Times, Feb. 5, 1967, p 44*

commuterville, *n.* a suburb where commuters live.

One cannot be categorical, but broadly speaking it is the Labour seats which get clobbered and the traditional Tory hinterland of owner-occupied commuterville which grows fat. *Harold Jackson, "Battles on the Boundaries," The Manchester Guardian Weekly, June 12, 1971, p 9*

compiler, *n.* a computer program which translates instructions written in a computer language to the internal code (machine language) of a specific computer.

The translation [source-language statement into the appropriate series of machine-language instructions] is accomplished by a computer program (set of instructions) previously written and stored in the machine's memory. This type of program is called a "compiler." A given source language is associated with a particular compiler. *Henry R. Lieberman and Louis Robinson, The New York Times, Jan. 9, 1967, p 137*

compiler language, the coding system of a com-

piler. Also called ASSEMBLER LANGUAGE or ASSEMBLY LANGUAGE. Compare COMPUTER LANGUAGE, MACHINE LANGUAGE.

For our purposes, the compiler language can also be translated into a logical form in which the computer can think. The machine can then make deductions and, more important, inductions.... *F. H. George, "Making Machines More Intelligent," New Scientist, June 15, 1967, p 657*

completist, *n.* one who sets completeness or completion as his goal. *Also used attributively.*

Among the veteran collectors [of science fiction]...was Gerry de la Ree, who identified himself as a forty-three-year-old "completist." "That means I buy everything that comes out in the field, and never throw anything away".... *"The Talk of the Town: Evolution and Ideation," The New Yorker, Sept. 16, 1967, p 38*

The "completist attitude," which has governed several projects, finds the company [Columbia Records] in the position of either having finished or nearing the end of the complete recorded works of Stravinsky, Varèse, Webern, Schönberg, and Copland.... *Robert Jacobson, "New Means for New Music," Saturday Review, Sept. 28, 1968, p 59*

compressed speech, speech reproduced at a faster than the normal rate without loss of understandability by being fed into a machine which automatically clips out certain sound segments.

Some 48 Virginia children with Negro dialects have learned to speak better English through compressed speech. They learned considerably faster than with normal language instruction.... All the children, ranging from kindergarten through third grade, made significant gains in articulating and hearing good English.... Lessons were initially presented at 100 words per minute, a little less than normal speaking rate, and then increased to 50 percent faster than normal. *Science News, Nov. 25, 1967, p 516*

com·pu- ('kam pyu:-), combining form for "computer," as in the following:

computalk, *n.:* Computalk...My article, "Talking to the Computer," (4 December, p. 498) was not intended as a learned paper describing and justifying all the techniques used in our recognition processes. *E. H. Lenaerts, London, England, in a Letter to the Editor, New Scientist, Jan. 8, 1970, p 76*

Computicket, *n.:* Another, about to be introduced, is Computicket which will link every kind of entertainment from baseball to ballet to local outlets like supermarkets.... *Time, May 31, 1968, p 51*

compuword, *n.:* Nevertheless, when questioned recently in fluent computalk at the House of Commons terminal by the leader of the Opposition, who asked about the implications of taking a strong policy against South Africa, the computer's only reply was the enigmatic compuword, "benn". *"Computer Diplomacy in Jeopardy," New Scientist, Jan. 1, 1970, p 19*

computational linguistics, the use of computers to collect and correlate linguistic information.

It [Communications Science Division] contends that what it calls computational linguistics—studies in parsing, sentence generation, structure, semantics and statistics, and including experiments in translation—deserves to be recognized and supported as a science. *The New York Times, Nov. 25, 1966, p 29*

computer dating, the arrangement of social engagements between single men and women by programming a computer to match their characteristics according to prescribed types; matchmaking by computer.

But the director, Brian De Palma, and the producer, Charles Hirsch, who wrote this movie [*"Greetings"*] together ...threw in another plot, about a computer dating service, that is very low-grade stuff. *Pauline Kael, "The Current Cinema," The New Yorker, Dec. 21, 1968, p 91*

computerese, *n.* **1** the terminology or jargon of scientists and others working with computers.

Ziegler [White House press secretary], who worked in Haldeman's advertising agency, mixes computerese into his briefings: he talks of "inputs" and "outputs," of "implementing" a policy within a "time frame".... *"How Nixon's White House Works: Muse Together," Time, June 8, 1970, p 18*

2 computer language.

It can be programmed in English, instead of "computerese." This means it can be re-programmed by your own staff to fit your expanding operations. *Advertisement by Friden (a division of Singer), Saturday Review, Jan. 13, 1968, p 35*

A book to get lost in, but not to despair of. One day we may all write computerese. The machine is neither master nor servant but friend—as in traffic-lights. *Cyril Connolly, "In the Beginning Was the Word," Review of "Cybernetics, Art and Ideas," edited by Jasia Reichardt, The Sunday Times (London), June 20, 1971, p 29*

computer graphics, art or design produced on computers.

The objective of most computer-graphics programs is easily stated: to represent objects of some kind and to provide a means for manipulating them. *Ivan E. Sutherland, "Computer Displays: The Logic of Displays," Scientific American, June 1970, p 65*

Computer graphics: new tool of industrial designers. Here the technique is used to visualize the Boeing 737 and to study human movements within the plane. *Picture legend, "Art and the Computer," Encyclopedia Science Supplement (Grolier) 1970, p 339*

computerizable, *adj.* that can be programmed for analysis, control, etc., by a computer.

The other main reason he [Dr. Kendall] gives for the Edwards committee appointment was that it needed someone who understood computer systems, and who could discern "the aspects of the organization which was computerizable". *New Scientist, May 15, 1969, p 368*

computerization, *n.* the use of computers; mechanization or automation by means of computers.

Some people in the trade believe that computerization will eventually result in great master lists of all magazine readers and all gadget buyers. *Calvin Trillin, "Onward and Upward with the Arts," The New Yorker, Sept. 24, 1966, p 158*

"...In a world of increasing mass production, automation and computerization, values based on a sense of extraordinary quality are irrelevant." *Art critic Toby Mussman, quoted by Harry Malcolmson, "Sculpture," Saturday Night (Canada), Jan. 1968, p 41*

computerize, *v.t.* to analyze, control, or equip with computers.

A computerized communications system will be in operation by 1970, giving the department centralized control over the entire police force. *The New York Times, March 16, 1968, p 30*

—*v.i.* to change to the use of computers in commerce, industry, etc.; adopt computerization.

It is vital if Britain is going to computerize that there should be a sufficient supply of people with experience, ingenuity—and genius—to programme our computers. *The Times (London), Jan. 7, 1965, p 14*

computer language, any of various alphabetical and numerical systems for programming computers according to rules of grammar or logic. Also called PROGRAMMING LANGUAGE. See the entries ALGOL, BASIC, COBOL, and FORTRAN for examples of computer languages. Compare COMPILER LANGUAGE, MACHINE LANGUAGE.

To apply computers to everyday problems, the user needs to know...: 1. What he wants to do and the specific logical steps necessary to perform that job. 2. The grammar and syntax (subsequently described) of a particular computer language, so he can communicate his desires to the machine. *Van Court Hare, Jr., Introduction to Programming: A BASIC Approach, 1970, p 110*

computerman, *n.* a computer scientist.

For the computerman or management theoretician it is tempting to design the ideal system, extracting the most from the computer, handling information in the most efficient way.... *Kenneth Owen, "Technology: Introducing a Non-system System," The Times (London), Sept. 25, 1970, p 26*

computer science, the science of computers, including computer design, devising of computer languages, programming, data processing, and related specializations.

D. L. Slotnick ("The Fastest Computer") is professor of computer science and director of the Center for Advanced Computation at the University of Illinois. *"The Authors," Scientific American, Feb. 1971, p 12*

computer scientist, a specialist in some aspect of computer science.

Effective work by computer scientists and behavioural psychologists is going on, but it is not to be learned about here. *Keith Oatley, Review of "Biology of Memory," edited by K. H. Pribram and D. E. Broadbent, New Scientist and Science Journal, May 20, 1971, p 478*

computery, *n.* **1** computer systems; computers collectively.

The problems for this Beckenham-based group, which has recently been adding computery and sophisticated mechanical filing systems to its staple lines of sales and book-keeping stationery and loose-leaf binders, were twofold. *Tony Aldous, "Management: For Twinlock, Decimalization Really Started Happening in 1967," The Times (London), March 16, 1970, p 24*

2 the use, manufacture, or operation of computers.

The key element in the campaign, though, will be straightforward economy, rather than any high-flown appeal to rationalisation and computery. *Peter Wilsher, The Sunday Times (London), Jan. 14, 1968, p 31*

comsat, *n.* **1** a communications satellite; an artificial earth satellite that transmits or relays electronic signals from one point to another on earth.

...Europe is at last beginning to develop real skill in building sensible space technology—comsats, navigation satellites, weather satellites.... *Nigel Hawkes, "The Month: Space Shuttle: NASA Leads Europe in Military Two-step," Science Journal, Oct. 1970, p 5*

2 Also, **Comsat** or **COMSAT,** the Communications Satellite Corporation, a U.S. government-sponsored commercial system for launching communications satellites.

Transmissions between the United States and Europe accounted for four hours and 45 minutes of satellite time, the company, known informally as Comsat, said. *The New York Times, April 2, 1968, p 31*

Through the National Aeronautics and Space Administration programs and the operation of the international communications satellite network by COMSAT, considerable experience has been amassed in this field. *Science News, Aug. 22 and 29, 1970, p 160*

[from *communications satellite*]

Comsymp, *n. U.S.* one who sympathizes with the Communist party or its aims.

Ron Gostick makes a living telling people Trudeau is a Comsymp. You'd be amazed how many people believe him. *Jon Ruddy, "Comsymp," Maclean's, Sept. 1968, p 56*

[from *Comm*unist *symp*athizer]

▶ This term is closest in sense to the earlier *fellow traveler.* A related term, *pink* or *pinko,* is applied to any political radical or leftist, as distinguished from *Red,* which is usually synonymous with Communist. *Comsymp* and *pinko* are terms of contempt.

COMUSMACV (ˌkɑm əs mæk'viː), *n.* acronym for *Com*mander *U*nited *S*tates *M*ilitary *A*ssistance *C*ommand, *V*ietnam. Compare MACV.

"There is no military solution to this problem of Vietnam," said General William C. Westmoreland to me. "The solution has to be one hundred per cent political." This was in August 1964 in Saigon. He had by then been COMUSMACV, the chief U.S. Military adviser, for about six months. *Blair Clark, "Westmoreland Appraised: Questions and Answers," Harper's, Nov. 1970, p 96*

▶ *COMUSMAC-* is like *Cinc-* (Commander-in-Chief). To both of these may be added numerous area designations: *V* for Vietnam, as in COMUSMACV; *Thai* for Thailand, as in COMUSMACThai; so also with *Eur* (Europe), *Pac* (Pacific), and *lant* (Atlantic).

concelebrant, *n.* a clergyman who celebrates the Mass jointly with another.

The office of the Most Rev. Terence J. Cooke, Roman Catholic Archbishop of New York, said yesterday that he would be the chief concelebrant at the requiem mass.... *Edward B. Fiske, The New York Times, June 7, 1968, p 21*

conceptual art or **concept art,** a form of art in which the works are intended to reflect an idea or concept in the artist's mind during the process of creation. For examples, see EMPAQUETAGE, EARTHWORKS. See also ANTIFORM. Also called PROCESS ART or IMPOSSIBLE ART.

"Conceptual Art and Conceptual Aspects" takes a reading on the proliferation of contemporary artists who reject art-as-object for what might be called art-as-idea. *Time, May 11, 1970, p 2*

Dada art of social confrontation and Bauhaus art-to-be-used-up have culminated in art as event, factory-made art, art-to-be-thrown-away, conceptual art, art as hearsay (the actual substance of most "earth" art, inasmuch as the public rarely sees it). *Harold Rosenberg, "The Art World: Thoughts in Off-Season," The New Yorker, July 24, 1971, p 62*

Some U.S. museums also began to document the avant-garde "process" or "concept" art, which involved only ideas and their realization in a situation, or a series of events, that did not always produce objects or traditional works of art. *Joshua B. Kind, "Museums," The 1970 Compton Yearbook, p 359*

conceptual artist, another name for CONCEPTUALIST.

As for the work of the conceptual artists—those who feel that the idea alone is what counts, and that the artist's idea, sketched or written down, need not necessarily be carried out—Geldzahler finds it provocative, but he doubts whether it will have much historical value. *Calvin Tomkins, "Profiles: Moving With The Flow," The New Yorker, Nov. 6, 1971, p 113*

conceptualist, *n.* an artist who creates works of conceptual art. Also called CONCEPTUAL ARTIST.

Such earthworkers, anti-formers, processors, and conceptualists as [Robert] Morris, Carl Andre, Walter de Maria, Robert Smithson, Bruce Nauman, Richard Serra, Eva Hesse, Barry Flanagan, Keith Sonnier, Dennis Oppenheim, and Lawrence Weiner have been enjoying increasing prestige. *Harold Rosenberg, "The Art World: De-aestheticization," The New Yorker, Jan. 24, 1970, p 62*

concerned, *adj.* involved in or troubled about current social or political problems.

And what of our idealistic, "concerned" youth? Do we see them demonstrating and protesting against the inhumanities perpetrated by the Viet Cong as they "liberate" Southeast Asia? No, Sir, they are much too busy ... finding fault with America's defense of democracy. *Dennis H. Martin, Scarborough, Ontario, in a Letter to the Editor, Time, July 13, 1970, p 4*

Students this year cannot believe even the most concerned politician much less move to help his election. *Philip Gennon Ryan, Brooklyn, in a Letter to the Editor, The New York Times, Oct. 8, 1970, p 46*

Con·corde (kɑn'kɔrd), *n.* the commercial supersonic aircraft produced jointly by Great Britain and France.

The British prototype of the new British-French Concorde made its debut at Bristol Airport this year. The jet transport is designed for commercial operation at 1,200 mph—twice the speed of sound. Passenger service is scheduled for 1974. *Picture legend, "Aeronautics," 1970 Collier's Encyclopedia Year Book, p 83*

A great moment in Concorde's history: that is what it seemed at 12.55 p.m. last Thursday. *The Sunday Times (London), April 16, 1972, p 8*

BAC admits that 250 Concordes each making 1,000 three-hour flights a year would pump out 12 million tons of water vapour, 12,000 tons of sulphur dioxide, and 150,000 tons of nitric acid. *The Sunday Times (London), April 16, 1972, p 8*

concrete poem, a combined poem and drawing. See also CONCRETE POETRY. Compare CALLIGRAMME.

[Ian Hamilton] Finlay's concrete poem is part of a wave of poetic experimentation that has been rising in Western Europe and South America recently. *Ronald Gross, "To* be Read and Seen," *The New York Times Book Review,* Feb. 25, 1968, p 4

concrete poet, a writer of concrete poetry. Also called CONCRETIST.

Concrete poets hammer words, syllables and individual letters into every conceivable permutation or physical shape. *Ronald Gross, "To be Read and Seen," The New York Times Book Review, Feb. 25, 1968, p 4*

...if there is a new avant-garde and a new aesthetic—based on, say, John Cage, William Burroughs, Samuel Beckett, the concrete poets, the novelists of the *anti-roman,* and for that matter drugs and negritude—isn't that simply a continuation of all that has been happening in art in our century, and in that sense a problem for art? *Malcolm Bradbury, "Books: Antennae," Review of "Innovations," edited by Bernard Bergonzi, The Listener, Sept. 1968, p 374*

concrete poetry, a form of avant-garde poetry in which words, letters, or fragments of words or letters are arranged in shapes and patterns to form a combined poem and drawing. Also called CONCRETISM.

Concrete poetry is all too often confused with the "Calligrammes" of Apollinaire and their modern equivalents in which lines of text are ingeniously manipulated in order to imitate natural appearances. *Cyril Connolly, The Sunday Times (London), Oct. 15, 1967, p 32*

In concrete poetry words are treated as signs, like forms in concrete painting, and this makes the poet as free to relate them as a concrete artist is to relate forms. *Guy Brett, The Times (London), Dec. 30, 1967, p 19*

Concrete poetry is difficult to describe but easy to recognize. The aim is to give words a new dynamism for the eye—to make the poem a kind of emblem or ikon of what is being said. *Edward Lucie-Smith, The Times (London), Nov. 2, 1965, p 13*

concretism, *n.* another name for CONCRETE POETRY.

Their main idea is to carry over the text of vanguardist poetic experimentation into popular songs; and their selection of lyrics ranges from Oswald de Andrade to Concretism. *Jose F. V. Amaral, "Literature: Latin-American," Britannica Book of the Year 1969, p 478*

concretist, *n.* another name for CONCRETE POET.

The dumbstruck poet may now make his mark as a "concretist," practicing a definition-defying new discipline derived in equal measure from pop art, typewriter doodles and the undeniable truth that a poem is, after all, just so many letters arranged on a page. *Time, April 12, 1968, p 59*

condominium, *n.* *U.S.* an apartment house in which each apartment is bought and owned individually as if it were a house. The land the building is on is usually held by a corporation.

The lack of concrete sensual apperceptions, the lack of interesting events in the lives of the twenty-thousand-a-year technical and professional intelligentsia in the garden suburbs and the highrise condominiums, lies at the root of their...truculent rhetoric. *Kenneth Rexroth, "Books and Men: William Golding," The Atlantic, May 1965, p 97*

Eight residential segments are planned to radiate from the core. The segments will contain private houses and rental or condominium apartments, and each segment will have its own golf course, park and marina. *The New York Times, Feb. 5, 1968, p 54*

[derived from the legal sense (in Roman law) of joint ownership of the same property with individual right of disposal]

conference call, a conference over the telephone between a group of people linked by a central switching unit.

Tuesday a bunch of us neighbors found ourselves being notified to stand by to come in for a conference call initiated by the White House. *Russell Baker, The New York Times, Nov. 19, 1970, p 47*

conformational, *adj.* of or relating to the three-dimensional forms or conformations assumed by molecules in various states.

Six-member ring of cyclohexane, C_6H_{12}, (a solvent used in paint remover) can exist in various shapes known as conformational isomers, or conformers. *Joseph B. Lambert, "The Shapes of Organic Molecules," Scientific American, Jan. 1970, p 59*

conformational analysis, the analysis of molecular shapes or conformations, especially to explain the chemical and physical properties of compounds.

Conformational analysis has revolutionized man's understanding of the structure of compounds. The properties of substances yet to be synthesized can be predicted with far more accuracy than previously. *"The 1969 Nobel Prizes for Physics and Chemistry," Encyclopedia Science Supplement (Grolier) 1970, p 298*

...conformational analysis has been invaluable in the synthesis of pharmacological agents, notably steroids and antibiotics of the tetracycline and penicillin families. *Joseph B. Lambert, "The Shapes of Organic Molecules," Scientific American, Jan. 1970, p 58*

confrontationist, *adj.* **1** seeking, supporting, or advocating confrontation.

...the confrontationist politicians of our time...have learned the value not of committing violence but of provoking it. *Richard Hofstadter, "The Future of American Violence," Harper's, April 1970, p 52*

2 clashing with traditional values, methods, etc.

Dubuffet...leads Ragon to wonder whether the part played by confrontationist artists is at all different from that of conformists. *Harold Rosenberg, "The Art World," The New Yorker, June 6, 1970, p 56*

Cong, *n.* short for *Vietcong,* the guerrilla forces in South Vietnam.

Wear him down. Wear the Cong down, and he'll quit. Put him through the meat grinder. Attrit him. He is hurting, said the American commander in mid-1967. *Ward S. Just, "Notes on Losing a War," The Atlantic, Jan. 1969, p 40*

On his left side, Kowalski wore a Bowie knife....He wanted the men to know that if the Cong ever attempted to overrun the airstrip, he Kowalski, would be out on the perimeter, meeting them hand-to-hand. *Alan Coren, "That Fell on the House that Jack Built," Punch, Feb. 21, 1968, p 256*

John, who turned out to have many unique ideas for ending the Vietnam war, said one quick method would be to turn 200 or so Central Park "gorilla fags" loose on the Cong. *Bruce Jay Friedman, "Lessons of the Street," Harper's, Sept. 1971, p 87*

conglobulate, *v.i.* to gather into a ball or globe.

By the time you've dropped fifteen or sixteen [cloves] into the sugary water reason cries out against such excess.

They resemble tadpoles. They conglobulate. *H. F. Ellis, "Cut Out This Receipt," Punch, Jan. 3, 1968, p 10*

► Only the variants *conglobate* and *conglobe* are found in current dictionaries. The *OED*, however, includes *conglobulate*, labeling it *rare* but citing its use by Johnson in Boswell's biography (1768): "A number of them [swallows] conglobulate together, by flying round and round, and then all in a heap throw themselves under water." The present-day form may be a new coinage since the related term, *conglobulation*, has no earlier record.

conglobulation, *n.* the act or result of gathering into a global mass.

What can I say about *Our World* (BBC-1, June 25)—the first-ever conglobulation by direct satellite of global simultaneities? *Anthony Burgess, "Television," The Listener, June 29, 1967, p 863*

Mergers, conglobulations, and joint failures. *Chapter heading in "Up the Organization" by Robert Townsend, Harper's, March 1970, p 81*

conglomeracy, *n.* the formation of commercial conglomerates.

In America the trend to diverse big business togetherness—otherwise known as conglomeracy—is sharply underscored by the announcement that the Weiss Noodle Company has been acquired by Iron Mountain Incorporated. *Philip Clarke, The Listener, April 6, 1969, p 53*

conglomerate, *n.* a huge business corporation formed by the acquisition and merger under unified control of many companies or industries operating in diverse and often entirely unrelated fields.

This was a rich man so vital that he had scarcely a moment to spare for fools.... he might have had me merged into a new conglomerate he was throwing together to forge a financial empire compounded of margarine, men's underwear, plastics, beefsteak and Sicily. *Russell Baker, "Observer: Daddy Warbucks's Secret Weapon," The New York Times, June 6, 1971, Sec. 4, p 15*

Mr. Pelham has been in Japan (a Japanese conglomerate is one of our clients). *John Casey, "Testimony and Demeanor," The New Yorker, June 19, 1971, p 26*

Like most conglomerates, once-glamorous Litton Industries has been struggling through troubled times lately. But last week the company regained some of its old luster by snaring one of the biggest defense awards in history—a $2.1 billion Navy contract to build 30 destroyers. *"Business: Defense," Time, July 6, 1970, p 62*

...many old-line publishers have surrendered their character to become part of a conglomerate empire.... *Edward Weeks, "The/Peripatetic Reviewer," The Atlantic, June 1970, p 125*

One more nice reminder of the past, in these days of conglomerates, is the still independent small shop. *M. M., "On and Off the Avenue," The New Yorker, July 4, 1970, p 58*

conglomerator, conglomerateer, or **conglomerateur,** *n.* the organizer or head of a conglomerate.

So it comes as a pleasant surprise to find this Scots conglomerator bringing Scottish, English and European textiles to the market on a modest, not to say downright low, forward P/E [price-earnings ratio] of 11.6. *Charles Raw, Richard Milner, et al., The Sunday Times (London), April 20, 1969, p 27*

To answer this question, 'Adam Smith' talked to all manner of experts, from "pressure performance" fund specialists (known as "gunslingers") to psychiatrists, from computer-happy economists to that Gnome of Zurich, from tape traders to conglomerateers—people who buy an old bra company, change its name to Space Age Materials and go public. *Eliot Fremont-Smith, The New York Times, June 3, 1968, p 43*

Conglomerateur Charles Bluhdorn figured that Evans was just the man to run Gulf & Western's new bauble, Paramount, and put him in charge. *Time, Jan. 11, 1971, p 31*

[from *conglomerate* + *-or, -eer,* or *-eur* (as in *entrepreneur*)]

conk, *v.t. Afro-American Slang.* to straighten (kinky hair) by rinsing it with lye, using pomade, etc.

First in Boston, then as a teen-ager in the early 1940s, he [Malcolm X] donned a zoot suit and painfully "conked" his hair. *Time, Feb. 23, 1970, p 88*

...street youths with elaborately straightened or "conked" hair, like the ones Dr. King had talked to in pool halls in Birmingham. *The New York Times, April 10, 1968, p 33*

[from earlier *conk, n.,* slang word for a hair straightener, the hair-straightening process, and ultimately the head]

conkout, *n. U.S. Slang.* a breakdown.

"Good morning, sweeties! I'm Sherri, your new Penn Central conductor. If any little old things like delays, derailments, engine conkouts, or fires make you feel icky-poo, you just come and tell little ol' Sherri." *Cartoon legend, The New Yorker, Nov. 14, 1970, p 55*

[from *conk out* to break down]

con-mannerism, *n.* action or bearing like that of a confidence man.

Though Chico's accent was an Italian defamation league all to itself, his shrewd con-mannerisms and manic assaults on the piano were often brilliant pieces of destructive art. *"Restoration Comedy," Review of "The Marx Brothers at the Movies" by Paul D. Zimmerman, Time, March 28, 1969, p 64*

[blend of *con man* and *mannerism;* apparently a *Time* coinage. *Time* also uses a derivative form, *con-mannerist.*]

conmanship, *n.* the art or skill of a confidence man or trickster.

The *Centre of the Action* is a confessional study of conmanship, in a New York jungle where rat eats rat and words are never wasted. *Norman Shrapnel, "Books: Refugees from Domesticity," Review of "The Centre of the Action" by Jerome Weidman, The Manchester Guardian Weekly, March 21, 1970, p 18*

Whether he was selling snake oil to farmers in the Southwest (his three-page sales pitch is a masterpiece of W. C. Fieldsian conmanship) or living it up in those all-purpose ashrams known as "studios" in Greenwich Village, [Kenneth] Rexroth was on top of the left-wing game. *Time, Feb. 25, 1966, p 76*

[from *con man* + *-ship,* probably influenced by *-manship* (see the entry -MANSHIP)]

consciousness-expanding, *adj.* another word for MIND-EXPANDING.

LSD has been called a "mind-expanding" or "consciousness-expanding" drug; its use has been advocated to increase human creative potential, since some people who have taken the substance report strong subjective feelings of creative drive. *John T. Goodman and Conrad Chyatte, "Psychology," Britannica Book of the Year 1968, p 652*

Consciousness I, II, and **III,** the designations given in Charles A. Reich's book *The Greening of America,* 1970, to three types of outlooks or perceptions of reality that predominate in America today. See also CORPORATE STATE.

Consciousness I is the traditional outlook of the American farmer, small businessman, or worker trying to get ahead.... Consciousness II represents the values of an organizational society. In the second half of the twentieth century, this combination of an anachronistic consciousness characterized by myth and an inhuman consciousness dominated by the machinelike rationality of the corporate state has proved utterly unable to manage, guide, or control the immense apparatus of technology and organization that America has built.... Consciousness III, which is spreading rapidly among wider and wider segments of youth, and by degrees to older people, is in the process of revolutionizing the structure of our society. *Charles A. Reich, "The Greening of America," The New Yorker, Sept. 26, 1970, p 74*

In recent times the games people played included Highbrow, Middlebrow, Lowbrow, U and non-U, Soul and no Soul. Now comes the first new pop-soc. parlor game of the '70s — Consciousness I, II, and III.... The game will be won, says Reich, when enough of his fellow citizens enter Consciousness III. Then a change of heart and spirit will set in all over America.... *"Opinion: Fuzzy Welcome to Cons. III," Time, Nov. 2, 1970, p 12*

What we have seen so far is a classic confrontation between what Charles Reich would call Consciousness I — the client as self-made man with primitive-American values — and Consciousness II, as represented by the college-trained, verbal, melioristic adman. *L. E. Sissman, "Innocent Bystander: High Wind on Madison Avenue," The Atlantic, July 1971, p 20*

consciousness-raising, *n.* a gaining or producing greater awareness of one's condition, needs, motives, etc., as a means to achieving one's full potential as a person. *Often used attributively.*

She [a member of NOW (National Organization for Women)] described consciousness-raising as "opening the door to the mind — questioning what is happening, why is it happening, does it have to happen that way?"... One young mother charged that marriage and motherhood had deprived her of her own identity. She feels consciousness-raising has been her salvation. *Peggy Voight, "Consciousness-raising, Suburban Style," The Herald Statesman (Yonkers, N.Y.), June 26, 1972, p 15*

Con·seil d'É·tat (kɔ̃'sei dei'ta), a French judicial body which investigates complaints of citizens against administrative rules of the government, often suggested outside of France as an alternative to an ombudsman; (literally) council of state.

The contrast with France lies not so much in the substance of the law as in its machinery. The Conseil d'Etat is the apex of a separate system of administrative courts, which have their own jurisdiction operating quite outside the ordinary system of civil courts. This makes French administrative law a distinct and conspicuous subject, with a special body of doctrine. In Britain, on the other hand, administrative law is submerged in ordinary law, administered by the ordinary courts along with everything else. *H. W. R. Wade, "Fettered Discretion: H. W. R. Wade*

Examines the Recent Milk Marketing Case," The Listener, July 4, 1968, p 17

constant-level balloon, the type of balloon used in the GHOST (Global Horizontal Sounding Technique) to collect atmospheric data.

Instead of rising vertically for a flight lasting only a few minutes, the constant-level balloon is designed to settle at a preselected altitude and to stay aloft for weeks or months, roving over the face of the earth. *Henry Lansford, "Meteorology," 1970 Collier's Encyclopedia Year Book, p 337*

con·sta·tive (kən'stei tiv), *adj.* implying the assertion or assumption of a wish, command, plan, etc., not its actual performance.

[Professor J. L.] Austin's first try was to call such sentences 'performative sentences', because the sentence itself is an integral part of whatever 'performance' is indicated by its main verb ('excuse', 'promise', 'demand'): saying 'I promise' is not something additional to promising, but rather in some central and intimate way it IS the promising. The sorts of statements which may be judged in terms of truth or falsity Austin called 'constative sentences'. *Alice Koller, University of Waterloo, Ontario, Review of "Speech Acts: An Essay in the Philosophy of Language" by John R. Searle, Language, March 1970, p 218*

[from *constate* to assert (from Latin *constat* it is certain) + *-ive*]

consumable, *n.* something that can be consumed.

Doris [Kenneth Doris, an engineer from the Mission Support and Evaluation Group at Houston] thought immediately of "Marooned," a science-fiction film he had seen recently, in which a group of astronauts stranded in a spaceship waited for rescue while their supplies of power, oxygen, and water — which engineers call "consumables" — dwindled. *"The Talk of the Town: Support," The New Yorker, April 25, 1970, p 28*

[noun use of *consumable, adj.*]

consumerism, *n.* public demand for greater safety and quality in consumer products; popular opposition to unsafe or defective goods. See also NADERISM.

Consumerism has caught on in Germany and is the going thing in Scandinavia today. It will unquestionably become a public issue in Britain and the rest of Europe during the next 10 years. The car makers will be put on their mettle. *Geoffrey Charles, "Cars and Drivers: 'Consumerism' to Dominate the 1970s," The Times (London), April 30, 1970, p 16*

The consumerism movement has also made customers more concerned about prices and less interested in change for the sake of change. *"Business: Autos; An End to Obsolescence?" Time, May 18, 1970, p 83*

"Consumerism" involves new approaches to judging and influencing corporate behavior; it presents new concepts of corporate responsibility, including protection of the safety and health of citizens and a meaningful choice for consumers in the products they buy. This movement seeks to develop forces representing the public interest to counter corporate power both in and out of government. *Ralph Nader, "Consumerism: Let the Seller Beware," The Americana Annual 1971, p 51*

consumerist, *n.* an advocate of consumerism.

Lately, not only the quantity but the quality of TV sales spiels for children have become targets of reform-minded parents' groups, consumerists and federal officials. *"Ad-*

vertising: Quieting the Children's Hour," Time, April 19, 1971, p 61

contact inhibition, the cessation of cell division when the surface of one cell comes into physical contact with the surface of another cell.

It has been suggested ... that one of the factors in the control of cell division is "contact inhibition." Abercrombie noted that cells in tissue culture continue to divide until they establish contact, at which point they stop dividing. ... no one knows how contact inhibition works. Some investigators have suggested that as the cells touch each other the distribution of electric charge on their surface changes, and that the change serves as a signal and halts growth. ... *Russell Ross, "Wound Healing," Scientific American, June 1969, p 49*

containerization, *n.* the shipping of cargo in large prepacked containers. Also called CONTAINER-SHIPPING.

The pioneer in containerization was the Sea-Land Line, created by Malcolm McLean. *Frank O. Braynard, "Ships and Shipping," 1968 Collier's Encyclopedia Year Book, p 485*

... if the container revolution moves along the path predicted, an enormous number of seamen and dockers will lose their jobs. McKinsey, for example, reckons that the number of dockers (whose main job is to handle the general traffic due for containerisation) could be reduced by ninety percent over the next fifteen years. *Lombard Lane, "In the City: Container Trouble," Punch, July 12, 1967, p 66*

containerize, *v.t.* to equip or design (a ship) to carry cargo in prepacked containers of a standard size.

Two factors are leading to present enthusiasm: the emergence of large, containerized vessels as the wave of the shipping future, and the development of propulsion reactors that are more efficient and smaller than those used in the Savannah. *Carl Behrens, Science News, March 29, 1969, p 316*

containership, *n.* a containerized ship.

Containerships, several of which are already in service and many more of which are on order, the study noted, have a big advantage over conventional freighters in that they spend much less time in port loading and unloading. *The New York Times, Feb. 4, 1968, p 82*

containershipping, *n.* another name for CONTAINERIZATION.

Containershipping, which is the most likely area of application, has already experienced more drastic upheavals in its methods of operation than nuclear propulsion. *David Clutterbuck, "Rough Passage for Nuclear Ships?" New Scientist and Science Journal, May 13, 1971, p 380*

continentalization, *n.* **1** *Geology.* formation of a continuous land mass.

As the Black Sea plate was forced beneath its northwesterly neighbour the ocean gradually closed. Metamorphism and granitisation then produced a "continentalisation" of the rocks which is virtually complete in Hungary but still happening in the Black Sea basin. *"Monitor: The Ocean That Closed up in Central Europe," New Scientist, Dec. 24, 1970, p 538*

2 the process of assuming the character of the European continent or mainland.

Another change obvious at a glance is what might be called continentalization. The town [London] is full of French, Italians, Spaniards, and you overhear strange accents on the streets — whiffs of exotic languages. *John Gunther, "Inside London," Harper's, July 1967, p 50*

contour-chasing, *n.* low-altitude flying that follows closely the contour of the terrain below.

At supersonic speeds, the effect of "bumps" on the occupants of an aeroplane can be more disturbing than that which occurs at slower speeds. Now that some military aircraft are being designed for contour-chasing to defeat radar defences, the likelihood of turbulence is greater than it is for aircraft operating at, say, 40,000 ft. *"Technology Review: Soft Ride for Pilots," New Scientist, Oct. 29, 1970, p 223*

contracept, *v.t.* to prevent the conception of.

The conventional excuse for contracepting and aborting babies is that catch-all cop-out, the "population explosion." *L. Brent Bozell, "Encouraging Murder," The New York Times, Oct. 14, 1970, p 47*

[back formation from *contraception*]

convenience food, canned, quick-frozen, dehydrated or other prepackaged food that is easy to prepare for eating.

But when foods become unrecognisable, what shall we do? The formulated, instantised, convenience foods will no longer look like meat, milk, cereal or vegetable. *Arnold E. Bender, "Nutrition Neglected?" New Scientist, Dec. 24, 1970, p 560*

The convenience food market continued to expand. To increase the flavour of these prepacked foods, processors used new flavour enhancers. The wider implications of the usefulness of convenience foods were shown in a cookery demonstration (by a blind woman) held in New York to celebrate the 1,000th copy of *The Braille Cookbook of Convenience Foods*. ... *Evelyn Gita Rose, "Domestic Arts and Sciences: Food Preparation," Britannica Book of the Year 1968, p 290*

conventional wisdom, the generally accepted attitude or opinion; popular belief.

The conventional wisdom about starting newspapers in New York City is that it can't be done. *"The Talk of the Town: Newspapers," The New Yorker, March 14, 1970, p 28*

The conventional wisdom insists that public financing of campaigns is inherently unpalatable to the voters. *Philip M. Stern, "The Politics of Money," The New York Times, June 11, 1971, p 35*

Sad to say, large chunks of these essays on contemporary America are conventional wisdom at its most conventional and least wise. *Jonathan Steele, "Books: Nothing More," Review of "The Crisis of Confidence" by Arthur M. Schlesinger, Jr., The Manchester Guardian Weekly, Oct. 18, 1969, p 19*

converger, *n.* a person who excels in close logical reasoning. Compare DIVERGER.

Many people of obvious intellectual ability gain low scores on conventional intelligence tests but high scores on tests containing questions to which there is no one correct answer. Such people are defined as divergers; convergers, on the other hand, gain higher marks on intelligence tests than on open-ended tests. When the two sets of tests were applied to English sixth forms, it was found that the science specialists tended to be convergers and the arts specialists divergers. *The Times (London), March 30, 1968, p 5*

Among the "trendy" biological subjects during the past few years have been both the psychological aspects of dreaming and the personality differences between convergers and divergers. By his work at Cambridge, Liam Hudson established in common coinage the terms converger and diverger to describe types of personality. The classical converger is a cool, analytical person with a "rational, unimaginative" approach to problems, and is probably a physical scientist. The diverger, on the other hand, has a grasshopper mind and sees connections between seemingly unrelated subjects. *"Monitor: Convergers Don't Like What They Dream About," New Scientist and Science Journal, May 13, 1971, p 367*

cool, *Slang.—n.* calm detachment; self-control or restraint.

A man was nothing in prison without his cool, for prison was the profoundest put-on of them all—it said, dig, man, you are here suffering for your crime. *Norman Mailer, "The Steps of the Pentagon: The Post Office," Harper's, March 1968, p 115*

...he ambled down Main Street in big town and small, flaunting his difference and his cool. The rag-tag generation finds no humor in the mistakes and cop-outs of the conforming armies. Sleeping, easily fooled, bigoted people are a travesty, they say, and are responsible for the relative chaos in which we live. Anything but cool, youth senses what is wrong and how things should be. *Burt Korall, "The Music of Protest," Saturday Review, Nov. 16, 1968, p 36*

Used especially in the phrases:

blow one's cool, to become emotional; get excited.

Twice a month, the troops got a newsletter from the boss [Thomas Reddin, Chief of Police in Los Angeles] with a one-paragraph message. One typical caveat: "Don't blow your cool and be the one who starts an incident." *Linda McVeigh Mathews, "Chief Reddin: New Style at the Top," The Atlantic, March 1969, p 92*

keep one's cool, to stay calm; control oneself.

I managed to keep my cool, however, and told him I wouldn't sign an exclusive contract with anyone. *The Times (London), Nov. 9, 1968, p 19*

As Democratic Senator Eugene McCarthy was addressing the group on the final night of the conference, three New Leftists arrived on the stage and started to heckle him.... "McCarthy kept his cool very well." *"Education: Students: Lessons in Mind Blowing," Time, Feb. 16, 1968, p 47*

lose one's cool, to become emotional; get excited.

He [Pierre Trudeau] "lost his cool" in London during the January meeting of Commonwealth prime ministers when reporters dogged his steps in public and showed insatiable curiosity about his personal life. *John S. Moir, "Canada," The Americana Annual 1970, p 148*

—*adj.* all right; satisfactory.

... Geraldine insinuates herself while feigning a search for a glass in my kitchen: "... I know the kinda scene you look for. You want to have it all your way, don't you, Colonel? That's cool with me." *Jack Richardson, "A Lively Commerce: From Jackson Heights to Las Vegas—the Compulsive Joys of Sex and Gambling," Harper's, Aug. 1970, p 84*

—*v.t.* **cool it, 1** to keep calm; calm down.

Several fist fights broke out, with some students shouting, "Cool it, cool it." *The New York Times, May 10, 1968, p 36*

But if Mr. Heath (and for that matter, Mr. Wilson) is really sincere about wanting "One Nation" then there surely is one obvious answer. Cool it. *Punch, Feb. 23, 1972, p 231*

2 to remain detached; not get involved.

...he [John Gielgud], like Dean Martin, only needs to

play on his public image—to cool it. *Pauline Kael, "The Current Cinema," Review of "Sebastian," The New Yorker, Jan. 27, 1968, p 108*

coop, *v.i. U.S. Slang.* to sleep during the night inside a parked police car while on patrol duty.

You recall reading about the policemen who like to sleep on duty? Well, it appears that while 'cooping,' as they call it, they tend to fall out of their prowl cars. *S. J. Perelman, "Out of This Nettle, Danger...," The New Yorker, Nov. 29, 1969, p 50*

[verb use of earlier noun, meaning a policeman's regular shelter, derived from chicken *coop*]

Cooper pair, a pair of electrons with equal and opposite momentum and spin, which attract each other and combine through an interaction involving the lattice of positive ions.

A Cooper pair can in a sense be regarded as a new particle, with twice the charge and mass of an electron, that can exist only in a metal. The effective diameter of a Cooper pair is called its coherence length and is on the order of a hundred-thousandth of a centimeter. The mechanism by which Cooper pairs are formed implies that all such pairs in a given superconductor are in the same state of motion. Either their centers of mass are at rest or, if the superconductor carries a current, they move with one and the same velocity in the direction of the current. *Uwe Essmann and Hermann Träuble, "The Magnetic Structure of Superconductors," Scientific American, March 1971, p 77*

[named after Leon N. *Cooper*, born 1930, an American theoretical physicist who was one of the proponents of a theory of superconductivity which posited the formation of electron pairs under certain conditions]

co-opt, *v.i.* to make additional appointments.

The Government, it was suggested, should press on with the production of a unified service with the establishment of area health boards having an elected membership with powers to co-opt. *The Times (London), Oct. 5, 1968, p 5*

—*v.t. U.S.* to take over; absorb.

Says Fred Kent, coordinator for New York's Environmental Action Coalition: "It is irresponsible for business to say that they [Continental Oil Co., Scott Paper Co., Sun Oil Co.] support us. They are just trying to co-opt us." *Time, May 4, 1970, p 16*

...a Republican Party based in the "Heartland" (Midwest), West, and South can and should co-opt the Wallace vote.... *Michael Janeway, "Reports: Washington: The Invisible Cities," The Atlantic, Oct. 1969, p 18*

The first order of business was to win approval of the new alliance with the Moratorium from the clamoring group, half of whom were muttering about being "coöpted by the liberals." *Francine du Plessix Gray, "A Reporter at Large: The Moratorium and the New Mobe" [New Mobilization Committee to End the War in Vietnam], The New Yorker, Jan. 3, 1970, p 39*

[extended from the earlier meaning of "commandeer, appropriate, preempt"]

coordinates, *n.pl.* clothing matched in color, fabric, design, etc., to produce a harmonious effect in combination.

You see, quite a lot of the range is made of striped ticking. And there's striped and plain co-ordinates and Him and Her outfits for brothers and sisters, and some of the little girls' dresses and little boys' shorts are completely reversible—they're awfully practical. *Alison Adburgham, "For Women: How Fashion Works," Punch, March 24, 1965, p 451*

cop, *v.i.* **cop out,** *U.S. Slang.* **1** to go back on a commitment; withdraw from involvement.

"A few Episcopal clergymen promised to go along, but at the last minute they copped out because of their big hangups on their families." *Francine du Plessix Gray, "Profiles: Acts of Witness," The New Yorker, March 14, 1970, p 118*

2 to give up a principle, a cause, etc.; to compromise.

"A man must be involved, engaged and committed." "And if he is not?"

"He is a fink. He has copped out. He has opted for middle-class affluence." *Russell Baker, The New York Times, May 28, 1968, p 46*

[from the earlier slang meaning "to plead guilty, especially to a lesser charge in order to avoid a trial," chiefly in the phrase *cop a plea,* from *cop* to take, seize, steal]

cop-out, *n.* *U.S. Slang.* an act of copping out; retreat; compromise.

An aphoristic ending is always a sign of structural flaws, and this book is weakened by incomplete thoughts and bad connections, and by the presence of a small crowd of inviting characters left standing on the edges of the story.... Davis comes close enough—close to Amis, anyway—to make his cop-out a real disappointment. *Susan Lardner, "Books: Tilt," Review of "Whence All But He Had Fled" by L. J. Davis, The New Yorker, April 20, 1968, p 189*

"That was no strategy," one of them observed bitterly, "that was a cop-out." *Warren Weaver, Jr., The New York Times, March 24, 1968, Sec. 4, p 1*

copper bracelet, a band of copper worn on the wrist in the belief that the copper will alleviate a variety of ailments, including arthritis, sciatica, and bursitis.

The Arthritis Foundation considers promotion of copper bracelets as an arthritis cure "part of the arthritis quackery racket...." *Time, July 6, 1970, p 56*

coprological, *adj.* of or having to do with obscenity in literature and drama; scatological.

It [Arrabal's "Le Jardin des Délices," a play] has some offensive scenes, for example, at the end of the first act, when an indecent word is translated into coprological action. *Harold Hobson, "Theatre: Pursuits of the Ideal," The Sunday Times (London), Jan. 11, 1970, p 53*

[from Greek *kópros* filth, dung, but directly derived from earlier *coprology*]

co-prosperity, *n.* mutual or cooperative prosperity. *Also used attributively.*

One guess from where the outside stimulus in the 1970s and 1980s might come: Japanese "protection" of Korea; "tutelage" for Indonesia; "co-prosperity" with the Philippines? *Ross Terrill, "Japan: The Land of the Re-rising Sun," The Atlantic, March 1971, p 80*

In some official quarters there is a mounting suspicion that Japan is a natural economic predator, committed to establishing its "co-prosperity sphere" by guile rather than force. *Creighton Burns, "Australia: Asia Fears Persist," The Times (London), March 31, 1970, p 11*

► This term, used in the 1930's and in World War II to describe Japan's economic policies toward occupied territories in China and the Pacific, has been associated in the West with Japanese economic expansion since World War II.

core city, *U.S.* another name for CENTRAL CITY.

... backlash is more pronounced among Jews who have not "made it" to suburbia and continue to live in the core city, in or near the ghetto, where they have regular contact with Negro life. *Irving Spiegel, The New York Times, July 8, 1968, p 20*

The core cities were left to decay, and local governmental agencies were left to fight the problems with minimal funds and few dedicated officials. *William H. Dougherty, Jr., "The Urban Redoubt: The Crucial Coalition," Saturday Review, Jan. 13, 1968, p 36*

...[Mayor] Lindsay did establish the principle...that commuters must at least pay something to the "core city" where they work. *The New York Times, June 19, 1966, Sec. 4, p 1*

core tube, a tube inserted into ground material to extract a sample.

Hence, in addition to trenching tools, scoops, core tubes, and a portable magnetometer, the Apollo-14 crew will be carrying a number of experiments designed to unravel deep structure. *Anthony Tucker, "Listening to the Moon," The Manchester Guardian Weekly, Jan. 30, 1971, p 5*

co-riparian, *n.* one that has rights to the use of a river jointly with another.

...India's indifference to East Pakistan's rights as a co-riparian to a fair share of the waters of the Ganges at Farakka places in dire jeopardy the future of over twenty million people. *S. N. Qutb, Press Attaché, Embassy of Pakistan, Washington, in a Letter to the Editor, The New York Times, Oct. 24, 1970, p 30*

cornrow, *v.t., v.i.* *U.S.* to arrange hair into flat braids or pigtails.

"We all suffered through our mothers cornrowing our hair when we were little," Miss Taylor said, "and we couldn't wait to get out of it." But cornrowing is back, although beauticians don't like to talk about that because you don't need to go to a beauty parlor to do it. *Barbara Trecker, "The Afro Versus the Dome," New York Post, March 8, 1972, p 15*

[originally southern Negro dialect; so called from the resemblance of a row of short pigtails projecting from the head to a row of cornstalks]

corporate state, 1 a term used by Charles A. Reich in *The Greening of America,* 1970: "The corporate state in which we live is an immensely powerful machine—ordered, legalistic, rational, yet utterly out of human control and indifferent to human values.... The corporate state, and not the market or the people or any abstract economic laws, determines what shall be produced, what shall be consumed, and how it shall all be allocated. The corporate state determines, for example, that railroads shall decay while highways flourish, that coal miners shall be poor and advertising executives rich." *Charles A. Reich, "The Greening of America," The New Yorker, Sept. 26, 1970, p 44*

Liberals who in some measure designed Reich's corporate state—its welfare system and its Keynesian apparatus—suffer unfairly at his hands. *John Kenneth Galbraith, "Who Minds the Store?" The New York Times, Oct. 26, 1970, p 37*

Cosa Nostra

2 the term has also been perhaps loosely applied to the *corporative state* of Fascist Italy and of Portugal, in which a limited group of corporations (representing both employers and workers) control the country's economy and in turn are supervised by certain political organs of the state.

Evidently the corporate state, which has been identified with fascism, can be arrived at as well through the quiet actions of civilized men as readily as through the tactics of a Hitler or a Mussolini. *Walter Pitkin, Jr., Weston, Conn., in a Letter to the Editor, The New York Times, June 25, 1971, p 38*

Co·sa Nos·tra (ˈkou sə ˈnous trə), a name for the Mafia crime syndicate in the United States, originally used as a secret name by its members but made public by the informer Joseph Valachi in 1962.

We understand and sympathize with the sentiment of a spokesman for the recent Italian-American Unity Day rally that "what we resent emphatically is this myth that anybody whose name ends in a vowel is Mafia or Cosa Nostra." *Arthur J. Scarzello, Bronx, N.Y., in a Letter to the Editor, The New York Times, July 6, 1970, p 30*

[from Italian *cosa nostra* our thing, our business]

cosmetic, *n.* something that decorates or embellishes, especially by covering up defects.

Attorney General John Mitchell's expressed preference for the term "quick entry" over the scorned catchword "no-knock" provides glaring evidence of the way in which Government currently uses words as cosmetics to delude the public and even itself. *James T. Connelly, Amherst, Mass., in a Letter to the Editor, The New York Times, July 27, 1970, p 26*

By the twentieth century artists were no longer performing a unique role: the creation of images which filled a deeply felt need of their culture, and which they alone could provide. Inevitably many people began to regard their work as "primarily decorative"—a cosmetic of society rather than food for its soul. *John Fischer, "The Easy Chair: Mark Rothko: Portrait of the Artist as an Angry Man," Harper's, July 1970, p 23*

If a 1965 graduate were to return today to Harvard—or Berkeley or Kent State—he would have no trouble in recognizing the old place.... Close scrutiny might reveal a few changes around the edges:...ROTC courses abolished, government research curtailed, black studies added, and probably a new president. But underneath the cosmetics, the bone structure of the university, the traditional departments, remain much as they were fifty years ago....*John Fischer, "The Easy Chair," Harper's, Feb. 1971, p 20*

—*adj.* **1** of the surface; superficial.

Environmental problems are cosmetic, not systemic. Unemployment and inflation, however unpleasant for those immediately involved, are technical faults and certainly nothing to justify any interference with the free price system. *John Kenneth Galbraith, "Who Needs the Democrats?" Harper's, July 1970, p 58*

2 of or for embellishment; decorative.

...there are cynical people who say Mr Nixon's tour [of Europe to discuss Middle Eastern problems with European political leaders] is done for its 'cosmetic value' to the Republican Party as it goes into its wrestling act to try and take the Senate and the House away from the Democrats.... "*A Real Old Western Hero—Alistair Cooke*

on the New Brinkmanship," The Listener, Oct. 1, 1970, p 450*

cosmeticize or **cosmetize,** *v.t.* to make more attractive or easier to accept. Compare SANITIZE.

He [Sir Val Duncan] promised that Rio Tinto would "cosmeticize" its opencast copper mine, and enthused on the miraculous abilities of modern earthmoving equipment. *Jon Tinker, "Snowdonia Cops It," New Scientist, Nov. 12, 1970, p 317*

"We have not Vietnamized the war; we have cosmetized it," the New York Republican [Senator Charles Goodell] said in his opening statement. "Behind the façade of this Potemkin village, the facts of Vietnam remain as ugly as ever." *Ian McDonald, "Vietnam War 'Cosmetized'," The Times (London), Feb. 4, 1970, p 6*

► In the literal sense of "to treat with cosmetics," *cosmeticize* was already used in the 1800's: "*1860 All Year Round No. 47. 493 The skins that were not hard red, were of a ghastly cosmeticised whiteness.*" *(OED)* The form *cosmetize* has no earlier record.

cos·mo- (ˈkɑz mou-), an old combining form meaning "universe" or "world," reborrowed from Russian *kosmo-* in the 1960's with the new meaning of "outer space," "space travel," and equivalent to English *astro-* (as used in *astronaut, astrospace,* etc.). Compounds with *cosmo-* were often taken whole from the Russian (with conventional adaptations of form and spelling), as the best-known one, *cosmonaut* (Russian *kosmonavt*); but the derivative *cosmonette* and compounds such as *cosmodog* are formed in English. The following are some examples:

cosmodog, *n.*: After 22 days in orbit in their Cosmos 110 satellite—longer than any other living beings have spent in space—Cosmodogs Veterok and Ugolyok were brought down to a safe landing in Russian Central Asia. *Time, March 25, 1966, p 43*

cosmodom, *n.*: After Soyuz 11's success, Soviet officials released drawings, pictures and descriptions of Salyut—which they called a "cosmodom," or space house. *The New York Times, June 13, 1971, p 6*

cosmodrome, *n.*: The landing stage of the station, called Cosmodrome, continued to send back to earth temperature and radiation measurements. "*Science News of the Week: Unmanned to the Moon and Back," Science News, Sept. 26, 1970, p 269*

cosmograd, *n.*: Soviet officials...emphasize the importance of space stations and, with Salyut's initial success, talk of it as a cornerstone for clusters of vehicles forming "cosmograds"—space cities. *John Noble Wilford, "Space: The Soviets Are Out There Building a 'City'," The New York Times, June 13, 1971, p 6*

cosmonautics, *n.*: Consistently, Soviet scientists—in the tradition of Ziolkowsky, the founder of Soviet cosmonautics—have spoken of the importance of manned space-stations in Earth-orbit. *Kenneth W. Gatland, "Space-Race After Apollo 204," New Scientist, Feb. 9, 1967, p 325*

cosmogenic, *adj.* originating from cosmic rays.

The possibilities that cosmogenic...He³ [an isotope of helium] in dust can be used for identification, can enable inference of an influx rate, and can contribute to atmospheric He³ were suggested by Mayne. *David W. Parkin and David Tilles, "Influx Measurements of Extraterrestrial Material," Science, March 1, 1968, p 941*

cosmonette, *n.* a Soviet spacewoman.

'In a Brussels radio interview, Professor [Marcel] Florkin [of Liege University] said: 'The very simple things I said during a luncheon meeting have been sensationalised.

'I am quoted as saying that "The Soviet Cosmonette Tereshkova is actually in a very abnormal psychic state."

'This is the first time that I heard of the word "Cosmonette," which until I read the newspaper report did not form part of my vocabulary,' *A. P. H., "Is Space Homicidal?" Punch, Jan. 20, 1965, p 85*

[from *cosmon*aut Soviet astronaut + *-ette* (feminine suffix)]

cost-benefit, *adj.* of or relating to cost-benefit analysis.

A power company contemplating a possible new plant or installation will reach its decision through the usual cost-benefit calculations. *Milton Katz, "Decision-making in the Production of Power," Scientific American, Sept. 1971, p 192*

Neither profit-and-loss nor cost-benefit accountancy reduces the operations of the megamachine, for the costs are magically converted into benefits, and the prospective losses through military obsolescence and outright destruction are the source of profits. *Lewis Mumford, "Reflections: The Megamachine," The New Yorker, Oct. 24, 1970, p 76*

cost-benefit analysis, an analysis or estimate of cost efficiency.

The prime difficulties of cost-benefit analysis manifest themselves as various aspects of the one central problem: how to place a monetary value on goods and services for which no market exists. *New Scientist, Aug. 20, 1970, p 374*

Mr. Justice Roskill and his colleagues have enlisted in their task that tool of modern social science, cost-benefit analysis. *Anthony Lewis, The New York Times, April 11, 1970, p 40*

cost efficiency or **cost effectiveness,** the efficiency of an operation, system, etc., in terms of the ratio of its cost to the benefit anticipated from it.

...a university is so much plant that should be kept in full production all the year round, its staff made to earn their living, and its management governed by strict cost-efficiency considerations. *Brian MacArthur, "Running Universities As Industrial Plant," The Times (London), April 23, 1970, p 12*

Today, when cost-effectiveness is all and image building for the general public is too expensive, the commercial giants are less lavish with their patronage and more careful of its destination. *Arthur Conway, "Books," Review of "Plastics Film Technology," New Scientist, May 14, 1970, p 345*

cost-efficient or **cost-effective,** *adj.* efficient in terms of the ratio of cost to anticipated benefits.

Mr. Heath and the Shadow Cabinet agreed that a vast amount of public money was being poured into development areas without producing a cost-efficient return. *David Wood, "SET Would Go: Emphasis on Indirect Levies," The Times (London), Feb. 2, 1970, p 1*

New category of cost-effective light-metal components with three to five times better strength and stiffness to weight ratio. Will help removing critical structural constraints in machines, vehicles and weapon systems. New category of cost-effective high-temperature components with higher creep strength and oxidation resistance. *Hans*

F. Wuenscher, a table in "Manufacturing in Space," New Scientist, Sept. 10, 1970, p 517

cost inflation, another name for COST-PUSH.

There are two quite different kinds of inflation: demand inflation, when, through credit expansion and tax reduction, money demand is allowed to rise much faster than productive capacity: and the cost inflation which follows. *Anthony Harris, The Manchester Guardian Weekly, June 6, 1970, p 23*

cost-push, *n.* Also called **cost-push inflation** or **cost inflation.** inflation in which rising costs of labor and production increase prices even when demand has not increased. Compare DEMAND-PULL.

For instance, the Radcliffe committee declared there was no limit to the increase in the velocity with which money could be made to circulate, and therefore no significance in the quantity of it. There was the never-ending debate between cost-push and demand-pull. *"Powell Sees Scope for £400m Tax Cuts," The Times (London), April 11, 1970, p 2*

Now that we are smarting under cost-push, the basic argument remains the same. *Henry C. Wallich, The New York Times, Dec. 16, 1970, p 47*

In South Africa, the international ailment of cost-push inflation is claiming another victim. In spite of a high average annual growth rate of around 6 per cent during the past decade, South Africa's retail price index inflated by a modest 2 per cent a year. *Stanley Uys, "Another Inflation Victim," The Manchester Guardian Weekly, Sept. 12, 1970, p 6*

costumey, *adj.* *U.S.* consisting of or characterized by clothing that is overly elaborate or affected to attract attention.

I have grown weary by now with the costumey aspect of Las Vegas. Everywhere, someone is dressed in a bastard version of some ancient or modern national dress. *Margot Hentoff, "Performing Arts," Harper's, Nov. 1969, p 36*

Stylish women throughout the world put the catch phrase "do your own thing" into practice by replacing the safe couture-approved dress with costumey, role-playing clothes that were outward projections of their inner selves. *Kathryn Zahony, "Fashion," The 1969 World Book Year Book, p 339*

cot death, *British.* another name for CRIB DEATH.

Breast-feeding could prevent cot death in very young babies, the report says. It criticizes the habit of propping up the baby unattended, in cot or pram, with a bottle of milk. *"Avoidable Factors in Many Infant Deaths," The Times (London), May 11, 1970, p 3*

cou·chette (ku:'ʃet), *n.* a train compartment with a sleeping berth.

There is no reason why B.R., with some imaginative timetabling, should not allow us to travel in comfort between London and Switzerland between 7 p.m. and 7 a.m. with dinner, breakfast and couchette thrown in for the price of the cheapest (and most uncomfortable) flight. *Pendennis, The Observer (London), July 5, 1964, p 12*

Mme Signoret plays the part of a touring actress who has spent the night in a couchette compartment where a woman has been discovered murdered. *Derek Prouse, The Sunday Times (London), Sept. 18, 1966, p 20*

[from French, literally, small bed]

counter-, a very productive prefix in the three senses listed below.

countercultural

The following selection reflects its widespread use:

1 opposing; in opposition.

countereffect, *n.:* The movie ["The Confession"] plays it very close and stays with the particulars, and at first the semi-documentary look and the bureaucratic realism have a counter-effect—the film seems to be non-involving. *Pauline Kael, "The Current Cinema: Stalinism," The New Yorker, Dec. 12, 1970, p 172*

counterexplanation, *n.:* Certainly it seems to be political activists or children of politically active families who are picked for trial on indictment in these cases. The authorities do not put forward any cogent counter-explanation of their methods of selection. *Stephen Sedley, "The Garden House Trial," The Listener, Oct. 8, 1970, p 470*

countergovernment, *n.:* In order to provide some opposition to the one-party government, and also to pacify the Cambodian left, Sihanouk took the extraordinary step of setting up a "countergovernment," a kind of shadow cabinet with no real power except to criticize, but nevertheless an opposition of sorts. *H. D. S. Greenway, "Cambodia," The Atlantic, July 1970, p 27*

countersorcery, *n.:* Sorcery and countersorcery were (and still are) prevalent in the Andean region. It was believed that sorcerers could cause illness and other misfortunes. Both public ceremonies led by priests, and private ceremonies led by shamans, were considered effective means of combating human misfortune. *Louis C. Faron, "The Inca," Encyclopedia Science Supplement (Grolier) 1970, p 27*

counterstimulus, *n.:* The troubled and turbulent times that this great Republic has been experiencing during the Vietnam war have brought about an atmosphere of discontent, disquiet and confusion. . . . As a counterstimulus, it would appear that we shall need a change in our national leadership that possesses those rare and essential qualities of dedication, humbleness and inspiration, a leadership that has the ability to think in simple direct terms, not in complicated or divisive terms. *Francis Keally, New York, in a Letter to the Editor, The New York Times, Sept. 9, 1970, p 46*

countertrend, *n.:* These nine chance birds do not constitute redress or a countertrend to a decade made hawkless by progress and chemicals and stupidity. . . . *"The Talk of the Town: Notes and Comment," The New Yorker, Aug. 15, 1970, p 19*

2 in return or retaliation; retaliatory.

counteraccusation, *n.:* To accusations of "Traitor!" and counter-accusations of "Reactionaries!", the communists and other political groups clashed in an unprecedented shouting match. *Peter Hazelhurst, "Overseas: Indian MPs Call for Nuclear Arms to Face China," The Times (London), April 29, 1970, p 6*

counterquote, *v.i.:* It is possible to go on counterquoting, but for a true understanding of the novel, one has to go beyond a superficial reading of the words on the printed page. *P. A. Tilley, London, in a Letter to the Editor, The Times (London), April 18, 1970, p 7*

counterstrike, *n.:* Much of Rand's reputation rested on its studies for the Defense Department on such harsh possibilities as various kinds of nuclear threat, strikes and counterstrikes, including calculations of projected casualties. *"Daniel Ellsberg: The Battle Over the Right to Know," Time, July 5, 1971, p 10*

3 corresponding or equivalent.

counterattractive, *adj.:* While it is true that there was virtually no counter-attractive facility to Hanover in a war-damaged Germany at the time it was built. . . . *Anthony Rowley, "Hanover: Centre of Attraction," The Times (London), Feb. 17, 1970, p 19*

counterlogic, *n.:* [Friedrich] Meckseper seems to demonstrate by creating a counter-logic, that the world is simply too complex and interesting to be perceived and classified in an inflexible, absolute way. He does so with wit, technical virtuosity, and a great deal of visual inventiveness. But this is only a partial interpretation of an artist whose alchemist's repertoire of symbols includes keys, rainbows, philosopher's stones, chalices, rays of light and puffs of smoke. *William Varley, "A Modern Bestiary," The Manchester Guardian Weekly, Oct. 17, 1970, p 21*

See also the main entries below for very current or specialized meanings.

countercultural, *adj.* relating to or characteristic of the counterculture.

We would create the *options* of communal living, of single women raising their children, and of women (not their doctors or the state) deciding whether to end an unwanted pregnancy. Some of our proposals are "countercultural," such as communal families or free medical care centers or abortions on demand. *Diana E. Richmond, Chicago, in "Backtalk: More About Women" (consisting of letters to the Editor about Women's Liberation Movement), The Atlantic, May 1970, p 96*

counterculture, *n.* the special culture made up of those, chiefly of the younger generation, who have rejected the standards and values of established society.

Members of the counter-culture said anything their parents ate must be bad. *Steven V. Roberts, The New York Times, June 5, 1971, p 34*

With its narcotics and hallucinogens, its electrically amplified noise and stroboscopic lights and supersonic flights from nowhere to nowhere, modern technology helped to create a counter-culture whose very disorder serves admirably to stabilize the power system. *Lewis Mumford, The Pentagon of Power, 1970, plate legend [27]*

According to Robert Glessing's recent book, *The Underground Press in America*, some 400 newspapers and magazines now serve the counter culture. There are probably as many like-minded radio stations; and more than one underground "wire service" exists, along with radical film and video-tape studios and street theater troupes and poster artists. The preferred name for this considerable activity is "alternative media." *Richard Todd, "Life and Letters: Alternatives," The Atlantic, Nov. 1970, p 112*

Of the many forms of Buddhism, the one best known in the West is Zen. Its guiding principles of inward meditation versus doctrine, of emphasis on the visceral and spontaneous as against the cerebral and structured, of inspiration rather than linear "logic", were seized on by the early beatniks, taken up by many of the young today, and were incorporated into the mystique of America's counterculture. *Robert Hughes, "Art: Sudden Enlightenment," Time, Dec. 14, 1970, p 76*

counterculturist, *n.* a member of the counterculture or one who is sympathetic to its standards and goals.

To the American counter-culturist, a telephone in the hand is as much a part of his uniform as denim, dried lentils and a coiffure from Michelangelo's Moses. *Russell Baker, "A Last Thread of Unity," The New York Times, June 13, 1971, p 13*

Ideally, the counter culturist seeks to enter a world of real experiences, where plastics, computers, sonic booms and acquisitive instincts, do not scar the primeval beauty of the human soul. . . . *"Sasthi Brata, A Challenge to*

Science and Technology," Review of "The Making of a Counter Culture" by Theodore Roszak, New Scientist and Science Journal, Jan. 21, 1971, p 142

counterdemonstrate, v.i. to demonstrate publicly in order to offset the effect of another public demonstration.

The desire for all and sundry to demonstrate and counterdemonstrate has made the police a permanent buffer at a time when recruiting to full strength has been disallowed.... "Police Chief Tells of Low Morale," The Times (London), Feb. 17, 1970, p 4

counterdemonstrator, n. a person who counterdemonstrates.

Boston marchers filed past counterdemonstrators carrying signs saying "Hardhats for Soft Broads." "The Nation: Women on the March," Time, Sept. 7, 1970, p 12

counterinsurgency, n. military action against guerrillas or other insurgents. Often used attributively.

The British effort in Malaya is a recent example of a counterinsurgency effort which required approximately ten years before the bulk of the rural population was brought completely under control of the government, the police were able to maintain order, and the armed forces were able to eliminate the guerrilla strongholds. Memorandum, "Vietnam Situation," from Secretary of Defense Robert S. McNamara to President Lyndon B. Johnson, Dec. 21, 1963, in "The Week in Review," The New York Times, June 13, 1971, Sec. 4, p 35

Counterinsurgency enters the high school ROTC curriculum. Dan Wakefield, "Supernation at Peace and War," The Atlantic, March 1968, p 101

"If the federal government handled Negro aspiration as it handles the revolt in South Vietnam," [I. F.] Stone writes at one point, "we would be sending counter-insurgency teams South to kill civil-rights agitators." "Checklistings: Books," Review of "In a Time of Torment" by I. F. Stone, Maclean's, March 1968, p 80

counterinsurgent, n. a person who engages in counterinsurgency.

They cannot invoke the Geneva Convention because as counterinsurgents trained to operate behind enemy lines or in hostile areas, they carry arms and use them in combat. Homer Bigart, The New York Times, June 2, 1967, p 7

—adj. of or relating to counterinsurgency.

Vietnam was consciously made into a test of liberal international policy by the Kennedy and Johnson Administrations—of liberal "nation building," carried on behind a shield of Green Beret counter-insurgent warfare, against the Asian Communist "model" of radical national transformation. William Pfaff, "Reflections: Vietnam, Czechoslovakia, and the Fitness to Lead," The New Yorker, July 3, 1971, p 36

counterintuitive, adj. running counter to intuition; not consistent with what one knows or perceives intuitively.

The point of this story is not to enter into a discussion of urban renewal policies but to illustrate what Forrester sees as a main characteristic of complex systems—that they are counter-intuitive; that they display complicated—and probably unpredictable—response patterns to simple system or input changes.... I find this hypothesis of counter-intuitive behaviour attractive, my own unaided intuitions having been inadequate to deal with more complex systems than I could enumerate. Joe Roeber, "Management: Against

Intuition," The Times (London), March 9, 1970, p 25

The models of social systems in the laboratory, as well as actual systems in real life, show that complex systems are counterintuitive. They behave in ways opposite to what most people expect. Jay W. Forrester, "Social-System Dynamics," McGraw-Hill Yearbook of Science and Technology 1971, p 32

counterproductive, adj. producing undesirable results.

...[There are] a number of interrelated problems in Africa which it is dangerous and counter-productive to deal with in isolation. Campbell Page, "On Safari for a Policy," The Manchester Guardian Weekly, Aug. 8, 1970, p 8

Bernardine Dohrn and the others on the top of the terrorist heap can only be moved to reconsider the role of violence if they are convinced it is tactically counter-productive. "The Recantations of a Reformed Berkeley Bomber," Time, Feb. 22, 1971, p 15

counterterror, n. opposing or retaliatory terror.

He reports on Israel's attempts to escape the fatal cycle of terror and counter-terror.... Murray Sayle, The Sunday Times (London), March 23, 1969, p 7

...Gene Browning, a moderate black intellectual, decides that the wanton killing of a black boy by a New York cop must be met with counterterror.... Irving Howe, "Books: New Black Writers," Review of "Sons of Darkness, Sons of Light" by John A. Williams, Harper's, Dec. 1969, p 135

counterterrorism, n. opposing or retaliatory terrorism.

There is a fear that Communist terrorism will provoke rightist counterterrorism until such tension is built up that the rightists, in conjunction with the army, will try to topple the Government on the ground that it cannot maintain security. The New York Times, Jan. 22, 1968, p 14

counterterrorist, n. a person who engages in counterterrorism.

Terrorists and counterterrorists trying to outwit each other in the calm setting of Geneva. "Goings on About Town: Motion Pictures, Le Petit Soldat," The New Yorker, Aug. 10, 1968, p 15

counterviolence, n. the use of violent methods to resist or put down violence.

The sickening cycle of violence and counter-violence that first ended in death at Kent State University may become more common. "Lunacy and Repression," The Manchester Guardian Weekly, May 23, 1970, p 1

The violence... exemplified by lynchings and other unlawful injuries, has provoked counterviolence in many quarters, and the time has come when the nation must restore good will and cooperation, regardless of race or color if we are to be a healthy nation. Earl Warren, "Centuries of Discrimination," The New York Times, Oct. 31, 1970, p 29

country-and-western, n. U.S. a stylized form of country, music, especially of the western U.S., played with electric guitars. Abbreviation: C & W or C-and-W Compare BLUEGRASS.

People say rock 'n' roll is a combination of rhythm and blues and country-and-western, but really it's just blues and country. Jaime Robertson, "The Band Talks Music," Time, Jan. 12, 1970, p 40

country rock, a blend of imitation folk music, especially western music, and rock 'n' roll rhythms.

Synthesis was the password for popular music in 1969. In an appropriate conclusion to the most eclectic decade in American popular music, the year was flooded with such new combinations as jazz-rock, folk-rock, and country-rock. *Don Heckman, "Recordings: Popular Records," The Americana Annual 1970, p 578*

His [Neil Diamond's] songs delve ingeniously into... blues, gospel, even country rock. *"Music: Tin Pan Tailor," Time, Jan. 11, 1971, p 40*

cow·a·bun·ga (ˌkau əˈbəŋ gə), *interj.* a surfer's cry when riding the crest of a wave.

Shouting... "Cowabunga!" they climb a 12-ft. wall of water and "take the drop" off its shoulder... till the wave carries them in to the hot white shore where gremmies, ho-dads and wahines watch in wonder. *Time, Aug. 9, 1963, p 49*

CPA, abbreviation of CRITICAL PATH ANALYSIS.

CPA is a technique for showing all the connexions and interrelations in time of the activities that make up a project. *Michael White, The Times (London), March 11, 1968, p 26*

crack, *v.i., v.t.* in various phrases:
crack on, *British Slang.* to go on; carry on.

... Big John with his immense experience had things under his personal control ("Crack on, lads!" was a favourite Big John order). *Murray Sayle, The Sunday Times (London), Jan. 5, 1969, p 11*

There she was cracking on about having colour TV so I said mmm, yes, isn't science wonderful.... *Advertisement by Imperial Metal Industries, Limited, Birmingham, England, Punch, Sept. 11, 1968, p iv*

crack up, *U.S. Slang.* to cause to laugh or to laugh uncontrollably; convulse with laughter.

Everybody wings it, and in that spirit the show's resident cast of bright young kooks often make the lines seem funnier than they really are. "If one gag goes completely over your head," says [Dick] Martin, "there'll be another along in a few seconds that'll crack you up." *"Television: Comedians: A Put-On Is Not a Put-Down," Time, March 8, 1968, p 47*

She wanted to go to Mexico, to a hot place, she said, where she could see something green.... "Hot? Something green? A billiard table in hell would answer the description."

"Oh. Wow! That really cracks me up," said Wallace. *Saul Bellow, "Mr. Sammler's Planet," The Atlantic, Nov. 1969, p 124*

And then Fred shouts: "I am the great pumpkin!" The whole room cracks up. Five minutes later, Ava announces Fred's enlightenment. As we applaud in disbelief, Fred claps his hands and punches them jubilantly over his head, like a boxing champ. "I just had a deepening enlightenment—I'm Chicken Little!" *Sara Davidson, "The Rush for Instant Salvation: Numerous Prophets and Travel Agents Advertise Round-trip Tickets to Nirvana, or to Wherever Else a Tourist Believes he Might Find God Consciousness," Harper's, July 1971, p 49*

crank, *v.i.* **crank up,** *U.S. Slang.* to get ready; prepare.

On the morning of March 10th [Senator Birch] Bayh instructed his staff to crank up for an all-out fight against the nomination.... *Richard Harris, "Annals of Politics: Decision," The New Yorker, Dec. 5, 1970, p 143*

crash, *v.t., v.i. U.S. Slang.* to sleep or lodge free. See also CRASH PAD.

"When a transient arrives looking for a place to crash," says one communard, "We send him to a motel." *Time, March 30, 1970, p 10*

... the man... said they could crash for the night at Love Inn. *Edward B. Fiske, "'Jesus People' are Happy with Their Life in Love Inn," The New York Times, June 15, 1971, p 45*

... a long-haired individual, spotting our rucksacks, approached and asked if we needed a place to crash. *Bill Sertl, "'A Communal Pilgrimage'—Along Canada's Highways," The New York Times, June 20, 1971, p 10*

crash barrier, *British.* a center guard rail of an express highway to prevent head-on collisions.

If international agreement can be achieved, he [Dr. J. P. Bull] believes, it will be possible to make direct comparisons between the hazards facing road users in one country with those in another. Controlled trials could then be held to test, for example, the optimum design of crash barriers, the control of pedestrian crossings.... *"Notes on the News: When is a Road Death?" New Scientist, April 18, 1968, p 110*

crash pad, *U.S. Slang.* a place in which one may sleep or lodge free or without invitation.

Lately, the Berkeley police have taken to dawn busts [raids] on the communal "crash pads" which litter any big university town. *Martin Walker, "Men Against The Man," The Manchester Guardian Weekly, Oct. 31, 1970, p 24*

One thing we discovered was that there were a series of hostels, or "crash pads," along our route, where it was even possible to get free meals. *Bill Sertl, "'A Communal Pilgrimage'—Along Canada's Highways," The New York Times, June 20, 1971, p 10*

crashworthiness, *n.* the quality of being able to withstand a crash; resistance to collision.

We are... concentrating on improved crash-worthiness which we believe to promise the greatest potential for saving lives in the event of school bus accidents. *John A. Volpe, Secretary, U.S. Department of Transportation, in a Letter to the Editor, The New York Times, Oct. 17, 1970, p 28*

crashworthy, *adj.* able to withstand a crash.

But [Ralph] Nader contended that automakers should build "crashworthy" cars that would not cause bodily injury in a "second collision" after the accident itself. *"Business: The U.S.'s Toughest Customer," Time, Dec. 12, 1969, p 65*

crawling peg, the price or rate maintained at a fixed level for a given period of trading, usually fluctuating in small amounts because of frequent change reflecting current market conditions.

... the crawling peg... would allow each parity to be moved up or down by a small amount each year. *Lombard Lane, "In The City: SDRs and Crawling Pegs," Punch, Dec. 11, 1968, p 852*

... it is difficult to open a paper here without seeing some reference to the negative income tax, crawling peg exchange rates, or the virtues of a free market a la Adam Smith, all of which have become articles of faith to the economists led by Friedman. *Adam Raphael, "Finance: Friedman—Money for the Root of Good," The Manchester Guardian Weekly, Feb. 21, 1970, p 22*

An esoterically named idea... is known as the "crawling peg." A nation's exchange rate would automatically change by small increments, upward or downward, if in actual daily trading on the foreign exchange markets it had persisted on the "floor" or "ceiling" established by the present rules for a specific period of time. *Edwin L. Dale, Jr., The New York Times, Dec. 1, 1968, Sec. 4, p 3*

crawlway, *n.* a passageway with a very low ceiling.

When the rocket is ready, the transporter will lift it and its launch tower, and clank onto a special crawlway, as wide as the New Jersey Turnpike and almost 8 ft. thick (to support the 17.5-million-lb. combined weight of the transporter and its load). *"Science: Space: Adventure Into Emptiness," Time, March 26, 1965, p 49*

crazy, *n. Slang.* a crazy or eccentric person.

Then waiting down in the subway . . . and being jammed in the car with all those faces looking at you, and maybe somebody in there shouting out loud to themselves or laughing or maybe *saying* something to you because there are so many crazies around now. *Roger Angell, "The Floto Letters," The New Yorker, Feb. 21, 1970, p 36*

Like the best of all goons, clowns or assorted crazies, he [Jerry Rubin] is deadly serious. "We are not protesting 'issues'; we are protesting Western civilization". . . . *Colin McGlashan, "Books: Other Nightmare," Review of "Do It!" by Jerry Rubin, The Manchester Guardian Weekly, Nov. 7, 1970, p 19*

[noun use of the adjective]

creative, *n. U.S.* a creative person.

. . . he [an adman named Jerry Della Femina] heads his own agency and is one of the more abrasive of the young "creatives" who have risen fast in a mercurial business. *"Business: Advertising," Time, June 22, 1970, p 78*

Maybe all this recent talk about creativity is pushing the creatives to the top. *Philip H. Dougherty, The New York Times, Feb. 5, 1968, p 53*

[noun use of the adjective]

► In English, adjectives in *-ive* are freely changed to nouns or noun equivalents, as has been the case with *captive, detective, derivative, explosive, fugitive, locomotive, sedative,* and *adjective* itself.

credibility gap, a gap or discrepancy between a government leader's public statements and positions on public affairs and his actual deeds, leading to a weakening of the government's or leader's credibility.

Nevertheless, he [Whitney M. Young, Jr.] added, the Administration "faces a credibility gap of enormous proportions" with blacks. He noted that Nixon had "asked black Americans to judge him by his deeds and not his words; we have done that—and we have been greatly disappointed." *"The Nation: Politics: A Northern-Southern Strategy," Time, Aug. 3, 1970, p 7*

As gaps have arisen they have been papered over, but the "credibility gap" between the regions and Whitehall has steadily widened and many of the people involved are now frustrated, disillusioned and increasingly cynical. *J. R. Atkinson, The Sunday Times (London), July 14, 1968, p 32*

► See the note under COMMUNICATIONS GAP.

creepy-crawly, *n. British. Used informally or as baby talk.* a crawling insect, or something likened to one.

And all this gentle safari in perfect safety—there are *no* poisonous snakes, *no* deadly creepy-crawlies, *no* tropical diseases. *Graham Norton, The Sunday Times (London), Sept. 7, 1969, p 50*

Any kind of revolutionary movement, whatever its cause

and methods, is fair game for infestation by the creepy-crawlies of Communist imperialism. *Dennis Johnson, "Rooks: Commie Plotters," Review of "Scotch on the Rocks" by Douglas Hurd and Andrew Osmond, The Manchester Guardian Weekly, Jan. 23, 1971, p 18*

► The adjective use of *creepy-crawly,* especially figuratively (as in *a creepy-crawly feeling*), is well-established in British English, attested since the 1890's.

cremains, *n.pl.* the ashes of a cremated corpse.

Any contact with the idea of dying takes place on a totally unrealistic level, buoyed up by semantic fiddling (the loved one passes into everlasting slumber, reposes in a casket, has his cremains hygienically dissolved, rests for all eternity in a memorial park). . . . *Alan Coren, "Booking Office: The High Cost of Leaving," Review of "The American Way of Death" by Jessica Mitford, Punch, Oct. 16, 1963, p 577*

[blend of *cremated* and *remains*]

crib death, the sudden death of an infant without any warning symptoms of known cause. Crib deaths have been attributed to viral infections, immune reactions to cow's milk, and other possible but so far unascertained causes. The technical name is SUDDEN INFANT DEATH SYNDROME. Also, *British,* COT DEATH.

In the United States, Dr Marie Valdes-Dapena of the School of Medicine at Temple University, a leading authority on cot deaths, published two maps of the city of Philadelphia, with crib deaths marked on one, and areas due for demolition on the other—the maps were virtually identical. *Donald Teare and Bernard Knight, "Death in the Cot," Science Journal, Jan. 1971, p 72*

criminalization, *n.* the act of making criminal.

There is evidence, too, that criminalization of the distribution of drugs has caused much collateral crime with drug addicts, "to support their habits," as the President's Crime Commission puts it, "stealing millions of dollars worth of property every year and contributing to the public's fear of robbery and burglary." *Norval Morris and Gordon Hawkins, The Honest Politician's Guide to Crime Control, 1970, p 9*

criminalize, *v.t.* to cause to become criminal; to declare (a person or activity) to be criminal.

. . . A President's Judicial Advisory Council Policy Statement (1964) has characterized the activities of the [Narcotics] Bureau as exceeding legal rightfulness in "criminalizing" by executive fiat and administrative dictum those addicted to addicting drugs who for decades have been prevented from going to a doctor for treatment unless it was under the aegis of Lexington Jail, and thru police channels. *Allen Ginsberg, "The Great Marijuana Hoax," The Atlantic, Nov. 1966, p 108*

crise de con·fiance ('kri:z də kɔ̃'fyɑ̃s), *French.* crisis of confidence.

This in turn provoked a *crise de confiance* in Britain, just as the earlier British decision had provoked a similar crisis of confidence in France. *Jean-Jacques Servan-Schreiber, The Times (London), July 16, 1968, p 23*

crise de con·science ('kri:z də kɔ̃'syɑ̃s), *French.* crisis of conscience.

An exposé of all these tumultuous recent troubles and power struggles was given to the Paris papers in a Party press communiqué, which has generated columns of news-paper comment. . . . This has been a *crise de conscience* in French Communist circles such as has never before been reported here to the public. *Genêt, "Letter from Paris," The New Yorker, Nov. 2, 1968, p 179*

critical path, short for CRITICAL PATH ANALYSIS.

. . . Discusses Critical Path Analysis and PERT scheduling technique by tracing a project from initial planning. Management attempts to maintain the project and target data by shifting of resources to critical areas as the critical path for the project shifts from one area of work to another. *"Films of the Week," Listing of "Critical Path in Use," Science News, May 17, 1969, p 468*

critical path analysis, a method of planning and controlling a complex operation by using a computer to show all the connections and interrelations in time that constitute the operation. *Abbreviation:* CPA Compare NETWORK ANALYSIS.

The key element is the techniques that take advantage of the computer's ability to handle vast masses of data and to solve large numbers of equations very quickly.
Among the techniques that have been applied most widely are critical path analysis (C.P.A.) and the closely related program evaluation and review technique (P.E.R.T.) . . . . *Harry Schwartz, The New York Times, Jan. 9, 1967, p 149*

crossbusing, *n.* *U.S.* the busing of children from two different districts to each other's schools.

People who wanted to live where there were blacks no longer wish to do so because of the hardening of racial attitudes caused by crossbusing to achieve racial balance. *Suzanne Brandeau, Winston-Salem, N.C., in a Letter to the Editor, The New York Times, Oct. 1, 1970, p 40*

cross-modal, *adj.* of or relating to the association of two different modes of perception in animals.

The experimental literature on cross-modal effects began to appear in 1960, and even at that early stage a possible relationship between these effects and language was postulated. *Susan Barnes, "Cross-Modal Effects and Language: An Analysis of the Literature," quoted by Emily Hahn, "A Reporter At Large," The New Yorker, Dec. 11, 1971, p 92*

. . . apes can match objects by touch to photographs of identical objects. To do this the brain must compare information from two senses, an operation called cross-modal integration. For instance, learning to read requires the association of sounds with written words, and the association of written words with their meanings. *"Thought Processes in Apes," Science News, Oct. 23, 1971, p 281*

crossply tire, a tire built up from plies laid across one another.

The new Terylene tyre cord is strong, durable and has a high stretch resistance. It is more resilient to impact than rayon and does not develop flat spots like nylon. Both crossply and radial-ply tyres can be made from Terylene. *"Technology Review: Terylene or Nothing for Tyre Cord," New Scientist, March 19, 1970, p 559*

crowd puller, a person, thing, or event that draws a crowd; an attraction.

Greyhound Racing is not the crowd-puller it was. *The Sunday Times (London), March 2, 1969, p 27*
Grange was the newest professional sensation, the prime crowd-puller whom George Halas had lured to the Chicago Bears. *Arthur Daley, The New York Times, July 5, 1968, p 30*

The word 'documentary' has never been a great crowd-puller, but I believe it still serves a purpose. It is a declaration of purpose to stick to the facts; and that puts the emphasis in the right place. . . . *Christopher Ralling, "The Truth About Documentaries—or Documentaries About the Truth," The Listener, Dec. 19, 1968, p 828*

Crow Jim, *U.S. Slang.* prejudice against whites by Negroes.

. . . blacks bullied whites, the smell of Crow Jim was in the air; one set of values had collapsed, as yet not replaced by anything else. *David Halberstam, "The End of a Populist: Senator Gore and a Journalist's Return to Tennessee," Harper's, Jan. 1971, p 36*
[reversed from *Jim Crow* prejudice against Negroes]

cru or **c.r.u.** (kru:), *n.* acronym for *collective reserve unit,* the name of an international currency or monetary unit for use along with other currencies in the reserves of the world's central banks.

France even came up with one version of a plan to establish the "cru"—for collective reserve unit—to be issued in proportion to each country's supply of gold, only to turn away from it again. *"Business: Money: International Monetary Fund," Time, March 29, 1968, p 55*
The c.r.u. would be controlled by a new international agency that would be tied to the I.M.F. [International Monetary Fund] and would operate under the same general rules. *Joseph R. Slevin, The Times (London), March 20, 1967, p 19*

crunch, *n.* **1** a tight squeeze; pressure between opposing forces.

"But we are caught in a crunch," Mr. [Edward A.] Schwartz said. "We are not a resistance group, we just present the alternatives. That's not radical enough for such campuses as Columbia and Michigan, but too radical for many others." *Steven V. Roberts, The New York Times, Feb. 26, 1968, p 26*

2 Usually, **the crunch. a** financial pressure; economic squeeze.

Both Drs. Hilst and Blair cautiously conceded that existing systems in Western Europe and Japan may be ahead of those in the United States—because, Dr. Hilst says, the crunch on resources came sooner in these more thickly populated areas. *"Science News of the Week: Environmental Monitoring: Slow Progress Worldwide," Science News, Oct. 10, 1970, p 301*

b the decisive or critical moment; turning point or crisis.

Bull suggests that such pragmatic considerations, in the crunch, are likely to prove an even more indispensable factor in the South African outlook than its precious racial exclusiveness, and he goes so far as to voice his confidence of this with the rather bold rhetorical question "Is there any reason to think that South Africa would feel bound to continue to support indefinitely an embattled white Rhodesia?" *Charles Miller, "UDI—Past, Present and Future," Review of "Rhodesia: Crisis of Color" by Theodore Bull, Saturday Review, Oct. 19, 1968, p 53*
Similarly, take this assurance on the palmy days of early 1957 of intention to maintain "free and innocent passage" for shipping through the Strait of Tiran, only to do nothing when the crunch came 10 years later. *Elizabeth Monroe, The Times (London), June 8, 1967, p 11*

crush barrier, *British.* a steel barrier for restraining crowds.

Crush barriers were overturned and town councillors

waiting to be presented were swept aside as they [15,000 people in Fiji] fought their way to meet the Queen. *"Fijians Pass Barriers to See Queen," The Times (London), March 5, 1970, p 6*

It is an old problem, tragically and suddenly revived but familiar. In 1946 at Bolton some thousands who had not been able to get into the Wanderers' ground broke down a fence. The newcomers caused people on the terraces to lose their footing, and 33 were suffocated or crushed to death against crush-barriers. *"Comment: The Ibrox Tragedy," The Manchester Guardian Weekly, Jan. 9, 1971, p 12*

cry·o·bi·ol·o·gy (ˌkrai ou bai'al ə dʒi:), *n.* the study of the effects of freezing and low temperatures on living things.

Robert Nelson, president of the [Cryonics] society, said it was a "nonprofit society formed to educate the public in the field of cryobiology, which encompasses freezing techniques on all biological matter." *The New York Times, Jan. 20, 1967, p 44*

[from *cryo-* freezing (from Greek *krýos* icy cold) + *biology*]

cry·on·ics (krai'an iks), *n.* the preservation of bodies from decay by a freezing process.

The body . . . of Stephen Jay Mandell . . . was frozen at a Long Island funeral home in cooperation with the Cryonics Society of New York, of which Mr. Mandell had been a member. . . . Cryonics derives from cryobiology — the study of life at extremely low temperatures. *The New York Times, Sept. 6, 1968, p 3*

The widespread application of cryonics might result in a sudden loss of population in an unpleasant year, to be followed by overpopulation when times improved. There is the question of how the thawed person would adjust to a strange society. One can also imagine staggering legal headaches. *Herman Kahn and Anthony J. Wiener, "Man and His Future: Some Technological Problem Areas: Dangerous Personal Choice," 1969 Britannica Yearbook of Science and the Future, 1968, p 408*

[from *cryo-* freezing (from Greek *krýos* icy cold) + *-nics*, as in *bionics*]

cryoprecipitate, *n.* a substance obtained by cryoprecipitation, now referring specifically to a concentrate of blood-clotting protein.

In its frozen state, this cryoprecipitate kept indefinitely and could be quickly processed for intravenous infusion in a solution averaging ten to 20 times the potency of plasma. *"Medicine: Hematology," Time, Aug. 16, 1968, p 36*

cryoprecipitation, *n.* chemical precipitation achieved by freezing, now used especially for a method of concentrating the blood-clotting protein needed in large amounts to treat hemophiliacs.

Cryoprecipitation, so-called because it is effected at low temperature, enables the antihemophilic factor from a pint of blood to be concentrated in a volume of only 10 ml. [milliliters]. *Martin C. G. Israëls, "Medicine: Hematology," Britannica Book of the Year 1969, p 498*

[from *cryo-* freezing + *precipitation*]

cryoprobe, *n.* an instrument for freezing tissues, usually with liquid nitrogen, in order to destroy, remove, or operate on them.

The central gas-cooled cryoprobe has a cap for treating wide, shallow areas, such as malignant skin lesions. *Picture legend, "The Unceasing Search for a Cancer Cure," The World Book Science Annual 1969, p 96*

Faced with cases that seemed beyond help, Dr. Bellows decided to try a cryoprobe chilled to a temperature of −65°C. *"Medicine: Ophthalmology: Icy Cure," Time, July 21, 1967, p 45*

[from *cryo-* freezing + *probe*]

cryosurgeon, *n.* a surgeon who specializes in cryosurgery.

Cryosurgeons use cold to kill the cells of a malignant rectal tumor. The frozen cells decay in 7 to 10 days. *Picture legend, "The Unceasing Search for a Cancer Cure," The World Book Science Annual 1969, p 96*

cryosurgery, *n.* surgery in which freezing temperatures are used to destroy or remove tissues.

He [Dr. John Milton McLean] was a leader in clinical research on the use of hormone ACTH [adrenocorticotropin] to treat inflammations of the eye and in the basic work on the new cryosurgery (freezing-surgery) of the eye, especially in retinal detachment. *The New York Times, May 3, 1968, p 47*

[from *cryo-* freezing + *surgery*]

cryosurgical, *adj.* of or relating to cryosurgery.

The significance of the introduction of this cryosurgical equipment was that cold could be safely and accurately applied to any part of the body to which the tip of the probe could be introduced, and the tissue surrounding the probe could be independently frozen and destroyed. *Sir James Fraser, "Special Report: Cold as a Treatment for Disease," Britannica Book of the Year 1970, p 517*

The Smith book produces a greater sense of immediacy by its expertise, detail and photographs. You can see the silver-tipped cryosurgical probe used to induce lesions at specific points in the brain for the relief of certain neurological disorders. *Philip Morrison, "Books," Review of "Current Trends in Cryobiology," edited by Audrey U. Smith, Scientific American, June 1971, p 133*

cryp·to- ('krip tou-), combining form formerly used chiefly in scientific and technical compounds with the meaning "hidden," "secret," but gradually extended to more general applications, especially in the sense of "veiled," "disguised," "not open and aboveboard." A sampling of recently formed compounds with *crypto-* includes the following:

crypto-censorship, *n.:* What is needed is not some form of crypto-censorship by external bodies but self-censorship, or self-inspection made by a body which is largely, but not wholly, composed of representatives from the several branches of television itself. *Ronald Butt, "Violence on TV," The Times (London), March 5, 1970, p 10*

crypto-colonial, *adj.:* Calling the house "weirdo," the neighbors sued on the ground that Eustice's dream was "inharmonious" with their own ranch-style and crypto-colonial homes. *"From Dream to Nightmare," Time, Sept. 26, 1969, p 56*

crypto-commercialism, *n.:* Let us have honesty, straight dealing, clean breasts, an end to subterfuge and shamateurism and crypto-commercialism. *H. F. Ellis, "Hypocritic Oaths, Etc.," Punch, Feb. 21, 1968, p 271*

crypto-opponent, *n.:* Opposition to the war has clinched the intellectual standing of Senator J. William Fulbright and perhaps even of Dr. Spock. War supporters who have been drummed out of the fraternity include Dean Rusk, John Roche and Eric Hoffer. As a crypto-opponent, Robert S. McNamara is slowly being reinstated, and the admissions

115

committee is eyeing a most impressive candidate: General David M. Shoup, a Marine hero who calls the U.S. "a militaristic and aggressive nation." *"The Tortured Role of the Intellectual in America," Time, May 9, 1969, p 36*

crypto-security, *adj.:* "I had an unblemished military record," he said. "I was up for promotion to sergeant, and I had a crypto-security clearance. I was due to leave Vietnam after being there 13 months, but I couldn't accept being part of an army that was doing those things to the Vietnamese people." *John M. Lee, The New York Times, July 15, 1968, p 6*

crypto-sexual, *adj.:* Looking like an eighteenth-century antecedent for the Ford Edsel, this uncomely wourche [a carriage] was designed to carry hunters from prey to prey in what was undoubtedly as uncomfortable a manner as possible. (Close scrutiny reveals the fan of a camp follower beneath the canopy; or, perhaps, then as now, she was sketched in merely as a piece of crypto-sexual salespitchery. We shall never know. *Illustration legend, "Carriages," Punch, Aug. 7, 1968, p 206*

CS, a symbol for a tear gas widely used in military and riot-control operations. Compare BZ, GB, VX.

The principal short-term incapacitant now in military use is CS (orthochlorobenzalmalonitrile). This compound was first synthesized in the U.S. in the 1920's. After World War II it was developed by the British government as a riot-control agent and named after its American discoverers, Ben Carson and Roger Staughton of Middlebury College. *Matthew S. Meselson, "Chemical and Biological Weapons," Scientific American, May 1970, p 21*

...CS is a lachrymator, a respiratory irritant, a sternutator, a vesicant and a lung irritant....*G. Robert N. Jones, "A Closer Look at CS Gas," New Scientist, June 18, 1970, p 579*

CSM, abbreviation of *corn, soya, milk,* used as the name of a powdered blend of corn meal, soybean flour, and dry milk marketed as a food supplement.

Although the U.S. Department of Agriculture has developed a food made of corn, soybeans and milk, called CSM, it is a gruel, really a baby food, Prof. Brownell says. *"Nutrition: Rice Substitute Developed," Science News, May 11, 1968, p 454*

CT, abbreviation of CELL THERAPY.

This book...is an exhaustive examination (with case histories) of the doctors of all stripes who deal in youth-giving formulas and operations—cell therapy (CT), facelifting.... *Katherine Gauss Jackson, "Books in Brief," Review of "The Youth Doctors" by Patrick M. McGrady, Jr., Harper's, Jan. 1969, p 106*

CTOL ('si:ˌtɒl), *n.* acronym for *conventional take-off and landing.*

Also, there are the greatly improved noise pollution characteristics of VTOL compared not only with conventional aircraft (CTOL) but with short takeoff and landing craft (STOL) as illustrated in the accompanying comparison of noise 'footprints'.... *Angela Croome, Science Journal, March 1970, p 5*

Cubanologist, *n.* an expert on Cuba and Cuban politics. Compare AMERICANOLOGIST, KREMLINOLOGIST, PEKINGOLOGIST.

But like other Cubanologists, who sit in Florida and observe Havana via the microfilms in a university library, Dr. Suarez does not assess Castro's achievements by reference to the past. *Jonathan Steele, "Books of the Year: Castro and Communism," Review of "Cuba: Castroism*

and Communism" by Andres Suarez, *The Manchester Guardian Weekly, Dec. 21, 1967, p 11*

cube, *n.* short for FLASHCUBE.

Flashbulbs were being partly replaced by flashcubes which were basically four bulbs in expendable reflectors, the cube turning after each shot. Even the cheapest cameras had some means whereby flashbulbs could be used or cubes could be plugged directly into the camera. *Victor G. C. Blackman, "Photography: Processes and Equipment," Britannica Book of the Year 1970, p 615*

cu·chi·fri·to (ˌkuː tʃiˈfriː tou), *n. American Spanish.* a cube of pork in batter and deep-fat fried.

One night over cold cuchifritos and a hot pinball machine, Willie had a vision of the triumph of love over induction. *Jeremy Larner, "They are Taking My Letters," Harper's, Oct. 1968, p 50*

cult-figure, *n.* a person or figure that is the object of a cult or popular adulation.

It is because she carried her instincts so miraculously intact from childhood into adult life that [the English painter Dora] Carrington is unique. There is some part of her in all of us, so that whatever our reaction to her, it cannot be one of indifference. It is easy to see how she could diminish into a fashionable cult-figure. *Michael Holroyd, "Love, Loneliness, Elation and Despair," The Times (London), Nov. 5, 1970, p 14*

Our TV commercials have popularized the figure of Lenny Lent and we are placing a number of articles on the history, theology and image of the Season in periodicals with wide readership spectrum.... We have not, so far, come up with a cult-figure to equal Father Christmas. Lenny Lent, while productive interimwise, lacks the folklore attributes we are looking for. *R. G. G. Price, "Forty Shopping Days," Punch, Feb. 23, 1966, p 269*

culturalization, *n.* the process of acquiring the ways, attitudes, and habits of a culture.

To become a human being, the hominid [animal resembling man] must acquire a human nature, and this he does through the culturalization process in which he is conditioned. Human nature, then, is what Homo sapiens learns from his culture. *Ashley Montagu, The New York Times Book Review, Feb. 25, 1968, p 14*

cultural revolution, 1 a complete transformation of the institutions of present-day culture or society.

We need an alternative program, an alternative both to development and to merely political revolution. Let me call this alternative program either institutional or cultural revolution, because its aim is the transformation of both public and personal reality. *Ivan Illich, "Revolution and Education in Latin America: The False Ideology of Schooling," Saturday Review, Oct. 17, 1970, p 57*

Legally sanctioned paths toward change, as far as Kate Millett is concerned, are simply not enough. She calls for a "cultural revolution, which must necessarily involve political and economic reorganization [but] must go far beyond as well." *"Who's Come a Long Way, Baby?" Time, Aug. 31, 1970, p 19*

The same social events that produced a sexist "cultural revolution" produced a sexist radical left, which, in turn, gave rise to the women's-liberation movement. Rock has been particularly resistant to the inroads of a resurgent feminism, but it is not impervious.... today there is a noticeable influx of female singers and composers, and they are finding a receptive audience. *Ellen Willis, "Musical Events: Rock, Etc.," The New Yorker, Oct. 23, 1971, p 173*

2 Usually, **Cultural Revolution**. the name of a major drive by Chinese Communists led by Mao Tse-tung, begun in 1966 and lasting several years, to enforce Maoist ideology and purge China of revisionist leaders and mandarin influences.

The Communist Chinese Threat was not rated as serious. The country's 2.75 million troops had their hands full stabilizing the countryside after the upheaval of the Cultural Revolution. *Lloyd Norman, "Armed Forces of the World," The 1970 World Book Year Book, p 217*

It is my impression that at long last the Great Proletarian Cultural Revolution has succeeded in generating a profound and fundamental transformation which is rejuvenating China. *Chester Ronning, "China's 700 Million Are on the Way," The New York Times, June 7, 1971, p 33*

cultural revolutionary, an advocate or supporter of cultural revolution.

The cultural revolutionary risks the future on the educability of man. *Ivan Illich, "Revolution and Education in Latin America: The False Ideology of Schooling," Saturday Review, Oct. 17, 1970, p 57*

Going beyond yoga, many cultural revolutionaries are adopting—or at least sampling—an imported version of the dietary discipline of the Zen Buddhists. *"Modern Living: The Kosher of the Counterculture," Time, Nov. 16, 1970, p 59*

cul·tu·ra·ti (ˌkəl tʃəˈrɑː tiː), *n.pl.* the cultured class; cultured people.

It is a measure of the isolation of the planning profession that its revolutionaries should be amiable culturati filled with nostalgia for "civilised" cities (especially Italian cities) of the past and with little grasp of the social pressures of today. *Colin Moorcraft, "Spoil-tip City," New Scientist and Science Journal, Dec. 16, 1971, p 180*

[formed in English from *culture* on the analogy of *literati* (the educated class)]

culture gap, a difference between cultures. See the note under COMMUNICATIONS GAP.

Its [the Peace Corps'] essential components are familiar enough—the primitive living conditions, the long working hours, the deep and abiding friendships across the culture-gap. *John Demos, The New York Times Book Review, March 3, 1968, p 38*

Oh dear, it seems that we are faced here with what the anthropologists call a culture gap, which can be crossed only by a certain stretching of the imagination on your side, a certain amount of deliberate explication on mine. *Dan Jacobson, "The Rape of Tamar," Harper's, Aug. 1970, p 60*

culture shock, the discomposure and disorientation a person experiences when thrust into a foreign culture or a new way of life. Compare FUTURE SHOCK.

[Alvin] Toffler argues: "Future shock arises from the superimposition of a new culture on an old one. It is culture shock in one's own society. But its impact is far worse. For most travelers have the comforting knowledge that the culture they left behind will be there to return to. The victim of future shock does not." *"The Diseases of the Future," Time, Aug. 3, 1970, p 13*

Mr. T. Dennison observed that a great deal of time, money and effort had been given by the steel industry to trying to interest British Schools in engineering but with little result. Able boys were repelled by the belief that they could only be "cogs" in industry, and they were also repelled by the "culture shock" they experienced on entering

it. *J. G. Crowther, "Spring Books: Treating Science as Creative Activity," Review of "Towards More Creative Science," edited by Donald Hutchings, New Scientist, April 27, 1967, p 232*

culturette, *n. Slang.* a woman engaged in cultural activities.

"The problem is how to build a permanent audience".... How to make the museum more than just a plaything for culturettes and dilettantes? *Russell Lynes, "After Hours: Atlanta's Culture for All Seasons," Harper's, Feb. 1969, p 30*

[from *culture* + *-ette*, as in *suffragette*]

culture-vulture, *n. Slang.* a person who is extremely or excessively interested in culture.

Long before my time the pioneer culture-vultures dismembered Charles Chaplin: some say he never got put together properly again. *J. E. Hinder, "Criticism: Television," Punch, Sept. 18, 1968, p 413*

But whether this awakening of public interest in the arts booms into vigorous, creative prosperity, or busts in a proliferation of culture centers inhabited by culture-vultures—but no culture—rests largely in the courage and wisdom of comparative newcomers to the field....*Emily Coleman, "The Councils [Arts Councils of America] Take Counsel," Saturday Review, April 30, 1966, p 59*

cup-tied, *adj. British.* participating in a cup-tie or tie-breaking match for a cup.

Wakeling, being cup-tied after playing for Corinthian-Casuals, will be missed in midfield, and Richards will probably replace him. *Norman Fox, "Football: Isthmian League Have Strong Hand," The Times (London), Nov. 20, 1970, p 18*

curate's egg, *British.* something that is of mixed quality; something good in parts only.

Purcell's *Dido and Aeneas* seems to be extraordinarily resistant to a wholly successful recorded performance. What we have had up to and including this one is a series of six curate's eggs. *Alec Robertson, "Reviews: Documentary," The Gramophone, April 1968, p 551*

With a business so diversified as Harrison & Crosfield's —which spans rubber and tea planting, tin mines, insurance broking, chemicals and general import-export—the average year tends to be something of a curate's egg. *The Times (London), Oct. 30, 1968, p 22*

► Originally used as a simile, as in "excellent in parts, like the curate's egg." The allusion, according to the *OED Supplement*, was to a story which first appeared in *Punch* concerning "a meek curate who, having been given a stale egg by his episcopal host, stated that 'parts of it' were 'excellent' (*Punch* 9 Nov. 1895, p 222)." The term is listed as a cliché in the latest edition of Fowler's *Modern English Usage* (revised by Sir Ernest Gowers), and though it continues to be much used in Great Britain it is not included in standard British and U.S. dictionaries. The only *OEDS* quotation is dated 1905.

cur·sus ho·no·rum (ˈkər səs həˈnɔr əm), *Latin.* course of honors; sequence of offices (originally referring to the series of offices leading up to the Roman consulate).

Indeed, some might find it remarkable that such a *cursus honorum*—Dean of King's College London, Dean of Exeter, Dean of St. Paul's—should have fallen to so liberal a thinker. *Joseph McCulloch, "Books: The Quest for Truth," Review of "Christian Humanist Memories and Meanings" by W. R. Matthews, The Times (London), March 14, 1970, p IV*

curtain-up, *n. British.* the rise of the curtain at the start of a performance.

Two bows before curtain-up for the conductor was a mark of honour from the Edinburgh audience for their fellow-countryman James Loughran, just appointed to the Hallé. *Alan Blyth, "James Loughran in Command: La Traviata," The Times (London), Dec. 22, 1970, p 11*

[from the phrase *curtain up!*, used as a warning call to the cast and crews]

curve ball, *U.S.* a trick or ruse.

... numbers of people will argue heatedly that Government half-truths, cover-ups, obfuscations, sophistries, euphemisms and curve balls are permissible tools of the trade so long as a "real lie" (meaning outright and provable) is not employed to gull the people. *Tom Wicker, "A Man to be Trusted," The New York Times, June 29, 1971, p 37*

[from the baseball term for a ball that swerves just before reaching the batter]

cushioncraft, *n.* a vehicle that travels on a cushion of air; an air cushion vehicle or hovercraft.

Britten Norman, the Isle of Wight aircraft manufacturer, has decided to sell its subsidiary making the ten-seat cushioncraft. *Arthur Reed, "World of Aviation: Britten Norman to Sell Subsidiary," The Times (London), Feb. 19, 1970, p 23*

cute·sy or **cute·sie** ('kyu:t si:), *adj. U.S.* self-consciously or affectedly cute.

Mozart: The Impresario (RCA Victor). Few new releases could possibly have a narrower appeal than Mozart's small squib about the tribulations of a Rudolph Bing of the 18th century.... the libretto was reworked in English by Dory Previn.... Her adaptation makes it a gossipy backstage operetta of fights, love affairs and campy humor. The music that interrupts the cutesy dialogue is standard Mozart.... *"Time Listings: Records," Time, June 7, 1968, p 4*

Start with the cutesie title [*Bashful Billionaire, The Story of Howard Hughes,* by Albert B. Gerber]. Pursue the mysteriously jumbled chronology. Endure a prose style whose principal interest is a rare, fossilized quaintness. *Michael Levitas, The New York Times Book Review, Feb. 25, 1968, p 10*

[from *cute* + *-sy* or *-sie*, as in *artsy, gutsy,* etc.]

cy·a·no·a·cet·y·lene (ˌsɑi ə nou ə'set əˌliːn), *n.* a large organic molecule discovered in cosmic gas clouds.

Cyanoacetylene (HC_3N), the most complex organic molecule found in space so far, has now come to light in the radio source as the galactic centre. *"Monitor: A Five-atom Molecule Turns up in Space," New Scientist, Aug. 6, 1970, p 270*

The five atoms of cyanoacetylene are the largest number so far found bound into a single molecule in interstellar space. *"Toward Life Between the Stars," Science News, Oct. 10, 1970, p 299*

Cyanoacetylene is the first interstellar molecule whose complexity approaches that required for amino acids. It contains 5 atoms: a hydrogen and a nitrogen connected to either end of a 3-atom carbon chain. *Jim Hampton, "Startling Discoveries in Astronomy," Encyclopedia Science Supplement (Grolier) 1971, p 56*

cy·ber·nat·ed ('sɑi bərˌnei tid), *adj.* automated through computers.

Papers and panel discussions on basic assumptions, computing machines and cybernated systems, and on the evolving and the future society. *"Books of the Week," Listing of "The Evolving Society," Science News, July 16, 1966, p 44*

[back formation from *cybernation*]

cy·ber·na·tion (ˌsɑi bər'nei ʃən), *n.* automation through the use of computers.

To begin with, I believe that cybernation—the complete adaptation of computer-like equipments to industrial, economic, and social activity—will represent a quantum jump in the extension of man. *Glenn T. Seaborg, "The Cybernetic Age: An Optimist's View," Saturday Review, July 15, 1967, p 21*

[coined in 1962 by Donald N. Michael, a U.S. communications expert, from *cybern*etics + autom*ation*]

cy·ber·net·ist (sɑi bər'net ist), *n.* an expert in cybernetics (the comparative study of complex calculating machines and the human nervous system).

Indeed, everything which a physicist does with energy, a cybernetist does with information: namely, he studies receiving, storing, transmitting, transforming and using information. *V. G. Drozin, "Cybernetics," Encyclopedia Science Supplement (Grolier) 1970, p 292*

▶ Earlier variant names are *cyberneticist* and *cybernetician*.

cy·borg ('sɑiˌbɔrg), *n.* a human body or other organism whose functions are taken over in part by various electronic or electro-mechanical devices.

The futuristic cyborg, or combination man and machine, will consist of a stationary, computerlike human brain, served by machines to fill its limited physical needs and act upon its commands. *"Man Into Superman, The Promise and Peril of the New Genetics: The Body," Time, April 19, 1971, p 27*

It is also possible that whenever biological life reaches the intellectual level at which the physiological organism can understand itself (i.e., the stage which Man has just attained), then inorganic components are used for the replacement of defective or worn-out biological ones. In fact, the Cyborg (which is the name recently coined for animal-machine integrations) is possibly the ultimate form for any race. *C. Maxwell Cade, "Books," Review of "Man Modified: An Exploration of the Man Machine Relationship" by David Fishlock, New Scientist, Sept. 11, 1969, p 541*

[contraction of *cybernetic organism*]

cyclic AMP, a chemical compound that acts as an intercellular messenger in carrying out the action of hormones, especially the hormones of the pituitary gland.

In a series of experiments she [Dr. Jane Shaw] is attempting to define the relationship between prostaglandins and a substance called cyclic AMP, a chemical widely recognized as a mediator of hormonal effects. *Barbara J. Culliton, "Prostaglandins: Something for Everyone," Science News, Oct. 10, 1970, p 306*

[*AMP*, abbreviation of *adenosine monophosphate* a compound of adenosine (a constituent of nucleic acid) and one phosphate group]

cyclo-cross, *n.* a sport which combines cycling and cross-country running.

Cyclo-cross was invented neither for the competitor nor the paying spectator but for the television viewer. *Michael Parkinson, The Sunday Times (London), Jan. 21, 1968, p 18*

cy·clo-pousse (ˌsi: klou'pu:s), *n.* (in Southeast Asia) a pedaled or motorized rickshaw; pedicab.

I have been pedalled uncomplainingly through a snow storm by a Hanoi cyclo-pousse boy clad in cotton shorts and singlet, and in the end he argued logically, at length, but without temper, about the fare. *Rawle Knox, "Talking to the Annamites," Punch, May 15, 1968, p 701*

[from French *cyclo-pousse*, from *cyclo-* bicycle or tricycle + *pousse* rickshaw, short for *pousse-pousse*, literally, push-push (though a rickshaw is pulled rather than pushed)]

cy·to·ki·nin (ˌsai tou'kai nən), *n.* a plant hormone that directs the differentiation of cells into the roots and shoots of young plants. Compare ABSCISIC ACID, BRASSIN, KINETIN.

The cytokinins are closely related to adenine, one of the bases found in nucleic acids, and compounds with strong cytokinin activity occur in transfer RNA. *New Scientist, Nov. 20, 1970, p 393*

There is good evidence that cytokinins are necessary for xylem differentiation, in addition to auxin and sucrose. *Donald E. Fosket, "Xylem," McGraw-Hill Yearbook of Science and Technology 1971, p 441*

[from *cyto-* cell + *kinin* a growth-promoting substance in plants (from Greek *kīnein* to move)]

D

dab, *Slang.* —*n.* a fingerprint.

Such a method, coding the sixteen points which must check with a scene-of-crime "dab" before being accepted in court, would cut search man-hours in certain circumstances, by days. *The Sunday Times (London), May 15, 1966, p 8*

—*v.t.* to fingerprint.

Wall Street firms are required to "dab" (fingerprint) every employee from messenger boy to president. *The Times (London), Feb. 6, 1970, p 25*

dal (da:l), *n.* a cooked dish of India, made with lentils and spices.

...Indian mothers deliberately withhold from their young children the only protein-rich food in the traditional diet, a lentil preparation called dal. *Joseph Lelyveld, The New York Times, Jan. 9, 1967, p 12*

Then there is *dal*, served separately in a great tureen, a yellow porridge-like gruel of curried lentils. *The Times (London), Aug. 6, 1963, p 10*

[from Hindi *dāl*]

dal·a·pon ('dæl ə,pɑn), *n.* a herbicide used especially against couch grass.

The results with herbicides have not all been positive, however. Dr. Kring and Dr. Ahrens reported that the highly water-soluble dalapon and highly active picloram required high rates of carbon application for detoxification. *Joan Lee Faust, The New York Times, July 31, 1968, p 52*

[probably from the chemical name, *di-alpha-chloropropionic* acid]

dammit, *n.* **as near as dammit,** *British Slang.* very nearly; almost.

That's bad enough, but with local taxation, insurance contributions and other items the public sector in toto relieves you of £20,000 million, as near as dammit. *George Schwartz, The Sunday Times (London), Oct. 19, 1969, p 28*

I am no longer a Reuters correspondent, but clearly this affectedly casual conversation was as near as dammit an apology for what had happened to me in Peking. *Anthony Grey, "East Berlin Revisited," The Manchester Guardian Weekly, May 15, 1971, p 6*

damp squib, *British Slang.* something that has no effect or that fails completely; anything ineffective.

In contrast there is a strong body of union opinion which believes the whole demonstration will be a damp squib. *Alan Hamilton, The Times (London), Jan. 9, 1971, p 2*

But with approximately £86 million spent on information services in 1966, by Federal authorities according to National Science Foundation, this does support the view that, compared with the damp squib that Dr Mellanby reports for scientific research, a real information firework display is going on in the technological development area. *Derek H. Barlow, London, in a Letter to the Editor, New Scientist, May 11, 1967, p 358*

[the earlier meaning was a joke or lampoon (a squib) that falls flat, as a squib (firecracker) whose powder is damp]

dan (da:n), *n.* one of several grades or ranks of proficiency in Japanese sports and games.

Brian is now 22 and a black belt third dan. *Dudley Doust, The Sunday Times (London), Dec. 1, 1968, p 22*

But then Iyeda has been playing the ancient Oriental board game constantly since he was eight, now ranks as a fifth Dan professional (ninth Dan is highest) in his native Japan, where GO has been the national indoor game for as long as anybody can remember. *Time, April 22, 1966, p 48*

D & D, *U.S. Slang.* abbreviation of *deaf and dumb* (in the sense of withholding information from the police for fear of reprisal).

Playing D. & D. (deaf and dumb) with cops was a lesson taught in the quiet back rooms of precinct houses. *Time, March 21, 1969, p 21*

dangle-dolly, *n. British.* a small doll hung in a car window as a charm or decoration.

A leading fancy goods manufacturer said that the industry had done "reasonably well" out of rattles, rosettes, and favours, but looked forward to an increasing Americanisation of British campaign methods, and saw no reason why, next time, Heath or Wilson dangle-dollies should not be hanging in the rear-windows of every car in the land. *Punch, March 30, 1966, p 457*

dark comedy, **1** another name for BLACK HUMOR.

The literary movement known as Black Humor or Dark Comedy, which achieved a certain inflated prominence in the early sixties, has lately shown signs of reaching some condition of impasse or exhaustion. *John W. Aldridge, "Dance of Death," The Atlantic, July 1968, p 89*

2 another name for BLACK COMEDY.

... there is scarcely any need to mention the vast terrain that has lately been opened up in the name of black comedy, sick comedy, or, more conventionally, dark comedy. *Walter Kerr, The New York Times, Oct. 16, 1966, Sec. 2, p 1*

► The term *dark comedies* has long been used by dramatic critics to describe several of Shakespeare's comedies, notably *All's Well That Ends Well, Measure for Measure,* and *Troilus and Cressida,* that are characterized by a pessimistic tone, an underlying seriousness of purpose, and unconventional endings. The American drama critic Walter Kerr, in the quotation under definition 2 above, probably uses the Shakespearian term as a catch-all for the genre of comedy that includes black comedy.

dar·o·bok·ka (ˌdær əˈbɑk ə), *n.* a drum struck with two hands, used in Egypt and North Africa.

... the atmosphere was charged by groups of musicians beating a variety of drums — tablas and darobokkas — giving a pulsating beat to accompany the eerie rhythm provided by reed and bamboo pipes. *Jim Railton, "Rowing: Where the Nile Flows a Lighter Shade of Blue," The Times (London), Dec. 18, 1970, p 20*

[from Arabic *darabukka* tambourine]

da·shi·ki (dəˈʃiː kiː), *n.* a loose, shirtlike, pullover garment originally from Africa, usually short-sleeved and having bright colors.

At Burroughs, there were several black students, wearing Afro haircuts and dashikis. *Calvin Trillin, "U.S. Journal: Missouri," The New Yorker, May 16, 1970, p 110*

More than a third of the participants are poor, black or both, and when they learn sewing they sometimes discuss black history and make African-style dashikis. *Time, Aug. 2, 1971, p 44*

data bank, **1** a collection of records stored in a computer system so that any data may be extracted from it or organized as desired.

In defence of databanks, one can point to major benefits in medicine, in research, in industry and in commerce which stem directly from the centralization of information. *Kenneth Owen, The Times (London), Nov. 18, 1970, p 12*

It was proposed ... that a computer data bank be established to provide prompt and comprehensive information for lawmakers who want to do their homework properly. *Time, Sept. 28, 1970, p 13*

2 *Transferred sense.* any data storage system.

The nucleic acid content of many of the extranuclear organelles makes sense on this theory, as do many special mechanisms for the transmission of organelle instructions that are not recorded in the central nuclear data bank. *Philip Morrison, "Books," Review of "Origin of Eukaryotic Cells" by Lynn Margulis, Scientific American, May 1971, p 128*

3 the place where such a collection is kept or stored.

... alarmed individuals fear that our rights to liberty and privacy will vanish. One target of criticism is the proposed central data bank in Washington, D.C., which is to contain important facts on all residents and citizens of the United States. *"Review of the Year—Man and His World," Encyclopedia Science Supplement (Grolier) 1970, p 238*

Also called DATA BASE.

data-bank, *v.t.* to put or store in a data bank.

As data banks proliferate, so will the indiscriminate use of the material they contain. And that raises the question whether an American citizen has a constitutional or legal right *not* to be data-banked, computerized, stored, exchanged and possibly damaged — materially or in reputation — by the process. *Tom Wicker, "In the Nation: A Right Not to be Data-Banked?" The New York Times, July 7, 1970, p 38*

data base, another name for DATA BANK.

The programs are written to retrieve and process information stored in a pre-arranged way in the computer's peripheral units — such as magnetic tape decks or discs. Any alterations to the way in which this store of information (the data base) is arranged ... usually requires alterations to all the relevant programs. *New Scientist, April 16, 1970, p 117*

dataphone, *n.* a telephone apparatus for transmitting data, such as information into a computer.

One of industry's main criticisms at the present time is of the weak marketing methods of the Post Office. Industry spokesmen say that if they were allowed to sell telephones, extension telephones, dataphones and other instruments direct to the public they could sell a lot more than they can now sell to the Post Office.... *Ron Brown, "Telecommunications: the Next 20 Years," New Scientist and Science Journal, July 1, 1971, p 14*

The telephone companies expected to continue ... activities in the area of data communications, including Data-Phone and private-line facilities that served more than 100,000 teletypewriters. *Walter Axelsen, "Communications," 1970 Britannica Yearbook of Science and the Future, 1969, p 150*

dating bar, *U.S.* a bar in which single men and women meet and date socially.

In city after city, run of the gin-mill bars have been turned into "dating bars." What converts an ordinary bar into a dating bar is a weekend admission fee (usually $1), a large welcome for single girls, and a good neighborhood. *Time, Sept. 15, 1967, p 37*

dawk, *n. U.S.* a person who disapproves of wars but is unwilling to oppose and propagandize actively against war; a compromiser who is neither a hawk nor a dove.

Toward that end, the House Republican Conference last

week issued a 37-page indictment of Lyndon Johnson's conduct of the war. In it, the Republicans did their agile best to sail with the doves and swoop with the hawks. The result was a dawk.... However, the Republican dawks could not convincingly square their criticism of U.S. war policy with their insistence that they still support the war. *"Dawk Talk," Time, Sept. 30, 1966, p 12*

[blend of *dove* and *hawk*; a *Time* coinage]

day-care, *adj.* U.S. concerned with the care of preschool children (usually of working mothers) outside their homes.

The board unanimously endorse a proposal to set up work incentives for welfare recipients and to expand counselling services, family planning and day-care services. *Martin Tolchin, The New York Times, May 22, 1968, p 1*

Although things have been getting progressively better for French women...they are still hampered by many thoughtless inequities. Day-care centers are scarce, businessmen are reluctant to hire women on a part-time basis. *Time, Aug. 17, 1970, p 24*

It is hard to understand why one must still struggle to persuade the general public and public officials of the need for homemaker services and day-care services. *Mrs. Marshall Field, New York, N.Y., in a Letter to the Editor, Harper's, Jan. 1966, p 6*

Day-Glo, *n.* the trade name of a fluorescent paint that gives off a variety of brilliant colors when exposed to light.

...the young master of protractor art fills the gallery with rainbow colors so hot and jumpy that they look like Day-Glo, though they are not. *Time, Feb. 2, 1970, p 2*

Under the impact of a very serious sun, the grass quite suddenly flushes green, especially on southfacing slopes, about the tenth. That green is unreal, almost a Day-Glo-poster color; if it lasted, it would make summer intolerably virid. But it is happily accepted as an outrider, as the first summer replacement for dead hay and grizzled mud. *L. E. Sissman, "Innocent Bystander: The City Shepherd's Calendar, April," The Atlantic, Feb. 1971, p 41*

The George Mitchell Choir, greasepaint and day-glo and soft-shoe, was hamming it up on the jetty. *Hugh Johnson, The Sunday Times (London), April 14, 1968, p 15*

d.b., abbreviation of *double-breasted* (suit, jacket, coat, etc.).

...a squat man in a shiny d.b. sharkskin equally engages my mother in a twenty-minute discursion on the philosophy of foot growth and persuades her to buy me shoes a half-size larger than she'd planned....*L. E. Sissman, "Innocent Bystander: In the Heart of Downtown 1935," The Atlantic, May 1971, p 30*

The broad check, the d.b. and the yellow shades are very, very Blass [a designer]. *Antony King-Deacon, The Times (London), Nov. 15, 1968, p 16*

dBA, abbreviation of *decibel A* (a unit for measuring noise in which A represents a weighting scale for loudness).

The PNdB [perceived noise decibel] is somewhat different from the dBA frequently used in assessing traffic and industrial noise because it contains a weighting factor dependent on the masking effect of high frequency noises in addition to the usual ear sensitivity frequency response. *Kenneth Mulholland and Keith Attenborough, "Predicting the Noise of Airports," New Scientist and Science Journal, March 18, 1971, p 605*

...Central London rush-hour street noise is 63 dBA.

Muriel Bowen, The Sunday Times (London), April 27, 1969, p 4

DDE, abbreviation of *dichlorodiphenyldichloroethylene* (a less toxic compound than DDT).

Almost no work has been done with DDE, the DDT compound that is present in food and in the environment. *Robert W. Risebrough, "Pesticide," McGraw-Hill Yearbook of Science and Technology 1971, p 320*

During the past few decades, residues of certain chlorinated hydrocarbons, such as DDT and DDE, have caused declines in populations of various birds by reducing their reproductive success. *Science News, March 6, 1971, p 166*

DDVP, abbreviation of *dimethyl dichlorovinyl phosphate*, the full chemical name of the insecticide DICHLORVOS.

Recent work by Swedish biochemist Göran Löfroth.... raises doubts about the wisdom of letting the organophosphorous insecticide DDVP be freely available in Britain. *"Probe: Domestic Nerve Gas?" New Scientist, Oct. 23, 1969, p 171*

de-, a very productive prefix, with various meanings shown below:

1 a to do the opposite of (an action).

debureaucratize, *v.t.:* Thus authority must be sweepingly decentralized and debureaucratized....*Edwin M. Yoder, Jr., Harper's, June 1970, p 114*

declericalise, *v.t.* The Church must be declericalised and run by ordained laymen. *Martin Jarrett-Kerr, The Manchester Guardian Weekly, July 3, 1971, p 18*

deconsolidate, *v.i.:* It sold control of W.S.F. [Westinghouse Saxby Farmer, a company] to the West Bengal Government for 1 rupee, and was able to deconsolidate. *John Carrington, The Times (London), July 1, 1970, p 27*

decouple, *v.t.:* ...study also provides strong evidence that the northeastern Pacific and the South Pacific were decoupled sometime during that period [the last 65 million years].... *Science News, May 9, 1970, p 458*

deglaciate, *v.t.:* ...the apparent presence of microblade groups in the southern Yukon around 7000 b.c. suggests that these groups were advancing into newly deglaciated territory hard upon the retreating Cordilleran ice. *Charles E. Borden, "New Evidence on the Early Peopling of the New World," Britannica Book of the Year 1969, p 102*

deideologize, *v.t.:* But the time has come: Unflinchingly to get down to the task of demythologizing and deideologizing the teaching office in the church. *Rev. Dr. Hans Kung, "Why Infallibility?" The New York Times, June 3, 1971, p 39*

de-isolate, *v.t.:* Now we are being urged to take the initiative to "de-isolate" Red China by entering into "scientific and technical cooperation" with Peking. *Bruno Shaw, "A Warning Against Mao," The New York Times, Nov. 13, 1970, p 37*

deparochialize, *v.t.:* "...He [Daniel Berrigan] had become ascetic, spiritual, unpriestly! It was a totally new vibration. He had finally become deparochialized." *James Forest, quoted by Francine du Plessix Gray, "Profiles: Acts of Witness," The New Yorker, March 14, 1970, p 70*

depenalize, *v.t.:* My vote is going to the Party—if any—that depenalizes the self-employed. *Mrs. M. E. Wykes, in a Letter to the Editor, The Times (London), June 1, 1970, p 9*

b opposite of.

deconsolidation, *n.:* Helped by the deconsolidations, by recovery in Australia, and by exceptionally high profits in semiconductors at home, the recovery in group profits last year was spectacular. *John Carrington, The Times (London), July 1, 1970, p 27*

decreation, *n.:* Miss Milford's book . . . is a study of the politics of a public modern marriage which was also a complex environment of creation and decreation, like any marriage. . . . *Malcolm Bradbury, "Books: The Beautiful and Damned," Review of "Zelda Fitzgerald: a Biography" by Nancy Milford, The Manchester Guardian Weekly, Oct. 17, 1970, p 18*

de-criminalization, *n.:* . . . societies may change their attitudes to crime. This has been demonstrated in the past decade by changes in the laws relating to attempted suicide, and to homosexual behaviour between consenting adults. This process has come to be somewhat inelegantly described by our American colleagues as de-criminalization. . . . *J. P. Martin, "Could Crime Cost Less?" Science Journal, Sept. 1970, p 57*

deculturalization, *n.:* . . . he [the French painter Jean Dubuffet] . . . proposes "institutes for deculturalization, nihilistic gymnasiums as it were, where particularly lucid instructors would give a course in deconditioning and demystification lasting several years, in such a way as to equip the nation with a thoroughly trained body of negationists who will keep confrontation alive. . . ." *Harold Rosenberg, "The Art World: Confrontation," The New Yorker, June 6, 1970, p 56*

de-isolation, *n.:* At stake, in the process of China's de-isolation, are questions of great significance to all nations: the control of nuclear weapons, the resolution of the Indochina war, peace in a quadripolar East Asia (U.S., U.S.S.R., Japan and China), scientific and technical cooperation, the war against poverty and hunger. *Edwin O. Reischauer, et al., Cambridge, Mass., in a Letter to the Editor, The New York Times, Oct. 28, 1970, p 46*

denormalization, *n.:* "A nurse sweeping abruptly into a resident's room commits an act of denormalization." Patients should also get up, eat and retire at normal hours. *Time, Oct. 12, 1970, p 57*

descrambler, *n.:* . . . industry is facing a serious problem in this area [guaranteeing privacy] and may be willing to pay for devices that limit access to any communications link to those with the correct "descrambler". *Richard C. French, "Electronic Arts of Non-Communication," New Scientist, June 4, 1970, p 470*

detrivialisation, *n.:* I understand that at a launching conference Mr. Day described this latest dispenser of understanding as a "step forward in the detrivialisation of broadcasting". . . . *David Wade, The Times (London), Oct. 31, 1970, p 18*

2 to remove or take away (something specified) from an object.

debarb, *v.t.:* [Senator] Muskie smiled, gulped a glass of water, showed his ability to debarb a question. *Time, Jan. 18, 1971, p 9*

deblur, *v.t.:* Any photograph which is out-of-focus or limited by an optical effect can be deblurred. *"Monitor: Sharpening up Viruses with Laser Light," New Scientist and Science Journal, May 6, 1971, p 304*

de-ink, *v.t., v.i.:* Scrap paper that is used to make some form of paperboard for packaging can be used as it is, but if the recycled paper must be white, the scrap must be de-inked. De-inking is an expensive process, and causes its own form of pollution. *Joseph Hanlon, "Cycling the Paper Round," New Scientist and Science Journal, April 29, 1971, p 259*

de-oil, *v.t.:* In the lab, both seem to de-oil feathers without affecting their waterproofing properties, and field trials are soon to be undertaken with five birds. *Jon Tinker, "How Birdlovers Kill Seabirds, Slowly," New Scientist and Science Journal, June 10, 1971, p 608*

depod, *v.t.:* At the same time it [the pea] is the most popular green vegetable, but particularly irksome to prepare fresh, involving all available members of the family in depodding operations. *Digby Brindle-Wood-Williams, The Times (London), Feb. 16, 1970, p III*

► For other entries beginning with *de-* look in the main listing of entries, e.g. *de-Americanize, de-capacitate* below.

dead-ee (ded'i:), *n.* a portrait of a dead person painted from a photograph.

There are "deadees" (painted after their lifetimes), and portraits from life. *Ada Louise Huxtable, The New York Times, Jan. 6, 1968, p 31*

Dead Hand, another name for RAYNAUD'S PHENOMENON.

Known as "Dead Hand" or "White Fingers" — and most recently as Vibration Syndrome — Raynaud's Phenomenon produces the same numbness and pain as a normal hand which is exposed to extreme cold for long periods but it occurs after only brief exposure to mild cold and takes much longer to overcome. *Tony Geraghty, The Sunday Times (London), March 23, 1969, p 5*

dead-head, *v.i., v.t. British.* Also spelled **dead head.** to remove or cut off the dead flowers of a plant.

He [Christopher Lloyd in *The Well-Tempered Garden*] deals with such necessary, if tedious matters, as weeding, pruning and dead heading. *Roy Hay, The Times (London), Sept. 19, 1970, p 21*

Lilacs, camellias, rhododendrons and azaleas should be dead-headed. *The Sunday Times (London), June 6, 1971 (page not recorded)*

dead-on-arrival, *n.* an electronic circuit which fails to operate when first used in equipment.

Even with this high pre-delivery rate [of rejected circuits] circuits received are not free from defects. To quote from a report by the Rome Air Development Center in the US: "Recent experience indicates that dead-on-arrivals constitute up to five per cent or more of the received product." *Geoffrey Dummer, "How Reliable is Microelectronics?" New Scientist and Science Journal, July 8, 1971, p 75*

[extended sense of the technical term (usually abbreviated as DOA) for a sick or injured person who is pronounced dead upon arrival at a hospital]

de-aestheticization, *n.* the removal of aesthetic qualities from art.

The movement toward de-aestheticization is both a reaction against and a continuation of the trend toward formalistic overrefinement in the art of the sixties, and particularly in the rhetoric that accompanied it. *Harold Rosenberg, "The Art World: De-aestheticization," The New Yorker, Jan. 24, 1970, p 62*

de-aestheticize, *v.t.* to rid (art or a work of art) of aesthetic qualities.

Di Suvero builds sculptures out of the beams of wrecked buildings, and Oldenburg de-aestheticizes bath fixtures by sewing them together out of cloth. The old idea of art as a mirror (fixed for desired distortions) held up to nature has in practice given way to the idea of art as a power of the free mind. *Harold Rosenberg, "The Art World: Retour de l'U.R.R.S., A Metaphysical Excursion," The New Yorker, July 1, 1967, p 73*

de-Americanize, *v.t.* to reduce American involvement in.

... Nixon chose to assume the operational responsibility for at least a limited de-escalation ... of the war, in which he seems to have lost faith and which he is in the process of "Vietnamizing" or "de-Americanizing." *Richard H. Rovere, "Letter from Washington," The New Yorker, Jan. 17, 1970, p 61*

Under the Johnson Administration, according to [Defense] Secretary Laird, "Vietnamization" meant "de-Americanizing" the war. *Senator Eugene J. McCarthy, "Topics: The Failure of Vietnamization by Any Name," The New York Times, Aug. 1, 1970, p 22*

deathplace, *n.* the place where one dies.

The messages were pouring in today to Bertrand Russell's anchorage and deathplace, Phas Penrhyn, the happy hillside home between the gaunt mountains and the sea. *Trevor Fishlock, The Times (London), Feb. 4, 1970, p 9*

[patterned after *birthplace*]

debby or **debbie,** *adj.* of or for debutantes; characteristic of debutantes.

"... We wore white tie and tails every night. We'd hit a few debbie parties and sink back into the Rue." *Thomas P. V. Hoving, quoted by John McPhee, "Profiles: A Roomful of Hovings," The New Yorker, May 20, 1967, p 114*

And "somewhere else" is mostly discothèques. Dolly's, with a membership limited to 600; Annabel's, very expensive and debby; and something actually called The In-Place. *Mordecai Richler, "Where It All Began: Has the Swing Lost Its Zing?" Maclean's, Aug. 20, 1966, p 28*

[shortening and modification of *debutante*]

deboost, *v.i.* to reduce thrust of a spacecraft, missile, etc., in flight, especially in order to lower the orbiting altitude of a spacecraft or to slow down a warhead before impact.

This combination would prevent anti-ballistic missile radar. ... from ascertaining the point of impact until the rocket "deboosts"—about three minutes and 500 miles from target. *Time, Nov. 10, 1967, p 15*

... the FOBS [Fractional Orbital Bombardment System] trajectory would avoid detection by the U.S. early-warning radar system and would make it impossible to determine the intended target until the "deboosting" rocket fires about three minutes before impact. *Scientific American, Jan. 1968, p 44*

— *n.* a reversing of thrust of an orbiting spacecraft, artificial satellite, etc. *Also used attributively.*

The second "de-boost" maneuver dropped Orbiter 2 from its taxiing orbit of 1,150 miles high and 130 miles low to a new orbit of 1,149 miles high and 31.3 miles low. *The New York Times, Nov. 17, 1966, p 15*

decametric, *adj.* of or equivalent to a decameter (10 meters) in wavelength.

... the satellite could clear up the puzzling problem of Jupiter's 'decametric' radiation bursts by studying their spectrum in a new frequency range. *"Development News: Space Radio Telescope Ready for Launching," Science Journal, May 1968, p 17*

Some observers see evidence that the decametric emissions are modulated by the passage of Jupiter's innermost satellite, Io. ... *Dietrick E. Thomsen, "Microwaves from the Planets," Science News, June 19, 1971, p 425*

decapacitate, *v.t.* to inhibit capacitation in (sperm).

There was a further theoretical difficulty in the way of the fertilization of human eggs, arising from the fact that it was necessary to use ejaculated sperm. The seminal plasma was believed to contain decapacitating factors, that is, substances that inhibit capacitation. *R. G. Edwards and Ruth E. Fowler, "Human Embryos in the Laboratory," Scientific American, Dec. 1970, p 48*

decapacitation, *n.* a process by which certain substances in seminal plasma inhibit capacitation.

The achievement of human fertilization in vitro ... has enlarged the stock of information on capacitation and decapacitation revealed by the fertilization of hamster eggs in vitro. *R. G. Edwards and Ruth E. Fowler, "Human Embryos in the Laboratory," Scientific American, Dec. 1970, p 48*

de·cath·lete (di'kæθ,li:t), *n.* an athlete who competes in a decathlon (a ten-event track and field contest).

Gerhard Auer, No. 3 in the West German boat, was once a decathlete, accumulating over 6,500 points. *Jim Railton, The Times (London), Sept. 7, 1970, p 11*

[blend of *decathlon* and *athlete*]

decision table, a tabular listing of conditions to be considered in defining a problem, together with the actions to be taken under each of the conditions.

Often easier to draw than a flow chart, a decision table still shows the essential conditional features of a computation sequence. Some users prefer decision tables because of their compactness and summary qualities. *Van Court Hare, Jr., Introduction to Programming: A BASIC Approach, 1970, p 109*

decontaminate, *v.t.* to remove the secret or sensitive parts of (a classified document) to make its publication harmless.

It was only when Secretary of Defense Laird refused to decontaminate and declassify the documents for the Foreign Relations Committee that men who had worked on the papers and reporters who had heard about them set out to expose the blunders and the cover-up. *James Reston, "Back to the Congress," The New York Times, June 20, 1971, p 13*

decrement, *v.t.* to show a decrease in or on.

Apart from becoming one of the main instruments to identify us electronically to the banking system, they [bank cards] may also be used as a sort of portable bank account. In this case it will be the card itself, not the account held at the bank's computer centre, which is decremented as we make our payments. *James Robertson, "Paying by Computer," New Scientist, July 23, 1970, p 181*

[verb use of *decrement, n.*]

deep space, space beyond the earth and the moon (as distinguished from *outer space* in the sense of the space immediately beyond the earth's atmosphere).

This will be the first time such a large, sophisticated mass has operated in the violent temperature ranges of deep space. What are the effects? To find out, the spacecraft will be positioned for some 4-1/2 hours with one side constantly facing the sun. *The New York Times, Oct. 8, 1967, Sec. 13, p 6*

deep space installation, a work of art in which objects are placed in certain positions within a relatively large and empty space.

These have not been announced as sculptures but as "deep space installations." . . . "Deep space" suggests that the room is being considered, not just as a place to put things in to be looked at, but as a single entire volume of space, rather as if it was a swimming pool filled with water. *Guy Brett, The Times (London), March 3, 1970, p 8*

deep structure, (in generative-transformational grammar) the basic or underlying structure of a sentence from which its surface or phonetic expression is generated. Compare SURFACE STRUCTURE.

Transformational-generative grammar assigns to each sentence a "deep structure" in attempt to generalize about language—and reproduce, from all constituent parts, all the possible sentences of a language. *"Lexicography (n.) the Controversial Art of Making a Dictionary," The New York Times, June 8, 1972, p 49*

de-escalate, *v.t., v.i.* to reduce in scale or size.

The debate followed the adoption of a resolution charging the Administration with failing to de-escalate the war and with pursuing a policy of redistributing bombing targets. *John H. Fenton, The New York Times, June 21, 1968, p 7*

Those who might be expecting in these excerpts some of the qualities imparted to this [musical] work by Elisabeth Schwarzkopf, Nicolai Gedda, and Erich Kunz in their famous Angel production are warned to de-escalate their expectations. *Irving Kolodin, "Recordings Report II: Miscellaneous LPs," Saturday Review, Nov. 25, 1967, p 90*

Then there is my favourite word "de-escalation." This is half Latin and half Greek—*scala*, staircase, ladder, scale. What fiend in human shape invented the horror? The birth rate no longer rises or falls: it escalates or de-escalates. *A. P. Herbert, "Liveliness of a Long-Distance Language," The Manchester Guardian Weekly, April 6, 1967, p 13*

de-escalation, *n.* a reduction in scale or size.

At the close of "Challenge '68," a poll of the students showed that sixty-five per cent favored de-escalation and cessation of the bombing of the North, and eleven per cent favored immediate withdrawal. *Calvin Trillin, "U.S. Journal: Iowa, The Last Peaceful Place," The New Yorker, April 20, 1968, p 175*

. . . a slow de-escalation of the warlike postures of Egypt and Syria behind a smokescreen of incidents not quite large enough to provoke a new Israeli riposte. . . . *Donald C. Watt, "Is There a Solution to the Middle East Problem?" The Listener, July 13, 1967, p 37*

de-escalatory, *adj.* designed to de-escalate.

. . . the hope was that if Washington made the first de-escalatory move, Hanoi might match it. . . . *Townsend Hoopes, "The Fight for the President's Mind and the Men Who Won It," The Atlantic, Oct. 1969, p 110*

"All they have to do," said Defense Secretary Clark Clifford last week, "is get word to us that they have reduced the level of combat and will continue to reduce the level of combat, and that that constitutes a de-escalatory step." *Time, Aug. 23, 1968, p 12*

deet, *n. U.S.* the commercial name of a widely used insect repellent.

The natural product and authentic deet showed identical repellency to *Aedes aegypti* mosquitoes. However, deet has been reported to show some attraction for pink bollworm moths in laboratory tests. *William A. Jones and Martin Jacobson, Science, Jan. 5, 1968, p 99*

[from the abbreviation *dt* of the chemical name *diethyl toluamide*]

defectology, *n.* the study of the causes and remedies of defects in human development or mechanical composition.

The Research Institute of Defectology is supported by faculties in Moscow, Kiev, Leningrad and other cities where teachers have been trained to care for handicapped children since 1920. *Science News, July 2, 1966, p 3*

Like corrosion science, welding defectology is not the most glamorous of spheres of scientific activity. *Tam Dalyell, New Scientist, March 13, 1969, p 565*

defuse, *v.t.* **1** to remove the critical element in (an explosive situation); exert a calming or moderating influence upon.

President Nguyen Van Thieu has defused chronic student protest by releasing jailed students. He also succeeded in mollifying the raucous disabled war veterans, who roll to their riots in wheelchairs, by granting them more liberal benefits. *"South Viet Nam: Return of the Lotus Blossom," Time, Sept. 7, 1970, p 17*

The tripartite declaration issued by Britain, France, and the United States in 1950 was, predictably, a total failure. Instead of trying to defuse the [Middle East] situation by controlling or eliminating the supply of arms into the area, it initiated an abortive attempt to maintain a military balance between two sides. *Lord Chalfont, "The International Arms Trade," Britannica Book of the Year 1971, p 254*

2 to lessen the force or effect of; weaken.

It would be nice to say the young girl puts up, as Anne Baxter did against Bette Davis, menacing competition. The truth is that Miss Bacall defuses and obliterates every other talent on stage. *Alistair Cooke, "[Lauren] Bacall in Her Private Heaven," The Manchester Guardian Weekly, April 11, 1970, p 16*

[figurative senses of *defuse*]

defuser, *n.* one who exerts a calming or moderating influence in a critical situation.

Why should a man so meticulously outspoken have fiercely attacked last week the work of reporters in Nigeria who merely wrote what they saw. Chiefly, it is because his style and skill as a public man is as a defuser of explosive predicaments. *Lewis Chester, "Profile: Lord Hunt, the Man Who Sold It Soft," The Sunday Times (London), Jan. 25, 1970, p 11*

degradability, *n.* susceptibility to chemical decomposition.

. . . in the wake of moves to ban DDT in several states and foreign countries. . . . The Federal commission will study the evidence of their "degradability and persistence, and the adequacy of our knowledge of their chronic and acute effects upon human health. . . ." *"Pesticides: Regulating a Monster," Science News, May 3, 1969, p 423*

degradable, *adj.* susceptible to chemical decomposition.

. . . there has been a reduction of the residual amounts of synthetic detergent material in the board's river sources of supply after the complete substitution in packets of washing powder retailed in Britain of anionic detergents which are biologically degradable. *Nature, May 30, 1968, p 1202*

In the past year or so, however, public indignation over litter and garbage has caused industry to ask chemists whether self-destroying, or quickly degradable, plastics might be devised to replace indestructible, unburnable and incompressible glass, aluminum and plastics, which comprise the largest segment of consumer waste. *"Photooxidation of Polymers," Science News, Aug. 7, 1971, p 92*

dehire, *v.t. U.S.* to discharge from hired employment. Compare DESELECT.

The pinched corporation... fires the chairman of the board. Fires is a rude word, but the bouncing of the boss is happening now on such a scale that Wall Street is mushrooming with firms bearing the weird names of "Dehiring Consultants, Inc." and "Executive Adjustment Advisers." Their function is to find painless ways of easing company presidents into "early retirement." In a depression, the boss is sacked and jumps from a window. In the "recedence," he is "dehired".... *Alistair Cooke, "Finance: Dehiring of the Boss," The Manchester Guardian Weekly, Sept. 5, 1970, p 22*

del·i ('del i:), *n. U.S.* short for *delicatessen*.

And it's time for lunch. He goes out and buys a pastrami sandwich at the deli. *Donald Barthelme, "City Life II," The New Yorker, June 21, 1969, p 37*

Delis are sold on the basis of volume, so when [Mr. Shapiro]... sells a store he commands a premium price. *Robert Metz, The New York Times, Feb. 14, 1967, p 59*

► See the note on clipped words under BINOCS.

deliver, *v.i. U.S.* to carry out or fulfill an expectation; make good.

Nixon will have to deliver spectacularly to retain his present thin edge, and it now looks as if he would be doing well to hold his own. *Richard H. Rovere, "Letter From Washington," The New Yorker, Oct. 23, 1971, p 158*

This autumn the President has a major opportunity to deliver on his pledge. *Edwin O. Reischauer, et al., Cambridge, Mass., in a Letter to the Editor, The New York Times, Oct. 28, 1970, p 46*

delta waves, large, slow brain waves marking the deepest level of sleep.

High-amplitude delta waves in sleep are almost typical of youth. With increasing age, however, the EEG [electroencephalogram] of the delta waves becomes smaller and flatter. *Julius Segal and Gay Gaer Luce, "Sleep and Dreams," 1970 Britannica Yearbook of Science and the Future, 1969, p 310*

demand inflation, another name for DEMAND-PULL.

There are two quite different kinds of inflation: demand inflation, when, through credit expansion and tax reduction, money demand is allowed to rise much faster than productive capacity: and the cost inflation which follows. *Anthony Harris, "Finance: Labour's Lost Innocence," The Manchester Guardian Weekly, June 6, 1970, p 23*

In short, on the domestic side, the Government dealt with the incipient renewal of inflation inherent in its own spending—what is known in the jargon as "demand inflation." *The Sunday Times (London), Jan. 21, 1968, p 10*

demand-pull, *n.* Also called **demand-pull inflation.** inflation caused by excessive demand for goods and services forcing the cost of production higher and therefore raising the market price. Compare COST-PUSH.

... demand-pull [is] an excessive pressure of demand on productive capacity—so that cost-push, or the rising cost of the factors of production, is seen simply as a consequence of demand-pull. *Anthony Harris, "Finance: Government Versus the People," The Manchester Guardian Weekly, Aug. 22, 1970, p 22*

The guidepost tax does not stop a businessman from paying wages beyond some guidepost level.... When I first wrote about it in a column, and testified about it before the Joint Economic Committee in 1966, we were in the early, fine flush of a demand-pull inflation. Now that we are smarting under cost-push, the basic argument remains the same. *Henry C. Wallich, Professor of Economics, Yale University, "Tax on Excess Wages?" The New York Times, Dec. 16, 1970, p 47*

demi-mini, *adj.* shorter than mini.

... they [five girls] all wore tiny, frothy demi-mini shifts, which barely covered their behinds and seemed designed to show even more leg than they had. *The New Yorker, Sept. 16, 1967, p 41*

—*n.* a skirt or dress shorter than mini.

... Designer Mary Quant, 32, grandam of Chelsea's [London] fashion hippies, decided to hike the hems still higher.... Mary has designed demure little matching boxer shorts for the birds to wear with their demi-minis. *Time, Nov. 18, 1966, p 26*

de·mi-pen·sion (də mi: pā'syɔ̃), *n. French.* an arrangement in a boarding house, hotel, etc., to eat only some meals, usually the noon meal; (literally) half-board.

... a regrettable tendency on insisting that his guests take at least demi-pension (from £2 10s. per head) which wouldn't be so bad if his restaurant were not mediocre compared with some of the others. *Mark Ottaway, The Sunday Times (London), Sept. 14, 1969, p 65*

demiworld, *n.* a world or sphere on the fringes of conventional, wealthy, or reputable society; demimonde.

Nor is there any need to make imaginative leaps into Crane's inner life since Crane himself reported what it was like for him to experience the demiworld of the city, the *Commodore* disaster, and the battlefields of Greece and Cuba. *R. W. Stallman, Storrs, Conn., in a Letter to the Editor, The Atlantic, Nov. 1968, p 48*

Home in New York, his *Scrutiny* byline and his impressive set of academic credentials opened the doors of literary society, a demiworld about which Podhoretz writes entertainingly and knowledgeably. *"Books: Little Norman," Review of "Making It" by Norman Podhoretz, Time, Jan. 19, 1968, p 67*

► *Demiworld* is a partial translation of French *demimonde*. The only earlier evidence for *demiworld* is an 1862 quotation from the London *Times* in the *OED*: "The bye-world... which the French call the *demi-monde*. The demi-world or bye-world is an alluring theme." The *OED* labels the entry *nonce-word*.

dem·o ('dem ou), *n.* short for *demonstration* (in any of several meanings): **1** a protest demonstration.

Just as the US Embassy provided a focus for an extreme Left 'demo' against 'fascist brutality' in Vietnam, so the public appearance of neo-fascist organisations has likewise provided alleged 'provocation.' *Robert Stanton, London, in a Letter to the Editor, The Listener, March 28, 1968, p 410*

Both the police and the students begin getting ready for the encounter days before a "demo" is scheduled to take place. *Robert Trumbull, The New York Times, Jan. 12, 1968, p 63*

2 a sample or type of record, play, etc., used for demonstration.

[Bernard] Purdie [a guitar and drum player] finally got a job with Lonnie Youngblood's orchestra, went on the road, returned, and went out again, with Les Cooper's band. "I stayed two years with Les, and we made 'Wiggle Wobble,' which turned out to be very good for me," he told us. Then he started making demos, or demonstration records. "When they make the demo the master, that's the big break. Mine came when they made the master of 'Mercy, Mercy' from our demo." *"The Talk of the Town: Pretty Purdie," The New Yorker, Nov. 18, 1967, p 56*

The American dirty-talk demo, *The Beard* at the Royal Court, starts at 10.30, is brief but soporific. *D. A. N. Jones, "Theatre," The Listener, Nov. 14, 1968, p 661*

demonology, *n.* a grouping of persons or things viewed by their opponents as evil, harmful, or disruptive influences.

Like his patron, the President, [Murray] Chotiner is one of the fixtures of liberal demonology, and one, as it happens, who can never be counted out. *Elizabeth B. Drew, "The White House Hard Hats," The Atlantic, Oct. 1970, p 52*

Prof. Amitai Etzioni's Sept. 5 "Topics" column "Genetic Manipulation and Morality" is another contribution to the demonology of genetic engineering that obscures the important dilemmas of health policy requiring open-ended public discussion and participation. *Joshua Lederberg, Stanford, Calif., in a Letter to the Editor, The New York Times, Sept. 26, 1970, p 28*

[figurative sense of the term for a belief in or a treatise on demons]

demystification, *n.* the act or process of demistifying; enlightenment.

... he [the French painter Jean Dubuffet] proposes "institutes for deculturalization, nihilistic gymnasiums as it were, where particularly lucid instructors would give a course in deconditioning and demystification lasting several years, in such a way as to equip the nation with a thoroughly trained body of negationists who will keep confrontation alive...." *Harold Rosenberg, "The Art World: Confrontation," The New Yorker, June 6, 1970, p 56*

In an age of unfolding rationality and demystification of the world, this numerical growth of scientists, technologists and technicians has been accompanied by the development of a new faith and a new priesthood. *Bob Fryer, "Unemployment, Myths and Science," New Scientist and Science Journal, Dec. 16, 1971, p 165*

demystify, *v.t.* to rid of mystifying elements; enlighten.

... what the mature William Blake fails to make clear can often be demystified with the help of the commentator and the textual exegesis. *The Sunday Times (London), Feb. 16, 1969, p 12*

[Robert] Morris, of course, maintains that his aim is to demystify the viewer. Says he of his sculpture: "You don't have to explore it. The information is given at once." *"Art: Sculpture," Time, May 17, 1968, p 60*

demythicization, *n.* the act or process of stripping a story, text, etc., of its myths or mythical aspects.

Italians are not, generally speaking, Romantics, and what we have in this opera [Rossini's "La Cenerentola," a version of the Cinderella story] is a curious Latin demythicization of the original: everything supernatural is reduced to realistic force.... *Winthrop Sargeant, "Musical Events: Latin Cinderella," The New Yorker, April 11, 1970, p 89*

demythicize, *v.t., v.i.* to strip or rid of myths.

We demythicize, we raise our trophies of excrement.
Let no one impede us or affront pigeons — winged shapely, having no talons —
Let no one contest our liberty to be empty, regimented into dirty grey, mocking the monuments which overshadow us.

Ugo Fasolo, "Pigeons" (a poem translated by Ezra Pound), The Atlantic, Nov. 1970, p 94

denticare, *n.* (in Canada) a government-sponsored program of free dental care for children.

There are no signs that denticare will stir up the militant professional opposition aroused by medicare. Dr. Campbell [of the Manitoba Dental Association] thinks most dentists accept denticare as inevitable but will try to gain a hand in controlling the plan. *Janice Tyrwhitt and Douglas Marshall, "Maclean's Reports," Maclean's, Jan. 1967, p 1*

[from *denti-* teeth, dental + *care,* patterned after *Medicare*]

denuclearization, *n.* the act or process of denuclearizing.

Restoration of Japanese sovereignty and denuclearization of the island [Okinawa] is long overdue. *C. L. Sulzberger, "Foreign Affairs: Removing an Argument," The New York Times, June 18, 1971, p 39*

denuclearize, *v.t.* to ban or remove nuclear arms from (a place or region).

Just this month the Soviet Government took the embarrassed step of associating itself with the Spanish Communist underground party in calling for the elimination of American bases and denuclearizing the Mediterranean. *C. L. Sulzberger, "Foreign Affairs: The Bull and the Bear," The New York Times, May 13, 1970, p 40*

... they "would agree not to manufacture, receive, store, or experiment with nuclear arms or nuclear launching artefacts," and to work jointly with the other Latin American republics for the area to be declared a denuclearized zone. *The Times (London), Nov. 25, 1964, p 11*

denucleate, *v.t.* to remove the nucleus or nuclei from (an atom, molecule, animal cell, etc.).

Fusion of mammalian eggs, in this case from mice, has been reported by Dr. Christopher Graham of Oxford. Using an influenza-like virus that for some unknown reason causes membranes to fuse, he has fused mouse egg cells with cells from mouse spleen and bone marrow, getting hybrid cells with double nuclei that may have undergone one cell division. But this has not yet been accomplished with denucleated egg cells, and no timetable is yet available. *"Clonal Reproduction: Closing in on Mammals," Science News, March 29, 1969, p 304*

denucleation, *n.* removal of a nucleus or nuclei from an atom, molecule, animal cell, etc.

... at the foot of the 17-metre suction pipe, just above the suction valve, is a pressure vessel designed to act as a denucleation chamber. The operating cycle of the pump is as follows: (1) Close the discharge valve and apply a pressure of 300 atm to the bellows, by pumping oil into the pressure vessel surrounding the bellows. Maintain this pressure for 10 seconds to ensure denucleation of the water in the denucleation chamber and suction pipe. *Alan T. J. Hayward, "New Law for Liquids: Don't Snap, Stretch!" New Scientist, Jan. 29, 1970, p 199*

de-orbit, *v.t.* to take out of orbit.

First of all, warheads de-orbited from satellites could reach their targets so quickly that a defending nation would lose the previous minutes of warning for which the United States has purchased such costly facilities as the Ballistic Missile Early Warning System. *Alton Frye, "Our Gamble in Space: The Military Danger," The Atlantic, Aug. 1963, p 49*

—*n.* the act of taking or coming out of orbit.

. . . the astronauts will make the eighth and final firing of their main rocket. This should begin the de-orbit, thrusting the spaceship earthward, its nose pointed downward at a forward angle. *The New York Times, Oct. 20, 1968, Sec. 4, p 11*

The critical factor will be to determine the moment of de-orbit. *James Strong, "The Soviet 'Space Bomb'," New Scientist, Nov. 16, 1967, p 424*

depollute, *v.t.* to free from pollution.

The money—our money—they and their friends in the Civil Service squander each year in the name of military continuity could equally well be used to provide scores of new hospitals, old folks' homes . . . or even to depollute a few of our rivers. *William D. Broadfoot, Shurdington, Cheltenham, England, in a Letter to the Editor, The Manchester Guardian Weekly, Aug. 7, 1971, p 2*

. . . May Christmas grow more comely and muted, And the world a fraction depolluted. *Frank Sullivan, The New Yorker, Dec. 26, 1970, p 23*

There is no question that just as technology has polluted the country, it can also depollute it. *Time, May 10, 1968, p 43*

The cheapest desalted water in the U S still costs 10 times as much as depolluted fresh water in water-short areas. *The Sunday Times (London), April 9, 1967, p 31*

depollution, *n.* the act or process of depolluting.

The air was cleansed, slums cleared, the desert on the wrong side of the tracks converted into the Golden Triangle, and a small beginning made in the depollution of the Allegheny and Monongahela rivers. *Edward Weeks, "Books: The Peripatetic Reviewer," The Atlantic, Feb. 1968, p 134*

The Trent River Authority at least is on the side of depollution. *Jon Tinker, "The Smug and Silver Trent," New Scientist and Science Journal, June 10, 1971, p 614*

depressurization, *n.* the removal or release of air pressure from a pressurized interior.

The explosion was caused by depressurization. It happened when the pressure inside the aircraft, kept at equivalent to that at about 8,000 ft., forced its way through the fuselage as the machine climbed into thin air at 25,000 ft. *Arthur Reed, "122 Safe as Explosion Rips Boeing," The Times (London), Sept. 25, 1970, p 2*

. . . "human error and mechanical failure between them caused creeping depressurization in the spacemen's nine-foot cabin and deprived the astronauts of life-supporting oxygen on the final phase of their journey." *Victor Louis, "Science: Triumph and Tragedy of Soyuz 11," Time, July 12, 1971, p 41*

depressurize, *v.t.* to remove or release air pressure from (a pressurized interior).

In their suits at last, the astronauts depressurized their cabin . . . and opened the hatch. It was 6-1/2 hours since the lunar module had landed. *Wernher von Braun and Frederick I. Ordway, "One Giant Leap for Mankind," The Americana Annual 1970, p 22*

dé·ra·ci·né (dei ra si:'nei), *adj.* uprooted from one's native or natural environment; displaced.

Being a déraciné white Russian refugee who came to Paris via Constantinople and Berlin and moved thence to London and New York, he [the Russian artist Pavel Tchelitchew] had to make his way socially as well as artistically to attain the position to which his birth and money would have entitled him. *Cyril Connolly, "Inside the Painter's Head," Review of "The Divine Comedy of Pavel Tchelitchew" by Parker Tyler, The Sunday Times (London), Jan. 18, 1970, p 59*

For if ever there was a nation that is *déraciné*, uprooted from its traditional ties and anchorages, it is post-war Germany. *Irving Kristol, "Germany 1967," The Atlantic, May 1967, p 48*

—*n.* an uprooted or displaced individual.

Not surprisingly he avoided marriage, explaining that although he could have married an American girl rich enough to give him leisure he would have been saddled with 'her whole background, her country, her family, her houses, her religion. Not that I had any fault to find with these things *for her*; but a *déraciné*, a man who has been torn up by the roots, cannot be replanted and should never propagate his kind.' *D. W. Harding, "Above the Tossing Waves," Review of "Selected Critical Writings of George Santayana," edited by Norman Henfrey, The Listener, Oct. 24, 1968, p 548*

[from French, uprooted]

derepress, *v.t.* to induce (a gene) to operate by disengaging the repressor.

The group . . . now hopes to find out how genes are repressed and derepressed—turned off and on—so that genes can be made to operate when required. *Charles S. Marwick, "Medicine," The Americana Annual 1970, p 437*

derepressor, *n.* another name for INDUCER.

There is evidence that molecules known as repressors and derepressors play a role in turning genes, and protein synthesis, on and off. *Science News, Feb. 28, 1970, p 215*

desalivate, *adj.* having the salivary glands removed.

In a second series of experiments, the researchers applied vaseline to the lips of desalivate pups every two hours during the daytime. *"Monitor: Sealed Lips Are Essential for Survival," New Scientist and Science Journal, Jan. 21, 1971, p 107*

deschool, *v.t.* to abolish traditional schools in (a society, etc.).

The radical deschooling of society begins, therefore, with the unmasking by cultural revolutionaries of the myth of schooling. *Ivan Illich, "The False Ideology of Schooling," Saturday Review, Oct. 17, 1970, p 68*

To eliminate the "social addiction" to attending school, his deschooled world would replace most formal classes with networks of "learning exchanges." *"Education: Should Schools Be Abolished?" Time, June 7, 1971, p 25*

descriptor, *n.* a symbol or group of symbols that identifies a particular subject in the storage unit of a computer.

To make the process totally computerized, the descriptors filed in the computer would also have to be obtained from the fingerprint by an automatic reading device. *"Computer Encoding of Fingerprints," Science News, May 25, 1968, p 495*

Each flight would be assigned a descriptor for use by the computer. As the flight proceeds, the computer would simultaneously calculate the plane's position, search its data bank for other aircraft in the area, operate the display screens of air route centers, and provide data for evaluation by the controllers. *Howard Bierman, "Electronics," 1969 Collier's Encyclopedia Year Book, p 234*

deselect, *v.t.* *U.S.* to discharge (a trainee) during training. Compare DEHIRE.

. . . I couldn't help recalling my own experience in the Peace Corps in Malawi. Nowhere else can a person be fired by being told he has been "selected out" or "deselected." *Delmarie P. Motta, Pasadena, Calif., in a Letter to the Editor, Time, Oct. 3, 1969, p 7*

The road from applicant to trainee to overseas volunteer is a hard one. Many individuals do not follow through. Many are "de-selected." *The New York Times, June 24, 1968, p 7*

desk study, *British.* a study made without extensive field and laboratory investigation.

Approval is being sought from the Government by the Water Resources Board to carry out a detailed survey for a new scheme to develop the Wash as a fresh water supply. The details are contained in a report published yesterday. Estimates made in the desk study put the cost of the first reservoir at £25m. *Pearce Wright, "Reservoirs Preferred to Barrage in Wash," The Times (London), Sept. 11, 1970, p 2*

desorb, *v.t.* to restore (an absorbed or adsorbed substance) to its original state.

Puraq's new process [of desalting seawater] uses a hydrophylic polymer solvent which can be made to desorb water by heat. The result is desalination nearly 50 per cent cheaper than by distillation. *Glen Lawes and Michael Kenward, "Technology Review: New Challenger for the Desalination Prize," New Scientist, Jan. 29, 1970, p 203*

despin, *v.t., v.i.* to neutralize the effect of revolving motion by revolving an attached object in the opposite direction at the same speed.

To maintain permanent radio illumination of the Earth the horn aerial mounted at one axis is mechanically despun in the opposite direction to spin stabilization. *Science Journal, Jan. 1970, p 18*

It also is essential that the satellite does not spin, for that would wrap the antennas around it. The "despinning" began on Monday. *Walter Sullivan, The New York Times, July 11, 1968, p 14*

destress, *v.t.* to eliminate excess strain on.

Immediate measures to guarantee the track's safety and eventual destressing (a heating process) of the entire existing mileage should prevent further serious trouble on these lines, Major Rose [Major C. F. Rose, an inspecting officer of railways] says. *"Weather Blamed for Welded Rail Crashes," The Times (London), April 2, 1970, p 2*

de·suete (di'swi:t), *adj.* outdated; outmoded.

. . . our artistic history and heritage we learn backwards, astonished to find what were once hailed as strokes of trenchant originality emerging from earlier now neglected and desuete masters. *Philip Hope-Wallace, "Strindberg,*

With or Without Water," The Manchester Guardian Weekly, May 1, 1971, p 19

[from French *désuète*, from Latin *dēsuētus*, past participle of *dēsuēscere* to disuse. As a direct borrowing from Latin *dēsuētus*, the form *desuete* existed in English during the 1700's. It is found in Bailey's *Universal Etymological English Dictionary* (1727) and defined as "out of use." The French form *désuète* (feminine of *désuet*) has been recorded only since the 1800's]

DET, abbreviation of *diethyltryptamine*, a hallucinogenic drug. Compare DMT, STP.

The group also includes some drugs, not used in medicine, generally referred to as STP, DMT and DET; these have not been controlled before. *David Wood, "Stiffer Drug Penalties in New Bill: Doctors May Face Gaol for Over-prescribing," The Times (London), March 12, 1970, p 1*

The use of LSD (lysergic acid diethylamide) appeared to decline during 1968, as did the use of some other hallucinogens, or psychedelics, such as STP, DMT, and DET. *Sidney Cohen, "Narcotics and Hallucinogens," The Americana Annual 1969, p 483*

deux-che·vaux ('dœ ʃə'vou), *n. French.* an automobile with a two-horsepower engine; (literally) two-horses.

Not long ago, on one of my infrequent trips to Los Angeles, I was riding down this profound hill, in the dark, in Miles Ackerman's *deux-chevaux. Gilbert Rogin, "You Say What I Feel," The New Yorker, July 12, 1969, p 29*

They come in battered *deux-chevaux*, creaking farm wagons, sleek Citröens, by chartered trains and buses. *"France: DeGaulle in a Crystal Ball," Time, Nov. 22, 1971, p 21*

deu·xième (dœ'zyem), *n. French,* a second performance (of a play, etc.), following the première.

Anyhow, Pulses is something truly new, even though this was the world deuxième. *The Sunday Times (London), Nov. 30, 1969, p 65*

devaluationist, *n.* a supporter or advocate of the devaluation of a currency.

. . . there is no doubt that Whitehall (and most devaluationists) hopelessly miscalculated the impact of devaluation on Britain's imports. *William Davis, "Waiting for the Surplus," The Manchester Guardian Weekly, Nov. 21, 1968, p 22*

developmental biology, the study of the development of organisms.

The research in which they are involved is nowadays fashionably called developmental biology—a term which will before long be as famous (or infamous) as molecular biology. . . . Specifically, the question developmental biology seeks to answer concerns the way in which a single fertilized cell can grow into an organized mass of millions of cells, of many different types, all functioning together as a whole. *Graham Chedd, "Interactions: Scientific Counter Culture," New Scientist and Science Journal, Jan. 28, 1971, p 174*

Dev·lin·ite ('dev lə,nait), *n.* a supporter or follower of Bernadette Devlin, born 1947, an Irish Catholic civil rights leader in Northern Ireland and member of the British House of Commons. Compare PAISLEYITE.

It must escalate. Blood must run in the streets. Ulster people must die like dogs. Unless they do, nothing will change. The British public cares deeply about dogs. It does not want to think about the Irish who are a centuries-old nuisance. We must, in the next year, get together, all of us, Paisleyites, Devlinites, civil rights groups, students, Orangemen, I.R.A. [Irish Republican Army] men, the lot, we must prove once and for all that we cannot be left any longer in the dead hands of our Unionist masters. . . . *Brian Moore, "Bloody Ulster," The Atlantic, Sept. 1970, p 62*

dex·am·phet·a·mine ('dek sæm'fet ə,mi:n), *n.* an amphetamine derivative widely used as a stimulant.

Preparations recently listed dexamphetamines as . . . having an unacceptable lesser degree of efficacy, or having an unacceptably greater toxicity than alternative preparations. *Oliver Gillie, "International Control Proposed for Slimmers," Science Journal, Feb. 1970, p 7*

[contraction of *dextroamphetamine*, from *dextro-* dextrorotatory chemical compound + *amphetamine* a drug for relief of congestion in colds, hay fever, etc.]

dex·tra·nase ('dek strə,neis), *n.* an enzyme manufactured by a fungus of the penicillium family, capable of preventing formation of dental plaque by streptococci.

. . . a certain enzyme, called dextranase, blocks the decay process by preventing the formation of dental plaque, a sticky substance deposited on the teeth by certain bacteria. *J. R. Porter, "Microbiology," The Americana Annual 1969, p 454*

[from *dextran* the bacterial product forming plaque + *-ase* enzyme]

di·a·bo·lus ex ma·chi·na (dai'æb ə ləs eks 'mæk ə-nə); *pl.* **di·a·bo·li ex ma·chi·na** (dai'æb ə,lai). *Latin.* devil from a machine; an evil person or thing introduced into a story or account to provide an explanation or resolve a problem. The term means the same as its model, *deus ex machina*, except that here the subject personifies evil rather than any (impersonal or benevolent) being.

He [Victor Alba] seems to have swallowed quite uncritically the propaganda of Argentine nationalists. Thus, he undertakes to explain Latin-American history with a *diabolus*, or rather *diaboli ex machina. Ronald Hilton, "Abajo la Oligarquia!" Review of "Nationalists Without Nations" by Victor Alba, The New York Times Book Review, Aug. 11, 1968, p 7*

[Jacques] Ellul appears to be without it [faith in humanity]. His analysis leaves him with no basis for rational optimism. His *diabolus ex machina* —technique— is greater than man. *A. Rupert Hall, "Books: An Unconvincing Indictment of the Evils of Technology," Review of "The Technological Society" by Jacques Ellul, Scientific American, Feb. 1965, p 128*

di·a·man·tane ('dai ə mən,tein), *n.* a hydrocarbon having the same spatial arrangement of carbon atoms as the diamond.

But a report (Tetrahedron Letters, 1971, p 1671) has now appeared . . . of the facile conversion of diamantane for the first time into functional derivatives suitable for the introduction of the diamantane nucleus into potential drugs. *"Diamond Fragments Make Potential Drugs," New Scientist and Science Journal, Aug. 5, 1971, p 301*

diamondoid, *adj.* having the form of a diamond.

However, the large diamondoid hydrocarbon diamantane, although known, was extremely difficult to prepare and has thus remained a chemical curiosity. *"Diamond Fragments Make Potential Drugs," New Scientist and Science Journal, Aug. 5, 1971, p 301*

di·az·e·pam (dai'æz ə,pæm), *n.* a chemical substance widely used as a tranquilizer.

Finally, hostile tendencies can often be remarkably controlled by drugs, like Librium and diazepam, which are *not* sedatives, and which do not depress the general level of cerebral activity, but which act specifically and selectively on the aggressive circuits. *Donald Gould, "Why Do We Act the Way We Do?" New Scientist, March 21, 1968, p 623*

[from *di-* two + *az-* nitrogen + *ep-* besides, distinctive + *-am* ammonia]

dibbler, *n.* an Australian mammal, regarded as extinct since the 1800's and rediscovered in 1967. See the quotations for details.

The animal is the rat-like marsupial, *Antechinus apicalis*, popularly known (to those who have even heard of it) as the Dibbler. Mouse-brown in colour with a long snout and a short tail it had apparently been dibbling away on the outskirts of a big city, undisturbed because nobody even suspected it was there. *New Scientist, "The Return of the Dibbler," June 8, 1967, p 577*

He set traps over the blossoms of Banksia trees, but caught instead a pair of dibblers, or freckled marsupial mice, fast-moving eight-inch long creatures, believed to be extinct and of importance as a link between the smaller phascogales [pouched mice] and the larger native cats. *Graham Pizzey, The Times (London), Jan. 23, 1968, p XIII*

di·chlor·vos (dai'klor vəs), *n.* an organic phosphate used as an insecticide in aerosol form or by impregnating a resin strip with it. Also called DDVP.

For example, one gallon of Dichlorvos, a chemical in common use for fly control, could, if applied with maximum efficiency, kill 100 square miles of dense locust swarm. *R. J. V. Joyce, "Radar Tracks Nomadic Swarms," The Times (London), Nov. 24, 1970, p 18*

[contraction of the full chemical name dimethyl *dichloro*vinyl ph*os*phate]

diet pill, *U.S.* any of various hormones, diuretics, etc., in tablet form, prescribed to reduce weight by speeding up metabolism.

According to the American Medical Association, the pills will not work and may cause death. At least 60 fatalities have been attributed to diet pills, and the figure may be substantially higher. *"Dangers of Diet Pills," Science News Yearbook 1969/1970, p 53*

Sam Fine, a Food and Drug Administration official, said today that the decision to seize large quantities of diet pills in Dallas and Abilene had been based on medical evidence that showed the pills produced insomnia, nervousness and symptoms of heart failure. *Harold M. Schmeck, Jr., The New York Times, Jan. 24, 1968, p 33*

Digger, *n.* any of a group of hippies devoted to helping others, especially other hippies, as by giving them free food and clothing.

"It doesn't matter what your ideology is; if you're doing something like cleaning up the Park, you're a Digger." *"The Talk of the Town," The New Yorker, Nov. 30, 1968, p 55*

. . . the Diggers with their hazy ideas about free stores and co-operative farms—whatever their failings, these are part of that utopian anarchist tradition which has always bravely refused to knuckle under to the proposition that life must be a bad, sad compromise with the Old Corruption. *Theodore Roszak, "The Visionary Sociology of Paul Goodman," The Listener, Dec. 5, 1968, p 755*

[named after the *Diggers*, a group of English idealists of the 1600's who applied communistic principles to agriculture, digging and planting publicly held lands]

dim sum ('dim 'səm), an appetizer of steamed, meat-filled dumplings.

Mrs. Grace Chu . . . is also the doyenne of Chinese cooking instructors hereabouts, and her classes for fall will include . . . Cantonese dim sum. . . . *Craig Claiborne, The New York Times, Sept. 12, 1968, p 60*

On the dim-sum list, note for instance pig's tripe . . . , fried fish in crab meat sauce, duck's feet and steamed roast pork in rice-flour roll. *"Chinese Cuisine With a Northern Accent," The Times (London), Jan. 15, 1972, p 12*

[from Cantonese]

ding-a-ling, *n. U.S. Slang.* a crazy person.

A generally staid, middle-class group, the jurors were unprepared for the grueling experience, which was enough to make ding-a-lings out of the most stable personalities. *Time, April 12, 1971, p 52*

Always wearing black tights under her dress and other kinds of kinky gear. . . . This kid is a dangerous ding-a-ling and I don't know why I handle her. *F. P. Tullius, "Billy Brown Shoes in West Hollywood," The New Yorker, May 27, 1967, p 33*

[so called from the idea of hearing imaginary bells]

dink, *n. U.S. Army Slang.* a derogatory name for a Vietnamese.

Young GIs soon learned that there were Army names for Vietnamese too: gook, dink, and slope. *Seymour M. Hersh, "My Lai 4: A Report on its Massacre and its Aftermath," Harper's, May 1970, p 55*

American boys become mass killers, firing at women and children. . . . And why not? These [Vietnamese] are not people, let alone allies. They are dinks and gooks and slant-eyed bastards. *Jonathan Steele, "Racist War," The Manchester Guardian Weekly, Aug. 8, 1970, p 19*

[of unknown origin]

di·ox·in (daɪ'ɑk sən), *n.* a very persistent and highly poisonous impurity present in herbicides. Its full name is 2,3,7,8-tetrachlorodibenzo-*p*-dioxin.

. . . extensive teratogenic, or fetus-deforming, effects were discovered in chick embryos when the dioxin, or a distillate predominantly consisting of it, was present at concentrations of little more than a trillionth of a gram per gram of the egg. *Thomas Whiteside, New York, in a Letter to the Editor, The New Yorker, March 14, 1970, p 124*

diplomaism, *n.* undue emphasis on the acquisition of an academic degree, especially as a qualification for hiring personnel.

The obvious question is whether a degreeless society would produce enough skilled people to bring technology under control. It is one thing to lambaste the tyranny of diplomaism, but quite another to expect nations to function without high standards of excellence. *"Education: Should Schools Be Abolished?" Time, June 7, 1971, p 26*

dir·et·tis·si·ma (ˌdir ə'tis ə mə), *n. Mountaineering.* direct ascent.

The first winter ascent by British climbers of the North Face of the Matterhorn (14,688 ft.) was achieved today by Dougal Haston, of Eiger *direttissima* fame, and Mike Burke, also an experienced mountaineer. *The Times (London), Feb. 13, 1967, p 1*

Harlin, who fell to his death in March, 1966, during the *direttissima* on the Eiger, was, like Terray, a remarkable physical specimen. *Jeremy Bernstein, "A Reporter At Large: Alpine Accidents and Rescues," The New Yorker, Oct. 30, 1971, p 122*

[from Italian, literally, most direct]

dirty, *adj.* being on drugs; using drugs. Compare CLEAN.

Two weeks ago four new men came into the group meeting and each admitted he was then "strung-out." Each was given 10 days to appear on the list as "clean." At the meeting 10 days later each was "dirty" and each swore that the agreement had been "clean *after* 10 days" and that therefore they should not be punished. *Victoria Brittain, "Curing Drug Addiction with Former Addicts' Help," The Times (London), May 2, 1970, p 9*

dirty pool, *U.S. Slang.* unfair or dishonest conduct; foul play.

They charged that officials of Harrison, a sprawling town of which Purchase is a small corner, had resorted to "dirty pool" by secretly presenting the bill in Albany and getting it passed by means of an exchange of favors among state legislators. *The New York Times, April 13, 1968, p 29*

disadapt, *v.t.* to make unable to adapt.

There were certainly consequences for concern from the latest *Soyuz 9* flight which set a new long duration space flight record for man—18 days. The two cosmonauts remained 'disadapted' to normal gravity for much longer than would have been predicted on a basis of the previous (American) longest duration flight—the 14-day *Gemini 7* mission. *Angela Croome, "Russia Embraces US with Hopes of Space Shuttle Deal," Science Journal, Dec. 1970, p 4*

disambiguate, *v.t.* to rid (a sentence, statement, etc.) of ambiguity.

Given a syntactically ambiguous grammar, it is possible to use semantic information to disambiguate its syntax and construct a similar unambiguous grammar. *Notice from the Department of Computer and Information Science, University of North Carolina, quoted in The New Yorker, Oct. 17, 1970, p 145*

disbenefit, *n.* a lack or absence of benefit.

It has not occurred to many that the argument should be about the superiority of SST [supersonic transport], all things considered, as a means of getting from here to there. It should be about the benefits to the thousands and the disbenefits to the millions. *Wilbur H. Ferry, "Must We Rewrite the Constitution To Control Technology?" Saturday Review, March 2, 1968, p 51*

The disbenefits are difficult to establish and easy to underestimate: how much is a clean river worth to the citizens along its banks? *Jon Tinker, "The Smug and Silver Trent," New Scientist and Science Journal, June 10, 1971, p 614*

disbound, *adj.* having a torn, loose, or poor binding; having come unbound.

As the author's trustee, the owner of a library has the moral responsibility of preserving his books in the best possible condition and thus to hand them on to posterity in a perfect state of preservation. Disbound copies should be rebound, new leather backs should be made where they have been cracked or been lost completely, and for exceedingly precious works, a box should be constructed by a competent craftsman. *Anthony Michaelis, "Collecting Scientific Books," New Scientist, Dec. 24, 1970, p 552*

disc, *n.* short for DISCOTHÈQUE. Less common than DISCO.

After that, how about a night on the town at one of the local discs. *Advertisement by The Five Very Different Hotels of Jamaica, The New Yorker, Nov. 22, 1969, p 115*

dis·caire (dis'ker), *n.* a person who selects the records to be played at a discothèque.

Upstairs, underneath the arches, couples shake, shuffle, or glide — depending on the whims of the discaire — from nine to three-thirty every night. *"Goings On About Town: Discothèques and Such," The New Yorker, May 9, 1970, p 6*

[from French]

dis·co ('dis kou), *n.* short for DISCOTHÈQUE.

There are some most luxurious and comfortable camp sites on the coasts of Europe, many with their own swimming pools, private beaches, supermarkets and even discos . . . . *Arthur Eperon, "Europe's Quieter Camping," The Times (London), June 6, 1970, p 26*

▶ *Disco* is often used attributively to form compounds, as in the following:

disco-beat, *n.*: . . . a couple of scantily clad girls swiveled and undulated to the disco-beat. . . . *Bernadine Morris, The New York Times, April 8, 1965, p 46*

discogirl, *n.*: . . . she is essentially a 3-minute discogirl, but her finale gave her a new dimension. *Derek Jewell, The Sunday Times (London), July 14, 1968, p 49*

disco-pub, *n.*: Rivals Watneys have had a great success with their Birds Nest disco-pubs and Charrington may just have learnt a lesson there. *"Business Diary: Bass Relief," The Times (London), June 17, 1970, p 27*

discoset, *n.*: The musical curiosity of the year was Tiny Tim, an almost middle-aged boy soprano . . . With an astonishing falsetto he rose to the top of "the charts" . . . He was on the Greenwich Village boîte circuit for a time until he improvised a gig at The Scene, a Manhattan nightery that adopted him as the darling of the discoset and launched his rise to broader public acclaim. *Philip Kopper, "Biography: Tiny Tim," Britannica Book of the Year 1969, p 166*

dis·co·thèque or **dis·co·theque** ('dis kə,tek), *n.* a nightclub or other place of entertainment where customers or performers dance, sing, etc., to recorded music.

The young generation loves the noisy nightclubs and the discothèques. *Jay Walz, The New York Times, April 29, 1967, p 16*

Neruda, who had spent most of the day meeting planes we had missed, shook hands amiably, gave the delighted hostess an abrazo and drove us to a *discothèque* which he had never visited before, but where the best folk-singers in Chile were reputed to be holding forth. *Selden Rodman, "A Day with Pablo Neruda," Saturday Review, July 9, 1966, p 17*

— *v.i.* to dance to recorded music at a discothèque.

Most older men will only react by trying doubly hard to prove how young they are, sweating it out on the tennis court or discothequing it way past their bedtime. *Time, Feb. 21, 1969, p 35*

Sportsman Saul Galin has scrutinized the best of European ski resorts — from the many picture-postcard villages . . . to chic resorts like St. Moritz and Mégève where, dressed to the hilt the Beautiful People congregate, discothequing and filling the gossip columns. *Betty Moore, Saturday Review, Dec. 2, 1967, p 36*

[from French *discothèque*, literally, record library, from *disque* disk, record + *-thèque*, as in *bibliothèque* library; originally applied to a record shop, then to a café or bar where customers chose records to be played from a selection]

discothèque dress, a short, low-necked dress, often black and with frills at the hemline, originally worn by go-go girls at a discothèque.

In a series of crepe dischotèque dresses, Miss Keenan dropped a flutter of fine pleats from a round yoke or pressed them flat on lowbelted dresses. *The New York Times, Nov. 16, 1966, p 46*

. . . there are no culottes, no knee breeches, no discotheque dresses. Knees are decorously covered. *Ernestine Carter, The Sunday Times (London), Aug. 30, 1964, p 33*

discrete, *n.* a separate piece of equipment, often a component part of a large system, such as a high-fidelity record playing system.

This is a bleak outlook when most manufacturers of discretes are — to quote an industry marketing manager — "up to our ears in transistors", having built up heavy stocks in expectation of sales that did not materialise. *New Scientist and Science Journal, Jan. 14, 1971, p 52*

▶ The *OED* includes a noun use of the adjective *discrete* in the sense of "a separate part": "1890 J. H. Stirling *Gifford Lect.* xviii 353 Break it up into an endless number of points . . . an endless number of discretes."

discriminance, *n.* a means or method of discriminating.

Existing seismic capabilities for the identification of underground nuclear explosions can identify, in the northern hemisphere, 50 kiloton events in hard rock. By the inclusion of other types of discriminance this identification could, in principle, be reduced by a factor of about five. *Frank Barnaby, New Scientist and Science Journal, April 15, 1971, p 131*

▶ The form *discriminance* was used last in the 1600's as a variant of *discrimination.*

disemplane, *v.i.* to get off an airplane.

There is a well-known story of how the Nawab [of Junagadh], a lover of dogs and many wives, decided to flee to Pakistan as the Indian army marched on his state. Arriving at the airport with his wives, animals . . . he was told that some of his favorite dogs would have to be left behind. One of his wives was promptly told to disemplane, the dogs were taken aboard the overloaded aircraft and the Nawab took off for Pakistan leaving his kingdom bankrupt and in chaos. *Peter Hazelhurst, "Sealing the Fate of India's Nawabs and Rajas," The Times (London), Oct. 16, 1970, p 10*

dishabituate, *v.t.* to cause to lose or give up a habitual action; disaccustom.

The first neural analysis of habituation was undertaken in the spinal cord of the cat. The spinal cord mediates the reflex responses underlying posture and locomotion in vertebrates. . . . Sir Charles Sherrington, the great British physiologist, found that certain reflex responses, such as the flexion withdrawal of a limb in response to stimulation of the skin, decreased with repeated stimulation and recovered only after many seconds of rest. The problem was reinvestigated by C. Ladd Prosser and Walter Hunter of Brown University, who found that the habituated flexion withdrawal can be restored to full size (dishabituated) by the application of a strong new stimulus to another part of the skin. *Eric R. Kandel, "Nerve Cells and Behavior," Scientific American, July 1970, p 63*

dishy, *adj. Slang.* desirable; comely.

Chabrol's "Les Bonnes Femmes" defined very exactly what it is to be a dishy girl bored stiff with selling electrical equipment. *Penelope Gilliatt, "The Current Cinema: The Other Third," The New Yorker, Sept. 14, 1968, p 194*

It was translated, years ago, by Sir Richard Burton, and it is performed on the record by a very dishy Indian girl named Chitra Neogy. *Philip Oakes, The Sunday Times (London), May 26, 1968, p 17*

Kaleidoscope: A fast-paced mod-style gambling story set in a glossy background of boutiques and casinos. Nifty plot and Susannah York as a dishy doll make up for Warren Beatty's lack of presence. *"Checklistings: Movies," Maclean's, March 1967, p 80*

[from *dish*, slang word for a comely girl or woman]

disinformation, *n.* distorted or false information designed to mislead foreign intelligence agents. *Often used attributively.*

Various branches of Moscow's intelligence and "disinformation" services have taken pains to leak indications that Brezhnev is firmly in the saddle, that his opponents have lost out, and prominent associates, such as Kosygin, may soon be quietly dropped by the wayside. *C. L. Sulzberger, The New York Times, April 17, 1970, p 36*

Cautious civil servants in Bonn who read their newspapers and think that a change of government could be around the corner are unwilling to inform on this "disinformation" network, and few people seem really quite sure how it is manipulated from inside the government. *The Sunday Times (London), May 7, 1972, p 7*

Can he not see that those who oppose the terrorist-bureaucratic communism of Hanoi may do so precisely because they have more knowledge of the whole system than can be obtained from dupes of the "disinformation" departments in Moscow? *Robert Conquest, The Times (London), Dec. 3, 1968, p 9*

[translation of Russian *dezinformatsiya*, a word used as part of the title of a special branch of the Soviet secret service]

disintegrant, *n.* a substance causing disintegration of a medicinal tablet.

A mixture of sodium bicarbonate plus tartaric acid also acts as a disintegrant by generating carbon dioxide when the tablet is placed in water. *Neiton Pilpel, "Tablets Are Not Pills," New Scientist and Science Journal, April 8, 1971, p 105*

disintermediation, *n. U.S.* heavy withdrawals from savings banks for direct investment in the securities market.

In addition, the refinancing got high marks from Wall Street because of the Government's effort to lessen "disintermediation". . . . *John H. Allan, The New York Times, May 2, 1968, p 67*

disposable, *n. U.S.* an object to be thrown away after it has served its purpose, such as a bottle or

container after its contents have been removed.

You toss away an average of 5.5 pounds of garbage per day. Use returnables. Not disposables. An incinerator just converts plastic and wax and aluminum containers into poisonous smoke. *Advertisement by Environmental Action Coalition, The New Yorker, April 18, 1970, p 127*

Using disposables of all varieties, including hypodermic syringes and needles, was saving hospitals large sums of money but had created new problems — how to dispose of some 18 lb of garbage per patient per day, and keeping the 1.2 billion stainless steel needles from being salvaged and used by drug addicts. *William Spector, "Medicine," 1971 Britannica Yearbook of Science and the Future, 1970, p 225*

disproduct, *n.* a harmful product, especially one that is the result of negligence on the part of the producer.

The National Bureau of Economic Research . . . is trying to revise the system of economic accounting so that it will gauge the cost of noxious factories, landscape wreckers, noise and other "disproducts." *Time, March 2, 1970, p 74*

district heating, a system by which all of a district's or community's heating and hot-water requirements are supplied from a central source.

Like colour television, district heating — supplying several consumers from one central source — has been around for years without being exploited on any scale in this country. *Gwen Nuttall, The Sunday Times (London), July 16, 1967, p 21*

District heating, of course, means fewer chimneys, less traffic to supply individual customers with fuel and therefore less pollution, less wear and tear. . . . *"Keeping Warm Cheaply," New Scientist and Science Journal, Dec. 16, 1971, p 175*

diverger, *n.* a person who excels in far-ranging and imaginative thought. Compare CONVERGER.

Many people of obvious intellectual ability gain low scores on conventional intelligence tests but high scores on tests containing questions to which there is no one correct answer. Such people are defined as divergers; convergers on the other hand, gain higher marks on intelligence tests than on open-ended tests. When the two sets of tests were applied to English sixth forms, it was found that the science specialists tended to be convergers and the arts specialists divergers. *The Times (London), March 30, 1968, p 5*

Among the "trendy" biological subjects during the past few years have been both the psychological aspects of dreaming and the personality differences between convergers and divergers. *New Scientist and Science Journal, May 13, 1971, p 367*

div·i ('div i:), *n. British.* short for *dividend*, especially a dividend paid to members of a local co-operative society.

Any connection between Jim Callaghan's statement on industrial subscriptions to Conservative election funds and the recent mild improvement in share prices? If the subs are out, there'll be more divi for the shareholders. *Punch, July 1, 1964, p 22*

The Rochdale Pioneers did make their idealism work and now we have the Cooperative Wholesale Society, though some think today's divi isn't really worth it. *Hunter Davies, The Sunday Times (London), April 4, 1971, p 10*

Dix·i·can ('dik si kən), *n. U.S.* a Republican of the southern United States.

As moderate Republicans appointed by Eisenhower retire from the Fifth Circuit and as Haynsworth prepares to leave the Fourth, the Nixon Administration is choosing segregationist Democrats or Dixicans to replace them. *Richard Harris, "Annals of Politics: Decision," The New Yorker, Dec. 5, 1970, p 78*

[from *Dixie* (the southern U.S.) + Republi*can;* patterned after *Dixiecrat* a southern Democrat, especially one opposed to Negro civil-rights legislation (coined in 1948). The related term *Republicrat* was current in the 1950's.]

D.I.Y., *British.* abbreviation of *do-it-yourself.*

The fact that not only the makers of shockers, but the garages which sell them, can do well out of the spares market is stressed in SAMA's promotional material for garages: "Sell shocks on your accessory counter and catch the D.I.Y. motorist as well. It's bouncing business! A new pair of shocks can make more profit than a pair of spotlamps or a pair of tyres or a new battery." *"The 30,000 Mile Shockers," The Sunday Times Magazine (London), May 30, 1971, p 29*

DMT, abbreviation of *dimethyltryptamine*, a hallucinogenic drug. Compare DET.

. . . there are chemists in laboratories in Toronto, Montreal and Vancouver who produce amphetamines and psychedelic drugs, LSD, STP, DMT and other molecular variations. *Sheila Gormely, "Youth Drug 'Witch Hunt'," The Times (London), Feb. 23, 1970, p IV*

DMZ, abbreviation of *demilitarized zone* (chiefly applied to the demilitarized zone between South Vietnam and North Vietnam situated on the 17th parallel).

. . . United States sources speculated that misinterpreted radar blips and sightings of "flying lights" might have caused the reports that enemy helicopters were operating around the DMZ. *The New York Times, June 24, 1968, p 10*

A film depicts, for example, US Marines carrying out a search and destroy mission near the DMZ. *The Listener, Jan. 18, 1968, p 68*

At the end of January, Honduras and El Salvador each sent three delegates to San José, Costa Rica, for the first of several bilateral peace talks mediated by the former secretary-general of the Organization of American States (OAS), José A. Mora. Finally, at an OAS-sponsored meeting of the Central American foreign ministers in Costa Rica on June 4, Honduras and El Salvador agreed to establish a demilitarized zone (DMZ) 1.8 mi. on either side of their common border. *Allen D. Bushong, "Honduras," Britannica Book of the Year 1971, p 376*

DNA pol·y·me·rase ('pɑl i mə,reis), an enzyme that promotes the formation of new nucleotides of DNA (deoxyribonucleic acid, the carrier of genetic information in the cells) by a process of replication. Compare RNA POLYMERASE.

. . . it has more recently been shown that besides its copying abilities, DNA polymerase can repair strands of DNA damaged by ultra-violet light. *The Times (London), May 25, 1970, p 5*

D Notice, *British.* a government memorandum requesting newspapers not to publish specific items of secret information in the interests of national security.

By accident, D Notices had given a vast amount of protection to national interests which the Government could

not have got in any other way. *Philip Rawstorne, The Manchester Guardian Weekly, July 13, 1967, p 4*

[*D*, abbreviation of *Defense*]

dock, *v.i.* (of a spacecraft) to connect with another orbiting spacecraft.

The manned orbital workshop was assembled yesterday when the three-man ferry craft Soyuz 11 docked with the Salyut, a big instrumented station that was sent aloft without a crew on April 19. *Theodore Shabad, The New York Times, June 9, 1971, p 20*

—*v.t.* to connect (orbiting spacecraft).

The space program puts great dependence on computers. . . . The machines are used to set orbiting patterns, dock vehicles and help perform many other functions — even help design spacecraft. *William D. Smith, The New York Times, Jan. 9, 1967, p 135*

[back formation from *docking*]

docking, *n.* the joining of orbiting spacecraft. *Also used attributively.*

Rendezvous and docking in orbit is a difficult operation; even with men in charge. The first Gemini attempt nearly ended in disaster. *Science Journal, Jan. 1968, p 10*

The simple task of clamping Agena's tether to Gemini's docking bar is an exhausting struggle. *Time, Sept. 30, 1966, p 54*

The view from command pilot John Young's window as Gemini 10 approached Agena 10 during the successful three-day Gemini mission. Docking collar of the Agena is at the right of the vehicle, and the upward-protruding column is the rendezvous radar antenna. At extreme right is the docking bar on Gemini 10. *Picture legend, The Times (London), July 25, 1966, p 8*

DOD, abbreviation of *Department of Defense* (of the United States).

Even allowing for growth in military-age population, DOD found that it could not expect to get more than 2,000,000 men, at least 700,000 short of pre-Viet Nam needs. *"The Case for a Volunteer Army," Time, Jan. 10, 1969, p 25*

doggy bag, *U.S.* a bag containing leftover food, given to a customer to carry home to feed his dog.

Asher's wife couldn't finish her turkey sandwich. The elderly waitress put it in a doggy bag for her. . . . *Gilbert Rogin, "The Regulars," The New Yorker, Nov. 7, 1970, p 44*

The guide also warns that a headwaiter will insist that a visitor take with him any food he orders and does not eat (but fails to mention if he will provide doggy bags). *Time, May 3, 1968, p 24*

do-it-yourselfer, *n.* a person who makes and repairs things at home.

To the do-it-yourselfer, shopping for lumber for a weekend carpentry project is often a confusing experience because sizes are never as stated. . . . *Bernard Gladstone, The New York Times, June 6, 1971, Sec. 2, p 30*

do-it-yourselfery, *n.* activity of a do-it-yourselfer.

Heywood's research had suggested that do-it-yourselfery allied to car ownership had a growth potential of its own. *Patricia Rowan, The Sunday Times (London), July 7, 1968, p 36*

do-it-yourselfism, *n.* the practice of being a do-it-yourselfer.

[Philip] Slater . . . is perceptive and provocative when analyzing American do-it-yourselfism and even the much-prized American family as devices that ensure further loneliness and isolation. *Time, June 1, 1970, p 87*

do·jo ('dou dʒou), *n.* a place where instruction is given in various Japanese arts of self-defense.

Special gymnasiums, called *dojos*, were set up to give private lessons in such martial arts as judo and karate. *Jonathan R. Eley and Martin P. Myrieckes, "Special Report: The Art of Self-Defense," The 1970 Compton Yearbook, p 444*

The Sixth Street *dojo* is on the top floor of the building—a former stable—above two social clubs. . . . *The New Yorker, March 30, 1968, p 26*

[from Japanese *dōjō*]

dol·ce vi·ta ('doul tʃei 'vi: tɑː), Often also **la dolce vita** (lɑː). *Italian.* a life of sensuous pleasure and luxury; (literally) the sweet life.

And now to the world of Greek yachts and the theatre and *dolce vita*, which we enter through the house of Maximilian. *Lois Long, The New Yorker, Oct. 31, 1964, p 206*

. . . the Swiss mistrust any kind of *dolce vita. Craig Claiborne, The New York Times, May 22, 1967, p 49*

A taste of *la dolce vita* is guaranteed on Italian Line's *Michelangelo, Raffaello, Leonardo da Vinci,* and *Cristoforo Colombo. David Butwin, "To Reach the Untaxable Ports," Saturday Review, March 9, 1968, p 86*

[from *La Dolce Vita,* title of an Italian film (1959) directed by Federico Fellini, dealing with the life of pleasure-seeking socialites]

dolly bird, *British Slang.* a young, slim, attractive, and usually fashionably dressed girl. Compare BIRD.

"You American Jews," she [an Englishwoman] said, "are so romantic. You think every little dolly bird is Delilah . . . ." *John Updike, Bech: A Book, 1970, p 147*

There is the unfairness, of course, that a man in his forties can get a dolly-bird (God help him, the one she provides him with) whereas a woman in her forties is more likely to be high and dry. *P. J. Kavanagh, "Home and Away," The Manchester Guardian Weekly, Oct. 23, 1971, p 21*

dolphinarium, *n.* an aquarium for dolphins.

Pittsburgh Zoo dedicated a $1-million bird house, and at Antwerp Zoo, performances began in a new dolphinarium. *George B. Rabb, "Zoos and Aquariums," The 1970 World Book Year Book, p 552*

Regardless of one's point of view on keeping wild animals in captivity . . . the fact remains that it is only by such close proximity that the general public can get to know, and perhaps appreciate, these animals for the beautiful creatures they are. It is with this in mind that we should perhaps welcome the establishment of the London Dolphinarium. *Arthur Bourne, "Exhibition," Review of "Dolphinarium" by Bob Stenuit, New Scientist and Science Journal, April 15, 1971, p 174*

domino, *n.* any of a group of things so positioned that if one of them should fall, all the others would fall in turn, like a row of dominoes. *Often used attributively.*

Most foreign policies proceed from certain perceived truths—Vietnam is a domino, Greece is the southern flank of NATO, Communism is monolithic. . . . *Elizabeth B. Drew, "Reports; Washington," The Atlantic, June 1970, p 4*

East Bloc representation [at the celebration of the UN's 25th anniversary] suffered from a domino sequence of dropouts. *Time, Oct. 26, 1970, p 36*

[abstracted from DOMINO THEORY]

domino theory, a hypothesis stating that if one thing or idea is disposed of, those allied or associated with it will be disposed of in turn, like a falling row of dominoes.

Chavez's next target was the Giumarra Vineyards, the largest table-grape growers in America, themselves controlling 10 percent of the annual crop, and a company not especially beatified by its enlightened view on the labor movement. His strategy was a San Joaquin Valley version of the domino theory: knock over Giumarra, and other growers will fall in line. *John Gregory Dunne, "To Die Standing: Cesar Chavez and the Chicanos," The Atlantic, June 1971, p 40*

. . . if there is "action" on the book in the shops, the owners will order more. Which means people calling up and ordering or coming in and buying it. It's the domino theory: One book bought is another book sold. *Goodman Ace, Saturday Review, Oct. 31, 1970, p 6*

[from the theory, first advanced in the administration of President Eisenhower in the mid-1950's, that if one country in southeast Asia falls to the Communists, the others will fall in turn]

don't-know, *n.* one who is undecided, especially an undecided voter. See also FLOATING VOTER.

. . . you're talking to your Aunt, and not to one of your slide-rule friends. I'm a don't-know, and everyone knows it's the don't-knows who decide the outcome of elections. *William Davis, "Grass Roots Bertha," The Manchester Guardian Weekly, May 30, 1970, p 22*

Both Labour and Conservatives report up to 33-1/3 per cent. "don't knows," even in some of the marginal seats, which looks as though a large protest vote could be garnered by the Liberals who are contesting every seat. *Muriel Bowen, The Sunday Times (London), April 9, 1967, p 4*

The D.K.s or "don't knows," along with the failures to match purchases and sales of securities, have ensnared many brokerage houses and have, in some cases, crippled their ability to operate. *The New York Times, July 11, 1968, p 53*

[from one of the responses (Yes/No/*Don't know*) listed in the forms which are circulated among voters in the public-opinion polls taken prior to elections]

don·to·pe·dal·o·gy (ˌdɑn tou pe'dæl ə dʒiː), *n.* a natural propensity or talent for putting one's foot in one's mouth (that is, for saying something indiscreet, foolish, or embarrassing). Compare FOOT-IN-MOUTH DISEASE.

At the other extreme, and refreshingly so, is her [Queen Elizabeth's] husband, Prince Philip, who looks remarkably like Stan Musial and is a self-confessed expert in the art of "dontopedalogy," as he calls it: opening his mouth and putting his foot in it. *Time, June 27, 1969, p 26*

[coined by Prince Philip, born 1921, the Duke of Edinburgh, from *donto-* (from Greek *odoús, odóntos* tooth) + *pedal* (from Latin *pedālis* of the foot) + *-logy* (as in *physiology, psychology,* etc.)]

Doomsday Machine, a hypothetical machine designed to trigger automatic nuclear destruction under certain conditions without anyone being able to stop it.

But weapons technology continues to "progress," and it is possible that the "ultimate" in weaponry, the so-called Doomsday Machine that can destroy all human life, will become not only technologically feasible but inexpensive. *Herman Kahn and Anthony J. Wiener, "Man and His Future," 1969 Britannica Yearbook of Science and the Future, 1968, p 402*

▶ The concept of the Doomsday Machine was popularized by Herman Kahn, the author of *On Thermonuclear War* (1960). The concept developed from studies of the use of nuclear weapons as deterrents to enemy attack. These studies suggested the Doomsday Machine as the ultimate deterrent, the irrational outcome of building increasingly more lethal instruments of destruction.

do·pa·mine ('dou pə,mi:n), *n.* a hormone produced by the adrenal glands that is essential to the normal nerve activity of the brain.

Some of the symptoms of parkinsonism may be due to lack of the neural chemical dopamine in the brain.... *Arthur Tye, "Drug Industry," 1970 Collier's Encyclopedia Year Book, p 214*

The use of L-Dopa is based on the belief that Parkinson's disease is the result of a deficiency of a substance called dopamine in the brain. L-Dopa is a naturally occurring substance that leads to the formation of dopamine. *The New York Times, May 8, 1968, p 49*

[contraction of *di*hydroxy*p*henylethyl*amine*]

dop·ant ('dou pənt), *n.* an impurity added in small quantities to a semiconductor to improve its conductive capacity.

The technique is now becoming increasingly important in making semiconductors, whose electrical properties are dominated by certain impurities ("dopants") in concentrations sometimes as low as one part in 10^8. *Geoff Dearnaley and J. Harry Freeman, New Scientist, Feb. 6, 1969, p 282*

A typical integrated circuit crystal . . . contains an acceptor dopant such as boron. The amount of dopant may be approximately one dopant atom for every 107 silicon atoms. . . . *W. J. Talbot and R. Naylor, "Computer Hardware for the 1970s," Science Journal, Oct. 1970, p 42*

[from *dope, v.*, to treat or coat one substance with another + *-ant* (noun agent suffix)]

dormin, *n.* another name for ABSCISIC ACID.

The story began several years ago when Professor P. F. Wareing, of the University College of Wales at Aberystwyth, found that the formation of dormant buds by sycamore trees in response to the shortening days of autumn was due to an increase in a growth-inhibitory substance in their leaves. He called this substance dormin. *New Scientist, Sept. 5, 1968, p 503*

[from *dorm*ant + *-in* (chemical suffix)]

do svi·da·nia (,dɔ: svi:'dɑ: nyə). Also spelled **dosvidanya, dosvedanya.** *Russian.* good-bye.

They [the Russian delegation to Czechoslovakia] . . . bade their hosts *do svidania*, climbed aboard their own train and sped a bare mile across the border to dine and sleep in the security of their own country. *Time, Aug. 9, 1968, p 20*

But it was time to return, before the Hotel Siberia shut its doors on me for the night. Dosvedanya, Galina—and

may Mother Russia grant you a few frivolities while you are still young enough to enjoy them. *Christopher Driver, "On the Town in Irkutsk," The Manchester Guardian Weekly, Nov. 22, 1969, p 7*

double, *n. U.S. Horse Racing.* a bet on the winners of the first two races of the day (the "daily double").

Of course I discovered some interesting possibilities in the first race, and interest soon grew into excitement. I hustled to the track, bet my "doubles," and prepared to take my place in the sun. *Sam Toperoff, "'They' Never Sleep," The Atlantic, Oct. 1967, p 78*

double-blind, *adj.* based upon a method of testing in which neither the identity of what is being tested nor its possible effects are disclosed to the subject or the one administering the test until its completion.

The ideal way to determine that two like products are equal in therapeutic action would be to compare them in extensive, double-blind clinical studies. *"Generic Equivalency: Testing the Me-too Drugs," Science News, Oct. 31, 1970, p 350*

Dr. Lawther also uses other members of his staff for "double-blind" experiments, in which neither the subject nor the technician knows exactly what is going on. If the subject knew what substance he was breathing, Dr. Lawther believes, there could be a psychological reaction that would affect his respiration, and if the technician knew what substances he was administering, he might unwittingly weight his findings. *Edith Iglauer, "A Reporter at Large: The Ambient Air," The New Yorker, April 13, 1968, p 83*

double-book, *v.t.* to accept two reservations for (the same hotel room) so as to help insure its occupancy in the event of a cancellation.

"Even when we double-booked the rooms once and had to turn people away, they said 'Never mind, dear, we know it's not your fault.'" *Mary Schofield, The Times (London), Aug. 17, 1970, p 5*

double-deal, *v.i.* to practice deception; cheat; deceive.

. . . it is Don Lope who is ill and she who double-deals pretending to call a doctor for him with her finger pressed firmly down on the telephone rest. *Penelope Gilliatt, "The Current Cinema: Buster Keaton," Review of "Tristana," The New Yorker, Sept. 26, 1970, p 124*

I am double-dealing once more by choosing only *new* recordings for the top ten. *Derek Jewell, The Sunday Times (London), Dec. 17, 1967, p 21*

[back formation from *double-dealing, n., adj.* or *double-dealer*]

double-helical, *adj.* consisting of two strands that coil around each other to form a double spiral or helix.

Until the dramatic announcement of the double-helical structure of DNA, there was complete ignorance of how a chemical substance could carry out the multifold activities needed for a genetic substance. *James D. Watson, "The Double Helix," The Atlantic, Feb. 1968, p 91*

double helix, the double-helical structure of a molecule of DNA. Compare ALPHA HELIX.

The irony was that the physicists-turned-biologists and their immediate collaborators promptly . . . discovered the double helix, and opened up vistas of genetic engineering that were anything but "safe." *Donald Fleming, "Big Science Under Fire," The Atlantic, Sept. 1970, p 98*

Chargaff's [the biochemist, Erwin Chargaff's] rules then suddenly stood out as a consequence of a double-helical structure for DNA. Even more exciting, this type of double helix suggested a replication scheme much more satisfactory than my briefly considered like-with-like pairing. Always pairing adenine with thymine and guanine with cytosine meant that the base sequences of the two intertwined chains were complementary to each other. *James D. Watson, The Double Helix, 1968, p 196*

The genetics of the living cell is more remarkable than capsule statements allow. Thus it is commonly said that the DNA—the molecular double helix—found in the nucleus of each cell of a plant or animal contains the complete genetic blueprint for reconstruction of the total organism. Geneticists have recognized for some time, however, that this statement cannot be rigorously true, since the cytoplasm (the nonnuclear region) of all plant and animal cells contains certain organelles, or subcellular structures, that have DNA of their own. *Ursula W. Goodenough and R. P. Levine, "The Genetic Activity of Mitochondria and Chloroplasts," Scientific American, Nov. 1970, p 22*

doubleknit, *n.* a fabric knitted with a double stitch to provide it with twice its usual thickness. *Often used attributively.*

...Adele Martin's eloquent understatement in wool doubleknit. *The New Yorker, Sept. 23, 1967, p 168*

Behind this huge production of Crimplene in Britain lies a modern and technically advanced doubleknit industry consisting of about 100 firms. *Stuart Taylor, The Sunday Times (London), April 30, 1967, p 27*

Save up to $2.33 on this special buy of polyester doubleknits. Scoop up anywhere from 1 to 5 yard lengths ... all first quality fabrics. *Advertisement by Singer Sewing Centers, Sunday News (New York), June 25, 1972, p 98*

dove, *n.* a person who is opposed to war or to confrontation of force; person who seeks accommodation with an enemy instead of making war. Compare HAWK.

In our opinion, the general run of Americans—whether hawks or doves, or neither—are deeply preoccupied with the war. *"The Talk of the Town," The New Yorker, Jan. 13, 1968, p 19*

...both Hawks and Doves are unanimous that the Vietnamese war must be brought to an immediate end if the United States economy is to avoid further disruption. *The Times (London), April 11, 1968, p 17*

On the basis of one definition (used in the latest Gallup Poll), about three Democrats in every 10 (27 per cent) are "doves." These are persons who think the United States should reduce its military effort in Vietnam, as opposed to 57 per cent of Democrats ("hawks") who think the nation should step up its military efforts. *The New York Times, Feb. 4, 1968, p 43*

One of the few points of agreement on Vietnam among all the current Presidential candidates—hawks Nixon and Humphrey, doves McCarthy and Kennedy, and moderate Rockefeller—is the recommendation that the burden of fighting the Vietcong and the North Vietnamese should be shifted back to the Saigon Government. *Daniel F. Halloran, The New York Times, May 27, 1968, p 46*

dovish or **doveish,** *adj.* opposed to war or to the use of force in a conflict; tending to seek accommodation with an enemy instead of making war. Compare HAWKISH.

Mr. Eban is widely regarded as the most "dovish" member of the Israel Cabinet, and one who would certainly

negotiate a real peace now, if he could. *The Times (London), Feb. 18, 1970, p 1*

...New Hampshire is considered hawkish and Wisconsin dovish.... *David Halberstam, "The Man Who Ran Against Lyndon Johnson," Harper's, Dec. 1968, p 53*

Actually, when set against the dovish temper of the country, the Congress, and the Cabinet, he [Henry Kissinger] works to reinforce and legitimize the President's hardline instincts on most major international business. *Joseph Kraft, "In Search of Kissinger," Harper's, Jan. 1971, p 54*

The President ... wants it on a schedule best calculated to enhance his political position while undermining that of hawkish spokesmen for escalation and doveish prophets of cataclysm. *Michael C. Janeway, "Washington," The Atlantic, Jan. 1968, p 6*

down, *n.* *U.S. Slang.* another word for DOWNER (def. 1).

In Hollywood, a boy of eleven ... has been pushing "ups" (amphetamine and methedrine pills) and "downs" (barbiturates, tranquilizers) since he was nine.... *Time, Feb. 16, 1970, p 36*

downer, *n.* *U.S. Slang.* **1** a sedative or depressant drug. Also called DOWN. Compare UPPER.

The series' intention, says [Andy] Griffith, is "to tell it like it is for the young people while remaining palatable to older audiences." The premiere involved a student who refused to pop "uppers" and "downers" like the rest of the kids. The comic relief, provided mostly by the school's bicep-brained athletic director (Jerry Van Dyke), was a downer. *"Television: The New Season: Perspiring with Relevance: Situation Comedies," Time, Sept. 28, 1970, p 66*

...Janis [Joplin, a rock singer], along with her famous Southern Comfort, harbored a sometime penchant for downers and hardstuff. *Jacob Brackman, "Overdosing on Life," The New York Times, Oct. 27, 1970, p 45*

2 a dull, tiresome person or thing.

...depressing people were "downers," a bad experience was a "bummer." *Bruce Jay Friedman, "Just Back From the Coast," Harper's, March 1970, p 69*

3 a lessening or decrease in force, intensity, etc.

This does not mean that America has seen the last of revolutionary violence. The movement has always been characterized by uppers and downers, and this spring may bring more uppers than anybody cares to see. *Jesse Birnbaum, "The Radicals: Time Out to Retrench," Time, Feb. 22, 1971, p 14*

downhiller, *n.* a downhill racer in a ski competition.

In particular, he learnt from the failure of the Swiss No. 1 downhiller, Jean-Daniel Daetwyler (he started fourth and finished fourteenth). *John Hennessy, The Times (London), Feb. 16, 1970, p 7*

Miss Chaffee, a product of the same ski country that had produced the great Andrea Mead, had been the team's outstanding downhiller. *Michael Strauss, The New York Times, Dec. 14, 1967, p 66*

Down's syndrome, a term replacing *mongolism* for a form of congenital disorder characterized by extreme mental deficiency and Mongoloid features such as slanting eyes and a round head. See the quotations for details.

The eighth week of human intrauterine life is particularly crucial. Injury at this time may leave the brain defective, the heart walls imperfect, or the bones of the nose and fingers maldeveloped.

The latter defects are among the conditions found in

babies suffering from mongolism, or Down's syndrome, as it is more often called today. *Harold M. Schmeck, Jr., "The Unborn Child," 1968 Collier's Encyclopedia Year Book, p 39*

... Down's syndrome, or mongolism [is] a genetic disease that results from an extra No. 21 chromosome in the child's cells. *Jane E. Brody, "Prenatal Diagnosis is Reducing Risk of Birth Defects," The New York Times, June 3, 1971, p 41*

[named after John L. H. *Down*, 1828-1896, an English physician who first described the characteristics of mongolism]

DP, 1 abbreviation of *data processing.*

As the report puts it: "Forecasting specific developments in the data processing (DP) field is far more difficult than predicting general trends." *New Scientist, Oct. 30, 1969, p 240*

2 abbreviation of DURABLE PRESS.

Durable press (DP) has touched off a revolution that is affecting the entire apparel industry and even such non-apparel commodities as sheets and blankets. *Duncan G. Steck, "Textile Industry," 1967 Collier's Encyclopedia Year Book, p 535*

drag, *Slang.* —*n.* a bore.

I don't like public transportation, and driving back and forth every day is a drag. The traffic and the traveling create tension, and who needs more tension? *Ernest Dunbar, The New York Times Magazine, May 3, 1968, p 108*

He thinks if I write about him, it's jolly, jolly good. And if I don't, it's a piece of badly-written drag. *Philip Oakes, The Sunday Times (London), Aug. 4, 1968, p 13*

—*v.t.* to bore.

I started lessons on drums six years ago, and on the side I played in rock groups. Both experiences dragged me. *Ray Fransen (a musician), quoted by Whitney Balliett, The New Yorker, April 25, 1970, p 123*

dragsville, *n. Slang.* something that is boring. Compare DULLSVILLE.

"Anti-smoking week will not be sanctimonious," Mr. Sidey promised last week. "In fact it will be anything but dragsville." *Michael Parkin, The Manchester Guardian Weekly, Dec. 19, 1968, p 4*

... University? That's just dragsville. *Mark Boxer, The Sunday Times (London), Sept. 24, 1967, p 35*

[see -VILLE]

drame à clef ('dram a 'klei), *French.* a play whose characters and situations represent real people and events; literally, a play with a key (i.e. a key to the actual people and events portrayed). The term was patterned after *roman à clef.*

Some English reviewers have interpreted the play ["The Hotel in Amsterdam" by John Osborne] as a *drame à clef....Time, Aug. 9, 1968, p 34*

Within the framework of Mr. Hay's skilfully wrought drame à clef, however, his dry performance is at times touching in the extreme. *The Times (London), Feb. 8, 1966, p 15*

drame à thèse ('dram a 'tez), *French.* a play with a thesis; play created for the purpose of expounding or illustrating an idea, doctrine, theory, etc.

He [Harold Pinter] was, however, responsible for the gelid direction of "The Man in the Glass Booth," the *drame à thèse* by the actor-novelist-playwright Robert Shaw that has now moved to Broadway. *Kenneth Tynan, "The Theatre*

Abroad: London," The New Yorker, Nov. 9, 1968, p 130

God knows there is room for the *drame à thèse*; perhaps America could do with one. *Maurice Wiggin, The Sunday Times (London), Oct. 15, 1967, p 30*

dram·ma gio·co·so ('dra:m ma: dʒou'kou sou), *Italian.* jocose drama; comedy.

Paisiello's little opera is a delicious sample of the older *dramma giocoso*—not a Himalayan masterpiece, but a masterly comedy of the second rank. *Herbert Weinstock, "Music to Other Ears," Review of Giovanni Paisiello's 1782 Opera "Il Barbiere di Siviglia," Saturday Review, May 11, 1968, p 54*

Felsenstein himself directed Mozart's *dramma giocoso* with his noted resourcefulness and fidelity to the score, to which Mr. Zdenek Kosler gave a well-paced though at first rather halting rendering. *The Times (London), Dec. 13, 1966, p 6*

drawback, *n.* withdrawal.

Representative Ogden Reid ... emphasized the need for President Nixon to have direct confrontation with party leader Leonid Brezhnev and Premier Aleksei Kosygin to arrange a drawback of the missile installations and stop the hijacking. *Phelps Phelps, New York, in a Letter to the Editor, The New York Times, Nov. 7, 1970, p 28*

► *Drawback* is here used literally and is derived from the verb phrase *draw back*. It is not connected with the noun *drawback* found in all dictionaries, whose chief meaning ("hindrance; shortcoming; disadvantage") is figurative.

drawdown, *n. U.S.* a reduction; cutback.

Last week, in what may be the beginning of a worldwide drawdown, the President announced that 14,900 troops will be brought home from various stations abroad. *Time, July 18, 1969, p 14*

There has been "draw-down," as the services call it, on military supply inventories throughout the world. *The New York Times, April 23, 1966, p 30*

[from the verb phrase *draw down*]

dreamscape, *n.* a dreamlike picture or view.

The book [*The Holy Well* by Valentin Katayev] is a dreamscape—Fellini is the unavoidable reference—as an old man in hospital, hearing his blood drip into a bottle, reviews his life. *Christopher Wordsworth, The Manchester Guardian Weekly, Aug. 17, 1967, p 11*

[from *dream* + *-scape* view, scene]

dreary, *v.t.* to make dreary.

... the high frequencies most people don't seem to notice are like to split my eardrums. Besides, it [television] drearies the ball game. *Jean Goldschmidt, "Pursuits: Bess," The Atlantic, June 1971, p 65*

► According to the *OED*, *dreary* was last recorded as a verb in the Middle English period (about 1300).

drillion, *adj., n. U.S. Slang.* an enormously large but indefinite number. Older slang words with the same meaning are *zillion* and *jillion.*

... a handful of bittersweet memories—plus about a drillion dollars from the dad who forgives him for marrying a Rhode Island Italian, now that she is dead. *Time, Jan. 11, 1971, p 24*

drin·a·myl ('drin ə,mil), *n.* a drug combining an amphetamine and a barbiturate, sold in Great Britain in tablet form and known as PURPLE HEART.

...his doctor had refused to prescribe any more of the drinamyl tablets he had been taking regularly for years and he was suffering from withdrawal symptoms. *The Times (London), Sept. 7, 1970, p 9*

drip, *n. British.* short for DRIP-FEED.

The hospital doctors promptly gave him emergency treatment by injection and followed it by a hydrocortisone drip and helium inhalations, but it was not possible to save his life. *The Times (London), April 23, 1966, p 8*

"I do not want to hear that the patient next door has had a Bad Turn and is on a drip." *Catholic Herald, May 5, 1972, p 8*

drip-feed, *British.* —*adj.* of or for feeding intravenously.

A baby was wheeled on a hospital trolley across a busy main road as a nurse held a drip-feed bottle because the men refused to turn out. *The Times (London), Oct. 19, 1970, p 2*

—*n.* a course of intravenous feeding. Also shortened to DRIP.

...every senior officer in the Sudanese command was stricken with a most terrible illness. The Ambassador, who is not a very young man, had to retire to bed for five days and was even on a dripfeed. *"Pop Goes the Market: Tuna War," The Manchester Guardian Weekly, July 17, 1971, p 11*

drip painting, 1 a form of action painting executed by dripping or splattering paint instead of by using brushstrokes.

In addition, he [André Masson, an artist] squeezed color directly onto his canvases from a special tube, thereby antedating the drip paintings of Jackson Pollock by 20 years. *"Art: Museums: Prophetic Approaches," Time, April 5, 1968, p 44*

2 the style or technique of making such paintings.

Pollock's modifications of painting tend toward an emulation of writing. In throwing, dribbling, and blotting his pigments, he brought paint into closer approximation of the resiliences of verbal utterance. The essential form of drip painting is calligraphy. *Harold Rosenberg, "The Art World: The Mythic Act," The New Yorker, May 6, 1967, p 168*

drive-up window, *U.S.* a window through which patrons can be served while seated in their cars.

Zip Food Stores in Denver adds drive-up windows at five of its seven small markets. *Wall Street Journal, April 8, 1965, p 1*

droit du seig·neur ('drwa dY sei'nyœr), *French.* right of the lord.

My stepfather seemed to think that he had a sort of *droit de seigneur* over all cheese in the house. *Oliver Woods, The Times (London), April 6, 1968, p 17*

However well Columbia goes, it will have to face up to Dartmouth, which exerting its *droit du seigneur* (a colossal crop of seniors and juniors) upon Princeton last weekend, made it 38-0 in its own favor without ever really exerting itself. *J. W. L., "Football: Help Wanted," The New Yorker, Oct. 17, 1970, p 146*

► The current use of this term suggests only faintly the historical sense of the feudal lord's *jus primae noctis* (right to have intercourse with a vassal's bride on her wedding night) recorded in dictionaries. In some earlier quotations the historical allusion is preeminent.

droop nose or **droop snoot,** an aircraft nose or foremost point that can be deflected to permit better visibility in landing.

Trouble with the development of the droop nose and fuel system of the Concorde has contributed towards additional costs of £1,700,000 during the current financial year, a parliamentary report disclosed yesterday. *Arthur Reed, The Times (London), May 9, 1968, p 3*

Both SST [supersonic transport] designs currently in competition have pivoted "droop-snoots," which swing down so pilots can see over the plane's long nose. *Science News, Nov. 19, 1966, p 422*

drop, *n. Slang.* a place used by spies to deposit secret messages or information.

Szolky [Gunmar Szolky, a secret agent] himself, in his forthcoming autobiography "Under Twelve Flags," maintains that he passed the entire period in Oslo managing a combination tobacconist's shop and foreign-agents' "drop," which was "blown" when a quisling agent found himself smoking a chart of harbor defenses. *Gordon Cotler, "Top Secret—Get Your Advance Copy Today," The New Yorker, April 6, 1968, p 38*

A Crime of One's Own [by] Edward Grierson—Amusing beginning in a bookshop...; funny espionage, with some genuine thrills when Mitty-ish bookseller decides that his lending library is a *drop* and that laundry list bookmarks may conceal microdots. *Leo Harris, "Unlawful Assembly," Review of "A Crime of One's Own" by Edward Grierson, Punch, March 1, 1967, p 321*

—*v.i.* **drop out,** to reject or withdraw from conventional society because of disillusionment with its standards and values.

The possibility that chronic cannabis users tend to become social dropouts Dr. McGlothlin finds quite plausible. "Chronic users of any drug, including alcohol, are liable to drop out," he says. *Lawrence Massett, Science News, Feb. 7, 1970, p 157*

Being a hippie, to them, means dropping out completely, and finding another way to live, to support oneself physically and spiritually. *Sara Davidson, "Open Land: Getting Back to the Communal Garden," Harper's, June 1970, p 94*

drop-in, *n.* 1 a person who drops in to a place; a casual visitor. Also called DROPPER-IN.

The pilot was Captain Itchy Bourne.... He despised all generals, especially drop-ins from Washington. *John Fischer, "The Easy Chair: War as Theater of the Absurd," Harper's, March 1970, p 18*

2 a place where people drop in or visit casually.

The rubbish came from Alice's Restaurant, a drop-in for dropouts built out of a deconsecrated church in Stockbridge, Mass. *Derek Malcolm, "The Arts: Alice in Hippy Land, London Cinema," Review of "Alice's Restaurant," The Manchester Guardian Weekly, Feb. 21, 1970, p 20*

—*adj.* designed to be inserted.

To prevent any possible confusion about which are the remains to be seen, each window has a drop-in name plaque. *Time, April 5, 1968, p 38*

The marketing drive centers on the "Single 8", a kit consisting of two 8 mm. cameras, a drop-in color-film cartridge and a projector. *Walter Carlson, The New York Times, March 2, 1966, p 51*

dropout, *n.* a person who withdraws from any segment or institution of established society to join groups of radicals, hippies, etc.

And by the end of the decade, there was a marked reaction among white middle-class Americans against the rebellious Negroes, the defiant university students, and the social drop-outs. *James Reston, "Focus on the Nation," 1970 World Book Year Book, p 25*

dropper-in, *n.* a casual visitor. Also called DROP-IN.

In the houses shared by groups of young people, the final onslaught of co-renters, dates, guests, and droppers-in kept the bathrooms constantly occupied and strewn with soggy towels.... *Morton Hunt, "Annals of Agriculture: The Three-Hundred-and-Nineteenth Growing Season," The New Yorker, Nov. 1, 1969, p 100*

I am not much inclined towards droppers-in; but sometimes one can't very well get out of providing a meal for the uninvited guest. *R. G. G. Price, "Chef of the Week," Punch, May 22, 1968, p 745*

drownproofing, *n.* a means of protection against drowning. See the quotation for details.

A new technique of water survival called "Drownproofing" has been in official use as part of the training program here since April. It has virtually superseded conventional swimming instructions in water survival courses.

The marine is taught to relax in the water and to allow the head and upper torso to sink beneath the surface at a 45 degree angle. Then, with a slow easy arm and leg motion, the head is raised above the surface; the man takes a deep breath and then relaxes again, exhaling slowly while under water. Marines in full combat uniforms with packs and rifles have stayed afloat using this method for an hour or more. *Hanson W. Baldwin, The New York Times, Oct. 15, 1967, Sec. 1, p 7*

druggy, *U.S.* —*n.* a person who takes drugs.

... the various student types ... joiners and doers, druggies and drunks.... *James Reston, The New York Times, Nov. 25, 1970, p 37*

More broadly, it [the new morality] is applied to various youth movements, and of course to the hippies and the new druggies. *Henry David Aiken, "The New Morals," Harper's, Feb. 1968, p 58*

Presumably they meant the movie to observe, without either condemning or condoning, some of the oddities in our midst—Hell's Angels, greasers, skinheads, druggies etc. *Derek Malcolm, "After Chandler," The Manchester Guardian Weekly, Dec. 18, 1971, p 21*

—*adj.* having to do with taking drugs.

"Can't You Hear Me Knocking" [a record], by contrast, is a stylistic meeting place for old and new. It begins with that familiar buzzing, distorted guitar sound and inimitable druggy sentiments.... *"Music: Return of Satan's Jesters," Time, May 17, 1971, p 34*

drugpusher, *n.* another word for a *pusher* (of narcotics).

In a routine part, nightclub proprietress in league with drugpushers, she [Patricia Neal] showed what real acting can do with the most unpromising, thin material. *R. G. G. Price, "Television," Review of "The Untouchables," Punch, Aug. 7, 1968, p 204*

drugster, *n.* a drug user or addict.

... injection of amphetamines has grown into an important procedure amongst drugsters. Injection of these drugs leads to a particularly dangerous form of addiction ending in certain early death if continued. *Oliver Gillie, "International Control Proposed for Slimmers," Science Journal, Feb. 1970, p 7*

[from *drug* + -*ster* one who uses, as in *trickster*]

▶ The form *drugster* was used during the 1600's and 1700's as a synonym of *druggist*, with the suffix -*ster* designating a trade or occupation (as also in *tapster, seamster, teamster,* etc.). Alongside this use there arose early a disparaging or derogatory application of -*ster* to any activity that suggested trafficking in a petty way, of which *huckster, trickster, rhymester* are some early examples. It is this use of -*ster* that has survived most prominently, producing *gangster, mobster,* and many other slang terms of contempt or deprecation. The term *drugster* is a current example of this use of -*ster*.

dru·zhin·nik (dru:ˈʒi: nik), *n.; pl.* **dru·zhin·ni·ki** (dru:ˈʒi: ni ki:). a civilian auxiliary policeman in the Soviet Union.

The Druzhinniki ... assist the police in preventing crime, combating hooliganism and drunkenness, and controlling crowds. They are also to be found guarding courtrooms during political trials. *David Bonavia, "Moscow Vigilante Reforms," The Times (London), June 27, 1970, p 7*

[from Russian *druzhinnik*, from *(Narodnaya) Druzhina* (People's) Patrol]

DRV or **DRVN,** abbreviation of the *Democratic Republic of Vietnam* (official name of North Vietnam).

Most of the DRV delegation are no strangers to Paris. They count French scholars and journalists who follow Vietnamese affairs among their friends, and with a sure touch they can direct a foreigner to good Parisian restaurants. *Ross Terrill, "Making Peace at Paris: A Special Report on the Negotiations," The Atlantic, Dec. 1968, p 6*

As far as Hanoi is concerned, the D.R.V.N. comprises all of Vietnam.... *John Van Laer, The New York Times, Oct. 6, 1968, Sec. 4, p 11*

DSRV, abbreviation for *Deep Submergence Rescue Vehicle*.

Your article "Hope for disabled undersea vessels" ... states that, despite Congressional criticism on costs of the DSRV, "the need for the vehicle was so great and so obvious that the program continues." *H. W. Adams, Deelmar, N.Y., in a Letter to the Editor, Science News, Oct. 3, 1970, p 282*

...expensive and sophisticated guidance control systems are built into the DSRV.... *New Scientist, June 25, 1970, p 629*

The U.S. Navy may have two prototype deep submergence rescue vehicles by 1972 or 1973. *DSRV-1* was launched on January 24 and is undergoing trials in shallow water. Ultimately the craft will be able to rescue 24 men at a time from a disabled submarine at depths of 5,000 feet (1,500 meters). *Myrl C. Hendershott, "Oceanography," The Americana Annual 1971, p 515*

Du·chenne dystrophy (du:ˈʃen), a form of muscular dystrophy.

Muscular dystrophy is in fact a group of diseases. In the best known, Duchenne dystrophy, which is inherited and affects only boys, the muscles start to waste away from an early age. *The Times (London), June 30, 1970, p 16*

[named after Guillaume Armand *Duchenne*, 1806-1875, a French neurologist who described the various forms of the disease]

duen·de ('dwen dei), *n. Spanish.* (literally) elf; demon. But see the quotations for other meanings.

... the quality of the Spanish character—which Michener sums up in one evocative word, *duende,* meaning "mysterious and ineffable charm." *"Books: The Infatuated Traveler," Review of "Iberia" by James A. Michener, Time, May 17, 1968, p 84*

... he has that essential flamenco ingredient which America's own great ethnic dance expert, La Meri, describes as *duende* (a "demon"), which means that "the dancer must be possessed." *Walter Terry, "World of Dance: Holiday Bounty," Saturday Review, Jan. 6, 1968, p 36*

As a Latin, Busoni approaches the idea of death through a feeling for what Lorca called *duende*—that Spanish apprehension of the dark magic of death which lurks behind life and behind all great works of art. *Ronald Stevenson, "BBC Music Review: Busoni's 'Turandot'," The Listener, April 14, 1966, p 556*

du·ka or **duk·ka** ('du: kə), *n.* a retail shop in Kenya and some other parts of eastern Africa. *Also used attributively.* See also DUKAWALLAH.

... the shops and garages were Indian-owned and the open-fronted bars, the dukkas selling every conceivable item from comic books to bicycles, the tea-rooms and the food stores were all Indian. *Anthony Pearson, "Coming to Terms with Africa," The Manchester Guardian Weekly, Jan. 23, 1969, p 6*

Turkana is far from here and full of naked men with spears, but my uncle Motidhai has a duka business there, and his sons, my cousins, adventure with lorries into that savage land. *Purshottam S. Patel, Nakuru, Kenya, in a Letter quoted by Edward G. Nash, Saturday Review, June 1, 1968, p 48*

[probably from Hindi *dukān*]

du·ka·wal·lah ('du: kə,wɑl ə), *n.* a shopkeeper in Kenya and some other parts of eastern Africa.

... Sam Fong became, after more than four years, a shopkeeper; or as Fakhru put it, "Now my friend you are a *dukawallah.* It should be abundantly clear that there is a place for you in East Africa to grow and prosper." *Paul Theroux, "Two in the Bush," The Atlantic, July 1968, p 84*

The first Asians went to East Africa well ahead of the British. ... They became the colony's 'dukawallahs' (or shopkeepers), running every kind of establishment from the smart shops in the capital to tiny stores in dusty African villages. *John Bierman, "Foreign News: The Middle Layer," The Listener, March 7, 1968, p 294*

[from *duka* + *-wallah* (Anglo-Indian suffix for one connected with). See also LABOURWALLAH.]

Dullsville or **dullsville,** *U.S. Slang. —n.* a condition of utter dullness; something very dull. Compare DRAGSVILLE.

... the thirty-seventh President tips ketchup on his cottage cheese. "Style-wise," a lady columnist impaled the new regime, "it looks like backward to Dullsville for the next four years in the nation's capital." *"Miscellany in Washington ... Stars and Strife: Pat-a-cake," The Manchester Guardian Weekly, Jan. 23, 1969, p 4*

—adj. very dull.

[President Lyndon] Johnson is square, folksy and dullsville, sounding just like dozens of boring politicians from the past. *Sally Slocum, St. Louis, in a Letter to the Editor, Time, Oct. 7, 1966, p 17*

dumdum, *n. Chiefly U.S. Slang.* a stupid person; a dumbbell. *Also used attributively.*

The police commissioner can expose himself in the middle of 42nd Street and no one'll pay attention to him. Yet all you need is one dumdum in the mayor's office pointing to a cop and saying, 'I like that boy,' and the next day he's got a promotion. *Bruce Jay Friedman, "Lessons of the Street," Harper's, Sept. 1971, p 87*

"Marooned," on the other hand, a sci-fi space epic, is total, straight Dullsville. ... At times this picture seems like a straight-faced parody of nice-guy, concerned-American stereotypes, and the dummies in space have left dum-dum wives below. *Pauline Kael, The New Yorker, Jan. 3, 1970, p 61*

dump, *U.S.* See the quotations for various specialized meanings.

—n. Computers.

When computers hit a snag they often print out dense reams of digits, which represent all the data that's been given to them. This is called a "dump." Searching out the error in a dump is referred to as "debugging," and it occupies much of any programmer's time. *Richard Todd, "You Are an Interfacer of Black Boxes," The Atlantic, March 1970, p 67*

—v.t. **1** *Motion Pictures.*

Finally, the movie was "dumped"—opened without the usual publicity and advance screenings. *Pauline Kael, "The Current Cinema: Mythmaking," Review of "Burn!" The New Yorker, Nov. 7, 1970, p 159*

2 *U.S. Football.*

A team is not "defended against" but "defensed," and he who would describe a quarterback caught behind the line of scrimmage as having been "dumped" rather than "sacked" reveals his status as a postulant before the mysteries. *Champ Clark, Time, Nov. 19, 1970, p 37*

—v.i. **dump on,** *U.S. Slang.* See the quotation for the meaning.

They [homosexuals] have also made it a practice to "trash" (wreck) restaurants, publishing houses, and other businesses that discriminate against the third world of sex; "dump on" (heckle) religious leaders, such as Billy Graham, who don't like them; and "zap" (confront) politicians until they express themselves one way or the other on equal housing and employment rights for homosexuals. *Faubion Bowers, "Homosex: Living The Life," Saturday Review, Feb. 12, 1972, p 24*

dune buggy, a small, lightweight car designed especially for driving on sand dunes and beaches.

To other users, the raffish vehicles offer instant fun at relatively little cost: $200 for the smallest trail bike, $1,000 for an average snowmobile, $1,200 for a dune buggy, $1,600 for an ATV. *"Environment: Mechanized Monsters," Time, Nov. 23, 1970, p 41*

A new and popular outdoor hobby was the building and driving of "dune buggies," cars modified especially for daring drives on sand dunes. *"Hobbies," The 1969 Compton Yearbook, p 269*

dunny, *n. Australian Slang.* a toilet.

They're so economically backward here [in England] ... what with all those tea-breaks and going to the dunny they never did a tap of work. *Jan Smith, "A Hard Day's Rest," The Sunday Times (London), May 2, 1971, p 42*

duorail, *n.* the conventional railroad consisting of two rails, as distinguished from the monorail.

Because the duorail is for the present favored, the new rapid-transit systems being built in the metropolitan areas of the Americas and Europe are underground railways powered by electric traction. *Ernest A. J. Davies, "Transportation, Special Report: Tomorrow's Transportation," The 1969 Compton Yearbook, p 450*

durable press, a textile-manufacturing process in which creases, pleats, etc., are set more or less permanently into fabric by the use of chemicals. *Abbreviation:* DP Also called PERMANENT PRESS.

In furnishings, the great growth of durable press and soil-resistant shirts made much of the older stock obsolete. *The New Yorker, Jan. 8, 1968, p 124*

The first limited success was an all-cotton durable-press shirt marketed this year. *"Cotton: Bad Days on the Plantation," Time, Oct. 10, 1969, p 61*

dustoff, *n. U.S. Military Slang.* another name for MEDEVAC. *Often used attributively.*

Wounded are picked up and shuttled away from enemy fire, then quickly evacuated on "dust-off" helicopters to the nearest U.S. hospital. *Time, Aug. 2, 1968, p 22*

. . . virtually all battlefield casualties are picked up by aerial ambulances, the so-called "dustoff" medical helicopters. *The New York Times, May 21, 1967, Sec. 1, p 22*

[so called from the dust they raise during their rapid descent and takeoff]

dy·ad ('dai₁æd), *n.* a meaningful dialogue, encounter, or relationship between two people or groups of people.

The T-group has a special lingo, a mixture of hippie talk and social science jargon. People are always "hung-up" or "uptight," trying to discover "where I'm at." They don't talk; they "have a dyad." *Ted J. Rakstis, "Sensitivity Training," Encyclopedia Science Supplement (Grolier) 1970, p 81*

dye laser, a chemical laser using the fluorescence of certain organic dyes, such as rhodamine and fluorescein, to produce intense coherent light over a wide range of possible frequencies.

The tunability of the dye laser is its most striking characteristic; therefore much work has been done in this area. The gross selection of wavelength can be achieved by properly choosing the dye. *Alexander Lempicki, "Liquid Lasers," McGraw-Hill Yearbook of Science and Technology 1970, p 234*

dyke, *n. Slang.* a lesbian. *Also used attributively.*

I am flipping vaguely through a pamphlet called *No More Fun and Games: A Journal of Female Liberation.* I say to her, forgetting, "What's this, some kind of dyke outfit?" *Edward Grossman, "In Pursuit of the American Woman," Harper's, Feb. 1970, p 48*

[of unknown origin]

dyk·ey ('dai ki:), *adj. Slang.* lesbian.

One interlude, however, is entirely free of stylistic ties. On the road, Robert and Rayette pick up two dykey hitchhikers. One is sullen. The other (Helena Kallianiotes) delivers a ten-minute broadside at "man." *Stefan Kanfer, "Cinema," Review of "Five Easy Pieces," Time, Sept. 14, 1970₄ p K 11*

dy·on ('dai₁ɑn), *n.* a hypothetical nuclear particle carrying both a magnetic charge and an electric charge.

. . . dyons effectively combined magnetic monopoles and quarks. A quark is another sort of hypothetical particle that was introduced into theoretical physics to explain certain regularities that appear in the properties of many of the elementary particles. *Dietrick E. Thomsen, "Searching for Monopoles," Science News, Aug. 22, 1970, p 183*

[coined by Julian Schwinger, born 1918, an American physicist, from Greek *dy-* two + *-on*, as in *electron, proton*]

dys·au·to·no·mi·a (dis₁ɔː təˈnou miː ə), *n.* an inherited disorder of the nervous system, found chiefly among Jews of European descent, in which sensory perception and many automatic functions are impaired.

Dysautonomia, transmitted through a recessive gene, affects the autonomic, or automatic, nervous system, which regulates such basic processes as respiration, digestion, blood circulation, and responses to pain, heat and cold. *Barbara Trecker, "Battling A Genetic Disease," New York Post, June 25, 1972, p 58*

[from *dys-* abnormal, defective + *autonomic* (nervous system) + *-ia* disease, as in *pneumonia, diphtheria,* etc.]

dys·bar·ism ('dis bə₁riz əm), *n.* paralyzing cramps caused by a sudden reduction of air pressure.

. . . farther up [than three miles], man becomes subject to "the bends," or dysbarism. Nitrogen in his tissues is released because of the low atmospheric pressure. *"Man's Venture into Space," The 1970 Compton Yearbook, p 564*

[from Greek *dys-* bad + *báros* weight, pressure + English *-ism*]

dysfunction, *v.i.* to cease to function properly or normally; to break down.

Looking at "the dysfunctioning of Arab society," Beirut Social Psychologist Halim Barakat says, "Men alienated from established orders have alternatives." *"The World: Arabs v. Communists: Thanks But No Thanks," Time, Aug. 9, 1971, p 23*

"I'm convinced that the next ruling generation is going to be all pillheads. I'm convinced of it. If they haven't dysfunctioned completely to the point where they can't stand for office." *Bruce Jackson, "White-Collar Pill Party," The Atlantic, Aug. 1966, p 40*

[verb use of *dysfunction, n.*]

dyslexic, *n.* a person affected with dyslexia (impairment in reading ability).

The conventional figure of the incidence of dyslexics in this country [Great Britain] is 4 per cent of backward readers. *Peter Lennon, "Lost In a World of Words," The Sunday Times (London), July 11, 1971, p 21*

To the parents of a dyslexic, the child's behavior may be profoundly perplexing. Often the child exhibits exceptional ingenuity and creativity, yet fails totally at school. *Robert Reinhold, The New York Times, Feb. 5, 1968, p 41*

[noun use of *dyslexic, adj.*]

dys·to·pi·a (disˈtou piː ə), *n.* the opposite of a utopia; place where all is bad or a condition in which all is evil. Compare KAKOTOPIA.

Only in two respects is Marcuse utterly lucid: in his desire to destroy our world, and in his yearning to be relieved of the tyranny of the genital in order to live in a nebulous, polymorphically perverse, anarchic dystopia. *Eliseo Vivas, "Marcuse as Torquemada of the Left," The New York Times, June 15, 1971, p 43*

dystopian

It may be that only a vision of Utopia can combat the dystopia of contemporary life. *Time, Jan. 18, 1971, p 15*

[from *dys-* bad + u*topia*]

► The coinage of *dystopia* (where all is bad) as the opposite of *utopia* (where all is good) suggests that the initial *u-* (from Greek *oú* not) has become associated with the prefix *eu-* (from Greek *eu-* good) although there is no historical connection; *dystopia* then contrasts with *utopia* as *dysgenic* with *eugenic*, *dyspeptic* with *eupeptic*, *dysphoria* with *euphoria*, and the like.

dystopian, *adj.* of or relating to a dystopia; the opposite of utopian.

Catherine, who takes after her mother, is also worried about life, and it seems that her friend Brigitte, a sensible little Jewess, is encouraging her to take the dystopian view. *Anthony Burgess, Review of "Les Belles Images" by Simone de Beauvoir, The New York Times Book Review, March 3, 1968, p 5*

. . . the deformed, the insane and the defective become the new elite. Madness and destruction ensue. . . . Despite such familiar dystopian details. *Intensive Care* has little in common with the average science-fiction novel, far more with social-commentary-as-critique such as Orwell's *1984* and Butler's *Erewhon. "Books: Back to Nightmare," Review of "Intensive Care" by Janet Frame, Time, May 18, 1970, p 88*

dys·tro·phi·ca·tion (ˌdis trə fəˈkei ʃən), *n.* the pollution of streams, lakes, etc., by domestic and industrial wastes and runoff from fertilized agricultural areas. See also EUTROPHICATION.

The sea can probably tolerate the runoff indefinitely but along the way the nitrogen creates algal "blooms" that are hastening the dystrophication of lakes and estuaries. *Ferren MacIntyre, "Why the Sea is Salt," Scientific American, Nov. 1970, p 115*

[from *dystrophic* depleted in nutrients (said of a lake) + *-ation*]

E

ear-catcher, *n.* something that attracts attention by its sound; a catchy tune, lyric, etc.

Demonstration records in my collection tend to sort themselves out into two changing piles: one predictably of ear-catchers designed to send listeners through the roof; the other, equally important, of "guess-whats." *Edward Greenfield, The Manchester Guardian Weekly, May 1, 1969, p 21*

[patterned after *eye-catcher*]

Earth Day, a day in April set aside by environmentalists to dramatize the need for pollution control. See also EARTH WEEK.

By the time Earth Day dawned on April 22, ecoactivists of all ages were suffused with quasi-religious fervor. *Time, Jan. 4, 1971, p 34*

The youngsters who coordinated Earth Day activities established a group called "Environmental Action" and set up headquarters in Washington, D.C. to lobby for conservation legislation. *A. L. Newman, "Conservation," The 1971 World Book Year Book, p 273*

earthday, *n.* the 24-hour day of the earth applied to measuring time on other celestial bodies, artificial satellites, etc.

For just over 14 earthdays the sun will not shine on the barren surface of the Sea of Rains, where the Lunokhod began its historic mission last Tuesday. *The Times (London), Nov. 24, 1970, p 6*

earthrise, *n.* a view of the earth from the moon or from a spacecraft orbiting about the moon, in which the earth seems to be rising above the moon's horizon.

The earthrise is seen over the lunar horizon from the Apollo 12 spacecraft. . . . *Picture legend, "Space Exploration," The 1970 Compton Yearbook, p 436*

[patterned after *sunrise*]

earth station, a station on earth equipped with electronic apparatus to receive and rebroadcast signals transmitted from outer space. Compare SATCOM.

Every single piece of equipment in the satellite must operate flat-out [at top capacity] in order to provide today's services, and their signals can be picked up only by giant 90- or 100-foot diameter Earth stations costing several million pounds. *Ron Brown, "Satellite Eye On All Aircraft," New Scientist, July 2, 1970, p 13*

Earth Week, a week in April set aside for expression of public concern over the pollution of the earth's atmosphere. Compare EARTH DAY.

To celebrate Earth Week (this year's version of Earth Day, spread over April 18-24), New York's Bronx Zoo set up this ominous "Animal Graveyard." Each of the 225 tombstones commemorates a species that has become extinct since 1600. . . . *Picture legend, Time, April 26, 1971, p 59*

earthwoman, *n.* a woman of the planet earth; a female earthling.

If the Apollo near-catastrophe warned earthmen and earthwomen that space travel was not without its dangers, there was plenty to remind them of the more routine hazards of flight. *E. C. Hodgkin, "Kidnapers, Hijackers and Cataclysms," The Times (London), Dec. 31, 1970, p 1*

[patterned after the older term *earthman*]

earthworker, *n.* an artist who makes earthworks.

The earthworkers may bring their massive mounds . . . into the galleries, or they may leave their sculptures far away, in the form of imprints inscribed in a desert, a dry lake, mud, and ice. *Picture legend, "Art: Process Art and Antiform," 1970 Collier's Encyclopedia Year Book, p 117*

earthworks, *n. sing.* or *pl.* **1** natural material, such as earth, mud, rocks, sand, and ice, shaped, altered, or treated so that it becomes a work of art. See also ECOLOGICAL ART.

Under the names of antiform, process art, earthworks, concept art, soft art, and impossible art, these manifestations emphasize ideas and processes rather than finished products. They are concerned with impermanence, and their makers seem to have rejected the idea of art as a salable commodity. *Benjamin de Brie Taylor, "Art: Process Art and Antiform," 1970 Collier's Encyclopedia Year Book, p 116*

2 earthwork, a particular work of this type, usually exhibited in photographs.

Earthworks protest against the constricting museum-gallery system organized around a handful of aesthetic platitudes by asserting the nostalgia of artists for invention, craftsmanship, and expressive behavior. *Harold Rosenberg, "The Art World: De-aestheticization," The New Yorker, Jan. 24, 1970, p 62*

easy meat, *British Slang.* an easy thing to do, obtain, etc.

. . . he himself says modestly, "It's easy meat, playing for England." *The Sunday Times (London), June 1, 1969, p 22*

► This is really a secondary sense. The earlier meaning implies a passive or impotent victim, e.g. "Unarmed citizens are easy meat for gunmen," to coin an example. Partridge (*Dictionary of Slang, 1950, p 1040*) gives " 'She's easy meat'—of a not invincible chastity," which is doubtless the origin.

Eaton agent, an organism resembling the virus of

pleuropneumonia (pleurisy with pneumonia), believed to cause various mild forms of pneumonia.

Mycoplasma pneumoniae, or Eaton agent, a microorganism intermediate in several respects between viruses and bacteria, is probably responsible for most cases of what used to be called primary atypical pneumonia or, loosely, virus pneumonia. *Maxwell Finland, M.D., "Medicine: Respiratory Disease," Britannica Book of the Year 1968, p 529*

[named for Monroe D. *Eaton*, born 1904, an American bacteriologist]

eb·ul·lism ('eb yə‚liz əm), *n.* the bubbling of body fluids resulting from a sudden reduction of air pressure.

The absence of an atmosphere on the Moon brings hazards of suffocation with a time of useful consciousness limited to a few seconds due to lack of oxygen and the ebullism—boiling of body fluids—due to lack of atmospheric pressure. *Charles A. Berry, "Lunar Medicine," Science Journal, May 1969, p 104*

[from Latin *ēbullīre* to bubble or boil up + English *-ism*]

ec·dy·sone ('ek də‚soun), *n.* a hormone that regulates growth and molting in insects.

Steroids, having substances similar to, and in some cases identical with, ecdysone, the hormone that causes moulting in insects, were discovered recently in bracken and a few other plants, sometimes in quite high concentrations. *The Times (London), Sept. 19, 1968, p 10*

The insect hormone ecdysone, which controls the metamorphosis of insects, achieves its effect by acting directly on DNA. *Alexander G. Bearn, "Genetics," Britannica Book of the Year 1967, p 511*

[from *ecdysis* the shedding of skin, molting + *-one*, as in *hormone*]

echo cardiography, the use of ultrasonic apparatus for diagnosing cardiac tumors, diseased valves, etc. See also ULTRASONOGRAPHY.

The principle underlying this technique is the graphic recording of high frequency sound waves as they bounce back to the recorder after striking an unusual structure within or outside the heart. This technique is also known as echo cardiography. *Johnson McGuire and Arnold Iglauer, "Heart Disease: Ultrasonics in Diagnosis," The Americana Annual 1970, p 339*

echo encephalography, the use of ultrasonic apparatus for diagnosing tumors and lesions in the brain. See also ULTRASONOGRAPHY.

Echo-encephalography got its start in 1954 when Lars Leksell, a Swedish neurosurgeon, reported the use of pulsed ultrasound to reveal lateral shifts in certain structures which normally lie in the medial plane of the brain. *Tom Weissman, Science News, Feb. 3, 1968, p 118*

echovirus, *n.* or **ECHO virus,** a type of virus associated with various kinds of meningitis, intestinal disturbances, and respiratory illnesses in human beings. See also REOVIRUS.

Polioviruses, reoviruses, echoviruses and infectious hepatitis virus still circulate widely. *Frank Fenner, New Scientist, Sept. 10, 1970, p 530*

[formed from its full name enteric *c*ytopathogenic *h*uman *o*rphan virus; called "orphan virus" be-

cause it is not known to cause any of the diseases it is associated with]

eco-. The prefix *eco-* (with the new meaning "of or dealing with ecology," "ecological and _____") has gained wide use growing out of the current concern over pollution of the environment. Some of the new words formed with *eco-* are listed here.

ecoalimental, ecometabolic, ecopathogenic, *adj.:* Ecological death manifests itself when animals die from starvation, dietary deficiencies or ingestion of "wrong" foods (ecoalimental), from infection by pathogens however transmitted (ecopathogenic), from the effects of foreign matter deposited in or on tissues (ecometabolic) or by lethal physical forces operating mechanically from outside the animal (ecophysical). *Don R. Arthur, New Scientist, March 21, 1968, p 625*

eco-atmosphere, *n.:* The scientists under Dr John Kirmiz have termed this mixture the "eco-atmosphere", in line with their previous studies of the jerboa's ecoclimate. *Science Journal, Sept. 1968, p 5*

ecocrisis, *n.:* The ecocrisis is as good an opportunity as any to start building a Brave New World, but for God's sake let's be careful how we go about it. *Graeme Garden, New Scientist and Science Journal, May 27, 1971, p 535*

eco-political, *adj.:* The Council on Environmental Quality has been in operation for only nine months, but it has already totally changed the eco-political situation in the United States. *New Scientist, Oct. 8, 1970, p 59*

eco-theologian, *n.:* The eco-theologians argue that man's despoliation of nature has drawn encouragement in part from mistaken or misapplied Christian concepts. *Time, June 8, 1970, p 49*

See also the entries below.

eco-activist, *n.* a person who is very active in matters pertaining to the protection of the environment from pollution.

Why the new vegetarian trend? It is inexpensive, for one thing. Moreover, the eco-activists are concerned by the amount of DDT and other chemicals in meat. *Time, Nov. 16, 1970, p 59*

eco-activity, *n.* any project or undertaking to combat pollution or improve the quality of the environment.

There are numerous "eco-activities" that can be performed by individuals or local school and community groups. . . . Right: old car tires are used in an experiment to stop soil erosion along Minnesota's Rum River. Local students furnished the labor and later planted trees inside the tires. *Picture legend, "Cleaning Up Our Environment," Encyclopedia Science Supplement (Grolier) 1970, p 172*

ecocatastrophe, *n.* a large-scale or world-wide disaster resulting from uncontrolled use of pollutants.

Gordon Rattray Taylor . . . suggests that overcrowding in the mushrooming cities of South America and Asia will eventually bring about social disruption followed swiftly by political and technological collapse. In his view, this is the form Doomsday will take, beating . . . ecocatastrophe by a short head. *Jon Tinker, New Scientist, Sept. 10, 1970, p 542*

ecocidal, *adj.* relating to or causing ecocide.

. . . beyond that lie the use of ecocidal weapons—herbicides in Vietnam—and "humane incapacitants." *Alex Comfort, "A Remedy for Poison," Review of "The Ultimate*

Folly: War by Pestilence, Asphyxiation, and Defoliation" by Richard D. McCarthy, *The Manchester Guardian Weekly, Aug. 15, 1970, p 18*

ecocide, *n.* the destruction of the earth's ecology through the uncontrolled use of pollutants. Compare BIOCIDE.

Professor Falk sees the mentality of our politicians confronted by these problems [the war system, population pressure, resource depletion and environmental overload] as archaic, even in their rhetorical efforts to be "fellow environmentalists"—as for instance in their belief that they can control the effects of the fourfold threat by improved technology and the profits from economic expansion. He diagnoses this as a desperate hope that survival can be assured without making any sacrifices. The irony of development is that to the extent that it succeeds, the world situation worsens and the dangers of ecocide are increased. *Robert Waller, "Global Eco-politics," Review of "This Endangered Planet" by Richard Falk, New Scientist and Science Journal, July 15, 1971, p 158*

Discarded automobiles, old newspapers and telephone books, tin cans, nonreturnable bottles—all add to the growing problems of solid-waste disposal. . . . The solution, ecologists say, is to use these wastes wisely so that they benefit the environment, not damage it. Such recycling would often be expensive, but, as ecologist David Gates says, "we're poisoning our world and we can't afford not to spend the money as soon as possible." . . . Ecocide—the murder of the environment—is everybody's business. *"Review of the Year: Environmental Sciences," Encyclopedia Science Supplement (Grolier) 1970, p 159*

[from *eco-* + *-cide* killing, as in *suicide, genocide,* etc.]

E. coli (ī: 'kou lai), partial abbreviation of *Escherichia coli,* a common rod-shaped bacillus of the intestinal tract, strains of which have been grown in large amounts and used extensively in experiments dealing with protein synthesis, genetic transmission, immunity, enzymology, etc.

The discovery of sigma factors in E. coli bacteria early last year caused considerable excitement in molecular biological circles, for the factors constituted the first control elements found in living cells that could act directly to turn on genes. *New Scientist, Dec. 3, 1970, p 363*

The relatively simple common intestinal bacterium *E. coli,* from which Beckwith and his associates isolated a pure gene, contains about 3,000 genes. *Harrison Brown, "Focus On Science," The 1970 World Book Year Book, p 35*

ecological art, the art of making or sculpturing earthworks.

If ecological art . . . sounds eccentric, it is. But it is also demanding. Its practitioners sweat and swim, dig trenches, hack through ice, suffer desert winds or the muscle ache of long climbs—all for the sake of a few photographs and a memory. *Time, June 29, 1970, p 62*

ecology, *n.* any balanced or harmonious system.

The introduction of a comprehensive computerized data base into a large company could well upset the 'ecology' of the firm to such an extent that it could take ages to re-establish a stable balance. . . . *A. S. Douglas, Science Journal, Oct. 1970, p 36*

[extended sense of the technical term for the balanced relationship between organisms and their environment]

economism, *n.* (in Marxist terminology) the seeking of material advantages at the expense of the revolution.

In early January, 1967, as the maelstrom China calls its Cultural Revolution swirled through virtually every section of the country, a fascinating term was added to the Chinese Communist lexicon. That term was "economism." *Arthur C. Miller, "China," The Atlantic, Aug. 1968, p 14*

The term "economism" comes from the history of the Russian Socialist movement around the turn of the century, when Lenin assailed a group called the "economists" for stressing improvement of the workers' lot rather than revolution to overthrow capitalism. *The New York Times, Jan. 14, 1967, p 3*

ecotelemetry, another name for BIOTELEMETRY.

Biotelemetry, or ecotelemetry, is an important new tool which enables the biologist to acquire information at a distance from an unrestrained living organism and its environment. *O. Z. Roy, "Biotelemetry," McGraw-Hill Yearbook of Science and Technology 1969, p 115*

ecumaniac, *n.* a fanatical or extremely enthusiastic promoter of ecumenism or the union of all Christian churches.

The 'ecumaniacs'—as hostile religious separatists like to call them—have come to believe that it is their religious duty to break down the barriers between denominations. *A. C. Forrest, Maclean's, July 6, 1963, p 26*

. . . Emmaus House [an underground church] was a hot-bed of zealous ecumaniacs, bent on building a new kind of parish with home rule and spontaneous liturgies. *Time, July 27, 1970, p 73*

ec·u·me·nop·o·lis (‚ek yu me'nap ə lis), *n.* the world viewed as one continuous city.

To emphasize its scholarly austerity, Constantinos Doxiadis concludes with an article (as unreadable as it is unbelievable) not on megalopolis, but on ecumenopolis —the world itself as a city—the ultimate end of man as a social animal. *J. H. Plumb, "Perspective: Look Books," Review of "The Cities of Destiny," edited by Arnold Toynbee, Saturday Review, Nov. 25, 1967, p 35*

Are we going to succeed in making the inevitable Ecumenopolis a tolerable habitat for human beings? *Arnold Toynbee, "The Coming World-City," The Times (London), July 18, 1970, p 5*

[coined by Constantinos A. Doxiadis, born 1913, Greek architect and engineer, from Greek *oikouménē* the world + *pólis* city. See also EKISTICS.]

E-Day, *n.* the day set for Great Britain's entry into the Common Market.

However, if the House of Commons votes "Aye" and we do take that historic step, then certain things will happen on January 1, 1973, which has been fixed as "E-Day," and a good deal more before January 1, 1978 when we become full members. *John Lambert and David Blake, "How E-Day Will Change Your Life," The Sunday Times (London), June 27, 1971, p 46*

[E, for *Entry,* patterned after *D-Day,* etc.]

edbiz, *n.* U.S. Slang. the business or industry of educational research and development.

But if educational technology is to be taken out of the hands of the fools and frauds, they say, there will have to be much more experimenting, financed on a long-term basis, and involving working teachers, which few current projects do. The folly of systems experts and curricular experts remote from the schools who attempt to build a canned "teacher-proof" curriculum is now apparent. Yet conferences on implementing all the new "innovations" continue to meet at tropical resorts; grants are proposed and disposed of, and the legions of the great edbiz go marching on. *Joseph Featherstone, "Classroom Gadgetry," New Republic, May 31, 1969, p 11*

[from *education* + *biz*, for *business* (as in *show biz*)]

edit, *n.* short for *editing* or *editorial*, used especially in journalism and film-making.

[Joseph] Strick tosses in so many starts of parades and tourist views that at times the movie ["Tropic of Cancer"] feels like a travelogue . . . luckily, the fast edit keeps the action from sagging. *Pauline Kael, "The Current Cinema," The New Yorker, March 7, 1970, p 96*

The 13-week-old New York Magazine has been running so light on ads recently that a friend of the ad director said, "It's just like Channel 13, just uninterrupted good edit." *Philip H. Dougherty, The New York Times, July 1, 1968, p 51*

As I read your edit in your issue of May 8, I felt like jumping up onto a soapbox and replying, "I'm glad you asked that question." *John A. Williamson, New Jersey, in a Letter to the Editor, Punch, June 19, 1968, p 893*

editionalize, *v.i.* to print several editions.

Indeed, where a national newspaper has no such connexion, it often tries to offset the handicap by editionalizing and by facsimile printing in more than one centre. *"The World's Press," The Times (London), Dec. 17, 1970, p I*

educational park or **education park,** *U.S.* a group of elementary and secondary schools built on a large tract of land, with many facilities used in common.

The most promising answer, said the Commission, is a new concept called education parks. . . . The parks replace several racially segregated schools with one wholly new establishment. Depending on the city, a park covers any range of grade levels, from the first grade through high school and serves from 5,000 to 30,000 students. *Science News, Feb. 25, 1967, p 185*

The commission called educational parks, or clusters of schools, a "revolutionary" technique that might provide common experiences for children of different backgrounds. *Gene Currivan, The New York Times, Feb. 14, 1966, p 27*

educationese, *n.* the jargon used by people associated with the field of education.

What kind of person is it who enjoys the aesthetics of a bell shaped curve, the rhetoric of educationese, or the poetry of the primer? *Peter Schrag, "Voices in the Classroom," Saturday Review, Jan. 21, 1967, p 74*

[from *education* + *-ese* language or jargon]

educrat, *n.* *U.S.* a representative or official of an educational system, agency, or institution.

. . . he [Governor Claude R. Kirk, Jr., of Florida] early exhibited a flamboyant affinity for newspaper headlines . . . and a remarkable talent for colorful invective (education leaders are referred to as "educrats" or wielders of "blackboard power"). *James Cass, "Politics and Education in the Sunshine State," Saturday Review, April 20, 1968, p 64*

[from *education* + *-crat*, as in *bureaucrat*]

-ee, a very productive suffix meaning "one who is _____ed"; freely added to verb stems to form

nouns paralleling agent nouns in *-er*; but also added to intransitive verbs and meaning "one who _____s" (as in *escapee*); and sometimes also added to adjectives (as in *deadee*). Originally a technical suffix in English law (adapted from the French past participle ending *-é*), *-ee* began to be used as a pseudo-legal and often humorous suffix in the 1700's, chiefly in forming nonce words (e.g. *laughee, sendee, educatee*). In current usage the suffix is often applied as formally and functionally as *-er* is, though sometimes the words created with *-ee* carry some connotation of whimsy from unnecessary formality (as in *meetee* below). Some examples of current use follow.

adaptee, *n.:* The adaptee then cannot tell the difference between yellow and white, ie is yellow-blind. *New Scientist, May 6, 1971, p 353*

blackmailee, *n.:* That you can't ever protect a man's reputation by invading his privacy; . . . that the underlying relationship of the FBI to passing Administrations—at least in the internal security area—is in part the relationship of the blackmailer to blackmailee. . . . *Victor S. Navasky, "The Government and Martin Luther King," The Atlantic, Nov. 1970, p 52*

curee, *n.:* Television, too, has had its go at portraying homosexuality as sober fact. Last year the most discussed of several network talk programs, the *David Susskind Show*, pitted "curees" against inveterates before thirty-two million viewers. Result? A draw. *Faubion Bowers, "Homosex: Living the Life," Saturday Review, Feb. 12, 1972, p 25*

deferee, *n.:* In any case, affluent college deferees do not compare in number with those who, often by the accident of poverty, unfortunately have physical or mental defects that cause deferment or rejection. *Clayton Fritchey, "Washington Insight: What The Draft Might Blow Up," Harper's, Aug. 1966, p 27*

embarkee, *n.:* From behind the plate-glass windows of the customs hall, British heart-teams peered through binoculars, waiting for deaths. Veins beat in their temples as from time to time, a weightless embarkee would reel before a sudden gust, fall, and be blown about the quay; then, infuriatingly, struggle to his meagre feet again. . . . *Alan Coren, "Towards the Four-Minute Heart," Punch, May 15, 1968, p 694*

meetee, *n.:* Some meetings should be . . . mercifully brief. A good way to handle the latter is to hold the meetings with everybody standing up. The meetees won't believe you at first. Then they get very uncomfortable and can hardly wait to get the meeting over with. *Robert Townsend, "Time: Three Thoughts on It," The Times (London), May 5, 1970, p 27*

See also DEADEE, FRANCHISEE, MERGEE.

eightfold way, *Nuclear Physics.* a theoretical classification of strongly interacting elementary particles into groups called multiplets and supermultiplets, whose relationship is established by their having nearly the same mass, hypercharge, and isotopic spin. Also called SU(3) SYMMETRY.

In the Eightfold Way, each combination of 3 fictitious objects, called quarks, makes a different baryon [heavy elementary particle]. *Yuval Ne'eman, "From Soldier To Scientist," The World Book Science Annual 1968, p 170*

The Eightfold Way, edited by Murray Gell-Mann and Yuval Ne'eman. W. A. Benjamin, Inc. ($9). A collection of research papers dealing with the classification of strongly interacting particles according to the "eightfold way" symmetry put forward by Gell-Mann and Ne'eman. *Kenneth E. Boulding, Scientific American, April 1966, p 139*

[from the Buddhist term for the eight paths to be followed to attain enlightenment; so called from the original suggestion that this classification would explain the relationship among a group of *eight* different elementary particles]

eighty-six or **86,** *v.t. U.S. Slang.* to refuse to serve (a customer).

On the evening of July 22, Mr. Mailer was filming a dream sequence at the house of Alfonso Ossorio in East Hampton, when Mr. Smith came into the house. "He told me, 'You're 86'd,' " Mr. Smith recalled yesterday. This is a barroom phrase that means "you're banned in here." *J. Anthony Lukas, The New York Times, July 31, 1968, p 29*

[originally rhyming slang for *nix*, used in the jargon of cooks, waiters, etc., to indicate that there is nothing left of an item ordered from the menu; later applied to a person who is refused service because he is disorderly, cannot pay, etc.]

ek·a·haf·ni·um (ˌek əˈhæf niː əm), *n.* a tentative name given to ELEMENT 104.

Using Mendeleev's naming scheme, some researchers have called the new element ekahafnium. The Russians gave it the name kurchatovium. The right to name new elements is given to the discoverers and the name is later approved by the International Union of Pure and Applied Chemistry. By year-end neither name has been adopted by IUPAC. *"Nuclear Chemistry," Science News Yearbook 1970, p 265*

[from *eka-* beyond (in the periodic table) + *hafnium*]

ek·a·lead (ˌek əˈled), *n.* a hypothetical chemical element beyond the transactinide series; element 114.

. . . element 114, which we have mentioned so often, proves to be homologous with that very stable element lead; it can therefore be called "eka-lead," using the terminology of Dmitri Mendeleev, the originator of the periodic table. . . . *Glenn T. Seaborg and Justin L. Bloom, "The Synthetic Elements: IV," Scientific American, April 1969, p 66*

[from *eka-* beyond (in the periodic table) + *lead*]

ekistical, *adj.* of or relating to ekistics.

The profound thing about the transition [from farm to town] is, and put this down in your ekistical notebook, it's rural-suburban. *Fran Buhler, quoted by Bill Moyers, "Listening to America: South Carolina," Harper's, Dec. 1970, p 103*

e·kis·tics (iːˈkis tiks), *n.* the study of communities and settlements of people, especially with a view to improving them by extensive planning.

. . . since we do not know what kind of life the future rural dewllers employed in agriculture would like to have, we should use the term "cities" as meaning all sorts of human settlements in the sense that ekistics, the science of human settlements, studies them. *Constantinos A. Doxiadis, "Ecumenopolis: Tomorrow's City," Britannica Book of the Year 1968, p 17*

[coined by Constantinos A. Doxiadis, born 1913, Greek architect and engineer, from Greek *oikistikós* of settlements or dwellings. See also ECUMENOPOLIS.]

Ekman layer, a layer of ocean water whose flow is at right angles to the wind's direction.

Thus the wind in the southern half of our square basin representing the North Atlantic transports water to the north in the thin Ekman layer. *D. James Baker, Jr., "Models of Oceanic Circulation," Scientific American, Jan. 1970, p 117*

[named after the Swedish oceanographer V. Walfrid *Ekman,* who first described it in the early 1900's]

elastohydrodynamic, *adj.* dealing with the elasticity of fluids under force.

Sometimes the film of lubricant is so thin, and the fluid pressures acting on the bearing surfaces are so high, that the elastic deformation of these surfaces cannot be ignored; the regime is then called elastohydrodynamic. *S. A. V. Swanson and M. A. R. Freeman. "Mechanism of Human Joints," Science Journal, Feb. 1969, p 74*

elastohydrodynamics, *n.* the study of elastohydrodynamic effects.

The sound introduction to elastohydrodynamics could readily have been extended to deal with realistic machine components to the advantage of the student. *Duncan Dowson, Review of "Basic Lubrication Theory" by A. Cameron, New Scientist and Science Journal, April 15, 1971, p 174*

electric, *adj.* played with electrically amplified guitars.

Joe Boyd, a brilliant young American record producer who was already doing exciting things with the Incredible String Band and was getting a reputation among artists for using studio techniques to give them room to manoeuvre. He had come here originally to run a British subsidiary for the creative Elektra company of America, at that time making the difficult transition from folk to electric rock. . . . *Karl Dallas, "Electric Folk," The Times (London), April 18, 1970, p III*

Gerde's Folk City is pondering a move to the West Village while two former centers of electric pop, the Night Owl and Generation, remain closed. *Robert Shelton, The New York Times, July 5, 1968, p 21*

electro-, a combining form with several meanings listed below, used with great frequency in technical terms.

1 electric (of, charged with, or run by electricity) or electrical (accompanied by, involved in, or relating to electricity).

electro-conductivity, *n.:* Compared with some other instruments, such as the electro-conductivity recorder for measuring SO_2, it [the instrument] offers the advantage of being insensitive to ammonia. On the other hand, its sensitivity to all sulphur compounds is a mixed blessing. *Jan Barynin, "Measuring Odour Pollution," New Scientist, Oct. 15, 1970, p 118*

electrodermal, *adj.:* The main significance of this finding, Dr. Mednick says, lies in its correlation with another group of data showing that the disturbed children were markedly abnormal in tests of their galvanic skin responses (GSR). The GSR is a measure of electrodermal conductivity regulated by the autonomic nervous system, which is largely in charge of regulating the body's internal stress reactions. *James Moriarty and Lawrence Massett, "Schizophrenia: Prenatal and Birth Complications Linked by Schizophrenia Research," Science News, July 4, 1970, p 15*

147

electroduct, *n.:* The Milan company was to have supplied and mounted high-tension wires in the tract of the electro-duct between Caboara Bassa and the South African border. *The Times (London), Dec. 19, 1970, p 4*

electro-engineering, *n.:* In the next three years Uljanik will deliver another four ships, each with a capacity of 225,000 tons for Norwegian shipowners, and two more of the Rig shipyards have similar developments. These de-velopments have given a significant impetus to marine en-gineering and electro-engineering. *Kresimir Dzeba, "Yugo-slavia: Switch to Manufacturing," The Times (London), April 14, 1970, p 18*

electrofilter, *n.:* As a result of his [Dr. Albert Parker's, a consultant] report the extensions were sanctioned, subject to a three-year abatement programme, which involved building a 350 ft. chimney, and installing electrofilters and other anti-pollution devices. *Tony Aldous, "Raising the Dust at Ivinghoe," The Times (London), May 21, 1970, p 8*

electromechanization, *n.:* The innovations will include large-scale, dual-purpose desalting plants; electromechani-zation of farms and of means of transportation; electrifica-tion of the metal and chemical industries, and more effec-tive means for utilizing wastes. *Scientific American, Nov. 1970, p 21*

electrosensory, *adj.:* ... influence of electric organ con-trol system on electrosensory afferent pathways in mormy-rids [African freshwater fishes]. ... *Advertisement by the "First International Symposium of the Institute for Bio-medical Research," Scientific American, March 1970, p 18*

2 by or with electrolytic decomposition.

electroslag, *adj.:* The purist would probably query the description of electroslag remelting as an arc process. ... *David Pocklington, "Books," Review of "Materials and Technology," edited by T. J. W. van Thoor, New Scientist, May 21, 1970, p 395*

3 a electronic.

electromusic, *n.:* The first part [of "Stages," a ballet] has electromusic by Arne Nordheim. *Richard Buckle, The Sunday Times (London), May 2, 1971, p 35*

b electron.

electrophile, *n.:* Then by dividing heterolytic [cell-destroy-ing] reagents into nucleophiles and electrophiles, he [Sir Christopher Ingold, F.R.S.] saw the basis of a scheme interrelating a great range of chemical reactions. *"Obit-uary," The Times (London), Dec. 10, 1970, p 10*

See also the entries below.

electrodelic, *adj.* producing a psychedelic effect through the use of electric lights.

Any swingers who have yet to shop in an "electrodelic environment" should race right over to Best's Fifth Avenue while the fuses hold out. *Joan Cook, The New York Times, Feb. 16, 1967, p 42*

[from *electro-* + psyche*delic*]

electrogasdynamic, *adj.* producing electric power by electrogasdynamics.

The U.S. Department of the Interior granted $680,500 to Gourdine Systems, Inc. ... to demonstrate the feasibility of transforming coal directly into cheaply transmittable electricity at the mine by using electrogasdynamic (EGD) generators. *James A. Pearre, "Engine and Energy," The 1967 World Book Year Book, p 330*

electrogasdynamics, *n.* the conversion of heat energy directly into electricity by sweeping charged particles through an electric field in a stream of gas.

Electrogasdynamics (egd for short) is a novel means of generating electricity. The principles involved are, how-ever, quite simple. Small particles of dust (or smoke, fog, etc.) are charged in a low-voltage region and then trans-ported by a gas stream to a high-voltage region, where the charges are removed. Work is done on the particles in mov-ing them against the electric field and electricity generated. *Peter J. Musgrove and Alan D. Wilson, "Power Without Pollution," New Scientist, March 5, 1970, p 457*

electrohydraulic, *adj.* producing mechanical or chemical energy by electrohydraulics.

The eight nozzles [of a rocket engine] are swivelled by electrohydraulic jacks to control pitch, yaw and roll. *Glen Lawes, "Into Space With a Golden Orb," New Scientist, Aug. 27, 1970, p 416*

electrohydraulics, *n.* the conversion of electrical energy directly into mechanical or chemical energy by the controlled discharge of high-voltage electric arcs submerged in water or another liquid.

For example, in the hard rock mining of copper an elec-trical energy system could replace explosives and thereby avoid the production of noxious fumes in the mine. We have built a system based on electrohydraulics and tested it both in the laboratory on three tonne boulders and in a copper mine. *W. R. Browne, M. Allen, and E. C. Schrom, "Elec-trohydraulics," Science Journal, March 1968, p 64*

electronic art, a form of art that uses electronic materials, such as moving and flashing light dis-plays, as the artistic medium. Compare LUMINAL ART.

Baudelaire's attack on Courbet [French painter, 1819-1877] on the ground that he sacrificed the imagination in behalf of external fact contains the ingredients of a Baudelairean judgment of Pop, Op, electronic, and kinetic art. *Harold Rosenberg, "The Art World: Discovering The Present," The New Yorker, Feb. 10, 1968, p 95*

Electronic music inspired him [Nam June Paik, a Korean] to make electronic art, just as the Russian composer Scria-bin made a motorized light display to accompany his *Prometheus* half a century ago. *"Art," Time, Jan. 28, 1966, p 49*

electronic countermeasure, an electronic device that misdirects the guidance system of an enemy missile.

By an electronic summer, [Israeli defense minister] Dayan meant clashes between Soviet-built, radar-controlled Egyptian surface-to-air missiles and Israeli jets equipped with electronic countermeasure (ECM) devices. *Time, July 20, 1970. p 18*

electronicize, *v.t.* to equip with electronic devices.

The stockbroker who signs his name Brutus and offers us, beginning on page 46, the first of two excerpts from his office diary, is not the gentleman shown at left amid the opulence and efficiency of his modestly electronicized and precomputerized downtown office. *Robert Manning, "The Editor's Page," The Atlantic, June 1971, p 4*

electronograph, *n.* **1** a device using an electron tube to produce images on a fine-grain photographic emulsion exposed to an accelerated beam of elec-trons.

It is remarkable that the ultimate in sensitivity, the stand-ard of comparison for a dozen ingenious up-to-date develop-ments, remains the electronograph. *Philip Morrison,*

"Books," Review of "Photo-Electronic Image Devices: Proceedings of the Fourth Symposium," edited by J. D. McGee, D. McMullan, E. Kahan, and B. L. Morgan, Scientific American, May 1970, p 139

2 an image produced by an electronograph.

Because the electron beam is focused, an 'electron picture' (electronograph) results. *"Spectracon Measures Range of Brightnesses," Science Journal, March 1970, p 14*

electronography, *n.* the use of electronographs.

The cost of electronography to the user is high. Every time an exposed photographic plate is removed, the air destroys the highly reactive photosurface. *Philip Morrison, "Books," Review of "Photo-Electronic Image Devices: Proceedings of the Fourth Symposium," edited by J. D. McGee, D. McMullan, E. Kahan, and B. L. Morgan, Scientific American, May 1970, p 139*

element 104, a radioactive chemical element with atomic number 104 in the periodic table and the first of the transactinide series. Also called EKA-HAFNIUM, KURCHATOVIUM, and RUTHERFORDIUM.

... Ghiorso and four associates announced in April 1969 their discovery of element 104—which the effervescent Ghiorso describes as the "hippie" element, because of what he called its somewhat hairy characteristics. *"The Hunt for Elusive New Elements," Encyclopedia Science Supplement (Grolier) 1970, p 277*

element 105, another name for HAHNIUM.

The high stability of element 105 surprised the team of scientists. It contradicted present nuclear theories predicting a half-life of only milliseconds for element 105. This will probably lead to a revision of existing nuclear theories. *Alfred von Smolinski, "Chemistry," The 1971 World Book Year Book, p 251*

É·ly·sée (ei li:'zei), *n.* the government of France.

The Elysee's creed is that the line laid down by M Harmel must be followed to the bitter end. *Rene Dabernat, "Finance: France Adamant on Farm Policy," The Manchester Guardian Weekly, July 11, 1970, p 22*

▶ Literally the *Élysée* is the official residence of the presidents of France, but like the *White House*, *Whitehall*, and the *Kremlin* the name is also used to designate the national government. The residence is really in full the Élysée Palace, but the 'Palace' part is usually omitted. (This phenomenon sometimes causes French people to refer to Buckingham Palace as "Buckingham.")

em·bar·ras de ri·chesse (ā ba'ra də ri:'ʃes), an embarrassment of riches; an excess or abundance that makes selection difficult.

... in spare part surgery—where the choice may be to replace a worn-out heart, lung or kidney with a mechanical implant or with a living tissue transplant—it [the choice between these two solutions] is already proving an *embarras de richesse*. *Donald Longmore, "Implants or Transplants?" Science Journal, Feb. 1968, p 78*

In his Preface, Robinson charges me with "misreading" documents and books, and on page 2 of his book he starts to pile up examples of what he understands by reading and what by misreading, until at the end one finds oneself overwhelmed by a unique *embarras de richesse. Hannah Arendt, "The Formidable Dr. Robinson: A Reply," The New York Review of Books, Jan. 20, 1966, p 28*

▶ This is an Anglicized form of the French idiom

embarras de richesses, which is also used in English, though less commonly, as in the following quotation:

... upon graduation from the University of California, he [Douglass Drumbeller] was offered seven jobs, averaging $8,000.... Drumbeller's *embarras de richesses* served as the occasion for a number of editors to reflect on the change that had come over the world of work since *their* days in school, when graduating students were glad to get any job at any price. *Robert L. Heilbroner, "No Room at the Bottom," Saturday Review, Feb. 19, 1966, p 29*

em·bour·geoise·ment (ā bu:r ʒwaz'mā), *n. French.* adoption of bourgeois or middle-class practices. Compare BOURGEOISIFICATION.

... the Soviet party, despite a new appearance of *embourgeoisement,* remained inherently Stalinist and the Italian party remained tightly faithful to Soviet discipline and loyal to Moscow as a "leading force." *C. L. Sulzberger, The New York Times, Feb. 11, 1970, p 46*

embryoid, *n.* a plant or animal form having the structure or function of an embryo.

These cells are then cultured, and from them are grown embryoids and eventually whole "pomatoes" [a hybrid plant produced from a potato and a tomato]. *Graham Chedd, "The New Botanists," New Scientist and Science Journal, April 29, 1971, p 263*

Many of the embryoids developed into structures simulating globular or heart-shaped stages of dicotyledonous embryos. *A. C. Hildebrandt, "Differentiation in Plants," McGraw-Hill Yearbook of Science and Technology 1967, p 308*

E-meter, *n.* a galvanometer that measures changes in the electrical resistance of a subject's skin, similar to devices used in lie detector tests, used by scientologists.

... Ron Hubbard's E-meter ... sets you completely free from all past conditioning—presumably so you won't question the conditioning then imposed by Hubbard's scientologists. *Julian Mitchell, The Manchester Guardian Weekly, April 25, 1970, p 16*

[contraction of *Electro*meter]

em·paque·tage (ā pak'taʒ), *n.* a work of conceptual art consisting of an object wrapped tightly in canvas or other material and tied to form a distinctive bundle or package.

Chicago's newest monumental "art work" was, for a few days, the entire Museum of Contemporary Art, which was "wrapped" by the master of *empaquetage,* Christo [a Bulgarian-born New York artist]. *Victor H. Miesel, "Art," The Americana Annual 1970, p 102*

[from French, packaging, package]

empty set, another name for NULL SET.

Every finite set of *n* elements has 2^n subsets if one includes the original set and the null, or empty, set. For example, a set of three elements, *ABC*, has $2^3 = 8$ subsets: *ABC, AB, BC, AC, A, B, C,* and the null set. *Martin Gardner, "Mathematical Games," Scientific American, March 1971, p 106*

en·ar·chist ('en,ɑr kist) or **en·arch** ('en,ɑrk), *n.* a high-ranking French civil service administrator selected from the top graduates of the École Nationale d'Administration (National School of Administration).

The first generation of *"enarchists"* now dominate at the policy level of government in the same way that *"polytechniciens"* [graduates of the École Polytechnique] for generations have held sway over top posts in industry and finance. *John Walsh, "France: After the Storm, Elite Schools Face Change," Science, July 19, 1968, p 249*

There have been constant complaints from outside that the "Enarchs" are arid technocrats and often precious with it. *Nesta Roberts, "Letter From Paris: The Quieter Revolution," The Manchester Guardian Weekly, Aug. 14, 1969, p 15*

[from French *énarque*, formed from *ÉNA*, initials of École Nationale d'Administration + *-arque* -arch (ruler or leader)]

enclave, *n.* a small isolated spot.

In a world where junior high school children "demand" to know everything, and to appoint the greybeards who will teach it to them, there are still one or two enclaves of expertise into which even the Panthers and the Weathermen refuse to rush. *Alistair Cooke, "Smoke Gets In Your Giro," The Manchester Guardian Weekly, Feb. 14, 1970 p 4*

No mother's son is safe from the insidious influence of longhair looks and habits and thoughts. Anti-Establishment ideas, once limited to the tiny circulation of sober little weeklies, are spread through a truly grass-roots underground press that is not restricted anymore to the intellectual enclaves of the two coasts, but springs up in places like Lansing, Michigan; Bloomington, Indiana; and Austin, Texas. *Dan Wakefield, "Arts and Letters: The War at Home," The Atlantic, Oct., 1969, p 119*

Wilson . . . looked out into a spacious studio with a tall thicket of microphones to the left and, directly in front, an enclave containing a music stand, two microphones, and an upright piano, and set off by a large screen. . . . *Nat Hentoff, The New Yorker, Oct. 24, 1964, p 64*

[extended sense of the term for a territory surrounded by that of another country]

encounter, *n.* *U.S.* an encounter group session.

As encounters multiplied and perspective deepened, Jane (Howard) found herself kicking pillows and hurling finger paint with the worst of them—and feeling, as a result, relieved of some fossil fears. *Brad Darrach, "Grope-shrink," Review of "Please Touch" by Jane Howard, Time, July 27, 1970, p 74*

encounter group, a group of people taking part in sensitivity training. Also called SENSITIVITY GROUP and T-GROUP. See also HUMAN POTENTIALS MOVEMENT.

Sensitivity training sessions . . . also known as encounter groups . . . share several common attributes. The programs are designed to place people in a group situation. Through a mixture of physical contact games and no-holds-barred discussions about each other's strengths and failures, each group member hopefully will feel less constricted. He will become more open, readily able to understand himself and others. If he is a member of an organization, it may enable him to become a more persuasive and influential participant in group decisions. *Ted J. Rakstis, "Sensitivity Training," Encyclopedia Science Supplement (Grolier) 1970 p 78*

Such feelings surely help to explain some of the cult phenomena that abound in the United States today; commune and encounter groups are the obvious examples, efforts to replace the old communities of family and village with a new kind of human contact: participants to talk to, even literally to touch, other human beings. *Anthony Lewis,*

"Notes on the New York Skyline, an Island Salt Pond, Chapel Market, etc.," The Atlantic, June 1971, p 61

endangered, *adj.* threatened with extinction.

A notable example: The signing by President Nixon of the Endangered Species Act "to prevent the importation of endangered species of fish and wildlife into the United States. . . ." *Peter T. Chew, "Rescuing Threatened Animals," Encyclopedia Science Supplement (Grolier) 1970, p 188*

The black rhino, of which there are about 300 in the reserve, is recognized as an endangered mammal and has been placed on the official list of threatened species compiled by the International Union for the Conservation of Nature. *Science Journal, April 1970, p 12*

The turtles are an endangered species and there is a $600 (£231) fine or one year in jail as a maximum penalty for possessing a turtle or its eggs in season (May 1 to Sept. 1). *Daily Telegraph (London), May 15, 1972, p 4*

end-consumer, *n.* the ultimate consumer of a manufactured product. Also called END-USER.

The result is that foreign business is faced in Japan with a global market, including the end-consumer, the complex distribution system, the powerful domestic competitors, and last but not least the Government. *Robert J. Ballon, The Times (London), June 17, 1970, p IV*

endgame, *n.* a contest in its final stage.

. . . the Viet Cong struck at Tet. It hit every provincial capital in South Vietnam, more than half the district capitals, seized the American Embassy for twelve hours, and held the city of Hué for twenty-two days. The American public never recovered, and from that point on, the Vietnam War was an endgame. *Ward Just, "Soldiers," The Atlantic, Nov. 1970, p 86*

[extended sense of the term for the final stage of a game, especially chess]

en·do·nu·cle·ase (,en dou'nu: kli:,eis), *n.* an enzyme that breaks up strands of DNA (deoxyribonucleic acid, the carrier of genetic information in the cells) into discontinuous segments. Compare EXONUCLEASE.

The enzyme is an endonuclease, able to clip—in the test tube at least—the newly formed DNA helix into fragments shorter than the original RNA template. *"The Secret Armoury of RNA Tumour Viruses," New Scientist, Nov. 5, 1970, p 257*

[from *endo-* inner + *nuclease* an enzyme that hydrolyzes nucleic acid]

endorse, *v.t.* **endorse out,** (in South Africa) to send away from an urban to a rural area as part of a system of controlling the influx of black Africans into the cities.

If an African is caught without his reference book, or violates one of a host of other restrictive regulations, he can be put in jail or fined or "endorsed out"—sent, that is, to a "homeland" that he may never have seen and to which he has no ties. *E. J. Kahn, Jr., "A Reporter At Large: South Africa: The Peace of the Grave," The New Yorker, Feb. 10, 1968, p 37*

Eye-witness reports from Johannesburg Station suggest that about 70 people a day were being "endorsed" out of that city alone at the end of last year, an increase over previous months. *Jonathan Steele, "Dumping-ground for Africans," The Manchester Guardian Weekly, March 21, 1970, p 6*

en·do·sul·fan (‚ɛn dou'səl‚fæn), *n.* a powerful insecticide containing chlorinated sulfate.

Endosulfan is extremely toxic to fish: concentrations in the water as low as 0 00002 parts per million cause death. *Norman Moore, New Scientist, April 16, 1970, p 114*

► German and Dutch spellings *(endosulvan* and *endosolvan)* have also appeared in English language publications *(Time, Manchester Guardian Weekly,* and *World Book Year Book).*

Endsville, *adj. U.S. Slang.* the largest, greatest, or most wonderful.

At the windup of his two-week tour, Soviet Cosmonaut Georgy Beregovoy announced that New York was strictly Endsville.... *Time, Nov. 21, 1969, p 46*

[from *end* (in the U.S. slang phrase *the end* the best or most exciting, often *the living end)* + *-ville* (see the entry -VILLE)]

en·dur·o (ɛn'dur ou), *n. U.S.* a race to test a runner's or driver's endurance.

Watkins Glen, the lovely 2 3-mile road course above Seneca Lake in upstate New York, is making a brave show this weekend in staging the best possible enduro under the circumstances. *John S. Radosta, The New York Times, July 10. 1968, p 32*

[probably from Spanish, from *endurar* to endure]

end-user, *n.* another name for END-CONSUMER.

Independent peripheral men in the US aren't happy with IBM's contention that the new price structure is in the end-user's best interests. The Computer Peripherals Manufacturers Association has announced that it will file with the US Department of Justice a request that it consider peripherals very seriously in its current anti-trust lawsuit against IBM. *"Technology Review: IBM Snaps Shut the Disc Umbrella," New Scientist and Science Journal, Feb. 4, 1971, p 244*

energy paper, a dry sheet of paper fiber impregnated with potassium persulfate and powdered carbon, that serves as the active material of a dry-cell battery and is easily replaceable when the battery runs out of power.

To the world of dry cells and storage batteries Dutch scientists have added a new concept: "energy paper." *Science Journal, Jan. 1968, p 13*

A potential use for this "energy paper" is to power cordless appliances such as electric shavers. *The New York Times, Aug. 2. 1968, p 45*

energy structure, a type of kinetic art structure having motorized, mechanical, or electronic parts.

Sculptors' work took many forms, from figurative to nonobjective, from funk to energy structures. *Victor H. Miesel, "Art," The Americana Annual 1970. p 99*

en·fant ché·ri (ã'fã ʃei'ri:), *French.* a cherished or pampered child (used chiefly figuratively in English).

Aix has entertained hope in recent years of purchasing a painting or two by the city's *enfant chéri,* Paul Cézanne, but the going rate is out of reach. *David Butwin, Saturday Review, Oct. 17, 1970, p 44*

...Ivory Coast had a trade balance of thirty-two million Central African francs in 1969. She is the *enfant chéri* of France, showered with loans and French capital that have helped her diversify her economy.... *Nadine Gordimer,*

"The Life of Accra, The Flowers of Abidjan: A West African Diary," The Atlantic, Nov. 1971, p 88

English disease, a term often used to describe various problems of labor management. first given widespread notice in Great Britain, such as excessive attention to work rules, apparent control of management policy by shop stewards, absenteeism, etc. Also called ENGLISH SICKNESS.

At the same time, rapidly rising costs of factory production—first noticeable in Britain and nicknamed "the English disease"—have become manifest in other countries of west Europe and in North America. *The Times (London), May 25, 1966, p 18*

► *English disease* and *English sickness* appear to be translations of French *la maladie anglaise* and German *die englische Krankheit* respectively. Formerly, *English disease* was sometimes applied to various ailments once associated with Great Britain, such as rickets and bronchitis. According to the *OED, English disease* or *English Malady* was used in the 1700's to mean low spirits or melancholy.

English English, English as spoken in England; British English.

It [a speech recognition machine] should be able to recognise English English, American English and what Mr. Pay called Continental English, which is a tall enough order. *"Notes On the News: Hopes of a Machine You Can Talk To," New Scientist, May 9, 1968, p 272*

It is not universal kernel sentences and transformational rules but a manifold context of specific political history and social sensibility that makes a man "stand" for office in English English and "run" for it in American. *George Steiner, "The Tongues of Men," The New Yorker, Nov. 15, 1969, p 230*

Englishment, *n.* an English rendering or version of a foreign work.

Aristophanes, with an easy Greek candor about bodily functions,... used a number of words unknown to Queen Victoria even in translation, and when Arrowsmith did translate them (in a larruping fine Englishment, an early draft of which Arrowsmith read to me and I read back to him one great evening years back in Rome) they turned out to be too colorful for the American stage.... *John Ciardi, "Manner of Speaking," Saturday Review, Aug. 13, 1966, p 22*

[from *English, v.,* to translate into English + *-ment*]

English sickness, another name for ENGLISH DISEASE.

In fact, "the English sickness" is a term widely used in Europe to describe high levels of absenteeism, restrictive practices and wildcat strikes.... *Peter Taylor, Science Journal, April 4, 1970, p 26*

enterobacteria, *n.pl.* intestinal bacteria, especially those belonging to a large family of rod-shaped bacteria that includes E. coli.

A permanent, vigilant body to monitor the epidemiology of enterobacteria would save time, money, anguish. and probably lives too, the next time danger arises. *New Scientist, Nov. 27, 1969, p 444*

[from *entero-* intestines + *bacteria*]

enterobactin, *n.* a substance produced by enterobacteria that has an inhibiting effect on other bacteria.

Pacifarin, found in certain batches of whole wheat and dried egg and produced by bacteria, protects mice infected with mouse typhoid. It was identified as enterobactin (a compound of known structure), recently discovered by biochemists at the University of California, Berkeley. *George M. Briggs, "Foods and Nutrition," 1972 Britannica Yearbook of Science and the Future, 1971, p 251*

[from *enterobacte*ria + *-in* (chemical suffix)]

enteropathogenic, *adj.* producing intestinal disease.

In particular, studies at the research station in Stock, Essex, on enteropathogenic strains of Escherichia coli ... and on bacterial drug resistance ... are unique, and unlikely to be taken over elsewhere. *Bernard Dixon, "A Sorry Sacrifice," New Scientist and Science Journal, April 8, 1971, p 68*

[from ε *ntero-* intestines + *pathogenic*]

environment, *n.* a work of environmental art.

... the $2.5 million Pepsi-Cola pavilion at the Osaka World's Fair in Japan ... will include among its features environments that can be manipulated by the viewer. *Benjamin de Brie Taylor, "Art: Process Art and Antiform," 1970 Collier's Encyclopedia Year Book, p 117*

Dada has contributed to every new technique employed in this century that it did not actually invent—collage, which is everywhere; its extension, assemblage, which includes junk sculpture, "found" objects and a hundred cousins; the "environment" as well as the Happening; kinetic sculpture, whether motorized or not, and on and on. *John Canaday, The New York Times Magazine, March 24, 1968, p 30*

environmental, *adj.* of or relating to environmental art.

From the desire to be totally encompassed by the work came the wall-size dimensions of the drip canvases, so suggestive to later "environmental" painters and sculptors. *Harold Rosenberg, "The Art World: The Mythic Act," The New Yorker, May 6, 1967, p 167*

environmental art, a form of art that encompasses the spectator instead of confronting him with a fixed image or object.

Luminal, minimal, and three-dimensional pop art have contributed to the development of environmental art in rejecting fixed walls and standard spaces and in becoming concerned with the commercial and urban world beyond the galleries. *Benjamin de Brie Taylor, "Art: Environments," 1969 Collier's Encyclopedia Year Book, p 115*

environmentalist, *n.* **1** a person concerned with problems of the environment and especially with the effects of uncontrolled pollution on the earth's atmosphere. Compare ANTIPOLLUTIONIST.

Some environmentalists reject all of modern technology and call for a return to a simple, pastoral life free of fumes, artificial chemicals and any noise but the chirping of birds and the croaking of frogs. *"Carets: Remote Sensing for Environmental Studies," Science News, June 19, 1971, p 413*

The concern of environmentalists for ecological hazards is justified. *Charles F. Raffaele, New York, in a Letter to the Editor, The New York Times, Sept. 25, 1970, p 42*

2 an artist who creates environmental art.

Other environmentalists see their works as means to

engage the viewer in a new kind of emotional release.... "People become part of the art object," [Tony] Martin explains. "They score it. They compose it. I supply the format." *Time, May 3, 1968, p 42*

environmental science, the group of sciences dealing with the environment and now especially with the effects of pollution.

As a group of marine biologists, we are actively involved in various facets of environmental science—a less emotive and more encompassing term than pollution studies. *J. R. Lewis, et al., in a Letter to the Editor, "The Polluters: Safeguarding Sea Food Supplies," The Times (London), March 31, 1970, p 9*

environ-politics, *n.* the politics of environmental conservation and ecology.

Telly pollution and doombooks, conservation-talk and environ-politics, are no substitute for eco-thought. This jaded and partial verdict is the result of attending a hot London week of environmental conferences. *Jon Tinker, New Scientist, Oct. 1, 1970, p 36*

enzyme detergent, a detergent containing water-soluble enzymes that break down protein and are derived from bacteria. The enzymes dissolve most stains, but are commonly regarded as dangerous skin and respiratory irritants.

In Sweden, manufacturers have voluntarily stopped putting enzymes into their best-selling *Tend* detergent. In Britain, failing any voluntary and urgent action, a total ban on the manufacture of enzyme detergents might well be in the public interest. ... *"Murky Washday Miracle," New Scientist, Oct. 15, 1970, p 108*

... the annual production of enzyme detergents and presoaks amounts to some two and a half billion pounds, resulting in retail sales of half a billion dollars. *Paul Brodeur, "The Enigmatic Enzyme," The New Yorker, Jan. 16, 1971, p 42*

episome, *n.* a genetic particle in the cells of bacteria that may exist autonomously in the cytoplasm or may be incorporated into the chromosomes. Also called PLASMID.

Infectious particles of this kind, called episomes, are known to carry factors determining fertility, the ability to produce particular bacterial antibiotics called bateriocins, and drug resistance. *Bernard S. Strauss, "Bacteriology," Britannica Book of the Year 1967, p 505*

[from *epi-* outer + *-some* body]

E-prime, *n.* a word coined by the American semanticist D. David Bourland, Jr., born 1929, for the English language without the verb "to be."

Bourland notes with some satisfaction that a number of scientific papers, not all done by [Alfred] Korzybski disciples, are now being written in E-prime; he is currently writing a book on how to speak or write without recourse to Isness. From personal experience, he claims that the use of E-prime can force a self-conscious but salutary revision in the speaker's outlook on life. *Time, May 23, 1969, p 36*

[abbreviation of *English-prime*]

Epstein-Barr virus, a virus found to be associated with various types of human cancers. It was first isolated by the British virologists M. A. Epstein and Y. M. Barr in 1964.

A recent development in the study of infectious mononucleosis is the evidence indicating that its cause may be a herpes-like virus, called the Epstein-Barr virus. *Alfred S. Evans, "Infectious Mononucleosis," McGraw-Hill Yearbook of Science and Technology 1970, p 220*

Added to the evidence linking the Epstein-Barr virus with Burkitt's lymphoma, and the burgeoning knowledge about animal cancer viruses, this result will strengthen the growing conviction that viruses are an essential causal determinant for human cancer. *New Scientist, Nov. 22, 1970, p 162*

equal time, *U.S.* **1** an equal amount of free air time given, usually at the same hour of another day, to an opposing political candidate, party, group, or citizen, to broadcast their views over radio or television. Compare FAIRNESS DOCTRINE.

Blair Clark, the Senator's campaign manager, announced his intention of requesting the three national television networks for equal time for the Senator before Tuesday's primary election in Wisconsin. *E. W. Kenworthy, The New York Times, March 31, 1968, p 57*

2 *Transferred sense.* an equal opportunity to reply to any charge or opposing view.

The request for equal time comes from Emma Wallop, a small-town Midwestern widow and retired nurse who wakes one day to discover that her former boarder, Randy Rivers, has published a bestselling novel entitled *Don't Look Now, Medusa.* A tin-plated *Spoon River Anthology,* it has as its main character a small-town Midwestern landlady, like Emma herself.... *R. Z. Sheppard, Time, Oct. 19, 1970, p 90*

e·quipe (ei'ki:p), *n.* a sports or racing crew and its equipment; team.

...Rothmans revealed yesterday that they are forming a full-time *equipe,* complete with four aircraft and pilots, which will tour round the air shows this summer. *"Smoke Wings," The Times (London), May 20, 1970 p 29*

[from French *équipe* gang, crew]

er·go·sphere ('ər gə‚sfir), *n.* *Astronomy* a hypothetical enclosed region that may surround a black hole.

...a body that enters this ergosphere can be influenced by the black hole without being completely captured by it. *Dietrick E. Thomsen, "Gravity Waves May Come from Black Holes," Science News, Dec. 26, 1970, p 480*

[from Greek *érgon* work, energy + English *sphere*]

eroduction, *n.* another name for SEXPLOITER.

Thus, of the 487 movies produced in Japan last year, 267 were so-called "eroductions"—a Japanese neologism combining "erotic" and "production" and referring to adults-only features with a strong tinge of blue. *Time, Oct. 17, 1969, p 33*

Crowded into insanitary homes or the dormitories run by their company, the Japanese seek escape through alcohol, television or *eroductions,* the sex films specialising in torture and disembowelment. *Richard West, "6: The Pacific," The Sunday Times (London), Oct. 31, 1971, p 77*

[from *erotic* pro*duction*]

erotologist, *n.* a specialist in erotology.

The Devil Drives: A Life of Sir Richard Burton by Fawn Brodie. The author maps the life of the flamboyant Victorian explorer, linguist and erotologist.... *"Books," Time, Aug. 11, 1967, p 3*

erotology, *n.* erotic literature and art.

Crammed down and spilling over with assorted entertaining gobbets of history, bibacity and erotology. *H. R. F. Keating, The Times (London), Aug. 1, 1970, p 7*

The board [of censors] bans about seven or eight hundred books a year.... The list of contraband includes "The Blue Negro and other Stories," "Classical Hindu Erotology," the "Gag Writer's Private Joke Book," "Gene Autry and Champion," "Peyton Place".... *E. J. Kahn, Jr., "South Africa," The New Yorker, Jan. 27, 1968, p 70*

ERTS (ərts), *n.* **1** acronym for *Earth Resources Technology Satellites,* a U.S. space program for studying earth resources by means of satellites.

...by the time the ERTS becomes a practical proposition it may be found that it has been pre-empted in many of the fields in which it was to have found use. *Edward Lavin, "Americans Delay Earth Resources Satellite," Science Journal, Dec. 1969, p 9*

2 any of the series of artificial satellites scheduled to be launched under this program.

The observations made aboard ERTS will be applied to agriculture, cartography, geology, geography, hydrology, hydrography and oceanography. *Science News, July 25, 1970, p 64*

America's own unmanned Earth Resources Technology Satellite (ERTS) should be launched in 1973. *Kenneth Gatland, New Scientist and Science Journal, April 29, 1971, p 257*

es·bat ('es‚bæt), *n.* a meeting of witches.

Alex Sanders, 44, likes to call himself the King of the Witches. . . . The attractions of Sanderian witchcraft appear to be many, and Sanders' own London coven (witch group) seems to hold the liveliest "esbats" (meetings) in town. . . . Esbats at the Sanderses' include dancing, chanting, feasting and the fondling of various ritual objects. *Time, April 27, 1970, p 96*

Apart from the festivals, the covens meet once a month as near as possible to the time of the full moon to celebrate a less important ceremony known as the Esbat. *Veronica Thomas, "The Witches of 1966," The Atlantic. Sept. 1966, p 120*

[probably from Old French *esbat* a frolic, gambol (French *ébats*), from *esbatre* to frolic, ultimately from Latin *ex-* out + *battere* to beat]

escalate, *v.t., v.i.* to increase or accelerate in scale or size.

We have escalated war and moral numbness; we cannot de-escalate in a day. *Edward M. Keating, "The New Left: What Does It Mean?" Saturday Review, Sept. 24, 1966, p 64*

Military analysts in Jerusalem are certain that the Syrians know that their topographical advantage on the Israeli border, where the Arabs control all the heights, declines as the military exchange escalates. *The New York Times, Jan. 15, 1967, Sec. 4, p 2*

escalation, *n.* an increase or expansion in scale or size, especially in the scale of a war.

The charge was made a dozen times by North Vietnamese officials in talks both formal and informal that every time the United States talked of peace, it was really preparing a further escalation. *Harrison E. Salisbury, The New York Times, Jan. 15, 1967, Sec. 4, p 2*

The North Koreans want the Communist Powers to play the game of escalation, but only Russia has the military resources needed for this. *Victor Zorza, The Manchester Guardian Weekly, Aug. 25, 1966, p 7*

escalatory, *adj.* leading to or involving increase in scale or size, especially of a war.

Simply to carry on as things stood was bound to lead to defeat; the U S had to make some sort of escalatory move. *Henry Brandon, The Sunday Times (London), April 13, 1969, p 50*

These escalatory measures may be necessary, it is argued, in order to strengthen our increasingly difficult position in South Vietnam. *The New York Times, March 13, 1968, p 46*

On the crucial points of escalation, *Quagmire*, which was written a year before the escalatory decisions, says that the bombing will not work. *David Halberstam, in a Letter to the Editor, Harper's, May 1971, p 8*

escapologist, *n.* **1** a performer who escapes or frees himself from specially devised restraints.

It took Timothy Dill-Russell, an escapologist. only 50 sec. to escape from a straitjacket while hanging upside down from a crane 75 ft. above Blackpool promenade yesterday. *The Times (London), Feb. 26, 1968, p 3*

2 a person who is adept at extricating himself from difficult situations.

. . . I can't help saluting the work put in by Alberto Lionello, a slippery *maestro* of comic embarrassment — not so much a born survivor as a born escapologist — who reminds me of Peter Sellers without the narcissism. *Kenneth Tynan, "The Theatre Abroad: Italy," The New Yorker, Oct. 21, 1967, p 108*

escapology, *n.* the skill or methods of an escapologist (literally and figuratively).

Every week there's that advertisement from the man in Cheshire offering handcuffs, leg-irons and manacles. It's too late now to try escapology. *E. S. Turner, Punch, Oct. 13, 1965, p 540*

Even by the high standards of Mr. Wilson [Harold Wilson, then British Prime Minister], who is no beginner when it comes to shooting himself out of a tight corner, this was one of his finest moments in the art of parliamentary escapology. *Hugh Noyes, The Times (London), Dec. 19, 1967, p 1*

-esque, 1 an adjective suffix, meaning "resembling or suggesting the style, ideas, etc., of _____," commonly attached to the names of famous or prominent people. Some recent examples of *-esque:*

Disneyesque, *adj.* [Walt Disney, 1901-1966, American film producer]: For openers, the Street *(Sesame Street)* looks as if a toy truck had overturned in Harlem. There is no Disneyesque nostalgia for the inaccessible past. *Time, Nov. 23, 1970, p 60*

Gershwinesque, *adj.* [George Gershwin, 1898-1937, American composer]: In this performance, too, the *Perpetuum mobile* sounded pleasantly acid, with the keyboard's Gershwinesque comments well pointed by Mr. Bampton. *Max Harrison, The Times (London), June 4, 1970, p 13*

McCarthyesque, *adj.* [Senator Eugene McCarthy, born 1916]: [John] Lindsay enlists a McCarthyesque volunteer army of the young. *Time, Feb. 16, 1970, p 13*

McLuhanesque, *adj.* [Marshall McLuhan, born 1911, Canadian communications specialist]: "It was a very moving occasion. It is not often one can say he has participated in turning a new page in history." — Henry Kissinger. The words seem slightly grandiloquent in a McLuhanesque age when all is known at once, the future long discounted, and uninformed options line up by the numbers. *"Nixon's Coup: To Peking for Peace," Time, July 26, 1971, p 7*

2 In the sense of "like a _____," "resembling that of a _____," the suffix appears in such words as the following:

goblinesque, *adj.:* An element of the goblinesque: the porcupine dome of the Parliament House . . .; the ubiquitous, unendearing cupids. . . . *Edmund Wilson, "Budapest," The New Yorker, June 4, 1966, p 90*

robotesque, *adj.:* Hanus Thein's production may once have had some point; here in Holland it was blunted and paralysed, as witness the stagnant grouping and robotesque movement of the company in the Hussite scenes. *William Mann, "July Festivals: Holland, Anti-hero," The Times (London), July 4, 1970, p 21*

es·sen·tic (e'sen tik), *adj.* showing emotion by outward expression.

Anger, for instance, has an "essentic form" characterized by a short duration and a strong outward thrust. . . . The essentic form of joy is a representation of a mental leap outward: there is a downward pressure followed by a rebound that exceeds the initial thrust. *Graham Chedd, Peter Stubbs, and Gerald Wick, "The Mathematics of Emotions," New Scientist. Dec. 31, 1970, p 580*

[from Latin *essent-* (stem of *essens* being) + English *-ic*]

establishment or **Establishment,** *n.* **1** Usually, **the Establishment.** the ruling groups or institutions of a country; a nation's power structure. Compare POWER STRUCTURE (definition 1), SYSTEM (definition 1).

If the Establishment means anything, it means big government and big business, and between them they pay most of the bills for big science. *Donald Fleming, "Big Science Under Fire," The Atlantic, Sept. 1970, p 97*

A whole new generation — the children of affluence — has taken up the cause of the black and the poor, not so much out of class feeling or shared experience, perhaps, as from recognition of a common enemy — the Establishment. It is the Establishment — the elders, the politicians, the military-industrial complex, the Administration, the press, the university trustees, the landlords, the system — that represses the black, exploits the poor, stultifies the students, vulgarizes American life. And it is the Establishment, of course, that wages the war in Vietnam — in the widespread protest against which the underlying class and generational clashes were dramatized and sharpened. *Tom Wicker, The New York Times, Aug. 9, 1968, Sec. 4, p 1*

2 the ruling circle of any institution (usually preceded by a modifier).

A sizable minority of senators tried unsuccessfully to reduce the size and influence of the military establishment by cutting the weapons procurement requests of the Department of Defense. *Robert M. Lawrence, "Defense Forces," The Americana Annual 1970, p 239*

In the years covered by Dos Passos' informal memoir, The Best Times, the underdog was anybody who did not belong to various Establishments such as Big Business or the various governments that had made World War I. *John Chamberlain, " 'Dos' and the Underdog," Harper's, Jan. 1967, p 97*

3 conventional society.

Now this has got to go both ways, not just from me — the middle-class, balding, middle-aged Establishment-type person — but from you young folks here who feel strongly on the other side. It's all right for some of you to tell us we've got to listen. But it's got to go both ways. *Robert*

Goldsworthy, quoted by Bill Moyers, "Listening to America," Harper's, Dec. 1970, p 80

The revival of pearls, downgraded in past years for representing the tired chic of the establishment, was one of the big accessory events. . . . *Ruth Mary DuBois, "Fashion," The Americana Annual 1970, p 290*

▶ In *The Changing English Language* (1968), Professor Brian Foster points out that *Establishment*, in the sense of "some well-entrenched group manipulating society from behind the scenes," had been used at various times in Great Britain long before the wide currency it attained during the 1960's. As a notable early instance of its use he cites a letter written in 1770 in which *establishment* was used to designate the religious ruling circles of the day. "Here we clearly see," he writes (page 162) "the religious origin, and in fact 'Establishment' was used as a synonym of the Established Church in the nineteenth century, e.g. by Dickens in *Dombey and Son* (chapter 32), though of course it is quite possible that the word was re-invented in the twentieth century after a period of disuse. It would clearly be easy to form it by analogy with the 'Established Church' of England."

establishmentarian or **Establishmentarian**, *adj.* of, belonging to, or favoring the Establishment.

In Pine Bluff, Ark., she [Martha Mitchell] was an average, Middle American high school girl. In wartime Washington, or postwar Forest Hills, or more recently in establishmentarian, suburban Rye, N. Y., she was little more than part of the background. . . . *Time, Nov. 30. 1970, p 31*

—*n.* a person who belongs to or favors the Establishment.

Call him wizard or weirdo, his [Richard J. Needham's] daily newspaper column of fables, waspish wisdom and homespun anarchy attracts worshipping women, admiring teenagers and bemused Establishmentarians by the thousands. *Nicholas Steed, "How to Cock A Snoot and Live, Live, Live," Maclean's, Aug. 20, 1966, p 18*

Galbraith himself has defined the true Establishmentarians as the pivotal Republicans who are given top posts in Democratic Administrations. *David Halberstam, "The Importance of being Galbraith," Harper's, Nov. 1967, p 54*

e·tham·bu·tol (e'θæm byu,tɔ:l), *n.* Also, **ethambutol hydrochloride.** a synthetic drug that inhibits the growth of tuberculosis bacilli.

New drugs studied included capreomycin, ethambutol and ethionamide. Their value would be determined by further study. *J. A. Myers, "Tuberculosis," Britannica Book of the Year 1963, p 799*

Two new antituberculosis drugs became available: ethambutol hydrochloride, a synthetic; and rifamycin, an antibiotic. These agents, when used in conjunction with the older, established drugs . . . delayed development of bacterial resistance to those compounds. *William Spector, "Medicine: Drugs," 1971 Britannica Yearbook of Science and the Future, 1970, p 224*

ethnic, *Especially U.S.* —*n.* **1** a member of a racial, cultural, or national minority group.

All sports are now saturated with ethnics. *Peter Schrag, "The Decline of the Wasp," Harper's, April 1970, p 89*

Just who are you anyway? Catholics, Protestants, Jews? Are you all from central and southern Europe? Then are Poles ethnics? Would Scandinavians consider themselves ethnics? *John A. Williams, The New York Times, Oct. 16, 1970, p 41*

If [Senator Edmund] Muskie gets the nomination, it will not be because of Vietnam or the economy or the King's Caucus or the governors or the big-city mayors or the ethnics, or the campaign organization or finances. *Joseph Kraft, "Reports & Comment," The Atlantic, June 1971, p 14*

2 ethnics, *pl.* racial, cultural, or national background.

. . . I think anyone whose parents were not intellectuals will have the same complete gap between his adult and highschool selves, even though class and ethnics don't seem to be involved. *Annette Mason, Los Angeles, Calif., in a Letter to the Editor, Harper's, Feb. 1968, p 6*

—*adj.* of or for ethnics.

Ethnic [Christmas] cards with black, brown or yellow Santas testify to the fact that the American melting pot is still bubbling, despite gloomy assertions to the contrary. *Time, Dec. 21, 1970, p 33*

ethno-, a combining form meaning "of or relating to racial or ethnic groups." *Ethno-* is used to form technical terms, chiefly in anthropology. Some recent examples of its use are:

ethno-law, *n.:* Biennial Review of Anthropology . . . appraises recent research papers in the areas of ethno-law . . . . *Science News, May 30, 1970, p 541*

ethno-political, *adj.:* If Nigeria's fifty million people are still a long way from solving their ethno-political problems, the end of a ruinous civil war seems at last to be in sight. *The Manchester Guardian Weekly, Oct. 12, 1967, p 8*

ethnopsychiatry, *n.:* As for the mission stations, Mr. Kerr read the commission a paper on ethnopsychiatry by Dr. Cawte, who had studied the Kalumburu mission station in the remote Kimberleys of Western Australia. *The Times (London), Sept. 30, 1965, p 11*

ethnoscience, *n.* and **ethnosemantics,** *n.:* . . . the following topics . . . surely ought to figure in an introductory text in anthropological linguistics, if only for historical reasons: . . . paralinguistics, kinesics [communication by gestures and facial expressions], ethnoscience, semiotics, ethnosemantics. . . . *Harvey B. Sarles, Review of "Anthropological Linguistics" by Joseph H. Greenberg, Language, March 1970, p 234*

See also the main entries below.

ethnomusicologist, *n.* a person who studies the music of different cultures.

Actually, as the ethnomusicologist Curt Sachs pointed out in his "World History of the Dance," there is evidence that primitive man may very well have started dancing in response to certain inner promptings long before he danced to audible rhythms, and the supposed unity of music and dance may not be "natural" at all. *Calvin Tomkins, "Profiles: An Appetite for Motion," The New Yorker, May 4, 1968, p 53*

ethnomusicology, *n.* the study of the music of different cultures.

The study of folk music—or ethnomusicology as it is commonly called—was given increased academic recognition, notably in the U.S. where regular courses were held in a number of universities. *Maud Karpeles, "Folk Music," Britannica Book of the Year 1968, p 573*

It was while he was doing graduate work in ethnomusicology at U.C.L.A. in 1962 that [Trumpeter-Composer

Don] Ellis grasped the jazz potential of the complex, repeated beat cycles underlying Asian and Middle Eastern music. *Time, May 26, 1967, p 46*

ethnomycological, *adj.* of or relating to ethnomycology.

This mushroom may represent possibly one of the oldest of the hallucinogens. Recent ethnomycological investigations have indicated the probability that *soma*, the ancient god-narcotic of the Aryan invaders of India 3500 years ago, was *A. muscaria. Richard Evans Schultes, "Psychopharmacological Drugs," McGraw-Hill Yearbook of Science and Technology 1971, p 357*

ethnomycologist, *n.* an expert in ethnomycology.

. . . a Mexican hallucinogenic-mushroom cult . . . was discovered several years ago by the Yankee ethnomycologist R. Gordon Wasson. *Winthrop Sargeant, "Musical Events: Homage," The New Yorker, April 25, 1970, p 130*

ethnomycology, *n.* the study of the use of hallucinogenic mushrooms and other fungi in various cultures and societies.

[Gordon] Wasson . . . began as an amateur mycologist and has since become the acknowledged founder of the huge and immensely important new science ethnomycology. *Robert Graves, "The Divine Rite of Mushrooms," The Atlantic, Feb. 1970, p 111*

e·tor·phine (i:'tɔr‚fi:n), *n.* a synthetic drug related to morphine.

Etorphine was first synthesised in 1963 and has been widely employed to immobilise game animals in Africa. *Bernard Dixon, "A Novel Competition," New Scientist and Science Journal, Sept. 23, 1971, p 664*

[from *et-* (perhaps from *ether*) + *morphine*]

eu·car·y·ote or **eu·kar·y·ote** (yu:'kær i: out), *n.* a cell with a visible nucleus. Compare PROCARYOTE or PROKARYOTE.

If the first eucaryotes arose 1.2 to 1.4 billion years ago, there would be about half of this time available for the evolution of soft-bodied multicellular organisms, since the first fossil animal skeletons were deposited around 600 million years ago at the beginning of the Cambrian period. *G. Evelyn Hutchinson, Scientific American, Sept. 1970, p 53*

The bacteria and their close relatives the blue-green algae comprise the so-called prokaryotic group; they are all micro-organisms. The second group, the eukaryotes, includes all other types of cell, whether animal, plant, protozoal or fungal. *Donald Williamson, New Scientist, Sept. 24, 1970, p 624*

[from *eu-* good, true + *caryote* or *karyote* cell nucleus (from Greek *káryon* nut, kernel)]

eu·phe·nics (yu:'fi: niks), *n.* a science dealing with ways of improving the human race by technological means, such as organ transplantation, prosthetics, and genetic engineering.

Attempts to control the basic characteristics of the organisms which develop under the influence of defective genetic constitutions have been spoken of by Lederberg as 'euphenics', in contrast to 'eugenics', which tries to change the genetic constitution itself. *John Newell, "Man's Growing Ability to Affect His Genetic Development," The Annual Register of World Events in 1966 (1967), p 422*

We now encourage certain measures for correcting the symptoms of genetic disease (euphenics) and for reducing their frequencies (eugenics). Both measures can be ex-

tended and should be with a generous measure of discretion and good judgment, especially in the case of eugenics. *George W. Beadle, "Anthropology: How to Transmit Culture," Science News Letter, Jan. 1, 1966, p 5*

[coined by the American geneticist Joshua Lederberg, born 1925, from *eu-* good + *phen-* appearance + *-ics*, on the analogy of *eugenics* (race improvement by hereditary control) and *euthenics* (race improvement by social and environmental control)]

euphorigenic, *adj.* inducing euphoria.

. . . R. S. Cahn . . . cast doubt on the euphorigenic activity of cannabinol. *Lester Grinspoon, "Marijuana," McGraw-Hill Yearbook of Science and Technology 1971, p 260*

Eurailpass, *n.* a tourist pass for traveling at a discount on European railroads.

All together, 104,000 Eurailpasses were sold in 1970, and travel agents expect sales to rise by 45% this year. *"Rites of Passage: The Knapsack Nomads," Time, July 19, 1971, p 56*

[contraction of *European rail*road *pass*]

Euro-, a combining form which has gained wide currency in several specialized meanings in recent years. It is now most often used in the three senses listed below.

1 of Europe, especially western Europe.

Eurodinner, *n.:* . . . however many Eurodinners Mr. Healy attends, and however many contingency plans and guidelines circulate through the defence Ministries of west Europe, there is only one man who can give the final authority to use nuclear weapons. *Lord Wigg, The Times (London), Feb. 19, 1970, p 11*

Eurofreeze, *n.:* The Eurofreeze created wartime-like refugee conditions for those caught on impassable highways, in crowded train stations and in befogged airports. *Time, Jan. 18, 1971, p 20*

Euroman, *n.:* The growing similarities between Europeans have enabled investigators for the first time to draw a sketch of the composite Euroman. . . . Euroman is roughly 34, married and has 1.5 children. He is employed by a company that has 50 or more employees, he earns about $50 a week in take-home pay. He quit school at 16, but he speaks one other language, most likely English. *Time, May 31, 1971, p 22*

Euro-politics, *n.:* . . . Mr. Heath himself has said virtually not a word about political Europe since he became Conservative leader: when he did talk Euro-politics he was speaking for the Macmillan administration. *Anthony Harris, "The Heath Adding Machine," The Manchester Guardian Weekly, Oct. 24, 1970. p 10*

Euroworld, *n.:* No other European financial centre has been able to provide that special combination of tradition, highly-developed markets and institutions, ease and speed of dealing, and predilection for international affairs which has established the City of London as the hub of the Euroworld. *S. M. Yassukovich, "Optimism In Eurodollar and Eurobond Markets," The Times (London), April 13, 1970, p II*

2 of or relating to the European money market.

Eurocapital, *adj.:* Of all the activities of the merchant banks today, possibly the most important internationally are the Eurocurrency markets and the Eurocapital markets which the London merchant banks created. *Lord Cromer, "Merchant Bankers' New Openings," The Times (London), April 13, 1970, p V2*

Eurofund, *n.:* ... various developments, not least the build-up of a vast, $30,000 million pool of hot, mobile and virtually-uncontrolled international Euro-funds, have strained the whole structure to its limits; and that the thing is only held together by string, tape and central bankers will-power. *The Sunday Times (London), Oct. 5, 1969, p 36*

Eurosterling, *n.:* It [Paris, as a deposit center] may not have achieved as much in this respect as London, which has pride of place as a Eurodollar centre, but it has certainly taken advantage of the growth of Eurocurrencies—especially Eurosterling. *Ian Morrison, "Harsh Controls Limit Appeal," The Times (London), July 6, 1970, p IV*

See also the main entries EUROBOND, EUROCURRENCY, EURODOLLAR.

3 of or relating to the European Economic Community or Common Market.

Euro-executive, *n.:* So much for the Euro-executive's remuneration; but what of the way he has to work in order to gain it? *Anthony Rowley, "Europe Leads the Pay Stakes," The Times (London), Aug. 18, 1970, p 21*

Euro-farmer, *n.:* Euro-farmers sink into the currency quagmire. *John Lambert, The Sunday Times (London), Oct. 5, 1969, p 30*

Euromerger, *n.:* Dunlop and Pirelli plan to amalgamate operating interest in the first substantial "Euromerger" since Royal Dutch Shell and Unilever were established before the war. *"The Logic of Dunlopirelli," The Manchester Guardian Weekly, March 7, 1970, p 24*

See also the main entries EUROCRACY, EUROPE.

Eurobond, *n.* a bond issued by an American or other non-European corporation for sale in European countries.

Issued abroad by both U.S. and foreign companies and usually payable in dollars, Eurobonds are used to tap the $60 billion in American money that is sloshing around Europe. *Time, Aug. 9, 1971, p 54*

The huge flood of Eurobond and other borrowing in Europe by American companies has not had any adverse effect in Europe, officials said. ... *The New York Times, July 25, 1968, p 47*

Eurocheque, *n. British.* a credit card used for obtaining goods and services in various European countries.

The Eurocheque cash card system discussed in Family Money-Go-Round (May 6) is, indeed, a most convenient system. *Daily Telegraph (London), May 16, 1972, p 21*

Eurocracy, *n.* the officials or administrators of the European Economic Community or Common Market.

The average Briton is sti l afraid of the EEC's [European Economic Community's] high food prices and fearful of losing British sovereignty to the Brussels-based Eurocracy. *"Common Market: Breaking Out the Bubbly," Time, July 5, 1971, p 19*

[from the earlier term *Eurocrat* (a Common Market official), formed on the analogy of *bureaucrat, bureaucracy*]

Eurocratic, *adj.* of or relating to the administration of the European Economic Community or Common Market.

... the process of unifying Europe through a common currency leading to a form of European parliamentary control has started. Britain could accelerate this process, to the security of all. But if under Eurocratic fostering it goes ahead with Britain outside instead of inside, Britain's prospects and position will be prejudiced by 1980, and probably even by 1975. *"A Priority Agenda: 2. Europe" (Editorial), The Times (London), June 19, 1970, p 11*

[from the earlier term *Eurocrat* (a Common Market official), patterned after *bureaucrat, bureaucratic*]

Eurocurrency, *n.* currency of various countries deposited in European banks and used in the European money market. Also called EUROMONEY.

... the volume of credit channeled in Eurocurrencies was something of the order of $19 billion. *Alan R. Roe, "Money and Banking: Eurocurrency and Eurobond Markets," Britannica Book of the Year 1969, p 535*

Last week a committee headed by Luxembourg's Prime Minister, Pierre Werner, handed in a report suggesting how the Common Market countries can create a new "Eurocurrency" that would acquire some of the privileges and powers of the dollar. *Time, Oct. 26, 1970, p 108*

Eurodollar, *n.* Eurocurrency in dollars.

... the Eurodollar [is] a U.S. currency that never goes home, because it is barred from the United States. *C. L. Sulzberger, The New York Times, July 29, 1970, p 38*

Euromoney, *n.* another name for EUROCURRENCY.

Today the defence possibilities in line with the market are much more favourable owing to the attraction of the Euromoney market which has since grown enormously. *Edwin Stopper, The Times (London), June 24, 1970, p 29*

Europe, European, Europeanism, Europeanist. This group of terms has gained recent currency (especially in Great Britain) in specific reference to the European Economic Community, better known as the Common Market. To join *Europe* means to gain entry into the Common Market; a *European* is one who favors such a move; *Europeanism* is either the advocacy of or the movement supporting such a move; and *Europeanist* means tending toward or supporting Europeanism.

Mr Shore has long been sceptical about the advantages of joining Europe, and Mr Hattersley is a passionate and long-standing European. *Ian Aitken, "Anti-Marketeers More Confident," The Manchester Guardian Weekly, April 4, 1970, p 8*

The highly uncertain future if Britain does not go into Europe has not yet been adequately explained or understood, according to some anxious pro-Europeans. *Mollie Panter-Downes, "Letter From London," The New Yorker, July 3, 1971, p 64*

We have insisted for too long on maintaining the status quo in NATO, ignoring the powerful trend toward Europeanism and the towering strength of the European Common Market. *Lt. Gen. James M. Gavin, USA, "Military Power: The Limits of Persuasion," Saturday Review, July 30, 1966, p 22*

Men under the age of 50 are more likely to be Europeanist than men over 50. *David Wood, "Shifts In British Opinion," The Times (London), June 30. 1970, p 6*

The Europeanists note that the nations of Western Europe contain 320 million people with a spending power of $385 billion, exports of $96 billion and imports of $102 billion. *Time, May 31, 1971, p 22*

europopocentric *adj.* having Europe as its center.

Bernal would surely agree that each man—including himself and Marx—must be a child of his time. How far

Marx's nineteenth century europocentric vision is totally applicable to the second half of the twentieth century is debatable. *Sarah White, Review of "Science in History" by J. D. Bernal, New Scientist, Feb. 27, 1969, p 473*

He [a historian] knows that for half a millennium the nations of Western Europe were destined to predominate. Thus, it is natural for him to have a Europocentric view of the modern world, to believe that non-Western cultures are below par if not permanently inferior. *Benjamin Quarles, "What the Historian Owes the Negro," Saturday Review, Sept. 3, 1966, p 11*

Europort, *n.* a European port serving as a major import and export harbor, especially for the Common-Market countries.

Rotterdam Europort is prepared to deepen its channel to 80 ft. to take 500,000-ton tankers, Franz Posthuma, managing director of the port, said in a paper read in London last night. *The Times (London), Jan. 9, 1968, p 18*

[translation of Dutch *Europoort*]

eu·tro·phi·cate (yu:'trɑf ə,keit), *v.i.* (of streams, lakes, etc.) to be or become polluted by the introduction of phosphates, nitrates, and other substances that promote growth of algae.

Even in the short run eutrophicating influences can greatly damage aquatic ecosystems. *"Water Pollution," Science News Yearbook 1970, p 297*

...the increased growth of vegetation in the water and the proliferation of algae in huge blotches of green slime ... causes lakes to eutrophicate, or age, before their time. *Richard D. Lyons, The New York Times, Nov. 15, 1970, Sec. 4, p 12*

[back formation from *eutrophication*]

eu·tro·phi·ca·tion (,yu: trə fə'kei ʃən), *n.* the pollution of streams, lakes, and other bodies of water by phosphates, nitrates, and other substances that cause rapid growth of algae, which deplete the water of oxygen. See also DYSTROPHICATION.

Eutrophication literally means "nourishing well," but in current usage it refers to the inadvertent nourishing of algae in lakes to the detriment of other living things. *"Science and the Citizen: Closed Cycle," Scientific American, Nov. 1970, p 46*

Scientists agree, however, that detergent phosphates are not the only cause of the accelerated eutrophication. Also implicated are the phosphates from human wastes and from agricultural fertilizer run-off, as well as nitrates and organic compounds that end up in the water. *John F. Henahan, "Phosphates Leave the Laundry," The World Book Science Annual 1972 (1971), p 285*

[originally used to describe a natural chemical enrichment process in lakes; from Greek *eútrophos* enriched, thriving]

eu·tro·phied ('yu: trə fi:d), *adj.* eutrophicated; polluted.

A group of University of Wisconsin scientists tried using alum applied directly to the surface of the eutrophied Horseshoe Lake in eastern Wisconsin. *"Eutrophication: Alum May Combat Algae," Science News, May 29, 1971, p 370*

...phosphates did the damage to the severely eutrophied Lake Washington, near Seattle. *John F. Henahan, "Phosphates Leave the Laundry," The World Book Science Annual 1972 (1971), p 285*

[from *eutrophy, n.,* well-nourished condition (in English in this sense since the 1700's) + *-ed* (adjective suffix), apparently with influence of *atrophied*]

evapotranspire, *v.t.* to cause the loss of (water) from soil by both evaporation and transpiration.

Water-use efficiency can be expressed in a variety of ways, such as tons of hay or bushels of potatoes per acre-inch of water evapotranspired, crates of marketable lettuce per acre-foot of water, or as a weight ratio, kilogram per kilogram. *E. G. Viets, Jr., "Efficient Use of Water," McGraw-Hill Yearbook of Science and Technology 1967, p 165*

[back formation from *evapotranspiration* the loss of water from soil by evaporation and transpiration]

é·véne·ment (ei ven'mã), *n. French.* event; incident (in the sense of a major social and political development).

Clouds of acrid tear gas hung over the chestnut trees of Left Bank boulevards, just as they had during the shattering *événements* of May 1968 that tore France apart and led directly to the fall of Charles de Gaulle. *Time, June 8, 1970, p 37*

During the evenements of May and June, 1968, the red flag of communism and the black flag of anarchism fluttered side by side on the occupied Theatre de l'Odeon. Inside, of course, the whole intelligentsia of Paris listened in on the discussions by day and by night. *Peter Laslett, "The Anarchist Revival," The Manchester Guardian Weekly, Aug. 7, 1971, p 18*

▶ This word came into English as a result of the events of 1968 in France referred to in the quotations, since this is the term used by the French for this and other happenings of a violent and controversial character. The attraction of the word is that in a partisan situation it is neutral, like the Irish "troubles." The word is Anglicized in the second quotation by the omission of diacritics.

exacta, *n. U.S.* (in horse racing) a method of betting in which the bettor picks the horses to win and to place in the exact order of the finish. Also called PERFECTA.

After all, for the price of a ride to the Big A [Aqueduct race track] and back you could have a couple of tickets on the daily double or a flutter on the exacta. *Audax Minor, The New Yorker, April 25, 1970, p 98*

Since exacta wagering calls for the bettor to pick the precise 1, 2 finish (unlike in quiniela gambling, in which 1, 2 or 2, 1 do not matter) two payoffs were in order to the holders of winning ninth-race exacta tickets. *Louis Efrat, The New York Times, Jan. 31, 1968, p 34*

[from American Spanish, short for *quiniela exacta* exact quiniela (*quiniela,* a bet on the first two finishers of a race in any order)]

ex·ci·plex ('ek sə,pleks), *n.* a complex or aggregate of excited states produced in a dye laser.

The key to such laser tunability lies in a reversible chemical reaction that forms the 'exciplex', or excited state complex. ... an exciplex reaction—unlike a normal chemical reaction—takes place only when the molecules of the dye are in an electronically excited state, just before the emission of light. The molecules are excited by directing light pulses into the dye solution (pumping). Once excited, the molecules of the dye react with a chemical present in the solution, and another form of the dye is created. This is the excited state complex, or exciplex. *Science Journal,* *Nov. 1970, p 17*

excitonic, *adj.* of or involving excitons (excited electrons in a crystal structure).

There is a variety of excitonic processes, however, that give rise to electrical conductivity. *Martin Pope, "Exciton," McGraw-Hill Yearbook of Science and Technology 1968, p 161*

In most cases excitonic fluorescence is quite efficient: In the substance anthracene, for example, 95 percent of the impinging light is reradiated as fluorescent light. *"The Fission of Nonparticles," Science News, April 19, 1969, p 378*

excitonics, *n.* the study of excitons (excited electrons in a crystal structure).

The recent developments in excitonics could have an important bearing on the study of energy-transfer mechanisms such as those involved in photosynthesis by living plants. *Scientific American, May 1969, p 56*

ex-directory, *adj. British.* not in the telephone directory; unlisted.

... manager Harry Catterick has the League's best kept ex-directory phone number. *The Sunday Times (London), Oct. 12, 1969, p 22*

exfiltrate, *v.i., v.t. U.S. Military Slang.* to get out of a hostile area stealthily or unnoticeably; slip out through the enemy lines.

During the night, the Vietcong remnants tried to "exfiltrate" (American jargon for to slip out), but ran up against the blocking force and were turned back after an exchange of fire. *David Bonavia, The Times (London), June 19, 1968, p 4*

... Corporal Courcey stays with the doomed native garrison instead of being exfiltrated (Army jargon for decamping) with the other Americans. *Julian Symons, The Sunday Times (London), Jan. 7, 1968, p 39*

[from *ex-* out + *infiltrate*]

exfiltration, *n. U.S. Military Slang.* a slipping out of a hostile area.

"Why don't you pick the best area for exfiltration?" the ground commander suggested.

"I really like that little knoll over to the west where you can see the exfiltration trails in the woods there," Captain Reese said. *Jonathan Schell, The New Yorker, March 16, 1968, p 83*

exoatmosphere, *n.* the outermost region of the earth's atmosphere.

The larger Spartan's [an antiballistic missile] job would be to provide an "area defence" by engaging enemy warheads in the exo-atmosphere—roughly 300,000 ft. up. *Howard Simons, "Side-effect of Mao's Bomb," New Scientist, June 29, 1967, p 772*

[from *exo-* outside, outer + *atmosphere*]

exoatmospheric, *adj.* of the exoatmosphere; designed for the exoatmosphere.

... some experts say the Moscow part of the Soviet missile defense system is based upon what is called an "exo-atmospheric" rocket, or a defensive missile designed to intercept incoming missiles above the atmosphere. *Hanson W. Baldwin, The New York Times, Feb. 5, 1967, p 76*

exobiologist, *n.* a specialist in exobiology.

Even Ponnamperuma, a highly respected exobiologist

(extraterrestrial biology) at NASA's Ames Research Center in California, admits that only a thumbprint on a beaker could introduce amino acids into a meteorite sample. *Time, Dec. 14, 1970, p 67*

exobiology, *n.* the study of life outside the earth.

As man enters the second decade of the Space Age, exobiology—that branch of planetary science concerned with the search for extraterrestrial life—will prove itself or be forgotten. It will not always be a science in search of a subject. *Norman H. Horowitz, "Life Beyond the Earth," 1970 Britannica Yearbook of Science and the Future, 1969, p 193*

exocytosis, *n.* a process by which cellular substances active in the transmission of impulses are released outside the nerve cells.

From ultrastructural and biochemical studies, it now seems certain that the tiny bag-like structures, or vesicles, seen in nerve endings, act as storage sites for transmitter substances. At the moment, interest centres around the mechanisms by which their contents are released into the extracellular space. The most plausible model is that of "exocytosis", in which the membrane of the storage granule fuses with the membrane of the cell, and the secretory products are lost through an opening in the fused membranes. *New Scientist, June 4, 1970, p 464*

[from *exo-* outside + *cyto-* cell + *-osis* process or condition]

exohormone, *n.* a hormonal secretion by an organism which affects the olfactory organ of another organism so as to alter its behavior in a certain way. Compare PHEROMONE.

If a goat's kid is taken away for only two hours from birth, the mother will reject it when it is returned. They probably become conditioned to its smell, or exohormones, at this time. *Gordon Rattray Taylor, Science Journal, Jan. 1968, p 31*

ex·o·nu·cle·ase (,ek sou'nu: kli:,cis), *n.* an enzyme that breaks up the strands of DNA which had been segmented by the enzyme endonuclease.

A circular structure for DNA was first described in 1962.... This conclusion was based on experiments showing the resistance of this viral DNA to digestion by exonuclease, enzymes which degrade DNA starting only at free ends of DNA molecules. *Margit M. K. Nass, "DNA Threads, Circles and Chains," Science Journal, Aug. 1969, p 46*

[from *exo-* outer + *nuclease* an enzyme that hydrolyzes nucleic acid]

exonumia, *n.* the study and collection of items other than coins and paper currency, such as tokens, medals, and coupons.

It is possible, but not likely, that rare pieces will turn up in junk boxes. It is more likely that the rare ones, such as the illustrated token from North Jellico, Tenn., will have to be purchased from one of the handful of dealers who specialize in exonumia. *Herbert C. Bardes, The New York Times, Nov. 27, 1966, Sec. 2, p 26*

[from *exo-* + *-numia,* extracted from *numismatics*]

exotic, *adj. Nuclear Physics.* highly unstable and hard to capture.

The newer exotic particles—K's [K mesons], sigmas and antiprotons—also respond to both [electromagnetic and strong nuclear] forces, and they will be especially useful in investigating the outer layers of the nucleus. *Dietrick E. Thomsen, "Building Exotic Atoms," Science News, Nov. 14, 1970 p 385*

expanded cinema, another name for INTERMEDIA.

Expanded cinema, sometimes called intermedia, the recent experiments in combining film with live actors and musicians, will be the subject of five of the 27 events, including two forums and a demonstration. *Vincent Canby, The New York Times, Sept. 7, 1966, p 51*

extra-, a very productive prefix, added chiefly to adjectives and meaning "outside (the area or province of)," "beyond (the scope of)," as in the examples below.

extrachromosomal, *adj.:* It appears . . . that enterobactereaceae [pathogenic bacteria that affect the intestinal tract] can transfer multiple resistance from one organism to another and even from one species to another by means of extrachromosomal hereditary factors. *Clifford R. Noll, Jr., "Biochemistry," 1967 Collier's Encyclopedia Year Book, p 124*

extramaternal, *adj.:* Our abiding image of Flaubert is of a mother's boy bachelor, working through the night, calling *"Maman!"* on waking, growing stout on huge Norman meals, finding his only extramaternal devotion in the self-imposed martyrdom of his art. *Anthony Burgess, "The Artist as Martyr," The Manchester Guardian Weekly, Sept. 7, 1967, p 10*

extraneural, *adj.:* Rabies virus is . . . generalized throughout the organism in every extraneural organ and tissue. *Colin Kaplan, Science Journal, April 1970, p 37*

extra-political, *adj.:* No doubt the lessening of a certain kind of partisan zeal can be attributed in part to a spreading disenchantment with the whole political order and a growing absorption with extra-political forms of expression. *Richard H. Rovere, The New Yorker, June 8, 1968, p 120*

extrareligious, *adj.:* The father, on the other hand, lives in northern New Jersey, where "temples, Hebrew schools and extrareligious facilities abound." *Time, Aug. 16, 1968, p 57*

extra-subjective, *adj.:* . . . philosophers who profess not to believe in the reality of the extra-subjective world admit the existence of other men and that they have the same subjective experience as themselves. *Edward R. F. Sheehan, "Conversations With Konrad Lorenz," Harper's, May 1968, p 74*

extralinguistic, *adj.* outside the province of language or linguistics.

'Thus the MEANING relation, particularly in the case of lexical designation—for example, that the English word *table* designates "table", has seemed to some not to be part of linguistics, since it involves references to extralinguistic events'. . . . *Harvey B. Sarles, University of Minnesota, Review of "Anthropological Linguistics: An Introduction" by Joseph H. Greenberg, Language, March 1970, p 234*

extralunar, *adj.* found or existing outside the moon.

A small fraction [of lunar breccias and fines] (1 or 2 percent) is an extralunar component of meteoritic or cometary origin, most readily identified by a relatively high content of nickel and platinum-group elements, which are found only in low concentrations in the crystalline rocks. *Brian Mason, "The Lunar Rocks," Scientific American, Oct. 1971, p 53*

extrapolability, *n.* the ability to extrapolate or make projections from available data.

We explored many traditional processes and sites, and from our observations are now trying to extrapolate what we can about ancient methodology. Obviously the degree of extrapolability from evidence or [from] crafts extant today must vary enormously from case to case. *Theodore A. Wertime, "A Metallurgical Expedition through the Persian Desert," Science, March 1, 1968, p 935*

extrasolar, *adj.* found or existing outside the solar system.

The search for extrasolar planets has been going on for 32 years, slowly, painstakingly, with none of the excitement of more glamorous fields of science. *Peter van de Kamp, "Barnard's Star and other Solar Systems," Encyclopedia Science Supplement (Grolier) 1971, p 54*

extraterrestrial, *n.* a creature from another planet.

"Much commotion was made over the discovery of the image of a 'Martian god' complete with space suit, found in cliffs overlooking the Sahara. . . . Such publicity is due, of course, to widespread popular interest in the possibility of contact with intelligent extraterrestrials. But for this very reason, we must examine critically any purported artifacts uncovered." *John Lear quoting from "Intelligent Life in the Universe" by I. S. Shklovskii and Carl Sagan, Saturday Review, Aug. 6, 1966, p 42*

[noun use of adjective *extraterrestrial* outside the earth]

extravehicular, *adj.* **1** outside an orbiting space vehicle.

Major Edwin Aldrin, the co-pilot of the Gemini 12 spacecraft, successfully completed his last extravehicular activity today when he stood up in the hatch to photograph two star clusters and experiment with a sextant. *The Times (London), Nov. 15, 1966, p 6*

2 of or for activity outside a space vehicle.

In the extravehicular configuration, the constant-wear garment is replaced by the liquid-cooling garment and four items are added to the intravehicular suit: extravehicular visor, extravehicular glove, lunar overshoe, and a cover over umbilical connections on the front of the suit. *"The Apollo Space Suit," Encyclopedia Science Supplement (Grolier) 1969, p 329*

ex-works, *adv.* British. directly from the factory.

It may be that some clerk has developed the habit of putting down the value ex-works and not the price at which it is being sold. *"Working Out the Trade Figures," The Times (London), Feb. 21, 1970, p 16*

eyeball, *n.* **eyeball to eyeball,** face to face.

. . . you had to get right in there with Williams, stand eyeball to eyeball, and plant the zinger on him, bang. . . . *John Corry, "The Return of Ted Williams," Harper's, June 1969, p 74*

The manager must always decide, or manage, in the selection of objectives and goals and the formation of basic policy. Personnel handling and 'eyeball to eyeball' negotiation are also not fit subjects for stimulation or modelling. *Robert K. Mueller, Science Journal, Nov. 1968, p 87*

eyewall, *n.* a layer of turbulent funnel-shaped clouds around the eye (calm center) of a storm. Also called WALL CLOUD.

. . . Hurricane Debbie . . . was some 800 miles east of Puerto Rico. Planes flew there to dump their crystals, in hopes of causing supercooled water droplets in the hurricane's eyewall to condense. *Science News, Aug. 23, 1969, p 153*

F

face, *v.t.* **face off,** *U.S.* to confront (an opponent) in a test of strength, will, endurance, etc.

Whether or not Dubček succeeds in facing off the Russians, says Professor William E. Griffith of M.I.T., he has unleashed "the most significant change in the European status quo since 1948." *Time, July 26, 1968, p 31*

facedown, *n.* *U.S.* a confrontation between opponents.

The eleven-man Czechoslovak Presidium has vowed to fight down the line for liberal reform and independence in the facedown with the eleven-member Politburo. *Time, Aug. 2, 1968, p 18*

The other cowboy in the electoral facedown, Barry Goldwater, will no doubt make the political counterblow of flicking the new coins into the air and putting six shots through them before they hit the ground. *Punch, Aug. 12, 1964, p 227*

[from *face down*, probably patterned after *showdown*]

face fly, a fly closely related to the common house-fly, found throughout the United States and Canada.

A serious problem in the United States is the face fly, which breeds on cattle dung, then attacks the eyes of cattle. *Science News, May 30, 1970, p 532*

face-off, *n.* *U.S.* a confrontation between opponents.

How elemental the face-off [between generations] can become was demonstrated last week in Monterey, Calif., when the state unemployment-insurance office ruled that jobless men with long hair can no longer collect unemployment benefits. *Time, June 8, 1970, p 12*

Mr. Soll tells us that the draft was the secret of American success in various cold war face-offs. *Aryeh Neir, in a Letter to the Editor, The New York Times, June 30, 1971, p 40*

[from FACE OFF]

fad·a·yeen (ˌfæd əˈyiːn), *n.* another form of *fedayeen*, an Arab commando. See FEDAI. *Also used attributively.*

"In our movement now," one fadayeen spokesman told him in a tense and almost worshipful murmur, "the only men who are photographed, the only ones who are spoken about, are the dead ones: the martyrs" — pronouncing the word like a soft fondling, "mar-tears." *Marshall Frady, "On Jordan's Banks," Harper's, Nov. 1970, p 108*

faggotry, *n.* *Slang.* homosexuality.

I remember what I used to hear about — the computer dating, the hectic beach resorts, the girls who complained that a wave of faggotry was upsetting the balance. *Edward Grossman, "In Pursuit of the American Woman," Harper's, Feb. 1970, p 64*

[from *faggot*, slang word for a homosexual, of unknown origin]

faggoty or **faggy,** *adj.* *Slang.* effeminate; homosexual.

The central character is a real motor-cycle fiend the *équipe* picked up somewhere, and in the course of the film he is put through a series of tests: first in a clothes shop where he has to cope with a couple of extravagantly faggoty assistants.... *John Russell Taylor, Review of "Bike Boy," a film by Andy Warhol, The Times (London), May 1, 1970 p 8*

Coco [a musical] is more of a bore than a bomb.... The production seems to squelch almost everyone connected with it. Only René Auberjonois as a faggy designer manages to filch an occasional moment of amusing exuberance. *Time, Dec. 26, 1969, p 31*

[from *faggot* or *fag*, slang words for a homosexual, of unknown origin]

fail-safe, *adj.* **1** designed to stop or alter an operation automatically in the event of a malfunction.

A fail-safe reel brake prevents accidental spilling of tape in case of power failure. *Science News, Jan. 27, 1968, p 102*

The authority said that subway trains were equipped with a fail-safe device that halts the train automatically if the brakes fail. *The New York Times, Feb. 7, 1968, p 51*

2 guaranteed not to fail; safe from failure; foolproof.

A master plan was worked out, beautifully turned and fail-safe on paper — and the team went bankrupt before lunch. *The Manchester Guardian Weekly, Sept. 26, 1968, p 6*

... her [Julie Andrews'] most recent effort *Star!*, directed by the fail-safe Robert Wise, looks as though it will wind up on the deficit side. *Hollis Alpert, "The Falling Stars," Saturday Review, Dec. 28, 1968, p 16*

— *v.i.* to stop or alter an operation automatically in case of some malfunction.

Those with gas central heating will have cursed the irony of a system which fails-safe when the electrical power supply is severed. *Anthony Tucker, "Showdown at Energy Gap," The Manchester Guardian Weekly, Dec. 19, 1970. p 13*

— *v.t.* to make or cause to be fail-safe.

The hope is that the Russians have better measuring equipment on these two probes than they had on Venera 4. One problem with Venera 4. says Dr. Drake, was that its equipment "was not fail-safed. If it failed and gave erroneous readings, there was no way to know." He hopes this one is fail-safed. *"To the Moon, To the Planets," Science News, May 31, 1969, p 525*

[from the *Fail-Safe* system developed by the U.S.

Strategic Air Command, in which bombers sent into enemy territory on the basis of an unconfirmed order can be prevented from completing their mission by withholding its confirmation or by other automatic safeguards]

fairness doctrine, *U.S.* a principle in licensed radio and television broadcasting of providing reasonable opportunity for different points of view in a controversial issue of public importance to be broadcast. Compare EQUAL TIME.

... the Federal Communications Commission ruled that under the so-called "fairness doctrine," all broadcasters who carry cigarette advertising must also carry announcements and programs telling of the possible perils of smoking. *The New York Times, Sept. 13, 1968, p 55*

faits di·vers (fe di:'ver), *n.pl. French.* news items; trivial happenings.

... a pattern exists, if we could but identify it, into which everything from international crime to parochial *faits divers* will fall. *Frank Kermode, "Britain's Decade That Was," The Atlantic, March 1971, p 98*

We are back in the high grazing country of the first novels, but the characters are more sharply colored or caricatured, the harmony of man with nature is missing, and the vicissitudes of the country folk are more in the line of *faits divers:* young Bernard is held prisoner on his *jas* (couch) for a week by a swarm of bees; Bouscarle's cadaver is dragged for two days by his gnawing dogs. *Robert J. Clements, "European Literary Scene," Saturday Review, May 4, 1968, p 23*

fake book, *U.S.* a book reproducing the melodies or similar shorthand versions of copyrighted popular songs without permission of the copyright owners.

... Burton Lane, a major Broadway composer ... sat at an upright in the well of the courtroom and played 15 popular songs from the original sheet music and from a "fake book" published by Rose and sold to musicians. *The New York Times, April 20, 1966, p 39*

fa·la·fel (fə'lɑ: fəl), *n.* a salad sandwich eaten in Israel and some Arab countries.

Falafel, popular with Israelis, is made with fava beans, chick peas, green peppers, onions, parsley and radishes ground up and seasoned with cumin, coriander, black pepper and salt. *Susan Rogers, New York Post, Nov. 1, 1971, p 46*

[from Modern Hebrew and Arabic]

fallout, *n.* a by-product or residue of something, usually unexpected. Compare SPINOFF.

A sublime piece of technological fall-out from space technology is a means of purifying foul-smelling sewage and converting it into sterile drinking water. *New Scientist, July 2, 1970, p 20*

From the research that produced the rocket motors, liquid propellants, space suits and other necessities of space flight emerged ... unexpected applications—in medicine, industry, and the home—for materials, equipment, and services that had been created for use in space. Such by-products are called "spin-off" or "fallout." *"Valuable By-Products of Space Research," The 1970 Compton Yearbook, p 574*

family, *n. U.S.* one of the operational units of the Cosa Nostra or Mafia.

A Mafia family is a group of individuals who are not necessarily blood relatives. *The New York Times, May 9, 1967, p 38*

The boss of one Cosa Nostra "family" is said to have given a half-million dollars in cash, divided five ways, to five of his lieutenants for Christmas. *Donald R. Cressey, "Theft of the Nation," Harper's, Feb. 1969, p 86*

The Luchese family ... was suspected of being in the narcotics traffic and because it had a large number of low-ranking members, called soldiers or button men, who might be induced to talk. *Charles Grutzner, The New York Times, Dec. 23, 1967, p 11*

family planning, regulation or limitation of the size of a family by birth control; planned parenthood.

Graft and corruption which permeate almost every sphere of life in India are now threatening to erode one of the most ambitious family planning ventures in the world. *Peter Hazelhurst, "Family Planners Fake Figures in India," The Times (London), May 7, 1970, p 6*

At the United Nations, the thirty-two delegates (all but four of them women) to the Commission on the Status of Women were debating a draft resolution that proposed the creation of regional seminars in family planning and the integration of women into economic life. *"The Talk of the Town," The New Yorker, Feb. 24, 1968, p 30*

Fanconi's anemia, a constitutional anemia of children, resembling pernicious anemia.

They have discovered that cells from patients with Down's syndrome (mongolism) and Fanconi's anaemia—two diseases which Miller had proved to predispose toward leukaemia—are more susceptible to SV40 transformation. *New Scientist and Science Journal, March 18, 1971, p 596*

Perhaps the mottled skin of individuals with Fanconi's anemia, in which chromosome breakage is frequent, is an expression of such mosaicism [unlike genetic characteristics in adjacent cells or tissues]. *Kurt Benirscheke, "Mosaicism and Chimerism," McGraw-Hill Yearbook of Science and Technology 1967, p 249*

[named after Guido *Fanconi*, 1882-1940?, a Swiss pediatrician who first described the disease]

fantasy, *n.* a coin of questionable origin or purpose, especially one issued by a country for sale to coin collectors rather than for use as legal tender. *Also used attributively.*

Growing concern over increasing activities in the manufacture and distribution of counterfeits, fantasies, and copies brought about the formation of an international committee to publicize these coins wherever found. *Elston G. Bradfield, "Philately and Numismatics," Britannica Book of the Year 1967, p 618*

Partly because of the appeal of the advertising and partly because so many collectors want to believe the claims, the "fantasy coin" business has grown to sizable proportions in recent years. *The New York Times, June 5, 1966, Sec. 2, p 27*

far-out, *adj.* **1** (literally) far removed in space; very distant in space.

Although Pluto, the solar system's most far-out planet, has appeared to be growing slightly dimmer for the past ten years, this is not a permanent change. *Science News, March 22, 1969, p 285*

2 (figuratively) far removed from the ordinary; very unconventional. Compare WAY-OUT.

I got away from writing vaguely autobiographical snips for the New Yorker market to writing some far-out, inventive pieces. *Josh Greenfeld, The New York Times Magazine, Jan. 14, 1968, p 41*

I'll put it this way. He was a brainy individual. He was smart. That impressed me. But he was a little far out for a small community like this. *Bill Moyers, "Listening to America," Harper's, Dec. 1970, p 75*

far-outer, *n.* one who is very unconventional; a nonconformist.

In 1965, when Joseph Tussman started his Experimental College Program, the far-outers soon discovered that Tussman . . . had some seemingly square notions — such as that learning involves hard work and that one aim of education is good citizenship. *Time, March 15, 1968, p 46*

For one thing, there's the question of warmth — after all, what are coats for — so only the most hardy far-outers wear them as short or shorter than their skirts. . . . *The Sunday Times (London), Jan. 8, 1967, p 40*

fastback, *n. U.S.* an automobile with lines that slope down from the midsection to the rear in an unbroken curve. Compare NOTCHBACK.

Ever-changing tastes of American car owners slowed the trend toward fastbacks. Motorists reiterated a preference for . . . rear fenders with pronounced bustles in the trunks. *Maynard M. Gordon, The Americana Annual 1967, p 109*

Fastback, *n.* a breed of pigs that are more economical and leaner than other breeds, first produced in 1971 in Great Britain.

We will have to wait another three years to enjoy the benefits of the "Fastback" . . . under what is the most intensive programme of its kind in the world. *New Scientist, Aug. 6, 1970, p 285*

Main customers for the Fast Back are the bacon curers and pork butchers, who sell whole sides of bacon, or joints of meat with the crackling and fat still intact. *The Sunday Times (London), May 16, 1971, p 52*

fast breeder or **fast-breeder reactor,** a breeder reactor (atomic power plant able to produce its own fuel as well as generate power with almost no loss of fissionable material) that uses fast or high-energy neutrons to produce fissionable material. Compare THERMAL BREEDER.

Two different breeder systems are involved, depending on which raw material is being transmuted. The thermal breeder, employing slow neutrons, operates best on the thorium 232-uranium 233 cycle (usually called the thorium cycle). The fast breeder, employing more energetic neutrons, operates best on the uranium 238-plutonium 239 cycle (the uranium cycle). *Glenn T. Seaborg and Justin L. Bloom, "Fast Breeder Reactors," Scientific American, Nov. 1970, p 13*

In a fast breeder reactor, atoms of nonfissionable plutonium are converted into fissionable atoms of plutonium-239. *James D. Lyman, "Nuclear Energy," 1969 Collier's Encyclopedia Year Book, p 403*

fast-food, *adj. U.S.* serving quickly prepared foods, such as hamburgers, frankfurters, french-fried potatoes, and other short-order dishes.

. . . frozen foods, packaged foods, TV dinners, fast-food franchises, preservatives and additives all stem from a culture that made pragmatism, step saving and time saving virtues in themselves. *Time, Nov. 16, 1970, p 63*

fat farm, *U.S. Slang.* a health resort or spa for over-weight people.

As waistlines keep expanding, so too do beauty resorts — the places that thin people like to call fat farms. *Time, March 2, 1970, p 64*

Last week the *First Tuesday* segments dealt with a weight-reduction "fat farm" and a Christian anti-Communist crusade. *Time, April 11, 1969, p 42*

faux na·if (fou nɑ:'i:f), *French.* falsely naïve; apparently but not actually simple or artless.

Dossena never admitted to being a forger, and no one ever managed to prove that he was deliberately trying to deceive. . . . It was others who claimed that his pieces were by Donatello or Simone Martini or an unknown Greek of the fifth century. He made a statement to a reporter . . . which may or may not have been *faux naïf. Russell Lynes, "After Hours: Forgery for Fun and Profit," Harper's, Feb. 1968, p 26*

Wood's work is very *faux naif* and Nicholson painted better when he was under the influence of Mondrian. *Paul Overy, "Art — Everyone is Talented," The Listener, June 20, 1968, p 818*

fa·vel·a (fə'vel ə), *n. Portuguese.* a shantytown or slum. Compare BARRIADA.

To this day, photographs of the Kennedys, torn from newspapers, hang on the walls of hovels in the *barrios* [districts] and *favelas* of Latin cities. The hatred of Latin Americans for the United States as the source of economic exploitation is matched only by their faith in United States leaders who fight our own oligarchs and their sometimes quixotic hope for the United States as a source of political idealism. *Arthur Schlesinger, Jr., "The Lowering Hemisphere," The Atlantic, Jan. 1970, p 87*

fa·ve·la·do (fɑ: ve'lɑ: dou), *n. Portuguese.* a person who lives in a favela; a slum dweller.

. . . one never knows whether a bus driver is drunk or sober, or a newspaper story has any verifiable connection with events, and one drifts away into the dreamy unreality of a Brazilian *favelado* who drank too much *cachaca. Richard Bourne, "The Cruel Continent," Review of "Summer At High Altitude" by Gordon Meyer, The Manchester Guardian Weekly, May 2, 1968, p 10*

Fed, *n. U.S. Slang.* the Federal government.

Professor Lekachman seems to construe a go-slow policy . . . for the Fed as indecision. I offer that there will be no inflation cum recession this year because we have gone slowly. . . . *James A. Sansoterra, Investment Manager, Detroit Bank & Trust, Detroit, Mich., in a Letter to the Editor, Harper's, Oct. 1970, p 16*

fed·a·i (ˌfed ɑ:'i:) or **fed·a·yin** (ˌfed ɑ:'yi:n), *n.; pl.* **fed·a·yin.** an Arab commando or guerrilla. Also spelled FADAYEEN.

Newsmen who had been trapped in the Jordan Intercontinental Hotel . . . told of seeing Bedouins shooting a wounded fedai to death. *Time, Oct. 5, 1970, p 27*

Suddenly a fedayin stepped around a corner from the rear of the house, his submachine gun leveled at them. . . . *Marshall Frady, "On Jordan's Banks," Harper's, Nov. 1970, p 112*

[*Fedai, fedayin,* and *fadayeen* are new spellings used to render the Arabic words *fidā'ī* and (plural) *fidā'īn.* The earlier spellings recorded in dictionaries are *fedayee* and *fedayeen.*]

Feebie, *n. U.S. Slang.* a member of the U.S. Federal Bureau of Investigation.

. . . on their left stands a man in a very dark suit, with very dark tie, very dark glasses, very white shirt, and very bald head; a cop, FeeBie, CIA, something like that. *Bruce Jackson, "The Battle of the Pentagon," The Atlantic, Jan. 1968, p 36*

...Secret Service agents derisively call the FBI men "Feebies." *Time, Feb. 28, 1969, p 14*

[from an irregular pronunciation of *FBI*, probably influenced by the U.S. slang word *feeb* a feeble-minded person]

feedback, *n.* a reciprocal effect of one person or thing upon another; a reaction or response that modifies, corrects, etc., the behavior of that which produced the reaction or response.

Primitives treat things and animals as people, and experience feedback from them. *The Manchester Guardian Weekly, March 21, 1970, p 18*

Outsiders are unable to penetrate the continuing feedback between the [Army Engineers] Corps and the congressional committees....*Elizabeth B. Drew, "Dam Outrage: The Story of Army Engineers," The Atlantic, April 1970, p 55*

Crisscrossing the country (as the saying goes), bringing joy through culture to the masses; testing opinion, acquiring "feedback" about one's subject—so difficult to obtain if you're an inmate of the Manhattan Island Intellectual Internment Camp. . . . *Richard Schickel, "Performing Arts," Harper's, Dec. 1971, p 30*

"It used to be called 'PIGS,' standing for 'Politically Involved Girls,' but they got a lot of feedback from that, so now it is called 'Sisters,' but, in any case, it stars Candy Darling and Holly Woodlawn and those people, and it's the very first major motion picture to probe in depth and *color* the timely question of Women's Liberation," our friend said. *"The Talk of the Town," The New Yorker, May 1, 1971, p 33*

Twelfth in a monthly series of 'open ended' problems featuring feedback from readers. *Edward de Bono, "Playback," Science Journal, Dec. 1969, p 30*

feedforward, *n.* the control of a feedback process by anticipating any defects in the process before it is carried out.

This more "intelligent" type of control is known as "feedforward" as opposed to feedback, and essentially it involves locating the sensor at the input end. *Kenneth Owen, "Instruments, Electronics and Automation," The Times (London), May 7, 1970, p 33*

Consider another and a peculiarly interesting example of feedforward: what you have it in mind to say *before* you have begun to put it into any sort of words. This feedforward can be very definite. It can unhesitatingly reject any and all of your efforts to say it. "No," you note, "that isn't it at all." *I. A. Richards, "The Secret of 'Feedforward'," Saturday Review, Feb. 3, 1968, p 16*

feed-in, *n.* a gathering of people to receive free food.

Even food, modest but nourishing, was provided for penniless but hungry travelers at the two or three daily "feed-ins." *Bill Sertl, "'A Communal Pilgrimage'—Along Canada's Highways," The New York Times, June 20, 1971, p 10*

Feed-ins happen each evening in Queen's Park, when about 100 hippies queue for a bowl of stew, made by the Diggers from food they either scrounged or bought. *The Sunday Times (London), July 23, 1967, p 4*

[see -IN]

feelie, *n.* an art object or medium which the spectator can feel as well as see, smell, and sometimes hear. *Also used attributively.*

Some of the confections are merely art-student capers, the "feelies" for example, where the visitor has to push himself through a narrow gangway of rotating sausages of soft foam. *The Sunday Times (London), April 14, 1968, p 11*

"You see, we asked a hundred and thirty-seven art consumers what they wanted in a work of art," Mr. Laing said.... "Women tended toward feelie things and free forms," Mr. Phillips called from across the room. *"The Talk of the Town," The New Yorker, April 30, 1966, p 35*

► The term *feelies* was first used in Aldous Huxley's *Brave New World* (1932) for a kind of escapist cinema of the future in which spectators could experience the sensations displayed on film with the aid of knobs attached to their chairs. The following quotation alludes to this in the context of a present-day "happening":

...with strobe lights [special lights for fast action photography], sounds, movies, and dancing all going on at once, we approach the "feelies" of *Brave New World. David McReynolds, "New York Letter," Saturday Night (Canada), March 1967, p 11*

feet, *n.* in various idioms:

die on one's feet, to collapse, fail, or break down.

When Rowan and Martin's Laugh In first hit our [British] screens, and before it died on its feet, there soon appeared a number of British imitations of its slick and snappy format. *New Scientist and Science Journal, May 27, 1971, p 538*

Now this most promising of African economies [Nigeria] is liable to die on its feet, even if it does not disintegrate into chaos. *"Britain, Nigeria, and Biafra," The Manchester Guardian Weekly, Aug. 17, 1967, p 1*

vote with one's feet, to show one's disapproval of a condition by leaving or escaping from it.

YAF [Young Americans for Freedom] and SDS [Students for a Democratic Society] combine in opposing the draft, and the 40,000 draft dodgers now in Canada have voted in the ultimate way—with their feet. *Martin Walker, "Looking for a New Utopia," The Manchester Guardian Weekly, March 27, 1971, p 6*

Some [East Berliners] continue to "vote with their feet" by climbing over, digging under or slipping through the Wall. *The New York Times, Jan. 2, 1966, Sec. 4, p 3*

Mr Edward Britton, general secretary of the NUT, said yesterday: "We are afraid teachers will vote with their feet by taking courses worth an extra £152 or £304, and not specialist qualifications." *"'Up to £228' Lost in Teachers' Pay Anomalies," The Times (London), Jan. 18, 1972, p 4*

fem, *adj. U.S. Slang.* effeminate.

Today's homosexual can be open ("come out") or covert ("closet"), practicing or inhibited, voluntary or compulsive, conscious or unaware, active or passive, manly ("stud") or womanly ("fem"). The difference between unconscious willingness and conscious unwillingness has thinned. Now the homosexual's variations are seen as such that he may act homosexually and not *be* homosexual, or be gay only off and on. *Faubion Bowers, "Homosex: Living The Life," Saturday Review, Feb. 12, 1972, p 24*

[probably an extended use of *fem, femme,* slang for female or feminine, from French *femme* woman]

Fem Lib or **Femlib,** *n.* another name for WOMEN'S LIB.

Jenkins loves the hooting and hollering and bashings and splatters of college football, Fem Libs be damned. *Larry L. King, Review of "Saturday's America" by Dan Jenkins, Harper's, Jan. 1971, p 95*

Should the conditions of Femlib take over, the cultural

fallout will be stupendous. *Fred Saidy, "Open Letter to Women's Lib," The New York Times, Nov. 11, 1970, p 45*

femto-, a prefix meaning one quadrillionth (10⁻¹⁵) of any standard unit in the international meter-kilogram-second system of measurements (SI UNIT).

There are international agreements about names and prefixes to be used, and it does not help understanding if in one line the authors adhere to the adopted usage (pg for picogram) and then in another call a femtogram (fg) an Emich. *L. Marton, "Identification Guide," Review of "The Particle Atlas" by Walter C. McCrone, Ronald G. Draftz, and John Gustav Delly, Science, May 24, 1968, p 872*

[from Danish *femten* fifteen]

fer·ro·pseu·do·brook·ite (ˌfer ouˌsuː douˈbrukˌait), *n.* a lunar form of the mineral pseudobrookite (a titanium iron oxide) brought back to earth by the crew of Apollo 11. See also KREEP.

Three new minerals were found in the lunar rocks. They are pyroxmanganite, ferropseudobrookite, and a chromium-titanium spinel, and they differ only in detail from terrestrial minerals. *S. K. Rincorn, "Lunar Dust," Science Journal, May 1970, p 29*

fertility drug, a drug that combats infertility in women by stimulating ovulation. See, for example, CLOMIPHENE.

The "fertility drugs" which have been so much in the news in recent years consist of FSH [follicle-stimulating hormone] or LH [luteinizing hormone] (or their analogues). *Graham Chedd, "Triggers of the Brain," New Scientist, Jan. 29, 1970, p 201*

Fertility drugs are useful when infertility is caused by failure of the woman's body to produce an egg each month that is capable of being fertilized. Failure to ovulate accounts for 20 per cent of infertility cases. *Jane E. Brody, "Multiple Births: How to Have a Baby or Nine," The New York Times, June 20, 1971, p 7*

fe·tol·o·gist (fiːˈtɑl ə dʒist), *n.* a specialist in fetology.

By being able to monitor growth and development continuously, fetologists would be able to catch, and perhaps treat, sickness that occurs in the natural womb but does not show up until after birth. *Edward Grossman, "The Obsolescent Mother," The Atlantic, May 1971, p 48*

fetology, *n.* the medical study of the growth, development, and diseases of fetuses.

In what amounts to a quiet medical revolution, a new specialty called fetology is being created, and with it a new breed of doctor whose main concern is caring for unborn patients. His art is clearly in an early stage, but he is learning fast. In little more than a decade he has gone far beyond determining the sex of the unborn infant—already a relatively simple task—into considerably more complex and revealing procedures. *Joseph R. Hixson, The New York Times, Jan. 9, 1967, reprinted from McCall's, Jan. 1967*

...researchers...have been devising ways to save babies when a woman's natural machinery fails and the fetus is born too soon. This new branch of medicine is called "fetology." *Edward Grossman, "The Obsolescent Mother," The Atlantic, May 1971, p 45*

[from *feto-* fetus + *-logy* study of]

fiberfill, *n.* synthetic fiber or filament used as filling in clothing, pillows, quilts, etc.

The arms alone have burlap, fiberfill, muslin and batting

back to back beneath the velvet. *The New Yorker, Nov. 18, 1967, p 249*

Prices of filament yarns, industrial yarns and fibrefill remain unchanged. *The Times (London), May 17, 1967, p 19*

fiberoptic, *adj.* of or relating to fiber optics.

Hemorrhage from the upper gastrointestinal tract remained a serious problem. Early diagnosis as to site and source, essential to successful treatment, was facilitated by prompt fiberoptic endoscopy, demonstrating erosive gastritis and hiatus hernia as causes additional to peptic ulcer and varicosities of the esophagus. *Joseph B. Kirsner, "Medicine: Gastroenterology," Britannica Book of the Year 1971, p 482*

fiber optics, 1 a bundle of flexible glass or plastic filaments which can transmit light around curves and into inaccessible locations.

Fiber optics have been fabricated from materials that transmit light in the ultraviolet to the infrared region; the frequent dependence of scientific instrumentation on responses in this spectral region should give impetus to using such fibers in the design of this equipment. *Morton Beroza, "Optical Fibers," McGraw-Hill Yearbook of Science and Technology 1971, p 308*

2 the branch of optics using fibers or filaments to transmit light.

Technological progress in fiber optics, especially during the past ten years, has given the engineer an important additional tool for transferring information by means of light. The medical investigator can use a bundle of flexible fibers both to illuminate internal parts of a living body and to return an image or other analytical information. Fibers assembled in the form of plates are surfaced with flat or curved faces for use in photographic or other optical systems or, when fused vacuumtight, in photoelectronic systems such as cathode ray tubes, image converters, and image intensifiers. The initial flexibility of the fibers is advantageous for producing image dissectors and scramblers. Fibers made of luminescent or lasing materials and excited to produce their own radiation are highly efficient in collecting and relaying this light. *G. G. Simpson, Science, Jan. 12, 1968, p 183*

Fi·bo·nac·ci numbers, series, or **sequence** (ˌfiː-bəˈnɑː tʃiː), the continuous series or sequence of numbers 1, 1, 2, 3, 5, 8, 13, 21, 34, 55, 89, 144, in which each number is the sum of the preceding two numbers.

It is interesting to note that since 1963 there has been an association solely concerned with Fibonacci numbers (the sequence each of whose members after the second, is the sum of the preceding two). In the quarterly journal of the association there are published numerous identities involving Fibonacci numbers and there is even a generalized plan to produce these. *Anthony Moresi, New Scientist, March 30, 1967, p 688*

To make a C-major chord, you can play the third note of the octave (E), the fifth note (G), and the eighth note (C). So your chord is made up of notes 3, 5, and 8, a Fibonacci series. *Diane Sherman, "Fun With Fibonacci," Encyclopedia Science Supplement (Grolier) 1970, p 377*

Note that the coefficients of *a* and *b* form two Fibonacci sequences. *Martin Gardner, Scientific American, April 1969, p 126*

[named for Leonardo (of Pisa) *Fibonacci*, a mathematician of the 1200's who first mentioned the series in his book *Liber Abaci*, published in 1202]

fi·bri·no·pep·tide (ˌfɑi brə nou'pep₁tɑid), *n.* a protein substance formed in the process of blood clotting.

The fibrinopeptides of man and chimpanzee have been found to be identical in all 30 of their individual chemical sub-units.... The fact that the genes of man and of the chimpanzee specify identical fibrinopeptides implies that the two species shared a common ancestor comparatively recently [five million years ago]. *The Times (London), Feb. 18, 1970, p 13*

fiche (fi:ʃ), *n.* a card, strip of film, etc., used in indexing or cataloguing data.

Although the PVC [polyvinyl chloride] paper used is only about a third of the thickness of a microfilm fiche (0.002 in against 0.006 in) it is sufficiently opaque to take printing on both sides.... *New Scientist, Dec. 31, 1970, p 601*

There is a strong possibility that a uniform, computer-supported fiche system will be developed over the next few years to prevent gaps from appearing in the records — not to "lose" people, as it were. *Nancy Fox, New Scientist and Science Journal, March 11, 1971, p 529*

[from French]

Fi·del·ism (fə'del₁iz əm), *n.* Anglicized form of FIDELISMO.

...that generation [the young people] is now trying out various kinds of anarchism, Trotskyism, Maoism, and Fidelism. *The Manchester Guardian Weekly, Oct. 10, 1968, p 6*

And there are aging, plodding Communists, holding on because they managed to step adroitly out of Stalinism and into Fidelism. *"Report on Cuba," The Atlantic, Nov. 1966, p 30*

Fi·de·lis·mo or **fi·de·lis·mo** (ˌfi: de'li:z mou), *n.* Communist revolutionary activity in Latin America based on the theories and practices of Fidel Castro, born 1927, Communist premier of Cuba. Also called CASTROISM.

It is too easy to dismiss *fidelismo* with the undoubtedly true judgments that the image of Fidel Castro in Latin America is not remotely as effective as it was in the first year or two of the revolution, and that no government in the hemisphere is under any immediate threat of Communism or of a radical leftist revolution, Cuban style. *Herbert L. Matthews, The New York Times, Jan. 2, 1967, p 18*

...the incident served to underline the widening differences between the traditional Latin-American Moscow-based Communism and the Cuban variety, often referred to as Fidelismo. *David Huelin, "Inter-American Affairs," Britannica Book of the Year 1968, p 436*

[from Spanish *Fidelismo*, from *Fidel* Castro + *-ismo* -ism]

Fi·del·ist (fə'del ist), *n., adj.* Anglicized form of FIDELISTA.

"All of these countries have been inspired by the success of the Cuban revolution", claims Desnoes, an introspective revolutionary who calls himself a Fidelist. *The Times (London), July 28, 1967, p 8*

The apparent solution of his difficulties with the Kremlin has removed the danger of a potentially ruinous split between "Fidelist" and the old-line Communist groups. *The New York Times, April 28, 1963, p 11*

Fi·de·lis·ta or **fi·de·lis·ta** (ˌfi: de'li:s tə), *n.* a supporter or advocate of Fidelismo. Also called CASTROIST or CASTROITE.

...if the *fidelistas* now accept the less revolutionary Soviet approach, Communism, as they have always said, becomes a relatively pallid force in contemporary Latin America. *Arthur Schlesinger, Jr., "The Lowering Hemisphere," The Atlantic, Jan. 1970, p 84*

— *adj.* favoring or supporting Fidelismo.

The colony is British.... At the same time, British Guiana is a part of South America. If it should go openly Fidelista, the whole of Latin America will feel the consequences. *The Wall Street Journal, April 16, 1963, p 34*

[from Spanish *Fidelista*, from *Fidel* Castro + *-ista* -ist]

field effect transistor, a transistor in which the effect of an electric field is used for current amplification.

A newer type of transistor element — the field-effect transistor — has come into use because it has better properties, occupies less area on the chip and therefore is less likely to be spoiled by a point fault. These newer kinds of transistor are produced by the metal-oxide-semiconductor (MOS) technique. *F. G. Heath, "Large-Scale Integration in Electronics," Scientific American, Feb. 1970, p 29*

field-ion microscope, an extremely powerful microscope in which the emission of electrons of positive ions is used to produce a magnified image of the emitting surface on a fluorescent screen.

In the field-ion microscope, it is possible not only to observe the positions of individual atoms on a metal surface at low temperatures, but also to follow the movement of the atoms when the specimen is heated. *New Scientist, July 30, 1970, p 224*

fightback, *n. British.* a return attack; counter-offensive.

Shrewsbury Town staggered Plymouth Argyle with a great second half fightback after being three down. *The Times (London), Nov. 12, 1970, p 15*

Preceded by the Beatles, the Liverpool pop-music group whose reception in New York on 7 February exemplified Britain's fight-back in mid-Atlantic culture, Sir Alex reached Washington on 12 February intent on battling, in his own way, for two threatened British interests. *"History of the United Kingdom," The Annual Register of World Events in 1964 (1965), p 7*

[from the verb phrase *fight back*]

filmlet, *n.* a short motion picture.

Where the Italian visual juke-boxes accompanied records with filmlets of the singer singing, or atmospheric three-minutes of landscape and happening, or a psychedelic play of coloured lights, film makers nowadays build whole feature films on the same principle. *The Times (London), March 10, 1970, p 16*

Students, most of whom borrow their parents' 8-mm. equipment, are required to make one filmlet a week which is subjected by Camiel to scathing professional criticism. *Time, Feb. 2, 1968, p 50*

filmography, *n.* **1** writings dealing with motion pictures.

This important book [*The Haunted Screen*, by Lotte H. Fisner]... is essential for any real follower of the cinema to add to their bookcase of filmography. *The Manchester Guardian Weekly, Jan. 3, 1970, p 18*

2 a list of the films of a particular actor, director, etc.

Citadel Press, for example, has been publishing for

several years now its *The Films of . . .* series, which includes complete filmographies of such performers as Bogart, Chaplin, Bette Davis, W. C. Fields, and, perhaps best of the lot, William K. Everson's perceptive annotations on the careers of Laurel and Hardy. *Arthur Knight, "The Literature of Film," Saturday Review, Nov. 4, 1967, p 51*

3 a book or article dealing with the films of a particular actor, director, etc.

Books about the movies are tumbling from the presses with the frequency of cookbooks: star autobiographies, illustrated filmographies of their careers. . . . *Richard Schickel, Review of "Stardom" by Alexander Walker, Harper's, Nov. 1970, p 130*

filmset, *n.* the set for a motion picture.

And a look at the bars and shops is almost like an Ealing filmset. . . . *Peter Nichols, "Britain's Monument in Malta," The Times (London), Jan. 3, 1972, p 10*

—*v.t.* to set type by photographic composition in which the image of a printing character is taken on film rather than made in hot metal.

The processes through which a filmset book passes from the moment when the author completes his manuscript to its appearance as a physical object are the main feature of the film while attention is also paid to the preliminaries of specification and copy preparation. *The Times (London), Feb. 8, 1965, p 16*

Final Solution, 1 the Nazi program for mass murder of the Jews of Europe. Compare HOLOCAUST.

Why was almost nothing done by the free countries to save Europe's Jewish population from the Nazi extermination machine between 1933 and the end of 1943, when the Final Solution was about nine-tenths completed? *Julian Moynahan, Review of "While Six Million Died" by Arthur Morse, The Listener, May 2, 1968, p 577*

2 Also, **final solution.** a systematic plan for the destruction of any people; genocide.

Objectively, one knew that no one in Lagos [capital of Nigeria] had consciously plotted a "final solution" to the Ibo question, however much the Ibo [an ethnic group in Nigeria] was detested. *The New York Times Magazine, March 31, 1968, p 54*

[translation of German *endgültige Lösung*]

fine-tune, *v.t.* to make fine adjustments in; regulate.

You just push a button to select a channel. And at the same time you get a perfectly fine-tuned picture, electronically. *Advertisement by General Telephone and Electronics, The New Yorker, Dec. 19, 1970, p 14*

Instead of "fine-tuning" monetary policy to respond to subtle or momentary changes in the economy, [Arthur F.] Burns was expected to adopt and adhere to long-range policies. *Norman S. Thompson, "Economy," The 1970 Compton Yearbook, p 231*

No single, central planning agency can fine-tune a diversified modern economy. *Time, March 29, 1971, p 24*

fingerprint, *n.* a distinctive identifying mark, trace, or impression.

Szell's musical memory, his knowledge of style and the composers' personal fingerprints, was quite remarkable. *The Manchester Guardian Weekly, Aug. 8, 1970, p 20*

Each geographic area apparently has its peculiar trace element fingerprint. Boston, for example, has far higher readings for vanadium than San Diego, Los Angeles or Honolulu. . . . *Science News, May 30, 1970, p 538*

When they [molecules] are bombarded by radiation from the stars, they respond in a precise and predictable way: they radiate electromagnetic waves at characteristic frequencies. Detected by radio telescopes, these waves are the "fingerprints" that scientists use to identify interstellar molecules. *Time, June 8, 1970, p 78*

The nuclear "fingerprint" of ancient pottery is an extremely precise chemical analysis of the material in that item by nuclear techniques. *Science News, June 13, 1970, p 570*

—*v.t.* to identify (something) through a distinctive mark, trace, or impression.

"We're now trying to purify the atypical cholinesterase, to fingerprint it, then perform amino acid sequencing to see if we're right." *Joan Lynn Arehart, "How Genes Control Drugs," Science News, June 26, 1971, p 438*

. . . a convenient, foolproof method was devised for "fingerprinting" missiles and other metal objects. In this method a photomicrograph or a replica of the metallic microstructure is used as a positive and unique means of identification. *A. V. Astin, "National Bureau of Standards," The Americana Annual 1968, p 473*

fink, *v.i.* **fink out,** *U.S. Slang.* to back out; retreat.

Naturally, ARENA [a Brazilian political party] dominated Congress and so when Castella Branco decreed that the next President would be elected by Congress, the opposition finked out. *Time, Oct. 7, 1966, p 38*

[from *fink,* *v.i.,* slang for "to act as an informer," from *fink,* *n.,* slang for "informer," originally, "strikebreaker," of unknown origin]

fink-out, *n.* *U.S. Slang.* an act or instance of backing out; retreat.

The cop-out is like a fink-out, only more graceful. It is getting away with a renege. *Jacob Brackman, "Onward and Upward with the Arts," The New Yorker, June 24, 1967, p 43*

Finlandization, *n.* the adoption by non-Communist European countries of a foreign policy like that of Finland, which aims to maintain friendly relations with the Soviet Union.

It would be idiotic to yield to political pressures and start weakening Nato's defense by pulling out U.S. troops just as the Russians have strengthened their forces. The psychological effect might produce the "Finlandization" of a free Europe that had come to doubt both itself and its greatest external friend. *C. L. Sulzberger, The New York Times, April 3, 1970, p 36*

. . . there is a foreign policy called Finlandisation, which allows more independence than Rumania has. *The Manchester Guardian Weekly, May 22, 1969, p 7*

firebase, *n.* a military base established especially to deliver heavy gunfire against an enemy.

The South Vietnamese came out of Sophia, one of their firebases near Tchepone, in a reasonably orderly fashion. *The Manchester Guardian Weekly, March 27, 1971, p 5*

Along the way, the raiders would set up permanent firebases to make sure that the trail was permanently closed. *"The World: Indochina: Blunting a Buildup," Time, Feb. 8, 1971, p 19*

Most of the casualties came at dusk when about 15 122mm Soviet-made rockets scored a direct hit on a bunker at firebase Charlie Two, four miles south of the strip dividing Vietnam. *The Sunday Times (London), May 23, 1971, p 6*

firebomb, *v.t.* to attack with incendiary bombs.

Since 1968 dozens of abandoned slum tenements in the East Village have been firebombed. *Shane Stevens, "Instant Urban Renewal," The New York Times, June 19, 1971, p 27*

In the meantime, attempts to firebomb the floating oil and burn it up were proving as unsuccessful as local efforts to dissolve it with detergents. *Science News, April 8, 1967, p 328*

[verb use of *fire bomb* an incendiary bomb]

fire brigade, *U.S. Military Slang.* a highly mobile military unit organized to handle emergency outbreaks or attacks.

The U.S. is likely to keep two airmobile divisions ... on hand after the other fighting units have been withdrawn. These units will serve as "fire brigades," taking advantage of their mobility to rush to any location where it appears that the ARVN ... is in trouble. *Time, Jan. 26, 1970, p 10*

[extended meaning of the term for a group of fire fighters]

firmware, *n.* the components of a computer that are neither hardware nor software, such as devices for storing data used in programming the computer. Compare HARDWARE, SOFTWARE.

Efforts also were made to transfer some of the functions of software — the programs of instructions to computers — to small, high-speed memories which could operate as "assistants" to computer processing circuitry. Both magnetic and LSI [Large-Scale Integration] memories were investigated for this function, which was given the new label "firmware." *James A. Pearre, "Computers," The 1968 World Book Year Book, p 274*

A modular construction, in which the basic computer consists of a standard box with wiring and power supplies capable of coping with the maximum memory capacity, to which is added the right hardware and firmware for the particular job.... *New Scientist, Jan. 7, 1971, p 27*

first-strike, *adj.* (of a nuclear weapon or deterrent) openly deployed and vulnerable to destruction, and therefore designed only for an initial attack that would reduce or eliminate the enemy's power to retaliate. Compare SECOND-STRIKE.

... the Poseidon [is] effective against hardened targets; it can, therefore, be regarded as a first-strike weapon. *Frank Barnaby, "Technology and the Myth of Deterrence," New Scientist, Sept. 24, 1970, p 619*

— *n.* an attack by first-strike weapons.

This means the 1000 silos will be capable of unleashing a deadly rain of 3000 MIRVs each guided with an accuracy of a quarter mile or less and exploding with the power of one-third megaton.

On such assumptioning, the Soviet ICBMs are certain to be vulnerable to a US first-strike. This may account for the continued deployment of SS-11 and SS-13 missiles on the philosophy that they are intended to provide a residual second-strike capacity should a US first blow be made. *Ralph E. Lapp, "Correcting Our Posture," The New Republic, March 28, 1970, p 14*

first-strike capability, the ability of a nuclear power to attack another power's missile silos with first-strike weapons, thereby reducing or eliminating its ability to retaliate. Compare SECOND-STRIKE CAPABILITY.

The Americans argued that the U.S. is not seeking a first-strike capability that could knock out the Soviet nuclear force in a surprise attack. *Time, Nov. 28, 1969, p 36*

The effect might be a period of dangerous nuclear nervousness, with each side tempted to shoot first if it thought the other was approaching a first-strike capability. *The New York Times, Feb. 6, 1968, p 42*

fish-eye, *adj. Photography.* **1** covering an extremely wide angle of view, usually such that a distorted image is created.

Several of the photographs, all of which are big enlargements, impressively displayed, are visually strong. A few, taken with so-called "fish-eye" lens, are attempts at interpretation to give an impression of the complete environment.... *The New York Times, Feb. 19, 1967, Sec. 2, p 30*

2 using or made with an extremely wide-angle lens.

The 160° "fish-eye" cameras were synchronized to less than a tenth of a second for each pair of eight-second exposures. *New Scientist, March 1968, p 540*

fishify, *v.t.* to supply with fish.

In about a week the Round Pond will be full, as well as fishified, and Kensington Gardens will have its focal point again. *The Times (London), March 18, 1970, p 5*

▶ The earlier meaning of this term, and the only one recorded, is "to turn (flesh) into fish." It was apparently first used by Shakespeare: "O flesh, flesh, how art thou fishified!" *(Romeo and Juliet II.iv.40).*

fish-in, *n.* a protest demonstration in which a group engages in illegal fishing at a particular body of water to force a confrontation with authorities who had banned fishing there.

Fish-ins, as the Duke of Devonshire discovered in Ireland last year when his famous stretch of the Munster Blackwater was invaded one Saturday morning by large numbers of rod-carrying demonstrators, are easy to organise and make a very effective publicity weapon. *Clive Gammon, "Fish-ins in Troubled Waters," The Sunday Times (London), Oct. 24, 1971, p 30*

Marlon Brando came here one or two winters ago to the Nisqually River to fish with the Nisqually Indians in their "fish-in" protest against unfair treatment by the state of Washington. *Mrs. Burton A. Lehman, Steilacoom, Wash., in a Letter to the Editor, The Atlantic, May 1966, p 36*

[see -IN]

fish protein concentrate, a tasteless, odorless, and durable fish flour made by pulverizing dried whole hake and similar species, used as food or as a dietary supplement.

Fish protein concentrate (FPC) is a second approach to feeding the world's hungry populations. FPC is on the verge of worldwide mass production except in the U.S. *Robert L. Davidson, "Engineering," 1970 Britannica Yearbook of Science and the Future, 1969, p 170*

fission-track dating, a method of determining the age of rocks and other geological formations by counting the number of characteristic tracks left by the spontaneous fission of uranium 238 during the lifetime of each sample. The number of tracks is proportional to the age of the sample.

Fission-track dating is direct and visual and has proved to be applicable to many materials and over an enormous range of ages. The critical factor is the uranium content of the material to be dated. A concentration of one part per million — which is common in rocks — provides enough tracks to date an object older than some 100,000 years easily. *R. L. Fleischer, P. B. Price, and R. M. Walker, "Nuclear Tracks in Solids," Scientific American, June 1969, p 34*

flack, *v.i.* *U.S. Slang.* to act as someone's press agent.

Bill Woestendiek, the newsman fired by Washington's WETA-TV because his wife was hired to flack for Martha Mitchell [wife of the then attorney general], has a new job.... *Time, June 15, 1970, p 40*

[verb use of *flack*, slang term for a press agent]

flackery, *n.* *Slang.* publicity; promotion.

There were also slogans minted by a Manhattan advertising agency and mimeographed press releases that smacked of big-city flackery. *Time, May 23, 1969, p 21*

...Belly-Button...happens to be a very funny book. Funny enough, perhaps, to sell well even without flim-flam or flackery. *Maclean's, April 1967, p 110*

[from *flack*, slang term for a press agent + *-ery*, noun suffix denoting occupation or profession]

flag, *v.t.* *U.S. Military use.* to put a flag of special color on a file folder or card to stop it from being altered or processed in any way.

...Wilson was able to order Colonel James D. Kiersey, chief of staff at Fort Benning, to "flag" Calley's records, an Army procedure freezing any promotion or transfer for a soldier. *Seymour M. Hersh, "My Lai 4: A Report on its Massacre and its Aftermath," Harper's, May 1970, p 81*

flak, *n.* *U.S.* **1** criticism; censure.

"... we now have a tough anti-pollution law, and the city is taking a lot of flak because its own incinerators won't be upgraded in time for the deadline set by that law." *Jeff Greenfield, assistant to Mayor John Lindsay, quoted by Nat Hentoff, "Profiles: The Mayor," The New Yorker, May 10, 1969, p 60*

2 exchange of criticism; a heated quarrel or argument.

In spite of the current flak between Mayor Lindsay and Edward Logue, the tough, intelligent, battlehardened former [urban] renewal administrator of Boston and New Haven who was picked to head the state corporation, the potential for the city is unlimited. *Ada Louise Huxtable, The New York Times, May 20, 1968, p 46*

[figurative senses of *flak* antiaircraft gunfire, from the German acronym formed from *Fliegerabwehrkanone* antiaircraft cannon]

flake¹, *n.* *U.S. Slang.* a very unconventional or eccentric person.

For kicks, [skier Jean-Claude] Killy races fast cars and jumps from airplanes; he has tried his hand at bullfighting, and he has a well-deserved reputation as something of a flake. *Time, Feb. 9, 1968, p 34*

He [Dizzy Dean] was a "flake" a full generation before that word came into use, and none of his fun-production exists today. *The New York Times, Aug. 2, 1968, p 36*

[probably from the idea of being flighty or light-headed]

flake², *n.* *U.S. Slang.* an arrest to meet a quota or to satisfy pressure for police action. See the quotation for details.

"An accommodation collar," he [Patrolman William R. Phillips] said, is an arrest, to satisfy superior officers, that is presented in court with such weak evidence that acquittal is assured. "A flake," however, is the arrest, on

known false evidence, of a person for something he did not do. *James F. Clarity, "Members of Panel Find Language is Corrupted," The New York Times, Oct. 20, 1971, p 36*

[probably so called from the flimsiness of the evidence submitted]

flake³, *v.i.* **flake out,** *Slang.* **1** to lose consciousness.

...what is the Greek national drink anyway? – oh, yeah, ouzo, and everybody eventually flakes out. *Bonnie Buxton, "The Unchaperoned Girl's Guide to Europe," Maclean's, June 1967, p 56*

Mr. Michael Nyman, a psychiatric worker at the unit, said that people taking the mixture "flaked out" after having hallucinations. *The Times (London), April 29, 1968, p 2*

2 to get out; leave; disappear.

By the way, both of us agree that *Norwegian Wood* and *Day Tripper* are not undecent. Where did you get that idea? Take our advice: state the right facts or flake out! *Patty Hutcheson and Susan Hutcheson, Fairview, Mass., in a Letter to the Editor, Time, July 15, 1966, p 9*

[the original meaning, still current, is to fall asleep or collapse from fatigue]

flak jacket, a padded jacket with small steel plates sewn in place to protect the trunk of the body from bullets or shrapnel, originally used by air force pilots.

On the corner of Tu Do and Le Loi, in the heart of Saigon, a military policeman in a flak jacket stood with a transistor radio pressed against his ear. *The New York Times, June 6, 1968, p 33*

fla·ko ('flei kou), *adj.* *U.S. Slang.* drunk.

Yet they greeted Harry with a fireside grudging gruffness that said, flako or otherwise, he was another daddy and welcome. *Ralph Maloney, "Intimacy," The Atlantic, Feb. 1971, p 81*

[from the phrase *flaked out* worn out (from drunkenness) + *-o*, as in *blotto, wino*]

flaky, *adj.* *U.S. Slang.* very unconventional; eccentric or crazy.

"Andy is a great guy to room with. He's flaky of course, but not quite as crazy as I am." *The New York Times, March 31, 1967, p 42*

If a kid can't take being in a class, it's pointless to force him to stay. He can get more out of figuring out why he wanted to leave – just as we can now talk to the kid who was punching me and ask why he acts so flaky. *Nicolas F. Hahn, "How to Teach a Delinquent," The Atlantic, March 1969, p 67*

[from FLAKE¹]

flannel, *British Slang.* –*n.* insincere talk or action used to cover up or deceive; bluff; blarney.

The Government wanted the power to put the troops in. The rest was all fairy tale and flannel. *"Docks Dispute: Pledge of Resolute Action to Keep Food Prices Stable," The Times (London), July 21, 1970, p 6*

...scientists are continually studying the effect of these substances [industrial wastes] on marine life, including matters such as the rate of dispersal in the sea. I don't think this is flannel, but I would like the scrutiny to be a bit tighter on the east coast, indeed all coasts. *New Scientist, May 28, 1970, p 436*

–*v.i., v.t.* to talk or act insincerely (about something); to bluff.

Some of the cast, I suspect were flanneling; but there

are two spellbinding performances by Ian Hogg and Pat Hartley. *Irving Wardle, "Electronic Experiment: Theatre Upstairs," Review of "Ac/Dc" by Heathcote Williams, The Times (London), May 15, 1970, p 16*

Where other men were prepared to flannel the issue for the sake of domestic or allied consensus or a quiet life, Kennan was not. *Alastair Buchan, The Sunday Times (London), Jan. 28, 1968, p 53*

flap, *n.* a concentration of sightings of unidentified flying objects in a small area within a short period.

A sharp increase in the total number of the U.F.O.s sighted during the past year has, of course, caused considerable excitement in local flying-saucer circles.... As for 1966, it got off to a very promising start with the U.F.O. flap in Michigan. We talked the Michigan flap over with three local ufologists and found them both elated and alarmed. *"The Talk of the Town: Saucer Flap," The New Yorker, April 9, 1966, p 32*

flappable, *adj.* tending to be excited or confused in a crisis.

As he demonstrated for a nationwide audience while he was being questioned by newsmen after the assassination attempt, Chief Reddin is not easily flappable. A round-faced man with dark eyes, he breaks into a wide, thin smile every few minutes, under normal circumstances. *The New York Times, June 6, 1968, p 21*

[back formation from *unflappable*]

flash, *v.i.* *U.S. Slang.* **1** to experience the effects of a psychedelic drug.

... if they [drug addicts] are not stoned out of their skulls or have not flipped or flashed or freaked out, they rap about the people over thirty who have ruined their lives.... *Jean Stafford, "Books," The New Yorker, Dec. 5, 1970, p 218*

2 Usually, **flash on.** to appreciate immediately; understand quickly.

"I really flashed on that song." *Time, Aug. 17, 1970, p 32*

If you "dig" something, you "flash on it," "turn on," "get into it." *Sara Davidson, "Rock Style: Defying the American Dream," Harper's, July 1969, p 60*

flashback, *n.* the recurrence of a hallucination originally experienced under the influence of a hallucinogenic drug.

This decline [in the use of LSD] has been due, in part, to the bad "trips" that terrified many users, the frequency of disturbing "flashbacks," and the prolonged anxiety states and psychotic reactions that were experienced. *Sidney Cohen, "Narcotics and Hallucinogens," The Americana Annual 1970, p 486*

[extended sense of the literary and motion-picture term for a return to an earlier occurrence in the midst of a chronological sequence of events]

flash-cook, *v.t.* to cook by a very short exposure to intense heat, such as infrared radiation.

Dairy Custard is the first test of a new technology called aseptic canning, which gives a fresher tasting product because cans are flash-cooked for six seconds rather than sterilised for 60 minutes. *The Sunday Times (London), July 4, 1971, p 38*

flashcube, *n.* a small disposable plastic cube containing a flashbulb on each of four sides that revolve into place as a photograph is taken.

Flashbulbs were being partly replaced by flashcubes, which were basically four bulbs in expendable reflectors,

the cube turning after each shot. *Victor G. C. Blackman, "Photography," Britannica Book of the Year 1970, p 615*

flash-forward, *n.* a motion-picture or literary technique, in which a scene of a future event is given ahead of its occurrence in a chronological sequence.

The hero . . . is killed in a flash-forward at the start of the story, and the movie that follows is a sort of drowning man's vision of everything that was ever dear to him. *Penelope Gilliatt, "The Current Cinema," Review of Claude Sautet's "The Things of Life," The New Yorker, Sept. 5, 1970, p 64*

Using flash-back and flash-forward from these prison reflections, Dennis Potter slowly built a believable picture of a complex personality. *Michael O'Donnell, "Voyeur," New Scientist and Science Journal, Dec. 23, 1971, p 229*

[patterned after *flashback*]

flat water, a lake or other similar body of water without turbulence and current.

They [canoemen] read the journal of the American Whitewater Affiliation. To them, a lake is not a lake but "flat water." *John McPhee, "The Sporting Scene," The New Yorker, March 21, 1970, p 128*

fleshette, *n.* one of a spray of darts exploded as an antipersonnel weapon.

In Vietnam there was added yet a third shell, the canister round, a blunt-nosed bullet which exploded on impact and distributed 9800 "fleshettes," which look like little roofing nails with barbs on the end; the canister round was for use against people, or personnel. *Ward Just, "Soldiers," The Atlantic, Nov. 1970, p 63*

[alteration (influenced by *flesh*) of *fléchette* a small dart-shaped projectile, from French]

flesh-printing, *n.* an electronic tracing or recording of the protein patterns found in the flesh of fish to help identify and study them.

Scientists and wildlife officials in Ohio are developing a method of electronic "flesh-printing" to help trace the migration patterns of fish. By making pictures of the protein patterns in walleye pike fillets, they hope to match the fish with their birth waters and thereby make it easier to chart, control and increase the walleye population. *William K. Stevens, The New York Times, July 16, 1968, p 36*

flightworthy, *adj.* capable of flight or of being used in flight.

. . . Shepard underwent surgery, and examination by National Aeronautics and Space Administration physicians found his condition flightworthy. *Science News, May 31, 1969, p 527*

But "a considerable amount of development is still necessary before these sensors become production, flightworthy hardware". *The Times (London), March 20, 1970, p 33*

flip, *v.i.* Often, **flip out.** *Slang.* to lose one's mind; go crazy.

"He goes to Notre Dame and that's all right, but he mustn't even hear about Chartres. Sheila, you've flipped." *George P. Elliott, "Tourist and Pilgrim" (a short story), Harper's, April 1968, p 71*

Kingsley Hall [is] an anti-hospital in London where "people who flipped out, or near to it, could stay and go through whatever they had to go through without drugs, electric shocks, or other psychiatric hocus pocus." *The Manchester Guardian Weekly, April 18, 1970, p 15*

[shortened from the slang expression *flip one's lid*]

flip chip, a microcircuit chip with an adhesive pad for fastening the chip to other components.

The technique has lately been used to bond transistor "flip chips" on to thin film patterns deposited upon glass or ceramic substrates to produce a versatile kind of hybrid micro-circuitry. *New Scientist, March 10, 1966, p 623*

flipping, *adj. Slang.* (used as a mild intensive) confounded; blooming.

"You seem to think you're in a flipping hotel, not in a hospital." *Mary Wood, "A Disregard For Human Dignity," The Times (London), Sept. 21, 1970, p 7*

If private business is so much more efficient than any Government agency why don't we farm out the whole flipping government operation to some private business? *Cloyd E. Suddoth, The Wall Street Journal, March 4, 1965, p 12*

flip side, 1 the back or second side of a phonograph record, especially the one with the recording of lesser importance.

On the flip side she sings "Where Have All the Flowers Gone?" Her voice is pleasant but not unusual; she sounds like the girl next door. *Sunday Telegraph (London), March 8, 1964, p 12*

2 *Transferred sense.* opposite number; counterpart.

Barbra's [Barbra Streisand's] marked resemblance to Fanny [Brice] is more than nasal. She is the flip side of Cinderella—the homely girl who made it. *"Cinema," Review of "Funny Girl," Time, Oct. 4, 1968, p 63*

float, *n. British.* a sum of small change with which a shopkeeper, tradesman, etc., begins the day's work.

"What's that, then?" I asked, pointing at the drawer. "That's my float," she grunted. "I'm not parting with that". *The Sunday Times Magazine (London), March 26, 1972, p 63*

floater, *n.* another name for FLOATING VOTER.

"To get a person to switch takes a little something extra," he added, noting that only about one in six are "floaters," ones who will switch. *The New York Times, July 2, 1968, p 64*

floating voter, a voter who is not committed to any political party, candidate, or issue; an undecided voter. Also called FLOATER. See also DON'T-KNOW.

What Harold [Wilson] is after is the floating voter. . . . The only other obvious course, meanwhile, is to win the floater's respect by getting tough with the unions, and by securing a balance of payments surplus. *Punch, April 23, 1969, p 587*

floor-through, *n. U.S.* an apartment that takes up an entire story of a building.

The trust she came into at twenty-one allowed her to live in a large floor-through, to decorate it, and to give dinner parties. *Edward Grossman, "In Pursuit of the American Woman," Harper's, Feb. 1970, p 48*

flower child, a young hippie carrying a flower as a symbol of love.

. . . *The Joshua Tree,* by Robert Cabot. It is about a meeting in the Mojave Desert of a rich old desert rat from the lost frontier, and a sort of psychedelic flower-child from California. *John Thompson, Review of "The Joshua Tree" by Robert Cabot, Harper's, Sept. 1970, p 96*

flower people, flower children.

This is the London of our day, Carnaby Street costumes,

flower people, pot, pop art and promiscuity. *John Hemmings, The Listener, Dec. 19, 1968, p 833*

"You see, I think the hippie type of dropping out is wrong," Father Kirk was saying. "I don't think you should stress the value of that type of dropping out. The flower people's dropout was always narcissistic, sensation-centered, passive." *Francine du Plessix Gray, "A Reporter At Large," The New Yorker, Jan. 25, 1968, p 66*

flower power, a slogan used by flower children, modeled on the term BLACK POWER.

. . . it soon became obvious that few hippies cared at all for the difference between political left and right, much less between the New Left and the Old Left. "Flower Power" (their term for power of love), they said, was nonpolitical. *Hunter S. Thompson, "The Hippies," 1968 Collier's Encyclopedia Year Book, p 79*

As they walked by to pick up their diplomas, many of the girls handed Mr. Lindsay a daisy or carnation and whispered: "Flower power." *Richard Reeves, The New York Times, June 3, 1968, p 33*

Well, perhaps not drugs, though it would not be hard to find support in the gospels for the Young Liberal doctrine "Make love not war," and perhaps even for flower power, if palms are allowable as flowers. *Christopher Driver, The Manchester Guardian Weekly, Aug. 31, 1967, p 12*

flu·er·ic ('flu: ər ik), *adj.* another word for FLUIDIC.

So far this "flueric" system has been tested only on a small scale, but Carl J. Campagnuolo and Allen B. Holmes seem to foresee no insurmountable difficulties. *Fred Wheeler, "Fluidics in the Air," New Scientist, May 16, 1968, p 351*

[from Latin *fluere* to flow + English *-ic* (adj. suffix)]

fluid fuel, liquid, gas, and chemical fuels collectively.

Throughout the world fluid fuels are replacing solid fuels because their technical advantages in transport, handling, storage, processing and use have a large monetary value. *The Times (London), April 22, 1970, p 26*

fluidic, *adj.* using the interaction of fluid streams of gas, air, or liquid to perform functions of instrumentation, control, etc., which would otherwise be performed by purely mechanical or electrical mechanisms. Also, FLUERIC.

The signal in fluidic devices is carried by the flow of a liquid, just as the signal in electronic circuits is carried by the flow of the electrons. . . . a fluidic device is not disturbed, as is an electrical device, by cold, heat, radiation, or minor vibrations. Fluid circuits can thus work in places where electronic circuits cannot, such as inside nuclear reactors and in the heart of a jet. *Foster P. Stockwell, "Fluid Devices Come of Age," The World Book Science Annual 1968, p 311*

fluidics, *n.* the science or technology of using fluid streams or fluidic devices instead of purely mechanical or electrical mechanisms to perform functions of instrumentation, the control of machinery, the processing of information, etc. *Also used attributively.*

. . . fluidics engineers are now thinking more in terms of integrating their devices into the whole system of operating a process or machine, rather than just mimicking electronic logic with fluids. *"Fluidics Digs In," New Scientist, March 26, 1970, p 612*

171

flukicide, *n.* a chemical substance that kills parasitic flatworms or flukes.

There has also been improvement in flukicides, while diethylcarbamazine has controlled parasitic bronchitis in cattle and sheep. . . . *Sam Hignett, "Control Achieved in Wide Range of Animal Diseases," The Times (London), Nov. 9, 1970, p VIII*

[from *fluke* + *-icide* killer, as in *germicide, herbicide*]

fluor·a·cet·a·mide (ˌflur ə'set ə,maid), *n.* the amide of fluoroacetic acid, used in Great Britain as a pesticide.

There are already sufficient safeguards that insist that such poisons as zinc phosphide and fluoracetamide are only used by trained pest control staff so there is little risk of them inflicting casualties among people. *New Scientist and Science Journal, June 17, 1971, p 714*

fluorescent, *adj.* of bright or glowing appearance.

Presently, a woman entered, a brown gamine with a certain look of money about her, like a faint shimmer along her limbs. She was already a trifle awash, on the arm of a pretty, perfumed, fluorescent youth whom she introduced to Fawzi by his first name and sang, "Isn't he beautiful?" *Marshall Frady, "An American Innocent in the Middle East," Harper's, Oct. 1970, p 72*

—*n.* a fluorescent light.

There [on Wall Street], mid the canyons of cold steel and glass . . . the plucky Californian [Nixon] worked hard and long under flickering fluorescents until he had achieved those legal and financial victories that were to prepare him for the presidency. *Edward Sorel, "The Richard M. Nixon Library," The Atlantic, Feb. 1971, p 86*

flu·o·res·cer (ˌflu: ə'res ər), *n.* a chemical substance which absorbs ultraviolet radiation and emits it in the form of visible light.

. . . what further inducement could be offered to the housewife to buy one brand rather than another? It had to be more than mere cleanliness, and so fluorescers . . . were incorporated in detergents to "add brightness to whiteness". *Margaret Hamilton, "Troubled Wake of the Washday Miracle," New Scientist, Oct. 16, 1969, p 122*

Fluorescers are molecules which absorb ultraviolet radiation, passing to an unstable high-energy level in the process, and emit visible light when they return to the stable state. *Martin Sherwood, "Film: Fluorescers," New Scientist and Science Journal, June 3, 1971, p 593*

fly-cruise, *n.* a pleasure cruise in which air travel is used to reach the cruise ship's port of embarkation and to return from the port of landing.

How much baggage am I allowed to take on a fly-cruise? Usually a little more than the regular airline allowance. But as every cruise differs on this point it is essential to check at the time of booking. There is, of course, no limit on traditional port-to-port cruises. *The Sunday Times (London), Oct. 19, 1969, p 63*

—*v.i.* to go on a fly-cruise.

The concept of fly cruising is, and was then, a familiar one, and some might say that Lord Mancroft was merely extending the idea to its logical conclusion, opening the cruise to a wider market. *John Carter, "Travel: Flying Out to the Nautical Carousel," The Times (London), Dec. 19, 1970, p 18*

flying squad, any highly mobile group organized for special tasks.

One approach is to equip and staff special ambulances as mobile coronary care units expressly for heart attack patients. . . . Such ambulance teams, called "flying squads," have now been introduced in many major Russian cities. *Bernard Lown, "Intensive Heart Care," Scientific American, July 1968, p 26*

. . . Alderman Frederick Hall, chairman of the education committee, said that one of the points brought up was a suggestion that a "flying squad" of teachers be set up to help schools where the staff problems were greatest. *The Times (London), Jan. 12, 1967, p 3*

▶ This term has long been used in Great Britain as the name of a police squad trained and equipped for rapid pursuit.

flypost, *v.t. British.* to post with bills or notices in haste, especially to avoid detection.

. . . someone has flyposted the area with yellow stickers reading "Jesus commands, Love one another." *The Sunday Times (London), Aug. 24, 1969, p 4*

[probably from the phrase "to post on the fly"]

FOBS (fɑbz), *n.* acronym for *Fractional Orbital Bombardment System,* a nuclear-weapon system in which warheads are delivered to targets on earth from an orbiting space vehicle in order to escape detection by conventional radar. Compare MOBS.

They [the Russians] sent aloft a giant SS-9 rocket, apparently carrying as its payload a mockup of an FOBS . . . , or space bomb, which could release its deadly cargo on virtually any terrestrial target. *"Soviet Union: Moscow's Better Mousetrap," Time, Oct. 12, 1970, p 33*

German substitutes often tend to be tongue-twisters, such as "atombombensatellitensystem" for fractional orbital bombardment system. Like their American colleagues, defense experts here simply call it "fobs." *The New York Times, Dec. 3, 1967, p 21*

In midsummer and late September the Soviet Union launched and recovered two FOBS, marking new tests of this vital system, which is capable of delivering nuclear bombs from outer space. *Flint O. DuPre, "Rockets and Missiles," 1971 Collier's Encyclopedia Year Book, p 465*

fo·co ('fou kou), *n.* a small guerrilla center radiating revolutionary activity throughout a country.

By going over to the counter-attack on the other hand, it [the guerrilla unit] catalyzes the people's energy and transforms the *foco* into a pole of attraction for the whole country. *Régis Debray, "Revolution in the Revolution?" Saturday Review, Aug. 24, 1968, p 18*

. . . the foco theory has never been disproved. The most serious criticism is that it does not necessarily bring warring revolutionary factions to coalesce around it. This was undoubtedly achieved by Castro's foco in the Sierra Maestra, but the experience has not been paralleled since. *The Manchester Guardian Weekly, May 23, 1970, p 19*

[from Spanish, focus]

fogbroom, *n.* a device to thin or disperse fog.

He [Wesley Bellis, of the New Jersey Department of Transportation] set up a research group, which finally evolved a "fogbroom," a 30-in. by 48-in. aluminum frame strung with a half mile of nylon thread and rotated at 86 r.p.m. by a base-mounted motor. *Time, July 14, 1967, p 38*

Foggy Bottom, an informal name for the U.S. State Department, often used with humorous or mocking intent in allusion to the supposed fogginess of its official statements or policies.

The promotion fight is merely one more front in Passport Director [Frances] Knight's longer, wider war. A Christmas card she mailed out last winter was a two-page tirade against her Foggy Bottom enemies. *Time, Oct. 19, 1970, p 17*

And so, while I may sound critical, my purpose is to shed some light on what goes on in the labyrinths of Foggy Bottom, and try to stimulate some concern about how to induce qualified and talented people to go to work for their government and help formulate and carry out an intelligent foreign policy. *William Attwood, "The Labyrinth in Foggy Bottom, A Critique of the State Department," The Atlantic, Feb. 1967, p 45*

[*Foggy Bottom* was originally a regional name applied to Hamburgh, a town which became part of Washington, D.C., and especially to its swampy southern portion with noxious nighttime fog. Later government buildings, including the headquarters of the State Department, occupied some of this area.]

fo·late ('fou,leit), *adj.* of or relating to folic acid, a constituent of the vitamin B complex.

. . . folate deficiency constitutes a considerable problem both in the U.S. and in the United Kingdom. It is particularly serious among alcoholics, . . . and the poor, especially those who are elderly and tend to neglect their meals. *Margaret Markham, "Foods and Nutrition," 1970 Britannica Yearbook of Science and the Future, 1969, p 252*

Drugs given to prevent epileptic seizures produce a certain degree of mental deterioration because they lower the level of folate chemicals in the patients' blood. Giving the patient folic acid will raise the folate level, but it also depresses the level of vitamin B-12, and depressing the B-12 precipitates convulsions. *Science News, July 11, 1970, p 35*

[from *fol*ic acid + *-ate* (adj. suffix)]

folkie, *n. Slang.* a folk singer.

. . . there is a minor cult of sensitive adolescent folkies like Tim Buckley and Steve Noonan, for no reason I can discern except that they are probably just like the kids who idolize them. *Ellen Willis, "Musical Events," The New Yorker, July 6, 1968, p 58*

"Pop" singers, disc jockeys, rock 'n rollers, bands, folkies, balladists and others will give free concerts in the open air. *The Times (London), Jan. 12, 1966, p 13*

. . . the bill included Kris Kristofferson, the first out-front early-sixties-type folkie to become a star in five years or so. . . . *Ellen Willis, "Rock, Etc.," The New Yorker, Sept. 25, 1971, p 120*

folknik, *n. Slang.* a devotee of folk songs or folk singers.

She [Mary Martin, a manager of singers] spent nights and Sundays in the company of various Toronto folkniks, including Ian Tyson, who was then designing labels for Resdan bottles. *Susan Dexter, Maclean's, April 2, 1966, p 21*

[see -NIK]

folk rock, a type of rock 'n' roll music with elements of folk-song melody and lyrics.

Musical mergers have bred mixtures that all but defy Mendel's law. Groups like Peter, Paul and Mary, and Simon & Garfunkel practice folk rock. . . . In such groups, the influence of classical has brought about blends of jazz and rock rhythms with composers as diverse as Satie and Bach. *Time, Jan. 12, 1970, p 39*

. . . the Byrds popularized folk rock, infusing a steady, driving rhythm into four-part harmonies overdubbed several times, electrified folk guitar picks and strums, and a steady, straight time bass line. *Ellen Sander, "Pop in Perspective: A Profile," Saturday Review, Oct. 26, 1968, p 82*

folk-rocker, *n.* a folk-rock musician.

At first glance, [Rudolph] Serkin looks more like a folk-rocker than he does like a concert pianist. His hair is modishly shaggy, his dress casually disheveled, his talk typically teen. *Time, Feb. 24, 1967, p 50*

folksay, *n.* the traditional speech and sayings of a people or social group.

Carl Sandburg . . . fashioned the speech, history, and folkways of the Midwest—what he called "folksay"—into a sparse, lean, rhythmic, free verse mixture of harsh beauty and delicate sensibility. *C. Hugh Holman, "Sandburg, Carl (August)," The Americana Annual 1968, p 587*

All jazz folksay, like all the anecdotal fragments of our literature, have become part of what we hand on to children and to older human beings who need to be educated or oriented. *Richard Gehman, "Mid-Month Recordings: 'Mildred'," Saturday Review, Jan. 14, 1967, p 105*

food science, the technical study of the preparation and processing of foods (sometimes including the science of nutrition and dietetics).

Designed primarily for students of home economics, catering and nutrition and what has in recent years been called food science, it is well suited to its purpose and demonstrates what good teachers who understand their subject can achieve. *Magnus Pyke, "Advancing Food Science," Review of "Food Science—a Chemical Approach" by B. A. Fox and A. G. Cameron, New Scientist and Science Journal, April 29, 1971, p 280*

Professor Alastair Frazer, who holds numerous posts in food-science and sits on the Health Ministry's own committee on drug-safety, declared that "chronic vitamin deficiency has never before been investigated or recognised as a disease." *The Sunday Times (London), May 5, 1968, p 1*

food stamp, a stamp issued by the U.S. government to recipients of welfare and unemployment benefits to purchase food.

My fellow Jerseyan, Melvin James Suplee (letter Oct. 18) has taken an angry pen in hand to protest the issuance of food stamps to General Motors strikers who desire to feed their families. "Outrageous," he says, for taxpayers to subsidize men on strike. *Joel R. Jacobson, Director of Community Relations of the United Auto Workers, Cranford, N.J., in a Letter to the Editor, The New York Times, Nov. 7, 1970, p 28*

foot-in-mouth, *adj.* characteristic of a person who "puts his foot in his mouth." See also FOOT-IN-MOUTH DISEASE.

. . . for the editors of Maclean's, charged with the onerous responsibility of selecting winners of the magazine's annual awards for achievement in such fields as ineptitude, utter gall, foot-in-mouth comment and plain, old-fashioned bone-headedness, it has been a difficult year. *Maclean's, Jan. 1968, p 1*

Treasury Secretary David Kennedy is becoming an increasing source of embarrassment to the Nixon Administration. His chronic foot-in-mouth habits, which are costly in terms of both dollars and prestige, began to be revealed the moment that he was appointed. *Time, Oct. 17, 1969, p 62*

foot-in-mouth disease, the habit or condition of

173

saying something awkward or embarrassing, that is, "putting one's foot in one's mouth." Compare DONTOPEDALOGY.

President Nixon's latest onset of foot-in-mouth disease unfortunately came just as the American Trial Lawyers' (barristers) Association was about to hold its annual meeting in Miami. . . . [The lawyers] unanimously agreed that calling any man guilty who is still sitting in the prisoner's box was "a very serious error." *Alistair Cooke, "Last Post," The Manchester Guardian Weekly, Aug. 15, 1970, p 5*

[formed as a pun on the technical term *foot-and-mouth disease*]

footpad, *n.* one of the cushioned or padded feet of a soft-landing spacecraft.

Extension is activated by a switch in the LM [lunar module]. . . . The footpads, about 37 inches in diameter, are made of 2 layers of spun aluminum bonded to an aluminum-honeycomb core. *Steven Moll, "The Flights of Apollos 8 and 9," Encyclopedia Science Supplement (Grolier) 1969, p 327*

The vehicle [an experimental lunar flying platform] will stand and land on four struts equipped with shock-absorbing devices and broad footpads similar to those on the LM. *Science News, Nov. 29, 1969, p 497*

footwell, *n.* the hollow space containing the accelerator, foot brake, etc., at the driver's feet in a motor vehicle.

Since I tested the car, additional cool-air vents have been provided in the footwells — I certainly found it too stuffy in warm weather unless a window was opened. *John Langley, "Safety Sets a Faster Pace," Daily Telegraph (London), May 17, 1972, p 13*

force de dis·sua·sion ('fɔrs də di: swa'zyɔ̃), *French.* another term for FORCE DE FRAPPE; (literally) force of dissuasion.

France continued to concentrate on development of its *force de dissuasion,* or independent nuclear deterrent force. *Robert E. Hunter and Geoffrey Kemp, "Defense: France," Britannica Book of the Year 1968, p 268*

Even the famous little nuclear *force de dissuasion* must now advance more slowly. *C. L. Sulzberger, The New York Times, July 3, 1968, p 34*

force de frappe ('fɔrs də 'frap), *French.* striking force, especially a nuclear striking force. Also called FORCE DE DISSUASION.

The French government, not pleased by the aggressive sound of *force de frappe,* prefers to call its creation a *force de dissuasion.* The theory behind the *force* is that not even a nuclear power would want to destroy France at the possible cost of the retaliatory death of even a few million of its own people. *Time, Nov. 17, 1967, p 34*

format, *v.t.* to lay out or specify the style or format of.

The signal processor formats the position data for readout in a manner similar to the technique used in the automatic position-determination system for Omega [a satellite navigation system]. *Eugene Ehrlich, "Omega-satellite Navigation System," The McGraw-Hill Yearbook of Science and Technology 1969, p 95*

FORTRAN or **Fortran** ('fɔr,træn), *n.* acronym for *Formula Translator,* a computer language used for writing programs involving scientific and algebraic computations. Compare ALGOL, BASIC, COBOL.

Designed as a basic text in computer programming for chemists, [*The Computer and Chemistry* by T. R. Dickson] presents rules and procedures for using FORTRAN, and shows how numerical methods may be applied to different chemical problems. *Science News, Sept. 14, 1968, p 273*

A computer is no better than the software that controls its operation. The BESM-6 can be programmed in Fortran and Algol, the two universal languages for scientific computer work. *Ivan Berengi, "Computers in Eastern Europe," Scientific American, Oct. 1970, p 107*

found, *adj.* (of artistic works or materials) appropriated from nature or the environment; not fashioned by the artist but taken as found and adapted for their aesthetic value or effect.

Basically, Pop Art is "found" art; its most potent effect is the hallucination of mistaking the street for a museum or the astonishment of Molière's character at learning that he has been speaking prose. *Harold Rosenberg, "The Art World: Marilyn Mondrian," The New Yorker, Nov. 8, 1969, p 168*

Dada has contributed to every new technique employed in this century that it did not actually invent — collage, which is everywhere; its extension, assemblage, which includes junk sculpture, "found" objects and a hundred cousins; the "environment" as well as the Happening; kinetic sculpture, whether motorized or not, and on and on. *John Canaday, The New York Times Magazine, March 24, 1968, p 30*

[abstracted from the term *found object,* translation of French *objet trouvé*]

found poem, a piece of prose rearranged to the form of a poem by breaking down a paragraph into rhythmical units, etc.

"Found poems" aren't a new idea: William Butler Yeats produced one thirty years ago from the prose of essayist Walter Pater. And the opposite process — presenting poetry as if it were prose — is as old as the Bible. *"Scratch a Rebel, Find a Poet: The Unintentional Verse of William Lyon Mackenzie," Maclean's, May 2, 1966, p 22*

fourth market, *U.S.* the trading of unlisted securities directly between investors. Compare THIRD MARKET.

Often talking simultaneously over two telephones — one connected to a buyer, the other to a seller — [Donald] Tomaso arranges direct trades between large institutional investors. He is one of the handful of entrepreneurs who run the "fourth market," so named because it bypasses the more conventional methods of trading securities: the stock exchanges, the over-the-counter market, and the market for listed stocks created by brokers who are not members of the exchanges. *Time, Oct. 26, 1970, p 110*

FPC, abbreviation of FISH PROTEIN CONCENTRATE.

FPC could be manufactured to meet a child's minimum daily protein requirement of ten grams for about one cent. *Edward Wenk, Jr., "Food for a Growing Population," 1970 Britannica Yearbook of Science and the Future, 1969, p 334*

If the consumption of contaminated sea-food or FPC seems somewhat remote, there is still little room for complacency. *"The Unseen Dangers of Oil," New Scientist, Feb. 4, 1971, p 228*

fracturation, *n.* the breaking or fracturing within a mass of rock.

There are several systems for describing the degree of fracturation of a rock. A widely used specification is known as RQD (rock quality designation). This is defined as the percentage of a rock core, usually in total lengths of about 3m (10 ft), naturally intact over lengths of 100mm (4 ins) or more. *Alan Muir Wood, "Faster Cheaper Tunnelling," New Scientist, Jan. 15, 1970, p 100*

frag, *v.t. U.S. Military Slang.* to kill or injure (a fellow soldier or superior officer), especially by means of a fragmentation grenade.

The lieutenant proceeded to make life miserable for the GI. Finally, the GI approached Karabaic and said, "I'm going to frag the bastard." Karabaic argued to no avail. In resignation, he said, "That's murder." The GI replied, "Don't mean nothing." But he hesitated, and as he walked away he handed Karabaic the grenade he had intended to use. *Eugene Linden, "Fragging and Other Withdrawal Symptoms," Saturday Review, Jan. 8, 1972, p 12*

In front-line companies, soldiers tell of "bounties" ranging from $50 to $1,000 being offered to the G.I. who will get rid of a "gung-ho" officer—one who is too eager for combat or too much of a stickler for trifling rules.... Fraggings are more frequent in rear areas, where boredom peaks and morale plunges. *Time, Jan. 25, 1971, p 30*

[from *frag*, short for *fragmentation grenade*, a type of hand grenade used in Vietnam and often employed in fraggings]

franchise, *n.* right to exercise control; jurisdiction.

So they—Robert Lovett, Paul Hoffman, John J. McCloy, the Dulles brothers (who began under the Democrats), William Burden, William Foster, Paul Nitze, and many others—were recruited. Quite a few continued under the Republicans. In time it came to be supposed, not the least by those involved, that such men had an exclusive franchise on foreign policy. *John Kenneth Galbraith, "Who Needs the Democrats?" Harper's, July 1970, p 49*

[extended sense of the term for the exclusive right of marketing a product or service in a particular territory]

fran·chi·see (ˌfræn tʃɑiˈziː), *n.* one who is franchised by a company to operate a retail store, branch, etc.

Visitors at the Start Your Own Business Exposition surrounded the Wonder Bakers exhibit. Samples of baked goods and frozen foods were given to potential franchisees. *The New York Times, Jan. 6, 1968, p 39*

Some may require considerable capital on the part of the franchisee, as in setting up a hotel in the Holiday Inns chain, or none at all beyond one's time in becoming a franchisee of a hearing aid company. *The Times (London), Oct. 16, 1967, p 22*

Fran·co·phone or **fran·co·phone** ('fræŋ kəˌfoun), *n.* a French-speaking native or inhabitant of a country in which French is only one of two or more official languages. *Often used attributively.* Compare ANGLOPHONE.

...the Francophones are worried about the patois spoken by some Canadians and cruelly call it *joual*, to represent the pronunciation in some places of *cheval. Terry Coleman, "Canadian Dream of the Sweet By-and-by," The Manchester Guardian Weekly, Aug. 7, 1969, p 15*

The troubles at Louvain center on insistence by the Flemish activists that the French-speaking or "francophone" section of the university be transplanted into French-speaking territory. *John Walsh, "Louvain: The University Incubates Belgian Political Crisis," Science, March 8, 1968, p 1084*

Mauritius also cultivated relations with France, French-speaking Africa, and its Francophone neighbors. Visits to Paris by Ramgoolam in February and Duval in September cleared the way for Mauritius' entry into associated status with the European Economic Community.... *Philip M. Allen, "Mauritius," 1971 Collier's Encyclopedia Year Book, p 333*

[from French *Francophone*, from *Franco-* French + Greek *phōné* voice, speech]

Fran·co·phon·ic or **fran·co·phon·ic** (ˌfræŋ kə-ˈfɑn ik), *adj.* French-speaking. Compare ANGLOPHONIC.

It should, after all, be remembered that the French not only continue to cherish their cultural, legal and social community of francophonic states, but are actively wooing new recruits such as Quebec. *Professor Thomas M. Franck, in a Letter to the Editor, The Times (London), Aug. 14, 1970, p 7*

Fran·co·pho·nie or **fran·co·pho·nie** (ˌfræŋ kou-ˈfou niː), *n.* **1** the French-speaking countries and communities of the world collectively.

When Gabon's conferring of sovereign attributes on Quebec at a Francophonie conference caused Ottawa to break relations, the Gabonese begged the Canadians to relent on the ground that they were sorry.... *The Times (London), Aug. 5, 1970, p 8*

2 the unification of French-speaking countries and communities into a commonwealth.

Francophonie, a term that emphasizes the common cultural elements in the French-speaking world, has largely replaced the stillborn "French Community" as the ruling concept, but important military and economic links remain in addition to the common culture. *Arthur C. Turner, "Africa," The Americana Annual 1969, p 43*

But the more enlightened among them recognize the value of a more open French-speaking community, and value the recognition of *francophonie* as a link between continents and peoples. *Edward Mortimer, The Times (London), Jan. 5, 1971, p 12*

[from French *Francophonie*]

fran·glais or **Fran·glais** (frɑːŋˈglei), *n., adj.* French containing many English words and expressions. Compare FRINGLISH.

The 1971 edition of the "Petit Larousse" has at last found room for [the entry] franglais. *The Manchester Guardian Weekly, Oct. 31, 1970, p 11*

Franglais permits a Frenchman to do *le planning et research* on *le manpowerisation* of a *complexe industrielle* before taking off for *le weekend* in *le country. Time, July 22, 1966, p 30*

Though her French [his mother's] was not so good as she supposed, and my own regrettably *Franglais*, we used to read the roles to each other, she taking female roles, I the male (the mother-son insults in Britannicus gave us both enormous pleasure). *Colin MacInnes, "French Fire," The Sunday Times (London), May 21, 1972, p 39*

[from French *franglais*, blend of *français* French and *anglais* English]

▶ The term *Franglais* was popularized in the mid-1960's by René Etiemble, a professor of comparative languages at the Sorbonne, especially in his book *Parlez-Vous Franglais?* in which he proposed French equivalents for Anglicisms to stop what he considered a misuse of the French language.

franglification, *n.* the introduction of English words and expressions into French.

Hugely enjoyable and informative survey of the French temper, from *le bébé boom* (which started it all)... to the monster-development of Languedoc and the franglification of language and social life. . . . *"Paperbacks: Europe," Review of "The New France" by John Ardagh, The Times (London), May 30, 1970, p 22*

[from French *franglification*, formed irregularly from *franglais* + the suffix -*fication*]

freak, *Slang.* —*n.* **1** a person who has broken away from conventional society, especially a hippie.

...the use of marijuana is extensive, and the number of freaks—people given to long hair, beads, and joss sticks—grows every year. *Peter Schrag, "Tennessee Lonesome End," Harper's, March 1970, p 66*

Imagine a random segment of two thousand Woodstock Festival freaks cut off and transposed into a vast, dark, rectangular auditorium, lying flat in clusters on long, colored mats or dancing, flailing without reserve (or, often, rhythm) to deafeningly amplified acid rock sounds from a live band. *James Toback, "Longhorns and Longhairs," Harper's, Nov. 1970, p 71*

2 a drug addict.

Parental and official concern, and anger too, is focused in Canada on amphetamine abuse, on the growth of a depression-ridden community of "speed freaks" (methedrine addicts). *Sheila Gormely, "Youth Drug 'Witch Hunt'," The Times (London), Feb. 23, 1970, p IV*

...the Skippy heiress is twenty-two and some kind of pill freak who busts up cocktail parties in New York. *Raymond Mungo, "If Mr. Thoreau Calls, Tell Him I've Left the Country," The Atlantic, May 1970, p 76*

3 *U.S.* an addict of anything; a devotee or enthusiast. Compare HEAD.

...this is a solid book. Something from which the casual moviegoer as well as the dedicated film freak can learn. *Richard Schickel, "Books in Brief," Review of "The Film Director as Superstar" by Joseph Gelmis, Harper's, April 1970, p 107*

I am also a Black Coffee freak, and have been known to drink fifteen to twenty cups in a day. *Raymond Mungo, "If Mr. Thoreau Calls, Tell Him I've Left the Country," The Atlantic, May 1970, p 81*

"I don't get it," confessed the good banker. "My son the bike freak." *Roger Angell, "Sad Arthur," The New Yorker, March 14, 1970, p 33*

"The Press Freaks should do their thing and the Radio Freaks should do their thing to turn people on," one man said, *The New Yorker, Feb. 14, 1970, p 32*

—*v.i., v.t.* **1** to get or make extremely excited, as if under the influence of a hallucinogenic drug.

"They [the Rolling Stones] won't do an encore," one of the crew said. "The kids didn't faint enough." *Sara Davidson, "Life and Letters: Mick Jagger Shoots Birds," The Atlantic, May 1971, p 98*

"A lot of kids from school on the bus were stoned too.... And it was really good for about an hour but then I started to freak. I felt like jumping off the bus.... I thought I was going insane and would have to be committed." *"Turning On: Two Views: A Teen-Ager's Trip," Time, Sept. 28, 1969, p 44*

None of their writing has the force of the classic texts.... None matches, say, those extraordinary paeans to self-disorientation found in Jerry's [Jerry Rubin's] touchstone parable of the Yippies freaking the college newspaper editors.... *Benjamin DeMott, "Looking Back on the Seventies," The Atlantic, March 1971, p 63*

2 freak out, *Slang.* **a** to come or put under the influence of hallucinogenic drugs.

The undergraduates attracted there [the University of California at Santa Barbara] might not be strong on scholarship but they would be... more given to surfing than freaking out on drugs. *Alistair Cooke, The Manchester Guardian Weekly, March 14, 1970, p 13*

Sebastian has a middle-aged leftist assistant (Lili Palmer) who objects to the Vietnam war, and a dipsomaniacal Saturday mistress (Janet Munro), who, in the service of a foreign power, freaks him out on LSD. *The New York Times, Jan. 25, 1968, p 33*

b to experience or produce sensations or reactions similar to those induced by hallucinogenic drugs; make or become extremely excited.

As a matter of fact, it's nonsense to listen to most good west coast rock unless you're prepared to let yourself break out emotionally and just wallow around in the sound, a cathartic procedure that's currently known on the coast as "freaking out." *Hubert Harrison, "The Pop Scene," Saturday Night (Canada), July 1967, p 41*

...Eddie Brigati... was freaking out the teenyboppers with the Cheshire cat grin. *The New York Times, Sept. 8, 1968, Sec. 2, p 34*

... Abbie Hoffman gleefully showered dollar bills onto the floor of the New York Stock Exchange... to freak out the straights. *"Americana: 'The World Is One Big Put-on'," Time, Feb. 2, 1970, p 13*

c to break away from the mores of conventional society, politics, etc.; to change radically.

Kudlow, who is twenty-five, worked for McCarthy in the early months of his campaign, became disillusioned, switched to the Kennedy campaign, and, after the assassination, "freaked out" and joined the S.D.S. [Students for a Democratic Society], because it seemed to be "the only ballgame in town." *Francine du Plessix Gray, "A Reporter at Large," The New Yorker, Jan. 3, 1970, p 37*

freak-out, *n. Slang.* **1** a person who is under the influence of a hallucinogenic drug.

Could it be that, like corn-cobs, wheat plants and bananas, the human seedlings of today are stimulated to loftier heights by the incessant accompaniment, walking, studying, eating and sleeping of their adhesive transistor sets? Have the vast quantities of decibels hammered into their bones by disc-jockeys, pop groups, and hippy-hippy freak-outs violently fertilized their growth buds and sent them shooting early for the ceiling? *"Last Word on Sonic Growth," New Scientist, May 16, 1968, p 329*

2 the action or conduct of a freak-out.

In my favorite bar in New York people theorized endlessly. The one-killer theory, the two-killer theory, the witchcraft theory, the LSD freak-out theory, etc. *Frank Conroy, "Manson Wins!" Harper's, Nov. 1970, p 55*

freaky, *Slang.* —*adj.* of or relating to freaks or freak-outs.

The crowd chanted with Ginsberg. They were of a generation which would try every idea, every drug, every action—it was even possible a few of them had made out with freaky kicks on tear gas these last few days.... *Norman Mailer, "Miami Beach and Chicago," Harper's, Nov. 1968, p 108*

Performance casts Mick as a freaky rock singer who has given it all up and lives in a cavernous house in Notting Hill with two handmaidens, a little girl, some draperies, a few pastel pillows and a lot of dope. *Time, Aug. 24, 1970, p 61*

—*n.* a person who has freaked out; a freak.

... most of the dwellings in the street had been painted in ... odd shades like cream and eau-de-nil, fraught, no doubt, with some underground significance in the secret codes of these peripheral freakies. *Alan Coren, "Shame in the Suburbs," Punch, Oct. 22, 1969, p 660*

free-associate, *v.i.* to say whatever words or ideas come to one's mind, usually in response to some stimulus (used both in psychology and generally).

To me, the whole experience was like watching and listening to a rather brilliant friend as he free-associated with no thought of whether he was making a fool of himself. *The New York Times, May 22, 1968, p 53*

... have the patient lie comfortably on his back, in a dark room, and free-associate while single numerals are projected in colored light on the ceiling. *Martin Gardner, "Mathematical Games," Scientific American, Jan. 1966, p 112*

[back formation from *free association*]

freebie or **freebee,** *n. Slang, Chiefly U.S.* **1** something obtained free of charge; something gratis.

... you can get a free dish of spinach (ugh) if you have a fresh haircut or a free cheese sandwich if you happen to be wearing white gloves.

These freebies and others—a different one each day—are part of a new series of signs appearing in the Horn & Hardart windows. *The New York Times, Aug. 9, 1968, p 46*

... I settled for a pair of freebees to an evening of Off Broadway theatrics. *Woody Allen, "A Little Louder Please," The New Yorker, May 28, 1966, p 40*

2 one who gets or gives something free of charge.

Third, there are the "freebees," the blue-chip gamblers who are transported and accommodated solely on their reputations as gamblers. ... *The Sunday Times (London), Oct. 27, 1968, p 4*

Rhonda ... sneers at the "freebies," girls who charge nothing for their favors. *The New York Times, Aug. 15, 1967, p 27*

[originally an adjective, *freebee* or *freeby*, meaning free of charge, with the endings *-bee* or *-by* unexplained]

free-fire zone, *Military use.* an area in which any moving thing may be fired upon or bombed.

To avoid hitting innocent civilians, most missions are carried out in "free-fire zones" designated by the Vietnamese province chief and kept under strict dusk-to-dawn curfew. *Time, July 21, 1967, p 25*

Incorporated into the design of each house is a mud-and-bamboo-reinforced block that is the entrance to the family's underground bunker. There is usually another bunker outside, which is connected by a tunnel to the house bunker. This is how these people survive in a "free-fire zone." *Ian Adams, "Operation Zippo," Maclean's, Feb. 1968, p 49*

free-for-aller, *n. British Slang.* one that ignores rules and restrictions to gain advantage.

Perhaps the next time the Prime Minister dilates upon the business world of ... private self-seekers with a conscious rejection of the spirit of humanity and social service, speculators, profiteers and free-for-allers, he will allow for a few exceptions. *The Sunday Times (London), Jan. 26, 1969, p 28*

"In the absence of a statutory incomes policy the trade union movement recognises the obvious. The unions are not free-for-allers." *Vic Feather, Trades Union Congress General Secretary, quoted by John Torode, The Manchester Guardian Weekly, April 18, 1970, p 8*

free-return trajectory, the trajectory of a spacecraft toward a lunar or planetary orbit which provides for an automatic return to earth if the spacecraft is unable to enter the proper orbit.

They had to be suitably placed to facilitate a "free-return" trajectory—in which the *Apollo* spacecraft would be able to coast round the Moon and return to Earth without using its propulsion system. *New Scientist, Feb. 22, 1968, p 429*

... reestablishment of a free-return trajectory was within the capability of both the service and the lunar modules' propulsion system. *Wernher von Braun and Frederick I. Ordway, "One Giant Leap for Mankind," The Americana Annual 1970, p 27*

free speecher, *U.S.* a student radical who agitates against the academic and political establishment.

There are some, of course, who'd like to make flag-raising compulsory, which would negate the very philosophy and spirit which gives the symbol meaning. Amongst them might be some "free speechers" who hiss and shout down the expression of opposing views. *R. E. Burlingame, Ann Arbor, Mich., in a Letter to the Editor, The New York Times, July 4, 1970, p 20*

The most ironic fate of all befell Brillo-bearded Jerry Rubin, 30, a former Berkeley free-speecher and now a yippie leader. *Time, Sept. 6, 1968, p 26*

[originally applied to members of the 1964 *Free Speech* Movement on the Berkeley (University of California) campus]

free university, an independent college or university organized chiefly by students to study subjects of interest to them without the usual academic restrictions of grades or credits.

... the so-called "free university," which eliminates the traditional boundaries between students and faculty, one academic discipline and another, the cognitive (knowing) process and the affective (feeling) process. *"Human Potential: The Revolution in Feeling," Time, Nov. 9, 1970, p 55*

The Free Universities springing up all over the country [Great Britain] are important here. For there is no distinction drawn between teacher and taught; ... the process followed is of sharing knowledge in equal partnership and of a mutual and difficult effort to make the vital connections. *Simon Hoggart, "Cambridge Anti-memories," The Manchester Guardian Weekly, Oct. 24, 1968, p 6*

freeze-etching, *n.* a method of preparing specimens for study under an electron microscope by freezing and then fracturing them to show internal structure in three dimensions.

... new methods of specimen preparation have been introduced into electron microscopy, particularly in connection with the technique of freeze-etching. *Ronald Reed, New Scientist, Aug. 21, 1969, p 377*

Branton used a new technique, called freeze-etching, to investigate the lamellas. He first quick-froze isolated chloroplasts and pieces of leaf in liquefied freon and then fractured them. The frozen specimens broke along natural planes of weakness, such as the interface between the surfaces of internal structures. This exposed a three-dimensional face with contours that revealed the surfaces of the structures. *William C. Steere, "Botany," The World Book Science Annual 1969, p 273*

freightliner, *n. British.* a train that carries a large quantity of freight packaged in containers.

The Eastern Region of British Railways said they felt they would be able to maintain all freightliner and company trains, but the London Midland Region had to cancel one freightliner, running from Manchester, Liverpool and Birmingham to Harwich. *The Times (London), June 25, 1968, p 21*

Friedmanite, *n.* a monetarist, especially one who supports the theories of the American economist Milton Friedman, born 1912, who advocates direct regulation of money supply by the government instead of manipulation of taxes, federal programs, etc., to regulate the economy. Compare NEO-KEYNESIAN.

For, although debate has raged passionately in the United States for years between the Friedmanites and the Keynesians, the British Keynesians have been markedly slow to take the Friedman challenge seriously or to respond to it in terms. *The Times (London), March 13, 1970, p 10*

. . . an orthodox Keynesian emphasizing fiscal measures, Dr. McCracken, is balanced by a semi-Friedmanite emphasizing monetary levers, Dr. Burns. *Joseph Kraft, "The Nixon Supremacy," Harper's, March 1970, p 46*

Fringlish or **fringlish,** *n., adj.* English containing or spoken with French words and expressions. Compare FRANGLAIS, HINGLISH, JAPLISH, SPANGLISH.

. . . Professor [Randolph] Quirk of University College, London, pointed out last weekend: "We shall perhaps hear retired colonels in Britain complain of 'Fringlish' . . . drowning the native wood notes wild." *New Scientist, April 23, 1970, p 198*

If they did not watch out, they thought gloomily, they would soon descend to using *fringlish* words like cul-de-sac instead of the proper French term *impasse. Peter Lennon, "Parlez-vous Franglais?" The Manchester Guardian Weekly, April 24, 1969, p 16*

[alteration of earlier *Frenglish,* blend of *French* and *English*]

Frisbee, *n.* Also popularly spelled **frisbee** or **frisby.** a trade name for a small plastic disk sailed in the air.

One of their jobs at Columbia is to chase people off South Lawn, where students like to play football and baseball, throw plastic flying saucers called Frisbees or just lie on the grass. *The New York Times, May 20, 1968, p 25*

My gaze passes beyond this student and through the dirty, mullioned windows to the lawn outside where a group of three seniors spin a frisbee in the spring air. The flying disk moves slowly, an easy target, I'm thinking, like a helicopter. *Stephen Minot, "On Aiding and Abetting: The Anguish of Draft Counseling," Harper's, Sept. 1968, p 50*

In streets all over the town students were gaily throwing frisbies—those fascinating saucer-like missiles, made of light plastic, which travel such a satisfactory distance with so little effort. *The Times (London), May 4, 1970, p 8*

fritz, *v.i.* **fritz out,** *U.S. Slang.* to go out of order; break down.

. . . when the television camera fritzed out on the lunar surface, Astronaut Alan Bean had a moment of atavism. Like any other 20th century man confronted by the perversity of nonfunctioning machines, he whacked it with his hammer. *Time, Nov. 28, 1969, p 18*

[from the slang phrase *on the fritz* in disrepair]

'Fro, *n. U.S.* short for AFRO.

One G.I. summed it up: ". . . The regs [Army Regulations] say you can grow your hair *this* long, but the first sergeant says he don't care what the regs say, because he don't like no black man with a 'Fro." *"South Viet Nam: Soul Alley," Time, Dec. 14, 1970, p 40*

fron·ten·is (frən'ten is), *n.* a Latin-American ball game resembling handball and consisting essentially of jai alai or pelota played with tennis rackets.

Mexico has been the world's leading frontenis power for seventeen years, and in Mexico City alone there are three thousand frontenis courts. *E. J. Kahn, Jr., "The Sporting Scene: The Olympics," The New Yorker, Nov. 2, 1968, p 191*

[from American Spanish *frontenis,* blend of Spanish *frontón* a jai alai court and *tenis* tennis]

frontlash, *n. U.S.* a reaction which offsets or neutralizes a backlash.

In 1964, a widely predicted "white backlash" against the Negro movement failed to materialize. It apparently was swallowed in what President Johnson called the "frontlash" against Barry Goldwater and the fear that he would drop nuclear weapons. . . . *Tom Wicker, The New York Times, Sept. 7, 1966, p 42*

Frontlash from the second Vatican Council, to borrow one of President Johnson's remarkable neologisms, is now being strongly felt among English Roman Catholics. *William Nicholls, Saturday Night (Canada), April 1967, p 42*

[from *front* + back*lash*]

frostbite boating, *U.S.* another name for FROST-BITING.

For frost-bite boating enthusiasts a mouton vest or parka would be heart-warming. *The New York Times, Feb. 9, 1968, p 31*

frostbiter, *n. U.S.* a sailboat used in frostbiting.

We've got everything here from ten-foot frostbiters, for winter racing, to fifty-foot yawls. . . . *Morton M. Hunt, "Profiles: The Inland Sea," The New Yorker, Aug. 22, 1964, p 69*

frostbiting, *n. U.S.* the sport of sailing or racing a sailboat in the winter months. Also called FROST-BITE BOATING.

Everett B. Morris, who died Tuesday at age 67, had fun writing about boats—from frostbiting in Port Washington, L.I., where his funeral service will be held this morning, to America's Cup drama off Newport, R.I., and ocean racing to Bermuda. *The New York Times, Feb. 17, 1967, p 31*

frostbitten, *adj.* coldly impassive; having an ice-cold or frigid personality.

Colonel Richard Meinertzhagen, the subject of this biography, was born in 1878 to a prosperous English financier and his frostbitten wife. *Phoebe Adams, "Short Reviews: Books," Review of "Duty, Honor, Empire" by John Lord, The Atlantic, Aug. 1970, p 114*

[patterned after *hard-bitten*]

frostbound, *adj.* lacking in warmth; frozen.

Relations with France seemed as frostbound as ever, despite the thaw in Guinea's relations with some French-speaking West African countries. . . . *"Organization of Senegal River States: Senegal, Mauritania, Mali, Guinea," The Annual Register of World Events in 1968 (1969), p 329*

froth, *v.t.* to cover or invest with something light and trifling.

The Church of Santa Maria della Salute, whose facade is frothed with baroque winged statues, has been closed, barriers keep visitors at a safe distance, and a warning sign is posted: "Pericolo Caduta Angeli" (in English, "Danger, Angels Dropping"). *Irving R. Levine, "Venice," The Atlantic, Jan. 1971, p 23*

The formula of a headline picture to open the bulletins is also deadening and can sometimes lead to unhappy associations. It seemed wrong to show Komarov's black bordered portrait laced with the teleprinty call sign and frothed up with the newsreel music. *Ian Rodger, "Television," The Listener, May 4, 1967, p 599*

[verb use of *froth*, n., something unsubstantial or of little worth]

frozen frame, a single image held momentarily still in the midst of a motion-picture sequence.

. . . the jump cut in which you see, for instance, a pickle shrinking bite by bite because the intervening film has been cut out; or the frozen frame, when the camera makes its point by stopping and holding a motionless shot of Sophia Western laughing, or a model wearing Supphose. *Janice Tyrwhitt, "What Do You Mean You Don't Like Television Commercials," Maclean's, Jan. 1, 1966, p 38*

frug (fru:g), *n.* a rock 'n' roll dance performed with little or no movement of the feet but with rhythmic motions of the hips, arms, head, and shoulders.

Under the direction of Mr. Fosse, the dancers are first-rate, whether they are mocking the muscular idiocies of the Frug or doing a turn as unwashed and pot-happy worshippers at an open-air church dedicated to the "Rhythm of Life". . . . *John McCarten, The New Yorker, Feb. 5, 1966, p 84*

. . . but the internal movements she had been detecting recently seemed a bit more like those of "a small, enthusiastic elephant dancing the frug." *Patrick Skene Catling, Punch, Aug. 18, 1965, p 232*

—*v.i.* to dance the frug.

. . . people grasped the sense of the youth movement by watching Mademoiselle's College Board members and other young things frugging in mini-dresses at Cheetah. *Marylin Bender, The New York Times, July 25, 1966, p 18*

[of unknown origin]

funabout, *n.* any of various small motor vehicles used to drive about for pleasure or sport.

Beach buggies, those curious bathtub-shaped funabouts based on Volkswagen Beetle components, are all the rage in the United States. *The Times (London), Sept. 10, 1970, p 15*

[from *fun* + run*about*]

fun and games, (often used ironically) playful or lighthearted activity, as at a party.

"There've been a lot of fun and games today," Assemblyman James T. McFarland, a Buffalo Republican, declared during the Assembly debate, "but we still don't have a budget." *The New York Times, April 2, 1968, p 8*

. . . some people said that he [Danny Reeves, owner of a football team] had become too difficult to work with. Danny could not understand that. As he often said, football was, after all, just "fun and games." *Time, Jan. 17, 1969, p 34*

Fun City, a nickname for New York City.

Only New York is different, but Fun City has enough troubles of its own. *Adam Raphael, "Exodus from the Cities," The Manchester Guardian Weekly, Aug. 14, 1971, p 17*

The Bell System is putting on a mini-revue at its business-communications exhibit, which has musical suggestions about how to enjoy Fun City. *The New York Times, Jan. 11, 1968, p 55*

fun fur, a garment made of an inexpensive or imitation fur or assembled furs, usually for casual wear.

The inexpensive items, commonly referred to as fun furs or young furs, were directed chiefly to the younger market. . . . They included rabbit, various types of lamb, raccoon, fox, calfskin, bobcat, bassarisk [a kind of civet cat], and muskrat. *Sandra Parker, "Furs," Britannica Book of the Year 1970, p 369*

At the Fillmore, about three hundred people had entered the hall by seven-fifteen. . . . They wore bell-bottom slacks, blue jeans, turtlenecks, boots, moccasins, capes, fun furs, bush hats, slouch hats, shoulder bags. . . . *Robert Kotlowitz, "Performing Arts: Into the Fillmore East," Harper's, May 1969, p 108*

funk art or **funk,** *n.* a type of pop art created from strange or bizarre objects, usually of a recognizable form, such as a huge toothbrush or a typewriter with finger-shaped keys.

"Funk Art" as epitomised last year in the Museum of the University of California in Berkeley, is an art of systematised irrationality and bad taste. Very much a part of it, and yet a stranger to its more boisterous manifestations, is the sculpture of Kenneth Price. . . . *The Sunday Times (London), March 24, 1968, p 48*

. . . San Francisco's William Wiley is, at 31, an elder statement-maker of the West Coast's cheerfully crude funk art movement. *Time, Feb. 28, 1969, p 41*

Sculptors' work took many forms, from figurative to nonobjective, from "funk" to energy structures. *Victor H. Miesel, "Art," The Americana Annual 1970, p 99*

In the living room, there was this thing floodlit
From up above; a funk-art statue of
A cop in a crash hat. . . .
L. E. Sissman, "N.Y., N.Y., 1970" (a poem), The Atlantic, Jan. 1971, p 49

funk artist, a person who produces funk art.

What they discovered . . . was regional groups with a common outlook, like the West Coast's "funk artists," whose gamy, gutsy assemblages have been shown in many national exhibits. *Time, Dec. 22, 1967, p 32*

funkiness, *n.* U.S. Slang. funky quality.

The Fillmore [a rock theater in New York City], patronized by the children of the bourgeoisie, strives for (and achieves) a certain level of funkiness. *"The Talk of the Town," The New Yorker, Jan. 23, 1971, p 25*

funky, *adj.* U.S. Slang. fine; excellent.

"That's a funky jacket, Kit Carson." *Time, Aug. 17, 1970, p 32*

Kathy [Kathy Buday, an American girl] scattered a handful of pants round the room—pants in different painted fabrics. "Persian, Indian, Tunisian, and this one's funky Marseilles." Everybody laughed. *Ernestine Carter, "Hip, Hip, Hooray," The Sunday Times (London), May 21, 1972, p 41*

▶ Originally a chiefly Negro jazz term:
In current jazz argot, "funky," which once meant malodorous, is a term of final approbation, meaning

earthy, unpretentious, and rooted in the blues. *Nat Hentoff, "Profiles: In the Mainstream," The New Yorker, March 28, 1959, p 47*

furry, *adj. U.S. Slang.* hair-raising; horrible.

...Mr. Conroy misses the whole point of the "furry fear" that gripped America after the murders [involved in the Manson case]. While it's true that the jet-set may have felt vulnerable for the first time, the rest of the country, and certainly the urban dweller, has been in the grip of that fear for at least ten years. *Barbara Hudgins, Madison, N.J., in a Letter to the Editor, Harper's, Jan. 1971, p 6*

fuse, *n.* **have a short fuse,** *U.S.* to get excited or angry easily; to "blow up" easily or quickly. See also SHORT FUSE.

The press is also now on to the fact that [Senator Edmund] Muskie can have a short fuse, and they poke and prod to see if he will explode. *Elizabeth B. Drew, "Reports and Comment: Washington," The Atlantic, April 1971, p 25*

"He's [Hartzog is] very hard on his people. He cracks the whip. And he has a short fuse." *John McPhee, quoting comments about George Hartzog, Director of the U.S. National Park Service, "Profiles: Ranger," The New Yorker, Sept. 11, 1971, p 60*

future shock, a state of stress and disorientation brought on by a quick succession of changes, especially in new standards of behavior and values, in society. Compare CULTURE SHOCK.

What brings on future shock ... is a rate of social change that has become so fast as to be impossible for most human beings to assimilate.... "Future shock arises from the superimposition of a new culture on an old one. It is culture shock in one's own society." *Time, Aug. 3, 1970, p 13*

Future shock, he [Alvin Toffler] says, can make us ill, physically and mentally; it robs us of the power to decide, deprives our children of the roots we took for granted, and it has ruptured marriage. *Edward Weeks, "The Peripatetic Reviewer," Review of "Future Shock" by Alvin Toffler, The Atlantic, Aug. 1970, p 112*

[coined by the American author Alvin Toffler]

futurist, *n.* another name for FUTUROLOGIST.

Some futurists, notably Alvin Toffler, author of *Future Shock* ... argue that TV cassettes will quicken the already bewildering pace of change in American life.... *Time, Aug. 10, 1970, p 40*

Such science fiction writers as Frederick Pohl and Arthur C. Clarke are prominent among the "futurists" who now speculate on the future, and it is difficult to believe that anyone engaged in such speculation for government and industry has not been deeply influenced by science fiction. *Isaac Asimov, "The Art of the Tomorrow Seekers," 1969 Britannica Yearbook of Science and the Future, 1968, p 42*

futurological, *adj.* of or relating to futurology.

The conference he [Arthur Bronwell, dean of engineering at the University of Connecticut] organised in 1959 with the US National Science Foundation, the Engineers' joint Council and many other learned bodies, sparked off a great deal of the systematic "futurological" thinking that was much a characteristic of the 'sixties. *John Wren-Lewis, "Old-fashioned Crystal-gazing," Review of "Science and Technology in the World of the Future," edited by Arthur Bronwell, New Scientist, Dec. 24, 1970, p 562*

futurologist, *n.* a person who studies or makes forecasts about the future developments in science and technology and their effect upon society. Also called FUTURIST.

The coming superpower is not China but Japan which, by late this century or early next one, will possess the largest gross national product in the world. Such is the considered opinion of Herman Kahn, futurologist.... *C. L. Sulzberger, "Foreign Affairs: Japan's Sun Also Rises," The New York Times, Aug. 5, 1970, p 34*

futurology, *n.* the art or practice of making forecasts about future developments in science and technology and their effect upon society.

Even bad futurology is better than no futurology and this book (plus the others which will inevitably follow) will have its uses for anybody attempting to answer such questions as: What has architecture done in the past? What of this is worth doing? How well has architecture done it? Will even a radically restructured architecture be able to continue to do it effectively? If not, how can these things be done? *Colin Moorcraft, Review of "Experimental Architecture" by Peter Cook, New Scientist, Dec. 31, 1970, p 612*

...the liberal high priests of futurology who avoid social analysis and deny the need for a revolutionary transformation of the world are so ineffectual in their prognostications despite their boundless imagination and their disarming faith in the natural sciences. *The New York Times, Aug. 19, 1968, p 12*

The tone is optimistic (is not all futurology?), though all the world's larger wild animals and its natural vegetation will be things of the past.... *Nicholas Guppy, "View to a Death," Review of "Mankind 2000," edited by Robert Jungk and Johan Galtung, The Sunday Times (London), Jan. 4, 1970, p 69*

fuzzbox, *n.* an attachment on an electric guitar that gives a fuzzy quality to the sound. *Often used attributively.*

There's a passage in one old song, "I Could Write a Book," when her voice turns sweetly gruff, an almost exact vocal gloss on modern fuzzbox guitar. *Derek Jewell, "Peak to Peak," The Sunday Times (London), May 9, 1971, p 31*

Screams, electric-guitar fuzzbox flights, cowbell-tappings against The Electric Circus's battery of stroboscopic lights all add up to kicks for the kiddies and footnotes for the ethnomusicologists. *The New York Times, Jan. 19, 1968, p 29*

G

GABA ('gæb ə), *n.* acronym for *gamma-aminobutyric acid*, an amino acid occurring in the central nervous system of mammals.

In mammals, GABA is a compound almost exclusively confined to the brain, where it is present in high concentrations. *New Scientist, July 23, 1970, p 174*

ga·ga·ku (gɑ:'gɑ: ku:), *n.* the classical ceremonial or court music of Japan.

Gagaku means "elegant music"; the term occurs in the *Analects* of Confucius in the fifth century B.C., and the tradition was introduced to Japan during the T'ang Dynasty in the eighth century A.D. *The Times (London), May 25, 1970, p 6*

[from Japanese]

gag strip, a comic-strip without a continuous story.

It [the Chicago Tribune-New York News Syndicate] had just started running a gag strip...based on "Laugh-In" and using black characters and now it was in the market for a continuity strip...featuring blacks. *"The Talk of the Town," The New Yorker, March 21, 1970, p 34*

gai·jin ('gɑi dʒin), *n.; pl.* **gai·jin.** *Japanese.* a foreigner; an alien.

...Mr Price is very much the *gaijin*—the foreigner—among the Chosen People. *David Holden, "Japan Reborn," The Sunday Times (London), Oct. 17, 1971, p 39*

The Japanese are fond of saying that there is a place for every person in their country—but manifestly not for foreigners, who are known as *gaijin* (literally, outside people) and who are discouraged from seeking citizenship or marrying Japanese. *Time, March 2, 1970, p 28*

I also learned that, according to visiting *gaijin*...Japanese bath water is inhumanly hot and impossible to endure. *Margaret Bennett, "Getting Boiled in Japan," Saturday Review, Jan. 20, 1968, p 40*

Galbraithian, *adj.* of or relating to the ideas and theories of the American economist John Kenneth Galbraith, born 1908.

There is a narrow sense, of course, in which corporations are to blame for the environmental crisis: Their products and factories are the direct producers of pollution and, in the Galbraithian sense, their powers of mass persuasion cause consumers to keep buying these products. *Science News, Jan. 2, 1971, p 14*

In the urban ghettos it [black power] calls for parental control of *de facto* segregated public schools...and for rent strikes against profiteering absentee landlords. This merely seems an extension of the Galbraithian principle of countervailing power into areas of American society where people previously had not known, in their poverty and distress, how to look after their own essential interests. *Julian Moynahan, The Listener, April 18, 1968, p 509*

—*n.* a supporter of Galbraith's theories.

By 1959 virtually all politicians in Britain were either Galbraithians or uneasily on the defensive against such of his phrases as "private opulence and public squalor". *The Times (London), Sept. 21, 1970, p 9*

game plan, *U.S.* a carefully planned course of action; strategy.

Now that there are signs of a change in the trend of the economy, it is timely to make a preliminary judgment on how the so-called "game plan"—the Administration's strategy for overcoming inflation without recession—has been going. *The New York Times, Oct. 20, 1970, p 45*

"By George, it looks like Nixon's game plan is beginning to work." *Cartoon legend, The New Yorker, Jan. 16, 1971, p 30*

[originally a sports term for the strategy to be used in a game]

gammasonde, *n.* a radiosonde (a radio-transmitting instrument package carried aloft by a balloon) designed to measure the intensity of gamma radiation in the upper atmosphere and relay the data back to the ground.

In the past two years there has been an increased emphasis on several aspects of antarctic meteorology,...albedo programs, meteorological studies aboard the Eltanin, and the inclusion of vertical coverage through radiometersondes, ozonesondes, and gammasondes. *A. P. Crary, Bulletin of the Atomic Scientists, Jan. 1964, p 29*

gamma surgery, a surgical operation in which gamma rays from pellets of radioactive cobalt are used to destroy cancerous cells, to relieve Parkinson's disease, etc.

Gamma surgery also opens up a new perspective in the surgery of pain. With only a bloodless procedure involved, a patient with advanced cancer can be spared the extra stress of a conventional operation, and could possibly be treated at a much earlier stage. *New Scientist, Dec. 3, 1970, p 377*

gangbang, *n. U.S. Slang.* sexual relations by a group of males with one female.

There were of course those other girls, demented atrocities who lay impassively in boiler rooms, behind schoolyard handball walls, or in the sand traps of the nearby golf course while a group of us would swagger our way through a gangbang....*Jack Richardson, "A Lively Commerce," Harper's, Aug. 1970, p 83*

gangle, *v.i.* to move awkwardly or loosely.

Men who go in for mime belong to a special physical type. They have tall, thin, long-boned bodies with joints made of some substance that combines the properties of rubber and angled steel. Their limbs can't be called gangling because they are controlled so efficiently but they would gangle if they could. *Punch, Feb. 12, 1969, p 247*

181

[back formation from *gangling, adj.,* awkwardly or loosely built]

garbologist, *n.* a garbage collector. Compare SANITATIONMAN.

Sanitation worker, Ronald Whatley, has suggested a new title for workers in his profession—"Garbologists." *The New York Times, Sept. 16, 1968, p 47*

One dustman in court last week called himself a garbologist. *New Scientist, Jan. 13, 1966, p 97*

[from *garbage* + -*ologist,* as in *biologist, zoologist,* etc.; perhaps influenced by Australian English *garbo* garbage collector]

gar·çon·niè·re (gar sɔ:'nyer), *n. French.* a bachelor's quarters.

The outside stairs lead to the *garconnière,* the quarters traditionally set aside for the young men in all Acadian families. *Horace Sutton, "Booked for Travel," Saturday Review, Jan. 8, 1966, p 95*

gar·da ('gɑr də), *n.; pl.* **gar·dai** (gɑr'di:). an Irish policeman or guard.

This [gun-running] alerted the Garda (police) and the Government through the Ministry of Justice. *The Times (London), May 29, 1970, p 11*

. . . for a drive around Kerry, they'd [reporters] follow him [General Charles de Gaulle] in their cars like a pack of hounds, only to be frustrated when the *gárdaí* would block the roads after he'd passed by. *John McCarten, "Irish Sketches," The New Yorker, Oct. 31, 1970, p 128*

[from Irish *gárda* (plural *gardaí*)]

gar·ri ('gɑr i:), *n.* a staple food of Nigeria, made of ground cassava.

. . . garri is regarded by relief doctors [in Biafra] as a mere "filler" without real nutrient value. *The Sunday Times (London), Jan. 11, 1970, p 13*

. . . Biafra's farmers have actually produced a surplus of yams and garri. *The New York Times, March 31, 1968, p 44*

gas, *n.* Usually, **a gas,** *U.S. Slang.* a great pleasure; a delight; a joy.

. . . as black Percussion Man Warren Duncan says, "It's a gas to ride the buses, see all the mountains and the jack rabbits and road runners. And the concerts are wild." *"Music: Prison Records," Time, Nov. 2, 1970, p 66*

gas chromatograph, the apparatus used in gas chromatography.

Complex mixtures of gases are more troublesome to analyse than is immediately obvious—the equipment required is either very complicated and costly, as with mass spectrometers, or very time consuming to operate, as with gas chromatographs. *New Scientist, July 25, 1968, p 184*

. . . the gas chromatograph . . . separates hydrocarbon molecules of different kinds according to their volatility. *Franklin J. Tobey, Jr., 1969 Collier's Encyclopedia Year Book, p 406*

gas chromatography, another name for GAS-LIQUID CHROMATOGRAPHY.

Gas chromatography is a procedure whereby a volatile mixture is separated into its components by a moving inert gas passing over a sorbent. . . . As a method of separating the individual components of a complex mixture gas chromatography has no equal. *F. W. Karasek, "Analytic Instruments in Process Control," Scientific American, June 1969, p 115*

gasdynamic laser, a gas laser in which the mixture of gases is energized by burning fuel instead of by means of electrical discharges. Compare GAS LASER.

A gasdynamic laser theoretically able to produce thousands of kilowatts of infrared light has been developed by Avco Corp. *Science News, May 30, 1970, p 529*

gas laser, a laser that produces its intense beam of light by exciting a tube filled with a mixture of gases, such as neon and helium or carbon dioxide and nitrogen. Compare GASDYNAMIC LASER.

Gas lasers are usually excited by electrical discharges. But this method has limitations, particularly when large volumes of gas are involved. In general, the energy generated by a gas laser increases as the volume increases. *"Gas Lasers Get Excited by Thermal Neutrons," New Scientist, Oct. 22, 1970, p 164*

gas-liquid chromatography, a method of analyzing the chemical substances of a mixture by combining it with a gas such as nitrogen and passing it through a liquid solvent. Also called GAS CHROMATOGRAPHY. Compare THIN-LAYER CHROMATOGRAPHY.

The extracts were . . . run through a gas-liquid chromatography device, a standard instrument used to detect and identify components of chemical mixtures. *The New York Times, March 24, 1968, Sec. 4, p 15*

Gast·ar·bei·ter ('gɑ:st₁ɑr bɑi tər), *n.sing.* or *pl.* a worker in West Germany who has come from another country (mainly Italy, Yugoslavia, Turkey, or Spain) to supplement the labor shortage.

In social terms, the gap between what the Germans call *Gastarbeiter* (guest worker) and his host has remained wide. *Time, June 8, 1970, p 39*

[from German, literally, guest worker]

gat (gɑ:t) or **gath** (gɑ:θ), *n.* a complex rhythmic passage that usually marks the final movement or section of a raga, the traditional Hindu musical form.

A typical *raga* . . . has two or three distinct phases. It may open with a slow, exploratory invocation *(alap),* which gives way to a melodic variation together with a rhythmic passage *(jor),* which, in turn, moves into a rapid flourish of runs *(jhala).* But this may be only an introduction to the second phase *(gat),* which is governed by one of a hundred and seventy-five *talas,* or rhythmic cycles. . . . *Ved Mehta, The New Yorker, Dec. 9, 1967, p 162*

An element of lively humour marked the *gat* when the percussionist, Manik Rao Popatkar, engaged the *sitar* in some brisk rhythmic dialogues with the *tabla. The Times (London), March 29, 1968, p 13*

Mr. [Ravi] Shankar himself is, of course, a prodigious virtuoso on the sitar, and to me the most memorable event of the evening was a *gath* performed by him, with tabla (drum) accompaniment by Alla Rakha. . . . *Winthrop Sargeant, "Musical Events," The New Yorker, Sept. 21, 1968, p 138*

[from Sanskrit]

Ga·tor·ade (₁gei tər'eid), *n.* a trade name for a soft drink containing glucose, citric acid, sodium bicarbonate, potassium chloride, etc., used by athletes and sportsmen instead of water to replenish rapidly lost body fluids and salts.

... Winnie Palmer, Arnold's [the golfer Arnold Palmer's] wife ... was carrying a container and explained that she had been dispatched at the ninth green to find some Gatorade. *Herbert Warren Wind, "The Sporting Scene," The New Yorker, July 5, 1969, p 70*

gau·ches·co (gɑu'tʃes kou), *adj.* of or having to do with a type of Spanish poetry whose character, language, and setting derive from the life of the gauchos of South America.

I travelled up and down Argentina and Uruguay, lecturing on Swedenborg, Blake, the Persian and Chinese mystics, Buddhism, gauchesco poetry. ... *Jorge Luis Borges, "Profiles: Autobiographical Notes," The New Yorker, Sept. 19, 1970, p 86*

[from American Spanish, from *gaucho* + Spanish *-esco* -esque]

gau·chist ('gou ʃist), *n.* Anglicized form of GAUCHISTE.

He [Eugene Ionesco] believes that the "gauchist" movement contains a fundamental Fascist element. *"Peter Lennon Interviews Eugene Ionesco," The Manchester Guardian Weekly, June 12, 1969, p 17*

gau·chiste (gou'ʃi:st), *n. French.* a political radical; a leftist. *Also used attributively.*

It was a mass demonstration ordered by La Gauche Proletarienne [The Proletarian Left], a militant Maoist group made up of amalgamated *gauchistes.* ... *Genêt, "Letter from Paris," The New Yorker, June 13, 1970, p 97*

Long-haired *gauchiste* (leftist) students in blue jeans and suede jackets stopped motorists in the Latin Quarter and flipped their cars over to form makeshift barricades. *Time, June 8, 1970, p 37*

gauchos, *n.pl.* baggy trousers usually reaching, and often gathered at, the ankles, similar to those worn by South American gauchos.

Knickers and gauchos, hip-huggers, bellbottoms and jeans—all are currently outselling dresses of any length. *"Modern Living: All in the Jeans," Time, Jan. 11, 1971, p 38*

gay, *n. U.S. Slang.* a homosexual.

... the signs being waved by City Hall's daily contingent of pickets had had nothing to do with appropriations or taxes. Instead, they read "Thomas Cuite Is Anti-Homosexual!" and "Cuite Oppresses 500,000 New York Gays"—messages inspired by the recent refusal of the Council, of which Brooklyn Councilman Thomas Cuite is majority leader, to take action on a bill outlawing discrimination against local citizens on the basis of their "sexual orientation." *"The Talk of the Town," The New Yorker, July 3, 1971, p 20*

[noun use of *gay, adj.,* homosexual]

Gay Liberation, *U.S.* a militant movement of homosexuals demanding greater civil rights and protesting discrimination in business, etc.

... a skinny, semi-hysterical young man lunged at him [Senator Edward Kennedy] with a placard, stumbling and shrieking, "What is your position on Gay Liberation?" *"The Talk of the Town," The New Yorker, Dec. 4, 1971, p 49*

Gay Liberation Odd man in and on top of everybody. *Bernard Rosenberg, "A Dictionary for the Disenchanted," Harper's, Nov. 1970, p 94*

Increasingly, homosexuals are creating their own para-institutions, including churches. And with the proliferation of such radical groups as the Gay Liberation Front, ... they are taking to the streets. *Time, July 13, 1970, p 6*

gay·o·la (gei'ou lə), *n. U.S. Slang.* undercover payments made by homosexual establishments for permission to operate without interference.

In June 1969, the New York City police raided the Stonewall Inn, a landmark homosexual bar in Greenwich Village, which has probably the world's largest "gay" ghetto. The police charged the bar with "after hours' liquor violations." This bust was at once gratuitous and hypocritical, for it is generally acknowledged that homosexual bars, steam baths, restaurants, and moviehouses everywhere in this country pay "gayola" to crime syndicates and to law enforcement agencies. *Faubion Bowers, "Homosex: Living The Life," Saturday Review, Feb. 12, 1972, p 23*

There is also a constant opportunity for blackmail and for shakedowns by real or phony cops, a practice known as "gayola." *Time, Jan. 21, 1966, p 41*

[from *gay, adj.,* homosexual + *-ola* (as in *payola,* U.S. slang word for graft, blackmail, or any similar payment)]

ga·zar (gə'zɑr), *n.* a gauzy silk fabric, often sequined with shiny metal.

Givenchy's turquoise gazar dress has white beading and bare midriff. *The New York Times, March 16, 1968, p 18*

... prettiest in purple gazar, ruffled at the high neck and sleeves, at Patou. ... *The Sunday Times (London), Aug. 25, 1968, p 39*

[from French, from *gaze* gauze]

ga·zump (gə'zəmp), *British Slang.* —*v.t.* to subject (the buyer of a house) to demands for a higher price after the purchase has been arranged.

The rapid increase in prices, the growing number of people with mortgages in their pockets, has meant that there is little time to be choosy before you are gazumped. *The Guardian (London), May 12, 1972, p 21*

—*n.* an act or instance of gazumping.

The brass-faced gazump is bad enough, but now the gazumpers are finding sneakier ways to dun the house-hungry. *News of the World (London), May 14, 1972, p 8*

► The origin of *gazump* is not known, though evidently it was at first part of the technical jargon of housing agents. The term has recently become a feature of the British housing scene, or rather of the English housing scene, since Scottish law prevents sellers from backing out of the sale of a house at the last moment to take advantage of a better offer. This is now (1972) legal in England, though regarded as very unsporting until the upsurge in house prices (20% for 1971 in the south of England).

GB, a symbol for a lethal nerve gas (fluoroisopropoxy methyl phosphine oxide), usually combined with an explosive for use as a bomb. The gas was formerly known by its German name, Sarin. Compare BZ, CS, VZ.

The U.S. Army planned to bury at sea some 27,000 tons of surplus chemicals including GB, an organic phosphorus nerve gas. ... *Theodor Benfey and Eugenia Keller, "Chemistry," The Americana Annual 1970, p 162*

According to a U.N. report, less than one drop of GB can paralyze and kill a victim within minutes of contact. *The New York Times, Aug. 6, 1970, p 32*

GDP, abbreviation of *gross domestic product.*

The need [in Trinidad] is to build up agriculture, which only accounts for 9 per cent of the gross domestic product, and manufacturing (16 per cent of GDP) as against petrol and asphalt which accounts for 25 per cent of the GDP and 80 per cent of the island's exports. *Malcolm Dean, "Black Outlook for Trinidad," The Manchester Guardian Weekly, May 2, 1970, p 4*

. . , GNP [gross national product] equals GDP plus net factor payments on foreign investments. . . . *Irving S. Friedman, "Economic Development," Britannica Book of the Year 1971, p 273*

gear, *n. British Slang.* high quality; style; class.

In the first cafe he went into someone sold him six librium [a tranquilizer] pills. "It was my sort of cafe, my sort of people – of course they had gear." *Victoria Brittain, "Amphetamines – The Teenagers' Basic Drug," The Times (London), Sept. 22, 1970, p 10*

[from earlier British slang *gear, adj.,* smart or fashionable, probably from the phrase *in top gear* in style]

geep (gi:p), *n.* the offspring of a goat and a sheep. Also called SHOAT.

Hundreds of people have claimed success in breeding shoats or geep (hybrids between sheep and goats). . . . A male goat cannot fertilise a sheep but a ram can easily fertilise a female goat; in fact the fertilisation rate is as high as normal. But after six weeks of normal development the foetus dies showing the. classical signs of rejection. *"Goats Have no Womb for Shoats and Geeps," New Scientist and Science Journal, July 8, 1971, p 66*

[blend of *goat* and *sheep*]

gel·e ('gel i:), *n.* a kind of African headdress worn by women.

The most visible signs of the new black consciousness are Afro hair-styles, dashikis and geles. . . . *Time, April 6, 1970, p 45*

GEM (dʒem), *n.* acronym for GROUND EFFECT MACHINE.

For mass transportation there are air cushion vehicles or ground effects machines (GEM) that use huge fans to draw air downward and up underneath the machine and create a cushion of air several feet high. GEM can travel over land, water, ice, marsh, mud or desert. . . . *Science News Letter, May 9, 1964, p 298*

gene deletion. See the quotation for the meaning.

Researchers are studying a number of possible techniques that might be used to remove unwanted genes (gene deletion), supply missing genes (gene insertion), or alter whole blocks of characteristics simultaneously (genetic surgery). *Nicholas Panagakos, "Biology of the Future," 1971 Collier's Encyclopedia Year Book, p 6*

gene insertion, the insertion of missing genes in the genetic inventory of a cell or animal. Compare GENE DELETION, GENETIC COPYING, GENETIC SURGERY.

For gene insertion, Professor Edward L. Tatum of Rockefeller University, a Nobel Prize winner, envisions the use of nuclear grafts from other cells; the feasibility of such additions has already been proven in experiments with microorganisms. More recently, other scientists have experimented with the use of viruses for gene insertion. *Nicholas Panagakos, "Biology of the Future," 1971 Collier's Encyclopedia Year Book, p 6*

gene pool, all the genes contained in the genetic makeup of a species. See also GENETIC LOAD.

Some of these collections of genetic stocks, or gene pools, have been carefully studied and documented and the material and information made freely available. *George Bell, "Books," Review of "Genetic Resources in Plants – Their Exploration and Conservation" by O. H. Frankel, E. Bennett, et al., New Scientist, Nov. 12, 1970, p 341*

Another approach is available owing to the peculiarity that American society treats as black anyone who derived even a relatively small portion of his genes from the African gene pool. Consequently it should be possible to obtain a series of I.Q. measurements from persons living under essentially identical social conditions but who have different portions of their genotype derived from the African gene pool. *Werner G. Heim, Colorado Springs, Colo., in a Letter to the Editor, Scientific American, Jan. 1971, p 6*

generate, *v.t.* to derive or produce (a grammatical sentence) from more basic forms by a set of rules of operation and transformation.

Surface structures – the sentences we actually speak and hear – are not "like" the kernels from which they are generated by transformational rules. *George Steiner, "The Tongues of Men," The New Yorker, Nov. 15, 1969, p 225*

generation gap, 1 the differences in social values, behavioral attitudes, and personal aspirations of one generation and that of the next generation, especially the generation of adolescents and young adults and that of their parents.

"What generation gap?" asks University of Michigan Psychologist Joseph Adelson, who argues that "an overwhelming majority of the young – as many as 80% – tend to be traditionalist in values." *Time, Aug. 17, 1970, p 35*

Do you want to bridge the generation gap? Have a look at some of the books now being written for today's teenagers. *The Guardian (London), May 18, 1972, p 13*

2 *Transferred sense.*

Meanwhile ICL [International Computers Limited] is finishing designs on a new series of machines that will make the 1900 series obsolete within 18 months or two years. Thus the generation gap between computers inside and outside eastern Europe seems likely to be perpetuated. *Ivan Berenyi, "Computers in Eastern Europe," Scientific American, Oct. 1970, p 106*

generative, *adj.* of or based on the derivation of grammatical sentences from more basic forms by operational and transformational rules.

. . . the phenomena of shape in grammar to be discussed below are characteristically ignored or perfunctorily dismissed . . . in authoritative works on grammatical theory, whether traditional, structural, descriptive, generative, or eclectic. *Paul Friedrich, University of Chicago, "Shape in Grammar," Language, June 1970, p 381*

He [Noam Chomsky] adds . . . that there will "definitely someday be a physiological explanation for the mental processes that we are now discovering." Does this confident assertion signify that generative linguistics is committed to materialism, to a view of consciousness as being purely or simply neurochemical? Some of its adherents seem to think so. . . . *George Steiner, "The Tongues of Men," The New Yorker, Nov. 15, 1969, p 227*

generative-transformational grammar, a system of rules of operation and transformation for deriving all the grammatical sentences of a language from more basic underlying strings of words. Compare TRANSFORMATIONAL GRAMMAR, PHRASE-STRUCTURE GRAMMAR.

The dominant linguistic influence at present is the theory of generative-transformational grammar developed by Noam Chomsky. This theoretical position taken by Chomsky has led to a great deal of psychological research in addition to reviving some traditional philosophical problems, particularly nativism versus empiricism, or competence versus performance. *K. F. Riegel, "Psycholinguistics," McGraw-Hill Yearbook of Science and Technology 1968, p 317*

generativist, *n.* a follower or advocate of generative linguistics. Compare TRANSFORMATIONALIST.

. . . theories come and go, and the linguists of the future may be better prepared by exposure to a broad range of issues, rather than to the hang-ups of tagmemicists, stratificationalists, generativists, or whatever. *Jane H. Hill, Wayne State University, Review of "Aspects of Language" by Dwight Bolinger, Language, Sept. 1970, p 667*

genetic alphabet, the set of symbols for the four chemical bases of DNA (deoxyribonucleic acid, the carrier of genetic information in the cells) that combine in various ways to form the genetic code.

Most DNA consists of sequences of only four nitrogenous bases: adenine (A), thymine (T), guanine (G) and cytosine (C). Together these bases form the genetic alphabet, and long ordered sequences of them contain in coded form much, if not all, of the information present in the genes. *Roy J. Britten and David E. Kohne, "Repeated Segments of DNA," Scientific American, April 1970, p 24*

genetic code, the biochemical code by which the four bases in the DNA molecule combine, usually in units of three, to specify the synthesis of particular amino acids and proteins that determine the hereditary characteristics of an organism. See also CODON.

The last of the 64 triplet "words" of the genetic code was deciphered by geneticists at the University of Cambridge. . . . It was found that the triplet UGA (the bases uracil, guanine, and adenine) . . . signals the end of a protein chain during protein synthesis in the cell. *Judith Cuddihy, "Review of the Year—Biology," Encyclopedia Science Supplement (Grolier) 1969, p 72*

genetic copying, the duplication of a genetic inventory.

Terms such as "genetic surgery," "genetic copying," "gene insertion," and "gene deletion" are beginning to appear in the scientific journals, and references to genetic manipulation and genetic engineering are common. The potential control of genetic material stems directly from the molecular biologists' fairly recently acquired ability to manipulate and experiment with the living cell rather than merely observe it. *Nicholas Panagakos, "Biology of the Future," 1971 Collier's Encyclopedia Year Book, p 6*

genetic engineer, a specialist in genetic engineering.

He [Dr. Edward Tatum, a pioneer of molecular biology] . . . hinted, at least, at the culture of embryos in the laboratory, destined to develop into adults whose physical and, possibly, intellectual characteristics had been chosen in advance by the genetic engineers. *New Scientist, June 23, 1966, p 762*

genetic engineering, 1 the scientific alteration of genes or genetic material to produce desirable new traits in organisms or to eliminate undesirable ones. Compare EUPHENICS.

The development of techniques for isolating pure genes brings us one step closer to practical genetic engineering . . . . Once the biological break-through arrives, genetic engineering, like nuclear engineering, can be used to attain both good and bad ends. *Harrison Brown, "Focus on Science," The 1970 World Book Year Book, p 35*

"Genetic engineering" implies that an alteration in the genetic complement of the fertilized egg is being effected. *The Times (London), Feb. 28, 1970, p 7*

2 any form of human intervention in hereditary processes to alter the character or nature of an organism.

. . . customs, like monogamy, primogeniture, prohibitions against incest, nationalism, war, and commerce have played their part in the de facto policy of genetic engineering of the human species. *Joshua Lederberg, "Humanics and Genetic Engineering," 1970 Britannica Yearbook of Science and the Future, 1969, p 82*

genetic load, the accumulated mutations in the gene pool of a species.

We are learning more about the gene pool and genetic load, but many questions remain unanswered. We know very little about . . . the relative proportions of balanced and mutational load produced by the common mutagenic agents. *Christopher Wills, "Genetic Load," Scientific American, March 1970, p 106*

genetic surgery. See the quotation for the meaning.

Researchers are studying a number of possible techniques that might be used to remove unwanted genes (gene deletion), supply missing genes (gene insertion), or alter whole blocks of characteristics simultaneously (genetic surgery). *Nicholas Panagakos, "Biology of the Future," 1971 Collier's Encyclopedia Year Book, p 6*

Gentle People, a term applied to any of various groups of people noted for their nonviolent creed, such as the flower children and certain American Indians.

It is the manners of the Gentle People that give their jamborees an air of prelapsarian innocence. *The Times (London), Aug. 31, 1970, p 7*

. . . the Gentle People refused a police order to stop playing bongo drums and reciting a Buddhist love chant on the grass of a small park. *The New York Times, June 4, 1967, Sec. 4, p 3*

If the Gentle People can't make any impact through poetry and unconventional dress, if the cheeky ones who try out the odd crude cartoon are battered down, both these groups will turn to those who offer them nail-bombs, and feel justified in returning violence for violence. *Mary Ann Ebert, Bromley, Kent, England, in a Letter to the Editor, The Manchester Guardian Weekly, Aug. 14, 1971, p 24*

geo-. The prefix *geo-* (meaning "of the earth" or "encompassing the whole earth") has generally been attached in the past only to technical terms, such as *geobotany, geomagnetism, geomorphology,* etc. Recent usage, as shown in the examples below, has extended it to less scientific and more socially oriented applications. See BIO- and ECO- for similar use of these prefixes.

geocide, *n.:* . . . Money has moved on, out of rails, into

geographical medicine

madness and real estate on the moon, futures in black air and dead waters, a corner on cobalt, a bull market in geocide. *Peter Kane Dufault, "Leaving a Station—Sunday, Feb. 1, 1970" (a poem), The New Yorker, April 18, 1970, p 44*

geohygiene, *n.:* The problem of geohygiene (earth hygiene) is highly complex and closely tied to economic and social problems. This problem can therefore not be solved on a national and especially not on a local basis. *The New York Times, July 22, 1968, p 15*

geoliterary, *adj.:* Stella Gibbons's skit is superbly funny, but to savour it fully one must be familiar with its target, those steamy and ridiculous west-of-Severn, sex-in-the-cowhouse novels that were the rage between the wars, and which, as a geo-literary phenomenon find a place somewhere between A. E. Housman and Dylan Thomas. *The Times (London), June 24, 1968, p 6*

geopoetry, *n.:* The theory [that the sea floor moves the land masses above it] was so unorthodox and tenuous that Hess [the American geologist Harry Hess] cautiously called it "geopoetry." It was soon to become geofact. *Time, Jan. 5, 1970, p 36*

geopolitical, *adj.;* As for the geo-political balance, that has been so changed by the rivalry between Russia and China that it is almost impossible at this stage to make an assessment. *Douglas Brown, "Vietnam and Armageddon," The Catholic Herald, May 12, 1972, p 4*

geo-warfare, *n.:* The final chapter [of *Physics of the Earth* by T. F. Gaskell] . . . introduces an entirely new viewpoint—geo-warfare—with melting ice-caps flooding major cities, artificially induced earthquakes and associated tidal waves (tsunamis) wreaking havoc and weather control bringing a new meaning to cold war. *Science Journal, April 1970, p 83*

geographical medicine, a branch of medicine dealing with the influence of geographical and climatological factors on general health, longevity, disease, etc.

Among the great advances in medical science since World War II has been the growth of a new discipline: geographical medicine. This field of investigation involves intensive study of populations, particularly of populations that have migrated from one environment to another. *Geoffrey Dean, "The Multiple Sclerosis Problem," Scientific American, July 1970, p 42*

geoscientist, *n.* an expert or specialist in any of the earth sciences, such as geophysics, geology, oceanography, or seismology.

. . . in Iceland, an excited conference of more than fifty local historians, geoscientists and applied scientists recently discussed the problems posed by the return of a most unwelcome visitor accompanying the cooling climate—the Arctic drift ice. *Leo Kristjansson, "The Ice Drifts Back to Iceland," New Scientist, March 6, 1969, p 508*

geostationary, *adj.* orbiting over a fixed position above the earth and therefore at the same rate as the earth moves.

The geo-stationary, or synchronous, satellite's speed is not 680 miles per hour as Shayon indicates but approximately 6,850 miles per hour. *Frederick Gail, Ottawa, in a Letter to the Editor, Saturday Review, Aug. 10, 1968, p 63*

geostationary orbit, the orbit of a synchronous satellite; an orbit in which a communications satellite moves at the same rate as the earth does, at an altitude of about 22,000 miles above the equator, so that it can act as a fixed relay station. Also called GEOSYNCHRONOUS ORBIT.

The third aerial system, Goonhilly 3, is expected to go into service early in 1972. It will meet the latest international standards and enable Goonhilly to work with the next generation of *Intelsat IV* satellites, the first of which is due to be placed in geostationary orbit over the Atlantic next year. *Science Journal, Nov. 1970, p 23*

geosynchronous orbit, another name for GEO-STATIONARY ORBIT.

This project should be seen as a possible first move towards a longer-term target which might be a European capacity equivalent to a two-ton-information-transfer satellite in geosynchronous orbit in the 1980s, providing this proves viable. *The Times (London), Nov. 22, 1968, p 23*

ger, *n.* a round tent stretched over a collapsible wooden framework, used in Mongolia.

They [Mongols] see nothing shameful in living in a Ger (a felt, canvas and wood tent, which is called a yurt in other parts of central Asia). *David Bonavia, "Mongolia," The Times (London), Oct. 27, 1970, p 8*

ger·ent·o·crat·ic (ˌdʒer ən təˈkræt ik), *adj.* of or relating to managers or administrators as a ruling class.

There is something to be said for a policy of gerentocratic redistribution of power and resources and even more for control against the commercial exploitation of the young through mass media. *A. H. Halsey, "Dr. Wilson's Elect," Review of "The Youth Culture and the Universities" by Bryan Wilson, The Manchester Guardian Weekly, April 25, 1970, p 18*

[from *gerent* manager + *-cratic,* as in *bureaucratic*]

ger·o·vi·tal (ˌdʒer ouˈvai təl), *n.* a drug related to the local anesthetic procaine (Novocaine), supposed to be effective in retarding old age or senility.

About 10,000 people in Britain are taking the Rumanian rejuvenation drug gerovital, according to a spokesman of the firm importing it. *The Times (London), April 14, 1970, p 2*

[from Greek *gérōn* old man + Latin *vītālis* vital]

Ge·samt·kunst·werk (gəˈzɑːmtˌkunst verk), *n. German.* an artistic work consisting of an amalgam of different art forms, such as drama, music, poetry, and stagecraft; (literally) total art work.

The Orff esthetic demands that his theater works be considered "stage pieces" or "world theater," not operas. They are to provide a ritualistic, theatrical experience, with music sharing an equal footing with the drama, movement, and staging—a new *Gesamtkunstwerk,* but in no way Wagnerian; epic theater, but not Brechtian. *Robert Jacobson, "Orff and His Esthetic," Saturday Review, Jan. 27, 1968, p 52*

I admired the way he [the Austrian conductor Erich Kleiber] saw opera as a *Gesamtkunstwerk*—taking an interest in everything—the costumes, make-up, lighting as well as the music. *The Gramophone, April 1968, p 527*

Ge·stalt therapy (gəˈʃtɑːlt), psychotherapy based on Gestalt psychology.

There are also numerous workshops in Gestalt therapy, an approach devised by the late German Psychiatrist Frederick S. Perls. One of the newest and most rebellious branches of psychology, Gestalt theory seeks to celebrate man's freedom, uniqueness and potential. *Time, Nov. 9, 1970, p 55*

Even among safely integrated, American middle-class adults, a subversive interest in psychedelic experimentation, non-verbal communication, sensory awareness, Gestalt therapy and contemplative disciplines begins to spread through the "growth centres" of America, threatening to erode the official reality of principle. *New Scientist and Science Journal, March 11, 1971, p 536*

ghe·ra·o (ge'rɑː ou), *n.* (in India and Pakistan) a form of protest demonstration in which the demonstrators surround a building, as of an office or plant, and prevent anyone from entering or leaving. Compare BANDH.

In West Pakistan, a wave of wildcat strikes continued to sweep the cities. . . . Some invoked *gherao*, a tactic borrowed from India in which workers barricade employers in their offices until wage demands are met. *Time, March 28, 1969, p 29*

The mob had imposed a *gherao* (political lock-in) on the local magistrate, the police and the owner of a factory, throwing stones and using bows and arrows. *The Times (London), July 13, 1967, p 5*

The first serious incident . . . was followed by more than 70 "gheraos"—a form of coercion by labor in which members of management are surrounded and denied freedom of movement. *Joseph Lelyveld, The New York Times, Sept. 11, 1967, p 3*

—*v.t.* to subject to a gherao.

The directors of one steel concern were "gheraoed" next to the blast furnace. . . . *Joseph Lelyveld, The New York Times, May 25, 1967, p 8*

[from Hindi, literally, encirclement]

GHOST (goust), *n.* **1** acronym for *Global Horizontal Sounding Technique,* a method of collecting data about the atmosphere by means of radio-equipped balloons launched to float at fixed altitudes.

In the Global Horizontal Sounding Technique (GHOST), balloons containing three-ounce (about 85-g) radio transmitters are launched to float at specified levels in the Southern Hemisphere. Tracked by the radio signals emitted, they provide data on winds at various levels in the atmosphere. *Frank Press, "Studying the Earth," 1969 Britannica Yearbook of Science and the Future, 1968, p 152*

2 any of the balloons used to collect atmospheric data.

Two GHOST flights of limited duration will be carried out over the United States in July and August to prove the balloons' ability to carry a heavy payload. *Science News, April 18, 1970, p 394*

ghost station, *British.* an unused or unstaffed railroad station.

. . . a three-dimensional "map" or model of the London beneath our feet, with its 550 miles of sewers, its railways, ghost stations, pipes, cables and hidden passages, and rivers such as the Fleet and the Walbrook. *The Times (London), Nov. 30, 1970, p 3*

gi·ga·bit ('dʒig ə‚bit), *n.* a unit of information equivalent to one billion bits or binary digits. Compare KILOBIT, MEGABIT, TERABIT.

The four-minute-mile for electronics engineers has been the gigabit computer, a computer that can process a billion bits of information per second. *Science News, April 4, 1970, p 345*

[from *giga-* one billion (from Greek *gígas* giant) + *bit*]

giggle-smoke, *n. U.S. Slang.* marijuana.

. . . the young soldier was saying that here in Vietnam cannabis, pot, the weed, giggle-smoke, grass, Mary Jane, call it what you will, is readily available and freely used. *Ian Wright, "Pot and the GI," The Manchester Guardian Weekly, June 20, 1970, p 6*

girlcott, *v.t.* (said of women, in humorous analogy to *boycott*) to join in a boycott against someone or something prejudicial to women.

The Y.W.C.A., Feminists in the Arts, Radicalesbians, National Organization for Women—and anyone of taste —will find much to girlcott in *Quiet Days in Clichy* [a motion picture]. *Time, Oct. 12, 1970, p J9*

Gi·ro ('dʒai rou; *German* 'ʒiː rou), *n.* a national service of the post office in various western European countries providing subscribers with a computerized system of money transfer similar to a checking account. *Also used attributively.*

For the "unbanked" millions, Giro would provide a simple, fast and cheap method for the payment and receipt of money and for keeping track of their monetary affairs. *The Times (London), Oct. 19, 1968, p 13*

The Giro system, which has been entrenched in Europe since it was developed in Austria in 1883, apparently derives its name from "gyration," in the sense of a rapid circulation of money. Giro is an international word, although the pronunciation varies from country to country. *The New York Times, Aug. 18, 1968, p 8*

[from German, ultimately from Greek *gŷros* a ring or circle]

given, *n.* something taken for granted; a fact.

Loneliness is a human given, and commitment and the public aspects of a relationship are probably things we'll always want. *Jane Kramer, "Founding Cadre," The New Yorker, Nov. 28, 1970, p 76*

The access of moneys to power is simply one of the givens in Washington. *Elizabeth B. Drew, "Stretching the Ends," The Atlantic, March 1971, p 22*

[noun use of the adjective]

► The noun has been formerly restricted in use to technical contexts.

give-up, *n. U.S. Stock Market.* a practice in which financial institutions, such as mutual funds, instruct brokers executing transactions for them to yield part of their commissions to other brokers, usually ones who have been performing services for the institution.

At issue was Fidelity's use of what are known as "give-ups." This is the cushion of the sales commissions on stock transactions that the broker actually handling the trade frequently gives to another broker on the instructions of his customer, generally a mutual fund. *The New York Times, July 24, 1968, p 53*

glas·phalt ('glæs‚fɔːlt), *n.* a material made from glass for paving roads.

. . . an experimental product called "glasphalt" . . . uses finely ground glass granules to replace the rock aggregates now used as a construction material for highways. *Time, March 16, 1970, p 62*

[blend of *glass* and *asphalt*]

glas·steel ('glæs‚stiːl), *adj.* made of glass and steel.

The only trouble is that the Sondheim score does not

187

have any integrity. It flirts with various styles, and is as neutral and eclectic as the glassteel skyscraper projections used as a backdrop. *Harold C. Schonberg, "The Broadway Musical: Getting Away with Murder," Harper's, July 1970, p 108*

gleamer, *n.* a cosmetic for making the skin of the face gleam.

Some [candidates for Miss Teenage America Pageant in Texas] wore pancake or foundation and blotches spread, islands of makeup holding up smaller islands of blusher or gleamer. *Kathrin Perutz, "Teenage America: Engagement in Fort Worth," Harper's, March 1970, p 98*

glisse·ment (gli:s'mã), *n. French.* sliding; gliding.

Sheer blind courage and what the French call *glissement* will not suffice, as they might do in the downhill, and the skills it [giant slalom] requires are of less artificial nature than the acrobatics demanded by the slalom. *John Hennessy, "Skiing Past and Future," The Times (London), Feb. 18, 1970, p 11*

glitch, *n. U.S. Slang.* a sudden mishap or malfunction.

Goofs and glitches always creep into the early blueprints for any new aircraft. . . . *Time, March 1, 1968, p 52*

. . . it appeared that for two of them [pulsars] at least the gradual slowdown was occasionally punctuated by jerks, sudden speedups, after which the slowdown resumed. These were called sudden events, or glitches, a word borrowed from the jargon of the astronauts. *Science News, Aug. 15, 1970, p 136*

Dr Jeffrey Scargle of the Lich Observatory and Dr Franco Pacini of the Laboratorio di Astrofisica, Frascati, have now proposed (Nature Physical Science, vol 232, p 144) a new explanation for sudden changes of all magnitudes which they call glitches, mini-glitches, and micro-glitches, depending on their size. *"Spinning Off Wisps Can Make a Pulsar Glitchy," New Scientist and Science Journal, Aug. 26, 1971, p 452*

[perhaps from Yiddish *glitsh* a slipping, *glitshen* to slip]

global tectonics, another name for PLATE TECTONICS.

"Analysis of the sedimentary, volcanic, structural and metamorphic chronology in mountain belts," they [Dr. John F. Dewey of Cambridge University and Dr. John M. Bird of the State University of New York] write, "and consideration of the implications of the new global tectonics (plate tectonics) strongly indicate that mountain belts are a consequence of plate evolution." *Kendrick Frazier, "Building Mountain Ranges: A Plate Tectonics Model," Science News, Aug. 15, 1970, p 143*

global village, a term coined by Marshall McLuhan (see MCLUHANISM) to designate the world of the late 1900's, in which the electronic communications media have radically reduced the distance and isolation of people from each other, restoring certain of man's original sense of being part of a village or tribe.

There are no boundaries in a global village. All problems will become so intimate as to be one's own. No problem can arise at one point without affecting all points immediately and emotionally, and world government will become a fact even if no one, due to past prejudices, particularly wants it. . . . *Isaac Asimov, "The Fourth Revolution," Saturday Review, Oct. 24, 1970, p 19*

With its steadily growing membership, the U.N. promises

to become an ever more faithful mirror of Marshall McLuhan's "global village." *Time, Oct. 26, 1970, p 39*

glue-sniffing, *n.* the habit or practice of inhaling the fumes of certain kinds of glue, for the intoxicating effect of the toluene present.

Dock C. Reeves Jr., 19 years old, a drugstore deliveryman with a medical history of glue-sniffing, died yesterday not long after his family found him lying beside a paper bag and an empty glue tube in their home. *The New York Times, May 24, 1968, p 23*

gnome, *n. Especially British.* a banker or financier, especially one doing business in the international money market.

. . . export prices rise, the balance of payments runs into trouble, the gnomes gather, the pound trembles, and the Government of the day deflates the economy. *The Manchester Guardian Weekly, Aug. 22, 1970, p 12*

There is all the difference in the world between keeping gold bars under your mattress — where it tends to stay, regardless of market fluctuations — and taking a receipt for gold held for you by your friendly Zurich gnome or London bullion dealer. *Malcolm Crawford, "Not Enough Gold to Go Around," The Sunday Times (London), May 21, 1972, p 57*

[abstracted from the phrase *gnomes of Zurich,* coined in 1964 by the former British Foreign Secretary George Brown to describe the international currency speculators located in Zurich, who he thought were determined to profit from their speculations on the value of the British pound]

gno·to·bi·ol·o·gy (͵nou tou bai'ɑl ə dʒi:), *n.* the branch of biology dealing with gnotobiotic animals and conditions. Compare GNOTOBIOTICS.

A highly specialized segment of the ultraclean technology is gnotobiology, the raising of germ free animals, largely for research purposes. *L. B. Hall, "Ultraclean Technology," Science Journal, April 1970, p 46*

[from *gnotobiotic + biology*]

gno·to·bi·ot·ic (͵nou tou bai'ɑt ik), *adj.* free of germs or associated only with known germs.

Recently, further investigation of gnotobiotic rats and mice has revealed that in the intestine of such animals there is an accumulation of at least two substances, one of which is a toxin. . . . *James G. Shaffer, "Microbiology," Britannica Book of the Year 1970, p 506*

[from Greek *gnōtós* known + English *-biotic,* as in *antibiotic*]

gnotobiotics, *n.* a field of science concerned with organisms or conditions that are either free of germs or associated only with known germs. Compare GNOTOBIOLOGY.

. . . gnotobiotics includes the study of both "germ-free" animals and animals whose microbial flora can be completely specified. The term also covers the various techniques used to obtain gnotobiotic animals and to maintain them in a gnotobiotic state. *Alan Betts, "Gnotobiotics — A Growing Technology," New Scientist, Jan. 15, 1970, p 101*

go, *adj. Slang.* **1** *Aerospace.* ready for launching; ready to start or use.

After conferring with launching crews, flight controllers, the far-flung tracking teams and the weatherman, William C. Schneider, the mission director, said: "Everything is at this time 'go.'" *John Noble Wilford, The New York Times, April 4, 1968, p 10*

2 ready for or favorable to a project or activity. Compare NO-GO.

"We're getting married next year." She was suddenly in a go condition with all the assurance of a woman on familiar ground. *Alexander Frater, Punch, Aug. 14, 1963, p 224*

But all systems are not "go" for the Nassau-Suffolk economy despite boosts of contracts.... *The New York Times, April 15, 1963, p 109*

go-aheadism, *n.* enterprise; initiative.

Part of the income from the antiquities of Herculaneum ... is going into the pockets of a few who show a kind of Neapolitan go-aheadism. *Terry Coleman, "Buried Treasure of Herculaneum," The Manchester Guardian Weekly, July 18, 1970, p 13*

[from *go-ahead, adj.*, energetic, enterprising + *-ism*]

► The use of this word in the 1800's is recorded in The *OED* with one citation: "1846 C. Kingsley in *Life* (1877) I. 143 It is the new commercial aristocracy, it is the scientific go-a-head-ism of the day, which must save us." The *OED Supplement* antedates the use with an 1838 citation using the form *goaheadism*. The word has probably been in continuous, though unrecorded, use since then.

gock, *n. Slang.* some foul, nasty substance.

... everybody's waiting for the bus, with the lumpy old wornout snow still there and all that's piled up on it since way back last month, and more black gock falling on it out of the sky.... *Roger Angell, "The Floto Letters," The New Yorker, Feb. 21, 1970, p 36*

[a variant of *guck*, both being words which, like *goo, gook, gunk*, are expressive of disgust, perhaps formed by influence of standard words like *glue* and *muck*]

Godardian, *adj.* characterized by a free and daring use of the camera, improvised scripts, and unconventional staging.

Partner is a Godardian exercise of repetitions, monologues, slogans, alienation effects, cheeky political symbolism. *Gavin Millar, "Films," The Listener, Oct. 8, 1970, p 497*

Of the directors who emerged in the 1960s, the most strikingly successful in 1970 was Bernardo Bertolucci, who seemed entirely to have overcome his phase of Godardian imitation *(Partner). David J. Robinson, "Cinema," Britannica Book of the Year 1971, p 195*

[from Jean-Luc *Godard*, born 1930, a French motion-picture director noted for his cinematic innovations + *-ian*]

gofer, *n. U.S. Slang.* an office assistant whose duties include running errands for the staff.

She plays an inadvertent career girl, jilted by the rounder she put through medical school, and working as a "gofer" at a Minneapolis TV station. *"Situation Comedies," Time, Sept. 28, 1970, p 66*

[alteration of *go-for*, so called from being told to *go for* coffee, newspapers, etc.]

goggle, *n.* Usually, **the goggle.** *British Slang.* television.

... there is no proof that watching the inflammatory material which appears on the goggle drives kids to rape, or arson, or flagellation.... *Donald Gould, "A Groundling's Notebook," New Scientist, May 28, 1970, p 432*

gogglebox, *n. British Slang.* television. Compare IDIOT BOX.

The very speed of television's development might have led to some initial resistance to it, even resentment of it. "'Gogglebox' and 'idiot's lantern' are hardly terms of affection and respect." *The Manchester Guardian Weekly, Jan. 9, 1969, p 8*

go-go, *Chiefly U.S. —adj.* **1** of or relating to the lively dancing and music performed at discothèques or similar nightclubs.

Besides skiing, most of the areas offer go-go bands, bars and terraces for sun bathing. But, most important, they offer "atmosphere." *The New York Times, March 11, 1968, p 43*

The heat seemed to have little effect on the enthusiasm of the guests or the hosts at the Georgia booth, which featured Jesse Jewell's Portion Controlled Pre-Cooked Chicken Drumettes (wrapped in Delta Airline napkins), hard-boiled eggs from the Georgia Egg Commission, Coca-Cola, and, on two platforms behind the serving line, a rock band and a go-go dancer. *Calvin Trillin, "U.S. Journal: Phoenix," The New Yorker, July 13, 1968, p 91*

Following the people will come supermarkets, golf courses, yacht clubs, and go-go girls. *Myron Roberts, "The Making of a City," Saturday Review, Sept. 23, 1967, p 72*

2 lively; energetic; enterprising.

There is a go-go spirit in Ford Motor offices that is unmatched in the auto industry. Company men feel that having a living, breathing Henry Ford around lends the firm a certain class that the hired managements of competitors cannot impart. *Time, July 20, 1970, p 66*

For overall appeal there's no one to beat [Canadian Prime Minister] Pierre Elliott Trudeau. Fortunately, he's no dandy because Canadians would never vote for him if he were, but he's a go-go young intellectual and dresses like it. *William Granger, "A Matter of Image, The Clothes," Maclean's, March 1968, p 35*

3 very fashionable; stylish; chic.

Only 26.1 per cent of the potential customers belonged to the under-20, or go-go set, and Rosensohn sees this as a sign that the Motorboard will not generate much bona fide ocean surfing. *The New York Times, Feb. 23, 1968, p 22*

... he was dressed for action, in a white polo shirt, red cardigan sweater (very go-go, being double-breasted) and tan slacks. *Jeannine Locke, "Health is Beauty, Baby," Maclean's, March 1967, p 52*

4 of or relating to go-go funds.

Stocks of franchising companies ... have been among the Street's latest go-go favorites. *Time, March 9, 1970, p 62*

Another offer of units is expected within the next week or two from Invan, Slater Walker's "go-go" unit trust which broke all records by attracting over £8m. [million] when it was first offered to the public in April. *The Times (London), July 5, 1968, p 21*

—n. **1** discothèque dancing.

It's golf and go-go, saunas and sunsets; paisleyed walls and chairs of patent leather. *Advertisement by El Conquistador Hotel and Club, Puerto Rico, The New Yorker, April 20, 1968, p 149*

2 short for GO-GO FUND.

... the go-gos constantly outperform everyone else. *Time, Sept. 22, 1967, p 17*

[shortened from earlier *a-go-go, adj.*, of or relating to discothèque dancing, from French *à-gogo* aplenty (used in the names of discothèques). The English meanings were influenced by the verb *go*, the French form *gogo* being often taken as a reduplication of the English verb.]

go-go fund, a type of investment fund that tries to accumulate large earnings in a short time and therefore may engage in risky, speculative stock-market operations. Also shortened to GO-GO.

Follow the go-go funds. "Anything they can buy you can buy too. Follow them into anything, computer leasing companies, conglomerates, etc. Price? You know that doesn't really matter when you're after performance." *The New York Times, June 8, 1968, p 40*

It has been this area of the market that has been patronised most heavily by the so-called "go-go" funds—the performance funds that show no hesitation to play the market like professional day-traders. *The Sunday Times (London), Oct. 15, 1967, p 46*

go-kart, *n.* a small, open, four-wheeled racing car for one person. Also shortened to KART.

A school that has its own land yacht, wind tunnel, go-kart and canoeing clubs . . . may sound like a well-endowed foundation or an expensive way to go about education. *The Times (London), Jan. 23, 1967, p 9*

[from *Go-Kart*, a trademark for such a racing car]

golden age club, *U.S.* any of various social or recreational organizations for elderly people.

Mrs. Mills continued to serve the A.W.V.S. [American Women's Voluntary Services] until recently. In 1962, as its national chairman, she directed the activities of its members, who work in nurseries and playrooms in children's hospitals, in golden age clubs and in veterans' and community hospitals. *The New York Times, May 2, 1968, p 48*

golden-ager, *n. U.S.* an old or elderly person.

There are no euphemisms in Dutch for being old—no "senior citizen," no "golden-ager". . . . *Anthony Bailey, "The Little Room," The New Yorker, Aug. 15, 1970, p 57*

GOM, abbreviation of *Grand Old Man*, used in describing an old and venerable person or thing.

For several years Mr. Heath [the British Prime Minister] has illustrated his Christmas card with a reproduction from his small collection of paintings, including Sir Winston's *Provence*, which is perhaps the best brushwork the G.O.M. ever did. *The Times (London), Dec. 18, 1970, p 6*

Second comes to the GOM of English racing, Lord Rosebery, born in 1882, the year after St Simon, and happily still going strong. *The Sunday Times (London), Nov. 2, 1969, p 21*

The Pennsylvania has been the G.O.M. of railroads, often a key to their mergers, gobbles, and grabs. . . . *The Atlantic, July 1968, p 87*

Gond·wa·na (gɑnd'wɑː nə), *n.* a supposed supercontinent comprising Australia, Antarctica, Africa, and sometimes including India and South America, believed to have existed for millions of years before splitting up during the Cenozoic era (about 60 million years ago). Compare LAURASIA.

Advocates of [continental] drift are challenged to say exactly how the present continents fitted together to form Pangaea, or alternatively to reconstruct the two later supercontinents Laurasia and Gondwana, which some theorists prefer to a single all-embracing land mass. *Robert S. Dietz and John C. Holden, "The Breakup of Pangaea," Scientific American, Oct. 1970, p 30*

[named after *Gondwana*, a region of central India inhabited by the Dravidian *Gond* people. The region is noted for its unusual geological formations.]

gospel, *n.* a form of Negro religious music combining elements of the spiritual, the blues, and jazz. *Often used attributively.*

His [Neil Diamond's, a composer of pop and rock songs] songs delve ingeniously into hard and soft rock, blues, gospel, even country rock. . . . *Time, Jan. 11, 1971, p 40*

By turning a small dial they can experience classical Indian music, jazz, folk songs of Appalachia, hard rock, blues bands, the Nashville and Detroit sounds, gospel music . . . anything. *The New York Times, Sept. 1, 1968, Sec. 2, p 12*

go-stop, *n. British.* another name for STOP-GO.

"If we are to consolidate our improved position and avoid a return to all the evils of stop-go, or go-stop as I prefer to call it, I am sure that any substantial or indiscriminate relaxation would be wrong." *Sir Leslie O'Brien, Governor of the Bank of England, quoted by Anthony Harris, The Manchester Guardian Weekly, Feb. 7, 1970, p 8*

Gothick, *adj. British.* characteristic of a lurid or gruesome medieval atmosphere; grotesque; macabre.

The point of *Dance Macabre* seems to be Gothick horror —a bit outmoded in the theatre, I thought, although in literature there is still a strong demand. *The Times (London), March 7, 1968, p 7*

. . . one is simply baffled that MGM should have wasted, on an absurd Gothick melodrama of the sort characteristic of Hammer Films, a cast including Deborah Kerr. . . . *Richard Mallett, "Criticism: Cinema," Review of "Eye of the Devil," Punch, March 13, 1968, p 396*

[deliberate archaic spelling of *Gothic, adj.*, in the sense of "medieval, suggestive of romance, the supernatural, etc." The Gothic novel, such as *Wuthering Heights*, was a genre of the 1800's, which has recently been revived.]

goulash communism, a form of communism emphasizing the production of more consumer goods and other means of raising the standard of living of the common people.

. . . Nikita S. Khrushchev had a point when he praised "goulash communism." The Soviet Premier . . . meant to laud his Hungarian Communist party hosts for providing their people . . . with material well-being in addition to ideology. *The New York Times, Aug. 6, 1968, p 10*

goulash communist, a supporter or advocate of goulash communism.

And China, unlike the goulash communists of the west, can pass herself off as a coloured, have-not nation sent by history to help the black world. *The Times (London), March 12, 1968, p 6*

grab, *v.t. Slang.* to cause (a person) to react; make an impression on.

. . . the Women's Liberation Front . . . is charging the Cormorants with discrimination in hiring practices. How does that grab you? *Roger Angell, "The Floto Letters," The New Yorker, Feb. 21, 1970, p 37*

gra·ma·dan (grɑː'mɑː dɑːn), *n.* See the quotation for the meaning.

. . . another Gandhian movement [is] already under way,

called *gramadan*.... Under *gramadan*—in intention a legalistic contrivance but in practice another visionary scheme—landowners in each village were asked to transfer the title to all their holdings to a village assembly, which was to represent all the families in the village and was to manage the affairs of the village in the interests of all. *Ved Mehta, "Indian Journal," The New Yorker, April 11, 1970, p 142*

[from Hindi *grām* village + *ādān* acquisition, receiving]

grammaticality, *n.* the degree of grammatical acceptability of a sentence.

"He didn't deny that 'Floyd broke the glass' could be made more explicit in, say, 'Floyd caused the glass to become broken,' but he said that the meaning was derived semantically. The argument is still raging, and other young linguists have joined in. Very often the debate turns not on any evidence—for there really isn't any evidence yet—but on intuitions of grammaticality...." *Janet Fodor, quoted by Ved Mehta, "Onward and Upward With the Arts (Linguistics)," The New Yorker, May 8, 1971, p 85*

Lakoff makes a very important point here regarding a non-native speaker's ability to make the sort of grammaticality judgements required for transformational research: far from being shaky and untrustworthy, it is unquestioningly relied upon by Latin composition teachers in correcting sentences they have never seen before. *Georgia M. Green, University of Chicago, Language, March 1970, p 150*

Grammy, *n.; pl.* **Grammys** or **Grammies.** *U.S.* a gold-plated replica of a phonograph record awarded annually by the National Academy of Recording Arts and Sciences.

...*The Lord's Prayer* and *The Glorious Sound of Christmas*...racked up more than a million dollars in sales, and thus received the highest accolade the Record Industry Association of America sees fit to bestow, a gold-plated "Grammy." *Herbert Kupferberg, "Music—Ormandy's Orchestra," The Atlantic, April 1969, p 142*

Another album, "Goin' Out of My Head," won a Grammy award as the best instrumental jazz performance of 1966. *The New York Times, June 16, 1968, p 68*

[from *gramophone* + *-y* (diminutive suffix)]

gra·na·de·ro (ˌgra: naː'ðei rou), *n.* a member of a special military or police force in Mexico, used especially to quell riots.

The crack regiment of *Granaderos* marched in and the college was put under military rule. *Alex Hamilton, "In Search of George Canning," The Times (London), April 18, 1970, p I*

[from Spanish, grenadier]

granny, *adj.* of or in the style of granny dresses.

Bluejeans, granny gowns, polka-dot clamdiggers, slouch hats, dashikis, and ponchos are not uncommon....*Andy Logan, "Around City Hall," The New Yorker, Oct. 30, 1971, p 106*

Girls in hot pants with granny shawls over bare breasts. *Patrick Campbell, "Wild Life in Cannes," The Sunday Times (London), May 23, 1971, p 12*

granny dress, a loose dress reaching from the neck to the ankles, similar to those formerly worn by elderly women or "grandmothers." Some granny dresses have long sleeves and ruffles at the neck and wrist; others have low scoop necks and high waistlines like the Empire style.

Some of the many teen-age girls in the audience wore long granny dresses. ... *The New York Times, Jan. 22, 1968, p 24*

Around her, bedecked with beads, boots, faded Levi's, granny dresses, stovepipe hats, bells and tambourines, 50,000 members of the turned-on generation celebrated the rites of life, liberty and the pursuit of hippiness. *Time, June 30, 1967, p 43*

granny glasses, gold- or steel-rimmed eyeglasses, similar to those often worn formerly by elderly women.

She [a young woman] was wearing gold granny glasses on her little heart-shaped face. He didn't know if her cheeks were flushed or rouged. *John Updike, Bech: A Book, 1970, p 148*

grantsman, *n.* an expert or specialist in obtaining grants of money, as for research.

To help communities, school boards, and others obtain federal funds for projects, a new kind of specialist has appeared—the "grantsman"—who is familiar with the technical forms and formal language. *Saturday Review, Dec. 17, 1966, p 82*

The institutional grant, money provided to colleges and universities for their own purposes, rather than to individual researchers.... would provide institutional stability as well as support for younger scientists now at a competitive disadvantage when pitted against experienced grantsmen. *Science News, July 27, 1968, p 77*

[back formation from *grantsmanship*]

grantsmanship, *n.* the art of obtaining grants of money, as for research, from various foundations or other donors.

On most U.S. campuses these days, grantsmanship—the fine art of picking off research funds—is almost as important to professorial prestige as the ability to teach or carry out the research once a grant is landed. *Time, March 17, 1967, p 34*

Gran Tu·ris·mo (ˌgræn tu:'riːz mou), a type of automobile built to the high standards required of racing automobiles. *Abbreviation:* GT

The waters are muddied ... by the only official definition of a GT, that of the Federation Internationale de l'Automobile. It sets the standards only for racing models, and doesn't include all the GTs that scoot around the U.S. and Europe. Roughly, a Gran Turismo: Must be very fast but still carry passengers in great comfort. Must handle well—partly because of tighter suspension, which gives a bumpier ride than most Detroit models, partly as a result of superior brakes, steering, shock absorbers, and tires. Should have distinctive styling. *Business Week, Jan. 21, 1967, p 56*

[from Italian, literally, grand touring]

graphoscope, *n.* a computer display unit on which the data displayed can be modified by the use of a light pen or similar device.

An exciting and recent development of the alphascope principle is the graphoscope. In this system, communication is by drawing and there are many clever devices to enable the user to draw on the scope as well as to obtain output from it. *Robert Parslow, "Thinking with the Machine," New Scientist, June 4, 1970, p 7*

[from *grapho-* writing or drawing + *-scope* instrument for viewing]

graphotherapy, *n.* the diagnosis and treatment of

mental or emotional problems through handwriting; the manipulation or alteration of handwriting as a form of therapy.

Like its parent, graphology, graphotherapy has many critics who equate it with such pseudo-sciences as phrenology and astrology. Both also have their advocates. *Time, Sept. 21, 1970, p 51*

[from *grapho-* writing + *therapy*]

GRAS (græs), *n.* acronym for *Generally Recognized as Safe*, used by the U.S. Food and Drug Administration as a label for food ingredients not considered to be harmful or dangerous.

Ralph Nader and his eager followers are now turning their angry attention to the list of food ingredients listed as GRAS—generally recognized as safe. *Magnus Pyke, New Scientist, July 30, 1970, p 232*

Heretofore saccharin has been on the agency's so-called GRAS list—a list of several hundred food substances "generally recognized as safe." *The New York Times, June 23, 1971, p 28*

grass[1], *n. Slang.* marijuana.

One youth held his grass out to me, and said, "Ain't it the weirdest. Get caught with this, and they can give you five years; drop napalm bombs good, and they give you a medal." *Bruce Jackson, "The Battle of the Pentagon," The Atlantic, Jan. 1968, p 39*

Where have all the hippies gone?.... Today Haight-Ashbury ("Hashberry") resembles a ramshackle holiday town when the season is over.... Nobody offers flowers now, or issues invitations to a pad for a free meal and a share of "grass." *Edward Thorpe, "On the Road from San Francisco," The Manchester Guardian Weekly, Oct. 17, 1968, p 19*

grass[2], *v.i. British Slang.* to inform against someone; turn informer.

Absurd is the highly professional mobster's verdict on a colleague who grassed—"He's finished for life; there's not one respectable criminal, inside or out, who'll ever trust him." *The Times (London), Feb. 21, 1970, p IV*

[from *grass, n.*, British slang term for a police informer, shortened from *grasshopper* policeman, rhyming slang for *copper*]

grass carp, a carp of the South China Sea and adjacent waters, noted for its ability to eat large quantities of aquatic weeds and imported for this purpose to various western countries.

The grass carp ... may soon be munching its way through Britain's weed-infested canals and drainage channels. *New Scientist, April 23, 1970, p 180*

grass skiing, the sport of racing down grassy or straw-covered slopes on specially designed skates.

Beachy Head is one of several sites being examined by a committee set up by the ski club to promote grass skiing. *The Times (London), July 27, 1970, p 2*

A new form of skiing called grass skiing used what looks like a cross between a roller skate and a tractor belt. *Picture legend, "Toys and Games," Britannica Book of the Year 1971, p 724*

gravitational waves, energy-carrying waves involving gravitational forces. The existence of such waves was considered hypothetical until 1969, when their discovery in laboratory experiments was announced. Also called GRAVITY WAVES.

When Einstein postulated his general relativity theory in 1916, he realized that it predicted the existence of gravitational waves. Similar to electromagnetic waves, which are generated by accelerating electric charges, gravitational waves would be radiated by accelerating masses, such as binary stars, and would travel through space at the speed of light. *Gerald Wick, "On the Crest of Gravitational Waves," New Scientist, Oct. 15, 1970, p 122*

graviton, *n.* a hypothetical particle of energy used as a unit for measuring gravitational force.

A graviton with mass would go slower than the speed of light, just as pions [pi mesons], the intermediate particle in strong interactions, are known to do. *Science News, Aug. 23, 1969, p 143*

[from *gravity* + *-on*, as in *electron, proton*, etc.]

gravity waves, another name for GRAVITATIONAL WAVES.

Gravity waves are thought to be a form of energy similar to electromagnetic radiation and travel at about the speed of light. *"Physics," 1970 Britannica Yearbook of Science and the Future, 1969, p 382*

gray-collar, *adj. U.S.* of or relating to workers who perform technical services of repair or maintenance.

Two decades ago, in 1948, the ratio of production to service jobs was just the reverse—55 to 45. By 1975, only one out of three jobs is expected to be in production.... Blue-collar, gray-collar, and farm employment combined will just barely exceed the white-collar total, a balance that economists would have pronounced ludicrously improbable half a century ago. *A. H. Raskin, "Where the Jobs Will Be," The 1968 World Book Year Book, p 105*

Great Leap Forward, the name of a large-scale economic program of rural collectivization and rapid industrialization instituted in China by Mao Tse-tung between 1958 and 1961.

The economic ideas with which Mao Tse-tung instituted the Great Leap Forward included the economic fallacy that as a man could produce more in a day than he could consume—by value—more manpower in China would be no handicap so long as everyone was a full-time producer—and this was one aim of the Great Leap. *The Times (London), April 17, 1968, p 8*

Like the Great Leap Forward of several years ago, Mao Tse-tung's Great Proletarian Cultural Revolution of 1966-1967 has come a cropper. *I. A. Sandoz, "Personalities: Mao Tse-Tung," 1968 Collier's Encyclopedia Year Book, p 433*

Great Society, 1 the name given to former President Lyndon B. Johnson's program of social welfare.

The New York Republican [Governor Rockefeller] said that recent inflationary pressures cutting into purchasing power might have done more to harm low-income persons than "the so-called Great Society" has helped. *The New York Times, May 23, 1968, p 23*

2 *Transferred sense* (to society as a whole).

Wheeler Ranch [a hippie commune] is a microcosm of Society as a whole. Just about everything that happens in Society happens here. After all, take away the long hair and we look like everyone else, with the same needs and basic desires. But the important thing to remember is that, like the Great Society, we are diverse. *Letter from Wheeler Ranch, Bodega Bay, Calif., Harper's, Aug. 1970, p 8*

Green Berets, 1 the nickname of a unit of the U.S. Army, officially called Special Forces.

The halycon years were 1964 and 1965. "Back then," one Special Forces sergeant major growled recently, "the Green Berets were Vietnam, baby." *The New York Times, Aug. 31, 1968, p 4*

2 Green Beret, a member of the Green Berets.

One stroboscopic sequence...starts out slyly as a somewhat tasteless spoof of suicidal Buddhists in Vietnam, then suddenly brings on miniskirted nuns, pursued by coolie-hatted VCs, who in turn are being hunted—and destroyed—by Green Berets. *Robert Kotlowitz, "Performing Arts—Hair: Side, Back, and Front Views," Harper's, Sept. 1968, p 108*

3 green beret, the beret worn by Green Berets as part of their uniform.

These are just a few items of a diversified trade that includes everything from aircraft to the famous green berets (which are made in Toronto). *Maclean's, Feb. 1968, p 13*

green card, 1 *U.S.* a green-colored permit which allows Mexican and other foreign workers to cross the Mexican border into the United States to do farm work. See also GREEN-CARDER.

The man had just come in from Mexico on a "green card," or visa, which is a symbol of the most serious obstacle that Chavez's organizing effort faces: the century-old effort of California farmers to depress wages and undercut resistance by pitting one group of poor people against another. *Peter Matthiessen, "Profiles: Organizer [Cesar Chavez]," The New Yorker, June 21, 1969, p 50*

2 *British.* a green-colored insurance document covering motorists against accidents in foreign countries.

Insurance companies have been known, however, to refuse to extend cover even for countries which recognise the green card as well as for those where it is not valid. *The Guardian (London), May 13, 1972, p 17*

green-carder, *n. U.S.* a Mexican or other foreign worker who holds a permit to work in the United States.

Workers pulled out on strike were readily replaced by scabs and green-carders—foreign nationals (in this case Mexicans) with U.S. work permits. *John Gregory Dunne, "To Die Standing: Cesar Chavez and the Chicanos," The Atlantic, June 1971, p 40*

"Green-carders" can become citizens after five years of residence—and pay taxes, be drafted, and qualify for Social Security while they wait. *Peter Matthiessen, "Profiles: Organizer [Cesar Chavez]," The New Yorker, June 21, 1969, p 55*

greenhouse effect, the absorption and retention of the sun's infrared radiation in the earth's atmosphere, resulting in an increase in the temperature of the earth's surface. The greenhouse effect is due to the accumulation of carbon dioxide and water vapor often caused by a cold-air mass trapping a warm-air mass underneath it much as the glass of a greenhouse traps underneath it the air that is heated by the sun. Also called HOTHOUSE EFFECT.

One of the most frightening bogeys with which environmentalists had become concerned was the "greenhouse effect." It was conjectured that the increased use of such fossil fuels as coal, oil, and gas would lead inexorably to an increase in the amount of carbon dioxide (CO_2) in the upper atmosphere. As the CO_2 content rose, there would be a commensurate increase in the tendency of the upper at-mosphere to retain the radiant energy from the sun. The consequence would be a steady and irreversible rise in the average mean temperature within the global envelope. This, in turn, would gradually melt the polar icecaps; the sea level would rise; and New York and other coastal cities would be inundated. *Howard J. Lewis, "Science," 1972 Britannica Yearbook of Science and the Future, 1971, p 329*

Will a further increase in carbon dioxide also have (or renew) a "greenhouse effect," leading to an increase in temperature (and thus to a rising sea level)? *Preston Cloud and Aharon Gibor, "The Oxygen Cycle," Scientific American, Sept. 1970, p 123*

greening, *n.* a renewal of youthful freshness; rejuvenation; rebirth.

The extraordinary thing about this new consciousness [Consciousness III] is that it emerged from the machine-made environment of the corporate state....For those who thought the world was irretrievably encased in metal and plastic and sterile stone, it seems a veritable greening of America. *Charles A. Reich, "The Greening of America," The New Yorker, Sept. 26, 1970, p 111*

Green Paper, *British.* a government document in which a proposal or idea is put up for discussion, usually printed on green paper to distinguish it from a White Paper, which presents fixed policy. Compare BLACK PAPER.

The Green Paper provides only skeleton plans for the new structure and its mode of action....*Science Journal, March 1970, p 11*

The Government's Green Paper on economic strategy, "The Task Ahead," presents a decidedly cautious assessment of Britain's economic prospects. *The Manchester Guardian Weekly, March 6, 1969, p 9*

Last week, the British government published a green paper (green for discussion) called "A Framework for Government Research and Development" (Cmnd 4814). *Sir Harry Nelville, "Rothschild v. Dainton: Who's Right?" New Scientist and Science Journal, Dec. 2, 1971, p 14*

green power, the power of money.

"We give the public what it wants," the theatre producers still cry, meaning of course they cater to the side of the public that has the most green power (that is, money). *The Manchester Guardian Weekly, April 11, 1968, p 12*

"'Green Power' is important for the Negro now. Pride and dignity come when you reach in your pocket and find money, not a hole." *Whitney Young, Time, Aug. 11, 1967, p 14*

green revolution, the recent large-scale development of inexpensive and high-yield varieties of wheat, rice, and other grains, especially to improve the economy of underdeveloped countries.

...the "green revolution" in the third world is at last showing results....There is a real chance that over the next ten years agricultural productivity will increase dramatically in the rice growing countries of South-East Asia. *The Manchester Guardian Weekly, Jan. 3, 1970, p 12*

...the Green Revolution [is] the development through "genetic engineering" of new cereal varieties whose introduction into developing countries has enormously increased crop yields and helped exorcise threats of famine. *The New York Times, Oct. 25, 1970, p 12*

Nonetheless, many U.S. environmentalists remain skeptical about the Green Revolution precisely because it depends so heavily on agricultural chemicals. *"Who's for DDT?" Time, Nov. 22, 1971, p 52*

gremmie, *n. U.S. Slang.* a surfer who is new or poor at the sport.

"A lot of gremmies come out just to impress girls, and all they do is sit on their popouts."

"What's a popout?" we asked. "A crummy board," the boy said. "Machine-made. And you can see the fibres going in all different directions in the resin." *"The Talk of the Town," The New Yorker, June 17, 1967, p 24*

[a diminutive of *gremlin*, a U.S. slang word for anyone annoying or troublesome]

grey area, *British.* a geographical area showing low employment but not poor enough to qualify for special government assistance.

The future of grey areas—places which have fallen between the two stools of prosperity and real depression—is of great importance in this corner of Britain. *The Times (London), June 1, 1970, p 7*

grok (grak), *v.i. U.S. Slang (chiefly hippie and student use).* to communicate meaningfully or sympathetically.

"I was thinking we ought to get together somewhere, Mr. Zzyzybyzynsky, and grok about our problems." *Roger Angell, "Life in These Now United States," The New Yorker, March 15, 1969, p 35*

Esalen [a growth center] T-groups frequently use the term grokking in their touch therapy.... *"Books: Future Grok," Time, March 29, 1971, p 61*

[from a "Martian" term for the power of perception and communication possessed by the hero of the science-fiction novel *Stranger in a Strange Land* (1961) by the American writer Robert Anson Heinlein, born 1907]

groove, *Slang.* —*n.* something very enjoyable, wonderful, or outstanding.

It's [a discothèque] in the vaults—below a crêpe-and-shish-kebab establishment of the same name—and it's generally considered to be a groove. *The New Yorker, April 27, 1968, p 7*

Asked how he felt about his release in exchange for the Krogers, Mr. Lorraine beamed: "It's a groove." *The Sunday Times (London), Oct. 26, 1969, p 2*

—*v.i.* **1** to enjoy oneself; have fun.

"Moovin' and groovin' with Big Daddy Madman Mathews on sooooooo-oulful 1600 WXKW 76 degrees in the big bag outside and time for: Muuuuu-sic!" *Disc Jockey Art Mathews, quoted by Richard Todd, The Atlantic, March 1970, p 67*

But as a black American, who is probably Black Beach Boy Fan No. 1, I close my eyes to their shoddy politics and simply groove on the music. *Alan Bell, New York, in a Letter to the Editor, Time, Sept. 27, 1971, p 2*

2 to be enjoyable; be fun.

"Life as it is ... really grooves." *John Updike, "The Hillies," The New Yorker, Dec. 20, 1969, p 35*

3 to associate (with), especially because an emotional bond has been formed.

... it is Radical Chic that prompts the Carter Burdens "to groove, as they say, with the Young Lords and other pet primitives from Harlem and Spanish Harlem...." *Time, June 15, 1970, p 87*

—*v.t.* to cause to groove.

"What better way to groove my contemporaries on earth than to decorate their material life with mind-expanding

design?" *Peter Max, The New Yorker, Nov. 28, 1970, p 157*

[from the slang phrase *in the groove* in perfect form]

grotty, *adj. British Slang.* mean; wretched; miserable.

She [Mrs. Joan Kay, a London telephone operator] said: "Telephonists are not allowed to move from their seats until the supervisor has given them permission, and if the supervisor feels grotty that day you can wait." *"Girl Telephonists 'In Tears,'" The Times (London), March 5, 1970, p 2*

Joe [Frazier] is sitting in his corner, and the obvious question is why on earth is the boxing champion of the world singing in a grotty London suburb in front of a house one third full. *"Soul with Stamina," The Manchester Guardian Weekly, June 26, 1971, p 17*

[alteration of *grotesque*, with the form perhaps influenced by *grotto* a cavern or crypt]

ground effect machine, another name for AIR CUSHION VEHICLE. Compare SURFACE-EFFECT SHIP.

Among the various novel craft that ride on a cushion of air is the class known in the United States as ... ground-effect machines—GEM is the usual acronym—and in the United Kingdom as hovercraft, because they are free of the Earth's surface. *S. R. Heller, "Air-cushion Vehicles," McGraw-Hill Yearbook of Science and Technology 1966, p 366*

[so called because of the effect of the ground in trapping the air to form a cushion]

ground-to-ground, *n.* a land-to-land rocket or missile.

"Tomorrow, we'll get three divisions in here, four, we'll get two hundred B-52s, we'll get ground-to-grounds, and whole batteries of Lazy Dogs, we'll get nuclear...." *Alan Coren, "...that Fell on the House that Jack Built," Punch, Feb. 21, 1968, p 258*

grouper, *n. U.S.* **1** a member of an encounter group.

When, for instance, the spirits of some grouper noticeably sag, he may be rocked tenderly in the air on the hands of the others. Tears are a summons to "cradle": the moist-eyed one is warmly and multiply embraced. *Time, Nov. 9, 1970, p 55*

2 one who takes part in group sex.

Many columns of ads for wife-swappers, lesbians, homosexuals, groupers, sadists, masochists.... *Edward Grossman, "In Pursuit of the American Woman," Harper's, Feb. 1970, p 54*

groupie, *n. Slang.* **1** a teen-age girl who is a fan of rock 'n' roll singing groups and follows them where they perform.

A true child of the 1960s, Lennon had it all—LSD, heroin, groupies and so much of the razzle-dazzle of superstardom that after a while, to hear him tell it, he no longer knew which end was up. *Time, Jan. 25, 1971, p 46*

It seems that rock bands prefer San Francisco groupies to New York groupies; the latter, being coldhearted Easterners, are only out for conquests; Bay Area chicks really dig the musicians as people, not just bodies, and stay afterward to do their housework. *Ellen Willis, "Musical Events," The New Yorker, Oct. 23, 1971, p 170*

2 a teen-age fan who follows any celebrity where he appears.

Flocks of pretty chess groupies gathered for a glimpse of

him outside the Presidente Hotel, but [Bobby] Fischer never breaks training. *"Sports: The Peacock vs. the Wren," Newsweek, Oct. 18, 1971, p 53*

Group of Ten, a group of leading financiers representing the United States, the United Kingdom, Canada, France, West Germany, Belgium, the Netherlands, Italy, Sweden, and Japan, organized in 1962 to support with loans the International Monetary Fund whenever required and to consider various reforms of the international financial system.

It became known today that the next such discussion will take place over the weekend at Basel, Switzerland, where representatives of the world's leading central banks, the so-called "Group of Ten," will meet for a new round of talks on the international monetary situation. *The New York Times, June 8, 1968, p 47*

group-think, *n.* the handling of any problem by a group, such as a commission, a board of directors, or a research team. *Also used attributively.* Compare THINK TANK.

The trend to group-think began earlier in this century when governments, along with universities and big businesses, decided that more progress could be made if assorted experts were brought together in one place to discuss a multidimensional question. *Time, Jan. 19, 1970, p 18*

Philanthropy, Ford-style, moreover, is a group-think affair. Decisions are shaped by over a hundred men. *Philip M. Stern, "An Open Letter to the Ford Foundation," Harper's, Jan. 1966, p 85*

group·us·cule ('gru: pə͵skyu:l), *n.* a very small or minor group.

He [Raymond Marcellin, the French Minister of the Interior] banned the "Gauche Proletarienne" [a leftist group], ostensibly because he considered it the most dangerous of the groupuscules. *The Manchester Guardian Weekly, July 11, 1970, p 6*

[from French, from *groupe* group + min*uscule* very small]

growth center, a center or institute providing sensitivity training, Gestalt therapy, or other means for the development of people's potentials.

One index of the rapid expansion of encounter groups has been the proliferation of "growth centers" that use various group methods designed to help individuals enhance their creativity, self-knowledge, and ability to work with others. *Irvin D. Yalom and Samuel Moffat, "Instant Intimacy," 1972 Britannica Yearbook of Science and the Future, 1971, p 410*

A similar event last year drew 850; last April, 6,000. Since January 1969, when Donald Clark counted 37 "growth centers"—established sites for the development of human or group potentials—the census has risen past 100. *Time, Nov. 9, 1970, p 54*

growth fund, a mutual-fund investment company whose stated goal is growth or appreciation in capital value.

Some giant growth funds have run into trouble over their asset valuations. *The Sunday Times (London), Feb. 9, 1969, p 32*

grun·gy ('grən dʒi:), *adj. U.S. Slang.* bad, inferior, or ugly.

". . . real people are pretty grungy actors when you come

right down to it. Like all those schlockmeisters on 'Candid Camera.'" *F. P. Tullius, "Ninety-Nine Years is Not Forever," The New Yorker, July 19, 1969, p 20*

The film ["McCabe and Mrs. Miller"] develops a striking ambience, thanks mostly to the talents of Production Designer Leon Ericksen, who constructed a Western town that is simultaneously grungy and beautiful. *Time, July 26, 1971, p 43*

[of unknown origin]

grunt, *n. U.S. Military Slang.* an infantry soldier or marine.

But it is his [Nixon's] support of the troops which is even more extraordinary. Were his motive genuinely that of wanting to praise the poor grunts in Vietnam, even according to the prevailing mythology of heroism (a mythology to which the grunts themselves no longer subscribe), it would be a motive worthy and deserving of worthy language. *David Halberstam, "American Notes: Mr. Nixon Meets The Language," Harper's, July 1970, p 31*

The sergeant grabbed the sleeping grunt by the throat and told him: "If I were a V.C., you would be dead." *Time, Jan. 25, 1971, p 31*

GT, abbreviation of GRAN TURISMO.

The Austin 1300 GT is neither high geared, quiet nor relaxing, but a quick and entertaining version of British Leyland's front-driven family car. *The Times (London), Sept. 10, 1970, p 15*

guaranteed annual income or **guaranteed income,** another name for NEGATIVE INCOME TAX.

For many years proposals have come from various positions in the political spectrum recommending a "negative income tax" or a guaranteed annual income. *Reo M. Christenson, "Poverty," The Americana Annual 1970, p 562*

The New York Democrat's position paper on welfare put him in opposition to Senator Eugene J. McCarthy on a guaranteed income. *The New York Times, May 19, 1968, p 41*

guerrilla theater, a type of dramatic presentation of short antiwar or antiestablishment plays, usually in pantomime and in any public place where an audience will gather. Also called STREET THEATER.

In Houston, . . . a Rice student who engaged in some guerrilla theatre during an antiwar demonstration was sentenced to six months for wearing the distinctive parts of an Army uniform. . . . *Calvin Trillin, "U.S. Journal: Houston, Not Super-Outrageous," The New Yorker, Dec. 12, 1970, p 166*

Schacht v. *United States* (90 S. Ct. 1555), decided by the Court this year, involved the applicability of a statute making it a crime to wear a uniform of the armed services without authority. The defendant, Daniel Jay Schacht, was a member of a "guerrilla theater" group which presented skits protesting the Vietnam war. In one skit he wore an army uniform as a costume. His conviction on the basis of this act was reversed by the Supreme Court. *Monrad G. Paulsen, "United States: Supreme Court," 1971 Collier's Encyclopedia Year Book, p 583*

guest worker, another name for GASTARBEITER.

Like the Swiss, the Germans have turned to foreign labour (here they are called guest workers) to help out. *The Times (London), Sept. 22, 1970, p 22*

Guevarist, *n.* a follower of the Argentine-born Latin American revolutionary Ernesto (Ché) Guevara, 1928-1967, or of his ideas of implementing revolution through terrorist guerrilla tactics to pave the way to social reform. *Also used attributively.*

Here in Germany student radicals have been variously described as Trotskyists, anarchists, Maoists, Guevarists, pacifists and utopians—all of which adds up to nothing. *C. L. Sulzberger, The New York Times, May 15, 1968, p 46*

In Ceylon, Government forces claimed they had crushed the revolt by Guevarist rebels in many parts of the island, but admitted the fighting was still going on in some provinces. *The Manchester Guardian Weekly, April 24, 1971, p 3*

gum·bah (guːmˈbɑː), *n. U.S. Underworld Slang.* a close friend; chum.

...the cops had collared a big gumbah of Frank Costello's and made a deal with him. *Marion K. Sanders, "Addicts and Zealots," Harper's, June 1970, p 78*

[alteration of Italian *compare*, literally, godfather; the spelling was influenced by the pronunciation]

gunboat diplomacy, the policy of using the threat of military intervention to enforce diplomatic treaties and alliances with other countries.

In former days international law was ultimately maintained by the threat of war, and gunboat diplomacy was supposed to teach lessons to nations whose own police departments failed. *C. L. Sulzberger, The New York Times, April 8, 1970, p 42*

In Macao they [Chinese Communist leaders] have displayed a savage skill for waging "gunboat diplomacy" against the miniscule Portuguese enclave, with as much finesse as the Western imperialists themselves ever played the ruthless game. *"Reports: Macao," The Atlantic, May 1967, p 14*

► This term came into wide use in 1965, when American troops landed in the Dominican Republic, presumably to help maintain order and protect U.S. citizens after left-wing elements had tried to seize power. In Great Britain the term had gained currency temporarily during the Suez crisis of October 1956, when Labourites attacked the Government's handling of the nationalization of the Suez Canal as "gunboat diplomacy." Originally the term was used in reference to the warships in which an American diplomatic mission went to China in 1844, after the Opium War, in order to establish a favorable treaty with the Chinese. In the early 1900's *gunboat diplomacy* was largely replaced by *dollar diplomacy*, which described the American goal of protecting American business interests in Latin America through the combined use of military and diplomatic power. The recent American experience in Indochina has kept *gunboat diplomacy* in the news through the 1960's and into the 1970's.

Gunn, *adj.* of or based upon the Gunn effect.

A Gunn device generates oscillations as a result of the curious manner in which the conduction electrons behave in n-type gallium arsenide. *New Scientist, March 20, 1969, p 643*

At top right is a cylindrical copper mounting for a Gunn oscillator, a tiny crystal of gallium arsenide that can be made to emit microwaves simply by applying a steady voltage across it. *Picture legend, "A Solid-State Source of Microwaves," Scientific American, Aug. 1966, p 23*

Gunn effect, the emission of microwaves and the simultaneous decrease of direct current flow in a semiconductor when it is subjected at a certain critical level to electrical voltage.

In the past year the emphasis in solid-state microwave devices has been on making practical Gunn effect microwave devices to replace the much larger and more clumsy microwave tubes used in radar and other applications. In addition, due to the interest inspired by the Gunn effect, different types of solid-state devices based on it are being developed and show considerable promise. *William E. Spicer, "Solid-State Physics," 1970 Britannica Yearbook of Science and the Future, 1969, p 380*

[named after Ian *Gunn*, of International Business Machines, who discovered the effect in 1963]

guns and butter, *U.S. Politics.* a policy of putting equal emphasis on both military and economic programs. *Often used attributively.*

...while it may be true technically and from a monetary point of view that you can have guns and butter, it is a fact of life that where your heart is there your money will go, and the heart of the Administration is in that war in Vietnam. *Dr. Martin Luther King, Jr., The New York Times, April 2, 1967, p 76*

President Johnson's guns-and-butter policy has produced an estimated $25,000 million to $35,000 million budget deficit, which must be covered by higher revenues. *The Sunday Times (London), March 24, 1968, p 32*

[originally the term was *guns before butter*, giving the highest priority to military expenditures]

gunship, *n.* a helicopter equipped with armament to support ground troops and protect transport helicopters from ground fire.

The man in the rear flies the helicopter and fires the rockets and Gatling-type six-barreled machine guns fixed on stubby wings on each side. The forward man fires a six-barreled minigun in a movable chin turret under the nose. "This is what we call a professional gunship," said Col. J. Elmore Swenson of Columbus, Ga. *The New York Times, Jan. 7, 1968, p 5*

This time a hail of fire from a battalion of U.S. defenders and the miniguns of circling American gunships stopped the assault short of the fort's outer fences. *Time, Dec. 8, 1967, p 30*

guru, *n.* **1** a leading figure in some field.

The object of all this praise from one of the gurus of the current fashion scene is an intense, red-headed, strong-willed high-school dropout who owns two shops in Toronto.... *Marjorie Harris, "The Susie Thing," Maclean's, Nov. 19, 1966, p 14*

2 an expert or authority.

The prime-time football and other changes lead some TV ratings gurus to predict that ABC, which reduced the Nielsen numbers gap about 4% last year, will make equal headway this season and approach parity with CBS and NBC, now in a virtual tie for first place. *Richard Burgheim, Time, Oct. 5, 1970, p 79*

3 a long, loose outer garment similar to the ones worn by Indian holy men. *Also used attributively.*

It seems like a wonderful idea for a play: a handsome young man with long blonde hair and beard, wearing a silver lamé guru, arrives in a Mediterranean city in the company of 12 lovely girls. *The Times (London), April 25, 1968, p 15*

While certain exhibitors focused on such items as Nehru jackets and the toga-like Guru shirts, others brought traffic through their doors with more conventional clothing and furnishings. *Leonard Sloane, The New York Times, April 3, 1968, p 69*

gut, *adj. U.S. Slang.* felt deeply or instinctively; emotional.

The welfare changes ... reflect the gut feeling of many Congressmen that large numbers of welfare recipients are either too lazy or too unmotivated to work. *Time, Aug. 25, 1967, p 17*

There is, as they would phrase it, little "gut reaction" in favour of trade unionism among American workers. *The Manchester Guardian Weekly, April 27, 1967, p 1*

The trick is to go where the people are, he went on, and "tackle the gut issues—jobs, substandard housing, education." *The New York Times, Jan. 21, 1968, p 84*

gutfighter, *n. U.S.* a hard-hitting, tough adversary.

President Nixon came to office convinced that he could govern only if he overcame his old reputation as a gut fighter and followed the politics of reconciliation.... *James Reston, The New York Times, Oct. 28, 1970, p 47*

To his detractors, he is "Facile" Frank Fasi, an arrogant gutfighter who shoots from the lip and to hell with the consequences. *Time, Feb. 23, 1970, p 44*

GVH disease, a condition in which grafted or transplanted tissue, especially of the bone marrow, attacks the tissues of the recipient's body, instead of the more common phenomenon in which the recipient's body rejects the graft.

Recent experience suggests that if donor and recipient have identically matched tissues, GVH disease will be mild and will subside of its own accord, but proof of this has yet to be established. *"Immunology," Science News Yearbook 1970, p 81*

[*GVH*, abbreviation of *Graft Versus Host*]

gyp·lure ('dʒipˌlur), *n.* a synthetic form of the sex attractant of the female gypsy moth.

Pheromones [olfactory hormones] control ant behavior and much insect mating. An artificial pheromone (gyplure) can be synthesised to attract gypsy moth males into an insecticidal trap. *Alex Comfort, "Communication May Be Odorous," New Scientist and Science Journal, Feb. 25, 1971, p 412*

gyppy tummy, *British Slang.* a common intestinal upset experienced by travelers.

Another sufferer was King Hussein, who followed talks with Nasser with a spell in a London hospital, due to a stomach ailment. Gyppy tummy? *Punch, May 8, 1968, p 657*

The joyless nature of the struggle is made grimmer because hundreds of people have been struck by a 48-hour virus which combines some of the worst features of influenza and "gyppy tummy." *The Times (London), Oct. 18, 1967, p 3*

[*gyppy*, a British Army slang term for *Egyptian*]

gypsy cab, *U.S.* a taxicab that may be hired by a passenger at its place of business but is not licensed to cruise the streets seeking passengers.

The law requires that the gypsy cabs be painted so that they do not resemble taxis operated with police medallions or that they carry letters six inches high saying that they are not licensed to pick up passengers while cruising. *The New York Times, July 15, 1968, p 21*

H

habitat, *n.* a vessel to house researchers or scientists under water over an extended period of time while they are conducting their work. See also AQUANAUT, SEALAB.

Four scientists from the U.S. Department of the Interior spent two months in a four-room habitat, Tektite I, nearly 50 feet below the surface of the sea.... Because internal and external pressures were identical, a floor hatch in the habitat's wet lab could be kept open permanently for ready access to the water. *Myrl Hendershott, "Oceanography," The Americana Annual 1970, p 517*

Diving from the barge Hugh Gordon, they were using a "habitat"—a watertight vessel that attaches to the pipe— to cut out the damaged section. *The Sunday Times (London), Dec. 15, 1968, p 41*

had·ron ('hæd,rɑn), *n.* a collective name for the pi meson and all heavier elementary nuclear particles.

Now more than 200 kinds of particles have been observed, mostly of the strong interacting kinds called hadrons.... *David Park, "Physics," 1970 Collier's Encyclopedia Year Book, p 431*

[from Greek *hadrós* stout + -*on*, as in *meson, proton*, etc.]

hadronic, *adj.* of or relating to a hadron or hadrons.

It has been found that a photon with a billion times as much energy as a photon of visible light behaves as hadrons do when it is allowed to interact with hadrons. The discovery that the photon has this hadronic character at very high energies, although it was unexpected, has now been incorporated into a new group of theories that make the hadronic photon respectable. *Frederick V. Murphy and David E. Yount, "Photons As Hadrons," Scientific American, July 1971, p 94*

haf·fir (hæ'fir), *n.* (in northern Africa) a temporary pond built to store rainwater and conserve the water table.

Adding to the number of points at which livestock can secure water helps to widen the area of grazing. This can be achieved by boring new wells and by constructing *haffirs* or artificial ponds in which seasonal rain water may be stored. *John and Anne Cloudsley-Thompson, "Prospects for Arid Lands," New Scientist, Nov. 5, 1970, p 286*

[from Arabic]

hahn·i·um ('hɑ: ni: əm), *n.* an artificial radioactive chemical element with the atomic number 105, atomic weight of 260, and half-life of 1.6 seconds. It is produced by bombarding californium with nuclei of nitrogen. Also called ELEMENT 105.

A new element, number 105 in the periodic table, has been synthesized by workers at the Lawrence Radiation Laboratory of the University of California. The element has

been named hahnium, after the late German physicist Otto Hahn. *Scientific American, June 1970, p 48*

haircurling, *adj.* causing or spreading terror; frightening; hair-raising.

The new book [*Pentagon of Power*, by Lewis Mumford] is an extended warning—warning is Mumford's specialty. It is serious but unhysterical. At the same time he has a proper awareness of the resilience of man—the haircurling school of Luddites tend to underestimate their audience: if people are that stupid, why write? Even the terrifying aspects of technopolitan society... are measures of the human capacity for achievement. *Alex Comfort, "The Shift in Awareness," The Manchester Guardian Weekly, June 19, 1971, p 20*

Passengers have hair-curling stories about many of the little lines, including engine failures, landings with the landing gear retracted, and even running out of gas. *Time, July 18, 1969, p 69*

hairtician, *n.* *U.S.* See the quotation for the meaning.

Competition among barbers is surely more intense today tĥan ever before. It has driven barbers to call themselves "hair stylists to men" and "hairticians".... *William Whitworth, "Profiles: Just A Little Off The Top," The New Yorker, Oct. 21, 1967, p 63*

[from *hair* + -*tician*, as in *beautician*]

hair-weaving, *n.* the weaving or sewing of a hairpiece or wig into a balding person's remaining hair.

The process is called "hair-weaving," and it was developed in Harlem several years ago to provide long straight hair for Negro women whose own hair had been damaged by frequent straightening treatments and who didn't want to wear wigs. *The New York Times, April 15, 1968, p 38*

hallucinant, *n.* something that produces hallucinations.

This is the core of last week's excitement in which... the sudden disclosure of a full military alert, official scare treatment given to threats at the borders, and the trumpeted arrest of a Communist Party leader served as somewhat unnerving hallucinants. *The Times (London), July 13, 1970, p 5*

hallucinate, *v.t.* to view or represent in the form of a hallucination.

No longer content with hallucinating his life story, he [the American novelist William Burroughs] has to crack open his fantasies to see what is inside. *Conrad Knickerbocker, The New York Times, March 22, 1966, p 43*

hallucinogenic, *n.* a drug that produces hallucinations.

Known medically as hallucinogenics or psychotogenics,

these drugs [LSD, mescaline, and psilocybin] are still subject to intense research. *Time, Sept. 26, 1969, p 46*

One is struck by student boldness in searching for pot and other hallucinogenics, and the comparative ease with which they secure them. *John Calam, Review of "The Poisoned Ivy" by William Surface, Saturday Review, Aug. 17, 1968, p 55*

[noun use of *hallucinogenic, adj.*]

hal·o·cline (hæl ə‚klɑin), *n.* a sharp discontinuity in the salinity of sea water, usually at a depth of about 180 feet.

There has been a marked decrease in the oxygen content of deeper waters, the report [on water pollution] states, and "if this development continues, the whole water mass below the halocline will probably turn into a lifeless 'oceanic desert' such as found in the Black Sea." *The Times (London), March 6, 1970, p 7*

[from Greek *háls, halós* salt + English *-cline* a layer (from Greek *klínein* to slope)]

hal·o·thane ('hæl ə‚θein), *n.* a nonflammable general anesthetic administered by inhalation.

One theory, supported by some evidence, is that halothane may undergo a chemical change in the body and produce a substance toxic to the liver in susceptible individuals. *Stanley A. Feldman, "Anesthesiology," Britannica Book of the Year 1970, p 495*

[from *halogens* (group of elements) + *ethane* (a gas)]

ha·mam (hæ'mɑːm), *n.* a public bathhouse in Iran.

Close by is a hamam or bath—the earliest of the Islamic period found in Iran—with a variety of rooms for dressing, relaxing and for hot and cold baths. *The Times (London), May 25, 1970, p 7*

[from Persian *hammām*, from Arabic]

H & I or **H and I,** abbreviation of *harassment and interdiction,* a term used by the U.S. command in Vietnam to describe random firing, especially at night, to deter enemy infiltration or attack.

The lunatic artillery strategy, called in Vietnam "harassment and interdiction," is illustrative of the dilemma: H & I fire was directed indiscriminately at trails, "suspected troop concentrations," and "suspected enemy base camps." *Ward Just, "Soldiers," The Atlantic, Nov. 1970, p 84*

hang, *v.i.* in various phrases:

hang in there, to hold on or hang on.

He [Richard M. Nixon] has a long history of coming from behind, they say, and of confronting adversities, and it would be in his nature to hang in there and fight. *Elizabeth B. Drew, "Reports and Comments," The Atlantic, May 1971, p 6*

let it all hang out, *Afro-American Slang.* to be carefree or uninhibited; let one's hair down.

Most whites can probably translate, even if they can't use, such terms as "rap" (talk), "rip off" (steal), "hangup" (pre-occupation) and "let it all hang out" (what J. Edgar Hoover did in that interview this week). *Russell Baker, The New York Times, Nov. 22, 1970, Sec. 4, p 11*

hangarage, *n. British.* space for housing aircraft; hangars collectively.

There is hangarage, a filling station, a restaurant—often servicing the motorway also—a motel, garage accommo-

dation and access to the motorway. *The Sunday Times (London), May 4, 1969, p 16*

[from *hangar* + *-age,* as in *cellarage, orphanage,* etc.]

hang five or **hang ten,** *Surfing Slang.* to curl the toes of one *(hang five)* or both *(hang ten)* feet over the edge of a surfboard.

Hanging Five, or Ten occurs when a surfer hooks his toes over the end of the board. *Sam J. Greller, "Surfing," The 1968 World Book Year Book, p 590*

hangup, *n. Slang.* **1** a psychological or emotional problem.

Aldous is the most interesting Huxley for moderns. That's because he touches modernity's hangups at so many points. *Charles Poore, The New York Times, June 27, 1968, p 41*

...man's racial hangups and his misconceptions about his evolution have led to aggression, violence, and war. *E. J. Kahn, Jr., The New Yorker, Nov. 2, 1968, p 192*

2 any problem or difficulty, especially that causes annoyance or irritation.

That big hangup for drivers caught in traffic lineups—the overheated engine—could soon become a thing of the past. *Maclean's, March 1968, p 4*

My hangup with Dr. Menninger and others who pontificate on violence is that they seem to be saying that they have answers. *Robert B. Miller, West St. Paul, Minn., in a Letter to the Editor, Saturday Review, Oct. 5, 1968, p 21*

[from the slang phrase *hung up.* See HUNG-UP.]

ha·ni·wa ('hɑː ni‚wɑː), *n. sing.* or *pl.* pottery with carvings of human, animal, or other figures which were placed outside ancient burial mounds in the Orient, especially Japan.

"After all," he [Saito, a Japanese artist] said, "up to then I had never done the likeness of a face except of Buddhist images and prehistoric *haniwa* figurines." *Time, Feb. 10, 1967, p 9*

[from Japanese]

happening, *n.* a spontaneous or improvised public performance, display, spectacle, or the like, often involving the audience or spectators.

The student protest movement continued in West Berlin and in many university towns in the Federal Republic, 'happenings' often being staged by the Socialist Students' Federation under the direction of the Federation's chief ideologist, Herr Rudi Dutschke. *"Western and Central Europe: Western Germany," The Annual Register of World Events in 1967 (1968), p 251*

The show is self-styled as a Happening, and, considered on its own terms—as an attempt to simulate spontaneity, that is—it is a failure.... *Edith Oliver, "The Theatre: Off Broadway," Review of Joseph Papp's production of "Hamlet," The New Yorker, Jan. 6, 1968, p 68*

What was happening was a Happening—a combination of artists' ball, carnival, charade, and a Dadaesque version of the games some people play. *"Modern Living: Resorts, Happening at the Hamptons [Long Island]," Time, Aug. 19, 1966, p 36*

haptic lens, a contact lens which covers the white of the eye. Compare MICRO-CORNEAL LENS.

The haptic lens is a part sphere designed to align with the sclera—the visible white part of the eye—and stabilised by evenly fitting the lens over the sclera so that it moves as the eye moves. *"UV [ultraviolet] Fit For Contact Lenses," New Scientist and Science Journal, Sept. 23, 1971, p 688*

[*haptic* from Greek *háptein* to fasten + English *-ic*]

ha·ram·bee (hɑː'rɑːm biː), *n.* a Swahili word meaning "pull together," used especially in Kenya as a rallying call for the people to work together for national betterment.

Hassanali Fakhru listened to the jerky Swahili, smiled, and answered, "The trouble with you foreigners is you're not interested in building a nation. You have no spirit of *Harambee." Paul Theroux, "Two in the Bush," The Atlantic, July 1968, p 76*

hard-core, *n. U.S.* a person considered as part of the nucleus of any group, especially one of a group who are consistently or chronically unemployed or who fail to meet standards in academic work.

...the Ford Motor Company, once praised for its social commitment, was forced to trim back production earlier in the year and in the process "quietly closed its two inner-city hiring centers in Detroit and even laid off some of the former hard-cores it had only recently hired." *Bayard Rustin, "The Failure of Black Separatism," Harper's, Jan. 1970, p 32*

[noun use of the adjective *hard-core*, as in *hard-core unemployment*]

hard drug, any drug that is considered physically as well as psychologically addictive, such as heroin and morphine. Compare SOFT DRUG.

...the maximum penalties are to be reduced for the use not only of cannabis but of heroin and other hard drugs as well. *The Times (London), March 13, 1970, p 11*

The money spent on gambling increased fourfold. Hard-drug usage—heroin, cocaine—multiplied ten times over. Gradually the plot of history and the quirks of society grew nastier—Suez, Profumo, and the 1966 Moors murder trial. *Time, July 6, 1970, p 71*

hard-edge, *n.* a form of abstract painting characterized by the use of austere, sharply defined, geometric forms, often set off by strong colors.

Pink and mauve are the dominant colors in the recent works of a second-generation Abstract Expressionist, who has stuck to his guns through Pop, hard-edge and minimal. *"Art In New York," Time, May 11, 1970, p 2*

Post-painterly or "hard-edge" abstraction cleaned up the gooey mess and substituted neatly defined geometrical shapes in chaste combinations. Optical art, also, is neatly defined and geometrical in its pattern. *John Canaday, The New York Times Magazine, Feb. 21, 1965, p 12*

hard-edger, *n.* a painter of hard-edges.

Peter Hutchinson...Another hard-edger with genes from shaped canvases and minimal sculpture....*John Canaday, The New York Times, Nov. 25, 1967, p 35*

hardened, *adj. Military use.* underground and especially protected against missiles or bombs by heavy concrete construction. Compare SOFT.

... the Poseidon [is] effective against hardened targets; it can, therefore, be regarded as a first-strike weapon. *Frank Barnaby, "Technology and the Myth of Deterrence," New Scientist, Sept. 24, 1970, p 619*

Hardened silos require a huge weight of explosives for their destruction. *John L. Steele, "The Russians Are Eight Feet Tall—But So Are We," Time, Aug. 3, 1970, p 11*

hardhat, *n. U.S.* **1** a construction worker.

When construction workers, some of them with crowbars, wade into a group of students, laying about them indiscriminately, not everyone joins in denouncing the hardhats. *Norman Cousins, "Explanations and Excesses," Saturday Review, Oct. 10, 1970, p 20*

2 an outspoken conservative or reactionary, especially one who believes in suppressing opposing opinions.

...the hard-hats who commit violence and spread a disregard for personal rights are as fanatical as any bomb-thrower. *Stephen L. Johnson, 5th Special Forces Group Nha Trang, Vietnam, in a Letter to the Editor, The New York Times, July 7, 1970, p 38*

Gradually, Gandhi's white-capped protégé became a hardhat on the Tibetan border question....*Time, June 14, 1971, p 41*

[extended senses of *hardhat*, the protective metal hat or helmet worn by construction workers]

hardhattism, *n. U.S.* the beliefs and practices of hardhats; the use of violent methods to suppress dissenters and radicals.

Vice President Agnew does not serve the whole community when he argues against permissiveness but permits himself to be permissive about hardhattism. *Norman Cousins, "Explanations and Excesses," Saturday Review, Oct. 10, 1970, p 20*

hard line, rigid adherence to an attitude or policy, especially in politics. Compare SOFT LINE.

French propaganda and French diplomacy encouraged the Biafrans to adopt a hard line and refuse a compromise. *C. L. Sulzberger, The New York Times, Jan. 23, 1970, p 46*

hard-line, *adj.* following a hard line; rigid and inflexible; uncompromising.

Albania also continued to express its opposition to the Soviet hard-line policy toward Czechoslovakia. *Nicholas C. Pano, "Albania," The Americana Annual 1970, p 72*

On the crucial issue of Vietnam, Clifford carries with him to the Pentagon an exceedingly hard-line philosophy. *Patrick Anderson, The New York Times Magazine, Jan. 28, 1968, p 20*

hard-liner, *n.* one who adopts or follows a hard line. Compare SOFT-LINER.

This campaign, and, even more, the present efforts of Dr. Husak to get rid, with Moscow's approval, of some of the more clumsy "hard-liners" only confirms what was stated in my article: that the economic paralysis caused by the purges is depriving the Soviet Union of important supplies. *Adolf Hermann, London, England, in a Letter to the Editor, New Scientist, Dec. 10, 1970, p 470*

hard-lining, *adj.* taking a hard line.

The government of Premier Lon Nol [of Cambodia], under increasing pressure from the harder-lining elements in the National Assembly to strengthen the war effort, declared national mobilization. *"The World: Indochina: Textbook Exodus," Time, July 6, 1970, p 24*

hard rock, the original hard-driving rock 'n' roll, played with a regular beat, often on electronically amplified instruments. Compare SOFT ROCK.

His [Neil Diamond's, a composer of pop and rock songs] songs delve ingeniously into hard and soft rock, blues, gospel, even country rock. ... *Time, Jan. 11, 1971, p 40*

By turning a small dial they can experience classical

Indian music, jazz, folk songs of Appalachia, hard rock, blues bands, the Nashville and Detroit sounds, gospel music . . . anything. *The New York Times, Sept. 1, 1968, Sec. 2, p 12*

hard science, any of the natural or physical sciences, such as physics, chemistry, biology, geology, and astronomy. Compare SOFT SCIENCE.

On the campuses, the people in the 'soft sciences' are arguing with the people in the 'hard sciences.' The physical sciences and engineering bring in more research money. *The New York Times, June 2, 1968, p 61*

hard scientist, a specialist in a hard science.

The numbers here differ from those previously published due to the increased number of total responses from "hard scientists" (569) now available due to questionnaires that came in late. *James A. Wilson and Jerry Gaston, "New Light on the Brain Drain," New Scientist, July 31, 1969, p 235*

hardstuff, *n.* a U.S. slang term for HARD DRUGS.

. . . Janis [Joplin], along with her famous Southern Comfort, harbored a sometime penchant for downers and hardstuff. *The New York Times, Oct. 27, 1970, p 45*

"They go to one of these hard-stuff parties. They get hooked — and they're done for. Done for! Done for!" *Sylvia Townsend Warner, "Truth in the Cup," The New Yorker, Dec. 7, 1968, p 62*

hardware, *n.* **1** the mechanical, electrical, or structural components of a computer or other automatic machine. Compare FIRMWARE, SOFTWARE.

In electromechanical systems, common control apparatus consists of hardware — an array of hundreds of relays wired together to do the switching jobs of a particular telephone exchange. *Advertisement by Bell Telephone Laboratories, Scientific American, June 1965, p 15*

2 the physical equipment of a rocket, missile, or other space vehicle, as distinguished from its design plans, its fuel, etc.

The AAP [Apollo Applications Program] was a much-desired plum for space industries, since NASA's most likely choices for the future would be ones making use of existing Apollo hardware. *Science News, June 18, 1966, p 490*

3 the physical equipment or facilities of any complex system.

While the Federal government, under the plan, would provide 90 per cent of the money for planning grants, research and pilot projects, it will only pay up to 60 percent of the cost of the programs in action, such as detoxication centers for alcoholics. And it will provide only 50 per cent of the costs of "hardware" — that is, new correctional centers, crime laboratories and police academies. *The New York Times, Feb. 12, 1967, Sec. 4, p 7*

Ha·re Krish·na ('hɑː re 'kriʃ nə), the title of a Buddhist love chant or mantra dedicated to the god Krishna, adopted as the name of a U.S. cult.

Paroled at 20, he [David Hoyt] drifted to the flowering world of San Francisco's Haight-Ashbury, where he became a member of the Hare Krishna cult and custodian of the Radha Krishna temple. *Time, Aug. 3, 1970, p 31*

. . . Senator Burdick introduced Ginsberg to his colleagues as the Pied Piper of the drug movement — from newspaper pictures of the poet chanting "*Hare Krishna*" at one of Leary's sellout psychedelic celebrations or marching across Sheridan Square with a big grin on his face and with a homemade sign saying "POT IS FUN!" pinned to his overcoat. *Jane Kramer, "Profiles: Paterfamilias" (a profile of the poet Allen Ginsberg), The New Yorker, Aug. 17, 1968, p 36*

ha·roosh (hə'ruːʃ), *n. U.S.* a commotion or noisy disturbance; a brawl.

. . . on May 21, 1969 he [President Nixon] announced the establishment of ten federal regions. . . . Some haroosh was of course inevitable. Originally Nixon had wanted eight regions, rather than ten. The biggest would have included all the Pacific Coast states, plus Arizona, Nevada, Alaska, Hawaii and Guam. *John Fischer, "The Easy Chair: Can the Nixon Administration be Doing Something Right?" Harper's, Nov. 1970, p 32*

▶ On the background of this word, John Fischer, Contributing Editor of *Harper's*, wrote us: "Haroosh is a fairly common colloquialism among cowboys of the southwest, where I grew up. It probably is of Irish origin; at least I've been told by a number of Irishmen that it is used in their country with much the same meaning."

hash, *n. Slang.* **1** hashish.

Should marijuana and hash (the leaf and resin of the cannabis plant) be subjected to severe penalties, while addictive drugs like alcohol and tobacco are passed by society? *The Sunday Times (London), April 4, 1971, p 11*

Heroin was present in both envelopes. Or it might be a bag of marihuana or "hash," or even barbiturates. *Russell Lynes, "After Hours: The People Vs. Some Persons," Harper's, April 1967, p 36*

2 marijuana.

The poster . . . begins: "This is an open letter to British visitors in Spain. It has just one thing to say — stay off the hash. Don't smuggle it, don't peddle it, don't carry it for others." *The Manchester Guardian Weekly, April 10, 1971, p 11*

hashhead, *n. Slang.* a person who is addicted to hashish or marijuana.

"The hippies come here for the pot, of course," says a young visitor from New York — and indeed Morocco is a hashhead's delight. *Time, Jan. 31, 1969, p 42*

[see HEAD]

hash-up, *n. British Slang.* any old material reworked to make it look new; a rehash.

. . . a style perilously close to certain Colour Supplement hash-ups and clearly aligned for Overground consumption. *Richard Holmes, "Books: Religion & Society: Priest of the Sugar Lump," Review of "Playpower" by Richard Neville, The Times (London), Feb. 28, 1970, p IV*

[from *hash up* to serve up in a new form, especially as a mixture or mess, ultimately from *hash, n.,* mixture of chopped-up food]

hassle, *v.t. U.S. Slang.* to abuse or harass.

I'd like to be able to . . . wear my hair long without getting hassled. *Tom McSloy, The New York Times, Oct. 15, 1970, p 47*

Jesus Christ loved, he took abuses and he would love some more. He wore long hair and a beard, and when they hassled him, he taught more love. *Calvin Hill, Time, April 6, 1970, p 79*

[from earlier *hassle, v.i.,* to fight or quarrel, from *hassle, n.,* a fight or struggle]

hatchback, *adj. U.S.* (of an automobile) having a hatch on the sloping roof.

The basic list price of the Vega 2300 is $1,950, which (with federal excise tax and dealer preparation) comes out to $2,091 for a two-door sedan, $2,197 for a "hatchback" coupe, and $2,329 for a station wagon. *"Debut for Subcompacts," Time, Sept. 21, 1970, p 92*

hatter's shakes, a trembling of the muscles and limbs formerly found among workers in hatmaking and now attributed to mercury poisoning. See also MINAMATA DISEASE.

The features in chronic mercurialism are an inflammation of the mouth, muscular tremors — the famous hatter's shakes — and a characteristic personality change. *Berton Roueche, "Annals of Medicine," The New Yorker, Aug. 22, 1970, p 68*

▶ Only the *OED* enters this term, in the form *hatters' shakes*, with a supporting quotation of 1902 from the British Medical Journal: "Muscular tremors ('hatters' shakes) are most often observed in those engaged in dusty post-carotting processes." Recent interest in the widespread occurrence of mercury poisoning, resulting from eating fish contaminated with mercury from industrial chemicals, has provided an explanation of the old idiom *mad as a hatter*, which, so far as we know, has never been satisfactorily explained before. The following quotations suggest the source of the idiom:

The bizarre mental symptoms of mercury poisoning gave rise to the phrase, "mad as a hatter," in the 19th century, when mercury compounds were used to treat felt in hatmaking. *"Mercury in Lake St. Clair," Science News, April 18, 1970, p 388*

In the eighteenth century, felt for hats was tanned by the use of mercury compounds. The hat makers in England absorbed into their bodies traces of the mercury, which produced mental aberrations — hence the expression "mad as a hatter". *"Mercury Mystery," New Scientist, Feb. 5, 1970, p 243*

hawk, *n.* a person who favors war or advocates military solutions in a conflict. Compare DOVE.

In our opinion, the general run of Americans — whether hawks or doves, or neither — are deeply preoccupied with the war. *"The Talk of the Town," The New Yorker, Jan. 13, 1968, p 19*

Politicians in Washington have often cited the emotive words "Munich" and "Czechoslovakia" in recent years, but only to draw an analogy useful to the hawks on Vietnam. *The New York Times, July 28, 1968, Sec. 4, p 3*

—*v.i.* to be or act as a hawk; be hawkish.

So in the early Seventies, with [Ronald] Reagan suddenly charging out of the West, hawking on the war, he may be able to play some of Nixon's older roles, talking about Victory, attacking No-win policies. . . . *David Halberstam, "The Questions Which Tear Us Apart," Harper's, Feb. 1970, p 76*

[shortened from *warhawk*, a term originally applied in the United States to one who favored war with France during the diplomatic crisis of 1798 and later to one advocating war against England in 1811; the current term *hawk* first appeared in 1962 in connection with the Cuban missile crisis, to characterize those who advocated demanding from the U.S.S.R. that it remove its missiles from Cuba, in contrast to the *doves*, who favored a peaceable approach]

hawkish, *adj.* warlike; favoring war or advocating military solutions in a conflict. Compare DOVISH.

An article about W. W. Rostow, the most "hawkish" of the President's advisers on Vietnam, quoted Rostow as saying, "The duty of men is to prevent war and buy time." *Richard H. Rovere, "Reflections: A New Situation in the World," The New Yorker, Feb. 24, 1968, p 43*

His [President Kennedy's] second year was climaxed by the Cuban missile crisis, which he handled with firmness, but without the bluster of some of his hawkish advisers who pressed him to bomb and invade the island. *Clayton Fritchey, "Washington Insight: A Tale of One City — and Two Men," Harper's, Dec. 1966, p 110*

hawkism, *n.* the principles or policies of hawks.

The comic muse was also represented by the play-writing debut of humorist Art Buchwald. His *Sheep on the Runway,* a satire on outmoded imperialism, poked fun at a Communist-baiting journalist trying to export American hawkism. *Harold Ferrar, "Theater," The Americana Annual 1971, p 672*

Hawthorne effect, an improvement in the performance of workers, students, etc., resulting from the attention of researchers seeking means to achieve such an improvement.

In the Oak School experiment the fact that university researchers, supported by Federal funds, were interested in the school may have led to a general improvement of morale and effort on the part of the teachers. In any case, the possibility of a Hawthorne effect cannot be ruled out either in this experiment or in other studies of educational practices. *Robert Rosenthal and Lenore F. Jacobson, "Teacher Expectations for the Disadvantaged," Scientific American, April 1968, p 23*

[named after the Western Electric Company's *Hawthorne* Works in Chicago, where experiments during the 1920's to improve working performance yielded this effect]

H-bomb, *v.t.* to bomb with a hydrogen bomb.

. . . can we really believe that the GPO [General Post Office] tower in Tottenham Court Road would continue to function if London is H-bombed? *Frank Barnaby, "Spine-chilling Prosperity," New Scientist, Dec. 31, 1970, p 610*

[from *H-bomb, n.,* patterned after *A-bomb, n., v.*]

head, *n. U.S. Slang.* **1** a drug addict.

"Why don't she and I, Mr. Bech, smoke some marijuana together as a dry run? That way she can satisfy her female curiosity and I can see if we could stand a trip together. As I size her up, she's much too practical-minded to be a head; she just wants to make the sixties scene, and maybe to bug you." *John Updike, Bech: A Book, 1970, p 83*

2 a devotee; fan.

. . . just how interested *are* people in film? It is assumed that the young think of nothing else, yet when Derek Hill organised an excellent collection of foreign films from the Counter Festival . . . in July, the cinema was nearly empty most of the time. . . . What was it that kept these young film-heads away? *Emma Cockburn, "Media: Cinema City," The Listener, Oct. 22, 1970, p 560*

[abstracted from compounds such as *acidhead, hashhead, pothead,* and *pillhead,* which, in turn, were patterned after older compounds such as *hothead, bonehead, sleepy head,* in which *head* had the general meaning of "a person whose head is filled with (heat, bone, sleep, etc.)"]

head-counter, *n.* one who takes polls; a pollster.

"I am afraid," said a Democratic head-counter recently, "that we have enough votes to override." *Tom Wicker, The New York Times, Jan. 27, 1970, p 42*

[from *head count*, colloquial term for a census or poll]

head-falsie, *n. Slang.* a wig.

Those pretenders who stick on their crowning glory with adhesive can be recognised in overheated carriages when the temperature raises itchy hell under their head-falsies .... *New Scientist, Jan. 7, 1971, p 5*

headhunt, *Slang.* —*v.i., v.t.* to recruit executives for a corporation.

. . . the board felt that a good consulting firm, with a strong track record for executive "headhunting," could assist in the normally chaotic selection process. *Warren G. Bennis, "Searching For The 'Perfect' University President," The Atlantic, April 1971, p 42*

. . . the new ex-Slater managing director Allan Baxter (head-hunted by K I M) wanted to carry out his own programme before coming back for consultation. *The Sunday Times (London), Nov. 2, 1969, p 30*

—*n.* an instance of headhunting.

There *must* be a dozen or so institutions out there seeking the strength and the imagination Bennis offers. They should be grateful for getting a headhunt for free. *Robert A. Lively, Buffalo, N.Y., in a Letter to the Editor, The Atlantic, June 1971, p 34*

headhunter, *n. Slang.* one who engages in headhunting, as a personnel agent or management consultant.

. . . you're hot and everything you do works and they're calling you for a job and the headhunters are crying for you .... *Time, June 22, 1970, p 78*

Julius Sakala is, temporarily at least, a municipal headhunter. *The Times (London), Dec. 30, 1970, p 13*

head shop, a shop selling psychedelic artifacts, such as glowing posters, sticks for burning incense, and paraphernalia used in drug taking. Also called PSYCHEDELICATESSEN.

The student . . . wants to come home for a sentimental weekend with the old crowd at the neighborhood head shop .... *Russell Baker, The New York Times, June 3, 1971, p 39*

The hippies represent a culture that pretends to deliver us from the malfeasances of affluence, but it does not, and the hippies are enchanted by nothing so much as the charm and grace they find in Georgetown. Nevertheless, if they stay on there they will destroy it. First there are the head shops, and then the tourists, and then the crummy gin mills. *John Corry, "The Politics of Style," Harper's, Nov. 1970, p 64*

Before long, we were double-parked on St. Marks Place in a colorful swirl of head shops and ice cream stores, advertising such flavors as Acapulco Gold and Panama Red. *Bruce Jay Friedman, "Lessons of the Street," Harper's, Sept. 1971, p 92*

[see HEAD]

headteacher, *n. British.* a person in charge of a school.

Hundreds of headteachers have been told that they could go on writing confidential reports on potential university entrants. *The Times (London), March 5, 1970, p 2*

► Headteacher is the generic term for all heads of state schools, used often by officialdom and unions. *Headmaster* is a more prestigious term for the same job. There is variety in the extent to which the *headteacher* teaches, even dissension as to how much he should do; as a rule, however, headteachers have no teaching obligations.

head-to-head, *U.S.* —*adj.* fought very closely.

In the offensive line, Southern Cal's huge tackle Ron Yary earned at least a draw in a head-to-head battle with Green Bay's All-Pro defensive end, Willie Davis. *Time, Aug. 9, 1968, p 56*

The Democratic primary in Nebraska May 14 was to have been a head-to-head match between the two anti-Administration candidates, perhaps driving the loser out. *The New York Times, May 3, 1968, p 30*

—*n.* a contest or fight at very close quarters.

It [the Sheridan tank] cannot stand against any of the Russian tanks in a head-to-head, and its highly sophisticated mechanisms make it difficult to use in places like jungles or deserts, where, on the one hand, the engine exhausts become clogged and overheated and, on the other, the combination of sand and heat makes it intolerable to operate. *Ward Just, "Soldiers," The Atlantic, Nov. 1970, p 65*

[patterned after *hand-to-hand*]

headwork, *n.* the use of the head to propel the ball in soccer.

Oxford generally looked the more dangerous, partly because the clearances of their defenders went to their own forwards with greater regularity and partly because their headwork was also better directed. *Norman Creek, "Cambridge Hold off Oxford Rally," The Times (London), Dec. 10, 1970, p 5*

heat, *n. U.S. Slang.* the police.

. . . out the door comes this great big porcine member of the heat, all belts and bullets and pistols and keys and flashlights and clubs and helmets. *F. P. Tullius, "Ninety-Nine Years is Not Forever," The New Yorker, July 19, 1969, p 20*

[extended from the U.S. slang term for intense police activity, especially in the phrase *the heat is on*]

heat pipe, a pipe containing fluid to transfer heat from one end to the other by a difference in pressures without external pumping or supporting mechanisms.

Heat pipes—first developed for space applications . . . may soon be used by electronics engineers. These devices can transfer heat from a component such as a high power transistor or valve to an external heat sink [device that absorbs heat] with fantastic efficiency. *Glen Lawes and Michael Kenward, "Heat Pipes Surge Forward," New Scientist, March 5, 1970, p 461*

heat pollution, another name for THERMAL POLLUTION.

Hot water pollution, often called thermal pollution, may act in much the same way as overfertilization. So far heat pollution has been more a threat than a fact. It was expected, however, to be a major unwanted legacy of nuclear power generation.... *"Thermal Pollution," Science News Yearbook 1970, p 300*

heave-ho, *v.i., v.t.* to heave or lift with force.

. . . the [Congolese] women who, apparently 12 months pregnant, nonetheless are constantly hauling and heave-hoing on this packing case of merchandise or that basket full of provisions. *Geoffrey Moorhouse, "That Old Man River," The Manchester Guardian Weekly, Aug. 7, 1971, p 17*

The distance from our court to the top of the hill was a full hundred yards of fairly steep incline and slippery footing, but the tires were chopped loose from the ground, and a groaning mass of men heave-ho'd the snow car up the ramp and onto the runway. *J. V. Whitey, "All The Prisoners Drove Away," The New Yorker, Jan. 18, 1964, p 84*

▶ The only previously recorded use of *heave-ho* as a verb (cited in the *OED*) appears in Richard Henry Dana Jr.'s *Two Years Before the Mast* (1840): "They were heave-hoing, stopping and unstopping, pawling, catting, and fishing, for three hours." In this quotation, however, the verb is used in the nautical sense of "to cry 'heave ho!'" A recent example of this use is found in the following quotation:

During a rehearsal of *Billy Budd*, a singer was asked why he was just lolling about in the wings, not heave-hoing with the rest of them. *D. A. N. Jones, Review of "Sailortown" by Stan Hugill, The Listener, Dec. 5, 1968, p 768*

heavy, *adj. Slang.* important or serious.

"Marcuse is heavy stuff." *Time, Aug. 17, 1970, p 32*

Something serious is "heavy," something relaxed is "laid back." *Sara Davidson, "Rock Style: Defying the American Dream," Harper's, July 1969, p 60*

—*n. Surfing Slang.* a very large wave.

We see them [surfers] in every size of wave, from the regular 4-ft. rollers off S. Africa to the house-size "heavies" off Hawaii, and their skill (and occasional accidents) are fascinating to watch. *Punch, March 6, 1968, p v*

hedge fund, *U.S.* an investment fund set up as a limited partnership for investing private capital speculatively.

A small hedge fund called, friends of mine who manage $2 million. They differ from mutual funds in the sense that they are *very* unregulated; operate with relatively little money; can go long, sell short, or write options. The managers of a hedge fund take 20 percent of the profits *if* there are profits. *Brutus, "Confessions of a Stockbroker," The Atlantic, June 1971, p 47*

The hedge funds, so-called, have been operating on borrowed money in order to concentrate the capital gains of their customers. *John Kenneth Galbraith, "1929 and 1969: Financial Genius is a Short Memory and a Rising Market," Harper's, Nov. 1969, p 56*

Hei·an or **Hei'an** ('hei'a:n), *adj.* of or relating to a period of Japanese history, 794-1185, marked by great artistic and literary development.

It [a book] stems from a culture, the Heian period in 11th-century Japan, that only an expert will feel at home in. *Thomas Lask, "A Stay Against Oblivion," The New York Times, June 11, 1971, p 31*

Sei Shonagon was a witty, malicious, free-loving lady of the Emperor's court in the great age of Hei'an literature. *Violet Powell, Review of "The Pillow Book of Sei Shonagon," Punch, Jan. 24, 1968, p 136*

heliborne, *adj.* carried or done by helicopter.

Man for man, the U.S. troops may lack some of their enemies' jungle skill, but the rapid availability of firepower

and heliborne mobility have tipped the scales decisively in their favor. *"The Atlantic Report: The War in Vietnam," The Atlantic, Oct. 1966, p 14*

[from *heli-* helicopter + *borne*, as in *airborne*]

he·lic·i·ty (hi:'lis ə ti:), *n. Nuclear Physics.* the direction of the spin of an elementary particle.

Depending on which way the spin turns, the particle [neutrino] can be compared to a left-handed or right-handed screw, and this combination of spin and forward motion is called helicity. *"Helicity of the Antineutrino," Science News, March 28, 1970, p 318*

Helicity can only be defined for particles with non-zero spin angular momentum; and stated very simply, a particle has helicity + 1 if it is seen as spinning counter-clockwise while approaching an observer, while if the observer sees the particle as spinning clockwise, it has helicity −1. *"How the Antineutrino Projects Its Spin," New Scientist, March 19, 1970, p 545*

[from *helic-* (for *helik-*, stem of Greek *hélix* spiral) + *-ity* quality or state]

helilift, *v.t.* to transport by helicopter, especially in an emergency.

Almost immediately, 1,000 reinforcements were helilifted to the heights commanding the battered town. . . . *Time, March 15, 1971, p 24*

[from *heli-* helicopter + *lift*, as in *airlift*]

he·li·o·sphere ('hi: li: ə,sfir), *n.* See the quotation for the meaning.

It [Pioneer Spacecraft] may even be able to detect the unknown limits of the heliosphere, the region in space influenced by the sun's gases and magnetic field, and chart the fringes of interstellar space. *Time, March 15, 1971, p 46*

[from *helio-* sun or solar + *-sphere*]

helipad, *n.* a landing and take-off area for helicopters.

Minutes later, two paratroop platoons from the 101st Airborne Division at nearby Bien Hoa landed on the embassy's rooftop helipad. *Time, Feb. 9, 1968, p 17*

[from *heli-* helicopter + *pad*]

helium speech, an unnatural, squeaky quality in the voice of undersea explorers, divers, etc., when communicating by telephone with the surface, due to interference by the helium gas contained in the pressurized mixture of gases breathed undersea to prevent nitrogen narcosis or "the bends."

There is an urgent requirement for speech converters to unscramble the extraordinary 'Donald Duck' noises of helium speech, and although these have been developed, they mostly at present require bulky equipment which has to be placed onboard the surface support vessel. *Science Journal, June 1968, p 25*

hell·u·va ('hel ə və), *Chiefly U.S. Slang.—adj.* **1** very difficult, unpleasant, etc.

"Once you get him [Gamal Abdel Nasser] out there, it's a helluva job to get him back to the fireplace again." *"The World: Egypt," Time, March 4, 1966, p 24*

2 very good, remarkable, outstanding, etc.

"Some demonstrations can only hurt our cause, you know what I mean. Like Dr. King says, our people've got to meet body force with Soul Force. He sets a good example. Like Joe Louis. He was a helluva fighter, huh? But he knew his place." *Jacob Brackman, "Onward and Upward with the Arts: The Put-on," The New Yorker, June 24, 1967, p 57*

3 great in extent; considerable.

"Money isn't everything, but it's a helluva way ahead of whatever comes in second place." *The Manchester Guardian Weekly, Oct. 20, 1966, p 16*

"We're in a helluva lot better financial position than the communities with higher ratings." *The New York Times, Jan. 8, 1968, p 25*

— *adv.* very; excessively.

. . . I think sourly that drowning on land is a helluva slow way to die. *A. W. Purdy, "Over the Hills" (a poem), Saturday Night (Canada), Feb. 1967, p 23*

[mildly euphemistic respelling (representing the pronunciation) of the slang phrase *hell of a*]

▶ *Helluva* is essentially an intensifier, like *terribly* (in "a terribly good play"), used to give force or emphasis to what is said. In Great Britain this spelling is rarely seen.

hembar, *n.* a hybrid variety of barley developed in 1969 by the U.S. Department of Agriculture.

Hembar yields 15 to 35 per cent more grain than other varieties with similar climate and soil requirements. *Sylvan H. Wittwer, "Agriculture: New Crop Varieties," The World Book Science Annual 1969, p 250*

[coined by Dr. Robert T. Ramage, research scientist of the U.S. Department of Agriculture in Arizona from arbitrary prefix *hem-* + *bar*ley]

hep·a·to·tox·in (ˌhep ə tou'tɑk sən), *n.* a substance poisonous to the liver.

Similarly, when the carcinogenicity of various biologically active compounds such as the aflatoxins and other hepatotoxins is considered, the rainbow trout has been shown to be by far the most sensitive biological system. *Lionel E. Mawdesley-Thomas, "Toxic Chemicals: The Risk to Fish," New Scientist, Jan. 14, 1971, p 75*

[from *hepato-* liver + *toxin* a poison]

hereditarian, *adj.* maintaining that individual traits are determined chiefly by heredity.

Eysenck shows his bias and wastes time by calling the second type of theory hereditarian and the third type environmentalist. *A. H. Halsey, "Heredity and the IQ Test," The Manchester Guardian Weekly, June 26, 1971, p 11*

. . . current studies do not support either an "environmentalist" or a "hereditarian" interpretation of differences in intelligence. . . . *John L. Fuller, "Letters to the Education Editor," Saturday Review, Nov. 16, 1968, p 96*

[adjective use of the noun *hereditarian*, in use since the mid-1800's]

her·ma·typ·ic (ˌhər mə'tip ik), *adj.* reef-building.

He [Thomas F. Goreau] experimentally demonstrated the supreme significance of the endozoic algae (zooxanthellae) present within all hermatypic corals in the necessarily high rate of calcification possessed by these reef builders. *Sir Maurice Yonge, "Professor T. F. Goreau Study of Coral Reefs," The Times (London), May 7, 1970, p 15*

[from Latin *herma* a square pillar (with the head of *Hermes* carved on top) + English -*typic* of the type]

het·er·o ('het ər ou), *adj.* attracted to members of the opposite sex; not homosexual.

The German boy is formal, rather earnest and inclined to homosexuality. The Englishman is a cocky landowner, romantic at heart and hetero. *Jeremy Kingston, "At the Theatre: Review of Robin Maugham's 'Enemy!'," Punch, Dec. 31, 1969, p 1101*

— *n.* a person who is hetero.

Now perhaps it is psychologically or even medically true that homosexual persons, in the nature of their persuasion, are somehow less trustworthy and stable than heteros. *Tom Wicker, "The Undeclared Witch-Hunt," Harper's, Nov. 1969, p 108*

[shortened from *heterosexual, adj., n.*]

heteroatom, *n.* an atom which substitutes for one of the atoms in a hydrocarbon aromatic structure.

Using spectroscopy, Ashe then found that the progressively heavier heteroatoms phosphorus and arsenic did partially disrupt the aromaticity of the rings; this explains the observed relative instability. . . . *"Success Smells of Fish and Onions," New Scientist, Sept. 2, 1971, p 501*

Another "heteroatom" that creates little distortion in the cyclohexane ring is nitrogen. *Joseph B. Lambert, "The Shapes of Organic Molecules," Scientific American, Jan. 1970, p 66*

[from *hetero-* other + *atom*]

heterojunction, *n.* another name for HETEROSTRUCTURE.

A heterojunction comprises a layer of gallium-aluminum-arsenide over gallium-arsenide leads. It serves to reduce the size of the region in which electronic interactions take place, thus reducing the operating current and, hence, the heat generation. *Charles Süsskind, "Electronics," 1971 Britannica Yearbook of Science and the Future, 1970, p 185*

Heterojunctions can be made between different semiconducting materials with the same or different conductivity types. *Morton B. Panish and Izuo Hayashi, "A New Class of Diode Lasers," Scientific American, July 1971, p 36*

heterophobia, *n.* sexual aversion to or fear of members of the opposite sex.

. . . there is strong evidence that many homosexuals suffer from a condition referred to as heterophobia — or fear of the opposite sex. *Peter Pringle, "Using Shock Tactics to Bend the Mind," The Sunday Times (London), May 9, 1971, p 8*

[from *hetero-* other + *phobia*]

heterostructure, *n.* a semiconducting device made up of several different types of semiconductors, used in lasers. *Often used attributively.* Also called HETEROJUNCTION.

Minute sandwich-like "heterostructures" composed of two or more different semiconducting materials show great promise as cheap, efficient carrier-wave generators for use in mass communications. *Morton B. Panish and Izuo Hayashi, "A New Class of Diode Lasers," Scientific American, July 1971, p 32*

The new laser, a double heterostructure diode, employs four thin alternating layers of gallium aluminum arsenide and gallium arsenide. *Science News, Sept. 12, 1970, p 219*

HGH, abbreviation of HUMAN GROWTH HORMONE.

HGH could be a boon to nursing mothers. Twenty-two Mexican women who complained of insufficient milk secretion were given daily injections of HGH for a week. All of their babies recorded significant weight gains during the period. . . . *Time, Jan. 18, 1971, p 23*

. . . HGH is used to treat dwarfism, which occurs in about 20,000 individuals in the United States. *Science News, Dec. 20, 1969, p 570*

hi·ba·ku·sha (hiˈbɑː kuː ʃə), *n. sing.* or *pl.* a survivor or survivors of the atomic explosions that destroyed Hiroshima and Nagasaki in 1945.

Dr. Fumio Shegeto, director of the Hiroshima Red Cross and Atomic Bomb Memorial Hospital, is himself a *"hibakusha"*—a person exposed to the bomb—and has dedicated himself to caring for the afflicted survivors. *Time, Aug. 10, 1970, p 27*

[from Japanese, literally, explosion-affected group]

hiccup, *n.* a short-lived decline in the stock market.

The Second Dual investment trust has already got off to a good start. The managers took advantage of the recent hiccup in the market to buy the dividend units at a lower price. *The Times (London), May 20, 1972, p 18*

hidden tax, an indirect tax; a tax paid by a person in a form other than conventional taxes.

. . . we have imposed a hidden tax on servicemen for years by requiring them to serve at considerably less than they could earn as civilians. *Richard S. Schweiker, U.S. Senator from Pennsylvania, in a Letter to the Editor, The New York Times, Feb. 20, 1970, p 40*

hi-fi, *v.i.* to listen to hi-fi (high-fidelity) recordings or record-playing equipment.

. . . all this wonderful luxuriation and mechanization of the mattress hasn't really lessened the popularity of the traditional *tataimi* [sleeping mat]. After a full Japanese night of swooping, gyrating, see-sawing, saki-sipping, hi-fi-ing, televiewing and general bed-frolicking under mobile mirrors, you're only too pleased to get a bit of sleep on the floor. *"Probe: And the Last Word . . . On Beddos," New Scientist, May 7, 1970, p 269*

[verb use of the noun]

► See the note under HI-RISE.

high, *adj.* **be high on,** to be excited about; be especially fond· of.

. . . Almond goes for obsessions and fatalities and an elliptical style—he's very high on portents. *Pauline Kael, "The Current Cinema," The New Yorker, Dec. 12, 1970, p 177*

'Well, the word is going round,' he [a press agent] says, 'that Zanuck is very high on you just now.' *Peter Fiddick, "Contemplating the Naval," Interview with William Fairchild [a Hollywood writer], The Manchester Guardian Weekly, May 23, 1970, p 15*

[from the phrase *be high on* be under the influence of (a narcotic drug)]

high camp, sophisticated use of the artistically banal or mediocre. Compare LOW CAMP.

[Michael] Sahl may have actually used a piece by Ernst, de Bériot, or one of the early nineteenth-century boys. That would make his score very high camp indeed. *"Discus," Review of "Mitzvah for the Dead," a Violin Composition by Michael Sahl, Harper's, Sept. 1969, p 34*

What we don't learn here is that Joan Crawford movies are now a symbol of High Camp. . . . *Wilfrid Sheed, "Fan Club in Session," The Atlantic, Nov. 1968, p 142*

We'll pay even more for 'Peyton Place'. And in return they [our American friends] will buy that appalling spy thriller Bernard Goldblatt describes as the epitome of high camp. *Cartoon legend, The Listener, June 13, 1968, p 770*

highlighter, *n.* a cosmetic used to highlight or emphasize facial features.

The natural look became the big thing, but it was not natural to produce—you had to learn how and where to put all the new subtly coloured highlighters, shadows, blushers and how to handle the battery of brushes that went with them. *Brigid Keenan, "Breakthrough for the Young," The Times (London), Oct. 22, 1970, p 16*

high profile, an attitude or position that is direct, open, and emphatic; a conspicuously clear-cut stance. Compare LOW PROFILE.

Following his inauguration, the President adopted what in current terminology might be called a fairly "high profile" on Biafran relief. *Elizabeth B. Drew, "Reports: Washington," The Atlantic, June 1970, p 6*

high-rise, *n.* a tall apartment or office building. *Often used attributively.* Also spelled HI-RISE. Compare LOW-RISE.

"We're abating taxes on the land, we're not going so heavy for high-rises. Nobody will be ashamed to live in the houses we're building." *John Lindsay, quoted by Larry L. King, "[Mayor] Lindsay of New York," Harper's, Aug. 1968, p 39*

Corbusier proposed to stack people vertically in high-rise towers so that the surrounding land could be freed for parks and playgrounds. *Time, Oct. 23, 1964, p 55*

high-riser, *n. U.S.* See the quotation for the meaning.

Demand rose to new heights in the mid-1960s with the introduction of high-risers—those small-wheeled children's bikes with elongated "banana" seats, tall "ape-hanger" handlebars, and moderate $30-$50 price tags. *Time, June 14, 1971, p 60*

high-voltage, *adj.* high-powered; dynamic.

Her [Nadine Gordimer's] principal problem, never really overcome, is how to join a low-key character to high-voltage politics without diminishing interest in either. Bray is too often a laboriously illustrated abstraction of honor and decency whom Miss Gordimer attempts to quicken with some peculiarly imprecise and subjective imagery. *"Books: Recessional," Review of "A Guest of Honour" (a novel) by Nadine Gordimer, Time, Nov. 16, 1970, p 103*

hijack, *n.* the act or crime of stealing or taking over by force a vehicle in transit, especially an airplane. Compare SKYJACK.

Michael said they were well looked after during the hijack but it was a frightening experience because the guerrillas filled the cockpit with explosives. *"Hijacking Crisis: Guerrillas Gave Their Autographs to Boy," The Times (London), Sept. 14, 1970, p 4*

[noun use of *hijack, v.*]

HILAC (ˈhɑɪˌlæk), *n.* acronym for *Heavy Ion Linear Accelerator*, a machine for accelerating ions of heavy particles, such as those of carbon and helium, to velocities capable of initiating nuclear reactions. Compare LINAC.

The rebuilt HILAC . . . at Berkeley [California] is also due for operation in 1972. It is expected to produce viable beams of particles as heavy as uranium. *New Scientist, July 2, 1970, p 8*

► HILAC has the appearance of having the ending *-ac* (or *-AC*) that is used in the names of computers

(*ENIAC, SEAC, UNIVAC*), in which it stands for *A*utomatic *C*omputer. Actually, the ending in *HILAC* is *-LAC*, for *L*inear *Ac*celerator, its linearity being what distinguishes it from the *-tron* type of circular accelerators, such as *cyclotron, bevatron, synchrotron*.

hinc·ty ('hiŋk ti:), *adj. U.S. Slang, chiefly Afro-American.* snobbish; conceited.

"I never did like Woolworth's," a fat lady said to us. "None of these stores hire colored, but the help are the hinctiest and now they done gone and killed that child." *Louise Meriwether, Daddy was a Number Runner, 1970, p 147*

...we were in this hincty little town in Georgia doing this flick about this rural pothead, called "Georgia High"....*F. P. Tullius, "Ninety-Nine Years is Not Forever," The New Yorker, July 19, 1969, p 20*

[of unknown origin]

Hinglish, *n.* a blend of Hindi and English spoken in India. Compare FRINGLISH, JAPLISH, SPANGLISH.

...now that the British-born teachers have gone home, English is on its way to becoming a native language—or, rather, native languages. (One native language has already been given the name Hinglish. It uses English parts of speech for more complicated functions, as in this Hinglish sentence: "Dekho great democratic institutions kaise India main develop ho rahi hain," which in English is "See how the great democratic institutions are developing here in India.") *Ved Mehta, "A Reporter at Large: Indian Journal," The New Yorker, Sept. 9, 1967, p 96*

hip, *U.S. Slang.* —*n.* the condition of being alert or wise to what is new, smart, stylish, etc.

Grooviness [at the discothèque "Yellowfinger's"] merges with aplomb, and hip attains a state akin to quiet well-being. *"Goings On About Town," The New Yorker, Sept. 19, 1970, p 7*

—*v.t.* to keep informed; alert; wise up.

When they [Bernadette Devlin and Peter Cush] reached Bootstrap [a black project in Watts], it was empty except for one woman, Eleanor Childs, the young education director, who said, "No one was hippin' us that this chick was coming." *Sara Davidson, "Bernadette Devlin: An Irish Revolutionary In Irish America," Harper's, Jan. 1970, p 83*

[noun and verb use of *hip, adj.*, alert, informed, up-to-date]

hipdom, *n.* another name for HIPPIEDOM.

The largest concentrations [of organic food stores] are in the capitals of hipdom: New York and California....*Time, April 12, 1971, p 60*

hip-hugger, *adj.* clinging to the hips. See also HIP-HUGGERS.

In performance, the Market offers no lights, no flash, and their clothes run to casual mixtures of epauletted jackets, Indian beads and hiphugger pants. *Jack Batten, "Canada's Rock Scene: Going, Going...," Maclean's, Feb. 1968, p 42*

There are separates, too, such as long jackets, stovepipe hip-hugger trousers, very full shorts, and box-pleated skirts that hook up with bridle bits of silver metal. *M. M., "On and Off the Avenue: This and That," The New Yorker, Aug. 26, 1967, p 82*

hip-huggers, *n.pl.* trousers that start about an inch and a half below the waistline and cling closely to the hips.

What time. Ten to ten. Her spindly model legs reach for the floor....From the tall closet beside her bed takes the hanger out with her gray hip-huggers. *Barbara H. Kevles, "In Search of Nan Page," The Atlantic, July 1970, p 78*

Knickers and gauchos, hip-huggers, bellbottoms and jeans—all are currently outselling dresses of any length. *"Modern Living: All in the Jeans," Time, Jan. 11, 1971, p 38*

hippie or **hippy,** *n.* a person who breaks away from conventional society, espousing complete freedom of expression, typically by wearing unconventional clothes and letting the hair go ungroomed, and maintaining a philosophy of love and fellowship. Hippies often live in communes and engage in free love and the free use of drugs. Compare FLOWER CHILD, YIPPIE.

A few wear the garb of hippies—beards, beads, jeans, long gowns—but most are simply young men and women dressed for midsummer comfort. *Howard Taubman, The New York Times, Aug. 6, 1968, p 25*

Robert Morley, playing a retired General, reacts to his children's strange behaviour by becoming a hippy himself and finally living up a walnut tree. *"The London Charivari: Theatre," Listing of "Halfway Up the Tree" (a play), Punch, March 6, 1968, p vi*

Young Canadians and Americans who want to get into Mexico are finding it hard these days to get tourist visas if they're hippies, or at least look like hippies. *Maclean's, June 1968, p 3*

—*adj.* of, relating to, or characteristic of hippies.

...although the youth at Woodstock had many hippie values, they were mainly college and high school students from middle-class homes. *Abigail L. Kuflik, "Woodstock," The Americana Annual 1970, p 484*

Almost every newspaper account emphasized the hippie dress and hair, yet I don't think more than a small fraction of the population there affected that style. *Bruce Jackson, "The Battle of the Pentagon," The Atlantic, Jan. 1968, p 39*

There appeared to be nothing of hippy disdain for convention evident in the hall and when two youths began to jive in the gangway this produced only embarrassment and a few girlish giggles around them. *The Times (London), Feb. 21, 1968, p 10*

[originally (1950's) "a person who is very or overly hip" (i.e., excessively eager to be ahead in the latest styles, extremely unconventional), from *hip, adj.*, alert, informed, up-to-date, + *-ie* or *-y*, diminutive suffix, probably formed for contrast with *hipster* one who is hip]

hippiedom, *n.* the realm or world of hippies; hippies as a group. Also called HIPDOM.

All in all *Hair* [a musical]...seems to be a truer and fairer representation of hippiedom than anything the theater has offered so far. *Henry Hewes, "The Theater of Shattered Focus," Saturday Review, Jan. 13, 1968, p 95*

The infernal glare that the Sharon Tate murders has thrown on hippiedom has produced a cease-and-desist order to television comics and their jokes about beads, LSD, and long hair. *Alistair Cooke, The Manchester Guardian Weekly, Dec. 20, 1969, p 4*

hippiness or **hippieness,** *n.* the quality or condition of being a hippie.

...I also liked the switched-on hippiness of Amanda Trees as Decibelle, smoothly prepared to make any scene, even matrimony. *Clive Barnes, The New York Times, Sept. 18, 1968, p 50*

You can make sense out of a [rock] group like Exodus — with their veneer of Dutch hippieness they bring to mind the Indonesians who waltzed around the Rembrandts-plein. . . . *Robert Stone, "There It Is," The Manchester Guardian Weekly, July 24, 1971, p 15*

hippyism or **hippieism,** *n.* adherence to the hippie cult; hippie practices and ideas.

Oppressed by a hippyism which seemed, in its elected rags, to mock the peasants in their enforced rags, I put on a collar and tie (the first ever seen in Deya) and spoke on Shakespeare, the ambitious, the money-getter, the ultimate bourgeois. *Anthony Burgess, The New York Times, Dec. 11, 1970, p 47*

. . . Another Approach to the youth market was to select themes and subjects, that, hopefully, would prove appealing. This was somewhat more risky, as Otto Preminger's grim attempt at hippieism, *Skidoo!,* devastatingly demonstrated. Young people are notoriously intolerant, and bad news travels fast. *Arthur Knight, "Motion Pictures," The 1970 World Book Year Book, p 425*

hi-rise, *n.* another spelling of HIGH-RISE.

. . . atop the hi-rise, treble-glazed flats that fringe Regent's Park, company directors nudge their mistresses on to the balconies of £50,000 penthouses to admire the view. . . . *Punch, May 7, 1969, p viii*

▶ *Hi-rise* is a current example of the use of the phonetic spelling *hi* instead of *high.* This spelling has wide currency in such words as *hi-fi* (for high-fidelity), *hifalutin,* and (chiefly in the U.S.) *hijinks.* The form *hijack* may also belong in this category if its first syllable originally represented *high,* but this is not known (the variant form *high-jack* being due to folk etymology). A similar simplified form often encountered in the United States is *nite* for night.

histocompatibility, *n.* compatibility of graft tissue; graft acceptance.

Organ transplantation has brought urgency to the problem of the genetics of histocompatibility. *Victor A. McKusick, "Medicine: Genetics," Britannica Book of the Year 1970, p 500*

[from *histo-* tissue (from Greek *histós* web) + *compatibility*]

histocompatible, *adj.* exhibiting histocompatibility.

Adoptive transfer of autoimmune encephalomyelitis between histocompatible guinea pigs has been regularly used recently to elucidate the mechanisms of autoimmune diseases. *Science, March 1, 1968, p 995*

histoincompatibility, *n.* incompatibility of graft tissue; graft rejection.

. . . these animals have virtually no immunological reactivity, so we felt confident that our test would not be complicated in any important way by histoincompatibility reactions between cells and hosts. *New Scientist and Science Journal, July 8, 1971, p 90*

hit, *Slang.* —*n.* an injection of a narcotic drug, especially heroin.

None of them will admit to an outsider that they are addicted but boast of the occasional sniff or "hit" as their elder brothers boasted of getting drunk — as a virility symbol. *The Times (London), March 13, 1970, p 11*

—*v.i., v.t.* to give oneself or another person an injection of narcotics; to shoot up.

I [Jeffrey, a nineteen year old boy] started hitting up once a day, and a couple of months later I started shooting two and three times a day. *Time, March 16, 1970, p 18*

How did he become an addict?

"You mean, who hit me first? My friend, Johnny." *The New York Times, Feb. 23, 1970, p 26*

hobbit, *n.* one of a fictitious race of genial, lovable, elflike creatures with furry feet created by the British writer John Ronald Reuel Tolkien, born 1882.

The saddest prospect is that the coming reaction will fall not only on these "new Fascisti" but also on a lot of innocents. Among them will be a good many students of the kind described by Nan Robertson of the New York Times as "intellectual hobbits — warm, lovable, and a little furry-minded." *John Fischer, "The Easy Chair: The Consequences of Peace," Harper's, Feb. 1968, p 18*

Few Nepalese or Tibetans have heard of it [the kingdom of Mustang] either: the Tibetans who have called it 'the land of Lo' — which makes it sound as if it were inhabited by Hobbits. *Gilbert Phelps, Review of "Mustang: A Lost Tibetan Kingdom" by Michel Peissel, The Listener, Dec. 26, 1968, p 864*

He is intensely vivid about Melbourne . . . its complex social structure, its railways and tramways, its hobos, hobbits and habits. *The Sunday Times (London), May 19, 1968, p 58*

ho-dad, *n. Surfing Slang.* a person who doesn't surf or who surfs poorly or amateurishly.

This book [*Surf's Up! An Anthology of Surfing*] assembles a couple of dozen pieces on this dazzling sport. . . . Cartoon columns from California papers make argot such as *ho-dad* and *cowabunga* clear to the uninitiate. *Scientific American, Dec. 1966, p 148*

[of uncertain origin]

hog, *n.* **low on the hog,** in a thrifty manner; without excessive or lavish spending.

"Compared to a Congressman, an M.P. lives lower on the hog, campaigns more quietly and takes fewer lavish junkets." *The Times (London), June 4, 1970, p 10*

[patterned after *high on the hog* in a lavish manner]

hoi chanh ('hoi 'cha:n), (in South Vietnam) returnees or defectors from Communist-controlled areas.

One American officer concerned with classification problems said, "We aren't going to accept them as *hoi chanh* if they don't turn themselves in until we come along and tell them we're going to blow up their hamlet and then they come running out waving their leaflet." *Jonathan Schell, "A Reporter at Large: The Village of Ben Suc," The New Yorker, July 15, 1967, p 88*

[from Vietnamese]

hoi-polloi ('hɔi pə'lɔi), *n. Slang.* clamor; fuss.

"New models every year and all this hoi-polloi about introductions and all that are becoming passé," says Henry Ford. *"Autos: Shifting Down for the '70's," Time, Feb. 23, 1970, p 80*

[possibly from confusion of *hoi polloi* the common people, the masses, with *hullabaloo* or *hoopla*]

holding pattern, a circular pattern flown by an aircraft above or near an airport while it waits to be cleared for landing.

Actually I was not over New York at all; I was in a "holding pattern" over Allentown, Pennsylvania. *Russell Lynes, "After Hours," Harper's, Oct. 1968, p 38*

holding tank, *U.S.* a tank on a boat for holding sewage to be pumped out at a dockside station.

Whatever the size of a holding tank, however, critics point out that its contents end up in municipal sewage plants—which in turn dump their often undertreated effluent into waterways. *Time, May 3, 1971, p 45*

hold time, a delay in the countdown or launching operations of a rocket or missile.

Fortunately, the countdown schedule had been padded with enough precautionary hold time to enable technicians to replace the oxygen without delaying the launch. *Time, Dec. 27, 1968, p 13*

Holocaust, *n.* **the Holocaust,** the Nazi destruction of European Jewry in World War II. Compare FINAL SOLUTION.

Before the Holocaust and the foundation of the state of Israel...the Zionist settlers in Palestine, the *"Yishuv,"* already thought of their return to the land...as having a quality of idealism so dedicated that it would symbolically purify Jewish existence....*Alfred Kazin, "In Israel: After the Triumph," Harper's, Nov. 1967, p 77*

hol·o·gram ('hɑl ə‚græm), *n.* a record or reproduction of an image produced on a photographic plate or film by holography.

...lasers alone can produce coherent beams strong enough to make holograms. *Science News, May 10, 1969, p 460*

Included in the exhibits displayed by International Business Machines at Edinburgh is a computer-generated hologram. *The Times (London), Aug. 9, 1968, p 17*

[from Greek *hólos* whole + English *-gram* record]

hol·o·graph ('hɑl ə‚græf), *v.t.* to make a hologram of; produce by holography.

The main purpose of the meeting, however, was to show the extent to which holography can be used to make accurate engineering measurements. This stems from the fact that a hologram stores a faithful three dimensional record of the object being 'holographed', and the reconstructed image can be matched against the object itself. *Science Journal, March 1968, p 86*

holographic, *adj.* of, relating to, or done by holography.

The original problem with holography was that whereas it is easy to record the square of the amplitude of the diffraction pattern, the phase is usually lost, and without a record of the phase the holographic reconstruction is poor except for very special objects. *Donald R. Herriott, "Applications of Laser Light," Scientific American, Sept. 1968, p 154*

ho·log·ra·phy (hɑ'lɑg rə fi:), *n.* a lensless method of photography in which a three-dimensional image is recorded on a photographic plate or film by means of laser light. The laser light is split into two beams that interfere with each other to form a pattern which depends on the shape of the photographed object. When the pattern on the plate or film is then exposed to visible light, a three-dimensional image of the object is formed. Compare ACOUSTICAL HOLOGRAPHY.

But still more spectacular is use of the laser as the basis for a new type of photography called holography. Laser light projected through a photographic film with holographic techniques, gives a real three-dimensional image with a wealth of detail and a remarkable depth of focus. *Science, Feb. 16, 1968, p 702*

Holography differs from photography in that it uses the coherent properties of laser light to record all the information in an arrangement of light rays on a piece of photographic film. *David Denby and John N. Butters, New Scientist, Feb. 26, 1970, p 394*

Fribram's hobby is photography, and when holography became a practical reality, he perceived its relevance to problems of brain function that had been baffling for many years. *Scientific American, Jan. 1969, p 18*

holophone, *n.* a device for recording an acoustical hologram.

A holophone records patterns in time in a manner analogous to the way an optical hologram records patterns in space. *"Trying to Get a Plasma to Remember Things," New Scientist and Science Journal, Jan. 21, 1971, p 105*

hol·o·scope ('hɑl ə‚skoup), *n.* an optical instrument for producing holographic images.

A suggestion to combine the optical non-linear effects with holography has led to a proposal that can in principle yield a "holoscope", a true three-dimensional microscope that could be used in much the same way as a normal two-dimensional one. *New Scientist, July 13, 1967, p 97*

[from Greek *hólos* whole + English *-scope* instrument for viewing]

holoscopic, *adj.* of or based upon complete or overall observation; comprising everything in sight.

Daiches found himself "licensed Platonist", i.e. ready to relate judgments on novels, literature, to the rest of creation—history, nature of man, etc.; "holoscopic" view. *Paul Jennings, "Great Scots," The Sunday Times (London), May 21, 1972, p 40*

[from Greek *hólos* whole + English *-scopic*, as in *microscopic* and *macroscopic*]

home and dry, *British.* safe.

"I don't want to sound too confident," he told us, "we cannot afford to assume that we are home and dry until the votes have been counted at the annual meeting." *The Times (London), Feb. 17, 1970, p 23*

home help, *British.* a woman who is hired to do housework.

There would be more staff, more home helps, more meals-on-wheels, more accommodation and clubs, more hostels for the mentally handicapped, more adult training centres. *John Roper, "Extra Funds for Health to Improve Care in Neglected Sectors," The Times (London), Nov. 12, 1970, p 4*

▶ *Help, n.* in the sense of a domestic servant or servants collectively) was originally and is still chiefly a U.S. use. But the phrase *home help* appears to be used only in Great Britain. In the United States, *help* is also applied to office, factory, or farm workers.

hominization, *n.* the act or process of making manlike in character or nature.

...dehumanization of the living worker was complemented, paradoxically, by the progressive hominization of the machine—hominization in the sense of giving the automation some of the mechanical equivalents of lifelike mo-

homme

tion and purpose.... *Lewis Mumford, "The Megamachine," The New Yorker, Oct. 17, 1970, p 131*

[from *homin-* (stem of Latin *homō* man) + *-ization*; formed on the pattern of *humanization*]

homme (ɔ:m), *n.* the French word for "man," used in English in various French compounds, as the following:

homme d'af·faires ('ɔ:m da'fer), a businessman; (literally) man of affairs.

Henri Micmacher is an homme d'affaires in the strict French sense. He is the founder-president of Pronuptia, the Paris-based marriage-gear multiple that in 1971 reckons to sell upwards of 46,000 wedding dresses. *Richard Milner, "Prufrock: Love and Profit," The Sunday Times (London), June 27, 1971, p 49*

homme de con·fiance ('ɔ:m də kɔ̃'fyɑ̃s), a man of trust; a right-hand man.

Around the death-bed of General Franco, an anxious crowd of would-be successors clusters: Admiral Carrero Blanco, the sometime submarine commander who has been the Caudillo's *homme de confiance* for 30 years.... *The Times (London), Oct. 30, 1970, p 10*

homme du monde ('ɔ:m dʏ 'mɔ̃d), a man of the world.

... Michel Piccoli [is a] good actor: one of those Frenchmen who excel at playing strong, not quite handsome, amused, interestingly jaded, middle-aged *hommes du monde*, a category nonexistent in contemporary American and English acting. *Penelope Gilliatt, "The Current Cinema: Coup de Foudre," Review of "The Things of Life," The New Yorker, Sept. 5, 1970, p 64*

homme du sy·stème ('ɔ:m dʏ si:'stem), a man of the system.

In turn unreconstructed Tory, ... Whig, and Liberal, he adapted to most major shifts in political ideas and practices. Party affiliation is in one sense irrelevant, for Palmerston was a great placeman on the eighteenth-century model, an homme du système who happily worked it without questioning its basic assumptions. *Angus Macintyre, "Books," Review of "Lord Palmerston" by Jasper Ridley, The Manchester Guardian Weekly, Dec. 12, 1970, p 18*

homo, *n.* the Latin word for "man," used in various Latin compounds to describe some essential characteristic or quality, on the analogy of established scientific terms such as *homo sapiens* ("rational man") and *homo faber* ("worker man"), including:

homo americanus, American man.

What Perosa finds in [F. Scott] Fitzgerald's fiction is a comedy of manners "with all its tragic implications," a way of writing through which he was able to define that unique creature, *homo americanus. Saturday Review, Oct. 26, 1968, p 42*

homo aquaticus, aquatic man.

... the name of Commandant Jacques-Yves Cousteau is so familiar, with his celebrated conception of *homo aquaticus*, which he predicted at the Congress of Underwater Activities in London in 1962. *New Scientist, Feb. 20, 1969, p 390*

homo insipiens, foolish man; the opposite of *homo sapiens*.

Thus, in dread of the fate of *homo insipiens*, more people, it would seem, are inclined to take time off to look again at the question: why? *The Times (London), Oct. 17, 1970, p 14*

homo ludens, playful or sportive man.

The Cyprus problem is anyway absorbingly complex. It embraces almost every aspect of the diplomatic game and *homo ludens* cannot fail to have an entertaining time delving into its subtleties on the spot. *David Gallagher, "Eat Kebab, Drink Othello," The Listener, Jan. 12, 1967, p 53*

homo maniacus, mad man.

Witnessing this worldwide obduracy, writers as disparate as Naturalist Konrad Lorenz and Novelist Arthur Koestler have redefined Homo sapiens as Homo maniacus.... *Time, June 7, 1968, p 30*

homo mathematicus, mathematical man.

This nearly perfect insulation of the national security managers leads them into the trap of collecting isolated facts and figures. McNamara was of course the leading specimen in the national security bureaucracy of *homo mathematicus*, i.e., men who behave, and believe that other men behave, primarily in response to "hard data," usually numbers (infiltration rates, "kill ratios," bomb tonnage). *Richard Barnet, "The Game of Nations," Harper's, Nov. 1971, p 57*

homo monstrosus, monstrous man.

When Carl von Linné (Linnaeus) worked out his monumental classification of natural things in the 18th century, he included the species Homo monstrosus. By Homo monstrosus he meant a species related to Homo sapiens but markedly different in physical appearance. *Scientific American, Oct. 1968, p 113*

homo neuroticus, neurotic man.

"Homo neuroticus," says Mrs. Szasz, "de-animalizes his pets in exactly the same way he de-humanizes himself." *Time, Feb. 14, 1969, p 50*

Ho·mo hab·i·lis ('hou mou 'hæb ə lis), an extinct species of man believed to have been the earliest toolmaker, about 1,700,000 years ago, whose fossil fragments were discovered in the early 1960's at the Olduvai Gorge in northern Tanzania.

Today one of the great questions is whether the earliest known manlike creature, Homo habilis, was actually a maker of tools. *Froelich Rainey, "Archaeology: Old World-New World Relationships," 1969 Britannica Yearbook of Science and the Future, 1968, p 232*

[from Latin *homō habilis* skillful man]

ho·mo·phile ('hou mə,faɪl), *n.* a person attracted to members of his own sex; a homosexual.

But to Dr. Ullerstam this [a Swedish law prohibiting homosexual contacts until the age of eighteen] seems unfair because "it causes the homophiles greater suffering than would appear at first sight [since] youths between fifteen and eighteen are often the most attractive and most available objects for the homosexual urge." *Robert J. Levin, Review of "The Erotic Minorities" by Lars Ullerstam, Saturday Review, July 9, 1966, p 30*

—*adj.* concerned with the rights or the welfare of homophiles.

Homophile activists contend that there would be more happy homosexuals if society were more compassionate.... *"Behavior: The Homosexual: Newly, Newly Understood," Time, Oct. 31, 1969, p 42*

There are, nowadays, increasing exchanges between the medical profession and the nonpatient—what Larry Littlejohn of San Francisco's homophile Society for Individual Rights (SIR) calls "impatient"—homosexuals. These exchanges are not always pleasant occasions.... *Faubion*

Bowers, *"Homosex: Living the Life," Saturday Review,* Feb. 12, 1972, p 28

[from *homo-* the same, of the same species + *-phile* (one) attracted to]

homo sap, short for *homo sapiens,* used humorously with allusion to *sap* (a fool).

Meanwhile, the solar system has been visited by aliens who seem to want to eliminate homo sap. *Edmund Cooper, "Science Fiction," The Sunday Times (London),* May 2, 1971, p 37

The earliest fact, and the latest, is differences increasing and multiplying, with *Homo sap* struggling to lasso and harness their circumambience for the varying uses of his struggle to keep on struggling. *Horace M. Kallen, "How I Bet My Life," Saturday Review,* Oct. 1, 1966, p 29

homosex, *n.* short for *homosexuality.*

The universe of homosexuality is so extraordinary that to know all its birds with their widely different plumage is to unknow it. Simultaneously shut and unshuttered, homosex exists in an overwhelming array of constellations and configurations. It defies logic, the way reason capitulates before love. The general public's recent awakening to the reality of homosexuality has, regrettably, not brought anything approaching ironclad understanding or sledge hammer conclusions. The questions who? what? why? bafflingly persist. *Faubion Bowers, "Homosex: Living The Life," Saturday Review,* Feb. 2, 1972, p 23

hon·cho ('hɑnt ʃou), *n. U.S. Slang.* chief; headman; boss.

Mr. Komer expects to be able to name these 45 key provincial *honchos,* and he hopes to place civilians in at least a quarter of the posts. *The New York Times,* June 4, 1967, Sec. 4, p 1

Nicholas Johnson, the [Federal Communications] commission's most outspoken liberal (who has also called for more public involvement in TV), recently criticized Nixon for clearing [Dean] Burch's appointment with broadcasting honchos before announcing it. *"Activist at the FCC?" Time,* Nov. 21, 1969, p 24

[originally U.S. Army use in Asia, from Japanese *hanchō* group leader]

Hong Kong flu, a variety of the Asian flu, caused by a virus first identified in Hong Kong, which spread throughout the world in 1969 and early 1970. Also called MAO FLU.

Army recruits at Fort Benning, Ga., wore face masks to cut the possibility of catching Hong Kong flu, which reached epidemic proportions in January. *Picture legend, The 1970 World Book Year Book,* p 365

hon·ky or **hon·kie** ('hɑŋ ki:), *n. U.S. Slang, used disparagingly.* a white man.

Mr. Lehman Brightman, a militant South Dakota Sioux who is now president of the United Native Americans in Berkeley, California, comments angrily: "Even the name Indian is not ours—it was given us by some dumb honky who got lost and thought he'd landed in India." *Ian McDonald, "Jane Fonda on the Warpath," The Times (London),* March 10, 1970, p 10

[originally used among Negroes in the U.S., of unknown origin]

hook, *n.* See the quotations for two specialized meanings.

The author of several how-to-do-it books (among them

Writing Articles that Sell, which she uses as the text for her course), she [Louise Boggess] points her students straight toward the mass writing market. In her streamlined, practical lessons the emphasis is unabashedly on formula writing that will sell. Her very first assignment is how to write a "hook," meaning an arresting opening sentence. What does she think of the word "The" for an opener? It doesn't exactly grab her, she admitted. *Jessica Mitford, "Let Us Now Appraise Famous Writers," The Atlantic,* July 1970, p 53

To the surfer each breaker has a "hook," or crest, a "shoulder," the calm portion behind the hook, and a "shore break," the final surge ending in the inevitable "soup," or foam. *Peter Bart, The New York Times,* Aug. 10, 1965, p 31

hoot, *n. British Slang.* something hilariously amusing or funny.

... 'The Projector' [a play] was a marvellous hoot, it was a very elaborate parody but everybody thought it was the real thing. *The Manchester Guardian Weekly,* June 5, 1971, p 16

After dinner, all the chaps chuck their clubs in a heap, and the wives have to pick a club and go off with the owner; it's going to be an absolute hoot! *Alan Coren, "Oh, Come All Ye Trendy!" Punch,* Dec. 17, 1969, p 990

hootch (hu:tʃ), *n. Slang, chiefly U.S. Military use in Asia.* **1** a thatched hut in which natives live.

They found in the village "undefended and unarmed women, children and old men in their hootches"—American soldiers' slang for grass-thatched huts. *The Times (London),* Nov. 18, 1970, p 6

At Phuoc Vinh, a black 1st Cavalry trooper recently dragged a wounded white from a rocketed hootch when no other black or white dared to venture in. *Time,* Sept. 19, 1969, p 19

2 (by extension) any house or dwelling.

It is a minor point, but if Mr. Dareff would have us believe that the term "hootches" is used to make fun of or belittle the Vietnamese for the way they live, I would like to point out that this term is used universally here in Vietnam to describe any dwelling, including our own, and that there is nothing "jocular" or malicious or belittling about the word at all. *John R. Cope, "Book Forum: Letters from Readers," Saturday Review,* Aug. 24, 1968, p 35

[from Japanese *uchi* house; the form was probably influenced by *hutch*]

hooter, *n. British Slang.* a nose.

... there are estimated to be over 500,000 people in this country [Great Britain] hooked on the ludicrous custom of impelling fermented tobacco-powder up their hooters. *New Scientist and Science Journal,* Feb. 4, 1971, p 229

hoo·ver ('hu: vər), *v.i., v.t. British.* to take up with or as if with a vacuum cleaner; to vacuum.

... we are and always have been a race of philistines. If this were not so the populace would not dissipate their lives watching professional pugilists and footballers or sit hoovering up the drivel poured out on television at peak viewing times.... *J. P. Brooke-Little, in a Letter to the Editor, The Times (London),* Nov. 2, 1970, p 9

"I have him in the baby bouncer while I'm practising after breakfast every morning, so he thinks it's like hoovering; just a part of life." *Suzy Menkes, The Times (London),* March 11, 1968, p 11

[from *Hoover,* trademark of a vacuum cleaner]

hopefully, *adv.* it is hoped (that).

Some day soon, we hope, he will combine the three books.

And, "hopefully," as current jabberwocky has it, make the reader's task just a trifle easier. *Charles Poore, The New York Times, Dec. 11, 1965, p 31*

Hopefully, listening will eventually lead to a desire on the part of the majority—as well as on the part of the minority—to correct injustices and change traditions, thus eliminating the need for a student like me, who has campaigned within the system and demonstrated peacefully, to turn to destruction of property, rock throwing and animalistic violence out of sheer frustration and despair. *Sherrill Cohen, Los Angeles, Calif., in a Letter to the Editor, Time, July 13, 1970, p 2*

Hopefully it has now passed the halfway mark. *Daily Telegraph (London), Oct. 5, 1971, p 16*

▶ The normal meaning of this adverb is "in a hopeful manner." Its new meaning, which came to be widely used in the 1960's, appears to have been patterned after German *hoffentlich*, which is used exactly the way the English word is. The new usage has been criticized or disparaged (as in the first quotation above) by many writers; nevertheless, it has become by now thoroughly established.

hormonology, *n.* the scientific study of hormones or internal secretions.

It used to be a shibboleth of hormonology that such messenger molecules were not affected by the chemical process they influenced but that they would emerge unscathed from the target organ; this is now known not always to be the case. *Arnold Klopper, "The Reproductive Hormones," Science Journal, June 1970, p 44*

horn, *n.* **the horn,** *U.S. Slang.* the telephone.

This morning, I got on the horn to Secretary Finch, just on a hunch, and asked him whether habitual ingestion of large portions of hominy might not have deleterious effects on the American stomach lining. *Roger Angell, "How They Brought the Bad News From Ghent (N.Y.) to Aix (Kans.)," The New Yorker, Jan. 3, 1970, p 26*

hors d'oeuvre, 1 (adverbial use) outside the major concern; apart from the main undertaking.

Adolfo ... was an important boutiquier when other custom milliners ventured no farther than hors d'oeuvre than an occasional scarf or handbag. *Lois Long, "On and Off the Avenue: Feminine Fashions," The New Yorker, Oct. 18, 1969, p 158*

2 (noun use) something beyond the main concern; something peripheral.

Restraints on free speech are usually hors d'oeuvres for the Supreme Court, but when Congress outlawed draft card burning to squelch antiwar dissent, the Justices backed the law, 7 to 1. *The New York Times, June 20, 1968, p 32*

... dictionaries ... of space and medical terms, and a number of other little compendia that look substantial in a table of contents but are essentially mere hors d'oeuvres. *Saturday Review, Nov. 19, 1966, p 49*

▶ The common meaning of *hors d'oeuvre* in both French and English is "appetizer," "side dish." In French the form is usually hyphenated and does not take a plural *-s.*

hors texte (or 'tekst), *French.* outside the text; printed on a separate leaf of a book, not with the text.

James A. Michener's text for *Facing East*, printed on Arches paper, with nine original in-text woodcuts by Levine, plus one *hors texte* original woodcut.... *Advertisement by Random House/Maecenas Press, The New Yorker, Nov. 14, 1970, p 107*

host-specific, *adj.* living on or in a particular species of host.

The plague bacterium is transferred from rat to rat by a particular flea which like all other fleas is host-specific; ordinarily it will feed on the blood of rats and rats alone. *The Times (London), Feb. 21, 1970, p IV*

hot dog, *U.S. Slang.* a very skillful athlete or sportsman, especially one able to perform stunts.

We had this one [basketball] player, Alston Mackintosh, from Oleander College in Nebraska, who could hit nine out of ten from the foul line with his back to the basket. He was a real hot dog, but when we had him move up to the pros he couldn't take the pressure. *Rudolph Wurlitzer, "The Boiler Room," The Atlantic, March 1966, p 131*

[probably from *hot dog!* exclamation used to show pleasure, admiration, etc.]

hot-dog, *adj.* *U.S. Slang.* very skillful; able to perform stunts.

I think I told you about Roscoe in one of my other letters. He's a hot-dog surfer and he used to be real wigged on Zen. *F. P. Tullius, "Season's Greetings from West Hollywood," The New Yorker, Dec. 31, 1966, p 28*

hothouse effect, another term for GREENHOUSE EFFECT.

... the Chief Inspector dismisses as "popular fantasies" the postulated "hothouse effect" of increased atmospheric carbon dioxide and the opposite cooling effect of extra dust in the air. *New Scientist, Sept. 3, 1970, p 451*

hot line, 1 a direct teletype line open for instant communication between leaders of different governments in case of an emergency.

Walt. W. Rostow, the President's national security adviser, was calling to report that the "hot line" was being activated from Moscow.

Since the hot-line link between Washington and Moscow was first put into operation on Aug. 30, 1963, it had conveyed nothing more dramatic than New Year's greetings and hourly testing messages. *Time, June 16, 1967, p 15*

2 a telephone line constantly open for communication in an emergency.

... drug abuse is a serious problem that can be dealt with only by a coordinated community effort. In such efforts a variety of orthodox and innovative services are interlocked to provide treatment and preventive services. Hot lines, storefront clinics, and rap sessions are backed up by emergency medical clinics and hospital facilities. *Sidney Cohen, M.D., "Drug Addiction and Abuse," The Americana Annual 1971, p 255*

3 *U.S. and Canada.* a radio or television program which broadcasts conversations with people who telephone the studio with questions, problems, etc.

About 20 orators arose, one after another, to espouse everything from (predictably enough) free university tuition to local night shopping and radio hot lines. *Ken Mitchell, "Speech So Free Nobody Wants It," Maclean's, Sept. 17, 1966, p 3*

[originally (early 1950's) a U.S. Air Force term for a direct telephone line between distant bases]

hot mooner, a scientist who believes there is thermal or volcanic activity in the moon's core and that this activity, rather than the impact of meteorites, produced the lunar craters. Also called VULCANIST. Compare COLD MOONER.

Hot mooners who believe that the moon has or once had a molten core like the earth's are still hot mooners. *The Sunday Times (London), Jan. 11, 1970, p 7*

The •meetings of GLEP [Group for Lunar Exploration Planning] are a little like auctions, with scientists whose instruments can be best set up on the lowland *maria* [flat areas originally thought to be seas] dickering with geologists who want rocks from the highlands — and even hot-mooners bargaining with cold-mooners to go to sites they think may be volcanic. *Henry S. F. Cooper, Jr., "Letter From the Space Center," The New Yorker, Jan. 9, 1971, p 69*

hot pants, close-fitting short pants, cut high on the leg, worn by women in place of a skirt or in combination with a split skirt.

The accepted generic term, hot pants, lends the style the leering inference of an adolescent joke. But short shorts are no joke; they are serious business.... *"Hot Pants: Legs Are Back," Time, Feb. 1, 1971, p 48*

When a fashionable acquaintance called Le Pavillon to ask whether that restaurant admitted women in shorts, its spokesman corrected her question before he answered it. "Madam," he informed her, "you mean hot pants." *Kennedy Fraser, "On and Off the Avenue: Feminine Fashions," The New Yorker, April 3, 1971, p 101*

[probably suggested by the slang expression "to have *hot pants*," meaning to be sexually aroused]

hot water pollution, another term for THERMAL POLLUTION.

Public controversy over hot water pollution was intense during 1969, mainly because of the many plans being promoted for nuclear power plants, which as presently conceived discharge much more waste heat in their condenser water per kilowatt hour than fossil-fuel plants. *"Thermal Pollution," Science News Yearbook 1970, p 300*

housebody, n. U.S. a person who stays mostly in or near the house; a homebody.

...[Graham] Greene hews to the comic conventions so strictly that it has to be a plan. The aunt is a heller, her nephew is a prim housebody who raises dahlias. *Wilfrid Sheed, "Life and Letters: Racing the Clock with Greene and Pritchett," The Atlantic, April 1970, p 109*

housebroken, adj. U.S. socially acceptable; tame.

She [Marian Anderson] used dreadful arrangements, sentimental and bathetic, and the housebroken, white-washed tunes she sang were designed to tweak the white conscience ever so slightly while perpetrating the stereotype of the black man as a shiftless creature but amiable, stupid, endowed with a natural lyric gift and a conviction that he is "Gwine to Hebbn." *Robert Evett, "The Critics And The Public," The Atlantic, Sept. 1970, p 120*

[figurative sense of the U.S. term applied to domestic animals trained to be clean indoors. The British equivalent is *housetrained*.]

househusband, n. U.S. a married man who manages a household (the correlative of *housewife*).

I Am a Househusband But Call Me Mister. *Title of article in Redbook, May 1971, p 80*

A trivial household chat between this column and the good husband? Maybe, but the President would err gravely if he took a cavalier attitude when millions of American househusbands [are] gathering in the barbershop and supermarket.... *Russell Baker, "Observer: A Tiny Dissent on Women's Lib," The New York Times, Sept. 3, 1970, p 32*

house of tolerance, a licensed brothel.

The last reliable statistics were from the year when they shut the "houses of tolerance" [in Italy]: 2,500 women living in the houses, and, throughout the country, 150,000 registered freelancers. *George Armstrong, "Letter from Rome: Fanfani the Historian," The Manchester Guardian Weekly, Dec. 19, 1970, p 6*

[translation of French *maison de tolérance*]

hoverbarge, n. British. a barge traveling across water on a cushion of air.

Hoverbarges could also carry goods to and from the airport cheaply, quickly and directly. *The Sunday Times (London), April 25, 1971, p 10*

hovercraft, n. sing. or pl. Chiefly British. a vehicle that travels above ground or water on a cushion of air produced by fans. Also called in the United States AIR CUSHION VEHICLE and GROUND EFFECT MACHINE.

...4,000 tons was unlikely to be the limit of size in hovercraft. They could travel faster than ships and carry cargoes more cheaply than aircraft, and so fall neatly between the two in operating costs. There might be a vast market for cargo hovercraft as large bulk carriers on the Atlantic and other trans-oceanic routes. *John Newell, "Science and Technology," The Annual Register of World Events in 1967 (1968), p 408*

hoverferry, n. British. a hovercraft to ferry passengers across water.

The world's first semi-amphibious hoverferry...showed its paces yesterday in special trials and sped along the Solent at 38 knots. *The Times (London), May 7, 1970, p 24*

hoverpad, n. British. a metal plate forming the base of a hovercraft or hovertrain.

The full scale test vehicle will be 24 metres long and will employ both the prototype hoverpads and linear motor envisaged for a 100-passenger commercial version.... *"UK Tracked Hovercraft to be Tested this Summer," Science Journal, May 1970, p 17*

hoverport, n. a port or terminal for hovercraft.

The new car ferry and hoverport at Dover will further enhance what is already, though few are aware of it, the world's leading port for international passenger traffic by sea. *The Times (London), May 1, 1970, p 15*

hovertrain, n. a high-speed train that rides on a cushion of air over a concrete track.

The promoters of hovertrains see their vehicles as providing a coarse, high-speed network, which, by allowing the ordinary trains to run at less diverse speeds, will vastly increase the capacity for goods and intermediate distance passengers, as well as enable the service to be improved. *New Scientist, Jan. 1, 1970, p 25*

hsien (ʃyen), n. Chinese. a county.

Each hsien [in China] has been given the target of becoming self-sufficient in food and light industrial products. *The New York Times, June 27, 1971, p 20*

...the central committee — as purged during the cultural revolution — will nominate ("elect") provincial committees who will choose *hsien* (county) committees and so down-wards. *The Times (London), April 18, 1968, p 11*

Hubble constant or **Hubble's constant,** an astronomical measure used in calculating the velocity at which galaxies recede according to HUB-BLE'S LAW.

... there still remains an uncertainty of perhaps 30% in the so-called "Hubble constant." This constant, H_0, is used to measure the rate of increase of the red shift of remote galaxies with increasing distance. *Jesse L. Greenstein, "A Gateway to the Future," 1970 Britannica Yearbook of Science and the Future, 1969, p 362*

Most astronomers agree that the universe is expanding, but they have never been able to get an accurate measure of the rate of that expansion, the so-called Hubble constant.... *Science News, Nov. 29, 1969, p 505*

Appropriately, the constant of proportionality relating distance and velocity is called Hubble's constant. *Peter Stubbs, New Scientist, April 29, 1971, p 254*

Hubble's law or **Hubble law,** the astronomical observation that the velocity of the recession of galaxies is proportional to their distance from our own galaxy, as shown by the systematic shift of lines in the spectra of the galaxies toward the red in linear proportion to their distance from us.

... in 1929, Hubble published his discovery of the apparent recession of the nebulae in accordance with what is now called Hubble's law. *W. H. McCrea, "Cosmology After Half a Century," Science, June 21, 1968, p 1296*

For some time Arp has argued that the extremely large red shifts of quasars — which according to the Hubble law indicates that they are the most distant known objects in the universe — did not arise entirely from their distance and recessional velocity but from some other cause. *"Science and Technology News: Quasars — Relatives of Compact Galaxies," Science Journal, Oct. 1968, p 9*

[named after the American astronomer Edwin P. Hubble, 1889-1953, who formulated the law]

hucksterize, *v.t.* to apply the high-pressure methods of a huckster to.

The students are told that it is wrong to be cynical about democracy — to think, in Kingman Brewster's words, that the Presidential election was a "hucksterized process" without a real choice. *Anthony Lewis, "Cry, the Beloved Country," The New York Times, May 2, 1970, p 32*

HUD (həd), *n.* acronym for *Housing and Urban Development* (full name, Department of Housing and Urban Development), a department of the U.S. government created in 1965.

When George Romney visited Warren, Mich., in July, he learned how sensitive community feelings are. Romney was cursed and hissed, as he explained HUD's aspirations to let more of the blacks who work in Warren's auto plants live in the town. *Time, Sept. 7, 1970, p 51*

huel·ga ('wel gɑ:), *n. Spanish.* a labor strike, often in the phrase *la huelga* (the strike).

... if [Cesar] Chavez is able to continue [the boycott against grape growers] despite his precarious health, there seems little doubt that, in the end, *la huelga* will prevail. *I. A. Sandoz, "Chavez, Cesar," 1970 Collier's Encyclopedia Year Book, p 405*

Here and there is the emblem of U.F.W.O.C. [United Farm Workers Organizing Committee, in Delano, Cali-

fornia], a square-edged black eagle in a white circle on a red background, over the word "HUELGA," which in Spanish means "strike." *Peter Matthiessen, "Profiles: Organizer [Cesar Chavez]," The New Yorker, June 28, 1969, p 43*

human growth hormone, a synthetic form of the pituitary hormone somatotropin, which regulates growth of the human body. *Abbreviation:* HGH

The creation of the synthetic "human growth hormone" (H.G.H.) was the work of Dr. Choh Hao Li and Dr. Donald Yamashiro, of the hormonal research laboratory of the University of California. *The Times (London), Jan. 7, 1971, p 7*

human potentials movement, a social movement to improve the self-respect of individuals and their relationships with others chiefly in group sessions that make people aware of their own feelings and sensitive to the feelings of others. See also SENSITIVITY TRAINING, ENCOUNTER GROUP.

The leaders of the human potentials movement should see this movement in a larger social context, and concentrate on the re-establishment of smaller social units and natural groups in society at large. Otherwise the movement becomes just another empty institution void of significance and meaning outside the four walls of the joy seminars.... *Else Weinstein, Glendale, N.Y., in a Letter to the Editor, Time, Nov. 30, 1970, p NY4*

hung-up, *adj.* Also, **hung up.** *Slang.* **1** having psychological or emotional problems.

The men who become prisoners are the most obvious criminals: clumsy, stupid, impulsive, hung-up. Some have gotten what they deserve, some are oversentenced, some belong in mental institutions, some shouldn't be in any institution. *Bruce Jackson, "Who Goes to Prison: Caste and Careerism in Crime," The Atlantic, Jan. 1966, p 52*

But she admits her songs are not yet very commercial. "I usually write them when I am very emotionally disturbed, really hung-up," she explains. *The Times (London), March 1, 1968, p 13*

2 hung up on, a obsessed or preoccupied with.

Each is hung up on his syndrome (which often takes the form of atavistic racial fears), unable to live without it. *The New York Times Magazine, Jan. 14, 1968, p 31*

b emotionally attached to; infatuated with.

"Solid citizen Albert," Harper says sardonically, "hung up on a chick — at *your* age".... *Richard Mallett, Punch, June 8, 1966, p 853*

[originally used in the sense of being delayed or stymied by a difficulty and unable to proceed]

hwyl ('hu: əl), *n.* great emotional fervor or eloquence, especially as a characteristic ascribed to the Welsh people.

The potential of forestry in social stabilization of the rural economy is arguably less than the "hwyl" of the foresters would have us believe. *New Scientist, June 5, 1969, p 517*

Then, after a dramatic entrance, Richard Burton complete with hwyl and a self-conscious Woodbine read a short poem by Dylan Thomas. *The Times (London), May 21, 1968, p 6*

—*adj.* filled with or characterized by hwyl.

... it [Swansea, Wales] is a fascinating, undervisited city, *hwyl* all through, an uninhibited place in which you feel that something unexpected might happen to you at any time. *Ian Nair, The Sunday Times (London), Nov. 14, 1971, p 13*

[from Welsh *hwyl*, the peroration of Welsh preachers, typically intoned in a sing-song fashion that rises to a high pitch of eloquence]

▶ The term is today widely used, chiefly by British writers. Its earlier occurrence as a noun is attested in the *OED Supplement*, with two quotations, one from the March 1, 1899 issue of the London *Daily News* and one from the London *Observer* of July 15, 1928.

hy·a·line membrane disease ('hai ə lən), a respiratory disease of newborn babies, especially when born prematurely, due to the formation of a hyaline or glassy film over the interlining of the lungs. Also called RESPIRATORY DISTRESS SYNDROME.

Each year, 50,000 U.S. infants die soon after birth—at least 25,000 of them from respiratory distress syndrome (RDS). Also called hyaline membrane disease, RDS is caused by the inability of an infant's lungs to extract oxygen from the air and pass carbon dioxide out of the body. *Time, Dec. 7, 1970, p 94*

[*hyaline* from Greek *hyálinos* of glass, from *hýalos* glass]

hydrogasification, *n.* the conversion of coal into gas by interacting it with hydrogen at high pressures to yield methane.

A $5.7-million pilot plan for hydrogasification of coal will be built by Procon, Inc., a subsidiary of Universal Oil Products, for the Institute of Gas Technology at a Chicago site, the magazine Chemical Week reports. *The New York Times, Aug. 15, 1968, p 62*

[from *hydro*gen + *gasification*]

hydrogasifier, *n.* an apparatus used in hydrogasification.

As an example, if Bituminous Coal Research is successful in developing a low-cost gas producer, it might be used with a steam-iron variation of the Institute's hydrogasifier to produce methane at an economically attractive price. Again, the Kellogg molten salt process might produce hydrogen for a hydrogasifier. *New Scientist, April 27, 1967, p 214*

hydronaut, *n.* (in the U.S. Navy) a person trained to work in undersea vessels engaged in search and rescue missions and in research projects. Compare AQUANAUT.

Hydronauts—the men who will operate the U.S. Navy's deep submergence vehicles—are being trained in a unique dry-land device that simulates operation of the bathyscaphe Trieste II. *Science News, March 25, 1967, p 286*

[from *hydro*- water + *-naut*, as in *astronaut*]

hydroplaning, *n.* the skidding of an automobile or truck on a wet road which results from the building up of a wedge of fluid between the moving tires and the pavement to a point where the tires lose contact with the road.

Film ["Grooving for Safety"] illustrates a new technique currently being employed to prevent tire hydroplaning, by putting narrow grooves in highways to provide an escape route for the water and improving tire traction. *"Films of the Week," Science News, Feb. 22, 1969, p 180*

[from *hydroplane, v.i.,* to glide on the surface of water]

hydropsychotherapy, *n.* treatment of mental or emotional disorders by techniques involving the use of baths, pools, etc.

...someone asked Lily Weiner, "Do hippies use hydropsychotherapy?" "No," she said, "but I wish I had a pool and could get them into the water with me." *Dan Wakefield, "Supernation at Peace and War," The Atlantic, March 1968, p 60*

[from *hydro*- water + *psychotherapy*]

hydroskimmer, *n. U.S.* an air cushion vehicle designed to travel over water.

Several ACVs called Hydroskimmers, have already been built for the U.S. Navy by Bell Aerosystems Company, Buffalo, N.Y. *Science News, June 4, 1966, p 445*

hydrospace, *n.* the space beneath the surface of the sea. Also called INNER SPACE.

Other categories of plot include a growing preoccupation with "inner space" or "hydrospace" (the word used, incidentally, in a recent advertisement in *New Scientist*)—the opening up of the watery four-fifths of our own planet. *New Scientist, Dec. 22, 1966, p 691*

...the boom ... is coming in the exploration and exploitation of what the hard men in the shipping world are learning to call hydrospace. *The Sunday Times (London), Oct. 13, 1968, p 33*

Hy·fil ('hai fil), *n.* a trade name for a plastic or resin strengthened with carbon fiber.

Rolls-Royce has had Hyfil fan blades fitted to some engines in Standard VC10s.... *The Times (London), May 7, 1970, p 2*

In the UK, 'Hyfil' compressor blades are an excellent example of such a carbon fibre/resin application. *New Scientist, July 10, 1969, p 68*

hype (haip), *Slang. —n.* **1** something that artificially stimulates sales, interest, etc., such as advertising or promotion.

Detached from hype and trend, almost entirely dependent upon their fine heads and solid musicianship, there are a few groups and a few individual performers in the new music who endure.... *Ben Hunter, Gates Mills, Ohio, in a Letter to the Editor, Time, Feb. 2, 1970, p 3*

2 any trick or stunt to attract attention.

The original plan [of the yippies] was to hold a vast free rock-folk festival and bring together in a Community of Consciousness 'technologists, poets, artists, community organisers and visionaries.' ... despite talks of plans the yippies were basically interested in improvising scenarios as they went along—using the Convention as a blank canvas for their revolutionary artistry. The talk, the publicity, the putting on, the 'hype' worked. *Richard Gilbert, "Television Shows the Politics of Ecstasy," The Listener, Oct. 31, 1968, p 566*

3 a person or thing publicized or promoted through hype.

...the performer who is written off as a hype becomes no longer the darling of the underground in-crowd, whatever his sincerity or intrinsic merit. *Karl Dallas, "The Arts: Back to Pop Roots, Marquee, Derek and the Dominos," The Times (London), Aug. 13, 1970, p 10*

—*v.t.* Usually, **hype up. 1** to stimulate artificially; promote, especially with tricks or stunts.

They're [producers of sports programs on television] so lacking in confidence in the attraction of the games they televise that they feel they have to hype them up with some hysterical commentator in order to get anyone to watch them. *Peter Gzowski, "Sports," Saturday Night (Canada), Aug. 1965, p 31*

2 to stir up in feeling; excite.

But Sandy . . . is so hyped up about the Boston opening Sept. 4 that some fear she may blow all the fuses. *Time, Sept. 1, 1967, p 47*

3 to trick or deceive.

Hype: to con ("Don't hype me, pig"). *Time, Aug. 17, 1970, p 32*

[from *hype*, U.S. slang term for a hypodermic injection (especially of a narcotic drug)]

hyped-up, *adj. U.S. Slang.* **1** artificial; fake.

A kind of psychedelic version of the Pied Piper, the ad is typical of the wild, hyped-up pitches aired in the "Saturday morning jungle." *"Television: . . . And Now a Word About Commercials," Time, July 12, 1968, p 52*

2 exuberant; excited.

Tom Wolfe is known for his frenetic, grammar-released, hyped-up tonal style. *The New York Times, Aug. 12, 1968, p 37*

[from the verb phrase *hype up*]

hyper, *n. Slang.* a promoter or publicist.

In Britain, the activities of pop managers and professional "hypers" have for a long time created doubts about the accuracy of the Top Thirty lists (there have even been questions in Parliament). *The Sunday Times (London), Aug. 11, 1968, p 5*

[from *hype, v.* + *-er*]

hy·per- ('haɪ pər-), a very productive prefix, meaning over; excessively; super-. Words formed recently with *hyper-* include:

hyperaggressive, *adj.:* The whole first part of the movie nags us with the author's exposure of his characters; the actively "normal" parents, for instance, have created a hyperaggressive daughter who wants to "mold" men, and a son who wants to be a girl and who winds up, literally, as a closet queen. *David Denby, "Movies: On Fracturing the Funny Bone," Review of "Little Murders," The Atlantic, April 1971, p 99*

hypercautious, *adj.:* Combined with ramifying bureaucratic muddle and the hypercautious instincts of the politically insecure youths who now occupy the upper reaches of the Administration, such frugality sometimes looks like a refusal to take any decisions at all. *The Manchester Guardian Weekly, March 6, 1971, p 4*

hyperfine, *adj.:* A useful property of the partially saturated maser is that the output strength will be responsive to any changes in internal conditions, and these may be causing the intensity variations. Apparent small shifts in the velocity may be attributed to hyperfine atomic structure because the 1.35-cm H_2O line is in fact a blend of six hyperfine energy transitions. *"Monitor: How Water Masers Mase in the Milky Way," New Scientist and Science Journal, July 29, 1971, p 243*

hyperinflation, *n.:* What a magnificent drain on our resources with the complex consequences of stock market boom and bust, uncontrolled inflation with its inherent danger of hyperinflation, chronic balance of payment troubles, the highest interest rates in decades, high unemployment. . . . *Oskar Morgenstern, "Vietnam: Who Profits from the War?" The New York Times, Nov. 7, 1970, p 29*

hyperslow, *adj.:* Duvalier affected the staring gaze, whispered speech and hyperslow movements recognized by Haitians as signs that a person is close to the voodoo spirits. *"The World: Haiti," Time, May 3, 1971, p 26*

hyperspecialization, *n.:* ". . . The remarkable thing is that at a time of overwhelming technical sophistication, expertise and hyperspecialization, professionals are discovering a common purpose—the well-being of people." *"Education: Graduates and Jobs: A Grave New World, Medicine," Time, May 24, 1971, p 45*

hypersuspicious, *adj.:* The hypersuspicious Thieu . . . preferred a fragmentation that he could control to a political unity that might be wrested from him. *Elizabeth Pond, "South Vietnam," The Atlantic, May 1971, p 22*

hyperverbal, *adj.:* He [Paul Newman as Rheinhardt in "WUSA"] is hyperverbal and is given to self-lacerating bitter tirades. . . . *Pauline Kael, "The Current Cinema: Mythmaking," The New Yorker, Nov. 7, 1970, p 165*

hyperbaric, *adj.* of or relating to the use of oxygen under high pressure, especially in medical operation and experimentation.

Still another way to increase the amount of oxygen available to human tissues is . . . to supply oxygen to him in a hyperbaric chamber, in which the total gas pressure is increased to two or three atmospheres. *Scientific American, Feb. 1966, p 63*

The revival of hyperbaric medicine in the mid-fifties contributed greatly to awaken interest in pressure physiology. *Karl E. Schaefer, "Diving Physiology," McGraw-Hill Yearbook of Science and Technology 1967, p 2*

[from *hyper-* + *-baric* (from Greek *báros* weight, pressure + English *-ic*)]

hypercharge, *v.t.* to charge to excess; supercharge.

Harold Wilson said in October 1965 that the atmosphere in Rhodesia was hypercharged with fear. If it was true then, it is even more true today. The events of the past months seem to have paralysed us. *"Rhodesian Letter: Living in a Land of Fear," The Manchester Guardian Weekly, Jan. 26, 1967, p 6*

—*n. Nuclear Physics.* a quantum number which is equal to twice the average electric charge in a group of strongly interacting particles.

Each eight-fold way multiplet consists of several subgroups of particles having the same mass, hypercharge and isotopic spin. *"Physics: Nucleus Action Probed," Science News Letter, Feb. 6, 1965, p 85*

hypermarket, *n. British.* a very large ground-floor store, usually built in the suburbs.

Hypermarkets—monster out-of-town shops, perhaps up to 10 times bigger than a big supermarket—are the latest challenge to traditional shopping. *James Poole, "Stores Hit Back at Hypermarkets," The Sunday Times (London), June 6, 1971, p 46*

. . . they commissioned an independent survey of the probable effects of the proposed hypermarket. *Alisdair Fairley, "Information," The Listener, Dec. 30, 1971, p 919*

hypersexual, *adj.* sexually aroused to an abnormal degree.

The drug puts the animals into a hypersexual state as well as making them more aggressive and disorienting their senses of perception. *The Times (London), May 4, 1970, p 11*

There have been studies where cats have been deprived of REM sleep for excessively long intervals. Such animals become hyperirritable and hypersexual. *Anthony Kales, "Sleep and Dreaming: Sleep Deprivation," McGraw-Hill Yearbook of Science and Technology 1969, p 22*

hypersexuality, *n.* the condition of being hypersexual.

The effect of LSD on serotonin is worrying, believes Nair, because of the association of this chemical with behaviour disorders including hypersexuality and abnormalities of sleep. *Science Journal, Nov. 1970, p 16*

In addition to these contraceptives, Schering leads in new hormone drugs—the anti-androgens, the first of which —against hypersexuality in men—is now being marketed. *James Poole, "Pills for Profit," The Sunday Times (London), Sept. 12, 1971, p 50*

hypervelocity, *n.* extremely high velocity, as that of spacecraft or of nuclear particles.

In this connection I would like to call to your attention the fact that I had independently and in advance of Harrison developed the idea of achieving controlled fusion by the impact of macroparticles accelerated to hypervelocities. *F. Winterberg, Reno, Nevada, in a Letter to the Editor, New Scientist, Oct. 5, 1967, p 47*

In the hypervelocity regions of boost and reentry flight, aerodynamic characteristics of lifting vehicles become highly sensitive to viscous drag effects at changing altitudes. *Scientific American, Oct. 1967, p 104*

The surfaces of the [lunar] glass spheres and rocks show minute craters, which are the result of hypervelocity impacts of tiny particles. . . . *Cornelis Klein, Jr., "Moon," McGraw-Hill Yearbook of Science and Technology 1971, p 274*

hyp·no·pe·di·a (ˌhip nəˈpiː diː ə), *n.* another name for SLEEP-LEARNING or SLEEP-TEACHING.

Research on sleep learning, or "hypnopedia", has been going on for more than 30 years—mostly in Russia. *The Times (London), June 5, 1967, p 7*

. . . the Soviets are quick to emphasise that hypnopedia is not a teaching method in itself, but only an important supplementary aid. *"Notes on the News: Sleep Learning Spreading in Soviet Schools?" New Scientist, Jan. 30, 1969, p 216*

[from *hypno-* sleep + Greek *paideíā* instruction]

I

-ian, a suffix now used chiefly to form adjectives of proper names in the sense of "relating to or characteristic of," and attached mainly to the names of well-known or famous persons. Primarily adjectival, *-ian* may be used also as a noun suffix; the variants *-an* and *-ean* are much less common. The following is a selection of currently common forms with *-ian:*

Beckettian, *adj.* [Samuel *Beckett,* born 1906, Irish playwright and novelist]: The painful story of a writer balancing his "obligation to express" against his conviction that there is, in the end, "nothing to express" is Beckettian drama of a high order. *Hilton Kramer, "The Anguish and the Comedy of Samuel Beckett," Saturday Review, Oct. 3, 1970, p 43*

Bergmanian, *adj.* [Ingmar *Bergman,* born 1918, Swedish film director]: Andreas Winkleman (Max von Sydow) is an inhabitant of that vital Bergmanian metaphor, an isle off the Swedish coast. *Time, June 8, 1970, p 74*

Borgesian, *adj.* [Jorge Luis *Borges,* born 1899, Argentinian writer]: Here are no visions and, in the Borgesian sense at least, no nightmares. *The Times (London), Dec. 24, 1970, p 5*

Brechtian, *adj.* [Bertolt *Brecht,* 1898-1955, German playwright]: *Edward II,* translated by Eric Bentley, has been called Brecht's only tragedy; a reworking of Marlowe's play, it has been transmuted through the Brechtian intelligence into a grimly poetic drama about a beleaguered king railing against an unanswering universe. *"Theater," Saturday Review, Nov. 26, 1966, p 41*

Chomskian, *adj.* [Noam *Chomsky,* born 1928, American linguist]: . . . Chomskian generative and transformational grammar is one of those specialized conjectures which, by sheer intellectual fascination and range of implication, reach out to the world of the layman. *George Steiner, "The Tongues of Men," The New Yorker, Nov. 15, 1969, p 217*

Crippsian, *adj.* [Sir Stafford *Cripps,* 1889-1952, British Labour Party leader]: For we in Britain have tried every conceivable version of such a [prices and incomes] policy from Crippsian exhortation (oddly, the most successful) through guide-lines and early warning to legislation and freeze. *Anthony Crosland, "The Price and the Prize of Sustained Growth," The Times (London), Sept. 26, 1970, p 12*

Dullesian, *adj.* [John Foster *Dulles,* 1888-1959, U.S. Secretary of State, 1953-1959]: Though steadily critical of the Dullesian effort to launch an ideological anti-Communist crusade, Rovere offers a qualified defense of the policy of "containment," especially the Marshall Plan. *Irving Howe, "Books: Torment and Therapy," Review of "Waist Deep in the Big Muddy" by Richard H. Rovere, Harper's, July 1968, p 98*

Hitchcockian, *adj.* [Alfred *Hitchcock,* born 1899, British film director]: Particularly risky is the idea of filming an old-fashioned Hitchcockian murder mystery in all its creaking intricacy. *Time, June 22, 1970, p 89*

Ivesian, *adj.* [Charles Edward *Ives,* 1874-1954, American experimental composer]: . . . "The Yale-Princeton Football Game," a little musical joke, with typically Ivesian quotations from popular marches. . . . *Winthrop Sargeant,*

"Musical Events: Good-Conduct Medals," The New Yorker, Dec. 12, 1970, p 178

Nabokovian, *adj.* [Vladimir *Nabokov*, born 1899, Russian-born novelist and poet]: Equally Nabokovian are the extremes of opinion about the master's Russian translation of "Lolita." To American buffs who can read it is the holy of holies, Nabokov's "crowning feat": to Soviet citizens who can, it appears written in a dead language. New Russians prefer their samizdat "Lolita" in genuine Nabokovese, and there may be a moral in that somewhere. *John Bayley, "Books: Nabokov Begins," Review of "Nabokov: Criticisms, Reminiscences, Translations and Tributes," edited by Alfred Appel, Jr. and Charles Newman, The Manchester Guardian Weekly, Feb. 27, 1971, p 18*

Wodehousian, *adj.* [Pelham Grenville *Wodehouse*, born 1881, British writer of humorous novels]: A Wodehousian phrase leaps to mind as the perfect description for Marin's educational philosophy: the most frightful bilge! *Robert L. Bates, Columbus, Ohio, in a Letter to the Education Editor, Saturday Review, Oct. 17, 1970, p 55*

Woolfian, *adj.* [Virginia *Woolf*, 1882-1941, British novelist]: Thus a lifelong love of technical language for its own sake pays off. The material isn't, as it were, orchestrated in a Woolfian way, nor is there anything like the immemorial moaning that Tennyson combines with geology. *Frank Kermode, "The Poet in Praise of Limestone," The Atlantic, May 1970, p 69*

IC, abbreviation of INTEGRATED CIRCUIT.

An IC is a circuit consisting of up to 20 transistors and diodes on a microscopic chip of silicon. . . . *Robert E. Stoffels, "Electronics," 1970 Britannica Yearbook of Science and the Future, 1969, p 167*

New integrated-circuit technology, and large-scale integration (LSI) in particular, should also have an impact on memory design—the report predicts that by 1975 superfast IC memories will be competitive with ferrite-core memories on the basis of cost considerations alone. *New Scientist, Jan. 7, 1971, p 20*

ice, *v.t. U.S. Slang.* **1** to kill.

When a white student broke a ban on drugs by giving LSD to an unprepared Ethiopian student, blacks threatened to "ice" him if he ever returned to Old Westbury. *Tom Powers, "Autopsy On Old Westbury: The Politics of Free-form Education," Harper's, Sept. 1971, p 61*

. . . a friend of his [Nathan Delaney, a drug addict] . . . had come to his apartment at about noon, in clothes that were spattered with blood, and announced, "I just iced two girls." *Fred C. Shapiro, "Annals of Jurisprudence: The Whitmore Confessions," The New Yorker, Feb. 15, 1969, p 51*

2 ice out, to ignore or exclude socially.

It [Washington] is not a big city, and when a lady is down and out and getting herself dumped from someone's guest list there, it is not the same as getting herself iced out in New York or Chicago. There are not that many guest lists that everyone wants to get on, and Washington is poorer for that. *John Corry, "Washington, Sex, and Power," Harper's, July 1970, p 66*

iceberg, *n.* **the tip of the iceberg,** a small or superficial part of something; that which appears only on the surface.

. . . the news article reported only the tip of the iceberg. Hidden is a serious situation for engineers in the United States and Great Britain. *Paul Harris, Los Angeles, Calif., in a Letter to the Editor, The Manchester Guardian Weekly, May 9, 1970, p 2*

. . . subclinical infection by the cholera vibrio, in which the host shows no sign of illness, is common. This situation is similar to that of poliomyelitis or viral hepatitis, where the manifest cases of illness represent only the tip of the iceberg, with a much larger number of persons carrying the infection and spreading it unknowingly. *Norbert Hirschhorn and William B. Greenough III, "Cholera," Scientific American, Aug. 1971, p 16*

. . . three unarmed black convicts at Soledad [were] shot to death in the exercise yard by a white guard stationed on a gun tower. The tip of the iceberg? Probably. Other allegations of mistreatment, smuggled out by inmates, are currently under investigation. . . . *Jessica Mitford, "Kind and Usual Punishment in California," The Atlantic, March 1971, p 50*

ice-out, *n.* the melting of the ice on the surface of a body of water.

. . . the big lake trout and pike are found on the surface for a short time immediately after ice-out. . . . *The New York Times, May 17, 1967, p 60*

[from the verb phrase *ice out* to melt away, thaw]

icescape, *n.* a landscape consisting of ice, especially the polar landscape.

The whole icescape was awash with light—a cold, weird winter light which has transformed the pressure ice into foaming white breakers and ice floes into tranquil lagoons. *The Sunday Times (London), Feb. 9, 1969, p 6*

[from *ice* + *-scape* view, scene]

ice-up, *n.* the freezing over of snow or water.

In southern France snow had stopped falling in most areas, but the low temperatures were bringing about an ice-up. *The Times (London), Dec. 31, 1970, p 5*

[from the verb phrase *ice up* to freeze, congeal]

iconize, *v.t.* to make an idol of; venerate uncritically.

In the land of his birth Lenin has been iconized and transmogrified into a sugary shibboleth. *Jan Halmstrom, Stockholm, Sweden, in a Letter to the Editor, New Scientist, May 14, 1970, p 348*

[form and meaning probably influenced by *idolize*]

i·dem·po·ten·cy (ai'dem pə tən si:), *n. Mathematics.* the property of remaining unchanged under multiplication by itself.

A similar triad of properties applies to operations: idempotency, which corresponds to reflexiveness and occurs if an operation produces no change in the number or set on which it operates; commutativeness, which corresponds to symmetry . . . and non-associativity, which corresponds to the transitive property. . . . *Leo Jolley, "Relation Codes: An Ordering of Ideas," New Scientist, May 16, 1968, p 339*

[from Latin *idem* the same + English *potency*]

i·dem·po·tent (ai'dem pə tənt), *adj. Mathematics.* having or characterized by idempotency.

Logical multiplication is said to be *idempotent*, signifying that all "powers" of a set are the *same*, and hence there is no need for the exponential symbolism of common algebra. *Edna E. Kramer, The Nature and Growth of Modern Mathematics, 1970, p 107*

identity crisis, a time of disturbance and anxiety when a person is in a self-conscious stage of personality development or adjustment, occurring especially during adolescence.

In the course of analyzing [George Bernard] Shaw's essay, [Erik] Erikson refers to Shaw's "identity crisis," and calls the long period of lonely, introspective writing a "moratorium"—an "interval between youth and adulthood" when one tries to achieve an inner and outer coherence. *Robert Coles, "The Measure of Man," The New Yorker, Nov. 14, 1970, p 75*

For Mrs. Frank Schiff, the former Gloria O'Connor, being an identical twin was never a problem in any sense. She and her sister, Consuelo, now the Countess Rodolfo Crespi of Rome, never went through an identity crisis. *The New York Times, June 21, 1971, p 34*

ideologism, *n.* conformity or adherence to an ideology, especially when excessive or extreme.

Vernon Bogdanor himself traces [Harold] Macmillan's success to his ready embrace of the improvisatory style of politics which was dictated by Keynesian economics: a flexibility which was denied to the Labour Party by its dead weight of "ideologism" (and not even up-to-date ideology at that). *The Manchester Guardian Weekly, Sept. 26, 1970, p 19*

idiot box, *Slang.* television. Compare GOGGLEBOX.

Anyone still wondering how the idiot box got its name hasn't been watching the TV commercials directed at housewives lately. Most are like messages from beyond Lewis Carroll's looking-glass. . . . *Maclean's, May 1968, p 34*

idiot's lantern, *British Slang.* television.

It is still fashionable in some circles to dismiss television as the idiot's lantern or the goggle-box and to condemn it as a purveyor of poor shadowy substitutes for the "real thing". . . . *Punch, Feb. 19, 1969, p 284*

igloo, *n.* a portable plastic structure having a dome shape, used as a protective covering.

The tariff applies to point-to-point consignments using the full 125 in. by 88 in. and 108 in. by 88 in. pallets with nets or igloos. *The Times (London), Dec. 3, 1970, p V*

i·ke·ba·na (i:'ke bɑ: nə), *n.* the Japanese art of arranging flowers for decoration in a vase or as models for still-life paintings.

The Japanese print is one of the principal sources of information on *ikebana*, or flower arrangement. *George Heard Hamilton, "Panorama from the Palette," Saturday Review, Dec. 3, 1966, p 33*

[from Japanese, literally, live flower]

image-builder, *n.* one engaged in image-building.

He [Robert T. Bartley, Commissioner of the U.S. Federal Communications Commission] warned of "the inherent danger of the broadcast operations' becoming a tool and image-builder for the corporate conglomerate. . . ." *Robert Lewis Shayon, "TV and Radio: The Quiet Merger," Saturday Review, Feb. 4, 1967, p 56*

image-building, *n.* the use of publicity and advertising to create or maintain a favorable impression before the public.

The program also gave a sympathetic hearing to policemen and showed the difficulties they labor under in a city the size of New York and some of the new techniques of image-building being employed to reach the communities they serve. *The New York Times, May 28, 1968, p 95*

It was only recently that a prominent firm of chartered accountants in London took the bold step of using film for image-building. *The Times (London), March 23, 1970, p 23*

Immobilon, *n.* a trade name for a drug used to immobilize wild animals.

These two forms of "Immobilon" are sold in packs together with the antagonist "Revivon", which is used to get the animal back on its feet quickly after Immobilon has been used for such operations as removing growths, tooth extraction, and foot trimming. *Bernard Dixon, "A Novel Competition," New Scientist, Sept. 23, 1971, p 664*

A rhinoceros injected with new drug Immobilon. *Picture legend, The Times (London), Nov. 9, 1970, p VIII*

im·mu·no- ('im yə nou-), a combining form now widely used in the physical sciences to denote any study, process, technique, etc., involving immunological or antibody-producing properties and reactions. See the examples below and the main entries which follow.

immunochemical, *n.:* Miles-Yeda, Ltd. . . . a subsidiary of Miles Laboratories, Inc. in the U.S., makes isotopes and immunochemicals. *David Perlman, "A Gateway to the Future," 1971 Britannica Yearbook of Science and the Future, 1970, p 385*

immunodiffusion, *n.:* He [Orjan Ouchterlony, a Swedish biologist] put a few drops of solution containing antigen in one well and a like amount of antibody solution in the other. The fluids diffused toward each other through the gelatinous agar and reacted at an intermediate zone. There a thin white crescent was precipitated in the otherwise clear gel. The crescent indicated the chemical neutralization of the antigen by the antibody. The technique is known as immunodiffusion. . . . *C. L. Stong, "The Amateur Scientist," Scientific American, Sept. 1969, p 248*

immunoparalysis, *n.:* . . . experience with protracted immunoparalysis maintained with the aid of immunosuppressant chemicals over periods of years to prevent destruction of transplanted organs was observed to be associated with a definitive increase in the frequency of cancer in these patients. *Michael J. Brennan, "Medicine," 1972 Britannica Yearbook of Science and the Future, 1971, p 291*

immunopharmacology, *n.:* The word immunopharmacology does not appear, between immunochemistry and immunotherapy, in any of the medical dictionaries that I have consulted but its use as the title of this book will probably cause it to be defined in their next editions. In the meantime, I take immunopharmacology to be the study of how and why applied chemical substances induce or modify immune processes. *H. O. J. Collier, "Chemicals and Rejection," Review of "Immunopharmacology," edited by H. O. Schild, New Scientist, Aug. 1, 1968, p 253*

immunoradioactive, *adj.:* . . . they [a team of researchers] are optimistic enough about their results, in experiments with . . . induced tumors in mice, to be talking about an immunoradioactive anti-cancer serum in the foreseeable future. *Science News, July 6, 1968, p 22*

immunoradiotherapy, *n.:* According to [Professor R. C.] Nairn, the results so far achieved with phosphorus-32 are "a very promising beginning to the exploration of possible immunoradiotherapy of cancer in human patients". *"Australians Are Developing Anti-Cancer 'Missile'," Science Journal, Aug. 1968, p 11*

immunoassay, *n.* analysis of the characteristics of a bodily substance by testing its immunological or antibody-producing reactions. Compare RADIOIMMUNOASSAY.

Gonadotrophins from chorionic tissue are produced mostly in early pregnancy and can be assayed either biologically or by immuno-assay. . . . *Geoffrey Chamberlain, "Monitoring the Human Fetus," New Scientist, April 9, 1970, p 66*

immunocompetence, *n.* the ability to produce or maintain immunity.

The best picture that could be assembled at this stage of the story was that the bursa and thymus, as "central" lymphoid tissues, secreted some hormone-like factor needed for the immunocompetence of lymphocytes in "peripheral" lymphoid tissues like the spleen. *Dr. Mel Greaves, "Cooperating in Immunity," New Scientist, Dec. 9, 1971, p 81*

immunocompetent, *adj.* capable of producing or maintaining immunity.

The antibody-forming cells are frequently designated as immuno-competent cells. *Felix Haurowitz, "Antibody Biosynthesis," McGraw-Hill Yearbook of Science and Technology 1969, p 104*

immunocyte, *n.* an immunity-producing cell that attacks other cells of the body.

Those pathogenic immunocytes that cause autoimmune disease are also curbed by the system of surveillance: in this instance the autoimmune process and the surveillance mechanism are both attributed to the same system of thymus-dependent immunocytes. *Philip Burch, Review of "Immunological Surveillance" by Macfarlane Burnet, New Scientist, Dec. 10, 1970, p 466*

[from *immuno-* + *-cyte* cell]

immunodeficiency disease, any disease caused by a deficiency in the immunity mechanism of the body.

The ability to transplant bone marrow material successfully . . . will mean a lot more than the treatment of relatively rare immunodeficiency diseases. Solving the graft-versus-host reaction will mean that virtually any congenital blood disorder . . . will be curable by simply replacing the patient's own blood-forming tissue with that from a donor. *Graham Chedd, "Immunological Engineers," New Scientist and Science Journal, May 13, 1971, p 397*

im·mu·no·e·lec·tro·pho·re·sis (,im yə nou i‚lek-trou fə'ri: sis), *n.* a method of identifying complex proteins through their immunological reactions after electrically induced separation from a substance such as blood plasma.

"Antigen and antibody preparations from many species, as well as from various individuals of a given species, have become available commercially in recent years. Hence numerous experiments involving . . . immunoelectrophoresis are within the reach of the enterprising amateur." *Richard La Fond, quoted by C. L. Stong, "The Amateur Scientist," Scientific American, Sept. 1969, p 258*

[from *immuno-* + *electrophoresis* electrically induced separation of substances]

immunoelectrophoretic, *adj.* of or relating to immunoelectrophoresis.

He [Dr. Tristram Freeman] was best known for his studies of a rare hereditary complaint . . . and of the dynamic exchanges of several plasma proteins and more recently for his modifications and application of the Laurell technique, an immuno-electrophoretic method for analyzing blood plasma proteins in terms of a dozen or more well-defined circulating proteins. *The Times (London), Nov. 23, 1970, p 10*

immunofluorescence, *n.* the labeling of antibodies with a fluorescent dye to reveal antigens, viruses, etc., when viewed under ultraviolet light.

Utilizing a technique of immunofluorescence, these investigators demonstrated gamma E [a type of immunoglobulin] antibody-forming cells in lymphoid organs of the tracheal mucosa, pharynx, and intestinal tract, although they were essentially absent in the spleen and lymph nodes. . . . *Robert Keller, "Immunology," 1970 Britannica Yearbook of Science and the Future, 1969, p 267*

immunofluorescent, *adj.* of or relating to immunofluorescence.

Indirect immunofluorescent techniques show cross immunity reactions. *Science News, May 11, 1968, p 462*

immunoglobulin, *n.* a globulin or protein in the blood that acts like an antibody and produces immunity.

Gamma globulin or immunoglobulin is one of the key antibody proteins which lymphocytes produce in response to microbial invasion. *"Molecular Biology," Science News Yearbook 1970, p 88*

A newborn pig has very little gamma globulin (the principal antibody protein) in its serum. Apparently it acquires gamma globulin and other immunoglobulins from its mother's colostrum when it begins to suckle. *Scientific American, June 1966, p 98*

immunohematologic, *adj.* of or relating to immunohematology.

Pathology of Sickle Cell Disease—Joseph Song-Thomas, C.C., 1971, 460 p., photographs, $26. A reference book to the multiphasic manifestations of sickle cell anemia, discusses the hemoglobin molecule, genetic mutation, biochemical aspects, immunohematologic manifestations, incidence, complications and therapy. *"Books," Science News, July 10, 1971, p 31*

immunohematology, *n.* the study of the immunological or antibody-producing properties of the blood.

Professor Jean Dausset is a member of the Faculty of Medicine at the University of Paris and is Director of Immunohaematology at the Georges Hayem Centre in Paris. *Science Journal, July 1968, p 51*

immunorepressive, *adj.* another word for IMMUNO-SUPPRESSIVE.

The doctors in charge increased the dosage of immunorepressive drugs as soon as it was discovered that the period of rejection was being experienced. . . . *The Times (London), Feb. 10, 1968, p 4*

immunosuppressant, *n.* an immunosuppressive drug. It is used especially to suppress rejection of grafted or transplanted tissue. Also called IMMUNOSUPPRESSOR.

. . . it is the lack of an effective immuno-suppressant, free of any deleterious effect on the bone marrow, which is a major difficulty in human organ transplantation. *H. E. Wade and D. A. Rutter, "Asparaginase—Treatment for Leukaemia," Science Journal, March 1970, p 66*

—*adj.* another word for IMMUNOSUPPRESSIVE.

. . . Hundreds of projects, ranging from cancer research, antibiotics and immunosuppressant drug research to cosmic radiation studies, are feeling the pinch. *Lennard Bickel, "Squeeze on Private Research," Science News, Nov. 23, 1968, p 530*

immunosuppression, *n.* the suppression by the use of drugs, radiation, etc., of the immunological reaction of the body to foreign substances, especially to prevent the rejection of grafts or transplants by the recipient's body.

In order to coerce the body into accepting a donor's organ, full immunosuppression has been necessary... often leading, unfortunately, to fatal secondary infection. *New Scientist, Nov. 6, 1969, p 281*

immunosuppressive, *adj.* causing immunosuppression. Also, IMMUNOREPRESSIVE, IMMUNOSUPPRESSANT.

Reports from transplant surgeons that immunosuppressive drugs given to their patients to suppress organ rejection foster the rise of cancer are additional evidence of the relationship between cancer and immunity and the need for moderation in drug therapy. *"Immunology: Tumors and Lymphocytes, Science News Yearbook 1970, p 76*

—*n.* an immunosuppressive agent or drug; an immunosuppressant.

The Development of Modern Surgery by Frederick F. Cartwright. A brief topically arranged history of surgery from the era before antisepsis and anesthesia to the present era of antibiotics and immunosuppressives. *Hilary J. Deason, "Books of Science," The World Book Science Annual 1968, p 283*

immunosuppressor, *n.* another word for IMMUNOSUPPRESSANT.

In a study of 400 patients who received kidney transplants, it was found that 15 of them developed lymphomas, cancer of the lymphatic system.... most of the patients who developed lymphomas had received antilymphatic serum in addition to chemical immunosuppressors. *Charles W. Young, "Cancer," The Americana Annual 1970, p 157*

impact crater, a crater produced by the impact of falling meteorites or of material ejected from volcanoes.

Evidently the maria are low-lying regions, in many cases enormous impact craters (judging from their roundness) that were filled with basaltic lava early in the history of the moon. *John A. Wood, "The Lunar Soil," Scientific American, Aug. 1970, p 17*

Impact craters can be observed on most of the material brought back from the Moon. *Picture legend, Science Journal, May 1970, p 29*

The men drove past a cluster of craters thought to be secondary impact craters (craters formed by ejecta from larger craters) to the base of the mountain and up part of the slope. *"Paydirt at Hadley-Apennine; Apollo 15 is Bringing Back a Lot for the Boys in the Back Room," Science News, Aug. 7, 1971, p 89*

On the earth there are two major types of crater: the volcano and the impact crater. *Cecilia Payne-Gaposchkin and Katherine Haramundanis, "The Moon," Encyclopedia Science Supplement (Grolier) 1970, p 46*

impacted, *adj. U.S.* **1** financially burdened by the demand on public services, especially schools, caused by the sudden influx of many new residents into an area.

Nixon... proposed that $1.5 billion in federal funds be made available to "racially impacted areas" over the next two fiscal years to help desegregating school districts meet their special needs.... *Time, April 6, 1970, p 12*

Funds were also earmarked for the following: federally "impacted" areas, that is, areas where the families of federal workers had swollen school enrollments ($1.026 billion).... *"Education," The 1967 Compton Yearbook, p 232*

2 designed to relieve an impacted area.

This is the $600 million included in the Democratic bill for the program ungrammatically called "impacted aid"—that is, Federal assistance to certain school districts to help them bear the impact of the children of Federal employees on their education costs. *Tom Wicker, The New York Times, Jan. 27, 1970, p 42*

impossible art, another name for CONCEPTUAL ART.

Happenings, "impossible art," auto-destruction art, multi-media events are alternative pursuits that can engage an artist's inventive powers.... *The Manchester Guardian Weekly, Jan. 10, 1970, p 20*

impulse buyer, a person who often buys on whim without much or any consideration of cost, quality, or utility.

While the Colts might be described as impulse buyers, they seem downright cautious compared to the Monacos, who bought their house without ever having seen the inside. *The New York Times, June 30, 1971, p 46*

A new range of McVitie and Price cake packages, designed by Richard Lonsdale-Hands Associates, will be on display in supermarkets this week, designed to attract the "impulse" buyer. *The Times (London), March 11, 1970, p 25*

in-¹, a combining form of the preposition *in*, meaning "within," "during," etc., frequently used in combination with a noun to form adjective modifiers. Such compounds are derived from corresponding prepositional phrases, as e.g., *in-college activities* derived from *activities in college*, *in-depth interview* from *interview in depth*. The compounds are ordinarily pronounced with a main stress on *in-* as well as on the normally accented syllable of the other member ('in-ca'reer, 'in-'cit y); but there may be a main stress only on *in-* when it is in contrast with *out-* ('in-,state 'stu dents). See the following examples as well as the main entries IN-COMPANY, IN-COUNTRY, IN-HOUSE.

in-car, *adj.:* Systems for improved highway safety, for instance, will include automatic guidance and control, in-car visual and audible hazard warnings.... *Science News, Aug. 3, 1968, p 107*

in-career, *adj.:* Whether in-career re-education will be best inside or outside universities is a matter for debate.... *New Scientist, Oct. 3, 1968, p 31*

in-city, *adj.:* It [a commuter railroad line] is not designed to stop every half-mile, nor to service in-city passengers. *Harper's, Jan. 1966, p 68*

in-home, *adj.:* Last year the three syndicated weeklies began a joint promotion campaign that promises to pay off, and they countered the research studies of regular magazines purporting to show an impressive pass-along readership with studies of their own, demonstrating a greater in-home readership and superior retention value. *Saturday Review, Jan. 8, 1966, p 111*

in-prison, *adj.:* With few exceptions, in-prison schooling had previously been limited to the high school level. *"Prisons," The 1967 Compton Yearbook, p 397*

in-process, *adj.:* The primary purpose of in-process measurement is to ensure that a workpiece is manufactured to the desired size. *New Scientist, April 20, 1967, p 140*

in-state, *adj.:* The land-grant colleges and state universities were founded as publicly supported institutions where in-state students would be able to obtain a college education for minimum rates. *The New York Times, Nov. 5, 1967, Sec. 1, p 85*

in-station, *adj.:* Demanding that their in-station hours be cut from 56 to 50 a week, 278 of Kansas City's firemen last month got around state laws by playing sick for four days.... *Time, Aug. 5, 1966, p 47*

in-², a combining form of the adjective *in,* used in the sense of "favored by connoisseurs as the latest, most up-to-date, or exclusive (item of its kind)" to form noun compounds. In compounds with *in-²* the main stress falls on the first syllable ('in, as 'in-,jargon, etc.). See the following examples and also the entry IN-CROWD.

in-jargon, *n.:* ... instead of teaching, the two speakers conducted a precious duologue of in-jargon. *The Sunday Times (London), Dec. 3, 1967, p 28*

in-language, *n.:* Of course this 'in-language' invariably provokes misunderstanding, or feigned misunderstanding, on the part of the sensible persons in the play. *T. E. Hope, "Language and Stereotype: a Romance Philologist's Parable," The University of Leeds Review, Oct. 1971, p 223*

in-thing, *n.:* ... if widows are the in-thing now, can unwed mothers be far behind? *Goodman Ace, "Top of My Head," Saturday Review, Oct. 19, 1968, p 8*

in-word, *n.:* Mr. Wilson, with the opinion polls leaning strongly towards him, has set his sights on 13 marginal seats—12 Tory and one Liberal.... It is not, of course, beyond the realms of possibility that the disclosure of these seats as the Prime Minister's top 13 is no more than an exercise to galvanize the party workers to new levels of achievement and to send yet another "frisson" (Mr. Wilson's latest in-word) through the Tory machine. *The Times (London), June 8, 1970, p 7*

-in, a combining form of the adverb *in,* introduced in the 1960's by the Negro civil-rights movement in a number of nouns formed from verb + *-in* on the analogy of *sit-in,* such as *kneel-in* (in segregated churches), *ride-in* (in segregated buses), *swim-in* and *wade-in* (in segregated swimming pools and beaches), and so on.

The original meaning was soon extended to the staging of any kind of public demonstration, as in *lie-in* and *stall-in* (blocking traffic), *smoke-in* or *puff-in* (for legalization of marijuana), and *teach-in* (by college professors criticizing government policies).

A third development was the weakening of the earlier meanings to cover any kind of gathering by a group, as for socializing. This meaning is exemplified by *be-in* (originally a social gathering of hippies or flower children), *love-in, sing-in,* and *laugh-in.*

Some of the abovementioned terms appear as main entries. Other main entries with *-in* are *fish-in, lie-in, paint-in, pray-in, sign-in, sleep-in, work-in.*

The following is a sampling of compounds not separately entered in the book:

bike-in, *n.:* Alternate modes of nonpolluting transportation called for "bike-ins," balloon ascensions and pedestrian parades. *Time, April 27, 1970, p 46*

camp-in, *n.:* As illustrated by the extra squads of policemen patrolling the Capitol, there is a latent fear in Congress that the camp-in will set off violence. *The New York Times, May 26, 1968, p 71*

eat-in, *n.:* Knives, forks and plates, not notepads and pencils, are set on the highly polished boardroom table at the weekly directors' meeting of W. Purdy Ltd. The weekly eat-ins are a vital part of quality control.... *Philip Clarke, The Sunday Times (London), April 18, 1971, p 53*

gay-in, *n.:* Last June's much-publicized "Gay-In" gathering in Manhattan's Central Park with smaller assemblages in other cities, had nationwide reverberations. As thousands of marchers paraded placards and chanted slogans— "Better Blatant than Latent," "An Army of Lovers Cannot Lose," pre-empting Plato's defense of love between Spartan soldiers—some "straight" bystanders urged, "Why don't you try women first?" "We have," answered many of the demonstrators. *Faubion Bowers, "Homosex: Living the Life," Saturday Review, Feb. 12, 1972, p 24*

mail-in, *n.:* The Ministers of Finance and Economy and of Agriculture were all victims of the chicken mail-in, which was organized in protest against a recent influx of imported eggs from Belgium. "Dead Chicken Mail-in," *The Times (London), July 29, 1970, p 4*

prance-in, *n.:* The quality of this Israeli prance-in often verges on the amateur.... *The New Yorker, April 13, 1968, p 7*

study-in, *n.:* The Youth Culture may be using big words to hide some facts—as in the battle against parietal rules which stand for boys' rights to have girls in dormitory rooms for individual study-ins and not, as the Yale Daily News stressed, for sleep-ins. *The New York Times, Jan. 7, 1968, Sec. 4, p 11*

in·cap ('in,kæp), *n. Military Slang.* an incapacitating chemical agent or drug; an incapacitant.

... the employment of "incaps" (i.e., incapacitating chemicals) which, if used against whole populations, will be bound to cause widespread deaths as well as general degradation. *New Scientist, April 4, 1968, p 42*

Considerable interest had focused on psychic or hallucinatory chemicals. Dubbed "incaps" (for incapacitating agents), they are designed to disorient temporarily rather than kill.... *Time, Sept. 6, 1968, p 40*

incapacitant, *n.* a chemical agent or drug designed to incapacitate a person or animal temporarily by inducing sleepiness, dizziness, disorientation, etc. See also INCAP.

How are we to ensure that the new wave of military morality is not simply due to obsolescence and still more pathological projects? It may take the death of a few human sheep around Dugway Proving Ground to make CBW a property too hot for any administration to harbour, and beyond that lie the use of ecocidal weapons—herbicides in Vietnam—and "humane incapacitants." *Alex Comfort, "A Remedy for Poison?" Review of "The Ultimate Folly: War by Pestilence, Asphyxiation, and Defoliation" by Richard D. McCarthy, The Manchester Guardian Weekly, Aug. 15, 1970, p 18*

Mr. Perry Robinson had traced a contract with the Shell Development Company dating from 1952, calling for an examination of synthetic cannabis derivatives, both for its incapacitating and its lethal properties. The military, however, may find it more effective to disturb or paralyze the body rather than the mind. BZ, one of the standard US incapacitants, produces dizziness, heart palpitation, urinary retention and constipation. *New Scientist, Feb. 29, 1968, p 465*

incendive, *adj.* capable of setting fire; incendiary.

A spark struck from such a surface [rusty steel smeared with aluminum] has a miniature thermite reaction which is exothermic [heat-releasing] and can prove more incendive to inflammable vapours than a spark struck from the impact of steel on steel. *R. J. Hartless, Hertford, England, in a Letter to the Editor, New Scientist, May 14, 1970, p 349*

[from Latin *incendere* to set on fire + English *-ive*]

in·cin·der·jell (in'sin dər,dʒel), *n.* jellied gasoline combined with napalm and used in flamethrowers and fire bombs.

The issues and living horror of the war disappear in a deadened, bureaucratic language—'incinderjell', 'the other side', 'body counts' of dead 'communists' reported with dream-like exactness. *Michael Rogin, "The American Dream," Review of "Abuse of Power" by Theodore Draper, The Listener, Feb. 22, 1968, p 244*

[alteration of *incendiary gel*]

in-company, *adj.* carried on within a company or business.

In-company supervisor training sessions should be arranged in order to improve the supervisor's understanding of his role in the management team and the functions of other departments. *The Times (London), Feb. 9, 1970, p 19*

[see IN-¹]

in-country, *adj.* carried on within a country, as distinguished from its borders or neighbors.

The Defence Department, he said, was not responsible for "in-country" activities in Laos. *The Times (London), March 4, 1970, p 5*

In South Vietnam, in what is called in Saigon the "in-country" war, development efforts have been concentrated upon types of weapons best utilized in jungles and rice paddies.... *Hanson Baldwin, The New York Times, May 1, 1966, Sec. 4, p 3*

[see IN-¹]

in-crowd, *n.* an exclusive set or circle of acquaintances; a group of insiders; clique.

...the magazine's [*New York* magazine] critics still point to its smug, In-crowd perspective. *Time, April 11, 1969, p 55*

...the performer who is written off as a hype becomes no longer the darling of the underground in-crowd, whatever his sincerity or intrinsic merit. *The Times (London), Aug. 13, 1970, p 10*

[see IN-²]

in-depth, *adj.* going deeply into a subject; very thorough; comprehensive.

. . . he has spent hours reading Government cables, memoranda and classified files to brief himself for in-depth discussions. *The New York Times Magazine, Jan. 28, 1968, p 70*

This time-lag is a serious handicap to Mr Nencini's book because he offers an in-depth report of the whole event in much the same way as he would cover it for his own Florentine paper. *The Sunday Times (London), Oct. 22, 1967, p 55*

[from the phrase *in depth*. See IN-¹.]

index, *v.t.* to adjust (income, rates of interest, etc.) to price changes in goods and services as reflected by the cost-of-living index.

As a social objective, it would seem that more and more

people feel that something better should be done for pensioners. That to index their pensions so that cost of living rises are compensated for at least once a year is a minimum. *The Guardian (London), March 25, 1972, p 18*

[verb use of *index, n.* (for *cost-of-living index*), probably patterned after French *indexer, v.*]

index crime, *U.S.* any of the most serious types of crimes on which statistical reports are published annually in the Uniform Crime Reports of the Federal Bureau of Investigation.

Of the seven index crimes in the Uniform Crime Reports, four are crimes of personal violence—murder, aggravated assault, rape, and robbery. They account for about 13 percent of all the index crimes in the country. The remaining three index crimes are burglary, larceny of $50 or more, and auto theft; these crimes against property make up the remaining 87 percent of serious crime. *Norval Morris and Gordon Hawkins, The Honest Politician's Guide to Crime Control, 1970, p 56*

Indian hay, *U.S. Slang.* marijuana.

...in the U.S. it is variously called the weed, stuff, Indian hay, grass, pot, tea, maryjane and other names. *Lester Grinspoon, "Marijuana," Scientific American, Dec. 1969, p 17*

Indianness, *n.* **1** the condition of being an American Indian.

...after mastering the meaning of Negritude and *machismo* they would have to grapple with the meaning of Indianness. *Calvin Trillin, "U.S. Journal: Los Angeles," The New Yorker, April 18, 1970, p 103*

2 a quality suggestive of India and its culture.

Gandhi always thought that a common thread of Indianness would somehow hold the two together. *"Hindu and Moslem: The Gospel of Hate," Time, Dec. 6, 1971, p 13*

inducer, *n.* a theoretical component of the operon that helps to activate genes. Also called DEREPRESSOR.

The French scientists advanced the theory, now substantially verified, that genes are controlled by a negative mechanism. That is, they are kept turned off by a "repressor" until another substance, an "inducer," comes along and disengages the repressor, thus allowing the gene to express itself. *Robert Reinhold, "Scientists Isolate A Gene," Encyclopedia Science Supplement (Grolier) 1970, p 108*

inertia selling, *British.* See the first quotation for the meaning.

"Inertia selling"—that is, sending unsolicited goods to potential customers and charging for them if not returned—has been under attack in the press. *Punch, March 27, 1968, p 460*

Mr. Weitzman, Labour member for Stoke Newington and Hackney, North, said inertia selling might not be carried out on a wide scale but something had to be done to stop it. *The Times (London), March 12, 1970, p 4*

infirmatory, *adj.* tending to invalidate or weaken; making infirm or insubstantial.

...a large number of papers have been published in the journals critical of Dr. Eysenck's [Hans J. Eysenck, a psychologist] thinking or infirmatory of his demonstrations in the field of introversion-extraversion studies. *Grahame Leman, London, England, in a Letter to the Editor, New Scientist, July 30, 1970, p 254*

223

► This word is labeled obsolete in the *OED* on the evidence of its only quotation from John Ayliffe's *Parergon* (1726). The current use may be a revival of the old word or a new independent formation patterned after *affirmatory, confirmatory*, etc.

inflatable, *n.* any of various functional structures or units made of strong plastic that can be inflated.

...what [Graham] Stevens is really concerned with is the activity of inflating. He works with air and gas, containing and concentrating it in many different ways within the bigger medium of the atmosphere and forces of gravity. They seem to share the property of the wind of sometimes being active and sometimes completely becalmed. These possibilities you never feel in inflatables that imitate the function of conventional buildings, like the Olivetti inflatable at Euston. *Guy Brett, "Underneath the Arches and Down at the Docks," The Times (London), Nov. 17, 1970, p 13*

The most popular toys are the inflatables: an 8-foot-long sausage and a 10-foot-square air mattress that looks like an upside-down wading pool. *Time, April 26, 1971, p 56*

Manufacturers of inflatables were quick to point out that their furniture had many advantages in addition to its unique design and light weight. It could be inflated or deflated with a vacuum cleaner or bicycle pump in a matter of minutes and, when fully inflated, could withstand the weight of a heavy man. *"Interior Decoration," The 1969 Compton Yearbook, p 284*

...Boat Shows at Earl's Court have given a boost to the inflatables.... These lightweight, easily transported and amazingly robust small boats are exactly what a certain type of British family has been wanting for years. *The Sunday Times (London), Dec. 29, 1968, p 39*

influence, *v.t.* to add alcoholic liquor to (a drink); to spike.

The old graduates kept the local bowling alley open all night. Next evening they assembled for a ham and beef banquet, looking prosperous for their ages and, because of state liquor laws, influencing their Cokes from brown paper bags. *William Friedman, "Nostalgic Reunion in Salina, Kansas," Time, July 13, 1970, p 14*

[probably from the legalistic phrase "under the *influence* of alcoholic liquor"]

informatics, *n.* another name for INFORMATION SCIENCE.

It was agreed in Amsterdam that an introduction to Informatics should form an integral part of general education in schools. *David Pegg, Cople, Bedfordshire, England, in a Letter to the Editor, The Times (London), Sept. 2, 1970, p 9*

information science, the study of the means by which information is processed or transmitted through computers and similar automatic equipment. Also called INFORMATICS.

The new chairs will bring the total to 47. Their professors will teach information science (a new field of study connected with computers), music, English, economics, pure mathematics, applied mathematics, and accounting. *The Times (London), Aug. 11, 1964, p 9*

infrasound, *n.* a very low-frequency sound wave produced in the atmosphere by phenomena such as thunderstorms, hailstorms, and tornadoes.

...the deflection of infrasounds at high altitude may well supply us with additional information about winds at these heights — heights which tend to be inaccessible to both balloon and satellite experiments. *"The Hailstorm's Unheard Growl," New Scientist, June 18, 1970, p 568*

[from *infra-* below + *sound*]

in-house, *adj.* being within or done within a business firm, organization, etc.

It [Bell System] employs, for example, as many PhDs as Britain produces annually and has an inhouse technical education programme equivalent in size and sophistication to a fair-sized university. *New Scientist, June 24, 1971, p 770*

Mr. Laird [Secretary of Defense] appears to have ordered what is known in bureaucratic jargon as an "in-house review." It will be conducted, that is, within the Department.... *Tom Wicker, The New York Times, Dec. 27, 1970, Sec. 4, p 11*

While a few companies — Ford is one — employ their own in-house anthropometric specialists, most rely on outside consultants. *Time, Nov. 15, 1968, p 62*

[see IN-¹]

initialism, *n.* an abbreviation formed from the initial letters of a phrase (such as *NATO* for *North Atlantic Treaty Organization* and *MRV* for *multiple reentry vehicle*), as distinguished from abbreviations formed by contraction *(doz.* for *dozen)* or by substitution *(lb.* for *pound* and *xtal.* for *crystal).*

By 1960, when the Gale Research Company of Detroit published the first edition of what is now called *Acronyms and Initialisms Dictionary* (lumping wordlike acronyms with unpronounceable abbreviations) 12,000 of both were already on the loose. *Time, July 20, 1970, p 61*

injectable, *n.* a drug or medicine that may be injected directly into the bloodstream.

...Dr. Kramer said the injectables are most often used by persons who formerly took amphetamines orally, as pep-pills. They graduated to main-lining to enhance the drugs' stimulating effects. *Jane E. Brody, The New York Times, Aug. 1, 1967, p 27*

Implantable time capsules, once-a-month pills and long-term injectables are also on the horizon, he says. *Science News, Dec. 23, 1967, p 615*

[noun use of *injectable, adj.*]

injection, *n.* the process of putting a satellite or spacecraft into a calculated orbit. Also called INSERTION.

"We were flying blind during lift-off and injection," says Bill Collier, ... Mariner II was safely delivered, apparently thriving in its adult environment, and on its way to Venus. *Time, March 8, 1963, p 79*

inner cabinet, *British.* a committee or other small group within an organization that performs unofficially the advisory function of a cabinet.

The one hope of avoiding an all-out inter-union dispute now lies with the Trades Union Congress. Its "inner cabinet," the finance and general purposes committee, hopes to call in all the parties next week to discuss the long drawn out row. *John Torode, "Union Rift Threatens Steel Production," The Manchester Guardian Weekly, Jan. 16, 1969, p 22*

The meeting was also told that Hebdomadal council, the university's "inner cabinet", had appointed a committee to listen to the views of the students' elected representatives. *"Student Injunctions to Continue," The Times (London), March 3, 1970, p 2*

Word that Mr. [Harold] Wilson has called the Parliamentary Committee of the Cabinet (the so-called Inner Cabinet) to a long meeting at Chequers tomorrow touched off a predictable spate of political and electoral speculation.... *The Times (London), March 7, 1970, p 3*

inner circle, a group of people who are closest to a center of power or influence.

Most of President Nixon's inner circle have been friends and confidants of the President's for years. *Hugh Sidey, "They Share the President's Power," The 1970 World Book Year Book, p 96*

A good number of NDP [West Germany's National Democratic Party] brass were Nazi party members.... These men constitute [Adolf] von Thadden's inner circle. They would run the government that "Bubi" von Thadden ... hopes to take over in 1973 or 1977, depending on how quickly the country's economy will deteriorate. *Peter Lust, "German Letter: The Other Adolf," Saturday Night (Canada), Feb. 1968, p 15*

inner city, *U.S.* the part of a city usually inhabited by large numbers of poor or disadvantaged people, viewed apart from other sections and suburbs where the middle-class groups live. Compare CENTRAL CITY.

... most outer-city integration has been restricted to areas contiguous to black sections of the inner city, leaving heavier concentrations of poorer blacks at inner-city lines, and a few in middle-income and upper-income suburbs farther away from the city. *Paul Delaney, The New York Times, June 1, 1971, p 28*

It is clear that the twin concepts of decentralization and community control of the schools developed in response to the failure of the schools in the inner city and have little or nothing to do with the sometimes excellent schools serving the city's middle-class, predominantly white students. *James Cass, "Education in America: Choose Your Own Brand of Disaster," Saturday Review, Nov. 16, 1968, p 95*

inner-city, *adj.* of or relating to an inner city.

In inner-city schools, 60% of the pupils who made the 10th grade dropped out before completing the 12th. *Lyndon B. Johnson, "Agenda for the Future: A Presidential Perspective," Britannica Book of the Year 1969, p 39*

The great drawbridge crisis turned out to be a minor, if dramatic, skirmish in the nationwide hostilities between inner-city and suburban residents, which, it now seems clear, will be the central American conflict of the nineteen-seventies. *Andy Logan, "Around City Hall," The New Yorker, June 26, 1971, p 81*

inner space, 1 another name for HYDROSPACE.

If technology makes it possible for Man to occupy the ocean depths it would be better to have come to some agreement in advance, if only to avoid the sort of grabbing which passed for national policy in the past.... In the House of Commons last week the Prime Minister told a questioner that the case for international control had still to be made out. Perhaps the British report on marine science and technology which is expected shortly will shed light on this and other problems arising from the new interest in what the Americans called "inner space". *"Editorial: An Omen From the Red Sea?" New Scientist, Oct. 24, 1968, p 174*

2 the subconscious part of the mind.

Three letters, on a drawing of three cubes, appeared not long ago on a fence at the University of Wisconsin with the slogan: Your Campus Travel Agent — One Trip Is Worth A Thousand Words. Just about everyone at Wisconsin knew what kind of "trip" that was: the voyage into "inner space," the flight into or out of the self, provided by LSD. *"LSD," Time, June 17, 1966, p 46*

3 the quality or suggestion of depth in an abstract painting.

Kandinsky and Malevich were 'diagonal invaders' of horizontal and vertical Renaissance space. They used diagonals to create 'inner space' by breaking down interiorising outer space. *Paul Overy, "Art: De Stijl," The Listener, March 7, 1968, p 318*

In·nig·keit ('in ix,kait), *n. German.* whole-hearted sincerity and warmth (applied in English only to musical works).

Later, perhaps conscious of the strained balance of the five movements, Mahler removed the short C major intermezzo, leaving the symphony as we now know it. *Blumine* has in fact a very characteristic innigkeit — a Mahlerian simple poignancy — which might well benefit a work whose progress from a child's heaven to a satanic hell has often seemed abrupt and unreal. *Stephen Walsh, The Listener, June 29, 1967, p 865*

In Beethoven's F minor quartet (the early C minor had been promised — one of those high-handed last-moment changes so regrettably popular with Russian visitors) their playing was smooth and thoughtful, portentous of the *innigkeit* rather than the urgency of the later Beethoven. *The Times (London), Nov. 21, 1966, p 14*

A conductor who insisted on emphasizing the *Innigkeit* of this work would have made it sheerly intolerable. *Harold C. Schonberg, The New York Times, April 30, 1965, p 41*

A quarter of a century ago it was generally accepted that Bruno Walter was pre-eminent as a Mozart conductor. Nobody, it was believed, so achieved the *Innigkeit* of the Mozart symphonies and operas. *Discus, Harper's, Aug. 1964, p 106*

input, *v.t., v.i.* to supply or be supplied with data fed into a computer or any system like that of a computer.

Part of the reason for the much faster rates at which data can be accepted by computers than by man is that data is carefully preprocessed before being input to a computer, whereas man has to extract information from the buzzing confusion of the real world. *N. S. Sutherland, "Machines Like Men," Science Journal, Oct. 1968, p 46*

... while one user is spending 5 seconds inputting some data (try and see how much data you can type in 5 seconds), the CPU [central processing unit] of a modern computer can execute as many as 1 million computations, or as many as 10,000 for each of 10 other users, and still not delay the person who is keying in his data. *R. Clay Sprowls, "Computers," Encyclopedia Science Supplement (Grolier) 1971, p 148*

"Just look at this report card! 'Accommodates enrichment data, inputs easily, and is generally self-programming.'" *Cartoon legend, The New Yorker, Nov. 28, 1970, p 44*

[verb use of *input, n.*]

insertion, *n.* another name for INJECTION.

Insertion: the process of boosting a spacecraft into an orbit round the Earth or moon. *The Sunday Times (London), July 13, 1969, p 13*

in·shal·lah (,in ʃɑ:l'lɑ:), *interj. Arabic.* God willing.

Every day 90 million Arabs intone the word *inshallah* —

God willing. It is Allah who will reform society, not a Brezhnev or a Mao, and the typical Arab has little enthusiasm for tinkering with changes himself. *"Arabs v. Communists: Thanks But No Thanks," Time, Aug. 9, 1971, p 23*

Statements like "We will succeed in doing such and such by A.D. 1985," or "A.D. 2000," etc. remind me of the Arab story of the little men underground trying to dig their way out to daylight and destroy the world. Every night they say, "Tomorrow we will break through," but God fills in their holes because they forgot to say *Inshallah* (God willing). Perhaps these superbiologists might find some way to say their equivalent of *Inshallah*, or to cross their fingers when they set their timetables. *Carleton S. Coon, Gloucester, Mass., in a Letter to the Editor, The Atlantic, March 1969, p 48*

[the Arabic original is a phrase, *'in shā 'llāh*, used as an interjection]

instant, *adj.* **1** produced or occurring in what seems to be an instant; involving little or no preparation, planning, thought, etc.

For present tastes, honed to instant violence, it is by no means obvious that Shakespeare outwrote Marlowe. [Ian] McKellen's Richard [II] is Shakespeare's, full strength and without eccentricity, a prince refined down to holy innocence.... *"The Stage Abroad: A Double Crown," Review of "Edward II," Time, Sept. 19, 1969, p 51*

The reorganization of the Army (the Socialists favour the creation of "instant soldiers" with basic training limited to six months). *Ritchie McEwen, "Austrian Parties in Deadlock on Coalition," The Times (London), April 10, 1970, p 6*

Mr. [Keith] Jenkinson pointed to a 1928 double-deck bus which has taken him eight years to renovate and is the third oldest in existence. "That's one bit of instant history the Americans are not going to get." *"Traffic in History," The Manchester Guardian Weekly, April 17, 1971, p 9*

2 characterized as being very quick, especially too quick to be of much value.

In this instant world of today people, sadly, have short memories.... *The Times (London), April 21, 1970, p 12*

[originally applied to premixed or precooked foods]

instantize, *v.t.* to make available in instant (premixed, precooked, etc.) form.

...the department contracted...for the purchase of "instantized" nonfat dry milk for distribution in welfare programs. *Joe Western, "Agriculture: Dairy Products," The Americana Annual 1970, p 58*

...when foods become unrecognisable, what shall we do? The formulated, instantised, convenience foods will no longer look like meat, milk, cereal or vegetable. *Arnold E. Bender, "Nutrition Neglected?" New Scientist, Dec. 24, 1970, p 560*

institutional revolution, another name for CULTURAL REVOLUTION.

I have shown in the case of education that a cultural or institutional revolution depends upon the clarification of reality. *Ivan Illich, Saturday Review, Oct. 17, 1970, p 68*

institutional revolutionary, another name for CULTURAL REVOLUTIONARY.

Thus, the Luddite blames the producer; the institutional revolutionary tries to reshape the design and distribution of the product. *Ivan Illich, Saturday Review, Oct. 17, 1970, p 57*

instructional television, *U.S.* closed-circuit television programs designed as courses for instruction within the classroom. *Abbreviation:* ITV

After more than a decade of intensive effort and the expenditure of hundreds of millions of dollars, instructional television seems to have arrived at a limbo of promise and partial success. *Judith Murphy and Ronald Gross, "The Unfulfilled Promise of ITV," Saturday Review, Nov. 19, 1966, p 88*

► British English seems to have no direct equivalent. *CCTV* (for *Closed-Circuit Television*) is often used to mean instructional television.

instrumental learning or **instrumental conditioning,** a form of conditioning in which the subject learns to respond according to the result of the effects (good or bad) of his previous responses. Also called OPERANT CONDITIONING.

Two types of learning are classical conditioning and instrumental learning. Classical conditioning begins with an unconditioned stimulus. The conditioned stimulus that is paired with it comes to substitute for it in producing the unconditioned response. In instrumental learning a conditioned stimulus is presented along with an opportunity to respond in various ways. The correct response is reinforced, or rewarded. *Leo V. DiCara, "Learning in the Autonomic Nervous System," Scientific American, Jan. 1970, p 31*

In a typical experiment, if a rat showed a slight increase in its heart rate, it would be rewarded by electrical stimulation of certain areas of the brain known to produce pleasure to the animal. This was then followed by a further increase in heart rate, which was called instrumental learning. *Ronald R. Novales, "Zoology," Britannica Book of the Year 1970, p 168*

Instrumental conditioning is also called *operant learning* because the learned response *operates* on the environment to produce some effect. *Ernest R. Hilgard and Leonard M. Horowitz, "Learning," The 1968 World Book Year Book, p 561*

integrated circuit, an electronic circuit hundreds of times smaller than a wired circuit, produced on a single chip of silicon in such a way that the components are completely integrated and cannot be grouped or redistributed in another way and still perform the same electronic function. *Abbreviation:* IC. Also called MICROCIRCUIT or MONOLITHIC CIRCUIT.

Integrated circuits have been used chiefly in computers and low-frequency instrumentation, but now they can be applied in VHF, UHF and microwave apparatus. *Michael Parkyn, "Microwave Circuits on the Beam," New Scientist, Oct. 15, 1970, p 13*

Integrated circuits have just reached the colour television business and are already vital components in the computer industry: electronics for mass-produced cars, desk calculators, and further ahead, the household computer, are on a long list of areas the industry would like to penetrate. *Peter Rodgers, "Finance: Competition in Miniature," The Manchester Guardian Weekly, April 11, 1970, p 22*

integrated circuitry, components or equipment consisting of integrated circuits. Also called MICROCIRCUITRY.

The effects of the rapidly falling price of integrated circuits can still surprise even those in close touch with this field. The W. German subsidiary of Texas Instruments exhibited integrated circuitry to replace the traditional string and pulley drive of radio receivers. *New Scientist, Nov. 12, 1970, p 329*

integrodifferential, *adj. Calculus.* containing or involving both integrals (area measurements) of a function and differentials (rate of change measurements) of a function.

In reactive gas dynamics problems, one has to include the effects of radiative heat transfer. This leads to a set of 11 coupled nonlinear scalar partial differential equations (actually some of the equations are integrodifferential equations). Because of the extraordinary complexity of these equations, this challenging subject is still in a state of development, and those problems which have been solved involve approximations the validity of which is often difficult to assess. *R. B. Bird, "Relative Gas Dynamics," McGraw-Hill Yearbook of Science and Technology 1967, p 413*

In·tel·sat (in'tel₁sæt), *n.* **1** acronym for *International Telecommunications Satellite (Consortium),* an organization of over 70 member nations formed to control and promote work in global communications by means of satellites.

... America is prepared to supply rockets to Europe even for communications satellites which would bring competition to US-comsats. The question of how this could be achieved without violating the *Intelsat* rules, however, has yet to be solved. *New Scientist, Oct. 1, 1970, p 16*

2 any of several communications satellites launched under the auspices of Intelsat.

The Intelsats launched by the Communications Satellite Corporation provide commercial service over vast areas by being stationed in synchronous orbits above the Atlantic and the Pacific oceans. *Steven Moll, "Review of the Year—Space Exploration," Encyclopedia Science Supplement (Grolier) 1968, p 298*

The Hughes satellites, including two Syncoms, three Intelsats (Early Bird, Lani Bird, Canary Bird), and two Applications Technology Satellites, now have a combined service life of over 17 years. Every satellite in synchronous orbit around Earth was built by Hughes. *Advertisement by Hughes Aircraft Company, Scientific American, April 1968, p 5*

intensive care unit, a medical unit equipped with life-saving and monitoring devices for providing 24-hour in-hospital care for severely ill patients, or immediate out-of-hospital care in emergencies, especially heart attacks.

Twenty years ago hospitals employed 1.5 persons to care for each patient. Today the ratio is almost 3 to 1 nationally and much higher in specialized intensive care units. *Howard A. Rusk, M.D., The New York Times, Feb. 25, 1968, p 51*

Doctors at the Royal Victoria Hospital, Belfast, are operating a new crash-call system which is saving the lives of people having coronary attacks at home, by sending a mobile intensive-care unit to the patient's own door. *Dr. Alfred Byrne, The Sunday Times (London), Aug. 6, 1967, p 2*

inter-, a prefix meaning "between" or "among," now used chiefly to form adjectives, as in the following recent formations:

interauthority, *adj.:* In the second case inter-authority arrangements could be made for recruiting pupils from outside the immediate area. *The Times (London), March 25, 1970, p 10*

intercentre, *adj.:* ... saturation signalling involves a large volume of inter-centre communication and with conventional techniques it can only be employed in networks of limited size and with limited traffic capacity. *New Scientist, Dec. 31, 1970, p 596*

interdealer, *adj.:* It appears to be technically feasible to use a central computer to record and report interdealer quotations for some or all over-the-counter securities on a continuing basis. *The New York Times, Feb. 19, 1968, p 60*

interfirm, *adj.:* The Stock Exchange yesterday announced details of price fractions for which inter-firm accounting computers will be programmed after decimalization. *The Times (London), March 11, 1970, p 28*

intersyllabic, *adj.:* Rhythmically, the production follows a metrical pattern as fixed as that of the metronome with which it opens. Lines are broken up with blows of a strap, or even split up with intersyllabic pauses. *Irving Wardle, "Ritual Takes Over," Review of "Arden of Faversham," The Times (London), May 22, 1970, p 6*

in·ter·a·bang (in'ter ə₁bæŋ), *n.* another spelling of INTERROBANG.

Thanks to the American Type Founders Co., Inc., an easy solution is at hand: the interbang (‽) a punctuation mark included in a new A.T.F. type-face called Americana. The symbol was invented by Martin K. Speckter, an advertising-agency president and hobbyist printer, who had long brooded over the proper punctuation for such rhetorical questions of daily life as "Who forgot to put gas in the car" or "What the hell." *Time, July 21, 1967, p 38*

interconceptional, *adj.* occurring between successive conceptions or pregnancies.

A second part of the volume [*From Conception to Birth: the Drama of Life's Beginnings*] verges on a manual, with a balanced regime for the times of pregnancy, the crisis of birth and the "interconceptional period." *Philip Morrison, "Books," Scientific American, Oct. 1971, p 118*

interdate, *v.i. U.S.* to go out on dates with members of a different religion or denomination.

Among the Catholic students 74 per cent interdated frequently and 66 per cent thought it likely they would marry non-Catholics. *The New York Times, Nov. 8, 1965, p 33*

in·ter·dit (æ ter'di:), *adj. French.* prohibited.

Karisimbi [a high peak in NW Rwanda, in central Africa] was strictly *interdit.* Provided, however, that I undertook to go straight up and down, he would in my case waive the rules. *The Times (London), Sept. 17, 1966, p 9*

There are hamburgers and hot dogs—and *quiche Lorraine* and *bifsteck tartare* as well: Moët et Chandon champagne and Coca-Cola are both on the menu. Empty seats are *interdit. Time, Nov. 2, 1970, p 56*

▶ In French there is a noun *interdit* as well as the adjective. The feminine of the adjective is *interdite,* a form recorded in the *OED* as an obsolete variant of *interdict, n.* and *v.* But *interdit, adj.* is an independent loan from modern French.

interface, *n.* something that serves to connect or coordinate different systems; the boundary joining any two parts, persons, or things.

"Interface" refers to anything that mediates between disparate items: machinery, people, thought. The equipment that makes the computer's work visible to the user is often called an "interface," and the word is used highly metaphorically, as in "the interface between man and the computer, between the scientist and society." *Richard Todd, "You Are an Interfacer of Black Boxes," The Atlantic, March 1970, p 66*

Last week, the Biological Engineering Society celebrated the tenth anniversary of this broad interface between medicine and technology with a conference in Oxford. *New Scientist, April 16, 1970, p 117*

And it is exactly at the "interface" between that Darwinian-Mendelian theory of random mutation and natural selection and the recent discoveries in genetics and biochemistry that one finds some of the most characteristic speculative arguments in current science. *George Steiner, "Books," Review of "Beyond Reductionism," edited by Arthur Koestler and J. R. Smythies, The New Yorker, March 6, 1971, p 108*

—*v.i., v.t.* to match, harmonize, or work together smoothly.

This was to be a full-dress affair, including inflated space suits, which have to "interface"—a space-age verb meaning, roughly, to coordinate—with equipment in the cabin. *Henry S. F. Cooper, Jr., "LM," The New Yorker, Jan. 11, 1969, p 42*

Putting the computer to work meant complex programming, interfacing of instrument and computer, of man and machine. *Advertisement by Hewlett Packard, Scientific American, May 1970, p 114*

I *like* big companies. They're very important. They have *money.* I'm offering them a chance to interface with new products right from the start. *"The Talk of the Town," The New Yorker, Feb. 27, 1971, p 34*

[extended senses of *interface, n.*, the touching surface of two objects that are joined]

in·ter·fer·on (ˌin tərˈfirˌɑn), *n.* a protein produced in the cells of many vertebrates that prevents the replication of viruses by its sensitivity to foreign nucleic acid.

... acute virus infection can be cured by stimulating the body's production of interferon. *Theodore F. Treuting, "Internal Medicine," The World Book Science Annual 1969, p 317*

Interferon, once hailed as a potential panacea for virus diseases, has fallen from grace in some scientists' eyes, and is a focus of controversy among those who continue to believe in its future. *"Viruses," Science News Yearbook 1970, p 112*

[from *interfere* + *-on* (chemical suffix)]

intergenerational, *adj.* occurring or existing between two or more generations of people.

Mothers in Poverty: A study of Fatherless Families.... An assessment of alternative explanations of the intergenerational transmission of poverty. *"Books," Science News, May 16, 1970, p 493*

They [most parents] may give a child the name of a relative to strengthen feelings of kinship, to keep alive an intergenerational awareness, or possibly to make a legacy more likely. *Mallory Wober, "Popular Images of Personal Names," Science Journal, Sept. 1970, p 39*

interleave, *n.* the correlation, by means of successive numbers, of physically separate locations of storage units in a computer.

One reason why Sigma 5 gets more efficient as it grows larger is that when memory modules are added interleave

and overlap occur. This not only increases the effective speed of the central processor but raises input/output capability too. *Advertisement by Scientific Data Systems, Scientific American, Feb. 1967, p 11*

intermedia, *n.* the use of many different devices and techniques from any artistic form to produce a show, exhibition, or other entertainment. This may include such a potpourri as exotic theatrical lighting combined with motion pictures and sound from tapes on a backdrop behind a full ballet. *Often used attributively.* Compare MIXED MEDIA, MULTIMEDIA.

That a great many Western artists for a great many years have quarreled with received definitions of artistic media, genres, and forms goes without saying: pop art, dramatic and musical "happenings," the whole range of "intermedia" or "mixed-means" art, bear recentest witness to the tradition of rebelling against Tradition. *John Barth, "The Literature of Exhaustion," The Atlantic, August 1967, p 29*

Lyla Hay, Gerald Hoke, Arthur Wagner, and Bronislav Radakovich perform well and strenuously amid the taxing conditions posed by this sort of experimentation. And there is no gainsaying the uniqueness of the event. Yet it does make the play much more difficult to follow, as well as compelling the theatergoer to sit on the floor for two hours. Since this form of environmental "intermedia" theater is in its early stages, one is inclined to forgive its imperfections and distractions. *Henry Hewes, "The Theater: For the Arkansas Traveler," Saturday Review, May 20, 1967, p 64*

► This term should not be confused with *intermedia* in the sense of musical or dance interludes, which is the plural of *intermedium* (a term with several technical senses, originally from Latin, in which it is the neuter of *intermedius,* from *inter-* between + *medius* middle). The term herein is a new English formation of *inter-* + *media* means of communication, expression, or entertainment (plural of *medium*).

intermediate, *n. U.S.* an automobile between the standard and the compact models in size. Compare SUBCOMPACT.

The intermediates, the Chevrolet's Chevelle and the Pontiac, Oldsmobile and Buick models received major changes for 1968 and get minor grille and trim facelifts for 1969. *The New York Times, March 26, 1968, p 32*

General Motors and Ford restyled their standard-sized cars for 1971, adopting the trend toward ventless front windows and concealed wipers that became paramount on the redesigned 1970 intermediates. *Maynard M. Gordon, "Automobiles," The Americana Annual 1971, p 130*

intermediate boson or **intermediate vector boson,** another name for W PARTICLE.

The disagreement between the Utah result and present theory suggests that additional sources of cosmic-ray muons exist. One possibility is the intermediate boson—a hypothetical particle never seen by experimenters. *New Scientist, Sept. 25, 1969, p 633*

The present theory of the weak interaction predicts that its quantum should be a so-called intermediate vector boson, which can come in two varieties, positively or negatively charged, designated W-plus or W-minus. *Dietrick E. Thomsen, "Weak Interaction Puzzle of the Fourth Force," Science News, Oct. 9, 1971, p 253*

intermodal, *adj.* **1** combining different ways of

transportation into one system.

Both vessels are part of an intermodal system in which United States Freight uses railroads to "piggyback" trailers and container vans to ports for delivery. *The New York Times, May 4, 1968, p 78*

2 used in an integrated system of transportation.

Unit trains are high-speed trains made up of about 100 permanently coupled flatcars, each able to carry two intermodal containers. *The Sunday Times (London), April 6, 1969, p 56*

internal pollution, the excessive and often harmful ingestion of a variety of synthetic substances in drugs and foods.

Dr. Beaconsfield, an American, is a specialist in the long-term effects of drugs upon various body tissues and cells. He earlier coined the term internal pollution and was instigator of this proposal for independent action by the scientific community. *Walter Sullivan, "Scientists Urging 'Pollution' Study," The New York Times, June 20, 1971, p 50*

interoperable, *adj.* capable of operating together or reciprocally.

In other respects the two nations' forces are working in parallel and Skynet [The Royal Navy's military satellite communications system] is compatible and interoperable with the US Defence Communication Satellite system.... *Science Journal, March 1970, p 13*

interpopulational, *adj.* occurring or existing between populations or between different groups, especially groups considered as separate species, cultures, etc.

I wonder whether he would agree that there are no known IQ tests which are capable of overcoming the *inter*populational cross-cultural barrier? *Ashley Montagu, The Listener, Dec. 30, 1971, p 907*

Interpopulational developmental comparisons ... helped to clarify what in the past seemed to be an aberrant course of leaf development. *Donald R. Kaplan, "Botany: Leaf," McGraw-Hill Yearbook of Science and Technology 1971, p 253*

in·ter·ro·bang (in'tər ə,bæŋ), *n.* a punctuation mark (‽) intended to express simultaneously a question and an exclamation, as in certain rhetorical questions (How about that?! Who needs him?!). Also spelled INTERABANG.

[Martin K.] Speckter's device, which he prefers to call the interrobang ("bang" is printer's slang for an exclamation point), remained just an idea until Detroit Graphic Artist Richard Ishbell casually included it in the Americana face he was designing. *Time, July 21, 1967, p 38*

[from *interrog*ation point + *bang*]

interrupt, *n.* **1** a temporary stop; interruption.

Sigma 5 can deal with foreground real-time interrupts in 6 microseconds without losing control of any of its other jobs, yet every background user will get his answers faster than he needs them. *Advertisement by Scientific Data Systems, Scientific American, Feb. 1967, p 11*

2 any breach, separation, or gap.

Wide though the interrupt be that divides us, runers [makers of runes] and counters, from the Old World of the Plants ... we nod them as neighbors.... *W. H. Auden, "The Aliens" (a poem), The New Yorker, Nov. 21, 1970, p 58*

intersensory, *adj.* involving the use of all or several senses at the same time.

... such is the power of intersensory whatever-it-is that any one of four golfers, sizing up to a simple chip shot of, say, 40 yards, knows suddenly that nothing can prevent him socketing it. *The Sunday Times (London), Nov. 26, 1967, p 20*

intersex, *n.* another name for UNISEX.

In our own culture, Winick sees intersex everywhere. Clothes and hair are the least of it. Sales of jewelry and fragrances for men have risen massively in the past three years. Since World War II, there has been a 66% increase in the number of women tennis players, a 1,000% rise in women golfers. Every third gun-owner is a woman, and so is every fifth skydiver. *"Behavior: Killing a Culture," Time, Oct. 12, 1970, p 57*

into, *prep.* **be into, 1** *Slang.* to be deeply involved or interested in.

"Yes, I *am* into a new thing, dear child. It's called embroidery." *Cartoon legend, The New Yorker, Aug. 1, 1970, p 21*

... he doesn't want to be President. He isn't into that. You know. Into power. *Penelope Gilliatt, "The Current Cinema: 'Woodstock,' or Synchronize Heartbeats," The New Yorker, April 11, 1970, p 161*

Career Plans [of 1971 Teen-ager]. Digs working in leather, wood, metal, and the cane fields of Cuba (for a month). Is also into making music, films, and videotapes. *Sherman B. Chickering, "Staying Hip: 1971, 18; Dropout from Senior Year of High School," Harper's, Sept. 1971, p 65*

2 to be in debt to.

... he [a Japanese truck driver] was a hi-fi nut who made his own equipment, which he could have got from Philco for $200 cheaper, and he was into us for several hundred dollars for some acoustical components. *Jon Ruddy, "Does It Pay to Go Bankrupt?" Maclean's, Oct. 1967, p 80*

▶ Definition 2 is an old slang usage just emerging into general use. Partridge (*Dictionary of Slang*, 1950) calls it a Canadian colloquialism, citing a 1932 source. It also occurs in Saul Bellow's *Adventures of Augie March*, 1949: "I said I'd stop Frazier's credit at twenty-five dollars. It was a lie; ... he was already into me for nearer to forty."

intra-, 1 a prefix used chiefly to form adjectives (both technical and nontechnical) with the sense of "situated, occurring, carried on, etc., within or inside," as in the following recent formations:

intracloud, *adj.*: Zeroing in on intracloud lightning ... lightning strokes between and within clouds are difficult to study and document because weather conditions usually prevent visual and photographic observations. *Science News, March 28, 1970, p 320*

intragovernmental, *adj.*: In what is fast becoming an ugly intragovernmental feud over the creation of an electronics and broadcasting giant, the Justice Department insisted that the FCC had violated the law by not holding more complete hearings. *Time, Feb. 10, 1967, p 58*

intraoffice, *adj.*: They were impatient with committees that took months to study proposals and with intra-office and interagency reports that delayed action. *The New York Times, April 14, 1968, Sec. 4, p 13*

intraregional, *adj.*: ... the remarkable rate of increase in intraregional trade cannot go on forever, and eventually there will be a need for wider markets. *Time, Feb. 3, 1967, p 29*

intraunion, *adj.*: The intra-union controversy, regarded as a bid by Negroes to gain more power within their union made idle half the fleet of 2,800 buses and drastically reduced service on elevated and subway rapid transit trains. *The New York Times, July 4, 1968, p 8*

intrazonal, *adj.*: The Chilean delegate—Pedro Daza—told startled delegates . . . that the only beneficiaries of tariff reductions to date had been foreign multinational companies. Intrazonal trade had increased, but so had the region's dependence on foreign capital. *Christopher Roper, "Foreign Investment in Latin America," The Manchester Guardian Weekly, Dec. 19, 1970, p 22*

2 in the following occurrence *intra-* has become an adjective modifying the noun with which it is combined, and meaning "inside, internal":

intra-trading, *n.*: The increase [in exports] of nearly 16 per cent was close to the average of 17 per cent for all countries covered, and virtually at the estimated average, if Common Market intra-trading is excluded. *"UK Stake in World Trade Maintained," The Times (London), May 6, 1970, p 26*

intrauterine device, a contraceptive loop, coil, ring, etc., placed within the uterus as a physical barrier to implantation of a fertilized ovum. *Abbreviation:* IUD See also LIPPES LOOP.

At the 14 municipal hospitals the free birth-control services will include provision of pills, intrauterine devices, and contraceptives as well as advice on the spacing of children. *The New York Times, June 17, 1968, p 41*

. . . the Pill and intra-uterine devices are not permitted. *The Times (London), June 2, 1967, p 9*

intravehicular, *adj.* of, relating to, or used inside a space vehicle. Compare EXTRAVEHICULAR.

The intravehicular space suit consists of: fecal containment subsystem, constant wear garment, biomedical belt, urine collection transfer assembly, torso limb suit, integrated thermal micrometeoroid garment, pressure helmet, pressure glove, and communications carrier. *"The Apollo Space Suit," Encyclopedia Science Supplement (Grolier) 1969, p 329*

intravenous, *n.* an injection or transfusion into a vein or an intravenous feeding or series of such feedings.

"Do you want me to rub your arm?" Ellie asked. "I don't think I dare. You have intravenouses going in both your hands." *Rachel MacKenzie, "Risk," The New Yorker, Nov. 21, 1970, p 66*

[noun use of *intravenous, adj.*, going into a vein]

introgressant, *n.* a gene of one species which is acquired by another species through hybridization.

The problem is to find a good scale to measure the proportions in which the parental species are represented in a sample of introgressants. *D. H. Valentine, "Biosystematics," McGraw-Hill Yearbook of Science and Technology 1968, p 121*

[from *intro-* into + *-gress* go (as in *progress, regress*) + *-ant* (noun agent suffix)]

Iof·fe bar (yɑf'i:), one of a set of current-carrying bars used to increase the strength of a magnetic field in a nuclear fusion reaction.

. . . by adding several current-carrying bars, called Ioffe

bars, around the plasma and parallel to the axis, a true magnetic well can be created. *Ernest P. Gray, "Plasma Physics," The World Book Science Annual 1969, p 345*

In addition extra current-carrying structures are often used to improve the stability of the plasma. These structures were originally proposed on theoretical grounds in 1955 by Harold Grad of New York University. They were first used successfully in an experimental test in 1962 by the Russian physicist M. S. Ioffe. The straight rods used by Ioffe in his experiment have come to be called Ioffe bars, but such stabilizing structures can assume various other shapes. *William C. Gough and Bernard J. Eastlund, "The Prospects of Fusion Power," Scientific American, Feb. 1971, p 52*

ion etching, the technique of eroding materials such as metals, glass, polymers, body tissue, etc., atom by atom, by bombarding them with high-energy ions, in order to reveal their smallest structural features.

The technique of ion etching has now been applied to a wide variety of specimens. Typical examples are metallurgical specimens usually polycrystalline and showing characteristic grain boundary formation. *New Scientist, Feb. 5, 1970, p 256*

ionicity, *n.* capacity for ionization.

Many of our present ideas about the degree of ionicity of the atoms in solids are based on the pioneering concepts introduced by Linus Pauling in the late 1920s and early 1930s. *Joseph I. Budnick, "Physics," The World Book Science Annual 1972 (1971), p 356*

ion implantation, a process of making semiconductor devices by implanting electronically the necessary impurities into silicon chips instead of diffusing them.

This month has seen the marketing of the first transistor device produced using the new technology of ion implantation. *"Ion Doped Transistors on the Market," New Scientist, Feb. 19, 1970, p 358*

Ion implantation in metal oxide semi-conductors would allow higher switching speeds, reduction in size, and will allow easier fabrication of three-dimensional devices. *Joseph I. Budnick, "Physics," The World Book Science Annual 1972 (1971), p 357*

irredeemable, *n.* a bond that cannot be redeemed before maturity.

Yields are temptingly high whether you are a low taxpayer going for the latest high coupon stock or the irredeemables like War Loan and Treasury 3 per cent. . . . *The Sunday Times (London), Sept. 28, 1969, p 27*

irrelevance, *n.* absence of contemporaneity; failure to address oneself to issues that are current. Compare RELEVANCE.

. . . writers like Mark Twain and Stephen Crane, despite their "irrelevance," were more important than Eldridge Cleaver and Rap Brown. *Arthur Mizener, "American Literature," 1970 Collier's Encyclopedia Year Book, p 105*

irrelevant, *adj.* having no bearing on issues that are current. Compare RELEVANT.

Ronnie, now 24, later chose not to join his father's "irrelevant" business, won a conscientious-objector status after a harrowing legal battle, and started writing a novel. *"When the Young Teach and the Old Learn," Time, Aug. 17, 1970, p 38*

ir·tron ('ər¸trɑn), *n.* a galactic source of strong infrared radiation.

To satisfy theoretical and observational constraints imposed by the shape of the spectrum shown in the figure, the size of the emitting region in the galactic center must be made much smaller than the observed diameter. Thus it is necessary to break up the source into many smaller sources. These sources must be nearly identical in all their physical properties, and have been named irtrons because of their characteristic infrared spectrum. *Frank J. Low, "Galaxy: Infrared," McGraw-Hill Yearbook of Science and Technology 1971, p 209*

Irtrons radiate fantastic amounts of energy, in some cases many times more than the total power emitted by all the stars in the largest galaxies. *Dietrick E. Thomsen, "Supporting Evidence for the Theory of the Steady State," Science News, May 9, 1970, p 464*

[from *infrared* spectrum + *-on*, as in *electron*, *neutron*, etc.]

i·so·en·zyme (¸ai sou'en¸zaim), *n.* one of two or more chemically different forms of the same enzyme. Also called ISOZYME.

Chymotrypsin-A and chymotrypsin-B [a pair of digestive enzymes] are the most closely related, their sequences differing only in about 20 per cent of the positions, and as their catalytic activities and specifications are practically identical they can correctly be considered as isoenzymes—"twins" in the family. *David Shotton, "Family Relationships Between Enzymes," New Scientist, March 19, 1970, p 547*

[from *iso-* equal + *enzyme*]

isolated camera, a television videotape camera that is focused on a single player or a single area of play during a game in order to permit immediate replay of any segment involving the player or area of play.

In the spring and summer it is baseball, and winter and fall it is football, beginning shortly after lunch on Saturday . . . and then the whole thing again on Sunday, a vast swirl of bats, swings, passes, kicks, touchdowns, stolen bases, shown again on instant replay, slow-motion, split-screen, and isolated camera. . . . The ball game is on. *Dan Wakefield, "Supernation at Peace and War," The Atlantic, March 1968, p 77*

isometrics, *n. pl.* or *sing.* exercises for strengthening muscles by tensing one set of muscles, especially against an immovable object.

Taking issue with those who dismiss high blood pressure as a hazard, [Dr. William S.] Breall draws attention to the danger of "weight lifter's hypertension." A man performing "severe isometrics," he explains, markedly increases his blood pressure because he tenses his arm or leg muscles and cuts down the flow of blood through them. *Time, July 20, 1970, p 46*

[from *isometric, adj.,* denoting muscular contraction occurring against resistance + *n.pl.* suffix *-s*]

isomorphic, *adj.* (of mathematical sets) having a one-to-one correspondence.

For example, suppose *P* and *Q* are not polygons but, say, some collections of numbers or vectors or other kinds of algebraic quantities on which operations like addition and multiplication can be performed. In such a setting, the appropriate notion of isomorphism would be a one-to-one correspondence, *s:* $P \rightarrow Q$, which preserves addition

[$s(x+y)=s(x) + s(y)$] and multiplication. When such an *s* exists, *P* and *Q* are isomorphic. *Hyman Bass, "Mathematics," 1972 Britannica Yearbook of Science and the Future, 1971, p 270*

isomorphism, *n.* a one-to-one correspondence between mathematical sets.

Both congruences and similarities are examples of what mathematicians call "isomorphisms." . . . Isomorphisms are interesting not only for comparing different objects but also for studying the internal symmetry of a fixed one. *Hyman Bass, "Mathematics," 1972 Britannica Yearbook of Science and the Future, 1971, p 270*

i·so·spin ('ai sou¸spin), *n. Nuclear Physics.* a quantum number based on the theory that the neutron and proton are different states of the same particle.

Drs. Berman, Fultz and Kelly suggest that the discrepancy is due either to a complicated and unexpected mixing together of isospin states (isospin is a number, with no simple physical meaning, that represents mathematically the difference between neutrons and protons) or to a component of the strong nuclear force whose action does depend on electric charge. *Science News, Oct. 17, 1970, p 320*

[contraction of *isotopic spin*]

i·so·ten·i·scope (¸ai sə'ten ə¸skoup), *n.* an instrument for measuring the pressure at which a liquid and its vapor are at equilibrium at a given temperature.

Chemists routinely measure the boiling point of certain fluids with an isoteniscope, an apparatus that excludes the atmosphere. With an isoteniscope the experimenter can investigate a number of properties of fluids, including their vapor pressure at any temperature, the theoretical boiling point of fluids that would be destroyed if heated to boiling, the individual pressures exerted by each gas in a mixture of gases and related information of interest, particularly to those who experiment with such instruments as gas lasers and gas chromatographs. *C. L. Stong, "The Amateur Scientist: How to Make an Isoteniscope," Scientific American, Dec. 1970, p 116*

[from *iso-* equal + *ten-* (stem of Latin *tenēre* to hold) + *-i-* (a connective vowel) + *-scope* instrument for viewing]

isozyme, *n.* another name for ISOENZYME.

Another enzyme being studied in assessing possible carriers is lactic dehydrogenase (LDH) which exists in five configurations—or isozymes—in normal muscle. In analyses of muscle samples, Dr Emery found an apparent shortage of one of these isozymes in six known carriers [of Duchenne dystrophy]. *New Scientist, Aug. 27, 1964, p 480*

isozymic, *adj.* of or relating to isozymes.

Population geneticists are presently having a field day describing isozymic variation in natural populations, however, and are finding a wide array of allelic diversity at many if not most loci of the genome. *Science, Jan. 5, 1968, p 72*

i.t.a. or **ITA,** abbreviation of *Initial Teaching Alphabet,* a system designed to teach the early stages of reading, consisting of 44 letters and code symbols, supposedly to give a closer phonetic regularity than traditional spelling.

Another difference was that, with the middle-class children, Bereiter tried out a phonetic alphabet called ITA.

Maya Pines, *"A Pressure Cooker for Four-Year-Old Minds,"* *Harper's, Jan. 1967, p 60*

She is one of those with the longest experience of i.t.a.— and as an employee of a school system at a high level. *Sir James Pitman, London, "Phonetic Alphabet," in a Letter to the Editor, Science News, March 25, 1967, p 274*

i·tai-i·tai ('i: tɑi'i: tɑi), *n.* a Japanese name for cadmium poisoning, a disease recently distinguished from lead and mercury poisoning.

By then, other Japanese were complaining of a strange disease called, for lack of a medical term, *itai-itai* (ouch-ouch). Seeking clues, health officials finally exhumed Takako's body last month and performed an autopsy. . . . By current Japanese standards, a reading of one part per million of cadmium is harmful to humans. Takako's liver contained 4,540 p.p.m. [parts per million], her kidneys 22,400 p.p.m. Scientists speculated that she breathed cadmium particles and fumes generated by the plant's smelting process. . . . *Time, March 8, 1971, p 34*

The classic instance of cadmium poisoning is among middle-aged women in a Japanese village near Toyama. Since 1962 some 223 cases have been reported, the disease being called itai-itai (translatable as ouchi-ouchi) from the extreme pain it causes. *New Scientist and Science Journal, April 22, 1971, p 186*

ITV, 1 abbreviation of INSTRUCTIONAL TELEVISION.

With certain honorable exceptions, ITV has merely transferred conventional teaching techniques to the screen or served as a conduit for other media: films, slides, etc. *Judith Murphy and Ronald Gross, "The Unfulfilled Promise of ITV," Saturday Review, Nov. 19, 1966, p 89*

2 *British.* abbreviation of *Independent Television* (the British commercial television network).

The real danger of a council . . . is that it would interrupt the direct dialogue between the BBC and its audience, and I should think that what I have said probably would be just as true of ITV. *Sir Hugh Greene, "Running the BBC," The Listener, April 7, 1966, p 498*

IUCD, abbreviation of *intrauterine contraceptive device.* See INTRAUTERINE DEVICE.

". . . Just today, I [a woman doctor in charge of a Family Planning Center in Delhi] have had a total of five patients, and I have had to remove the I.U.C.D.s from three of them, because of the bleeding." *Ved Mehta, "A Reporter at Large: Indian Journal," The New Yorker, Sept. 9, 1967, p 86*

It is claimed in official circles that the IUCD or the Loop has come to stay in India. *New Scientist, Feb. 16, 1967, p 408*

▶ *IUD* is the current preferred abbreviation. *IUCD* is the older form.

IUD, abbreviation of INTRAUTERINE DEVICE. See also IUCD.

Vasectomies and IUDs can make the future a bit brighter. It's the present that bothers me. *New Scientist, May 1, 1969, p 262*

Although oral contraceptives, when well used, are the most effective method and require only the taking of a tablet for three weeks out of four, in practice in many communities the use-effectiveness (i.e. method and patient failures) is no better than that of the intra-uterine device (I.U.D.). *Max Elstein, "The Present Status of Contraception," The Practitioner, April 1972, p 486*

J

jackboot, *n.* **1** rough, bullying measures to achieve compliance or submission; jackboot tactics.

The writers' trials and the jackboot on Prague have made it quite clear that Brezhnev and Kosygin's views on liberalism are akin to Stalin's. *J. H. Plumb, "Perspective," Saturday Review, Oct. 26, 1968, p 36*

2 a person who uses rough, bullying measures.

Makarios, now President of Cyprus, considers Grivas a trigger-happy jackboot bent on grabbing full power on the island. *Time, April 1, 1966, p 24*

—*v.t.* to make by using rough, bullying measures to achieve compliance or submission.

German (Communist) troops were jackbooting their way around the northwestern section of Czechoslovakia for the first time in 23 years. . . . *The New York Times, Sept. 1, 1968, Sec. 4, p 3*

jackboot tactics, rough, bullying measures to achieve compliance or submission.

"With this first attempt by the Government to bludgeon this Bill through with jackboot tactics in the face of a one-day strike called solely over the issue we are discussing, it would be quite improper for this committee to continue its sitting," he [Edward Taylor, leader of the Opposition] said. *Ian Church, "Ports Bill MPs Clash Over Strike 'Duress'," The Times (London), March 18, 1970, p 26*

jack-up, *n.* **1** *U.S.* an increase.

Summing it all up, Eliot Janeway, the economist, gave this assessment in his weekly newsletter: "We see very little practical hope of avoiding another jack-up in short-term rates at the very time when foreign pressure on the dollar comes back on hard." *The New York Times, May 17, 1968, p 73*

2 a type of rig for off-shore oil drilling, on which legs are lowered to the sea bed from the operating platform.

There are three main methods for drilling and maintaining wells: from a platform (fixed, jack-up, or floating) or a ship; from remote-controlled equipment on the sea floor; or from manned equipment on the sea floor. . . . *Nicholas Fleming, "Man Under the Sea," New Scientist, Dec. 3, 1970, p 366*

[from the verb phrase *jack up* to increase, raise]

Ja·cob-Mo·nod ('dʒei kəb mə'nɑd; *French* ʒa'kɔːb-mɔː'nou), *adj.* of or relating to the theory that genes are controlled by the mechanism called the operon, first advanced by the French scientists François Jacob and Jacques Monod.

The achievement [isolation of the lac operon] clears the path for a detailed study of the workings of the Jacob-Monod mechanism in the test tube under controlled con-

ditions. *Robert Reinhold, "Scientists Isolate A Gene," Encyclopedia Science Supplement (Grolier) 1970, p 109*

While the phage DNA is integrated it betrays its presence only by a small number of proteins which function as typical Jacob-Monod repressors keeping its infective genes shut off and dormant. *"Monitor: Pinning Down the Virus Genes that Cause Cancer," New Scientist, Jan. 22, 1970, p 145*

Jag, *n. Slang.* a Jaguar sports car, especially the classic two-seater coupe.

Again, only the most pig-headed of the heavy-drinking brigade—the "I can handle the Jag at 80 after half-a-dozen doubles with one arm behind my back, old boy" type—would argue with the intentions of the 1967 Act, which has demonstrably saved lives. *Graham Chedd, "The Hazards of a Pin-prick," New Scientist, March 14, 1968, p 577*

The police streak past: important ones in Mercedes, middle ones in Jags, plain coppers in Volkswagen beetles with blue lights on top. *Corinna Adam, "Romania," The Sunday Times (London), Oct. 17, 1971, p 62*

jams, *n.pl.* **1** a clipped and contracted form of *pajamas.*

He went among the people and took on the people's ways . . . he bought six-packs and electric back-yard rotisseries, he wore His-'n-Hers flowered at home jams, he joined the Thursday Evening Swingin' Couples League at the Nutley Bowlmor Lanes. *Roger Angell, "Sad Arthur: Go Hesse, Young Man," The New Yorker, March 14, 1970, p 34*

2 swim trunks with a pajamalike drawstring around the waist, used by male surfers. Compare BAGGYS.

There will also be ascots (which can double as belts), walking shorts, swim trunks and surfers' "jams," knee-length trunks with drawstring waists. *The New York Times, Jan. 22, 1968, p 36*

Jane Crow, *U.S. Slang.* discrimination against women.

Men hate an "uppity" woman; they also hate an "aggressive" woman. Ours has been a Jane Crow society for several thousands of years. *Margaret Bernard, East Chicago, Ind., in a Letter to the Editor, Time, Jan. 18, 1971, p 2*

[patterned after *Jim Crow* (discrimination against blacks), with *Jane* as in *Jane Doe* (fictitious name for any female)]

Japlish, *n.* a blend of Japanese and English spoken in Japan. Compare FRINGLISH, HINGLISH, SPANGLISH.

A great many Japanese speak English nowadays (or at least "Japlish," as the American colony calls it), and their words are usually understandable. *Maya Pines, "Lucky American Women," Harper's, Jan. 1963, p 54*

Perhaps one of the most indicative—and amusing— effects of American influence has been the infiltration of American English into other languages. Japanese sometimes sounds like Japlish: *masukomi* for mass communications, *terebi* for TV, *demo* for demonstration and the inevitable baseballism *pray bollu, storiku* and *hitto. Time, July 22, 1966, p 30*

—*adj.* of or in Japlish.

A word of warning to tourists and others: the Japlish veneer can be deceptive. The Japanese may use more English words, but they still think like Japanese. *Michael Hornsby, "Japlish—the English Intrusion into Japanese," The Times (London), Nov. 26, 1970, p 12*

[blend of *Jap*anese and Eng*lish*]

ja·po·nai·se·rie (ʒa pɔ: neˈzriː), *n.* a style or work of art characteristically or distinctively Japanese.

Mr. Helpmann's most recent ballet, "Yugen," is a piece of japonaiserie based on a Noh play.... *Clive Barnes, The New York Times, May 29, 1967, p 28*

The book's milieu of intellectual decadence ... has more or less faded from our own tradition. It comes, after all, from the transition from aristocratic to bourgeois world, one in which the artistic powers seem to afford the only way of living in an otherwise meaningless universe. But it has long been there in the Japanese mind (the English revival of *japonaiserie* went with our own decadence movement).... *Malcolm Bradbury, "Aesthetic Decadence, Japanese-style," Review of "Forbidden Colours" by Yukio Mishima, The Manchester Guardian Weekly, Sept. 12, 1968, p 14*

The interwoven warmth in the blue of "Méditerranée", the play of warm and cool colour in the "Plat de Fruits", added to its effective contrast of the vertical and horizontal, the subtle japonaiserie of "La Plage à Arcachon", and typical window views are examples. *The Times (London), Oct. 18, 1966, p 6*

[from French *Japonais* Japanese + *-erie* -ery]

▶ Introduced by French writers in the late 1800's, *japonaiserie* was used in English at the turn of the century, but only in the plural form *japonaiseries* and with the specific sense of "Japanese ornaments." The preferred English form for the latter sense has been *Japanesery* (since the 1880's), formed from *Japanese* + *-ery* but probably on the model of the French word.

ja·wan (dʒəˈwɑːn), *n.* a common soldier of India.

Across the forbidding landscape, some 125,000 to 150,000 Chinese troops and more than 300,000 Indian *jawans* (infantrymen) are positioned in edgy, continuous confrontation. *Time, Aug. 9, 1968, p 24*

[from Hindi *jawān*]

jawbone, *U.S. Slang.* —*v.t.* to use jawboning on; influence by jawboning.

... every price increase that happens to catch the public's eye must be "jawboned" to death by the Government. *The New York Times, Jan. 2, 1966, Sec. 4, p 2*

The showdown came when Victor Feather, the T.U.C.'s [Trades Union Congress'] earthy new chief, warned that labor might just let labor go it alone at the polls next time.... Since June, Feather has been jawboning his union chiefs on the virtues of labor discipline on the shop floor. *Time, Sept. 19, 1969, p 32*

—*adj.* using or characterized by jawboning.

So many workers in so many industries have already got such big increases that those still on the waiting list won't pay any heed to jawbone appeals. *Bert C. Goss, New York, in a Letter to the Editor, The New York Times, June 16, 1970, p 46*

[back formation from *jawboning*]

jawboning, *n. U.S. Slang.* strong urging or warning by an influential person to leaders in industry, labor, etc., to comply with certain regulations and restraints.

As for jawboning, Nixon's Republican advisers consider it unfair and almost immoral to single out individual companies or industries.... *Time, Oct. 10, 1969, p 57*

Lloyd Bentsen, in his victorious Texas senatorial campaign, frequently advocated "jaw-boning" or Presidential persuasion, and voluntary wage-price guidelines, as anti-inflation weapons. *Tom Wicker, The New York Times, Dec. 20, 1970, Sec. 4, p 11*

Lecturing business and labor on their responsibilities to hold down prices and wages—jawboning as it was called in the Johnson Administration—has been foregone. *Joseph Kraft, "The Nixon Supremacy," Harper's, March 1970, p 48*

"Please, can I have the thirty cents this week without the jawboning?" *Cartoon legend, The New Yorker, March 13, 1971, p 34*

[from *jawbone, n.,* the bone of the jaws + *-ing*]

jaw-jaw, *British Slang.* —*v.i.* to talk at great length; to engage in a long discussion.

So the novelty of the reaction to the latest call for a European Summit is not in any changed assessment of the super-Powers' intentions, but in the feeling that it is time at last to start jaw-jawing. *"Comment: A Decision of Conscience," The Manchester Guardian Weekly, Dec. 13, 1969, p 12*

—*n.* drawn-out or lengthy talk; long discussion.

The Conference of the Committee on Disarmament (CCD)—the major forum for international negotiations on disarmament—held 46 formal and five informal plenary sessions during 1970, and there were frequent informal multilateral consultations on disarmament questions between members of the committee. And the main result of all this jaw-jaw was merely the finalising of a draft treaty on the prohibition of the emplacement of nuclear weapons, and other weapons of mass destruction on the seabed.... *Frank Barnaby, "A Dismal Year for Disarmament," New Scientist, Dec. 31, 1970, p 588*

[reduplication of the slang verb *jaw* to talk, which the *OED* calls "A vulgar, contemptuous, or hostile equivalent for speak." The first quotation cited is dated 1748 and is from Smollett's *Roderick Random*, xxiv: "He swore roundly at the lieutenant ... whereby the lieutenant returned the salute, and they jawed together fore and aft a good spell."]

jaz·zo·thèque (ˈdʒæz əˌtek), *n.* a night club where both jazz music and recorded music for dancing are played.

The success of the dancing policies at the Rainbow Grill and the Riverboat has led the Half Note, which has been a nondancing jazz club for 10 years, to clear some space for dancers. The club is now calling itself a "jazzothéque". *The New York Times, Jan. 6, 1968, p 24*

[from *jazz* + disco*thèque*]

jazz-rock, *n.* a blend of jazz and rock 'n' roll rhythms.

Synthesis was the password for popular music in 1969. In an appropriate conclusion to the most eclectic decade in American popular music, the year was flooded with such new combinations as jazz-rock, folk-rock, and country-rock. *Don Heckman, "Popular Records," The Americana Annual 1970, p 578*

Neither jazz-rock nor soul-jazz is the pure, uncut stuff of mainline jazz; both belong to what an earlier, more idealistic age would have called "commercial" music. *Albert Goldman, "Jazz Meets Rock," The Atlantic, Feb. 1971, p 105*

jelly bomb, an incendiary bomb made with jellied gasoline; a fire bomb.

"Stones is nothing. You've got to wait till the jelly bombs come over. Half the time you've got time to throw them back." *James Fox, quoting an unidentified British soldier in "After Another Night of Rioting in Belfast...," The Sunday Times Magazine (London), April 11, 1971, p 17*

je-m'en-fi·chis·me (ʒə mã fi:'ʃi:z mə), *n. French.* lack of concern or interest; literally, "I-don't-care-ism."

With most of the old skills and decisions taken out of the worker's hands by automatism and centralized control, what human qualities remain are mostly negative ones: balkiness, mindless indifference, resentment, *jem'enfichisme*—or, in a phrase, psychological absenteeism. *Lewis Mumford, "Reflections: The Megamachine: Human Walkouts," The New Yorker, Oct. 31, 1970, p 60*

je-m'en-fou·tis·me (ʒə mã fu:'ti:z mə), *n. French.* another name for JE-M'EN-FICHISME.

... here is the terrible harvest of those years of mutual mistrust, disunity and despair at the losses of 1914-18, *je-m'en-foutisme* and defeatism in France. *John Terraine, "New Books: The Freak War," Review of "To Lose A Battle: France 1940" by Alistair Horne, Punch, April 9, 1969, p 545*

Jenny McDade, who wrote it, caught very accurately the mixture of indifference and paralysing rigidity in adults and its opposition to the high aims and plain contrary *je-m'en-foutisme* of Kathy her heroine, the school-leaver in question. *David Wade, "Radio Drama: A Spiritual Pilgrimage," Review of "Leaving School" by Jenny McDade, The Listener, May 18, 1967, p 666*

Jesus freak, *U.S. Slang.* a person who is enthusiastic about or infatuated with the person and message of Jesus Christ; especially, one of the Jesus People.

Todd Henning, 20... turned from "freaked-out motorcycle addict" to "Jesus freak" when he visited the Love Inn.... *Edward B. Fiske, The New York Times, June 15, 1971, p 45*

Jesus Movement or **Jesus revolution,** a Protestant Christian movement in the United States, consisting chiefly of young people who worship and spread the teachings of Jesus Christ independently of any of the established churches or denominations. Compare CHILDREN OF GOD.

The sect [Children of God] had its origins among a small group of conservatives within the Jesus Movement, a nationwide Fundamentalist movement among youth, and served only as a reactionary facet of that group until early 1970, when it mushroomed into a full-fledged sect. *James*

T. Wooten, "Ill Winds Buffet Communal Sect," The New York Times, Nov. 29, 1971, p 41

The Jesus revolution, like the others, has a flavor peculiarly American. Its strong Pentecostalism emphasizes such esoteric spiritual gifts as speaking in tongues and healing by faith. *Time, June 21, 1971, p 39*

Jesus People, the people who make up the Jesus Movement; the body of chiefly young people who emphasize an intense personal relationship with Jesus Christ.

The Jesus People, also known as Street Christians or Jesus Freaks, are the most visible; it is they who have blended the counterculture and conservative religion.... Some, but by no means all, affect the hippie style; others have forsworn it as part of their new lives. *Time, June 21, 1971, p 39*

Mr. Ross and fellow occupants of Love Inn are "Jesus People," part of a nationwide movement of youths who are "turning on to Jesus" and dressing up the old-time religion in hippie garb. *Edward B. Fiske, " 'Jesus People' Are Happy With Their Life in Love Inn," The New York Times, June 15, 1971, p 45*

Jesus shop, (in the United States) a store specializing in popular religious articles used by members of the Jesus Movement, such as posters, buttons, and shirts inscribed with Biblical verses and religious messages.

It [Telegraph Avenue] now looks little different from many another street in the San Francisco Bay area (except for its Jesus shops, symbols of the brand of freaked-out Christianity that has replaced Flower Power as a culture).... *"Feedback: Graham Chedd on the Coast," New Scientist and Science Journal, June 3, 1971, p 588*

jet belt or **jet flying belt,** a special belt equipped with flying gear and attached to a small jet-powered engine, designed to enable a person to take off in flight to a height of about 25 feet and fly short distances.

Under development since 1965, the... Jet Belt logged its first manned free flight on April 7, 1969, when Robert F. Courter, Jr., lifted off a runway apron at Niagara Falls International Airport and piloted the system over a 300-foot elliptical course. *"The Jet Flying Belt," Encyclopedia Science Supplement (Grolier) 1970, p 373*

A Buck Rogers-style Army "jet-flying belt" that is expected to transport a soldier over the treetops at 60 m.p.h. for as far as ten miles. *Time, July 15, 1966, p 21*

jetboat, *n.* a boat propelled by a jet engine.

I had walked for many miles beside the central section of this river and considered it good jetboat water, but I had not seen the first 15 miles and the map indicated an ominous rise in height. *Sir Edmund Hillary, The Times (London), Oct. 26, 1968, p 11*

jetborne, *adj.* carried or transported by jet aircraft.

It [The Hilton's "Day-Hour Plan" ($12 for the first three hours, $3 an hour thereafter)] is intended to make life easier and less expensive for today's jet-borne businessman, who often zips in and out of two or three cities in a single day. *Time, Aug. 9, 1968, p 55*

... [President] Johnson's real purpose was to address a much wider audience and he revealed that purpose an hour before he climbed aboard his jetborne White House for the flight back to his Texas ranch. *Max Frankel, The New York Times, April 21, 1968, Sec. 4, p 1*

jet fatigue, another name for JET SYNDROME.

The popular name for this disruption of rhythmic biological function on flights spanning many time zones is jet fatigue, a temporary affliction known not only to tourists but also to wide-ranging businessmen and government officials. *The New York Times, Sept. 15, 1968, Sec. 4, p 11*

jet-hop, *v.i.* to travel from place to place by jet aircraft.

. . . he announced a series of surprise summit meetings that will have him jet-hopping from island to island and coast to coast over the next two months. *"Nixon: A Fresh Burst of Summitry," Time, Dec. 6, 1971, p 22*

jet-lag, *n.* another name for JET SYNDROME.

. . . jet-lag remains a medically unsolved problem with doctors urging that the best thing that any business man can do with his few hours saved by flying supersonically is to have a few more Martinis in his New York hotel when he arrives. *Nicholas Valéry, "Comment: Concorde's Icicle in Hell," New Scientist and Science Journal, April 15, 1971, p 133*

"I don't generally do this sort of thing, actually I have as low an opinion of interviews as you do—" "How do you know I have a low opinion?" Jet-lag was getting to Bech; irritability was droning in his ears. *John Updike, Bech: A Book, 1970, p 139*

jet-set, *n.* Also, **jet set.** the wealthy social set that gathers in fashionable places in many parts of the world, often traveling by jet plane.

With dismay the magazine also reported that Mrs. Kennedy had actually been seen in Shepheard's, the Manhattan discotheque that is "one of the jet-set's favorite rendezvous." *Time, Jan. 22, 1965, p 42*

. . . Mr. Conroy misses the whole point of the "furry fear" that gripped America after the murders. While it's true that the jet-set may have felt vulnerable for the first time, the rest of the country, and certainly the urban dweller, has been in the grip of that fear for at least ten years. *Barbara Hudgins, Madison, N.J., in a Letter to the Editor, Harper's, Jan. 1971, p 6*

—*adj.* of or relating to the jet set.

. . . his campaign managers created a new image of him [Pierre Trudeau] as the youthful, debonaire, "with-it" man of the jet-set age. *John S. Moir, "Trudeau, Pierre Elliott," The Americana Annual 1970, p 694*

That [lead poisoning] is not a jet-set or beautiful-people concern—but a simple matter of life and death for the children of poverty. *Jeff Greenfield, New York, N.Y., in a Letter to the Editor, Harper's, Jan. 1971, p 6*

► This term made its appearance in the early 1960's and quickly replaced such older terms of similar meaning as *café society* and *smart set.* Though it may have been a felicitous coinage by a society news reporter, there is evidence indicating that the term was used during the 1950's in a special sense that may have foreshadowed the current meaning. The sense in which *jet set* was used between 1956 and 1958 was that of a group of youngsters in the Soviet Union, especially in Moscow, who had adopted a "fast" Western style of life. The following two 1956 quotations use the term in this sense; the second quotation suggests the possible origin of the term.

Orders for the crackdown on the Soviet "jet set" of

juvenile delinquents came straight from Communist boss Khrushchev because his own son was mixed up in the scandals. The story told here is that Khrushchev came home one day and found his son togged out in a green coat and narrow trousers. He blew up, whaled his son, and got the lurid story out of him. Then the crackdown was on. *Newsweek, Sept. 3, 1956, p 12*

This is the Soviet "Jet Set," an element of the younger generation that is causing great concern to the country's leaders and to the Communist party. The term was originated by a young member of a foreign embassy staff in Moscow and refers to the Soviet youth who are attracted by things foreign—specifically Western things and especially clothing, hair styles, jazz, movies, automobiles—and who go in for restaurants, hard drinking, wild parties and the gay life generally. *William J. Jorden, The New York Times, Nov. 4, 1956, p 14*

jet-setter, *n.* a member of the jet set.

We can condone photographic safaris as a means through which the jet-setters can escape their intolerable boredom. *The New York Times, May 5, 1968, Sec. 4, p 15*

jet syndrome, the symptoms of an upset of the body clock. Also called JET FATIGUE, JET-LAG.

Symptoms of biorhythm upset, known popularly as the jet syndrome, are experienced by jet airplane travelers who fly through several time zones in 12 hours or less. The local time between their place of departure and their destination may differ by 5, 6, or even as much as 10 hours. *Arthur J. Snider, "The Rhythm of Life," The World Book Science Annual 1968, p 115*

jha·la ('dʒɑ: lə), *n.* a heavily cadenced passage ending the second movement of a typical raga, the traditional Hindu musical form.

[Ravi] Shankar delighted his audience with an exquisite alap, jor and jhala in raga Darbari Kanad: music great enough to send even the initiates into ecstasies. *The Times (London), Nov. 19, 1968, p 14*

[from Sanskrit]

jingo, *v.i.* to sound of jingoism; express loud or aggressive patriotism.

The flags waved and the speeches jingoed when the United States embarked on its first armed adventure in Asia. *Herbert Mitgang, "As American as Antiwar Dissent," The New York Times, May 25, 1970, p 32*

. . . he never descends into the loathsome smocks-and-ale jingoing that infected the essays of his contemporaries, such as Hilaire Belloc. *Robert Hughes, The Sunday Times (London), March 9, 1969, p 58*

[verb use of *jingo, n.,* a chauvinist]

jin·kai sen·jit·su ('dʒin kɑi sen'dʒit su:), the Japanese strategy of throwing waves of men into action.

In any market that arouses their interest, the Japanese use *jinkai senjitsu* (human-sea tactics), inundating the area with trade delegations and survey groups. *Time, May 10, 1971, p 50*

[from Japanese *jinkai-senjutsu*]

job action, *U.S.* a protest by workers without undertaking a general strike, such as a slow-down or work-to-rules action.

The Uniformed Fire Officers Association yesterday voted a "job action"—the refusal to perform nonfirefighting duties—to back up demands for more manpower. *The New York Times, July 26, 1968, p 16*

During the afternoon, the city had applied for and been granted an injunction against the firemen's job action. *Andy Logan, "Around City Hall," The New Yorker, Jan. 16, 1971, p 83*

job-hop, *v.i.* to go from job to job; change jobs frequently.

After leaving Washington in the mid-1950s, he [Najeeb Halaby, President of Pan-Am] job-hopped, serving briefly as operating vice president of Servo-mechanisms Inc. and later organizing his own law firm in Los Angeles. *"The Pilot-President," Time, Jan. 19, 1970, p 43*

[patterned after *table-hop, island-hop,* etc.]

job-hopper, a person who job-hops.

Boyden's prospects are rarely aware that Boyden is aware of them as potential job hoppers. *Time, Oct. 13, 1967, p 63*

Employers don't like early job-hoppers. *Thomas Hickman, "School Leavers," The Sunday Times (London), July 25, 1971, p 45*

jock, *n.* *U.S. Slang.* an athlete, especially at a college. *Often used attributively.*

Dubbed "Claustrophobia Manor" by the athletes, the barracks-style housing for the 4,000 competitors [at the Pan-American Games] was woefully overcrowded. Wary of trouble from students who had protested the amount of money that Colombia was spending on the games, security-minded officials turned the athlete's village into a kind of jock concentration camp. *Time, Aug. 16, 1971, p 42*

The only funny performance is by Michael Meyer as Brenda's jock brother, a big, gregarious, simple-minded, good-hearted lug who has exactly the right moves of the athlete—shoulder-rolling, ass-slapping, gum-chewing—all down pat. *Dan Wakefield, "Movies: More Sad Young Men," Review of "Stolen Kisses," The Atlantic, July 1969, p 108*

An obstacle to such trust is the attitude of some students and faculty members who, for example, smear all anti-strike students with the blanket label of "jocks." *The New York Times, May 12, 1968, Sec. 4, p 13*

[extended sense of *jock* an athletic supporter or jockstrap]

jockette, *n.* *U.S.* a female jockey.

Officially recognizing the female entries, Delaware's new Dover Downs scheduled the world's first fully mixed event this week, billing it as the "Jack and Jill race" and identifying the female riders as "jockettes." *Time, April 4, 1969, p 48*

[from *jockey* + *-ette* (feminine suffix)]

jogging, *n.* the exercise of running at a slow, regular pace, often alternately with walking.

Jogging has become fashionable, and its devotees have adopted "Run for your life" as their slogan. *Charles Marwick, "Medicine: Heart Disease," The Americana Annual 1969, p 442*

John, *n.* *U.S. Slang.* See the quotations for the meaning.

Despite the fact that a recent New York law makes the "John," or customer, guilty as well as the prostitute, the New York District Attorney's office sees fit not to prosecute the male customer but only the woman he exploits. *Diane Schulder, "Women and the Law," The Atlantic, March 1970, p 104*

... a prostitute is arrested after having committed a sex act with her customer, known in the trade as a "John,"

after "John Doe." *J. Anthony Lukas, The New York Times, Aug. 15, 1967, p 27*

John Bircher, another name for BIRCHER.

... the bitterness with which they [Negroes] are pursued produces its own reaction. The ultra-conservative Governor, Mr Ronald Reagan, is part of this. So are the John Birchers, who are at their strongest in the red-neck South of this enormous State [California]. *John Cole, "Of Pigs and Panthers," The Manchester Guardian Weekly, Oct. 3, 1968, p 10*

jo·lie-laide (ʒɔ: li:'led), *French.* —*n.* a plain-looking woman or girl who has charming ways or other attractive features of personality.

His [Raffaele Viviani's] creation of the blind musicians' band, with one of them a proud man misguidedly jealous about his homely wife (superb Rosita Pisano is, in fact, like Massina, a *jolie-laide*)—this image has been powerfully realised.... *D. A. N. Jones, The Listener, May 23, 1968, p 679*

The starting point this week is Princess Anne's hats. Underneath them is the pleasant face of a *jolie laide* who exemplifies the distinct changes that are taking place in the British monarchy and its relations with the people. *William Hardcastle, "Crown and People," Punch, June 4, 1969, p 828*

—*adj.* (of a woman or girl) plain-looking yet charming or attractive; (literally) nice-plain.

Mrs. Bedford, an approachable, jolie-laide woman with exuberant blue eyes, has never written any biography before, and does not intend to write any more after this. *The Times (London), Oct. 11, 1968, p 10*

Jo·mon or **Jō·mon** ('dʒou̯ˌmɑn), *adj.* of or belonging to a Japanese culture of the Stone Age noted for its hand-made decorated pottery.

... much controversy has arisen as to the relation, if any, between the Ainu [a light-skinned aboriginal people of Japan] and the so-called Jōmon culture. Jōmon means literally "corded pattern", and the name is derived from the remarkable pottery which, in five distinct periods, was made by a people who knew neither the potter's wheel nor the arts of agriculture. *E. W. F. Tomlin, "The 'Hairy People' of Northern Japan," New Scientist, June 15, 1967, p 666*

The discovery of pottery in Ecuador decorated in almost identical manner to the Jomon pottery of Japan, made at the same time, about 2,500 B.C., led to a hypothesis that a Japanese reached there. *Walter Sullivan, The New York Times, May 19, 1968, Sec. 4, p 14*

As you would expect, the potters' craft has progressed since the Jomon ware of Neolithic Japan. *Advertisement in Scientific American, April 1968, p 45*

[from Japanese *jōmon*]

jor (dʒɔr), *n.* the rhythmic second movement of a typical raga, the traditional Hindu musical form. Compare ALAP, GAT.

In the second movement, jor, a pulse or beat is introduced against which the musician constructs his phrases. *N. A. Jairazbhoy, "Music: The Music of the Mughal Courts," The Listener, April 11, 1968, p 480*

Jazz and rock 'n' roll periodicals have run involved disquisitions on the technicalities of the tabla, the tamboura, the alap and the jor. *The New York Times, Dec. 20, 1966, p 58*

[from Sanskrit]

Josephson effect, the effect produced by a Josephson junction.

...the Josephson effect (a quantum phenomenon whereby, near absolute zero, current can flow without resistance across an insulating gap). *"Low Temperatures in Practice," New Scientist, May 23, 1968, p 407*

The Josephson effect, one of the most important in solid state physics, can be used for detecting microwave radiation and low voltages, among many other purposes. *The Times (London), April 15, 1970, p 13*

[named for Brian D. *Josephson*, an English physicist who predicted this effect in 1962]

Josephson junction, the junction formed by two superconductors separated by a thin insulating layer, across which current will flow without resistance and generate radio waves when subjected to a certain voltage.

A Josephson junction is a unit in which two superconductors are joined by an electrically bad connection. That is, there may be some insulator between them, or a narrow air gap, or their surfaces may be rough so that there is only contact at certain points and not over the whole surface. If a driving voltage is applied to such a junction, an oscillating current will flow across it, and it will emit microwave radiation. *Science News, Sept. 6, 1969, p 172*

jostle, *v.i.* *U.S. Slang.* to pickpocket.

Robert Baldwin, charged with "jostling,"... was convicted by a single judge and sentenced to one year in prison. *Time, July 6, 1970, p 42*

jostler, *n.* *U.S. Slang.* a person who pickpockets.

A woman detective picked a prosecutor's pocket in Queens Criminal Court Monday to demonstrate how "jostlers"—the police terminology for pickpockets—work. *The New York Times, June 2, 1965, p 33*

jou·al (ʒuː'al), *n.* a dialect or patois of Canadian French, used chiefly by uneducated French Canadians.

Nor is it a question of slang. French-Canadian slang [as spoken in Quebec] is called *joual*—a corruption of the word *cheval*—and is as different from the correct French Canadian as Cockney is from English. *Jeff Holmes, "Argument," Maclean's, March 5, 1966, p 44*

He [Jean Drapeau, Q.C., Mayor of Montreal] speaks fluent English and a French that bears no trace of *joual*—an archaic and affectedly rustic way of speaking French that is common to many citizens of the province [Quebec], of all classes, and that purists are currently trying to discourage. *"The Talk of the Town: Mayor," The New Yorker, April 29, 1967, p 33*

—*adj.* of or like joual.

Because the language [used in a popular radio and TV show, "Seraphin"] is very *joual*, it's a very popular language, and the situations are so true to the myth.... *Wendy Michener, "The Very Irreverent Crusade of Ti-Pop," Saturday Night (Canada), Feb. 1968, p 30*

[from Canadian French *joual*, a rendition of the joual pronunciation of French *cheval* horse]

judoist, *n.* an expert in judo.

...Mr. Gleeson [is] one of the most experienced judoists in this country, and national coach to the British Judo Association. *The Times (London), Nov. 29, 1966, p 4*

▶ See the note under JUDOMAN.

judoman, *n.* a person who participates in judo wrestling matches or competitions.

The *Black Belt Yearbook* listed 102,569 judo players in the United States and named Seino, Graham, and Coage among the top 10 judomen in the nation. *Bob Posen, "Judo: Individual Honors," 1969 Collier's Encyclopedia Year Book, p 527*

▶ This term seems to be interchangeable with the older term *judoka* (from Japanese *jūdōka*), which appears in dictionaries. *Judoka,* however, is used both in the sense of a judo wrestler and an expert in judo. Another term for the latter meaning is *judoist.*

jugular, *n.* the most vulnerable point of an opponent (especially in the phrase **have an instinct for the jugular**).

His detractors often accuse Vice President Spiro Agnew of having an instinct for the jugular. *Time, June 1, 1970, p 6*

The chief virtues in a political machine are plodding patience, an utter lack of imagination, unsqueamishness in the face of greed and brutality, and a feel for the jugular. *Richard Harris, "Books," Review of "Boss" by Mike Royko, The New Yorker, May 8, 1971, p 138*

—*adj.* aiming for the jugular; cutthroat; murderous.

...Mr. Scranton will not get far in the jugular combat of national politics without a more lionlike approach.... *Tom Wicker, The New York Times, July 28, 1965, p 30*

[from the *jugular (vein),* in which a puncture or break may prove fatal]

juice, *n.* *U.S. Slang.* **1** alcoholic liquor.

...parents respond by taking a kindlier view of early drinking, in hopes that their children will find liquor an acceptable alternative to pot. That ploy often fails, mainly because so many youths are convinced that marijuana is less harmful than "juice." *"Modern Living: The Family," Time, Aug. 30, 1968, p 35*

But they need their juice, for their kind of tension would not be relieved by the head-lightening stuff, they need the down-deep sleep of the intelligence that comes with liquor. *Stephen Erhart, "As The Hippiest Doctor Almost Grooved," Harper's, May 1971, p 83*

2 a usurious loan or the exorbitant interest rates exacted on it.

One proposal, being drafted by the Justice Department, would grant the feds [federal agents] jurisdiction over "juice"... by which sharks and syndicates have milked and bankrupted laboring men and businesses. *Time, March 19, 1965, p 21*

At least two murders and perhaps more have been connected with the loan shark, or "juice" racket, as it is called here, as well as beatings and threats. *The New York Times, June 9, 1968, Sec. 1, p 29*

3 favorable standing; position, power, or influence.

This Las Vegas is a jet-age Sodom, a venal demimonde in which the greatest compliment that can be paid a man is to say that he has "juice" (influence in the right places). *"Las Vegas: The Game is Illusion," Time, July 11, 1969, p 24*

"The important thing now is I got juice as an actor," [Steve] McQueen went on. "That means you choose your material, you pick your situations." *Peter Bart, The New York Times, Dec. 4, 1966, Sec. 2, p 13*

juiced, *adj.* *U.S. Slang.* drunk.

Later Marvin apologized: "I'm sorry I was so rotten this afternoon. I was a little juiced." *Time, Oct. 24, 1969, p 70*

juicehead, *n. U.S. Slang.* a habitual drinker of alcoholic liquor; tippler.

If anybody wanted to get stoned the guy who owned the pad made them go up on the roof. Juice-heads drank Red Mountain.... *F. P. Tullius, "Frog Week at the 7-11, Near West Hollywood," The New Yorker, Sept. 9, 1967, p 41*

[from *juice* (def. 1) + *head* (see the entry HEAD)]

juice man, *U.S. Slang.* a person who lends money at exorbitant interest rates; a loan shark.

...a professional criminal...often must make a loan from a "juice man," a loan which may involve an interest rate of 20 per cent a week. *The New York Times, Aug. 20, 1967, Sec. 1, p 35*

juicer, *n. U.S. Slang.* a heavy drinker of alcoholic liquor.

... "A lot of people are worn out from last night, especially the juicers. The difference between the juicers and the heads is that the juicers sometimes get a little obstreperous but the heads go sit quietly in a corner someplace." *"The Talk of the Town: Abolafia for President," The New Yorker, May 13, 1967, p 40*

jumbo, *n.* short for JUMBO JET.

When the Concordes are delivered to BOAC on 1975 the airline will have a fleet of five supersonic and 60 subsonic jets, which will include at least a dozen Jumbos. *Daily Telegraph (London), May 26, 1972, p 1*

At the new Kansas City, Mo., jetport, one of the few in operation to have been specifically designed for the jumbos, passengers walk only 175 ft (or a minimum of 85 ft) from bus or car door to aircraft. *Joseph Gies, "Transportation," 1971 Britannica Yearbook of Science and the Future, 1970, p 278*

jumbo jet, a jet aircraft with a passenger capacity of about 500 people and a freight capacity of about 200 tons. Also shortened to JUMBO. Compare MEGAJET.

Discussing high-capacity airliners ("jumbo jets") the director-general said a matter of prime concern was the problems on the ground they would bring with them. *The Times (London), May 24, 1966, p 8*

The design of the terminal buildings, runways, and other facilities of civil aerodromes, to meet the problems created by the introduction of jumbojets, is one of the most complex puzzles of modern life. *Sir Harold Hartley, "150 Years of the 'Civils'," New Scientist, July 11, 1968, p 72*

Planning is in progress at the 102-acre base for an $11 million...maintenance facility for the 747 jumbo jet and the supersonic jetliners of the nineteen-seventies. *The New York Times, June 19, 1968, p 94*

jump cut, an abrupt transition from one filmed shot or scene to another due to the excision of intervening film.

...French director Jean-Luc Godard...cut directly from scene to scene without fades or dissolves, and even introduced jump cuts—unmatching actions—within a scene. *Arthur Knight, "Look What's Happening to the Movies," The 1969 World Book Year Book, p 115*

jump-cut, *v.i.* to make jump cuts.

He [William Conrad, producer-director of the motion picture "Brainstorm"] recklessly jump-cuts from scene to

scene, using gimmicky transitions or linking one sequence to another with trick dialogue. *Time, June 18, 1965, p 80*

jump jet or **jump-jet,** *n. British.* a jet aircraft designed for short vertical take-off and landing. Compare V/STOL.

A Hawker Siddeley..."jump jet" aircraft, piloted by Flight-Lieutenant John Farley, coming in to land in a forest clearing during a demonstration yesterday at Royal Aircraft Establishment, Bedford. *Picture legend, The Times (London), Sept. 27, 1966, p 20*

Can't think why King Hussein wants to buy Harrier jump-jets. Isn't the Jordanian Air Force nervous enough as it is? *"People," Punch, June 26, 1968, p 907*

jump suit or **jumpsuit,** *n.* a one-piece garment resembling a parachutist's uniform, used especially for casual wear.

She's lithe, but you wouldn't mistake her for a man, and the sky-blue driver's jump suit matches her eyes. *Alan Edmonds, "Go Kill Me a Tiger, Darling," Maclean's, Sept. 17, 1966, p 19*

The fashions include jumpsuits for both men and women .... *The New York Times, July 11, 1968, p 40*

jump-up, *n.* (in the British West Indies and Guyana) an informal dance.

"...You go for a swim with the local leader. You have some rum and a bloody good lunch, then you have a jump-up, and a proper shindig." *Joseph Godber, British Minister of State for the Colonies, quoted in "The Anguilla Story: Running Jump-ups," The Sunday Times (London), June 13, 1971, p 9*

Georgetown, Guyana, Dec. 10—The pale leaves in the American Ambassador's garden shone moistly last night in the colored lights set up for his pre-Christmas jump-up. *The New York Times, Dec. 12, 1966, p 24*

junk sculptor, an artist who makes junk sculptures.

Long before the *tachiste* painter [action painter] or the junk sculptor, the American Indian shaped art from sand, bone, feathers—whatever he had at hand. *Time, Jan. 14, 1966, p E1*

junk sculpture, the art of making three-dimensional figures from material usually found in junkyards, such as scrap metal, broken glass, pieces of wood and rubber, and other discarded items.

Students interested in musicology, junk sculpture, the Theater of the Absurd, and the literary *dicta* of Leslie Fiedler can go somewhere else. *John Fischer, "The Easy Chair: Survival U: Prospectus for a Really Relevant University," Harper's, Sept. 1969, p 14*

jurimetricist or **jurimetrician,** *n.* an expert in jurimetrics.

Being, in this enterprise, jurimetricists and not legal historians, they [the authors] chose the molds of analytic rather than historical jurisprudence for the ordering of their materials. *Mark DeWolfe Howe, "Books," Review of "The American Jury" by Harry Kalven, Jr. and Hans Zeisel, Scientific American, Sept. 1966, p 296*

...econometricians, polimetricians, psychometricians, jurimetricians are all rapidly proliferating species of a genus of mathematically minded scholars who are infiltrating the academic world armed with computers and many of the analytical tools of higher mathematics. *"Math Penetrates the Social Sciences," Encyclopedia Science Supplement (Grolier) 1970, p 287*

239

jurimetrics, *n.* a branch of law using scientific tools and research in dealing with legal matters.

This ambitious project [a nationwide study of the jury system] brings lawyers and social scientists together in the search for truth and understanding. . . . The two worlds of discourse have become one. This fruit of the union of jurisprudence and social science has inevitably been christened "jurimetrics." *Mark DeWolfe Howe, "Books," Review of "The American Jury" by Harry Kalven, Jr. and Hans Zeisel, Scientific American, Sept. 1966, p 295*

[from *juris*prudence + *-metrics,* as in *biometrics,. psychometrics,* etc.]

juvenile hormone, 1 a hormone, secreted by the corpus allatum (a gland behind the brain of insects), that controls the metamorphosis from the larval to the adult stage.

Juvenile hormones play a regulatory role in the molting process of insects. They are of much interest because of the possibility of their application to the selective control of insect populations. *Ajay K. Bose, "Chemistry," 1972 Britannica Yearbook of Science and the Future, 1971, p 216*

A chemical analogue of the juvenile hormone has now been produced at Mysore, and large scale treatment of pests with this chemical would reduce their numbers, while avoiding problems of residual toxicity, or the development of resistant strains. *New Scientist, Dec. 5, 1968, p 560*

2 a synthesized form of this hormone, used to prevent development of maturation of insect pests.

Juvenile hormone is a possible DDT substitute in killing insects. *"Science and Technology News: Growth Hormones Help Produce m-RNA," Science Journal, Feb. 1970, p 20*

juvie or **juvey,** *n. U.S. Slang.* **1** a juvenile delinquent.

First, Los Angeles County police went after the "juvies" (minors under 18), began carting them off by the busload last summer for violating a 10 p.m. curfew dating back to 1939. *Time, Dec. 2, 1966, p 52*

2 a detention home for juvenile delinquents.

Dot and Meg . . . had sculpted a large eye together in an art class, and they had asked for permission to take it with them' when they left. "But the teacher at juvey said, 'You have to finish it,' " Meg said. *Renata Adler, "A Reporter at Large: Fly Trans-Love Airways," The New Yorker, Feb. 25, 1967, p 128*

K

kak·o·to·pi·a (ˌkæk əˈtou piː ə), *n.* the opposite of a utopia; a misplanned, ugly, and unhappy place to live in. Compare DYSTOPIA.

A monstrous habitat, in short, in which only monsters could be at home.... If this nightmarish conclusion were peculiar to Kepler, it might be treated as a personal aberration; but as it happens, it has been a recurrent theme of later technological kakotopias. In H. G. Wells' 'The Time Machine' the narrator realizes that the technological progress toward leisure and luxury had proved self-destructive: and he travels farther into time only to find all life gradually waning on the planet. *Lewis Mumford, The Pentagon of Power, 1970, p 49*

[from Greek *kako-* bad + English u*topia*]

▶ As in the case of *dystopia,* the coining of *kakotopia* to name a place where all is bad suggests the understanding of *utopia* ("nowhere") as *eutopia* ("a place where all is good"). The same opposition was made by Jeremy Bentham, but he used the traditional spelling with *c*'s: *cacotopia,* recorded as a nonce word in the *OED* in an 1818 quotation from him: "As a match for Utopia (or the imagined seat of the best government), suppose a Cacotopia (or the imagined seat of the worst government) discovered and described."

ka·lash·ni·kov (kəˈlɑːʃ niˌkɔːf), *n.* a Soviet submachine gun, used especially by Arab guerrillas.

A ragtag group of *fedayeen* bearing *kalashnikovs,* hand grenades and often Pepsi-Cola bottles, swarms around the headquarters area. *C. L. Sulzberger, "Foreign Affairs: The Kalashnikov Kid," The New York Times, Oct. 30, 1970, p 41*

They consist of forays across the border by from 40 to 100 men armed with Russian mortars, rockets, recoilless guns and kalashnikov automatics.... *Michael Calvert, "Portuguese Guinea: Where Silence Answers Noise," The Times (London), Jan. 12, 1972, p 10*

[from Russian]

ka·lim·ba (kəˈlim bə), *n.* a small, hollow piece of wood, usually about eight inches long, with metal strips inserted along it lengthwise that vibrate when played with the thumbs. This modern version of the tribal instrument is tuned to play Western music and is held in both hands with the palms upward. Compare MBIRA.

Buckley blends unusual "noises" into the music: clinks, kalimba, calliope, gunfire, and an odd assortment of rhythm instruments. *Ellen Sander, "Pop in Perspective: The Underground Establishment," Review of "Goodbye and Hello" by Tim Buckley, Saturday Review, Oct. 26, 1968, p 89*

[from a Bantu word]

ka·ma·graph (ˈkɑː məˌgræf), *n.* **1** a type of printing press that can reproduce exactly an original painting specially made for it.

Max Ernst, the well-known dada and surrealist painter; Edouard Pignon, a French abstractionist; and the late René Magritte, the extraordinary Belgian surrealist who died this year, have all executed special work for the kamagraph. *Benjamin de Brie Taylor, "Art: Reproductions: New Processes," 1968 Collier's Encyclopedia Year Book, p 131*

2 a reproduction of a painting made by the kamagraph.

Kamagraphy faithfully produces 250 perfect copies of a painting on a special press, destroying the original in the process.... Each kamagraph looks as though the artist had painted it by hand. *"Art: Techniques, Multi-Originals & Selected Reproductions," Time, June 23, 1967, p 49*

[back formation from *kamagraphy*]

ka·ma·gra·phy (kəˈmɑː grə fiː), *n.* a method of reproducing an original painting so that both the color and raised brush stroke on canvas are duplicated. The canvas has to be specially made for the type of press used in kamagraphy.

A French process called kamagraphy has been developed by engineer André Cocard, with the backing of art collector and vintner Alexis Lichine. It is capable of reproducing 250 copies of a painting, each of which looks as if it had been painted by hand. *Benjamin de Brie Taylor, "Art: Reproductions: New Processes," 1968 Collier's Encyclopedia Year Book, p 131*

[from French *kamagraphie,* probably from Sanskrit *kāma* pleasure + French *-graphie* representation or record of something]

Ka·ma·ku·ra (ˌkɑː məˈkuː rə), *adj.* of or relating to a period in Japanese art and architecture, about 1170-1350, characterized by the introduction of Zen Buddhist styles.

The sale of Japanese works of art also included an extremely fine Buddhist wood sculpture of the Kamakura period at 3,200gns. and brought £25,783. *The Times (London), June 24, 1970, p 12*

[from *Kamakura,* a town in southeastern Honshu, which was the seat of the military government or shogunate of Japan from 1192 to 1333]

ka·on·ic (keiˈɑn ik), *adj.* containing or producing kaons (K mesons, heavy nuclear particles weighing over 960 times more than electrons). Also called K-MESIC. Compare MUONIC, PIONIC.

To date Wiegand has been able to put kaons in orbit around 24 different elements ranging in mass from lithium to uranium. The X rays emitted by the "kaonic" atoms are analyzed by a nuclear X-ray spectrometer.... *Scientific American, July 1969, p 52*

ka·ra·te (kə'rɑ: ti:), *v.t.* to strike or beat with blows used in karate. See also KARATE-CHOP.

Wow, dearie, did you miss the action! A wolf was bugging me, so I gave him a shot of Mace, karated him, and called the fuzz. *Cartoon legend, The New Yorker, Sept. 14, 1968, p 129*

[verb use of the noun]

karate-chop, *n.* a sharp slanting stroke with the hand used in karate (a Japanese system of self-defense using the hands and feet to deliver strokes, punches, blocks, and kicks to vulnerable parts of the body).

"I'm Larry Taylor," a breathless, sharp-featured young man said, offering a karate-chop handshake to Jay Steffy. "I'm Jay Steffy," Jay Steffy said, karate-chopping back. *"The Talk of the Town," The New Yorker, Dec. 5, 1970, p 49*

—*v.t., v.i.* to strike with a karate-chop.

... the wife ... can karate-chop hell out of her husband. *Time, May 11, 1970, p 62*

ka·ra·te·ka (kə'rɑ: ti: kɑ:), *n.* a karate expert.

Karatekas, those fearsome exponents of the Japanese technique of self-defence called Karate—a sort of tougher version of Judo—often display their prowess by breaking plates, blocks of wood and even bricks with their bare hands. *"Notes and Comments: Courage Breaks the Brick," New Scientist, July 7, 1966, p 8*

[from Japanese]

kart, *n.* short for GO-KART.

A second hand Class One kart can be picked up for £20 or £30. *The Sunday Times (London), Oct. 16, 1966, p 17*

karting, *n.* the sport of driving or racing a go-kart.

Followers of a fairly new pursuit are also being wooed, and on July 12 a karting week is being held. From what I am told, karting is becoming skilled and highly competitive and can also be a fine spectator sport. *The Times (London), March 30, 1968, p 26*

Kart racing is for the young, and for the not so young—a happy way to taste the thrills of speed, even at 25 m.p.h. Now a competition sport, karting attains sensational speeds of 60, 70 and even 100 m.p.h. *Advertisement by the Swiss Watch Industry, Time, May 21, 1965, p 5*

ka·tyu·sha (kə'tyu: ʃə), *n.* a Czech rocket launcher of great range and accuracy, used especially by Arab guerrillas. Compare KALASHNIKOV.

Palestine guerrillas fired three Katyusha rockets into Amman airport today as three French relief aircraft landed, damaging one of the aircraft with a few shrapnel splinters. *The Times (London), Sept. 28, 1970, p 1*

To talk of demilitarization in the days of katyushas is obsolete. *Ted R. Lurie, "How We [the Israelis] See Nasser," The Manchester Guardian Weekly, Feb. 7, 1970, p 6*

[from Czech, from *Katyusha* "Katy"]

kbar, abbreviation of KILOBAR.

Experimentally, Walsh and Rice found no evidence for a phase transition during shock compression of water to pressures up to 100 kbar. *M. N. Plooster, Nature, March 30, 1968, p 1247*

Ken·ya·pith·e·cus (ˌki:n yə'piθ ə kəs), *n.* either of a pair of humanoid apes believed to have lived from 14 to 20 million years ago, identified by the British paleontologist Louis S. B. Leakey from several skeletal fragments he discovered in the vicinity of Lake Victoria in Kenya between 1962 and 1967.

Moreover, a stratum at Fort Ternan, Kenya, containing the bones of *Kenyapithecus*, an ape-like creature probably in the line of human development, has been dated at 14 million years old. *Froelich Rainey, "Dating the Past," 1971 Britannica Yearbook of Science and the Future, 1970, p 397*

Though Leakey still insists that *Kenyapithecus* is a hominid, most other scientists now believe that he is an ape. *Time, Aug. 29, 1969, p 38*

[from *Kenya* + New Latin *pithecus* ape]

kernel sentence, (in generative-transformational grammar) a primal or irreducible sentence from a small number of which all other sentences may be generated by transformations.

Chomsky argued that all possible grammatical sentences in English (or any other tongue) could be derived, or "generated," from a small number of basic, or "kernel," sentences, plus a set of rules of operation and transformation. *George Steiner, "The Tongues of Men," The New Yorker, Nov. 15, 1969, p 223*

key, *n. Slang.* a kilo of a drug, especially hashish.

There are profits aplenty. A $10 or $20 "key" of Lebanese hash can fetch $1,500 or more in the U.S.... *Time, April 13, 1970, p 36*

[a respelling of *ki* in *kilo* based on the pronunciation]

keyboard, *v.t.* to feed (information) by the use of a keyboard.

After the encyclopedia, consisting of many volumes, has been keyboarded into the computer, the computer under instruction withdraws the material on a specified subject from its memory storage and sets it up for publication as a separate book or pamphlet.... *Gerard O. Walter, "Typesetting: Electronic Typesetting," Scientific American, May 1969, p 68*

A shortage of keyboarding staff in typesetting encouraged several printers, notably newspapers where typesetting capacity requirements tend to concentrate in a few hours a day, to employ part-time (and mainly female) staff. *W. Pincus Jaspert, "Industrial Review: Printing," Britannica Book of the Year 1971, p 404*

khur·ta ('kur tɑ:), *n.* a long, loose-fitting, collarless shirt worn in India. Also spelled KURTA.

In the West, with his [Ravi Shankar's] sitar, *khurta*, and *agarbatti* (incense), he is a confirmed trendsetter, and the trend is toward wild nonconformity that is actually conformity, Indian style. *A. S. Raman, "Ravi Shankar at Home and Abroad," Saturday Review, Oct. 10, 1970, p 46*

[from Hindi *kurtā*]

kHz, abbreviation of KILOHERTZ.

The principal sound frequency may be as high as 150 kHz or as low as 20 kHz, having wavelengths of approximately 2.2 to 15 mm. *David Pey, "The Diversity of Bats," Science Journal, April 1969, p 48*

kicky, *adj. U.S. Slang.* lively; spirited; racy.

... Bergdorf was taking no chances. As a postscript, it brought out some kicky styles to preview its new fur boutique. *The New York Times, Aug. 15, 1968, p 42*

... we've added kicky new nightlife to all the land/water sports, unstinted luxury and loving Personal Service. *Advertisement by Balmoral Club, Nassau, The New Yorker, April 20, 1968, p 139*

[from *kick*, *n.*, slang word for energy, excitement, stimulation, etc., + -*y* (adj. suffix)]

kidney machine, a machine which operates as a kidney substitute.

Much has been written of the medical, social and ethical problems which have stemmed from the advent of the kidney machine. Recently, too, the psychological difficulties of the patients, who depend totally upon regular blood-cleansing hook-ups with the machines, have received a good deal of attention. *New Scientist, Nov. 21, 1968, p 418*

ki·fi ('ki: fi:), *n.* (in northern Africa) a narcotic drug; an opiate.

The dope market was somewhat less covert. Half a dozen times a day I was asked: "Hey, you American? Where you from, California? You want hashish? You want kifi?" *Mike Booth, "Moroccan Disenchantment," The Times (London), May 9, 1970, p 26*

[from Arabic]

kill ratio or **kill rate,** the proportion of combat casualties on either side, used as a yardstick for estimating military effectiveness or success, especially in antiguerrilla warfare. Compare BODY COUNT.

... those Nigerians who had escaped the cross-fire had fled northward into the forest, leaving behind 41 dead, the Biafrans said. They put their own losses at three killed and a dozen wounded.
The lieutenant was pleased with the kill ratio. *The New York Times, Aug. 11, 1968, Sec. 1, p 3*

Israeli reconnaissance watched them [Soviet-made SA-2s within eleven miles of the west bank of the Suez Canal] but no effort was made to bomb them for fear Russian MIGs would respond. In North Viet Nam the same type of SA-2s had a "kill" rate of less than one success per 1,000 firings. *Time, July 20, 1970, p 18*

kilobar, *n.* a unit of pressure equal to one thousand bars. *Abbreviation:* kbar.

The element phosphorus has been found to become superconducting near 4.7 degrees Kelvin at pressures exceeding 100 kilobars, one bar being atmospheric pressure at sea level. *Science News, June 15, 1968, p 573*

[from *kilo-* 1000 + *bar* unit of pressure]

kilobit, *n.* a unit of information equal to one thousand bits or binary digits. Compare GIGABIT, MEGABIT, TERABIT.

Pulse code modulation (PCM) gives very high quality speech reproduction but is an expensive and highly complex system requiring a digit rate of about 64 kilobits/second. *Science Journal, March 1970, p 12*

[from *kilo-* 1000 + *bit* binary digit]

kilohertz, *n.* a term replacing the older *kilocycle* as the name of the unit of frequency equal to one thousand cycles per second. *Abbreviation:* kHz Compare MEGAHERTZ.

The key that will open the door to low prices is the development of new techniques for manufacturing the microcircuits that divide down the vibration frequency of the quartz crystal from 8 kilohertz to the few hertz needed to

drive the hands. *Ron Brown, "Short Circuit to Cheap Electric Clocks," New Scientist and Science Journal, Feb. 11, 1971, p 310*

[from *kilo-* 1000 + *hertz* one cycle per second]

kin·e·the·od·o·lite (ˌkin ə θiːˈɑd əˌlait), *n.* a device consisting of a camera attached to a theodolite, used for tracking missiles and aircraft.

The ... target aircraft are ... tracked by kinetheodolites or radar or both, but even when the most advanced smoothing techniques are used on trajectory data the miss-distance information given by comparing trajectories is not precise enough. *The Times (London), May 25, 1967, p XIII*

It [apparatus to permit measurements of controls of new aircraft] consists of two kinetheodolites, one on each side of the runway and so trained that they keep an aeroplane in view throughout its approach to the landing or during its take-off and climb. *New Scientist, Nov. 16, 1967, p 403*

[from *kine-* motion or motion picture + *theodolite*]

kinetic, *adj.* of or relating to kinetic art; involving motion or the suggestion of motion produced by mechanical parts, colors, lights, etc.

The University of Iowa dedicated its new museum and commissioned for it a large kinetic fountain by the Belgian surrealist Pol Bury. *Victor H. Miesel, "Art: Museums and Collections: New Museums and Additions," The Americana Annual 1970, p 101*

Dada has contributed to every new technique employed in this century that it did not actually invent—collage, which is everywhere; its extension, assemblage, which includes junk sculpture, "found" objects and a hundred cousins; the "environment" as well as the Happening; kinetic sculpture, whether motorized or not, and on and on. *John Canaday, The New York Times Magazine, March 24, 1968, p 30*

kinetic art, a form of art involving any sort of movement or motion, whether through the use of mobile parts, motor-driven mechanisms, and the like, or through the use of light effects, optical illusions, etc. Also called KINETICISM. Compare LUMINAL ART.

Of particular interest was the use of light and motion in sculpture, especially in constructions designed for spectator participation. ... "Options," a large group show that originated at the Milwaukee Art Center ... featured kinetic art that reacted to touch, weight, and body heat. *Victor H. Miesel, "Art: New Dimensions," The Americana Annual 1969, p 95*

kineticism, *n.* another name for KINETIC ART.

Manhattan's avant-garde Jewish Museum is currently showing 102 works by kineticism's established practitioners, Jean Tinguely and Nicolas Schöffer. *Time, Jan. 28, 1966, p 44*

ki·ne·tin ('kai nə tən), *n.* a plant hormone, a type of cytokinin, originally derived from yeast. Compare ABSCISIC ACID, BRASSIN.

Cultured plant cells normally need the hormone kinetin in order to divide and grow. *Walter G. Rosen, "Botany," The World Book Science Annual 1967, p 268*

... kinetin, the first growth factor isolated, promotes growth by a "stop-and-go" signal and by affecting a plant's growth habits. ... *David E. Fairbrothers, "Botany: Cytokinins," The Americana Annual 1969, p 130*

[from *kinet-* motion + -*in* (chemical suffix)]

kinky, *adj. Chiefly British Slang.* **1** involving or appealing to sexually unconventional or perverted tastes.

. . . the current "The Right Honourable Gentleman," on which Littler collaborated, contains references to a man sleeping with two women at once and other kinky behaviour. *The Observer (London), Aug. 30, 1964, p 4*

The whole thing reminded me of Otto Preminger's 1965 movie, *Bunny Lake Is Missing,* in which the heroine found herself alone with a man who fondled a black whip and announced that it once belonged to "The Great One," the Marquis de Sade himself. Movies, I suddenly notice, are kinkier than ever. *Marshall Delaney, Saturday Night (Canada), July 1966, p 39*

With nude girls appearing in *The Times,* with explicitly sexual acts being performed nightly on the public stage (matinees on Wednesdays and Saturdays), and with copulation in living color, accompanied by a full symphony orchestra, dominating the screens of neighborhood movie theaters, London's pimps, panders and pornographers have had to repackage the product and redefine their traditional markets. The general effect of the permissive society has been to turn the industry decidedly kinky in its attempts to stay on the wrong side of conventional morality — sado-masochism is definitely "in" this year — and to concentrate its marketing effort for basic services on the out-of-town visitors' trade — tourists and businessmen with no time for preliminaries. *Donald Goddard, Blimey! Another Book About London, 1972, p 100*

2 sexually deviant.

Obscenities, it was complained, had been introduced by "kinky" authors into television plays. *The Times (London), April 12, 1966, p 6*

3 odd; queer; eccentric.

. . . after several gruesome murders and a lot of kinky goings-on the police finally come to the correct solution. *The Times (London), June 1, 1967, p 8*

4 unconventional in a sophisticated way; offbeat.

". . . there's the danger of making everything the same in an effort to be way out," she [the actress Susannah York] added thoughtfully. "I loathe really kinky clothes." *Joan Cook, The New York Times, Oct. 4, 1966, p 44*

But today they report huge sales of bed jackets for bedtime television, kinky underwear and the . . . leg-o'-mutton blouse. *The Times (London), March 21, 1966, p 13*

[extended senses of *kinky* twisted]

► *Kinky* in reference to clothing (see definition 4 and also the entry *kinky boot*) is used especially to suggest the type of feminine attire or accessory that is associated with fetishism and sexual stimulation.

kinky boot, *British.* a knee-length or thigh-length boot, especially of black leather, worn by women.

It was the year that satire became an industry; that the Derby winner, Relko, was tested for dope; that women adopted the fashionable long 'kinky' boot. *The Annual Register of World Events in 1963 (1964), p 1*

. . . these tiny intangibles sticking in the mind as they do, not even the headiest of cultural exchanges, not even . . . Brigid Brophy doing a maypole dance in kinky boots, will be able to clear the air. *Alexander Frater, Punch, March 30, 1966, p 464*

kinship family, a family unit consisting of several closely related families (as father, mother, sons,

their wives, and their children) all living together.

In the less complicated, less urbanized days, the average U.S. family was an "extended" or "kinship" family. This meant simply that the parents and their children were surrounded by relatives: in-laws, brothers, sisters, aunts, uncles, grandparents, cousins. If the relatives did not live within the same household, they were next door or down the block or on the next farm. But as Americans became more mobile, the kinfolk have been gradually left behind. *Time, Dec. 28, 1970, p 34*

► This term is synonymous with the more commonly used term *extended family.*

ki·rin ('ki: rin), *n.* a mythical animal of a composite form, shown especially in Japanese carvings and porcelains. It is the Japanese form of the *kylin* or "Chinese unicorn."

A boxwood carving of a wasp in a rotten pear by Kogetsu made 90 guineas . . . , a kirin, the Japanese equivalent of the western unicorn, also carved in ivory, 65 guineas. . . . *The Times (London), Feb. 22, 1966, p 12*

[from Japanese, from Chinese *ch'i lin*]

kiss of life, *British.* an act that gives back life; something that revitalizes.

The Government's kiss of life for Rolls [-Royce] could be very misleading if it is seen as a sign of a volte face by the Government over propping up ailing companies. *Victor Keegan, "Flightpath to Ruin?" The Manchester Guardian Weekly, Nov. 21, 1970, p 22*

The question of Britain's possible entry into the Common Market, for long declared to be a dead issue in the House of Commons, was given the kiss of life today by Sir Alec Douglas-Home. *The Times (London), June 2, 1965, p 12*

► Since the early 1960's *kiss of life* has been a popular term in Great Britain for *mouth-to-mouth resuscitation.* The model was probably the earlier figurative phrase *kiss of death,* meaning a seemingly friendly act that results in betrayal or ruin.

kitemark, *n.* the registered certification mark of the British Standards Institution, indicating compliance of a manufactured product with the Institution's standards of performance.

But the new regulation comes at a time when the B S I "kitemark" standard — set with the aid of belt manufacturers — is coming under expert criticism. *The Sunday Times (London), Jan. 15, 1967, p 8*

kitschy, *adj.* artistically shallow or vulgar, but slickly professional; gaudy or ostentatious.

Flamboyant orange hat, half-blouse breaking into white tassels below full breasts lent a kitschy, high-school-queen quality. *Don Mitchell, "Alcohol Tripping," Harper's, Sept. 1969, p 84*

I am jealous of the scenery here for the Gibichung Palace, but the trees by the Rhine are Kitschy. . . . *William Mann, "The Arts: The Ring Completed," The Times (London), March 25, 1970, p 17*

. . . those of us who are writers, teachers, community leaders, makers of opinion can bury our outmoded, liberal, laissez-faire ideas about freedom of expression at any cost — and help to cramp and cripple the mass appeal of pornography by making it *démodé,* by pointing out its kitschy insipidity, by exposing its infantilism, by laughing it to scorn. *L. E. Sissman, "Innocent Bystander: The Sex Biz," The Atlantic, Aug. 1971, p 26*

[from *kitsch* inferior works of art or literature, from German *Kitsch*]

kitten, *v.i.* to act coyly or coquettishly.

...there are, I suppose, women who have sold themselves as "sexual objects" and must slink and kitten before their masters. *Irving Howe, "Books," Review of "Sexual Politics" by Kate Millet, Harper's, Dec. 1970, p 128*

▶ *Kitten* as a verb has been in use at least since the time of Shakespeare, but only in the sense of "to bring forth kittens." The form recorded here is new, derived by back formation from *kittenish*.

ki·wi fruit ('ki: wi:), an edible fruit resembling a large gooseberry, produced by a New Zealand vine and sold in the United States as a delicacy.

Chinese gooseberries, also known as kiwi fruit, are in metropolitan markets for the third season in increased quantities. *The New York Times, Aug. 13, 1966, p 12*

[from *kiwi*, a nickname for a New Zealander, originally the Maori name of the apteryx, a New Zealand bird]

Kleinian, *adj.* of or relating to the theories of Melanie Klein, 1882-1960, a German pioneer in child psychology who emphasized infant sexuality and argued that the psychoanalytic technique could be applied to very young children.

This is something that psychoanalytic thought itself has often failed to grasp; wherever psychoanalytic theory stops short at tracing back human ills to an aboriginal calamity, whether in the tribal life of our remote ancestors, as in Freud's own early work, or in the early life of the individual child, as in much Kleinian theory, then at this point the psychoanalytic movement does less than justice to its own insights, and takes over the outlook of the fatalistic religions whose neurotic character it has been instrumental in exposing. *John Wren-Lewis, "The Cosmic Enemy," The Listener, May 18, 1967, p 650*

—*n.* a follower or supporter of Melanie Klein's theories.

... "Kleinians" maintain that paranoia is full-blown in the first year of life. *Donald M. Kaplan, "Since Freud: The Youngest Dreamer," Harper's, Aug. 1968, p 57*

Freudians believe the Kleinians overemphasize the early months of life and neglect adult experience and environmental factors. *"Review of the Year: Psychology," Encyclopedia Science Supplement (Grolier) 1969, p 276*

kleptocracy, *n.* government by thieves.

In the course of a quite long digression about the Federal Republic of Cameroon, which he seems to regard as one of the less wicked kleptocracies, Mr. Barnes makes no reference to the part played in its history by the Union des Populations Camerounaises. *Thomas Hodgkin, "Back to Africa," Review of "Africa in Eclipse" by Leonard Barnes, The Manchester Guardian Weekly, July 10, 1971, p 18*

[from *klepto-* theft + *-cracy* government]

klick or **klik,** *n. U.S. Military Slang.* (in Indochina) a kilometer.

Sipping lemonade or good Russian vodka, they trade experiences. Nothing to the north for 20 klicks (kilometers). All quiet at Kompong Speu, but the city [Phnom Penh] is deserted and still smoldering from a Communist mortar attack that morning. *Time, July 6, 1970, p 24*

"O.K., well, there's one hootch down there about a klik south of us that we want you to get," the ground commander said. *Jonathan Schell, "A Reporter at Large: Quang Ngai and Quang Tin," The New Yorker, March 16, 1968, p 86*

Klinefelter's syndrome, a congenital disorder of males resulting from the presence of an extra female chromosome (XXY instead of XY) in the cells. Compare XYY SYNDROME.

The boy had Klinefelter's syndrome, a condition characterized by small testicles, other sexual abnormalities and an extra X chromosome. *Science News Letter, Jan. 8, 1966, p 32*

... accidents may produce, in approximately 1 out of 400-600 "male" births, an XXY sex-chromosome constitution that gives rise to Klinefelter syndrome—sparse body hair, long legs, enlarged breasts, and sterility. *Samuel H. Boyer, "Medicine: Genetics," Britannica Book of the Year 1969, p 495*

[named for Harry F. *Klinefelter*, Jr., born 1912, an American physician who described the syndrome]

klutz (kləts), *n. U.S. Slang.* a clumsy, awkward person.

Candice [Bergen] is generally hailed as heiress apparent to Grace Kelly, but the princess role does not quite fit. Says she: "Basically I'm the klutz who makes a terrific entrance to the party and then trips and falls and walks around with food in her hair." *Time, Nov. 2, 1970, p 83*

[from Yiddish *klots*, literally, a block or lump, corresponding to German *Klotz*]

klutz·y ('klət si:), *adj. U.S. Slang.* awkward and clumsy.

... the sad, klutzy ballerinas of the Music Hall pollute children's first live experience of dance. *Pauline Kael, "English Bull," The New Yorker, Jan. 17, 1970, p 72*

K-mes·ic ('kei,mes ik), *adj.* another word for KAONIC.

... in 1952 physicists at Rochester and Pittsburgh identified X-rays originating from pi-mesic atoms. Since then muonic atoms (mu mesons in atomic orbit) and K-mesic atoms were discovered. *"Unusual Matings Discovered at CERN," New Scientist, Sept. 17, 1970, p 566*

knee-jerk, *adj.* reacting without much thought or in a predictable or automatic way (like the reflex of the foreleg produced when a light blow is delivered to the knee).

Rauh was instantly denounced by some for responding in the usual knee-jerk liberal fashion. ... *Richard Harris, "Decision," The New Yorker, Dec. 5, 1970, p 83*

Erwin [Frank C. Erwin, Jr., Chairman of the University of Texas Board of Regents] is hardly a knee-jerk reactionary. Like many a Texas Democrat, he is coldly conservative on some issues, warmly liberal on others. When it comes to education, he is all populist, believing that every Texas youngster deserves a shot at college. *"Education: The Emperor of U.T.," Time, Aug. 10, 1970, p 54*

The board seems to encourage the local state of political apathy, depending on entrenched hacks and knee-jerk Republicans to turn out the winning vote. *Samuel Kaplan, "The Balkanization of Suburbia: If It's Impossible to Read the Maps, then How Can the People Find the Government?" Harper's, Oct. 1971, p 74*

... in his [Arthur Schlesinger, Jr.'s] own essay on American violence, we read that "reason cannot always disentangle the log-jam into which history may thrust the structures of society." "But," he adds—guess what—"violence is justified only when the resources of reason are demonstrably exhausted and when the application of force remains the only way of achieving rational ends." This is "knee-jerk liberalism" at its worst. *Jonathan Steele, "Books," Review of "The Crisis of Confidence" by Arthur M. Schlesinger, Jr., The Manchester Guardian Weekly, Oct. 18, 1969, p 19*

—*n.* a person whose reactions are predictable or automatic, especially in politics.

The most notorious Congressman from Iowa is cranky old H. R. Gross, a seventy-year-old knee-jerk best remembered for castigating the Reverend Bill Moyers for dancing the frug in the White House. . . . *Larry L. King, "Harold E. Hughes: Evangelist From the Prairies," Harper's, March 1969, p 52*

kneeroom, *n.* enough room in front of a seat of an automobile, airplane, etc., to keep one's knees in a natural, comfortable position when seated.

More people are buying Rolls-Royces today than ever before. . . . More front headroom and rear kneeroom could be devised by reducing the bulk of their cushions and backrests, without detracting from comfort. *Geoffrey Charles, "Cars and Drivers: More Join the Rolls-Royce Queue," The Times (London), April 16, 1970, p 18*

knee-slapper, *n. U.S.* a hilarious joke.

If T. R. [Theodore Roosevelt] is President when he is fully dressed, went one knee-slapper, what is he with his clothes off? *Time, Dec. 5, 1969, p 56*

"How's the World Treating You," an English comedy at the Music Box, is full of knee-slappers like that one, but it does have the benefit of a couple of rowdy music-hall performances by Patricia Routledge and Peter Bayliss. *John McCarten, "The Theatre: Look, Ma, I'm Playwriting," The New Yorker, Nov. 5, 1966, p 128*

knocker, *n. British.* **1** a door-to-door salesman.

A knocker was a specially trained salesman working, not under the authority and generally not in the pay of a district sales agent, but for the company itself, out of the Dayton executive offices. *"When the Law Caught Up with America's Two-Armed Bandits," Excerpt from "Think: A Biography of the Watsons and IBM" by William Rogers, The Sunday Times (London), Jan. 18, 1970, p 37*

2 on the knocker, from door to door.

I was working on the knocker when *Love on the Dole* was published and got those wonderful reviews. *Walter Greenwood quoted by D. G. Bridson, "Manchester in the Thirties," The Listener, Nov. 28, 1968, p 714*

Selling gemstones on the knocker will soon become a familiar feature of suburban life, if "James Bond" merchandiser Mervyn Brodie has his way. *The Sunday Times (London), Sept. 14, 1969, p 25*

knocker-up, *n.; pl.* **knockers-up.** *British.* a person who brings the resident of a house to the door in order to prepare the ground for someone else to solicit, canvass, etc.

Three hundred yards away, Michael Whincup, the candidate, is canvassing with six knockers-up. *The Times (London), March 11, 1966, p 8*

▶ In old industrial areas, especially mining, houses used to have a slate outside on which was written a time. A "knocker-up" would then tour the streets rousing workers for a shift of work,

acting as an alarm clock. A *knocker-up* as used in the quotation would rouse the resident and ask if he/they would like to meet the candidate. The candidate would be called across to those who said yes.

knockoff, *n. U.S.* a copy or reproduction of the design of a textile or apparel product.

[Coco] Chanel had long since refused to join the cabal of Paris designers who tried to prevent style piracy. . . . Private customers paid $700 for the original; buyers, intent on knockoffs, paid close to $1,500. *"Modern Living: Chanel No. 1," Time, Jan. 25, 1971, p 38*

Copying designs to sell for less has a name in the industry. It is called the "knockoff." *Robert E. Dallos, The New York Times, Jan. 25, 1966, p 44*

knuckle-walk, *v.i.* to walk as chimpanzees and gorillas do, with the knuckles of the hands touching the ground.

Orangutans adjust to walking on a cage floor with a variety of hand postures, but they cannot knuckle walk. *Russell H. Tuttle, "Chimpanzee," McGraw-Hill Yearbook of Science and Technology 1967, p 132*

Russell Tuttle, also of the University of Chicago, suggested that the initial divergence between man and ape may have occurred in the arboreal habitats through differential use of forelimbs and hind limbs and before the evolution of knuckle-walking. *John G. Lepp, "Zoology," 1971 Britannica Yearbook of Science and the Future, 1970, p 291*

ko·bo ('kɔː,bɔː), *n.* a unit of money in Nigeria. See the quotation for details.

The naira will be made up of 100 kobo . . . the name is a corruption of the word "copper" and the popular term here [in Nigeria] for the penny, a copper coin. . . . The kobo, symbolized by a lower-case k, will be produced in coins of one-half kobo, 1, 5, 10 and 25 kobo. A 50-kobo paper bill will be produced. *The New York Times, Aug. 9, 1972, p 14*

ko·gai ('kou gɑi), *n. Japanese.* pollution of the environment.

Although *kogai* is one of the most controversial and thoroughly covered topics in the Tokyo press, the daily seminars [on pollution] were closed to Japanese reporters . . . . *Fred C. Shapiro, "Our Far-Flung Correspondents," The New Yorker, May 23, 1970, p 94*

After 48 schoolchildren were felled by photochemical smog in Tokyo last summer, *kogai* (environmental disruption) became the nation's top issue. *Time, Jan. 4, 1971, p 34*

Japan's growth was attended by heavy social cost. Some Japanese began to refer to GNP as "gross national pollution," and the new word "kogai" ("public nuisance") gained wide currency. *Ardath W. Burks, "Japan," Britannica Book of the Year 1971, p 427*

Ko·jah ('kou dʒɑː), *n.* a mutant variety of mink. See the quotations for details.

Last year, too, there appeared Kojah mink (rare and expensive), a mink so long-haired that it resembles sable. Nobody I have asked knows whence it sprang, and the thing is a real mystery, because I hear that neither minks nor sables believe in miscegenation. *Lois Long, "On and Off the Avenue: Feminine Fashions," The New Yorker, Nov. 8, 1969, p 179*

Called "Kojah" for reasons best understood by the trade (although the name does have a bit more class than "mable" or "sink"), the fur is much thicker and softer than conventional mink and less bulky than sable. *Time, Jan. 31, 1969, p 47*

[of uncertain origin]

kook (ku:k), *n. Slang.* an odd, crazy, or eccentric person. *Often used attributively.*

"Don't think that just because he talked about those way-out rockets he's a kook," cautioned a fellow officer. *Time, Oct. 4, 1963, p 37*

To rate even the thinnest chance of winning, Murphy not only had to hold onto all factions of the G.O.P., from rabid-right kooks to solid moderates, he also had to pick up some 20% of Democratic and Independent votes. *Time, Nov. 13, 1964, p 22*

"Has it ever occurred to you that the kook market has grown?" said a United States auto executive when asked to explain the growing sales of foreign cars. *The New York Times, March 26, 1968, p 32*

[probably shortened and altered from *cuckoo, adj.,* U.S. slang word meaning crazy]

kooky, *adj. Slang.* odd; crazy; eccentric.

. . . this study of a kooky girl [Petulia] is also, from the orthodox point of view, kookily narrated. . . . Seldom has the kooky girl character been seen in anything but a comedy; almost for the first time here we are made to realise the havoc she can cause. *Richard Mallett, "Cinema: Petulia," Punch, June 19, 1968, p 899*

The first group includes *Vogue, Harper's Bazaar* and *Queen,* and shows expensive clothes mainly for the thirties and upward age-group, although pressure of the so-called swinging image has resulted in space for young 'kooky' clothes. *Gillian Freeman, The Undergrowth of Literature, 1967, p 16*

krad, *n.* a unit of gamma-ray radiation.

The procedure is carefully planned beforehand, with all the essential information required for the localization of the target and the creation of the lesion in the brain marked on a transparent programme operation chart. A typical dose is 25 krads and the procedure lasts about 2 hours. *"Gamma Rays Cut Out the Brain Surgeon's Scalpel," New Scientist, Dec. 3, 1970, p 377*

[from *k-rad*iation, a form of radiation obtained by bombarding certain elements with high-speed electrons]

KREEP (kri:p), *n.* a yellow-brown glassy mineral obtained on the moon, noted for its unusual chemical composition. See also FERROPSEUDOBROOKITE.

Another Apollo 12 find of general agreement was that of an exotic component called KREEP by some—for high content of potassium, rare earth elements and phosphorus—found in rock 13 and in other material dated about 4.5 billion years old. *Science News, Jan. 23, 1971, p 62*

The Apollo 12 finds also show some enrichment in calcium and aluminum, but they are mainly distinguished by an additional component known by its acronym as KREEP, signifying material enriched in potassium (K), rare-earth elements (REE) and phosphate (P). *Brian Mason, "The Lunar Rocks," Scientific American, Oct. 1971, p 53*

The lunar regolith has been found to contain particles of unusual chemical composition, high in potassium, phosphorus and certain metals known as rare-earth elements. These mineral fragments have been dubbed *kreep* (from *K,* the chemical symbol for potassium, rare-earth elements and *P,* the chemical symbol for phosphorus). *Paul D.*

Lowman, Jr., "The Geology of the Moon," Encyclopedia Science Supplement (Grolier) 1971, p 43

Kremlinologist, *n.* an expert student or observer of the Soviet government. Also called SOVIETOLOGIST.

"Will they be content to stop at that point, or will they continue to grind out more ICBM's? We simply don't know," one top Kremlinologist in Washington conceded. *The New York Times, Feb. 25, 1968, Sec. 4, p 2*

Kremlinology, *n.* the study of the policies, practices, etc., of the Soviet government. Also called SOVIETOLOGY. Compare PEKINGOLOGY.

If the West had grasped at that time [the post-Stalin thaw of 1953-1957] the opportunity provided by the division among the Soviet leaders on the problem of Germany, the two halves of Germany might by now have been unified. There were many other equally promising avenues to explore, as the diplomatic cliché has it, but the diplomatists were not interested, because this was "Kremlinology"—an inexact science if ever there was one. *Victor Zorza, "Secrets of the Moscow Embassy," Review of "The Kremlin and the Embassy" by Sir William Hayter, The Manchester Guardian Weekly, Nov. 3, 1966, p 10*

kur·cha·to·vi·um (ˌkər tʃəˈtou vi: əm), *n.* the name given by Soviet scientists to ELEMENT 104. See the quotations for details.

Russian physicists had reported . . . that they had succeeded in synthesizing element 104, which they named kurchatovium in honor of the Russian physicist I. V. Kurchatov. The Berkeley group then synthesized element 104 by a different method and challenged the Russian finding, naming their discovery rutherfordium in honor of the British physicist Lord Rutherford. *"Science and the Citizen," Scientific American, June 1970, p 49*

. . . the Soviet scientist G. N. Flerov announced the creation of element 104 by the bombardment of plutonium atoms (atomic mass 242) with neon nuclei (atomic mass 22). The Soviets called this element kurchatovium, after a famous Russian physicist. However, there is some dispute as to whether or not the Soviet scientists actually succeeded in producing element 104, and the name "kurchatovium" has not been officially accepted. *Theodor Benfey and Eugenia Keller, "Chemistry: Chemical Elements," The Americana Annual 1970, p 162*

kur·ta (ˈkur tɑ:), *n.* another spelling of KHURTA.

Over a black *kurta* and black pajamas Mr. Bande sports a handsome black *achkan,* or tunic. He wears the traditional skullcap, and his beard is neatly trimmed according to the specifications of a Moslem divine. *Ved Mehta, "A Reporter at Large: Indian Journal," The New Yorker, June 8, 1968, p 103*

ku·ru (ˈku: ru:), *n.* a fatal disease of the human nervous system similar to scrapie in sheep. Kuru, occurring in natives of the New Guinea highlands, is characterized by tremors and fits of giggling followed by loss of muscular coordination and speech, inability to swallow, and other degenerative symptoms.

Kuru . . . was found to be caused by a virus that persists in the tissues for long periods of time before symptoms appear. *Thomas C. Merigan, "Medicine: Infectious Diseases," 1970 Britannica Yearbook of Science and the Future, 1969, p 271*

Kuru, one of the strangest and most insidious diseases known, is fading away in its New Guinea habitat, apparently because of a ban on ritualistic cannibalism. *Walter Sullivan, "Fatal Nerve Disease Wanes as Cannibalism Is Banned," The New York Times, June 12, 1971, p 33*

[from the native name of the disease, roughly meaning "shivers"]

Ku·ta·ni (kuːˈtɑːniː), *adj.* of or designating a type of Japanese pottery valued for its designs.

The dramatic bronze castings were discovered in Hong Kong, the hand-decorated Kutani porcelains in Japan, and others originally came from old China. *The New York Times, Oct. 22, 1967, Sec. 1, p 10*

[from *Kutani*, a village in Honshu, Japan where such ware has long been produced]

kvell, *v.i. U.S. Slang.* to enjoy oneself thoroughly.

The New York Spy is a useful and terribly bright guide to New York, conscientiously kvelling through 'the city's pleasures', charmed alike by brutal manners, as chronicled by Tom Wolfe, and the Jewish takeover (London swings but Jewish New York *kvells*). *Frank Kermode, "Travel Books: Americas," Review of "The New York Spy," edited by Alan Rinzler, The Listener, Dec. 28, 1967, p 849*

[from Yiddish *kveln*]

kvetch, *U.S. Slang.* —*n.* a habitual complainer or faultfinder.

The subway graffiti had begun to include phrases like "Medea Is a Yenta" and "Kafka is a Kvetch." *Calvin Trillin, "Lester Drentluss, a Jewish Boy from Baltimore, Attempts to Make it Through the Summer of 1967," The Atlantic, Jan. 1968, p 43*

—*v.i.* to whine, complain, or find fault.

. . . what is a Jewish mother for, except to *kvetch* a little? *Jack Newfield, "Goodbye, Dolly!: A Reminiscence of The New York Post," Harper's, Sept. 1969, p 92*

"Stuyvie is a reactionary," said one of the classmates. But he is an amiable one, not given to angry kvetching, a twinkly-eyed bachelor who'd rather talk about pot-smoking escapades in Mexico, his efforts at preserving the California backland from suburban tractation. . . . *Nicholas von Hoffman, "The Class of '43 Is Puzzled," The Atlantic, Oct. 1968, p 70*

One day, after listening to Kashouk *kvetch* for a couple of hours, Sol Hurok, who was just beginning to make a name for himself as an impresario, put the question direct. "Tell me, Kashouk," Hurok wanted to know. "If you always lose so much money, why do you stay in business?" *Harold C. Schonberg, "Music," Harper's, Feb. 1971, p 111*

[from Yiddish *kvetsh*, *n.* or *kvetshn*, *v.*, literally, squeeze]

kwa·cha (ˈkwɑːtʃə), *n.* the new monetary unit of Zambia (since 1969) and of Malawi.

Malawi's decimal currency was to be introduced in March 1971; the new unit, the kwacha, is divided into 100 tambolas. *Elston G. Bradfield, "Coin Collecting," The 1970 Compton Yearbook, p 188*

. . . Zambia changed to a decimal currency and replaced the pound, shilling, and pence with the kwacha (meaning "dawn"), which equals US $1.40, and the ngwee (meaning "bright"), which is one-hundredth of a kwacha. *Franklin Parker, "Zambia: Currency Change," 1969 Collier's Encyclopedia Year Book, p 624*

KWIC (kwik), *n.* acronym for *key-word-in-context.*

A second type of bibliographic information retrieval device is the key-word-in-context (KWIC) index, which has become widely used, particularly as a device for retrieving information from current materials. *Frederick G. Kilgour, "Information Retrieval: Developments," McGraw-Hill Yearbook of Science and Technology 1967, p 16*

kyu·do (ˈkyuːdou), *n.* a Japanese method of archery used to develop concentration and coordination.

Those who prefer a less physically demanding exercise may use their weekly practice time for kyudo. . . . *The New York Times, June 25, 1967, p 7*

[from Japanese *kyūdō* archery]

L

labor-intensive, *adj.* requiring great expenditure of labor to increase productivity or earnings.

. . . a labor-intensive textile mill in Arusha, or an agricultural project, would in theory be preferred to a modern, highly mechanized factory in Dar es Salaam. *Anthony Lewis, "Brook Farm Below the Equator," The New York Times, Jan. 5, 1970, p 36*

The service sectors have in common the fact that they are disproportionately labor-intensive rather than capital-intensive, even though some sectors (particularly transportation and communication) have extremely high ratios of capital to output. *W. Halder Fisher, "The Anatomy of Inflation: 1953-1975," Scientific American, Nov. 1971, p 20*

La·bour·wal·lah ('lei bər,wɑl ə), *n.* (in Kenya and some other parts of eastern Africa) a prominent member of the Labour movement.

. . . the Britain with which they [Britons in Kenya] had "genuine ties" had disappeared long ago, and particularly with the advent of the "communist Labourwallahs". *Naurali Peera, University of Salford, Salford, Lancashire, England, in a Letter to the Editor, The Times (London), March 19, 1970, p 11*

[from *Labour* + *-wallah* (Anglo-Indian suffix for "one connected with"). See also *dukawallah*.]

lac, *adj.* of or relating to the lac operon.

. . . the *lac* repressor binds to DNA that contains the *lac* genes but not to DNA without *lac* genes. *Mark Ptashne and Walter Gilbert, "Genetic Repressors," Scientific American, June 1970, p 43*

lack-in-office, *n.* one who seeks to gain public office; an office seeker.

The Davidsons sell dogs through advertisements in newspapers, giving their telephone number. Mrs. Davidson said: "I know what I am doing, because I have worked with dogs all my life. I would not like to see legislation brought in to control places like this. That would just give power to a lot of lacks-in-office." *Trevor Fishlock, "RSPCA Concern Over Slum Dog Breeding Farms," The Times (London), May 28, 1970, p 4*

lac operon, the operon which controls the metabolism of lactose (milk sugar). Lac operon was isolated in 1969.

. . . the first isolation of a single gene unit — the lac operon from the common intestinal bacteria called *Escherichia coli (E. coli). "Genetics," Science News Yearbook 1970, p 104*

Boston: The isolation in pure form of a set of six bacterial genes known as the *lac* operon has been accomplished by a group led by Dr. Jon Beckwith of the Harvard Medical School. . . . *Science Journal, Jan. 1970, p 14*

ladder polymer, a high-temperature polymer consisting of two molecular chains which are intermittently linked like the two sides of a ladder.

The use of conventional straight-chain polymers seems to be restricted by an upper temperature limit of about 550°C, but the ladder polymers (so-called because of their integral cross-linked structure) offer more exciting possibilities. *John Howard, "Plastics to Withstand the Heat," New Scientist and Science Journal, June 24, 1971, p 761*

La·ko·da (lə'kou də), *n.* a shorn fur-seal skin resembling glossy suede.

A midicoat of Lakoda in its natural caramel uses black beaver for the collar and cuffs, the hem, and the edging of the deep slits that go up the sides to the hips. . . . *Lois Long, "On and Off the Avenue: Feminine Fashions," The New Yorker, Nov. 8, 1969, p 179*

[from the name of an area on the Pribilof Islands in the Bering Sea, where the skin is obtained]

La·maze (lə'meiz), *adj.* of or relating to a form of painless childbirth obtained through psychoprophylaxis.

. . . they heard a lecture by Dr. I. Chabon . . . followed by a French film showing the birth of a baby by natural childbirth using the Lamaze technique. *Joan Cook, The New York Times, March 25, 1965, p 40*

The method is known as . . . the Lamaze Method of "natural" childbirth, a misnomer, its advocates claim, because "the method helps the woman cope with nature." The mother is given little or no anesthetic and relies on her knowledge of the psychology of childbirth and of specially developed breathing rhythms and relaxing techniques to make the delivery easier. *Sally Olds and Linda Witt, "Fathers in the Delivery Room," Encyclopedia Science Supplement (Grolier) 1971, p 265*

[named after Fernand *Lamaze,* a French obstetrician who developed this form of childbirth in the 1950's from Pavlov's studies of the conditioned reflex]

lame, *adj.* U.S. Slang. not up to date, or naive.

Anyone who does not know that [he (Mark Lindsay) is the positively super-fab lead singer of Paul Revere and the Raiders] is obviously lame . . . or perhaps just over 25 and into the twilight of life. *Time, June 2, 1967, p 26*

lander, *n.* a space satellite or vehicle designed for landing instead of orbiting. Also called LANDING VEHICLE. Compare SOFT-LANDER.

The 30 kg lander was released from a hovering helicopter and allowed to free fall to the lake bed. In the thin atmosphere of Mars, the lander would be slowed to the same velocity by a six metre parachute; no parachute was used in this test. *"Development News: Model of US Mars Lander Tested Successfully," Science Journal, July 1968, p 13*

The Mars 3 lander also took to the surface instruments for measuring atmospheric temperature and pressure, for mass-spectrometric determination of the chemical composition of the atmosphere, for measuring wind velocities and for determining the chemical composition and physical and mechanical properties of the surface layer. *"A Tale of Trouble with Mars Lander," Science News, Dec. 25, 1971, p 422*

Next day, the third foray from the lunar lander *Falcon* provided more scientific treasures. *"Apollo 15: A Giant Step for Science," Time, Aug. 16, 1971, p 28*

land freeze, a government restriction on the sale and transfer of land.

The old mining and homesteading laws should be reformed to prevent continuation of the present system of irrational first-come, first-served claims. In addition, a partial land freeze should be continued until present surveying and assessing programs by federal agencies can be completed. With 20 more planners, the U.S. Bureau of Land Management estimates, it can classify all Alaska by 1980. *Time, July 27, 1970, p 50*

landing vehicle, another name for LANDER.

The most impressive signal was produced by the impact of the spent upper stage of the Apollo 12 landing vehicle. *Peter Gwynne, "The Moon Retains Its Mysteries," Science Journal, March 1970, p 83*

land-to-land, *adj.* launched from the ground at a target on the ground. Compare GROUND-TO-GROUND.

The Jordanian Ambassador alleged that in the attack on the town and neighbouring villages Israel used land-to-land rockets for the first time. *"30 Die in Israeli Attack," The Manchester Guardian Weekly, June 6, 1968, p 3*

► The term is used in contrast to *air-to-air, air-to-ground, surface-to-surface*, and similar collocations.

land yacht, another name for SAND YACHT.

A school that has its own land yacht, wind tunnel, go-kart and canoeing clubs—and plans to build a hovertrain and submarine—may sound like a well-endowed foundation or an expensive way to go about education. *The Times (London), Jan. 23, 1967, p 9*

Lang·muir probe ('læŋ myur), a device to measure plasma density by calculating the potential of electric discharge along a probe in a plasma-filled tube.

Existing techniques for measuring density all suffer from various drawbacks. To achieve a measurement with high resolution it is necessary to insert a Langmuir probe which means disturbing the plasma to an unknown extent....*Graham Chedd and Peter Stubbs, "Monitor: A Powerful New Technique for Probing Hot Plasmas," New Scientist, May 29, 1969, p 454*

The oscilloscope traces represent the signals picked up by a Langmuir probe, a small wire used to detect the local value of the plasma density or the electric potential. *Francis F. Chen, "The Leakage Problem in Fusion Reactors," Scientific American, July 1967, p 81*

[named after Irving *Langmuir*, 1881-1957, an American chemist]

lan·gous·tine (ˌlã gu:'sti:n), *n.* a prawn or small lobster, especially of the European North Atlantic waters.

The langoustines, served with a dark sauce gingerly seasoned with shallots, are excellent and so is the chicken breast with champagne sauce. *Craig Claiborne, The New York Times, Feb. 3, 1967, p 20*

...the langoustines which several boats are taking out of the Sound of Raasay and the Minch make anything found in the Mediterranean tasteless by comparison. *The Times (London), Nov. 9, 1968, p 20*

[from French, diminutive of *langouste* lobster]

► Sometimes known as a Norway lobster. The *langouste* is not the ordinary lobster which would be *homard* in French, but the "spiny lobster" or "crayfish."

language, *n.* short for COMPUTER LANGUAGE.

NEAT/3, a language with built-in simplicity, incorporates simple English instructions with powerful tools that enable the computer to generate its own program. Complicated logic and coding are eliminated because flexible procedural instructions and pre-programmed major computer functions are combined in one language. *Advertisement by National Cash Register Company, Dayton, Ohio, Scientific American, April 1968, p 149*

language laboratory, a room or rooms equipped with interconnected tape recorders having one permanent master track and one erasable student track for receiving language instruction.

Recent developments in the use of the language laboratory for programmed learning and practice drills have made possible the more efficient use of the teaching resources of the school at the same time as reducing the tedium for students faced with the task of acquiring, often from scratch, a completely new set of skills. *The Times (London), Jan. 16, 1967, p II*

languor, *v.i.* to grow weak; languish.

America languors with an illness of euphoria brought on by our leaders who have proclaimed an international détente in the struggle against Communism. *General Curtis E. LeMay, "The Ideas by Which We Are Ruled," Harper's, June 1969, p 37*

[verb use of the noun. The verb (taken from Old French *langorer*) existed in English about 1350 to 1550 but thereafter became obsolete.]

lan·sign ('læn,sain), *n.* (in semantics) a word, character, sound, etc., that stands for or represents a thing or idea.

In the 1930s C. K. Ogden, I. A. Richards and A. Korzybski, and more recently C. E. Osgood, D. H. Mowrer and others, tried to show how language symbols and signs (lan-signs, as they are sometimes called) are associated with their referents in much the same way as conditioned stimulus becomes associated with an unconditioned stimulus, as in the classical conditioning theory of Pavlov. *Frank George, Science Journal, Jan. 1970, p 57*

[from *lan*guage *sign*]

Lan·tian Man ('læn'tyæn). See the quotation for the meaning.

The Lantian Man from Shensi Province, discovered in 1964 in south central China, is earlier [than Peking Man], possibly dating from 500,000-600,000 years ago, and also more like Java Man in form. *William Howells, "The Beginnings of Man," 1968 Collier's Encyclopedia Year Book, p 48*

[revised spelling of earlier *Lantien Man*, named for the county of *Lantien*, in Shensi province, China, where its fossil remains were discovered]

lap·a·ro·scope ('læp ər ə,skoup), *n.* an optical instrument that can be inserted through the abdominal wall for direct examination of organs, etc.

Human ovaries may be inspected by inserting a tube (laparoscope) through the body wall which both illuminates the internal organs and transmits an image back to the observer. *Picture legend, "General View of Uterus and Ovaries," Science Journal, June 1970, p 57*

Delicately, the surgeon lifts the cyst. . . . He inspects it from all sides by means of the laparoscope. *Françoise Tournier, "The Inside Story," The Sunday Times Magazine (London), Sept. 12, 1971, p 38*

[from Greek *lapárā* flank + English *-scope* instrument for viewing]

lap·a·ros·co·py (,læp ə'ras kə pi:), *n.* an operation using a laparoscope.

An acceptable surgical method for recovering the oöcyte was developed by Steptoe and others. Called laparoscopy, it is a relatively minor operation; even though it requires general anesthesia the patient seldom remains in the hospital for more than 24 hours. The abdomen is artificially distended with an inert gas to provide room to view and work on the internal organs, and minor incisions are made in the abdominal wall to allow the passage of instruments. *R. G. Edwards and Ruth E. Fowler, "Human Embryos In the Laboratory," Scientific American, Dec. 1970, p 50*

This lump, independent of the womb, can be traced very early thanks to laparoscopy, the method of examination used by young gynaecologists as often as their grandfathers used the speculum. *Françoise Tournier, "The Inside Story," The Sunday Times Magazine (London), Sept. 12, 1971, p 42*

lapbelt, *n. Chiefly U.S.* an automobile seat belt.

The shoulder harnesses, like the lap belts, which are also on all new cars now, are aimed at preventing riders from pitching about in accidents and colliding with the car inside. *The New York Times, Sept. 15, 1968, p 46*

lap·i·des·cent (,læp ə'des ənt), *adj.* resembling a stone, especially a stone monument; stonelike.

He [Thomas Hudson, a character in Hemingway's book] is curiously apart, a lapidescent presence, half man, half monument, adored but unapproachable, given to periods of almost hieratic muteness and immobility. *Tony Tanner, "Hemingway: Mens Morbida In Corpore Sano," Review of "Islands in the Stream" by Ernest Hemingway, The Times (London), Oct. 12, 1970, p 6*

[from Latin *lapidēscentem*, present participle of *lapidēscere* to become stony. Compare *lapidescent, adj.* in the *OED*, meaning "having a tendency to solidify into stone," with citations from 1644 through 1811.]

larger-than-life, *adj.* of epic or legendary proportions; exalted.

In U.S. folklore, nothing has been more romanticized than guns and the larger-than-life men who wielded them. *Time, June 21, 1968, p 13*

The larger-than-life political figures thunder their dogmas through the act. *The Sunday Times (London), April 23, 1967, p 49*

In 1867, another partisan, the naturalist John Burroughs, published a similar larger-than-life document, *Notes on Walt Whitman as Poet and Person. . . . Justin Kaplan, "Nine Old Bones: Walt Whitman's Blue Book," The Atlantic, May 1968, p 64*

large-scale integration, a miniaturization technique for fabricating a hundred or more integrated circuits as a unit on a chip of silicon. *Abbreviation:* LSI

Computer Memory Circuit, incorporating 1,244 transistors, 1,170 resistors and 71 diodes, is an example of large-scale integration (LSI). The term is usually reserved for integrated circuits whose density is 50,000 or more devices per square inch. *Picture legend, Scientific American, Feb. 1970, p 23*

An extension of the integrated circuit is seen in the developing technology of large-scale integration — LSI. Instead of components being tied together, as in an integrated circuit, complete circuits will be wired together on a chip into a piece of equipment such as a communications subsystem or a computer. *"Technology: Review of the Year," Encyclopedia Science Supplement (Grolier) 1967, p 331*

large-statured, *adj.* consisting of relatively tall trees and shrubs.

Large-statured forests (moist forests of the Temperate Zone, where nutrients are abundant, and certain tropical rain forest) have a net productivity [of solar energy fixed by green plants] ranging up to several thousand grams per square meter per year. *George M. Woodwell, "The Energy Cycle of the Biosphere," Scientific American, Sept. 1970, p 70*

lasable, *adj.* capable of being lased.

He is therefore working on the seemingly impossible ideal of sourceless illumination, and hopes to exploit the laser principle in which a molecule excited by higher-energy radiation can amplify an incident beam by adding its energy to it. His scheme is to introduce into the room traces of a "lasable" gas chosen so that its excitation-frequency lies in the invisible ultraviolet, and its emission frequency in the visible. *Ariadne, New Scientist, Nov. 17, 1966, p 369*

lase (leiz), *v.i.* to emit the intense light beam of a laser.

Many lasers, as I have described, are excited (or "pumped," as we say in the laboratory) by light. Others may be made to lase by radio waves, or by an electric current, or by chemical reactions. *Thomas Meloy, "Laser's Bright Magic," National Geographic Magazine, Dec. 1966, p 864*

—*v.t.* to subject to laser light beams.

. . . bean sprouts appeared at the soil surface seven days after planting in the lased samples and nine days in the control sample. *"Laser Speeds Seed Growth," New Scientist, Feb. 5, 1970, p 261*

Compare MASE.

▶ Derived by back formation from *laser*. The following early quotation describes this development.

Everybody is his own etymologist, and almost overnight the acronym LASER becomes the noun laser and, finally, the verb to lase. *John Maddox, "Is the Literature Worth Keeping?" Bulletin of the Atomic Scientists, Nov. 1963, p 16*

laser surgery, the destruction of living cells by the beam of a laser.

. . . a multi-disciplined team of surgeons, physicists, engineers and technicians is required if laser surgery is to be conducted effectively and safely. *Ronald Brown, "Practical Lasers," New Scientist, July 27, 1967, p 190*

LASH or **lash,** *n.* a system of shipping in which barges loaded with cargo are placed on board the ship directly instead of being unloaded. *Often used attributively.*

With the inauguration of a new route, a special containerization method called LASH has crossed from Europe to America. LASH stands for Lighter Aboard Ship; lighter refers to a 380-ton, 61-foot-long barge, which carries the cargo. *"America Gets the LASH," Science News, May 2, 1970, p 424*

Shipowners also hastened the introduction of combined oil-bulk carriers, able to take advantage of the best charter rates or work triangular routes more profitably; liquid gas carriers, and lash vessels in which laden barges are floated directly into a large hull. *The Times (London), Aug. 12, 1970, p 18*

L·as·pa·rag·i·nase (ˌel æs pəˈrædʒ əˌneis), *n.* a bacterial enzyme used in inhibiting the growth of certain forms of cancer.

A new drug was added to the list of agents deterrent to, but not curative of, acute leukemia. An enzyme, L-asparaginase, seems to starve leukemic cells of certain nutrients and thereby kill them. *Frank P. Mathews, 1968 Collier's Encyclopedia Year Book, p 354*

The cells of some leukemias need an outside supply of the amino acid L-asparagine. This means they are vulnerable to treatment with the enzyme L-asparaginase, which destroys the amino acid. *Lloyd J. Old, Edward A. Boyse, and H. A. Campbell, "L-asparagine and Leukemia," Scientific American, Aug. 1968, p 34*

It took Cornell's Dr. John D. Broome eight years to ferret out the guinea pigs' secret. These animals, and a few closely related species such as the agouti, have in their blood the enzyme L-asparaginase, so called because it effects a chemical breakdown of the amino acid L-asparagine. *Time, April 14, 1967, p 56*

[from *L-asparagine* (the *L-* or levorotatory form of the amino acid asparagine) + *-ase* enzyme]

Las·sa fever (ˈlɑːs ə), a highly contagious and usually fatal virus disease believed to be transmitted by mice, first identified in 1970 in Lassa, a village in western Nigeria.

The infection, being called Lassa fever, involved almost all the body's organs. The virus produced fever as high as 107 degrees, mouth ulcers, a skin rash with tiny hemorrhages, heart infection and severe muscle aches. *Science News, March 21, 1970, p 288*

Lassa fever had already proved so deadly that one of the world's most expert virologists had fallen ill of the disease, a lab assistant and two nurses had died of it, and research with the virus had been abandoned until more exacting safety precautions could be devised. *Time, Feb. 23, 1970, p 42*

latchkey child, a child whose parents are away at work all day.

Millions of "latchkey" children, for instance, find nobody at home when they get home from school in the afternoon. *The New York Times Magazine, Jan. 7, 1968, p 74*

[so called from the child's having to carry with him the key to his house or apartment]

late-blooming, *adj.* late in developing or reaching full potential.

The reasons for Nixon's increased pace were clear.... He needed more than ever to hold the spotlight lest it wander to the late-blooming Rockefeller write-in campaign. *Time, March 15, 1968, p 13*

I K A had been the absolute pioneer in Argentina's late-blooming mass production motor industry. *The Times (London), April 9, 1967, p 30*

lateral thinking, thinking which seeks to avoid being caught up in details in order to range as widely as possible to include all aspects of a problem or topic.

Lateral thinking, which, being interpreted, means thinking about the sides of things, is all the rage at present. So here is a small problem which involves thinking about the sides of squares. *Martin Hollis, "Tantalizer: Lateral Thinking," New Scientist, July 24, 1969, p 187*

... there is another way. This involves 'lateral thinking' and the assumption that no existing way of doing anything is likely to be the best. This means that adequate is not the end of the search but the beginning. It is a matter of trying to do things in a different way and then seeing whether that different way offers any advantages. If not, then the exercise in flexibility is its own reward. *Edward de Bono, "Play Back: Improving the Familiar," Science Journal, July 1969, p 31*

lat·er·ize (ˈlæt əˌraiz), *v.t.* to convert to laterite (reddish bricklike soil resulting from weathering, leaching, etc.).

Complete defoliation could also cause laterization, the destructive process that occurs in some tropical soils when removal of vegetation exposes them to erosion and sunlight.... As yet, there is no evidence of laterizing of similar soils in Viet Nam after defoliation, probably because the ground cover is never completely destroyed and grass and weeds reappear. *Time, Feb. 23, 1968, p 46*

[back formation from *laterization* conversion into *laterite* (from Latin *later* brick)]

lat·i·fun·dism (ˌlæt əˈfənˌdiz əm), *n.* the practice or condition of holding land in large estates.

The great landholdings—the latifundia—were broken up at the time, but a new latifundism has arisen. *The New York Times, July 10, 1967, p 28*

[from American Spanish *latifundismo*. See the etymology of LATIFUNDIST.]

lat·i·fun·dist (ˌlæt əˈfən dist), *n.* the owner of a latifundium or large estate.

It is necessary for every urban guerrilla to keep in mind always that he can only maintain his existence if he is disposed to kill the police and those dedicated to repression, and if he is determined to expropriate the wealth of the big capitalists, the latifundists and the imperialists. *Carlos Marighella, "Minimanual of the Urban Guerrilla," quoted in Time, Nov. 2, 1970, p 20*

Over 200 000 peasant families were landless, yet nine million acres lay idle in the grip of latifundists and private corporations. *Walter D. Ryder, "Lessons of Castro's Cuba," New Scientist and Science Journal, Dec. 30, 1971, p 262*

[from American Spanish *latifundista*, from Spanish *latifundio* a latifundium (large landed estate) + *-ista* -ist]

Latin rock. See the first quotation for the meaning.

This quintet, spearheaded by two sharp-voiced girls... from Ipanema could begin a rush to what's been called Latin rock—a striking compound of bossa nova, rock and jazz. *The Sunday Times (London), Jan. 19, 1969, p 58*

One reason may be the group's [Santana Group's] abhorrence of the common journalistic practice of putting labels on things—especially the tag Latin rock, so often and justly used to describe Santana's music. "It would take a gun to make me call it Latin rock," says [Gregg] Rolie. "The only thing revolutionary about us is that we have guitars rather than horns. Otherwise, it's just feeling and timing." *"Music: Latin Rock," Time, Sept. 21, 1970, p 68*

laugh-in, *n.* a situation or event marked by hilarity, often one staged for this purpose.

As part of their demonstration against the Defence Minister, Mr Healey, the other week, students at Cambridge proposed to organise a "laugh-in." The idea, apparently, was that the participants in the demonstration should disperse themselves in various parts of the hall, and then, in the course of Mr Healey's speech, first one and then another would burst into peals of laughter. *Harry Whewell, "Laughter in a Cold Climate," The Manchester Guardian Weekly, March 21, 1968, p 6*

At an airport, Fielding's baggage check-in is a laugh-in. *Time, June 6, 1969, p 56*

[see -IN]

laugh line, 1 a wrinkle at the outer corner of the eye supposedly formed from habitual smiling or laughing.

We sat next to Ralph Brasco, a rangy man with plenty of laugh lines around his eyes, who has been with the Department of Sanitation for ten years. *"The Talk of the town," The New Yorker, Aug. 15, 1970, p 20*

2 a brief quip or joke; a one-liner.

One of the laugh-lines floating around the London headquarters of Amoco (one of the toughest bargainers) is: "Now we know where the Middle East guys learned their trading techniques—from the British." *New Scientist, Aug. 22, 1968, p 366*

laugh track, a recording of audience laughter added to a sound track, especially of a previously filmed television show.

Perhaps symptomatic of the quiet corrosion around "The Jean Arthur Show" is the "laugh track" or "canned laughter" on the show. "That 'laugh track' was the most deplorable thing I ever heard in my life," says Mr. Quine. "It was even laughing on the straight lines!" *The New York Times, Nov. 20, 1966, Sec. 2, p 19*

Any writer worth his laugh-track is eager to contribute to this master of all comedians [Jack Benny], knowing it will get the most skilled delivery. *Goodman Ace, "Top of My Head: Shoulda Said," Saturday Review, Oct. 5, 1968, p 12*

launching pad, a place from which something starts; springboard.

Then came the Kennedys. John burst onto the political scene using vast sums of money, clever exploitation of television, cadres of advance men, personality-projection techniques, and the launching pad of Presidential primaries. *Harvey Wheeler, "The End of the Two Party System," Saturday Review, Nov. 2, 1968, p 20*

Secondly, we expect to be the launching pad for British manufacturers who are coming into the United States market for the first time and wish to do so from a base on the east coast. *The Times (London), July 11, 1966, p IV*

[figurative sense of the term for a rocket- or missile-launching platform]

launch vehicle, a rocket used to propel a spacecraft, artificial satellite, etc., into an orbit or trajectory.

The earliest launch vehicles were derived from the ballistic missiles developed by the United States and Russia after World War II. *"Space Travel: Reaching into Space," The 1970 Compton Yearbook, p 556*

Because of various failures in the launch-vehicle guidance system and in the spacecraft itself, a lunar landing was not accomplished. *H. M. Schurmeier, R. L. Heacock, and A. E. Wolfe, "The Ranger Missions to the Moon," Scientific American, Jan. 1966, p 54*

launch window, the time when astronomical conditions permit the launching of a spacecraft under the most favorable conditions.

...the 20-day period centered around the launch date allowing travel between planets on an orbit requiring the least amount of energy. This is the so-called "launch window" used to hurl space vehicles from earth to the moon, or to Venus or Mars. *Science News, Sept. 3, 1966, p 165*

Opportunities for flights from the earth to the moon occur only once every 28 days, for a period of two or three days. One of these "launch windows" was open last week.... *The New York Times, Oct. 30, 1967, p 5*

After blast-off and ascent through the atmosphere, SATURN will place its third stage, with the APOLLO spacecraft on top, into a "parking orbit" about 100 miles high. The two will circle the earth until they are at the "launch window," the right position at the right time to go for the moon. *John Gellner, "Putting a Yank on the Moon," Saturday Night (Canada), Aug. 1967, p 15*

laundry list, *Chiefly U.S.* a detailed and usually long list.

Four brief paragraphs...describe the President's proposed welfare reforms and revenue-sharing program, as well as a laundry list of social concerns (health, education, housing, transportation, equal voting rights, etc.). *Tom Wicker, "In the Nation: Mr. Nixon and the Environment," The New York Times, Feb. 3, 1970, p 42*

The at-large ballot is a bewildering laundry list of 75 names.... *Time, May 10, 1968, p 22*

[so called from the practice of keeping an itemized list of the items sent to a commercial laundry]

Lau·ra·sia (lɔːˈreiʒə), *n.* the name given to a supercontinent comprising North America, Europe, and Asia which is believed to have existed for millions of years before splitting up during the Cenozoic era (about 60 million years ago). Compare GONDWANA.

The northern rift split Pangaea from east to west along a line slightly to the north of the Equator and created Laurasia, composed of North America and Eurasia. The Laurasian land mass evidently rotated clockwise as a single plate around a pole of rotation that is now in Spain, creating a western "Mediterranean" that ultimately became part of the Gulf of Mexico and the Caribbean Sea. *Robert S. Dietz and John C. Holden, "The Breakup of Pangaea," Scientific American, Oct. 1970, p 36*

[from *Laur*entian (Mountains of North America) + Eur*asia*]

la·ver·bread (ˈlei vərˌbred), *n.* a breadlike food prepared from dried laver (a kind of seaweed) in various British localities, especially in western Britain.

253

The excellent market, where all the world shops, is a paradoxical modern hangar sheltering hundreds of tiny peasant stalls, some selling local delicacies such as laver bread.... *Prys Morgan, The Times (London), April 2, 1970, p V*

In addition to being a holiday resort, metallurgical metropolis of Britain, birthplace of Beau Nash and Dylan Thomas, Swansea is also the centre of the laver-bread industry. *Patrick Ryan, "Round Britain with Gun and Camera: Wales, Wales," Punch, Feb. 15, 1967, p 221*

law and order, a slogan calling for a curb to the increase in crime and violence.

Here, I shall say only that the term "law and order" has become, for many whites, a code word for enforcing separation between the races—or worse, a means of justifying brutal suppression and disregard of civil liberties. That, to my mind, is a perversion of the term. *Lyndon B. Johnson, "Agenda for the Future: a Presidential Perspective," Britannica Book of the Year 1969, p 35*

The current emphasis on law and order distresses me because the phrase appears to mean only the stringent regulation of the disadvantaged and rebellious. *R. Hobart Ellis, Jr., New York, in a Letter to the Editor, The New York Times, March 11, 1970, p 46*

The published motions cover a wider and more immediate political field than usual—from the economy and unemployment to the media, Ulster and law and order. *Daily Telegraph (London), May 24, 1972, p 15*

▶ During the mid-1800's the phrase *Law and Order* was used in the United States to designate various political parties, especially those opposing the extension of the suffrage demanded by a rebellious group called the Dorrites and those insisting on States' rights and the extension of slavery into new territories. Thus historically the term has long been associated with extreme conservatism and opposition to radicals and dissidents.

law-and-order, *adj.* supporting or advocating stringent measures to suppress violence and crime, including rioting and other forms of violent demonstrations.

Burger was best known for his views on the handling of criminal prosecutions, which had often caused him to be classified as a "law and order" judge. *C. Herman Pritchett, "Supreme Court: Warren Earl Burger," The Americana Annual 1970, p 661*

Though the 110-member [Democratic Party] Platform Committee was preparing to draft a stern "law-and-order" plank in hopes of neutralizing a similarly tough G.O.P. [Republican] statement, Attorney General Ramsey Clark warned against allowing the phrase to become a slogan for repression. *Time, Aug. 30, 1968, p 13A*

One of the President's advisers argues that whatever one might say about the drawbacks of the law-and-order campaign of 1970, it took people's minds off the economic issue, which could have been still more damaging for the Republicans. *Elizabeth Drew, "Reports & Comment: Washington: Hard-hat Blues," The Atlantic, May 1971, p 12*

Lazy Dog, *U.S. Military Slang.* a type of bomb that explodes in midair and scatters steel pellets at high speed on the target area.

"... Tomorrow, we'll get three divisions in here, four, we'll get two hundred B-52s, we'll get ground-to-grounds, and whole batteries of Lazy Dogs, we'll get nuclear...."

Alan Coren, "... That Fell on the House that Jack Built," Punch, Feb. 21, 1968, p 258

The Lazy Dog is an advanced antipersonnel weapon introduced last spring. *Harrison E. Salisbury, The New York Times, Jan. 13, 1967, p 8*

lazy-eye blindness, another name for LAZY EYES.

One preventable scourge is amblyopia, or "lazy-eye blindness." This disease results from crossed eyes or muscle imbalance. Double vision sets in, the young brain stops using one eye, and partial blindness results. *Roul Tunley, "America's Unhealthy Children: An Emerging Scandal," Harper's, May 1966, p 43*

lazy eyes, dimness of sight in which no organic defect of the eyes is found, technically called amblyopia. Also called LAZY-EYE BLINDNESS.

The tests also yield useful information concerning children with "lazy eyes" and elderly people suffering from cataract. *Science News, Sept. 3, 1966, p 150*

L-band, *n.* a band of ultrahigh radio frequencies ranging between 390 and 1550 megahertz. Compare S-BAND.

The use of L-band gets round the increasing vhf [very high frequency] congestion in the continental United States and Europe, and will give an order of magnitude improvement in accuracy when the satellites are used for position fixing, as is planned for later in the decade. *Ron Brown, New Scientist and Science Journal, May 13, 1971, p 366*

lbf, abbreviation of *pound force* (a force whose acceleration equals that of gravity on a mass of one pound).

Some 15 Olympus engines have already done 5000 hours of running on the test bench and the type is rated to yield 32 850 lbf thrust with the prospect of successive upratings to an ultimate maximum of 40 000 lbf. *New Scientist, Feb. 27, 1969, p 440*

L.D.C., abbreviation of *less developed country.*

World food production is increasing at 1 per cent yearly but the world population is growing at 2.5 per cent yearly so the greatest danger is looming precisely in the so-called "L.D.C.'s".... *The New York Times, Sept. 24, 1967, Sec. 4, p 4*

There is no doubt that the speedy economic advancement of the less developed countries (L.D.C.s) would benefit the whole world economy.... *The Times (London), Sept. 25, 1967, p xiv*

L-Do·pa ('el'dou pə), *n.* drug that raises the level of dopamine in the brain, found effective in relieving the rigidity, tremors, and other symptoms of Parkinson's disease. Also called LEVODOPA.

The Food and Drug Administration (FDA) now permits more than 200 clinical investigators and hospitals across the country to use L-Dopa in treating patients. *Israel Shenker, "The Remarkable Effects of L-Dopa: Drug Brings Parkinson Victims Back Into Life," Encyclopedia Science Supplement (Grolier) 1970, p 212*

The substance, reported to have resulted in "modest to dramatic" easing of Parkinson symptoms, is an amino acid known as L-Dopa, a short form for L-Dihydroxyphenylalanine. *The New York Times, May 8, 1968, p 49*

L-driver, *n. British.* short for *learner-driver,* a person learning to drive who must be accompanied in the car by a qualified driver and display the two

"L-plates" on the back and on the front of his vehicle.

...the motorways...were built specially to carry fast traffic, and from which pedestrians, cyclists, moped riders and L-drivers are specifically excluded. *Dudley Noble, Chief Executive, Institute of Advanced Motorists, in a Letter to the Editor, Punch, Dec. 6, 1967, p 866*

lead-free, *adj.* another word for NONLEADED.

True or false: lead-free gasoline is the best thing to come down the freeway since the V-8 engine. True, according to the oil companies that recently switched to unleaded or low-lead fuels and are promoting them as an antipollution measure. False, from the viewpoint of the Ethyl Corp., the nation's largest producer of lead additives for gasoline. *Time, Sept. 14, 1970, p 51*

Two British oil companies and the American Gulf yesterday said they were ready to market a lead-free petrol in the United Kingdom. *The Times (London), March 9, 1970, p 1*

leadless, *adj.* another word for NONLEADED.

...oil companies have begun to market leadless gas. *"Review of the Year—Environmental Sciences," Encyclopedia Science Supplement (Grolier) 1970, p 159*

lead·swing·ing ('led,swiŋ iŋ), *n. British Slang.* the practice of shirking work; malingering. The equivalent U.S. term is *goldbricking.*

...the right of low paid workers to choose unemployment on modern scales of benefit rather than a job at inadequate wages....Mr. Crossman...insisted that "lead swinging" among the unemployed was confined to a very small minority and that the real problem was caused by the very low wages in some jobs compared with the scale of social security benefits. *Ian Aitken, "Mr. Crossman Raises Some Problems," The Manchester Guardian Weekly, Sept. 12, 1968, p 9*

...detailed examination of the facts showed that lead-swinging is quite rare and that most of those specifically accused are the innocent victims of dreadful circumstances. *Bernard Hollowood, "Criticism: On the Box," Punch, Nov. 5, 1969, p 760*

[from the British slang (originally nautical) phrase *swing the lead* or its derivative *leadswinger;* in allusion to the laziness of the man who was supposed to be taking soundings with the lead line but contented himself with swinging it idly]

leaflet, *v.i.* to distribute leaflets.

Leafletting on New York's Lower East Side for ten years would not reach the housewife in Escanaba, Mich. but thirty seconds on the six o'clock news would. *Robin Morgan, The New York Times, Dec. 22, 1970, p 33*

They moved out on to the streets leafletting and selling lapel buttons and bumper stickers. *The Sunday Times (London), June 23, 1968, p 10*

[verb use of the noun]

league table, *British.* a tabulated comparison of performance in any field.

It is possible to make a league table of top jobs now and see whether specializations contribute directly to incomes, using the quarterly salary survey tables of the *Cornmarket Careers Register. The Times (London), June 24, 1968, p 26*

At a time when "growthmanship" and "league tables" matter, inorganic chemicals, taken together, have performed badly. *L. F. Haber, "European Chemistry: 1. The Inorganic Scene," New Scientist, May 23, 1968, p 391*

[so called from the tables of performance records of athletic or sports associations]

learning curve, a graphic representation, usually S-shaped, of the progress shown in acquiring adeptness or practical experience in a field.

In order to evaluate properly the cost estimates submitted by the two final bidders, both of which were unreasonably optimistic, the Secretary would have needed a compilation of experience statistics, based largely on so-called learning curves, which was simply not available at that early stage in his administration. *Adam Yarmolinsky, "How the Pentagon Works," The Atlantic, March 1967, p 60*

The airline that will be first with the most 747s, and thus must cope with every one of the bumps in what airmen call a new plane's "learning curve," is Pan American. *Time, Jan. 19, 1970, p 40*

leather, *n.* **hell-bent for leather,** as fast as possible; very fast.

General Tolson said that he had expected initial resistance to be light but that he had told his commanders to advance cautiously. "The worst trap we could get into here would be to go hell-bent for leather, thinking we've got it easy," he said. *The New York Times, April 4, 1968, p 19*

▶ Reference is made to this phrase in Harold Wentworth's *American Dialect Dictionary* (1944) as a variant of *hell for leather,* for which it supplies citations from several sources. The *ADD* gives for *hell-bent for leather* the date 1919 and locates it in western Massachusetts. However, the earliest quotation in our files is from a British source ("Perhaps it is no wonder that so many of us are hell-bent for leather." *The Sunday Times (London), April 12, 1959, p 19*) and we have confirmed its current use among both American and British speakers.

Lea·vis·ite ('li: və,sait), *n.* a follower or supporter of the English literary critic Frank Raymond Leavis, born 1895, noted for his controversial attacks on current literary values.

...in his memoirs, he [a Cambridge ex-professor] makes his historical reference to the notorious nuisance the "Leavisites" were in his time. *F. R. Leavis, Cambridge, England, in a Letter to the Editor, The Times (London), April 28, 1970, p 11*

—*adj.* of Leavis or the Leavisites.

They [Dr. Leavis and his followers] argue that in the era of the breakdown of values, and in the absence of religion, our only connection with the past of the "organic community" is through the English books of the Great Tradition, as chosen by the Leavisite priesthood. *Stephen Spender, "The Age of Overwrite and Underthink," Saturday Review, March 12, 1966, p 21*

lech, *v.i.* to be a lecher; to lust.

The last American musical adapted from a film, *Sweet Charity* from *Cabiria,* proved to be a wretchedly vulgar show...the plot merely an excuse to parade a set of middle-aged married men leching after sexy secretaries half their age. *Jeremy Kingston, "Criticism: At the Theatre," Punch, Oct. 15, 1969, p 639*

—*n.* **1** a lecherous desire; lust.

...once a month he draws his state dole. Otherwise, no purpose, no curriculum beyond some half-hearted physical jerks and a vague lech for the daily cleaner. *Christopher*

Wordsworth, "Word Out of Cuba," Review of the novel "Inconsolable Memories" by Edmundo Desnoes, The Manchester Guardian Weekly, Feb. 22, 1968, p 10

2 a lecher.

One of these was Dr. Fritz Sigismund Fassbender, a florid, heavy-set man in his early fifties — a man with a huge mop of unruly hair, and a soul seething with unruly passion for tender young females. In simple language Fritz was a lech. *Marvin H. Albert, quoted by Wendy Michener from his book, "What's New, Pussycat," Maclean's, March 19, 1966, p 66*

— *adj.* lecherous.

The question can be taken or left for what it is as long as Friedman sticks to the mimicry of detective-story dialogue, journalism clichés, police-blotter prose, and the series of burlesque lech-skits that give *The Dick* its basic shape. *R. Z. Sheppard, "Books," Review of "The Dick" by Bruce Jay Friedman, Time, Sept. 7, 1970, p 62*

[back formation from *lecher* and *lechery*]

leching, *adj.* given to lechery; dissolute.

He [Whittaker Chambers] felt guilty for his painful birth, guilty for his "hatred" of his parents, and guilty for his love of his brother Richard, a wild, leching lad who committed suicide at 22. *"Books," Review of "Friendship and Fratricide: An Analysis of Whittaker Chambers & Alger Hiss" by Meyer A. Zeligs, Time, Feb. 10, 1967, p 66*

leftfield, *n. U.S.* a position outside the center of action; the sidelines.

Ambitious sons of famous fathers are hardly unique in politics. With personality continuing to outweigh party loyalty as a political asset, an increasing number of candidates are emerging from leftfield to give voters surprising options. *Time, March 9, 1970, p 19*

...the anxious look of the Yugoslav guide suggested that we were on the verge of another diplomatic incident. In this kind of country [Albania] inadvertent ironies keep coming out of left field. To utter is to criticize. *Peter Ustinov, "The Atlantic Report: Albania," The Atlantic, Nov. 1966, p 18*

[figurative sense of the baseball term (usually spelled *left field*); from the fact that the left field is far off from the home base]

leftist, *n. U.S.* a left-handed person; a lefty.

A recording of Ravel's Piano Concerto for the Left Hand and posters of such famous leftists as Rock Hudson, Tiny Tim, and David are also for sale at this unusual shop, whose owner, a young southpaw named June Gittleson, never lets the word "right" cross her lips. *"On and Off the Avenue: Gifts for Men," The New Yorker, Dec. 19, 1970, p 101*

▶ Both in America and Britain the standard meaning of *leftist* (a term attested since the 1920's) is that of an adherent of the left (liberal or radical) wing of a party, movement, etc. The term *lefty* is used in the United States only in the sense of a left-handed person; in Great Britain *lefty* is chiefly used as a colloquial variant of *leftist*, usually in the specific sense of a socialist or communist.

LEM (lem), *n.* acronym for *lunar excursion module* (the earlier name of the LUNAR MODULE). Compare LM.

The simulation technique, using a team of digital and analog computers, gives scientists accurate information about the LEM's future performance on or near the

moon's surface. *Science News Letter, July 16, 1966, p 38*

Sitting on its four stilted and saucer-footed legs, the all-white LEM resembles a weird, buglike denizen from outer space. *William R. Shelton, "Midway to the Moon," The World Book Science Annual 1965, p 52*

leptonic, *adj.* of, relating to, or belonging to the class of elementary particles called leptons. See the quotation for details.

...the number of known leptons has remained constant at four for the last decade, while the number of known strongly interacting particles, or hadrons, has been increasing rapidly. The basic leptonic quartet consists of the muon, the electron, and the neutrinos associated with these two particles. Many experimental searches have attempted to add to this list, but without success. *"New Weakly Interacting Particle Found at CERN [European Council for Nuclear Research]," Science Journal, Dec. 1970, p 12*

Lesch-Ny·han syndrome ('leʃ'naɪ hən), a genetic disorder of male children. See the quotations for details.

...the Lesch-Nyhan syndrome [is] a severe neurological disease of males characterized by mental retardation, involuntary writhing motions called choreoathetosis and compulsive self-mutilation of the lips and fingertips by biting. *Theodore Friedmann, "Prenatal Diagnosis of Genetic Disease," Scientific American, Nov. 1971, p 35*

The Lesch-Nyhan syndrome was first described in 1964. *The Times (London), Aug. 19, 1970, p 10*

The lack of the IAP [inosinic acid pyrophosphorylase] gene in humans causes the Lesch-Nyhan syndrome, a distressing disease in children resulting in early death. *New Scientist and Science Journal, March 11, 1971, p 532*

Skin cells from patients with a genetic defect known as the Lesch-Nyhan syndrome lack an enzyme essential for incorporation of purine bases into new nucleic acids. *Science News, Oct. 11, 1969, p 327*

let-out, *n. British.* a way out; means of escape; loophole. *Also used attributively.*

But it has also said it would like a "representative organization" and the association leaders believe this is the let-out that would enable them to get recognition on a national basis. *The Times (London), Feb. 2, 1968, p 21*

...I am wondering how to deal with political canvassers. For example, if they trick you into saying you are going to vote for them, is it legally binding or is there a let-out clause? *Joy Melville and Angela Milne, "For Women: Answer Your Election Problems," Punch, March 23, 1966, p 438*

[from the verb phrase *let out* to release]

letterform, *n.* **1** the design of a letter in printing type.

By enlarging what is known as the body of each letterform and fractionally but effectively reducing the ascenders and descenders of the lower-case letter-forms, he triumphed in that most difficult task open to any artist or craftsman. *The Sunday Times (London), Oct. 15, 1967, p 8*

2 a sheet of stationery for writing letters.

A sturdy lined letterform for children will surely induce the most recalcitrant to get down to the "thank-you" letters which they have to be bullied into writing after birthdays and parties. *The Times (London), Sept. 11, 1970, p 8*

letter stock. See the first quotation for the meaning.

Letter stock is unregistered stock, which a company

dares not offer on the open market for fear of driving down the price of the company's publicly-traded stock. *The Sunday Times (London), Feb. 9, 1969, p 32*

Mates may yet scrape by, but his Omega holdings have been double trouble. Not only were they backed by a company under investigation, but they were "letter stock." Such stock is sold privately by a company, usually at a price well below the going market value, when it wants to avoid time-consuming registration with the SEC and costly underwriting by investment bankers. *Time, Jan. 3, 1969, p 62*

lev·al·lor·phan (ˌlev əˈlɔr fən), *n.* See the quotation for the meaning.

Morphine is a powerful analgesic; codeine a mild analgesic; thebaine is a central nervous stimulant and levallorphan is an antidote to morphine poisoning. They all have very similar structures; the differences in their pharmacological effects can be explained by differences in the ability to form hydrogen bonds. *Illustration legend, "The Hydrogen Bond," New Scientist, March 21, 1968, p 630*

[contraction of the full chemical name *lev*-N-*allyl*-3-hydroxy*morphinan* bitartrate]

level-peg, *v.i. British.* to maintain a balanced condition or position, as between rivals.

Conversions have been level-pegging with repurchases, while the trust is about 40 per cent. liquid to meet further possible encashments. *The Sunday Times (London), May 26, 1968, p 26*

England and Wales have met 74 times, and it is as nearly level-pegging between them as makes no odds, with 32 victories to England, 31 to Wales, and 11 drawn. *U. A. Titley (Rugby Correspondent), "England Three-quarters Look Stronger," The Times (London), Feb. 28, 1970, p 10*

► This term occurs invariably in the form *level-pegging* and appears to be used largely among journalists and radio and television commentators.

leverage, *v.i., v.t. U.S. Finance.* to speculate or cause to speculate on borrowed money in the expectation that the profits will exceed the interest rate.

. . . as the prospectus warns: ". . . short-term trading, investing in put and call options written by others, the purchase and sale of warrants, selling short and leveraging through borrowing are all speculative techniques which carry with them greater risk of loss and which will result in greater turnover of the fund's portfolio. . . ." *The New York Times, Feb. 20, 1968, p 64*

I unloaded her on a doctor. Even better than an ordinary doctor—a surgeon. The world's most expert person on every subject. Especially investments. He gave her the benefit of his experience, leveraging her up to the ears in convertible bonds, which he got her to hock at a bank, then come back with the money, and buy *more* convertible bonds on margin (putting up only half of the purchase price). *Brutus, "Confessions of a Stockbroker," The Atlantic, July 1971, p 49*

[verb use of *leverage, n.,* the property which a security has of showing a relatively large increase in profits in relation to a small change in its price]

le·vo·do·pa (ˌle vouˈdou pə), *n.* another name for L-DOPA.

Antiparkinsonism drugs. Levodopa (L-dopa, levodihydroxyphenylalanine) has been found effective in relieving the distressing rigidity, tremors, and mental depression of Parkinson's disease. *Arthur Tye, "Economic Review:*

Drugs," The 1970 Collier's Encyclopedia Year Book, p 214

lexis, *n.* vocabulary; lexicon.

Its [the Oxford English Dictionary's] twelve volumes provided the most thorough and lively account of a language ever attempted, a definite canon of the English lexis. *The Sunday Times (London), March 24, 1968, p 10*

[from Greek *léxis* word, speech]

LGP, abbreviation of *liquefied petroleum gas.*

Liquefied petroleum gas (LGP), which contains somewhat heavier fractions than natural gas, is more convenient as it can be liquefied at normal temperatures. *Glen Lawes and Michael Kenward, "Stepping on the Gas to By-Pass Exhaust Pollution," New Scientist, March 12, 1970, p 508*

liaison, *v.i.* to make a liaison.

. . . typically, a half-day of lifeseeing, a half-day of conventional sightseeing or shopping, then half-the-night (depending on one's constitution) liaisoning with the natives at nightclubs. *Jon Ruddy, "Maclean's Reports: Now You Can See the REAL Scandinavia," Maclean's, April 1968, p 4*

[verb use of the noun]

Lib or **lib,** *adj.* of or relating to WOMEN'S LIB.

The Lib Movement was rich in documentation of the conditioning processes. Writer after writer rummaged in her past, hunted out childhood details with a bearing on the making of modern femininity. *Benjamin DeMott, "In and Out of Women's Lib," The Atlantic, March 1970, p 116*

There are now 24 girls in the lib lobby, but the deal is still the same as was worked out at that famous dormitory feast in Houston. They won't play unless the tournament guarantees minimum prize money. . . . *Vincent Hanna, "The Liberation of Women's Tennis," The Sunday Times (London), June 27, 1971, p 20*

liberate, *v.t.* to free from social biases or restrictions, now especially those based on sexual differences.

In nearly half a dozen cities, women swept past headwaiters to "liberate" all-male bars and restaurants. *Time, Sept. 7, 1970, p 12*

Li·ber·man·ism (ˈli bər mənˌiz əm), *n.* the economic ideas and theories of the Russian economist Yevsei Grigorevich Liberman, born 1897, especially his advocacy of less bureaucratic planning and control of marketing and his stress on profit sharing for workers and management.

The revisions, grouped together in Russia under the term Libermanism, permit everything from market pricing of some consumer goods to incentive bonuses in factory piecework and decentralized planning—all untouchable in Marxist dogma. *Time, May 10, 1968, p 38*

The ludicrous assumption of Harrington that "the best of the young" are against bureaucracy, corporations, profit, Libermanism (Russian version of profit), and the whole apparatus of power is without much substance. *George S. Odiorne, Ann Arbor, Mich., "Comments on Michael Harrington's 'Great Society,'" in a Letter to the Editor, Harper's, Feb. 1967, p 84*

Lib-Labbery, *n. British.* alliance between the Liberals and Labour supporters.

First, the absence of an unequivocal declaration by Liberal leaders that in the event of a close finish there would be no Lib-Labbery in the new parliament and second, Mr. Thorpe's echo of the Labour gibe at Mr.

Heath's reference to a possible devaluation of the pound if Labour came to power. *J. S. MacArthur, Highbridge, England, in a Letter to the Editor, The Manchester Guardian Weekly, June 27, 1970, p 2*

[from *Lib-Lab* (the name given in the early 1900's to a member of the British Liberal Party who favored the policies of the Labour Party, and more recently used to describe anything involving both Liberals and Labour supporters) + *-ery* actions or activity, here also having a connotation of shady dealings, as in *skulduggery*]

Lib·ri·um ('lib ri: əm), *n.* Popularly spelled **librium.** the trade name of a drug, used especially as a tranquilizer.

I called the psychiatrist, but his answering service told me he was away on a month's vacation. I dined forlornly on hot milk and Librium and was asleep before ten ... and awake before three. *Roger Angell, "Ainmosni," The New Yorker, May 31, 1969, p 34*

In the first cafe he went into someone sold him six librium pills. "It was my sort of cafe, my sort of people — of course they had gear." *Victoria Brittain, "Amphetamines — the Teenagers' Basic Drug," The Times (London), Sept. 22, 1970, p 10*

li·chen·o·met·ric (ˌlɑi kə nə'met rik), *adj.* of, relating to, or based on lichenometry.

... a growing number of carbon-14 and lichenometric dates for moraines from southern Alaska and the western U.S. leaves open the possibility that one or more episodes of glacier expansion, as yet unrecognized in most areas, may have occurred during this interval. *George H. Denton and Stephen C. Porter, "Neoglaciation," Scientific American, June 1970, p 109*

li·chen·om·e·try (ˌlɑi kə'nɑm ə tri:), *n.* the measurement of the diameter of lichens to establish their age or the age of the area in which they grow.

Although not as precise or reliable as other methods of dating neoglacial moraines, lichenometry has proved to be particularly useful in certain nonforested arctic and alpine regions and, under ideal circumstances, is applicable over intervals as great as 4,000 years. *George H. Denton and Stephen C. Porter, "Neoglaciation," Scientific American, June 1970, p 109*

lid, *n.* *U.S. Slang.* a small package containing from 22 grams to one ounce of marijuana.

... the high price of "commercial" marijuana ($10 to $15 for a "lid" from which some 40 cigarettes can be rolled). *Time, Sept. 8, 1967, p 18*

Day or night, it is crowded with hippies, feeding the hunger that follows a smoke of marijuana, coming down off an LSD trip, or looking for a lid of "pot" or a tab of "acid." *The New York Times, Jan. 8, 1968, p 1*

li·dar ('lɑiˌdɑr), *n.* a radarlike device that uses light beams to detect objects or changes invisible to the eye.

Experiments carried out at Williamsburg, Virginia, now show that lidar is a really effective tool in detecting these potentially dangerous regions of CAT [clear air turbulence]. *New Scientist, May 9, 1968, p 300*

Essentially, lidar is an instrument analogous to radar in that it is composed of a transmitter which emits energy to space and a receiver which detects that portion backscattered by obstacles in its path. Recent applications in the lower atmosphere include cloud height measurements,

haze layer and visibility determinations, dimensions of plumes and clouds of particulates, water vapor profiles, accurate distance measurements, clear-air turbulence, and other aeronautical problems. *Robert M. Brown, "Atmosphere," McGraw-Hill Yearbook of Science and Technology 1971, p 109*

[blend of *li*ght and ra*dar*]

Lie algebra (li:), an algebraic system that reduces independent quantities to groupings whose relationships are then subject to algebraic operation. It was developed by Marius Sophus Lie, 1842-1899, a Norwegian mathematician, and is used especially in studying behavior of fundamental atomic structure.

The study of "Lie groups" and "Lie algebras" is receiving the attention of the best mathematical minds. *Edna E. Kramer, The Nature and Growth of Modern Mathematics, 1970, p 489*

lie-down, *n.* another name for LIE-IN.

The final report now being prepared by the Planning Council may disclose a recognition of aspects of the equal rights movement that have impeded this "enlistment" thus far.... These impeding aspects are: (1) The toleration by leaders of the movement of violence in the pursuit of their goals, including sit-ins, lie-downs and civil disobedience of existing law, that has infringed the principle of equal rights for all members of the American society. *Arthur Krock, The New York Times, June 5, 1966, Sec. 4, p 13*

Lie group (li:), a mathematical group with a continuous operation in which it is possible to label the group elements by a finite number of coordinates.

The quark came into physics as a result of physicists' attempts to find some order among the dozens of subatomic particles that had been discovered. They found that if they arranged the known particles in an orderly fashion according to certain characteristics, they came up with certain symmetrical patterns in which each particle had its assigned place, rather like pieces on a chessboard....

The mathematical name of these patterns is Lie groups or unitary symmetry groups. They have been used to predict the existence of new particles.... *H. N. Schwartz, "Letter from Geneva: Quark Hunt Still Fruitless," Science News, May 31, 1969, p 538*

lie-in, *n.* a lying down of a group of people in a public place to disrupt traffic, etc., as a form of protest or demonstration. Also called LIE-DOWN.

Last week pollution protesters staged a lie-in at government offices in Tokyo. *"Kicking the Growth Cult," Time, Dec. 27, 1971, p 40*

[see -IN]

lifer, *n.* *U.S. Military Slang.* a career officer or soldier.

This means "them" — the men over 30, career officers or senior NCOs, whom they call "lifers." Because the American Army has been so inflated by draftees and young college graduate officers, who are civilians only in the service for the minimum length of time, lifers are in the minority. *Ian Wright, "Pot and the GI," The Manchester Guardian Weekly, June 20, 1970, p 6*

The old ones, the lifers, know everyone in the Army, from four-star generals on down, and an extraordinary bond grows between them. *Ward Just, "Soldiers," The Atlantic, Oct. 1970, p 82* [extended from the original meaning of *lifer* a person sentenced to prison for life (attested since the early 1800's)]

life science, any of the sciences dealing with living organisms, including biology, biochemistry, medicine, psychology, and the like.

More general objections are that proper instruction in the life sciences requires the study of living things and that the high school level is by no means too early a starting point for such studies. *"Science and the Citizen: Antivivisection for High Schools?" Scientific American, Oct. 1964, p 58*

life scientist, a scientist who specializes in one or more of the life sciences.

Many groups tried to build machines for scanning real images or photographs with a view to automating tedious laboratory processes such as cell counting.... Unfortunately the life scientists, who first drew attention to the possibilities, were unable to make very wide use of the limited systems available. *Colin Fisher, "Analysing Images by Computer," New Scientist and Science Journal, Sept. 23, 1971, p 676*

life-support system, any system designed to support the physiological processes essential to life.

All submersibles require life-support systems, and those on the small oceanographic types take into consideration the following services for atmospheric control and monitoring: breathing mixture supply system; carbon dioxide removal system; hydrogen, carbon monoxide, and toxin removal systems; air purification and filtering system; atmospheric monitoring system; and emergency breathing supply system. *E. S. Arentzen, "Oceanographic Submersibles: Life-support Systems," McGraw-Hill Yearbook of Science and Technology 1970, pp 280-281*

... the annual production of between 150 and 200 billion tons of dry organic matter ... includes both food for man and the energy that runs the life-support systems of the biosphere, namely the earth's major ecosystems: the forests, grasslands, oceans, marshes, estuaries, lakes, rivers, tundras and deserts. *George M. Woodwell, "The Energy Cycle of the Biosphere," Scientific American, Sept. 1970, p 64*

Each astronaut has a life-support system to supply him with breathing and suit-pressurizing oxygen and water for the liquid-cooled garment. For added safety, the secondary system has been improved for the Apollo 14 mission. *"Buddy Life-Support Systems," Science News, Jan. 2, 1971, p 2*

lifting body, a gliderlike wingless spacecraft with sufficient aerodynamic lift and maneuverability to reenter the earth's atmosphere in the manner of a conventional airplane.

The HL-10 manned lifting body, the leading candidate to become the much-talked-about space shuttle plane of the middle or late 1970's, has reached its greatest height and speed while investigating the stability of its controls in the thin upper atmosphere. *Science News, Aug. 16, 1969, p 124*

lig·ase ('lig,eis), *n.* an enzyme with joining properties, important in the synthesis and repair of deoxyribonucleic acid (DNA).

... all newly made DNA is synthesized in a discontinuous manner. These discontinuous segments are then joined by an enzyme, ligase, to produce a continuous strand. *James C. Copeland, "Molecular Biology: Molecular Genetics," 1970 Britannica Yearbook of Science and the Future, 1969, p 299*

They [Howard Temin and his colleagues at Wisconsin] found, in addition to the reverse transcriptase, three other enzymes—two nucleases and one DNA ligase. One of the nucleases, an endonuclease, can clip the host's DNA chain in two; this allows the exonuclease to nibble away at the two ends. The DNA ligase could fit the virus-produced DNA into the gap left and join it up with the loose ends. *New Scientist and Science Journal, April 29, 1971, p 247*

[from Latin *ligāre* to bind + English *-ase* enzyme]

light-day, *n.* the equivalent of a day in a light-year. See also the quotation under LIGHT-MONTH.

If a quasar's radiation varies with a period of, say, four days, then the radius of the quasar can be no greater than four light-days. *Dietrick E. Thomsen, "Radio Astronomy: East-West Baseline," Science News, Nov. 8, 1969, p 437*

light-month, *n.* the equivalent of a month in a light-year. See the quotation for details.

We pointed out in a previous footnote that a light-year is the distance traveled by light in a year. The units light-month, light-week and light-day have been derived in the same way. A light-month is about 500,000,000,000 miles; a light-week, about 115,000,000,000 miles; a light-day, about 16,000,000,000 miles. *"Quasi-Stellar Objects (Quasars)," Encyclopedia Science Supplement (Grolier) 1968, p 62*

light pen, a small photoelectric cell in the form of a pen, used to put new information into a computer by sensing light from the screen of a cathode-ray tube and transmitting the light impulses to the computer.

The engineer in charge can then correct the diagram with a single light-pen, and the machine will re-translate the diagram into numbers. *Jean-Jacques Servan-Schreiber, The Times (London), July 18, 1968, p 24*

Light pen is another device that can put drawings into a computer. The pen contains a photocell that responds to spots of light displayed by a computer on a cathode ray tube. *Picture legend, "Computer Inputs and Outputs," Scientific American, Sept. 1966, p 90*

The most common graphic input is the light pen. This does not emit light but is a hand held light detector, effectively just a photocell with a limited field of view. When it detects light from the screen it sends a signal to the computer. *R. Elliot Green, "Interactive Computer Graphics," Science Journal, Oct. 1970, p 71*

light show, a display of colored lights in kaleidoscopic patterns usually accompanied by music.

Arthur, 154 E. 54th St.... Tiny tables, a minimal light show, and rampant recorded rock that shifts to the rampant live sounds of the Bubble Gum Machine. *"Goings on About Town: Discothèques and Such," The New Yorker, July 6, 1968, p 4*

light water, ordinary water, H_2O, as distinguished from *heavy water* (deuterium oxide, D_2O).

Most nuclear power plant reactors operate on enriched uranium—which has a higher proportion of fissionable U-235 atoms in comparison to nonfissionable U-238. This makes it possible to use easily available graphite or light water as the moderator to slow down neutrons to the point where they can cause U-235 to split. *"Light on Heavy Water," Science News, July 25, 1970, p 58*

light-water, *adj.* of, using, or relating to light water.

While American technology of light-water reactors becomes progressively adopted in western Europe—Britain remaining for the time being faithful to the technology that she herself developed—future generations of reactors are being investigated. *Nicholas Vichney, "What Future for Advanced Reactors in Europe?" New Scientist, Dec. 10, 1970, p 434*

light-week, *n.* the equivalent of a week in a light-year. See also the quotation under LIGHT-MONTH.

So there is now evidence for the existence of a continuous sequence of objects which generate energy by means as yet unknown.... These objects appear to produce up to 100 times the luminosity of a normal galaxy in a volume which does not exceed light-weeks in diameter. *J. B. Oke and W. L. W. Sargent, "Seyfert Galaxies," Science Journal, Feb. 1970, p 61*

Light Whiskey, an American whiskey of a lighter body and fewer natural flavor components than traditional whiskeys.

Ten months from now, on July 1, 1972, with the grudging consent of the U.S. Government, a new whiskey will be born. It will be the first new whiskey type in 40 years, taking its place with Bourbon, Scotch, Canadian, Irish and "Blended." Its name: Light Whiskey.... What then does "light" mean? It means simply that the new whiskey will have a light body and a light taste. Indeed, the major reason for its development is that—in contrast with a full-bodied Bourbon or a decently smoky Scotch—it should please our present-day penchant for "lightness," light-bodied and light-flavored whiskies like the delicate Canadians and the popular pale Scotches. *Robert J. Misch, "Light Whiskey—Will it be Your Cup of Tea?" House Beautiful, Sept. 1971, p 114*

like, *conj. U.S. Slang.* Used without a definite meaning chiefly to understate or deemphasize the word or phrase that follows or precedes it.

"Afterward, a girl came up to me and said, 'You look kinda interested in this; did you know there are civil rights for women?' And I thought like wow, this is for me." *Kate Millett, quoted in Time, Aug. 31, 1970, p 19*

"Man, when I'm high (snapping his fingers)... like, I'm inside myself, I'm outside myself (snap, snap)." *John Kifner, The New York Times, Jan. 11, 1968, p 18*

"... you're one of those who will never like cop out on the true scene and split for the Establishment bread." *Cartoon legend, The New Yorker, Oct. 25, 1969, p 61*

li·ku·ta (li'ku: tə), *n.; pl.* **ma·ku·ta** (mə'ku: tə). one hundredth of a zaire, the unit of money in the Zaire Republic (the former Democratic Republic of the Congo).

Currency: The monetary unit [of The Democratic Republic of the Congo] is the Zaire (Z.) divided into 100 makuta (K.) each worth two American cents. "Makuta" is the plural form of the word "likuta." One Z. equals two U.S. dollars. *The New York Times, June 27, 1971, Sec. 11, p 5*

L.I.M., abbreviation of LINEAR-INDUCTION MOTOR.

The TACRV [tracked air cushion research vehicle] propelled by the L.I.M. will ride on thin cushions of air on a fixed U-shaped guideway which contains a central vertical aluminium reaction rail. *Kenneth Owen, "Cushioned Ride for U.S.," The Times (London), May 29, 1970, p 29*

lim·o ('lim ou), *n.* short for *limousine.*

One night ... a black limousine rolled up to the front portico [White House] at the appointed hour.... Out of the limo stepped Spiro Agnew. *Time, March 30, 1970, p 20*

Weyman hopped out, shook hands with Siegel, and introduced the young lady as his wife. "You ride in the limo, dear," he said to her breezily, helping her out of the Daimler and into the back seat of the Pierce-Arrow while she nodded and smiled acquiescence. *St. Clair McKelway, "Annals of Imposture: The Big Little Man from Brooklyn," The New Yorker, Nov. 23, 1968, p 96*

limousine liberal, *U.S.* a wealthy liberal.

Canada is most fortunate to have a Premier who is willing to tell the bleeding hearts and limousine liberals what he thinks of them and who will also take whatever strong measures are necessary to rid his country of Communist murderers. *Michel Porges, New York, in a Letter to the Editor, The New York Times, Oct. 26, 1970, p 36*

The Lindsay supporters that Mario Procacino used to sneer at as "limousine liberals" during the mayoral campaign would have probably been more accurately described as "Raleigh Three-Speed liberals." *Calvin Trillin, "U.S. Journal: Manhattan," The New Yorker, Oct. 9, 1971, p 124*

lin·ac ('lin,æk), *n.* acronym for *linear accelerator* (particle accelerator constructed in a straight line).

... construction work has begun on a $5 million storage ring called the Stanford Positron-Electron Asymmetric Ring (SPEAR). This new device, oval-shaped with an average diameter of about 65m, will be located at the end of the two-mile linac. *"Superconductors Make the High-Energy Scene," New Scientist, Dec. 3, 1970, p 365*

► See the note under HILAC.

li·nar ('lai,nɑr), *n.* See the quotation for the meaning.

Radio astronomy, having coined the words quasar and pulsar, has now added linars to the growing list of strange objects inhabiting the visually dark areas of space. Linars—based on the words line and star—are point sources which emit with extraordinary energy, at wavelengths characteristic of the spectral line of particular chemical compounds. *Anthony Tucker, "A New Word for the Astronomers," The Manchester Guardian Weekly, Aug. 15, 1970, p 15*

lin·co·my·cin (,lin kə'mai sən), *n.* an antibiotic derived from a kind of streptomyces (soil microbe), found effective against certain bacteria that are resistant to penicillin.

Although not a broad-spectrum antibiotic, Lincomycin is effective against the most important gram-positive organisms, including resistant staphylococcus. It is effective by mouth and by injection, which is essentially painless. *Arthur Tye, "Drug Industry: Antibiotics," 1966 Collier's Encyclopedia Year Book, p 195*

For some 18 months now, Upjohn Ltd have been advertising the antibiotic lincomycin by a series of impressive colour advertisements. *"Probe: Drugs and Ads," New Scientist, May 8, 1969, p 277*

[from *linco(lnensis)*, name of the variety of streptomyces from which the drug is derived + *-mycin*, as in *streptomycin, actinomycin*, and other names of antibiotics]

linear-induction motor, an electric motor that produces thrust directly without torque by the movement of the magnetic field which creates a linear impelling force rather than a rotating force. *Abbreviation:* L.I.M. Also called LINEAR MOTOR.

A linear induction motor is like a regular rotary motor that has been sliced open and laid out flat. Both rotary and linear motors produce force by the interaction of a magnetic field and a current induced by the field. The movement of the rotor inside the stator of a rotary motor produces torque (a twisting force) which then must be transformed to thrust, usually through the form of gears connected to a wheel. The interaction of the magnetic field in a linear-induction motor, however, produces thrust directly. *Lowell K. Bridwell, "Transportation: Ground Transportation," 1970 Britannica Yearbook of Science and the Future, 1969, p 390*

Vehicles with linear induction motors float above the rail or rails, and may achieve speeds of 300 miles per hour or even more. In Britain, Professor Eric Laithwaite's prototype vehicle is expected to run in Cambridgeshire in 1970. *Dennis Gabor, Innovations: Scientific, Technological, and Social, 1970, p 29*

linear motor, short for LINEAR-INDUCTION MOTOR.

Laithwaite pioneered the renewed development of linear motors, which are like normal induction motors, cut across the circumference and rolled out flat, with the rotor laid down as a metal rail, and the stator clamped beneath the moving field which impels it along. . . . *Glen Lawes, "Hovertrain Comes on Apace," New Scientist, July 9, 1970, p 69*

Their major contribution to date is the linear motor, which has streamlined the design of three products and will be spread right across the range. *Keith Richardson, The Sunday Times (London), April 18, 1971, p 49*

lingua franca, any standard language that is widely used as a general medium of communication.

This is exactly the same thing as happens in certain countries where register switching may involve different languages: the mother-tongue may be used in the home, but a *lingua franca* such as English, French, or Russian in the schools, the lawcourts, and government offices. *M. A. K. Halliday, The Listener, Jan. 13, 1966, p 53*

Back when Erasmus and Grotius wrote in Latin, they had readers throughout the Continent. With the disappearance of that lingua franca, writers in the emerging major languages lost little; but Holland's writers were left with a parochial vernacular. *Robert J. Clements, Saturday Review, July 2, 1966, p 23*

[extended sense of the term for a hybrid language used as a common trading jargon]

lin·gui·ne (liŋ'gwi: ni:), *n.* long, thin, flat noodles.

The kitchen produces first-rate linguine with clam sauce, spaghetti with marinara sauce, squid with tomato sauce . . . . *Craig Claiborne, The New York Times, Jan. 26, 1968, p 22*

"Great linguine with white clam sauce," he said when we had been seated at a table for four. . . . *Gilbert Rogin, "You Say What I Feel," The New Yorker, July 12, 1969, p 29*

[from Italian *linguine*, plural of *linguina*, diminutive form of *lingua* tongue]

linkman, *n. British.* **1** (in soccer, rugby, and field hockey) a player who acts as a link between the center forwards and backs.

Using Brindley as a deep-lying linkman, Staffordshire set up the openings, only for Goh and Flood to turn them back time after time. *Brian Lewis, "Staffordshire More Than One Goal Better," The Times (London), Nov. 9, 1970, p 12*

2 a moderator or coordinator, especially of a radio or television discussion program.

Tommy Steel will appear as linkman and commentator. *Kenneth Pearson, The Sunday Times (London), May 5, 1968, p 51*

3 an intermediary; a go-between.

The new setup at Broadcasting House [appointment of Charles Curran as Director-General of BBC] looks a little as though the Director-General is in risk of being downgraded to the role of link man between the Governors (more specifically the chairman) and the staff. *"Comment: Change at the Top," The Manchester Guardian Weekly, Aug. 15, 1968, p 8*

linksland, *n.* See the first quotation for the meaning.

A linksland—a links, for short—is a stretch of sandy soil deposited by the ocean and whipped into dunes and fancifully shaped sand hills by the winds off the sea. *Herbert Warren Wind, "Two Opens to Remember," The New Yorker, Aug. 1, 1970, p 60*

Carnoustie, however, like so many seaside links . . . is nothing much to the eye, being on a comparatively flat expanse of reclaimed linksland. *The Sunday Times (London), July 7, 1968, p 24*

Link trainer, a trade name for a set of audio-visual aids for training people to drive a motor vehicle.

In the Link trainer, the pupil finds that it is like being in the cinema, with a wide screen. The film shows a driver's view of real traffic. The pupils respond to the conditions shown in the film, and to instructions. . . . *Glen Lawes and Michael Kenward, "Computer As A Back-Seat Driver," New Scientist, June 11, 1970, p 527*

▶ The original *Link trainer* was a flight simulator for giving flying instruction on the ground.

Lip·pes loop ('lip is), a loop-shaped plastic intrauterine device, named after its inventor, the American physician Jack Lippes. Also called THE LOOP.

The Lippes loop, for example, has shown infection rates of only 0.4 and 0.7 per 100 woman-years, and the few pelvic infections that have occurred cleared up quickly. *Science News, Feb. 1, 1969, p 117*

lip print, the impression made by the lines of the lips on a surface.

. . . Kazuo Suzuki and Yasuo Tsuchihashi suggest "the novel possibility that the lip-groove pattern (lip print) is dissimilar in different individuals", and may be used as a means of identification in the same sort of way as fingerprints. *"A Warning to Criminals—Wipe Away Those Lip Prints!" New Scientist, Sept. 3, 1970, p 455*

literarism, *n.* emphasis on literary or humanistic values.

Dr. [Frank R.] Leavis's lecture at Bristol on " 'Literarism' versus 'Scientism' ", printed in The Times Literary Supplement this week, is a heartening sign. *Editorial in The Times (London), April 25, 1970, p 9*

lithogenous, *adj.* produced by or originating from stone or rock.

Excluding extra-terrestrial components, which are not quantitatively important, the material of which deep-sea sediments are composed is either derived from the continents (lithogenous), or is produced within the marine environment itself by organisms (biogenous) or by inorganic reactions (hydrogenous). *Roy Chester and Henry Elderfield, "Dust Over the Oceans," New Scientist, Aug. 27, 1970, p 433*

[from *litho-* stone + *-genous* produced by]

lithoprint, *n.* a print reproduced by lithography.

His enchanting drawings (transformed into big, clear-coloured lithoprints in limited editions of 100 each) are in a gallery run by his mother in the purlieus of his architect father's office. *The Sunday Times (London), April 6, 1969, p 30*

—*v.t.* to print by lithography.

The several hundred local natural history publications, often duplicated or lithoprinted, offer an easy outlet for young artists. *Jon Tinker, "Wildlife Painting Booms," New Scientist and Science Journal, Jan. 28, 1971, p 206*

lithospheric, *adj.* of or belonging to the solid rock part of Earth.

According to the theory of plate tectonics, lithospheric slabs spread apart at mid-ocean ridges and thrust under other slabs at ocean trenches. *Illustration legend, "Earth: The Dynamic Earth: Plate Tectonics," Science News Yearbook 1970, p 154*

[from *lithosphere* the part of the Earth's crust consisting chiefly of solid rock + -*ic* (adj. suffix)]

litmusless, *adj.* neutral; neither positive nor negative.

It's a disarming neutrality in the Swedes themselves that lends to one's own rather litmusless attitude to the country. *Ian Breach, "The Swedish Way of Motoring," The Manchester Guardian Weekly, Sept. 5, 1970, p 16*

[from *litmus (paper)* + -*less*. Since litmus paper is used to indicate whether a solution is acid or alkaline, something litmusless would be neutral.]

litmus test, a decisive test.

. . . Israel wants the planes now, while it can still get them. At the same time, the sale, which has the support of sizable groups in both the House and Senate, is regarded in Israel as a kind of litmus test of U.S. intentions. *"Israel and Its Enemies," Time, June 22, 1970, p 28*

But the litmus-test of a liberal regime must surely be the freedom of the individual from arbitrary arrest and punishment, and in this respect France has become not more liberal but less. *Edward Mortimer, "Risk of Arrest Grows for French Militants," The Times (London), May 4, 1970, p 4*

[so called from the use of *litmus* paper to test a solution for acidity or alkalinity. An older term with the same meaning is *acid test.*]

litter bag, *U.S.* a plastic or paper bag, often sealable, in which litter can be put.

Continental Can, whose products—often used, can often be spotted in America's lush countryside, is this month launching "a massive anti-litter program" throughout its plants and district sales offices. They've handed out over 100,000 litter bags as well as a lot of print and promotional material. *The New York Times, June 6, 1968, p 78*

litterbin, *n.* *British.* a trash basket, especially on a street, in a park, or other public place.

The trip, worth over £1,500, will involve long hours on the sands of California, Vancouver, New South Wales and New Zealand, gazing at overflowing litterbins. *The Times (London), Feb. 7, 1970, p 3*

litterbug, *v.i.* *U.S.* to litter a public place with wastepaper, refuse, etc.

. . . Arlo Guthrie launches into 18 minutes and 20 seconds of wildly seriocomic semitrue narrative-plus-song about

how he helped a friend named Alice clean out her place in Stockbridge, Mass., dumped the refuse over a cliff, was arrested for litterbugging and fined $50. . . . *"Music: Recordings: Woody's Boy," Time, Jan. 15, 1968, p 45*

[verb use of *litterbug, n.*]

Little Neddy, *British.* one of a number of industry-wide committees under the National Economic Development Council (popularly called *Neddy*); any one of the Economic Development Committees.

The Little Neddy for the hotel and catering industry has just published the result of a survey it commissioned among foreign travel agents. *Lombard Lane, "In the City: Wooing the Tourist," Punch, May 24, 1967, p 766*

If ever a Writers' Little Neddy, for literary "economic development," gets set up, Anthony Burgess will surely be leading it. His productivity, which we have all learned by now is not the same thing as mere production, is a lesson to us all. *Norman Shrapnel, "Books of the Week: Productivity, Burgess and Others," Review of "Enderby Outside" by Anthony Burgess, The Manchester Guardian Weekly, June 6, 1968, p 11*

The likelihood of increased demand in private housing and public building other than housing has caused the little Neddies for building and civil engineering to step up their output forecasts for this year and next. *The Times (London), Sept. 25, 1968, p 24*

live-in, *adj.* **1 a** living in the place where one is employed. Compare LIVE-OUT.

. . . the Hetheringtons have no live-in maid. A woman comes three days a week to clean. Alec uses the maid's room as a study. *Anthony Bailey, "Profiles: Through the Great City," The New Yorker, July 29, 1967, p 37*

b requiring one's living in the place where one is employed.

The nine-member faculty-student committee proposed that Miss LeClair be denied several campus privileges because she had lied to the college when she said she had an off-campus live-in job, and violated the housing regulations. *The New York Times, April 19, 1968, p 53*

c living in another's quarters.

Steve McQueen's live-in girl friend in *Bullitt* will probably need some fancy footwork to escape agony in her new film . . . *Time, Feb. 7, 1969, p 33*

2 relating to or involving living in a particular place as an inhabitant, resident, etc. Also, LIVING-IN.

They are taking part in a community organizing project called Neestow (from a Cree word meaning "brother-in-law"). . . . In fact the Neestow project . . . is patterned on the "live-in" principles used by civil rights workers in the southern United States. *Ken Mitchell, "Maclean's Reports: The Trouble with Helping the Metis," Maclean's, June 18, 1966, p 1*

. . . Dr. Jastrow went on from a discussion of the moon to a discussion of the live-in prospects on Mars (quite promising; colonies likely). . . . *"The Talk of the Town: Travel Plans," The New Yorker, Jan. 10, 1970, p 17*

—*n.* See the quotation and the entry -IN.

Twenty-two social workers who have been staging a protest live-in at the office of the City Department of Labor were arrested last night after seven days of sleeping, washing clothes and cooking in the halls of the building. *The New York Times, Oct. 18, 1966, p 47*

live-out, *adj.* not living in the place where one is employed. Compare LIVE-IN (def. 1 a).

He [Arthur Ochs Sulzberger] has a live-out cook, but he likes to bend over the stove himself, and sometimes prepares family meals. *Geoffrey T. Hellman, "Profiles: Viewer from the 14th Floor," The New Yorker, Jan. 18, 1969, p 41*

living-in, *adj.* another word for LIVE-IN (def. 2).

Apart from caring for its five living-in patients and the 15 to 20 who visit it from home, Dr Kelleher believes that the unit still has a vital role to play. *The Sunday Times (London), June 11, 1967, p 2*

LM (lem; so pronounced from the former spelling LEM, for *lunar excursion module*), abbreviation of LUNAR MODULE.

After more than two hours on lunar ground, Armstrong and Aldrin returned to the LM, lifted off the moon, and reentered lunar orbit. *Picture legend, "Space Exploration: Moon Mission," 1970 Collier's Encyclopedia Year Book, p 492*

The LM was perched at an angle of 8° in a small valley of the rolling Fra Mauro highlands, on the eastern rim of the Ocean of Storms, just south of the lunar equator. *Steven Moll, "The Flight of Apollo 14," Encyclopedia Science Supplement (Grolier) 1971, p 340*

LNG, abbreviation of *liquefied natural gas.*

Technology is currently being developed for the use of liquefied natural gas, LNG, as a motor fuel. *The New York Times, Jan. 13, 1967, p 22*

As a fuel for internal combustion engines, L.N.G. has a high resistance to pre-ignition and detonation. *"The World of Technology: Liquid Natural Gas—The Fuel of the Future?" The Times (London), Feb. 27, 1970, p 27*

loadmaster, *n.* a crew member of a heavy transport aircraft who is responsible for the cargo.

The aircraft [Douglas C-47s] carry a crew of eight—pilot, co-pilot, navigator, flight mechanic, load master (who also drops the flares), two gun loaders, and a Vietnamese Air Force liaison officer. *"Notes on the News: Airborne Firepower Against the Vietcong," New Scientist, Aug. 17, 1967, p 328*

load-shedding, *n.* the cutting off of electric power in a particular area to prevent a large-scale blackout.

The small black-out the other day, however, was not a failure of the system but a prudent control of it: the man could not let the load gauge go much higher than seven million kilowatts or we should have had November 1965 all over again. He was performing a routine known as load-shedding—in this case, deliberately cutting off power in the less densely populated areas in and around New York. Load-shedding is one of the last and most drastic steps which the power companies advise in an emergency. *Alistair Cooke, "Brown-Out," The Listener, Oct. 15, 1970, p 503*

lobby-fodder, *n.* a politician regarded as one primarily serving the needs of lobbyists.

It is the first portent in this Parliament that Conservative backbenchers will no more be lobby-fodder on some issues than 30 or 40 Labour backbenchers were in the last Parliament.... *David Wood, "Birth of a Backbench Campaign," The Times (London), Nov. 2, 1970, p 9*

lobotomized, *adj.* dulled or sluggish, suggesting the aftereffects of a lobotomy.

It was the life and times of a tightly clustered and rather faceless group, which ended with a robotlike square dance. Mr. Sheppard's lobotomized shuffle was a joy to watch. *The New York Times, Feb. 5, 1968, p 29*

... Acting President [Peter Regan of The State University of New York at Buffalo] was explaining his reasons for calling the police onto the campus, a speech greeted for the most part with a lobotomized silence. *Warren G. Bennis, "Searching For The 'Perfect' University President," The Atlantic, April 1971, p 50*

local group, a group of relatively close galactic systems, especially the one including the Milky Way galaxy, the two Magellanic Clouds, and the Andromeda Nebula.

Our own galaxy is a member of the "local group," an association of about 20 galaxies, only one of which, the Andromeda galaxy, has a mass comparable to that of ours. *Martin J. Rees and Joseph Silk, "The Origin of Galaxies," Scientific American, June 1970, p 28*

The Local Group containing our galaxy lies at the edge of this supercluster, which is slowly rotating. *"Structure of Universe Obscures Age," The Times (London), March 9, 1970, p 13*

lock-away, *n. British.* a long-term security.

At this level and in view of the prospects the shares should be regarded as a widows' and orphans' lock-away rather than a performance stock. *The Times (London), April 9, 1970, p 28*

locked, *adj.* **locked in,** not open or susceptible to changes; committed.

... most of the senators who were finally to vote for Carswell [as a Supreme Court justice] had already announced their intention, and they were, as the Washington saying goes, "locked in." *Richard Harris, "Decision," The New Yorker, Dec. 12, 1970, p 58*

"The Extra campaign had to be aggressive because people are so locked in to coupons," says John Pearce of C D P. *The Sunday Times (London), March 3, 1968, p 51*

lock-in, *n. U.S.* a protest demonstration in which a group locks itself within a building, office, etc.

In their maneuvering over the bill, the Democrats staged a lock-in in the House, and the Republicans held a sit-out in the Senate. *Time, Oct. 18, 1968, p 27*

They have organized petitions, demonstrations, sit-ins, lock-ins and progressively more violent means to protest causes as diverse as the coming of an official of Dow Chemical Co. (proscribed because it makes napalm for the war) and a proposed increase in Boston subway fares.... *The New York Times Magazine, March 3, 1968, p 16*

lock-on, *n.* **1** the automatic tracking of an object by radar.

On previous missions the on-board landing radars that control the descent rate of the LMs had locked onto the moon's terrain when the craft were about 30,000 ft. above the surface. As *Antares* swooped below that altitude, its radar remained inactive. "C'mon, radar," Mitchell implored. "Get the lock-on." No response. Up from Houston came instructions to flick a circuit breaker off and on. Then, at 23,500 ft., the radar suddenly came alive. *Time, Feb. 15, 1971, p 8*

When an air-to-air training missile "sees" its target, a new microminiaturized signal amplifier developed by Hughes tells the pilot that lock-on has been achieved. *Advertisement by Hughes International, Hughes Aircraft Company, Scientific American, May 1967, p 83*

2 the forming of an airtight connection for underwater passage between submarines, rescue and exploration craft, etc.

And, as it [rescue craft] will need to contend with the underwater currents playing around the submarine, it will need extremely sensitive means of controlling its position just before lock-on if damage is to be averted. *Peter Williams, "The Quest for Scorpion," New Scientist, June 6, 1968, p 509*

Back at the surface, a lock-on device enables divers to transfer to a larger chamber on board, releasing the sub to return to work with a fresh diving team. *The Sunday Times (London), April 23, 1967, p 8*

[from the verb phrase *lock on*]

lock-out, *n.* an underwater compartment in which the air pressure is sufficient to prevent water from entering through the compartment's open port.

Some of the modifications which are being considered, are as follows: a lock-out which will allow entry and exit of divers at work sites down to 1000 feet. . . . *Peter Williams, "Adrift Within the Gulf Stream," New Scientist, Nov. 17, 1966, p 341*

lockstep, *n.* a rigid pattern or arrangement.

When Manning came to Stanford in 1964, he was determined to break the traditional lockstep of three-year law school curriculums. *"Stanford's Dean Steps Down," Time, Oct. 5, 1970, p 69*

So let us in these next five days start a long march together, not in lockstep, but on different roads leading to the same goal. *"President Nixon in Pekin," Daily Telegraph (London), Feb. 22, 1972, p 28*

—*adj.* rigid; unbending.

Mrs. Handy's lockstep methods (copy the great novelists, read the "Masters of the Far East," stay away from girls) produced a handful of published novels. . . . *"Books: General," The New Yorker, Oct. 30, 1971, p 155*

[from *lock step* a mode of marching in close order]

locust years, years of deprivation and hardship.

Yet before these locust years of Labour, we had the Conservative years of rising prosperity. *"More Homes Promised: Value-added Tax Defended," The Times (London), May 27, 1970, p 8*

Those were terrible years—'the locust years,' Churchill has called them. *Hans Koningsberger, "Poland's New 'Far West'," Harper's, July 1965, p 90*

► The phrase used by Winston Churchill (see the second quotation) was in reference to the depression years preceding World War II. Its origin is the biblical verse (Joel 2:25) "And I will restore to you the years that the locust hath eaten. . . ."

lo-fi ('lou,fai), *adj.* of a standard or inferior quality of sound reproduction; not hi-fi.

. . . most of the hi-fi sound that Cole created for next week's Andy Williams special will be wasted when it is fed through the nation's strictly lo-fi TV sets. *Time, April 26, 1968, p 38*

—*n.* lo-fi sound, reproduction, or equipment.

Finally, despite Mr. Kolodin's warning of the "lo-fi," we would "urge" the purchase of this set [Allan Berg's *Lulu*] as a significant item in Toscanini's recorded legacy, and as a definite contribution to any collection in which these selections are of interest. *Brian L. Wallen, Champaign, Ill., in a Letter to the Recordings Editor, Saturday Review, July 29, 1967, p 53*

loft, *v.t.* to launch into space.

The more I hear about the McGeorge Bundy Foundation's plan for lofting communications satellites into space in order to extend the scope of Educational TV broadcasting, the more I wish it (and him) well. . . . *Michael Arlen, "The Air," The New Yorker, Jan. 7, 1967, p 80*

LOFT (lɔ:ft), *n.* acronym for *low frequency radio telescope.*

LOFT would be designed for observation at frequencies between 0.5 and 10 megahertz, a range that is reflected by the ionosphere and cannot be observed from the ground. *Science News, Sept. 5, 1970, p 202*

log, *v.t.* **log in,** to register, especially with a computer as an authorized operator.

The user gives his password (which, to preserve privacy, is not printed) and the machine logs him in and reports the number of seconds used by the central processor in the exchange. *Illustration legend, "Time-Sharing on Computers," Scientific American, Sept. 1966, p 132*

logic, *n.* the logical operations performed by a computer by means of electronic circuitry, such as comparing, selecting, and sorting. *Often used attributively.*

In the 1970s we shall see the introduction of LSI [large-scale integration] for electronic logic where the volume of that logic in production justifies the high tooling costs. *W. J. Talbot and R. Naylor, "Computer Hardware for the 1970s," Science Journal, Oct. 1970, p 47*

The computer logic is so fast that it has to loaf at several intervals while the input and output devices—the peripherals—are printing information. *"The Talk of the Town," The New Yorker, April 11, 1970, p 34*

A content-addressable memory of the same capacity would require 2000 identical logic circuits in its response store, one for each word. *Ron Brown, "A Ground Computer to Direct Air Traffic," New Scientist, Dec. 10, 1970, p 448*

In the past 20 years, the cost of a logic element (for example, a flip-flop) for use in a central processor has gone down from about £3 to 2d—a drop of 36,000 per cent. *Earl Masterson, "The New Peripherals," Science Journal, Oct. 1970, p 76*

lognormal, *adj.* having a normal or symmetrical logarithmic distribution.

Distributions that are not normal come in for genuine attention (although not enough time is spent on the lognormal case), and tests of significance and regression methods are given brief but quite usable explanations. *Kent V. Flannery, "Books," Review of "Principles of Statistics" by M. G. Bulmer, Scientific American, Aug. 1967, p 126*

[from *log*arithm + *normal*]

loid (lɔid), *Slang.* —*n.* a strip of celluloid used by a burglar to push back the bolt of a spring lock. *Also used attributively.*

A "loid" expert wiggles a celluloid or piece of Venetian blind strip in a door crack to open a spring lock. *John Bowers, "Big City Thieves," Harper's, Feb. 1967, p 51*

—*v.t.* to unlock (a door) with a loid.

It takes an experienced thief to "loid" (open with a strip of celluloid) a door if it is fitted with a spring lock that is not double-locked. *The Times (London), Nov. 4, 1968, p 8*

[from cellu*loid*]

lol·i·gin·id (,lɑl ə'dʒin id), *adj.* of or belonging to a family of long-bodied cylindrical squids.

In addition, LaRoe's work has proved that tropical loliginid squid grow much faster than previously believed. His squid reached maturity within five months after hatching, contrary to the belief that it would take three years. "*Squid Reared in Aquarium,*" *Science Journal, Feb. 1970, p 14*

[from Latin *lōlīgō, lōlīginis* cuttlefish + English *-id* (adj. suffix)]

lollipop, *n. British.* a pole bearing a large disk, used as a sign to stop the traffic by a person assigned to help children cross the streets at schooltime. *Often used attributively.*

Mr. Blackmore, holding the lollipop that stops most traffic, said: "That offside brake seems to be pulling." *Peter Dunn, The Sunday Times (London), Jan. 25, 1970, p 13*

Top-hatted they stream from the school, one boy picks up the lollipop sign — which is hidden in a bush — and traffic is brought to a halt. *The Sunday Times (London), March 9, 1969, p 5*

lon·geur (ɔːŋˈgər), *n.* a variant spelling of *longueur,* meaning a long or tedious passage in a book, play, etc. The original spelling was taken directly from French, and was apparently first used by Lord Byron in his epic poem *Don Juan* (1821). However, evidence showing the use of the simplified English spelling has been accumulating since the late 1950's, as the following sampling of quotations indicates:

In our contemporary life we had the battle of Passchendaele and the Russian Revolution, but taking things by and large, and month by month, one was aware of extensive stretches in which nothing historically worth while seemed to be going on — longeurs which the Director of History (with a capital H) would not have tolerated in his scenario. *Claud Cockburn, The Guardian (London), Nov. 2, 1959, p 7*

All of the Irish critics welcomed the play as a fine piece of historical drama. . . . Sean White wrote The Irish Press that "it has great strength despite its central longeurs." *The New York Times, May 24, 1963, p 16*

The last part of the book (and the first written) is much less interesting and has many longeurs. . . . *Bernard Bergonzi, "Bouillabaisse," Review of "A True Story" by Stephen Hudson, The New York Review of Books, March 17, 1966, p 22*

The piece [*Grande pièce symphonique* by César Franck] is loose in construction and, as so often with Franck, one feels that its *longeurs* could do with a little pruning. *Stanley Webb, The Gramophone, April 1968, p 540*

However, despite the show's contradictions and longeurs, it does at least attempt something audacious and original and for that I respect it. *Michael Billington, "Media Satire," The Times (London), May 29, 1970, p 7*

longhair, *n. Slang.* a person wearing long hair, especially a male hippie.

As some of the young earnestly and tearfully sought to move Congress with their message against the war, a longhair pranced naked before the Capitol. *Time, May 17, 1971, p 15*

. . . rampaging hardhats . . . have been hunting down longhairs in the canyons of downtown Manhattan. *A. H. Raskin, "Reuther's Legacy for Social Stability," The New York Times, May 18, 1970, p 28*

► The earlier and still current meanings of *longhair* are (1) a devotee of the arts, especially classical

music, and (2) an intellectual or scholar. The term in any of its senses is usually used somewhat disparagingly.

longstop, *n. British.* a person or thing that serves to check, hold back, or prevent something undesirable.

In fact, session after session major Bills are sent to the Lords so late that the peers cannot be expected to act as efficient longstops. *The Times (London), March 30, 1970, p 6*

[from the *long stop* in cricket, who stops the balls that pass the wicketkeeper]

► During the Anglo-American campaign in northern Tunisia in the winter and spring of 1942-1943 there was a commanding hill known as Longstop near Medjez-el-Bab. French writers coming across this name invariably misunderstood it. See the following quotations referring to this name:

With the fall of Longstop the outer defence perimeter ought to fall easily despite really magnificent resistance by the enemy. *Philip Jordan, Jordan's Diary, 1943, p 238*

Longstop (really Djebel el Ahmera) was known as Longstop Hill to the Americans, since for them it was presumably a meaningless name. Thus 'Longstop Hill, the objective of this initial phase of the attack, is not quite seven miles to the northeast of Medjez el Bab'. *George F. Howe, Northwest Africa: Seizing the Initiative in the West, 1957, p 339*

lon·guette (lɔːŋˈget), *n.* another name for MIDI.

. . . strangers busied themselves with . . . the bulging dossier of *Women's Wear Daily* evidence of the arrival of its "longuette." *Kennedy Fraser, The New Yorker, Oct. 10, 1970, p 167*

Along Belgrade's Terazije, maxicoats and Longuettes, velvet knickers and leather gaucho pants abound, as do swinging discothèques, modish *butiks* and the most daring skin magazines. *Time, March 29, 1971, p 29*

[from French *longuette,* adj., somewhat long; longish]

looking-glass, *adj.* completely inverted or reversed; topsy-turvy.

T.U.C. [Trades Union Congress] leaders will find themselves in a looking glass world when a delegation visits West Germany in 10 days' time, a world where most things are the opposite way round from what they are used to. *The Times (London), Oct. 18, 1968, p 30*

How long do we think the looking-glass politics and Marie Antoinette economics that Faisal practises can serve in Saudi Arabia? The cracks in the façade are still tiny but they are clearly to be seen. *Harold Jackson, "Faisal Through the Looking-glass," The Manchester Guardian Weekly, May 11, 1967, p 5*

[in allusion to Lewis Carroll's *Through the Looking Glass.* Compare ALICE-IN-WONDERLAND.]

loop, *n.* **the loop,** another name for LIPPES LOOP.

The loop is unsuitable for girls who have not been pregnant. *The Sunday Times (London), March 30, 1969, p 10*

Three years ago, family-planning experts here thought the intrauterine device, the loop, would be the answer to a population increasing at the rate of more than a million a month. *The New York Times, Aug. 16, 1968, p 8*

loosey-goosey, *adj. U.S. Slang.* uncoordinated because of excessively loose or supple movement of the body.

He is long off the tee, and he uses an unorthodox, cross-handed style for putts because "I'm too loosey-goosey doing it the regular way." *"Sport: Golf," Time, June 27, 1969.*

[from the rhyming slang phrase *loose as a goose*]

Lorentz force, a force acting on an electrically charged particle moving through a magnetic field.

Negative mass—inertial and gravitational—need not, however, predicate the abandonment of either principle provided we allow the Lorentz force on a particle to depend on the sign of its mass as well as that of its charge. *J. W. Gardner, Whetstone near Leicester, England, in a Letter to the Editor, New Scientist, Sept. 4, 1969, p 487*

Lorentz force, named for the Dutch physicist H. A. Lorentz, tends to make a charged particle entering a magnetic field travel at right angles to both the direction of its original motion and the lines of force. *B. J. O'Brien, "Radiation Belts," Scientific American, May 1963, p 88*

[named after the Dutch physicist Henrik Antoon Lorentz, 1853-1928]

lossmaker, *n. British.* a business or industry that shows consistent losses or deficits.

What happens when two companies, both lossmakers, merge into one? The answer, as often as not, is one big lossmaker. *Derek Malcolm, "Finance: The Lion and the Fox," The Manchester Guardian Weekly, Jan. 23, 1971, p 22*

lossmaking, *adj.* showing consistent losses or deficits.

He started by picking up a 40% stake in the lossmaking Carson's chocolate business in March 1964. *Richard Milner, "The Rise of Mr. Goldsmith," The Sunday Times (London), Aug. 15, 1971, p 41*

lotus position, a sitting position with the legs folded and the arms resting on the knees, used in yoga.

His thing, once he discovered the lotus position can work up an appetite, included four scrambled eggs, ham, the half chicken, bread and butter, and a quart of milk. *John Ciardi, "Manner of Speaking," Saturday Review, Oct. 24, 1970, p 10*

[so called in allusion to the lotus leaf which, though it rests on water, does not become wet, and thus symbolizes detachment]

love beads, colored beads worn about the neck as an ornament and symbol of brotherly love.

[Charles] Reich, who "does a good deal of smiling" and "continues to smile even when his book is being attacked," who "had left off his love beads, which are usually strung around his neck wherever he goes".... *Thomas Meehan, quoted by L. E. Sissman, "Innocent Bystander: I-Less in Gaza: The Greening of Charles A. Reich," The Atlantic, June 1971, p 30*

. . . a group of bright, radical interns . . . sported the abundant hair, bell bottom trousers, love beads, and other symbols of the disaffected young. . . . *Harry Schwartz, "Medicine: Lincoln Hospital," The New York Times, Nov. 29, 1970, Sec. 4, p 8*

love-crossed, *adj.* ill-fated in love.

But there is a final scene in which the hopelessly love-crossed Elaisa taunts her beloved Viscardo into stabbing her to death, and blesses him and Bianca with her dying breath. *Winthrop Sargeant, "Musical Events," Review of "Il Giuramento," The New Yorker, May 23, 1970, p 76*

[apparently formed by alteration of the phrase *star-crossed love,* in allusion to Shakespeare's famous line in Romeo and Juliet: "A pair of star-crossed lovers take their life."]

love-in, *n.* a gathering of hippies, flower children, etc., for the purpose of celebrating or expressing love.

The electronic band made the floor jump, and everybody was happy, sniffing the incense, smoking pot. It was a real love-in. *"Modern Living: Hippies, Within the Tribe," Time, Aug. 25, 1967, p 46*

Only once in a while did he have time to remember that there was a crowd in the jails of New York with blacks and Puerto Ricans overcrowded in their cells, and ghettos simmering on the American stove, a world of junkies, hippies, freaks, and freaks who made open love at love-ins, be-ins, concerts, happenings, and on the stage of tiny theaters with invited guests. *Norman Mailer, "Prisoner of Sex," Harper's, March 1971, p 44*

One of them [the prospective rebels] managed, all the same, to puncture descriptions of the Parliamentary Party meeting the same day as a "love-in." It was, he muttered, not so much a love-in as a lot of people in a tight spot huddling together for warmth. *The Manchester Guardian Weekly, Dec. 5, 1968, p 4*

[see -IN]

lovestruck, *adj.* affected strongly with love.

But the production keeps it [Ugo Benelli's performance in *Giovedi Grasso*] in the perspective of a coherent ensemble where all characterizations are balanced, even to the scatty, lovestruck housemaid (Janet Hughes) and the dimwitted reluctant elderly seductress (Johanna Peters in best form). *William Mann, "Miners and Minors at Wexford," The Times (London), Oct. 27, 1970, p 11*

[patterned after *moonstruck, thunderstruck,* etc.]

low camp, (used as both a noun and adjective phrase) unconscious or unsophisticated use of the artistically banal or mediocre. Compare HIGH CAMP.

In his novel *A World in the Evening* Christopher Isherwood gave the first literary definition. He divided camp into two schools, 'high' and 'low'. Low camp he defined very accurately as a female impersonator 'imitating Marlene [Dietrich] in a seedy nightclub', but by inventing high camp he liberated the word from its purely homosexual connexions.... *George Melly, Revolt Into Style, 1970, p 177*

► See the note under CAMP.

low profile, 1 a deliberately low-keyed or understated attitude or position; a restrained, inconspicuous stance. Also called LOW SILHOUETTE. Compare HIGH PROFILE.

...the "low profile" our policymakers have sought to maintain had been elevated considerably even before the President's speech on Cambodia by our shipment of arms to Phnom Penh and by our troops' increasing involvement in operations around the Cambodian border. *Robert Shaplen, "Letter From Indo-China," The New Yorker, May 9, 1970, p 130*

Ultimately, a far more vexatious issue than any of Japan's economic problems is the nation's future role in Asia and the world. Japan today simply stands too tall and too rich to maintain a low profile.... *"Toward the Japanese Century," Time, March 2, 1970, p 37*

An Ivy League degree or a "low profile" is not in itself going to ensure the bearer of success in dealing with an adamant board or angry students. *Warren G. Bennis, "Searching For The 'Perfect' University President," The Atlantic, April 1971, p 50*

2 a person who shows or cultivates a low profile.

We now have a government of "low profiles," gray men who represent no identifiable place, no region, no program. *Peter Schrag, "The Decline of the WASP," Harper's, April 1970, p 87*

low-rise, *adj.* (of a building) having few stories and no elevator. Compare HIGH-RISE.

Another example of this [resistance to technical innovation] has occurred in low-rise industrialized building. Hitherto the architect has been completely responsible for the design of the housing he is concerned with.... No longer is the local architect the designer of the building. His function has been to an extent usurped by the architects employed by the manufacturer. *Eric Shankleman, "The Wampanoag Effect," New Scientist, Feb. 22, 1968, p 428*

In a layout of predominantly "low-rise" (not tall) new buildings there would be a larger element of private housing than had been usual in new towns. *The Times (London), June 24, 1967, p 3*

low silhouette, another term for LOW PROFILE (def. 1).

The Soviet military men, as well as the civilians, generally try to maintain an extremely low silhouette. *"Moscow-on-the-Nile," Time, June 22, 1970, p 33*

LRL, abbreviation of *Lunar Receiving Laboratory,* a sealed, germ-free building where astronauts and lunar samples are quarantined for a given period after returning from the moon.

The LRL, first conceived some five years ago to protect both the samples from earthly contamination and the earth from possible lunar germs, is a fiendishly difficult place in which to work. *Science News, Aug. 2, 1969, p 95*

Some rocks in the moonscapes are circled in red — the rocks that the geologists have found in the L.R.L. *Henry S. F. Cooper, Jr., "Letter From The Space Center," The New Yorker, April 17, 1971, p 127*

LRV, abbreviation of *lunar roving vehicle.* See also LUNAR ROVER.

Certainly the lunar Rover was a high-cost vehicle, but it was a pilot-research vehicle. The LRV made possible one of the most prolific scientific explorations ever attempted. *Ronald F. Smith, Winnipeg, Manitoba, in a Letter to the Editor, Science News, Sept. 18, 1971, p 184*

LSI, 1 abbreviation of LARGE-SCALE INTEGRATION. Compare MSI.

LSI...involves building up very complex electronic networks on tiny chips. A major step beyond current solid-state technology, it would permit packaging the entire circuit for a high-performance radio in a space one-thousandth the size of today's typical transistor. *Irwin Stambler, "1968: The Year in Review: Aerospace," 1969 Collier's Encyclopedia Year Book, p 80*

2 a unit or array of integrated circuits.

...the central processor for a high-capacity computer could be built from perhaps 100 LSI chips, making such a computer readily portable. *F. G. Heath, "Large-Scale*

Integration in Electronics," Scientific American, Feb. 1970, p 29

ludd·ite ('ləd,ait), *n.* one who is strongly opposed to increased mechanization or automation in any field.

...join our small group [*Medical Consumer Group*] and help the campaign for medical quality control as a measure for preventing medical accidents. These unfortunate human errors are not inevitable. They can be prevented by improved systems and organization. But first it is necessary to overcome the professional and official luddites. *W. A. Marshall, in a Letter to the Editor, New Scientist, Sept. 10, 1970, p 549*

In American estimates, however, port capacity can be greatly increased by quick installation of modern equipment — if the Indian Government is really determined to override the Luddite resistance of the wharf labour. *The Times (London), Dec. 29, 1965, p 5*

[from the proper name *Luddite*, applied in the early 1800's to any of a group of English workers who went about destroying manufacturing machinery for fear that the use of the machines would put them out of work; ultimately from Ned *Ludd*, a Leicestershire "village idiot" who in the 1790's broke some stocking frames]

ludd·it·ish ('ləd,ait iʃ), *adj.* characteristic of a luddite; showing Ludditism.

Not many years ago it was considered regressive and ludditish even to suggest the need for control of technology. *Wilbur H. Ferry, "Must We Rewrite the Constitution to Control Technology?" Saturday Review, March 2, 1968, p 53*

Ludd·it·ism ('ləd ə,tiz əm) or **Ludd·ism** ('ləd iz əm), *n.* strong opposition to increased mechanization or automation in any field.

In an uprising against ignorance and psychopathology Ludditism has no place.... *Alex Comfort, "The Shift in Awareness," The Manchester Guardian Weekly, June 19, 1971, p 20*

There is the Dataf low project, aimed at increasing their productivity: "Though systems men are just as susceptible to Luddism as anyone else," McQuaker comments. *The Sunday Times (London), April 16, 1967, p 24*

[originally used in the sense of "the beliefs and practices of the 19th-century Luddites"]

lu·dic ('lu: dik), *adj.* of or relating to play; playful.

I open one of our weightiest quarterlies, and confining myself to the particular literary essay I open at, I encounter — along with many of the words just listed — *rebarbarize, ephebic,...authentification, anamnesis, pseudocausality, eld, ludic, logoi,...* and *liberative. Louis Kronenberger, "American Lingo," The Atlantic, Sept. 1970, p 109*

Despite the time-worn example of kittens chasing blown leaves as if they were mice, it remains to be proved that "ludic behaviour" (play) is directly related to superiority in the adult animal. *John Hillaby, "Animals That Play," New Scientist, Nov. 25, 1965, p 566*

[from Latin *lūdus* game, play + English *-ic*]

luminal art, a form of art that uses the arrangement or projection of colored electric lights to create images, moving patterns, flashing designs, etc. Also called LUMINIST ART.

Along with everything else, art has gone electric.... The new luminal art has suddenly emerged as both international and popular. A record 42,000 visitors showed up when Kansas City's Nelson Gallery staged a month-long "Sound Light Silence" show last November. *"Art: Techniques," Time, April 28, 1967, p 36*

Kinetic art deals with movement, with which a great deal of contemporary work—including most luminal art—is concerned, directly or indirectly. *Benjamin de Brie Taylor, "Art: Kinetic and Luminal Art," 1968 Collier's Encyclopedia Year Book, p 129*

luminist art, another name for LUMINAL ART.

Although interest in kinetic and luminist art remained high in 1969, there was a reaction against the technologically elaborate and sensation-rich work of recent years. Many artists turned to projects designed to give subtle aesthetic experiences devoid of sophisticated engineering or aggressive electronics. *Victor H. Miesel, "Art," The Americana Annual 1970, p 99*

lunabase, *adj.* relating to or designating the low, flat surfaces of the moon. Compare LUNARITE.

The lunabase valleys have parted the mountains, and the overlay of ash, clearly visible on the foothills, is absent from them. The valleys are younger than the mountains. *V. Axel Firsoff, "Water Within and Upon the Moon," New Scientist, March 7, 1968, p 530*

lunanaut, *n.* another name for LUNARNAUT.

A member of the White House space council gives firm assurance that "neither side" had, until recent accidents, killed an astronaut or cosmonaut (but why, at the present stage, not lunanaut?). *The Times (London), Oct. 5, 1967, p 8*

[from Latin *lūna* moon + English astro*naut*]

lunarite, *adj.* relating to or designating the upland surfaces of the moon. Compare LUNABASE.

The least four of the largest craters in the bright (lunarite) mountain flows are conical or "dimple" craters, which suggests collapse following withdrawal of lava. *Ian Ridpath, "Are the Moon's Craters Volcanic?" New Scientist, Feb. 2, 1967, p 263*

lunar module, a lightweight manned spacecraft carried by a larger spacecraft and detached while in lunar orbit so that it may land on the surface of the moon. *Abbreviation:* LM Compare COMMAND MODULE, SERVICE MODULE.

The lunar module is the first of its kind, a new generation of spacecraft too weak to lift itself from the earth, too vulnerable to fly through the atmosphere without burning up. So specialized is the strange vehicle that it even is designed in two sections—one to land on the moon and the other to take off again. *Jonathan Eberhart, "Space Engineering: Moonward by Jungle Gym," Science News, March 1, 1969, p 218*

Tucked in the nose of the third stage of the 363ft Saturn-V rocket for the first time will be the lunar module, which will provide the vital link for the astronauts between the moon's surface and the command spacecraft. Standing 23 ft high, weighing 16 tons, the LM looks at first glance like some vast aluminum daddy-long-legs. *Adam Raphael, "The Riskiest Space Flight Yet," The Manchester Guardian Weekly, Feb. 20, 1969, p 7*

lunarnaut, *n.* an astronaut who travels to the moon; a lunar astronaut. Also called LUNANAUT.

...deprivation of nasal satisfaction may prove irksome and nerve-ragging to future long-stay lunarnauts and the provision of an interesting aromatic background may be as necessary to their well-being as the maintenance of an artificial atmosphere. *"Probe: And the Last Word...On Smells," New Scientist, Aug. 14, 1969, p 316*

[from *lunar* + astro*naut*]

lunar rover or **lunar roving vehicle,** a vehicle for exploratory travel on the lunar surface. Also called MOON CAR, MOON CRAWLER, MOON ROVER. Compare LUNOKHOD.

Scott and Irwin will take three field trips (one a day) in the lunar rover to numerous craters, the mountain and the rille. *Everly Driscoll, "Mission Into The Moon's Past," Science News, July 10, 1971, p 30*

The Lunar Roving Vehicle looks like a two-tone buckboard; the chassis is silvery, and the four plastic fenders (which will prevent the astronauts from being sprayed with dust) are brown. *Henry S. F. Cooper, Jr., "Letter From the Space Center," The New Yorker, July 17, 1971, p 42*

Apollo 15 was first of three missions to transport heavier payloads than the earlier flights and to carry an electric-powered vehicle resembling a golf cart, called Lunar Rover. With the added mobility afforded by the Rover, crews of these missions can make extensive trips away from the lunar module—up to a theoretical maximum of 35 miles. *William Hines, "Space Exploration," The World Book Science Annual 1972 (1971), p 367*

lunarscape, *n.* a view of the lunar surface.

The moon began to show out over the North Sea. It was huge, and through my powerful binoculars I was able to study its face. The lunarscape looked like some great contoured globe. Would Spadeadam [rocket station] ever contribute to a landing on that frozen-looking orb? *Henry Tegner, "Country Diary," The Manchester Guardian Weekly, Aug. 15, 1970, p 12*

These [paintings] include some dramatic lunarscapes and a painting of Spacelab Q-4 (an impression of a joint UK-USA space station of the future in orbit). *Colin Moorcraft, "Astronomy and Art," New Scientist and Science Journal, April 22, 1971, p 224*

[from *lunar* + *-scape* view, scene]

▶ *Lunarscape* is another name for the more established *moonscape*, apparently influenced by the current use of *lunar* in compounds descriptive of the Apollo space flights.

lungs, *n.pl.* breathing spaces, such as small parks that might be placed in overpopulated or traffic-congested areas.

Designs for urban living provide for "Landscaped areas," created either as "lungs" or to resolve an architectural dissonance. *Dennis Johnson, "Blessed Plots," The Manchester Guardian Weekly, April 18, 1970, p 11*

lu·ni·log·i·cal (ˌlu: nəˈlɑdʒ ə kəl), *adj.* of or relating to study of the moon, especially its geology.

The winning lunar roving vehicle concept consists of a collapsible four-wheel vehicle to provide surface transportation on the Moon for two astronauts, their hand tools, other equipment, lunilogical samples and experiments. *Science Journal, Jan. 1970, p 16*

Lu·no·khod (ˌlu: nəˈxɔ:t), *n.* a vehicle designed by Soviet scientists for scientific exploration on the lunar surface, powered by solar cells and directed by radio signals from earth. Compare LUNAR ROVER.

The news agency called the Lunokhod "a self-propelled scientific laboratory", and said that it "fundamentally extends" the area of exploration. *David Bonavia, "Soviet*

Eight-wheeled Vehicle Moves Across Surface of Moon: Forerunner of Machines to Explore Planets," The Times (London), Nov. 18, 1970, p 1

There are real advantages in carrying out X-ray astronomy from the lunar surface, but why this should have been thought sufficiently important to justify inclusion in the first Lunokhod was not made clear. *Science, Jan. 1971, p 15*

[from Russian *Lunokkhod*, literally, moonwalker]

lu·te·o·ly·sin (ˌlu: ti: ouˈlɑi sən), *n.* a chemical substance which destroys the corpus luteum even if an egg has been fertilized, studied to develop an effective contraceptive pill.

A further method — impossible at the moment — would be to use synthetic analogues of the gonadotrophins as specific antagonists to them. Luteolysins, as yet unknown in man, could be used to prevent the formation or growth of the corpora lutea. *Christopher Newall, "Blocking the Reproduction Machinery," Review of "Symposium on Antifertility Agents," Science Journal, March 1968, p 87*

[from *(corpus) luteum* a ductless gland important in maintaining pregnancy in animals + *lysin* a substance causing dissolution]

lym·phan·gi·og·ra·phy (ˌlimˌfæn dʒi:ˈɑg rə fi:), *n.* the process of X-raying the lymphatic vessels.

In another procedure, called lymphangiography, a radiopaque dye is injected into a lymph vessel, after which an X ray is taken of the area normally drained by that vessel. Using this technique, the doctor can determine whether the lymph nodes in the area have been affected by the tumor. *Irwin H. Krakoff, M.D., "Cancer: Detection and Diagnosis," Encyclopedia Science Supplement (Grolier) 1968, p 82*

[from New Latin *lymphangion* lymphatic vessel + English *-ography*, as in *radiography*]

ly·so·cline (ˈlɑi səˌklɑin), *n.* a layer of water in the sea where certain chemical substances undergo dissolution.

When marine organisms die and sink to about 4,000 meters, they cross the "lysocline," below which calcium carbonate redissolves because of the high pressure. *Ferren MacIntyre, "Why the Sea is Salt," Scientific American, Nov. 1970, p 106*

[from *lyso-* dissolution + *-cline* layer (as in *thermocline* and *syncline*)]

ly·so·som·al (ˌlɑi səˈsou məl), *adj.* of or relating to lysosomes.

The membrane serves to protect the rest of the cell from the contents of lysosomes, because uninhibited action of lysosomal enzymes causes cell death. *The Times (London), Sept. 23, 1968, p 6*

ly·so·some (ˈlɑi səˌsoum), *n.* a cellular granule containing enzymes which cause the chemical decomposition of substances entering the cell.

Virtually all animal cells contain lysosomes to perform breakdown and digestive processes within them. *Picture legend, "The Body's Deadly Defenses," The World Book Science Annual 1968, p 109*

...in arthritis the damage to the joints might be caused by some agent rupturing the lysosomes and allowing enzymes to leak out.... *"Science and Technology: Medicine," The Annual Register of World Events in 1968 (1969), p 377*

[from *lyso-* dissolution + *-some* body]

ly·so·staph·in (ˌlɑi səˈstæf ən), *n.* an enzyme that destroys staphylococcal bacteria by disintegrating the bacterial cell wall.

Enzymes may offer an alternative to antibiotic therapy in treating staph infections that cannot be blocked by known antibiotics. Preliminary research on dogs with acute staph infections of heart valves suggests an enzyme called lysostaphin is a potential cure for such infections in human beings. *"Life Sciences Notes: Microbiology, An Alternative For Treating Staph," Science News, Nov. 11, 1967, p 469*

[from *lyso-* dissolution + *staph*ylococci + *-in* (chemical suffix)]

Lys·tro·sau·rus (ˌlis trəˈsɔr əs), *n.* a small reptile of the Triassic period (about 200 million years ago), whose fossil remains were recently discovered in Antarctica.

...*Lystrosaurus*, a small mammal-like reptile found previously in South Africa, India, China, and Russia ... lived around rivers and lakes, feeding on aquatic vegetation in the Early Triassic.... *"Earth: The Restless Ocean Floors, Supporting Evidence," Science News Yearbook 1970, p 151*

Just off Antarctica's Ross Ice Shelf, for example, an Ohio State University expedition recently discovered the fossilized bones of a hippopotamus-like reptile called *Lystrosaurus* that had been thought to live only in prehistoric South Africa and Asia. *Time, Jan. 5, 1970, p 36*

[from *Lystro* (of uncertain origin) + Greek *saûros* lizard]

M

Mace (meis), *n.* Also spelled **mace.** the trade name of a nerve irritant with a tear gas base, which produces a burning sensation in the eyes, throat, etc., used in the form of an aerosol spray as a temporary incapacitant. Also called CHEMICAL MACE.

... the police authorities in the US are frequently accused of being slap-happy in the use of such weapons. One of the latest — Mace — which attacks the eyes and the facial muscles, is the subject of a deepening controversy. *New Scientist, May 29, 1969, p 489*

Mace temporarily incapacitates, but it contains no toxic ingredient other than tear gas and the risk with Mace is negligible when compared with conventional weapons, the team reported. *The New York Times, June 8, 1968, p 18*

—*v.t.* to attack or disable with Mace.

I've been maced in the face and tear-gassed and hit on the head. *Ralph Maloney, "The War Was Two Years Ago," The Atlantic, March 1970, p 62*

...[Relevant Teen-ager 1971] fired when he responded to foul and abusive language by Macing an old woman's hot dog. Currently sells bootleg record albums and still deals dope whenever it falls his way. *Sherman B. Chickering, "Staying Hip: 1971," Harper's, Sept. 1971, p 63*

machine art, a form of art that uses mechanical, electronic, magnetic, or similar devices as objects of art. Compare MACHINE SCULPTURE. See also AUTO-DESTRUCTION ART.

Machine Art. A related trend in constructions and environments was inspired by science and industry as artists turned to electronic experts and computer specialists for assistance. Barely two years after its inception, E.A.T. (Experiments in Art and Technology) became an international organization. Its more than 35 chapters encouraged the development of machine art all over the world. The trend was traced in a historical survey of modern technology, "The Machine," mounted by the Museum of Modern Art. *Victor H. Miesel, "Art," The Americana Annual 1969, p 95*

machine language, 1 the coding system that a computer uses to process information. Compare COMPILER LANGUAGE, COMPUTER LANGUAGE.

Machine languages are typically specific to a particular class or type of computer and frequently are entirely numeric, thus difficult for a human to understand. *Van Court Hare, Jr., Introduction to Programming: A BASIC Approach, 1970, p 411*

Programming in machine language is a dying art because it is too intimately involved with the machine design and with numeral systems that are not easy to handle. *R. Clay Sprowls, "Computer Programming," Encyclopedia Science Supplement (Grolier) 1971, p 159*

2 information or instructions in the physical form which a computer can handle without conversion, translation, etc.

There is generally agreed to be an essential equivalence between formal logical systems and Turing machines, so that Gödel's theorem can be expressed thus: Given a Turing machine, a question can be asked, in "machine language", which the machine will not be able to answer, and yet it can be proved, by using mathematical English, that the answer to the question is "yes." *I. J. Good, "Logic of Man and Machine," New Scientist, April 15, 1965, p 183*

machine-readable, *adj.* able to be processed directly by a computer.

In a temporary clinic set up in Rotherham last month, 2500 people were screened, at a rate of one per minute, for a wide variety of abnormalities. The information gathered was produced in machine-readable form to be processed by a computer.... *R. J. Donaldson, New Scientist, Dec. 7, 1967, p 587*

These [information-handling] functions all involve the manipulation of digital information. Therefore they can be handled by machines, with great savings in time and labor over manual techniques, provided that the basic records are available in a machine-readable medium such as punched cards. *Ben-Ami Lipetz, "Information Storage and Retrieval," Scientific American, Sept. 1966, p 228*

machine sculpture, a sculpture in the form of a mechanical, electronic, or similar device. Compare MACHINE ART.

But the ultimate comment on technology came from the American artist Tinguely who built machine-sculptures that could be exhibited only once — because they destroy themselves. *Gerald L. and Marsha J. Wick, "Of Artists and Atoms," New Scientist, March 12, 1970, p 513*

machine time, the amount of time a computer or other machine is in operation on a specific job.

In my environment the majority of user time, not machine time but user time, is spent in writing and running short programs. *S. Michaelson, "Bringing Your Computer to Life," New Scientist, Sept. 12, 1968, p 548*

machine translation, translation from one language into another by an electronic computer.

Information stored in microfilm, microdots, magnetic tape, computers, and in other machine-manipulatable form, can be retrieved from any distance. Access will be speeded up by the use of advanced techniques in classifying and indexing, machine translation, and electronic scanning. *George E. Callahan, "Communication Aids in Education," McGraw-Hill Yearbook of Science and Technology 1970, p 82*

ma·chis·mo (mɑ:'tʃi:z mou), *n.* manly self-assurance; masculine drive; virility.

You cannot really know anyone unless you know their pleasures, and a chief pleasure on Mulberry Street is food, which also stands for warmth, and affection, and for a man with a really big appetite *machismo. John Corry, "The Best Bartender in New York," Harper's, Aug. 1970, p 49*

No one, of course, has mentioned birth control, although in an officially anticlerical country the taboo is not so much religious as emotional. Having many sons is proof of virility, of *machismo* ("maleness"), that quality prized above all others in Latin America. *Gladys Delmas, The Atlantic, March 1964, p 92*

Another factor is *machismo*, a he-man complex that makes sexual prowess and large families—in or out of wedlock—a matter of male pride. *Time, Aug. 20, 1965, p 30*

[from American Spanish, from *macho*. See MACHO below.]

ma·cho ('ma: tʃou), in Spanish America, especially Mexico:

—*n.* a vigorous, robust man.

The one who knows how to fight and win is a real "*macho*." *Sergio Gutierrez Olivos, The New York Times, April 16, 1967, Sec. 4, p. 13*

—*adj.* robust; manly.

Tequila, the *macho* drink of Mexico, has made rapid sales gains in the United States in the past few years. *John Revett, "Tequila: The Sour Taste of Success," The Times (London), Aug. 19, 1970, p 19*

[from Spanish, literally, male *(n.* and *adj.)*]

macro-, combining form meaning "large" or "large-scale." A sampling of recently formed compounds with *macro-* includes:

macrochange, *n.*: Revolutions, including the Russian one, made the mistake of insisting that the macro-change, of the whole system, should come before micro-change, of the life style. *Terry Coleman, "The Unquiet American," The Manchester Guardian Weekly, April 18, 1970, p 15*

macrocontract, *n.*: With a macro-contract worth some £30 million, neither side can afford to make mistakes. *Richard Milner, The Sunday Times (London), Oct. 19, 1969, p 37*

macro-energy, *n.*: ...few scientists would aver that either quantum theory or relativity is wrong. It is thought instead that both must be incomplete, missing some essential facts about nature. The incompleteness must lie somewhere in the interface between the macro-world and macro-energy and the micro-world and micro-energy. *Tom Alexander, "Science Rediscovers Gravity," Encyclopedia Science Supplement (Grolier) 1970, p 64*

macrofluidics, *n.*: Another aspect of fluidics technology, which might be called "macrofluidics", is in directing flows of fluids in chemical plant etc. without moving valves, using the switching effects of bistable fluidic elements. *Glen Lawes and Michael Kenward, "Fluidics Dig In," New Scientist, March 26, 1970, p 612*

macrofouling, *adj.*: The principal macro-fouling species include barnacles, molluscs, hydroids, algae, sea-squirts, tubeworms and polyzoans. *David Houghton, "Foul Play on the Ship's Bottom," New Scientist, Dec. 3, 1970, p 383*

macrolevel, *n.*: A moving spaceship, on the ultimate microlevel, may be essentially the same as one of Conway's spaceships, appearing to move on the macrolevel whereas actually there is only an alteration of states of basic space-time cells in obedience to transition rules that have not yet been discovered. *Martin Gardner, "Mathematical Games," Scientific American, Feb. 1971, p 116*

macrophallic, *adj.*: Freedom from constraint has not resulted in any great efflorescence of erotic art, but merely a dreary duplication of commercial porn, meaty, masturbatory, with its inevitable distortions, brutalised women and macrophallic faceless men. *Germaine Greer, "The Scandinavian Myth," The Sunday Times (London), April 23, 1972, p 43*

macroplan, *n.*: Whatever the macro-plan, every graduate has a right to be considered in terms of what he needs to get out of his job and how he will be utilized by it. *Geoffrey Brown, "Britain's Other Brain Drain," New Scientist, May 28, 1970, p 418*

macroscale, *n.*: Meteorology is one of the few sciences which continually and consistently acquires a mass of reliable data on a macroscale. *L. P. Smith, "Meteorology Applied," Encyclopedia Science Supplement (Grolier) 1968, p 113*

macrosociology, *n.*: At a session devoted to macro-sociology, papers were presented on "The Comparative and Evolutionary Study of Macro-Institutions".... *Emory S. Bogardus, "Sociology," The Americana Annual 1968, p 603*

macrostrategy, *n.*: But it is impossible for a government nowadays to have no macro-strategy; and Mr. Heath's Carshalton speech in 1967 gave a glimpse of one in embryo. *Peter Jay, The Times (London), Nov. 1, 1968, p 27*

macroworld, *n.*: The illustrations—and it is hard to leave them alone—cover both the micro and macroworld of nature. *Thomas Lask, The New York Times, Aug. 3, 1968, p 27*

mac·ro·bi·ot·ic (ˌmæk rou bai'at ik), *adj.* of or relating to macrobiotics.

The young waitress who brought us a cup of tea (made with a tea bag and sweetened with honey) said that she herself was a vegetarian but that the girl behind the counter was "macro," and went on to explain, "Macrobiotic. That means she'll eat fish." *"The Talk of the Town," The New Yorker, Feb. 10, 1968, p 22*

Macrobiotics, like other panaceas, can be many things to many people. Some think that it confers superhuman strength.... For many, yoga and macrobiotic diets have become a substitute for drugs. *Time, Nov. 16, 1970, p 60*

Detectives are one group with a legitimate right to paranoia—there really are a lot of bad people hiding in the bushes—but what in the world was next—Nixon joining a commune? Hoover opening a macrobiotic restaurant? *Bruce Jay Friedman, "Lessons of the Street," Harper's, Sept. 1971, p 95*

—*n.* a follower or adherent of macrobiotics.

Most macrobiotics, as Ohsawa's devotees call themselves, try to follow his other nine diets, which are graduated from six to minus three to include increasing amounts of fish and vegetables—organically grown—along with brown rice. *Time, Nov. 16, 1970, p 59*

[from Greek *makrobiotos* long-lived, prolonging life; so called from the belief that a macrobiotic diet confers longevity]

macrobiotics, *n.* a dietary system based on the Zen Buddhist division of the world into the opposite and complementary principles of *yin* and *yang*, in which a balanced diet consists of a 5 to 1 proportion of yin (organically grown sugar, fruits, vegetables) to yang (meat, eggs, etc.).

"Rice, unpolished rice, is the basis of macrobiotics.... It is a cleansing diet. Physically, mentally, and spiritually." *Muriel Spark, "The Driver's Seat," The New Yorker, May 16, 1970, p 46*

mac·ro·lide (ˈmæk rəˌlaid), *n.* any of a class of antibiotics made by species of streptomyces, characterized by a ring structure of large size.

There exists a class of antibiotics known as the polyene macrolides, which have been known for some 15 years as potent and effective therapeutic agents against a wide variety of fungal infections of Man. *"Editorial: A Versatile Rostrum," New Scientist, Oct. 17, 1968, p 120*

[probably from *macro-* large + *-ol* + *-ide*, chemical suffixes]

MACV (mækˈviː), *n.* acronym for *Military Assistance Command, Vietnam,* the official name of the U.S. military command in South Vietnam. Compare COMUSMACV.

We have also recently told MACV that we have a high priority requirement for night photorecce of key motorable routes in Laos. *Excerpt from a cablegram from Admiral U. S. Grant Sharp, The New York Times, June 13, 1971, Sec. 4, p 37*

Mad Hatter's disease, another name for MINAMATA DISEASE. Compare HATTER'S SHAKES.

Two American physicists, however, have sifted the evidence and offer the explanation that Newton had a classic case of Mad Hatter's disease—mercury poisoning. *"Mercury, Not Mum?" New Scientist and Science Journal, Dec. 30, 1971, p 274*

Maf·fe·i galaxy (mɑːfˈfeiː), either of two galaxies which are part of the local group.

The Maffei galaxies, obscured by the Milky Way dust, appear as small, faint, diffuse patches. *Hyron Spinrad, "Science Year Close-Up," The World Book Science Annual 1972 (1971), p 266*

According to preliminary estimates, Maffei 1 and Maffei 2 appear to be about three million light-years away, or not quite twice as distant as the Andromeda galaxy.

The identification of the new galaxies began in 1968 when Paolo Maffei, a young Italian astronomer working in the Laboratory of Astrophysics in Frascati, reported finding two strange objects quite close together in infrared photographs of one of the dustiest regions of the Milky Way, between the constellations Perseus and Cassiopeia. *"Science and the Citizen," Scientific American, March 1971, p 45*

mafia or **Mafia,** *n.* any secret or exclusive society; a closed circle or clique.

Angkor has been particularly close to French hearts since Andre Malraux put the temple area and its twelfth-century sculptures on the map in 1924. Malraux and his wife, Clara, hacked their way through the jungle to help themselves to these masterpieces of Khmer art. They successfully made off with seven sandstone Buddhas, but were captured and arraigned in Phnom Penh. Clara was released, Malraux stayed to stand trial. Back in Paris she drew support from Andre Gide, Andre Maurois, Francois Mauriac, and others from the Twenties literary mafia. *"Their Man in Angkor," The Manchester Guardian Weekly, Aug. 22, 1970, p 11*

The composers' Mafia, with its dedication to atonality and the production of new noises, holds no terrors for him [Gian Carlo Menotti]. *Winthrop Sargeant, "Musical Events," The New Yorker, Jan. 3, 1970, p 44*

Camp's supporters, younger party workers in constituency organizations across the country, started organizing delegates for the November convention. And although their alliance was loose and informal, Diefenbaker men soon began referring to them as "the Eglinton Mafia." *Alexander Ross, "Dalton Camp: The Man Who Finally Belled the Cat," Maclean's, Feb. 1967, p 74*

[extended use of the name of the secret criminal society]

ma·fi·o·so (ˌmɑː fiːˈou sou), *n.; pl.* **ma·fi·o·si** (ˌmɑː fiː-ˈou siː). a member of the Mafia (secret society of criminals).

The *mafiosi* were recognizable, too, by their uncanny success in everything they touched. The Mafia doctor got all the patients and could always find a hospital bed in a hurry.... By tradition, members of the Mafia did not themselves seek election to Parliament, but everybody knew that the political boss who arranged for a candidate's election was a *mafioso. Norman Lewis, "The Honored Society," The New Yorker, Feb. 22, 1964, p 35*

...Santo Sorge [is] a naturalized citizen who is under indictment in Palermo, Sicily, for criminal conspiracy as an alleged member of an international ring of Mafiosi.... *The New York Times, March 20, 1968, p 35*

magic acid, an acid with remarkable properties as a reagent. See the quotation for details.

...the strength of an acid is...judged by the readiness with which it loses the ion to an alkali. G. A. Olah and R. H. Schlosberg...now report that even methane, a hydrocarbon gas not normally considered an alkali at all, can act as an acceptor to "magic acid," probably the strongest acid known.

Magic acid is made from fluorosulphonic acid (FSO_3H, a very strong acid in its own right) by dissolving antimony pentafluoride in it: its strength derives from the great drive behind the reaction.... *New Scientist, July 4, 1968, p 41*

Magic Marker, *U.S.* the trade name of an instrument for marking and drawing, consisting of a metal tube which holds quick-drying, waterproof ink and a thick felt tip which transmits the ink onto a surface.

Poring all day over legal tomes, scrawling notes with a Magic Marker on a clip board, using Latin phrases, he [Lenny Bruce] experienced a heady pleasure. *Albert Goldman, "What Lenny Bruce Was All About," The New York Times Magazine, June 27, 1971, p 22*

magic number, one of a group of numbers, each representing the number of protons or neutrons in certain nuclei of relatively high stability, the most stable nuclei being those having the highest possible number of protons or neutrons in their shells.

...it was shown that certain nuclei would be extremely stable when they contained a "magic" number of neutrons or protons. The magic number was associated with nuclei having closed shells of neutrons or closed shells of protons, or perhaps both.

Computer calculations are able to spot several of these elements among the superheavy group yet to be discovered. Both elements 110 and 114 seem to exhibit this quality, and in the case of 114, the elements may have a double magic number, with both its neutron and proton shells closed. *"Nuclear Chemistry: The Magic Numbers," Science News Yearbook 1970, p 266*

Indeed, certain numbers of neutrons or protons, called magic numbers—2, 8, 20, 50, 82, and 126—correspond to particularly stable structures, like the completed electron shells in the noble gases of chemistry. *D. Allan Bromley, "Physics," The World Book Science Annual 1967, p 339*

Nuclei having magic numbers of protons and neutrons

possess great stability and half life periods of even a few days. If 114 is a magic number, then we shall be able to study the chemical properties of 'eka-lead'. *G. N. Flerov and I. Zvara, "Synthesis of Transuranium Elements," Science Journal, July 1968, p 69*

magnesium pemoline, a combination of the stimulant pemoline and magnesium hydroxide, used as a drug to stimulate the nervous system.

The Abbott researchers reasoned that learning and memory might be improved by boosting the supply of RNA, and hit upon a seemingly harmless chemical, magnesium pemoline (tradenamed Cylert), which increases RNA synthesis twofold or threefold. *Time, Jan. 7, 1966, p 41*

Tests on student volunteers in America have shown that a drug, Magnesium Pemoline, increases the speed and accuracy of their work when they are tired. *The Sunday Times (London), Oct. 27, 1968, p 3*

magnetic anomaly, a pattern of alternating bands of rock having normal and reversed magnetization.

The age of the rocks lying 40 miles west of the ridge implies that they have travelled at an average rate of 0.8 centimetres a year since the time they were extruded from the ridge. This agrees well with the figure estimated from the magnetic anomalies of the ocean floor. *The Times (London), Oct. 3, 1968, p 13*

Because young lavas are frequently found at the centers of the ridges, it was concluded that the positive magnetic anomaly over the center represented the present epoch of normal magnetization, and the pattern of positive and negative anomalies on the flanks of the ridge represented earlier periods in the history of a reversing magnetic field. *Charles L. Drake, "Earth Sciences: Geophysics," 1970 Britannica Yearbook of Science and the Future, 1969, p 162*

magnetic bottle, a magnetic field or fields to confine plasma (highly ionized gas) in a controlled thermonuclear reaction.

... no one yet knows how to confine a hot plasma in a "magnetic bottle" long enough for the energy liberated by relatively infrequent thermonuclear reactions to overcome the inevitable loss from electromagnetic radiation and from plasma escaping from the bottle. *Ernest P. Gray, "Physics: Plasma Physics," The World Book Science Annual 1967, p 341*

More than a hundred kinds of microinstabilities have been identified, and fusion researchers have been trying to find magnetic-bottle configurations that will be able to reduce the microinstabilities to acceptable proportions. *Alvin M. Weinberg, "Curbing The Energy Crisis," The World Book Science Annual 1972 (1971), p 222*

magnetocardiogram, *n.* the record or tracing made by a magnetocardiograph.

Using careful shielding that excluded magnetic disturbances from outside sources, [Dr. Cohen] ... produced what he called magnetocardiograms, which are symmetrical with electrocardiograms taken from the same subjects. *The New York Times, May 30, 1967, p 18*

Such "magnetocardiograms" might make mass screening programmes a cheap and practical proposition. *"Monitoring the Heart Without Electrodes," New Scientist, March 10, 1966, p 635*

magnetocardiograph, *n.* a cardiograph that records heart action in the magnetic field around the heart.

Dr. Cohen said ... it is ... too early to assess the long-range potential of the magnetocardiograph. *Richard D. Lyons, The New York Times, May 6, 1967, p 33*

magnetogasdynamics, *n.* the study of the interaction of magnetic fields and plasma (highly ionized gas).

Elements of Magnetogasdynamics—[by] L. E. Kalikham.... Deals with the theory of magnetogasdynamics, various problems involved in the motion of plasma, the investigating methods employed and selected applications. *Science News, Jan. 7, 1967, p 22*

magnetopause, *n.* See the first quotation for the meaning.

The outer boundary of the magnetosphere, where there is a transition from the terrestrial to the interplanetary magnetic field, is called the magnetopause. *A. J. Dessler, "Magnetosphere," McGraw-Hill Yearbook of Science and Technology 1968, p 239*

The space probes show that at about ten earth radii, the earth's geo-magnetic field ends its conflict with the interplanetary environment. The magnetic field goes through a series of rapid fluctuations at that distance from earth. This is known as the magnetopause. *Sir Bernard Lovell, "The Pollution of Space," The Listener, June 27, 1968, p 829*

magnetoplasmadynamic, *adj.* using plasma (highly ionized gas) in magnetic fields to generate power.

NASA's engine, being tested at Lewis Research Center in Cleveland, is called a magnetoplasmadynamic (MPD) arc thruster. An electric arc heats the argon or xenon propellant until it is ionized into a plasma, which is then forced through a "nozzle"—is actually a cone-shaped magnetic field—to produce thrust. *Science News, April 1, 1967, p 298*

magnetosphere, *n.* **1** an area of radiation formed by the earth's magnetic field which extends up to 40,000 miles from the earth and protects it from dangerous particles.

The moon, unlike the earth, is not protected from the solar wind—it has no magnetic field and, therefore, no shielding magnetosphere. *Science News, Dec. 23, 1967, p 611*

2 any similar area around a heavenly body.

This low-frequency electromagnetic radiation, which was suggested first by Pacini and later by James E. Gunn and myself at Princeton, is inevitable if the pulsars are magnetic neutron stars spinning in a vacuum. Peter Goldreich and William Julian at the California Institute of Technology have shown, however, that such a star must have a magnetosphere, a plasma-filled region surrounding the star. *Jeremiah P. Ostriker, "The Nature of Pulsars," Scientific American, Jan. 1971, p 56*

magnetospheric, *adj.* of the magnetosphere.

The length of the magnetospheric tail is uncertain. It has been observed by Norman Ness and John Wolfe to extend at least 10^3 R_e in the antisolar direction. *A. J. Dessler, "Magnetosphere," McGraw-Hill Yearbook of Science and Technology 1968, p 239*

magnetotelluric, *adj.* of or relating to the magnetic areas of the earth.

There were also two outstanding sessions on paleo- and archeomagnetism, which included some interesting new results. New studies are underway on ... magnetotelluric phenomena. *Waldo E. Smith, "Meetings: International Union of Geodesy and Geophysics: 14th General Assembly," Science, March 1, 1968, p 1002*

magnicide

[from *magneto-* magnetic + *telluric* of the earth]

magnicide, *n.* the murder of an important person.

Suddenly, faceless men sought fame by magnicide, the killing of someone big. In April the murder of Martin Luther King.... In June came the second Kennedy assassination, an unbelievable replay of the first, including a blind-chance killer.... *Time, Aug. 30, 1968, p 17*

[from Latin *magni-* (stem of *magnus* great) + English *-cide* killing, as in *homicide*]

mag·non ('mæg nɑn), *n. Nuclear Physics.* a quantized wave propagated by the deviation of a nuclear spin in a magnetic field.

...nuclear spins relax by interacting with the electronic spin system—through the emission or absorption of spin waves (magnons). *Advertisement by Ford Motor Co., Scientific American, July 1969, p 65*

[from *magnetic* + *-on*, as in *electron, neutron*, etc.]

mag·nox ('mæg,nɑks), *n.* a British type of nuclear reactor fueled by rods of natural uranium encased in magnesium alloy cans.

At the end of its program of magnox-type reactors, the U.K. abandoned this system in favour of the ACR (advanced gas cooled, graphite-moderated reactor) type.... *Lucien Chalmey, "Fuel and Power: Electricity," Britannica Book of the Year 1970, p 365*

[from *Magnox*, trade name of the magnesium alloy]

Ma·ha·ri·shi (,mɑː həˈriː ʃiː), *n.* **1** the title of a Hindu guru or spiritual guide.

...the Maharishi Mahesh Yogi inhabits a rather splendid bungalow, full of plate-glass and classy carpeting. He has come a long way and back since he took the Western world by transcendental meditation and had his brush with the Beatles. *Geoffrey Moorhouse, "Maharishi's Progress," The Manchester Guardian Weekly, March 20, 1969, p 19*

2 Often spelled **maharishi.** any guru.

Like our maharishi-seeking hippies of today, St. Francis of Assisi considered dirtiness as among the insignias of holiness.... *"And the Last Word...On Baths," New Scientist, Sept. 18, 1969, p 565*

[from Sanskrit *mahā* great + *rishi* sage, seer; the form of the compound in Sanskrit is *mahārshi*]

mail cover, *U.S.* the screening and holding up of certain types of mail by postal officials, especially at the request of the recipient of such mail.

When a person is subjected to a mail cover, the Post Office records the name and address of anyone sending mail to him, as well as the postmarking and the class of mail. First-class mail is not delayed or opened, the department says. *C. P. Trussell, The New York Times, Feb. 24, 1965, p 26*

main, *v.t. Slang.* to inject (heroin or a similar drug) into a vein; mainline.

...all my friends were on heroin. I snorted a couple of times, skinned a lot, and after that I mained it. *"Kids and Heroin: The Adolescent Epidemic," Time, March 16, 1970, p 17*

mainframe, *n.* the central processor and immediate access store of a computer.

The emphasis during the year was on small computers and calculators and on peripheral equipment; the latter

grew at twice the pace of the "mainframe" business. *Marcelino Eleccion, "Electronics," Britannica Book of the Year 1970, p 321*

mainstreet, *v.i. U.S. and Canada.* to campaign for election along the main streets of towns and districts.

Though she [Olive Diefenbaker] refuses to speak in public she mainstreets better than The Chief [John Diefenbaker] himself. Perhaps, being a woman, she seems more sincere, more fragile, less "political," and certainly she conveys an image of great warmth. *Susan Dexter, "How The Chief Lost (and Won) the Election," Maclean's, Jan. 1, 1966, p 31*

From the Irish and black community of Dorchester to the Italian North End, Boston has witnessed a merry binge of mainstreeting, leafletting and parties with some of the excitement of a mayoral election. *"POVERTY—A Vote in the Action," Time, June 14, 1971, p 20*

[verb use of *main street*]

Majoritarian, *n. U.S.* a person who belongs to the Silent Majority.

Joseph C. Goulden [author of the *Harper's* article "Voices from the Silent Majority"] went to the White House bureaucracy not too long ago; he requested a sampling of "representative" letters from the four hundred thousand or so members of the "Silent Majority" who wrote President Nixon after his Vietnam speech last November. Then he embarked on an unusual trip around the country to get to know a few of Mr. Nixon's Majoritarians. *Harper's, April 1970, p 4*

major-medical, *n. U.S.* a broad form of health insurance, providing coverage for large surgical, hospital, and other medical expenses.

But a man who had *almost* died could need a haven, and surely the room was that. His own and yet not his own. Enclosed, privileged, paid for by major-medical, suspended below the roof and above the street. *Robert Henderson, "The Unknown Rooms," The New Yorker, June 5, 1965, p 36*

ma·ku·ta (məˈkuː tə), *n.* the plural of **likuta.**

The Congo devalued its currency by about two-thirds yesterday and introduced a new currency system of zaires, makuta and senghi. *The Times (London), June 26, 1967, p 17*

mal de sie·cle (,mal də ˈsye klə) or **mal du siè·cle** (,mal dy ˈsye klə), a term denoting weariness of life or pessimism of a melancholy sort, roughly equivalent to *Weltschmerz* and *taedium vitae.*

All the belief systems that have served society for hundreds of years have gone, resulting in the modern *mal de siecle*—a frustration which has "led to the rejection of science as a pursuit and objectivity as a moral attitude." *Graham Chedd, "Biology Stirs its Social Conscience," New Scientist, Dec. 10, 1970, p 431*

A sombre self-portrait included some years ago in an anthology of French drawings at the Orangerie gave its evidence of early symptoms of the *mal du siècle*, the Romantic disquiet, not entirely hidden by an air of affectation. *William Gaunt, The Times (London), Jan. 31, 1967, p 6*

[from French *mal du siècle*, literally, sickness of the age. The *de* form is a partial Anglicization.]

male chauvinism, excessive male pride or exaggerated loyalty to members of the male sex. Compare SEXISM.

...thousands of women across the country turned out for the first big demonstration of the Women's Liberation movement.... In Los Angeles, H.O.W. (Happiness of Womanhood) members paraded posters proclaiming "Communists Have Done It Again" and "Women's Lib is a Society of Man-Eaters." Historically hampered by archaic laws and antique moral codes, European women have accepted their lot much more readily than their American counterparts. Recently, however, growing numbers, taking a cue from their more combative sisters across the Atlantic, have launched their attack on male chauvinism. *"Women's Lib, Continental Style," Time, Aug. 17, 1970, p 23*

male chauvinist, a person who exhibits male chauvinism; a man who regards himself as superior to women. Compare SEXIST.

On rare occasions the women replied in bitter kind: "Male Chauvinists Better Start Shakin'—Today's Pig is Tomorrow's Bacon." *"Women on the March," Time, Sept. 7, 1970, p 12*

During the past several years higher education has experienced a series of crises. The newest, and in the long term perhaps the most significant, development is the issue of discrimination against women.... Male chauvinists would like to think that the current uproar is the work of a few militant troublemakers. They may hope that, if they are cautious and patient, the storm can be counted on to dissipate. The odds are, however, that we are witnessing a major movement that will persist until it has brought forth substantial changes, not only in the universities, but also in the professions. *Philip H. Abelson, "Women in Academia," Science, Jan. 14, 1972, p 127*

mal·i·bu board ('mæl ə,bu:), a streamlined plastic surfboard, usually about 9 feet long.

Then, when the swell brought in good surf, it was malibu boards, skegs, and washouts as the surfers took over the place. *Anthony Smith, "The Pensioners Take Over: Operation Seashore," The Times (London), Sept. 21, 1970, p 3*

[named after *Malibu* Beach, on the Pacific, in southern California, much frequented by surfers]

ma·ma-san ('mɑ: mə'sɑ:n), *n.*; *pl.* **ma·ma-san** or **ma·ma-sans.** a matronly native woman in Japan, Korea, Vietnam, etc., often the head of a family or other group.

Known as Soul Alley, this 200-yd. back street is located just one mile from U.S. military headquarters for Viet Nam. At first glance, it is like any other Saigon alley: mama-sans peddle Winston cigarettes and Gillette Foam Shaves from pushcarts, and the bronzed, bony drivers of three-wheeled cycles sip lukewarm beer at corner food stalls as children play tag near their feet. *"Soul Alley," Time, Dec. 14, 1970, p 39*

On another occasion we [hostesses at a Tokyo bar] were visited by two enormous Sumo wrestlers, with their equally large Mama-San. They were jolly, and never stopped laughing as they downed huge quantities of beer. *Margaret Hollingsworth, "Ten-Per-Cent Hostess," The Manchester Guardian Weekly, Jan. 4, 1968, p 10*

[from Japanese *mama* mama, mother + *-san*, an honorific title]

mammogram or **mammograph,** *n.* an X-ray picture of the breast.

The film image can be switched from positive to negative (black to white) as an aid in determining configuration and relationship. This function appears particularly valuable in the study of mammograms and angiograms [X rays of the blood vessels]. *"Production News: Enhancing Difficult X-radiographs," Science Journal, June 1968, p 27*

This image Dr. Wolfe and many other radiologists agree is far clearer and more detailed than film mammographs because there are sharp lines between areas of differing tissue density, such as between cancerous and normal tissues. *Robert Reinhold, The New York Times, March 25, 1968, p 25*

mammography, *n.* See the quotation for the meaning.

X-ray examination of the breast called mammography is now revealing cancer undetectable by ordinary means. *Faye Marley, "Progress in Medical Research," Science News, Dec. 24, 1966, p 554*

[from *mammo-* breast + *-graphy* representation or record]

mammoplasty, *n.* plastic surgery of the breast.

He said the mammoplasty in the first case involved the transplant of adipose (fatty) tissue, in the second case the operation involved the implantation into the breasts of what was described as "probably silicone rubber." *Alvin Shuster, The New York Times, April 4, 1968, p 26*

[from *mammo-* breast + *-plasty* plastic surgery]

man, *n.* **the Man,** *U.S. Slang.* **1** the white man; white society personified.

The Man systematically killed your language, killed your culture, tried to kill your soul, tried to blot you out.... *Calvin Marshall, "The Black Church: Three Views," Time, April 6, 1970, p 71*

"In fact," she [Miss Ruth Eisenbraun] was saying, "the society as a whole is loosening up. If I were black, the South is where I'd prefer to be. Nobody in the North believes now in integration because they've never had it, but here, in an economic and social way, they've had integration all along, though of course entirely on the Man's terms...." *John Updike, Bech: A Book, 1970, p 122*

2 the Establishment in general; the system.

Kent and Cambodia were made to order for radicals. Something like Dowdell's death was made for them: 'The pigs got Tiger. You can't trust the Man. Come on with us.' I can hear them now. *Bill Moyers, quoting Chancellor Laurence Chalmers of the University of Kansas, "Listening to America," Harper's, Dec. 1970, p 59*

3 the police.

"...I catches up with one fella in an alley after he put my TV in a truck. He keeps denyin' what I seen him do with my own eyes, so I blasts him and takes him bleedin' down to the Man." *Nathaniel Folmar, quoted in "The Beautiful People of Detroit," Maclean's, Dec. 1967, p 27*

To the bombers and kidnappers the Man is Authority. He is every policeman. *"The Politics of Gelignite," The Manchester Guardian Weekly, Nov. 7, 1970, p 1*

[originally used by Southern blacks to counteract the whites' use of "boy" in addressing or referring to black men]

managerialist, *n.* one who believes in managerial planning or control in business, government, etc. *Also used attributively.*

"No doubt some cynics and managerialists will deride them [local city councils] as 'mere talking-shops.' It is perhaps more likely ... that they will make local government a reality to many people who now ignore or stand aside from it." *John Ardill, quoting a White Paper on Local Government Reform in England, The Manchester Guardian Weekly, Feb. 14, 1970, p 8*

While serious economic problems beset the country, many remained caught in the irrelevancies of such questions as whether the Sovet Union was a "degenerate workers' state" or a "managerialist bureaucracy." *Steven Kelman, "The Feud Among the Radicals," Harper's, June 1966, p 67*

man amplifier, a mechanical device which can be attached to a person's body and maneuvered by him so that he may exert much greater strength or force than he is physically capable of by nature.

General Electric has a family of other augmentor robots, including...Hardiman, which is worn by its human operator as a sort of outside skeleton enabling him to lift a 1,400-pound load exerting 30 pounds of force. The Hardiman exoskeleton is typical of a whole class of augmentors, called man amplifiers. *Jonathan Eberhart, "Robots: Sim, Sam and the Beast," Science News, March 9, 1968, p 238*

manifold, *n. Mathematics.* a topological space or surface. See the quotations for details.

Manifolds are objects of primary interest in present-day topology. They are spaces built by pasting together pieces that look like ordinary Euclidean space. If the dimension of the Euclidean space is *n*, the manifold is called *n*-dimensional. One way to study a manifold is to try to break it into simple pieces resembling triangles; if the procedure is successful, it is said that the manifold has been triangulated. *Irving Kaplansky, "Mathematics," Britannica Book of the Year 1970, p 491*

In a pure mathematical sense, we can have manifolds with any number, *n*, of dimensions. *Edna E. Kramer, The Nature and Growth of Modern Mathematics, 1970, p 460*

man-on-man, *adv., adj. U.S. and Canada.* (in team sports) of or in a defensive position in which one defenseman is assigned to one offensive player.

. . . they were "gambling," trying to cover Green Bay's wide receivers too tightly—mostly because they were forced into single man-on-man coverage by the blitzing tactics of the Kansas City linebackers. *Time, Jan. 27, 1967, p 52*

"He's always at the outer edge of the rulebook anyway," says Eric Nesterenko of the Chicago Black Hawks, a veteran who has played frequently against Howe [Gordie Howe, a hockey player with the Detroit Red Wings] man-on-man. *Peter Gzowski, "Gordie Howe, Hero," Maclean's, Dec. 14, 1963, p 21*

man-rate, *v.t.* to certify (a rocket or spacecraft) as safe for manned flight.

After it [a new Soviet booster] has been man-rated, however, and used in orbital rendezvous and docking missions, the USSR will have achieved a major platform for further advance. . . . *Kenneth W. Gatland, "Russia's Moon Programme," New Scientist, March 21, 1968, p 631*

The general question of the reliability of unmanned spacecraft has always been a thorny problem for NASA. Manned spacecraft have redundant systems—back-up systems in case one fails. This method, called "man-rating a spacecraft," is costly. *Science News, June 19, 1971, p 416*

-manship, combining form meaning the art or tactic of using (something specified) to gain an advantage. The form was abstracted from *gamesmanship, lifemanship,* and *one-upmanship,* terms coined by the English humorist Stephen Potter,

born 1900, on the model of *sportsmanship.* Some recent examples of its use are:

growthmanship, *n.:* Like President Nixon, who used to poke fun at growthmanship, Lekachman seems to hold that the New Economists exaggerate the importance of growth and GNP [gross national product]. *Seymour E. Harris, in a Letter to the Editor, Harper's, Oct. 1970, p 9*

Housemanship, *n.:* It was by a stroke of sheer Housemanship—not normally his best asset—that the Secretary for Trade and Industry managed to sail through the debate with such surprisingly little personal damage. *Norman Shrapnel, "Davies Rides Commons Storm," The Manchester Guardian Weekly, Aug. 7, 1971, p 7*

Marxmanship, *n.:* Like ten others whose Marxmanship was slightly off target, he was able, unlike Ali, to cite a passage about the mole from Marx, but not the right one. *"The Times Diary," The Times (London), March 13, 1970, p 10*

quotemanship, *n.:* . . . Mr. Boller . . . has identified no less than 22 distinct varieties of quotes currently used in the art of quotemanship, not counting the nonquote or out-of-context or spurious quotes. *Eliot Fremont-Smith, The New York Times, May 31, 1967, p 45*

ringmanship, *n.:* [Boxer Henry] Cooper's finest bit of ringmanship seems to have gone unnoticed by the British press. *Michael Katz, "Henry Cooper A Pro's Pro Who Could Never Make the Top," The Times (London), Nov. 13, 1970, p 17*

stockmanship, *n.:* Some farmers are working far too hard themselves and haven't been able to pay attention to details, like concentrating on stockmanship and keeping down wastage. . . . *Peter Dunn, "The Muddy Truth About Farms," The Sunday Times (London), Jan. 25, 1970, p 13*

winemanship, *n.:* Winemanship has long held the status of an art in Europe, and when fine French and German wines began flowing across the Atlantic, the expertise came too. Vines, vineyards and vintages were soberly debated. Wine-tasting sessions became social events and the sniffy phrases of oenology became part of the language. *Time, Oct. 19, 1970, p 51*

Mao flu, another name for HONG KONG FLU.

. . . I discover that the Russians refer to the flu, which is allegedly advancing westwards from Asia as—"Hong Kong" flu. In the West, of course, it has become known as "Mao" flu. *Ariadne, New Scientist, Dec. 12, 1968, p 632*

[named after *Mao* Tse-tung, born 1893, the Chinese Communist leader]

Mao·ism ('mɑu͟ɪz əm), *n.* strict adherence to the doctrines of Marx and Lenin, as expounded by the Chinese Communist leader Mao Tse-tung.

Mao Tse-Tung's "cultural revolution" has been defeated, in spite of Peking's repeated claims that it is victorious. . . . The "triple alliance"—that is, the combination of the recently condemned "leading cadres," the local Army commanders, and the inert so-called "revolutionary" masses—took over in the provinces. The other Communist parties denounce "Maoism" and pretend not to understand what is going on in China—but their leaders know perfectly well what it was all about. *Victor Zorza, "Mao's Revolution that Failed," The Manchester Guardian Weekly, March 16, 1967, p 7*

Mao·ist ('mɑu ɪst), *adj.* of or relating to Mao Tse-tung or to Maoism.

In the event, the North Vietnamese turned first to China, but the disastrous and costly failure of Maoist solutions left them disenchanted. The agrarian reform, which sought to collectivise all land, so outraged the peasants that they rose in revolt. *P. J. Honey, "North Vietnam," The Listener, Feb. 22, 1968, p 242*

—*n.* a follower or supporter of Mao Tse-tung or of Maoism.

The young Maoists, more influenced by the idea of Götterdämmerung than perhaps they know, are for burning down and starting over. *Renata Adler, The New York Times, April 4, 1968, p 58*

Mao·ize ('mɑu‚aiz), *v.t.* to bring under the influence of Mao Tse-tung; convert to Maoism.

Mao demolished...others who did not share his own mystical concept of the revolution. He hoped to replace them with freshly radicalized, totally Maoized youth who would be prepared to spend their lives in permanent struggle. *"Mao's Attempt to Remake Man," Time, July 12, 1971, p 22*

Mao jacket, another name for NEHRU JACKET.

Mr. Lanvin expressed his disapproval of "extravagances" such as the Mao jacket, the evening turtle neck, and pendant and chain jewelry. *Enid Nemy, The New York Times, May 22, 1968, p 50*

mar·ag·ing steel ('mɑr‚ei dʒiŋ), a very strong iron alloy containing little or no carbon and consisting chiefly of nickel with lesser amounts of other metals.

A relatively new steel, known as maraging steel, has been used in extremely thin gauge in the making of the case of the third stage of the Black Arrow rocket for putting British research satellites into orbit. This is an age-hardened steel which avoids the risk of distortion and scaling associated with high-temperature heat treatment and quenching. *New Scientist, July 25, 1968, p 185*

[*maraging*, from *martensite* (the hard component of quenched steel) + *aging*]

marginalize, *v.t.* to omit, exclude, or ignore, especially by leaving on the fringes of society or isolating from the course of progress.

In three countries the challenge to an emerging Latin American type of socialism . . . to solve towering economic and social problems which effectively leave half the populations marginalized has already begun. *Richard Wigg, The Times (London), Oct. 31, 1970, p 12*

mariculture, *n.* the cultivation of marine plants and animals for food and raw materials. Also called SEA FARMING.

If we are very optimistic and assume for a moment that the yield of the traditional fishery will not change, mariculture could perhaps lead to an increment in the crop produced from the sea from the present 1% to 1.1%. *Pieter Korringa, "Mariculture," McGraw-Hill Yearbook of Science and Technology 1971, p 23*

[from *mari-* sea + *culture*]

▶ The related older term *aquiculture* encompasses all bodies of water, including the sea.

mariculturist, *n.* one who engages or specializes in mariculture.

The man who studies agriculture stands in a different place from the man who studies mariculture. There are other differences between the two fields but not so basic as the need for the mariculturist to swim. *Edward de Bono, Science Journal, Dec. 1969, p 30*

marine science, all the sciences dealing with the sea and its environment, including marine biology, oceanography, and similar specializations.

However, for any MP interested in marine science, a study of what the Canadians are attempting would be well worth while. For example, there is the project for control of the ice-cover on the Gulf of St Lawrence. *Tam Dalyell, MP, New Scientist and Science Journal, Jan. 28, 1971, p 195*

Mar·kov chain ('mɑr‚kɔːf), *Statistics.* a system of discrete states in which the transition from one state to another is a fixed probability that is not affected by the system's past history.

Mathematicians insist on analyzing anything analyzable. The random walk is no exception and (mathematically speaking) is as adventurous as the wanderings of the man of La Mancha. Indeed, it is a major branch of the study of Markov chains, which in turn is one of the hottest aspects of modern probability theory because of its increasing application in science. *Martin Gardner, "Mathematical Games," Scientific American, May 1969, p 118*

In its simplest form, a Markov chain states that the probability of a succeeding event occurring is dependent upon the fact that a preceding event occurred. For example, if the letter Q is known to exist, what is the probability of it being followed by the letter U? *John P. Dowds, "Oil Field Model," McGraw-Hill Yearbook of Science and Technology 1971, p 307*

[named after A. A. *Markov*, 1856-1922, a Russian mathematician who first investigated such systems]

Markov process, any process based on a Markov chain.

The interconnection between classical potential theory and Brownian motion [motion of particles suspended in a fluid] depends heavily on the fact that Brownian motion is a Markov process, that is, its present behavior is not influenced by its past behavior. *Reuben Hersh and Richard J. Griego, "Brownian Motion and Potential Theory," Scientific American, March 1969, p 74*

Mar·mes man ('mɑr mis), a prehistoric man whose fossil bone fragments were discovered in 1965 in the state of Washington and dated as being over 11,000 years old.

More skull fragments of the Marmes man—believed to be the oldest find of human remains in the Western Hemisphere—have been unearthed by a Washington State University archeological team. *The New York Times, May 4, 1968, p 10*

Preliminary study of the skull bones, finger and wrist bones, teeth, and fragments of rib and long bones indicates that Marmes man was a Mongoloid, having a broad-cheeked, flat face. Most of the human bones are charred and split like those of the animals with which they were found, which suggests that human beings were eaten by occupants of the site. *Bert Salween, "Archaeology," 1969 Collier's Encyclopedia Year Book, p 107*

[named for R. J. *Marmes*, a rancher on whose property the bones were discovered]

Mar·so·khod (‚mɑr sə'xɔːt), *n.* a vehicle designed by Soviet scientists for scientific exploration on Mars. See also LUNOKHOD, PLANETOKHOD.

In addition to discussing future Lunokhod explorations of the moon, the Soviets also described similar automated stations and robots for Venus, Mars and Mercury. These they call "planetokhods" or "marsokhods." *Science News, Nov. 21, 1970, p 397*

[patterned after Russian *Lunokkhod*, literally, moonwalker]

Martianologist, *n.* a person who engages in scientific study of or who is an expert on scientific study of the planet Mars.

Notably absent in all the Mariner pictures are the networks of "canals" that some Martianologists began putting into their drawings a hundred years ago. *Picture legend, "The Surface of Mars," Scientific American, May 1970, p 26*

marvie or **marvy,** *interj. U.S. Slang.* a shortened and altered form of *marvelous.*

"O Sad Arthur, how marvie!" cried the entranced Lambie. *Roger Angell, "Sad Arthur," The New Yorker, March 14, 1970, p 34*

When Donna heard the news, she clapped her hands. "Marvy—now we can go on the trip together!" *S. J. Perelman, "Missing: Two Lollapaloozas—No Reward," The New Yorker, Oct. 17, 1970, p 39*

Mary Jane or **maryjane,** *n. U.S. Slang.* marijuana.

Known as *khif* or hashish in the Middle East, bhang or ganja in India, *ma* in China, *maconha* or *djama* in South America, pot, grass, boo, maryjane and tea in the U.S., it is ubiquitous and easily grown, can be smoked in "joints" (cigarettes), baked into cookies or brewed in tea ("pot likker"). *Time, July 7, 1967, p 19*

. . . the young soldier was saying that here in Vietnam cannabis, pot, the weed, giggle-smoke, grass, Mary Jane, call it what you will, is readily available and freely used. *Ian Wright, "Pot and the GI," The Manchester Guardian Weekly, June 20, 1970, p 6*

mas·con ('mæs,kɑn), *n.* **1** a massive concentration of dense material lying about 30 miles below the lunar surface, and characterized by a higher-than-average gravity.

Most scientists believe that the moon has mascons, large concentrations of material beneath the surface which alter the orbital paths of spacecraft. By tracking the satellites, scientists will be able to measure these perturbations. *Science News, Sept. 1970, p 216*

The most remarkable property of the mascons is that the five most pronounced examples coincide with circular lunar seas, such as Mare Imbrium; none lies under the large, irregular maria. *Joseph Ashbrook, "Astronomy: The Moon," 1970 Britannica Yearbook of Science and the Future, 1969, p 120*

2 a similar feature on the planets or their moons.

We have already noted the detection on the Martian surface of mascons, analogous to the lunar areas of especially high gravity. *"Mars May Sport Active Volcanoes and Glaciers," New Scientist and Science Journal, Dec. 30, 1971, p 247*

[from *mass* concentration]

masculinist, *n.* a person in favor of male rights or privilege.

Economic discrimination against women has a direct parallel in the unfair treatment accorded the Negro. Lest old-fashioned masculinists panic, all that the new-style feminists really demand is the opportunity for a mediocre woman to get as far as a mediocre man. *Marilyn Bender, The New York Times, July 18, 1968, p 31*

No militant masculinists stooped to conquer; indeed

almost the only men to be seen on the premises, apart from the staff, were male journalists invited to help celebrate the occasion. *The Times (London), Oct. 13, 1967, p 8*

[patterned after *feminist*]

mase (meiz), *v.i.* to generate and amplify microwaves. Compare LASE.

Many substances have been made to "mase" and "lase" —that is, to behave like masers or lasers. *"Masers and Lasers," Encyclopedia Science Supplement (Grolier) 1964, p 308*

No significant overestimation of the mass of the coronal clouds would result from this small degree of masing and no significant selections of incoming clouds would occur. *S. H. Storer and D. W. Sciama, "Is Interstellar Hydrogen Capable of Maser Action at 21 Centimetres?" Nature, March 30, 1968, p 1238*

[back formation from *maser* a device that generates and amplifies microwaves]

mask, *n.* the arrangement of components of an integrated circuit.

The end product from an integrated-circuit design service is the mask itself. Even now most IC masks are produced by a draughtsman who first lays out the masks hundreds of times full size on a board about four feet square. The final mask is made by a process of successive photo-reductions. This mask, which might be about one eighth of an inch across, is repeated several hundred times across a two-inch silicon slice. *"Big Advance in Small Circuits," New Scientist, Dec. 10, 1970, p 441*

. . . if one is designing the mask for an integrated electronic circuit, the objects to be represented are the transistors, resistors, gates, wiring and other elementary components from which the circuit is to be built. *Ivan E. Sutherland, "Computer Displays," Scientific American, June 1970, p 65*

masscult, *adj.* of or relating to drama, art, music, and other forms of culture spread by the mass communications media, especially television.

Their [literary magazines'] golden age lasted from World War I to the communications, or "masscult," revolution of the mid-1950's. . . . *Eliot Fremont-Smith, The New York Times, Sept. 11, 1967, p 47*

[contraction of *mass* cu*lture*]

massless, *adj.* lacking mass; having a mass of zero.

In a neutron-star collapse, gravity converts up to 10 per cent of a star's mass into energy, which appears as the supernova's light and other electromagnetic radiation, plus gravity waves and neutrinos (massless particles, virtual seeds of pure energy, that travel through the universe at the speed of light). *Tom Alexander, "Science Rediscovers Gravity," Encyclopedia Science Supplement (Grolier) 1970, p 63*

According to the uncertainty principle, virtual photons can have a nonzero mass, unlike real photons, which are massless. *Frederick V. Murphy and David E. Yount, "Photons As Hadrons," Scientific American, July 1971, p 97*

matching fund, 1 a sum of money given by some individual or institution, usually in proportion to that raised by public contribution. The matching fund is an inducement to obtain enough money in total to pay for some project.

Along with such institutional changes, the European science ministers endorsed an international matching fund for support of four-or-five-year, pilot interdisciplinary research programs, as well as establishment of reserve funds in each participating nation for projects approved by international committees. *Science News, March 30, 1968, p 303*

2 matching funds, *pl.* the sums of money contributed to match the individual contributions.

The New York Philharmonic was still without a permanent music director for the 1970s, while in many cities, efforts were underway to raise matching funds to meet the 1971 deadline set by the monumental Ford Foundation program to increase orchestral endowments. *Robert C. Marsh, "Music," The 1969 World Book Year Book, p 420*

materials science, the study of the properties and uses of materials, such as glass, metals, polymers, etc.

Materials science is a very wide subject since it includes metals, ceramics, glasses and polymers, together with a great deal of solid state physics, and it is a difficult task to write about these related topics with equal ease, as Fishlock has done. *Leslie Holliday, "Books: Of Whiskers and Fatigue," Review of "The New Materials" by David Fishlock, Science Journal, Jan. 1968, p 85*

Efforts are now being made to see the subject in the broader background of materials science and there are signs that this name [soil mechanics] is slowly passing out of use in favour of soil engineering or some similar appellation. *R. L. S. Taylor and I. J. Smalley, "The Subsidence of Buildings," Science, Jan. 1971, p 81*

ma·tière (ma'tyer), *n. French.* artistic material; (literally) material.

In a series called "Los Espejos" (The Mirrors), he [Manuel Rivera] once again uses his unusual *matière* to trap light as if in a mammoth spider web and spin all manner of bewitching effects. *Time, Nov. 25, 1966, p E1*

Lecture Four. The matiere of verse demonstrated further in Wallace Stevens; who isn't my poet. *Geoffrey Grigson, Review of "Owls and Artificers: Oxford Lectures on Poetry" by Roy Fuller, The Manchester Guardian Weekly, Aug. 7, 1971, p 19*

matrix, *n.* **1** an ordered table or two-dimensional array of variables, especially for use in computer programming.

Dr. Warner's group has been working for two-and-a-half years on computer diagnosis. They have set up a "matrix"—a device for statistical analysis—that comprises some thirty-five different disease entities and fifty-seven symptoms known to be associated with congenital defects. The symptoms include a group of twenty-two heart murmurs; seven electro-cardiographic findings, eleven X-ray findings, three age group categories and six findings from physical examination. *The New York Times, May 28, 1963, p 19*

2 an array of circuit elements designed to perform a particular function, especially in a computer.

The diodes on each character unit are connected to a matrix of seven horizontal wires. . . . The other side of each diode is connected to one of five vertical wires. In this way, any one diode can be switched on individually by applying a voltage across selected horizontal wires and vertical wires in the matrix. *"The News, New Data Display Needs Less Wiring," Science Journal, Nov. 1970, p 16*

matrix isolation, *Chemistry.* the trapping of molecules in an inert solid (the matrix or background material) to observe them in isolation.

. . . Illinois researchers went back more than 100 years . . . to trace the steps leading to the video tape recorder, oral contraceptive pills, the electron microscope, magnetic ferrites . . . the matrix isolation—a technique for 'freezing' chemical reactions to study intermediate products. *Peter Gwynne, Science Journal, April 1969, p 9*

mau-mau, *v.t. U.S. Slang.* to terrorize.

. . . his [Norman Mailer's] demonstration of the inadequacies and distortions of Kate Millett's *Sexual Politics* is convincing and indicates that the English Department of Columbia University had been mau-maued by that termagant of Women's Lib. *John V. Hagopian, in a Letter to the Editor, Harper's, June 1971, p 9*

[popularized by the American journalist Tom Wolfe, author of *Radical Chic and Mau-mauing the Flak Catchers*, from *Mau Mau* a secret society of Kikuyu terrorists in Kenya, also used in Afro-American slang as a name for a militant member of the Black Muslims or Black Panthers]

ma·vin ('mei vən), *n. U.S. Slang.* an expert or connoisseur.

Much of the credit for the Cinderella publishing story goes to Robert Gottlieb, then the editorial genie in residence at Simon & Schuster, now the mavin at Alfred Knopf. *Time, Sept. 12, 1969, p 78*

[from Yiddish *meyvn*, from Hebrew *mēvīn*]

max·i ('mæk si:), *n.* **1** a skirt, dress, coat, etc., reaching to the ankle or just above it; a maxiskirt, maxidress, maxicoat, etc. Compare MICRO, MIDI, MINI.

When you have seen one maxi, you have seen them all, though Saint Laurent makes his droopier than ever with mufflers and downdragged crochet berets, but pants-suits have infinite variations. *Ernestine Carter, The Sunday Times (London), Feb. 2, 1969, p 58*

2 the ankle-length style of fashion.

In their desperation to whet consumer demand by the good, old American economic device of forced obsolescence, the industry's merchants, manufacturers and editors have been touting the midi, the maxi and other varieties of lowered hemlines. *Marylin Bender, The New York Times, July 5, 1968, p 50*

—*adj.* **1** reaching to the ankle or just above it; ankle-length.

Teen-agers and college girls rushed for maxi coats and shops reported good sales in the style. *Ruth Mary DuBois, "Fashion," The Americana Annual 1970, p 287*

2 larger or longer than usual.

As fashions grow minier, accessories are waxing maxier. Witness the popularity of superwatches—huge, outsize timekeepers that measure 3 in. across and come with round, square and octagonal faces. *Time, Nov. 10, 1967, p 47*

In the Dublin suburbs there is a mini-car in nearly every garage, and downtown the traffic jams are becoming very maxi. *John F. Henahan, "Still Life in the Ould Turf," Saturday Review, Sept. 23, 1967, p 4*

[from *maxi-*]

maxi-, a new prefix derived from *maximum* (on the analogy of *mini-*), currently used with the two meanings given below:

1 reaching down to the ankle; long.

maxicoat, *n.:* Along Belgrade's Terazije, maxicoats and Longuettes, velvet knickers and leather gaucho pants abound, as do swinging discothèques, modish *butiks* and the most daring skin magazines. *Time, March 29, 1971, p 29*

maxidress, *n.*: To relieve the sterile monotony of nurses' uniforms, Fashion Designer Pierre Cardin recently unveiled three new creations at a London showing. Two of his designs—nunlike wimples with white maxidresses—were harmless affairs that might make ward nurses look functional if not fashionable. *Time, Nov. 16, 1970, p 67*

maxilength, *n.*: Both in Paris and in the United States, couturiers showed maxilengths (almost floor-sweeping) but were commercially cautious and kept enough of their styles short. *Kathryn Zahony Livingston, "Fashion," The 1970 World Book Year Book, p 342*

maxi-shorts, *n.pl.*: The middle-aged American who waddled down the steps of the expensive Spinzar Hotel in his rainbow maxi-shorts would hardly have glanced at the woman who came towards him from out of the shadows, her hands cupped, her face haggard and vacant. *The Listener, Feb. 29, 1968, p 270*

2 very large.

maxi-order, *n.*: After announcing his latest orders last week in New York, Pao hopped a plane for Tokyo to look for shipyards interested in another maxi-order. *Time, July 5, 1971, p 53*

maxi-taxi, *n.*: Those most favoured by your correspondents seem to be the post-bus and the mini-bus (or maxi-taxi). *D. W. Glassboro, London, in a Letter to the Editor, The Times (London), Oct. 8, 1970, p 11*

may·o ('mei ou), *n.* short for *mayonnaise*.

Dottie . . . said gently, "So sorry. Then run down to the corner and get me a ham and cheese on rye and tell them to hold the mayo." *Lillian Hellman, "An Unfinished Woman," The Atlantic, April 1969, p 118*

We were sitting at a luncheonette counter the other day, just about to bite into a b.l.t. down, with mayo, when a familiar voice addressed us from an adjacent stool. *"Undivided Attention," The New Yorker, July 10, 1971, p 20*

mbi·ra (əm'bi: rə), *n.* a hollow piece of wood, usually about eight inches long, with metal strips, inserted lengthwise, that vibrate when played with the thumb. The instrument is tuned to play tribal music while held in both hands with the palms upward.

. . . he was making music with a mbira, a kind of African hand-piano. His brother, who is three years his junior, was accompanying him on a kalimba, he said, which is a modern version of the mbira and was designed by his father, Dr. Hugh Tracey, a well-known South African musicologist. *The New York Times, June 4, 1966, p 27*

[from a Bantu word]

Mc·Lu·han·ism (mək'lu: ən‚iz əm), *n.* **1** the ideas and theories of the Canadian writer and communications specialist Marshall McLuhan, born 1911, especially his emphasis on the influence of electronic communications and the mass communications media in radically reshaping society.

On a superficial level Joel Lieber's provocative novel bears out the basic precept of elementary McLuhanism: the medium is the message. *Samuel I. Bellman, "In a Darwinian Nightmare," Review of "How the Fishes Live" by Joel Lieber, Saturday Review, May 6, 1967, p 36*

2 a word or expression peculiar to Marshall McLuhan.

These movies are all "non-linear", to use a favorite McLuhanism; they refuse to follow A-to-Z patterns. . . .

Marshall Delaney, "Movies," Saturday Night (Canada), Oct. 1968, p 56

McLuhanite, *n.* a follower or supporter of Marshall McLuhan and his ideas.

As the McLuhanites are so fond of pointing out, television—and particularly the commercials—had accustomed them [audiences at movie houses] to seeing more, and faster. *Arthur Knight, "The Now Movie: Engaging the Eye-Minded," Saturday Review, Dec. 28, 1968, p 18*

McLuhanites and Orwellians are likely to block our view of their masters' arguments. . . . *D. A. N. Jones, The Manchester Guardian Weekly, Jan. 23, 1971, p 18*

. . . you are happy to take your children away for a week or two in the middle of the summer term, on the McLuhanite principle that a child at school is merely interrupting his education anyway. . . . *Christopher Driver, "Cottages or A La Carte," The Manchester Guardian Weekly, Sept. 26, 1970, p 16*

Also, there is some kind of joke on McLuhanite coolness; Chance [the central character of *Bad News*, by Paul Spike] is a walking television screen. . . . *John Updike, "Books," The New Yorker, Sept. 25, 1971, p 133*

McLuhanize, *v.t.* to put under or subject to the control or influence of television, computers, and other forms of electronic communications media.

Among the nonelectronic press, a gnawing feeling grows that their efforts are becoming obsolete. This is hardly so, as the sales of Theodore White's books can attest. But the fear of being McLuhanized into irrelevance has forced the pen-and-pencil men to fight back. *Martin F. Nolan, "Speak Into the Cupcake, Please: A Primer On How to Read the Pols and the Press," The Atlantic, Oct. 1968, p 124*

The thesis of Australia in the seventies as a model McLuhanized society is fervently denied by publishers. *Max Harris, "Arts Boom Insecure," The Times (London), March 31, 1970, p VI*

meals on wheels, a service that brings a hot meal daily to an elderly or disabled person in his home. It is usually a private service subsidized by government.

Islington council said: "We have heard that from tomorrow our refuse collectors, sewermen, baths plant operators and drivers, except those on meals on wheels and health and welfare vehicles, are on strike." *The Times (London), Sept. 29, 1970, p 4*

means-test, *v.t. British.* **1** to examine the financial means of (an unemployed or disabled person) to determine eligibility for welfare benefits.

. . . anyone who qualifies for free welfare milk will not have to be separately means-tested for ophthalmic or dental treatment or for free prescription charges. *"Comment: Can We Beat Karl Marx?" The Manchester Guardian Weekly, Nov. 14, 1970, p 3*

2 to make (benefits) dependent upon the outcome of such an examination.

The state retirement pension is below what is commonly regarded as the poverty line and many old people do not claim the means-tested benefits to which they are entitled, either because they are not aware of them or because they find the process of claiming too cumbersome or too humiliating. *The Times (London), April 20, 1970, p 9*

The means-tested state which we are now entering may have a profoundly disturbing long-term effect on incentives and attitudes to work. *Daily Telegraph (London), May 5, 1972, p 9*

meat and potatoes, *Slang.* **1** the most important or basic part.

Publishers counter most of the criticism thrown at them with hard economic facts. Fiction, they say, is currently a drug on the market everywhere. "We only buy fiction for prestige, as an investment in the writer or out of a sense of duty," says [Jack] McClelland. Other trade books do better but only sensational best-sellers can recover production costs on the Canadian market alone. Textbooks remain the meat and potatoes of publishing in Canada. *Douglas Marshall, "Maclean's Reviews: The Rapid $50 Advance of Canadian Publishing," Maclean's, July 1967, p 65*

2 Often, **meat-and-potatoes.** basic; fundamental.

Chapter six discusses very briefly equipment and methods of observation. It is a pity these subjects are so perfunctorily covered, for this is the kind of "meat and potatoes" information amateur astronomers . . . are eager to glean from an experienced observer. *P. Lancaster Brown, "Books: The Southern Sky," Review of "Astronomical Objects for Southern Telescopes" by E. J. Hartung, New Scientist, Aug. 15, 1968, p 351*

mechanical, *n.* **1** a mechanical part or structure; a mechanism.

Sigma factors were found when the RNA transcribing enzyme, RNA polymerase, was thoroughly purified. The "core" enzyme (minus the sigma factor) consists of four subunits, which seemed originally to be little more than rude mechanicals doing the enzymatic hard work, the sigma factor telling them where to do it. *"After Sigma Comes Psi to Turn Genes On," New Scientist, Dec. 3, 1970, p 363*

2 mechanicals, *pl.* the operational or functional parts; mechanics.

Many regulations, particularly in relation to TV, prevented advertisers from using international campaigns if the basic mechanicals—artwork, films, and so on—were not produced in Italy by Italians. *Murray Leask, "Advertising," Britannica Book of the Year 1967, p 66*

3 any nonessential participant.

Frivolity seems to me the only, precarious excuse for this novel—a let-out, for instance, for treating the income-earning group as characters and the rest as 'mechanicals'. *Robert Taubman, "Not Caring," Review of "The Nice and the Good" by Iris Murdoch, The Listener, Feb. 1, 1968, p 148*

[noun use of the adjective]

mechanoreceptor, *n.* a sense organ that is sensitive to mechanical stimuli.

These sense organs differ from previously reported mechanoreceptors of the small intestine which, activated by movement in the mucosa, signal distension. . . . *Dwight J. Ingle, "Medicine: Physiology," Britannica Book of the Year 1967, p 524*

medallion, *n. U.S.* **1** a license or permit to operate a taxicab, issued in the form of a medallion which is purchased by the licensee.

. . . a government contract is awarded to the bidder who will best serve the government's interest or to the one who submits the lowest bid. The theory is extended to taxicab medallions and turnpike concessions. . . . *Charles A. Reich, "The Greening of America," The New Yorker, Sept. 26, 1970, p 56*

2 a taxicab driver with such a license.

"If medallions want to start a fight, all right, but don't go looking for trouble," he said. *Homer Bigart, The New York Times, July 10, 1968, p 36*

med·e·vac ('med ə, væk), *U.S.*—*n.* military helicopter used to carry the wounded from combat areas to hospitals.

The two wounded Aid Men continued to crawl about and administer care. There would be no medevac; there was no landing zone for it. . . . *S. L. Marshall, "The Truth About The Most Publicized Battle Of Vietnam," Harper's, Jan. 1967, p 77*

—*v.t.,* **med·e·vacked, med·e·vack·ing.** to transport by a medevac.

At My Lai, Ridenhour reported, one soldier shot himself in the foot so that he would be Medevacked out of the area. *Time, Nov. 28, 1969, p 23*

[from *medical evacuation*]

Medicaid, *n. U.S.* a joint state and federal program that provides financial benefits for medical service to the poor or disabled. *Often used attributively.*

Generally, a family of four with one wage earner is now eligible for Medicaid if it has an income of $6,000 or less. *Martin Tolchin, The New York Times, Jan. 9, 1968, p 31*

[from *Medical aid*]

Medicare, *n. U.S. and Canada.* a government health-insurance program providing low-cost hospital and medical care, especially for people over sixty-five. *Often used attributively.*

Medicare, which became effective on July 1, 1966, offered inexpensive health care for most of the nation's elderly citizens. *"Health," The 1967 Compton Yearbook, p 289*

In Florida, a general practitioner was paid $191,000 from the Medicare treasury in a single year. *Science News, May 24, 1969, p 497*

[from *Medical care*]

medichair, *n.* a chair with electronic sensors to monitor the physiological activity of a person.

. . . scientists have developed an instrumented chair that gives a person a quick basic medical check-up in one sitting.

. . . This medichair was demonstrated for the first time yesterday at the opening session of the annual meeting of the Aerospace Medical Association in Las Vegas. *John Noble Wilford, The New York Times, April 19, 1966, p 37*

[from *medical chair*]

me·dul·lin (mə'dəl ən), *n.* a prostaglandin isolated from the medulla of the kidney, used in the treatment of high blood pressure.

A kidney substance called medullin, which at St. Vincent Hospital, Worcester, Mass., was first tried on a patient with high blood pressure and reduced it to a normal level, was found to be a member of the prostaglandin family. *Science News Letter, June 18, 1966, p 481*

[from *medulla + -in* (chemical suffix)]

mega-, *combining form.*

1 very large; bigger than most of its kind.

mega-association, *n.:* The closer links which are already developing within the personal finance industry, could be logically developed into a mega-association for all parties. *Margaret Stone, The Times (London), June 27, 1970, p 13* megacity, *n.*: And among the new moralists analogous doubts exist concerning . . . the noisy, ugly, chaotic, increasingly dangerous and ever-spreading mega-cities. . . . *Henry David Aiken, "The New Morals," Harper's, Feb. 1968, p 61*

megadestruction, *n.*: The U.S. alone has enough nuclear megadestruction stored in warheads to equal the explosive power of ten tons of TNT for every person on earth. *Time, Dec. 8, 1967, p 23*

megagame, *n.*: However, there are plenty of people who like tennis the way Ashe and Graebner play it. It is the megagame. *John McPhee, "Profiles: Levels of the Game," The New Yorker, June 7, 1969, p 56*

megahallucinogen, *n.*: A successor to LSD in 1967 was so-called megahallucinogen, STP. Users say the letters stand for serenity, tranquility, and peace, but doctors call it "a real mind-bender," and "the caviar of psychedelics." *Betty Jo Tricou, "Drugs," The World Book Science Annual 1967, p 286*

megamillionaire, *n.*: Nelson Aldrich Rockefeller, 59, a megamillionaire via the Rockefellers, a political patrician through the Aldriches. . . . *Time, March 8, 1968, p 21*

megaministry, *n.*: Peter Walker, Secretary of State for the Environment, scoffed last week at the suggestion that this new megaministry's powers were bringing it into conflict with other departments in Whitehall. *New Scientist and Science Journal, Feb. 18, 1971, p 385*

megapark, *n.*: . . . [August] Heckscher has a fondness for dramatic ideas. We asked whether the supermegalopolis would have megaparks in it, and he said, "Certainly. We'll see the National Park System not as way out *there* but as an integral part of the supermegalopolis." *"The Talk of the Town: New Commissioner," The New Yorker, March 4, 1967, p 32*

megatanker, *n.*: The step to a million tons or the "megatanker" involves considerable technical problems, in particular as regards stress and strain on the hull and the ratio of underwater displacement. Nevertheless, a working design is expected towards the end of 1971. The megatanker will have a length of 1620 ft, a width of 250 ft, and a draught of 105 ft. *New Scientist, Oct. 22, 1970, p 176*

2 one million (in units of measurement).

megabar, *n.*: The pressure needed to produce metallic hydrogen may well be less than a megabar; laboratory equipment will just about stretch to 600 kilobars at the moment. *New Scientist, Jan. 9, 1969, p 81*

megadecibel, *n.*: The controversy over Viet Nam was raised several megadecibels by widespread speculation that the Johnson Administration was considering use of tactical nuclear weapons in the war. *Time, Feb. 23, 1968, p 10*

meganewton, *n.*: . . . the stress, measured in meganewtons per square metre, is that required to rupture a specimen in 100 hours when all the materials have been corrected to a common density. *Noël Penny, Illustration legend, "Gas Turbines for Land Transport," Science Journal, April 1970, p 59*

megaparsec, *n.*: . . . a reasonable interpretation of the statistics suggests the presence of at least one quasar within a few Megaparsecs from us (1 Mpc = 3.26 x 10^6 light years) with other quasars spaced roughly equally throughout the universe. *Science Journal, Oct. 1969, p 17*

megarad, *n.*: With simple calibration the radiation dosage can be read off directly in megarads. *New Scientist, March 21, 1968, p 638*

[from Greek *mégas* large, great]

See also the main entries below.

megabit, *n.* a unit of information equivalent to one million bits or binary digits. Compare GIGABIT, KILOBIT, TERABIT.

In the lower band the system will provide 16 high speed digital broadband channels, each capable of supporting a data rate of 500 Megabits/sec. *"Narrow Waveguide for Multiconversations," Science Journal, Oct. 1970, p 19*

[from *mega-* one million + *bit*]

megabuck, *n.* *U.S. Slang.* a million dollars.

Dr Lawrence Hafstad, in charge of reactor development for the US Atomic Energy Commission, is quoted as saying that nuclear power would cost "a megabuck per megawatt". *New Scientist, June 20, 1968, p 615*

megahertz, *n.* a term replacing the older *megacycle* as the name of the unit of frequency equal to a million cycles per second. *Abbreviation:* MHz Compare KILOHERTZ.

Around noon, for example, the best frequency for communicating between South America and the UK might be near 22 megahertz. *New Scientist, Jan. 14, 1971, p 71*

[from *mega-* one million + *hertz* unit of one cycle per second]

megajet, *n.* a jet aircraft larger and faster than a jumbo jet. Compare JUMBO JET.

Compared with today's Boeing 747, for instance, these new 'megajets' would cruise 40 per cent faster with some 250 per cent more payload. *Peter Masefield, "Aviation, Airports and Technology in the 1970's," Science Journal, Sept. 1970, p 47*

megamachine, *n.* a term coined by Lewis Mumford to describe a social system so dominated by technology that it resembles a gigantic machine which functions without any regard for human needs and objectives. See also MEGATECHNICS.

What is needed to save mankind from the megamachine — or whatever controls the megamachine — is to displace the mechanical world picture with an organic world picture, in the center of which stands man himself. *Lewis Mumford, "The Megamachine," The New Yorker, Oct. 31, 1970, p 85*

The megamachine was "invisible" because its tens of thousands of intricately interacting parts were human. *Allan Temko, "The New Books," Review of "The Myth of the Machine: Technics and Human Development" by Lewis Mumford, Harper's, Oct. 1967, p 110*

megastructure, *n.* a very large building.

Arcology is architect Paolo Soleri's master city of the future. Integrating architecture with ecology, it is a total planned environment — dwellings, factories, utilities, cultural centers — within a single megastructure 1·2 miles wide and up to 300 stories high. *Estie Stoll, "Arcology," Encyclopedia Science Supplement (Grolier) 1971, p 287*

megatechnics, *n.* a term coined by Lewis Mumford to describe the large-scale mechanization of a highly technological society. See also MEGAMACHINE.

Under the impulsion of unprecedented "megatechnics" — "nuclear energy, supersonic transportation, cybernetic intelligence, and instantaneous distant communication" — the far-flung settlement patterns of Megalopolis are resistlessly expanding in many parts of the world, transforming man and the earth. *Allan Temko, "The New Books," Review of "The Myth of the Machine: Technics and*

Human Development" by Lewis Mumford, Harper's, Oct. 1967, p 108

meg·a·ton·nage ('meg ə,tən idʒ), *n.* the total destructive force in megatons (one megaton = one million tons of TNT).

In a queer display of morbid mathematics Defense Secretary Melvin Laird has summed the megatonnages of strategic nuclear explosives possessed by the United States and the Soviet Union, and he has concluded, quite absurdly, that Russian infinity is a greater quantity than American infinity. *Joseph C. Lausier, Freeport, Me., in a Letter to the Editor, The New York Times, Nov. 19, 1970, p 46*

megaversity, *n.* a very large university, with an enrollment of many thousands of students. Compare MULTIVERSITY.

Under [John A.] Hannah, M.S.U. [Michigan State University] has grown from a sleepy agricultural college of 6,390 students into a 5,000-acre "megaversity" with an enrollment of 42,541 and an annual budget of more than $100 million. *Time, March 21, 1969, p 34*

[from *mega-* very large + uni*versity*]

megavitamin, *adj.* of or based upon the ingestion of very large dosages of vitamins.

The use of very large amounts of vitamins in the control of disease has been called megavitamin therapy. Megavitamin therapy is one aspect of orthomolecular medicine. It is my opinion that in the course of time it will be found possible to control hundreds of diseases by megavitamin therapy. *Linus Pauling, Vitamin C and the Common Cold, 1970, p 70*

me·lit·tin (mə'lit ən), *n.* a substance extracted from the poison of honeybees which affects the red blood cells but has antibiotic properties.

They found the antibacterial effect of one milligram of the bee substance, called "melittin," was the equivalent of as much as 93 units of penicillin. *The New York Times, Aug. 22, 1968, p 28*

[from Greek *mélitta* bee + English *-in* (chemical suffix)]

mel·lo·tron ('mel ə,trɑn), *n.* an electronic musical instrument programmed by computer.

... the cold, windswept string tone of the Mellotron. a keyboard instrument which simulates — but not quite — the sound of an orchestra. *Richard Williams, The Times (London), Dec. 22, 1970, p 11*

[apparently formed from *mello*w + *electronic*]

melodica, *n.* a small wind instrument resembling a harmonica but having a pianolike keyboard.

There was a service on Sunday conducted by the captain, with music provided by the senior technical officer on the flute, and an engineer officer with his melodica. *Basil Gingell, The Times (London), April 26, 1967, p 3*

[from *melodic*, on the analogy of *harmonic, harmonica*]

memory bank, the memory unit of a computer with its data.

Participating entertainment enterprises like theaters and sports arenas are linked by sales outlets in such spots as railroad stations, travel agencies, department stores and even supermarkets. At most of those locations, buyers tell a sales clerk what event they want to see and when. By pushing buttons on a console, the clerk queries a regional computer's "memory bank" and gets an instant reading on what seats are available. Customers then can have their tickets printed electronically on the spot. *Time, Aug. 29, 1969, p 57*

memory drum, a reel of magnetic tape or a cylinder on which data are recorded in the memory unit of a computer.

The memory drum of a computer at a medical college holds millions of pieces of evidence regarding the results of certain types of treatment based on particular symptoms. *Walter Buckingham, "Automation," The Americana Annual 1967, p 104*

memory switch, an Ovonic device which requires a pulse of electricity to close it. See the quotation.

The threshold switch is a two-terminal component that can have two states in an electrical circuit: an almost nonconducting ("off") state and a conducting ("on") state. Normally the device is in the "off" state, but when the voltage across it reaches a certain threshold value, it flips over to the "on" state and thus acts as a switch. On removal of the applied voltage the "off" state is immediately restored. The memory switch behaves in much the same way, except that it will remain in the "on" state once it has been switched on, even though the applied voltage subsequently drops below the threshold value. *H. K. Henisch, Scientific American, Nov. 1969, p 30*

memory trace, a chemical change occurring in the brain when new information is absorbed and remembered.

The two most popular chemical contenders for this elusive "memory trace" ... have been ribonucleic acid (RNA) and protein. The learning process is assumed to produce changes in these molecules which then, on recall, alter in some way the properties of the neural synapses and allow the memory to be expressed. *"Trends and Discoveries," New Scientist, July 27, 1967, p 206*

men·a·zon ('men ə,zan), *n.* a systemic insecticide used widely because of its low toxicity to mammals.

...Dr. A. Calderbank, already a veteran of insecticide and herbicide research... was jointly responsible for the discovery of the powerful aphicide menazon.... *New Scientist, Sept. 25, 1969, p 665*

[irregularly formed from the names of some of its chemical components: di*me*thyl, tri*az*in, thi*on*ate]

mensch (mentʃ), *n.* *U.S. Slang.* a respected person; a decent human being.

The Warren Commission unleashed an army of investigators to dredge up the facts about [Jack] Ruby (né Jacob Rubenstein, alias J. Leon Rubenstein), the seedy Dallas strip-joint owner who yearned to be a *mensch*, a pillar of the community.... *Time, Jan. 13, 1967, p 16*

As the candidate was finishing his sandwich, someone called out, "Hey, McGovern, you're a *mensch!*"

The candidate turned to one of his table companions. "Abrams," he said, "what is a *mensch?*"

"It's good, Senator," Mr. Abrams said. "It means you're a substantial human being." *"The Talk of the Town," The New Yorker, June 24, 1972, p 26*

[from Yiddish *mentsh*, literally, a person, human being, from German *Mensch*]

Men's Lib or **Men's Liberation**, *U.S.* an organization of males whose aim is to free men from their traditional image and role in society.

We recently read in the *Times* about a group called Men's Liberation, Inc., whose aim is to free men from their traditional role of "all-powerful provider" and embolden them to cry, complain, feel sorry for themselves, and change their minds. The members of Men's Lib say they are tired of "having to prove our masculinity twenty-four hours a day" and believe that if their cause should prevail, "outmoded concepts would disappear in the face of reality." *"On and Off the Avenue: Gifts for Men," The New Yorker, Dec. 19, 1970, p 101*

To the Women's Liberation Movement the sex-role distinctions mean pressure to conform to separate and unequal rewards for being a woman. To the Men's Liberation Movement they mean pressure to conform to the "ego ethic"—or conform to perform. *Warren T. Farrell, "The Human Lib Movement," The New York Times, June 17, 1971, p 41*

[patterned after *Women's Lib, Women's Liberation*]

merchants of death, a term of opprobrium for manufacturers or sellers of arms, who presumably profit more than others from war.

The company's [Lockheed's] press releases...speak about the "free world" unnecessarily often. Given that basic philosophy, it may be noted that Lockheed are sensitive about their image as merchants of death. They point out that none of their products is at present being used to kill people in Vietnam. *Michael Leapman, "Passions High in Dispute Over the Rising Cost of a US Defence Contract," The Times (London), Sept. 21, 1970, p 6*

The military-industrial complex is at once more and less than the name implies. As a catch phrase, it may be on its way to surpassing in notoriety "merchants of death," the term that grew out of Senator Gerald Nye's investigation of the arms industry in 1934. *"What Is the Military-Industrial Complex?" Time, April 11, 1969, p 21*

► As the second quotation suggests, this term had its origin in the years between World Wars I and II. It was revived during the 1960's, first in connection with the investigation of mail-order sale of firearms that grew out of the assassination of President Kennedy in 1963, and more recently in relation to the war in Indochina.

merde (merd), *n. French.* excrement; filth.

Today is my thirtieth birthday...and knowing less than I ever knew before, having learned only to recognize merde when I see it, having inherited no more from my father than a good nose for merde....*Alfred Kazin, "The Pilgrimage of Walker Percy," Harper's, June 1971, p 85*

...he was the one from Aspreys, tried to sell me a Colt repeater....his salesmanship was merde. *John Hall, The Manchester Guardian Weekly, Dec. 12, 1970, p 15*

...no, we cannot have that kind of pornographic *merde* in this majestic and high-minded sentence....*Donald Barthelme, The New Yorker, March 7, 1970, p 36*

mergee, *n.* one party to a merger.

Royal Little, retired founder of Textron, Inc., counsels...students on the pitfalls of getting together [in mergers]. These include such dangers as whether the mergee's inventory is all he says it is....*Time, Nov. 24, 1967, p 60*

Elsewhere in the motel—we learn later—the rival corporation, Penta, has chosen a more ingenious method: they tell their mergees that it seems important only that the change be comfortable for everyone; why not just divide into pairs of compatible people, and Penta will choose among these two-man teams. *Richard Todd, "Notes on Corporate Man," The Atlantic, Oct. 1971, p 85*

mer·i·toc·ra·cy (ˌmer ə'tak rə si:), *n. British.* **1** a ruling class in society consisting of those who are most talented or have the highest intellect.

[Michael] Young is most widely known as the author of *The Rise of the Meritocracy* [first published in 1958]. The book portrays a 21st-century Britain in which the social revolution has thrown up a ruling elite selected, not by birth or wealth, but by intellectual ability as demonstrated in examinations. *John Walsh, "Social Science: British Council Has Key Role in Research Support," Science, April 26, 1968, p 403*

2 a system of education which stresses advancement of those who are most talented or have the highest intellect.

Selection of pupils by ability is not so much a device of meritocracy as an accepted method of increasing teaching productivity. *E. Connell, The Times (London), Feb. 17, 1965, p 13*

[from *merit + -ocracy,* as in *aristocracy*]

mer·i·to·crat ('mer ə tə,kræt), *n.* a member of a meritocracy.

It urges a programme of action for the children—the potential drop-outs who are too often ignored in an education system which often seems devoted only to the able and the clever—the meritocrats. *Brian MacArthur, The Times (London), May 8, 1968, p 10*

mer·i·to·crat·ic (ˌmer ə tə'kræt ik), *adj.* of or belonging to a meritocracy.

The managerial revolution has been much more thorough in America and on the Continent than in Britain, where nepotism and the old boy network still hamper progress towards meritocratic rule in the Civil Service, industry, commerce and finance. *Bernard Hollowood, "Honours Even," Punch, Oct. 19, 1966, p 572*

meson factory, a particle accelerator designed to produce intense beams of mesons with which to probe atomic nuclei.

A new generation of machines, called meson factories, should yield a sharper dimension in the study of what goes on in atomic nuclei.... The Los Alamos facility is the most energetic of the meson factories now under construction. It will be a linear accelerator, 1,800 feet long, that will accelerate protons or negative hydrogen ions to energies between 100 million and 800 million electron volts. The protons, striking various targets, will produce pi and mu meson beams. *Dietrick E. Thomsen, "Probing the Depths of the Nucleus," Science News, Oct. 11, 1969, p 332*

mes·o·scale ('mes ou,skeil), *adj.* intermediate between large-scale and small-scale.

Basic research continued into cyclonic storms and other aspects of the mesoscale or so-called secondary circulation of the atmosphere, including tropical cyclones (hurricanes and typhoons), mid- and high-latitude lows, and tornadoes. *Francis W. Reichelderfer, "Meteorology," Britannica Book of the Year 1969, p 518*

Dr. H. A. Panofsky, a Pennsylvania State University meteorologist, pointed to weaknesses in the knowledge of mesoscale meteorology, the meteorology of areas 10 to 20 miles in diameter, or about the size of many urban areas. Such knowledge, in the form of sophisticated mathematical models, is badly needed, he says, so that meteorologists can help air pollution control officials. *Science News, Jan. 30, 1971, p 81*

[from *meso-* middle + *scale*]

mes·o·scaph or **mes·o·scaphe** ('mes ou‚skæf), *n.* an undersea vessel designed for medium depth exploration of the seas.

The existence of these many portholes, with the possibility of looking in virtually every direction, is a principal characteristic of the mesoscaph and distinguishes her from naval or combatant submarines. *Jacques Piccard, "Drifting in a Silent World," Encyclopedia Science Supplement (Grolier) 1970, p 145*

The mesoscaphe can drift along with the Gulf Stream at depths ranging from 500 to 2,000 feet, as the scientists aboard study their environment with cameras, hydrophones, water samplers, and plankton nets. *Bruce C. Heezen and Paul J. Fox, "Deep-Sea Exploration," Encyclopedia Science Supplement (Grolier) 1969, p 144*

[from French *mésoscaphe*, coined by its inventor, the French deep-sea explorer Jacques Piccard, born 1922, from Greek *mésos* middle + *skáphē* vessel]

mesosome, *n.* a structure on cell membranes that is concerned with the formation of the cross wall when a cell divides.

The key to their theory [as to how DNA enters bacteria] is the mesosome, a structure which can be observed in electron micrographs of bacteria.... It is the point at which DNA is attached to the cell membrane. *New Scientist, Oct. 16, 1969, p 113*

[from *meso-* middle + *-some* body]

message, *n.* a unit of the genetic code which specifies the order or sequence in which amino acids synthesize a particular protein.

The genetic message is carried from the nucleus to the cytoplasm in the form of messenger ribonucleic acid (messenger RNA). *Robert Cox, "The Ribosome—Decoder of Genetic Information," Science Journal, Nov. 1970, p 57*

messenger, *n.* a chemical substance which carries or transmits genetic information.

A theory of messenger-RNA (mRNA) was offered, designating one type of RNA as a messenger between the DNA templates in the nucleus and the protein-manufacturing RNA in the cytoplasm. *"Trends and Discoveries in the Search for Life," Encyclopedia Science Supplement (Grolier) 1965, p 40*

messenger RNA, a ribonucleic acid which carries genetic messages from the DNA (deoxyribonucleic acid) in the nucleus of a cell to the ribosomes in the cytoplasm, specifying the particular protein or enzyme to be synthesized. *Abbreviation:* mRNA Compare RIBOSOMAL RNA, TRANSFER RNA.

Because coding experiments are done with RNA, genetic codes are usually given in terms of messenger-RNA rather than DNA. *James F. Crow, "Genetics," The World Book Science Annual 1967, p 300*

meta-, combining form meaning "going beyond or transcending the usual kind of (a specified person or thing)," used chiefly in technical terms. Compounds recently formed with *meta-* include:

metaculture, *n.:* Activities such as reading, writing, private communication, learning, previously framed with silence, now take place in a field of strident vibrato. This means that the essentially linguistic nature of these pursuits is adulterated; they are vestigial modes of the old "logic."

Yet we are unquestionably dealing with a literacy, with codes of recognition so widespread and dynamic that they constitute a "meta-culture." *George Steiner, "A Future Literacy," The Atlantic, Aug. 1971, p 41*

metahistorian, *n.:* A historian writes the history of a period, a metahistorian compares different periods in order to derive common rules. *C. R. Wason, Stevenage, England, in a Letter to the Editor, New Scientist, March 12, 1970, p 525*

metamaterialist, *n.:* ...*Artforum* contains interviews with ... the meta-materialist Richard Van Buren, a former box builder who contributes the following sample of the new vocabulary of active materials: "The wood was at one speed, at one sense of time, and the resin was at another sense of time. That was one of the problems." *Harold Rosenberg, "De-aestheticization," The New Yorker, Jan. 24, 1970, p 64*

metaprogram, *n.:* When you take hold of ecology, it will help if you have a firm understanding of the order of nature and if you have a good metaprogram. *"The Talk of the Town," The New Yorker, May 2, 1970, p 30*

metavolcanic, *adj.:* Westmoreland [Westmoreland Minerals (mining)] and its partners have said the banded iron formation adjoins 2,000 ft. to 3,000 ft. wide metavolcanic zones.... *Berry Ritchie, "Westmoreland Could Still be a 'Flyer'," The Times (London), Feb. 2, 1970, p 23*

met·al·lide ('met ə‚laɪd), *v.t.* to subject (a metal) to metalliding.

Molybdenum, for example, is a relatively soft metal; when boron is metallided into it, the resulting surface alloy is apparently second in hardness only to diamond. *Science News, July 15, 1967, p 66*

[verb use of the noun *metallide*, variant of *metalloid* a nonmetal used in alloys]

met·al·lid·ing ('met ə‚laɪ dɪŋ), *n.* a process of strengthening the surface of metals by diffusing the atoms of one metal through high-temperature electrolysis into the surface of another. The resulting surface alloy is harder than any mechanically applied coating or plating.

Metalliding, a process patented by General Electric Company, creates alloys at the outer layer of a wide variety of metal substances. The process places both the alloying and base metals in a bath of molten fluoride salts and applies direct current electricity between them. Ions of the *anode* (alloying metal) flow to the *cathode* (base metal) and diffuse into it, forming the alloyed surface. *Frederick C. Price, "Chemical Technology: Surface Alloys," The World Book Science Annual 1968, p 290*

[gerund of *metallide, v.*]

meter maid, *U.S.* a policewoman who patrols metered parking areas and gives traffic summonses for parking violations.

The city [New York] itself is hazardous for me now. I started on a walk one afternoon during my last visit, but the wind was so strong I had to lean against walls and hold on to No Parking signs. A Meter Maid was soon watching me censoriously, no doubt thinking I was drunk. *Igor Stravinsky, "On Manners, Music, and Mortality," Harper's, Feb. 1968, p 41*

meth, *n. U.S. Slang.* methamphetamine (a stimulant drug). Also called SPEED.

"It sounds like I'm knocking her. I'm not. She was a good kid, if she hadn't been so freaked out on meth." *J. Anthony Lukas, The New York Times, Oct. 16, 1967, p 53*

meth·i·cil·lin (ˌmeθ əˈsil ən), *n.* a synthetic penicillin that has proved effective against penicillin-resistant staphylococci.

Another six days later there were signs of bacterial infection in the lungs, and the doctors prescribed methicillin. *New Scientist, Jan. 18, 1968, p 118*

[contraction of the full name di*meth*oxyphenyl-pen*icillin*]

meth·o·trex·ate (ˌmeθ ouˈtrekˌseit), *n.* a drug that is an antagonist of folic acid and is used in the treatment of leukemia.

If a doctor has at hand a drug he believes to be beneficial, it is hard to dissuade him from using it. A case in point is a drug called Methotrexate, a highly toxic anti-cancer drug. Physicians have been prescribing it in the treatment of psoriasis, even though the Food and Drug Administration has not approved it for such use. Some 20 years ago physicians stumbled onto the fact that, though Methotrexate does not cure psoriasis, the drug suppresses the scaly, itchy symptoms of the skin disease ... chronic use of Methotrexate may cause severe liver damage, including cirrhosis, which could appear without warning. *Science News, June 6, 1970, p 549*

[probably irregularly formed from the full chemical name *meth*ylamin*o* p*te*r*o*ylglutamic acid + *-ate* (chemical suffix)]

meths, *n.pl. British.* methylated spirits (denatured alcohol).

But what are the other problems we shall have to deal with in ten years time if we do not take measures now? According to Patrick Clivego, go-ahead director of Rescue, one of them will be meths drinking among the aristocracy. *Punch, March 27, 1968, p 448*

methyl atropine, a chemical compound that inhibits the transmission of nerve impulses.

... Smith and his colleagues applied methyl atropine to the lateral hypothalami of killer rats. This chemical, which blocks the action of acetylcholine, turned the formerly deadly rats into harmless pacifists. ... *Graham Chedd, Peter Stubbs, and Gerald Wick, "A Chemical Control of Killing," New Scientist, Feb. 1970, p 342*

methylmercury, *n.* a highly toxic compound of mercury widely used in technology and as a pesticide.

Ultimately, scientists fear, its [mercury's as a fungicide] hazard to human beings may prove equally great. The Swedes solved their problem by banning the use of one extremely pervasive compound, methylmercury, and shipping it to the United States, where it is now used to treat wheat seed. *Frank Graham, Jr., "Pesticides," The Atlantic, Sept. 1970, p 25*

Poisoning by methylmercury compounds, as exemplified by Minamata disease and other sporadic outbreaks, has been characterized by the permanence and irreversibility of the injury to the nervous system. *Leonard J. Goldwater, Durham, N.C., in a Letter to the Editor, The New York Times, June 2, 1971, p 40*

Since these fish [pickerel and perch] are prized by fishermen, the suspected ultimate poison (methyl mercury) is a clear threat to human health. *Time, May 4, 1970, p 85*

meth·yl·phen·i·date (ˌmeθ əlˈfen əˌdeit), *n.* a drug used as a stimulant, especially in the treatment of mental disorders.

The idea that hyperactivity has a biological basis is further strengthened by the dramatic change in behavior produced in many of these children by a stimulating drug (such as amphetamine or methylphenidate). *Mark A. Stewart, "Hyperactive Children," Scientific American, April 1970, p 98*

Army medical researchers reported a "dramatic" new treatment to bring would-be suicide victims out of comas brought on by overdoses of drugs.

The treatment involves "hitherto unreported dosages" of a mild psychomotor stimulant, methylphenidate. *Science News Letter, July 24, 1965, p 64*

[from *methyl* + *phenyl* + *-id* + *-ate*, chemical suffixes]

meth·y·ser·gide (ˌmeθ əˈsərˌgaid), *n.* a drug derived from the fungal nerve poison ergot.

A newer drug, methysergide, also derived from the nerve poison, is effective in reducing the number and severity of migraine headaches in about 70 per cent of patients. *Jane E. Brody, "Headaches," Encyclopedia Science Supplement (Grolier) 1969, p 167*

[apparently from *methyl* + blend of *serotonin* and *ergot* + *-ide* (chemical suffix)]

metric, *adj.* **1 go metric,** to adopt the metric system of measurement.

Going metric will not deprive us of the use of fractions where they are convenient: we can continue to count in halves and quarters as well as in twos, tens, and dozens. *Gordon Bowen, "The Merits of Going Metric," The Manchester Guardian Weekly, Aug. 29, 1970, p 15*

2 (of a country or person) using or accustomed to a metric system of measurement.

In a metric Britain, Manchester will be 296 km from London, not 184 miles. The motorist will have to drive within speed limits of 50 and 120 km per hour, and will have to think of his car as doing 0.354 km per litre, instead of a mile per gallon. His weight will be 68 kg instead of 150 lb. His wife's vital statistics will turn out to be 92-61-92 instead of 36-24-36. *David Hamilton, New Scientist, April 30, 1970, p 247*

met·ri·cate (ˈmet rəˌkeit), *v.t., v.i.* to convert to the metric system; change to metric units. Also, METRIFY.

The cost of metricating road signs, which the Government were examining, would eventually have to be considered by local authorities. *Sir John Eden, The Times (London), Oct. 28, 1970, p 7*

metrication, *n.* conversion to the metric system. Also, METRIFICATION.

Mr Benn said he no more approved or disapproved of metrication as such, than he approved or disapproved of having ten fingers. But three quarters of our exports (he said 75 per cent) were to metric countries. It was good to share the same calendar, to agree on Greenwich Mean Time, and to have common units of measurement. *Terry Coleman, "People and Places," The Manchester Guardian Weekly, March 7, 1970, p 14*

metrification, *n. British.* another word for METRICATION.

The crowning glory of all was decimal coinage, but there was still time to retract. He [Lord Somers] had not heard a good word for it. Now there was a threat of metrification of weights and measures. That was the last straw. Before long there would be a move to drive on the right. *"Parliament:*

Progressive Moves in the Wrong Direction," The Times (London), April 17, 1970, p 6

met·ri·fy ('met rǝ,faɪ), *v.t., v.i. British.* another word for METRICATE.

Although the Confederation of British Industry hopes that 75 per cent. of Britain's industries will have metrified by 1975, there is as yet no official equivalent of the Decimal Currency Board, charged with supervising the change. *Colin Bell, The Sunday Times (London), March 31, 1968, p 10*

Metroliner, *n. U.S.* a high-speed train of the Amtrak railroad network.

The metroliner, electrically propelled with aluminium coaches, has neither quite the panache nor the speed of the Japanese Tokkaido Line, but it has cut the travelling time from Washington to New York, a distance of 226 miles, by nearly ninety minutes to two and a half hours. *Adam Raphael, "A Great American Railway," The Manchester Guardian Weekly, Jan. 31, 1970, p 6*

Metroliners are capable of speeds up to 160 mph but cruise at 120 mph. *Walter E. Jessup, "Civil Engineering," 1970 Collier's Encyclopedia Year Book, p 182*

MHz, abbreviation of MEGAHERTZ.

Other arguments for L-band (390 to 1550 MHz) is that there is room frequency there whereas the VHF wavebands (30 to 300 MHz) now in use are heavily congested and are prone to interference. *Angela Croome, "Satellites to Police the Atlantic's Busy Air Lanes," New Scientist and Science Journal, Aug. 12, 1971, p 363*

mickey, *n.* **take the mickey out of,** *British Slang.* to take the starch out of, especially by mocking or ridiculing.

...there [on television] were Bird, Wells, Fortune, and Barry Humphries taking the mickey out of Kenneth Harris, Lord Devlin, Mark Lane, etc., and the next thing I knew I was laughing. *Stanley Reynolds, "Timing of TV Satire," The Manchester Guardian Weekly, Feb. 16, 1967, p 14*

[probably originally used with *Mickey* in the sense of Irish spirit or bravado, the name being applied facetiously or offensively to any Irishman]

Mickey Mouse, *U.S.* **1** *Military Slang.* **a** anything that is unnecessary or unimportant.

A central concern now is the steady leak of talented officers, most of them young captains, majors, and lieutenant colonels. A study is under way to find the causes, but the most sensitive army officers already know them. They are four: the repeated Vietnam tours, the antimilitary atmosphere in the country, the low pay, and (for the younger men) the anachronistic spit-and-polish, the Mickey Mouse. *Ward Just, "Soldiers," The Atlantic, Nov. 1970, p 81*

b a muddled situation; a mix-up; foul-up.

Logistically so far, the only big Mickey Mouse, in G.I. parlance, was a brief shortage of canvas-and-rubber jungle boots (leather footgear rots in Viet Nam's steamy climate); they were flown in directly from Stateside manufacturers. *Time, Dec. 10, 1965, p 15*

2 *Student Slang.* an easy or simple college course.

Some popular opinion persists, of course, that college courses in "the movies" are a kind of trade-school apprenticeship or something easy to relax with ("Mickey Mouse" in today's campus parlance). *David C. Stewart, "The Movies Students Make: New Wave on Campus," Harper's, Oct. 1965, p 68*

3 simple; easy; unimportant.

"This is no Mickey Mouse business," said E. James Strates.... "In the old days you put together a funhouse for $3,000, now it can cost $40,000." *Richard F. Shepard, The New York Times, Sept. 25, 1967, p 41*

[named for the Walt Disney animated cartoon character, in allusion to its childish appeal, its simplicity, triviality, etc.]

mickey-mouse, *v.i.* to synchronize the background music with the action, as in an animated cartoon.

The choreography, by Norman Maen, is the feeblest element in the film, with too much unimaginative "Mickey-mousing", matching each note in the score with some movement rather than creating an overall style of dance. *John Russell Taylor, The Times (London), July 6, 1967, p 8*

micro, *adj.* shorter than mini; mid-thigh or higher.

The hem was the same place it was last year—everywhere. Couturiers pegged it all the way from micro to floor level. *Edith R. Locke, "Fashion: A Year for All Looks," 1970 Collier's Encyclopedia Year Book, p 232*

—*n.* a skirt, dress, or other garment that is shorter than mini. Compare MAXI, MIDI, MINI.

Hemlines go to all lengths. In extremes, there are micros, which barely cover the buttocks; minis, maxis and the nineteen-thirties length, which is well below the knee but still shows some shin. *Gloria Emerson, The New York Times, Jan. 22, 1968, p 36*

[from *micro-* very small]

micro-, *combining form.* **1** miniature.

microbreccia, *n.:* Souvenir from the moon: a large microbreccia. This is a rock composed of fragmental material. Note the glass-lined pits on the rock's surface. *Picture legend, "The Lunar Rocks: Scientists Report Exciting Discoveries," Encyclopedia Science Supplement (Grolier) 1970, p 51*

microchip, *n.:* Because the construction of these "microchips" was extremely complex, it was much more difficult to eliminate some of the procedural difficulties in the monolithic than in the hybrid IC's. *Robert E. Stoffels, "Electronics," 1970 Britannica Yearbook of Science and the Future, 1969, p 166*

microdevice, *n.:* ... automation is increasingly used in the production of the micro-devices and circuits which in turn are assembled into further automation systems. *Kenneth Owen, The Times (London), May 7, 1970, p 33*

microexplosion, *n.:* It may be possible to get thermonuclear power from the very sudden heating of pellets of fuel, or microexplosions. *Dietrick E. Thomsen, Science News, Oct. 17, 1970, p 323*

microfile, *n.:* Having selected the appropriate microfile from his folder, by means of one of 65 keywords (eg "filter"), the engineer inserts it into a reader and selects the page he wants by scanning down the first column. *Glen Lawes, "Technology Review: Hard Sell for the Desk-Top Library," New Scientist, July 10, 1969, p 71*

microinstability, *n.:* More than a hundred kinds of microinstabilities have been identified, and fusion researchers have been trying to find magnetic-bottle configurations that will be able to reduce the microinstabilities to acceptable proportions. *Alvin M. Weinberg, "Curbing The Energy Crisis," The World Book Science Annual 1972 (1971), p 222*

micronuclear, *adj.:* Only by thorough and candid discussion of these "micro-nuclear" weapons can valid conclusions be drawn about a realistic defence policy for this country and Nato. *C. B. Joly, Winchester, England, in a Letter to the Editor, The Times (London), March 23, 1970, p 11*

microsystem, *n.:* One early form of life could have been a thermodynamically open, self-assembled, proteinaceous microsystem, capable of propagating its own kind through the use of preformed polyamino acids. *Sidney Fox, "In the Beginning...Life Assembled Itself," New Scientist, Feb. 27, 1969, p 452*

microzone, *n.:* No one regional center can be pinpointed as the place from which agriculture emerged. Rather, there were a series of agricultural developments stemming from a number of environmental niches or microzones. *Gordon R. Willey, "Archaeology," The World Book Science Annual 1968, p 267*

2 microscopic.

microcrater, *n.:*...Mr. Gold [Thomas Gold, an astrophysicist at Cornell University]...had found microscopic craters—three or four craters, sometimes, to a speck of dust—and he was certain these microcraters proved that much of the dust on the moon came from space....*Henry S. F. Cooper, Jr., "Letter From the Space Center," The New Yorker, April 4, 1970, p 92*

microfungus, *n.:*...high protein foods such as skimmed milk powder, leaf protein, micro-fungi and yeasts or soy proteins are enthusiastically promoted. *Philip Payne and Erica Wheeler, "What Protein Gap?" New Scientist and Science Journal, April 15, 1971, p 148*

microorgan, *n.:* These microscopic collections consist of both blood lymphocytes and epithelial cells which make up the various linings of the body. The microorgans were found in the mastoid gland, pancreas, gullet, bronchia, larynx and different parts of the skin. *"New Organ Discovered," Science News, Oct. 25, 1969, p 376*

microparticle, *n.:*...the search continues for facts about the similarities and differences between "organized elements," microfossils, and microparticles formed from amino acid polymers. *S. W. Fox and R. J. McCauley, "Could Life Originate Now?" Encyclopedia Science Supplement (Grolier) 1969, p 78*

microworld, *n.:* Chemists and molecular biologists have unraveled many of the intricate processes needed to create the microworld of the living cell. *Bert Bolin, "The Carbon Cycle," Scientific American, Sept. 1970, p 125*

[from Greek *mikrós* small]

See also the entries below for compounds in *micro-* having specialized meanings or greater-than-average frequency.

microanalyzer, *n.* an apparatus for microscopic analysis of the composition of chemical elements, compounds, minerals, etc.

An ion microanalyzer provided instant photomicrographs of a specimen's chemical distribution by combining a mass spectrometer with an ion-emission microscope. *Jacob Kastner, "Molecular Biology," Britannica Book of the Year 1970, p 543*

microbeam, *n.* a finely focused electron beam.

Chromosome mapping and investigations of chromosome structure could be extended by the laser microbeam. *Michael W. Burns and Donald E. Rounds, "Cell Surgery by Laser," Scientific American, Feb. 1970, p 108*

microblade, *n. Archaeology.* a thin sliver chipped delicately from a prepared flint core, usually with parallel edges.

Late in the Upper Paleolithic and during the ensuing

Mesolithic, it became the fashion to make smaller and smaller bladelettes. Commonly inserted as "side blades" into lateral grooves in antler and bone projectile points, such "microblades" lacerated the flesh of wounded game animals and thus promoted free bleeding and rapid death. *Charles E. Borden, "New Evidence on the Early Peopling of The New World," Britannica Book of the Year 1969, p 101*

microbody, *n.* See the quotation for the meaning.

Ever since the electron microscope became available, microscopists have noted little particles within cells which they were unable to identify with any particular function. In a fit of divine inspiration, they named these particles "microbodies." Over the past few years, [Professor Christian] de Duve has discovered that these microbodies contain an enzyme system which could conceivably constitute the primitive respiratory system of the cell. The particles always contain an oxidase enzyme of some type, capable of indirectly converting oxygen to hydrogen peroxide. They also contain a catalase enzyme, which can convert hydrogen peroxide to water. *Graham Chedd, "The 'Micro-Kitchens' of the Cell," New Scientist, June 27, 1968, p 675*

micro book, a very small book which requires the use of a magnifying glass for reading.

The micro book is already much more than an idea. A company called Micro & Cine Books Ltd has been set up in Jersey and has taken premises to make the hardware—the readers and covers. Davies and his co-worker are intending to form their own publishing company in Alderney, which they have recently adopted as their base. *Edward Owen, "The Dawn of Micro-Publishing?" New Scientist, Dec. 31, 1970, p 601*

microcalorie, *n.* one millionth of a calorie.

Heat flow through the ocean crust is on average 1.2 microcalories/cm²/s except in active regions such as mid-ocean ridges. *David Davies, "The Red Sea: Development of an Ocean," Science Journal, Aug. 1969, p 42*

The heat flux of the moon is about two-tenths to three-tenths of a microcalorie per square centimeter per second, or about a sixth to a third that of the earth. *Science News, Nov. 28, 1970, p 414*

microcapsule, *n.* a very small or microscopic capsule of a chemical substance, drug, etc.

Chang showed that his microcapsules of asparaginase broke down asparagine [an amino acid] when suspended in an asparagine solution, and so he tested the technique in animals. *New Scientist and Science Journal, Jan. 28, 1971, p 171*

microcircuit, *n.* another name for INTEGRATED CIRCUIT.

Ferranti have introduced a new and advanced airborne computer known as the Argus 400—the first machine incorporating fully integrated silicon microcircuits to be developed and built in Europe. *The Times (London), Aug. 10, 1965, p 10*

microcircuitry, *n.* **1** another name for INTEGRATED CIRCUITRY.

If they can get a transmitter into that fabled olive in the vodkatini, then they could pack a fine old array of microcircuitry into a mouse's saddle-bags. *New Scientist, June 10, 1965, p 702*

2 microscopic circuits.

Ganglion cells, however, fall into certain classes, indicating considerable order in the microcircuitry between them and the receptor cells. *Peter Gouras, "Vision," McGraw-Hill Yearbook of Science and Technology 1969, p 344*

microcirculation, *n.* circulation of the blood through the capillary vessels.

But in the microcirculation, other factors—chemical messengers—seem to be at work. The red of a sunburn, for example, doesn't come from reaction of the brain or nerves. Ultraviolet light striking the skin causes it to release a compound called histamine. That body drug causes tiny arteries and capillaries to dilate so that blood suffuses the skin—sunburn. *Joe Hixson, "Microcirculation: 60,000 Miles of Blood Vessels," Science News, Dec. 2, 1967, p 547*

micro-corneal lens, a contact lens covering only part of the cornea of the eye. Compare HAPTIC LENS.

Micro-corneal lenses cover only two thirds of the surface area of the cornea—the transparent bulge in front of the pupil—and must be aligned with its curvature. *"UV [ultraviolet] Fit for Contact Lenses," New Scientist and Science Journal, Sept. 23, 1971, p 688*

microcrack, *n.* a microscopic crack in a material such as glass or chrome.

The low strength of glass is attributed to the presence of microcracks in the glass surface which drastically reduce the overall stress needed to cause fracture. *New Scientist, Feb. 27, 1969, p 457*

—*v.i., v.t.* to produce microcracks (in a material).

At low thicknesses the deposits of chrome thrown by the new method are microporous, while thicker coatings are microcracked, which according to concentrated testing, gives a far greater resistance to corrosion. *Kenneth Owen, "The World of Technology: Metal Processing," The Times (London), May 22, 1970, p 27*

microculture, *n.* **1** a small, narrowly confined geographical area, whose inhabitants are considered to have their own ways and fashions that form a cultural unit within a nation, state, or other larger area.

That part of Texas where I first lived was some microculture. Puritanism in theory. Tobacco Road in practice. *E. T. Gibbons, quoted by John McPhee, "Profiles: A Forager," The New Yorker, April 6, 1968, p 58*

2 a culture of microscopic organisms, tissue, etc.

"To clean the specimens I used a microculture slide in the form of a glass plate containing 12 depressions, each approximately one centimeter wide and four millimeters deep...." *Pete Rowe, quoted by C. L. Stong, "The Amateur Scientist: How to Study Learning in the Sow Bug and Photograph Tiny Live Crustaceans," Scientific American, May 1967, p 144*

microdot, *n.* **1** a photograph of a letter, page, or other document reduced in size to a dot for purposes of secrecy or economy in processing or storage.

He would also hold a current set of the micro-dot films on which would be recorded all the information "known" to the centralized computer about properties in the market. *The Times (London), Nov. 10, 1966, p 9*

2 *Slang.* a small pill containing the hallucinogenic drug LSD in highly concentrated form.

...one senior officer said last night: "I am deeply concerned about the use of this completely new form of LSD.

Normally the drug produces hallucinations, but these microdots create fear, terror and suicidal tendencies." *Terence O'Hanlon, "Terror Tablets Hit Britain," New York Post, Jan. 3, 1972, p 5*

microearthquake, *n.* a small earthquake, of magnitude of less than 2.5 on the Richter scale.

The first seismological station near downtown Los Angeles specifically to monitor very small earth tremors is being developed at the University of Southern California. It should be installed by late summer.... improved electronic equipment and modern developments in seismometer design should enable the new instrument to sort out artificial vibrations from those caused by local microearthquakes.... *Science News, March 28, 1970, p 320*

Italian researchers making seismic measurements at and around the [Bay of Pozzuoli] area found evidence of only a few microearthquakes. *Science News, March 13, 1971, p 181*

"Before a volcano erupts it generates micro-earthquakes, which we are able to detect on our seismographs," Dr. Robson says.... *The New York Times, May 23, 1967, p 29*

microecology, *n.* a branch of ecology concerned with environmental conditions in very small areas.

Too little is still known about microecology to allow for meaningful generalizations about the significance of impenetrable microsites for the protection of polluting chemicals against attack. *Martin Alexander, "Pollutants That Resist the Microbes," New Scientist, Aug. 31, 1967, p 440*

microelectronic, *adj.* of or relating to microelectronics.

And without the voracious demand of the computer industry we would not have seen such a rapid advance in electronic, and especially microelectronic, technology. *W. J. Talbot and R. Naylor, "Computer Hardware for the 1970s," Science Journal, Oct. 1970, p 42*

microelectronics, *n.* the branch of electronics dealing with integrated circuits.

Tiny "throw away" packages of instruments that could be dropped into the sea, then left there when the job is done, may soon make oceanographers pardonable litter bugs. The hot-dog-shaped package could contain as many as three or four instruments and make a number of measurements at the same time, cutting costs and increasing the accuracy of scientific data, an oceanographer reported.... Microelectronics, the use of extremely small circuits to replace larger and more costly tubes and transistors, will make such throw-away devices "economically useful," he [James M. Snodgrass] said. *William McCann, "Disposables Scan Sea," Science News Letter, April 3, 1965, p 213*

microencapsulate, *v.t.* to enclose (something small) in a microcapsule.

Numerous metabolic diseases, many of them fatal in early infancy, have their roots in a lack of an appropriate enzyme in the liver, and all are presumably targets for liposome therapy. The technique has the advantage over other attempts that are being made to microencapsulate enzymes for therapy in that liposomes are constructed of "natural" materials. *"Parcel Post for Missing Enzymes," New Scientist and Science Journal, July 15, 1971, p 122*

microencapsulation, *n.* encapsulation in microcapsules.

But today striped paint is no more ridiculous than... copying paper that needs no carbon, or drugs that taste pleasant yet later (according to a precisely designed time

289

schedule) release unpalatable medicants into the body, or packaged perfume painted invisibly on to paper for release months or years later, or petrol in the form of an apparently solid brick that can be sliced with a knife. These and many other equally startling but useful products all owe their existence to microencapsulation. *A. C. Watson, "Micro-encapsulation," Science Journal, Feb. 1970, p 62*

microform, *n.* **1** any material on which something can be reproduced in greatly reduced form.

The master files of the more than 3.2 million patents issued since 1790 will be put on microfilm, videotape or another microform for quick retrieval and public sale. *Stacy V. Jones, The New York Times, Jan. 25, 1966, p 55*

Paper would be impracticable but microform might be the answer. *Bryan Silcock, The Sunday Times (London), Sept. 24, 1967, p 2*

—*v.t.* to reproduce on microfilm or other material; make copies of on microform.

The Massachusetts Institute of Technology ... is planning to "microform" its entire engineering library. *J. C. R. Licklider, The New York Times, Jan. 9, 1967, p 139*

microlens, *n.* a lens for photography on a microscopic scale.

Walon Green, who directed the picture and shot a good portion of the photography as well, used microlenses and extreme slow motion to get awesome footage of mayflies living out their brief lives. ... *Jay Cocks, "Bug's-Eye View," Time, July 19, 1971, p 48*

micromachining, *n.* the machining of very small parts, such as the components of microcircuits.

Micromachining has received much publicity in the past, and forms the mainstay of Laser Associates' range of systems. ... An example of this would be the drilling of a very fine hole in a hard material to a depth many times the diameter. *"Profits from Lasers?" New Scientist, April 16, 1970, p 101*

micrometeoroid, *n.* a tiny meteoroid; a meteoroid so small that it will not disintegrate upon entering the earth's atmosphere.

To date the methods of measuring the number of micro-meteoroids that strike satellites have employed either microphonic techniques to count the impacts, or some system whereby the perforations in a material are scored electronically. *New Scientist, Oct. 17, 1963, p 160*

A satellite is being developed to reach 172,000 miles into space and gather data on micrometeoroids, tiny bits of matter no larger than grains of sand. *Science News Letter, Aug. 29, 1964, p 133*

microminiaturization, *n.* the production of microminiaturized objects or parts.

Now, microminiaturization has entered the field; large-scale integrated (LSI) circuits are smaller and more complex than their predecessors. *"Technology: Review of the Year," Encyclopedia Science Supplement (Grolier) 1971, p 27*

microminiaturize, *v.t.* to reduce (electronic circuits, etc.) to a size smaller than miniature. Also, SUBMINIATURIZE.

The transistorized lock ... could be microminiaturized and adapted to any number of combinations. *Stacy V. Jones, The New York Times, May 20, 1967, p 49*

micropopulation, *n.* the population of microorganisms living in a particular habitat.

Bdellovibrio bacteriovorus, discovered in 1962 by H. Stolp of Berlin-Dahlem, is the only bacterium so far known which lives as a parasite on other bacteria. It is not a virus bacteriophage but a true bacterium. First discovered in Berlin, it was found later by Dr. Stolp in soil samples from Mexico, Venezuela, Greece, Malta, Australia, Ceylon, Japan and from other countries. It can be considered therefore as a common member of the micropopulation of soil and water. *New Scientist, Feb. 2, 1967, p 282*

microprobe, *n.* an instrument using a very fine-focused electron beam, usually in combination with optical apparatus, to analyze the chemical composition of rocks, minerals, glasses, alloys, etc.

In the laboratory, I have seen a laser instrument called a microprobe that permits quick and easy analysis of any object without damaging it. *Thomas Meloy, National Geographic Magazine, Dec. 1966, p 868*

... microprobe analysis of three [suspected contaminants] gave a composition (99 percent iron, 1 percent manganese, < 1 percent nickel) similar to steel. *David W. Parkin and David Tilles, "Influx Measurements of Extraterrestrial Material," Science, March 1, 1968, p 938*

microprogram, *n.* special data in the memory of a computer, used as part of a more complex program or to control the operations of a subordinate computer.

In the 1970s, Babcock believes, writable control stores and loadable microprograms will become common. *"Increased Dividends in Plug-in Software," New Scientist and Science Journal, June 17, 1971, p 685*

We can also expect to see new devices, possibly based on the use of amorphous materials, employed in very fast semi-fixed stores used for micro-programmes. *Kenneth Owen, The Times (London), March 6, 1970, p 29*

—*v.t.* to provide (a computer) with a microprogram.

... a given micro-programmed machine may be easily adjusted to duplicate the characteristics of another machine, so that programs written in machine language for other computers can be handled without reprogramming. *Van Court Hare, Jr., Introduction to Programming: A BASIC Approach, 1970, p 413*

micropulsation, *n.* an extremely small fluctuation in the earth's magnetic field.

Micropulsations are small quasi-sinusoidal oscillations of the Earth's field having periods ranging from about 1/5 sec to several hundred seconds. *A. J. Dessler, "Magnetosphere," McGraw-Hill Yearbook of Science and Technology 1968, p 241*

Hydromagnetic waves have proved essential to the explanation of geomagnetic micropulsations, and of the close relation between magnetic disturbances at magnetically linked points of the Earth's northern and southern hemisphere. *Thomas Cowling, New Scientist, Nov. 5, 1970, p 270*

microskirt, *n.* a skirt that is shorter than a miniskirt.

The trouble is that with maxicoats, culottes, microskirts and trousersuits all in vogue, even the Hemline dictate is just a matter of personal predilection. *Graham Searjeant, The Sunday Times (London), Oct. 12, 1969, p 27*

microsleep, *n.* See the quotations for the meaning.

They [people deprived of sleep for a few days] lapsed into momentary blackouts called microsleeps and were beset by ... a sense of disorientation. *Julius Segal and*

Gay Gaer Luce, "Sleep and Dreams," 1970 Britannica Yearbook of Science and the Future, 1969, p 313

... the subjects developed serious anomalies in brain wave pattern accompanied by 'microsleep'—a compulsive tendency to drop off unless kept constantly active. "Science and Technology News: RN [Royal Navy] Deep Dives Beat Compression Syndrome," Science Journal, May 1970, p 14

microslide, n. a microscopic slide used in ultramicroscopic study or experimentation.

They [the individual droplets of a supercooled drop of water] fell on his microslide in large numbers for approximately 50 seconds until the drop was completely frozen. New Scientist, Jan. 14, 1971, p 54

A rapid detection method for the major components of cannabis by J. Karlsen involves the use of microslides for thin-layer chromatography. Albert R. Sperling, "Psychopharmacological Drugs," McGraw-Hill Yearbook of Science and Technology 1971, p 359

microstate, n. another name for MINISTATE.

Other events included ... proposals that a special UN membership category be created for "microstates." Neville M. Hunnings, "Law," Britannica Book of the Year 1970, p 463

microsurgery, n. surgery performed on cells, tissues, etc., with the aid of a microscope.

Informed researchers believe that as equipment grows more sophisticated, tomorrow's surgeons will use such mind-defying techniques as nanosurgery, 10,000 times finer than the microsurgery now employed in pediatrics, and dependent on improvements in electron-microscopy and laser instrumentation now under study in the United States and France. James C. G. Conniff, "Fetology: New Medical Specialty," Encyclopedia Science Supplement (Grolier) 1967, p 181

microtektite, n. a microscopic variety of tektite found deep in ocean sediments.

But ocean sediments in some regions, notably near Australia and the Ivory Coast, contain small glassy objects called microtektites which are reckoned to be the fine-grained components of the so-called "strewn fields" of larger tektites. "A Hint of Global Pollution A Million Years Ago?" New Scientist and Science Journal, Aug. 5, 1971, p 299

Checking with other research, they found that another major concentration of these microtektites had settled around Australasia during another reversal that took place 700,000 years ago. "Science: The Comets Did It," Time, Sept. 6, 1971, p 48

microtubule, n. a long, straight tubular structure, of uncertain function, in many cells of the body.

Microtubules are now generally recognized as an almost ubiquitous component of the cytoplasm of cells. D. Frisch, "Microtubule, Cell," McGraw-Hill Yearbook of Science and Technology 1968, p 262

The microtubules are very fine tubes averaging 250 angstroms in diameter. They are found in cilia, in the tail of sperm cells, in the mitotic spindle of a dividing cell and in the cytoplasm of many types of cell (where they have been studied by Keith R. Porter, Lewis G. Tilney and J. Richard McIntosh of Harvard University). Norman K. Wessells, "How Living Cells Change Shape," Scientific American, Oct. 1971, p 77

microvascular, adj. of or relating to the very small vessels of the circulatory system, such as the capillaries.

Precise formations of the microvascular system and other spaces in organs of dead animals are revealed in detail when this liquid silicone compound is injected. Science News, Sept. 9, 1967, p 262

microvilli, n.pl. microscopic hairlike parts growing on the surface of a cell.

... partly digested food is finally broken down on the surface of the small intestine which, he [Dr. A. M. Ugolev] claims, forms a "living porous reactor", the pores being formed by microvilli, where adsorbed enzymes complete the process of hydrolysis. Science Journal, Jan. 1969, p 19

The photographs from the scanning electron microscope show that on day 4 of the reproductive cycle the epithelium is covered by a regular carpet of thread-like microvilli.... "Sperm's Eye View of Implantation," New Scientist and Science Journal, Aug. 12, 1971, p 356

midcourse, adj. for or during the middle part of the course of a spacecraft, aircraft, etc.

During the uneventful, 73-hour coast [of Apollo 11 toward the moon], only one of the four planned midcourse corrections was necessary. After breakfast Thursday, Collins prepared for the minor course-correction maneuver. William J. Cromie, "... One Giant Leap for Mankind," The 1970 World Book Year Book, p 66

—n. the middle part of the course of a spacecraft, aircraft, etc.

... the small rocket engine which can manoeuvre the space craft slightly in mid-course was needed only to direct Ranger to the sunny rather than the dark side of the moon. The Times (London), Aug. 1, 1964, p 6

midcult, n. cultural characteristics associated with the middle class, typified by conventional and moderately intellectual values and ideas.

If there is any clerical rival to Dr Billy Graham in President Nixon's affections, Fr Hesburgh is the man. In their different ways, all three men exercise a ministry to Midcult. Christopher Driver, "Most Powerful Priest in America," The Manchester Guardian Weekly, April 17, 1969, p 5

[contraction of middle-class culture]

Middle America, a broad cross section of the American population conceived as politically middle-of-the-road or moderate, belonging to the middle-income class, and geographically situated chiefly in the midwestern states. Compare SILENT MAJORITY.

Laid out like a sheet of rolled steel on the Great Miami River, a major industrial center plopped down on the placid, undulating farmland of southwestern Ohio, Dayton is about as Middle America as you can get. Paul Hemphill, "Merle Haggard: When you're runnin' down our country, hoss, you're walkin' on the fightin' side of me," The Atlantic, Sept. 1971, p 98

What is seriously wrong with Mr Nixon's new Middle-America is that it is virtually all white. Henry Brandon, The Sunday Times (London), Sept. 29, 1968, p 8

To call Salina Middle America, however, would not be entirely accurate. "We have some pockets of intolerance," says Whitley Austin, editor of the Salina Journal, "but most of the people simply try to be fair." Salina is an accumulation of American eras. Ladies wait for men to open doors for them. William Friedman, "American Scene: Nostalgic Reunion in Salina, Kansas," Time, July 13, 1970, p 14

Middle American

► The term *Middle America* has long been used by geographers in an entirely different sense, to denote the region between the United States and South America which includes Mexico, Central America, and the West Indies.

Middle American, 1 a person belonging to Middle America.

Who precisely are the Middle Americans? . . . They make up the core of the group that Richard Nixon now invokes as the "forgotten Americans" or "the Great Silent Majority," though Middle Americans themselves may not be a majority of the U.S. All Americans doubtless share some Middle American beliefs, and many Middle Americans would disagree among themselves on some issues. . . . Although a hard figure is not possible, the total of Middle Americans probably approaches 100 million, or half of the U.S. population. *Time, Jan. 5, 1970, p 9*

2 of or belonging to Middle America.

. . . *Newsweek* wrote on December 2, 1968: "Her [Mrs. Richard Nixon's] looks and taste are classic Middle American, even as her husband's are." *David Halberstam, "Richard M. Nixon," 1969 Collier's Encyclopedia Year Book, p 3*

mid·i ('mid i:), *n.* **1** a skirt, dress, or other garment reaching to the calf, usually the mid-calf. Also called LONGUETTE. Compare MAXI, MICRO, MINI.

If I died, what would they bury me in? A mini? A midi? Pants? I know, this isn't important. *Jean Goldschmidt, "Pursuits," The Atlantic, June 1971, p 66*

2 the style or length characterized by hemlines at the calf.

What you seemed to miss is that for the individual, fashion should be FUN! In variety and change there is that fun. As for the midi, let's hope it helps to bring back those qualities so sadly lacking from the recent sartorial scene: grace, elegance and good taste. *Barbara Pixley White, in a Letter to the Editor, Time, Oct. 5, 1970, p 4*

—*adj.* reaching to the calf.

The mid-calf-length midi had, according to one fashion expert, "become merely an extra, whether as coat, cape, pants, or late-day dress." U.S. designer Anne Klein had shown midi coats in her fall collection but cut them shorter "after getting the message from the stores' buyers." *Phyllis West Heathcote, "Fashion and Dress," Britannica Book of the Year 1969, p 337*

In this case, it is a series of sandwich-board capes in midi and maxi lengths. *Enid Nemy, The New York Times, July 11, 1968, p 40*

[from *mid* + -*i*, as in *mini* and *maxi*]

militaria, *n.pl.* a collection of objects having to do with the military, such as firearms, decorations, uniforms, etc.

During his last years he spent much of his time in trying to gather together writings, militaria and other possessions left by the Field-Marshal. *The Times (London), Dec. 23, 1970, p 10*

[from Latin *mīlitāria*, neuter plural of *mīlitāris* military]

military-industrial complex, the combination of a strongly entrenched military establishment and a large war matériel industry, viewed as a powerful interest group controlling American economic and foreign policy.

This basic issue [the neglect of domestic problems] aroused intense emotion and led to vigorous denunciations of the "military-industrial complex," which presumably had a stake in a high level of international tension to justify more arms for soldiers, greater profits for businessmen, and reelection of congressmen who brought jobs and money to their constituents. *John W. Spanier, "United States," The Americana Annual 1970, p 729*

► The term was apparently first used by President Dwight D. Eisenhower in his Farewell Address, delivered on January 17, 1961. It appears in the following passage: "In the councils of government, we must guard against the acquisition of unwarranted influence, whether sought or unsought, by the military-industrial complex. The potential for the disastrous rise of misplaced power exists and will persist."

mim·e·o ('mim i:,ou), *n.* a mimeographed bulletin, newsletter, memorandum, etc. *Often used attributively.*

Why Sandra Peredo's patronizing attitude toward the little magazines? She states, for instance, that the mimeo mags are interested in dirty words and anti-Establishment statements as their main themes. *George Bowering, London, Ontario, in a Letter to the Editor, Maclean's, Jan. 1967, p 56*

—*v.t.* to mimeograph.

We learn later that the statement was mimeoed and a few reporters were walking off with it when the secretary came after them and snatched it out of their hands. *Jeremy Larner, "Reflections on the McCarthy Campaign," Harper's, May 1969, p 82*

[shortened from *mimeograph*]

Min·a·ma·ta disease (,min ə'mɑ: tə), poisoning by ingestion of methylmercury. Also called MAD HATTER'S DISEASE.

In the early 1950's fishermen and their families around Minamata Bay in Japan were stricken with a mysterious neurological illness. The Minamata disease, as it came to be called, produced progressive weakening of the muscles, loss of vision, impairment of other cerebral functions, eventual paralysis and in some cases coma and death. The victims had suffered structural injury to the brain. *Leonard J. Goldwater, "Mercury in the Environment," Scientific American, May 1971, p 15*

Poisoning by methylmercury compounds, as exemplified by Minamata disease and other sporadic outbreaks, has been characterized by the permanence and irreversibility of the injury to the nervous system. *Leonard J. Goldwater, Durham, N.C., in a Letter to the Editor, The New York Times, June 2, 1971, p 40*

[from *Minamata*, a town in western Kyushu, Japan]

mi·nau·diè·re (mi: nou'dyer), *n.* a small metal case, often jeweled, in which a woman carries cosmetics and other small items.

Rare shells . . . have been fashioned into exquisite minaudières for the hand, pill boxes for the purse, and unique pendant-lockets for chain, pin or belt. *Advertisement in The New Yorker, March 8, 1969, p 17*

"I found that my regular minaudière was terribly small and I always had to stuff things in my pocket," . . . [Mrs. Butler] said. *Enid Nemy, The New York Times, June 22, 1967, p 43*

[from French, literally, coquettish]

mind, *n.* **blow one's mind,** *Slang.* **1** to experience or cause to have drug-induced hallucinations.

... he regularly turned on with marijuana or blew his mind with LSD. *John Corry, The New York Times, March 21, 1966, p 1*

In one episode, some hippies offer him coffee and "blow his mind" with the new mind-expanding drug. *Iain Ewing, "The Paste-Pot Press That Blows Its Readers' Minds," Maclean's, Sept. 1967, p 89*

"In this place," said the soldier with a grin, "you can blow your mind every night of the year." In the language of the marijuana subculture familiar to most Americans under 30 but sadly baffling to most of the rest, the young soldier was saying that here in Vietnam cannabis, pot, the weed, giggle-smoke, grass, Mary Jane, call it what you will, is readily available and freely used. *Ian Wright, The Manchester Guardian Weekly, June 20, 1970, p 6*

2 to cause to lose control over one's mind; to excite, stir, shock, etc., to an extreme degree.

Then [at the annual conference of U.S. Student Press Association held in Washington], on screens on three walls, flashed gory Viet Nam scenes from Communist propaganda movies.... The film was meant to blow the minds of the viewers, but they blew their cool instead. Some raced around trying to pull the plugs of the projectors; others tried to get their hands on the organizers. *"Lessons in Mind Blowing," Time, Feb. 16, 1968, p 47*

The old-fashioned beggar with tin cup and violin is being pushed off the stage by long-haired kids with a bold sophisticated line in cadging. The Hippie will stop passers-by and explain that he is fifty cents short on his fare to New Jersey. Could they help? Less commercially minded but equally thick-skinned characters are content with "blowing people's minds." One I met gets his kicks walking up to somebody and saying: "Would you hold this dollar for me while I go in that store and steal something?" *William Davis, Punch, Oct. 22, 1969, p 658*

"His duplicity blew our minds." *Time, Feb. 16, 1970, p 62*

mind-bender, *n.* *Slang.* **1** a hallucinogenic drug.

STP is a new, untested drug, resembling both ampheta-mine pep pills and the active ingredient in mescaline, the cactus-derived mind-bender. *Science News, July 22, 1967, p 80*

2 a user of drugs, especially hallucinogenic drugs.

In recent years, youthful mind-benders have tripped (or thought they did) on everything from airplane glue to morning-glory seeds, from nutmeg to black tea. *Time, April 7, 1967, p 60*

3 something which boggles the mind.

Apart from any benison it may bring to science writers by giving them a glimmering of what on earth they are writing about, the glossary brings more simple comfort to those of us who have previously lived under the vague belief that a quasar was a queer type of laser. The booklet leads with its full name of *Quasi Stellar Radio Source* which mouthful, swallowed with the other 86 mindbenders, produces heartfelt gratitude for the mercy of occupying this particular column where no equipment is needed more technical than a lard-bladder. *New Scientist, March 18, 1965, p 694*

4 a person who uses subtle means to influence, persuade, or bend others to his will.

What the Republican mind-benders are thinking about is individualized communication—computerized mail and telephone on a scale new to politics—and subtle use of television, all designed to touch basic attitudes, the voter's "value profile," rather than change his idea about old Dick Nixon. *Richard Reeves, "Nixon's Secret Strategy," Harper's, Dec. 1971, p 97*

mind-bending, *adj.* *Slang.* **1** causing hallucina-tions; hallucinogenic.

In dealing with student dissidents, perhaps a more effective coolant might be the joint (marijuana cigarette), which has sealed many a youthful alliance. Indeed there is a precedent for such get-togethers in the American Indian ceremony of the peace pipe, which was often filled with "kinnikinnick"—a mind-bending admixture of hemp and the inner bark of dogwood. *"The Need for Conciliation," Time, June 7, 1968, p 31*

2 distorting the perception; causing mental stupor or derangement.

Already "mind-bending" gases for military purposes are said to be at an advanced stage of development, if not actually on the active lists; their proponents suggest that they are more humane than bullets. *New Scientist, April 21, 1966, p 151*

3 boggling the mind; overwhelming.

The theoretical mathematics of the situation [mining metals] are positively mind-bending. Howarth and Cham-bers claim that 300,000 tons of ore has already been stock-piled at El Sobrante. If this assays "only" 20 ounces of platinum per ton, this means that they have the equivalent of four times the total American stockpile of platinum ... and rather more than four times the annual US production. *The Sunday Times (London), Jan. 25, 1970, p 29*

mind-blow, *v.t.* *Slang.* to blow the mind of; excite, stir, shock, etc.

It can mind-blow a long-haired GI to know he'll have to live straighter to survive in Sweden than in the Army or in America. *Clancy Sigal, "I am an American Military Deserter and I Ask for Political Asylum," The Listener, Oct. 22, 1970, p 540*

[see MIND, def. 2]

mind blower, *Slang.* **1** a hallucinogenic drug.

Psychedelic drugs not only have a bewildering range of subjective effects on human perception but their chemistry is pretty baffling too. There are at least three different classes of psychedelic drugs, each with very different molecular structures. To complicate matters further, two chemicals with almost identical structures can have very different psychedelic properties: one might be a real mind-blower and the other as ineffective as a sugar lump. *"What Makes a Molecule Blow Your Mind?" New Scien-tist, June 27, 1968, p 703*

2 a user of drugs, especially hallucinogenic drugs.

For most of the 19th century's mind blowers, opium meant laudanum, an alcoholic solution of the drug used as a common painkiller. *Time, May 30, 1969, p 55*

3 a mindblowing experience.

There is the hysteria of The Who and the pure rhythmic orgasm of Ten Years After. They all help to make *Wood-stock* as unique on film as it was in fact, "the mind blower," as John Sebastian puts it, "of all time." *Time, April 13, 1970, p 103*

mindblowing, *Slang.* —*adj.* **1** hallucinogenic.

... the poet celebrates the mindblowing effects of LSD and laments at the same time his lost childhood. *Bill Byrom, The Times (London), May 4, 1968, p 21*

2 exciting, stirring, shocking, etc., to an extreme degree.

The underground journals range ... from the transcendental theory of Avatar to the "mind-blowing" visual effects and kinky sex ads of The East Village Other. *John Leo, The New York Times, Sept. 4, 1968, p 39*

My doctor and I agreed that while I was in the hospital I would not hang around with my friends outside anymore. I only saw them for an hour or so in the evenings on the way home, and they thought it was very mystical and mind-blowing to be in the hospital. *Jonathan Strong, "Patients," The Atlantic, March 1969, p 43*

— *n.* the act of blowing one's mind.

... the editors [of *Krazy Kat*, a selection of George Herriman's comic strips] ... try to acclimatize the work into the world of "mind-blowing" and "psychedelia;" as usual, the strip evades all such Kategories. *"Books," The New Yorker, March 14, 1970, p 156*

mind-expander, *n.* a mind-expanding or hallucinogenic drug.

Today Dr. Laverne said that the effects of Vietnamese marijuana were sometimes surprisingly similar to those induced by hallucinogenic and psychotogenic agents such as L.S.D., mescaline and other so-called mind-expanders that have been used experimentally, illicitly, and proved harmful to the body and central nervous system of humans. *Louis Heren, "Drugs as My Lai Defence," The Times (London), March 26, 1970, p 7*

mind-expanding, *adj.* intensifying and distorting perception; psychedelic.

LSD has been called a "mind-expanding" or "consciousness-expanding" drug; its use has been advocated to increase human creative potential, since some people who have taken the substance report strong subjective feelings of creative drive. *John T. Goodman and Conrad Chyatte, "Psychology," Britannica Book of the Year 1968, p 652*

min·i ('min i:), *n.* **1** a short skirt, dress, etc., especially one ending 2 to 4 inches above the knee; a miniskirt, minidress, etc. Compare MAXI, MICRO, MIDI.

The setting: Kärntner Strasse (Vienna's Fifth Avenue) .... and the atmosphere is as gemütlich as ever.... The passing girls, dressed in their gray, tan, and dark-blue conservatively cut suits, look as if they were afraid to wear minis. *F. Yorick Blumenfeld, "Reports: Austria," The Atlantic, Feb. 1968, p 34*

2 the style or length of fashions characteristic of the miniskirt.

"The midi will get time, but not equal time with the mini," predicts Henri Bendel [a fashionable women's clothing store in New York] President Geraldine Stutz. *Time, May 12, 1967, p 68*

3 anything miniature in size.

The Micro 16 does not pretend to be a pale imitation of a large machine: it is intended to be, and indeed is, a highly effective mini. It is no accident that the machine should be "highly thought of" by active users in the small machine field, myself included. *L. Molyneux, Newcastle-upon-Tyne, England, in a Letter to the Editor, New Scientist and Science Journal, May 20, 1971, p 484*

4 *British.* short for *minicar* (a small automobile). See MINI-.

A mini and a Cadillac belong to different species which may require different rules. When it comes to exhaust

gases, anyway, the exhalations of a mini are negligible compared with a Cadillac's. The argument will presumably end later this month when the Department of Commerce publishes its final specifications. When that happens the carmakers will have to stop protesting and make whatever changes the United States requires. *"Safer Cars," The Manchester Guardian Weekly, Nov. 3, 1966, p 9*

— *adj.* **1** reaching well above the knee; very short.

Minis, which ruled city streets all summer, were still applauded in fashion shows.... The maxi coat, worn over the mini dress, was symbolic of the times. *Ruth Mary DuBois, "Fashion," The Americana Annual 1970, p 287*

2 very small; miniature.

Increasing interest in equipment for camping was evidenced by the great variety of improved camping stoves and the number of "mini" refrigerators and stoves suitable for outdoor and trailer use. *Carol L. McCabe and Evelyn G. Rose, "Domestic Arts and Sciences," Britannica Book of the Year 1967, p 289*

But not to be too gloomy, there was a bright spark in the "World of Wodehouse," and that ... from (of all things!) a child actress. Miss Gaynor Jones. This little girl played a sort of mini Eliza Doolittle and she alone breached the wall around Blandings Castle. *Stanley Reynolds, The Manchester Guardian Weekly, March 2, 1967, p 13*

[from MINI-]

mini-, *prefix.* currently used with the two meanings given below.

1 of very small size, duration, or importance; miniature or minor.

miniboom, *n.:* After enjoying a miniboom for nearly a decade, the economy, which manages to combine capitalistic profit incentives within a Communist framework, has run into a severe inflationary problem. *"Yugoslavia: Tito's Daring Experiment," Time, Aug. 9, 1971, p 21*

minicomputer, *n.:* The Apollo Systems Division of General Electric has designed the security system, which consists of a vast array of sensors on-line to a minicomputer, to watch everything. *New Scientist and Science Journal, June 3, 1971, p 597*

minicrisis, *n.:* Two weeks ago, rumors swept the continent that several strong European currencies would be revalued upward, in effect devaluing the dollar.... But, like a stabbing pain that passes quickly, the minicrisis was a warning that the dollar faces more trouble. *"Money: The Dollar's Dilemma," Time, April 19, 1971, p 60*

minicruise, *n.:* For a fortnight's cruise on an ocean liner — as opposed to the much less expensive mini-cruise around the coasts — prices start at around £70.... *Michael Baily, The Times (London), Jan. 5, 1968, p III*

minidiscourse, *n.:* The producers want to get away from "talking heads" (minidiscourses by scientists in their labs) and let the pictures carry as much information as they can. As a man on the programme put it. "We want to show the beauties of science". *"Television Marathon," New Scientist and Science Journal, Jan. 21, 1971, p 122*

minidose, *n.:* ... the contraceptives of the next generation may include a minidose pill taken once a day every day.... *Jane E. Brody, The New York Times, Nov. 12, 1967, Sec. 4, p 7*

minigun, *n.:* Ground commanders requested artillery strikes, and they also called in the principal weapon for air support at night — the AC-47 (this was the military version of the DC-3, and was nicknamed Spooky) armed with three 7.62-mm. machine guns, called miniguns, which could fire a hundred rounds per second. *Jonathan Schell, "Quang*

Ngai and Quang Tin," *The New Yorker*, March 16, 1968, *p 43*

minimovie, *n.:* Gidget, that synthetic gadget of girlyness, winds up at the UN too, no less, in the week's minimovie, Gidget Grows Up, with Karen Valentine taking over where those starlets left off in the realm of the cutesy-poo. *Judith Christ, "This Week's Movies," TV Guide, Dec. 27, 1969, p A-3*

minipark, *n.:* A plan to create "100 vest-pocket or mini-parks" in the city's slum areas was reported last night by the New York Urban Coalition.... *The New York Times, June 24, 1968, p 32*

minirecession, *n.:* Another aspect of the current apprehension is linked to the "mini-recession" in the American motor industry.... *Geoffrey Charles, The Times (London), March 17, 1970, p 27*

minisurvey, *n.:* A thousand and one eccentric facts, odd anecdotes, shaggy dog stories, and mini-surveys about the Bolton pubs are here poured lovingly forth. *Jeremy Tunstall, "Pub Sociology," Review of "The Pub and the People" by Tom Harrison, The Manchester Guardian Weekly, Jan. 2, 1971, p 19*

minitractor, *n.:* The cost of a mini-tractor will be about £300: a more conventional tractor can cost more than three times as much. *New Scientist and Science Journal, Jan. 21, 1971, p 120*

miniwar, *n.:* The showdown in Jordan was all but inevitable. Since 1968, Hussein's successive Cabinets and the eleven guerrilla organizations that make up the Palestine Liberation Organization (PLO) have been in chronic conflict.... Three times since 1968, disagreements between sides have resulted in actual miniwars. Three months ago, 200 people were killed in three days of fighting. *"Jordan: The King Takes on the Guerrillas," Time, Sept. 28, 1970, p 16*

2 reaching well above the knee; very short.

minicoat, *n.:* Designed to reflect the spirit of the times, furs were young, gay, new looking, offbeat. Rabbit had been dyed in new and heady shades—orange, mauve, navy, shocking pink, bright green—to fashion double-breasted minicoats and pea jackets. *Phyllis West Heathcote, "Fashion," Britannica Book of the Year 1967, p 338*

minidress, *n.:* Marbel Junior, who showed up in a periwinkle blue and white flowered dinner jacket, had the last word in the show—a bridal minidress with a veil twice as long as the dress. *Myra MacPherson, The New York Times, May 13, 1968, p 50*

minikilt, *n.:* Of course, describing these as mini-kilts makes the purist splutter in his porridge. *Philip Clarke, The Sunday Times (London), April 6, 1969, p 53*

minishorts, *n.pl.:* In Paris, minishorts are an every-night, run-of-the-disco affair. *Time, Feb. 1, 1971, p 32*

minisuit, *n.:* "Come to the point," Trudeau said, eager to quit Gray's office, slide down the polished oak bannisters of St. Martin's House, and vault over the stacks of remaindered Canadiana in the hall, to where Elaine Bedard, wearing a flared pink leather minisuit, awaited him in his Mercedes-Benz. *Mordecai Richler, Saturday Night (Canada), Sept. 1968, p 36*

[from *miniature*. The form first became popular in Great Britain through the appearance of the *Mini Minor*, a small car produced in 1960 by the British Motor Corporation. The consequent appearance of other *minicars* and of the *minicab*, a small taxicab, furthered the use of *mini-* as a prefix.]

See also the entries below for compounds in *mini-*

having specialized meanings or greater-than-average frequency.

minibike, *n.* *U.S.* a small motorcycle. See the first quotation for details.

That the minibike owners cut a funny figure is due not only to their physique but also to the new bike's low frame, small wheels and elevated handle bar, which are designed to drastically reduce the amount of necessary agility. *The New York Times, May 30, 1968, p 35*

Shawn [Moran] is a minibiker, one of the thousands of American kids who in the past two years have embraced half-size (or even smaller) motorcycles, the replacement for the tricycle in the age of opulence. Recession or no, mini-bikes seem to be all over, but nowhere are they more visible than in Los Angeles. *Time, Nov. 2, 1970, p 56*

One faction, for example, favors the 18-in.-wheel mini-bike, which, according to its advocates, is more maneuverable than the 27-in. English model that others prefer. *"Polo on Wheels," Time, Aug. 23, 1971, p 33*

minibus, *n.* a small vehicle with the seats arranged as in a bus, designed to take more passengers than an automobile.

Travel Director Simon Thuo Kairo ... to start Kenya's first African-owned safari operation. Kairo's safaris, however, are not designed for big-game hunting. Equipped with five Volkswagen minibuses, he takes his clients to "meet the people in the villages and let them enjoy African dishes." *"Kenya," Time, Aug. 16, 1968, p 52*

There were two charter flights full of United supporters, to say nothing of 16 intrepid voyagers through the snows on a 4,000-mile round trip from Manchester in a minibus. *Geoffrey Green, The Times (London), March 23, 1968, p 8*

minicell, *n.* a small bacterial cell produced by an abnormal division process and able to transfer episomes (extra-chromosomal particles) from or into normal cells.

The scientific palm of the week must undoubtedly go to that bizarre little object the minicell. For no fewer than three papers have appeared in different journals of the past few days, describing how these tiny cells, formed by a pinching off of one end of *Escherichia coli* bacteria, have been used to package up specific portions of the microbes' DNA. *New Scientist, Aug. 13, 1970, p 325*

minimal, *adj.* of or relating to minimal art.

Minimal forms still massively demand their unrewarding space, but they are countered by weirdly eccentric shapes that are frankly frivolous, at least unpredictable. *Time, Jan. 3, 1969, p 42*

The inherent detachment of Pop's aestheticized banalities prefigures the "pure" objects of Minimal sculpture.... *Harold Rosenberg, "The Art World," The New Yorker, Nov. 8, 1969, p 169*

—*n.* **1** minimal art.

Ironically, though current trends in United States art are unrepresented at the American Pavilion, they are in evidence at "foreign" pavilions, where the echoes of pop, op, and minimal resound. *Grace Glueck, The New York Times, June 22, 1968, p 29*

2 a work of minimal art.

On the ground floor [of the Guggenheim Museum], Robert Morris' I-beam minimals; on the first tier, Fukushima's arched *Blue Dots. Picture legend, Time, Oct. 27, 1967, p 43*

minimal art, a form of art that reduces shape, color,

etc., to its simplest or most basic elements, avoiding embellishment or dramatization. Also called MINIMALISM, REDUCTIVISM, REJECTIVE ART.

[William] Turnbull's sculpture would surely qualify as an exemplary form of Minimal art. But the whole category of Minimal art seems to have been created around the least important aspect of the work: its use of simple "primary" shapes, as in the critic Barbara Rose's term "ABC art," with its implication of going back to the basic alphabet. The best Minimal art, like some of Donald Judd's, for example, is in a sense explosive, carrying a charge of compressed energy behind its blank surfaces. *Guy Brett, "Simply Vertical," The Times (London), March 18, 1970, p 15*

minimal artist, a painter, sculptor, or other artist who works in minimal art. Also called MINIMALIST.

Minimal artists whose works were seen in one-man shows in New York included Sol Lewitt, Robert Smithson, Charles Ross.... *Victor H. Miesel, "Art: Sculpture," The Americana Annual 1969, p 95*

minimalism, *n.* another name for MINIMAL ART.

Art keeps running away from illusion. "Ideas of truth are the foundation," wrote Ruskin some time ago, "and ideas of imitation the destruction of all art." Not to use art to imitate visual reality is relatively easy, but how do you reach truth? One way, and a sensible one, is to make a work that asserts its simplicity.... Call it minimalism if you like, but the real point is that the thing insists on being just itself and nothing more. *Norbert Lynton, "Working to Rule," The Manchester Guardian Weekly, May 1, 1969, p 20*

But he [Andy Warhol] gives dramatic clarification to Minimalism by minimalizing the artist, too, and the world he inhabits. *Harold Rosenberg, "The Art World: Art's Other Self," The New Yorker, June 12, 1971, p 105*

minimalist, *n.* another name for MINIMAL ARTIST.

Minimalists do the minimum. That's it with the minimum waste of words. *Maurice Wiggin, The Sunday Times (London), Feb. 26, 1967, p 50*

Nonetheless it [representational and figural sculpture] is outclassed numerically and formally by the minimalists, a useful term but essentially as misleading as nonobjective once was for the positive statements of geometrically abstract art. *George Heard Hamilton, "Of Art and Anti-Art," Saturday Review, Nov. 25, 1967, p 42*

The moral would seem to be that minimalists should stay minimal; it is safer for them that way. *Richard Roud, "Year of the Fuzz," The Manchester Guardian Weekly, Dec. 18, 1971, p 20*

—*adj.* of or relating to minimalists or minimal art.

Tony Smith, usually taken as the original minimalist sculptor (after the pyramids and Goethe's sphere on a cube) is well represented by large sculptures and ill served by some barely adequate paintings. *Norbert Lynton, "Working to Rule," The Manchester Guardian Weekly, May 1, 1969, p 20*

In her [Gertrude Stein's] remarks on the Cubist object stripped of association or feeling, she spotted, decades in advance, the principle of the Minimalist "art of the real" and the "thingish" novel of the nineteen-sixties. *Harold Rosenberg, "The Art World: Paris Annexed," The New Yorker, Jan. 30, 1971, p 74*

minimax, *adj.* of, relating to, or based on the minimax theorem.

They [moves in mathematical games] will depend not on chance but on decisions by the players, each of whom is trying to minimize his opponent's utility (that is, payoff) and

maximize his own.... This decision rule is known as the minimax rule. *Anatol Rapoport, "Escape from Paradox," Scientific American, July 1967, p 53*

The efficiency of a new product launch would depend, of course, upon the advertising campaign and all the other preparations, as well as upon its actual production. This part of the process of evaluation depends on "games against nature". The idea is that you should be able to assess the risk entailed in providing a new product and think of it at worst in terms of deciding what you would lose if you were wrong. This is the process of minimax regret. *Frank George, "Cybernetics to Aid the Manager," New Scientist, July 9, 1970, p 87*

—*v.i.* See the quotation for the meaning.

... such games [Matching Pennies] always have a solution—a 'best strategy', and a calculable pay-off, for each player—if both players try to attain as high a security level as possible. Each player, then, is minimaxing—minimising maximum loss, or maximising minimum profit; making the most unfavourable outcome as acceptable as he can. *Michael Lipton, "A Game Against Nature: Strategies of Security," The Listener, April 4, 1968, p 437*

[from *mini*mum + *maxi*mum]

minimax theorem, a theorem in the mathematical theory of competitive games which states that in an optimal strategy one player plays so as to minimize his maximum losses and the other plays so as to maximize his minimum winnings.

Game theory, one of the most elegant and useful branches of modern mathematics, was anticipated in the early 1920's by the French mathematician Émile Borel, but it was not until 1926 that John von Neumann gave his proof of the minimax theorem, the fundamental theorem of game theory. *Martin Gardner, "Mathematical Games," Scientific American, Dec. 1967, p 127*

minipill, *n.* a pill containing a very low dose of a drug, especially an oral contraceptive having only one-tenth of the progesterone and none of the estrogen present in larger pills.

The minipill was developed for one reason alone: because it was believed to provide safe contraception. *"Minipill Crushed," New Scientist, Jan. 29, 1970, p 187*

... Syntex Laboratories, after consultation with the FDA [Food and Drug Administration], has suspended all human trials of its minipill because breast tumors developed in five dogs. *"Minipill in Limbo," Science News, Jan. 24, 1970, p 93*

Researchers are working upon minipills, injections or implants that might be good for a year, pills that would induce abortion if a woman had conceived but didn't yet realize it, and pills for men. *Alton Blakeslee, "Safer, One-a-Month Pill is Nearly Ready," New York Post, Aug. 4, 1971, p 70*

mini-ski, *n.* a short ski worn by beginners or in ski bobbing.

Mini-skis, they [a group of West German physicians] claimed, would help the beginner learn faster; reduce the skier's fear of falling; in case of falling, result in fewer sprains and fractures. *Sidney Katz, "What's Happening in Medicine," Maclean's, Dec. 1968, p 80*

For added balance, ski bobbers wear mini-skis fitted with breaking crampons on both feet. *Time, March 17, 1967, p 36*

miniskirt, *n.* a skirt that reaches well above the knee; a mini. Compare MICROSKIRT.

Miniskirts are more than just provocative, according to British revenue authorities—they are tax evaders as well.... A tax official explained that a 12 1/2 per cent purchase tax is charged only on skirts longer than 24 inches from waist to hem. Anything shorter is classified as children's clothing and hence is not taxable. *The New York Times, July 16, 1968, p 28*

ministate, *n.* a very small country, especially one of the recently established independent small states of Africa or Asia. Also called MICROSTATE.

South Africa's economic predominance radiates from here to the three ministates of Botswana, Lesotho and Swaziland. *The New York Times, Jan. 26, 1968, p 70*

A U.S. resolution on mini-states was shelved when smaller countries indignantly opposed the idea that very small states should take associate rather than full membership, thus relinquishing the right to vote, and the obligation to pay dues. *Betty Flynn, "United Nations," The 1970 World Book Year Book, p 537*

If past experience is any guide, the new ministates will be using their debating privileges to the maximum, a stupefying—and increasingly serious—problem for the U.N. *"United Nations," Time, Oct. 26, 1970, p 39*

minisub, *n.* a very small research submarine equipped to explore and monitor the underwater environment.

While the new mariners may not know what makes a shark tick, they know enough not to trust so-called shark repellent.... Two scientists cruising by in a Mini-Sub, an underwater observatory, watched wide-eyed as the sharks swam through the repellent to devour the tuna chunks. *Wesley Marx, "Exploring the World's Last Frontier," Maclean's, April 2, 1966, p 15*

minitanker, *n. British.* a small ship or truck carrying some liquid; a small tanker.

Whisky is to be exported from Scotland by pipeline and "minitanker", the shipping firm of Christian Salvesen and Co., of Leith, announced yesterday. *The Times (London), May 18, 1967, p 23*

Petrol is supplied free, either by the client filling up at the company's garage or from a mini-tanker which regularly visits the special parking places. *"Driverless Taxis—A Token of the Future," New Scientist and Science Journal, Sept. 2, 1971, p 520*

miracle rice, a recently developed hybrid rice seed that yields twice or three times the amount per harvest as traditional varieties.

The new strains of "miracle rice" that have brought self-sufficiency in food supply to many other Asian nations have failed to take hold in North Viet Nam, partly because workers assigned to collective farms are unwilling to give the new strains the intensive care they require. *Time, Aug. 24, 1970, p 24*

The introduction of U.S.-supplied "miracle rice" notwithstanding, the country [Laos] was still unable to produce enough rice for its own people. *Richard Butwell, "Laos," The Americana Annual 1969, p 408*

MIRV (mərv), *n.* acronym for *Multiple Independently-targeted Reentry Vehicle,* an offensive missile having multiple warheads that can be guided within a pattern to different targets so as to penetrate an enemy's antiballistic missile shield. Compare MRV.

MIRV's threaten the viability of the fixed land-based missile component of the strategic force and provide pressures for the development and deployment of new systems. A Russian MIRV capability presents a much greater potential threat to the U.S. than vice versa because of the greater payload of the Russian missiles. Therefore it should be an extremely important U.S. objective to see that MIRV's are controlled. *Herbert Scoville, Jr., "The Limitation of Offensive Weapons," Scientific American, Jan. 1971, p 24*

—v.t. to equip with a MIRV.

MIRVing the Polaris system allows a dozen warheads to be fitted to a single Poseidon missile. *R. E. Lapp, The New York Times, Nov. 3, 1968, Sec. 4, p 17*

Since each MIRVed rocket is capable of carrying a number of warheads, and each warhead is capable of being delivered to a separate target, the system vastly increases the destructive power of an individual missile. *Time, April 20, 1970, p 22*

miscode, *v.t.* to provide with a wrong or faulty genetic code.

... any factor altering the formation of membrane proteins would also serve to disrupt the normal lipo-protein lattice. Experiments with a mutant of a microorganism, Neurospora, show, for example, that the mutant DNA miscoded a single amino acid in the sequence of structural protein in the membrane. As a result of this seemingly minor alteration, the entire membrane was defective. *Barbara J. Culliton, "Expanding On a Classic View: Membranes Play An Active Role in Cellular Structure and Functioning; They May Hold a Key to the Understanding of Cancer," Science News, May 23, 1970, p 510*

misorient or **misorientate,** *v.t.* to place in the wrong direction; to arrange or position badly; misdirect.

Adjacent grains are misoriented with respect to one another, the extent of the misorientation depending on the thermal and mechanical history of the specimen. *"A Look at the Stitching that Holds Metals Together," New Scientist, Oct. 8, 1970, p 65*

We have the uneasy suspicion that our communal sense of values had become misorientated; and so it has. *Fred Hoyle, The Sunday Times (London), April 9, 1967, p 52*

Mister Charley or **Mister Charlie,** *U.S. Slang, chiefly Afro-American,* the white man. Also spelled MR. CHARLEY or MR. CHARLIE.

"What Congress did to Adam [Clayton Powell] was a direct insult to the entire black community. It was 'Mister Charley' saying, 'Out you go, niggah!' It's a very emotional issue around here." *The New York Times, March 3, 1968, p 109*

And if his [the Negro student's] education does open the world to him, he may find himself cut off from his old community. He is an "Uncle Tom," the most dread and spirit-shattering of epithets, not because he laughs at Mister Charlie's jokes but because he is interested in mathematics. *Charles Merrill, "Negroes in the Private Schools," The Atlantic, July 1967, p 39*

mixed media, a combination of various media, such as tapes, films, phonograph records, photographs, and slides, used in an artistic or educational presentation. Also called MULTIMEDIA. Compare INTERMEDIA.

Mr. Rubin was propelled into mixed media, he said, by seeing so many bad but interesting examples, including some of Andy Warhol's work in Greenwich Village. *Vincent Canby, The New York Times, Aug. 19, 1967, p 17*

mixed-media, *adj.* using mixed media. Also called MULTIMEDIA.

Gallery-going became more and more popular in 1970 as exhibitions proliferated everywhere. . . . More galleries experimented with mixed-media exhibitions making use of the wonders of modern technology. *Sandra Millikin, "Art Exhibitions," Britannica Book of the Year 1971, p 105*

. . . the composer . . . felt, in the thirties, that he had to write fugues; in the early forties, sweet-tempered, folksy music; in the later forties, music with a heavy saturation of dissonance; in the early fifties, what they called "twelve-tone" music, which was as often as not a parody of Schoenberg; in the late fifties, pointillistic music in imitation of Webern; then, in the sixties, aleatoric music, electronic music; and now, mixed-media stuff. . . . *Robert Evett, "The Anatomy of Pretentiousness," The Atlantic, Jan. 1971, p 78*

MOBS (mɑbz), *n.* acronym for *Multiple Orbit Bombardment System,* a nuclear-weapon system in which earth satellites carry warheads that may be released from space upon earth targets, thus escaping detection by conventional radar. Compare FOBS.

Some observers here fear that the recent Russian shots may represent a step upward from this FOBS system to the so-called MOBS — multiple-orbit bombardment system — that Soviet officials have discussed publicly since 1961. *Evert Clark, The New York Times, April 3, 1968, p 1*

mo·camp ('mou,kæmp), *n.* a tourist camp providing various facilities for campers.

If you're touring Turkey, stay at BP Mocamps. Here's a welcome for campers and caravanners. And more. Like hot and cold water, toilets, showers, kitchen, laundry and ironing facilities. *The Times (London), Nov. 1, 1967, p II*

[from *mo-* (as in *motor, motel,* and *mobile*) + *camp*]

mod, *adj.* extremely up-to-date and fashionable in style of clothes, makeup, music, art, etc.; avant-garde.

With a fever to be relevant, priests and ministers are bringing religious services into the coffeehouse, the factory, the supermarket. More often than not, the music that enhances these mod liturgies comes from an electric guitar pulsating to a rock beat. *Melvin Maddocks, "Rituals—The Revolt Against the Fixed Smile," Time, Oct. 12, 1970, p 43*

Carnaby Street, in the West End in London, as every teen-ager who knows anything knows, is the Mecca of the "mod" fashions which became so popular that nearly every department store in America which caters to the young opened special shops for them. *Russell Lynes, "After Hours: What Revolution in Men's Clothes?" Harper's, May 1967, p 28*

—*n.* **1** a mod person.

These are the mods — short for moderns — who care more about looking "smart" than any other segment of the population, male or female. The British public became aware of them when the Beatles were first popular. *Gloria Emerson, The New York Times, Feb. 24, 1965, p 43*

Starting out as an adjective to describe clothing, "mod" has continued on to become a noun denoting an extremely up-to-date person or group, as well. *Ruth O'Brien, "Whirl of Words," Springfield [Mass.] Republican, July 15, 1967, [page not recorded]*

2 mod style or fashion.

The look of "chic mod" she says she is trying to achieve starts with a pointed doll's face engulfed in brass gold hair, and with caramel colored eyes rimmed with the thinnest line of black pencil. *Marylin Bender, The New York Times, Feb. 7, 1968, p 50*

[originally *mod, adj.,* "of or relating to the *Mods,*" a group of young British working-class boys in the late 1950's who acted like dandies and wore ultra-fashionable clothes, *Mods* being a shortened form of *moderns*]

mo·del·lo (mou'del ou), *n.* a small version or model for a large work of art.

The painting is the "modello," or sketch, for "The Immaculate Conception," one of the masterpieces of El Greco's mature years. *Martin Arnold, "El Greco Stolen in Spain in '30's Found Here," The New York Times, June 17, 1971, p 1*

[from Italian, literally, model]

mode-locked, *adj.* (of a laser) having its light phases modulated so as to produce pulses of extremely short duration.

The development of the "mode-locked" pulsed laser perhaps offered the single most important technological advance in chemical dynamics of excited states. This type of laser generally consists of a standard pulsed laser (of, say, pulse duration of about 10^{-9} sec) and a crystal that "coordinates" the phases of light from the pulse and then generates a series of very narrow pulses whose individual lifetimes are only about 10^{-12} sec. *Nicholas J. Turro, "Chemistry," 1972 Britannica Yearbook of Science and the Future, 1971, p 211*

The extremely high peak powers that can be got in picosecond pulses from such "mode-locked" lasers promise fresh insights into interactions of light and matter. *Arthur L. Schawlow, Scientific American, Sept. 1968, p 121*

mo·dem ('mou,dem), *n.* an electronic device for converting signals from one form to another to facilitate transmission.

Handling data on conventional speech circuits requires the conversion of digital information into analog form, by modulators and demodulators (modems) which also protect the telephone circuits from damage. *D. L. A. Barber, "Computer Networks," Science Journal, Oct. 1970, p 62*

[blend of *modulator* and *demodulator*]

mod·u·lar·i·ty (,mɑdʒ ə'lær ə ti:), *n.* the use of modules in building computers and other machines.

It will be more rational in the future to evolve digital transmitters directly adaptable to digital computers. These will be of more complex construction than existing equipment and impose the need for modularity in design to ease servicing and for more extensive servicing by the instrument manufacturers themselves. This trend will encourage the evolution of digital transmitters probably linked to the digital computer by a form of telemetering or data highway. Modularity, to ease maintenance and increase reliability, will be a feature of such transmitters. *Peter Prior, "Trend Towards Supervision by Computers," The Times (London), May 7, 1970, p 35*

modularize, *v.t.* to make modular or break into units; build (something) into modules or units.

We are an anxious people. Our cosmetic media and modularized lifestyles attempt to hide this fact but it haunts every feature of existence. *Joseph Rhodes, The New York Times, Oct. 8, 1970, p 47*

module, *n.* **1** a self-contained, standardized, and

interchangeable unit or component in a computer or other machine.

One reason why Sigma 5 gets more efficient as it grows larger is that when memory modules are added interleave and overlap occur. *Scientific American, Feb. 1967, p 11*

2 a unit in an aircraft or spacecraft, that has a specific function and is often designed to function apart from the main craft as a self-contained, self-supporting unit.

An operational crew module which could be used in an emergency for escape and survival is to be fitted to the American F111 fighter-bomber, 50 of which will be supplied to the R.A.F. by January, 1970. *The Times (London), March 29, 1966, p 5*

mo·gul ('mou gəl), *n.* a moundlike elevation on a ski slope.

Becky's eyes and face hesitated, but she obeyed. Easily, solid on her skis, she swung down among the moguls and wind-bared ice, and became small, and again waited. *John Updike, "Man and Daughter in the Cold," The New Yorker, March 9, 1968, p 35*

[probably from Norwegian *muge, mugje* (feminine *muga*) a heap or mound; form influenced by English *mogul* a prominent person]

moldy fig, *U.S. Slang.* an old-fashioned or outmoded person or thing.

Holden Caulfield [hero of J. D. Salinger's *The Catcher in the Rye*] is a moldy fig; the Lord of the Flies has been swatted. This year, the unquestioned literary god on college campuses is a three-foot high creature with . . . the improbable name of Frodo Baggins [hero of J. R. R. Tolkien's *The Lord of the Rings*]. *Time, July 15, 1966, p 54*

[originally (1940's) applied by progressive jazz fans to lovers of traditional jazz]

mol·e·chism or **mol·e·cism** ('mal ə,kiz əm), *n.* any virus, viewed as an infective agent possessing the characteristics of both a living microorganism and a nonliving molecule. Also called ORGANULE.

Outside the cell, the virus may lie inert like a crystal or bit of dust. It comes alive only when it invades an intact living cell in order to reproduce. Yet while in the cell, it is no longer a virus since it has become part of the genetic material of the cell. For most virologists, viruses fall between the smallest living organism and the largest inert chemical molecules. According to the late Dr. Thomas Rivers of Rockefeller University, a virus could be appropriately described as a "molechism" or an "organule." *Newsweek, Jan. 20, 1969, p 63*

Organule or molecism?
. . . Whether viruses are molecules or organisms depends on how you look at them, and it is always important to have more than one point of view. *F. Kingsley Sanders, Science Journal, March 1968, p 90*

[*molechism*, from *molecule* + *chemical* + *organism*; *molecism*, from *molecule* + *organism*]

molecular astronomy. See the quotation for the meaning.

Molecular astronomy is a science only a few years old. Its purpose is to determine what chemical molecules can be found in interstellar space and, if possible, how they got there and what their being there means for theories of galactic and stellar evolution and of cosmology. *"Molecular Astronomy," Science News Yearbook 1970, p 225*

molecular fossil, a molecule of organic material extracted from rocks older than the oldest known fossils, used to study the early evolution of life on earth.

The exciting studies of Calvin, who has attempted to prove the existence of what he calls "molecular fossils," have not, however, firmly established the biogenic nature of these substances. *Jules Duchesne, "Meteorites and Extraterrestrial Life," Science Journal, April 1969, p 36*

Both the organic geochemical approach and the micropaleontological approach have identified remnants of living organisms either in the form of molecular fossils or microfossils, providing evidence for life forms around 3×10^9 years ago. *Eugene D. McCarthy, "Origin of Life," McGraw-Hill Yearbook of Science and Technology 1971, p 11*

molecular genetics. See the quotation for the meaning.

. . . molecular genetics, which accounts for heredity in terms of nucleotide base sequences, had become established as a separate discipline. . . . *Gunther Stent, "The 1969 Nobel Prize for Physiology and Medicine," Encyclopedia Science Supplement (Grolier) 1970, p 123*

moment of truth, the decisive or critical moment at which one must confront a challenge or ordeal without evasion.

As the excruciatingly painful moment of truth nears on voting a half-billion dollars of new taxes, a rash of substitute proposals can be expected from lawmakers. . . . *The New York Times, March 1, 1966, p 34*

Owen's [movie director Don Owen's] moment of truth came after the screening of his first rough version of the film ["The Ernie Game"]. *Wendy Michener, "Maclean's Reviews: The Best Fiction Movie Canada Ever Made," Maclean's, Oct. 1967, p 111*

[originally meaning the moment in a bullfight when the matador confronts the bull with the final sword thrust, probably first used in this sense by Ernest Hemingway in his book *Death in the Afternoon* (1932) as a translation of Spanish *momento de la verdad*]

mon·e·ta·rism ('man ə tə,riz əm), *n.* the economic doctrine or theory of the monetarists.

The lecture was a full-blooded onslaught on "the new monetarism", the doctrines of the Chicago school of economists led by the celebrated Professor Milton Friedman. *Peter Jay, "Monetary Swallows," The Times (London), March 13, 1970, p 10*

Monetarism, the belief that the state of the economy can be decisively manipulated through regulating the flow of money, became an accepted cult in the White House after Dr Burns had left it to assume the chairmanship of the Federal Reserve Board. *"Henry Brandon in Washington: The Dollar Dilemma," The Sunday Times (London), Aug. 8, 1971, p 4*

mon·e·ta·rist ('man ə tər ist), *n.* an advocate or supporter of the theory that a balanced economy depends on the money supply. Compare NEO-KEYNESIAN. See also FRIEDMANITE.

Alaric Shepherd there reveals himself as an uncompromising monetarist . . ., insisting that "as John Stuart Mill once said, nothing is more important than money." He is, he confessed to our man, well advanced with his own magnum opus, a definitive 1,000-page *Monetary His-*

tory of the United Kingdom and Europe. "Business Diary," The Times (London), April 21, 1970, p 25

—*adj.* of monetarists or monetarism.

Broadly, the monetarist school remains confident that a recovery cannot be far off, since the monetary policy of the Federal Reserve Board remains expansionary. *Anthony Harris, "Obstinate Recession," The Manchester Guardian Weekly, Nov. 28, 1970, p 22*

monoamine oxidase, an enzyme which neutralizes amines by oxidation, thus acting as a tranquilizer, protecting the organism from bacterial amines, etc.

Among the factors believed responsible for making these amino compounds harmless in foodstuffs is detoxification after consumption through the action of a naturally occurring human enzyme, monoamine oxidase (MAO). *Science News, May 27, 1967, p 500*

monocrystal, *n.* a very strong filament made of a single piece of synthetic crystal. See also WHISKERS.

Our group at the Academy of Sciences' Institute of Physical Chemistry in Moscow has succeeded in producing threadlike monocrystals or whiskers in these low-pressure conditions. *Boris Vladimirovich Deriaguin, "Low-Pressure Diamond Whiskers," New Scientist, Oct. 30, 1969, p 228*

monocrystalline, *adj.* composed of monocrystals.

Scientists were also exploring the possibility of incorporating monocrystalline fiber composites, called whiskers, into filling materials, such as silver amalgam, silicate cement, and acrylic resin. *Clifford H. Miller, "Dentistry," The World Book Science Annual 1967, p 315*

monohull, *n.* a sailing vessel with a single hull. Compare MULTIHULL.

Well, the design of the monohull can be improved—there is constant experiment with materials—and the multihull, with everything in its favour, could do the voyage extremely quickly. *Sir Francis Chichester, The Sunday Times (London), Feb. 2, 1969, p 50*

Slowly multihull boats are gaining ground against the traditional monohulls. *Peter Laurie, "Taking the Maverick Out of the Multihull," The Sunday Times Magazine (London), April 11, 1971, p 20*

monokini, *n.* **1** a one-piece bikini.

Hand-loomed Orlon yarn "monokini" has top and bottom joined by a band. *Angela Taylor, The New York Times, May 30, 1966, p 20*

The one-piece got briefer and briefer until it reached the limit with the topless swimsuit, or as the French called it, the "monokini." *Sandy Boler, The Sunday Times (London), May 5, 1968, p 60*

2 a man's bikini.

. . . Young and amazingly inventive Spanish "coiffeur-architect" Truderro, whose recently launched black-and-yellow salon (he works wearing only a jet monokini, a trained canary perched on his shoulder) has attracted EVERYONE. *Colleen Brooks, "Invitation to the Harvest," The New Yorker, April 10, 1965, p 92*

▶ The coiners of *monokini* obviously contrast *mono-* ("one; single") whimsically with *bi-* in *bikini* as though this *bi-* were the word element meaning "two"; *bikini* of course is from the name of a Pacific atoll; but since the bikini is in fact a two-piece bathing suit, the pun on *bi-* is inescapable.

monolithic, *n.* a monolithic circuit.

Monolithic integrated circuits are used for arithmetic and logic functions in the new computers. The central processors use what is called monolithic systems technology (M.S.T.). . . . Monolithics are also used as storage devices in the high-speed buffer memories. *Kenneth Owen, "Automation: Setting the Computer Pace," The Times (London), July 3, 1970, p 27*

monolithic circuit, another name for INTEGRATED CIRCUIT.

In the next five or ten years we may well expect to see the development of automated methods for the manufacture of monolithic circuits and very large-scale integrated circuits which will further increase the reliability and speed of tomorrow's computers as well as cut their cost. *Van Court Hare, Jr., Introduction to Programming: A BASIC Approach, 1970, p 19*

mononucleate, *adj.* having only one nucleus in a cell.

Here I shall be concerned with the mononucleate hybrid cells that are produced when the nuclei of two cells (and occasionally three) fuse together as the heterokaryon [cell in a fungus] divides. *Henry Harris, "Cell Fusion and the Analysis of Malignancy," New Scientist and Science Journal, July 8, 1971, p 90*

monopole, *n.* a hypothetical north or south magnetic pole existing in isolation from its opposite.

A magnetic monopole is a hypothetical particle that would have only a single magnetic charge, either a north or south pole alone. All known magnetic bodies have at least one north and one south pole, but theory predicts that monopoles should exist. *Science News, May 2, 1970, p 436*

It is at one point claimed that there is a feeling that there are no more challenging problems in physics: the very opposite is true, what with the possibilities of quarks and magnetic monopoles, particles travelling faster than light and black holes. *John Taylor, "Views," The Listener, Nov. 11, 1971, p 643*

. . . physicists have searched for monopoles in just about every accessible nook and cranny. They have searched in the heavens above; in the depths of the oceans; in those things of the Earth, on the Earth, and surrounding the Earth. As yet, all their efforts have proved futile. *New Scientist, April 30, 1970, p 218*

monosexual, *adj.* of, relating to, or for one sex only. Compare UNISEXUAL.

Or, when uninhibited, do the younger women of all tribes perform ritual monosexual dances to satisfy some urge of which we yet know little? *Colin Bertram, The Times (London), Jan. 21, 1967, p 11*

monotechnic, *adj.* specializing in one discipline or field of endeavor.

Sir John Frederick William Herschel, Baronet, who died 100 years ago this week, was a well-known member of perhaps the most well-known astronomical family. Illustrious monotechnic families like this one are more common in the field of music, so it is interesting to note that Herschel's grandfather was a musician in the Hanoverian guard, who sent his son Friedrich Wilhelm to England as a professional musician. Astronomy became a major enthusiasm of William Herschel (as he came to be known). . . . *Eric Deeson, "Perseverance Strikes the Mark," New Scientist and Science Journal, May 13, 1971, p 392*

—*n.* a monotechnic school.

We could learn much from the American system of higher education, . . . and also from the Russian model where *monotechnics* of high educational as well as vocational standing greatly outnumber the traditional universities. *Alexander King, "Revolution in Education," The Listener, Sept. 1, 1966, p 297*

. . . the modern mode of monotechnics . . . boasts of effacing, as fast and as far as possible, the technical achievements of earlier periods. . . . *Lewis Mumford, "Reflections: The Megamachine," The New Yorker, Oct. 17, 1970, p 112*

monounsaturate, *n.* a monounsaturated oil or fat, often used in diets. Compare POLYUNSATURATE.

For the first time, a group of nationally recognized physicians, drawn from dozens of different disciplines, urged all Americans to drastically reduce their intake of high-fat, high-cholesterol foods. The Federally funded *Intersociety Commission for Heart Disease Resources* also called for an over-all national policy to prevent premature heart disease. . . . The commission's diet calls for . . . keeping polyunsaturated fats (corn oil, safflower oil, soybean oil and cottonseed) at less than 10 per cent of calories with the rest of dietary fats consisting of monounsaturates (peanut and olive oil). *Jane E. Brody, "Medicine: Cholesterol," The New York Times, Dec. 20, 1970. Sec. 4, p 7*

monounsaturated, *adj.* (of a fat or oil) free of hydrogen bonds at one point in its carbon chain.

Most fats that remain solid at room temperature are derived from land animals and classed by chemists as "saturated" because they have hydrogen atoms attached at all available points in their carbon chains. Some vegetable fats have one such point with two fewer hydrogen atoms and are "monounsaturated." Many vegetable and seed oils and all fats from fish and marine mammals, lack the full complement of hydrogen atoms at two or more points and are "polyunsaturated." These fats are liquid at room temperature. *Time, Jan. 10, 1969, p 60*

mon·stre sa·cré (mɔ̃ strə sa'krei), *pl.* **monstres sacrés.** a celebrity whose eccentric or unconventional behavior is excused or admired by the public.

Jean Cocteau: The Man and the Mirror is most vivid in recounting the great friendships that linked the writer-artist to such fascinating figures as the aviator Roland Garros; Edith Piaf; Anna de Noailles and her fellow poet, Cocteau's lifelong friend Max Jacob; Madame Francine Weisweiller, whose devotion and admiration (which he reciprocated) warmed his declining years; Picasso, and Colette, as much of an individualist and a *monstre sacré* as Cocteau himself. *Thomas Bishop, Saturday Review, May 25, 1968, p 22*

[from French, literally, sacred monster]

Mon·ta·gnard (ˌmɑn tə'nyɑrd), *n.* one of an aboriginal people living in the highlands of South Vietnam. Also called YARD.

But there are still great numbers of Vietnamese for whom French is a second language, particularly the mountain tribesmen (the so-called Montagnards)—and the Vietcong. *Bernard B. Fall, "Vietnam: The Undiscovered Country," The New York Review of Books, March 17, 1966, p 8*

When 600 montagnard tribesmen graduated recently from the Pleiku Montagnard Training Center, they each took back to their mountain villages some new concepts in farming, a saw, a knife—forged from the leaf of an old truck spring—and a gun. *Thomas A. Johnson, The New York Times, Jan. 2, 1968, p 2*

[from French, literally, mountaineer]

Monte Carlo method, the use of tables of random numbers to solve mathematical problems involving complex physical processes.

The five million models were generated using what is known as the Monte Carlo method; that is, the known measurements were fed into the computer on a completely random basis, as when dice are thrown, and the resulting figures then tested to see how closely their mathematical structure resembled the real earth. *Science News, June 8, 1968, p 551*

Writing in a recent issue of *Science* . . . Press [geologist Frank Press] describes how previous models of density distribution [in Earth] have been based on certain assumptions. . . . By using a Monte Carlo method Press believes that his distributions have been derived quite independently of such assumptions. *"Six Models Describe Earth's Interior," Science Journal, Sept. 1968, p 15*

[named after *Monte Carlo,* city in Monaco famous as a center of gambling]

mood drug, a drug, such as a stimulant or tranquilizer, that affects or alters one's state of mind.

There is some opposition to the use of mood drugs for children. Traditionalist Freudian psychiatrists believe that behavior and learning problems are psychological, not physical or chemical in origin. *"Drugs for Learning," Time, Aug. 10, 1970, p 44*

"Overuse of mood drugs is becoming increasingly acute," he said recently. . . . *Adam Hopkins, "Red Scare Raised in the US Battle of the Ads," The Sunday Times (London), Oct. 24, 1971, p 6*

Moog synthesizer (moug), an electronic keyboard instrument for generating a large variety of sounds.

Following the impact of "Switched-on Bach" in 1968, the Moog synthesizer quickly became instrument of the year, both for popular music and adaptations of the classics. *Robert C. Marsh, "Music," The 1970 World Book Year Book, p 431*

Baroque composers did not write for these great outsized modern harpsichords, anymore than they did for the piano, or the Moog Synthesizer. *Robert Evett, The Atlantic, May 1970 p 124*

[named after the American engineer Robert A. *Moog,* who invented it]

moon car, another name for LUNAR ROVER.

Its hollow, wire-mesh wheels snapped into place, and the moon car was lowered to the ground. *"From the Good Earth to the Sea of Rains," Time, Aug. 9, 1971, p 6*

mooncraft, *n.* a spacecraft for traveling to the moon. Also called MOONSHIP.

When the Russians are ready they may launch a fully-fuelled propulsion module and join the two components of a mooncraft in Earth-orbit. *Kenneth W. Gatland, "Russia's Moon Programme," New Scientist, March 21, 1968, p 631*

moon crawler, another name for LUNAR ROVER.

Lunokhod-1, Russia's moon crawler, this week became the first vehicle to travel across the lunar surface. *Anthony Tucker, "Russia's Moon Rover," The Manchester Guardian Weekly, Nov. 21, 1970, p 3*

"Moon mobiles" and an unmanned "moon crawler" that looked very much like the current Russian Lunokhod were being considered until the manned Apollo outran the unmanned Surveyor. *Everly Driscoll, "Moon Mobile Debut On Apollo 15," Science News, June 12, 1971, p 404*

moonport, *n.* a launch complex for preparing spacecraft to travel to the moon.

The board of inquiry was expected to order the entire spacecraft removed from its booster and taken to the Merritt Island, Fla., moonport for step-by-step disassembly. *Science News, Feb. 18, 1967, p 161*

moonrock, *n.* a rock sample from the moon. See FERROPSEUDOBROOKITE and KREEP for examples.

There is something bizarre about the exchange in Moscow recently of a minute quantity of Apollo moonrock for an even more minute quantity of Luna 16 moonrock. *New Scientist and Science Journal, June 24, 1971, p 766*

moon rover, another name for LUNAR ROVER.

As an example of sheer technological innovation, however, nothing aboard Apollo 15 quite beats NASA's new LRV (for Lunar Roving Vehicle), more commonly known as the "moon rover." *"Roving the Moon," Time, July 26, 1971, p 38*

moonship, *n.* another name for MOONCRAFT.

Dropping into the calm seas 300 miles north of Hawaii several feet per second faster than planned, the moonship created a mighty splash. *"Apollo 15: A Giant Step for Science," Time, Aug. 16, 1971, p 28*

moonwalk, *n.* an exploratory walk on the moon's surface.

They [the astronauts] will leave Intrepid twice for 3 1/2-hour moonwalks, which will be televised in colour. *The Sunday Times (London), Nov. 9, 1969, p 8*

During their 66 hours on the moon—twice the duration of Apollo 14's lunar stay—they plan to venture out of their LM on three moonwalks for periods of up to seven hours and distances as far as five miles. *Time, Feb. 22, 1971, p 37*

moonwalker, *n.* a person who takes a moonwalk; a moon explorer.

The board, chaired by Edgar Cortright, Director of NASA's Langley Research Center and including Earth's first moonwalker Neil Armstrong, spent seven weeks studying photographs of the crippled service module taken by the Apollo 13 astronauts. . . . *Peter Gwynne, "Apollo Disaster Causes NASA Rethink," Science Journal, Sept. 1970, p 4*

morning-after pill, an oral contraceptive that could prevent pregnancy even if taken one or several days after intercourse.

Dr. Chang and Dr. Pincus had been working recently on a new pill, known popularly as the "morning-after" pill. It affects the egg after ovulation. *The New York Times, Aug. 24, 1967, p 35*

morph, *n.* a variant form of an animal or plant species.

There were also differences between the various "Morphs", i.e., winged or wingless, viviparous or oviparous; between the sexes; and between aphids of the same type collected on different dates. *New Scientist, July 29, 1965, p 283*

[from Greek *morphé* form]

MOS, abbreviation of *metal oxide semiconductor,* used in integrated circuits, especially of the large-scale integration or LSI type.

A more recent metal-oxide-semiconductor (MOS) technology can produce upward of 500,000 transistors per square inch. . . . *Scientific American, April 1970, p 46*

. . . more circuits are being fabricated on a single silicon slice, with the trend from MOS devices to MSI (medium scale integration, applied to devices with up to 100 circuits or so on one chip) and then to LSI (large scale integration), with more than 100 circuits on one chip. *Geoffrey Dummer, "How Reliable Is Microelectronics?" New Scientist and Science Journal, July 8, 1971, p 78*

mostest, *n.* the mostest, *Slang.* the greatest amount or degree of something; the most.

Manufacturers are confident that several thousand compulsive trendsetters will rush to be in the firstest with the mostest. *Geoffrey Sumner, The Sunday Times (London), April 30, 1967, p 5*

[from *most, n.* + *-est* (superlative suffix)]

moto-cross, *n.* a cross-country motorcycle race.

But to listen to him [TV commentator Murray Walker], particularly in moto-cross as he shouts his heroes home through fields of liquid mud, is to hear a dedicated man. *J. E. Hinder, "Television," Punch, Sept. 14, 1966, p 413*

[from French, from *moto* motorcycle + *cross,* short for *cross-country* (taken from English)]

motor hotel or **motor inn,** a motel, especially one situated in a city and built like a hotel but providing parking and other facilities for motorists.

It is Trust Houses' first "purpose-built" motor hotel, with 28 double bedrooms, good parking space, and service and petrol filling stations. *The Times (London), Feb. 9, 1965, p 16*

Though outwardly in strong shape, with 46 restaurants and six motor inns as well as its food-processing, the company has recently been having trouble keeping earnings up to snuff. *Time, April 21, 1967, p 25*

moxibustion, *n.* the use of moxa (a Japanese wormwood) in medicine, especially as a cauterizing agent.

Next, the doctor resorted to another traditional Chinese treatment called moxibustion: he lit two pieces of an herb called *ai* or *ngai* (*Artemisia vulgaris,* or wormwood) and held the smoldering wads near Teston's abdomen. *"Yang, Yin and Needles," Time, Aug. 9, 1971, p 48*

[from *moxa* + connective *-i-* + com*bustion*]

Mr. Charlie or **Mr. Charley,** variant spellings of MISTER CHARLEY and MISTER CHARLIE.

Tipped off that some other farmers were confused and might vote for white-sponsored candidates, he [Mr. Ickes] asks them: "You going to vote for Mr. Charley (the white man)? What's Mr. Charley ever done for you?" *James C. Tanner, The Wall Street Journal, Aug. 10, 1965, p 1*

"Adam Clayton Powell is the vicar for the man who always wants to spit in Mr. Charlie's face," says John Morsell, assistant executive director of the N.A.A.C.P. *"The Future of Black Leadership," Time, April 4, 1969, p 19*

mri·dan·ga (mri:ˈdæŋ gə), *n.* an ancient drum of India with a long, conical shape and two heads, one larger than the other.

Palghat Raghu on the mridanga and Alla Rakha on the tabla got so much into the spirit of the tala that as the piece progressed it was like a tala in search of a raga. *Narayana Menon, The New York Times, Sept. 12, 1968, p 56*

[from Sanskrit]

► See the note under SARANGI.

mRNA, abbreviation of MESSENGER RNA.

...mRNA in DNA may also be the basis for the timing cycle that regulates cell activity. They isolated unique classes of protozoan mRNA whose concentrations varied periodically. *Jacob Kastner, "Molecular Biology," Britannica Book of the Year 1970, p 543*

MRV, abbreviation of *multiple reentry vehicle.* Compare MIRV.

... MRVs (for multiple re-entry vehicles) ... land in a pre-planned pattern, but they cannot be steered to widely separated targets. *"Moscow's Military Machine: The Best of Everything," Time, May 4, 1970, p 40*

Just recently [Defense] Secretary Laird announced that the Russians were testing an SS-11 system with three multiple reentry vehicles (MRV's), which lack the capability for being independently targeted. *Herbert Scoville, Jr., "The Limitation of Offensive Weapons," Scientific American, Jan. 1971, p 16*

Ms. (miz), abbreviated title used instead of *Miss* or *Mrs.*

The proliferation of Women's Lib-oriented journals has served to standardize the movement's special jargon.... Others are also playing the game. Unliberated honorifics like "Mrs." and "Miss" are replaced by the noncommittal "Ms." *"Who's Come a Long Way Baby?: Liberation and Language," Time, Aug. 31, 1970, p 18*

"How come no woman heads a super-agency?" demanded Ms. Komisar. *"The Talk of the Town," The New Yorker, Sept. 5, 1970, p 27*

As an old-fashioned man, the President prefers the old conventions, such as addressing a woman as "Miss" or "Mrs." rather than the new, liberated, statusless "Ms."—not pronounced "Muss" or "Mess," as certain fastidious male chauvinists have suggested.

No, for reasons that elude me, "Ms." is pronounced "Miz." Miz as in Miz Scarlett, misanthrope and *Miserere mei Deus,* which we may translate today as "God have mercy on all us women" because our President isn't likely to. *Harriet Van Horne, "Nixon & Children," New York Post, Jan. 3, 1972, p 26*

The elections committee of the California Senate has passed a Bill allowing women to sign the electoral roll as Ms. *Daily Telegraph (London), Feb. 12, 1972, p 6*

MSI, abbreviation of *medium-scale integration,* a method of producing a number of integrated circuits on a single chip of silicon. Compare LSI.

... more circuits are being fabricated on a single silicon slice, with the trend from MOS [metal-oxide-semiconductor] devices to MSI (medium scale integration, applied to devices with up to 100 circuits or so on one chip) and then to LSI (large scale integration), with more than 100 circuits on one chip. *Geoffrey Dummer, "How Reliable Is Microelectronics?" New Scientist and Science Journal, July 8, 1971, p 78*

MSR, abbreviation of *missile site radar,* an electronic radar used at antiballistic missile sites.

The Sentinel system would also include some short-range Sprint missiles, which were originally to be deployed to defend the five or six perimeter acquisition radars, or PAR's, which were to be deployed at five sites located across the northern part of the country. Missile-site radars, or MSR's, were to be deployed at every ABM [antiballistic missile] site. *Herbert F. York, "Military Technology and National Security," Scientific American, Aug. 1969, p 24*

muck-up, *n. British Slang.* a mess or muddle; a foul-up.

... "You cannot get away from the fact that Anzio was a bit of a muck-up and the person in overall charge was Alexander." *Field Marshal Lord Montgomery, quoted by Basil Gingell, "Authors Blame Lord Alexander Over Anzio," The Times (London), Oct. 15, 1970, p 4*

mu·co·pep·tide (ˌmyu: kouˈpepˌtaid), *n.* a complex protein in the cell wall of bacteria, whose synthesis is thought to be inhibited by the action of antibiotics.

The cell envelope, the outer portion of the bacterial cell, is a complex structure consisting of an inner plasma membrane and a rigid mucopeptide layer, the cell wall proper, that confers strength and shape. *Richard Losick and Phillips W. Robbins, "The Receptor Site for a Bacterial Virus," Scientific American, Nov. 1969, p 121*

[from *muco-* mucous + *peptide* a combination of amino acids]

multi-, a productive combining form with the sense of "many" in adjective compounds (*multichannel, multicultural,* etc.) and "multiple" in noun compounds (*multiprocessing*). Some recently formed compounds follow:

multibillion, *adj.:* What would be the practical and scientific benefits of a multibillion dollar space station? *Brian O'Leary, "Behind the Scenes at NASA," New Scientist and Science Journal, Jan. 28, 1971, p 184*

multichannel, *adj.:* This new technique, which can carry multi-channel telephony, telegraphy and all forms of data information, was proved feasible by the experimental Telstar satellite in 1962. *W. H. Kennett, The Times (London), Dec. 13, 1967, p V*

multicultural, *adj.:* After years of bi-bi [bilingual, bicultural, etc.] talk, I am delighted to understand from your Editorial that Canadians are encouraged to preserve our society as a multilingual and multicultural one. *Vilma Eichholz, Clarkson, Ontario, in a Letter to the Editor, Maclean's, March 1968, p 72*

multidirectional, *adj.:* Since small lengths of fiber can be used, pieces of material can be built up (and given multidirectional strength) with layers consisting of matrix and short fibers. *Anthony Kelly, "The Nature of Composite Minerals," Scientific American, Sept. 1967, p 166*

multi-ethnic, *adj.:* Black, brown, red and yellow faces are rapidly surrounding the white faces of Dick and Jane, the two textbook youngsters who introduced reading to generations of Americans.

They represent a growing nationwide effort to develop what educators and publishers call "multi-ethnic textbooks"—that is, classroom literature that depicts blacks and other minorities in a different and more equal perspective. *Paul Delaney, "The Outer City: Negroes Find Few Tangible Gains," The New York Times, June 7, 1971, p 28*

multipoint, *adj.:* Coach passengers will proceed by escalator to a first-floor multipoint immigration lounge for rapid examination while their luggage comes up by airport-type carousel. *Michael Baily, The Times (London), May 1, 1970, p 15*

multirole, *adj.:* ... the Continentals realised their dependence on the survival of Rolls Royce (whose engines power the Concorde, the multi-role combat aircraft, and many other European projects).... *David Fairhall, "Airbus Plan Rejected," The Manchester Guardian Weekly, Dec. 12, 1970, p 9*

multiscreen, *adj.:* Taking his cue from the multiscreen effects exhibited at the 1964 New York World's Fair, John

Frankenheimer shot many of the sequences for *Grand Prix*, his auto racing extravaganza, to make the vast, curving Cinerama screen contain three or more separate images working in counterpoint. *Arthur Knight, "Motion Pictures," 1968 Collier's Encyclopedia Year Book, p 372*

multistable, *adj.:* Perceiving is not just sensing but rather an effect of sensory input on the representational system. An ambiguous figure provides the viewer with an input for which there are two or more possible representations that are quite different and about equally good, by .whatever criteria the perceptual system employs. When alternative representations or descriptions of the input are equally good, the perceptual system will sometimes adopt one and sometimes another. In other words, the perception is multistable. *Fred Attneave, "Multistability in Perception," Scientific American, Dec. 1971, p 63*

multi-track, *adj.:* Recording studios also offer new technical means of composing, through such devices as the echo chamber, multi-track recording and tape superimposition. *Time, Aug. 29, 1969, p 47*

multi-access, *adj.* of or relating to the sharing of one computer by two or more users simultaneously. Also, MULTIPLE-ACCESS.

The centre, using an ICT Atlas 2 installed in premises rented from the University, will offer industrial firms, universities and the Ministry itself the chance to gain experience in using multi-access techniques, which allow a number of designers to use the computer together, each communicating with it from a separate terminal. *New Scientist, July 13, 1967, p 78*

multiband, *adj.* combining two or more wavelength exposures.

Vertical aerial view of part of the Carrizo Plains, California, at near right was taken using ordinary Ektachrome film and reveals little trace of the phenomena rendered starkly visible in the enhanced multiband photograph at far right. Such pictures are produced by combining two or more narrow band exposures. *Picture legend, "Earth Resource Satellites," Science Journal, June 1969, p 64*

multicompany, *adj.* controlling or operating diverse companies or a variety of companies.

Litton, which prefers to be known as a multicompany company rather than a conglomerate, says the new unit will not only give counseling in the marketing of products and services but also will prepare the graphics. *Philip H. Dougherty, The New York Times, July 9, 1968, p 61*

multihull, *n.* a sailing vessel having two or more hulls joined by a common deck, as a catamaran. Compare MONOHULL.

Slowly multihull boats are gaining ground against the traditional monohulls.... What is the point of multihulls? They are an alternative to the basic boat problem of stability. *Peter Laurie, "Taking the Maverick Out of the Multihull," The Sunday Times Magazine (London), April 11, 1971, p 20*

multi-industry, *adj.* involved or operating in widely different industries.

The men who are challenging established firms with exuberance and even effrontery are the builders of conglomerates — those multipurpose, multi-industry companies that specialize in hodgepodge acquisitions. *Time, March 7, 1969, p 55*

multilingualism, *n.* the use of more than one language by a cultural or national group.

The discovery that multilingualism was cultivated as a way of life among certain South American Indians rendered the familiar concepts of society, tribe, and ethnic group elusive and difficult. *Ward H. Goodenough, "Linguistic Anthropology," 1969 Britannica Yearbook of Science and the Future, 1968, p 226*

multimarket, *adj.* involved or operating in various widely different markets.

[Assistant Attorney General Richard Wellington] McLaren is becoming the most active — and visible — trustbuster since the days of Teddy Roosevelt; his broadsides have helped chill investor enthusiasm for multimarket companies. *Time, May 23, 1969, p 61*

multimedia, *adj.* **1** using a combination of various media, such as tapes, film, phonograph records, photographs, and slides, to entertain, communicate, teach, etc. Also called MIXED-MEDIA.

The twenty-fourth Edinburgh International Festival opens this year on August 23 when Sir John Barbirolli conducts Beethoven's ninth symphony, and ends on September 12 with the last late-night performances of the Military Tattoo and of the multimedia rock musical *Stomp. The Times (London), April 28, 1970, p 7*

2 involving the use of different communications media in the same place.

These standards apply both to multimedia information centers with print and audiovisual materials and to schools with separate libraries and audiovisual centers. *Dan Bergen, "Libraries," The Americana Annual 1970, p 420*

— *n.* the use of more than one medium of communication or entertainment at one time. Also called MIXED MEDIA.

Concerts and demonstrations of multimedia were given in schools, colleges, theatres, museums, warehouses, and barns, in a variety of musical, nonmusical, unmusical, and antimusical presentations. *Nicolas Slonimsky, "Music," Britannica Book of the Year 1969, p 549*

multipack, *n.* a package containing two or more individually packaged products, sold as a unit. *Often used attributively.*

But the really significant development is the appearance in the stores of multi-packs, and extra-large quantity assortments. *The Times (London), July 11, 1967, p 17*

Despite the increasing number of "multipack" foods, such as Chef Boy-ar-Dee's lasagna with canned meat sauce, canned grated cheese, and packeted pasta, frozen foods continued to be eaten in the U.S. at the rate of 68 lb. per person per year. *Evelyn Gita Rose, "Domestic Arts and Sciences: Food Preparation," Britannica Book of the Year 1969, p 289*

multiple, *n.* a mass-produced painting, sculpture, or other artistic work.

...present-day American artists have tried to project themselves directly into the surroundings of the majority through products midway between art and supermarket ornaments and spectacles, such as light displays and Happenings, posters, color prints, banners, and multiples. *Harold Rosenberg, "The Art World: Keeping Up," The New Yorker, Feb. 21, 1970, p 87*

The artist who becomes interested in multiples takes the first step towards involving himself with the demands of technology. *Edward Lucie-Smith, The Times (London), March 26, 1968, p 7*

multiple-access, *adj.* another word for MULTI-ACCESS.

This "multiple-access time-sharing" arrangement does much more than place additional computational ability at the command of the engineer. *The Sunday Times (London), May 14, 1967, p 33*

multiplet, *n.* a group of nuclear particles that have approximately the same mass, hypercharge, and isotopic spin. Compare SUPERMULTIPLET. See also SU(3) SYMMETRY.

Early in 1964 order was brought to the nuclear "jungle" by the SU-3 theory under which the 100 or so known nuclear particles are grouped into families, or multiplets, of eight or ten members. *Science News Letter, Feb. 6, 1965, p 85*

multiprocessing, *n.* the use of two or more computer processors which have access to a common memory and can execute several programs simultaneously.

Multiprocessing, like multiprogramming, got off to a slow start because of the associated complexities in coordination and control, but a number of multiprocessing systems are now in operation and many more are planned. *I. Auerbach and J. R. Hillegass, "Digital Computer Equipment," McGraw-Hill Yearbook of Science and Technology 1967, p 151*

Magnetic tape, line printer, card-handling, and bulk storage equipment are all necessary for present requirements. Multiprocessing capability is also very important. *Theodore J. Williams, "Process Computer Control," McGraw-Hill Yearbook of Science and Technology 1971, p 351*

multiprocessor, *n.* a computer unit consisting of several processors, used in multiprocessing.

In construction, ours will be a memory-oriented multiprocessor system—that is, it will be able to carry out a number of operations, simultaneously, around the same memory.... *Katsuhiko Noda, "A National Model for Computers," New Scientist, Nov. 16, 1967, p 20*

multiprogramming, *n.* the handling of several programs concurrently by a single computer.

System 370 Models 155 and 165, the company states, have been developed to meet emerging needs such as large data bases, remote-access computing and high-throughput multiprogramming. *Kenneth Owen, The Times (London), July 3, 1970, p 27*

At its cleverest, it uses a Univac operating system to do more multiprogramming than seems decent. *Headley Voysey, "Emulation Is the Name of the Game," New Scientist and Science Journal, Dec. 2, 1971, p 30*

multiracialism, *n.* a political or social system in which all racial groups are accorded equal rights and opportunities.

What progress there was toward multiracialism during the 1953-63 period when Southern Rhodesia was federated with what are now Zambia and Malawi is now being reversed. *Alfred Friendly, Jr., The New York Times, March 24, 1968, Sec. 4, p 9*

multiresistant, *adj.* resistant to various antibiotics.

In the right environment such as the intestinal tracts of cattle being fed a number of different antibiotics, multiresistant strains develop very rapidly. *Anthony Tucker, The Manchester Guardian Weekly, Jan. 18, 1968, p 7*

multispectral, *adj.* capable of sensing emissions from several spectra, especially from parts of the visible, infrared, and microwave spectra.

All available evidence suggests an extensive scientific programme which includes placing the Earth under the most detailed observation with multispectral cameras and other sensing equipment. *Kenneth Gatland. New Scientist and Science Journal, April 29, 1971, p 256*

The possibility of aerial survey lies in multispectral photography, especially with infrared or "false" colour photography using a line scanner. *"Mapping Geobotanical Anomalies from the Air," New Scientist and Science Journal, July 15, 1971, p 122*

multiversity, *n.* *U.S.* a very large university made up of various divisions, extensions, campuses, etc. Also called POLYVERSITY. Compare MEGAVERSITY.

The rebellion at Berkeley centered on the indifference of multiversity's mechanism to the personal needs of the students. *Wilbur H. Ferry, Saturday Review, March 2, 1968, p 53*

[coined by Clark Kerr, born 1911, former president of the University of California, from *multi-* + *university*]

mu·on·ic (myu:'ɑn ik), *adj.* of, containing, or producing *muons* or *mu mesons* (unstable nuclear particles weighing over 200 times more than the electron). Compare KAONIC, PIONIC.

Extensive studies of the sizes and shapes of nuclei have been made using muonic atoms. *E. H. S. Burhop, "Books," Review of "Muons" by A. W. Weissenberg, New Scientist, April 11, 1968, p 92*

mu·o·ni·um (myu:'ou ni: əm), *n.* an isotope of hydrogen consisting of a positively charged mu meson and an electron.

In many respects the muonium atom resembles the simplest ordinary atom, the atom of hydrogen which consists of a proton (p^+) and an electron. In fact muonium can be considered a lighter isotope of hydrogen. In both atoms the nucleus is a comparatively heavy positively charged particle (either a proton or a muon) that is surrounded by a much lighter negatively charged particle (an electron). *Vernon W. Hughes, "The Muonium Atom," Scientific American, April 1966, p 93*

... the positive muon has been observed to collect a negative electron when coming to rest in pure gases, and the resulting "atom," muonium, has been studied with great precision. *Leon M. Lederman, "Muon," McGraw-Hill Yearbook of Science and Technology 1971, p 275*

Murphy game or **Murphy,** *n.* *U.S. Underworld Slang.* See the first quotation for the meaning.

"The Murphy game" is underworld argot for a slick maneuver in which a victim puts his cash in an envelope and gives it to the con man, who makes a fast sleight-of-hand switch and hands back an identical envelope stuffed with newspaper strips. It was named after an Irishman who was arrested many times for perpetrating such tricks. *Time, April 16, 1965, p 16*

Everybody should have a car.... How are you going to get it? You can get it selling drugs. You know, you can get it playing the Murphy. *The New York Times, Sept. 4, 1966, Sec. 4, p 5*

Murphy's Law, any of various humorous rules of thumb. See the quotations for examples.

Your reference to Murphy's Law touches on only part of

that ancient Irish potentate's laws.... His set of the laws of life refer with circularity to nothing, everything and anything. They are: 1) nothing is as easy as it looks; 2) everything takes longer than you think it will; and 3) if anything can go wrong, it will. *Daniel C. McCarthy, Manhattan, in a Letter to the Editor, Time, April 13, 1970, p 6*

Murphy's Law states that if it is possible to connect two things together the wrong way round. then someone will do it that way. *Marcus Langley, "The Profit Motive and Practical Realities," New Scientist, Sept. 21, 1967, p 601*

"Recently," [Roger] Baker writes, "I learned of a governing principle known as Murphy's first law of biology. It states: 'Under any given set of environmental conditions an experimental animal behaves as it damn well pleases.'" *C. L. Stong, "The Amateur Scientist," Scientific American, June 1970, p 143*

mu·si·cas·sette ('myu: zə kæˌset), *n.* a small cassette of musical tape recordings.

As yet, of course, musicassettes are more for the uncritical listener to popular music (as the preponderance of pop in the cassette repertoire would indicate), the background-music listener, and those who want compact recordings they can play on battery portable machines. *Ivan Berger, "Cassettes for Music," Saturday Review, May 25, 1968, p 50*

Muslim, *n.* *U.S.* a member of the *Black Muslims,* an American organization of blacks who observe a form of the Islamic religion and are advocates of black nationalism.

He knows the alternatives: the Muslims and the black nationalists or, on the other hand, the ageless kind of self-abasement and self-delusion which he and others associate with the effort to beg and pray for a pittance here and there from the white man. *Robert Coles, The New York Times Magazine, April 21, 1968, p 135*

mu·ta·gen·ic·i·ty (ˌmyu: tə dʒəˈnis ə ti:), *n.* the inducement of mutations; the use of agents (mutagens) that cause genetic aberrations.

... chemical mutagenicity promises to become a boiling issue in the 1970's with controversies already having erupted over cyclamates, pesticides ... and many other substances. *"Toxicity and Mutagens," Science News, March 28, 1970, p 314*

mu·ta·gen·ize ('myu: tə dʒəˌnaiz), *v.t.* to induce mutation in.

Their approach was systematically to make individual tests on each of several hundreds of colonies from a heavily mutagenized stock of *E. coli.* This technique had already been successfully used to locate a mutant of *E. coli* lacking a ribonuclease activity. *Science Journal, March 1970, p 14*

MVP, *U.S.* abbreviation of *most valuable player.*

[Carl] Yastrzemski ... was named the American League's MVP. *Bill Braddock, "Sports: Baseball," The Americana Annual 1968, p 626*

my, abbreviation of *million years.*

Previously, evidence for rocks older than about 3400-3500 my, has been sketchy, with an age for a Minnesota gneiss of 3550 my.... *"Greenland Yields the Oldest Rocks in the World," New Scientist and Science Journal, Dec. 2, 1971, p 11*

my·co·tox·in (ˌmai kouˈtak sən), *n.* a poison produced by a fungus.

At the second [symposium of the Third International Congress of Food Science and Technology] participants discussed ... the significance of aflatoxin and other mycotoxins. *Magnus Pyke, "Food Science and the Voice of Reason," New Scientist, Sept. 17, 1970, p 578*

[from *myco-* (from Greek *mýkēs* fungus) + *toxin*]

my·o·e·lec·tric (ˌmai ou iˈlek trik), *adj.* using electric currents produced by muscular contraction to actuate movement of an artificial limb, such as an arm or a hand.

Most other myoelectric controlled prostheses require two sets of electrodes, one for opening and another for closing. *Science, Jan. 1971, p 13*

[from *myo-* (from Greek *mŷs* muscle) + *electric*]

mysterium, *n.* a hydroxyl radical identified as emitter of a distinctive pattern of radio frequencies in several regions of the Milky Way.

In fact, one of the first groups to discover the hydroxyl line named it "mysterium" because they did not believe it could be hydroxyl emission. *"Is 'Mysterium' the Message?" Scientific American, Oct. 1967, p 50*

[from *mystery* + *-ium* (suffix of chemical radicals)]

myth, *v.t.* to make mythical; turn into or contrive a myth.

Edward Plowman also observes that "in the drug scene many kids develop a spiritual awareness.... They believe in a spiritual reality. They've seen visions and demons. Thus a conservative Christianity, which hasn't mythed away God and angels, appeals to them." *Time, Aug. 3, 1970, p 31*

[verb use of the noun]

mythogenic, *adj.* of or having to do with the forming of myths.

Religious institutions are now disintegrating, the two researchers believe, because religion has cut itself off from its "principal sources of nourishment—the soul, the symbolic and mythogenic process, the psychic energy resources." *Time, Oct. 5, 1970, p 73*

N

NAA, abbreviation of NEUTRON ACTIVATION ANALYSIS.

NAA has already been used in the crime laboratory to detect counterfeit ancient Roman and Greek coins, which are a lucrative field for forgers. The procedure can also detect coins that are genuinely ancient but were forgeries when they were first made. In addition, NAA can detect forged stamps. *Anthony Standen, "Chemistry: Neutron Activation Analysis," 1969 Collier's Encyclopedia Year Book, p 164*

NAD, abbreviation of *nicotinamide adenine dinucleotide,* an electron-carrying coenzyme necessary for the conversion of glucose to alcohol and for the removal of hydrogen from compounds.

During alcohol metabolism, the ratio of $NADH_2$ to NAD increases. Since the availability of the hydrogen acceptor NAD is important for the dehydrogenation of alcohol to acetaldehyde, the resulting $NADH_2$ must be continually reoxidized back to NAD by other oxidation-reduction reactions. *Gaston Pawan, "When the Pubs Have Shut," New Scientist, Nov. 30. 1967, p 540*

Na·der·ism ('nei dǝr,iz ǝm), *n.* another name for CONSUMERISM.

The phenomenon [consumerism] was also called "Naderism," because of the successful crusades of a young lawyer, Ralph Nader, against unsafe automobiles, industrial hazards, and environmental pollution. *Richard Harwood, "United States: Congress," The Americana Annual 1970, p 725*

... it will be interesting to see whether the thinking behind the Sherman and Clayton Acts (to say nothing of militant Naderism) eventually penetrates the Brussels bureaucracy. *New Scientist and Science Journal, Aug. 19, 1971, p 431*

Naderism was not for Britain. *Lady Burton of Coventry, "Britain Does Not Want Ralph Nader Methods," The Times (London), March 2, 1972, p 10*

Na·hal (naː'haːl), *n.* **1** a branch of the Israeli army. See the quotation for details.

The casualties were soldiers belonging to Nahal, an élite corps which combines military training with the establishment of agricultural settlements in exposed or remote areas. *The Times (London), Dec. 31, 1970, p 6*

2 Also spelled **nahal.** a settlement established by Nahal.

In practice, Israel has already founded six "Nahals" — agricultural settlements manned by soldiers—at points in or near the Jordan Valley.... *Alastair Hetherington, "A Path to Peace for Jews and Arabs," The Manchester Guardian Weekly, March 28, 1970, p 13*

For that reason, the government has established there a necklace of *nahals,* fortified camps manned by young

Israelis who are equ lly able to farm or to fight. *Time, Jan. 4, 1971, p 28*

[from Modern Hebrew]

nai·ra ('nɑi rǝ), *n.* a unit of money in Nigeria. See the quotation for details.

On Jan. 1, 1973. Nigeria will scrap her system of Nigerian pounds, shillings and pence, borrowed from her colonial ruler, Britain, and begin a decimal currency system with units of money called the naira and the kobo.... The naira—the name is adapted from the word Nigeria—will be the major unit of exchange and will have a value about half that of the current Nigerian pound, or $1.53. *The New York Times, Aug. 9, 1972, p 14*

naive, *adj.* **1** not having or showing formal training, techniques, etc., in art; lacking artistic sophistication.

"Curious paradox: the youngest among the world's great powers ... the United States possesses the oldest, the most original, and just about the most authentic naive painters," admitted Paris' *Figaro Littéraire* with an air of astonishment. The show consisted of 111 naive American paintings from the collection of Edgar William and Bernice Chrysler Garbisch.... *"Art: Unknown Masters," Time, Feb. 9, 1970, p 54*

2 not previously subjected to a test, experiment, etc.; unconditioned.

The experiments just described have shown that fear of the dark, acquired by training, can be transferred to naïve animals by material extracted from the brain of trained donors. *G. Ungar, L. Galvan, and R. H. Clark, "Chemical Transfer of Learned Fear," Nature, March 30, 1968, p 1261*

naked ape, a human being.

Honest adults who can still remember themselves when young will probably have difficulty recalling anyone more revolting whom they met in later life. The transient ambition of the adolescent naked ape is to live a life of high tragedy. Parents, therefore, should never try to understand their offspring. *"And the Last Word ... On Youth," New Scientist, Oct. 22, 1970, p 161*

[a term popularized by the British anthropologist Desmond Morris in his book *The Naked Ape* (1967)]

name, *n.* **the name of the game,** the essential thing; the thing that really counts.

Well, all right, I said. The name of the game is trust; you've got to trust things. *James Dickey, Deliverance, 1970, p 206*

"Some of them [refugees] have slipped back to the Pathet Lao," said an American official at the time, "but we have rounded up most of the population, and the name of the game is control of the population." *H. D. S. Green-*

way, "Reports & Comment: Laos," *The Atlantic, July 1971, p 10*

In the rough and tumble world of professional basketball, survival is often the name of the game. *Time, May 18, 1970, p 76*

[from the fact that in certain games, especially card games, the game's object is expressed by its name, as in the expressions *to have gin, to get twenty-one, to call rummy*, etc.]

Na·mib·i·an (nə'mib i: ən), *adj.* of or belonging to Namibia, the name by which African nationalists call the territory of South-West Africa (after *Namib*, the coastal desert area) in the Republic of South Africa.

Proponents of Namibian independence accuse South Africa of genocide and racial extermination, claiming that blacks are herded into "concentration camps" to be killed off as a result of inadequate medical attention. *"South Africa," Time, July 5, 1971, p 27*

—*n.* a native of Namibia.

We as sponsors of the Friends of Namibia Committee, on the third anniversary of the Namibians' imprisonment, appeal for their release and repatriation. *John W. Pardoe, Andrew Faulds, David Steel, Trevor Huddleston, Bishop of Stepney, in a Letter to the Editor, The Manchester Guardian Weekly, Feb. 20, 1971, p 2*

na·no- ('nei nou- *or* 'næn ou-), combining form meaning "one billionth," used in units of measurement involving submicroscopic objects, velocities, etc., as in the following examples:

nanoequivalent, *adj.:* Coulometric analysis is the quantitative determination of materials by measuring the amount of electricity necessary for their complete reaction.... Accuracy and precision compare favorably with other methods and range from a few hundredths of a per cent at the hundred microequivalent level under ideal conditions to approximately 10% at the five nanoequivalent level. *D. A. Aikens, "Coulometric Analysis," McGraw-Hill Yearbook of Science and Technology 1967, p 146*

nanohenry, *n.:* The capacitors...are 28 microfarads, 5 nanohenries, 2 milliohms, and a sample has given 1.8 million amps three times without failure. *A. MacAulay, Aldermaston, England, in a Letter to the Editor, New Scientist, Feb. 29, 1968, p 484*

nanometer, *n.:* The structure of clay comprises very small particles, usually crystalline platelets less than 0.001 millimeter in diameter, arranged to give a certain amount of structural rigidity.... A typical clay particle could be shaped like a flat plate 100nm × 1000nm × 10nm covered by a water layer 200nm thick (1 nanometer is 10^{-9}m). *Science, Jan. 1971, p 79*

nanomole, *n.:* Most, if not all, effects result from block of conduction in nerve axons. Conduction is blocked in isolated, desheathed frog sciatic nerves by a solution [of tetrodotoxin, a poisonous compound] containing about 3 nanomoles per liter. Excitation is abolished in skeletal muscle also. Depolarization does not occur and the block may be reversed by washing. *Frederick A. Fuhrman, "Tetrodotoxin," McGraw-Hill Yearbook of Science and Technology 1968, p 387*

nanovolt, *n.:* The other problem is how to take just a few microvolts from the national standard of one volt, and to infer its correctness to a few parts of a nanovolt (10^{-9}V). *Ian Firth, "A Cold Way to Voltage Standards," New Scientist, Aug. 22, 1968, p 391*

nanowatt, *n.:* The new COS/MOS units, on the other hand, operate on nanowatts of power in the quiescent state and use greater power only during the instant of switching information. *Advertisement by RCA, Harrison, N.J., Scientific American, March 1968, p 17*

[from Greek *nânos* (and Latin *nānus*) dwarf]

nanosurgery, *n.* surgery performed on microscopic parts of cells, tissues, etc., under an electron microscope.

Informed researchers believe that as equipment grows more sophisticated, tomorrow's surgeons will use such mind-defying techniques as nanosurgery, 10,000 times finer than the microsurgery now employed in pediatrics, and dependent on improvements in electron-microscopy and laser instrumentation now under study in the United States and France. *James C. G. Conniff, "Fetology: New Medical Specialty," Encyclopedia Science Supplement (Grolier) 1967, p 181*

Napoleonism, *n.* the policy of a ruler or a country of assuming unlimited control over subject peoples or nations.

...the traditional Latin American leader's custom of renouncing ultimate power as soon as he had won it (for fear of accusations of "Napoleonism"), were less significant than the internal political and social divisions. *Bill Luckin, The Sunday Times (London), April 6, 1969, p 27*

Without our nation standing up against Russia's modern day mad dog Napoleonism Europe itself would not remain independent through the 1970s. *George A. Nicholson, Jr., Grosse Pointe, Mich., in a Letter to the Editor, The Manchester Guardian Weekly, June 6, 1970, p 2*

[originally (1800's) applied to Napoleon I and his dynasty]

narc or **nark** (nɑrk), *n. U.S. Slang.* a federal narcotics agent.

I guess you know this town is on a bum trip—narcs everywhere and no good weed going unpunished. *Roger Angell, "The Floto Letters," The New Yorker, Feb. 21, 1970, p 34*

Most speed freaks get to a point where they're seeing narks in the trees with cameras.... *John Kifner, The New York Times, Oct. 17, 1967, p 44*

When I heard on television one day that undercover agents of the Daytona Beach police force were working the beach disguised as hippies, I realized that if an oldie came upon two people talking in youth jargon so thick it was totally unfathomable he would probably be in the presence of a narc and an evangelist. *Calvin Trillin, "U.S. Journal: Florida," The New Yorker, May 1, 1971, p 109*

[shortened from *narcotic agent* or *detective*]

► By coincidence the British slang term for a police informer is also *nark*. The latter, however, came from Romany (the Gypsy language) *nâk*, meaning nose, and has been used since the 1800's.

nasty, *n.* a nasty person or thing.

It's brave of Paramount to put *Borsalino* on at the Paramount in an undubbed version. Starring Jean-Paul Belmondo and Alain Delon as two lovable crooks in prewar Marseilles, the film has had enormous success in Paris and elsewhere and hits London while the iron is hot. Nice nasties are de rigueur these days. *Derek Malcolm, "Bergmania in Close-up: London Cinemas," The Manchester Guardian Weekly, Aug. 8, 1970, p 21*

...Nasties—they're the newest social force, waiting in

the wings to displace the last 1960s social force, the Flower People. They've always been around, the Nasties—disguised as merely unpleasant people, as persons with hateful, mean, offensive characters. *Anastasia Erland, Saturday Night (Canada), Feb. 1968, p 27*

[noun use of the adjective]

nationist, *n.* a person who favors nationhood or nationalistic aspirations. *Also used attributively.*

Each town and village in the East Bank, under its mayor or mukhtar, exists in atomised isolation. Between a cunning provincialist like Sheikh Ja'abri of Hebron, a nationist firebrand like Mayor Ma'asri of Nablus, and the Christian collaborationists of Bethlehem there is no scope for concerted action. *David Caute, "Little Europe in the Sands," The Manchester Guardian Weekly, July 18, 1970, p 7*

natural language, any language that has evolved naturally over the ages, as distinguished from an artificially devised language.

Almost all the things we say to one another are fearfully fuzzy in meaning, and it is only our common non-linguistic experience which saves us from mutual incomprehension. It is a fallacy, therefore, to suppose that the layman can be enabled to use a computer properly simply by designing a computer language to look like a natural language. *Christopher Longuet-Higgins and Stephen Isard, "The Monkey's Paw," New Scientist, Sept. 3, 1970, p 478*

... the only formalized languages that seem to be of real interest are those which are fragments of natural languages (fragments provided with complete vocabularies and precise syntactical rules) or those which can at least be adequately translated into natural languages. *Alfred Tarski, "Truth and Proof," Scientific American, June 1969, p 68*

Nax·a·lism ('næk sə‚liz əm), *n.* the beliefs and practices of the Naxalites.

Although secure in power Mrs. Gandhi faces many difficulties. The menace of Naxalism, the Maoist movement in West Bengal, may be less virulent than before but a daily reign of murder, arson, and terror in Calcutta continues....*Inder Malhotra, "Power Without Glory: India," The Manchester Guardian Weekly, Dec. 26, 1970, p 16*

Nax·a·lite ('næk sə‚lait), *n.* one of a group of Communist revolutionaries, originally of West Bengal, that engage in terrorist activities in India.

Confusion has been caused in Calcutta by a sudden spurt of activity by the Maoist extremists known in the city as Naxalites. *The Times (London), April 20, 1970, p 6*

—*adj.* of or belonging to the Naxalites.

...Naxalite violence, accompanied by the chanting of Maoist slogans and the plastering of Calcutta walls with Mao's portrait, has been so unremitting that police patience has been exhausted. *Inder Malhotra, The Manchester Guardian Weekly, May 9, 1970, p 6*

[from the *Naxal(bari)* district of West Bengal + *-ite*]

NC, abbreviation of NUMERICAL CONTROL. Compare APT (def. 3).

Milling and drilling operations were the most common NC applications, followed by turning operations. Many other NC systems were used in wire manufacturing, flame cutting, gas and arc welding,... plating, metal grinding, glass cutting... and complex metal contouring. *Orland B. Killin, "Industrial Review: Machinery and Machine Tools," Britannica Book of the Year 1970, p 421*

neb·bish ('neb iʃ), *n.* a person who is pitifully unfortunate.

...the center of the play is Mr. Gammell's black comedy Hitler. He starts as a bandy-legged nebbish: jumpy, up tight, the least-likely-to-succeed mobster you have ever seen. *Dan Sullivan, The New York Times, Aug. 8, 1968, p 28*

—*adj.* pitifully unfortunate.

The central character is so nebbish he has not even a name. *The Times (London), April 6, 1968, p 21*

...a perversion, a monstrous contained exultation...is manifested in certain daredevils, paranoid psychopaths who, after nebbish lives, suddenly feel themselves invulnerable in the certain wooing of sweet death.... *Howard Luck Gossage, "Tell Me Doctor, Will I Be Active Right Up to the Last?" The Atlantic, Sept. 1969, p 57*

[from the Yiddish interjection *nebekh*, probably from German *nie bei euch* may it not happen to you]

Neddy, *n. British.* nickname for the National Economic Development Council of Great Britain. Compare LITTLE NEDDY.

A Neddy-sponsored questionnaire sent out to 2.000 firms in the wool trade, is the first phase of a £80,000 survey designed to establish the competitiveness of the British wool textile industry and how it can increase profitability. *The Times (London), April 18, 1968, p 21*

[alteration of the abbreviation *NEDC* for National Economic Development Council]

needle, *n.* **1** a spur, goad, or stimulus.

...there is plenty of time for the newer helmsmen to come to the fore. One hopes they do, for without the constant needle of improving competition the men at the top will find it difficult to improve any further. *John Nicholls, The Times (London), March 16, 1970, p 8*

2 a barbed or sarcastic remark.

More than [Will] Rogers, [Bob] Hope has become the friend of politicians and statesmen, tycoons and sportsmen.... He kids the starch out of them, and they feel better for it; a needle from Hope becomes an emblem instead of a scar. *Time, Dec. 22, 1967, p 48*

3 the needle, *Especially U.S. Slang.* narcotic drugs.

James Baldwin also told him [Daniel Snowman]: 'When I was growing up in the streets of Harlem, most of my generation—for reasons I had no difficulty to discover—perished on the needle... by and by, white kids—sons and daughters of Pan Am, sons and daughters of General Electric—bored to death with their lives and their luxury and ashamed of their parents, trying to arrive at what they thought of as reality, they hit the needle, too.' *The Listener, Oct. 17, 1968, p 505*

"She is inscrutable. How she managed to protect her children is a mystery. None of us has been in prison. None has been on the needle." *The New York Times, June 3, 1963, p 19*

4 thread the needle, to accomplish a difficult task.

... Mr. Udall... expressed hope that the committee "can succeed in making the compromises and threading the needle" to get authorization for the central Arizona plan, which conservation groups have fought successfully so far. *William M. Blair, The New York Times, Jan. 27, 1967, p 13*

needle time, *British.* (in radio broadcasting) the

programmed air time devoted to recorded music.

The pirate radio broadcasters, who escaped the restrictions of "needle time" (limitation on the broadcasting of records imposed under British copyright legislation), claimed large audiences among young listeners for their round-the-clock output of "pop" music interspersed with advertising. *James Magee, "Television and Radio," Britannica Book of the Year 1967, p 723*

negative income tax or **negative tax,** direct payments by the government to any family or individual whose income falls below a specified level, often proposed as a replacement for present welfare programs in the United States. *Abbreviation:* NIT Also called GUARANTEED ANNUAL INCOME or GUARANTEED INCOME.

...the unemployed in the United States have begun to demand not just the right to work but a guaranteed annual income whether they work or not. Far from being considered a shocking proposal, the idea has been advanced independently by middle-class reformers under the somewhat specious label of the "negative income tax." *Lewis Mumford, "The Megamachine," The New Yorker, Oct. 31, 1970, p 54*

This coupled with his [the Chancellor of the Exchequer's] proposal to investigate and discuss publicly the tax-credit system, more commonly known as negative income tax. *The Times (London), May 5, 1972, p 17*

né·go·ciant (nei gɔ:'syã), *n. French.* dealer; merchant.

It used to be practicable for French negociants to hold wines in their cellars until they had matured and could be sold for almost immediate drinking. *John Arlott, "High-pitched Wine," The Manchester Guardian Weekly, May 16, 1970, p 17*

► As used in English, the meaning of the word is close to being "a wine dealer," equivalent to French *négociant en vins.*

neg·ri·tude ('neg rə‚tu:d), *n.* **1** the distinctive qualities or characteristics of Negroes, especially African Negroes. Also called NEGRONESS or BLACKNESS.

...the whole-hearted attempt by other Negroes to emphasize their Negroid features and hair texture shows their pride in their "negritude"—a word currently in fashion in Negro communities. *Time, Aug. 27, 1965, p 19*

2 pride in the cultural and artistic heritage of Negroes, especially African Negroes.

If any one idea has dominated the talk of Dakar's first World Festival of the Negro Arts, it is the controversy over "negritude," a word that is said to signify that the creative process of the Negro artist is unique. *Lloyd Garrison, The New York Times, April 24, 1966, p 17*

One is forced to conclude that the noble doctrine of négritude, the poetizing of what is best in the Black African tradition to achieve a world-wide communion among Negroes meanders all too frequently into this area of racial hatred. *Robert J. Clements, "Poetry on the Campus," Review of "Poems From Black Africa," edited by Langston Hughes, Saturday Review, June 11, 1966, p 69*

[from French *négritude,* literally, the condition of being a Negro]

negritudinous, *adj.* characterized by or exhibiting negritude.

...to continue to create works that will be Nigerian and African and Negritudinous, I must respond to this call to say something, even as an artist. *Ben Enwonwu. The Times (London), Oct. 4, 1968, p 11*

Negroness, *n.* the condition or quality of being Negro. Also called BLACKNESS or NEGRITUDE.

"The Negroness that we are is there. There's no way to get out of it." *Lloyd Garrison, The New York Times, April 24. 1966, p 17*

Nehru, *n.* a Nehru jacket or coat.

Mr. Goring will sell the men's bags, but he will "emphatically not" wear them. "On the other hand, I wouldn't wear Nehrus or those damn beads either, so you can't go by me," he said. *Enid Nemy, The New York Times, June 6, 1968, p 50*

Nehru jacket or **Nehru coat,** a long, narrow jacket or coat with a high collar. Also called MAO JACKET.

Variations on the narrow "Nehru" jacket with the stand-up collar continue.... *Angela Taylor, The New York Times, May 24, 1967, p 46*

Those who feel that tuxedos are old-fashioned are trying out the long mandarin-collared Mao or Nehru coats. *Time, March 1, 1968, p 43*

[named after Jawaharlal *Nehru* 1889-1964, prime minister of India, who wore this type of jacket or coat]

Nehru suit, a suit consisting of a Nehru jacket and tight pants.

Mr. Tillotson, a tall, mustached man, appeared unperturbed in black Nehru suit with gold neck chain and white ruffles at cuffs and neck.... *The New York Times, June 24, 1968, p 42*

nellie, *adj. Slang.* feminine; effeminate.

...it ["The Boys in the Band"] was also fu'l of lachrymose seriousness about the miseries and heartbreaks of homosexuality. It was like "The Women," but with a forties-movie bomber-crew cast: a Catholic, a Jew, a Negro, a butch faggot, a nellie faggot, a hustler, and so on.... *Pauline Kael, "The Current Cinema," The New Yorker, March 21, 1970, p 166*

[from the feminine name *Nellie,* nickname of *Helen*]

Nelly, *n.* **not on your Nelly,** *British Slang.* certainly not; not likely.

...Home said "that would mean me investing in another man's career. Not on your Nelly!" *The Sunday Times (London), May 15, 1966, p 9*

[shortened from *not on your Nelly Duff,* rhyming slang for *not on your puff,* "puff" being a little-known slang word for "(breath of) life." There is a vulgar tinge to *not on your Nelly,* probably because of some dubious meaning ascribed to "Nelly."]

neo-, combining form meaning "new" or "new version of," attached chiefly to names or designations of doctrines, beliefs, theories, systems, etc. Compounds formed with *neo-* which appeared recently include:

neoconservative, *adj.:* Judaism and Christianity have always placed primacy in man. Now this primacy is being attacked by what I call the neoconservative ecological approach to life. *James Schall, "Is Ecology Heresy?" Time, Aug. 23, 1971, p 31*

neoexpressionist, *adj.:* Landscape and other subjects

are handled by Miss Rosenberger as a series of neoexpressionist clichés. *Hilton Kramer, The New York Times, Jan. 20, 1968, p 25*

neofeminist, *n.:* "Are you still against abortion?" [Ellen] Willis [a rock critic] asks, alluding to a position I had once taken which gave me, for a time, some small notoriety among the rest of the neo-feminists. *Margot Hentoff, "Performing Arts," Harper's, Nov. 1969, p 28*

neo-Maoist, *adj.:* If a neo-Maoist China is to take shape after the cultural revolution and the ninth congress one can say that it is still very murky and that its institutional life is not in sight yet. *Richard Harris, "Peeping Through the Bamboo Curtain," The Times (London), Feb. 21, 1970, p 7*

neonationalism, *n.:* . . . that signs that "middle-class radicalism and neo-nationalism" were growing in West Germany could no longer be denied. *Philip Shabecoff, The New York Times, May 11, 1968, p 13*

neopopulism, *n.:* Once dismissed as a racist demagogue, Alabama Gov. George Wallace brings a quirky but potent neopopulism to 1972 Presidential politics—as witnessed by his triumph in the Florida Democratic primary. *Newsweek, March 27, 1972. p 3*

neorevisionist, *adj.:* One of the Maoists' main targets is the Marxist Communist Party, branded by Peking as neorevisionist to distinguish it from the pro-Moscow Communist Party. *"Indian Students Riot," The Times (London), Feb. 26, 1970, p 6*

neorevisionist, *n.:* . . . the Indian Marxists have often been denounced by Radio Peking as "neo-revisionists." *Inder Malhotra, "Marxists Hit Back at Mrs. Gandhi," The Manchester Guardian Weekly, July 18, 1970, p 5*

See also the main entries below.

neocolonial, *adj.* supporting or practicing neocolonialism.

At one session with the press—before the discovery of the Vietcong camp—he [Prince Sihanouk] passionately denounced the United States for ever coming to Vietnam as "a military and neo-colonial power". . . . *Robert Shaplen, "Letter from Cambodia," The New Yorker, Jan. 13, 1968, p 86*

— *n.* a neocolonial power.

For many Africans, he [Moise Tshombe, then premier of Katanga, Republic of the Congo] became a symbol of the "neocolonials" (the Belgians) and the "imperialists" (the Americans). *The New York Times, July 5, 1967, p 12*

neo-Dada, *n.* another name for ANTI-ART. Also called NEO-DADAISM.

Abstraction, neo-Dada and other up-to-date tendencies can be seen flourishing among "unofficial" works of the younger generation. *Hilton Kramer, The New York Times, Oct. 13, 1967, p 24*

. . . it has always seemed to me a little incongruous to record, analyze, and teach such gestures of "anti-art" with the very solemnity, not to say pomposity, they had set out to ridicule and abolish. Be that as it may, the appeal of "anti-art" was irresistible to many young art students, and critics now gravely talk about neo-Dada. . . . however, it is not the label that matters but the wit and talent that may go into these assemblages of discarded objects. *E. H. Gombrich, "Art and Anti-Art," The Atlantic, Feb. 1966, p 94*

neo-Dadaism, *n.* another name for NEO-DADA.

Perhaps a change in the air encouraged . . . the recent revival of surrealism and neo-Dadaism. *The Times (London), July 16, 1966, p 7*

neoglacial, *adj.* of or relating to neoglaciation.

Carbon-14 dates of vegetation, peat or soil overrun by glacier ice provide direct ages for neoglacial advances, and dating of organic matter in recessional or advance deposits associated with neoglacial moraines may provide important limiting ages. *George H. Denton and Stephen C. Porter, "Neoglaciation," Scientific American, June 1970, p 105*

neoglaciation, *n.* the formation of new glaciers.

Historical records of the latest glacier fluctuations during neoglaciation are available from many Alpine regions. *George H. Denton and Stephen C. Porter, "Neoglaciation," Scientific American, June 1970, p 102*

neoimperial, *adj.* of or characterized by neoimperialism. Also, NEOIMPERIALIST.

This analysis could embrace not just neoimperial China and neoimperial Russia. *C. L. Sulzberger, The New York Times, March 17, 1968, Sec. 4, p 12*

neoimperialism, *n.* a revival or recurrence of imperialism.

Their [the Moorish kings'] rule was broken by the French conquest in the 19th century, but Morocco still claims its former lands, including much of the Algerian Sahara, the northern parts of Senegal and Mali and all of Mauritania. Morocco's territorial claims are plainly unacceptable to its neighbors, who brand them "neo-imperialism," and embarrassing to its friends. *"Morocco," Time, Feb. 17, 1967, p 24*

neoimperialist, *n.* one who supports neoimperialism.

I believe that, in fact, we are in danger of seeing the isolationists of the 1920s and 1930s replaced by the neo-imperialists, who somehow imagine that the United States has a mandate to impose an American solution the world around. *George McGovern, "Viewpoint: Foreign Policy and the Crisis Mentality," The Atlantic, Jan. 1967, p 55*

neoisolationism, *n.* a revival or recurrence of isolationism.

More than one high official has expressed concern that disillusionment about the Indochina War and preoccupation with domestic ills wi'l bring on neoisolationism in the United States. *Robert Manning, "The Editor's Page," The Atlantic, Jan. 1971, p 4*

He [Richard M. Nixon] is still very much the internationalist . . . at a time when neo-isolationism is spreading through the country. *Rowland Evans and Robert Novak, "The Road to Miami Beach," Harper's, Jan. 1968, p 23*

neoisolationist, *adj.* of or characterized by neoisolationism.

This month's magazine offers a considerable dose of anti-neoisolationist nourishment: two articles on Egypt and the Middle East situation, reports on Berlin, Canada, and China policy; as well as a lighthearted exercise in the ways of England. . . . *Robert Manning, "The Editor's Page," The Atlantic, Jan. 1971, p 4*

— *n.* one who supports neoisolationism.

Isolationism, it would seem, is once again on the rise. President Nixon has used the term neo-isolationist to describe certain of his senatorial critics who wou'd alter U.S. foreign policy or who seek a greater role for the Congress in shaping it. *John L. Steele, "How Real Is Neo-Isolationism?" Time, May 31, 1971, p 18*

neo-Keynesian, *adj.* of, characterized by, or based upon government spending and tax adjustment as

311

the major influential factors in economic growth.

[Senator Hubert H.] Humphrey pledges to continue the neo-Keynesian policies that have helped stimulate the nation to 7-1/2 years of unprecedented growth in jobs, wages and production. *"Those Little-Discussed Campaign Issues," Time, Oct. 25. 1968, p 31*

—*n.* a supporter of a neo-Keynesian fiscal policy. Compare MONETARIST, FRIEDMANITE. See also NEW ECONOMICS.

It was also recognized that monetary policy could be effectively exploited for purposes of stabilization policy, and this position is accepted by Neo-Keynesians and monetarists alike. *Karl Brunner, "Controlling the Money Supply," The Times (London), Sept. 7, 1970, p 19*

ne·o·phil·i·a (ˌniː əˈfil iː ə), *n.* a love of novelty; a great interest in anything new.

What was best in the dream — the idealism of the Ban the Bomb movement, a general exuberant impulse toward freedom — finally went mad. . . . Booker mainly blames the communicators — the fad-conscious journalists, the telly talkers, the trendy film makers — who turned Neophilia into an industry. *"Books: The End of the New," Review of "The Neophiliacs" by Christopher Booker, Time, July 6, 1970, p 71*

Indeed, the opportunity to explore a complex area can be used instead of food or water as a reward to induce a rat to choose one passage rather than another. This well-developed neophilia has led some writers to use the term "curiosity drive" to refer to it. . . . *S. A. Barnett, "Rats," Scientific American, Jan. 1967, p 85*

neophiliac, *n.* a person characterized or affected by neophilia.

What on earth do the Beatles, Harold Wilson, Twiggy, and Kenneth Tynan have in common? . . . They are Neophiliacs — lovers of "the new" — and they are doomed to live out the damnation of all ultramodern men: "Keeping pace with pace." *"Books: The End of the New," Review of "The Neophiliacs" by Christopher Booker, Time, July 6, 1970, p 71*

neph·a·nal·y·sis (ˌnef əˈnæl ə sis), *n.* analysis of maps of cloud formations made from photographs of clouds taken by artificial earth satellites.

In September a long-awaited daily exchange of cloud-cover (nephanalysis) charts based on satellite photographs was begun between Moscow, Russia, and Washington, D.C. *The 1967 Compton Yearbook, p 485*

[from Greek *néphos* cloud + English *analysis*]

neph·e·loid layer (ˈnef əˌlɔid). See the quotation for the meaning.

Several years ago Drs. Maurice Ewing and Edward M. Thorndike detected turbid layers in the deep waters several kilometers off the East Coast of the United States. They called these areas nepheloid layers and found them to be a suspension of clay-sized mineral particles. *Science News, Oct. 4, 1969, p 304*

[from Greek *nephélē* cloud + English *-oid*]

nerve agent, a gas or other substance used in chemical warfare that attacks the nervous system.

Work on toxins is "too expensive", studies of the operational feasibility of incapacitating agents (such as LSD) have stopped, and there is no further interest in carbamates. Stocks of five nerve agents (T-2715, GB, GD, GF and VX) are kept at Nancekuke and, at present, a total

of about 100 lb is in the store. *Frank Barnaby, "Open Day in Nancekuke," New Scientist, Nov. 5, 1970, p 281*

nettle, *n.* **1** something vexing or nettlesome; irritation; vexation.

The Minister [Dr. Hillery, the Irish Republic's Minister of External Affairs] said that someone had to deal with the nettle of the Orange Order. *The Times (London), July 9, 1970, p 1*

. . . I made a lot of money but spent every cent, and the commuting was an endless nettle. *Whitney Balliett, "Our Far-Flung Correspondents," The New Yorker, Oct. 18, 1969, p 188*

2 grasp the nettle, to attack a difficulty boldly; deal promptly and firmly with a problem.

Still, with the audacity that has made the Warren Court the most fascinating institution in this usually predictable Capitol city, the Justices grasped the nettle on Monday and announced that they will rule on Mr. Powell's case. *Fred P. Graham, The New York Times, Nov. 24, 1968, Sec. 4, p 11*

And with John Davies about to grasp the Ministry of Technology end of the nettle with characteristic brusqueness, the laboratories of the Atomic Energy Authority, especially Harwell, are suffering renewed and damaging queasiness. *Anthony Tucker, "Splitting the Atom Men," The Manchester Guardian Weekly, Aug. 8, 1970, p 10*

▶ *Nettle* in the sense of "something vexing" represents a new meaning, most likely derived from the verb *to nettle,* "to vex or irritate," rather than by extension from the noun's literal meaning ("a plant with stinging leaf hairs").

The idiom *grasp the nettle* (attested in the *OED* since 1884) may be a distant echo of Shakespeare's "Out of this nettle, danger, we pluck this flower, safety" (King Henry IV, II.iii.10). The idiom must have originated among country dwellers, who were aware that the nettle is harmless if grasped tightly and quickly.

nettle-grasper, *n.* a person who attacks a difficulty boldly.

The trip [to Somalia] was planned long ago, but now the President . . . has been assassinated, his Prime Minister . . . is in prison, and the young — or not-so-young — colonels running the place have still to surface. The problem for the Foreign Office is what you do about such regimes. The nettle-graspers are all for firm decisions and quick recognition, the slitherers for "playing it long." The technique is to let the coup cool and tactfully look the other way till you can be sure who has won and what you think of him. *"Miscellany: Tripwire," The Manchester Guardian Weekly, Nov. 1, 1969, p 11*

[from the idiom *grasp the nettle*]

network, *v.t., v.i.* British. to broadcast or telecast over a network.

More than ever this year's American elections are being fought over the airwaves — especially on television. . . . First there's the great set-piece networked from coast to coast and paid for by the candidate, an operation not to be embarked on very often. *Gerald Priestland, "Foreign News: Just a Lot of Broadcasting," The Listener, Oct. 10, 1968, p 461*

It became one of Scottish Television's most popular programmes and was the first originating in Scotland to be networked. *The Times (London), April 26, 1968, p 9*

network analysis, the mathematical or statistical study of networks and their connecting lines, points, branches, etc. Compare CRITICAL PATH ANALYSIS.

A modern society is to a large extent a system of networks for communication, transportation, and the distribution of energy and goods. The complexity and cost of these networks demand that existing networks be effectively used and that new networks be rationally designed. To meet this demand there has evolved a new discipline called network analysis. *Howard Frank and Ivan T. Frisch, "Network Analysis," Scientific American, July 1970, p 94*

. . . the application of scientific techniques in government as in business management is very useful. It is enough to mention operational research, network (critical path) analysis, etc. *T. Boniszewski. Southampton, England, in a Letter to the Editor, New Scientist, July 9, 1970, p 96*

network analyst, a specialist in network analysis.

Network analysts rely heavily on graph theory, a branch of mathematics that was founded with Leonhard Euler's formulation and solution of the first graph-theory problem in 1736. *Howard Frank and Ivan T. Frisch, "Network Analysis," Scientific American, July 1970, p 94*

neur·a·min·i·dase (‚nur ə'min ə‚deis), *n.* an enzyme that hydrolizes neuraminic acid (a fatty acid in the spinal cord) and attacks mucous cells and substances.

The enzyme neuraminidase, injected into mice as a postcoital contraceptive, seemed to be the most effective base for a "morning-after pill" of any yet tried. *New Scientist, Dec. 31, 1970, p 608*

The enzyme, known as neuraminidase, can attack the mucus of saliva, nasal secretion, sputum or egg white and so on. *C. H. Stuart-Harris, Science Journal, Jan. 1970, p 40*

neurobiological, *adj.* of or relating to neurobiology.

As work in this field frequently forms part of a wider programme of neurobiological research, it is not possible to isolate a figure for expenditure on research into epilepsy alone. *Tam Dalyell, "Westminister Scene: Problems of Epilepsy," New Scientist and Science Journal, Jan. 28, 1971, p 195*

neurobiologist, *n.* a specialist in neurobiology.

. . . neurobiologists . . . uncovered a link between calcium and the establishment of the classic Pavlovian conditioned response. Drs. Robert Grenell and Eduardo Romero . . . elicited responses at will by manipulating the cellular chemical in a living brain. *"Calcium Link Found," Science News, March 7, 1970, p 246*

neurobiology, *n.* the branch of biology that deals with the nervous system.

. . . much basic research is being carried out by the council and the universities, particularly in the field of neurobiology, and may well throw light on the problems of epilepsy. *Tam Dalyell, "Westminister Scene: Problems of Epilepsy," New Scientist and Science Journal, Jan. 28, 1971, p 195*

neurochemical, *n.* a chemical substance that affects the nervous system or some part of it.

Several neurochemicals, when applied to a specific area of the brain, appear to control killing behavior in laboratory rats. . . . *"Modifying Murderous Rats," Science News, Feb. 21, 1970, p 197*

— *adj.* of or relating to neurochemistry.

The most logical direction for neurochemical research is perhaps to carry forward the work of neurophysiologists by elucidating the chemical changes that accompany action potentials and synaptic transmission. *Alan Boyne, "The Shadow of Brain Research," New Scientist and Science Journal, Aug. 26, 1971, p 462*

neurochemist, *n.* a specialist in neurochemistry.

Probably one of the most baffling aspects of brain research concerns the nature of consciousness. Neurophysiologists and neurochemists have yet to find the exact seat of consciousness or to explain how it functions. *J. Edward Tether, "Brain Research," Encyclopedia Science Supplement (Grolier) 1968, p 105*

Chemical transmitters are attracting a good deal of attention from neurochemists at the moment. *"More Clues About the Brain's Chemical Messages," New Scientist and Science Journal, Dec. 16, 1971, p 145*

neurochemistry, *n.* the chemistry of the nervous system.

As a basic science, neurochemistry has continued to advance, and many of its observations have been of great clinical importance. It has been found that disturbances of vitamin B_6 (pyridoxine) may cause seizures. This vitamin is an essential nutritional cofactor, without which the brain enzyme which produces gamma-aminobutyric acid (GABA) fails to function. It is highly probable that this is a key point in the problem of seizures. *Francis M. Forster, "Nervous System," The Americana Annual 1962, p 528*

neurodepressive, *adj.* acting as a nerve depressant.

When pregnant rats are treated with atropine, a neurodepressive drug, no later than the third day of pregnancy, implantation of a fertilized egg is delayed. . . . *Science News, Jan. 17, 1970, p 63*

neuroendocrinologist, *n.* a specialist in neuroendocrinology.

These organic compounds [amines], which were thought to act as chemical mediators (neurohumors) at synaptic junctions (where the endings of nerve cells come into contact) in the central nervous system, were of interest to neuroendocrinologists. Most of these compounds are found in high concentration in the hypothalamus. *Albert Wolfson, "Zoology: Adaptive Physiology," 1969 Britannica Yearbook of Science and the Future, 1968, p 389*

neuroendocrinology, *n.* the endocrinology of the nervous system.

Neuroendocrinology research was expected to establish the pathways in the brain that regulate the hypothalamic hormones and the role of the amines in the control of these pathways. *Albert Wolfson, "Zoology: Adaptive Physiology," 1969 Britannica Yearbook of Science and the Future, 1968, p 389*

neu·ro·he·mal organ (‚nur ou'hi: məl), an organ of the circulatory system having neurological importance.

According to Bruce Johnson, in the cockroach *Periplaneta* secretory material is released from the granules in the axons along the whole length of the cardiac nerves; that is, the nerves themselves act as neurohemal organs where the hormone is released into the circulating blood . . . . *Sir Vincent Brian Wigglesworth, "Zoology," Britannica Book of the Year 1967, p 173*

[from *neuro-* nerve or nervous system + *hemal* of or relating to the circulatory system]

neu·ro·ki·nin (‚nur ou'kai nən), *n.* a protein substance that causes dilation of blood vessels and has an undertermined effect on nerves.

In 1960 a polypeptide, neurokinin, was isolated by Wolff and his colleagues in the USA, from the subcutaneous tissues near the temporal blood vessels in patients during an attack of migraine. *Robert Smith, "The Attack on Migraine," New Scientist, Jan. 27, 1966, p 208*

. . . substances around the headache site, referred to as "headache fluid," . . . among which are two miniature proteins called bradykinin and neurokinin, are believed to make nerves sensitive to pain. *Jane E. Brody, "Headaches," Encyclopedia Science Supplement (Grolier) 1969, p 166*

[from *neuro-* nerve or nervous system + *kinin* any of various proteins involved in dilation and contraction of tissue, from Greek *kīneîn* to move]

neuroleptic, *n.* a tranquilizing drug, especially one used to treat schizophrenics.

Schizophrenics treated over long periods with neuroleptics have sometimes shown symptoms typical of endogenous depression and have attempted suicide. *"A Law to Help the Suicidal," New Scientist, Nov. 21, 1968, p 417*

[from French *neuroleptique*, from *neuro-* nerve or nervous system + *-leptique* -leptic (as in *epileptic*)]

neuropharmacological, *adj.* of or relating to neuropharmacology.

Apart from their clinical effects these various poisons have proved novel tools in neuropharmacological research, especially in elucidating the mechanism of nervous conduction. *Alan N. Davison, "For Student and Specialist," New Scientist and Science Journal, Dec. 9, 1971, p 119*

neuropharmacologist, *n.* a specialist in neuropharmacology.

The effects of the new drug [magnesium pemoline] on rats are impressive. Those given the compound learned from four to five times faster than untreated rats. They also retained what they had learned longer, Dr. N. P. Plotnikoff, an Abbott neuropharmacologist, reported. *"Drug Improves Memory," Science News Letter, Jan. 1, 1966, p 6*

neuropharmacology, *n.* the study of the effects of drugs on the nervous system.

. . . brain-control chemistry (neuropharmacology) is making very rapid progress. I see no reason for assuming that the human brain will lose its individuality after losing contact with its body. . . . Even when the body is very weak and ailing, the brain continues its active life if it is not exhausted by physical pain. *Nikolai Amosov, "Brain Without a Body," Encyclopedia Science Supplement (Grolier) 1969, p 233*

Chronicles the development of neuropharmacology during the past 10 years. Of particular importance are the chapters on central nervous pharmacology with the micro-iontophoretic technique of drug application. *Review of "The Pharmacology of Synapses" by J. W. Phillis, Science News, Jan. 16, 1971, p 38*

neuroscience, *n.* any of the sciences dealing with the nervous system, such as neurology, neurochemistry, etc., or these sciences collectively.

Although the prospects of, for example, greater self-knowledge through neuroscience, are exciting, we know that self-knowledge does not necessarily give rise to wisdom and that there is fear that neuroscience will be misapplied in mind-control. *Maurice Wilkins, "Making Science*

More Socially Responsible," The Times (London), Nov. 26, 1970, p 12

neurotransmitter, *n.* a chemical substance that transmits impulses between nerve cells.

Norepinephrine is a neurotransmitter, a substance responsible for carrying a signal across the gap between two neurons. Neurons that use norepinephrine as a neurotransmitter have a role in the control of mood, learning, blood pressure, heart rate, blood sugar and glandular function. *"Nutrition: Malnutrition and Brain Damage," Science News, April 17, 1971, p 266*

In the brain, as elsewhere in the body, the transmission of nervous impulses from one cell to another is due to the release at nerve endings of chemicals called neuro-transmitters; these include acetylcholine and noradrenalin. *"Royal College of Physicians' Report on Smoking: Smoke Peril," The Times (London), Jan. 6, 1971, p 4*

neutron activation analysis, a method of analyzing the composition of a substance by radioactive bombardment with neutrons to identify the elements present by their characteristic radiation. *Abbreviation:* NAA Compare ACTIVATION ANALYSIS.

. . . neutron activation analysis, [is] a technique which detects trace elements by bombarding them with neutrons so they give off characteristic gamma rays. . . . *"Cystic Fibrosis Detection," Science News, March 7, 1970, p 245*

. . . neutron activation analysis offers a sensitive method for comparing bearing wear. The method can detect wear due to a few minutes' running, as well as abnormal wear. *"Neutrons Measure Bearing Wear," New Scientist, July 30, 1970, p 241*

neutron radiography, a technique for producing an X-ray type picture on photographic film by exposing an object to a stream of neutrons.

. . . neutron radiography gives promise of complementing X-ray radiography. X-rays emphasize the contrast between bone and soft tissue, while neutrons emphasize tissue differences and void spaces. *Frank B. Baranowski, "Californium," McGraw-Hill Yearbook of Science and Technology 1970, p 131*

neutron star, a hypothetical heavenly body that is the source of powerful X-rays and consists of a mass of very densely packed neutrons probably formed by the collapsed atoms of a large star.

After two years of frantic study, pulsar research has now settled down and most workers in the field agree that they are neutron stars behaving somewhat peculiarly. *Nicholas Valery, Science Journal, Oct. 1970, p 10*

If white dwarfs [small stars of great density] resemble giant atoms, neutron stars (if they exist) would be more like giant atomic nuclei. They could exist at a temperature of absolute zero and would have mean densities in the range from 10^{11} and 10^{15} grams per cubic centimeter. In other words, the mean density in a neutron star would be on the order of a billion tons per cubic inch! *Jeremiah P. Ostriker, "The Nature Of Pulsars," Scientific American, Jan. 1971, p 50*

never, *adv.* **never ever,** an emphatic form of *never.*

However, if we enter the Common Market the British electorate (unlike any other of the enlarged ten) will never ever have had, nor ever will have, the opportunity of passing their opinion on this subject. *Daily Telegraph (London), April 14, 1972 [page not recorded]*

new economics, the policy, based on Keynesian theory, of a flexible adjustment of taxes and government spending to influence or improve the economy; the policy of the neo-Keynesians.

In the thirty-odd years since Roosevelt and the peacetime New Deal, the national Democratic Party has won elections on five major policies. And the spillover from these policies has won a legion of local contests. The policies were:

(1) Implementation of the New (or Keynesian) economics. This insured, as all liberal Democrats believed, that the economic system worked. *John Kenneth Galbraith, "Who Needs the Democrats?" Harper's, July 1970, p 44*

New Federalism, a policy of federal decentralization and revenue-sharing with the states, advocated by President Nixon.

Two years of liberal encomiums to decentralization have intellectually legitimized the concept, if not the name, of states' rights and have set the stage for the widespread acceptance of Nixon's "New Federalism." *Bayard Rustin, "The Failure of Black Separatism," Harper's, Jan. 1970, p 32*

What if the Federal Government provides money and lets the states provide services to people? A cornerstone of the Nixon Administration's domestic policy, the "New Federalism," proposes to shift responsibility and power from the Federal Government to the states by providing more state and local control and decentralization of decision-making. *Irving J. Lewis, "Government Investment in Health Care," Scientific American, April 1971, p 21*

New Federalist, a supporter or advocate of New Federalism.

To the New Federalists, morality in a nation is determined not by government policy, church decree, or social leadership—what is moral is what most people who think about morality at all think is moral at a given time. *William Safire, quoted by Elizabeth B. Drew, "Reports: Washington," The Atlantic, May 1970, p 22*

New Left, a movement of political radicals opposed to the traditional liberals of the left and calling for revolutionary changes in government, civil rights, foreign policy, education, and other areas affecting society. Also called RADICAL LEFT. Compare OLD LEFT.

The "New Left," represented by groups such as the National Mobilization Committee to End the War in Vietnam and the Students for a Democratic Society, had no doubt that the nation had become a sick society, characterized by poverty, racism, violence, and war. *Richard S. Kirkendall, "United States: A Time to Mourn," The Americana Annual 1969, p 714*

New Leftist, a member of the New Left.

The New Left thinks of the poor as victims and believes that the conservatives think of them only as failures.... The New Leftists have a mystical faith in the purity and wisdom of the poor, "uncorrupted" by the Establishment— an idea that the New Right rejects as nonsense. *"The New Radicals," Time, April 28, 1967, p 15*

An Irishman from California, he [Jack Quarry, a boxer] has a pale, hard, sullen, lower-class face that. in the mind of a New Leftist, would seem most apposite peeping out from behind a police visor or supporting a flag-decaled construction hat. *Jack Richardson, "Ali on Peachtree," Harper's, Jan. 1971, p 49*

new penny; *pl.* **new pence.** the British penny in the newly established decimal system (effective February 15, 1971), equal to one 100th of a pound and corresponding to 2.4 pence in the old system. A new penny is worth 2.4 American cents. *Abbreviation:* p

The economic crux of the matter...is to be found in that shoppers' table, which turns both nine and ten old pence into four new pence—an anomaly brought about by the necessity of "rounding up" or "rounding down" the old sums to convert them to the nearest equivalent in new coins. *John Brooks, "Our Far-Flung Correspondents: By Tens," The New Yorker, Nov. 21, 1970, p 192*

The minimum cost of a call would go down from 6d.— the equivalent of 2 1/2 new pence—to 2 new pence with a compensating adjustment in the length of the call. *The Times (London), Feb. 20, 1970, p 13*

▶ Since the appearance of this term it has been noticed that many people in Great Britain, some of them highly literate, have been using the plural form *new pence* in the singular, as "one new pence." This is a remarkable development, since few would ever have said "one pence" under the old system. Thus in a circular letter sent out in February 1972 by the managing director of a London unit trust (mutual fund), the following appears:

"After careful consideration of all the relevant facts and costings we have come to the conclusion that we can offer our existing unit holders the opportunity of increasing their investment at a discount of 1 new pence per unit."

New Politics, a development in American politics, associated especially with the figures of Senators Eugene J. McCarthy, the late Robert F. Kennedy, and George S. McGovern, in which emphasis is placed upon intense participation of voters in the political processes rather than on party machinery.

The young radicals are probably not nearly so important as they sometimes seem, and what is called the New Politics may matter even less than they do. *John Corry, "The Many-sided Mr. Meany," Harper's, March 1970, p 58*

New Right, a political movement standing for conservatism and nationalism in response to both the New Left and the traditional or established conservatives.

"I belong to the New Right in Japan,...and I agree with the New Left on one thing—that what the Japanese were taught after the war about American peace and democracy was not true." *Christopher Driver, The Manchester Guardian Weekly, Dec. 12, 1970, p 7*

True to its ideal of detachment, the Voice avoids the excesses of partisan politics.... And the paper that claims to have discovered the New Left has recently discovered a New Right, rebelling against the upper-class gentility of Bill Buckley. *"The Press: Newspapers: Voice of the Partially Alienated," Time, Nov. 11, 1966, p 52*

newsmaker, *n. U.S.* a newsworthy person or event.

Scatterbrained, overstimulated, and insecure in her role as a newsmaker, Martha likes to tell herself and others about her "projects" and "accomplishments." "I've done a great deal for the Salvation Army. I attend a lot of fun-making functions." *"Martha Mitchell's View From the Top," Time, Nov. 30, 1970, p 33*

Such pictures as these made in the frontline of combat reveal field photojournalism itself as one of the real newsmakers of the year. *Margaret R. Weiss, "Photography in The Front Line," Saturday Review, March 11, 1967, p 134*

newsreader, *n. British.* a news announcer.

Robert Dougall, the B.B.C. newsreader, has been nominated as president-designate of the Royal Society for the Protection of Birds, an organization in whose affairs he has taken an active interest for the past 20 years. *The Times (London), Sept. 14, 1970, p 8*

new town, a planned urban community, often situated near a large city, built to contain the housing, business, and other facilities necessary to make it self-sufficient. Also called SATELLITE TOWN or SATELLITE CITY.

The first wave began in England with Ebenezer Howard's ideas on garden cities (1898). . . . The second wave, the so-called "New Town" movement, began in Western Europe — especially England and Sweden — after World War II and is today spreading in the United States and some other countries. *Constantinos A. Doxiadis, "Ecumenopolis: Tomorrow's City: Escape Cities," Britannica Book of the Year 1968, p 24*

The high hopes that "new towns" . . . could provide a solution to congestion, high population densities, and the erosion of public services have collapsed. *Lewis Herber, "Cities and Urban Affairs," The Americana Annual 1970, p 176*

N galaxy, a galaxy distinguished by a starlike central nucleus. Compare SEYFERT.

A program of photographic monitoring of quasars, N galaxies and Seyfert galaxies has been carried out over the last two years at the University of Florida. . . . *Science News, Dec. 5, 1970, p 424*

[N for *nuclear*]

ngwee (əŋ'gwi:), *n.* a new monetary unit of Zambia (since 1969). See the quotation for details.

Zambia changed to a decimal currency on January 16, replacing pounds, shillings, and pence with kwacha (1 kwacha = $1.40) and ngwee (100 ngwee = 1 kwacha). *Franklin Pierce, "Zambia: Currency Change," The Americana Annual 1969, p 756*

Nibmar or **NIBMAR** ('nib,mɑr), *n.* acronym for *no independence before majority African rule,* a statement by Great Britain and members of the British Commonwealth demanding proportional representation for the black population in white-ruled dependencies before granting independence, especially applied to the conflict between Rhodesia and Great Britain.

Afraid that [Prime Minister Harold] Wilson might come to terms with the Rhodesian regime, they [the Commonwealth leaders] demanded that he agree to something called NIBMAR — an acronym standing for "No Independence Before Majority African Rule." *"The Commonwealth," Time, Sept. 23, 1966, p 31*

Britain, he [Sir Colin Crowe, Britain's chief representative to the United Nations] said, had never accepted a commitment to Nibmar from the United Nations. *Michael Knipe, "Afro-Asians Dissatisfied with British UN Veto," The Times (London), Nov. 12, 1970, p 6*

niggle, *n. British.* a petty or trifling complaint.

The chapter on media gives some useful analytical data

but does not describe how different constituents should be sterilized. I would like personally to have seen more on the turbidostat and other types of culture vessel. . . . However, these are just niggles. *Julian Wimpenny, Review of "Materials and Methods" by G. L. Solomons, New Scientist, March 19, 1970, p 575*

[noun use of *niggle, v.*]

nightside, *n.* **1** the side of a planet, moon, etc., that faces away from the sun and is thus in darkness.

Temperatures on the nightside of the planet [Mars] were very low, dropping down to −85° F. *Jenny Elizabeth Tesar, "Portrait of Mars," Encyclopedia Science Supplement (Grolier) 1970, p 322*

2 the dark or unilluminated side of anything.

[Elias] Lönnrot awoke the nightside of the nineteenth-century professional and middle-class mind, represented by himself, and connected it with the prehistoric culture of subarctic medicine men. *Kenneth Rexroth, "Classics Revisited: The 'Kalevala,'" Saturday Review, Aug. 19, 1967, p 73*

night-sight, *n.* a gun sight for use under adverse lighting conditions, especially at night.

Our marksman, who saw him clearly through his night-sight, asked the platoon commander for permission to fire at him. *Simon Winchester, The Manchester Guardian Weekly, Nov. 6, 1971, p 12*

nighttown, *n.* a town at night, as a subject of a painting, as the scene of nightclub activity, etc.

True, sleep-walking Mickey gets mixed into a cake by the giant bakers of the Night Kitchen. . . . And where all seeing readers join is in delight at the architecture of his [Maurice Sendak's] Manhattan nighttown of towering pots and packets and jars. . . . *Shelagh Webb, "A Flutter of Shock," Review of "In the Night Kitchen" by Maurice Sendak, The Manchester Guardian Weekly, June 5, 1971, p 18*

After private talks with Deputy Foreign Minister Gheorghe Macovescu and intensive briefings from U.S. Ambassador Richard Davis and his staff, [John] Gronouski [U.S. Ambassador to Poland] swept out on a tour of Bucharest's nighttown with his wife, the Davises, and other embassy types. *"Diplomacy: The Bridge Builder," Time, April 15, 1966, p 43*

nightviewer, *n.* See the quotation for the meaning.

Information on nightviewers — which as the name implies are devices which can provide excellent daylight viewing conditions in almost pitch dark, has been restricted because of their obvious military applications. *Roger Vielvoye, "New Techniques Could Mean the Return of Airship Travel," The Times (London), May 8, 1970, p 29*

nightwatchman, *n. Cricket.* a usually second-rate batsman sent in to defend the wicket until the close of play, late in the day.

In the fifth over Holder trimmed Aftab's bails with his second ball and the fifth was caught by Turner off the nightwatchman Wasim Bari's glove and shoulder. *Robin Marlar, "Exemplary Turner Hits Tourists," The Sunday Times (London), May 2, 1971, p 24*

-nik, a slang suffix used to form nouns. *Sputnik,* whose successful launch in 1957 heralded the birth of the Space Age, was the model for *beatnik,* which became widely current in the late 1950's. *Beatnik* inspired the coinage of a number of nouns ending with the Russian personal suffix -*nik*, meaning "one who does or is connected with something." Most of the new -*nik* words closely followed the meaning of *beatnik* in denoting a person who rejects standard social values and becomes a devotee of some fad or idea or takes part in some mode of life. This class of words included *folknik* (folk-song devotee), *peacenik*, *protestnik*, *jazznik*, *filmnik* or *cinenik* (movie fan), and *Vietnik* (one who opposes U.S. involvement in Vietnam). Many words in -*nik* are in some degree derogatory, inviting disparagement or ridicule.

cinenik: Secter chose the 1965 Commonwealth Film Festival in Wales for the movie's ["Winter Kept Us Warm"] world premiere and it enchanted the ciné-niks there. *John Bernard, Maclean's, Nov. 19, 1966, p 23*

citynik: A kibbutz is a collective settlement, where all are equal, each giving according to his abilities and receiving according to his needs.... The day starts at dawn—in mid-summer this means four o'clock. It is surprising how quickly a reasonably healthy citynik adjusts to the hours and graft. *Denis Herbstein, "Working Holiday: Kibbutzim," The Sunday Times (London), Jan. 4, 1970, p 67*

computernik: Despite the alarums of the computerniks and the current promulgation of the notion (from over the Canadian border) that bound volumes are doomed to obsolescence, the book would appear to be here to stay. *William Tarz, Review of "Rare Books and Royal Collectors" by M. L. Ettinghausen and "A Primer of Book Collecting" by J. T. Winterich and D. A. Randall, Saturday Review, Oct. 22, 1966, p 59*

filmnik: Another favorite is urbane, eccentric Woody Allen, who is currently flipping the filmniks by writing a Japanese movie in which the dubbed-in sound track is totally different from what is occurring on-screen. *Time, March 4, 1966, p 27*

goodwillnik: This editor didn't once ask me if I knew anything about music or had any right to write about it. Or, for that matter, whether I could write about anything. He wanted a goodwillnik, and whatever my feelings about this man's regulations, I think it was most admirable of him to spell them out. *Robert Evett, "Music: The Critics and the Public," The Atlantic, Sept. 1970, p 117*

jobnik: For any serviceman, the proudest insigne is the unit crest with a red background designating a battle unit. The "jobnik"—a soldier with a desk job—is looked down on. *Time, June 22, 1970, p 30*

no-goodnik: Lew Archer's job is to find a 17-year-old girl who has run off with a 19-year-old nogoodnik. *Anthony Boucher, The New York Times, March 3, 1968, p 37*

protestnik: ... Tom Lehrer [a satiric singer] plinks away at targets ranging from air pollution to nuclear proliferation. Among his bull's eyes: those guitar-plunking protestniks *(The Folk Song Army)* whose St. Joan is Baez as they "strum their frustrations away." *"Records," Time, Nov. 12, 1965, p 4*

See also the main entries PEACENIK, VIETNIK.

nil norm, *British.* a standard of minimum wage and price increases set by the government, limiting increases of a specified maximum to underpaid workers or where the increase results in a rise in productivity. Also called ZERO NORM.

But for all the traditional wage demands some principle does need to be hammered out to establish who will be permitted to breach the nil norm. *The Sunday Times (London), Aug. 14, 1966, p 8*

There can be little doubt that the £1 a week rise would not qualify as an exception to the nil norm laid down in the summer. *The Manchester Guardian Weekly, Feb. 1, 1968, p 8*

ni·mo·nic (ni'mou nik), *adj. Metallurgy.* designating any of a group of nickel-chromium alloys with a very high tolerance of heat and stress due to varying and minute quantities of titanium, carbon, aluminum, or cobalt.

For some time scientists within the UKAEA [United Kingdom Atomic Energy Authority] had been studying a selection of nickel-based alloys, and in particular a nimonic alloy called PE 16. *R. Stuart Nelson, "Filling the Voids in Fast Reactor Technology," New Scientist and Science Journal, March 25, 1971, p 667*

[from *nickel* + *Monel* (a nickel alloy named after Ambrose *Monel*, who introduced the metal) + -*ic* (adj. suffix)]

nine-ball, *n. U.S. Slang.* a variety of pocket billiards. See the quotation for details.

For the hustler, nine ball is the best game. The first nine balls—eight solid-colored balls and the nine ball with a yellow stripe—are racked in a diamond with the one ball in front and the nine ball in the middle. The rules are simple: the lowest numbered ball on the table must be hit first, and whoever makes the nine ball wins. *James Morgan, "The Big Jamboree at Johnston City, Ill.," The Atlantic, April 1970, p 67*

1984, *n.* a date symbolizing a totalitarian society of the future in which all truth and freedom is suppressed and people live in a totally regimented and dehumanized state.

Throughout the campaign, the political uses of television advertising and packaging of candidates were heralded by proponents as the inescapable wave of the future and by doomsayers as the ominous forerunner of 1984. *Time, Nov. 16, 1970, p 14*

[from the novel *1984* by George Orwell, 1903-1950, which is set in such a society]

nine-to-fiver or **nine-to-five,** *n. Slang.* a person who holds an office job with regular hours, usually nine in the morning to five in the evening.

At Grand Central you can't tell the action crowd from the nine-to-fivers. Singapore Sammy stopped there to put a saw on Carry-Me-Back in the fifth, at Roosevelt and wound up on the 5:14 to Greenwich. *Time, April 19, 1971, p 12*

Almost all hippies are white and this is significant. They are the children of the "haves" who are rejecting the values and rewards of the society—the same values and rewards that Negroes are struggling to obtain. In the course of their rejection, they have created a new way of looking at things and a new context in which to live. Dedication to the work ethic has produced the alienation that the hippies see all around them in the "nine-to-fives." *Ralph J. Gleason, "The Flower Children," Britannica Book of the Year 1968, p 790*

nit, *n.* a unit of brightness in the meter-kilogram-second system. See the quotation for details.

I have an obscure feeling that modern, enlightened methods of teaching mathematics or science... are a pretty shaky bridge across an enormous gap.... let's look at some of the units you get on to when you have sorted out mass and weight.... I noticed wild things like the *Nit* "a unit of luminance in the MKS system which is the equivalent to one candela per square metre"; and the *Slug* "a unit of mass in the foot pound system.... The slug is also called a gee pound." *Paul Jennings, "Glugs, Puffs, Googols, and Porns," Punch, Sept. 11, 1968, p 364*

[from Latin *nitēre* to shine]

NIT, abbreviation of NEGATIVE INCOME TAX.

Under the NIT, the tax scales would be continued downward past the zero-tax line.... *Time, Feb. 8, 1971, p 15*

Nit·i·nol ('nit ə,nɔ:l), *n.* a nonmagnetic alloy of titanium and nickel. See the quotations for details.

In 1968 a nickel-titanium alloy, 55-Nitinol, was discovered to have the ability to regain its original shape after being heated and then cooled below a certain temperature, crushed, and subsequently reheated. This "memory" property is expected to make Nitinol a valuable component of fire-extinguisher activators. *Donald F. Clifton, "Metals," The 1969 Compton Yearbook, p 324*

One of the fascinations of the behavior of plastics is that when certain kinds of plastic are molded in a distinct form, then melted so that the form is lost and then allowed to cool, they resume much the same form. Called "plastic memory," the phenomenon has an analogue in a little-known metallic alloy. The metal is named Nitinol from its constituents (nickel and titanium) and the place where it was discovered 10 years ago (the Naval Ordnance Laboratory). *"Science and the Citizen," Scientific American, March 1971, p 47*

ni·trog·en·ase ('nɑi trə dʒə,neis), *n.* a natural enzyme that activates the conversion of nitrogen to ammonia by nitrogen-fixing bacteria.

Nitrogenase itself was isolated in the early 1960's, but scientists did not know exactly how it converted nitrogen to ammonia. By producing their simple inorganic catalyst, the two chemists have proven what had been suspected, that the element molybdenum is a key to the process. *"Nitrogen Fixation: Starting with the Simple," Science News, Sept. 12, 1970, p 218*

[from *nitrogen* + *-ase* enzyme]

nitty-gritty, *n.* **1** the practicalities or details.

But they got bogged down in the nitty-gritties of negotiation.... *The Manchester Guardian Weekly, April 10, 1971, p 1*

How many meetings, finally at the nitty-gritty, are interrupted by your secretary asking if you want to take a call.... *Robert Townsend, Harper's, March 1970, p 87*

2 get down to the nitty-gritty, to get down to the fundamentals or details.

...Dr. Swanson... can really understand people in a gutsy way. And he's not afraid to get down to the nitty-gritty of unpleasant problems.... *The New York Times, June 27, 1967, p 20*

Nixon Doctrine. See the first quotation for the meaning.

...the Nixon Doctrine [was] enunciated by the President on Guam last July, that the U.S. from then on would avoid military commitments that might lead to ground-combat interventions similar to Viet Nam. *Time, April 13, 1970, p 17*

...the so-called Nixon Doctrine... has been understood to be an approach to Asia that would support its developing nations against attack or subversion with money, advice, equipment and cheers, but not with American troops. *Tom Wicker, "In the Nation: Is There a Nixon Doctrine?" The New York Times, Jan. 6, 1970, p 40*

The Nixon Doctrine, however interpreted and applied, can do little to help Southeast Asia or any of the rest of Asia solve the problems that have grown out of Asian history and—in part, at least—out of the history of the Western role in the East. *Richard H. Rovere, "Letter from Washington," The New Yorker, Jan. 23, 1971, p 90*

The Nixon Doctrine, although not officially applicable to Europe, has some worrying implications for Europe. It implies that America is ready to expend money and technology on behalf of her allies but no longer ready to shed her own blood. It also implies that American help is conditional on self-help. *Peter Jenkins, "Come Home America," The Manchester Guardian Weekly, Aug. 12, 1972, p 15*

Nixonomics, *n.* President Nixon's economic policies, especially from an opposing political viewpoint.

Nixonomics means that all the things that should go up—the stock market, corporate profits, real spendable income, productivity—go down, and all the things that should go down—unemployment, prices, interest rates—go up. *Lawrence F. O'Brien, Chairman of the Democratic National Committee, on May 21, 1970, quoted by Rowland Evans, Jr., and Robert D. Novak, "Nixonomics: How the Game Plan Went Wrong," The Atlantic, July 1971, p 66*

Some economists, of course, were disposed to give Nixonomics little or no credit for this rosy outlook. *"The Economic Outlook: Boomy," Newsweek, Oct. 18, 1971, p 29*

[blend of *Nixon* and *economics*]

NLF, abbreviation of *National Liberation Front* (the name of the political arm of the Communist guerrilla force in South Vietnam).

My own view is that negotiations could begin with a step that does not require the approval of either Saigon or the N.L.F.—namely a reciprocal, phased disengagement of North Vietnamese and American troops from South Vietnam. *Donald S. Zagoria, The New York Times Magazine, April 21, 1968, p 74*

NOAA ('nou ə), *n.* acronym for *National Oceanic and Atmospheric Administration* (of the United States).

Specifically, NOAA will be concerned with determining atmospheric conditions that make for pollution, the effects of pollution on weather, and contaminants in fish. *"Environment Uppermost: NOAA Charts a Course," Science News, March 27, 1971, p 212*

Formed in 1970, NOAA absorbed the activities of the Environmental Science Services Administration, which was abolished. *F. C. Durant III, "Astronautics and Space Exploration," 1972 Britannica Yearbook of Science and the Future, 1971, p 174*

nod, *n.* **on the nod,** *British.* without formality; by tacit agreement or acknowledgment.

The agenda, usually the cause of great friction, was accepted "on the nod". *The Sunday Times (London), Jan. 12, 1969, p 4*

With the Royal Exchange will die more than two centuries of tradition of trading mostly done "on the nod," with scarcely a written contract to be seen. *Geoffrey Whiteley, "Two Centuries of Cotton Tradition to End," The Manchester Guardian Weekly, July 11, 1968, p 10*

no-fault, *adj. U.S.* of or relating to a form of automobile insurance by which an accident victim is compensated for damages or expenses by his own insurance company, whether the accident was his fault or not.

Neither the [insurance] industry nor the federal government had reached a conclusion about the recent proposal of "no-fault" insurance, designed to reduce costs and eliminate prolonged court cases, by requiring drivers to carry insurance that would cover injury to themselves, regardless of who caused the accident. *Edwin W. Darby, "Insurance," The 1970 World Book Year Book, p 377*

No-fault auto insurance substitutes certainty for uncertainty, promptness for delay, fairness for inequity, and efficiency for wastefulness. *Robert N. Gilmore, General Counsel, American Insurance Association, New York, in a Letter to the Editor, The New York Times, June 14, 1971, p 36*

Specifically, the hearings were to focus on a modified no-fault bill introduced by Senator Bernard G. Gordon, a Peekskill Republican. The bill is designed to end much of the current reliance on litigation-oriented settlements for auto accidents. *"The Nation: No Fault: It all Depends On Whose Ox Is Gored," The New York Times, March 5, 1972, Sec. 4, p 4*

no-go, *adj.* **1** *Slang.* not in a favorable condition for proceeding. Compare GO.

... in space jargon this was potentially a "no-go" situation; with no alternative open except to abort the mission. *Adam Raphael, "All Go—Mascons Permitting," The Manchester Guardian Weekly, June 19, 1969, p 13*

Children's performances of plays, movies and sports events must end half an hour before curfew. Any child who wants to go may have to walk ... because bicycles are forbidden at all times to youngsters under 14, motorbikes to all under 16. Also no-go in most of the snowbound capital are sleds and skis, because they "disturb public order." *"The World: Russia," Time, Jan. 14, 1966, p 32*

2 *British.* not to be entered without special allowance; barred to designated persons, groups, etc.

Is it a form of UDI [Unilateral Declaration of Independence] at Liverpool, or is Liverpool to be a no-go area? *Daily Telegraph (London), May 5, 1972, p 9*

noise, *n.* **1** energy that varies in its characteristics.

"The presence of these domains can be detected and their size determined by means of a sensitive thermometer. As air in the first few feet of the atmosphere drifts past the sensing element of the instrument the pointer fluctuates constantly in response to 'temperature noise.' At my geographical location the daytime fluctuation ranges from a maximum of about one degree F. in bright winter sunlight to 10 degrees in June." *Douglas A. Kohl, quoted by C. L. Stong, Scientific American, June 1967, p 136*

2 make noises, to express or indicate (certain feelings, thoughts, etc.) vocally.

General Electric and Alcoa, for example, are making noises about getting into city building. *Howard Simons, New Scientist, June 22, 1967, p 718*

Meanwhile the Canadian government is making hurt little noises about the treatment of its citizen. *Gordon Donaldson, Maclean's, June 18, 1966, p 3*

... left-wing Liberals have made neutralist noises in the past. *The New York Times, Sept. 15, 1965, p 42*

... it didn't surprise me when she [Elsa Maxwell] said, "... you should go to Hollywood ... nobody out there knows how to speak except Ronald Colman."

Norah and Lefty made encouraging noises, so she went on, "Next week I'm giving a party for Ernst Lubitsch ... so you be here about twelve and I'll introduce you to Ernst and tell him to do something about it." *David Niven, The Moon's a Balloon, 1972, p 147*

noise pollution, 1 the production of noise by motor vehicles, jet planes, machinery, etc., viewed as harmful to man and his environment.

Man is an adaptable animal. Without realizing it, he has become accustomed to excessive noise pollution in his environment. But Dr. Alexander Cohen of the U.S. Public Health Service's National Noise Study says, "This sonic boom is not something you adapt to easily." *Theodore Berland, "Up to Our Ears in Noise," The 1970 World Book Year Book, p 132*

2 the loud sound or noise itself.

Also, there are the greatly improved noise pollution characteristics of VTOL compared not only with conventional aircraft (CTOL) but with short take off and landing craft (STOL) as illustrated in the accompanying comparison of noise 'footprints'.... *Angela Croome, "Civil VTOL Designs Await Government Funds," Science Journal, March 1970, p 5*

no-knock, *adj.* *U.S.* of or deriving from legislation granting police the authority to enter upon premises without announcing or identifying themselves.

... John Mitchell puts on a happy face and suggests that the name of the "no-knock" law be changed to something more felicitous, like "quick-entry." *Elizabeth B. Drew, "The White House Hard Hats," The Atlantic, Oct. 1970, p 57*

The "no-knock" and "preventive-detention" provisions of the District of Columbia Crime Control Act have violated, respectively, the public's right to be secure against unreasonable searches and seizures and the traditional presumption of innocence. *"The Talk of the Town," The New Yorker, April 10, 1971, p 30*

no-load, *adj., n.* See the quotations for the meaning.

The mutual savings bank industry is preparing a pilot test of its long-discussed plan to offer mutual fund shares to the public.

As things now stand, the savings bank plan calls for a "no-load" fund, in which shares would be sold without sales commissions, and investment management fees would be closely related to the actual cost of managing the fund. *H. Erich Heinemann, The New York Times, Dec. 16, 1966, p 73*

A handful or so Canadian funds are "no-loads"—are offered without any sales charge and are generally available through investment dealers. *Alexander Ross, "The Canadian Funds: a Checklisting," Maclean's, Oct. 1968, p 22*

non-. **1** *Non-* in its original sense of "not," "lacking," or "opposite of" continues to be freely used to form noun and adjective compounds. A sampling of such recent formations includes:

nonaerospace, *adj.:* To counter that, some 100 unemployed have come together in a group called Talent Plus Inc., with the aim of finding new jobs partly by helping each other to write résumés that stress as much nonaerospace background as possible. *Karsten Prager, "Seattle Under Seige: The Troubles of a Company Town," Time, Jan. 4, 1971, p 22*

nonastronaut, *n.:* The ability to fly nonastronauts on space missions will allow the research scientist, whether his field be medicine, chemistry, metals, geology or what have you, to pursue the potential of his discipline as a space passenger without having to master the techniques of space flight. *Wernher von Braun, "After Apollo, What?" Encyclopedia Science Supplement (Grolier) 1970, p 313*

319

nonbiodegradable, *adj.:* Landfills should be limited to the minimum number and acreage necessary to dispose of the nonbiodegradable materials that have no resource value, such as broken concrete, earth materials, and similar rubble. *Percy H. McGauhey, "Buried in Affluence," 1972 Britannica Yearbook of Science and the Future, 1971, p 361*

non-black, *n.:* At the University of Natal, non-white students . . . refer to whites as "non-blacks." *Stanley Uys, The Manchester Guardian Weekly, Aug. 22, 1970, p 7*

noncolor, *n.:* In interior decoration, the most popular hue is a noncolor, beige. Names too are sexually equivocal; one child out of five has a name like Robin or Leslie or Dana. *Time, Oct. 12, 1970, p 57*

noncommitted, *adj.:* . . . what the KGB [secret service agency of the Soviet Union] consciously fears is bad publicity in the West and among non-committed nations. *The Sunday Times (London), Jan. 12, 1969, p 50*

nondegradable, *adj.:* For centuries man's nondegradable waste materials have generally been hauled, along with the degradable wastes, for disposal in open gulleys or abandoned pits. *Richard B. Engdahl, "The Solid Waste Problem," Encyclopedia Science Supplement (Grolier) 1971, p 233*

nondisposable, *adj.:* The people of Bowie, Md., want action. As a result, the Bowie city council has recently enacted an ordinance banning the sale of nonreturnable and nondisposable containers within city limits. *Time, Aug. 24, 1970, p 37*

nondisruptive, *adj.:* The contract would forbid widespread new modes of student protests — such as the occupation of Warwick University registry earlier this year — because these disrupt academic life. But the colleges on their side would agree to permit non-disruptive occupations and boycotts of classes. *"Student Charter Plan," The Manchester Guardian Weekly, Oct. 24, 1970, p 9*

nonelectronic, *adj.:* This process of using magnetic tape to record and recompose sounds gathered from "nature" is called *musique concrète*. Sounds from city streets, factories, beaches and bird-filled forests are treated electronically; the nonelectronic sounds are transformed into new, electronic sounds. *Gershon Kingsley and John Watts, Encyclopedia Science Supplement (Grolier) 1970, p 345*

nonestablishment, *adj.:* However, it is widely held that Mr. Trudeau became the darling of the Liberals, and now their champion, because he was a lone outsider, a non-establishment man who spoke coolly and directly on fresh ideas. No candidate was so divorced from the party regulars. *Jay Walz, The New York Times, April 14, 1968, Sec. 4, p 10*

nonethnic, *adj.:* . . . non-regional and non-ethnic minorities have been proliferating and functioning both as social classes and as political blocks — students, intellectuals, suburbanites, welfare clients, pensioners, a growing *Lumpenproletariat*, newly unionized and militant civil servants, and so on. *Richard H. Rovere, "Letter from Washington," The New Yorker, July 18, 1970, p 78*

nonfriend, *n.:* While making a final break with the administration, the white radicals also cut themselves off from much of the rest of the student body. On the first day of the sit-in they announced to the large group of students crowded into Wofford's office, "There are people here who are not our friends." The nonfriends were expelled. *Tom Powers, "Autopsy on Old Westbury: The Politics of Free-form Education," Harper's, Sept. 1971, p 57*

noninvolved, *adj.:* The wily and elusive Hjalmar Schacht, who died June 4 at 93, was far less the noninvolved Nazi than he liked to claim after the war. *Roger Alden, New York, in a Letter to the Editor, The New York Times, June 10, 1970, p 46*

nonmusician, *n.:* Is it not precisely through intervals of selective appropriation, via pictorial analogies which are often naïve in the extreme, that the nonmusician assimilates the complex, ultimately technical realities of music? *George Steiner, "A Future Literacy," The Atlantic, Aug. 1971, p 44*

nonpolluting, *adj.:* The Fishmans believe that biking is a healthy, friendly, quiet, inexpensive, non-polluting, fast, and practical means of transportation, and apparently a lot of New Yorkers agree with them. *"The Talk of the Town," The New Yorker, Sept. 26, 1970, p 28*

nonstick, *adj.:* The Hotpoint 6150 free-standing cooker, for example, is equipped with four high-speed rings set in a lift-up hot top; two auto-timed ovens — one fitted with non-stick coated panels, and a Pan-guard device to prevent liquids boiling over. *Hilary Gelson, "Gas Versus Electricity," The Times (London), March 12, 1970, p 8*

nontrivial, *adj.:* I have given the impression, I fancy, that in private he [G. H. Hardy] was a conversational performer. To an extent, that was true, but he was also, on what he would have called nontrivial occasions (meaning occasions important to either participant), a serious and concentrated listener. *C. P. Snow, "G. H. Hardy: The Pure Mathematician," The Atlantic, March 1967, p 113*

2 An extension of *non-* appearing with increasing frequency indicates not so much the opposite or reversal of something as rather that that "something" is not true, real, or worthy of the name. In this use, *non-* is prefixed to a noun and often carries such connotations as "sham; pretended; pseudo-; mock; fraudulent." In the older use *non-* is part of a yes-or-no classification: a statement is either *sense* or *nonsense;* but here *non-* makes a comment or a criticism: a *non-book* pretends to be a book; a *nonpolicy* is a vacuum where a policy should be. Apparently the first popular term in which *non-* bore this meaning was *non-book,* as the following early quotation suggests:

. . . we owe to Professor Daniel J. Boorstin of Chicago the concept of the pseudo-event, which is an event taking place only in order to be reported in the newspapers, just as we owe to *Time* magazine the notion of the non-book, which is a book published in order to be purchased rather than to be read. *Eric Larrabee, "Jazz Notes," Harper's, April 1964, p 117*

nonactor, *n.:* Mitchum is simply and gloriously himself in spite of everything — one of the most powerful and expressive non-actors in the business. *Derek Malcolm, "Films: Ill Met by Leanlight," The Manchester Guardian Weekly, Dec. 19, 1970, p 17*

nondebate, *n.:* The debate on the amendments to end the Indo-China war was the usual non-debate. *Louis Heren, "Cloakroom History-making on Capitol Hill," The Times (London), May 21, 1970, p 8*

nonevent, *n.:* The most stupendissimo non-event of the Fall Publicity Season so far was the big, big Sophia Loren press conference at Radio City Music Hall. *"The Talk of the Town," The New Yorker, Oct. 3, 1970, p 30*

nonhappening, *n.:* Inside the hall are people looking at TV cameras and TV cameras looking at people. It is a nonevent, a nonhappening. *Clive Barnes, The New York Times, Aug. 6, 1968, p 20*

noninformation, *n.:* There is another view of question time which is especially prevalent among those who believe that the conviction has gone out of party politics and that what we see at Westminster nowadays is a political charade. To them, question time is merely part of the pseudo-struggle or, as it was once cleverly, if unfairly, described "the ritual exchange of non-information." *Ronald Butt, "Question of Time," The Times (London), April 16, 1970, p 5*

nonissue, *n.:* The "voting machines" fiasco [in Trinidad] has always been a major non-issue which has said more about the sterility of official opposition than the corruption of the Government. *Malcolm Cross, Trinidad, in a Letter to the Editor, The Manchester Guardian Weekly, May 23, 1970, p 3*

nonplay, *n.:* Jimmy Shine—Dustin Hoffman does his brave best to make us believe that this non-play by Murray Schisgal is a touching comedy about the ignominy of young manhood; for all his bravery and talent, it is not enough. *"Goings on About Town: Plays," The New Yorker, Dec. 28, 1968, p 2*

nonpolicy, *n.:* Flora Lewis (Report on "The U.S. and Indochina," March issue) cogently reveals some of the contradictions in American nonpolicy toward "Indochina." *Earl L. Heuer, Grand Haven, Mich., in a Letter to the Editor, The Atlantic, May 1971, p 37*

nonstory, *n.:* It [the current Kennedy inquiry] is a nonstory, held behind closed doors, to repeat old tales, which few people quite believe anyway. . . . *James Reston, "Edgartown, Mass.: The Strange Case of Senator Kennedy," The New York Times, Jan. 7, 1970, p 42*

See also the entries below.

nonaddict, *n.* a drug user who is not addicted to drugs.

By design the counsellors are hard on the addicts. . . . "If you all want to use drugs, you don't *want* to function in the street. . . . You want the South Walk (prison) and, man, I can send you right back there." These threats and the harsh lack of intimacy (it is always *Mr.* Turner with Christian names rarely heard) seems shocking to a nonaddict and to new addicts in the group. *Victoria Brittain, "Curing Drug Addiction with Former Addicts' Help," The Times (London), May 2, 1970, p 9*

nonaddicting or **nonaddictive,** *adj.* not causing addiction.

The U.S. Food and Drug Administration was ready to approve release of a new analgesic that New York's Winthrop Laboratories say is "in the morphine range of potency" but is nonnarcotic—and, they hope, nonaddicting. *Time, July 7, 1967, p 45*

We would prefer to use a heroin antagonist (a non-addictive drug which makes the addict ill if he takes heroin), but the best one available . . . just can't be had in this country yet. *Tony Clifton, The Sunday Times (London), Oct. 29, 1967, p 9*

nonaligned, *n.* one that opposes political alignment with a larger power; a neutralist.

The two groups in Indonesia opposing each other are the "nonaligneds" and the "interventionists." *"War Behind the Embassy Walls," The Manchester Guardian Weekly, May 30, 1970, p 6*

noncandidacy, *n.* the status of a noncandidate.

In addition to repeatedly asserting his non-candidacy, [Senator Edward M.] Kennedy had made some forceful speeches in recent months. *"The Talk of the Town: Kennedy on Fifth Avenue," The New Yorker, Dec. 4, 1971, p 47*

noncandidate, *n.* a person who has not announced or is unwilling to announce his candidacy for an office.

Mr. Goldberg has never stood for public office. His performance as a candidate—if measured by his performance as a noncandidate—may be distant, arrogant, haughty and, what is far worse for the state's Democrats, unsuccessful. *Thomas H. Baer, New York, in a Letter to the Editor, The New York Times, March 25, 1970, p 46*

One of the most maddening candidates in a political race is the non-candidate.

He is the fellow who is being talked for a race but who will just never admit his candidacy until the last minute. *Don F. Wasson, "'Movement' for Wallace," The Tuscaloosa News [Alabama], March 25, 1969, p 4*

no-net (nou'net), *n.* a group of nine nuclear or subatomic particles.

There are other resonances with quantum numbers similar to the A2 meson. Under the SU(3) scheme they form a nine-particle configuration: three A2 mesons, four K* (pronounced K-star) mesons, and two f⁰ mesons. To reconcile the A2 meson with current theory, it is necessary to show that the other members of its SU(3) nonet display similar double structure. *"A2 Meson Splits and Shatters High-energy Theories," New Scientist, Oct. 29, 1970, p 211*

► The only previously recorded sense of this word is "a group of nine musical instruments or voices." As used in nuclear physics, the term was probably adopted on the analogy of *quartet, sextet, octet,* etc., where the meaning "any group of_____" is well established.

nongraded, *adj.* **1** without a proficiency rating.

[Robin] Widdows, as the second highest non-graded driver, gains six points. *Maxwell Boyd, "Motor Racing: Rindt Still Top of Formula II," The Times (London), March 31, 1970, p 13*

2 *U.S. Education.* not divided into grades.

Nongraded classes, for example, permit a precocious five-year-old to take some classes with six-, seven-, and eight-year-olds, and the rest with youngsters his own age. *Samuel G. Sava, "When Learning Comes Easy," Saturday Review, Nov. 16, 1968, p 104*

nonleaded or **nonlead,** *adj.* containing no tetraethyl lead (an antiknock additive which is a contributor to air pollution). Also, UNLEADED, LEAD-FREE, LEADLESS.

The two most desired types of gasoline components for nonleaded gasolines are highly branched paraffins and the common aromatic components such as benzene, toluene, and xylene. *F. F. Farley, "Gasoline," McGraw-Hill Yearbook of Science and Technology 1971, p 212*

News that British Petroleum and Shell are to produce non-lead petrol for cars in Britain will revolutionize the engineering side of car manufacture in the next year or two. *Geoffrey Charles, "Clean Petrol Will Raise Costs," The Times (London), March 10, 1970, p 5*

non-nuclear, *n.* a non-nuclear power; a nation with an arsenal of only conventional weapons. Compare NUCLEAR.

So far, negotiation under the heading 'nonproliferation' has virtually been between the Americans and the Russians and it has been about Germany. This is indeed something, but negotiation between nuclears and non-nuclears has scarcely begun. *Elizabeth Young, "No Alternative to Politics," The Listener, Feb. 9, 1967, p 186*

no-no ('nou,nou), *n. U.S. Slang.* something one must not do, say, use, etc.; something forbidden.

321

From now on, drugs are a no-no for revolutionaries, said [Black Panther leader Eldridge] Cleaver.... Cleaver read out of the movement "the whole silly, psychedelic drug culture, quasi-political movement of which we have been a part in the past." *Time, Feb. 15, 1971, p 28*

... some people ... have had a lifelong problem keeping their weight down. With some of these individuals, desserts are all-time "no-nos." *Nancy Goldstein, "Obesity," Encyclopedia Science Supplement (Grolier) 1971, p 247*

nonproliferation, *n.* the halting of the spread of nuclear weapons among nonnuclear powers by common consent. *Often used attributively.*

The Soviet Union would like the solution of nonproliferation to add dimensions and a sense of realism to the problems of outlawing nuclear weapons. *Raymond H. Anderson, The New York Times, June 28, 1968, p 1*

nonproliferation treaty, a treaty signed by 93 nations as of December 1969 and ratified by more than 43 nations on its effective date, March 5, 1970, whereby countries not possessing nuclear weapons agreed never to produce or acquire them in order to halt their proliferation. *Abbreviation:* NPT See also SALT.

For more than a year the United States delayed testing a peaceful nuclear device called Cabriolet in order not to complicate negotiations on the nuclear nonproliferation treaty. *Science News, May 11, 1968, p 449*

nonsense, *adj.* **1** that does not specify a particular amino acid in the genetic code.

The experiment was undertaken on the hypothesis that there would be no complementary stretches in the two heavy strands of the two phages except those provided by the sense and nonsense bases of the *lac* operon. The hypothesis was confirmed. *"Science and the Citizen," Scientific American, Jan. 1970, p 50*

2 that results from the presence of nonsense sequences in the genetic code.

They [Drs. J. and M. Gross] also demonstrate that the mutation is recessive to the wild type gene in partial diploids, that it is the result of an amber nonsense mutation and that the polymerase lesion has little or no effect on the ability to carry out genetic recombination. *"DNA Polymerase Not Active in Replication," Science Journal, March 1970, p 14*

nose, *n.* **rub one's nose in,** to cause one to experience closely (something unpleasant, especially as a punishment).

In the view of one leading Republican who finally cast a crucial vote against [appointment to the Supreme Court of George H.] Carswell, the choice was also an attempt to rub the Senate's nose in the mess it had made of the [Judge Clement F.] Haynsworth nomination. *Richard Harris, "Annals of Politics," The New Yorker, Dec. 5, 1970, p 61*

Robert Carr, in an attempt to show that he is not rubbing deregistered noses in the dirt, has indicated that they can set up separate friendly societies to get these tax advantages. *John Fryer, The Sunday Times (London), Nov. 14, 1971, p 60*

nosh, *Slang,* —*v.t., v.i.* to nibble or snack.

The politician, equipped with a trowel and the Fixed Smile, gobs mortar on a cornerstone, or noshes his way along the campaign trail. *Melvin Maddocks, "Rituals—The*

Revolt Against the Fixed Smile," *Time, Oct. 12, 1970, p 42*

Nor could any of it have been described as dainty noshing. *Patrick Campbell, The Sunday Times (London), Dec. 7, 1969, p 49*

—*n.* **1** *U.S.* a snack.

Advertising copy will stress that the company makes everything from "soup to nosh." (A nosh is a snack.) *Walter Carlson, The New York Times, April 9, 1965, p 40*

2 *British.* food.

While on the subject, couldn't one of the dining-rooms be turned into a Chinese restaurant, sort of? I've always found Chinese nosh both cheap and filling—tasty, too. *Colin Howard, "Maiden Speech," Punch, Feb. 14, 1968, p 220*

[from Yiddish *nashn, v.,* to nibble, *nash, n.,* a nibble, snack]

nosher, *n. Slang.* a person given to eating snacks.

. . . hot meal vending machines in the lobby for late night noshers, help yourself breakfasts and make-your-own-beds. *The Sunday Times (London), March 23, 1969, p 28*

no-strings, *adj.* free of conditions or obligations.

Following the February £13m no-strings pay deal, which gave manual employees rises of £4 to £5 15s. a week, union officials have been conducting a wages and conditions survey of motor plants in Britain. *Paul Routledge, "Ford Facing £14 a Week Pay Demand," The Times (London), Aug. 18, 1970, p 15*

[from the phrase *with no strings attached*]

notchback, *n. U.S.* an automobile with a sloping or slanting roof and a pronounced rear bumper. Compare FASTBACK.

Chevrolet's new Camaro, Mercury's Cougar, and Cadillac's front-drive Eldorado appeared in "notchback" versions but did not emulate the slower-selling fastbacks offered by competitors. *Maynard M. Gordon, "Automobiles: The 1967 Models," The Americana Annual 1967, p 109*

notes i·né·gales ('nɔ:t i: nei'gal), *n.pl. French.* (literally) unequal notes. See the first quotation for the meaning.

Chief among these "errors" is the convention of *notes inégales,* which decreed that, with certain specified or understood exceptions, pairs of stepwise quavers (or, in some time-signatures, semiquavers) were to be played unevenly, the first note rather longer than the second. *The Times (London), July 9, 1965, p 16*

Mr. Weaver shows a commendable awareness of performance practice, even though scholars are not unanimous —namely the *notes inégales* in the finale of No. 3 where he adjusts the left hand to the triplet meter in the right. *Boris Schwarz, "Virtue and Virtuosity in Bach," Saturday Review, Oct. 31, 1970, p 55*

nou·veau pau·vre (nu:'vou 'pou vrə); *pl.* **nou·veaux pau·vres.** *French.* one who has become poor recently.

One of every four Americans 65 or over lives at or below "the poverty line." Some of these 5,000,000 old people were poor to begin with, but most are bewildered and bitter *nouveaux pauvres,* their savings and fixed incomes devoured by spiraling property taxes and other forms of inflation. *"Behavior: The Old in the Country of the Young," Time, Aug. 3, 1970, p 49*

[patterned after *nouveau riche*]

nou·veau ro·man (nu:'vou rɔ:'mã); *pl.* **nou·veaux ro·mans.** a type of novel developed chiefly in France in the 1960's by such writers as Alain Robbe-Grillet, Michel Butor, Marguerite Duras, and Claude Mauriac, characterized by lack of moral, social, or psychological comment and by precise descriptions that suggest the mental state of the person experiencing or seeing them. Also called ANTI-ROMAN.

The detailed objectivity of the narration, giving every event movement by movement, the device of addressing the reader by the vocative . . . and the drifting plotlessness of the book, are hallmarks of the *nouveau roman. The Times (London), May 19, 1966, p 18*

The characters are many and the story jumps from one to another, often (in the manner of the *nouveau roman*) with no names other than "he" or "the boy" to tell you whose episode it is. *Katherine Gauss Jackson, Harper's, July 1965, p 112*

Some French critics allege that Alain Bosquet's *Confession méxicaine* (1965) first transplanted to Mexican soil the techniques of the *nouveau roman. Robert J. Clements, Saturday Review, Jan. 27, 1968, p 27*

[from French, literally, new novel]

now, *adj. Slang.* very fashionable or up-to-date; belonging to the Now Generation.

Despite the "now" tendency—derived in part from Frantz Fanon—to regard violence as psychological therapy and revolution as an act of theater, Hofstadter says, the young, apocalyptically impatient revolutionists operate on the latent, unexamined assumption that "violence *will* deliver" practical reforms. *Timothy Foote, Time, Nov. 23, 1970, p 108*

. . . sure as God made little green banknotes, you're bound to find that someone's been doing something you didn't, something more In, something more Now. *Alan Coren, Punch, Dec. 17, 1969, p 990*

Bullitt, I find, is completely typical of the "now" look in American movies—a swift-moving, constantly shifting surface that suggests rather than reveals depths. *Arthur Knight, "Engaging the Eye-Minded," Saturday Review, Dec. 28, 1968, p 18*

Now Generation, a name applied to the generation of young people of the late 1960's to characterize their concern with current trends, fashions, issues, etc.

The more mature of the unmarried in the Now Generation say that, far from promoting promiscuity, the pills impose a sense of responsibility. *"Medicine: Contraception," Time, April 7, 1967, p 20*

"The police don't understand the now generation and the now generation doesn't dig the fuzz." *Judy Stone, The New York Times, Sept. 22, 1968, Sec. 2, p 32*

NPT, abbreviation of NONPROLIFERATION TREATY.

As of Dec. 9, 1969, the NPT had been signed by 93 governments, 22 of which had ratified it. *Ernest W. Lefever, "Disarmament," The Americana Annual 1970, p 248*

NTA, abbreviation of NITRILOTRIACETATE, a nitrogen-based ingredient of some detergents.

. . . there is some concern in both the United States and Canada that this very ability to chelate the heavy metal ions may be an environmental hazard; the NTA may take up the heavy metals from sediments and make them available in toxic amounts to organisms. *Science News, April 25, 1970, p 408*

Because of the danger to pregnant women, the detergent industry stopped putting NTA into detergents. *John F. Henahan, "Phosphates Leave the Laundry," The World Book Science Annual 1972 (1971), p 285*

Dr. Samuel S. Epstein, the Boston toxicologist, who wrote the report, said that, with or without NTA, the environment would still be polluted with excessive amounts of phosphates from both detergents and human wastes. *Richard D. Lyons, The New York Times, Nov. 15, 1970, Sec. 4, p 12*

nuclear, *n.* **1** a nuclear weapon, especially a missile armed with an atomic warhead.

The highest common interest on either side of the Iron Curtain is in survival. A strategic nuclear exchange would have a catastrophic effect on both. The West, moreover, is unlikely to initiate the use of nuclears. The Russians have a superiority in conventional forces at their disposal which is unlikely to diminish. *General John Hackett, London, in a Letter to the Editor, The Times (London), Feb. 27, 1970, p 9*

2 a nuclear power; a nation with an arsenal of atomic weapons. Compare NON-NUCLEAR.

So far negotiation under the heading "nonproliferation" has virtually been between the Americans and the Russians and it has been about Germany. This is indeed something, but negotiation between nuclears and non-nuclears has scarcely begun. *Elizabeth Young, "No Alternative to Politics," The Listener, Feb. 9, 1967, p 186*

nuclearism, *n.* emphasis on nuclear weapons as a deterrent to war or as a means of attaining political and social goals.

The most extreme state of contemporary deformation is a pattern which may best be called "nuclearism." By this term I mean to suggest the passionate embrace of nuclear weapons as a solution to our anxieties (especially our anxieties concerning the weapons themselves), and as a means of restoring a lost sense of immortality. That is, one turns to the weapons, and to their power, as a means of restoring boundaries. Nuclearism, then, is a secular religion, a total ideology in which grace, the mastery of death, is achieved by means of a new technological deity. *Robert Jay Lifton, The Atlantic, Oct. 1970, p 106*

nuclearist, *n.* a person who supports nuclearism.

An instant myth seems to be emerging that nuclear threats are highly effective. Recently ex-President Eisenhower referred to some he had made at a time of stalemate in negotiations to end the Korean War, and which he is quoted as believing conjured an immediate settlement. . . . President Eisenhower's threats must have been a godsend to China's nuclearists. . . . *Elizabeth Young, London, "Are Nuclear Threats Effective?" in a Letter to the Editor, The Manchester Guardian Weekly, Oct. 20, 1966, p 15*

This deity is seen as an all-powerful force, capable of both apocalyptic destruction and unlimited creation, and the nuclear believer, or nuclearist, allies himself to that force and feels thereby compelled to expound the virtues of his god. *Robert Jay Lifton, The Atlantic, Oct. 1970, p 106*

nuclear magnetic resonance, the interaction of atomic nuclei with an external magnetic environment. It is used as an instrument of structural analysis in chemistry and physics.

F. W. Cope reports that the nuclear magnetic resonance (NMR) spectra of deuterium oxide in such cells is not that of ordinary D_2O water but that of a more organized water

. . . . This cannot be due merely to the physical presence of macromolecules inside the cells. Therefore they concluded that water must interact with these macromolecules in order to restrict the motion of the water molecules. *S. R. Erlander, "The Structure of Water," Science Journal, Nov. 1969, p 65*

nuclear medicine, the use of radioactive materials and of instruments detecting nuclear radiation in the diagnosis and treatment of diseases.

. . . nuclear medicine [is] a new medical specialty which has developed largely under the support of the Division of Biology and Medicine of the AEC [Atomic Energy Commission]. The main accomplishment of this discipline is a vast improvement in the diagnosis of cancer and many other diseases. *Gould A. Andrews, M.D., Oak Ridge, Tenn., in a Letter to the Editor, The Atlantic, April 1971, p 32*

nucleophile, *n.* a substance that is strongly attracted to atomic nuclei.

Then by dividing heterolytic reagents into nucleophiles and electrophiles, he saw the basis of a scheme interrelating a great range of chemical reactions. *"Obituary: Sir Christopher Ingold," The Times (London), Dec. 10, 1970, p 10*

nucleosynthesis, *n.* the process by which chemical elements are created from the nuclei of hydrogen.

Further points in favour of lunar water, free or combined, are that the universe consists practically entirely of hydrogen and helium — hydrogen being the starting material for nucleosynthesis in stars — and that oxygen is now known to be abundant in the Moon's crust. . . . *P. D. Lowman, Jr., "The Moon's Resources," Science Journal, May 1969, p 92*

For more than a decade astronomers have agreed that the heavy elements which are built up in stars by nucleosynthesis are dispersed throughout galaxies by supernova explosions. *"Supernovae Get Together to Share Out the Goodies," New Scientist and Science Journal, March 25, 1971, p 663*

Dr Teruaki Ohnishi of Tokyo University proposes that the nucleus of our Galaxy exploded several hundred times soon after its formation. He assumes that some nucleosynthesis occurred in these explosions. . . . *New Scientist, April 30, 1970, p 217*

nudie, *Slang.* — *n.* **1** a motion picture or play in which actors perform in the nude. Compare SKIN FLICK.

One imagines that for a certain percentage of the audience nudies are a harmless substitute for following women in the streets or arranging to bump against them in subways. *Richard Schickel, "Performing Arts," Harper's, July 1970, p 36*

2 a magazine or newspaper featuring photographs of nudes.

Non-book books, including nudies comprise 20 per cent. of their turnover. *Philip Oakes, The Sunday Times (London), Oct. 15, 1967, p 13*

On newsstands now inundated with naughties, nudies and assorted onetime no-noes, the bestselling hard-sex publication is *Screw*, the tabloid that has inspired imitation by more than a dozen equally raunchy rivals. *Time, April 19, 1971, p 48*

— *adj.* relating to or showing people in the nude.

It opens with an unseen director screen testing girls for the lead in a nudie murder mystery, which without the nudie element, becomes the frame for the film itself. *Vincent Canby, The New York Times, May 2, 1968, p 57*

nuke (nu:k), *U.S. Slang.* — *n.* **1** a nuclear weapon.

The guessing game of "enoughness" goes on unabated, its premise being "We must not have too many nukes or the enemy will feel threatened, but we must not have too few or he will attack." *Daniel Lang, "A Reporter At Large," The New Yorker, Jan. 9, 1971, p 60*

If possible, the U.S. would like to use nuclear explosives to dig the trench. Nukes are faster than dynamite, run one-tenth the cost. . . . *"Panama: Dig We Must," Time, Dec. 25, 1964, p 14*

"I worked with the people, so I knew what they were doing," Walkley [James Walkley, a former Air Force sergeant, who used to work on target planning at Hickam Field in Hawaii] said. "With a nuke, you'd have to drop a certain type on a certain type of target." *Jack Anderson, "Washington Merry-Go-Round: Nuke Targeting Being Updated," The Cleveland Press, April 7, 1972, p 2*

2 a nuclear-powered electrical generating station.

According to the Hudson River Fishermen's Association, the nuke was directly responsible for the death of between 310,000 and 475,000 fish in a six-week period last year alone. *"Environment: Delaying Nuclear Power," Time, Sept. 13, 1971, p 49*

— *v.t.* to attack with nuclear weapons.

". . . if we felt hemmed in, we would have a right-wing government that would — "

"Yes, that we would have one group of people who would say, 'We have to get ready to nuke 'em to kingdom come and stand guard.' But that's a futile policy anyway. And you would have another group who would say, '. . . What they propose is reasonable, after all. Let's just accommodate ourselves to them and stop being hostile to Communism.'. . ." *William Whitworth, "A Reporter at Large: Some Questions About the War (an interview with Eugene V. Rostow)," The New Yorker, July 4, 1970, p 52*

null set, *Mathematics.* a set with no members. Also called EMPTY SET.

Mathematics has available for this purpose [an *impossible* event] the *null* or *empty* set, symbolized by Ø. The null set is a subset of every aggregate and hence is useful in connection with many other issues. *Edna E. Kramer, The Nature and Growth of Modern Mathematics, 1970, p 261*

Every finite set of n elements has 2^n subsets if one includes the original set and the null, or empty set. For example, a set of three elements, ABC, has $2^3 = 8$ subsets: ABC, AB, BC, AC, A, B, C, and the null set. *Martin Gardner, "Mathematical Games," Scientific American, March 1971, p 106*

number runner or **numbers runner,** *U.S. Slang.* a person who collects bets in the form of an illegal lottery known as a numbers game.

Mother played the numbers like everyone else in Harlem but she was scared about Daddy being a number runner. Daddy started working for Jocko on commission about six months ago when he lost his house-painting job, which hadn't been none too steady to begin with. *Louise Meriwether, Daddy was a Number Runner, 1970, p 21*

number two, *Slang.* second; not in the most important or powerful position.

As long as Russia feels the understandable necessity to catch up in the arms race, the language of economic priorities is distorted for her in a way that need not be for the US as number one super-Power. It just does not pay to be number two. *Jonathan Steele, "Super-Powers," Review of "The Emergence of the Super-Powers" by Paul*

Dukes, The Manchester Guardian Weekly, April 25, 1970, p 17

num·é·raire (nY mei'rer), *n. French.* standard for currency exchange rates.

The Bretton Woods agreement, hammered out by an international panel of experts, headed by Harry Dexter White, of the United States, and John Maynard Keynes, of Britain, established the dollar as the *numéraire,* or measuring rod, against which the value of other currencies was set, and also as the principal currency in which the reserves, or national savings accounts, of other nations would be held. *John Brooks, "A Reporter At Large," The New Yorker, Oct. 23, 1971, p 118*

Not only can they [SDRs] be used as the numeraire for currency values, they can also be modified to form the basis for further increases in national reserves in the future. *"Reserves: A Case for Reform," The Times (London), March 3, 1972, p 17*

numerical control, a method of machine-tool automation using perforated tape carrying coded instructions. *Abbreviation:* NC

Numerical control means a fully automatic control system which works from numerical information, of the kind found on an engineering drawing. . . . A digital computer is used to prepare punched or magnetic tape containing full machining instructions. *H. Tipton, "Turning From a Tape," New Scientist, May 12, 1966, p 362*

numerically-controlled, *adj.* automated through numerical control.

Now, numerically-controlled machine tools have been developed which offer a 5-axis capability and could do everything that Molins [Machine Company] required, without any movement of the workpieces from one machine to another. *Fred Wheeler, "Automatic Machining: A System Approach," New Scientist, Sept. 14, 1967, p 563*

nun·cha·kus (nu:n'tʃɑ: ku:z), *n.pl.* See the quotation for the meaning.

The radical taste tends . . . to nunchakus, which go back more than 500 years. They were . . . invented by Japanese peasants for self-defence when metal weapons were forbidden to all but the Samurai, and have been revived by Tokyo students for their frenzied battles with the police.

Nunchakus are two hardwood sticks, about 14 inches long and 1 1/4 inches in diameter, connected by a rawhide or nylon cord. Eight stick-men abreast, it is claimed, can clear a street in no time. The sticks have 30 inches of reach, making frontal assaults impossible. *The Manchester Guardian Weekly, May 2, 1970, p 11*

nuoc mam ('nwɔ:k 'mɑ:m), a spicy Vietnamese fish sauce.

Bits of rice and *nuoc-mam* are what they're used to, and jungle sounds at night do not make them jump. *Johanna Kaplan, "Dragon Lady," Harper's, July 1970, p 83*

For the Oriental community there is the pungent *Nuoc Mam* so prized by the Vietnamese. . . . *Horace Sutton, "Booked for Travel," Saturday Review, Oct. 31, 1970, p 45*

For there is nothing in either Chinese or French cooking that exactly corresponds with the Vietnamese thin sauce or relish called nuóc mam, formed—like the ancient Roman *garum*—from the liquor of decomposing fish, but tasting (at least in Paris) pleasant enough, like a garlic-flavoured Fino sherry. *"Good Food Guide: Paris Varieties," The Times (London), March 25, 1972 p 11*

[from Vietnamese]

nuplex, *n.* a nuclear-powered complex of industrial manufacturers.

The obvious answer is to initiate, or promote, energy-consuming industries in the vicinity of these stations, creating at each point a nuclear powered agro-industrial complex—or "nuplex". *Sanat Biswas, "India's Nuclear Dawn," New Scientist, July 10, 1969, p 60*

Dr Finniston mentioned the building of large industrial complexes in arid coastal regions; of "nuplexes" centred on large nuclear reactors using seawater. *"Shaping Things to Come," The Manchester Guardian Weekly, Sept. 13, 1969, p 9*

nurturance, *n.* the action or process of nurturing; the providing of sustenance and care.

Reverence for such neglected "feminine" values as gentleness and nurturance becomes an excuse to bad-mouth women who display "masculine" characteristics like self-assertion or who don't want to preside as goddess of the organic kitchen. *Ellen Willis, "Musical Events," The New Yorker, Oct. 23, 1971, p 170*

nurturant, *adj.* providing sustenance and care.

Social scientists apply the term "nurturant" to typical female professions such as child care, teaching, nursing or social work. *Tom Alexander, "There Are Sex Differences In the Mind, Too," Encyclopedia Science Supplement (Grolier) 1971, p 81*

nut, *n.* **1** core; basic part.

The nut of [Jeremy] Bray's argument . . . is that the government's role in managing the economy would be more effective if the blanket approach were replaced by a new structure providing two kinds of centres of analysis and demand management: management agencies for each industry and also for each locality. *"Dr. Bray and His Book," New Scientist, Oct. 2, 1969, p 4*

. . . you go and do your thing and we'll go and do ours—just the way it's always been, but without tackling the nut of the problem, effective politics. *John A. Williams, "An Open Letter to the Ethnics," The New York Times, Oct. 16, 1970, p 41*

2 do one's nut or **do one's nuts,** *British Slang.* to act or work like one who is crazy.

[Ian] Macdonald's fears of famine [in East Pakistan] are well justified. East Pakistan imports more than 10 percent of its total food supply. . . . Macdonald has been doing some extra-mural lobbying of the Home Office to spread the word of his famine warnings. In his own words: "I've been doing my nut about saying why do we have to wait for the house to be on fire. . . ." *Peter Pringle, "The Hungry Monsoon," The Sunday Times (London), April 18, 1971, p 9*

Don't tell us, after the rich crop of British Rail announcements about increased seat reservation fees, and another five shillings on sleepers, that they aren't doing their nuts to get themselves out of the red. *William Davis, Punch, Aug. 20, 1969, p 286*

—v.t. *British Slang.* to strike with the head.

While they [skinheads] favor the boot as a primary weapon, they also use their heads to "nut" or butt a victim, and whatever other weapons come to hand: bricks, rocks, bottles, knives and razors. *Time, June 8, 1970, p 37*

I jumped up and nutted him, and this other kid jumped on his back. *Norman Harris, The Sunday Times (London), Sept. 21, 1969, p 22*

nuts and bolts, the basic features or components.

While Laird has immersed himself in day-to-day Pentagon business in order to learn the nuts and bolts of the Defense Department, Packard has taken on the long-range tasks. *Time, March 28, 1969, p 15*

With that philosophic fundamental out of the way, what of the nuts and bolts of printed news in the years ahead? . . . Here those two columns of *What's News* on the front page of *The Wall Street Journal,* and the news-magazines, point the way. *Herbert Brucker, "Can Printed News Save a Free Society?" Saturday Review, Oct. 10, 1970, p 64*

nuts-and-bolts, *adj.* basic; practical.

The National Research Council is more a nuts-and-bolts operation. Established in 1916, the NRC is, for the time being, a working conglomeration of some 450 panels of scientists, by-and-large not Academy members, convened

to mull over specific scientific questions. *Barbara J. Culliton, Science News, Aug. 15, 1970, p 147*

nutter, *n. British Slang.* a crazy or eccentric person.

Much of this is born of solitariness, a detached curiosity, and affection for the shabby and odd, the nutters of the species. *Caroline Tisdall, The Manchester Guardian Weekly, Feb. 20, 1971, p 20*

NVA, abbreviation of *North Vietnamese Army.*

. . . millions of people in Vietnam . . . have risked their lives, their fortunes, and their sacred honor to fight off the NLF, the VC, the DRV, the NVA, and all the others with alphabetical tags that simply spell "the enemy." *Edward G. Lansdale, Alexandria, Va., in a Letter to the Editor, The Atlantic, March 1969, p 28*

O

OAO, abbreviation of *Orbiting Astronomical Observatory,* an unmanned scientific satellite of NASA, designed for astronomical research from a circular orbit around the earth. Compare OGO, OSO.

The OAO satellite was planned as a general observing facility as well as for the specific experiments mentioned. Three months before the satellite was launched, NASA placed notices in general astronomical publications announcing that the satellite, like earth-based observatories, would be made available to guest observers for their own research. *"Astronomy: New Observation Opportunities," Science News Yearbook 1969, p 148*

Although the first OAO malfunctioned, the second one (launched on Dec. 7, 1968) has been an outstanding success and has produced a wealth of important new astronomical data. *George L. Withbroe, "Observatory, Astronomical," McGraw-Hill Yearbook of Science and Technology 1971, p 300*

obdurability, *n.* physical hardness and resistance.

Because of the apparent obdurability of bone it was supposed until very recently that once the skeleton of a vertebrate has been formed it ceases to partake of metabolism, or to have any appreciable breakdown. *Howard Rasmussen and Maurice M. Pechet, "Calcitonin," Scientific American, Oct. 1970, p 45*

▶ This word may have been formed on the analogy of *durability.* The term that would seem more likely as the root form, *obduracy,* has a continued use chiefly in the figurative sense of "stubbornness," though there is evidence, principally in the 1600's and 1700's, of its use to mean physical hardness, now considered rare or obsolete.

O·bie ('ou bi:), *n.* an annual award given by a newspaper for the best off-Broadway plays and performances presented in the American theater.

Meanwhile, he [James Coco] was acting (six Broadway shows, 25 off-Broadway), collecting two Obies for off-Broadway performances . . . and being entirely forgotten by audiences and casting directors when his shows were over. *"The Theater: Adventures of the Fat Man," Time, Jan 12, 1970, p 37*

[from the pronunciation of the letters *OB,* abbreviation of *off-Broadway*]

o·bit·u·ar·ese (ou,bitʃ u ər'i:z), *n.* the style, language, or content of obituaries.

. . . much orthodox obituarese only adds to the great corpus of bogus history enshrined in the printed word. When we read that "He was a ready and sympathetic listener, always ready to give advice, whether to his senior colleagues or to a first-year student", we all know that the truth is quite otherwise: "Because he did neither worthwhile research nor teaching during much of his career, he spent his time urging his quaint and outdated views on anyone who would listen." *New Scientist, June 18, 1970, p 594*

ob·jet de ver·tu (ɔ:b'ʒe də ver'tY); *pl.* **objets de vertu.** *Art.* an object of value because of its workmanship, antiquity, or rarity.

Auctions—At the Parke-Bernet Galleries . . . Friday, April 17, at 2: *Objets de vertu,* from various collectors. *"Goings On About Town: Auctions," The New Yorker, April 18, 1970, p 19*

With other objets de vertu (small, precious ornaments), the cup [of enameled gold, made in Vienna and dated 1665] was auctioned from the collection of the late Mrs. Helen de Kay of New York and Greenwich, Conn. *Sanka Knox, The New York Times, Dec. 10, 1966, p 33*

▶ *Objet de vertu* is an English coinage made up of French words to dignify what in English would have been the presumably inelegant phrase "object of virtu." The result is a misnomer, however, since the word *virtu* has no equivalent meaning in the

French form *vertu*. The English word *virtu* means a curio, antique, or the like, and was taken from Italian *virtù;* the French word simply means "virtue."

ob·jet trou·vé (ɔːbˈʒe truːˈvei); *pl.* **objets trouvés** *French.* any object found in nature or the environment that is adapted for its aesthetic value as a work of art; (literally) found object. See also FOUND.

Like an *objets trouvés* sculptor, Director Claude Chabrol *(La Femme Infidele)* likes to give commonplaces a classic aspect. Is coincidence a cliché? *Stefan Kanfer, Time, Sept. 7, 1970, p 63*

Ob·lo·mov·ism (ɑbˈlou məvˌiz əm), *n.* overwhelming sluggishness; inertia; sloth.

It was the cocktail hour in Bel-Air, but John Ford, seventy-five, wasn't having any. In fact, he was already in bed. He spends a lot of time there these days, though friends hint there may be a touch of Oblomovism combined with whatever real ills his aging flesh may be heir to. *Richard Schickel, "Performing Arts," Harper's, Oct. 1970, p 44*

[from *Oblomov*, the main character of a novel of the same name by Ivan Goncharov, 1812-1891. Oblomov was a Russian landowner whose chief characteristic was profound indolence. In Russia his name came to symbolize a strain of apathy and passivity in the national temperament.]

obviosity, *n.* something obvious; a plainly evident remark, inference, detail, etc.

The recent *Preliminary Report on Soccer Hooliganism,* prepared by a Birmingham research group under Dr J. A. Harrington for the Minister of Sport, contains so many obviosities, and betrays so little knowledge of the game (not to speak of group psychology), that it has irritated people inside it (not to speak of psychologists). *Hans Keller, "Sport: Violence," The Listener, Feb. 29, 1968, p 286*

Who says there's nothing charming about obviosities, clichés and an 1890 style? . . . In this book Smith is openly sentimental, seldom hesitates to use a cliché, and isn't afraid of being obvious. As a result "Shelter Bay", though written in 1964, seems to have been written in the 1890's— and badly at that. . . . it has the kind of touching charm that a less unsophisticated author couldn't have given it. *James Bannerman, "A Book So Bad It's Quite Good," Review of "Shelter Bay" by Harvey H. Smith, Maclean's, March 6, 1965 p 46*

[from *obvious*, on the pattern of pairs such as *porous, porosity*]

OC, abbreviation of *oral contraceptive.*

Much of the publicity has centered on the safety of the oral contraceptives (OC's). OC's cause a number of metabolic changes in a woman's body. . . . These changes appear to be reversible: when a woman stops using OC's, these conditions revert to their pre-OC state. There is . . . one serious disorder that has been linked with OC's: thromboembolic disease. *"Oral Contraceptives: How Safe Is the Pill?" Encyclopedia Science Supplement (Grolier) 1970, p 234*

oceanaut, *n.* another name for AQUANAUT.

Food, clothing and shelter used to be enough to get explorers to their goals. In the deep oceans, however, as in space, the most important consideration is air. Oceanauts can only begin their quests encumbered by the huge air tanks to which they are presently bound. . . . *Jonathan Eberhart, "Aquanauts Get Liquid Air," Science News, Aug. 5, 1967, p 138*

[from *ocean* + *-naut*, as in *astronaut*]

oceanics, *n.* the scientific exploration and study of the ocean.

A science of the seas is rapidly emerging. It's called oceanics. Through research in this vital and promising field, Bendix has already made a number of interesting and significant contributions. . . . We have developed techniques for operating electronic systems at depths of 18,000 feet, and transmitting data from these systems to the surface. *Advertisement by The Bendix Corporation, Time, May 8, 1964, p 80*

OCR, abbreviation of *optical character recognition,* the ability of a computer unit to optically "read" printed material and convert it into computer code without manual keyboard operation.

Optical character recognition (OCR), as practiced by the new generation of machines that read, is one of filtering, selecting and reducing from the detail present in each character on the paper just sufficient information to allow the correct identity to be decided with certainty. *J. A. Weaver, "Machines That Read," Science Journal, Oct. 1968, p 67*

oc·to·push (ˈɑk təˌpuʃ), *n.* a form of hockey invented in Great Britain, played in a swimming pool. See the quotation for details.

Octopush, for the benefit of unaquatic land-lubbers and ignoramuses, is a new form of underwater hockey. . . . The game is played by teams of six. . . . The object of the game is to propel or shovel the puck . . . along the bottom of the pool and into the opponents' gull [goal]. *Philip Howard, "Take a Deep Breath—It's Octopush," The Times (London), Feb. 18, 1970, p 11*

[blend of *octopus* and *push*]

OD or **o/d,** abbreviation of *overdose* (applied to narcotics taken in excess or to drug users sick or dead from an overdose).

"When I was shooting up, . . . I liked to hear about the ODs [overdose cases], and I'd think I was brave for taking it." *"Kids and Heroin: The Adolescent Epidemic," Time, March 16, 1970, p 25*

The doctor released them as not o/d . . . and I said they could sit in the waiting room, but one took some more pills in there and the doctor got mad and said we should put them out. *Victoria Brittain, "Government Concern at the Rise in Barbiturate Addiction," The Times (London), Aug. 17, 1970, p 6*

—*v.i. Slang.* to become sick or die from an overdose of a narcotic. Compare OH-DEE.

. . . they were just about to start shooting a film called *Zaccariah,* a rock, shlock, cowboy musical turn-of-the-century thing starring Ginger Baker, when the drummer OD'd and had to be replaced. *Albert Goldman, "Jazz Meets Rock," The Atlantic, Feb. 1971, p 104*

off, *n.* **from the off,** *British.* from the beginning; from the start.

My employer, Mrs. Heyley, was a woman of seventy. . . . She had spent forty formative years in India, and after twenty-four hours I had new insight into why the natives were so keen to see the sun set on the Empire. Heredity had thrust our roles on us from the off: behind her lay

off-Broadway

generations of sahibs and a direct link with Clive of India. *Catherine Drinkwater, "Girl Wanted: A Series of Seven Off-Beat Jobs," Punch, Jan. 4, 1967, p 32*

—*v.t. U.S. Slang.* to kill.

Then he described how [Alex] Rackley was taken from the bed to a car and then to the river. "At the swamp, Alex was offed," said Sams. "Warren [Kimbo] shot him first. Lonnie [McLucas] hit him a second time. We were told not to come back unless he was dead." *"The Panthers on Trial," Time, May 11, 1970, p 29*

off-Broadway, *n.* the segment of the New York professional theater outside of Broadway (the traditional theatrical center), noted for its introduction of experimental plays, often by unknown playwrights. Compare OFF-OFF-BROADWAY.

The hope of the American theater has sometimes been placed in off-Broadway: in terms of sustained achievement this amounts to wistful thinking. Of the several playwrights who got their start off-Broadway, only Edward Albee has remotely fulfilled his promise. *"The Theater: Dramatic Drought," Time, May 17, 1968, p 63*

Theatre began to happen. Broadway was sick and timid, unwilling and unable to put on daring new works or revive the classics. Off-Broadway, basing itself in and around the [Greenwich] Village area, began to rock the American theatre with [Edward] Albee's plays and the latest works from Europe. *David McReynolds, Saturday Night (Canada), Oct. 1966, p 25*

—*adj.* of or relating to off-Broadway.

Vinie Burrows, who plays Bobo in "The Blacks," the long-running Off Broadway play by Jean Genet, has been invited to appear on June 26 at Antioch College. *The New York Times, June 18, 1963, p 33*

offenseful, *adj.* full of offense.

Self-control, silence. But with each year,
to the murmur of trees and the clamor of birds,
that separation seems more offenseful
and the offense more absurd.
Vladimir Nabokov, "How I Love You" (a poem), The New Yorker, May 23, 1970, p 44

▶ The last recorded use of this word was by Shakespeare in *Measure for Measure* (II.iii.26): "So then it seems your most offenceful act was mutually committed?"

off-island, *n.* an off-shore island.

The off-islands may seem to be just across the nautical street but the journey can still be an experience on a rough day. *Ian Nairn, The Sunday Times (London), Feb. 23, 1969, p 63*

—*adj. U.S.* visiting or temporarily residing on an island; being an off-islander.

The Guam Democrats had regularly dominated the island's unicameral legislature until last November's local elections, when the rival Territorial Party—more conservative than its opposition but by no means a political outpost of the Republican Party—administered something of a drubbing to the Democrats. This upset afforded small comfort to off-island Republicans here, though, because while the Guamanians are American citizens, they cannot vote in our Presidential elections. *E. J. Kahn, Jr., "Letter from Guam," The New Yorker, Feb. 13, 1965, p 42*

—*adv.* See the quotation for the meaning.

. . . one islander was heard to remark recently that he never carried more than 30 cents in his pocket unless he planned to go off-island. *Phyllis Meras, "Travel," The New York Times, June 27, 1971, p 3*

off-islander, *n. U.S.* a temporary or seasonal resident of an island. Compare ON-ISLANDER.

. . . local businessmen gladly pocket the $20 million a year spent annually on bus trips, post cards and clam chowder. In fact, the tourist trade is growing so rapidly that many "off-islanders," the regular summer residents, are concerned lest their historic hideaway lose its charm. *"Business: Trading Up Nantucket," Time, July 26, 1968, p 67*

off-line, *adj.* not in direct line with or under direct control of a central computer. Compare ON-LINE.

The first of the three computers is an "off-line" machine that is used for production planning. It receives orders for specific sizes, amounts and types of steel and groups them according to quantity and composition. . . . It calculates about three weeks ahead. . . . It stores for this period detailed information on each item ordered and on the progress made with those orders that are actually in hand. *Fred Wheeler, "Computer Chain of Command in a Steelworks," New Scientist, July 9, 1964, p 84*

The off-line approach is one in which the experimental data from an analytical device is entered into a computer by manual intervention. *Max Tochner, "Computer-Assisted Analytical Chemistry," McGraw-Hill Yearbook of Science and Technology 1971, p 59*

off-off-Broadway, *n.* the segment of the New York professional theater producing low-budget and often highly experimental plays that would not be presented in Broadway and off-Broadway theaters. Compare OFF-BROADWAY.

For proof that the theme of sexual diversion can be honestly and yet dramatically treated, one has to go, not to off Broadway, but to what is called Off-off Broadway. Actually the distinction between the two is quite real. Off Broadway still comes under the jurisdiction of the actors union (although at reduced rates). Off-off Broadway is completely outside the union because it never takes place in a "real" theatre; instead, Off-off Broadway uses cafés, rooms, lofts, churches, and in the case of two plays I saw recently the back room of a saloon in the East Village [Greenwich Village]. . . . *Richard Roud, "On the Off-Broadway Bandwaggon," The Manchester Guardian Weekly, Oct. 17, 1968, p 21*

—*adj.* of or relating to off-off-Broadway.

The farthest off-Off Broadway theater of them all is the Firehouse Theater, which has been doing avant-garde plays in Minneapolis nearly as long as the Tyrone Guthrie Theater has been doing the other kind, and with much less help from the Establishment. *Dan Sullivan, The New York Times, June 23, 1968, Sec. 1, p 74*

It would seem that these off-off Broadway playwrights are emerging in a period when no producer can expect to present their unconventional works except at a financial loss. *Henry Hewes, "Bests of the 1966-67 Theater Season," Saturday Review, June 10, 1967, p 20*

offput, *v.t. British.* to disconcert; embarrass.

. . . the peculiarity of a faith that can revel in medieval plumbing in the 1970s and be so offput by the female of any species that not even a cow is allowed to pasteurise here. *Geoffrey Moorhouse, "Zorba's Place," The Manchester Guardian Weekly, Nov. 7, 1970, p 15*

[back formation from *off-putting* disconcerting, which was formed from the phrase *putting off*]

off-sale, *n.* the sale of alcoholic liquor for consumption off the premises. Also called TAKE-HOME SALE.

M. & B. [Mitchells and Butlers public houses] wants to stop off-sales in favour of the 23 Wine Sellers off-licences it has opened in Birmingham. *"Strike by Midland Pub Managers Planned," The Times (London), Aug. 18, 1970, p 20*

A plan to boost off-sales of wine to £245 million by 1973-74 was launched last week by the Wine and Spirit Trade Association. *The Sunday Times (London), May 29, 1966, p 41*

off-the-job, *adj.* **1** not on the job; done or happening while away from one's work.

Douglas [a training officer] says the off-the-job study is essential because it removes the pressures and distractions of the shop-floor. *Tony Aldous, "Case Book: How Training Boards Can Help Small Businesses," The Times (London), Feb. 9, 1970, p 19*

2 being off one's job; laid off or unemployed.

In addition to the usual demands . . . he [Walter Reuther] is insisting on a "guaranteed annual income." As a starter, that would mean increasing the industry's unemployment benefits. And for union members with seniority, it would involve some sort of new company-financed plan enabling an off-the-job worker to maintain "his normal living standard" for up to a year. *"U.S. Business: Labor," Time, July 21, 1967, p 51*

OGO, abbreviation of *Orbiting Geophysical Observatory*, an unmanned scientific satellite of NASA, designed for gathering physical data about the earth. Compare OAO, OSO.

The satellite, OGO-IV (Orbiting Geophysical Observatory), was put into a polar orbit for a study of the relationship between particle activity, aurora and airglow, the geomagnetic field, and the effects of sources of electromagnetic energy in the atmosphere. *The Times (London), Jan. 19, 1968, p 13*

oh-dee, *v.i. Slang.* to be killed by or as if by an overdose of a drug. Compare OD.

"I'm worried that the commission [President Nixon's Commission on Campus Unrest] is close to oh-deeing. Mississippi almost did them in, and Kent State will put them over." So said Joseph Rhodes Jr., 23, before setting off for a hearing last week at Kent State University in Ohio, the scene of one of the bloodiest episodes in the recent history of campus disorder. *"Education," Time, Aug. 31, 1970, p 51*

[pronunciation of *OD*, abbreviation of *overdose*]

oilberg, *n.* an oil tanker with a capacity of 200,000 tons or more; a very large oil-carrying ship.

But the oilbergs have made at least as big an impact on shipbuilding as they have on the oil industry. *Robin Sanders, The Sunday Times (London), May 4, 1969, p 37*

[from *oil* + ice*berg*]

Old Left, the leftist movement, predominantly Marxist in ideology, that represented the radical element in politics before the emergence of the New Left. *Often used attributively.*

The New Left is, of course, an enormously diverse group, ranging from slightly disguised representatives of the Old Left to political fauna so bizarre as to defy classification. *Joseph W. Bishop, Jr., "The Reverend Mr. Coffin, Dr. Spock, and the ACLU," Harper's, May 1968, p 65*

The Old Left had a program for the future; the New Left's program is mostly a cry of rage. The Old Left organized and proselyted, playing its part in bringing about the American welfare state. But it is precisely big government, the benevolent Big Brother, that the New Left is rebelling against. *"The New Radicals," Time, April 28, 1967, p 14*

And just as Establishment becomes a devil-image, so do other terms, such as (in different ways) "confrontation" and "youth" become god-images. It is true that these god- and devil-images can illuminate many situations, as did such analogous Old Left expressions as "the proletarian standpoint," "the exploiting classes," and "bourgeois remnants". . . . *Robert Jay Lifton, "Notes on a New History: The Young and the Old," The Atlantic, Oct. 1969, p 86*

. . . Daniel instead produces notes toward an autobiographical novel about his Old-Left parents, Paul and Rochelle Isaacson, who in the early 1950's were electrocuted for passing atom-bomb secrets to the Russians. . . . *Christopher Lehmann-Haupt, "No Handwriting on the Wall," Review of "The Book of Daniel" by E. L. Doctorow, The New York Times, June 7, 1971, p 31*

Old Leftist, a member of the Old Left.

En route to the United Nations, a handful of anti-antiwar demonstrators managed to pelt the peace parade with eggs. New York police on horseback—in contrast with the "Cossack" image so many Old Leftists apply to them—kept the countermarchers from breaking up the parade. *"The U.S.: The People, The Dilemma of Dissent," Time, April 21, 1967, p 15*

oleophilic, *adj.* attracting oil to itself.

The French authorities used . . . chalk treated with a film of stearate to make it "oleophilic" or oil-attracting. *"Is Sand the Answer to the Large Oil Slick?" New Scientist, June 11, 1970, p 529*

Sawdust treated with appropriate silicones is water repellent but strongly oleophilic and will soak up many times its weight of oil. *"Patents," Science Journal, Feb. 1970, p 21*

[from *oleo-* oil + *-philic* attracting]

olfactronic, *adj.* of or relating to olfactronics.

Another aspect of the olfactronic approach to detecting sources through their airborne signatures is the variety of possible ways in which this can be done. Any set of measurements, together with the numerical values, that adequately characterizes an airborne effluent in the presence of irrelevant impurities in air, can be used as an olfactronic signature. *Andrew Dravnicks, "Odours as Signatures," New Scientist, Sept. 15, 1966, p 623*

olfactronics, *n.* the analysis and detection of odors by sensitive instruments and techniques.

Eventually olfactronics may be used to guard bank vaults against burglars, . . . as well as to stand guard as fire alarms and sentries against the Vietcong. *Richard D. Lyons, The New York Times, July 16, 1967, Sec. 4, p 8*

[from *olfactory* + *-tronics*, as in *electronics*]

o·lig·o·mer (ou'lig ə mər), *n.* a chemical compound with a few recurring subunits, in contrast with a polymer which has many recurring subunits and a monomer which has no recurring subunits.

If conditions are chosen carefully, an oligomeric enzyme can be dissociated into its sub-units; by changing the conditions again, the original active oligomer is reformed. *"Enzymes that Piece Themselves Together," New Scientist, May 14, 1970, p 320*

[from *oligo-* few + *-mer*, as in *polymer* and *monomer*]

o·lig·o·mer·ic (ou,lig ə'mer ik), *adj.* of or characteristic of an oligomer.

The best understood enzymes contain only one protein chain; but most enzymes are in fact composed of a small number of protein sub-units associated together. This oligomeric structure is useful in allowing certain control functions to operate. . . . But it generates some interesting problems. How is the oligomer put together? How do the sub-units recognize each other? *"Enzymes that Piece Themselves Together," New Scientist, May 14, 1970, p 320*

o·lig·o·nu·cle·o·tide (ou,lig ou'nu: kli: ou,taid), *n.* a substance composed of a small number of nucleotides (constituents of nucleic acid).

Since the sequence of nucleotides in many RNA molecules is known, specific oligonucleotides with three or four monomers may be designed to bind to a selected part of the molecule by complementary base pairing. *"New Techniques Devised to Study RNA," Science Journal, April 1970, p 14*

[from *oligo*- few + *nucleotide*]

o·lim (ou'li:m), *n.pl. Hebrew.* Jewish immigrants to Israel. Compare ALIYAH.

The founders of modern Israel called themselves *olim:* pilgrims, "those who ascend." *Melvin Maddocks, "Books: Dream into Nightmare?" Review of "The Israelis" by Amos Elon, Time, June 7, 1971, p 52*

Positively, the nation feels refreshed by *olim*, the homecoming immigrants, justified in its deepest purpose, and strengthened to build a new life on its corner of the earth. *David Spanier, The Times (London), Sept. 16, 1967, p 10*

om·buds·man ('am,bədz mən), *n.* **1** a government official appointed to investigate the grievances and protect the rights of private citizens.

Now, at last, we have the Ombudsman, whose business it is to investigate charges of bad administration, and lay reports which the Commons can accept as thorough market research among the consumers of politics. *David Wood, The Times (London), March 4, 1968, p 8*

If it is argued (as it is in the President's Crime Commission task force report on the police) that it is "unreasonable to single out the police as the only agency which should be subject to special scrutiny from the outside," we would give two answers. First, we agree: the ombudsman inquiring into the citizens' complaints of excess or abuse of power by *all* state authorities, covering the police as well as other officials, works well in the countries where such a system now exists. There is practically unanimous agreement that both citizens and government officials including the police are well satisfied ("generally enthusiastic" according to the task force report on the police) with the work of the ombudsman. We do not doubt that the ombudsman system would work well here, and that it is needed. *Norval Morris and Gordon Hawkins, The Honest Politician's Guide to Crime, 1970, p 100*

New Zealand has installed an ombudsman; several American states are talking about doing the same thing; and now four Canadian provinces as well as the federal government are either looking at bills, or being urged to look at bills, that would make federal and regional *ombudsmen* part of our own parliamentary system. *Ken Lefolii, Maclean's, April 18, 1964, p 6*

The perfunctoriness with which the Government recently rejected the conclusions of the unofficial inquiry conducted by Justice into the Scandinavian *ombudsman* procedure was disappointing. *The Times (London), April 23, 1963, p 13*

2 someone to complain to or report a grievance to.

There came to the office a tall highboned man in his late forties named Harvey Schmedemann, a local liquor dealer. He had come to protest to the newspaper, his only ombudsman that day, a mimeographed newsletter thrust by a hippie into the hand of his eleven-year-old son as the boy walked across the University of Kansas campus. Schmedemann was angry. "Look at this," he said, holding up the newsletter. "Full of obscenities and put in the hands of an eleven-year-old kid. A kid! What is going on up there? Can't someone do something about that place? . . ." *Bill Moyers, "Listening to America: Kansas," Harper's, Dec. 1970, p 59*

3 any person who champions or defends individual rights.

Like many of my generation, I knew her [Eleanor Roosevelt] somewhat, not well. How could one not know her, since she was everywhere, doing everything — columnist, lecturer, traveler constantly crisscrossing the country, ombudsman for every injustice, agitator for every cause that needed help, one-woman lobby? *Max Lerner, "Eleanor," New York Post, Nov. 15, 1971, p 46*

[from Swedish, literally, commissioner]

ombudsmanship, *n.* the position or authority of an ombudsman.

The series of programmes under the heading, The Scientists, now being shown on commercial television are the best of their kind so far to emerge from the perennial funfair. Late on Saturday night is scarcely the ideal time for such viewing but one must be thankful for small mercies especially since the opposition at that hour is devoted to football and the loquacious ombudsmanship of Bernard Braden. *New Scientist and Science Journal, June 3, 1971, p 597*

om·buds·wom·an ('am,bədz,wum ən), *n.* a female ombudsman.

I am looking forward with impatience to the appointment of the proposed Parliamentary Commissioner for Administration. . . . Of course, if people felt closer to their councillors they might be able to wrest more expansive replies from the town hall. Perhaps the only answer is for more councillors to see themselves as Ombudsmen and Ombudswomen, and to leave less discretion to the routine decisions taken by officials. I am looking through this week's letters. *Lena Jeger, "Parcel of Grievances," The Manchester Guardian Weekly, Oct. 21, 1965, p 6*

omega, *n.* or **omega meson,** a highly unstable and short-lived elementary particle with a mass 1540 times that of an electron. Compare PHI, RHO.

Physicists had supposed that the photon, or light particle, was the sole intermediary of electromagnetic forces. But experimental evidence has shown that photons approaching hadrons tend to turn themselves into one of the mesons called phi, rho or omega. Thus, it appears that electromagnetic forces are mediated to leptons directly by photons and to hadrons by phi, rho or omega. *Dietrick E. Thomsen, "New Mathematics in Field Theory," Science News, April 10, 1971, p 250*

omnifaceted, *adj.* covering all facets.

The Great Depression! In these troubled times, how could more words about those troubled times become a national bestseller? The answer is that Studs Terkel's omnifaceted study of the latest major societal breakdown in the U.S. seems remarkably relevant to 1970. *Time, July 20, 1970, p 76*

omnifocal, *adj.* (of a lens) having a focal length that varies imperceptibly from one part to another.

Now an optical company in Ohio offers to solve this problem with an "omnifocal" lens which has power that's gradually increased from top to bottom with no blurred area or transition zone. *"Forecast: About Bifocals," Maclean's, Feb. 20, 1965, p 1*

on, *adj. British Slang.* **1** having a favorable potential; easily possible.

. . . the candidate . . . recovered sufficiently to win a storm of applause with "So you see, old boy, that while I agree with you denationalisation just isn't on: Labour's made such a howling mess of these industries that no one in his senses would ever buy them back!" *Bernard Hollowood, Punch, Sept. 25, 1968, p 421*

2 all right; seemly.

[Brett] Whiteley [a London painter] himself is now in the U.S., at the start of a $500-a-month Harkness Foundation scholarship. . . . and is already hard at work on an American series, including a collage portrait of Folk-Rock Singer Bob Dylan. Says Whiteley: "Dylan is the outsider. He's the most on person in America." *Time, Nov. 10, 1967, p 42*

on-board, *adj.* installed or carried aboard a craft or vehicle.

In the satellite, they [special frequency-control devices] would decrease the frequency of incoming signals to a frequency band in which they could be efficiently amplified by on-board equipment before being increased again and radiated back to Earth. *"Tuning in With Mixed Frequencies," New Scientist, Oct. 22, 1970 p 178*

Lufthansa, the West German airline, is considering the abolition of on-board food service on short domestic flights. . . . *The New York Times, May 20, 1968, p 93*

on·co·gene ('aŋ kə₁dʒi:n), *n.* a tumor-producing gene.

The [Robert Heubner] theory itself states that human cancer is viral in origin and is caused by a more or less hypothetical entity called the oncogene. This, according to Heubner, is an extra piece of genetic material (presumably DNA) passed on from generation to generation. Originally the oncogene was part of an RNA virus but at some unspecified time it incorporated itself into someone's DNA and has been passed on ever since; a tiny time bomb implanted in the nucleus of each cell. *Lucy Eisenberg, "The Politics of Cancer," Harper's, Nov. 1971, p 101*

[from Greek *ónkos* tumor + English *gene;* influenced by *oncogenic* tumor-producing]

on·co·ge·nic·i·ty (₁aŋ kou dʒə'nis ə ti:), *n.* the quality or condition of being oncogenic (tumor-producing).

. . . SV40 could induce cellular changes in human fibroblasts, thus providing one of the first laboratory demonstrations of the potential oncogenicity of a virus for human cells. *Stuart A. Aaronson, "Transformation, Cell," McGraw-Hill Yearbook of Science and Technology 1971, p 421*

one-liner, *n. U.S.* a very brief joke or witty remark.

. . . your mass audience doesn't laugh at that kind of stuff. . . . See if you can think up some one-liners. *Russell Baker, The New York Times, Oct. 11, 1970, Sec. 4, p 13*

[Senator Eugene] McCarthy had a one-liner for everyone in Washington, and the reporters who found favor were those who learned to leer and feed straight lines. *Jeremy Larner, "Nobody Knows . . . Reflections on the McCarthy Campaign," Harper's, May 1969, p 84*

one-off, *British.* —*adj.* made or intended for only one time, occasion, or person.

The relationship of the unit holder to his management group is . . . of the same kind as that between the policy holder and the insurance company, the bank depositor and his bank, and the building society member and his society. All these relationships involve money and are on a continuing basis rather than a one-off purchase. *Margaret Stone, "Unit Trusts: When There's a Merger, Who Looks After the Unit Holder?" The Times (London), March 28, 1970, p 21*

University technicians are often the real backroom men of academic research. It is they who devise the intricacies of "one-off" apparatus, adapting, devising, and generally manipulating standard apparatus for fresh uses. *"Lab-Man Elevated," New Scientist, March 26, 1970, p 596*

—*n.* anything made or intended for one time, occasion, or person; something special.

Another technique dating from the early days of fluidics is based on a photosensitive plastic material (Dycril). . . . Provided care is taken with the processing this technique is very useful; it is simple and calls for no expensive equipment, and for this reason is a convenient laboratory method for the rapid production of 'one-offs'. *B. J. Cooper, "Fluidics Grows Up," Science Journal, Dec. 1968, p 56*

onetime, *adj.* on only one instance; occurring only once.

. . . unlike police who deal with homicide or other major crimes, who have onetime or rare contact with their customers, the police who handle problems of morality rather than injury, crimes like prostitution and drug addiction, tend to develop a peculiar rapport with the people with whom they war. *Bruce Jackson, "Exiles from the American Dream: 'The Junkie and the Cop'," The Atlantic, Jan. 1967, p 44*

▶ The older meaning of *onetime, adj.* (since the 1880's) is "of some earlier time; former," as in *a onetime history teacher.*

one-time pad, a cryptographic method in which a secret message is coded in a cipher system devised especially and only for use on a single occasion.

. . . the main cipher-using Powers began to shift over to the one system that even Friedmann's methods cannot readily break: one-time pad. The German diplomatic service was using this in the early 1920s; the Russians took it up from 1930; even the British were using it by 1943. Mr Kahn shows, indeed, that it is theoretically unbreakable. Messages in it are prepared from a page of random figures, of which only the sender and the receiver have copies; no page is ever used twice. *M. R. D. Foot, "The Medium is the Secret," Review of "The Code Breakers" by David Kahn, The Manchester Guardian Weekly, Feb. 22. 1968, p 10*

one-up, *adj.* ahead of another, as by one point; in a position of advantage.

Ky is likely to be a stickler on these questions, anxious to get one-up on the N.L.F. any way he can. *Hedrick Smith, The New York Times, Dec. 1, 1968, Sec. 4, p 1*

Another trap the psychiatrist must strive to avoid is the mistake of being one-up. The psychiatrist is in the perfect position to be the one-up man and it's an easy habit to acquire. *Murray Wilson, "Help Me, Doctor, For I Am Sick," Maclean's, Oct. 1967, p 46*

—*v.t.* to score an advantage over; go one better.

The Liberals have had a variety of plans. John Wintermeyer, the party's 46 year old leader, first one-upped the socialists by endorsing the Saskatchewan plan, dithered, finally about-faced and produced a Tory-like scheme at the Liberal convention a month ago. *"Medicare in Ontario Now Irresistible," Canada Month, March 1963, p 10*

When she offers Jill an apple and Jill remarks that this reminds her of Snow White, but apologizes saying she knows that Mrs. Baker is not a witch, Mrs. Baker one-ups her neatly by replying, "And I know you're not Snow White." *Saturday Review, Nov. 8, 1969, p 28*

Trying to be funny, he said to the salesgirl: "That horse is a fake." She one-upped him: "Yes, so was the original." *Saturday Review, Dec. 21, 1968, p 6*

Since murder is illegal and it isn't always convenient to escape, sometimes you have to stand and fight. I have found the best defense to be an attack. Pin the snob down. Demand specific evidence to support his opinions, but never admit that the evidence is adequate (most of the time it won't be anyway). Turn the knife in the wound by one-upping his tastes, if you are able to get him to express them. No matter what they are, attack them. *Fred Gossen, University of Alabama, Tuscaloosa News, July 26, 1970, p 36*

[partly from the sports phrase *be one up on* (an opponent), meaning to lead in a game by one point, but chiefly a back formation from *one-upmanship* (the art or practice of being one up on one's friends), a term coined by the English humorist Stephen Potter, and the title of one of his books, published in 1952. See also -MANSHIP.]

one-upman, *v.t.* to one-up; go one better.

A few weeks later, Osborn, about to take a holiday, one-upmanned the director with a "My address while abroad will be: c/o J. S. Morgan & Company, 22 Old Broad Street, London. But I really do not wish to hear anything about Museum affairs unless absolutely necessary." *Geoffrey T. Hellman, "Profiles: The American Museum," The New Yorker, Dec. 7, 1968, p 72*

[back formation from *one-upmanship*. See the etymology under ONE-UP.]

on-islander, *n. U.S.* a permanent resident of an island. Compare OFF-ISLANDER.

Traditionally, the Vineyard...has been a haven of tranquillity, offering respite from the cares of the metropolis—a place where...tourists, especially day-trippers, were tolerated rather than sought. This is how the "on-islanders" want to keep it. On the other hand, there is much to attract "off-islanders." *Phyllis Meras, "Martha's Vineyard: Birthdays But No Parties," The New York Times, June 27, 1971, Sec. 10, p 3*

on-line, *adj.* in direct line with or under direct control of a central computer. Compare OFF-LINE.

PSA [Pacific Southwest Airlines] has an on-line automated reservations system that helps make sure all its seats are filled with passengers and all its passengers have seats. *Advertisement by the National Cash Register Co., Scientific American, Feb. 1965, p 89*

In not too many years, it is hoped, entire steel plants will be under the control of on-line computers, supervised with the help of a central computer which will deal with customers' orders. *"Tidying Up for the Computer," New Scientist, Oct. 8, 1964, p 79*

—*adv.* in line with an actual process or operation; in real-time.

The Wantage Research Laboratory of the United Kingdom Atomic Energy Authority were showing the latest version of their X-ray device for measuring the ash content of coal quickly and accurately. The 15 minutes or so needed for measurements with the first instruments developed has been reduced to perhaps 100 seconds—fast enough for the device to be used "on-line" for blending coals of different ash content at the pit head. *New Scientist, May 23, 1968, p 402*

op or **Op,** *n.* short for OP ART.

'Op' was a form of abstract design depending largely on optical illusion to create its effects. This could at times be combined with movement and thus become a type of kinetic art. *"The Arts: Art," The Annual Register of World Events in 1965 (1966), p 427*

—*adj.* of or characterized by op art.

In the new Op paintings and textile designs, discussed here in July, squares, circles, rectangles and ellipses jangle against one another as violently as they do in daily life. *Martin Gardner, "Mathematical Games: The 'Superellipse': a Curve that Lies Between the Ellipse and the Rectangle," Scientific American, Sept. 1965, p 222*

op art or **Op art,** a form of abstract art that relies heavily on optical illusion. Also called OPTICAL ART.

There is an obvious but superficial sense in which Op art (discussed in this department last July) can be called mathematical art. This aspect of Op is certainly not new. Hard-edged, rhythmic, decorative patterns are as ancient as art itself, and even the modern movement toward abstraction in painting began with the geometric forms of the cubists. *Martin Gardner, "Mathematical Games: The Eerie Mathematical Art of Maurits C. Escher," Scientific American, April 1966, p 110*

[shortened from *optical art*, on the analogy of *pop art*]

op artist, a person who produces op art. Also called OPTICAL ARTIST.

Now, hard on the heels of op artists, who address their work to the retina, has come a widespread number of "kinetic" artists, who try to combine mechanics and art. *"Art: Styles, The Movement Movement," Time, Jan. 28, 1966, p 44*

Op-Ed page, *U.S.* a newspaper page featuring articles by columnists and other writers.

The Op-Ed page—so named because it runs opposite a newspaper's editorial page—became a journalistic tradition with the rise of the personal column. Pioneered by the Pulitzers in the old New York morning *World*, the Op-Ed provides a variety of viewpoints in dozens of major metropolitan dailies. *Time, Aug. 10, 1970, p 32*

[shortened from *Opposite Editorial page*]

open admissions, *U.S.* another name for OPEN ENROLLMENT.

With surprising fervor, the City University of New York (CUNY) has set out to help break the poverty cycle of young people—both white and black—who graduate with serious educational deficiencies from the city's high schools each year. Under its new "open admissions" policy, CUNY was taking such students despite their academic shortcomings, even admitting some of them directly into its four-year colleges. *"Education: Gambling on Open Admissions," Time, Sept. 28, 1970, p 36*

open classroom, *U.S.* a classroom, especially at the elementary-school level, in which the activities are informal, individualized, and centered on open-ended investigation and discussion of subjects instead of formal instruction.

An open classroom means nothing to me unless it means that a child learns in that classroom that learning is not dependent at every level on the presence of a teacher. *Ned O'Gorman, The New York Times, June 8, 1971, p 39*

Critics ... claim that the open classroom fails to equip children with basic skills and facts, and that it will result in placing students at a disadvantage in selective examinations for jobs and college entrance. *Linda Gail Lockwood, "Education," The World Book Science Annual 1972 (1971), p 307*

open corridor, another term for OPEN CLASSROOM.

... children wander through their classrooms like free souls — sprawling on the floor to read library books that they themselves have chosen, studying mathematics by learning how to cope with family food bills, chattering and painting and writing, writing, writing. Their teachers glide purposefully from group to group and from child to child, guiding, correcting, encouraging. All this adds up to a new style of elementary instruction that has been called "informal education" or "open classrooms" or "open corridors." *"Does School + Joy = Learning?" Newsweek, May 3, 1971, p 60*

open-ended, *adj.* having no fixed time limit.

... the Government was proposing to introduce "open ended" drinking hours, so that we can behave like real members of the Common Market.... *Dennis Johnson, "Britain in Focus: Time for a Change," The Manchester Guardian Weekly, Nov. 21, 1970, p 11*

She [Mrs. Lyndon Johnson] agonized for her exhausted husband, slept fitfully and suffered from a recurring nightmare in which she wandered lost through endless rooms. The months before L.B.J.'s [President Lyndon B. Johnson's] decision not to run again were the worst; to her, the thought of another campaign seemed like "an open-ended stay in a concentration camp." *"Historical Notes: Recollections of the Fishbowl," Time, Nov. 9, 1970, p 18*

open enrollment, *U.S.* a policy of unrestricted admission to a college or university that permits poor or unprepared students to matriculate. Also called OPEN ADMISSIONS.

The open enrollment policy for the city universities will be a mistake. In order to maintain the high academic standards of this city, it is imperative that the existing standards of CUNY be maintained. *Barbara Feldman, New York, in a Letter to the Editor, The New York Times, Jan. 7, 1970, p 42*

open-heart, *adj. Surgery.* performed on the interior of the heart while maintaining circulation by means of a heart-lung machine.

For many years, surgeons were unable to operate successfully on the interior of the heart in spite of frequent need to do so. Then, in the 1950s, with the development of the heart-lung machine — a mechanical device which substitutes temporarily for the heart and lungs — the procedure known as open-heart surgery became feasible. *"A Footnote on the Heart," Saturday Review, July 1, 1967, p 50*

Since last March at the National Heart Hospital alone he has performed 219 "open heart" operations. *Elizabeth Gough-Cooper, The Sunday Times (London), March 30, 1969, p 6*

open housing, *U.S.* prohibition of racial or religious discrimination in the sale or rental of a house,

apartment, or other dwelling. *Often used attributively.*

"You have to earn at least $10,000 or $12,000 a year to move to the Cleveland suburbs," remarked Gerta Friedheim, young, petite Cleveland Heights housewife who heads the Suburban Citizens for Open Housing, an organization pushing for integration of the outer city. *Paul Delaney, "The Outer Cities: Negroes Find Few Tangible Gains," The New York Times, June 1, 1971, p 28*

... in defiance of the white majorities of Michigan, he [George Romney] has fought for open housing that would not end at the edge of a slum. *Margaret L. Coit, "The Dream Nobody Wanted to Hear," Review of "The Concerns of a Citizen" by George Romney, Saturday Review, April 6, 1968, p 38*

Ending overt discriminatory practices in existing and planned accommodations — the goal of most open-housing statutes — is primarily an enforcement problem. *Time, Sept. 7, 1970, p 51*

Nova Scotia's open-housing laws prohibit racial segregation only in overcrowded tenements and in apartments too expensive for Negroes. *Murray Barnard, "For Negroes in Halifax, Black Power v. Ping Pong," Maclean's, Nov. 1967, p 1*

open-loop, *adj.* of or relating to an automatic control process which has no feedback or self-corrective mechanism. Compare CLOSED-LOOP.

... almost all skilled muscular activities seem to exhibit many "open-loop," pre-programmed characteristics. An open-loop system (one that draws little or no information from the thing it governs) can always be operated more effectively than a closed-loop one, provided that its task is well defined and not subject to major disturbances. *J. H. Milsum, "The Control Engineer's View of Medical Problems," New Scientist, June 30, 1966, p 830*

open sentence, *Mathematics.* an equation containing one or more unknown quantities.

Decision procedures — sometimes called algorithms — are familiar in everyday mathematics. For example, the technique of long division represents a decision procedure for the predicate "x is divisible by y," where x and y can be any natural number. (A predicate is an open sentence: one that can be completed by assigning names to its variables.) *Howard de Long, "Unsolved Problems in Arithmetic," Scientific American, March 1971, p 55*

operand, *n.* any of the items of information involved in a computer operation.

By means of a fine-grained separation of the computer's functional units a high degree of overlapping has been attained. Current efforts in "pipelining" the processing of "operands" will allow a further significant increase in speed. *D. L. Slotnick, "The Fastest Computer," Scientific American, Feb. 1971, p 76*

operant conditioning, 1 another name for INSTRUMENTAL LEARNING.

The other type of learning — clearly subject to voluntary control and therefore considered superior — is instrumental, or trial-and-error, learning, also called operant conditioning. *Leo V. DiCara, "Learning in the Autonomic Nervous System," Scientific American, Jan. 1970, p 31*

... R. K. Siegel and W. K. Honig report how they set out to establish whether or not pigeons could form the broad concept of "human being." They used as subjects eight naive homing pigeons, which had been established on a food regime which kept the pigeons at 70 per cent of their normal body weight. At daily intervals they were placed in operant conditioning chambers and trained to peck at keys, the reward being occasional access to grain. *"Man in the Mind of the Pigeon," New Scientist, Sept. 3, 1970, p 455*

2 another name for REINFORCEMENT THERAPY.

Victims of mental illness, especially long-term patients, often have their abnormal patterns of behavior "rewarded" by people, doctors included, who humor the patients' delusions. This is wrong, according to psychologists who believe in reinforcement therapy, or operant conditioning. These psychologists believe that responses that are followed by rewards will increase. Therefore, only "good" responses should be rewarded. *"Review of the Year: Behavioral Sciences: Psychotherapy," Encyclopedia Science Supplement (Grolier) 1970, p 71*

In the language of operant conditioning, these people [drug addicts] have lived in decayed and fragmented social subcultures, have received little in the way of stable schedules of reinforcement, and have often been subjected to conflicting stimulus control. *John R. Smythies, "Drug Addiction," McGraw-Hill Yearbook of Science and Technology 1971, p 171*

operator, *n.* the part of the operon that activates and regulates the structural genes. Also called REGULATORY GENE.

According to a now classic hypothesis in genetics, there are two classes of genes. The first consists of structural genes that, through RNA, determine the sequence of the amino acids and thus the structure of protein. The second class of genes, called operators, control the first, turning them on and off to regulate gene expression. Working as a unit, a package of structural and operator genes is called an operon. *"A Single Gene: Molecular Tour de Force," Science News, Nov. 29, 1969, p 494*

The promoter and operator sites are adjacent parts of the same DNA duplex. The promoter is the site to which the transcribing enzyme (RNA polymerase) binds in order to start transcription, and the operator is the site to which the specific repressor protein binds to stop gene expression (possibly by preventing transcription). *Lorne A. MacHattie, "Gene," McGraw-Hill Yearbook of Science and Technology 1971, p 213*

op·er·on ('ap ə‚ran), *n.* a cluster of linked genes functioning as a unit in controlling the production of proteins. Compare LAC OPERON.

An operon is a chromosomal unit consisting of a group of adjacent structural genes, which are regulated together, and the operator, which coordinates their activities. *Clifford R. Noll, Jr., "Biochemistry: Control of Protein Biosynthesis," 1968 Collier's Encyclopedia Year Book, p 149*

The group ... now hopes to find out how genes are repressed and derepressed — turned off and on — so that genes can be made to operate when required. This concept, known as the operon concept, was first formulated by the French scientists François Jacob, André Lwoff, and Jacques Monod, who won the 1965 Nobel Prize. *Charles S. Marwick, "Medicine," The Americana Annual 1970, p 437*

OPM, 1 abbreviation of *other people's money.*

No institution manages more "O.P.M.," or Other People's Money, than Manhattan's 116-year-old United States Trust Co., one of whose few advertising themes is "Planned silence is essential to a trust company's character." *Time, Aug. 15, 1969, p 60*

2 abbreviation of *output per man.*

... the UK with much higher R & D [Research and Development] spending (1.5 per cent of GNP) had only a third of Japan's growth in output per man (OPM) employed. *S. K. Guha, Watford, England, in a Letter to the Editor, New Scientist, June 5, 1969, p 543*

opster, *n. U.S. Slang.* an op artist. Compare POPSTER.

"Sculpture: New York Scene," a bright, concentrated little group show ... ranging from the intricate light-and-shadow wall reliefs of the opster Ben Cunningham to the ingenious carved wood mechanical devices of Robert Zakarian.... *Grace Glueck, The New York Times, March 18, 1967, p 25*

opt, *v.i.* **opt out,** *Chiefly British.* to choose to withdraw from something; to back out; beg off.

These could be considered (in Malta) among the risks of opting out. *Daily Telegraph (London), May 10, 1972, p 16*

Morgan has no cures for society so he opts out, even if his Mum does call him a class traitor. *Wendy Michener, Maclean's, Aug. 20, 1966, p 43*

... the children actually provide a useful excuse to opt out of tasks which can well be performed by someone other than the rector's wife but which she is usually expected to assume. *Geoffrey Moorhouse, Manchester Guardian Weekly, March 5, 1964, p 13*

optical, *adj.* of or relating to op art.

Leaving aside the question of the contemporary fashion for "optical" painting, Vasarely's work shows — indeed it largely created — two important trends in abstract art today. *"Father of 'Op' Art," New Scientist, May 20, 1965, p 491*

optical art, another name for OP ART.

There is the Klee of the early 1930s, the precursor of optical art, in whose canvases flickering and apparently changing patterns of iridescent colours dance around firm linear designs whose strength creates a high degree of tension between colour and form. *The Times (London), July 22, 1965, p 15*

optical artist, another name for OP ARTIST.

The Manhattan optical artist [Josef Levi] has devised several new dizzying exercises with illuminated shadow boxes superimposed on black and white perforated metal screens. *Time, Feb. 7, 1969, p 4*

optical astronomer, a specialist in optical astronomy.

Now, the optical astronomers turned to one of their most powerful tools: the spectrograph, which separates light into its component wave lengths by passing it through a prism or a series of fine lines etched on a glass plate. *Time, March 11, 1966, p 51*

Before 1960 radio astronomers had identified and catalogued hundreds of radio sources: invisible objects in the universe that emit radiation at radio frequencies. From time to time optical astronomers would succeed in identifying an object — usually a galaxy — whose position coincided with that of the radio source. Thereafter the object was called a radio galaxy. *Maarten Schmidt and Francis Bello, "The Evolution of Quasars," Scientific American, May 1971, p 56*

optical astronomy, the branch of astronomy that uses telescopes for direct observation of the heavens (as distinguished from *radio astronomy, X-ray astronomy,* etc.).

The first machine to automate completely one of the

important processes of optical astronomy has been commissioned at the Royal Observatory, Edinburgh. The machine, called GALAXY, is used to locate and measure the star images on photographic plates from the Observatory's 400 mm Schmidt telescope. A single plate taken by the Schmidt may contain tens of thousands of star images, all in perfect focus. *"GALAXY Extracts New Star Data," Science Journal, March 1970, p 14*

optical fiber, one strand of fiber optics.

Optical fibers are a means of manipulating light that is rapidly finding use in many fields. Some recent developments are their use in chromatography, automatic titrations, and control of chemical reactions. *Morton Beroza, "Optical Fibers," McGraw-Hill Yearbook of Science and Technology 1971, p 308*

Equally, nobody has yet produced glass which meets all the challenging requirements of optical fibres.... *W. T. Gunston, Science Journal, Dec. 1970, p 68*

optoelectronic, *adj.* using a combination of optical and electronic systems or devices.

Electrons and photons are in any case intrinsically linked so there is nothing very strange in the fact that for 15 years research teams have been trying to develop new types of device or system in which a flow of the one is coupled with an emission of the other, generally in the visible part of the spectrum.... the underlying reason for the lack of production hardware seems to be that, as soon as a function has been performed by an opto-electronic device, another research team has found a way to do the same thing without using light at all. *W. T. Gunston, Science Journal, May 1970, p 43*

optoelectronics, *n.* the combined use of optical and electronic systems or devices.

A shaft of light is a neat way of coupling electronic circuits together in such a manner as to suppress "noise" passing from one to another. Here, then, is an application for opto-electronics in computers, data transmission and communication systems, where the trend towards miniaturization is meeting problems with the bulkiness of the transformers normally used to isolate bits of the system. *"Optical Coupling for Miniature Circuits," New Scientist, Aug. 12, 1965, p 387*

Optoelectronics, albeit using incoherent light, has also found its way into the video cassette field via a new video disc system being developed by Philips. *New Scientist and Science Journal, April 29, 1971, p 266*

orbital, *n. British.* a highway going around the suburbs of a city.

First priority for roads, after the orbitals outside Greater London, is Ringway 2 (North and South Circular Roads). *The Times (London), Feb. 3, 1970, p 2*

orbital steering. See the first quotation for the meaning.

... orbital steering [is] a process in which atoms within enzymes are held at precise angles to permit them to join and form new molecular compounds in biochemical reactions. *"Enzymes, Orbital Steering," Science News, June 27, 1970, p 618*

A new concept that enzymes facilitate chemical reactions by precisely guiding the angles of approach of atoms in the reacting compounds has been proposed by Daniel E. Koshland, Jr., of the University of California at Berkeley. Koshland presented evidence for this concept, which he calls orbital steering.... *"Orbital Rendezvous," Scientific American, Aug. 1970, p 46*

Oreo, *n. U.S. Slang.* a derogatory name for a black man who is part of the white establishment or is in favor of working within the white establishment.

Trouble is Negroes been programmed by white folks to believe their products are inferior. We've developed into a generation of Oreos — black on the outside, white on the inside. *Richard Levine, Harper's, March 1969, p 61*

[from the trade name for a chocolate cookie with a vanilla cream filling]

organization chart, a chart showing the structure of an organization in the form of a diagram.

Although there are many kinds of organizations, the same type of organization chart is used to describe them all. This is the familiar pyramid of lines and boxes arranged in ascending order of importance. *Donald Winks, "How to Read an Organization Chart for Fun and Survival," Harper's, Jan. 1967, p 38*

According to the tidy White House organization charts, the key influence on presidential decisions in all but foreign affairs ought to be the Domestic Affairs Council, headed by John Ehrlichman. But the Shultz franchise of supervising the cash enmeshes him in policy decisions. *Time, Aug. 10, 1970, p 8*

organo-, combining form for "organic," now used especially in forming adjective compounds designating organic insecticides, fungicides, bacteriocides, etc., as in the following examples:

organochlorine, *adj.:* In one of the most competent surveys ever of the organochlorine scene, the report points out that by 1963 Britain used only 1 per cent of the 60 000 tons of organochlorine insecticide used in the United States, a position which has probably improved since then. *New Scientist, Nov. 5, 1970, p 255*

organomercuric, *adj.:* This disease [smut disease of barley] cannot be treated by organo-mercuric compounds, probably because it is so deep seated in the seed. *Richard Warren, "Systematic Attack on Fungi," New Scientist, Nov. 20, 1969, p 403*

organomercury, *adj.:* This has been an important weakness in the armoury for pollution control because the toxicity of the organomercury compounds varies widely. *Pearce Wright, The Times (London), Sept. 30, 1970, p 2*

organophosphate, *adj.:* Organophosphate pesticides, although highly toxic, are being used in increasing amounts because they are far more biodegradable than chlorinated hydrocarbons such as DDT. *Science News, Feb. 20, 1971, p 130*

organophosphorous, *adj.:* The organophosphorous insecticides inhibit the enzyme cholinesterase, which normally breaks down acetylcholine following the transmission of the nerve impulse across the synapse. *Robert W. Risebrough, "Pesticide," McGraw-Hill Yearbook of Science and Technology 1971, p 319*

organule, *n.* another name for MOLECHISM or MOLECISM.

Organule or molecism?... Whether viruses are molecules or organisms depends on how you look at them, and it is always important to have more than one point of view. *F. Kingsley Sanders, "Books," Review of "The Natural History of Viruses" by C. H. Andrewes, Science Journal, March 1968, p 90*

[from *organ*ism + molec*ule*]

org-man, *n. U.S.* short for *organization man,* one who gives himself up wholly to the business or to the institution with which he is associated.

They [white Anglo-Saxon Protestants] grew great as initiators and entrepreneurs. They invented the country, its culture and its values; they shaped the institutions and organizations. Then they drew the institutions around themselves, moved to the suburbs, and became org-men. *Peter Schrag, "The Decline of the Wasp," Harper's, April 1970, p 86*

orienteer, *n.* a person who engages in orienteering.

Furthermore, Swedish orienteers bled their way into medical history a few years ago following an epidemic of the disease. *"Inside Track, The Viral Hepatitis," The Sunday Times (London), Oct. 10, 1971, p 30*

orienteering, *n.* the sport, developed in Scandinavia as a combination of map-reading and cross-country running, of competing with others to get first through an unknown area with the use of a compass and topographical map.

During the summer the Army has staffed and run an Adventure Training Centre on the shores of Lough Foyle for boys from Belfast and Londonderry. When it closes in October, over 200 boys from all types of school will have completed 12-day courses there, with rock-climbing and orienteering in the Mourne Mountains, and canoeing at sea and in the rivers. *Hugh Hanning, "Ulster Looks to Its Youth," The Times (London), Oct. 7, 1970, p 8*

orogenics, *n.* the process of mountain formation.

Because the book is primarily concerned with the effects of the Caledonian, Hercynian, and Alpine orogenics in Europe, no detailed stratigraphy is given. Caledonian movements are seen only on the Scandinavian Peninsula, but without any comparison or correlation with the British Isles the account is rather brief. *Dan Greenberg, Review of "The Geology of Western Europe" by M. G. Rutten, Science Journal, Dec. 1970, p 82*

[from *orogenic*, *adj.*, relating to mountain formation]

orthodox sleep, the dreamless part of sleep, during which the body undergoes no marked changes. Compare PARADOXICAL SLEEP.

There are two basic kinds of sleep: 'orthodox' sleep and 'paradoxical' sleep. During orthodox sleep there are no dreams and measurements of brain waves show a slow 'alpha' rhythm. *Oliver Gillie, "Drug Addiction — Facts and Folklore," Science Journal, Dec. 1969, p 78*

After about an hour of this orthodox sleep phase, a change occurs and paradoxical sleep begins and lasts about 10 minutes before orthodox sleep is resumed.... I believe that orthodox sleep (non-rapid eye movement, non-dreaming, or slow wave sleep) serves a function for the growth and renewal of general bodily tissues, and that paradoxical sleep (rapid eye movement or dreaming sleep) is important for brain growth and renewal. *Ian Oswald, "Sleep, the Great Restorer," New Scientist, April 23, 1970, p 170*

orthoferrite, *n.* a wafer of crystalline material in which specific areas of magnetism can be induced by the application of electric current, used especially in computers to store and transmit data.

For several years, Bell scientists have been experimenting with thin wafers of crystalline materials known as orthoferrites, which are compounds of iron oxides and such rare-earth minerals as ytterbium, thulium and samarium-terbium. *"Computers," Time, Sept, 5, 1969, p 37*

Bubble domains were first found in a class of materials called orthoferrites, compounds of rare earths, iron and oxygen. They have the general chemical formula $RFeO_3$, where R is any of the rare earths or the element yttrium. *Dietrick E. Thomsen, "The Magnetic World of Bubble Domains," Science News, May 8, 1971, p 318*

[from *ortho-* straight + *ferrite* an iron compound]

or·tho·ker·a·tol·o·gy (ˌɔr θou͵ker əˈtɑl ə dʒiː), *n.* a method of correcting or improving the eyesight by altering the cornea through the periodical application of new contact lenses.

Dr. Harry Hollander of the center [The Sight Improvement Center Inc. of New York] said that "normally a contact lens is fitted exactly to the curve of the cornea of the eye. In orthokeratology, the cornea is made to change its shape to match the lens curvature." *Ernie Johnston, Jr., "New Lenses Shape Eyes, Aid Vision," New York Post, June 14, 1972, p 74*

[from *ortho-* correct + *kerato-* cornea + *-logy* study, system]

orthomolecular, *adj.* of or based upon a theory formulated by the American chemist Linus Pauling, born 1901, according to which disease may be caused by deficient molecular concentrations of essential substances in the body, so that cures may be effected by combining medical treatment with dietary and vitamin therapy to overcome the molecular deficiency.

Another way in which the disease [diabetes] can be kept under control, if it is not serious, is by adjusting the diet, regulating the intake of sugar, in such a way as to keep the glucose concentration in the blood within the normal limits. This procedure also represents an example of orthomolecular medicine. *Linus Pauling, Vitamin C and the Common Cold, 1970, p 66*

His [Linus Pauling's] approach, which he calls orthomolecular psychiatry, involves giving the brain "the right molecules in the right amounts," and he is currently trying to discover the optimum concentrations for specific individuals. This is a radical approach to mental health, one not endorsed by most medical researchers. *Joseph N. Bell, "Linus Pauling: A Man of Science," The World Book Science Annual 1969, p 382*

Orthomolecular treatment, then, would involve carefully measuring the concentrations of vital substances in the body ... and then providing the individual with the right substances to bring him up to scratch. *New Scientist, May 16, 1968, p 329*

[coined by Linus Pauling from *ortho-* straight, correct, exact + *molecular*]

orthotic, *adj.* of or relating to orthotics.

The list of practical factors that prevail against myoelectric systems is long and specialized. It led me to the conclusion that the short-term control of remote manipulators is easier to achieve than the long-term control of orthotic arms by a paralyzed patient in a wheelchair. *Alex K. Godden, Oxford, England, in a Letter to the Editor, New Scientist, March 26, 1970, p 629*

or·thot·ics (ɔrˈθɑt iks), *n.* the rehabilitation of injured or impaired joints or muscles through artificial support.

... shortages existed in all of the other rehabilitation disciplines: occupational therapy, prosthetics and orthotics, social work, speech pathology and audiology, rehabilitation counseling.... *Howard A. Rusk, "Medicine," Britannica Book of the Year 1969, p 510*

[from *ortho-* straight, correct + *-tics*, as in *prosthetics*]

orthowater, *n.* another word for ANOMALOUS WATER.

The substance, variously called orthowater, anomalous water, polywater, and superwater, differs radically from ordinary water. *Arnold E. Levitt, "Chemistry," The 1970 Compton Yearbook, p 176*

Orwellian, *adj.* characteristic or suggestive of the British author George Orwell, 1903-1950, of his works, or of Orwellism.

There is an Alice in Wonderland quality (or is it Orwellian?) to the Nixon Administration's continued insistence that the Cambodian invasion is a success. *Richard J. Walton, West Redding, Conn., in a Letter to the Editor, The New York Times, June 29, 1970, p 36*

But it is, unhappily, not simply a matter of abolishing nuclear weapons. They and the knowledge of how to make them are permanent facts of power. They exist, as finally as computers and radio-telescopes exist. We cannot, with some convulsive Orwellian gesture, expunge a whole area of human knowledge and experience. *Lord Chalfont, "Dimensions of Violence," The Listener, Jan. 20, 1966, p 84*

Orwellism, *n.* the manipulation or distortion of facts for propaganda purposes. See also 1984.

President Nixon may have been wounded in the midterm elections but his election night insistence that the blood on his face was nothing less than the blush of victory can now be seen as a triumph of public relations. At least, an interesting example of the progress of Orwellism in national politics. *Alistair Cooke, "Austerlitz Turns Out as Waterloo," The Manchester Guardian Weekly, Dec. 5, 1970, p 5*

[so called in allusion to a society of the future completely controlled by propaganda in the novel *1984* by George Orwell. The adjective *Orwellian* has been much used to describe such a totalitarian society.]

os·mo·lal·i·ty (ˌαz məˈlæl ə ti:), *n.* degree of the pressure operative in osmosis.

...X-ray diffraction studies of hemoglobin spacing in human red cells showed that...when the cells shrank, the spacing changed much more slowly with external osmolality, presumably because the molecules were so close together that they could not easily become more tightly packed. *Arthur K. Solomon, "The State of Water in Red Cells," Scientific American, Feb. 1971, p 95*

[from *osmolal* of or relating to the *osmol*, a unit of osmotic pressure (from *osmosis* + *mol* molecular weight in grams) + *-ity* (suffix denoting quality, condition, or degree)]

os·mo·lar·i·ty (ˌαz məˈlær ə ti:), *n.* the quality or tendency characteristic of osmosis.

The most important functions of the kidney are to keep constant the volume, osmolarity and composition of the fluid which surrounds the cells of the body. *H. E. de Wardener, "The Fluid Environment," New Scientist, June 24, 1965, p 868*

[from *osmolar* of or relating to osmosis (from *osmol*, a unit of osmotic pressure + *-ar*, adj. suffix) + *-ity*. See the etymology of OSMOLALITY.]

OSO, abbreviation of *Orbiting Solar Observatory*, an unmanned scientific satellite of NASA, designed for solar research from a circular orbit around the earth. Compare OAO, OGO.

The OSO weighs about 500 lb, of which 200 lb are scientific experiments. They are launched at the rate of about one per year by a Delta rocket from Cape Kennedy into a 300-nautical-mile circular orbit at an inclination of 33°. *John E. Naugle, "Space Probes: Geophysical Experimentation," McGraw-Hill Yearbook of Science and Technology 1968, p 363*

In addition to picture-taking experiments, each OSO contains instruments that monitor the UV and x-ray radiation emitted by the entire solar disk. *George L. Withbroe, "Observatory, Astronomical," McGraw-Hill Yearbook of Science and Technology 1971, p 301*

os·te·o·ar·thro·sis (ˌαs ti: ou αrˈθrou sis), *n.* a degenerative disease of the joints occurring in middle and old age.

Professor [Vernan] Wright says the amazing thing is not that the human joint goes wrong occasionally, but how often it sees its way through a long life of stress and strain without giving trouble. When it does give trouble, however, as in osteoarthrosis (as osteoarthritis is now known), life can become very unpleasant and difficult. *"Football Players Cooperate with Medical Team to Seek Cure For Arthritis," The Times (London), Nov. 3, 1970, p 4*

[from *osteo-* bone + *arthr-* joint + *-osis* diseased condition]

Ost·po·li·tik (ˈɔːst pou liːˌtiːk), *n.* **1** a policy of the West German government to establish normal diplomatic and trade relations with the Communist countries of eastern Europe. Compare WESTPOLITIK.

In the West, the big change was Willy Brandt's narrow victory in the West German elections last October, and the formation of a new Bonn coalition government dominated by the Social Democrats, prepared to abandon the rigidities of the Adenauer foreign policy of the last twenty years and embark on an entirely new and dynamic course of Ostpolitik. In no time at all, Brandt's government changed all of the old terms of reference, and tossed out all of the clichés and dogmas in which discourse about West Germany had been locked. *Don Cook, "Brandt's New Deal," The Atlantic, July 1970, p 26*

2 a similar policy of any western nation.

Nixon as a risk-taker is something of a surprise.... But his Ostpolitik is daring. It is a repudiation of his entire past. *Richard H. Rovere, "Letter From Washington," The New Yorker, Oct. 23, 1971, p 156*

[from German, Eastern policy]

OTB, abbreviation of *off-track betting*, a state-licensed system in the United States for placing bets away from the track where the horses are racing.

Seems that the OTB computers that are linked with those at the race track developed a colic or something, and wagers at the fourteen shops around town had to be recorded manually. *Audax Minor, "The Race Track," The New Yorker, July 31, 1971, p 65*

ōutachieve, *v.t.* to surpass in achievements; do better than.

In fact, getting along with parents has never been easy

in the U.S. America has almost begged for trouble by expecting children to out-achieve their parents, yet wanting them still to look up to them. *"When the Young Teach and the Old Learn," Time, Aug. 17, 1970, p 39*

out·a·site or **out·a·sight** (ˌaut əˈsait), *adj. U.S. Slang.* **1** very advanced or unconventional; far-out.

The new film surrealists (the outasite ones) can make you suddenly think of a very large, strong, cheery wrestler, with thumbs the size of most people's wrists, trying with all his might to thread a needle. *Penelope Gilliatt, "The Current Cinema," The New Yorker, Aug. 29, 1970, p 51*

2 out of this world; incomparable; wonderful.

Chances are that parents will never like Janis Joplin or Country Joe and the Fish, no matter how many times you insist they're outasight. So save your confrontations for topics that you consider important. *Henry Muller, "Some Tips on Coping with Parents," Time, Aug. 17, 1970, p 38*

[from the phrase *out of sight*]

outer city, *U.S.* the outskirts of a city; the suburbs.

A small, growing number of black families is increasingly able to penetrate the new Outer Cities of America, the swelling bands of suburbs that ring the stagnating inner cities. *Paul Delaney, "The Outer City: Negroes Find Few Tangible Gains," The New York Times, June 1, 1971, p 1*

outgun, *v.t.* to surpass; outdo; be better than.

... I should now go on ... with a "ten best" list full of incontrovertible masterpieces. I can't do it; but I can and do suggest that my 10, whittled down despairingly from an initial list of 30, comfortably outguns Philip Hope-Wallace's for the theatre in sheer talent and the proper use of the medium's widening possibilities. *Derek Malcolm, "Cinema: Movies for Minorities," The Manchester Guardian Weekly, Dec. 26, 1970, p 18*

out-party, *n.* a political party not in power.

At the moment, then, Hubert Humphrey is under the cloud of age and the memory of battles long ago. An out-party would have to be at its last gasp to announce, even if it were true, that it has no one to turn to but a man in his sixties. *Alistair Cooke, "United States: Democrats in Line for 1972," The Manchester Guardian Weekly, Nov. 14, 1970, p 6*

For a minority out-party, any position except "me too" almost inevitably is going to become simple opposition.... *Tom Wicker, The New York Times, July 18, 1965, Sec. 4, p 8*

out·place (aut'pleis), *v.t. U.S.* to place in a new job before actual discharge from a company; help secure new employment.

Instead of simply bouncing a subordinate, the boss can send him to a firm that specializes in helping unwanted executives to find new jobs. The practitioners have even coined a euphemistic description for the process: "outplacing" executives who have been "dehired." *"Personnel, Outplacing the Dehired," Time, Sept. 14, 1970, p 83*

outplacement, *n.* the act or process of outplacing. *Also used attributively.*

The outplacement firms have their critics. Some industrial psychologists feel that an executive who has been fired needs the determination to reassess his abilities and find a job on his own. *"Personnel, Outplacing the Dehired," Time, Sept. 14, 1970, p 83*

outseg, *v.t. U.S. Slang.* to be more segregationist than; to surpass in degree of segregationist policy.

Governors Spiro Agnew of Maryland and Winthrop Rockefeller of Arkansas won office even though their Democratic opponents "outsegged" them.... *"Mississippi, More Toward Moderation," Time, Oct. 13, 1967, p 19*

[Albert] Brewer ... acquired a reputation as an effective administrator, and, most important, he has no intention of being "Out-segged" by [George C.] Wallace. *Adam Raphael, "Crow of a Bantamweight," The Manchester Guardian Weekly, April 4, 1970, p 14*

overachieve, *v.t., v.i.* to do or perform better than expected.

... this succinct yet passionate ballet overachieves its immediate purpose by choreographically summing up the Dumas story with a series of brilliantly visualized cinematic-style vignettes. *Clive Barnes, The New York Times, May 2, 1968, p 58*

When the "morning after" rolls around, many an overachieving boozer prays for a hangover cure. *Time, Feb. 15, 1971, p 33*

[back formation from *overachiever* a student whose grades surpass expectations]

overbook, *v.t., v.i.* to make more reservations for accommodations than are actually available in an airplane, ship, hotel, etc.

When Mr. Humphries continued to protest a senior official told them the aircraft was overbooked and that they had been taken off the flight on his orders. *The Times (London), Aug. 14, 1967, p 2*

And let the CAB [Civil Aeronautics Board] look closely at the custom of making passengers wait on stand-by only to be put aboard half-empty planes at the last minute — yes, I know people overbook and then fail to show up, but that knowledge does nothing for my personal convenience when some clerk has snarled my reservation.... *John Ciardi, "Manner of Speaking," Saturday Review, Aug. 31, 1968, p 7*

overcentralization, *n.* **1** the excessive concentration of political authority in a national government.

Now the country [Poland] is tense but quiet, as [Edward] Gierek attempts to consolidate his position and cope with an appalling economic mess caused by years of overconcentration on heavy industry, overcentralization and postponement of reforms. *"East Europe: The Restless Empire," Time, March 29, 1971, p 26*

2 any similar concentration of power or influence.

"It's a good lesson," one said, "of what can happen from overcentralization of economic means. Hundreds of thousands of people were tied to one company. I have a friend in the sign business who was expanding when we began to lay off. 'Your layoffs won't affect me,' he said. But now he has let half his work force go and he may have to close." *Bill Moyers, "Listening to America," Harper's, Dec. 1970, p 92*

overchoice, *n.* excessive choice; too many choices.

He [Alvin Toffler] describes the explosive growth of choice in the field of consumer goods, education, art and music, and the life-styles of a myriad of diverse social subcults which are springing up. Indeed it is the problem of overchoice, as he sees it, that helps to explain the identity crisis about which so much has already been written. *Anthony Wedgwood Benn, "Ad-hocracy," Review of "Future Shock" by Alvin Toffler, The Listener, Oct. 29, 1970, p 588*

overcontain, *v.t.* to contain or check to excess.

If a Negro writer . . . overcontains his emotions, he becomes a white Negro writer, in the long gray line from Phillis Wheatley to Frank Yerby. *Stanley E. Hyman, "Life & Letters: Richard Wright Reappraised," The Atlantic, March 1970, p 130*

overculture, *n.* a dominant culture.

In America, where the melting pot and conflict of cultures and life-styles replace a strong overculture, we lack rituals and strong agreed-upon traditions to deal with the horrors of life. *John Bart Gerald, "Conventional Wisdoms," Harper's, July 1971, p 70*

overdub, *v.t.* to add (one or more vocal or instrumental parts) to a recording.

Apparently Crosby, Stills and Nash went back to the studios to overdub their vocals on "Suite: Judy Blue Eyes", but the rest are left as originally played. *Richard Williams, "Records: Second Thoughts on Woodstock," Review of "Woodstock — Music from the Original Soundtrack," The Times (London), July 18, 1970, p 7*

She also prefers to use her own voice, overdubbed several times, as a backing choir. . . . *Richard Williams, The Times (London), Jan. 5, 1971, p 9*

overeducate, *v.t.* to provide with more education than is required for a job.

Finally, critics contend that C.U.N.Y.'s [City University of New York's] new students are being "overeducated" for nonexistent jobs, and would do better at technical training institutes. *"Education: Open Admissions: American Dream or Disaster?" Time, Oct. 19, 1970, p 66*

overexploitation, *n.* the exploiting of a natural resource beyond the level of natural replenishment.

Improved technology of fishing existing stocks ought to be accompanied by increased knowledge of the biology of commercially important fish so that natural fluctuations in stocks may be understood. Moreover, improved international cooperation should limit overexploitation of important stocks. *Ian Morris, "Restraints on the Big Fish-in," New Scientist, Dec. 3, 1970, p 374*

overhit, *v.i.* to hit too hard or too far.

Her tennis was sounder than Miss Wade's in both conception and execution. Miss Wade overhit too often in the first set but settled down to outclass Miss Krantzcke in the second, profitably examining the Australian's backhand. *Rex Bellamy, "French Championships: Miss Wade Falls to Australian," The Times (London), June 4, 1970, p 7*

over-housed, *adj.* having more space than necessary in which to live.

In 1965 they found themselves over-housed and decided to sublet the fourth floor. . . . *The Times (London), March 14, 1970, p 3*

overinflated, *adj.* too large; oversized.

It [the report] coupled this recommendation with a suggestion urging voluntary retirement after 20 years' service — regardless of age — thus opening up the ranks to younger officers presently stymied by the overinflated bureaucracy. *"The Administration, State Looks at Itself," Time, Dec. 21, 1970, p 15*

overinspirational, *adj.* excessively or self-consciously inspirational.

It ["The Virgin and the Gypsy"] is in some ways what one might term a small film, not over-ambitious or over-inspirational. *Derek Malcolm, "Miles Ahead: London Cinema," The Manchester Guardian Weekly, July 11, 1970, p 21*

overinterpretation, *n.* interpretation beyond a necessary or justified point.

Like most cosmogonic conjectures, Gamow's model is not strictly "scientific". There are traces of metaphysical speculation, of over-interpretation, of pictorialized facile concepts, and perhaps, even of suppressed religious memories. Yet no original thinker can resist the temptation to make gigantic extrapolations. *Wolfgang Yourgrau, "The Cosmos of George Gamow," New Scientist, Oct. 1, 1970, p 39*

overkill, *n.* **1** the ability to annihilate an enemy or objective several times over.

What does being ahead mean when possessing more or less overkill cannot be translated into anything that is militarily or humanly meaningful? *Seymour Melman, Columbia University, in a Letter to the Editor, The New York Times, Nov. 2, 1970, p 47*

2 something that causes harm by exceeding the required or safe limits.

This prospect of recession raised fears in certain quarters that the nation's fiscal and monetary authorities, in their desire to correct inflation, might pursue restrictive policies too long, leading to economic overkill. *Clifton H. Kreps, Jr., "Banking," The Americana Annual 1970, p 125*

[Theodore] Kheel feels that the crunch is demanded by the very nature of representative bargaining. He readily concedes that bargaining under deadline pressure can lead to miscalculations, contract inequities, and in what he calls "overkill," meaning long and bitter strikes. . . . *Fred C. Shapiro, "Profiles: Mediator," The New Yorker, Aug. 1, 1970, p 44*

— *v.i.* to kill or destroy several times over.

We maintained armed forces to defend a non-existent Empire and spent uselessly and prodigally in a vain attempt to keep abreast of the titans in capacity to kill and overkill, and in doing so we saddled ourselves with expensive commitments that hindered industrial re-equipment and social spending on housing and education. *Bernard Hollowood, "I'm Backing Idealism," Punch, Nov. 27, 1968, p 751*

overmark, *v.t.* to mark or grade too generously.

By contrast, one judge admitted that she had overmarked Wood, for no good reason that I could discover other than sympathy for a champion in distress. *John Hennessy, "Skating: Startling Decline," The Times (London), March 5, 1970, p 13*

overnutrition, *n.* ingestion of too much or unnecessary food, especially in an unbalanced diet of more fat, calcium, or other food substance than the body can effectively use.

The neglect of this branch of science is little short of a tragedy, because enormous problems of malnutrition and overnutrition remain unsolved and untackled. *Roger Lewin, "Facelift for Nutrition in the 70s," New Scientist and Science Journal, Feb. 25, 1971, p 407*

overoccupied, *adj.* too crowded; not providing sufficient space.

Its [Mexico City's] street scenes off the massive dual carriageways have an impressive shabbiness — that stained and damaged identity of overoccupied housing and underoccupied people. *Arthur Hopcraft, "The Man Who Can't Lose," The Manchester Guardian Weekly, June 6, 1970, p 5*

over-perform, *v.t.* to perform with interpretation not justified in the score or script.

Monteverdi's late four-part Mass also seemed slightly over-performed for what is basically a fairly austere work: a lot of detail was pressed to our notice, and the character of some movements was almost parodied. . . . *Stanley Sadie, "The Arts: Thrilling Monteverdi," The Times (London), March 2, 1970, p 13*

overprescribe, *v.i., v.t.* to prescribe medicine unnecessarily or in excess of what is required.

There are rogues in any profession, and in this situation there are three possible culprits apart from the farmer himself. There is the agricultural merchant who bends the regulations, there is the veterinary surgeon who overprescribes, and finally there is the unscrupulous retail pharmacist. . . . *Bernard Dixon, "Devaluing a Drug," New Scientist, March 28, 1968, p 679*

I cannot tolerate the overprescribing of unnecessary and expensive drugs which in my opinion is largely due to this pressure. *The Times (London), Oct. 12, 1967, p 9*

overprescription, *n.* the act or practice of overprescribing; unnecessary or excessive prescription of medicines.

Dr. [Ian] Hindmarch blames overprescription by doctors as the main source of illicit amphetamines. He added: "Some doctors to me are pushers. They give out up to 100 at a time to avoid being pestered weekly." *"Drug-Taking at Every School In Country," The Times (London), Nov. 4, 1970, p 6*

overqualified, *adj.* exceeding the minimum requirements for eligibility; being overly qualified.

. . . applications are flooding colleges across the country. The problem is how to cull the lucky few from the overqualified many. Forced to refine their criteria, admissions directors now seek "high-energy" students (basal metabolism readings may be next) and especially "interesting people." *"Colleges, How to be Interesting," Time, March 28, 1969, p 41*

. . . it is often hard to get the message across to personnel men "who make points hiring overqualified people for less than they're worth" and plant managers who get promoted by cutting costs. *David R. Jones, The New York Times, Feb. 3, 1968, p 30*

overquantification, *n.* too much reliance on quantity in a system of values.

The main mischiefs of megatechnics are due not to its failures and breakdowns but to its unqualified successes in overquantification. These defects were present in the very conception of the mechanical world picture, which ignored organic needs and the processes of feedback and overemphasized quantity and speed, as if quantity in itself guaranteed value in the product quantified. *Lewis Mumford, "Reflections: The Megamachine," The New Yorker, Oct. 31, 1970, p 59*

overshoot, *n.* a miss of an intended objective resulting from aiming too high or trying for too much.

He [the Soviet cyberneticist Vadim Alexandrovich Trapeznikov] sees the market economy as a system with high gain and strong feedback, possessing self-regulation, but troubled by overshoots; in contrast, in the Soviet system there is low gain and very weak feedback, "depriving it of automatic functioning and correction for minimum losses." *Zdzislaw Antoni Siemaszko, "Amplifying Human Intellectual Activity," New Scientist, Dec. 17, 1970, p 515*

oversing, *v.i.* to sing more loudly or with more interpretation than is justified.

. . . Marenka and Jenik, though, both tended to over-sing in what is, after all, London's smallest regular opera house. *Stephen Walsh, "Talent is Displayed," The Times (London), July 27, 1970, p 5*

oversophisticate, *n.* an overly sophisticated person.

. . . the formation of the Young Vic is an important event . . . . It also amounts to the first sign that Britain may at last be coming round to treating youth theatre with the respect it has long received on the Continent: and ceasing to view its artists as professionally inferior to those working for the adult public. . . . And it would be fatal if it fell into the control of . . . those over-sophisticates who turn to children as raw primitive material with which they hope to revitalize their own work. In any youth theatre policy, the young must come first. *Irving Wardle, "Children's Hour," The Times (London), March 7, 1970, p I*

overstability, *n.* excessive stability; resistance to change, fluctuation, or upset.

No segment of modern man's environment and organization as yet shows any signs of fixation or overstability, except automation itself. *Lewis Mumford, "Reflections: The Megamachine," The New Yorker, Oct. 24, 1970, p 117*

oversteering, *n.* the necessity to steer more than usually to maintain or change a course.

Surveys showed American Motors that buyers liked imported cars for their size, economy, reliability, and fun-to-drive handling. They disliked the lack of power, sensitivity to side winds, oversteering, poor ventilation, noise and lack of space. To add stability, A.M.C. made the Gremlin heavier than the average import, with a weighty rear end that should minimize oversteering. *"Autos: Shifting Down for the '70s," Time, Feb. 23, 1970, p 81*

overstretch, *n.* overextension of military forces.

By concentrating Britain's role in the European defence theatres the Navy was increasingly able to match commitments and meet the problem of overstretch. *The Times (London), March 10, 1970, p 9*

overstructured, *adj.* too elaborately planned or arranged; overorganized.

In the fifties, one was expected to play the game and *then* lie about the results. I suppose the undergraduates of today would consider our game "overstructured." But I don't mean to quibble. Bladderball [an annual ball game] is bladderball. *Calvin Trillin, "New Haven, Return of an Overstructured Bladderballer," The New Yorker, Nov. 21, 1970, p 172*

overswing, *v.i.* to swing too hard and with too much follow-through.

When he is up against a long course like the Augusta National, [Gary] Player, who is not a big man, has a tendency to overswing in search of added yardage, and as a result, he is far off balance more than occasionally at the finish of a full shot. *Herbert Warren Wind, "The Sporting Scene: A New Fifteenth and the Old Casper," The New Yorker, May 2, 1970, p 100*

overtalk, *n.* excessive talkativeness.

If forced into a June primary, [Arthur] Goldberg would still be a heavy favorite. Perhaps the only thing that could seriously hurt his chances now is his Humphreyesque penchant for overtalk. *Time, March 30, 1970, p 19*

overtechnologize, *v.t.* to make excessively tech
nological.

We asked Father [Daniel] Berrigan how he and his
friends had managed to prevent the F.B.I. from discovering his whereabouts.

"Because the F.B.I. are overtechnologized and dehumanized," he answered, with a smile. ". . . You could say that
my survival is a triumph of the love and the humanity of the
people who shelter me over the F.B.I., who are merciless
but extraordinarily unimaginative men. . . ." *"Notes From
the Underground," The New Yorker, July 25, 1970, p 22*

O·von·ic (ou'van ik), *adj.* of or relating to the
Ovshinsky effect; using glassy material for a semiconductor.

Commercial switches, known as Ovonic devices, have
been developed, which will drop their resistance rapidly
by several orders of magnitude when suitably biassed.
They will either stay "on" when the voltage is removed,
or snap "off" again—although not quite so rapidly—when
the current falls below some holding value. The type which
stays "on" is usually termed a memory switch. It can be
restored to the "off" state by a suitable pulse of current.
*John Male and Anthony Warren, "Through a Glass Easily,"
New Scientist, July 16, 1970, p 128*

The Ovonic switch is an inherently symmetrical semiconductor which can be changed instantaneously from a
high-impedance blocking state simply by increasing the
voltage or current above a given threshold level. *Kenneth
Owen, "The World of Technology" The Times (London),
Feb. 13, 1970, p 27*

[from *Ov*shinsky effect + *-onic,* as in *electronic*]

Ovonics, *n.* the use or application of Ovonic devices or of the Ovshinsky effect in electronics.

Other fields of application for Ovonics lie in a.c. control
where the bidirectionality of Ovonic switches will be of
prime importance. *Stanford R. Ovshinsky, "Amorphous
Semiconductors," Science Journal, Aug. 1969, p 78*

Ovshinsky effect, the property exhibited by certain amorphous glass-based compositions of
switching from a state of high resistance to one of
low resistance depending on the level of the voltage
applied with reference to chemical composition of
glass or a glasslike substance.

By experiment with glass, he [Ovshinsky] discovered
that if a particular voltage of electricity were introduced,
the electrons in the glass would race out of their individual
sequestrations collectively, like tribesmen hidden in the
hills awaiting a chieftain's signal to attack. The signal to
the electrons is now known as "the Ovshinsky effect." To
achieve "the Ovshinsky effect" the voltage must be
matched precisely to fit each combination of chemicals in
the glass; the voltage must also be varied with the thickness of the glass. *John Tebbel, "Twenty Years of Transistors," Saturday Review, Dec. 14, 1968, p 68*

. . . the so-called Ovshinsky effect . . . is exhibited by
amorphous glass films containing certain amounts of
arsenic, germanium, silicon, and tellurium. The resistance
of such films is voltage-sensitive, that is, the resistance is
high when the voltage across them is below a certain threshold level. When the voltage exceeds the threshold, the
resistance abruptly switches to a low state. The threshold
can be preselected by adjusting the mixture of elements in
the glass. This mechanism has applications ranging from
simple alternating or direct current switching to logic and
memory functions in computers. *Samuel Weber, "Electronics," The World Book Science Annual 1969, p 298*

His discovery of the Ovshinsky effect is especially
startling because Ovshinsky is a self-taught scientist who
went no further in his formal education than Akron's
Buchtel High School. *Mort LaBrecque, "The Ovshinsky
Effect," Encyclopedia Science Supplement (Grolier) 1971,
p 369*

[named after the American inventor Stanford R.
Ovshinsky, who discovered it]

own-brand, *adj.* bearing the name or brand of the
store which sells it instead of the manufacturer's
name.

The principles of own-brand groceries date back to the
turn of the century when stores such as Lipton and Home &
Colonial did much of their own packaging. *Patricia Tisdall,
"Own Brands are Money-savers," The Times (London),
Feb. 16, 1970, p IX*

owner-occupation, *n. British.* occupation of a
house by its owner; homeownership.

The truth is that less homes have been built for owner-
occupation in the last six months than in the same period
a year ago. *Arthur Jones, "General Election Broadcasts,"
The Listener, March 24, 1966, p 431*

"Freedom to choose between tenancy and owner-occupation over a wide range of rents and prices is . . . (an)
essential ingredient in the satisfaction of housing needs",
the plan says. *Tony Aldous, The Times (London), Sept. 25,
1970, p 3*

owner-occupied, *adj. British.* lived in by the
owner.

And gains on owner-occupied houses are not subject to
tax. *Charles Ashe, The Sunday Times (London), March 23,
1969, p 28*

owner-occupier, *n. British.* a person who owns the
house he lives in; a homeowner.

A house does not disappear from use just because it
changes ownership from a local authority to an owner-
occupier. *The Times (London), Feb. 8, 1967, p 14*

ox·a·cil·lin (ˌɑk sə'sil ən), *n.* a semisynthetic form of
penicillin that is resistant to neutralizing by penicillinase (the enzyme which destroys natural penicillin). Compare AMPICILLIN, CLOXACILLIN.

He was also given heavy doses of antibiotics, including a
gram of chloramphenicol, a gram of oxacillin, two million
units of penicillin. . . . *Michael Crichton, "The High Cost
of Cure: How a Hospital Bill Grows 17 Feet Long," The
Atlantic, March 1970, p 50*

Oxbridgean or **Oxbridgian,** *n.* a student or graduate of Oxford or Cambridge University.

His [John Ney's] evidence is personal observation,
engagingly wicked gossip, and literary quotation, with
which he is as apt as an eighteenth-century Oxbridgean
with the Latin tag. *Phoebe Adams, Review of "The European Surrender" by John Ney, The Atlantic, May 1970,
p 132*

—*adj.* of or relating to Oxford or Cambridge Universities. Compare REDBRICK.

Hard on the heels of the US ping pong team were Arthur
Galston and Ethan Signer, respectively professors of
biology at Yale and MIT, and the first American scientists
to visit China for two decades. . . . Galston I encountered
during and after a mini press conference in the ivy-covered,
Oxbridgian atmosphere of Yale. *Graham Chedd, New
Scientist and Science Journal, June 17, 1971, p 706*

[from *Oxbridge*, a blend of *Ox*ford and Cam*bridge*, used as a collective name to distinguish this type of traditional institution from the newer British universities. *Oxbridge* was apparently first used by Thackeray in *The History of Pendennis* (serialized in 1848-1850) as the name of the university which Arthur Pendennis, the novel's hero, attends. In 1928 Virginia Woolf revived the name in a series of lectures published in 1929 as *A Room of One's Own.*]

o·zone·sonde ('ou,zoun,sand), *n.* a radiosonde (a radio-transmitting instrument package carried aloft by a balloon) designed to measure the distribution of ozone above the earth and transmit the data back to earth.

In the past two years there has been an increased emphasis on several aspects of antarctic meteorology,... albedo programs, meteorological studies aboard the Eltanin, and the inclusion of vertical coverage through radiometersondes, ozonesondes, and gammasondes. *A. P. Crary, "Antarctica: Meteorology," Bulletin of the Atomic Scientists, Jan. 1964, p 29*

P

p, abbreviation of *penny* or *pence* in the newly established British decimal system (effective February 15, 1971) in which a pound equals 100 new pence, as in *4p, 53 1/2p*, etc. See also NEW PENNY.

The urgency of facing that prospect needs emphasizing. The unfamiliarity of the new coinage, with pence abbreviated to "p" rather than "d", at 100 to the pound, will be the least distressing aspect of the change. *Adam Fergusson, The Times (London), April 17, 1968, p 11*

pa'an·ga (pɑː'ɑːŋ gə), *n.* the monetary unit of the kingdom of Tonga, at par with the Australian dollar. 2.14 pa'angas equal $2.40 or £1 sterling.

Tonga has decided against calling its new decimal currency unit the dollar because the native word, "tola", also means a pig's snout, the soft end of a coconut, or, in vulgar language, a mouth. The new unit, to be introduced next year, will be called "pa'anga", which has only two alternative meanings—a coin-shaped seed and, not surprisingly, money. *The Times (London), May 21, 1966, p 8*

pablum, *n.* **1** a source of sustenance; fuel.

In one week Spiro Agnew ascribed moral decay to the universities, Dr Spock, and the Presidential Commission on Campus Unrest, which, he said, had produced a report which 'was sure to be taken as more pablum for the permissivists'. *Clive Irving, "Views," The Listener, Oct. 22, 1970, p 538*

2 something intellectually watered down or insipid; pap.

"You can go to Hollywood as a second assistant unit manager for ten years, make the long, stultifying climb, and finally turn out predigested pablum." *The New Yorker, "Talk of the Town: Horror Comedy," July 23, 1966, p 24*

[from *Pablum*, trade name of a bland but very nourishing cereal for infants, with meaning (especially of def. 1) influenced by *pabulum* food, nourishment (from Latin *pābulum* fodder)]

pach·y·os·te·o·morph (,pæk iː'ɑs ti: ə,mɔrf), *n.* an evolutionary level characterized by heavy bone structure. *Also used attributively.*

As a number of separate lineages approached and attained the pachyosteomorph level of organization in the late Middle and early Upper Devonian, arthrodires underwent a remarkable burst of secondary adaptive radiation, to become the dominant fishes of the time. *Roger S. Miles, "Paleozoic Fish," McGraw-Hill Yearbook of Science and Technology 1971, p 313*

[from Greek *pachýs* thick + *ostéon* bone + *morphé* form]

pa·cif·ar·in (pə'sif ər ən), *n.* a bacterial substance that prevents certain germs from causing disease while permitting them to survive within the organism they have invaded.

Pacifarin, found in certain batches of whole wheat and dried egg and produced by bacteria, protects mice infected with mouse typhoid. It was identified as enterobactin (a compound of known structure), recently discovered by biochemists at the University of California, Berkeley. *George M. Briggs, "Foods and Nutrition," 1972 Britannica Yearbook of Science and the Future, 1971, p 251*

[from *pacifier* + *-arin*, as in *heparin*]

pacification, *n.* the elimination of guerrilla or terrorist activity in an area, especially by removal of the inhabitants and often destruction of the buildings, food supplies, crops, and other things useful to guerrillas operating in the area.

Whatever its name, the object of pacification for nearly two decades has been to wrest rural areas from Viet Cong control and bring them under the aegis of the Saigon government. *Time, Oct. 26, 1970, p 48*

Although substantial parts remained under Vietcong control, rural development teams were making progress in their dual task of pacification and social and agricultural uplift. *Roland Challis, "Foreign News: Starving Them Out," The Listener, March 7, 1968, p 294*

In order to accelerate the realization of pacification and particularly in order to denigrate the morale of the Viet Cong forces, it may be necessary at some time in the future to put demonstrable retaliatory pressure on the North. *Memorandum, "Vietnam Situation," from Secretary of Defense Robert S. McNamara to President Lyndon B.*

Johnson, Dec. 21, 1963, The New York Times, June 13, 1971, Sec. 4, p 36

It [the book] draws critical distinctions between true peacekeeping (dogged holding of the ring) and the sort of "pacification" the British Army considers itself expert in: no more than heavy-handed police operations in support of the civil government. *Peter Preston, "Partial Peace," Review of "The Impartial Soldier" by Michael Harbottle, The Manchester Guardian Weekly, June 6, 1970, p 15*

package, *n.* a compact assembly of various units or elements. Compare ARRAY.

Its substitute on *Apollo 11* was a package of three experiments—a passive seismometer, laser reflector and solar wind sensor. *Peter Gwynne, "NASA Asserts Lunar Flights Good for Science," Science Journal, Feb. 1970, p 4*

pad, *n. U.S. Slang.* **1 the pad,** graft which is received by and shared among various members of a police precinct or department for ignoring illegal activities.

When a cop was transferred to a new post, the pad from his old station kept up for another two months. *"Investigations: Guarding the Guardians," Time, Nov. 1, 1971, p 23*

Mr. Armstrong said the testimony would show how the gamblers of the city paid off the policemen on a regular monthly basis after they had been placed on what is called "the pad." Narcotic bribes, the counsel said, usually "are made on an individual score basis." *The New York Times, Oct. 19, 1971, p 47*

2 on the pad, sharing in the graft collected by policemen of a precinct or department for ignoring illegal activities.

"I never knew a plainclothesman," said Phillips, "who wasn't on the pad." And yet for years it went further than that: it was as if the whole town was on the pad, as if a sidewalk couldn't be cleaned without grease, as if the garbage could not be carted without paying grease. . . . *Pete Hamill, The New York Post, Oct. 20, 1971, p 47*

The Knapp Commission investigating police corruption in New York City has added a new phrase to the public lexicon: "On the pad." It refers to lists of policemen paid to ignore illegal activities. As the Commission begins two weeks of public hearings, it has also underscored an old truth: The public plays a role in setting public policies, even those unofficial policies followed by policemen on the pad. *The New York Times, Oct. 21, 1971, p 46*

[so called from the secret pad on which the names of policemen accepting graft were listed]

paint-in, *n.* an undertaking by a group of people to paint or decorate the exterior of buildings or other structures to improve, or show the need to improve, the appearance of a run-down area.

What is a Paint-In? Well, it's a protest, like a sit-in, except that people paint and other people gather round and the mayor and the newspapers and the civic boosters and the provincial government all stop swinging at each other and start swinging together. *Barry Broadfoot, Maclean's, May 14, 1966, p 3*

Across the street from the White House, the Nixons have permitted what may well be the sprightliest exhibition of contemporary art in town. There, a plain plywood fence had been built around Lafayette Park while construction work is going on. Depressed by the sight, Jane Shay, a staffer at the nearby National Trust for Historic Preservation, organized a one-day paint-in by a group of Washington high school art students. The result was a half-mile mural

in which [were] green trees, pink pigs. . . . Tricia [Nixon] even walked down on the day of the paint-in and added a few dabs herself. *Time, "Art: Patrons," June 20, 1969, p 64*

[see **-in**]

pair bond, a prolonged and exclusive union between a male and female pair of a species; a monogamous bond or union.

Ritual "Dance" of the wandering albatross is actually the agonistic responses of an unmated male and female that are not familiar with each other. The signals, both visual and vocal, alternately attract, repel and appease the potential partner until eventually the birds are at ease in each other's presence and a pair bond is established. *W. L. N. Tickell, "The Great Albatrosses," Scientific American, Nov. 1970, p 90*

pair bonding, the act or condition of forming a pair bond.

Similarly pair-bonding, which is the ornithologists' in-phrase for procreative conjunction between sexually ardent cocks and hens, can be welded by the formal presentation of food (courtship feeding) or duetted songs which, in certain African bush-shrikes, reach a state of harmonic perfection rarely matched by human vocalists. *John Hillaby, "The Anatomy of Behaviour," New Scientist, June 17, 1965, p 768*

Pais·ley·ism ('peiz li:,iz əm), *n.* a movement in Northern Ireland founded by Ian Paisley, born 1926, head of the Free Presbyterian Church of Ulster, directed against ecumenical and other efforts to draw together Catholics and Protestants.

Whether or not one agrees with all aspects of Brian Moore's analysis of the unhappy Ulster situation, he is correct in perceiving that its solution lies in bringing this festering evil to a head and performing the necessary surgery. . . . Once this is done and the evil spirits of Paisleyism exorcized, I think that the "Wearers of the Green" and their largely Scot protagonists of the Six Counties will rediscover their common humanity and basic Celtic heritage. *Joseph E. Hickey, Jr., Wethersfield, Conn., in a Letter to the Editor, The Atlantic, Dec. 1970, p 34*

Pais·ley·ite ('peiz li:,ait), *n.* a follower of Ian Paisley; a supporter of Paisleyism. Compare DEVLINITE.

Two Irish independents already have broken through and taken their seats in the Commons, and on June 18 there are to be Paisleyites and Devlinites in the field. . . . *David Wood, The Times (London), May 19, 1970, p 1*

—*adj.* of or relating to Paisleyites or Paisleyism.

Martin Waddell's whimsical portrait of an Ur-Protestant Ulster bigot is a bad case of bandwaggonry. . . . Augustus Harland, the Paisleyite monster whose diary this purports to be, is a grotesque parody of a human being. *Derek Mahon, "Beyond Justice," Review of "A Little Bit British" by Martin Waddell, The Listener, Oct. 22, 1970, p 555*

Paki, *n. British Slang.* a Pakistani.

"Cruising" by Gerald Walker is a sharp, terse piece of work, half novel and half thriller. . . . Whether the hated object is queers, blacks or Pakis, the inadequacies breeding the hatred are faithfully put down here. *Julian Symons, "The Other Island," Review of "Cruising" by Gerald Walker, The Sunday Times (London), June 6, 1971, p 32*

Palaeosiberian, *n.* any of a number of aboriginal peoples of northeastern Siberia speaking languages that do not belong to any of the large language families.

. . . the Palaeosiberians and a small Mongol enclave in Afghanistan . . . use these two methods of taking Soma. *Robert Graves, "The Divine Rite of Mushrooms," The Atlantic, Feb. 1970, p 111*

pa·laz·zo pajamas (pə'lɑːt sou), a woman's garment for lounging or semiformal wear, consisting of loose, wide-legged trousers and a matching jacket or blouse.

All these varieties continued into the nineteen-sixties, when they were joined by such other forms as palazzo pajamas (wide enough to sweep around a palace in), culottes, pants dresses and pants suits. *Bernadine Morris, The New York Times, April 30, 1968, p 52*

pa·le·o- ('pei liː ouˑ) or *(British)* **pa·lae·o-**, combining form meaning "ancient," "prehistoric," or "of geological times," usually attached to names of established branches of science or to words describing some measurable physical phenomenon or activity. Compounds formed recently include:

palaeoanthropology, *n.:* Palaeoanthropology is now an exciting and fast developing science. . . . New fossil discoveries modify our ideas about human evolution every year, and new techniques for dating and evaluating the fossils themselves cause us to revise our interpretation. *Bernard Campbell, New Scientist, June 11, 1970, p 544*

palaeochronology, *n.:* All dating methods based on counting the ridges of fossil shells and corals are necessarily hazardous because the animals may miss out growth ridges in a systematic fashion and many species of fossil "clock" have no exact living counterpart against which to be regulated. In spite of these and other pitfalls, which further research may be expected at least to make more evident, the subject of palaeochronology is one of the most promising and least well trodden fields of science. *The Times (London), June 4, 1970, p 13*

palaeoengineering, *n.:* In flying animals, engineering requirements are particularly stringent. . . . The problems of strength and powered flight become more severe as the animal becomes larger, although increased size makes it easier to achieve a good performance in gliding flight. We have been examining the palaeoengineering of Pteranodon ingens, the largest pterodactyl and also the largest flying creature ever to exist. . . . *George Whitfield and Cherrie Bramwell, "Palaeoengineering: Birth of a New Science," New Scientist and Science Journal, Dec. 23, 1971, p 202*

paleoclimate, *n.:* . . . a new independent method has been developed to study paleoclimates based on deep ice cores from the ice sheets in Antarctica and Greenland. *W. Dansgaard, "Paleoclimatology," McGraw-Hill Yearbook of Science and Technology 1971, p 311*

paleoenvironmental, *adj.:* After a basic introduction from the geologist's viewpoint, the book discusses the occurrence of organic residues in freshwater sediments and sedimentary rocks, and evaluates both the importance of these residues in paleoenvironmental and related problems, and their role as biochemical fossils. *Review of "Non-Marine Organic Geochemistry" by Frederick M. Swain, Science News, Feb. 6, 1971, p 101*

paleozoogeography, *n.:* . . . hope has been entertained that major gaps in knowledge of the fossil record will be filled . . . by new finds in Antarctica, China, and Australia. But the presence of North American and European genera in these faunas poses new problems of paleozoogeography. *Roger S. Miles, "Paleozoic Fish," McGraw-Hill Yearbook of Science and Technology 1971, p 312*

See also the entries below.

paleobiochemistry, *n.* a branch of paleontology (the study of fossils) that deals with the biochemical constituents of fossil animals and plants.

In one of the first applications of paleobiochemistry it has been found that hydrocarbon compounds in rocks 3 billion years old may be composed of fossilized chlorophyll. *Franklin J. Tobey, Jr., "Nuclear Physics: Radioactive Fallout," 1969 Collier's Encyclopedia Year Book, p 406*

paleogenetics, *n.* the study of the genetics of fossil animals and plants.

Cytochrome c is a key molecule in the final stages of the "burning" of foodstuffs for the provision of energy in living cells, forming part of a chain along which electrons are passed—eventually—to water. It has also become the star of the young science of chemical palaeogenetics, enabling evolution to be studied at the molecular level. *New Scientist, "A Secret Role for Cytochrome c?" July 16, 1970, p 119*

paleogeophysics, *n.* the study of the physical phenomena within or upon the earth in geological times.

The rapidly growing subject of palaeogeophysics has an immediate appeal because of the apparent unlikelihood of being able to measure the Earth's physical properties in the dim and distant past. *New Scientist, March 21, 1968, p 649*

paleoichthyologist, *n.* an ichthyologist who specializes in fossil fish.

The Gogo fish fauna thus offers excellent opportunities for studies in sedimentary petrology and paleoecology, fields which are usually ignored by paleoichthyologists. *Roger S. Miles, "Paleozoic Fish," McGraw-Hill Yearbook of Science and Technology 1971, p 312*

paleolimnology, *n.* the study of the condition of lakes, ponds, etc., especially fresh-water lakes and ponds, in geological times.

Techniques for the analysis of the evidence from sea-level changes, desert evolution, ocean sediments, and lake sediments (paleolimnology) have not been applied or perfected to the point where these disciplines can contribute reliably to the picture of Holocene climate, although all four disciplines give promise of significant potential contribution. *Hurd C. Willett, "Climatic Evolution," Science, March 15, 1968, p 1221*

paleomagnetic, *adj.* of or relating to paleomagnetism.

Eighteen scientists and engineers, supported by 16 officers and men of a military aviation detachment, made geological, biological, topographic, geophysical, and paleomagnetic observations. . . . Paleomagnetic investigations of rocks of Jurassic age were compared with those of rocks of the same age in other regions of Antarctica to evolve the tectonic history of the continent. *Laurence M. Gould, "Antarctica: Scientific Programs," Britannica Book of the Year 1968, p 95*

paleomagnetism, *n.* a branch of geophysics dealing with the earth's magnetic fields in geological times, especially through the study of magnetism in ancient rocks.

Recent studies of paleomagnetism (the determination of the location of the earth's magnetic poles in past eras) have brought renewed interest in the theory of continental drift. *George R. Tilton, "Geochemistry," The World Book Science Annual 1967, p 301*

paleomagnetist, *n.* a specialist in paleomagnetism.

A stern criticism which palaeomagnetists have always had to face from their colleagues in physics working purely on present-day magnetism is over the long-term stability of the magnetic minerals within their rock samples. *New Scientist, Dec. 17, 1970, p 491*

...the results are important because what the palaeomagnetist might interpret as a magnetisation produced by cooling in a field of given strength could have a completely different origin. *New Scientist and Science Journal, April 29, 1971, p 248*

paleotemperature, *n.* the temperature of oceans and seas in geological times, obtained by measuring or analyzing the chemical components of fossil sediments. *Also used attributively.*

Fifteen years ago Dr. Cesare Emiliani, now at the University of Miami's School of Marine and Atmospheric Sciences, published what he called a generalized paleotemperature curve. As extended further in 1966, it shows how surface temperatures in the equatorial Atlantic Ocean and adjacent seas have varied over the past 425,000 years. *Science News, May 23, 1970, p 505*

pal·y·tox·in (ˌpæl ə'tɑk sən), *n.* a highly poisonous substance discharged by polyps, especially as protection against octopuses.

The scientists collected some of the polyps [limumake-o-Hana], ground them up, and extracted some of the poison, which is called palytoxin. They learned several things about the palytoxin, but its incredible potency was the most interesting. *Richard J. Goss, "Zoology," The World Book Science Annual 1972 (1971), p 376*

[probably from Greek *palýnein* to strew, sprinkle + English *toxin*]

PAN (pæn), *n.* acronym for:
1 peroxyacetyl nitrate.

...the principal constituents of smog...include ozone, an unstable toxic form of oxygen; nitrogen dioxide, an irritating reddish brown gas; peroxyacetyl nitrate (PAN), an explosive liquid; aldehydes; and acrolein, a poisonous, colorless or yellowish liquid. *John T. Middleton, "Air Pollution," Encyclopedia Science Supplement (Grolier) 1971, p 244*

2 polyacrylonitrile (a polymer of acrylonitrile, used for making synthetic fibers).

While in principle a number of precursor fibres could give rise to carbon fibres with very good mechanical properties, this has yet to be established. PAN (polyacrylonitrile) may have special advantage, in that the nitrogen atoms may play a part in stabilizing the structure. *Dwarakanath V. Badami, "Carbon Fibre: A Question of Structure," New Scientist, Feb. 5, 1970, p 254*

Pan-Africanist, *n.* an advocate or supporter of the political union of all African nations.

Since its independence in September 1966, Botswana has sought to steer a balanced course between the political pressures of Pan-Africanists and the pressures resulting from strong economic ties with the Republic of South Africa. *Marion E. Doro, 1968 Collier's Encyclopedia Year Book, p 157*

—*adj.* of or relating to Pan-Africanists or their policies.

He did not refer to the split between the A.N.C. [African National Congress] and another organization in South Africa, the Pan-Africanist Congress, but said that the A.N.C. intended to wage war from within, not invade from outside. *David Yudelman, The Times (London), March 11, 1968, p 2*

Pan-Asianism, *n.* a movement or policy seeking the political union of all Asian nations.

It would be more than a half truth to say that his [Nehru's] pan-Asian feelings were a product of his British education rather than of his actual experience. How else could a man see India and China as brothers except from an overlay of western socialist idealism? Besides this reflection of the western concept 'Asia', there has been the nationalist aftermath, an attempt to keep pan-Asianism alive the better to deal with major outside powers. *Richard Harris, "What is Asia?: Leadership in Asia," The Listener, June 30, 1966, p 932*

Pan-Asianist, *n.* an advocate or supporter of Pan-Asianism.

"To my father it was completely different—he was a pan-Asianist who believed in a unified Asia free of colonialist rule", says Miss Maw. *The Times (London), April 13, 1968, p 10*

pan·chres·ton (pæn'kres ˌtɑn), *n.* an explanation designed to cover or to fit all possible cases equally well; a catch-all explanation or proposition.

Finally I would like to suggest that there has been a tendency in psychoanalysis for the concept of infantile psychosexuality to have lost the original freshness and vigor with which it was presented, and to have become a dogma, and even a panchreston, a kind of vacuum cleaner gobbling up many varieties of behavior and reducing them all to the same tired explanations....*Paul Chodoff, Washington, D.C., in a Letter to the Editor, Science News, Feb. 25, 1967, p 178*

[an extended sense of obsolete English *panchreston* universal medicine, panacea (recorded in the *OED* with citations from 1632 through 1706), from Greek *pánchrēston*, neuter *adj.*, good for everything, from *pan-* all, everything + *chrēstós* useful, good]

panda car, *British.* a police prowl car.

Five children, who formed a "secret five club" and helped catch two thieves, are to be given a ride in a police panda car as a reward. *The Times (London), March 17, 1970, p 2*

The Panda car got on to us. *Clive Borrell, The Times (London), Feb. 3, 1972, p 5*

[from the color configuration of the cars]

Pan·gae·a (pæn'dʒi: ə), *n.* a hypothetical continent that included all the land masses of the earth before the Triassic period (about 200 million years ago) when continental drift began with the breaking away of the northern group (Laurasia) from the southern group (Gondwana).

According to our reconstruction, Pangaea was a land mass of irregular outline surrounded by the universal ocean of Panthalassa: the ancestral Pacific. *Robert S. Dietz and John C. Holden, "The Breakup of Pangaea," Scientific American, Oct. 1970, p 35*

[coined in the 1920's by Alfred L. Wegener, a German geologist, from Greek *pan-* all + *gaîa* land]

pangram, *n.* a sentence made up to include all the letters of the alphabet.

The pangram, an ancient form of word play, is an attempt to get the maximum number of different letters into a sentence of minimum length. *Martin Gardner, "Mathematical Games," Scientific American, Sept. 1964, p 222*

[from *pan-* all + *-gram* letter, as in *anagram*]

pangrammatic, *adj.* of or relating to a pangram.

Also represented: Sotadic [palindromic] verses, pangrammatic rubaiyat and problems in alphametics (alphabet arithmetic). *Time, Sept. 17, 1965, p 72*

pantdress, *n.* a dress with a skirt divided and sewed like trousers; a dress with culottes. Compare PANTSKIRT.

At far left, a Persian pantdress in pure wool (with a matching mini-nightie, about $60). *Maclean's, Dec. 1967, p 35*

This time, it is a more coordinated trend—pant-skirts, pant-dresses, pant-suits, tops and pants, and so on, as contrasted with the single item it used to be, he said in a recent interview here. *Isadore Barmash, The New York Times, July 15, 1968, p 43*

Panther, *n.* short for BLACK PANTHER.

His [Bobby Seale's] trial in New Haven for complicity in the murder of a fellow Panther kept the campus in a state of near-hysteria throughout the last term. *John Fischer, "The Easy Chair: Black Panthers and Their White Hero Worshipers," Harper's, Aug. 1970, p 18*

. . . the alleged bias for "activists," typically meant that delegates were presidents of youth organizations or youth members of town councils, not Weathermen or Panthers as the word suggests. *Don Mitchell, "Letter From a Cold Place: Heavy Snow and Cheerless Rhetoric in the Mountains of Colorado," Harper's, Aug. 1971, p 26*

Pantherism, *n.* the extremist or militant doctrines of the Black Panthers.

'Hair,' is probably the most vicious, counter-revolutionary play going. It promotes a kind of integrationist, dope-above-hope, psychedelic Pantherism. *LeRoi Jones, The New York Times Book Review, June 27, 1971, p 27*

panti-, Also spelled **panty-.** a combining form designating panties worn with some other garment as one piece.

panti-slip, *n.:* She has introduced a . . . "panti-slip," a bit of nylon tricot edged with lace and worn with a matching camisole. *Joan Cook, The New York Times, Jan. 8, 1966, p 16*

panti-tights, *n.pl.:* "Sorry," the man in overalls said. "We're right out of them. What about a pair of panti-tights?" *William Davis, The Manchester Guardian Weekly, April 11, 1970, p 14*

pantyleg stocking: Gold and silver pantyleg stockings (at $4 each) are selling so fast stores can't keep them in stock. *Time, Dec. 2, 1966, p 53*

pantshoes, *n.pl.* shoes designed to be worn with flaring or bell-bottomed trousers.

Pants had to be worn with staunch pantshoes to avoid looking wobbly. *Edith R. Locke, "Fashion," 1970 Collier's Encyclopedia Year Book, p 232*

pantskirt, *n.* a divided skirt resembling trousers; culottes. Compare PANTDRESS.

The pants and pantskirt as shown by Marc Bohan at Dior are for the country and around the house. *The Times (London), Aug. 3, 1964, p 11*

This time, it is a more coordinated trend—pant-skirts, pant-dresses, pant-suits, tops and pants and so on, as contrasted with the single item it used to be, he said in a recent interview here. *Isadore Barmash, The New York Times, July 15, 1968, p 43*

pantsuit, *n.* Also spelled **pants suit.** a woman's suit with matching jacket and trousers.

The people strolling down Kasr el Nil, Cairo's most fashionable shopping district, look better dressed than in past years. There is only an occasional miniskirt or pant-suit, but the clothes generally seem more stylish and the shop windows brighter and better stocked with locally made shoes, purses, textiles. *Hedrick Smith, "Where Egypt Stands," The Atlantic, Jan. 1971, p 40*

Partisans of the pants suit argued that women were wearing pants anyway and the suit was neater than haphazard tops and slacks. *Angela Taylor, "Women's Fashions," 1967 Collier's Encyclopedia Year Book, p 210*

pan·ty·hose ('pæn ti:,houz), *n. pl.* or *sing.* Also spelled **pantihose.** a woman's garment worn from the waist down to replace both panties and stockings, originally made for wear with miniskirts.

There are now not only government dollar stores [in Cairo, Egypt] but a string of busy boutiques on Sharwabi Pasha Street as well, openly offering Parisian perfumes, German pantyhose, British woolens, Italian slacks and bras, American Techmatic razors, fancy French cravats, all at outrageous markups. *Hedrick Smith, "Where Egypt Stands," The Atlantic, Jan. 1971, p 40*

"The stretchiest stockings and panti-hose yet, resulting from a new concept of hosiery manufacture," were announced by the British firm Pretty Polly. *Phyllis West Heathcote, "Fashion and Dress," Britannica Book of the Year 1969, p 339*

pa·pa·raz·zo (,pɑ: pə'rɑ:t sou), *n.; pl.* **pa·pa·raz·zi** (,pɑ: pə'rɑ:t si:). *Italian.* an aggressive free-lance photographer who pursues celebrities to take their pictures wherever they go.

Off for a month's vacation from the attentions of Rome's *paparazzi* went Sophia Loren, 35, with her husband, Italian Film Producer Carlo Ponti, and their 18-month-old son Cheepy (C. P. Jr.). *Time, July 20, 1970, p 32*

They are the *paparazzi* of the London picture market, a wheeling horde of newly self-styled impresarios of the arts, past masters of the coolly imperceptible bid, fur-coated, felt-hatted, and above all, undercapitalised. *Benita Egge, The Sunday Times (London), April 13, 1969, p 60*

United States District Court Judge Irving Ben Cooper ruled yesterday that the activities of Ronald E. Galella, the self-styled "paparazzo" photographer, had "relentlessly invaded" the right to privacy of Mrs. Aristotle Onassis and had interfered with the protective duties of the Secret Service. *The New York Times, July 6, 1972, p 1*

paper factor, a terpene of the balsam fir which is a naturally occurring insect juvenile hormone.

Paper factor is highly effective in killing the cotton stainer bug, which destroys up to half the cotton crop in Asia, Africa and South America each year. *Jane E. Brody, The New York Times, Nov. 29, 1966 [page not recorded]*

The tree synthesizes what we named the "paper factor," and this substance accompanies the pulp all the way to the printed page. *Carroll M. Williams, Scientific American, July 1967, p 17*

[so called for the fact that it was first discovered in newsprint]

paper gold, another name for SPECIAL DRAWING RIGHTS.

When it was first proposed that the world's reserves be supplemented by new drawing rights in the IMF [International Monetary Fund]—a matter of giving the fund the right to print "paper gold" in carefully controlled quantities—the Americans launched the idea that the rights should be awarded in the first place to the poor countries. *Anthony Harris, The Manchester Guardian Weekly, Sept. 27, 1969, p 22*

... the far from reassuring phrase "paper gold" became the common nickname for S.D.R.s. *John Brooks, "A Reporter At Large," The New Yorker, Oct. 23, 1971, p 130*

paperless, *adj.* transferring information or data without the use of paper.

An experimental paperless service in San Francisco already provides computer transfer of funds from the accounts of industrial corporations to those of their employees.... *New Scientist and Science Journal, May 13, 1971, p 386*

Pap smear, short for *Papanicolaou smear,* a diagnostic test chiefly for cervical or uterine cancer.

The time may come when urinalysis as a test for breast cancer may become as common—and effective—as the Pap smear for early diagnosis of uterine malignancy. *Faye Marley, Science News, Dec. 16, 1967, p 595*

[named after George *P*apanicolaou, 1883-1962, a Greek-born American anatomist who developed the test]

PAR (pɑr), *n.* acronym for *perimeter acquisition radar,* a radar forming the outermost part of an antiballistic missile system. See also MSR.

Theoretically, enemy missiles would be picked up soon after launch by PAR (perimeter acquisition radar), which would inform the central control system. *Robert J. Ranger, "Defense," Britannica Book of the Year 1970, p 253*

par·a ('pær ə), *n.* short for *parachutist, paratrooper, paracommando,* etc.

But these days the image of Saint-Cyr [French military academy] is that of an electronic scientist rather than that of a future cavalry officer, or even "para." *Nesta Roberts, "Letter from Paris: The Caged Finch," The Manchester Guardian Weekly, March 21, 1970, p 7*

The Belgian paras sustained only seven casualties in rescuing the hostages. *Time, Dec. 4, 1964, p 28*

[from French]

para-, a combining form abstracted from *paramilitary, paramedical,* etc., and meaning "related to but not quite," "supplementary to," "subordinate to." In this sense, extended from *para-,* meaning "beside" or "near," the form has recently become very productive in various professional circles forming such new compounds as the following:

para-academic, *adj.:* [Paul] Goodman has, in great measure, become the spokesman of the alienated and the rebellious, and he has become a sort of roving prophet for the independent students who are establishing free universities and similar para-academic organizations. *Peter Schrag, "Education's 'Romantic' Critics," Saturday Review, Feb. 18, 1967, p 82*

para-academic, *n.:* We who spoke at the counter-commencement are not, in Mr. Hechinger's words, "camp-

followers to the youth movement," or "para-academics," nor are we supporters of force and violence against anyone in the conduct of university affairs. *Erich Fromm, Dwight MacDonald, and Harold Taylor, The New York Times, June 17, 1968, p 38*

parabanking, *n.:* ... banks overseas, stimulating parabanking enterprises, and arranging banking mergers. *João Sousa da Câmara, The Times (London), Nov. 3, 1970, p 19*

parabiospheric, *adj.:* ... as a terrestrial envelope the biosphere obviously has a somewhat irregular shape, inasmuch as it is surrounded by an indefinite "parabiospheric" region in which some dormant forms of life are present. *G. Evelyn Hutchinson, "The Biosphere," Scientific American, Sept. 1970, p 45*

para-book, *n.:* ... books that looked like books but weren't books—that is to say, para-books, with titles like *Le Petomane, Fanny Hill's Cookbook, Private Eyesores, A Book of Bloomers. Robert Robinson, The Listener, Nov. 4, 1971, p 618*

para-church, *n.:* ... groups that don't attract or seek publicity, that meet in upper rooms.... This is sometimes called the para-church, the church of the future which is beginning to take shape.... *Auriol Stevens, The Manchester Guardian Weekly, Dec. 12, 1970, p 14*

paracompact, *adj.:* Modern General Topology ... includes, besides regular material, also recent theories, especially on metric space, paracompact space, and mapping. *Science News, June 27, 1970, p 616*

para-governmental, *adj.:* It seems that the Viet Cong set up a much more efficient political and para-governmental structure in certain areas than was previously realised. *David Leitch, The Sunday Times (London), Feb. 25, 1968, p 8*

para-institution, *n.:* Increasingly, homosexuals are creating their own public para-institutions, including churches. And with the proliferation of such radical groups as the Gay Liberation Front and the Gay Activists Alliance, they are taking to the streets. *Time, July 13, 1970, p 6*

para-party, *n.:* The General, who is 71, said in an interview with a reporter of the Athens newspaper Ethnos: "Give me a whip and I will show you what I can do. What is all this? Parties, para-parties, warring cliques and para-state organizations? Let them give me a whip and we shall see." *"Grivas Says Whip is Needed," The Times (London), March 19, 1970, p 7*

para-police, *adj.:* ... the Rangers can, in many instances, be considered a kind of spontaneous para-police force.... *James Alan McPherson, "Chicago's Blackstone Rangers," The Atlantic, June 1969, p 94*

parapolitical, *adj.:* To elucidate the parapolitical function of modern spying, Hagen explores the development of espionage agencies and re-examines most of the outstanding cold war spy cases.... *"Books: The Balance of Espionage," Review of "The Secret War for Europe" by Louis Hagen, Time, April 4, 1962, p 62*

parareligious, *adj.:* For instance, the religious or parareligious sects of the West Coast may seem as mysterious to an East Coast observer as primitive societies. *Sanche de Gramont, The New York Times Magazine, Jan. 28, 1968, p 37*

para-theatre, *n.:* ... what has been called para-theatre: many people in America feel that some of the best "theatre" can be found in the dance recitals of people like Yvonne Rainier, Paul Taylor, or Merce Cunningham, as well as in various attempts at mixed-media.... *Richard Roud, "What's the Point?" Review of "The Third Theatre"* by Robert Brustein, The Manchester Guardian Weekly, July 11, 1970, p 18

par·a·ce·ta·mol (ˌpær əˈsiː təˌmɔːl), *n.* a drug used to relieve headaches and reduce fever.

Mrs McKee died in hospital a week after taking an overdose of the drug paracetamol at her home in Highbury Hill, north London. *"Warning On Painkiller Drug," The Times (London), March 4, 1972, p 2*

And a terribly natural-looking box of Healthcraft Pain Relief Tablets which in fact are powerfully laced with Paracetamol — which is the modern form of headache drug, the aspirin *de nos jours. Nicholas Tomalin, The Sunday Times (London), July 4, 1971, p 17*

[from *para-* near, related to + the chemical name *acetam*idophen*ol*]

paradoxical sleep, any of about five periods in a night's sleep, each period lasting about ten minutes, during which dreams occur and the body undergoes marked changes, including rapid eye movement, loss of reflexes, and increased brain activity. Also called REM SLEEP. Compare ORTHODOX SLEEP.

After about an hour of this orthodox sleep phase, a change occurs and paradoxical sleep begins and lasts about 10 minutes before orthodox sleep is resumed.... in paradoxical sleep, unlike orthodox sleep, the blood flow through the brain is increased far above waking levels. *Ian Oswald, "Sleep, the Great Restorer," New Scientist, April 23, 1970, p 171*

parafoil, *n.* a combination of parachute and airfoil.

The U.S. Navy's "parafoil" performs like an airfoil in providing a gliding descent permitting the parachutist to guide it — quite different from the vertical descent of conventional parachutes. *Picture legend, The 1969 Compton Yearbook, p 345*

... a revolutionary parachute invention ... known as the para-foil, would enable pilots bailing out over enemy territory to glide like birds until they reached safety.... *The New York Times, Aug. 13, 1967, Sec. 1, p 15*

paragraph loop, a loop in figure skating in which a series of turns are introduced at various points of the circles.

He kept his head, and laid down a final paragraph loop which, while not faultless, was better than anything either Curry or the third skater Michael Fish produced. *Dennis Bird, The Times (London), Dec. 3, 1970, p 16*

parajournalism, *n.* unconventional journalism. See also UNDERGROUND PRESS.

... perhaps the current fad for first person parajournalism, where the reporter — me, say — looks into his own heart for information about politics, war, or suffering, and tells what he finds there in long loping sentences all stuffed with literary allusion and neighborhood bar slang — I'm a scholar and good fellow, too — may have gone too far. *Herbert Gold, "Life & Letters: On Epidemic First Personism," The Atlantic, Aug. 1971, p 85*

parajournalist, *n.* a practitioner of parajournalism.

It is difficult to pinpoint exact and usable definitions of this parajournalism. But let us try, following MacDonald as he castigates a Wolfe review of Mailer's latest novel and berates the reviewer as again playing parajournalist because his technique was "to jeer at the author's private life and personality — or rather his persona...." *Dan Wakefield, "The Personal Voice and the Impersonal Eye," The Atlantic, June 1966, p 89*

parajournalistic, *adj.* of or relating to parajournalism or parajournalists.

A wave of parajournalistic publications, the so-called underground press, was mounting a serious challenge to established dailies. *Richard T. Baker, "Newspapers," The Americana Annual 1970, p 503*

par·a·kit·ing (ˈpær əˌkɑi tiŋ), *n.* the act or sport of soaring in a parachute while being towed by a motorboat, car, or other fast vehicle.

In parakiting, the water skier becomes airborne when his trailing parachute pops open. *Time, March 30, 1970, p 42*

[from *parachute + kite + -ing*]

paralanguage, *n.* the paralinguistic parts or aspects of language.

Language Today A Survey of Current Linguistic Thought *written and edited by* Mario Pei.... Renowned linguistics scholar Mario Pei and his colleagues provide the reader with illuminating discussions of modern grammar, semantics (including propaganda), paralanguage, and gesture. *The New York Times Book Review, Oct. 22, 1967, p 21*

paralinguistic, *adj.* of or relating to factors connected with but not essentially part of language, such as tone of voice, tempo of speech, gestures, facial expressions, etc.

Wolfram ... rejects the possibility of distinguishing 'careful' and 'casual' speech, as Labov had done, on the grounds that interpretation of paralinguistic cues is open to subjective bias; but this is to throw out the baby with the bathwater. *R. K. S. Macaulay, Pitzer College, Review of "A Sociolinguistic Description of Detroit Negro Speech" by Walter A. Wolfram, Language, Sept. 1970, p 772*

paralinguistics, *n.* the study of paralinguistic factors in language.

And there seem to be no references to the following topics, all of which surely ought to figure in an introductory text in anthropological linguistics, if only for historical reasons: cultural relativity ..., paralinguistics, kinesics, ethnoscience, semiotics, ethnosemantics, componential analysis.... *Harvey B. Sarles, University of Minnesota, Review of "Anthropological Linguistics: An Introduction" by Joseph H. Greenberg, Language, March 1970, p 234*

paramedic, *n. U.S.* a medical technician or other auxiliary worker in medicine. *Also used attributively.*

In a fresh and growing trend, more than 40 training programs for doctors assistants are under way across the country. The graduates, already numbering in the hundreds, are tagged with clumsy names — paramedic, clinical associate, health practitioner.... Started by Duke University in 1965, paramedic studies are wide-ranging — from community health to bacteriology and psychosomatic medicine, plus techniques such as regulating intravenous infusions and operating respirators. *Time, Nov. 9, 1970, p 38*

▶ This term should not be confused with the military term *paramedic,* meaning a parachuting medical corpsman in the armed forces and deriving from *parachute + medic.* The word entered here is a back formation of *paramedical,* which means related to medicine in an auxiliary capacity.

paramenstrual, *adj.* of or relating to the paramenstruum.

...the para-menstrual failure rate in "O" level candidates was 17 per cent. for girls whose menstrual loss lasted up to four days....*Alfred Byrne, The Sunday Times (London), Dec. 29, 1968, p 3*

par·a·men·stru·um (ˌpær əˈmen stru əm), *n.* a period of eight days comprising the four days preceding menstruation and the first four days of menstruation.

Recent studies have shown that in women half of all medical and surgical admissions to hospital occur during the paramenstruum.... At this time women appear to have a lowered pain threshold, lowered resistance to infection, and an increased tendency to fever and allergy. *Penny Hunter Simon, The Times (London), Sept. 30, 1970, p 14*

[from New Latin *para-* beside, near + *menstruum* menstruation]

parameter, *n.* **1** a measurable factor which helps with other such factors to define a system.

Various individual experiments have climbed past various obstacles to reach positions close to the break-even level. In fact, in some instances two of the three essential parameters (density, temperature and confinement time) have already been achieved. *Wm. C. Gough and Bernard J. Eastlund, "The Prospects of Fusion Power," Scientific American, Feb. 1971, p 63*

2 any defining or characteristic factor.

...the President should "use the moral influence of his office in new ways designed to reduce racial tensions and help develop a climate of racial understanding." None of those things can be done overnight, but the fact that Nixon was willing to make his chastisement public suggests—as Finch put it in bureaucratese—that the President at least understands "the parameters of the problem." *Time, Aug. 3, 1970, p 9*

The mind with all its parameters and limits ingrained through years of constant failure to aim beyond the "feasible" and "allowable," the "probable." I read Timon of Athens today....*Ward Just, "Soldiers," The Atlantic, Nov. 1970, p 65*

pa·ram·e·trize (pəˈræm əˌtraiz), *v.t.* to determine the parameters of.

...the nuclear charge distribution...can be parametrized directly using a suitable mathematical form which does not necessarily have fundamental significance. *Daphne F. Jackson, "How Complex are Atomic Nuclei?" New Scientist, April 9, 1970, p 76*

paramilitarism, *n.* the ideals and spirit of militarism among paramilitary groups (i.e. civilian groups organized on a military basis).

Parties for the Panthers have become fashionable in New York in the last three weeks—ever since the Leonard Bernsteins gave one and were denounced for doing so in an editorial in the Times...[which] talked about the Panthers' "Mao-Marxist ideology and Fascist paramilitarism".... *"The Talk of the Town: Three Gatherings," The New Yorker, Feb. 14, 1970, p 33*

par·a·myx·o·vi·rus (ˌpær əˌmik səˈvai rəs), *n.* any of a group of viruses that includes the viruses causing mumps and various respiratory diseases.

The presence of intranuclear inclusions distinguishes measles virus (and the closely related distemper and rinderpest viruses) from paramyxoviruses such as mumps, parainfluenza, and Newcastle disease virus, which are morphologically very similar but produce only cytoplasmic inclusions in infected cells. *A. F. Howatson, "Measles," McGraw-Hill Yearbook of Science and Technology 1971, p 263*

The two workers point out that cases of diabetes have been reported in man after an attack of mumps, a disease which is caused by one of the paramyxo-viruses. *The Times (London), Nov. 27, 1968, p 9*

[from *para-* + *myxovirus* the virus causing influenza]

paraphernalia, *n.pl. Slang.* See the quotation for the meaning.

In the argot of the drug world, it is "paraphernalia": the necessary accouterments to merchandising heroin. The small glassine envelopes or "bags," used to package heroin are paraphernalia. So, too, are the legal, harmless powders used to dilute the drug, usually quinine, dextrose, lactose or mannite. *Time, July 20, 1970, p 15*

paraprofessional, *n.* a person engaged to assist the work of professionals, as in teaching, nursing, social work, etc.; an aide or assistant in a professional field who does not have full professional training. Also called SUBPROFESSIONAL.

I know of communities where school authorities declined, on the basis of nonexistent need, munificent sums allotted them under titles of various educational acts, to purchase equipment for instance, or hire "paraprofessionals." *Leon Mones, East Orange, N.J., in a Letter to the Editor, The New York Times, Feb. 11, 1970, p 46*

...classes were proceeding, with regular teachers and "para-professionals," mostly mothers, to help out with classes in reading and in English, which is taught by modern adult methods of language instruction. *"The Talk of the Town: I.S. 201 Complex," The New Yorker, Oct. 5, 1968, p 44*

—*adj.* acting as a paraprofessional; being an aide or assistant to professionals.

There is some talk now of using para-professional help, trained on the job like interns. In some schools, mothers already are supervising lunch hours and study periods. Eventually they may be accepted into classrooms, with other assistants such as qualified volunteers or unemployed artists, peace workers, the retired, almost anyone with a BA and common sense. *June Callwood, "Why Good Teachers Don't Teach Anymore," Maclean's, May 1967, p 64*

pararuminant, *n.* an animal whose digestive system is similar to a ruminant's.

Eight m.p.h. is a more usual speed for red kangaroos. They can sometimes clear a six-foot fence; there is a record leap of 27 feet, over a pile of wood 10 feet high. They do not chew their cud, although they have a complex stomach structure that harbors a rich microbial community; they are pararuminants. *Philip Morrison, Scientific American, March 1971, p 118*

par·a·sta·tal (ˌpær əˈstei təl), *adj.* serving the state or government indirectly or in an auxiliary capacity; working with the state though not officially a part of it.

The [Uganda] Government monopoly of importing is to be exercised through parastatal bodies, such as the National Trading Corporation, and the Uganda Development Corporation. *Michael Wolfers, The Times (London), May 19, 1970, p 22*

—*n.* a parastatal group.

...the parastatals were still almost wholly outside central control; and little had been done to curb the penchant of the STC [State Trading Corporation] for importing luxury goods. *Richard Gott, The Manchester Guardian Weekly, Oct. 23, 1971, p 6*

parawing, *n.* a glider which incorporates a sail-shaped, parachute-like device that unfurls to act like a wing during descent.

The National Aeronautics and Space Administration said...that it would negotiate a contract...for research flight testing on an all-flexible combination of parachute and wing called a parawing. *The New York Times, May 30, 1967, p 23*

pa·ri·e·tals (pə'rai ə təlz), *n.pl. U.S.* visitation rules in a dormitory for members of the opposite sex.

... Yale students ... have rejoined the nationwide battle for liberalized "parietals" — campus term for women's visiting hours in male dormitories, or vice-versa. *The New York Times, Dec. 17, 1967, Sec. 4, p 9*

[noun use of *parietal, adj.*, of or relating to visiting hours within college walls, ultimately from Latin *pariēs* wall]

parking orbit. See the first quotation for the meaning.

The United States has used "parking" orbits on its Ranger shots to the Moon. Under this technique, the probe and a booster rocket are "parked" in orbit around the earth. At the appropriate point in the orbit, the booster is re-ignited, sending the vehicle toward its goal. *The New York Times, April 3, 1963, p 14*

After getting away satisfactorily from its "parking orbit" round the Earth, *Lunik IV* was slated to be functioning quite as planned and the 250 ft. radio telescope at Jodrell Bank picked up its signals when the vehicle was above the horizon. *New Scientist, April 11, 1963, p 73*

Parkinson's Law, any of various observations made by the English satirical writer, C. Northcote Parkinson, born 1909, especially concerning time and work. See the quotations for details.

Alone among the great institutions in Washington, the Court seems to have escaped Parkinson's Law, which holds that the number of employees in any office increases constantly and that the work expands to occupy the new hands. *Anthony Lewis, "Annals of Law: The Gideon Case," The New Yorker, April 25, 1964, p 160*

Parkinson's Second Law is that Government expenditure rises to meet revenue. *Edwin L. Dale, Jr., The New York Times, March 24, 1967, p 43*

And, as Parkinson's Law conclusively shows, once the numbers in any committee or group have increased beyond a certain point, the decision-making function falls into the hands of a much smaller inner circle of powerful figures. *Canada Month, June 1963, p 30*

park·y ('par ki:), *n. British Slang.* a park guardian or keeper.

It's just coats on the ground and the parkies chase us at least once a month for doing something wrong. *Hunter Davies, The Sunday Times (London), May 9, 1971, p 34*

I have seen many an old pensioner, bending to touch the petals of a fine gladiolus, jump back full of alarm and guilt as he saw the parkies' tell-tale armband appear round a curve in the gravel. *Dennis Johnson, The Manchester Guardian Weekly, May 23, 1970, p 10*

[shortened from *park-keeper*]

parochiaid, *n. U.S.* governmental aid to parochial schools.

Litigation on parochiaid is likely to go on for several years. But lawyers are fairly sure that *Lemon's* broad principles, plus the anti-aid line-up reflected by the court's near unanimity, will eventually require a drastic rearrangement of Catholic education. *"Education: Untangling Parochial Schools," Time, July 12, 1971, p 53*

[patterned after *Medicaid*]

par·the·nog·e·none (ˌpar θə'nadʒ əˌnoun), *n.* an organism that can reproduce without fertilization.

The human population, by virtue of its enormous size, could indeed contain a few parthenogenones. These would be very difficult to distinguish from normal individuals: they would of course be female and they would resemble their mothers very closely but otherwise they need show no distinctive features. *C. R. Austin, Science Journal, June 1970, p 42*

[from *parthenogenesis*]

participational, *adj.* (of a show or exhibit) involving the participation of the spectators or the audience.

In spite of its premature closing, the participational section of the Morris exhibition was valuable because of the discussion and thought it provoked among artists and public alike. *Caroline Tisdall, "Waiting Till it's Safe," The Manchester Guardian Weekly, June 19, 1971, p 12*

The $30 million Ontario Science Center opened in September in Toronto. The Center features hundreds of "participational" exhibits that are operated by push buttons. *Frederick H. Armstrong, "Toronto," The Americana Annual 1970, p 687*

participatory democracy or **participant democracy.** See the quotations for the meaning.

Therapeutic-community patterns also have relevance for current social change. Young people alienated from established social institutions are experimenting with such ventures as communal living, organizations for political activism and encounter groups. These "alternate institutions" frequently emphasize values similar to those of a therapeutic community: group cohesion and commitment; open communication, particularly about personal problems; helping and being helped by peers, and "participant democracy," meaning involvement of the entire group in decision-making. *Richard Almond, "The Therapeutic Community," Scientific American, March 1971, p 42*

Both the Negroes and the antiwar groups have made use of the politics of marches, sit-ins and mass demonstrations. But those who practice this "participatory democracy" can ultimately achieve their objectives only if they work through electoral processes and win control of Congress and the Presidency. *William V. Shannon, The New York Times, May 6, 1968, p 46*

participatory theater, a form of theater in which the plays include participation or physical involvement by the audience.

[The contemporary theater] is trying to rediscover its pre-verbal origins, and it is trying to isolate what it is that theater can uniquely do that films and television cannot do. This has led in two directions, one sacred, the other profane.... With Jerzy Grotowski and the Polish Laboratory Theater, the emphasis is on the sacred.... With *Hair* and *Oh! Calcutta!* the emphasis is on the profane.... A reverse movement is also present, with Grotowski illuminating the profanation of the soul.... These ventures in dramatic exploration are also intimately related to an attempt to bridge the we-they gap in the actor-audience relationship—what is popularly called "participatory" theater. *Time, Feb. 23, 1970, p 68*

particle physicist, a specialist in particle physics.

Even particle physicists and molecular biologists would be hard put to point to new discoveries, insights and ideas rivalling those in the field of astronomy in the near-miraculous 10 years since 1961. *Bill Gunston, "Astronomy," New Scientist and Science Journal, Aug. 5, 1971, p 334*

particle physics, a branch of physics dealing with elementary particles (protons, neutrons, electrons, positrons, neutrinos, mesons, etc.).

One of the basic hypotheses of particle physics is that nature should be symmetrical with regard to three basic characteristics of particle interaction: electric charge, parity (right or left handedness), and direction of motion in time.... *Science News, June 28, 1969, p 616*

par·ton ('par,tan), *n.* any of certain concentrated charges into which a proton or neutron may break up under nuclear bombardment. Compare SUB-NUCLEON.

Richard P. Feynman of Cal Tech has been developing a theoretical model of the nucleon that may explain the inelastic-scattering results. He has given the name "parton" to the unknown constituents of the proton and the neutron that inelastically scatter high-energy electrons. Feynman assumes that partons are point particles. He and others have examined the possibility that partons may be one or another of the great array of previously identified subnuclear particles. *Henry W. Kendall and Wolfgang K. H. Panofsky, "The Structure of the Proton and the Neutron," Scientific American, June 1971, p 73*

The partons may rapidly recombine to make another proton, in which case the scattering will be elastic. Alternatively, they may recombine to make one or more other particles, in which case the scattering will be inelastic. *Gerald Feinberg, "Physics: High-energy Physics," 1970 Britannica Yearbook of Science and the Future, 1969, p 375*

[from *particle* + pro*ton* or neut*ron*]

partwork, *n.* a book or set of books published one part or fascicle at a time.

Purnell's three most successful part-works [were] *The History of the Second World War* (launched in October 1966 and extended from 96 to 120 parts), *The History of the Twentieth Century* (launched in 1968), and *The History of the First World War* (launched in 1969)....*William A. Katz, "Publishing," Britannica Book of the Year 1970, p 644*

An architect who started doing illustrations for the IPC partwork *Birds of the World* has since abandoned the set-square and become a full-time artist....*Jon Tinker, New Scientist and Science Journal, Jan. 28, 1971, p 206*

par·y·lene ('pær ə,li:n), *n.* a plastic derived from an isomer of xylene (paraxylene) by polymerization.

The product, named parylene, has been successfully used as a dielectric, or insulation, on capacitors....*The New York Times, Feb. 18, 1965, p 43*

It's a skintight plastic coat so thin you would never know it's there. Yet it covers the bee completely, right down to the individual hairs on the bee's knees. It was done to protect specimens in a natural history museum. But we didn't spend 12 years on a new plastic just to protect bees. We developed parylene to protect things like bees—fragile, complex things so intricate in shape they are next to im-

possible to coat. *Advertisement by Union Carbide, Scientific American, Nov. 1966, p 33*

[from *paraxylene*]

pass-fail, *adj.* of or relating to a system of crediting academic work in which a student passes or fails but otherwise is not graded.

There has been much discussion of grading reforms; but the only major change, if it can be called that, has been the introduction of some options to take a certain number of courses on a pass-fail basis, without any indication of the actual quality of the work performed. *Fred M. Hechinger, The New York Times, Aug. 9, 1970, p 7*

"I believe we have gained a great deal in suggesting grading instead of somewhat more rigid pass-fail standards," he said. *Denis Taylor, The Times (London), April 20, 1970, p 2*

passive, *adj.* used to reflect but not record or amplify energy pulses.

The method, proposed six years ago by Drs Duane Muhleman and Irwin Shapiro of Massachusetts Institute of Technology, involves measuring the relativistic time delay produced in a radar beam passing through the strong gravitational field of the Sun. Previous investigators, including Shapiro, have done this by so-called passive radar —bouncing signals off planets when they were close to the Sun's limb—achieving precisions of around 5 per cent. *New Scientist, Dec. 3, 1970, p 362*

The package [ALSEP: Apollo Lunar Surface Experiments Package], containing a magnetometer...and solar wind experiment, actually flew aboard the *Apollo 12*. Its substitute on *Apollo 11* was a package of three experiments —a passive seismometer, laser reflector and solar wind sensor. *Peter Gwynne, "NASA Asserts Lunar Flights Good for Science," Science Journal, Feb. 1970, p 4*

paste job, something made up of collected bits and pieces; a pastiche.

Your story "The Malpractice Mess"... wasn't your usual incisive approach but rather a superficial paste job. To begin with you lifted a case...from my book "The Negligent Doctor" without realizing that although the story was true enough, her name was fictitious. But most important, the article recites all the clichés advanced by the American Medical Association without taking the trouble to check them out. *Charles Kramer, New York, in a Letter to the Editor, Time, Nov. 23, 1970, p 2*

[shortened from *scissors-and-paste job*]

pastiche, *v.t.* to combine (various works, styles, etc.) into a mixture or hodgepodge.

...the unfortunate Victorian habit of "reviving", that is, pastiching, the Renaissance, the Baroque and just about every other style of the past. *Bevis Hillier, The Times (London), Oct. 17, 1970, p 20*

[verb use of *pastiche, n.*]

past·ies ('pei sti:z), *n.pl.* a pair of small adhesive coverings on the nipples of female performers, worn chiefly to comply with laws against indecent exposure.

Orgiastic rock music, go-go girls (some of them topless, which in Toronto means with pasties), surly waiters, raw prole [proletarian] vitality. *Alexander Ross, "A Status Guide to Toronto: The After-Dark Scene," Maclean's, Nov. 1968, p 76*

Typical of the elaborate revues being offered by the hotels is "Toujours Paris".... Among the performers are

...a long line of tall, beautiful, plastic-looking showgirls who wear rhinestone pasties instead of brassieres. *Vincent Canby, The New York Times, Aug. 5, 1968, p 20*

pataphysical, *adj.* of or relating to pataphysics.

"They [the Czech producers of Alfred Jarry's play "Ubu Roi"] had a perfectly good program printed up, a ten-page job including a detailed description, in the best 'pataphysical' jargon, of that crazy machine you saw giving off sparks as the curtain went up. The idea being to get the spectator into the proper 'pataphysical' spirit Jarry believed in — you know, anarchist, antiscientific, irreverent." *Curtis Cate, "Footlose in Prague," The Atlantic, Feb. 1965, p 114*

pataphysics, *n.* an imaginary science satirizing scientific and scholarly thought and writing, invented by the French surrealist writer Alfred Jarry, 1873-1907.

Pataphysics was defined by its founder, who died of absinthe and under-nourishment in 1907, as a science that will 'examine the laws governing exceptions', and describe 'a universe which can be — and perhaps should be — envisaged in the place of the traditional one'. *John Lehmann, "Alice at the Sorbonne," The Listener, Sept. 22, 1966, p 425*

By creating its own, contiguous, reality, the novel both illuminates the current desire to live by the moment and fulfils the stringently nebulous requirements of Pataphysics, the "science of the particular." *John Whitley, The Sunday Times (London), Nov. 12, 1967, p 56*

[coined by Alfred Jarry as French *pataphysique*, from *pata-* (an arbitrary prefix probably suggested by *meta-*) + *-physique*, as in *métaphysique* metaphysics]

patchboard, *n.* a removable panel in a computer or other electronic equipment having multiple electric terminals into which wires may be plugged in various ways according to the operation desired. Also called PATCH PANEL.

Expressly designed for multiple circuit industrial control applications, this new Tape Reader combines the durability of toggle switches, the flexibility of a patchboard, the repeat accuracy of a cam timer, with the advantage of punched tape programming. *Scientific American, March 1967, p 52*

patch panel, another name for PATCHBOARD.

Basically, an analog computer consists of an assembly of individual electronic computing elements that can be interconnected by means of a "patch panel" outside the machine. This panel is a terminal board with holes, each hole facing an interval contact. The computer operator uses "patch cords" (wire connectors) to interconnect specific holes for the kind of operation he wants the machine to perform. *Robert Vichnevetsky, The New York Times, Jan. 9, 1967, p 140*

pathotype, *n.* a pathogenic or disease-producing type of organism.

The organism [*Pseudomonas solanacearum*], earlier considered to be a soil inhabitant and an omnivorous root invader, primarily of solanaceous species such as tobacco, tomato, and potato, has revealed itself as a "species" comprising different races and pathotypes, each with its own specific disease-causing characteristics. *Ivan W. Buddenhagen, "Plant Disease," McGraw-Hill Yearbook of Science and Technology 1971, p 331*

patienthood, *n.* the quality or condition of being a patient.

Miss MacKenzie obviously cannot report, except by hearsay, on the operation itself, but about the painful explorations prior to it and about the trip back, complete with a couple of frightening detours, she is brilliantly precise. Hers is the best account of the psychology of patienthood in a modern hospital I've ever read. *Richard Schickel, "Books in Brief," Review of "Risk" by Rachel MacKenzie, Harper's, May 1971, p 111*

Millions of boys . . . live, as Captain Ahab says, with half of their heart and with only one of their lungs, and the world is the worse for it. Now and again, however, an individual is called upon . . . to lift his individual patienthood to the level of a universal one and to try to solve for all what he could not solve for himself alone. *Erik H. Erikson, quoted by Robert Coles, "Profiles: The Measure of Man," The New Yorker, Nov. 14, 1970, p 108*

patriality, *n.* the condition of being a native or natural-born subject or citizen of a country.

Patrials are defined as "all people who are citizens of Britain by being born here, or become citizens by adoption, registration, or naturalisation in the UK, or who have a parent or grandparent who was born here or acquired citizenship by adoption, registration, or naturalisation." . . . In some cases, where patriality depends on ancestral connection, a certificate issued through the British High Commissioner in his own country will be needed as proof of that right. *Francis Boyd, "Britain to Impose Tighter Controls," The Manchester Guardian Weekly, March 6, 1971, p 8*

[from *patrial* of one's native country + *-ity*]

patterning, *n.* a form of physical therapy in which brain-damaged or brain-deficient children are guided through the individual movements of creeping, crawling, walking, etc., on the theory that following the pattern of those functions that the brain has failed to develop will help to develop them through therapy. *Also used attributively.*

"Patterning" is a rigid physical treatment for children handicapped by brain damage, mental retardation or reading disabilities. *"Medicine: Rehabilitation," Time, May 31, 1968, p 42*

The "patterning" treatment for retarded and brain-damaged children, the efficacy of which was questioned by a group of medical and health organizations recently, has been vigorously defended by its developers. *The New York Times, May 26, 1968, p 55*

Pax Americana, peace enforced by American power. The term was modeled on *Pax Romana*, the peace imposed by Roman might under the Caesars, and *Pax Britannica*, a later term with the same connotation applied to the British Empire.

Mr. Steel's final advice to America should warm British hearts — at any rate nostalgically. It is that *Pax Americana* should model itself on *Pax Britannica* which although often "insufferably smug and hypocritical" reserved its power "for situations it could hope to control and which were directly related to the national interest." *Francis Williams, "Innocents Abroad," Review of "Pax Americana" by Ronald Steel, Punch, Feb. 28, 1968, p 321*

In the opinion of many European experts, the Kremlin has a more ambitious objective: to alter the status quo by exchanging the *Pax Americana* for a *Pax Sovietica. Arnaud De Borchgrave, "The Kremlin's Grand Design," Newsweek, Oct. 18, 1971, p 17*

Pursuing a *Pax Americana* as leader of the so-called "free world" (the term invariably appears in quotes in this book), the United States seeks to impose its will and its ways whether the rest of the world wants them or not. *Joan Rothschild, "A Necessary Violence vs. the Status Quo," Review of "Struggle Against History: U.S. Foreign Policy in an Age of Revolution," edited by Neal D. Houghton, Saturday Review, Nov. 2, 1968, p 45*

Pax Sovietica, peace enforced by Soviet power.

In the opinion of many European experts, the Kremlin has a more ambitious objective: to alter the status quo by exchanging the *Pax Americana* for a *Pax Sovietica. Arnaud De Borchgrave, "The Kremlin's Grand Design," Newsweek, Oct. 18, 1971, p 17*

There won't be a Pax Sovietica or anything like it, because the world is too big to be governed by anybody. *Walter Lippman, The Sunday Times (London), Oct. 19, 1969, p 49*

payload, *n.* the cargo, warhead, bombs, etc., carried by a rocket or aircraft, having to do with its objective but not related to its operation.

The Lunik series perfected and proved Russia's ability to propel heavy payloads through and beyond the restraining gravity of earth. *Joseph L. Zygielbaum, "Soviet Launch Sites and Tracking Stations," The World Book Science Annual 1965, p 69*

pa·zazz (pə'zæz), *n.* another spelling of PIZZAZZ.

His [John Turner's] campaign manager, John Claxton, son of Brook Claxton, the Liberal Minister who held the seat from 1940 to 1953, mounted a campaign that has had few equals anywhere for sheer *pazazz. Mungo James, Saturday Night (Canada), May 1966, p 34*

"I don't see what's wrong with the floor we have," said the King.
"Square," said the Queen. "Square, square, square. Montina Corlon's different. It's got pazazz." *Advertisement, The New Yorker, Jan. 16, 1965, inside cover*

PCPA, abbreviation of *para-chlorophenylalanine,* a drug which reduces the level of serotonin and is widely used in clinical research to treat a variety of conditions, including intestinal tumors and schizophrenia.

The drug, known as PCPA or para-chlorophenylalanine, is commonly used to interfere with the synthesis in the brain of another chemical which affects mood and sleep. *The Times (London), May 4, 1970, p 11*

peace feeler, a probe made by one country of another country's receptivity to peace, usually through diplomatic channels.

Foreign Minister Abba Eban said today in Jerusalem that peace feelers toward the Arabs were being put out in several ways, and he mentioned Dr. Gunnar V. Jarring, the United Nations special envoy, as one of them. *The New York Times, Feb. 27, 1968, p 1*

It is now probable (Sir Robert told the Cabinet) that we are about to be the object of an American peace-feeler, perhaps even of a peace-offensive; and all our own loose-thinkers are on the scent. *Mark Arnold-Forster, The Manchester Guardian Weekly, Jan. 9, 1971, p 10*

peaceful coexistence, the absence of open hostility between ideological adversaries; the maintenance of formal, bilateral relations between countries of opposing social systems.

Peaceful coexistence between the United States and the People's Republic of China is not only desirable but also feasible. Although serious differences of principle separate the two countries, the presence of ideological struggle does not jeopardize the development of normal state relations .... peaceful coexistence is by definition reciprocal. As spelled out in the Feb. 28, 1972, U.S.-Chinese Shanghai communiqué, the principles of peaceful coexistence consist of mutual respect for sovereignty, territorial integrity and political independence; mutual nonaggression; mutual noninterference in each other's internal affairs; equality and mutual benefit. *Peter S. H. Tang, "As for Peaceful Coexistence," The New York Times, April 13, 1972, p 43*

[originally the name of the post-Stalin Soviet foreign policy formulated in 1961 by Nikita Khrushchev, 1894-1971, who headed the Soviet government from 1958 to 1964]

peacekeeper, *n.* a person or group that arranges or implements the cessation of hostilities between belligerent countries.

. . . if an international truce force went to the island, Turkey would forgo its right to intervene [in Cyprus] for three months. Considering the number of Turks who have been killed by Greeks in Cyprus since Christmas, this is a generous offer, as well as a rare declaration of faith in the United Nations as a peace-keeper. *"Tasks of a Truce Force in Cyprus," The Manchester Guardian Weekly, March 5, 1964, p 1*

Lieutenant-General Burns . . . was the first of a new breed of international trouble-shooters who now try to halt the escalators of war by policing cease-fires — the Canadian peacekeepers. *Terence Robertson, Maclean's, Dec. 1, 1965, p 16*

peacekeeping, *n.* the action or function of a peace-keeper.

The Ruskian [Dean Rusk, former U.S. Secretary of State] logic of collective security and peacekeeping as applied to Vietnam, the nation's faith in its unlimited capacities; these were falling apart in 1969. *Michael Janeway, "The Politics of Quackery," The Atlantic, Dec. 1970, p 72*

—*adj.* charged with maintaining or implementing peace between belligerents; acting as a peace-keeper.

Top U.S. officials dream of inveigling the Japanese into an important role in any international peace-keeping force sent to Indochina to guarantee a future settlement. *Flora Lewis, "Reports: The Nixon Doctrine: Japan's Soft Step," The Atlantic, Nov. 1970, p 16*

peacenik, *n. U.S. Slang.* a person who engages in peace demonstrations; an active opponent of war. Compare VIETNIK.

What is the real offense of a long-haired peacenik who holds his fingers in a V as the hardhats come marching by? *Peter Schrag, "America's Other Radicals," Harper's, Aug. 1970, p 45*

When Barbara Howar was asked on the CBS special how somebody with her peacenik views could keep going out with Kissinger, she said, in a reply cut from the show, "Politics make strange bedfellows." *Joseph Kraft, Harper's, Jan. 1971, p 61*

[see -NIK]

peace sign, 1 a V-shaped sign made with the fingers as an expression of peace.

. . . an admiring article by Tom Cawley, a reporter for the Binghamton *Press,* which was flanked by a large, smiling picture of [Mayor John] Lindsay giving the peace sign .... *Andy Logan, "Around City Hall," The New Yorker, Dec. 25, 1971, p 54*

2 another name for PEACE SYMBOL.

Peter Stowe, an economics professor at Southern Illinois University, was haled into court under the law. In their car's rear window, his wife had stuck a [U.S.] flag decal with a peace sign where the stars should have been. *Time, July 6, 1970, p 14*

▶ The V-shaped sign with the fingers was formerly (especially in World War II) called the *victory sign* and represented the *V* in Victory. The current use of the sign to indicate peace represents an adaptation of the upside-down *V* in the peace symbol.

peace symbol, the sign ⊕ used as a symbol of peace. Also called PEACE SIGN.

American Opinion magazine, published by John Birch Society Founder Robert Welch, compared the familiar peace symbol to an anti-Christian "broken cross" carried by the Moors when they invaded Spain in the 8th century .... Any resemblance, however, is probably coincidental. The peace design was devised in Britain for the first Ban-the-Bomb Aldermaston march in 1958. The lines inside the circle stand for "nuclear disarmament." They are a stylized combination of the semaphore signal for *N* (flags in an upsidedown *V*) and *D* (flags held vertically, one above the signaler's head and the other at his feet). *Time, Nov. 2, 1970, p 6*

peace talks, negotiations for effecting peace between two or more belligerent countries.

Israeli Premier Golda Meir declared on television: "Had we known that things would develop as they have, with the Egyptian contravention of the cease-fire, we would not have agreed to enter into the peace talks. We have been bitterly disappointed." *Time, Sept. 7, 1970, p 16*

Another professor, who attempts a humor column on the front page of *Le Monde* each day, noted the drop in Wall Street prices occasioned by peace talks in the UN and concluded that America needs the war as a means of expending surplus bombs and blood. *Herbert R. Lottman, "The Newspaper deGaulle Has to Read," Harper's, Jan. 1967, p 62*

Peck's Bad Boy, *U.S.* a person who behaves recklessly or indiscreetly; an enfant terrible.

. . . the book [*From Those Wonderful Folks Who Gave You Pearl Harbor*] is an earnest effort by Della Femina to buttress his reputation as the Peck's Bad Boy of Advertising. *"Advertising," Time, June 22, 1970, p 78*

[Governor George] Wallace's motives—ego, a Peck's-bad-boy desire to make trouble, a yen to see just what would happen if a presidential election were thrown into the House of Representatives, or a combination of all these—do not actually matter. *Douglas Kiker, "Washington," The Atlantic, Feb. 1967, p 4*

▶ Though long a popular phrase in the American common vocabulary, *Peck's Bad Boy* has not been recorded anywhere as a meaningful expression. Reference books cite it only as a book title, which is what it was originally, in part. The book's full title was *Peck's Bad Boy and His Pa*. It was a collection of sketches, published in 1883, about the pranks played by a mischievous boy on his father. The sketches had been written by George Wilbur

Peck, 1840-1916, and published in his own newspaper, the Milwaukee *Sun*.

peculiar galaxy, any of a group of galaxies having highly unusual shapes.

Many of the peculiar galaxies look as though they were normal in shape at one time, but were subsequently distorted in appearance by some unusual event. In all the cases that have been examined thus far, the unusual event that altered the appearance of the peculiar galaxy seems to have been either a *collision* with another galaxy, or a gigantic *explosion* within the galaxy that literally blew it apart. *Robert Jastrow and Malcolm H. Thompson, Astronomy: Fundamentals and Frontiers, 1972, p 213*

ped·a·lo ('ped ə,lou), *n.* a kind of raft with a paddle wheel operated by working pedals, used especially as a sports or pleasure craft.

There are two swimming pools (one of them shallow enough to make child-sacrifice unlikely) and sail-boats and pedalos are available. *Ian Crawford, The Sunday Times (London), Dec. 29, 1968, p 33*

Under the lashing rain, the Yellow Sea becomes very unlike the Mediterranean—a wild, inimical sea reminiscent of pirate ships rather than *pedalos. Hans Koningsberger, "A Reporter at Large: China Notes," The New Yorker, April 30, 1966, p 94*

pedestrianization, *n.* the act or process of pedestrianizing.

The scheme to ban cars from Bond Street is essentially to make it a parade, although pedestrianization can have a commercial appeal. *Suzy Menkes, The Times (London), March 18, 1968, p 7*

pedestrianize, *v.t.* to convert (a street, etc.) to use by pedestrians; make free of vehicular traffic.

Eventually it intends to pedestrianise Low Street and turn the whole centre into a traffic-free area. *Robert Troop, The Sunday Times (London), Nov. 19, 1967, p 30*

peel, *v.i.* **1** Also, **peel off.** to remove or detach oneself from a group.

They engineered a splendid try for Morgan, Griffiths kicked a short penalty and Wiltshire peeled from the line-out for a try after five minutes of incessant pressure. *David Parry-Jones, The Times (London), April 13, 1970, p 6*

I worked for a sad, nervous little outfit called Pied Piper [ice cream] . . . Mel [the owner] would leap into the oldest truck . . . and, ringing his bells, screech out of the hangar and into the summer sunlight. The rest of us would follow, and we'd all rattle along for a mile or so in a rinky-dink parade of Pied Piper trucks, before each of us in turn, ringing his bells in salute, peeled off and headed out alone for his own territory. *Thomas Meehan, "The Pied Piper," The New Yorker, July 4, 1970, p 25*

2 peel out, *U.S. Slang.* to accelerate sharply in an automobile so that the tires leave rubber marks on the pavement.

As an adolescent man is freer to drive a car carefully rather than "peel out" and display the "horsepower" of his car—a vicarious display of his own power. *Warren T. Farrell, The New York Times, June 17, 1971, p 41*

Pekingologist or **Pekinologist,** *n.* other names for CHINA WATCHER.

. . . professional China watchers—often referred to as Pekingologists, or, more flippantly, as dragonologists—are constantly sifting through the raw material that Hong

Kong provides them with. *Robert Shaplen, "A Reporter at Large: The China Watchers," The New Yorker, Feb. 12, 1966, p 44*

. . . Fleet Street is said to be desperate for reliable Pekinologists who can churn out a thousand weekly words on the Chinese enigma. *Punch, April 2, 1969, p 478*

Pekingology or **Pekinology,** *n.* the study of the policies, practices, etc., of the Chinese Communist government in Peking. Compare KREMLINOLOGY.

. . . practitioners of the recondite art of Pekinology say that if Chairman Mao died tomorrow the party leadership probably would fall. . . . *Seymour Topping, The New York Times, April 3, 1966, Sec. 4, p 6*

pem·o·line ('pem ə,li:n), *n.* **1** a drug used to relieve depression; a stimulant.

Pemoline has been known sometime to be a mild brain stimulant, midway in strength between Amphetamine and coffee. *The Sunday Times (London), Oct. 27, 1968, p 3*

2 a shortened form of MAGNESIUM PEMOLINE.

Widely hailed as a memory-improving drug, pemoline —tradenamed Cylert by Abbott Laboratories—has been the focus of several independent studies since it was first publicized two years ago. *Science News, Jan. 6, 1968, p 14*

[perhaps from its chemical components phenyl-imino—oxaz*o*lidin*o*n*e*]

pence, *n. sing. or pl.* See the footnote under NEW PENNY.

pend, *v.t.* to leave undecided; postpone a decision on.

. . . the United States Atomic Energy Commission has spread a security blanket over what may be a basic innovation in controlled fusion technology. It has done this by "pending" the settlement of nine patent applications filed by KMS Industries Inc. . . . *New Scientist, July 16, 1970, p 134*

[verb use of *pending, adj.,* as in *with cases still pending, patent pending,* etc.]

pen·e·tra·li·um (,pen ə'trei li: əm), *n.* the most secret or hidden part.

The Penetralium of Mystery. *Title of an article on extrasensory perception by Cecil King, The Times (London), Aug. 1, 1970, p 12*

One accedes to the League, as it is called in "The Journey to the East" . . . by mysterious invitation—a tap in the night, a sudden summons from one of the hieratic brethren. . . . The novice keeps anxious vigil over his own soul and learns the cabalistic lore of the sanctified ones. He may be found unworthy of acceptance in the inner *penetralium* and be rejected. *George Steiner, "Books: Eastward Ho!" Review of "The Journey to the East" by Hermann Hesse, The New Yorker, Jan. 18, 1969, p 87*

[a new singular form derived in English from the old plural noun *penetralia,* which came from the Latin neuter plural of *penetrālis* inmost, deepest]

penguin suit, *Slang.* an astronaut's space suit.

. . . the astronauts donned the tight-fitting overalls, known as a penguin suit, in which tension is produced by several layers of rubberized material. The suit forces the wearer to exercise his muscles despite the state of weightlessness that exists in space. *Theodore Shabad, "Soviet Astronaut, on TV, Demonstrates Spacesuit for Keeping Trim," The New York Times, June 10, 1971, p 18*

penny, *n.* **1 two a penny,** *British.* very plentiful or common and therefore not valued. The equivalent U.S. phrase is *a dime a dozen.*

It is, of course, an isolated church in many ways, and foreign theologians, two a penny in Oxford or in Boston, are curiosities in Sofia. *Patrick C. Rodger, The Times (London), April 4, 1970, p 10*

Winston Churchill had little money of his own, hardly enough to keep him living in the style demanded in the 4th Hussars. He found in India that subalterns were two a penny and invited nowhere. Life in cantonment offered less than no opportunity. *Noel Annan, "Winston Churchill," Review of "Winston S. Churchill" [biography] by Randolph Churchill, The Listener, Oct. 27, 1966, p 612*

2 See the footnote under NEW PENNY.

►*Ten a penny* is also used in England in the same sense.

pen·ta·ton·ism ('pen tə,toun,iz əm), *n.* the use of a pentatonic or five-tone musical scale.

Pentatonism exists only on the frontier with Bolivia, but an archaic tritonic [three-tone] song, the *Baguala,* sung to the *caja,* can still be heard in the high mountains of the north-west. *Bruno C. Jacovella, The Times (London), July 4, 1970, p 30*

pen·tom·i·no (pen'tam ə,nou), *n.* a polyomino (many-sided piece) made to cover five squares on a game board.

The reader may enjoy experimenting with the 12 pentominoes (all patterns of five rookwise-connected counters) to see what happens to each. *Martin Gardner, "Mathematical Games," Scientific American, Oct. 1970, p 122*

[from *pent-* five + d*omino*]

people mover, any of various means for transporting people quickly between two fixed points.

. . . a "people mover," a vehicle smaller than a streetcar, for West Virginia University in Morgantown . . . will provide continuous service between the old campus in town and the new campus in the suburbs of this small mountain city. *James P. Romualdi, "Transportation," The World Book Science Annual 1972 (1971), p 375*

. . . rail-oriented, change-of-mode centers will be strategically located throughout the region. They will enable commuters to change from car to rail transportation and, possibly, in the New York City center, to change from subway to a noiseless pedestrian conveyor called a "people mover." *Thomas Fleming, The New York Times, June 20, 1971, p 22*

people's, *adj.* (reflecting the designation of institutions in Communist countries) of or belonging to the proletariat; socialist or communist.

First newspaper reports [from Communist China] . . . said "350 production brigades of 30 people's communes in the district suffered losses of varying degrees." *The New York Times, March 12, 1966, p 1*

"One must recognize that after twenty years the people's democracies move toward greater independence, while the contrary happens in countries tied to the United States . . . ." *A report in the French newspaper Le Monde, quoted by Herbert R. Lottman, "The Newspaper De Gaulle Has to Read," Harper's, Jan. 1967, p 66*

Peking's leaders won power by the gun. They have always felt threatened by U.S. encirclement. At any moment it may have been necessary once more, as against Japan, to mount "people's war." Soldiers are in this way central to China's revolutionary drama. *Ross Terrill, "The 800,000,000: Report From China," The Atlantic, Nov. 1971, p 119*

people sniffer, the nickname of a portable chemical and electronic apparatus that can detect the presence of hidden persons.

United States troops refer to the gadget as the "people sniffer." It leads American officers here in the Mekong delta to enemy hide-outs by "sniffing out" the kind of ammonia odors given off by the human body. *Gene Roberts, The New York Times, Aug. 18, 1968, Sec. 1, p 3*

people's park, *U.S.* a park for the use of people as they see fit, without regulatory or other impositions on its use by government officials.

For six years, Berkeley's chancellor, Roger Heyns, 52, did his best to cool down the original hotbed of U.S. student activism. Last year he was unfairly blamed for the way police handled student demands that one of the university's empty lots be turned into a "people's park." *Time, Nov. 23, 1970, p 81*

Pepper Fog, a trade name for a PEPPER GAS.

After a decade of assorted riots, the nation's 400,000 policemen are armed with more lethal weapons than some of history's major wars required plus Mace and Pepper Fog, undercover agents, computers and helicopters. *Time, July 13, 1970, p 34*

pepper gas, a riot-control gas that forms a thick haze and causes irritation of the throat and nasal passages. Also called by the trade name PEPPER FOG.

About 225 state and city policemen, armed with pepper gas, submachine guns, rifles and shotguns, repelled the mob, at first with truncheon blows. *The Times (London), July 9, 1970, p 5*

per·bro·mate (pər'brou₁meit), *n.* a salt of perbromic acid.

Preliminary studies showed that the perbromate ion has physical and chemical properties between those of the perchlorate and periodate ions. *William L. Jolly, "Chemistry: Inorganic Chemistry," 1970 Britannica Yearbook of Science and the Future, 1969, p 141*

per·bro·mic acid (pər'brou mik), a compound of bromine in its highest oxidation state ($HBrO_4$), first synthesized in 1968. It lies between the analogous perchloric and periodic acids.

An inconsistency in the reactions of members of the halogen family that has plagued inorganic chemists since the middle of the nineteenth century was cleared up this year at Argonne National Laboratory, Argonne, Ill., by Dr. Evan H. Appleman. He synthesized perbromic acid in which bromide has a valence equal to that of seven hydrogen atoms. *Science News Yearbook 1969, p 181*

perceived noise decibel. See the quotation for the meaning. *Abbreviation:* PNdB or PNdb

Flight tests of 707 and DC-8 aircraft have shown that fan noise can be decreased 10-15 perceived noise decibels by the use of such [sound-absorbing] linings. The perceived noise decibel is a unit of measurement of the human annoyance caused by noise exposure. *James J. Kramer, "Turbojet," McGraw-Hill Yearbook of Science and Technology 1971, p 425*

perfecta, *n. U.S.* another name for EXACTA.

For horseplayers who hopefully bet on exactas, perfectas, quinellas, doubles, and such, I can report that one afternoon last week at the Fair Grounds in New Orleans, an exacta paid $25,257. *Audax Minor, The New Yorker, Feb. 20, 1971, p 107*

[from American Spanish, short for *quiniela perfecta* perfect quiniela]

performative, *adj.* implying the actual performance of a wish, command, plan, etc.

Unlike Westerners, the Vietnamese do not clearly differentiate between what the philosopher Professor J. L. Austin calls "performative" and "constative" utterances, between for example, the marriage contract "I do" (take the woman to be my lawful wedded wife), and the statement "This is my lawful wedded wife." *Frances FitzGerald, "The Struggle and the War: The Maze of Vietnamese Politics," The Atlantic, Aug. 1967, p 75*

per·i·ap·sis (₁per i:'æp sis), *n.* the point in the orbit of a satellite body closest to the center of the heavenly body around which it is orbiting.

. . . its [faster-orbiting vehicle's] companion, in a 50° orbit with apoapsis 20 500 miles and periapsis 530 miles, undertakes the scrutiny of selected areas of Mars to gain a better idea of surface and atmospheric changes, seasonal variations, and the still enigmatic dust storms and Martian clouds. *New Scientist and Science Journal, May 6, 1971, p 305*

[from *peri-* near + *apsis* orbit]

per·i·cyn·thi·on (₁per i:'sin θi: ən), *n.* another name for PERILUNE. Compare APOCYNTHION.

. . . as the moon travelers neared pericynthion—their closest approach to the lunar surface—Mission Control radioed a "go" for lunar orbit. *John H. Glenn, Jr., "Focus on Space," The 1969 World Book Year Book, p 48*

[from *peri-* near + *Cynthia* goddess of the moon]

perilune, *n.* the point in a lunar orbit nearest to the center of the moon. Also called PERICYNTHION. Compare APOLUNE.

After being tracked for several days the spacecraft would be further slowed so that its perilune, or closest approach, would be reduced to about 28 miles above the lunar surface, which would be the primary altitude for photography. *Ellis Levin, Donald D. Viele, and Lowell B. Eldrenkamp, "The Lunar Orbiter Missions to the Moon," Scientific American, May 1968, p 60*

[from *peri-* near + French *lune* moon (from Latin *lūna*)]

peripheral, *n.* any part of the electromechanical equipment of a computer, such as magnetic tape, high-speed printers, keyboards, and displays.

The first peripherals were highly mechanical and not well matched to the demands of the electronic computer. There has been a gradual conversion from these all mechanical peripherals to the electro-mechanical and onwards to the electro-mechanical-optical. *Earl Masterson, "The New Peripherals," Science Journal, Oct. 1970, p 75*

"The computer logic is so fast that it has to loaf at several intervals while the input and output devices—the peripherals—are printing information." *Jim Hendershot, Vibrac Corporation, quoted in "The Talk of the Town: Synchrotrons and Peripherals," The New Yorker, April 11, 1970, p 34*

Peripherals include a card reader operating at three

cards per minute, a line printer operating at 300 lines per minute and a paper tape reader. *"Cost of Mini-computers Could Tumble Next Year," New Scientist and Science Journal, June 3, 1971, p 572*

—*adj.* of or relating to computer peripherals.

It is likely that Poland will produce small central processors, tape readers, line printers and other components; East Germany will probably supply peripheral equipment; Hungary, magnetic memories and software (programs). Czechoslovakia, which has large electronics plants, will be a major source of integrated circuits. Romania and Bulgaria may contribute various subcomponents and some software. *Ivan Berenyi, "Computers in Eastern Europe," Scientific American, Oct. 1970, p 102*

periphonic, *adj.* of or relating to an omnidirectional or multispeaker sound system.

A little of Third Ear Band's nursery doodling goes a very long way indeed, with or without electronic backing. . . . But the French pieces were almost as uneventful, even with benefit of this excellent multi-channel, so-called periphonic, sound. *William Mann, "The Arts: Summer Encounter," The Times (London), June 25, 1970, p 7*

[from *peri*- all around + *phonic* producing sound]

pe·ri·tus (pe'ri: tus), *n.; pl.* **pe·ri·ti** (pe'ri: ti:). one of the theological experts serving as consultants at the Second Vatican Council (1962).

Father Baum, a *peritus* (adviser) at the Second Vatican Council, believes that condemnation of contraception is a matter of discipline that involves neither the church's infallibility nor divine revelation, and thus is subject to change. *Time, April 22, 1966, p 43*

. . . Charles Davis, Britain's leading Roman Catholic theologian, . . . was . . . one of the "periti," the experts who gave bishops advice on theological and intellectual issues during the Vatican Council. *Dana Adams Schmidt, The New York Times, Jan. 12, 1967, p 10*

[from New Latin *peritus*, from Latin *perītus*, *adj.*, skilled, expert]

permanent press, another name for DURABLE PRESS.

Recently a completely new process emerged, and is rapidly gaining ground in the USA, Europe and Japan. It is known by a variety of names, but possibly the most general is "permanent press". *Peter Lennox-Kerr, "Making the Creases Stay In," New Scientist, July 20, 1967, p 151*

Foreign competition is most severe in man-made-fiber textiles, the most rapidly growing segment of the industry since advancing technology gave the world wash-'n'-wear shirts and permanent-press pants. *Time, April 18, 1969, p 61*

per·me·ase ('pər mi: eis) *n.* an enzyme that concentrates lactose in cells.

Early studies on the way the bacterium *Escherichia coli* utilizes lactose showed that a specific component was necessary for the accumulation of the sugar. This so-called "permease" has since been found to be a protein, located in the cell membrane. *New Scientist, Jan. 1, 1970, p 8*

. . . many specific permeases (a type of enzyme) are known to be associated with the inner mitochondrial membrane and it should be possible to reveal their identity on acrylamide gels in the future. *Robert L. Hill, "Molecular Biology," 1972 Britannica Yearbook of Science and the Future, 1971, p 301*

[from *permea*te + -*ase* enzyme]

permissionist, *n.* another word for PERMISSIVIST.

Mr Justice Megarry went on: "The permissive society is one in which the permissionists have unlimited rights but no duties, and others have unlimited duties and no rights." *"Judge Attacks Permissive Society," The Times (London), March 23, 1972, p 2*

permissive, *n.* another word for PERMISSIVIST.

It [a proposal for a world-wide cricket tour] also irritates the extreme cricket-establishment people, some of whom seem to relish the thought of the tour, barbed wire and truncheons and all, to show that they are not going to be dictated to by the long-haired permissives. *Alan Gibson, The Times (London), Feb. 5, 1970, p 9*

permissivism, *n.* the beliefs and attitudes of permissivists.

But the most impressive tributes to "the high priest of permissivism," as he [Dr Spock] once described himself, were casual. Not a single baby cried during the 90 minutes of protest. *The Manchester Guardian Weekly, Oct. 17, 1968, p 3*

permissivist, *n.* a person considered excessively indulgent toward unacceptable behavior or attitudes. Also called PERMISSIVE or PERMISSIONIST.

In one week Spiro Agnew ascribed moral decay to the universities, Dr. Spock, and the Presidential Commission on Campus Unrest, which, he said, had produced a report which 'was sure to be taken as more pablum for the permissivists'. *Clive Irving, The Listener, Oct. 22, 1970, p 538*

So theatrical permissivists should ask themselves whether, if there must be censorship, it is not better from their point of view that it should remain with a rationally indefensible institution, which is in no position to enforce for long unpopular or unjustifiable standards. *The Times (London), Feb. 16, 1966, p 13*

per·ox·i·some (pə'rɑk sə,soum), *n.* See the quotations for the meaning.

Recently the cells of higher organisms have been found to contain organelles called peroxisomes, whose major function is thought to be the protection of cells from oxygen. The peroxisomes contain enzymes that catalyze the direct reduction of oxygen molecules through the oxidation of metabolites such as amino acids and other organic acids. *Preston Cloud and Aharon Gibor, "The Oxygen Cycle," Scientific American, Sept. 1970, p 113*

Peroxisomes, tiny enzyme packages that may be a key to control of plant and animal growth, have been discovered in plants. They were previously known to exist in human cells; . . . peroxisomes appear to break down glycolic acid molecules that would otherwise play a role in growth. Slow-growing crops, including spinach, wheat and tobacco, are abundant in peroxisomes, while fast-growing crops such as corn have few. *Science News, Feb. 8, 1969, p 141*

[from *peroxide* + -*some* body]

peroxyacetyl nitrate, a highly toxic element in smog.

Activated by sunlight, nitrogen oxides combine with waste hydrocarbons from automobile exhaust to produce the noxious final product of photochemical smog, peroxyacetyl nitrate, often referred to as PAN. *Barry Commoner, "A Reporter At Large: The Closing Circle," The New Yorker, Oct. 2, 1971, p 78*

Volume I . . . describes the web of photochemical reactions that desert sunlight spins daily in the warm pool of Los Angeles air out of the hydrocarbons and nitric oxide from a million manifolds. It is a remarkable story: the reducing agents turn into fierce oxidants that crack rubber, irritate the eyes and yellow the citrus groves. The products are many, the reagents not few. Ozone and peroxyacetyl nitrate are two recognizable and voracious oxidants. *Philip Morrison, "Books," Review of "Air Pollution," edited by Arthur C. Stern, Scientific American, Sept. 1970, p 240*

persistent, *adj.* (of toxic chemicals, especially insecticides) hard to decompose; chemically stable and therefore degradable only over a long period of time.

As 1969 came to a close, the bureaucratic infighting had begun, with makers of DDT carrying on a delaying action on Hardin's [Secretary of Agriculture Clifford Hardin's] first ban. Action against other persistent pesticides, such as aldrin, dieldrin, and endrin, and those containing lead and mercury, is also in prospect. *"Ecology: Poisons at Large: Government Restrictions," Science News Yearbook 1970, p 310*

DDT belongs to a class of biocides that are chlorinated hydrocarbons. The chlorine-carbon bond is rare in nature and is comparatively stable. Few bacteria and fungi are equipped to break it. These biocides are therefore relatively persistent, much more so than are the carbamates and the organophosphates. *Robert W. Risebrough, "Pesticide," McGraw-Hill Yearbook of Science and Technology 1971, p 319*

personal distance. See the quotation for the meaning.

The advocate spoke from three distances. . . . The psychologists had expected their spokesman to be most persuasive from the middle distance, five to six feet. Any nearer approach would invade what Northwestern University Anthropologist Edward T. Hall and others have called "personal distance" — an invisible sphere that most animals, as well as man, consider off limits to strangers. *"Behavior: Distant Persuasion," Time, Sept. 7, 1970, p 27*

person-day, *n. Statistics.* a unit of time designating one average day of one person's normal activities.

In that year [1960] people in California spent some 235 million person-days in specified outdoor recreational activities, primarily swimming, picnicking, fishing and boating. *R. Merton Love, "The Rangelands of the Western U.S.," Scientific American, Feb. 1970, p 91*

personhood, *n.* the distinctive personal quality or characteristics of a human being; individuality.

The nation . . . possesses little knowledge, if any, of the steps by which the human being becomes itself, the separate, private acts of imagination on which the achievement of personhood depends. *Benjamin DeMott, quoted by Richard Todd, "Notes on Corporate Man," The Atlantic, Oct. 1971, p 92*

The United Church of Christ has in hand a statement written by six Christian education executives which maintains that sex is moral if the partners are committed to the "fulfilling of each other's personhood" — pointedly omitting marriage as a prerequisite. *"Religion," Time, Dec. 13, 1971, p 36*

PERT (pərt), *n.* acronym for *Program Evaluation and Review Technique*, a method of network analysis for planning a complex operation by using a computer. See the quotations for details.

The manager is confronted with such a bewildering array of linked decisions that could stem from the same set of facts in front of him that it would be impossible for him to be sure of selecting the *best* set of decisions to take; but the computer can trace the outcome of each of a very large number of logical paths and so arrive at the optimum path. This is the basis of such techniques as PERT and Critical Path Analysis. *E. Eastwood, New Scientist, Oct. 21, 1965, p 176*

More than anything else, Raborn made use of a then-obscure management system known as PERT (for Program Evaluation Review Technique). Using PERT, Raborn set precise timetables for each phase of the enormously complicated program, thus assured that everything would mesh without time-wasting gaps or overlaps in the schedule. *Time, April 23, 1965, p 20*

perturbative, *adj. Astronomy.* of or relating to the perturbations (disturbances in the motions) of planets.

The introduction by Dr W. J. Eckert explains that the tables of both Jupiter and Saturn contain systematic errors of the sort that would be caused by the omission of perturbative terms of appreciable size or by incorrect values of them. The discrepancies were read from a smooth curve drawn from the residuals (observation tables). *Edward J. Gunn, New Scientist, Nov. 12, 1970, p 345*

pe·se·wa (pə'se wə), *n.* a unit of money in Ghana. See the quotation for details.

The pesewa means a penny in the Ghanaian Fante language, and the cedi, which is worth 100 pesewas, is derived from a word meaning a small shell. *The Times (London), July 14, 1965, p 11*

Peter Principle. See the first quotation for the meaning.

Everybody has heard of Educator Laurence Peter's "Peter Principle," which holds that employees advance until they are promoted to their level of incompetence. *Time, April 13, 1970, p 13*

. . . much blame must attach to the [U.N.] administrative system, which has not only set out to prove Parkinson's Law, but which religiously follows the Peter Principle of promoting mediocrities. *Hella Pick, The Manchester Guardian Weekly, July 25, 1970, p 6*

petnapper, *n. U.S.* one who practices petnapping.

With the increasing number of animal care bills before Congress, medical researchers are worried that they might get hog-tied along with the petnappers. *"General Science: Researchers Fear Animal Restrictions," Science News, April 30, 1966, p 317*

petnapping, *n. U.S.* the kidnaping of pet animals.

The United States acted in 1966 to curb "petnapping." Under a federal law signed by President Lyndon B. Johnson in August, animal dealers who steal pets and sell them to research laboratories may be fined up to $1,000 and sentenced to a maximum of one year in jail. *"Animals," The 1967 Compton Yearbook, p 111*

► Though *petnapping* and *petnapper* are formed on analogy with *kidnaping* and *kidnaper* the traditional American forms *-naping* and *-naper* have been supplanted by the spellings *-napping* and *-napper*, which are more usual in Britain.

petrol bomb, *British.* a bomb made with a bottle filled with petrol and fitted with a wick; an incendiary bomb; Molotov cocktail.

The most common is still the petrol bomb—milk bottles filled with petrol with a wick stuffed into the mouth. *Brian Moynahan, "Battle of the Ulster Bombs," The Sunday Times (London), Oct. 31, 1971, p 104*

PG, abbreviation of PROSTAGLANDIN.

Prostaglandin (PG) was discovered in crude form in 1930 in human seminal plasma and material from sheep seminal vesicles. Various PG's have since been found in almost every tissue. *Robert B. Greenblatt, "Medicine: Endocrinology," Britannica Book of the Year 1970, p 498*

Their [doctors'] experience is too limited, the researchers concede, for them to recommend routine use of prostaglandins for abortion, and they urge a more extensive trial. . . . when the technique of PG abortion is simplified and improved, it is likely to be more acceptable than surgery—both emotionally and aesthetically—to many women. *"Medicine: Abortion Without Surgery?" Time, Feb. 9, 1970, p 40*

pharmacogenetic, *adj.* of or relating to pharmacogenetics.

A major advance pharmacologists are now serving up to physicians has to do with "pharmacogenetics," the study of genetically triggered individual responses to drugs. More and more clinicians are tuning in to pharmacogenetics. It should help them prescribe more rationally. . . . Known pharmacogenetic conditions appear to adhere to the general principles established for inborn errors of metabolism. *Joan Lynn Arehart, "How Genes Control Drugs," Science News, June 26, 1971, p 438*

pharmacogeneticist, *n.* a specialist in pharmacogenetics.

Some pharmacogeneticists advocate screening individuals who are to receive succinylcholine [a muscle relaxant] before surgery for their pseudocholinesterase activity. *Joan Lynn Arehart, "How Genes Control Drugs," Science News, June 26, 1971, p 439*

pharmacogenetics, *n.* the study of the interaction of genetics and drugs.

A body of knowledge, called pharmacogenetics, was accumulating that showed that the fate of a drug in the body, or even the nature and extent of its therapeutic effect, depends in certain cases upon a discrete genetic trait. *Sumner M. Kalman, "Pharmacology," 1970 Britannica Yearbook of Science and the Future, 1969, p 278*

A major advance pharmacologists are now serving up to physicians has to do with "pharmacogenetics," the study of genetically triggered individual responses to drugs. More and more clinicians are tuning in to pharmacogenetics. *Joan Lynn Arehart, "How Genes Control Drugs," Science News, June 26, 1971, p 438*

phase, *v.t.* **phase down,** to reduce gradually; reduce by phases.

The secretary said that the programme to phase down American air operations in Indo-China and turn over more of the air effort to the South Vietnamese "is solidly based and progressing, if anything, ahead of schedule." *The Times (London), Nov. 6, 1970, p 8*

[patterned after *phase out* to end or discontinue by phases]

phased-array, *adj.* having or based on a complex of electronically steerable radiating elements in place of a mechanically rotated antenna.

These phased-array radars, with computer complexes, could sight incoming missiles more than 1,000 miles

away. . . . *Heather M. David, "The Great ABM Debate," The Americana Annual 1970, p 464*

"Phased-array" aerials scan by means of a pattern of controlled delays between the signals passing through the different elements of the aerial. *New Scientist, Sept. 23, 1965, p 738*

phasedown, *n.* the gradual reduction of a program or operation.

. . . I believe we should proceed with our phasedown forthwith and carry it through expeditiously to completion—that is, until *all* U.S. Army, Navy, Marine Corps and Air Force personnel, except Embassy guards, are out of Vietnam. *Matthew B. Ridgway, "Disengaging from Vietnam," The New York Times, June 27, 1971, Sec. 4, p 15*

The best scope for achieving economies in clerical staff will probably come on the female side, where the turnover is rapid and any required phasedown can thus be acquired easily in a relatively short time. *Keith Payne, The Times (London), Feb. 12, 1968, p 17*

[from PHASE DOWN]

phe·naz·o·cine (fə'næz ə sən), *n.* a synthetic pain reliever more powerful and less addictive than morphine.

Another family of synthetic analgesics . . . is the one represented by methadone. . . . Still another, recently developed by Everett L. May of the National Institutes of Health, is the group of substances called benzomorphans. The best-known member of this group, phenazocine, is seven to 10 times more potent than morphine as an analgesic. . . . *Marshall Gates, "Analgesic Drugs," Scientific American, Nov. 1966, p 133*

[from *phen-* benzene derivative + *azo-* nitrogen + *-cine* (perhaps as in *medicine*)]

phe·net·ic (fi:'net ik), *adj.* of or relating to a method of classification of organisms based on overall or relative degrees of similarity among the organisms to be classified. Compare CLADISTIC.

A good example of new phenetic data was provided by C. G. Sibley who summarized his thousands of pieces of data on proteins in bird muscle and eggs. The protein data were treated in the same way as the more classical morphological data; a classification was derived based on degree of similarity. This phenetic approach was carried to its logical endpoint by R. R. Sokal who used computers to add up the number of characters held in common among taxa and then applied statistical techniques as a means to quantify degrees of similarity. The assumption is that those taxa with more characters in common are (probably) more closely related to each other than to others. *Thomas J. M. Schopf and Peter L. Ames, "Meetings: Systematics Workshop," Science. Feb. 9, 1968, p 659*

[from *phen-* (from Greek *phaínein* to show forth) + *-etic*, as in the term *phyletic* (based on phylum or line of descent), with which *phenetic* is contrasted]

phenetics, *n.* the phenetic system of classification.

This is a cladistic (or branching) approach toward forming a classification and markedly differs from the methodology of phenetics which emphasizes the degree of similarity independent of the way in which similarity was achieved. *Thomas J. M. Schopf and Peter L. Ames, "Meetings: Systematics Workshop," Science, Feb. 9, 1968, p 659*

pher·o·mo·nal ('fer ə,mou nəl), *adj.* of or relating to pheromones.

Her [Dr. Martha McClintock of Harvard] investigation threw up the bizarre observation that, precisely as in mice, the cycles of close friends, like those of mice caged together, fall into synchrony. Many possible influences could affect this. Is it a result of suggestion? . . . Room-mates tend to work late or sleep early by agreement: was it an effect of similar light-dark patterns? Apparently not. Of all the likely influences, a pheromonal communication, by subliminal odour, seemed biologically the most likely. *Alex Comfort, "Communication May Be Odorous," New Scientist and Science Journal, Feb. 25, 1971, p 413*

pher·o·mone ('fer ə,moun), *n.* any of a class of complex chemical substances secreted especially by insects to produce a specialized response in other insects of the same species.

These chemical messages have been termed phero-mones, and in insects they have a wide range of functions, from sex attractants and trail markers to alarm phero-mones and those which participate in maintaining the social structure of a colony. *James S. Kittredge, "Pheromones," McGraw-Hill Yearbook of Science and Technology 1971, p 323*

Virgin female roaches exude one of the most powerful sex lures in nature. Called pheromone, it sends male roaches into a frenzied priapic jig. *Douglas Marshall, Maclean's, July 1967, p 4*

[from *phero-* (from Greek *phérein* to carry) + *hormone*]

phi, *n.* or **phi meson,** a highly unstable and short-lived elementary particle with a large mass and zero charge.

Physicists had supposed that the photon, or light par-ticle, was the sole intermediary of electromagnetic forces. But experimental evidence has shown that photons ap-proaching hadrons tend to turn themselves into one of the mesons called phi, rho or omega. Thus, it appears that electromagnetic forces are mediated to leptons directly by photons and to hadrons by phi, rho or omega. *Dietrick E. Thomsen, "New Mathematics In Field Theory," Science News, April 10, 1971, p 250*

Phillips curve, a curve showing a correlation be-tween rates of unemployment and rates of inflation. See the quotation for details.

The Phillips curve . . . lays it down that the rate at which wages rise is inversely proportional to the level of unem-ployment—that is, that the greater the pressure on the labour market (and hence the lower the level of unemploy-ment), the faster the price of labour will rise. *Anthony Harris, The Manchester Guardian Weekly, March 14, 1970, p 22*

[named after A. W. H. *Phillips*, born 1914, a British economist]

phil·lu·men·ist (fi'lu: mə nist), *n.* a collector of match-box labels.

But the label is treated with a self-renewing adhesive, of special appeal to Britain's mounting army of phillumen-ists. *Basil Boothroyd, "A Little Extra Something," Punch, Sept. 8, 1965, p 341*

[from *phil-* lover, devotee + Latin *lūmen* light + English *-ist*]

phil·lu·me·ny (fi'lu: mə ni:), *n.* the hobby of a phil-lumenist.

Little did John Walker foresee that his invention would

become a great blessing to mankind, or that it would give rise to a popular hobby—phillumeny—the collecting of match-box labels. *Doreen Thomas, "Flash-back," The Listener, April 13, 1967, p 493*

phone-in, *n.* another name for CALL-IN.

One of the most exciting potentials this year has been the phone-in—not so much for anything it's yet achieved, but for the developable importance and excitement of ac-quiring presently-participating listeners. *Marghanita Laski, "Radio," The Listener, Dec. 30, 1971, p 915*

. . . last week he proposed reducing transit fares for San Franciscans over 65 to 5¢ and, on a subsequent TV "phone-in," said he would try to get buses closer to the curb at pickup. *Time, March 29, 1968, p 16*

pho·no·an·gi·og·ra·phy (,fou nou,æn dʒi:'ɑg rə fi:), *n.* examination of blood vessels by monitoring the sound made by the bloodstream.

Phonoangiography, which picks up sound just as a stethoscope does, is being used to detect hardening of the arteries. A normal artery is silent. *Science News, Nov. 7, 1970, p 368*

The sound of blood flowing through the vessels is picked up by a sensitive microphone, recorded on magnetic tape, and analyzed by phonoangiography—a new method of locating and estimating size of arterial obstructions. *Michael E. DeBakey, "Medicine," The World Book Science Annual 1972 (1971), p 326*

[from *phono-* sound + *angiography*, examination of the blood vessels]

pho·rate ('fou,reit), *n.* a highly toxic, organic phos-phorous compound used as a systemic insecticide.

Germination is also delayed, and with 125 ppm [parts per million] of Phorate or Thionazin, germination is reduced to 60 to 70 per cent of controls without these chemicals. . . . Weeds, however, were always less frequent in treated field plots, and in those treated with 250 ppm of Thionazin, no weeds grew for a year after application. *"Trends and Dis-coveries: Plant Growth Affected by Insecticides," New Sci-entist, April 17, 1969, p 133*

[contraction of *pho*sphorodithioate, a part of its chemical name]

pho·to·au·to·troph (,fou tou'ɔ: tə,trɑf), *n.* an auto-troph (self-nourishing organism) that obtains its nourishment or energy from light. Compare PHOTO-TROPH.

The majority of blue-green algae are aerobic photo-autotrophs: their life processes require only oxygen, light and inorganic substances. *Patrick Echlin, "The Blue-Green Algae," Scientific American, June 1966, p 76*

Once advanced oxygen-mediating enzymes arose, oxy-gen generated by increasing populations of photoauto-trophs containing these enzymes would build up in the oceans and begin to escape into the atmosphere. *Preston Cloud and Aharon Gibor, "The Oxygen Cycle," Scientific American, Sept. 1970, p 116*

photobotany, *n.* the branch of botany that studies the effects of light on plants.

The author starts with the basic physics of radiation and rightly emphasizes the importance of using frequency (or wave-number) rather than wave-length as an independent variable. He then moves on to techniques, to radiotoxic effects, shuns photobotany (chlorophyll doesn't appear even in the index), and then speeds to photo-reception and its underlying mechanisms. *Robert Weale, "Books: For*

Student and Specialist," Review of "An Introduction to Photobiology: The Influence of Light on Life" by Yves Le Grand, New Scientist, July 2, 1970, p 39

photochemical, *n.* a chemical produced by the action of light on a substance.

. . . the Environmental Protection Agency, created in December, 1970, set air-quality standards in 1971 for six principal pollutants of urban areas. These were sulfur oxides, carbon monoxide, particulates (soot and smoke), hydrocarbons, nitrogen oxides, and photochemicals. *Ralph E. Lapp, "The Cultivation of Technology," The World Book Science Annual 1972 (1971), p 34*

photochromic, *adj.* of or exhibiting photochromism.

Instead of a phosphor layer on the inside face of the tube, the R.C.A. device has a "photochromic" layer. Instead of emitting light, such a layer changes colour when struck by an electron beam. *The Times (London), May 24, 1968, p 25*

Photochromic materials, which are light sensitive organic dyes, change color upon exposure to near-ultraviolet light. The process reverses itself when the dyes are exposed to heat or certain other wavelengths of light. Developing is eliminated, and the change is instantaneous. *Science News Letter, July 25, 1964, p 56*

photochromism, *n.* the property of changing color when exposed to light; sensitivity to light.

. . . when dyes (notably fluorescein) are dissolved in a rigid medium such as glass and are exposed to a strong light, the dyes change color. When the light is removed, the dyes revert to their normal color after a second or so. This general phenomenon is called photochromism. *Gerald Oster, "The Chemical Effects of Light," Scientific American, Sept. 1968, p 164*

photocoagulating, *adj.* inducing photocoagulation.

Drs J. Marshall and J. Mellerio . . . have found that when the retina is subjected to a photocoagulating laser pulse (an ophthalmic surgical technique) the transient pressure waves which reverberate through the eyeball resemble the seismic records following an earthquake. *Science Journal, July 1969, p 16*

photocoagulation, *n.* coagulation induced by laser beams.

Photocoagulation with lasers has improved the treatment of visual loss in central serous retinopathy (any noninflammatory disease of the retina), macular lesions, exudative choroiditis, and some retinal vascular changes due to atrophy of the optic nerve. *Roland I. Pritikin and M. L. Duchon, "Eye Diseases: Treatment Advances," The Americana Annual 1970, p 286*

In laser photocoagulation, for example, one of the problems has been that the red light of the ruby is not well absorbed by the red color of hemoglobin, thus limiting its effectiveness in treating blood vessel diseases of the retina. *Scientific American, Sept. 1967, p 37*

photocoagulator, *n.* a laser device used in photocoagulation.

Among the few practical applications of laser beams has been their development as photocoagulators for "spot-welding" detached retinas back into place inside the human eye. *New Scientist, March 30, 1967, p 679*

photocube, *n.* a transparent plastic cube usually filled with a piece of spongy material to hold a photograph up against the inside of each surface so that it may be displayed.

Perspex photocube — an ingenious way of displaying six

different photos, price £2, postage 1s.6d. extra, from Presents of Sloane Street, London, S.W.1. *The Times (London), Nov. 13, 1970, p 15*

photofabrication, *n.* the use of photography in the manufacture of integrated circuits by photoengraving semiconductor surfaces on a small silicon wafer or chip.

Photofabrication starts with drawings and by chemistry and optics transforms them into the objects, usually with a reduction in linear scale. *Scientific American, April 1967, p 47*

photopigment, *n.* a pigment whose characteristics are changed by the action of light.

The details of the coupling between the absorption of light by a photopigment and the subsequent changes in membrane conductance await further study. *Joel E. Brown, "Eye (invertebrate)," McGraw-Hill Yearbook of Science and Technology 1971, p 205*

. . . the photochemist cannot study the photopigments of a single receptor in living animals and the finest microelectrode is gross in size when compared with the diameter of some of the processes which we assume to carry electric potentials in the nerve net. *Kit Pedler, Science Journal, Feb. 1970, p 53*

photopolarimeter, *n.* an instrument combining telescopic, photographic, and polarimetric (measuring polarized light) apparatus for producing detailed images of planetary features.

The Jovian atmosphere will be analyzed by an ultraviolet photometer and an infrared radiometer; the latter will also record temperatures on the surface of the planet. Finally, the disk of the planet will be photographed by a novel mechanism: an imaging photopolarimeter. It will consist of a telescope of one-inch aperture that will sweep out a cone as the spacecraft spins slowly at about five revolutions per minute. *"Science and the Citizen: Pioneers to Jupiter," Scientific American, Oct. 1971, p 44*

Most intriguing of all, light measurements by Pioneer's imaging photo-polarimeter will enable computers on earth to construct about ten pictures of the planet [Jupiter] that will show features as small as 250 miles across. *Time, March 15, 1971, p 46*

pho·to·rec·ce (ˌfou tou'rek iː), *n.* *U.S. Military Slang.* reconnaissance by aerial photographs.

We have also recently told MACV [Military Assistance Command, Vietnam] that we have a high priority requirement for night photorecce of key motorable routes in Laos. *Excerpt from a cablegram from Admiral U. S. Grant Sharp, The New York Times, June 13, 1971, Sec. 4, p 37*

[shortened from *photoreconnaissance*]

pho·to·re·sist (ˌfou tou ri'zist), *n.* a plastic material that hardens to varying degrees depending on the intensity of the light to which it is exposed, used especially as a protective coating on the surface of silicon wafers or chips in the manufacture of integrated circuits.

The next step is to make the holographic master, which consists of one hologram for each frame. This is done in the conventional way except that the hologram is formed in a layer of a photoresist material a few micrometres thick. The laser light softens the photoresist and the more intensive the light at any given point the softer the photoresist becomes. *Ron Brown, "Television in the Can," New Scientist, Oct. 1, 1970, p 19*

photorespiration, *n. Botany.* respiration induced or stimulated by the presence of light.

. . . genetic variability was found for several physiological components of yield: the efficiency with which light is utilized in photosynthesis (net photosynthesis); rate of carbon dioxide release in light (photorespiration); rate of carbon dioxide release in darkness (respiration). . . . *Henry R. Fortmann, "Agriculture," 1971 Britannica Yearbook of Science and the Future, 1970, p 109*

Physiological features of C-4 plants. . . . Their CO_2 compensation points are very low, and they do not exhibit the light-induced stimulation of CO_2 production which is termed photorespiration. *W. M. Laetsch, "Photosynthesis," McGraw-Hill Yearbook of Science and Technology 1971, p 324*

photoscanner, *n.* a device that reproduces on X-ray film the distribution of a radioactive isotope injected in the body for diagnostic purposes.

The gamma rays coming from the abnormal portions of bone are detected by a photoscanner that is passed externally over the body. Any portion of bone that gives off gamma rays is considered diseased. X-rays, in contrast, work by showing changes in bone density. . . . *"Medicine: Tumor Detection Aided by Radioactive Chemical," Science News, Nov. 12, 1966, p 400*

photoscanning, *n.* the use of a photoscanner. Compare SCANNING.

Photoscanning using radioactive isotopes can tell us if cancer is present in such organs as the thyroid gland, the liver and the brain. *R. W. Raven, The Times (London), Sept. 19, 1967, p 9*

photosensor, *n.* a device that is sensitive to light.

In a study of commonly used type fonts, for instance, it has been found that 24 rows of photosensors are necessary to recognise unambiguously a typical character. In contrast, the number of vertical columns in the photosensor array is determined primarily by psychological considerations: many columns lead to a higher reading rate. *New Scientist, Dec. 24, 1970, p 554*

photosurface, *n.* photographic surface.

The cost of electronography to the user is high. Every time an exposed photographic plate is removed, the air destroys the highly reactive photosurface. *Philip Morrison, Scientific American, May 1970, p 139*

pho·to·troph ('fou tou₁traf), *n.* an organism that uses light to break down carbon dioxide. Compare PHOTOAUTOTROPH.

Norris and Ribbons have been concerned to choose for special coverage those organisms which are not well described in other publications or which involve, because of their unusual physiology, special techniques. Hence the fascinating collection of autotrophs, phototrophs, anaerobic and rumen bacteria. . . . *Louis Quesnel, "Books: For Student and Specialist," Review of "Methods in Microbiology," Volumes 1, 3A, and 3B, edited by J. R. Norris and D. W. Ribbons, New Scientist, Sept. 10, 1970, p 545*

phrase marker, a linguistic marker or signal representing one of the phrasal components of a construction.

"Now, the fundamental idea of transformational grammar is that the bracketed and labelled representation of a sentence is its surface structure, and associated with each sentence is a long sequence of more and more abstract representations of the sentence—we transformationalists

call them phrase markers—of which surface structure is only the first. . . ." *Noam Chomsky, quoted by Ved Mehta, "Onward and Upward with the Arts: Linguistics," The New Yorker, May 8, 1971, p 53*

phrase-structure grammar, a grammar consisting of phrase-structure rules. Compare GENERATIVE-TRANSFORMATIONAL GRAMMAR.

Considerable progress has been made . . . in using computers to manipulate languages, both vernaculars and programming languages. Grammars called phrase-structure grammars and transformational grammars supply the theoretical backdrop for this activity. *Anthony G. Oettinger, "The Uses of Computers in Science," Scientific American, Sept. 1966, p 166*

phrase-structure rule, one of the rules governing the construction of the phrasal constituents of a sentence.

During the past five years it has become clear that phrase structure rules and transformations provide a grossly inadequate characterization of the notion 'rule of grammar'. The problem is this: phrase structure rules and transformations are local; they define well-formedness conditions on individual phrase-markers and on pairs of successive phrase-markers. However, certain rules of grammar are global in nature; they extend over entire derivations, or parts of derivations, and cannot be stated in full generality (if at all) by local operations. I have proposed that rules of grammar be considered as well-formedness conditions on derivations (or 'derivational constraints'). In the most general case, rules of grammar will be global in nature. Phrase structure rules and transformations turn out to be special cases of derivational constraints. *George Lakoff, University of Michigan, "Global Rules," Language, Sept. 1970, p 627*

phy·tane ('fai₁tein), *n.* a complex hydrocarbon ($C_{20}H_{42}$), a product of the breakdown of chlorophyll, the presence of which in oil-bearing rocks is believed to be evidence of the existence of living matter 3 billion years ago.

Two specific hydrocarbons, a C_{20} hydrocarbon, phytane . . . and a C_{19} hydrocarbon, pristane, which is present in marine organisms, seem to occur ubiquitously in ancient sediments. *Eugene J. McCarthy, "Origin of Life," McGraw-Hill Yearbook of Science and Technology 1971, p 3*

For one thing, the chemical analysis of organic material from the Gunflint cherts in several laboratories reveals the presence of the hydrocarbons pristane and phytane: two "chemical fossils" that can most reasonably be regarded as being breakdown products of chlorophyll. *Elso S. Barghoorn, "The Oldest Fossils," Scientific American, May 1971, p 38*

[from Greek *phytón* plant + *-ane* (chemical suffix)]

phy·to·chrome ('fai tə₁kroum), *n.* a protein pigment in plants. See the quotations for details.

Phytochrome is a protein having two forms which are interconvertible by radiation. One form, which has an absorption maximum near 0.73 micrometres wavelength in the far-red, and is thus known as P*fr*, is biologically active. *New Scientist, March 18, 1965, p 719*

Phytochrome molecules regulate such processes as germination, growth, and flowering, turning these functions on and off in response to the length of days and nights. *James A. Pearre, "Botany," The 1967 World Book Year Book, p 247*

phytohemagglutinin, *n.* any of various protein

substances extracted from plants that cause cells to change in shape, divide, or clump together.

The search for inducers in a number of laboratories turned up many different kinds of substances that stimulated interferon production in animals. These included bacteria, parasites, viruses, polysaccharides, agents such as phytohemagglutinin that promote cell division, bacterial endotoxins, synthetic plastics and other substances. *Maurice R. Hilleman and Alfred A. Tytell, "The Induction of Interferon," Scientific American, July 1971, p 27*

[from *phyto-* plant + *hemagglutinin* antibody that causes red blood cells to agglutinate]

phytotoxicant, *n.* a substance toxic to plants.

. . . O₃ has been recognized as a phytotoxicant for at least 100 years. Primary sources of O₃ include the upper atmosphere and electrical storms. *Francis A. Wood, "Air Pollution," McGraw-Hill Yearbook of Science and Technology 1971, p 91*

phy·to·tron ('fai tə,trɑn), *n.* a laboratory for the study of plant growth under controlled climatic conditions.

At the Gif-sur-Yvette Phytotron (the word is apparently due to the late R. A. Millikan) Dr. J. P. Nitsch is trying to grow pine-apples in glass wool. *New Scientist, March 30, 1967, p 670*

. . . CalTech has recently invested something approaching £3 million in a so-called "phytotron"—an Orwellian word for a highly technologically sophisticated greenhouse. *New Scientist, Oct. 1, 1970, p 2*

[from *phyto-* plant + *-tron* an instrument or device]

Pi·a·get·ian (,pi: ə'ʒei ən), *adj.* of or relating to the Swiss psychologist Jean Piaget, born 1896, or his theories of child development.

The child is being cared for in an experimental nursery school for the children of graduate students run, I understand, in accord with the best Piagetian principles. *Donald Barthelme, "Critique De La Vie Quotidienne," The New Yorker, July 17, 1971, p 29*

Collection of articles representative of the theoretical and empirical research derived from Piagetian theory, focus is on intellectual development of the young elementary school child. . . . *"Books of the Week," Listing of "Logical Thinking in Children: Research Based on Piaget's Theory," edited by Irving E. Sigel and Frank H. Hopper, Science News, Aug. 17, 1968, p 171*

—*n.* an advocate or supporter of Jean Piaget and his theories.

Quite possibly, Piagetians sometimes speculate, adolescents' fascination with their ability to visualize alternatives is what makes them so eager to test new life-styles and utopian ideals. *Time, Dec. 12, 1969, p 42*

pi·clor·am (pai'klɔr əm), *n.* a highly active and persistent herbicide, used extensively for defoliation in Vietnam.

Dr. Arthur W. Galston, professor of biology at Yale, has described Picloram as "a herbicidal analog of DDT," and an article in a Dow Chemical Company publication called "Down to Earth" reported that in field trials of Picloram in various California soils between eighty and ninety-six and a half percent remained in the soil four hundred and sixty-seven days after application. *Thomas Whiteside, "A Reporter at Large: Defoliation," The New Yorker, Feb. 7, 1970, p 34*

The recently introduced chemical, picloram, is one of the longest-lived pesticides and would contaminate the ground for years. *Richard Scott, The Manchester Guardian Weekly, Feb. 21, 1970, p 6*

[formed backwards from the chemical name *amino-*trich*loro*pic*olinic* acid]

pi·cor·na·vi·rus (pi,kɔr nə'vai rəs), *n.* any of a group of viruses containing ribonucleic acid, including the poliovirus, rhinovirus, and similar viruses.

The picornaviruses are a third category. "Pico" stands for very small, and "rna" is added because they contain ribonucleic acid, which is conventionally abbreviated to rna. *The Times (London), Sept. 3, 1965, p 14*

FMD [foot-and-mouth disease] is caused and transmitted by a picorna virus (one of the smallest known disease-producing organisms) of which there are seven major types and at least 50 subtypes. *George C. Poppensiek and Howard E. Quirk, "Veterinary Medicine," 1969 Britannica Yearbook of Science and the Future, 1968, p 339*

pi·co·sec·ond ('pai kou,sek ənd), *n.* one thousand billionth (10⁻¹²) of a second; a trillionth part of a second.

Laser pulses lasting about a trillionth of a second, or one picosecond, can now be measured accurately for the first time, making it possible to measure picosecond events in atoms and molecules. *Science News, Dec. 2, 1967, p 537*

Closely spaced picosecond pulses have been observed in Q-switched ruby and neodymium/glass lasers. *New Scientist, Dec. 28, 1967, p 767*

[from *pico-* trillionth (from Spanish *pico* peak) + *second*]

Picturephone, *n.* a trade name for the VIDEO-PHONE.

As befits an executive in a communications company, however, Thomas has a Picturephone on his desk, and takes part in conferences by TV; "if you have something critical to do, you have to get in an aeroplane and go". *New Scientist, Dec. 24, 1970, p 565*

picture telephone, another name for the VIDEO-PHONE.

. . . the life of existing television cameras may now be extended by forming the tube at higher temperatures. The manufacture should be cheaper, involving only silicon and silicon compounds. The development of picture telephones, which many electrical companies believe may come into popular use in the 1980s, is brought a step nearer with this advance. *"Science Report: Discovery Paves Way for Picture Phones," The Times (London), March 30, 1970, p 8*

pierced earring, *U.S.* an earring made for insertion in a pierced ear.

Employed by a costume jewelry company, Miss Robbe travels all over the country promoting the company's earrings. The package deal includes the purchase of a $6 pair of pierced earrings. With this purchase, the customer may sign a permission slip and have her (or his) ears pierced free of charge. *Sally Tucker, "The Brave Ones Left With Pierced Ears . . . The Cowards Stood And Trembled," The Tuscaloosa News (Alabama), Dec. 31, 1971, p 8*

pig, *n. Slang.* a policeman.

Nothing is more hampering to a man with dogmatic opinions than the evidence of the public opinion polls. . . . Now we have the instructive example of the so called

363

student rebellion.... The news that in only 19 per cent of the riots were the police called in also makes nonsense of the New Left's equally mulish contention that the "pigs" are the Establishment's unfailing resort. *Alistair Cooke, "Cooke's Column: The Students," The Manchester Guardian Weekly, Jan. 24, 1970, p 5*

... Jake was murdered in a shoot-out in Chicago where three pigs were killed and seven were wounded. *Edward Jay Epstein, "Report from The Black Panther Newspaper," The New Yorker, Feb. 13, 1971, p 72*

Though many radicals still think of police as "pigs"—with some justification in a number of cities—liberals who used to minimize crime are now recognizing that police have a serious task on their hands. *Time, July 13, 1970, p 34*

In a year when policemen were out of favor with many students—when "pig" had replaced "cop" in the typical academic vocabulary—the Longfellow seniors voted to invite Patrolman Sanders to deliver their commencement address. *John Fischer, Harper's, Dec. 1970, p 22*

► *Pig* is a hostile or insulting epithet used especially by radicals to describe policemen and sometimes other law-enforcement officers. The use of *pig* in this sense was part of British underworld slang throughout the 1800's. The current use may be a re-emergence of a very old expression.

piledriver, *n.* **1** a person who hits or strikes with great power or impact.

Hill, a 6-ft. 3-in. 212-lb. pile driver, rewarded them by leading the league in rushing.... *Time, April 6, 1970, p 79*

Her [Jeanne-Marie Darré's] piano playing has immense vitality, propelled by a phenomenal technique. But she is made of blood, bone and brain... and she is not a piledriver. *Harold C. Schonberg, The New York Times, Aug. 22, 1966, p 41*

2 (in wrestling) a slamming downward of an opponent so that the top of his head hits the canvas.

I was coerced into becoming wrestling correspondent.... Friday night became Majestic night, a night immersed in grapevine, arm and head lock, body slam and press, piledriver, full and half nelson, Boston crab, head scissors, flying mare, leg snatch and folding press, bear hug, knockout and submission. *Eric Todd, The Manchester Guardian Weekly, Dec. 26, 1970, p 23*

pill, *n.* **the pill,** an oral contraceptive in pill form.

The pill is an extremely effective means of birth control, but it can only work if the patient remembers to take it. *Science Journal, Nov. 1970, p 14*

"Laughing test-tube baby,
Scientific coup,
Could you tell me, maybe,
What's the point of you?"
"I'm the demonstration
Life will burgeon still,
I'm the incarnation
Of how to dodge the Pill." *William Davis, Punch, Feb. 26, 1969, p 292*

Newspapers, magazines, television and even newsreels have carried on a noisy debate over the last year on whether the Pill, by far the most popular contraceptive, is safe. *Alison and David Stein, Saturday Night (Canada), March 1967, p 17*

pillhead, *n. Slang.* a person addicted to taking pills, such as tranquilizers, barbiturates, and amphetamines, to combat depression, insomnia, anxiety, etc.

There were five other patients "in residence" when I arrived and during my six-month stay, the population totalled only nineteen—fourteen narcotic addicts, two marijuana smokers and two "pillheads," including me. *Maclean's, Sept. 4, 1965, p 31*

Mr. Leech told the children, in group discussions, using the slang of the "pillheads" and "junkies", that on Tuesday he buried an addict of 23.... *The Times (London), March 28, 1968, p 3*

[see HEAD]

pin-fire, *v.t.* to treat (a horse) for splints and other leg ailments by anesthetizing and applying electric needles to the affected part.

Woodlawn was pin-fired below the knee last spring after injuring himself just before Cheltenham. The Hennessy Gold Cup is his next objective, and all being well he will be trained in the new year for the Grand National. *Michael Phillips, The Times (London), Nov. 4, 1967, p 7*

pinholder, *n.* a device for holding cut flowers, consisting of a mounting or base studded with pins.

Most of them, like the pink daisies in *Through the Looking Glass* who turned white with shock when Alice threatened to pick them would, one feels, quite rightly faint at the sight of a pin-holder. *Betty Massingham, The Times (London), March 22, 1967, p 11*

pink spot, a chemical substance (DMPEA or dimethoxyphenylethylamine) that is closely related to the hallucinogenic drug mescaline, discovered in the urine of non-paranoid schizophrenics, where its presence may be a biochemical indication of schizophrenia.

Dr. Arnold J. Friedhoff of the New York University School of Medicine, one of the first to identify DMPEA, or the pink spot, in the urine of schizophrenics, presents further evidence on its metabolic pathways. *Science News, May 25, 1968, p 503*

[so called because the presence of the substance is indicated by the appearance of a pink spot on the porous chromatographic paper used in the analysis of urine]

pin·ta ('pɑin tə), *n. British.* a pint of a beverage, especially milk.

The National Dairy Council, while properly warning that if you intend to drive you should stick to milk, is mounting a campaign which urges the consumption of a pinta (milk) before a pinta (beer) over Christmas. *New Scientist, Dec. 26, 1968, p 723*

[from the advertising slogan "drinka *pinta* milka day" introduced by the National Dairy Council of Great Britain in 1958, perhaps on the analogy of *cuppa* a cup of tea (a colloquialism, according to Eric Partridge, by 1940, and in Australian English [since circa 1905)]

pi·on·ic (pɑi'ɑn ik), *adj.* of or relating to pi mesons.

The existence of such exotic atoms was predicted on theoretical grounds as early as 1947. Five years later the first ones were observed; because negative pi mesons, or pions, were used to take the place of the electrons in this case, the resulting exotic atoms were called pionic atoms. Subsequently both muonic atoms and kaonic atoms were discovered. *Scientific American, Nov. 1970, p 45*

[from *pion* pi meson + *-ic*]

pipe bomb, a home-made bomb encased in an iron or steel pipe.

There are unquestionably many people, both in and out of the Weatherman faction, who still believe that the way to salvation is a pipe bomb and a fuse. *Jesse Birnbaum, Time, Feb. 22, 1971, p 14*

Pipe bombs are another favourite anti-personnel bomb. *Brian Moynahan, "Battle of the Ulster Bombs," The Sunday Times (London), Oct. 31, 1971, p 10*

pipeline, *n.* **in** or **into the pipeline,** in the works; under way.

But there are plans in the pipeline for converting more forest land to parkland.... For the parks themselves, and for those delegates of 1972, it might just mean that tents, not trucks, will nestle round the slopes.... *Martin Walker, "National Park or Concrete Jungle?" The Manchester Guardian Weekly, Dec. 12, 1970, p 16*

Air Force advocates gingerly say that to perform any future death-dealing missions this mighty bomber must be put into the defense pipeline now. *Herbert Mitgang, The New York Times, June 7, 1971, p 33*

Pis·ce·an ('pis i: ən, 'pɑi si: ən, *or* 'pis ki: ən), *n.* a person born under the sign of Pisces, February 19-March 20.

Other personalities, selected "at random" for proof that they are just as at home in the traditional horoscope, include such "hardly wishy-washy" Ariens as Warren Beatty, Debbie Reynolds and Schmidt's brother, Jack (obviously better off as "strong-willed ambitious" Pisceans). *"Modern Living: The Revised Zodiac," Review of "Astrology" by Steven Schmidt, Time, Nov. 23, 1970, p 44*

—*adj.* of or relating to Pisceans.

Mr. Morgan—Pisces, as the children called him, whose journeys were all of the mind (a Piscean trait), that possibly being the reason that he resisted any other kind of travel.... *Katinka Loeser, "The Houses of Heaven," The New Yorker, April 3, 1971, p 35*

pis·ci·cide ('pis ə‚said), *n.* the extermination of fish, especially all fish in a given area.

Yet I was unable to detect any evidence of mass piscicide in the Sonic's track. The only dead fish I saw was a 6 in. specimen pointed out by Mr. Tolar himself. *The Times (London), Aug. 21, 1963, p 5*

[from *pisci-* fish + *-cide* killing, as in *genocide*]

pi·ta (pi:'tɑ:), *n.* a flat, round barley or flour bread eaten in the Middle East.

Now a smaller size is in vogue for sandwiches, and despite its ethnic overtones, Syrian bread, also called pita, shows every indication of becoming as American as pizza pie. Just witness the recent growth of Greek and Israeli sandwich stands. *Susan Rogers, "An Ancient Staff of Life," New York Post, Nov. 1, 1971, p 46*

pix·el ('pik səl), *n.* one of the photographic elements of a television image or picture.

The Vidicon converted each picture into an image consisting of 200 lines with 200 picture elements ("pixels") per line, making a total of 40,000 pixels per picture. *Robert B. Leighton, Scientific American, May 1970, p 28*

The image of Phobos studied most closely by Smith falls within a rectangular array of picture elements (pixels) measuring eight by 10 pixels. Each pixel ... is about 13 microns on a side. To clean up the image, Smith reports in *Science,* "first-order noise removal, geometric correction, and photometric decalibration [were] applied by hand, pixel by pixel." *Scientific American, July 1970, p 50*

[from *pix* (picture) *element*]

piz·zazz or **pi·zazz** (pə'zæz), *n. U.S. Slang.* **1** liveliness; vitality; pep.

Jazz and soul food, soul food and jazz, are thought to generate pizzazz. *"Goings On About Town," The New Yorker, Aug. 28, 1971, p 4*

2 showy quality; flashiness.

In a high-rolling state [Florida] that likes politics with pizazz, [Governor Reubin] Askew is a nonsmoking teetotaler who devotes most of his spare time to Presbyterian Church activities. *Time, May 31, 1971, p 15*

Also spelled PAZZAZZ, BIZZAZZ.

[of unknown origin]

PKU, abbreviation of *phenylketonuria* (an inherited condition in which the body cannot metabolize the amino acid phenylalanine, resulting in brain damage and mental retardation in infancy).

Dr. David Y. Hsia, a professor of pediatrics at Northwestern University, reported yesterday findings that confirm that a special diet permits normal brain development in children born with the defect called phenylketonuria, or PKU. *Richard D. Lyons, The New York Times, May 3, 1968, p 18*

Among other things, the testing revealed that two of the babies had the metabolic ailment phenylketonuria, commonly called PKU, which can lead to severe mental retardation unless the infant is put on a special diet at an early stage. The discovery of two cases of PKU among three thousand babies was surprising because the disease commonly occurs only once in every ten thousand infants. Today, both the babies are alive and healthy. *"A Safer Start for 50,000 Newborn Babies," Maclean's, March 6, 1965, p 1*

placebo effect, the beneficial effect which placebos (medications without active ingredients) seem to have on certain patients or their ailments.

Some disorders, and some patients, are more susceptible to placebo-effect than others—arthritics particularly. *Brian Inglis, The Sunday Times (London), July 2, 1967, p 8*

planeside, *n.* the area beside an airplane.

I arrive back at Kennedy Airport a veritable Adonis of virility and hedonistic masculinity. But by the time I walk from planeside to a taxi, a cold wind sweeps across the airport and wipes away the whole four weeks' work. *Goodman Ace, "Was This Trip Necessary?" Saturday Review, Aug. 31, 1968, p 6*

—*adj.* at the planeside; beside an airplane.

In a planeside interview, General Abrams said that, although the Communists had the ability to launch new offensives, "I don't know about" the magnitude of such ability. *The New York Times, March 28, 1968, p 3*

Pla·net·o·khod (plə'net ə‚xɔ:t), *n.* a vehicle designed by Soviet scientists for scientific exploration of the planets. See also LUNOKHOD, MARSOKHOD.

The vehicle is called Lunokhod-1. The hybrid Russian word means "moon vehicle" or "moon walker", and Soviet scientists are predicting that other such vehicles, named Planetokhod or Marsokhod, will eventually move over the surface of the Planets. *David Bonavia, The Times (London), Nov. 18, 1970, p 1*

planetologist

[patterned after Russian *Lunokkhod*, literally, moon walker]

planetologist, *n.* a specialist in planetology.

"For earth scientists and planetologists," declared MSC's [Manned Spacecraft Center's] Dr. Robin Brett, as Warren cut through the inner plastic bag enclosing the rocks, "This is a very, very exciting time." *"Apollo Returns: the Work Begins," Science News, Aug. 2, 1969, p 96*

planetology, *n.* the study of the planets in the solar system.

The next section deals with "general planetology", a term defined as being a branch of astronomy that deals with the study and interpretation of the physical and chemical properties of planets. *Patrick Moore, "Books: Living Space," Review of "Habitable Planets for Man" by Stephen H. Dole, New Scientist, June 25, 1964, p 827*

planholder, *n.* a shareholder in a pension plan.

When the planholder reaches retirement, he draws a pension expressed in units—helping to offset subsequent rises in the cost of living. *Richard Milner, The Sunday Times (London), Aug. 20, 1967, p 18*

planned obsolescence, the manufacture of products designed to deteriorate or become outdated after a shorter period of time than might normally be expected.

"Our whole economy is based on planned obsolescence." Bloomingdale's, obviously, is leaning Fairchild's way; so, for example, are Stanley Korshak in Chicago, Sakowitz in Houston, Erlebacher in Washington. *"Out on a Limb with the Midi," Time, Sept. 14, 1970, p 77*

After about two years, the makers wisely claim, the bracelets lose their power and must be replaced—a sort of magical planned obsolescence. *Time, July 6, 1970, p 56*

plasma jet, a jet of extremely hot plasma or ionized gas.

Plasma jets, the white-hot streams of gas used for such tasks as cutting and welding, may soon have yet another use, "steering" satellites through space. A plasma jet system, using helium as fuel, would be able to keep an orbiting satellite pointing in the right direction for long periods and would out-perform chemically fueled jets in fuel economy, ease of starting and stability, researchers say. *"Engineering," Science News Letter, Sept. 12, 1964, p 163*

plasmapause, *n.* the upper limits of the region above the atmosphere that contain layers of plasma or highly ionized gas. Compare PLASMASPHERE.

But the spacecraft will be far beyond the plasmapause, the outer boundary of the ionosphere, and beyond the magnetosphere for most of the time. *R. G. Stone, Science Journal, March 1970, p 73*

When the Sun is quiet, the plasmapause is able to force its way out from its usual position; but when the Sun is unusually active it is pushed down to lower altitudes. *"Io Shows Up Jupiter's Plasmapause...," New Scientist and Science Journal, July 1, 1971, p 8*

A sounding rocket meets the right conditions as it goes through the ionosphere; as does a satellite in an eccentric orbit when, at its apogee, it goes through the plasmapause. *New Scientist and Science Journal, Jan. 28, 1971, p 198*

plasma physicist, a specialist in plasma physics.

Typically, plasma with a density of 10^{14} nuclei per cu.cm must be held together for about one second. To bring this about is the dream of plasma physicists. *Larry Miller,*

"*Another Rung on the Fusion Ladder," New Scientist, Oct. 24, 1968, p 186*

plasma physics, a branch of physics dealing with plasma or highly ionized gas, especially as it appears in a wide range of cosmic phenomena and as it is used in controlled thermonuclear reactions.

Hydrogen bombs achieve fusion from the extraordinary temperatures and enormous pressures generated by atomic explosions, which are clearly untenable for peaceful thermonuclear power: controlled fusion must meet the stringent demands of plasma physics nonviolently. *Mort LaBrecque, "Power without Pollution," Encyclopedia Science Supplement (Grolier) 1971, p 367*

... plasma physics [is] the study of balanced mixtures of free ions and electrons. *Mikhail D. Millionshchikov, "Physical Sciences in the Soviet Union: The Growing Interest in Plasma Physics," 1970 Britannica Yearbook of Science and the Future, 1969, p 421*

Plasma physics in Sweden is a small affair despite the award of half this year's Nobel prize for physics to its leading theoretical exponent, Professor Hannes Alfven. *New Scientist, Dec. 3, 1970, p 400*

plasmasphere, *n.* an envelope of highly ionized gas about a planet. Compare PLASMAPAUSE.

Since none of Jupiter's outer satellites seems to affect the planet's radiation, the plasmasphere evidently does not have a long tail extending to satellite orbits beyond Io. *"Io Shows Up Jupiter's Plasmapause...," New Scientist and Science Journal, July 1, 1971, p 8*

plasma torch, a device that produces plasma or ionized gas for vaporizing, melting, or reducing any substance, such as metal or waste products.

In addition to vaporizing solids, plasma torches could also be used to heat liquids. *Science News, March 7, 1970, p 250*

plasmid, *n.* another name for EPISOME.

... minicells may be used to isolate from *E. coli* those small pieces of DNA, independent of the bacterial chromosome, known as plasmids or episomes. *New Scientist, Aug. 13, 1970, p 325*

[from cyto*plasm* + *-id* structure, body]

plastic, *adj.* not natural or real; synthetic; artificial.

Live television can be quite lively, as viewers of the British version of David Frost's talk show discovered last week. In mid-interview with Yippie Jeer-leader Jerry Rubin, some 30 Yippie yahoos stormed the studio stage, screeching obscenities, knocking over equipment, squirting Frost with water and insults ("You are a plastic man. You have been dead for years"). *Time, Nov. 23, 1970, p 36*

Now that so many of the young seem to wear their hearts on their sleeves, it is hard to tell which ones are real and which ones are plastic. *Russell Lynes, "After Hours: Highbrow, Lowbrow, Middlebrow Reconsidered," Harper's, Aug. 1967, p 19*

plastic memory. See the quotation for the meaning.

One of the fascinations of the behavior of plastics is that when certain kinds of plastic are molded in a distinct form, then melted so that the form is lost and then allowed to cool, they resume much the same form. Called "plastic memory," the phenomenon has an analogue in a little-known metallic alloy. The metal is named Nitinol from its constituents (nickel and titanium) and the place where it was discovered 10 years ago (the Naval Ordnance Laboratory). *"Science and the Citizen," Scientific American,* March 1971, p 47

plate, *n.* **1** one of a number of vast crustal blocks that comprise, according to the theory of plate tectonics, the land masses of the earth and that are believed to produce the drift and fragmentation of continents. Also called TECTONIC PLATE.

Earthquakes occur because each plate is rigid and moves against another plate with great resistance. *Richard M. Pearl, "Earth Sciences," Encyclopedia Science Supplement (Grolier) 1971, p 13*

The plates, which are layers of rock several miles thick and thousands of miles long, are driven sideways by underlying forces which may be convection currents kept in motion by the earth's internal heat. *The Times (London), Feb. 9, 1970, p 10*

Both of these plates [the Caribbean and Atlantic] are moving westward, but the Atlantic plate is moving faster and is being forced under the Caribbean. . . . *Louise Purrett, Science News, March 6, 1971, p 170*

According to the sea-floor-spreading hypothesis, large plates of the Earth's crust are slowly moving relative to one another, like giant slabs of floating ice. *Robert W. Decker, "Volcano," McGraw-Hill Yearbook of Science and Technology 1971, p 430*

By 1971 scientists realized that the earth's upper layer, consisting of the crust and upper mantle to a depth of about 100 km, is divided into six relatively rigid, migrating plates that have spread apart and come together to form many of the major geological features on the earth. Because continental drift is only part of the story, "plate tectonics" is a more appropriate term to describe this process. *J. M. Dennison, "Earth Sciences," 1972 Britannica Yearbook of Science and the Future, 1971, p 232*

2 on a plate, *British.* without effort or exertion. The U.S. phrase is *on a platter* or *on a silver platter.*

. . . if New Zealand has the EEC door slammed in her face . . . car factories of Japan, to take one immediate example, would have a new market handed to them on a plate. *Patrick Keatley, The Manchester Guardian Weekly, July 11, 1970, p 4*

plate tectonics, a theory of the structure of the earth's surface, according to which the land masses of the earth consist of vast crustal blocks called plates, which are bounded by seismically active trench systems, mountain chains, etc., and which are slowly driven sideways by convection currents or other forces kept in motion by the earth's internal heat.

In accordance with plate tectonics, the Pacific Ocean is spreading apart along the East Pacific Rise, much like the sea-floor spreading that is occurring along the Mid-Atlantic Ridge. *John M. Dennison, "Earth Sciences," 1972 Britannica Yearbook of Science and the Future, 1971, p 232*

It would therefore be well to lay out the rules of plate tectonics—the set of conditions which are believed to govern the behaviour of features on the Earth's surface. . . . Plate tectonics has been adequately tested in other parts of the world and has shown its ability to predict, amongst other things, the direction of the movement accompanying earthquakes. *David Davies, "The Red Sea: Development of an Ocean," Science Journal, Aug. 1969, p 39*

platform, *n.* a navigation system or radio-signal device to determine location.

. . . he [Astronaut John Swigert] charged up *Odyssey's* small re-entry batteries, closed off its four back-up oxygen tanks, and transferred the precise alignment of the command module's "platform"—its complex of navigational gyroscopes and accelerometers—to a similar platform in the lunar lander. *"Apollo 13: Ill-Fated Space Odyssey," Time, April 27, 1970, p 15*

platform tennis, *U.S.* a form of tennis played with paddles and a heavy rubber ball on a wooden platform surrounded by walls of wire netting, off of which the ball can be played.

For platform tennis, more commonly called paddle tennis, is not only the newest addition to the family of tennis-type court games: it is unique in that it is played primarily in winter and always outdoors. *Time, March 3, 1967, p 45*

More than 250 players on 128 teams will gather at the "home of platform tennis," the Fox Meadow Tennis Club in Scarsdale, N.Y., on Friday to compete in the 38th annual United States men's doubles championship. *"Platform Tennis Is Top Draw," The New York Times, Feb. 27, 1972, Sec. 5, p 6*

platoon, *v.t., v.i. U.S. Sports Slang.* to specialize in a particular play or position.

Later, [Gil] Hodges [manager of the New York Mets] decided to "platoon" him [Cleon Jones] by playing him only against lefthanded pitchers. *Time, Sept. 5, 1969, p 52*

[verb use of the noun *platoon* a group of football players specializing in either offensive or defensive plays]

playbook, *n.* a book containing the diagrams of a football team's plays.

On the field, Plimpton did the calisthenics and learned the playbook cold, but when the test came during an intrasquad scrimmage before a large crowd, his reflexes scattered and every play was botched. *Time, Jan. 6, 1967, p 64*

They spend most of their time watching films of their next opponents or studying the 'play-book' which sets out the dozens of moves they have to learn before the next match. *Vivian Jenkins, The Sunday Times (London), Sept. 28, 1969, p 22*

playgroup, *n.* a type of improvised nursery school for preschool children, privately formed and supervised usually in some neighborhood facility.

Mothers find difficulty in getting baby-sitters, but the playgroups in church premises and the adventure playgrounds are welcomed. *Rt. Rev. Oliver Tomkins, Bishop of Bristol, The Times (London), March 20, 1970, p II*

Most of the volunteers will be given work designed to protect the environment, to help old people, to organise playgroups, and to do the most pressing kind of community work in their own areas. *Simon Hoggart, "Social Work for Jobless," The Manchester Guardian Weekly, Oct. 2, 1971, p 11*

playpit, *n. British.* a small pit, sometimes filled with sand, for children to play in.

Columbia [Maryland] . . . is America's showpiece city of the future. . . . This private enterprise venture into community creation is a regular weekend draw. . . . The village shopping centres have good stores as well as sculpture and playpits for the children. *Judy Hillman, "Maryland Showpiece," The Manchester Guardian Weekly, May 8, 1971, p 15*

PL/1, abbreviation of *Programming Language One,*

367

a very simple computer language for general programming needs.

Although there is a proliferation of languages already—such as Cobol, devised by the United States Department of Defence for commercial work, and I.B.M.'s Fortran (scientific) and PL-1 (general purpose)—they are costly investments and are beginning to look clumsy. *Pearce Wright, The Times (London), April 26, 1968, p 25*

Contrasted with machine language, the PL/I program is almost self-explanatory. (PL/I is an abbreviation for Programming Language One.) R. *Clay Sprowls, "Computer Programming," Encyclopedia Science Supplement (Grolier) 1971, p 158*

plotter, *n.* a peripheral output component of a computer system for analysis of data.

Another output device is the plotter, which can make plots from computer-generated data. *R. Clay Sprowls, "Computers," Encyclopedia Science Supplement (Grolier) 1971, p 146*

PLSS (plis), *n.* acronym for *Portable Life-Support System.*

A backpack portable life-support system (PLSS) provides moon-walking astronauts with oxygen and temperature control for up to four hours of activity outside the spacecraft. *The 1970 Compton Yearbook, p 567*

plug, *v.t.* **plug into,** to use electronic equipment, especially to listen to something or be in communication with someone.

A third-grade classroom in Minot, North Dakota's third largest city, population 33,477. Five children were plugged into a tape recorder, listening to a story and following it in the books in front of them. *Charles E. Silberman, "Murder in the Schoolroom: Some New Hopes for Life in the Primary Schools," The Atlantic, July 1970, p 88*

The place is completely wired for closed-circuit television, so anybody in any of the rooms can be plugged into what's going on in any other room. We'll also be able to do live telecasts from here over national hookups. *"The Talk of the Town: Automation House," The New Yorker, March 14, 1970, p 30*

PNdB or **PNdb,** abbreviation of PERCEIVED NOISE DECIBEL (a standard unit for measuring noise, based on the type of sound and its intensity).

Although both the Douglas company and the airlines contend that the new aircraft [jumbo jets] will be within the noise standard of 112 PNdb (Perceived Noise decibels), the authority has maintained that its information shows the craft will be noisier on take-off and landing than the present jets. *The New York Times, Dec. 28, 1966, p 66*

For instance the monitored noise limits for jet take-offs which are designed to ensure that the first major built up area does not receive noise above 110 PNdB (perceived noise decibels) by day or 102 PNdB by night, often mean that the aircraft's engine power must be reduced as soon as a safe height is reached. . . . *Michael Noble, The Times (London), Aug. 28, 1970, p 7*

pocket, *n. U.S. Football.* a small, heavily protected area in the backfield for the passer, usually the quarterback.

. . . Myers seldom runs a roll-out; he is a drop-back "pocket" passer, throws what the pros call a "soft ball"—a pass that reaches the receiver slightly nose up, is therefore easier to catch. *Time, Oct. 18, 1963, p 94*

point, *n. U.S.* a charge or fee discounted by a lender from a loan, usually one percent of the loan's face amount, by which the effective interest rate is substantially increased.

"Points" are a means by which a lender, operating under a legally fixed ceiling, can get a mortgage interest rate equivalent to other market rates on invested money such as on safe corporate bonds, which now yield better than 6.5 per cent. *Edwin L. Dale, Jr., The New York Times, May 8, 1968, p 17*

point man, *U.S. Military.* the man in front of a patrol.

Cisneros survived 42 patrols in Viet Nam, mostly as the exposed point man, and saw his unit chewed up behind him several times. *Time, Jan. 5, 1970, p 14*

The cost of being too militant was to be sent to serve as a point man on the Demilitarized Zone. *"Armed Forces: Black Powerlessness," Time, Nov. 29, 1971, p 28*

point of no return, a point reached in a course beyond which it is no longer possible to reverse or turn back to an earlier condition.

The majority of the children have passed the dreaded "point of no return," in this case medical phraseology for a victim of malnutrition who has become so dehydrated that death is only a matter of time. *Lloyd Garrison, The New York Times, Aug. 7, 1968, p 24*

[figurative sense of the aviation term for a point in a flight course at which the gas supply is insufficient to return safely to base]

pokesy, *adj.* slow-moving; easygoing.

The relationship between these two belated western outlaws (time of the Spanish-American war) is very well hit off in William Goldman's pokesy, cooler-than-cool script. . . . *John Russell Taylor, "The Arts: A Star is Born," Review of "Butch Cassidy and the Sundance Kid" (a motion picture), The Times (London), Feb. 6, 1970, p 13*

[variant of *pokey,* probably influenced in spelling by *folksy, bluesy, cutesy,* etc.]

po·lem·o·log·i·cal (pə‚lem ə'ladʒ ə kəl), *adj.* of or relating to polemology.

There is a French Institute of Polemology in Paris and a Polemological Institute at Groningen in the Netherlands. *Walter Sullivan, The New York Times, Aug. 26, 1968, p 35*

po·le·mol·o·gy (‚pou lə'mɑl ə dʒi:), *n.* the study of conflicts, especially of war among nations.

"War is one aspect of the human experience with which we in Europe are extremely familiar, alas." The man who shared these sentiments with me recently is Professor Gaston Bouthoul of the *Ecole des Hautes Etudes Sociales* in Paris. As the founder of Polemology (a word he coined), or the study of war, he has spent a good deal of time thinking about this particular folly which man shares with certain social insects. *Friedel Ungeheuer, "Foreign Report: Who's Afraid of War?" Harper's, Dec. 1970, p 28*

Students of polemology will not find anything startlingly original in what he has to say. His thesis is that America should not disarm since "the war system" is necessary to preserve her social and political stability. *Michael Howard, The Sunday Times (London), Feb. 4, 1968, p 53*

[from Greek *pólemos* war + English *-logy* study]

pole position, an advantageous position.

Berlin-based Schering is one of those companies with a

US twin of the same name formed by confiscation of its American interests in the war. The German company retained a pole position in hormone research which led to the Pill. *James Poole, "Pills for Profit," The Sunday Times (London), Sept. 12, 1971, p 50*

[figurative sense of the racing term for the position of a contestant who is on the inside (near the infield) of a track, which gives him the advantage, since his opponents must cover a larger circumference in attempting to pass him]

polimetrician, *n.* a political scientist who specializes in mathematical and statistical methods of study and research.

. . . econometricians, polimetricians, psychometricians, jurimetricians are all rapidly proliferating species of a genus of mathematically minded scholars who are infiltrating the academic world armed with computers and many of the analytical tools of higher mathematics. *"Math Penetrates the Social Sciences," Encyclopedia Science Supplement (Grolier) 1970, p 287*

poliovirus, *n.* one of three types of RNA-containing viruses that cause poliomyelitis. Compare PICORNAVIRUS.

Oysters and clams can quickly rid themselves of *poliovirus* and bacteria when transplanted from polluted water into clean water. *Science News Letter, Dec. 4, 1965, p 363*

politic, *n.* a relationship in which one person or group governs or exerts power upon another.

One of the problems here may be that primates physically have intercourse with females that they can dominate. It may just be that the phenomenon of sexual encounter depends on a sexual politic. And that without this politic, in the way it has been contrived for several million years, there may not be any sexual encounter. *Lionel Tiger, "An Unchauvinist Male Replies," Time, Aug. 31, 1970, p 21*

political animal, a person with drive, gifted or knowledgeable as a politician.

He [the Rev. Wilfred Wood] has the command of language and certainly the understanding. But he lacks the wish of the true political animal to act for effect. *Peter Evans, The Times (London), April 20, 1970, p 4*

[The phrase was originally applied by Aristotle to man in the sense of his being a social creature.]

politicization, *n.* **1** the act or process of making something a political issue or involving something in politics.

M. André Bergeron, of the Force Ouvrière group of unions, has pointed out that this reform is liable to encourage precisely that politicization of the trade unions which the President himself deplores. *Edward Mortimer, The Times (London), Sept. 11, 1968, p 5*

2 training in political skill; a making politic, prudent, or civil.

"People who would be very polite to each other meeting face to face in a doorway will turn into aggressive idiots behind the wheel." The solution: "To complement the three big Es (engineering, enforcement, education) with two big Ps—personalization and politicization." *Helmut Schelsky (a German sociologist), quoted in "Behavior: Behind the Auto Mask," Time, Oct. 26, 1970, p 63*

pollutive, *adj.* causing pollution.

The diesel engine has a similar amount of development work behind it and is a naturally less pollutive engine than the spark ignition one. *Glen Lawes, New Scientist, July 2, 1970, p 12*

polyacrylamide, *n.* a polymer of acrylamide $(CH_2CHCONH_2)$, widely used as a thickening agent in chemistry.

Another method used for binding enzymes is to trap them in a gel—most commonly a polyacrylamide gel. *Alan Wiseman and Barry Gould, "New Enzymes for Industry," New Scientist, April 11, 1968, p 68*

Marked differences in the effectiveness of different water-soluble polymers can be found. Apparently partially hydrolyzed polyacrylamides are best. These polymers alter the flow of water without altering the flow of oil. *Hendrik K. Van Poollen, "Petroleum Secondary Recovery," McGraw-Hill Yearbook of Science and Technology 1971, p 322*

George G. Guilbault and Joseph H. Montalvo of Louisiana State University have applied such an enzyme electrode to the measurement of urea in body fluids. In their device the enzyme urease is embedded in a polyacrylamide membrane coated in a layer about .1 millimeter thick on an electrode sensitive to ammonium ions (NH_4+). *Klaus Mosbach, "Enzymes Bound to Artificial Matrixes," Scientific American, March 1971, p 31*

polycentric, *adj.* characterized by polycentrism.

After the success of Tito's revolt against Moscow [Palmiro] Togliatti conceived of "polycentric" Communism. This means adjusting party methods in each country to national traditions and requirements. *C. L. Sulzberger, The New York Times, Jan. 18, 1965, p 34*

polycentrism, *n.* the existence or establishment of a number of independent political centers within the framework of a single political movement or ideology.

No longer was Moscow the undisputed centre of all Communist thought and policy. Polycentrism, as the new trend was called, corroded the once strictly unified command position and ideological faith. *Hans Kohn, "Communist Movement," Britannica Book of the Year 1968, p 230*

polycentrist, *n.* an advocate or supporter of polycentrism.

Many more responsible non-communists were becoming polycentrists, including General de Gaulle. *The Times (London), July 7, 1966, p 7*

pol·y·chlor·in·at·ed bi·phen·yl (ˌpɑl iːˈklɔr ə‚nei·tid baiˈfen əl). Also shortened to **polychlorobiphenyl,** *n.* one of a group of chemicals widely used in industry as electrical insulators and in plastics manufacture, recently detected in wildlife at levels approaching the concentration of DDT and similar insecticides.

Polychlorinated biphenyls, another group of chlorinated hydrocarbons that are industrial pollutants, have become similarly dispersed throughout the global ecosystem. *Robert W. Risebrough, "Pesticide," McGraw-Hill Yearbook of Science and Technology 1971, p 320*

Scientists have recently become concerned over contamination of the environment by polychlorinated biphenyls (PCB'S), industrial compounds which have much in common with chlorinated pesticides. The PCB'S are persistent poisons, they are attracted to fatty tissues of organisms and they are concentrated up the food chain. *Science News, July 25, 1970, p 69*

polyether, *n.* See the first quotation for the meaning.

A polyether is a thermoplastic material that contains ether-oxygen linkages, —C—O—C—, in the polymer chain. *William J. Bailey, "Chemistry," 1972 Britannica Yearbook of Science and the Future, 1971, p 216*

All three versions [of furniture] are available in either Burma teak, or prime beech and are fitted with specially composed polyether foam cushions. *Hilary Gelson, The Times (London), March 28, 1968, p 9*

polyglass tire or **polyglas tire,** an automobile tire with polyester fiber cord and a double fiberglass ply belt molded around the outside, designed for better traction and longer tread wear.

A new "polyglass" tire of bias-belted construction became widely used on U.S. 1970-season models. *Maurice Platt, "Industrial Review: Automobiles," Britannica Book of the Year 1970, p 417*

[from *poly*ester + fiber*glass* or fiber*glas*]

pol·y I:C ('pɑl i: 'ɑi'si:), a synthetic chemical compound that stimulates the production of the antivirus protein interferon by its resemblance to the RNA (ribonucleic acid) core of infectious viruses.

... several groups reported that poly I:C, a synthetic double-stranded RNA, that induces the production of interferon, an antiviral protein produced by animals, was effective as a protective agent against some viral diseases. *Robert G. Eagon, "Microbiology," 1971 Britannica Yearbook of Science and the Future, 1970, p 239*

Perhaps the most exciting prospect is that a recently-recognised compound, known for short as polyI:C, induces the body's own cells to create the natural anti-viral agent called interferon....*Alfred Byrne, The Sunday Times (London), Jan. 4, 1970, p 8*

[shortened from the chemical name *poly*inosinic:-polycytidylic acid]

pol·y·im·ide (ˌpɑl i:'im,ɑid), *n.* any of a class of tough, heat-resistant polymeric resins used as ablators, adhesives, semiconductors, insulators, etc.

Plastics like the polyimides and fluorocarbons will give special properties like high temperature resistance, inertness, and low friction without lubricants. *Dennis Gabor, Innovations: Scientific, Technological, and Social, 1970, p 13*

By printing a conducting circuit on to a polyimide film, and then fixing an integrated circuit on to the film Philips Research Laboratories, Eindhoven, Netherlands, has developed a new way of mounting integrated circuits in electronic equipment. *New Scientist and Science Journal, March 4, 1971, p 488*

polyoma virus, a virus containing DNA and associated with various tumors formed in mammalian animals.

A number of viral agents of cancer in lower animals, such as the polyoma virus in mice, Rous sarcoma virus in chickens, and certain leukemia viruses in mice and hamsters, provide models for the study of related human diseases. *James G. Shaffer, "Microbiology," Britannica Book of the Year 1968, p 515*

[from *poly*- many + *-oma* tumor]

polyomino, *n.* a many-sided piece so shaped that it can cover a number of-squares on a game board

and join other similar pieces. See, for example, PENTOMINO.

The word "polyomino" was invented—by the author [Solomon W. Golomb] of this book—to describe all the flat shapes which can be produced by joining sets of equal squares edge to edge. Two squares must then join in the shape of a domino: larger numbers allow different modes of connection, in increasing variety. *T. H. O'Beirne, New Scientist, April 13, 1967, p 103*

[from *poly*- many + d*omino*]

polyribonucleotide, *n.* a nucleotide (constituent of nucleic acid) synthesized by either DNA polymerase or RNA polymerase.

The exciting discovery of M. Nirenberg and J. Matthaei that polyribonucleotides of known and random composition and sequence would stimulate protein synthesis when added to extracts of bacteria presented a strange paradox. *Norton D. Zinder, "Protein Synthesis," McGraw-Hill Yearbook of Science and Technology 1967, p 321*

polyribosomal, *adj.* of or relating to polyribosomes.

In the unaltered cytoplasm surrounding these areas ribosomes were gathered into polyribosomal aggregates, indicating very active synthesis of protein. *Colin Kaplan, "Rabies," Science Journal, April 1970, p 36*

polyribosome, *n.* a cluster of ribosomes linked by messenger RNA functioning as a unit in synthesizing proteins. Also called POLYSOME.

The ribosomes on the surface of the endoplasmic reticulum are arranged as polyribosomes with a spiral configuration. *J. Cronshaw, "Xylem: Endoplasmic Reticulum and Ribosomes," McGraw-Hill Yearbook of Science and Technology 1967, p 426*

A cluster of ribosomes translating a given strand of mRNA forms a polyribosome. *"Carcinogen Produces Giant Polyribosomes," New Scientist and Science Journal, June 24, 1971, p 735*

polysome, *n.* another name for POLYRIBOSOME.

Working with R. B. Freedman and D. J. Williams at University College, London, Rabin has been studying the surface structure of the rough endoplasmic reticulum of rat liver cells. This reticulum is a series of intracellular membranes which carry on them the polysomes (messenger RNA and ribosomes) thought to be responsible for the biosynthesis of proteins destined for export from the cell. *New Scientist, Oct. 15, 1970, p 113*

What probably happens is that there is a regular cycle of association and dissociation of subunits, so that the 30S and 50S subunits meet upon the mRNA molecule and progress along the message as 70S ribosomes among a whole string of them, called a polysome. *New Scientist and Science Journal, Feb. 25, 1971, p 410*

polysulfone, *n.* a hard, rigid, corrosion-resistant synthetic polymer used widely in the manufacture of mechanical and electrical equipment.

In the case of ethylene and sulfur dioxide, the compound produced is a polysulfone, a heat-moldable, resistant material desirable for electrical circuits. *Science News, March 29, 1969, p 308*

Polysulphone moulded components perform satisfactorily in various aircraft parts. *John Howard, "Plastics to Withstand the Heat," New Scientist and Science Journal, June 24, 1971, p 761*

polyunsaturate, *n.* a polyunsaturated oil or fat, such as certain vegetable oils or fish oil, often used in low-cholesterol diets. Compare MONOUNSATU-RATE.

...the phrase "high in polyunsaturates" on a can of shortening doesn't tell the consumer how high or in comparison to what. *Jane E. Brody, The New York Times, Dec. 20, 1970, Sec. 4, p 7*

Richest of all in polyunsaturates are vegetable oils from corn, cottonseed, safflower, soybeans, and (if not artificially hydrogenated) peanuts and some olives. *Time, June 19, 1964, p 66*

polyunsaturated, *adj.* (of a fat or oil) free of hydrogen bonds at several points in its carbon chain.

Their experiments on brain development in chick embryos show that polyunsaturated fatty acids from fish and vegetable oils are necessary for normal brain development. *Science News, Sept. 30, 1967, p 316*

polyversity, *n.* another name for MULTIVERSITY.

Once an idea supported only by a few, notably Mr. Eric Robinson and Professor Robin Pedley, the development of the comprehensive university or "poly-versity" has been supported this year both by the National Union of Students and the National Union of Teachers. *Brian MacArthur, The Times (London), April 6, 1970, p 2*

[from *poly-* extensive + uni*versity*]

polywater, *n.* another name for ANOMALOUS WATER.

Recent work suggests that anomalous water does exist, and that it is a polymer of the water molecule H_2O. The formula of this so-called polywater is $(H_2O)n$. *Gary Mitchell, "Physics: Polywater," The Americana Annual 1970, p 546*

If polywater could be made—or found in nature—in large amounts, scientists envisioned several possible uses. It might serve as a high-temperature lubricant, as feed water for steam engines, or as a control fluid in nuclear reactors. *Arnold E. Levitt, "Chemistry: Properties and Preparation," The 1970 Compton Yearbook, p 177*

ponce (pɒns), *v.i. British Slang.* **1** to live on the earnings of a prostitute; to be or act as a pimp.

The Judge commented: "Anybody who has sat here day after day and listened to the evidence must have realized as the days went by that the prosecution case was crumbling away." The judge referred to "the deadly harm which springs from the addiction to cannabis." He said: "You have seen and heard how it has destroyed character, led to lying and a wanton disregard for the law, and you have had to listen to tales of pimping and poncing, prostitution, lying, and planting of evidence." *"Three Vice Squad Detectives Acquitted," The Times (London), Nov. 24, 1970, p 4*

2 to go (*around* or *about*) in a flashy, showy way.

"I was invited to Cannes, but what do I want to go poncing about Cannes for?" *Hunter Davies, The Sunday Times (London), May 29, 1966, p 11*

[from *ponce, n.,* an earlier slang term for a pimp; def. 2 derives from the idea of a ponce having plenty of money to spend on flashy clothes and riotous living]

poof, *n.; pl.* **pooves** or **poofs.** *British Slang.* an effeminate male, especially a passive homosexual.

Jill: ...John always wears whichever [perfume] I have on. He never bothers with after shave.

John: After shaves are for pooves. *"Look! His Clothes and Hers: Jill Bennett and John Osborne," The Sunday Times (London), Oct. 10, 1971, p 42*

"You made all your money out of pushing heroin to schoolchildren and investing the proceeds in the white-slave traffic, which is run for you by a gang of psychopathic poove murderers you've smuggled in from Trinidad." *Alan Coren, Punch, Oct. 29, 1969, p 703*

Blokes who put on too much are frightened they'll be thought poofs and ladies who do the same could be thought to be over-advertising themselves. *Molly Parkin, The Sunday Times (London), Dec. 14, 1969, p 54*

[ultimately from French *pouffe* puff]

poor-mouth, *v.i., v.t. U.S.* to claim or complain of poverty.

Elliott Gould's complaints do run on.... Only his young son seems to have been spared such compulsive poor-mouthing—so far. Gould's irresponsible childishness on and off the screen may give a vicarious thrill to many who share his petulant self-pity.... *John Moore, Washington, D.C., in a Letter to the Editor, Time, Sept. 28, 1970, p 2*

[Eugene] McCarthy's advertising campaign, despite the McCarthy camp's constant poor-mouthing on the subject, wasn't exactly modest.... *Michael J. Arlen, "The Air: Nixon in Illinois," The New Yorker, Sept. 21, 1968, p 169*

"I sell a few hides to pay the taxes," he poor-mouthed, suggesting an improbable picture of himself in a dinner jacket leading a tallowy cow down a dusty arroyo to keep the sheriff from foreclosing on his splendid Palo Corona Ranch at Carmel, California. *Nicholas von Hoffman, "The Class of '43 is Puzzled (25th Class Reunion of Harvard University)," The Atlantic, Oct. 1968, p 70*

poovey or **poovy,** *adj. British Slang.* of or like pooves; homosexual.

Ralph fell in love with Carrington and Lytton fell in love with Ralph, so they all joined in a *ménage à trois....* Volume one ended with Lytton severed from his protracted idyll of intellectual and poovey bliss at Cambridge.... *Kenneth Alsop, "A Kind of Loving," Review of "Lytton Strachey: The Years of Achievement" by Michael Holroyd, Punch, Feb. 21, 1968, p 282*

You could not possibly prefer the poovy drips on the moon, or the thick skinheads of Hussite Prague in this production. *William Mann, The Times (London), July 4, 1970, p 21*

pop¹, *adj.* of or relating to the popular arts and fashions, especially those reflecting the values and mores of the younger generation.

...I just don't believe that many young persons in this swinging pop society are left ignorant of the facts of life because of inertia or reticence on the part of our official guardians. *Donald Gould, New Scientist, Oct. 29, 1970, p 232*

The attraction was the assembly of American pop groups and singers whose names may not be well known to a wide public, but who have great drawing power in the pop world. *David Wilsworth, The Times (London), June 29, 1970, p 2*

He believes in little except himself. Unfortunately, that self is mainly composed of pop-culture fragments, miscellaneous emotions and loose social ties. *"Books: The Wattage of Inertia," Review of "The File on Stanley Patton Buchta" (a novel) by Irvin Faust, Time, July 6, 1970, p 74*

[shortened from *popular,* originally in such terms as *pop music, pop singer, pop song* and later especially in the phrase *pop culture*]

pop² or **Pop,** *n.* short for POP ART.

There were about a hundred and fifty paintings on view in the huge Main Hall, reduced in size and otherwise modified by draperies, and they ranged from Op and Pop to Picasso. *John McCarten, "Irish Sketches," The New Yorker, Feb. 24, 1968, p 100*

—*adj.* of or characterized by pop art.

The works of pop painter Roy Lichtenstein were among those chosen to represent the United States at the Venice Biennial, one of the world's most prestigious exhibitions. *"Fads of 1966," The 1967 Compton Yearbook, p 250*

pop³, *v.t.* **1** *Slang.* to swallow (a drug in pill form), especially habitually.

The word from Wall Street is that executives of finance and insurance companies are popping pills these days to tranquilize their nerves as they watch the news for the latest take-over attempts in their industries. *Robert Metz, The New York Times, Aug. 2, 1968, p 46*

Cambodia is granting asylum to two American seamen who apparently mutinied on the munitions-carrying ship ... and forced her to sail to Cambodia.... [Members of the crew] described the two hijackers as anti-Vietnam war hippies who signed on in the United States. For the whole of the voyage they were "popping pills and blowing marijuana". *Ian McDonald, "Cambodia Granting Asylum to Hijackers of Ship," The Times (London), March 17, 1970, p 1*

2 *British.* to fasten with poppers.

The invaders don midi leather skirts popped up the side with three-quarters of the poppers undone.... *Prudence Glynn, The Times (London), July 21, 1970, p 7*

pop art or **Pop art,** an art form that uses everyday objects, especially popular mass-produced articles such as comic strips, soup cans, and posters, as its subject matter and sometimes also as the artistic material or medium itself. Also shortened to POP or Pop.

Pop art is thought to be the art of everyday things and banal images—bathroom fixtures, Dick Tracy—but its essential character consists in redoing works of art. Its scope extends from Warhol's rows of Coca-Cola bottles to supplying the "Mona Lisa" with a mustache. *Harold Rosenberg, "The Art World," The New Yorker, Nov. 8, 1969, p 167*

pop artist, an artist who produces works of pop art.

Discarding all subtleties, the pop artists commented on life today by bombarding us with its most familiar images. Cans of Campbell's soup, neon signs, billboard blowups all combine to reproduce the face of the contemporary United States. *Katharine Kuh, "The Happening of Art: Snap, Crackle and Pop," The 1969 Compton Yearbook, p 53*

popout, *n. Surfing Slang.* a poorly made surfboard.

"A lot of gremmies come out just to impress girls, and all they do is sit on their popouts." "What's a popout?" we asked. "A crummy board," the boy said. "Machine-made. And you can see the fibres going in all different directions in the resin." *"The Talk of the Town," The New Yorker, June 17, 1967, p 24*

popper, *n. British.* a snap fastener or gripper. The traditional term in Britain is *press-stud.*

It fastens with poppers sewn under the buttons so that you do not have the bother of making tiny buttonholes. *Moira Keenan, The Times (London), Feb. 18, 1970, p 12*

If your body is a tall one, these body shirts simply don't work, especially if, like the one I tried last week, the only fastening is at the crotch, with poppers. Take one breath,

the poppers unpop, the garment slides upwards relentlessly. *Daily Telegraph (London), May 15, 1972, p 12*

popster, *n. U.S. Slang.* a pop artist. Compare OPSTER.

... a "Floating Biennale" yacht, anchored in the Grand Canal at the '64 Venice Biennale ... was raided by the police. They made off with a giant anatomical detail, rendered on canvas by popster Harold Stevenson. *Grace Glueck, The New York Times, Oct. 16, 1966, Sec. 2, p 3*

pop-top, *adj.* having a ring attached to a metal tab in the top, that can be pulled to open the can. Compare RING-PULL, ZIP-TOP.

Insert finger, tug and quaff: in those few seconds, the aluminum ring atop a pop-top can of beer or soda fulfills its function and becomes instant junk. Garbage men hate the rings because the sharp edges can cut. *Time, Sept. 21, 1970, p 84*

popular, *n.* a newspaper or magazine written, often in a sensational style, to appeal to the general public. Compare QUALITY.

There were perplexing shifts in public taste which seemed to benefit the "quality" papers at the expense of the "populars." *Dennis Johnson, The Manchester Guardian Weekly, July 25, 1970, p 11*

popularist, *adj.* seeking popular interest or participation; appealing to or involving the general public.

What emerged was a popularist outlook (Hightower called it "human") and the determination to dissolve painting and sculpture into broader aesthetic streams. *Harold Rosenberg, "The Art World: Dilemmas of a New Season," The New Yorker, Oct. 10, 1970, p 150*

There is no doubt that, after two years of passive and effacingly popularist administration, the President of All the People [Mr. Nixon] tried to become President of Most of the People; a President who saw an opening to the bilious, ulcerated right. *The Manchester Guardian Weekly, Nov. 14, 1970, p 3*

population explosion, the rapid increase in world population resulting from better care for the young and the old.

... suddenly, almost everyone, rich, poor and in between, is concerned about choking to death, or dying lakes and rivers, or the ice-cap melting, or the population explosion.... *Tom Wicker, The New York Times, Feb. 3, 1970, p 42*

population inversion. See the first quotation for the meaning.

... population inversion ... is a situation in which enough gas molecules are brought down to a lower energy level to prevent the loss of energy all at once. *Science News, May 30, 1970, p 529*

... the thermally excited gas molecules undergo a temporary "population inversion," which is the essential prerequisite for laser action. *Scientific American, July 1970, p 52*

porn or **porno,** *Slang.* —*n.* **1** pornography.

Printed matter is still the most common form of porn, much of it supplied by such relatively new publishing houses as Los Angeles' Oxford Bindery and Manhattan's Olympia. *Time, Nov. 16, 1970, p 92*

2 a pornographic movie.

People who wouldn't ordinarily go to pornos go to porno-spoofs, which always have an adolescent anti-establishment air about them. *Pauline Kael, "The Current Cinema," The New Yorker, Nov. 6, 1971, p 189*

3 a writer of pornography.

The right-wing National Democratic Party derides [Gunther] Grass as a "porno," because his works are peppered with four-letter words. *Time, Sept. 5, 1969, p 27*

— *adj.* pornographic.

So busy are the makers of porn films in San Francisco that they have depressed the market for imported sex movies, and are now selling their own products abroad — a small victory for the nation's trade balance. *Time, Nov. 16, 1970, p 92*

Foreigners now provide 60 per cent. of the customers in Denmark's porno business and one difficulty is getting the country's sexport through the customs barriers of less liberal countries. *Antony Terry, The Sunday Times (London), Oct. 19, 1969, p 24*

But Randolph would always take his profits *out* of the market and let the losses sit. Eventually, it meant whittling down his principal, when he'd be forced to sell to keep up with mortgage payments, light bill, and his porno habit, which was getting expensive to satisfy. *Brutus, "Confessions of a Stockbroker," The Atlantic, July 1971, p 52*

pornobiography, *n.* a pornographic biography.

The mildly lascivious may be grateful that he gives the longest plot summary of *Genarvon* I know of, and prints the entire text of *Don Leon*, a not very titillating piece of pornobiography. *Harvey Curtis Webster, Review of "The Uninhibited Byron: An Account of His Sexual Confusion" by Bernard Grebanier, Saturday Review, Oct. 17, 1970, p 32*

The Music Lovers — Ken Russell seems to have invented a new genre of pornobiography. In this film, Tchaikovsky is the chief victim of Russell's baroque vulgarity. *"Goings On About Town," The New Yorker, Dec. 11, 1971, p 24*

pornography, *n.* a description or portrayal of any activity regarded as obscene.

In recent years the movies and television have developed a pornography of violence far more demoralizing than the pornography of sex, which still seizes the primary attention of the guardians of civic virtue. *Arthur Schlesinger, Jr., Saturday Review, Oct. 19, 1968, p 23*

pornotopia, *n.* an ideal place or setting for the activities envisioned in pornographic literature.

Both kinds of writing tend to regard the world as a pornotopia. Reality is conceived as the scene of exclusively sexual activities and human and social institutions are understood to exist only insofar as they are conducive to further sexual play. *Steven Marcus, The Other Victorians, 1966 (British edition), p 194*

[from *porno*graphic + u*topia*]

porny, *adj. Slang.* pornographic.

Partly because of the visual quality and the use of pastels, you don't get that depressed, crummy feeling that usually settles in with the first shots of porny pictures. *Pauline Kael, "The Current Cinema," The New Yorker, Nov. 6, 1971, p 188*

po·ro·mer·ic (ˌpɔr ə'mer ik), *n.* an extremely porous polymeric plastic material, used for shoe uppers instead of leather.

Nevertheless, the poromerics — because they "breathe" and thus simulate the properties of leather — are still the only suitable alternative to natural leather in men's footwear. *Dale Littler and Alan Pearson, New Scientist and Science Journal, April 1, 1971, p 37*

— *adj.* made of poromeric; very porous.

The leading entry is Du Pont's leather-like poromeric material, Corfam, introduced in shoe uppers in 1964. *Lawrence Lessing, The Sunday Times (London), Jan. 15, 1967, p 53*

[from *poro*sity + poly*mer* + *-ic*]

porridge, *n.* do (one's) porridge, *British Underworld Slang.* to serve time in prison.

Eddy could do his porridge because of his bottle. If you want that translated, this petty crook could put up with prison because he got the thrill from crime that came, he thought, from having the right guts. *Leonard Buckley, "Crime Bristol Fashion: Thick as Thieves," The Times (London), March 1, 1972, p 13*

pos·i·grade ('pɑz ə,greid), *adj.* **1** producing thrust in the direction in which the vehicle is moving. Compare RETROGRADE.

It was also necessary to take into account time delays in the spacecraft and booster for relays, valves, and mechanical equipment to operate, a figure for the last boost of thrust from the engines as they "tail-off" after shutdown, and another figure for the thrust of the small, posigrade rockets that give the spacecraft a gentle separation push away from the booster. *John H. Glenn, Jr., "Focus on Space," The 1965 World Book Year Book, p 48*

2 of or from a posigrade rocket.

Command Pilot Schirra made a number of ground-computed corrective maneuvers. To change his elliptical orbit into a circle that reached up closer to Gemini 7, he made several "posigrade" burns — bursts from his forward thrusting rockets. *Time, Dec. 24, 1965, p 35*

[from *posi*tive + retro*grade*]

position paper, a document which presents the position of a political group, government, trade union, etc., on an important issue.

They got out an eleven-page policy statement, called a "position paper," which after performing the vulgar necessity of attacking President Johnson and the Administration for "laxity" in enforcing the fair (i.e. equal) employment laws, went on to say something on their own account. *Alistair Cooke, "Republicans Seek Philosophy," The Manchester Guardian Weekly, Sept. 9, 1965, p 2*

positive eugenics, eugenics (race improvement by hereditary selection) which attempts to increase the genetic transmission of favorable traits rather than decrease transmission of unfavorable ones.

. . . scientists and non-scientists alike have a powerful aversion to positive eugenics — the controlled breeding of 'better' children. *R. A. Beatty, "The Future of Reproduction," Science Journal, June 1970, p 99*

Conceivably a changed social climate and increased knowledge will make it possible for positive eugenics to be practiced on man. I suspect that the only rational course would be to select for genetic diversity. *Christopher Wills, "Genetic Load," Scientific American, March 1970, p 107*

Possum, *n. British.* a nickname for an electronic device or equipment by means of which a paralyzed person may telephone, type, or operate certain types of machines.

Basically Possum is an electronic aid which enables very severely disabled persons to exercise control over electric and electro-mechanical equipment. *Wendy Hughes, "Doctors Ignore the 'Possum'—The Waste of A Miracle Aid," The Sunday Times (London), June 13, 1971, p 11*

[from Latin *possum* I am able, used because of its resemblance to the initials of the technical name of this device, *P*atient *O*perated *S*elector *M*echanisms]

postcode, *n. British.* a combination of letters and numbers identifying a postal area in Great Britain, used for accelerating mail deliveries. The corresponding system in the U.S. is called ZIP CODE.

. . . a postman at the letter-coding desk has each envelope put in front of him and types out its postcode on a keyboard at his fingertips. *Peter Laurie, "The Power of the Post Office," The Sunday Times Magazine (London), June 20, 1971, p 17*

postconciliar, *adj.* existing or occurring after the Vatican ecumenical council of 1962-1965. Compare PRECONCILIAR.

During the first decade of the 20th century, Modernists like French Abbé Alfred Loisy, who championed scholarly Biblical criticism, and British Jesuit George Tyrrell, who urged the revision of old dogmatic formulas, were excommunicated for beliefs that have become commonplace in the post-conciliar church. *Time, May 23, 1969, p 40*

The post-conciliar attitude seems to draw attention above all to the value of personal and social relationships as the expression of the pattern of God's love on earth. *Harold R. Pearce, The Times (London), Feb. 24, 1968, p 9*

. . . the doctrinaire course being steered by church authorities in the postconciliar period [is] a course which in many issues (birth control, mixed marriages, celibacy, episcopal election, the Dutch church, the creed of Paul VI) has been paid for by serious burdens to individuals and to the church. *Rev. Dr. Hans Kung, "Why Infallibility?" The New York Times, June 3, 1971, p 39*

postfigurative, *adj.* of or designating a form of society in which the values of the adult or older generation predominate.

Dr. Mead distinguishes three types of culture:
1) Post-figurative—in which the old are models for the young.
2) Co-figurative—in which the peer group is the model for the young.
3) Pre-figurative—in which the children become the model for parents, who must "learn how to alter adult behavior." *Ernest van den Haag, "One Man's Mead, Another Man's Poison," Review of "Culture and Commitment: A Study of The Generation Gap" by Margaret Mead, The Atlantic, June 1970, p 118*

post·ne·o·na·tal (ˌpoust niː ouˈneiˈtəl), *adj.* of, relating to, or occurring during the first year of infancy.

Deaths in the postneonatal period appear to be roughly in step with the increased number of births. . . . The authors call for more research into the phenomenon, which caused two deaths a thousand live births in the areas concerned. *"Avoidable Factors in Many Infant Deaths," The Times (London), May 11, 1970, p 3*

[from *post-* after + *neonatal* newborn]

post-painterly, *adj.* of or characterized by a style of painting that uses traditional painterly qualities of color, form, and texture in producing nonobjective works, such as hard-edges.

There was Abstract Expressionism, and then there was Post-Painterly Abstraction, and meanwhile there were Pop and Op and Kinetic art. *Norbert Lynton, "Books," Review of "Movements in Art Since 1945" by Edward Lucie-Smith, The Manchester Guardian Weekly, Nov. 1, 1969, p 19*

At the Metropolitan, the largest displays are by so-called object-makers—"post-painterly" canvases: that is to say, smooth-surfaced, cool, and tending to blend with their setting. *Harold Rosenberg, "The Art World: Ecole de New York," The New Yorker, Dec. 6, 1969, p 184*

The primary structures themselves seemed to come out of a kind of painting that Clement Greenberg called "Post-Painterly Abstraction" but that was more frequently referred to as "color-field painting." *Calvin Tomkins, "Profiles: Moving With The Flow," The New Yorker, Nov. 6, 1971, p 106*

pot culture, a way or style of life centered around the use of pot or marijuana.

And what is there in the new Pot Culture to distinguish it from the *qat* chewers of Aden or Rabat, which allows men to wane into sexual impotence, or the philosophical apathy of the Indian slum dweller? *Friedel Ungeheuer, "Foreign Report: Who's Afraid of War?" Harper's, Dec. 1970, p 31*

pothead, *n. Slang.* a person who regularly smokes marijuana.

. . . the implied assumption that the pothead, *through the influence of marijuana alone*, stands a 10 per cent chance of being drawn ineluctably on to the "hard" drugs is an example of tendentious reasoning masquerading as hard fact. . . . *D. Hamm, New Scientist, Oct. 31, 1968, p 267*

Pot being no worse than alcohol, they [college kids] know the insanity in an alcoholic judge's sending a pothead to jail on the word of a drinking prosecutor slowly murdering his own liver—while Washington subsidizes tobacco growers and cancer research from the same pocket. *Larry L. King, Harper's, Oct. 1970, p 98*

[from *pot* marijuana + *head* (see the entry HEAD)]

pothole, *v.i.* to explore caves as a sport or hobby.

Four potholers were found suffering from exposure yesterday after being missing for more than 12 hours. They were with 10 others potholing on the Pennines at Casterton, near Kirkby Lonsdale, Westmoreland. *The Times (London), Oct. 26, 1970, p 4*

[verb use of *pothole* a cave entered from the surface]

pov·e·ra (ˈpɑv ər ə), *adj.* of or relating to a form of art that regards the artistic idea or process as more important than the finished product.

Apart from metaphysics, however, the program of de-aestheticization has been of practical importance in the art of the past few years in that it has promoted among *povera* artists a salutary disregard for prevailing aesthetic dogmas. *Harold Rosenberg, "The Art World: De-aestheticization," The New Yorker, Jan. 24, 1970, p 65*

[from Italian (arte) *povera* impoverished (art)]

poverty line, a minimum level of income set as the standard of adequate subsistence or livelihood, below which a person or family is classified as living in poverty.

Actually, the number of Americans living below what the Department of Labor calls the "poverty line" declined sharply in the '60s, but a better educated nation knew more about the poverty that was left, and many felt that it was intolerable in so rich a country. *James Reston, "Focus on the Nation," The 1970 World Book Year Book, p 24*

The number of persons with incomes below the Government's poverty line has decreased dramatically from 39 million to 25 million in the last eleven years. *Wilbur J. Cohen, "First Priority: Welfare Reform," The New York Times, June 9, 1971, p 43*

Powellism, *n.* a movement in British politics led by (John) Enoch Powell, born 1913, Conservative Member of Parliament, characterized especially by advocacy of laissez-faire economics and exclusion of black immigrants from Great Britain.

Powellism is a combination of racism, archconservative economics, and a touch of prickly isolationism. *Time, June 29, 1970, p 21*

What the press calls Powellism, as though it were already a rightist political pressure group for discontented small people, as Poujadism was in France in the fifties, is having the immediate effect of filling the mailbags of M.P.s and the newspaper correspondence columns with letters of violent approval or condemnation. *Mollie Panter-Downes, "Letter from London," The New Yorker, May 11, 1968, p 98*

Powellist, *adj.* another word for POWELLITE.

. . . the Conservatives, refreshed in Opposition from their ideological wellsprings, are likely for a year or two to be more Powellist in economics and more disposed to fasten legislative chains on the unions. *The Manchester Guardian Weekly, Sept. 5, 1968, p 12*

Powellite, *n.* a follower or supporter of Enoch Powell; an adherent of Powellism.

He [Mr. Maudling] has long been at odds with the extreme free-market views of the Powellites, and now his friends at Westminster and in the City are hearing his scornful dismissal of the doctrine of the "high-wage, low-cost economy" that Mr. Heath uses to justify Tory opposition to incomes legislation and all the parliamentary Orders that flow from it. *The Times (London), March 18, 1968, p 8*

—*adj.* of or relating to Powellites or Powellism. Also, POWELLIST.

. . . a massive Conservative majority would bring back to Westminster a lot of members who, if not overtly Powellite, would sympathise with the kind of conservatism for which Mr Enoch Powell stands. *The Manchester Guardian Weekly, Sept. 27, 1969, p 12*

power, *v.t., v.i.* **1 power down,** to reduce the power consumption (of a spacecraft).

"I would like to make sure that the LM [lunar module] is okay before we power down the CSM [command and service modules]." *Glynn Lunney, Apollo 13 mission controller, quoted in The Times (London), April 18, 1970, p 6*

2 power up, to increase the power consumption (of a spacecraft).

Because of the cold which had restricted the astronauts' sleep to only two or three hours and caused them considerable discomfort, the lunar module was powered up three hours earlier than planned—nine hours before entry into the earth's atmosphere. *Ian McDonald and Michael Knipe, "Perfect Splashdown for Apollo Crew," The Times (London), April 18, 1970, p 1*

power base, *U.S.* a foundation of political support for a campaign, a policy, etc.

These progressives are young and ambitious, confident of their ability to build an effective power base in Georgia without the rural white supremacists. *Walter Rugaber, The New York Times, May 19, 1968, p 49*

. . . Percy was suggested as a favorite-son candidate, largely to keep the delegation free of commitments less easy to shake. He may now emerge as a vice presidential possibility, but his power base in Illinois is in fact weak. *George A. Ranney, Jr., "Reports: Illinois," The Atlantic, May 1968, p 26*

Thieu is now left alone with his military and administrative powerbase—and the United States. *"Hazards Ahead for Thieu," The Manchester Guardian Weekly, Sept. 11, 1971, p 12*

. . . his [Mr. Faulkner's] power-base in the Unionist right might have been used to make successful reform where O'Neill was bound to fail. *The Sunday Times (London), Nov. 14, 1971, p 16*

power broker, *U.S.* a person who manipulates power by influencing people in positions of power.

Politicians, on the other hand, know exactly where he stands, and another of the contradictions of [Senator Henry] Jackson's candidacy is that it disturbs a number of Democratic and Republican power brokers alike. *Time, Nov. 22, 1971, p 28*

. . . it is difficult to think of such faculty persons as anything but cynics or fanatics to whom the ends of power justify the means. The means, alas, include the students, black and white, who serve as cannon fodder for the "cause." . . . the power brokers among the faculty will be busy at the same old stands, ready as ever to seduce the innocent. *Stanley W. Page, New York, in a Letter to the Editor, The New York Times, April 17, 1970, p 36*

power point, *British.* an electrical outlet; a wall socket.

The basic plan of a kitchen is not governed merely by four walls and the location of power points and plumbing outlets. . . . *Hilary Gelson, The Times (London), Sept. 25, 1970, p 12*

power structure, **1** the structure of established groups or institutions that hold power in a country. Compare ESTABLISHMENT (def. 1), SYSTEM (def. 1).

But the Congress cannot be expected to submit passively to the processes of decay, however far advanced these may seem to be. It still represents what in America would be called "the power structure." *Joseph Lelyveld, "Reports: India," The Atlantic, Feb. 1968, p 20*

"You struggle to make it as a *person*—not a white or a Negro—in the white world, inside the white power structure, and then you go back to the ghetto when you're in a position to *do something*." *Durward Taylor, quoted by Bonnie Buxton, Maclean's, March 1968, p 39*

2 the ruling circle of any institution.

[Sam] Massell [candidate for mayor of Atlanta] countered with charges of anti-semitism and claimed that his opponents were members of a business "power structure" trying to keep control of Atlanta. *Gene Stephens, "Georgia: Atlanta Election," The Americana Annual 1970, p 316*

PPB or **PPBS,** abbreviation of *Planning-Programming-Budgeting (System)*, a system of planning in business, government, research, etc., in which benefits are measured in relation to final costs and alternative ways of reaching goals are examined to select the least costly method.

The basic idea is Planning, Programming and Budgeting, or PPB. Rand worked on the system for the Defense Department and the initials PPB are firmly lodged in the Rand vocabulary. PPB means that the initial research and analysis is tied firmly and logically to the final budget in terms of benefit received, not just output. *David Bird, The New York Times, April 29, 1968, p 32*

The PPBS, which began in the Defense Department and now is the rule throughout the Government, has these aims, as set forth by President Johnson. . . . *Howard Simons, "American Newsletter: Science for Living," New Scientist, July 14, 1966, p 81*

pram park, *British.* an area reserved for parking baby carriages.

Interest in the development of new shopping centres is not confined to this country [England]. . . . The scheme [for a shopping centre at Ridderker, near Rotterdam] will include the usual public amenities such as seats and plants in the concourse, and a pram park. *Gerald Ely, "British in Dutch Project," The Times (London), Feb. 23, 1970, p 13*

[patterned after *car park*]

pray-in, *n.* the gathering of a group of people to listen to sermons, improvise prayers, etc., as a form of protest or demonstration, especially in a church, synagogue, or other house of worship.

More than 3,000 Roman Catholics went to Westminster Cathedral yesterday for a "pray-in" called by an ad hoc group of laity, opposed to the Pope's ruling. *Anthony Cowdy, Muriel Bowen, and Tony Dawe, The Sunday Times (London), Aug. 18, 1968, p 1*

They relied on persuasion, oral and written, and experimented with such non-violent techniques as preach-ins and pray-ins. . . . *Review of "Black Freedom: The Nonviolent Abolitionists from 1830 Through the Civil War" by Carleton Mabee, The New Yorker, May 2, 1970, p 127*

Early today policemen entered the Church of the Jesuit Fathers in Madrid and evicted 116 demonstrators who had planned a peaceful pray-in protest against the Burgos trial. *The Times (London), Nov. 16, 1970, p 4*

prebiotic or **prebiological,** *adj.* before the appearance of living things.

. . . James P. Ferris of the Salk Institute for Biological Studies . . . assumes that the earth's atmosphere in prebiotic times contained methane, nitrogen, and water. *Leonard Nelson, "Biochemistry: The Atmosphere," The World Book Science Annual 1967, p 263*

The interface from prebiological to biological evolution is more likely to be recognized in terms of molecular structural changes rather than morphological remains. *Eugene D. McCarthy, "Origin of Life," McGraw-Hill Yearbook of Science and Technology 1971, p 5*

. . . a great deal of prebiological organic synthesis occurred on the earth under reducing conditions at an early stage in our planet's history. *G. Evelyn Hutchinson, "The Biosphere," Scientific American, Sept. 1970, p 52*

. . . these two simple chemicals [formaldehyde and ammonia] have recently been detected in space; and a reaction between them to yield amino acids is assumed to be an essential step in the chemical evolution that preceded the emergence of life. Ergo: such pre-biotic evolution could have occurred elsewhere in the Galaxy. *New Scientist, Dec. 10, 1970, p 425*

prebiotic soup, another name for PRIMORDIAL SOUP.

There is a big gap between any of the postulated "prebiotic soups" and the simplest organism subject to natural selection. To narrow the gap a little, many people have suggested that the first organisms did not use all the current amino acids. *New Scientist, Dec. 29, 1966, p 740*

precensorship, *n.* censorship imposed, especially by the government, on secret or classified information prior to its being printed or published by a newspaper, magazine, etc.

The original understanding of the First Amendment was probably the Blackstonian view that a publisher was not to be subjected to "previous restraint" — that is, precensorship — but would be liable civilly or criminally for a publication that violated the law, whether of defamation or incitement to crime or disclosure of state secrets. *Paul A. Freund, "On 'Prior Restraint'," The New York Times, June 25, 1971, p 35*

The Times knew about the U-2 overflights of Russia before Powers was shot down, and The Times knew of the plans for the Bay of Pigs invasion. Bowing to implicit precensorship and to the argument of "national security," The Times did not publish its knowledge. *Peter G. Stillman, "Documents on Vietnam Excursion," The New York Times, June 27, 1971, p 14*

preclear, *v.t.* to clear in advance; certify as safe beforehand.

At the present time, FDA [Food and Drug Administration] approval is somewhat academic because the agency does not regulate IUDs before they appear on the market, though if legislation giving FDA broad authority to preclear all types of medical devices materializes, the situation may change. . . . *Barbara J. Culliton, "Contraception: Improving Mechanical Birth Control Methods," Science News, Aug. 8, 1970, p 121*

preconciliar, *adj.* existing or occurring prior to the Vatican ecumenical council of 1962-1965. Compare POSTCONCILIAR.

I am theologically a profound conservative. I could teach with deep relish a course in preconciliar theology. I would like to have lived in the Middle Ages, one of the high points of man's spirit. *Francine du Plessix Gray, "Profiles: The Rules of the Game" [Ivan Illich], The New Yorker, April 25, 1970, p 68*

Everyone tends to exaggerate the mutual isolation of pre-conciliar days and to forget what two world wars accomplished in bringing Christians together. *Cardinal John Heenan, The Sunday Times (London), Jan. 22, 1967, p 10*

preconsciousness, *n.* the unconscious mental activity just under the consciousness level.

Osip Mandelstam . . . was one of the master poets of Russian, perhaps of world literature. . . . We learn of the "hum" in the literal deeps of the poet's consciousness or pre-consciousness. . . . The "hum" sometimes came to Mandelstam in his sleep, but he could never remember it after he awoke. *George Steiner, "Books: Death of a Poet," Review of "Hope Against Hope" by Nadezhda Mandelstam, translated by Max Hayward, The New Yorker, Dec. 26, 1970, p 61*

prediabetes, *n.* the period or condition in prediabetic persons that precedes the onset of overt diabetes.

Prediabetes in man — the stage from conception to the first evidence of disturbed carbohydrate metabolism — was extensively studied. *Howard F. Root, "Diseases: Diabetes," Britannica Book of the Year 1966, p 246*

prediabetic, *adj.* exhibiting metabolic changes that indicate a predisposition to diabetes.

In addition, a blood sugar test showed that the twins were "prediabetic." *Science News Letter, Jan. 22, 1966, p 51*

—*n.* a prediabetic person.

The reason for the poor performance of the cells taken from prediabetics is not yet known but it may be due to more rapid aging of the diabetic cells. *Barbara Ford, "Biology: Diabetic Cells Less Efficient," 1970 Collier's Encyclopedia Year Book, p 138*

pre-emptive, *adj.* launched to prevent the enemy from attacking first; initiated on the basis of evidence that an enemy attack is imminent.

But our offensive ICBM's (the Minutemen) will scarcely avail us if Soviet strategy calls for a Soviet pre-emptive (surprise) attack. *Albert L. Weeks, New York, in a Letter to the Editor, The New York Times, July 14, 1970, p 36*

No less ominous than an American or Israeli intervention in Jordan is the threat . . . of a preemptive strike against the missiles installed by the Russians and Egyptians in breach of the military standstill agreement. *Peter Jenkins, The Manchester Guardian Weekly, Sept. 26, 1970, p 3*

prefigurative, *adj.* of or designating a form of society in which the values of the younger generation predominate. Compare POSTFIGURATIVE, CO-FIGURATIVE.

In her [Margaret Mead's] "prefigurative" culture the young are "natives" in the new world in which their parents are "immigrants." *Ernest van den Haag, "One Man's Mead, Another Man's Poison," Review of "Culture and Commitment: A Study of The Generation Gap" by Margaret Mead, The Atlantic, June 1970, p 118*

preg·gers ('preg ərz), *adj. Chiefly British Slang.* pregnant.

"I would only offer my seat to a woman if she were carrying a baby, if she were preggers, or if she were obviously infirm, and for no other reason that I can think of", one Home Counties citizen said. *The Times (London), Feb. 4, 1964, p 7*

"The wife is preggers again." *Sean O'Faolain, "The Heat of the Sun" (a short story), The Atlantic, Sept. 1966, p 72*

► The *-ers* ending is a vestige of the British upper-class slang use of *-er* and *-ers* with clipped words, such as *champers* for *champagne,* the *Pragger Wagger* for the *Prince of Wales,* etc. The usage originated at Rugby School and was introduced in the late 1800's into Oxford University. Notable examples of the usage are *Rugger* (for *Rugby*) and *soccer* (for association football). *Starkers* and *bonkers* also have this ending but the origin of *bonk* in *bonkers* is obscure.

prehormone, *n.* a rudimentary or incipient hormone.

A description of the nature of the skin hormone naturally released by irradiated skin was finally provided in 1936 by Adolf Windaus of the University of Gottingen. He demonstrated that 7-dehydrocholesterol is the natural prehormone that is found in the skin and showed how it becomes calciferol on ultraviolet irradiation. *W. F. Loomis, "Rickets," Scientific American, Dec. 1970, p 82*

prenuclear, *adj.* **1** before the age of nuclear weapons.

In earlier, prenuclear times, American Presidents responded to such depredations with fleets, Marines and righteous cannon fire—as when Thomas Jefferson dispatched U.S. frigates under Stephen Decatur to clean out the Barbary pirates who menaced American trade in the Mediterranean. *Time, Sept. 21, 1970, p 12*

2 lacking a visible nucleus.

These other organisms have cells with nuclei and specialized organelles or specialized intracellular structures; they are called eukaryotic (truly nucleated), whereas bacteria and blue-green algae are prokaryotic (prenuclear). It would be surprising if the autotrophs on the lowest rungs of the evolutionary ladder were anything but prokaryotic. *Elso S. Barghoorn, "The Oldest Fossils," Scientific American, May 1971, p 30*

preppie, *n. U.S. Slang.* a student or graduate of a preparatory school.

No longer believe that Harvard students are all rich preppies tracing their Harvard histories back almost as far as the Saltonstalls.... *Larry L. King, "Blowing My Mind at Harvard," Harper's, Oct. 1970, p 103*

pre·preg ('pri:,preg), *n.* a plastic or other synthetic material impregnated with the full complement of resin before it is molded. *Also used attributively.*

One impressive development is the scaled-down aircraft fuselage section which Union Carbide has built for the Bell Aerospace Co. entirely out of carbon-fibre "pre-preg" —a tape of aligned fibres loaded with resin. *Glen Lawes and Michael Kenward, New Scientist, April 30, 1970, p 228*

. . . these sketches are intended merely to suggest the main principles. They show a possible method for continuously turning polyacrylonitrile fibre to carbon, bonding the carbon fibres into a prepreg sheet and then using this to form the skins on each side of a light alloy honeycomb core. *W. T. Gunston, Science Journal, Feb. 1969, p 42*

[shortened from *pre-impreg*nated]

preprogram, *v.t.* to program beforehand for automatic control.

How does one reconcile the known malleability of behavior with a preprogrammed and rigidly "wired" nervous system? *Eric R. Kandel, Scientific American, July 1970, p 58*

presence, *n.* troops of one country stationed in another by mutual agreement.

"Liberal" intellectuals and "conservative" politicians both shared the unthinking assumption behind Johnson's words to the AFL/CIO that the American "presence" abroad is by definition always good. *Jonathan Steele, "Books: Last Straw," Review of "No Hail, No Farewell: The Johnson Years" by Louis Heren, The Manchester Guardian Weekly, Nov. 14, 1970, p 18*

[probably translation of French *présence,* as in *la présence française*]

presoak, *n.* a stain-removing substance put into water to soak laundry before washing.

The difference between a pre-soak and a detergent is mainly a difference in the concentration of active ingredients. However, both products contain essentially the same ingredients—enzymes, phosphates and surfactant, a cleaning agent. *"Consumerism," Time, Feb. 16, 1970, p 86*

...the annual production of enzyme detergents and pre-soaks amounts to some two and a half billion pounds, resulting in retail sales of half a billion dollars. *Paul Brodeur, "A Reporter At Large," The New Yorker, Jan. 16, 1971, p 42*

presort, *v.t.* to sort mail before delivery to the Post Office.

Bulk posting and direct mail firms which pre-sort their letters for the Post Office are protesting against the new proposed postal charges.... *The Times (London), July 25, 1970, p 18*

... he would relent and extend the deadline for the mandatory zip-coding of mail and mandatory pre-sorting of business mail.... *Walter Carlson, The New York Times, Feb. 9, 1966, p 59*

press baron, a powerful newspaper publisher.

Two newspapers, *Der Kurier* in West Berlin and the Hamburg *Abendecho*, recently ceased publication, and Axel Springer, the German press baron, recently forecast that the day is not far off when German cities as large as half a million will be unable to support more than one newspaper. *Richard L. Tobin, Saturday Review, March 11, 1967, p 123*

Is it not remarkable that sterling should be affected far more by the speeches or articles of a press baron than by the announcement of a multi-million pound order gained in America by Rolls-Royce? *The Times (London), May 14, 1968, p 14*

press-show, *v.t.* to show to the press before public presentation; to preview.

"So far I have press-shown 18 films, to the first four of which only one critic turned up. It seems they are only interested in festivals when they are flown south with all expenses paid. The whole thing is an example of English conservatism and French curiosity." *Derek Hill, quoted in "The Times Diary: Film Flop," The Times (London), July 16, 1970, p 10*

press-up, *n. Especially British.* another word for *push-up* (calisthenic exercise).

We kept the hi-fi booming pop, we danced, we had trials of strength: one-arm press-ups, handstands, somersaults.... *A. Alvarez, "Attempt," The Atlantic, April 1971, p 85*

prêt-à-por·ter (pre ta pɔr'tei), *n., adj. French.* ready-to-wear.

"How much?" said the princess. "I haven't a clue." The poodle was hauled up on to the palazzo pijama lap, the fur on his cheeks blown into, and Francesca asked to find a price for the pret-a-porter. *Terry Coleman, "The Princess, the Poodle, and the Palazzo Pijama," The Manchester Guardian Weekly, July 25, 1970, p 16*

If a lady of style has gobs of money, she can still find all the exclusive, just-for-you creations her heart desires, in Paris' high-fashion houses. But the designers these days trend more to mass-market ready-to-wears, known as prêt à porter.... *Time, Aug. 9, 1968, p 30*

And more ironically still, French prêt-à-porter designers are being invited ever more frequently to design for our famous ready-to-wear.... *Alison Adburgham, "Fashion: Fall of the House of Paris," Punch, May 14, 1969, p 715*

pretax, *adj.* another word for BEFORE-TAX.

They forecast a sales gain of 8 to 10 per cent but see an almost dramatic improvement in margins as pretax earnings rise 15 to 20 per cent above those of 1967. *Robert Metz, The New York Times, Jan. 12, 1968, p 38*

pre-teen, *Especially U.S.* —*n.* a person close to his teens; a boy or girl between ten and twelve.

... the texts of many popular songs are so obviously coital that one wonders how they get on the radio and are sold openly to pre-teens. *Richard Schechner, "Pornography and the New Expression," The Atlantic, Jan. 1967, p 77*

—*adj.* close to the teens; approaching adolescence.

... Darlene [is] mother of two pre-teen children. *Austin C. Wehrwein, The New York Times, Jan. 6, 1966, p 33*

preventive detention, *U.S.* the jailing of a criminal suspect without bail to prevent his committing any possible criminal acts before his trial is held.

The "no-knock" and "preventive-detention" provisions of the District of Columbia Crime Control Act have violated, respectively, the public's right to be secure against unreasonable searches and seizures and the traditional presumption of innocence. *"The Talk of the Town," The New Yorker, April 10, 1971, p 30*

But even if the courts uphold preventive detention ... the net result would be to put more prisoners into a prisons system that is already overcrowded, understaffed, underfinanced, and a breeding-ground for professional criminals. *Tom Wicker, The New York Times, May 28, 1970, p 38*

► In British law, the term *preventive detention* refers to the imprisonment of persistent offenders under the Criminal Justice Act of 1948. The term as used in the United States applies to the detention of alleged or suspected offenders whom a judge considers potentially dangerous; this form of detention is not considered constitutionally legal by many in the United States.

primary structure, a minimal sculpture.

Terms such as "primary structures" and "minimal art" are used rather loosely and interchangeably. In relation to current work, they imply a concern with basic structures and with constructions unelaborated in the traditional sense of sculpture. *Benjamin de Brie Taylor, "Art: Primary Structures and Minimal Art," 1968 Collier's Encyclopedia Year Book, p 129*

primary structurist, a minimal sculptor. Compare STRUCTURIST.

In his recent works (at the Waddington Galleries) he has moved away from the elemental forms of the Situation period to elementary geometric forms, similar to those used by the Primary Structurists in America. *Paul Overy, The Listener, April 20, 1967, p 528*

primordial soup or **primordial broth,** the mixture of chemicals which gave rise to life on earth. Also called PREBIOTIC SOUP, PROTOBIOTIC SOUP. Compare SOUP.

Polymers of amino acids forming primitive proteins are formed much more readily in those dramatic laboratory reconstructions of the primordial "soup" than are crude nucleic acids constructed from nucleotides. *Graham Chedd, New Scientist, Jan. 23, 1969, p 174*

Threadlike filament of organic matter resembling decomposed plant tissue is another kind of fossil that appears in electron micrographs of the Fig Tree cherts. Some specimens are nine microns long. Not identifiable with any known organism, the filaments might conceivably be polymerized abiotic molecules from the "primordial broth." *Picture legend, "The Oldest Fossils" by Elso S. Barghoorn, Scientific American, May 1971, p 32*

printout, *n.* the printed output of a computer, an offset printing press, etc.

More and more medium-sized papers are already being printed, with clearer pictures and neater type, on offset color presses. And before long we shall begin to see print-outs issuing from that little box hitched to the TV-hi-fi console in the living room. *Herbert Brucker, "Can Printed News Save a Free Society?" Saturday Review, Oct. 10, 1970, p 55*

Robert Craig, of the University of New Hampshire and a delegate on the McCarthy slate, made available to the volunteers the computer print-outs of his study of New Hampshire voters. *The New York Times, March 17, 1968, Sec. 4, p 1*

[from the verb phrase *print out*]

prisoner of conscience, a political prisoner.

A great many prisoners of conscience, it claims, are sent with or without trial "to the so-called special psychiatric hospitals, where they are given forcible treatment for their supposed mental ailments". *"Europe's Prisoners of Conscience," The Times (London), April 20, 1970, p 6*

privatism, *n.* the pursuit of privacy; withdrawal from publicity or involvement in public matters.

Few observers of the U.S. scene foresaw that political passions on the campuses would become muted in a new emphasis on "privatism." *Time, Dec. 28, 1970, p 6*

privatistic, *adj.* **1** given to or fond of privacy; seclusive.

At Harvard he [Banfield] is known for his privatistic ways. Though he lunches regularly at the faculty club, he scrupulously avoids faculty committees and politics. *Richard Rodd, "A Theory of the Lower Class: Edward Banfield: The Maverick of Urbanology," Review of "The Unheavenly City" by Edward C. Banfield, The Atlantic, Sept. 1970, p 6*

2 favoring or based upon the use of private enterprise, as distinguished from collectivism.

I cannot say in blanket fashion whether this Mao Myth is "good or bad." For the ordinary Chinese it seems to give meaning to things. . . . The "privatistic" alternative, anyway, in a country with *per capita* income perhaps one twentieth of America's, is not a glittering one. *Ross Terrill, "The 800,000,000: Report From China," The Atlantic, Nov. 1971, p 119*

proactive, *adj.* *Psychology.* characterized by the dominance of first-learned material over material learned subsequently.

The word-recall experiments also reveal that, 24 hours after having learned List I and List II, a subject's recall of List II words diminishes but his recall of List I words does not. This phenomenon, which demonstrates that interference by List I can affect recall of List II is termed "proactive inhibition." *John Ceraso, Scientific American, Oct. 1967, p 118*

[from *pro-* forward + *active*, patterned after *retroactive*]

pro-am ('prou'æm), *adj.* **1** including both professional and amateur players; professional and amateur.

. . . a great last round of 68 enabled Dickson and his partner, Jack Ging, who received nine strokes against Bonallack's four, to win the pro-am section also by a stroke. *Pat Ward-Thomas, The Manchester Guardian Weekly, Jan. 30, 1969, p 22*

2 of or relating to pro-am competition or competitors.

In fact, I would not recognize the usual pro-am dinner at all—with its familiar climax of applause and the day's low-ball team sauntering up to the awards table to receive silver bowls and sets of matched irons. *George Plimpton, "The Alex Karras Gold Classic," Harper's, May 1971, p 64*

—*n.* a pro-am game, match, or tournament.

"They send helicopters to take me from one pro-am to another. Last year I waited at airports and wondered how I would get out to a golf course." *Lincoln A. Werden, The New York Times, July 11, 1968, p 46*

pro·car·y·ote (prou'kær i:,out), *n.* a cell without a visible nucleus. Also spelled PROKARYOTE. Compare EUCARYOTE.

Procaryotes were found in the Beck Spring Dolomite in association with the primitive eucaryotes. . . . A mat of threadlike procaryotic blue-green algae, each thread of which is about 3.5 microns in diameter. . . . Cells of this kind, among others, presumably produced photosynthetic oxygen before eucaryotes appeared. *Picture legend, "The Oxygen Cycle," Scientific American, Sept. 1970, p 112*

[from *pro-* before + *caryote* cell nucleus (from Greek *káryon* nut, kernel)]

pro·car·y·ot·ic (prou,kær i:'at ik), *adj.* not having a visible nucleus. Also spelled PROKARYOTIC. Compare EUCARYOTIC.

Procaryotic cells, which lack a nucleus and divide by simple fission, were a more primitive form of life than the eucaryotes and persist today in the bacteria and blue-green algae. *Picture legend, "The Oxygen Cycle," Scientific American, Sept. 1970, p 112*

Cells that contain a membrane-bound nucleus are termed eucaryotic (plants and animals), while those without nuclei are known as procaryotic (bacteria and blue-green algae). *Ian Craig, "Chloroplasts: Little Green Slaves?" New Scientist and Science Journal, Aug. 5, 1971, p 313*

process art, another name for CONCEPTUAL ART.

Some U.S. museums also began to document the avant-garde "process" or "concept" art, which involved only ideas and their realization in a situation, or series of events, that did not always produce objects or traditional works of art. *Joshua B. Kind, "Museums," The 1970 Compton Yearbook, p 359*

Process art is primarily concerned with acts and effects. Richard Serra, for example, has dripped hot lead along wall intersections and leaned objects against each other in precarious positions. Bill Bollinger has spread floors with graphite and a sawdust-like compound to be disturbed by the viewer's feet and has stretched rope between various points in a room. *Benjamin de Brie Taylor, "Art: Process Art and Antiform," 1970 Collier's Encyclopedia Year Book, p 117*

processor, *n.* an artist who creates works of process art.

Such earthworkers, anti-formers, processors, and conceptualists as Morris, Carl Andre, Walter de Maria, Robert Smithson, Bruce Nauman, Richard Serra, Eva Hesse, Barry Flanagan, Keither Sonnier, Dennis Oppenheim, and Lawrence Weiner have been enjoying increasing prestige. *Harold Rosenberg, "The Art World," The New Yorker, Jan. 24, 1970, p 62*

Prod, *n.* (in Ireland) a derogatory term for a Protestant.

"Why don't I go down South?" asked a Belfast long-shoreman. "That's just what the Prods want us to do." *Time, April 5, 1971, p 21*

"But it isn't just the Papist agin the Prods, Joe." *Patrick Campbell, The Sunday Times (London), Sept. 21, 1969, p 12*

The British soldiers quickly detoured McCurrie's cortege, but not before the two groups of mourners had caught sight of one another. There were jeers, fist shakings and muffled epithets, like "Bloody Prods" and "Dirty Papists." *Time, July 13, 1970, p 17*

pro·ette (prou'et), *n.* a female professional in sports, especially golf.

. . . even a lady "proette" has lost the U S Women's Open through signing for a correct total but a 5 and a 4 when she meant a 4 and a 5. . . . *Henry Longhurst, The Sunday Times (London), Oct. 5, 1969, p 20*

For obvious reasons, the LPGA [Ladies Professional Golf Association] objects to its members being called "pro" golfers, and is trying to popularize the description "pro-ettes". . . . *Alan Edmonds, "And Sandra Post Makes Three . . .," Maclean's, Sept. 1968, p 39*

And while no proette has ever topped $50,000 for a season, Jack Nicklaus for one has picked up that much in a single tournament. *"Sport—Whoopee for the Proettes," Time, June 28, 1971, p 41*

[from *pro* a professional + *-ette* (feminine suffix)]

pro-European, *adj.* **1** supporting or advocating the social, cultural, or economic unification of western European countries.

Maurice Schumann, 58, Minister of Foreign Affairs, combines impeccable Gaullist credentials with a pro-European outlook. *Time, July 4, 1969, p 23*

2 favoring Great Britain's entry into the European Common Market.

The well-known differences of attitude between members of the Government over Britain's application to join the Common Market received yet another airing at the weekend with a strongly pro-European speech from Mr Roy Hattersley, the Minister of Defence for Administration. *Ian Aitken, The Manchester Guardian Weekly, April 4, 1970, p 8*

—*n.* one who is pro-European.

Even Mr. Heath, the dedicated pro-European, did not often introduce the great controversial subject of Britain's approach to membership in the European Economic Community. . . . *Mollie Panter-Downes, "Letter from London," The New Yorker, July 4, 1970, p 61*

prog, *n.* British Slang. **1** a progressive; a person who favors progress or reform.

'Chaps like us,' observes Frank's PR cousin Adam, 'who don't believe in change, do far more for the Church than a thousand bloody progs like Pope John.' *John Hemmings, "Books: Sin is the Spur," Review of "The Crying Game" by John Braine, The Listener, Aug. 29, 1968, p 280*

The "progs" or progressives believe Tewkesbury lives too much in the past. . . . *The New York Times, June 1, 1965, p 33*

2 a member of a progressive group, especially one in a political party.

By European standards the "progs," as they are known, are a moderate party which might feel most at home in the British Liberal Party, or perhaps among the west German Free Democrats. *Dan Van Der Vat, The Times (London), March 26, 1970, p 6*

program or *(British)* **programme,** *v.t.* to cause to follow a planned sequence of steps or operations; to direct, control, or channel in accordance with a plan, schedule, or code.

To what extent can astronauts, environmentally be-suited, rigidly programmed, and electronically guided to their destination, be said to resemble the courageous explorers of the past—Marco Polo, Magellan, or Amundsen, say—who travelled, in all things, hopefully? *New Scientist, Dec. 19, 1968, p 653*

There could hardly be a more convincing demonstration of the existence of an internal clock operating independently of the environmental conditions. Quite evidently an annual cycle of feeding and fasting is also programmed in the animal. *Eric T. Pengelley and Sally J. Asmundson, "Annual Biological Clocks," Scientific American, April 1971, p 75*

Mr. Carter said the project hoped to show that "the legitimate hostilities and aggressions of black youth" could be "programed" to benefit the slum community. *Donald Janson, The New York Times, Feb. 24, 1968, p 14*

This thing is so instinctively, plus manipulatively, engineered to leave 'em crying that it could hardly fail commercially even if the actors were programmed . . . to make obscene gestures at the audience at ten-second intervals. *Pauline Kael, "The Current Cinema," Review of "Love Story" by Erich Segal, The New Yorker, Dec. 26, 1970, p 53*

—*v.i.* **1** to construct or provide for a sequence of steps or operations, as for a computer.

The ability to write a computer program will become as widespread as the ability to drive a car. Not knowing how to program will be like living in a house full of servants and not speaking their language. *John McCarthy, "Information: Presenting an Issue About Its Processing by Computers," Scientific American, Sept. 1966, p 72*

2 to follow a prearranged plan, schedule, scheme, etc.

Also, it is broadly hinted by the casework staff [in the penitentiary] that if the inmate "programs," the U.S. Board of Parole will look more favorably at his case. *Steve Routhier, Brunswick, Me., in a Letter to the Editor, The Atlantic, May 1971, p 34*

programmable, *adj.* capable of being programmed.

. . . at the moment, a highly simplified programmable logic system is more economic than stored programme control. *John Pollard, New Scientist, July 16, 1970, p 20*

The mathematician's abstract world does not contain such realities—which leads mathematicians, such as Minsky, dogmatically to assert that everything which cannot be programmed cannot exist (and the corollary that everything that does exist must be programmable). *Ian Benson, "Machines That Mimic Thought," New Scientist and Science Journal, Sept. 2, 1971, p 528*

prog·ram·met·ry ('prou,græm ə tri:), *n.* See the quotation for the meaning.

There are measurements as to errors found per shift of operators and per programmer, the size of files, and the use of other parts of the configuration. Yet perhaps the most exciting is in the area known as programmetry—the measurement of program performance. *A. d'Agapayeff, "Software Engineering," Science Journal, Oct. 1970, p 98*

programming language, another name for COMPUTER LANGUAGE.

The next development was to devise "programming

languages", in which programmers could represent their directives to the computer in a form convenient for scientific or commercial work. A program in such a language is processed by another program called a "compiler", which translates it to the instruction code of the specific machine for execution. *"Towards a Common Computer Language," New Scientist, April 28, 1966, p 226*

The authors appear to have a strange conception of what computer programming languages are. They write as though programming languages come ready-made with identifiers, so that they approve of attempts to "purge them of arbitrary restrictions and unpronounceable identifiers"! *Andrew Ortony, New Scientist, Oct. 8, 1970, p 83*

prokaryote, *n.* another spelling of PROCARYOTE.

Bacteria and blue-green algae are known as prokaryotes, meaning they lack the membrane-limiting nucleus possessed by nucleate organisms, or eukaryotes. (*Karyon* is Greek for nucleus.) *Ursula W. Goodenough and R. P. Levine, "The Genetic Activity of Mitochondria and Chloroplasts," Scientific American, Nov. 1970, p 24*

prokaryotic, *adj.* another spelling of PROCARYOTIC.

The bacteria and their close relatives the blue-green algae comprise the so-called prokaryotic group; they are all micro-organisms. The second group, the eukaryotes, includes all other types of cell, whether animal, plant, protozoal or fungal. *Donald Williamson, "Where Did Mitochondria Come From?" New Scientist, Sept. 24, 1970, p 624*

Only the prokaryotic blue-green algae can employ chlorophyll that is not packaged into the layered plastids of the green leaf; some bacteria, also prokaryotes, photosynthesize even without the green stuff. *Philip Morrison, "Books," Scientific American, May 1971, p 128*

promoter, *n.* a functional genetic element in the Jacob-Monod model of the operon.

... a gene consists of 3 elements, together called an operon. The elements are a "promoter" that produces the repressor; an "operator" that starts the gene operating but is normally dampened by the repressor; and a "structural" portion, which is placed into action by the operator and does the main work of the gene. *Robert Reinhold, "Scientists Isolate A Gene," Encyclopedia Science Supplement (Grolier) 1970, p 108*

The promoter and operator sites are adjacent parts of the same DNA duplex. The promoter is the site to which the transcribing enzyme (RNA polymerase) binds in order to start transcription, and the operator is the site to which the specific repressor protein binds to stop gene expression (possibly by preventing transcription). *Lorne A. MacHattie, "Gene," McGraw-Hill Yearbook of Science and Technology 1971, p 213*

pro·sage ('prou sidʒ), *n.* See the quotation for the meaning.

Prosage is a sausage which doesn't have any pork in it. As a matter of fact it doesn't even have any meat in it—only pure vegetable protein. *Philip Clarke, The Sunday Times (London), Jan. 11, 1970, p 35*

[from *pro*tein sau*sage*]

pros·ta·glan·din (ˌprɑs təˈglæn dən), *n.* any one of 16 or more hormonelike substances produced in the tissues of mammals by the action of enzymes on certain fatty acids, found in high concentrations in seminal fluid of the prostate gland, and thought to have a variety of important functions in reproduction, nerve-impulse transmission, muscle contrac-

tion, regulation of blood pressure, and metabolism. *Abbreviation:* PG

In a 1968 report, E. J. Corey and his associates at Harvard University announced that they had developed methods for the total synthesis of five biologically potent prostaglandins.... *James S. Sweet, "Molecular Biology: Biochemistry," 1970 Britannica Yearbook of Science and the Future, 1969, p 293*

In Sweden, Britain and Uganda 200 women are using prostaglandins (instead of contraceptives) to induce abortion as soon as they miss a period. *"Prostaglandins: Rapid Research Advances," Science News, April 3, 1971, p 230*

[coined by the Swedish physiologist Ulf S. von Euler from *prostate gland* + *-in* (chemical suffix)]

protectionist, *n.* one who seeks to protect wildlife; a wildlife conservationist.

Jack Berryman, who directs Wildlife Services ... deeply resents the attacks of what he calls "the wild-eyed protectionists," who, he says, portray him and his field men as "bloodthirsty killers." *Faith McNulty, "A Reporter at Large: The Prairie Dog and the Black-Footed Ferret," The New Yorker, June 13, 1970, p 57*

proteinoid, *n.* a peptide-chain molecule resembling a protein molecule.

... the relatively small amino acid molecules combined to form protein-like macromolecules, which we called proteinoids because their building blocks were amino acids and their size was comparable to that of small protein molecules. *S. W. Fox and R. J. McCauley, "Could Life Originate Now?" Encyclopedia Science Supplement (Grolier) 1969, p 75*

In the past, Fox and others have demonstrated that these proteinoid microspheres can have catalytic activity, so that they take up small molecules and perform chemical reactions, that they can grow and divide.... *"Communication in Early Chemical Evolution," New Scientist and Science Journal, June 10, 1971, p 613*

Protestant ethic, a set of values held by some social scientists to be the ideological basis of the capitalistic system, including the ideas of strict personal compliance with the law, the necessity and desirability of work and thrift, and encouragement of competition and the profit motive in everyday life.

To some the Protestant Ethic—hard work is a virtue for its own sake—appears to have been replaced by an almost Mediterranean spirit, a spreading belief that men should work no more than they must to enjoy the good life and worldly pleasures. *Time, March 23, 1970, p 77*

The Protestant ethic and tradition of capitalism have made most middle-class Americans cherish their privacy and independence, and the dread of relinquishing them dies hard. *Lynne and Jack Waugh, "The New Communes," Encyclopedia Science Supplement (Grolier) 1971, p 310*

... Mrs. Dollart is well known to put aside her Protestant ethic to attend the Tuesday-night bingo in St. Mary's Catholic Church basement.... *Anthony Bailey, "Profiles," The New Yorker, July 24, 1971, p 40*

protobiont, *n.* an elementary or primordial organism.

As a preliminary stage in the total process of organic evolution, chemical evolution of course reaches its climax when lifeless organic molecules are assembled by chance into a living organism. This first form of life is what the

Russian biochemist A. I. Oparin calls a "protobiont." *Elso S. Barghoorn, "The Oldest Fossils," Scientific American, May 1971, p 30*

protobiotic soup, another name for PRIMORDIAL SOUP.

...the constituents of Haldane's soup (a "protobiotic soup of amino-acids, ribose, four purine and pyrimidine bases, and a source of high-energy phosphate"). *Cyril Connolly, "The Proper Study," The Sunday Times (London), Oct. 3, 1971, p 40*

protocontinent, *n.* another name for SUPER-CONTINENT.

The Hegira Of The Indian Subcontinent About 60,000,000 Years Ago is suggested on the above map of earth's protocontinent, as Professor J. Tuzo Wilson has pictured it. *Map legend in "Baptism of a Mountain" by John Lear, Saturday Review, March 2, 1968, p 48*

The abundance of these [igneous] rocks in the equatorial mid-Atlantic Ridge, says Dr. Enrico Bonatti of the University of Miami, indicates that there is either a continuous layer or large blocks of continental type mantle imbedded in the mantle under the ridge. Dr. Bonatti proposes, in the June 10 Journal of Geophysical Research, that this mantle material was originally part of a layer of continental-type mantle below the protocontinent Pangaea. *"Continental Mantle Under the Sea," Science News, July 10, 1971, p 26*

protogalaxy, *n.* See the first quotation for the meaning.

A galaxy in the process of formation, before any stars have formed in it, is called a *protogalaxy*. In the course of time the protogalaxy contracts and its density rises, as a result of the continuing inward force of its own gravity. *Robert Jastrow and Malcolm H. Thompson, Astronomy: Fundamentals and Frontiers, 1972, p 208*

A protogalaxy consisting of an irregular cloud of gas and probably some dust, with a mass of a little less than a million times that of the sun, existed in intergalactic space somewhat more than 10 billion years ago. *Paul W. Hodge, Scientific American, May 1964, p 83*

pro·to·na·tion (ˌprou təˈnei ʃən), *n.* the addition of a proton to an ion.

The hydride complexes are usually obtained by reduction or protonation of suitable metal complexes. All the positively charged species listed in Table 1 were obtained by protonation, usually in very strong acid. . . . *Joseph Chatt, Science, May 17, 1968, p 724*

proton decay, the radioactive transmutation of one chemical element into another by the emission of a proton from an unstable nucleus.

Called proton decay, it is a process in which a nucleus emits a proton and decreases both atomic number and atomic weight by one. *Science News, Oct. 31, 1970, p 349*

A consortium of nuclear physicists from America, England and Canada have discovered a new mode of nuclear disintegration—proton decay. The three modes already known are: emission of a beta particle (electron or positron), emission of an alpha particle (helium nucleus), and spontaneous fission (occurring only in very heavy nuclei). *New Scientist, Nov. 5, 1970, p 259*

protovirus, *n.* a primary or prototypical virus that serves as a model for others of the same kind.

According to his hypothesis, normal cells manufacture RNA, which moves to neighboring cells in the form of a protovirus, or template, and stimulates the production of a new form of DNA. *Time, April 19, 1971, p 28*

RNA tumor viruses may have evolved when RNA coded for by one cell was transferred to a second cell, where it produced new DNA that the host DNA incorporated. In time, a DNA "protovirus" region might be established and might code for a complete RNA tumor virus particle. *Robert L. Hill, "Molecular Biology," 1972 Britannica Yearbook of Science and the Future, 1971, p 301*

Provisional or **provisional,** *n.* a member of the so-called Provisional wing of the Irish Republican Army, consisting of militant extremists. Also nicknamed PROVO.

The Provisionals are more aptly defined by the things they are against. *"Ireland's Odd Men Out," Newsweek, Oct. 18, 1971, p 18*

What is known is that the arms were destined for the breakaway I.R.A. group in the North—the so called provisionals. *The Times (London), May 15, 1970, p 5*

If that is so, however, there are other questions: why and how did the nucleus of the Provisionals come into existence —ready ruthlessly to exploit inside their community the real and imagined grievances that these policies induced? *Ulster, by the Sunday Times (London) Insight Team, 1972, p 255*

pro·vo or **Pro·vo**[1] (ˈprou vou), *n.* any of a group of Dutch or German political activists that engage in agitation, rioting, and disruptive activities.

The youthful protesters, who used to be known as Provos (for provocateurs), rioted over almost everything from Crown Princess Beatrix's lavish wedding in 1966, when they tossed smoke bombs at the royal carriage, to the country's critical housing shortage. *Time, June 15, 1970, p 37*

...Frankfurt's notorious Provos, [are] members of a group of youths who, as their name indicates, like to provoke the public. *The New York Times, Aug. 8, 1967, p 35*

[ultimately a short form of French *provocateur* agitator]

Pro·vo[2] (ˈprou vou), *n.* a nickname for a PROVISIONAL.

Mothers, egged on by the Provos, swore their lasses had been raped, especially by the black men in the army. *Simon Winchester, The Manchester Guardian Weekly, Feb. 13, 1971, p 24*

Nevertheless, he believes, like any good Provo, that the fight must go on until Stormont is abolished not just suspended, British soldiers have left the streets of Ulster, *all* internees have been released but there are significant moves towards a United Ireland. *Brian Moynahan, "Facing a Terrible Freedom," The Sunday Times (London), May 14, 1972, p 15*

pseu·do·cho·lin·es·ter·ase (ˌsu: douˌkou ləˈnes təˌreis), *n.* an enzyme present in the liver and blood plasma of man. It is chemically similar to the enzyme cholinesterase in nerve tissue but its exact physiological function is not known.

Pseudocholinesterase catalyzes hydrolysis of aspirin, succinylcholine [a muscle relaxant] and other drugs. *Joan Lynn Arehart, "How Genes Control Drugs," Science News, June 26, 1971, p 438*

pseudo-event, *n.* a staged or contrived event; something arranged so that it may be publicized or reported in the news media.

I sometimes wonder what memories today's children will retain of the big pseudo-event (defined by sociologist Daniel Boorstin as a news event planned in advance) of Canada's electronic age. *Jocelyn Dingman, Maclean's, March 1967, p 78*

psi·lo·cin ('sai lə sən), *n.* a hallucinogenic drug related to DMT, derived from the mushroom *Psilocybe mexicana.*

Included by name as "drugs having a potential for abuse because of their hallucinatory effect," were ... two other agents called psilocybin and psilocin.... *Richard D. Lyons, The New York Times, July 2, 1967, Sec. 4, p 8*

...*Conocybe, Panaeolus,* and *Stropharia* ... contain the extraordinarily biodynamic compound psilocybin, a hydroxy indole alkylamine with a phosphorylated side chain (the only indole compound with a phosphoric acid radical known from the plant kingdom) and sometimes the unstable derivative psilocin. *Richard Evans Schultes, "Psychopharmacological Drugs," McGraw-Hill Yearbook of Science and Technology 1971, p 357*

psi·lo·cy·bin (,sai lə'sai bən), *n.* a hallucinogenic drug derived from the mushroom *Psilocybe mexicana.*

...psilocybin, which is found in certain mushrooms, was in use by Indians when the Spanish conquerors first came to Mexico. *Jerome H. Jaffe, "Drug Addiction and Abuse," Encyclopedia Science Supplement (Grolier) 1969, p 188*

...modern work with the hallucinogenic drugs such as mescalin, LSD-125, psilocybin and others which induce dreamlike states in waking subjects has also attracted research interest to the chemistry of fantasy. *Norman Mackenzie, "Sleeping and Dreaming," The Listener, May 12, 1966, p 680*

psych (saik), *v.i., v.t. Slang.* **1** to lose or cause to lose resolve; break down psychologically (especially in the phrase **psych out**).

"What about it, buddy?" Lewis said, looking at the two empty slots in the quiver. "I got a shot." "You did?" Lewis said, straightening. "I did. A spectacular miss at fifteen yards." "What happened? we could'a had meat." "I boosted my bow hand, I think. I psyched out. I'll be damned if I know how." *James Dickey, "Two Days in September" (part of a novel), The Atlantic, Feb. 1970, p 84*

Having discovered psychology, the cops induce "truth" by psyching the subject. *Time, April 29, 1966, p 35*

2 to stimulate or excite (especially in the phrase **psych up**).

We were all psyched up, and as a result when we got there the shooting started, almost as a chain reaction. *Seymour M. Hersh, "My Lai 4," Harper's, May 1970, p 65*

Ficker said yesterday: "I don't believe in getting the crew all psyched up." *The Times (London), Sept. 15, 1970, p 6*

"He's [Harry Parker, a Harvard crew coach, is] deadly honest," said Canning. "He's never tried to psych us, or insult us with a pep talk. Before a race, we get a briefing, an appraisal. Only that." *Roger Angell, "The Sporting Scene: 0:00.05," The New Yorker, Aug. 10, 1968, p 78*

psy·che·del·i·a (,sai kə'del i: ə), *n.* **1** the realm or world of psychedelic drugs.

...Dr. Timothy Leary, 49, the guru of psychedelia, heard a Laredo, Texas, jury convict him for the second time of smuggling marijuana from Mexico.... *Time, Feb. 2, 1970, p 28*

2 artifacts associated with the effects induced by psychedelic drugs.

The kit costs $6.50 and contains a roller applicator, paint pan and three three-ounce bottles of pastel psychedelia. *Sandra Peredo, Maclean's, Sept. 1967, p 91*

[from *psychedelic* + *-ia*, as in *schizophrenia*]

psy·che·del·ic (,sai kə'del ik), *adj.* **1** mind-expanding; hallucinogenic; chemically altering the psyche so as to intensify perception.

Graham B. Blaine Jr., chief of psychiatry of Harvard University's Health Services, wrote in his recent book, "Youth and the Hazards of Affluence," that even a single dose of such psychedelic drugs as LSD may result in recurring episodes of psychosis, often resulting in depression and suicidal or homicidal impulses. *Fred M. Hechinger, The New York Times, Oct. 9, 1966, Sec. 4, p 9*

It is everything for everybody, and everyone—they argue —has the inalienable right to pursue ecstasy via unlimited access to the "psychedelic" (mind-manifesting) drugs—a name they prefer to "hallucinogens," which they regard as too negative. *Sidney Cohen, "LSD And the Anguish of Dying," Harper's, Sept. 1965, p 71*

2 of or relating to psychedelic drugs or their use.

In the U.S.A., Dr. Timothy Leary, the best-known spokesman of the "psychedelic revolution". has admitted the grave danger in the uncontrolled use of LSD. Indeed, nobody in his senses would deny it. *Kenneth Leech, The Times (London), July 25, 1966, p 11*

To quote from Masters' and Houston's admirable study "The Varieties of Psychedelic Experience": It is frequent and funny, if also unfortunate, to encounter young members of the Drug Movement who claim to have achieved a personal apotheosis when, in fact, their experience appears to have consisted mainly of depersonalization, dissociation, and similar phenomena. *"The Talk of the Town," The New Yorker, Oct. 1, 1966, p 41*

3 suggesting or resembling the effect of psychedelic drugs; loud, bright, kaleidoscopic, etc.

Robert Wyatt, the drummer; Michael Ratledge, organist, and Kevin Ayers, bassist, are explorers of the ultimate fringe of psychedelic music, jazz, conscious distortion, electronic dadaism and shock-rock. *Robert Shelton, The New York Times, July 12, 1968, p 16*

This [THX 1138] design has been characterized as "psychedelic" by several critics—as if brilliant colors and rapid cutting invariably produced an example of drug-induced visions. *David Denby, "The Inhuman Future," The Atlantic, June 1971, p 98*

...Jon Eby took the opposite approach—and put Stanfield in the middle of what we fondly believe to be the first psychedelic political poster in the history of the Tory party. *Douglas Marshall, Maclean's, March 1968, p 23*

—n. 1 a psychedelic drug.

When I wrote these lines LSD and its chemical relative, mescaline, were the only hallucinogenic agents known. Today the number has proliferated to include psilocybin, DMT, ... and many more now being synthesized or tested. They have a new name, the "psychedelics," meaning mind-revealing, mind-expanding or consciousness-expanding drugs. *Sidney Katz, Maclean's, June 20, 1964, p 9*

Perhaps I am being overly solemn about Dr. Leary, psychedelics, and, by extension, Murray the K's world. *Robert Kotlowitz, Harper's, July 1966, p 99*

383

2 a person who is addicted to psychedelic drugs.

Such dangers do not deter the acid heads or "psychedelics"—even though some users are willing to admit that they found no great "show," or had a "freak trip" (a bad one), or "tripped out" (the worst kind). *Time, March 11, 1966, p 43*

[from Greek *psȳchḗ* soul, mind + *dēloûn* to reveal, manifest + English *-ic*]

psychedelically, *adv.* In a psychedelic manner; with psychedelic effects of color, sound, etc.

Long before Expo '70 was more than an idea, Canadians began promoting it by means of a psychedelically painted school bus that travelled around both Canada and Japan. *E. J. Kahn, Jr., The New Yorker, June 6, 1970, p 101*

psychedelicatessen, *n. U.S.* another name for HEAD SHOP.

The paraphernalia of the mind drugs was everywhere—all the sorts of things that crowd the "head shops" and "psychedelicatessens" of the Lower East Side and, of course, certain areas of the U.S. west coast. *Saturday Night (Canada), June 1967, p 24*

In Los Angeles, the leading psychedelicatessen is the Headquarters, not far from the gates of the U.C.L.A. campus. *Time, Feb. 24, 1967, p 55*

[blend of *psychedelic* and *delicatessen*]

psychic energizer, a drug that relieves mental depression.

Monamine oxidase (MAO) inhibitors, currently used largely as "pepper-uppers" or "psychic energizers", also tend to reduce blood pressure, but the doses needed are generally considered too dangerous for clinical purposes. *Britannica Book of the Year 1964, p 653*

psychoactive, *adj.* acting on the mind; affecting or altering the mental state.

Lebanese hashish contains only one important psychoactive chemical according to a report in Science (169, 3945, p 611) from an Israeli team.... *Science Journal, Nov. 1970, p 27*

...marijuana is a psychoactive drug and can certainly cause problems if the basic personality structure of the user is weak.... *Roger Jellinek, The New York Times, June 4, 1971, p 31*

psychoactivity, *n.* potency as a psychoactive agent.

These tribesmen [in western and northeastern Siberia], having discovered that the narcotic constituent of the mushroom is excreted with almost undiminished psychoactivity, incorporated a ritual urine-drinking ceremony in order to take full advantage of the biodynamic principle in a region where the mushroom is rare. *Richard Evans Schultes, "Psychopharmacological Drugs," McGraw-Hill Yearbook of Science and Technology 1971, p 357*

psychochemical, *n.* a psychoactive chemical agent.

The national and international pattern of drug abuse during 1969 reflected a continuing increase in the use of most psychochemicals. *Sidney Cohen, "Narcotics and Hallucinogens," The Americana Annual 1970, p 486*

psychogeriatric, *adj.* of or relating to mental illness among the elderly.

A better measure of a man's age than the state of his arteries may be the degree of his solitude, Dr. J. P. Junod, of the Geneva psycho-geriatric centre, said at an international conference on community psychiatry. *The Times (London), Dec. 1, 1966, p 8*

psychohistorical, *adj.* of or relating to the psychological aspects of history.

And further efforts at deepening our psychohistorical insight could in turn help us to create new kinds of political, institutional, and legal structures appropriate to our unprecedented situation. *Robert Jay Lifton, "False God," The Atlantic, Oct. 1970, p 110*

psychopharmaceutical, *n.* a psychoactive drug.

One advantage of doxepin [an antidepressant drug] is its apparently low toxicity compared to other psychopharmaceuticals. *Jeanne Bockel, Science News, Dec. 20, 1969, p 581*

psychoprophylaxis, *n.* a method of preparing women for natural childbirth by psychological conditioning. See also LAMAZE.

A gynaecologist once pointed out to me that a fundamental difference in approach to tasks—any tasks—may be one reason among many others why "psycho-prophylaxis" works so well for some women in childbirth and so badly for others.... *Gillian Tindall, The Manchester Guardian Weekly, Jan. 9, 1969, p 17*

...Mrs. Karmel and Elisabeth Bing, a Berlin-born physical therapist, founded the American Society for Psychoprophylaxis in Obstetrics.... *Marylin Bender, The New York Times, May 16, 1967, p 42*

The Childbirth Education Association of Toronto is presently sponsoring classes in psychoprophylaxis. *Susan E. M. Porter, Maclean's, Dec. 1967, p 86*

[from *psycho-* psychological + *prophylaxis* treatment to preserve health]

psy·cho·so·mat·ry (ˌsaɪ kou səˈmæt riː), *n.* the influence of the mind on the body, especially in causing certain ailments.

He never makes promises, and ridicules the sort of magic that grows hair on billiard balls. Nevertheless, extraordinary cures do happen, which he attributes more to the mysterious working of psychosomatry. *Ted Simon, "A Fringe Profession," The Times (London), May 11, 1970, p 12*

[from *psychosom*atic of both the mind and body + *-atry*, as in *psychiatry*]

psy·chot·o·gen (saɪˈkɑt ə dʒən), *n.* a drug that produces a psychotic state; a psychotogenic drug.

Herbert Weingartner, assistant professor of medical psychiatry and behavioral science at the School of Medicine, and a psychologist at Phipps Clinic, foresees a future in which some hallucinogens, more precisely those described as psychotogens, will be used in ways that will benefit the functioning of the human brain. *"Hopkins Study Shows Small Doses of Certain Drugs Can Benefit Behavior," Johns Hopkins Journal, March 1970, p 1*

psychotogenic or **psychotogenetic,** *adj.* producing a psychotic state; causing psychosis or mental derangement.

...the effects of Vietnamese marijuana were sometimes surprisingly similar to those induced by hallucinogenic and psychotogenic agents such as L.S.D., mescaline and other so-called mind-expanders that have...proved harmful to the body and central nervous system of humans. *Louis Heren, The Times (London), March 26, 1970, p 7*

Dr. Weingartner bases his conclusions on extensive research with several members of the psychotogenetic family, primarily with what has been labeled DOET (2,5-dimethoxy 4-ethylamphetamine) and DOM (2,5-dimethoxy

4-methylamphetamine), commonly called "speed." *"Hopkins Study Shows Small Doses of Certain Drugs can Benefit Behavior," Johns Hopkins Journal, March 1970, p 1*

psychotomimetic, *adj.* imitating or reproducing a psychotic state; affecting the mind psychotically.

A psychotomimetic snuff, *rapé dos indios,* is said to be prepared from fruits of the central Amazonian moraceous tree *Olmedioperebea sclerophylla,* but nothing is known of its chemistry. *Richard Evans Schultes, "Psychopharmacological Drugs," McGraw-Hill Yearbook of Science and Technology 1971, p 357*

— *n.* a psychotomimetic drug.

Though much more has been found out about the psychotomimetic effects of the older drugs, and new ones have been discovered (e.g., psilocybin, the active ingredient of Mexico's "magic mushrooms"), LSD remains preeminent — partly because it was the first of the "modern" psychotomimetics but chiefly because it produces the most powerful psychological effects from the smallest doses. *Hannah Steinberg, "Science Probes The Effects of Mind Expanding Drugs," Britannica Book of the Year 1968, p 521*

psychotomimetically, *adv.* in a psychotomimetic manner.

The Δ^1-isomer is the major constituent. It appears to be quite active and is currently being advertised as "the psychotomimetically active constituent of hashish", although the evidence for this claim is far from substantial. *Andrew T. Weil, Science Journal, Sept. 1969, p 38*

psychotoxic, *adj.* regarded as harmful to the mind or personality.

Late last year the Senate whisked through a bill directing the FDA [Food and Drug Administration] to police the sales records of all firms distributing any drugs that may induce "psychotoxic effects or anti-social behavior" if taken in excessive quantities. *Joseph W. Sullivan, The Wall Street Journal, Jan. 27, 1965, p 8*

psy·chro·tol·er·ant (ˌsɑi krou'tɑl ər ənt), *adj.* able to endure cold.

Slime is caused by cold resistant, or psychrotolerant, bacteria which are not a health hazard but which produce an objectionable smell and change the colour of the meat. *Science Journal, May 1970, p 19*

[from *psychro-* cold (from Greek *psȳchrós*) + *tolerant*]

psy·op ('sɑiˌɑp), *n. U.S. Military Use.* an action or operation in psychological warfare.

"With national elections over and the new Government in operation, U.S. Psyop personnel should devote priority attention to assisting the GVN [Government of Vietnam] in projecting a positive image to the RVN [Republic of Vietnam] public," a United States Mission directive states. *The New York Times, Jan. 21, 1968, p 9*

At Bragg, the psywar department is hopeless, a grab-bag of highly sophisticated instruments to, as they say, "use communications to influence the behavior of the target area." To that end, psyops operatives at Bragg are studying the world's religions, "group dynamics," and "the social system." It is sociology gone berserk. *Ward Just, "Soldiers," The Atlantic, Nov. 1970, p 79*

[from *psychological operations*; patterned after *psywar* (psychological warfare)]

pul·sar ('pəlˌsɑr), *n.* an astronomical source of powerful radio and light waves emitted in short, intense bursts or pulses at very precise intervals. Compare QUASAR.

In current theory a pulsar is the core of a star that had exploded into a supernova. It is condensed, magnetic, and spins rapidly. It is surrounded by a plasma of charged particles which gives off the optical and radio waves and also serves as a drag to slow rotation. *Science News Yearbook 1970, p 218*

Pulsars have been found in all parts of the sky, but lie primarily in the Milky Way near the symmetry plane of the galaxy. *J. P. Ostriker, "Pulsar," McGraw-Hill Yearbook of Science and Technology 1971, p 362*

Instead he told of his visit to Kitt Peak Observatory, Arizona, a few days before, where astronomers were in the act of discovering a pulsing, visible star in the Crab Nebula, the site of the fastest pulsing (and most rapidly decelerating) of the pulsars.... This is the first identification of an optical star with a pulsar. *Fred Wheeler, "We Don't Really Know: Quarks Refuted by Pulsars?" New Scientist, Feb. 13, 1969, p 332*

[from *pulse* + quasar]

pump, *v.t.* to provide (a laser) with the energy to raise atoms in its active medium (ruby, helium, etc.) to an excited state.

Many lasers, as I have described, are excited (or "pumped," as we say in the laboratory) by light. Others may be made to lase by radio waves, or by an electric current, or by chemical reactions. *Thomas Meloy, National Geographic Magazine, Dec. 1966, p 864*

punji stick or **punji stake,** a sharp bamboo spike, often dipped in excrement, which is set in camouflaged holes in the ground to pierce the legs of enemy soldiers.

A Green Beret points out to the journalist some American-made punji sticks (the movie is obsessed with punji sticks). *Renata Adler, The New York Times, June 20, 1968, p 49*

The instructors' wives wove grass rugs and made clay cooking pots, while children helped to fashion the village's huts and whittled vicious punji stakes of bamboo. *Time, Feb. 4, 1966, p 18*

[*punji* from Vietnamese]

purple heart, *British.* a popular name for a tablet of the drug DRINAMYL.

Control over the sale of amphetamines was first tightened up in the UK with the passing of the Drugs (Prevention of Misuse) Act 1964. This act was a result of public concern over the growing use of 'pep pills' such as purple hearts, which are a mixture of amphetamine and barbiturate. *Science Journal, Feb. 1970, p 7*

[so called from the original color and shape of the tablet, allusion to the American military award]

purserette, *n.* a female purser on a ship or aircraft.

The amount of labour involved in manufacturing clothes could be cut by a new technique that British Rail is using to make uniforms for hovercraft purserettes — the low-flying equivalent of the air hostess.... Moulded uniforms have so far been made in small batches — about a dozen purserettes are trying them out to see how they wear.... *New Scientist, May 28, 1970, p 431*

put, *v.t.* **put down,** *Slang.* **1** to reduce in size or importance; belittle; deflate.

. . . one 19-year-old had started putting Harvey down in front of the others. "You know, Harvey," the kid had said, "sometimes I think you're a real phony." *Alexander Ross and Michael Valpy, Maclean's, Aug. 1967, p 26*

The zingers that do get through [the NBC censor's scissors] may bruise tender sensibilities, but as [comedian Dan] Rowan says: "We put everybody on but we never put anybody down." *Time, March 8, 1968, p 47*

2 to criticize.

The history of the motion-picture industry might be summed up as the development from the serials with the blade in the sawmill moving closer and closer to the heroine's neck, to modern movies with the laser beam zeroing in on James Bond's crotch. At this level, the history of movies is a triumph of technology. I'm not putting down this kind of movie: I don't know anybody who doesn't enjoy it more or less at some time or other. *Pauline Kael, "Marlon Brando: An American Hero," The Atlantic, March 1966, p 72*

"This beauty [Vivien Leigh] and I had one hell of a scrap the other night, and it was all on account of you." "How so?" asks Maugham. "Well," I explain, "we were talking about *Then and Now* and I referred to the play as mandra-GOla, which is the way we say it in America. Maugham's eyebrows are arched. Vivien wants to talk, but I will not let her. "I know it's said differently in England and differently in Italy. But *we* say mandraGOla. So, of course, my friend here put me down pretty sharply—" Vivien interrupted. "Not sharply enough," she said. *Garson Kanin, "From 'Remembering Mr. Maugham'," Saturday Review, Oct. 1, 1966, p 59*

put-down, *n. Slang.* an act, statement, etc., meant to put down someone or something.

This growing power has made Fairchild the most feared and disliked man in the fashion-publishing field. Despite his wide blue eyes and guileless countenance, he and his No. 1 hatchet man, *WWD* [Woman's Wear Daily] Publisher James Brady, have chalked up—and delighted in—a long string of personality assassinations, cutting insults and crushing putdowns. *Time, Sept. 14, 1970, p 77*

. . . the rebellion has broken out. Predictably, the response to it is a gradual escalation involving a more naked use of the tactics that were supposed to prevent, but which also helped to provoke, the crisis in the first place: patronizations, put-downs, and tongue-lashings. . . . *Richard Poirier, The Atlantic, Oct. 1968, p 55*

put-on, *n. Slang.* an act, statement, etc., meant to fool someone naive or credulous; a prank, hoax, or spoof.

First, Genet has a very rare capacity for psychological self-revelation. He can make the reader believe in his integrity even though it is clear that much of what he says is a put-on. *Tom F. Driver, "An Exaltation of Evil," Review of "Miracle of the Rose" by Jean Genet, Saturday Review, March 11, 1967, p 36*

My Chinese buddy, Roscoe Yi just came back from Haight-Ashbury. . . . Roscoe is pure Baroque; *everybody* else is "Whitey" to him. He claims he's designing a sports car, using the "Quotations of Chairman Mao" as a blueprint, but you never know—he's pretty good with the put-on. *F. P. Tullius, "Frog Week at the 7-11—Near West Hollywood," The New Yorker, Sept. 9, 1967, p 40*

The Beatles ran out of put-ons, and John Lennon took to bed. In accordance with Aubrey's Law, sitchcom has swamped or drowned television's handful of comic talents. *Some Like it Hot* shuddered into M*A*S*H, and the situation of cinematic comedy became a question of semantics. *Melvin Maddocks, Time, July 20, 1970, p 30*

[from the verb phrase *put (someone) on*]

put-on artist, an expert in the put-on.

Also, though he [Henry Ford II] is usually forthright, he occasionally stirs suspicions that he is a bit of a put-on artist. Asked about his favorites in his art collection, he replies: "I've got a Toulouse-Lautrec; then I've got a Degas and a Manet and a Gauguin"—all the names uttered in the tones of a bored auto dealer listing the cars he cannot sell. *Time, July 20, 1970, p 66*

We remember the kidder as a good-natured, teasing sort—that moment when he rendered his victim absurd was quickly dissipated in the general laughter that followed. . . . Occasionally, a victim will try to explain away his confusion by assuming that the put-on artist is "just being ironical"—that he really means precisely the reverse of everything he says. *Jacob Brackman, "Onward and Upward with the Arts: The Put-On," The New Yorker, June 24, 1967, p 35*

PVS, abbreviation of *Post-Vietnam Syndrome.*

. . . a significant number of Vietnam veterans are encountering serious readjustment problems on return to civilian life that, for some at least, is as severe a test of emotional stability as any stress they encountered in the service.

The ailment has been called the post-Vietnam syndrome, or PVS, but the term is not sufficiently broad to encompass the wide range of emotional problems that some of the veterans are experiencing. *Jon Nordheimer, "Postwar Shock Besets Veterans of Vietnam," The New York Times, Aug. 28, 1972, p 1*

Q

Q, a symbol for the unit of heat energy equal to one quadrillion British Thermal Units (10^{18} BTU).

The U.S. Geological Survey estimates that the country contains 5,162 Q of oil, 3,317 Q of natural gas and 32,000 Q of coal. *Time, April 19, 1971, p 58*

qa·nat (kɑ:'nɑ:t), *n.* an underground tunnel dug in the hills to convey water to the plains below.

The desert counterpart of the Dutch dikes is the marvelous *qanat*, the artificial spring made by digging a gently sloping tunnel from the ground-water level deep below the broken gravelly stuff at the edge of the mountains to the valley far below. *Philip Morrison, "Books," Review of "Polderlands" by Paul Wagret and "Arid Lands: A Geographical Appraisal," edited by E. S. Hills, Scientific American, July 1969, p 135*

The tunnel-well, or qanat, is an ancient method of irrigation which is still widely used in Iran, Cyprus, and Morocco. Professor Paul English, of Texas University, has traced the spread of qanats throughout the Old World from the borders of Persia, where they were probably first developed about 2,500 years ago. *The Times (London), Aug. 2, 1968, p 6*

[from Arabic *qanāt* pipe, duct]

QC, abbreviation of QUICKCHANGE.

QC jets can expand air cargo service to small cities. . . . citing new technology such as the QC jets, CAB [Civil Aeronautics Board] Chairman Charles S. Murphy predicted that air cargo might surpass passenger volume by 1980. *Kenneth E. Schaefle, "Transportation: Airlines," The 1967 World Book Year Book, p 527*

Another useful cargo carrier is the so-called QC or quickchange aircraft or convertible passenger-freighter. *J. M. Ramsden, The Times (London), Dec. 3, 1970, p IV*

Qi·a·na (ki:'ɑ: nə), *n.* the trade name of a washable and wrinkle-resistant synthetic fabric chemically related to nylon.

Qiana is said to have color, clarity, and luster equal to or better than most luxurious silks. *Frederick C. Price, "Chemical Technology," The World Book Science Annual 1969, p 274*

In the lingerie sector of Lord & Taylor, those of us known to the profession as mature women (and not in the psychiatrists' sense) will come upon the commendable and reasonably sedate bathing suits produced by Edith Lances of sea-blue Qiana, which is a man-made silk —brassière top, shorts, and long overskirt. *"This and That," The New Yorker, July 10, 1971, p 69*

qiv·i·ut ('kiv i:,u:t), *n.* the underwool of the arctic musk ox.

Many woolen manufacturers are enthusiastic about the principal product of the musk ox, its underwool, which the Eskimos call "qiviut." The fiber is similar to that of cashmere but about twice as long and half as thick. It can be prepared with the same machines as those used for cashmere. *Science News Letter, June 12, 1965, p 370*

She [Marianne Moore] quotes from "The Arctic Ox," perhaps her favourite poem:

"To wear the arctic fox
you have to kill it. Wear
qiviut—the underwool of the
arctic ox—
pulled off like a sweater;
your coat is warm, your
conscience better."

Willa Petschek, The Manchester Guardian Weekly, March 7, 1968, p 13

[from the Eskimo name]

Q scale. See the quotation for the meaning.

On earth, such rubble would be a very poor conductor of tremors; on the geologist's "Q" scale, a measure of how long vibrations in the earth take to die down, it would rate about 10. By contrast, the moon rubble scored at least 2,000. The difference is that the earth rubble would be filled with gases and liquids that would let the vibrations travel at high speeds, enabling them to penetrate far down into the planet. *"Apollo 12: Return to the Moon," Science News Yearbook 1970, p 45*

[Q, abbreviation of German *Querwellen* transverse waves]

QSE, *British.* abbreviation of *qualified scientist and engineer.*

An average Q.S.E. in the Atomic Energy Authority is assumed to earn about £2,300, £3,350, £3,700 or £4,000 at ages 30, 40, 50, or 55 respectively. *Lord Rothschild, The Times (London), July 21, 1970, p 21*

But the number of qualified scientists and engineers (QSEs) in the world is between five and eight million. *G. D. W. Smith, "Information by the £," New Scientist and Science Journal, Aug. 5, 1971, p 342*

QSO, abbreviation of QUASI-STELLAR OBJECT.

Some well-reproduced spectra of QSOs show clearly the difficulties involved in observing these objects. *R. C. Smith, New Scientist, April 18, 1968, p 140*

The first quasars that were discovered were identified by their combination of radio and optical properties. After these first discoveries, astronomers found numerous other starlike objects that had the same unusual optical properties as quasars—that is, very large red shifts, and unusual emission spectra—but were not strong radio sources. These objects received the separate name of "Quasi-Stellar Objects, or QSO's." *Robert Jastrow and Malcolm H. Thompson, Astronomy: Fundamentals and Frontiers, 1972, p 229*

QSTOL ('kyu:ˌstoul), *n.* acronym for *quiet short takeoff and landing.* Compare CTOL, STOL.

Now companies which have promoted the vertical take-off and landing (VTOL) airliners for years are studying other projects. Instead of talking about "technological breakthroughs" they stress quietness. The word even gets into the title of the latest British Aircraft Corporation project, which is known as QSTOL.... *Tony Dawe, "The Man Who Killed VTOL," The Sunday Times (London), June 13, 1971, p 11*

Q-switch, *n.* any of various devices for causing a crystal laser to produce a high-energy pulse of extremely short duration.

Q-switches are employed to obtain a very powerful pulsed output from a laser by allowing the laser to store up energy; when it reaches a maximum the blockage is quickly removed, and an intense pulse of laser radiation is emitted. *R. F. Pearson and R. Cooper, New Scientist, Oct. 20, 1966, p 93*

—*v.t.* to cause (a crystal laser) to emit a high-energy pulse by means of a Q-switch.

Saturable absorbers have recently been used very successfully to Q-switch ruby and neodymium-doped lasers . . . *.Michael Hercher, "Laser: Saturable Absorbers," McGraw-Hill Yearbook of Science and Technology 1968, p 223*

[*Q,* abbreviation of *quantum*]

Q-switched, *adj.* capable of emitting an extremely short, high-energy pulse by means of a Q-switch.

. . . they used the 104-inch telescope to transmit and detect pulses of 50-nanosecond duration produced by a "Q-switched" (short-pulse) ruby laser. *James E. Faller and E. Joseph Wampler, "The Lunar Laser Reflector," Scientific American, March 1970, p 41*

Q-switching, *n.* the use of a Q-switch to obtain extremely short, high-energy laser pulses.

Q-switching is a technique for producing giant laser pulses by preventing lasing action until a large amount of energy has been pumped into the atoms responsible. *New Scientist, Oct. 24, 1968, p 205*

quadriphonic or **quadrophonic,** *adj.* of or relating to high-fidelity sound reproduction involving signals transmitted through four different channels. Also, QUADRISONIC.

. . . the interesting quadriphonic disc system . . . puts the sums of the two left and the two right channels into the frequency range from 30 Hz to 15 kHz, and multiplexes in the band from 20 to 45 kHz the difference signals needed to decode them. *Ivan Berger, Saturday Review, Oct. 31, 1970, p 57*

This year may well mark the end of the stereophonic age and the beginning of the new, all-exciting and even more complex quadrophonic age. *New Scientist and Science Journal, April 8, 1971, p 88*

[from *quadri-* (or *quadro-*) four + *phonic* of sound]

quadrisonic, *adj.* another word for QUADRIPHONIC.

Now Davis is looking forward to Columbia's further development of quadrisonic sound, a kind of double-stereo system that was introduced last year by Vanguard. *Time, Sept. 28, 1970, p 73*

[from *quadri-* four + *sonic* of sound]

quad·ro ('kwɑːdˌrou), *n.* a square section of a planned city or urban development, functioning as a residential unit with at least one apartment house and shopping center.

Within the one city he [Arnold J. Toynbee] envisages *quadros* (single units of settlement) as in Brazilia, which will be of a small enough scale to engender community spirit. *Misha Black, "Books," Review of "Cities on the Move," by Arnold Toynbee, New Scientist, Oct. 15, 1970, p 141*

[from Portuguese, literally, a square]

quality, *n.* a newspaper or magazine usually of limited circulation because of its appeal to a sophisticated or specialized group of readers. Compare POPULAR.

The Newspaper Publishers' Association, to which all the nationals belong, seems now to be married, at least in principle, to the idea of joint action to solve some of its problems. Not all the problems, however, are the same for all papers. The "qualities," for example, need to earn a greater percentage of their income from advertising than the "populars," which rely more heavily on mass sales. *Dennis Johnson, "Britain in Focus: A New Light on the Darker Days," The Manchester Guardian Weekly, July 25, 1970, p 11*

quality of life, a phrase now frequently used to suggest the fundamental conditions of everyday living which make life satisfactory and rewarding, but which increased material production and improved technology have either failed to provide or actually helped to erode.

From all accounts the visitor was not amused nor, like President Pompidou, delighted with the fair's evidence of growing concern for "the quality of life" in France. *Daily Telegraph (London), May 15, 1972, p 9*

quan·ta·some ('kwɑːn təˌsoum), *n.* one of the granules containing chlorophyll found inside the chloroplast of plant cells.

Through the electron microscope, small leaf particles, quantasomes, resemble the stipples on the rubber surface of a table-tennis paddle. *Picture legend, "Botany," The World Book Science Annual 1969, p 273*

Studies of shadowed, isolated grana have revealed a 200-A subunit in these membranes. These 200-A subunits appear to be an aggregate of four smaller units, which might correspond to the globular structures seen in thin sections. The 200-A units have been termed quantasomes and are possibly related to a basic photosynthetic unit, that is, the smallest physiological unit capable of photosynthesis. *W. W. Thomson, "Cell Plastids: Chloroplasts," McGraw-Hill Yearbook of Science and Technology 1968, p 131*

[from *quanta* (plural of *quantum* smallest unit of energy) + *-some* body; so called from its being regarded as the smallest unit or elementary particle of the cell]

quantifier, *n.* **1** a person who is skilled in quantifying or counting.

Deutsch and his colleagues agree that "both types of scientific personalities, the quantifiers and the pattern-recognizers—the 'counters' and the 'poets'—will continue to be needed." *Time, March 29, 1971, p 32*

2 a person whose primary concern is with the quantification of data or an activity.

Near the end of his tour he had gone to Harvard, where in another and gentler time he might have been revered but now was first almost captured by the radical students and later, speaking to a group of professors, [was] asked to explain about the two McNamaras, McNamara the quantifier, who had given us the body count in Vietnam, and McNamara the warm philosopher, who had delivered a speech at Montreal that had seemed to contradict his and Johnson's actual policies. *David Halberstam, "The Programming of Robert McNamara," Harper's, Feb. 1971, p 38*

quantum chemist, a specialist in quantum chemistry.

Since the introduction of the fundamental wave equation of quantum mechanics by Erwin Schrodinger in 1926, much of the work of quantum chemists has been focused on its solution for specific chemical systems; in other words, on the problem of constructing adequate mathematical models of atomic and molecular structure in order to obtain reliable nonexperimental information about chemical processes and to unify existing information. *Arnold C. Wahl, "Chemistry by Computer," Scientific American, April 1970, p 54*

quantum chemistry, the application of the laws of quantum mechanics (the mechanics of atomic and molecular changes) to chemistry.

The difficult stage of a new theoretical development is always at the beginning—getting started—but at last, after a rather long incubation period, the new subject of "quantum chemistry" has got into its stride and is gaining rapidly in strength. *H. C. Longuet-Higgins, "Electrons in Molecules," New Scientist, March 14, 1963, p 582*

quantum electronics, the application of the laws of quantum mechanics to electronic systems and interactions.

Dr. Silin mentioned the following distinguished scientists as having taken part in the process of re-examining the institute's political work: . . . Professor Alexander Prokhorov, a pioneer of quantum electronics and a 1964 Nobel Prize winner. *David Bonavia, The Times (London), Dec. 3, 1970, p 6*

quantum jump or **quantum leap,** a sudden spectacular advance; a major breakthrough.

At this point commercial pressures led to one of those quantum jumps . . . which have been so characteristic of the history of computing. The argument was very persuasive. It had been realized that it should be possible to design complete languages, with a syntax and semantic definition, for the writing of programs. *A. d'Agapayeff, "Software Engineering," Science Journal, Oct. 1970, p 95*

. . . the ability of marine technology to take "quantum" leaps in innovation means that a laissez-faire approach to the ocean mineral resources can no longer be tolerated. *Tony Loftas, New Scientist, Dec. 3, 1970, p 372*

[figurative sense of the term in physics denoting the sudden jump of an electron, etc., from one energy level to another]

quantum physics, physics according to the quantum theory; modern or contemporary physics.

In classical physics the particle should lose all its energy on entering the barrier and remain there forever. In quantum physics a small probability packet gets temporarily trapped inside the barrier while most of the packet is reflected. *Illustration legend, "Computer Displays," Scientific American, June 1970, p 69*

The principle of complementarity is important because it contains deep insight into the questions of unity of observer and observed, and also the language of quantum physics. *Constantine Philippidis, "Books," Review of "Atomic Order: An Introduction to the Philosophy of Microphysics" by Enrico Cantore, New Scientist, June 11, 1970, p 543*

A few years ago, in our laboratory at the Max Planck Institute for Metal Research in Stuttgart, we set out to investigate the possibility of making a photograph of a quantum effect. Since quantum physics normally deals with natural phenomena on a submicroscopic scale, the effect we were interested in was obviously a special one. *Uwe Essmann and Hermann Träuble, "The Magnetic Structure of Superconductors," Scientific American, March 1971, p 75*

quap (kwap), *n.* a hypothetical nuclear particle consisting of an anti-proton and a quark.

Quarks, quaps, Stuff and Other Stuff are the essential ingredients of a new energy-producing process thought out by three astrophysicists at the Institute of Advanced Study, Princeton. They are the first group to derive estimates for the rates at which plausible quark-fusion reactions may proceed. *"Burning Quarks to Exorcise Quasars," New Scientist, Aug. 6, 1970, p 272*

[from *quark* + *anti-proton*; perhaps influenced by *quap*, the name of a valuable radioactive substance in H. G. Wells's novel *Tono-Bungay*, 1909, which Edward Ponderevo, the narrator's uncle, obtains in Africa]

quark (kwark), *n.* a hypothetical electrically charged nuclear particle proposed as the basic component of known particles such as protons and neutrons.

Dr. [Murray] Gell-Man's next major contribution came in 1961 when he theorized that subatomic particles consist of still more fundamental particles. All matter, he said, is actually made of 3 basic building blocks. He called these building blocks "quarks" (from a line in James Joyce's *Finnegans Wake*: "Three quarks for Muster Mark!"). A quark, if it exists, would have a fractional electrical charge, something previously unheard of in physics. Scientists around the world have been hunting for proof that these particles exist. In 1969, four scientists from Australia's Sydney University claimed that they detected quarks. If this discovery is substantiated, the field of atomic physics will be revolutionized. *"The 1969 Nobel Prizes for Physics and Chemistry," Encyclopedia Science Supplement (Grolier) 1970, p 297*

The quark was back. Professor Charles McCusker of the University of Sydney said he'd found their tracks and while the pooh-poohing was in progress up came a bubble chamber picture from the Argonne National Laboratory containing a track. *"Ariadne's Record of the Year," New Scientist, Dec. 31, 1970, p 706*

Quarks are supposed to come in three configurations, each with an antiquark: one with two-thirds the charge of an electron and two with one-third the charge each, one a plus and one a minus. Dr. McCusker's five tracks are described as being of the two-thirds variety. *"Particle Physics: Theories—Quark and Scattering," Science News Yearbook 1970, p 242*

It may be, however, that quarks do not exist as separate physical entities. They may be only a mathematically convenient parameter in the model, or they may be disallowed by some law of nature yet unknown. *Lawrence W. Jones, "Hadron," McGraw-Hill Yearbook of Science and Technology 1971, p 215*

quarter, *adj.* less than half; far from complete;

very imperfect *(used with a hyphen in combinations).*

Some quarter-liberals in South Africa feel that oppression against the black man in white-ruled South Africa would be less intolerable if each black man did have a black-ruled homeland nearby to which he could return if he grew too miserable under white oppression. *Norman Macrae, "Foreign Report," Harper's, March 1970, p 36*

But to take effective steps to discourage the purveying of such quarter-truths, such as the Indian Government has taken, is described in your editorial columns as "censorship", a threat to "the freedom and the integrity of documentary producers". *Trevor Ling, The Times (London), Aug. 29, 1970, p 11*

qua·sar ('kwei,zɑr), *n.* another name for QUASI-STELLAR OBJECT. Compare PULSAR.

The third group of abnormal galaxies or galaxylike objects are the quasars. These objects release enormous amounts of energy that dwarf the energy released by the Seyfert galaxies. Unlike the Seyfert galaxy, the typical quasar is also a radio galaxy. In a sense, the quasars combine the properties of radio galaxies and Seyfert galaxies, but they carry the unusual properties of these two objects to an extreme. They are the most difficult objects of all to explain in terms of the properties of stars. *Robert Jastrow and Malcolm H. Thompson, Astronomy: Fundamentals and Frontiers, 1972, p 227*

The puzzling quasars are believed to be less than 10 light-years in diameter—compared with the 100,000-light-year diameter of a typical galaxy—yet they are pouring out 100 times more light than a typical galaxy of 100 billion stars. *Robert Jastrow and Nicholas Panagakos, "The Birth of the Universe," 1969 Collier's Encyclopedia Year Book, p 74*

The term quasar, a contraction of "quasi-stellar radio source," was originally applied only to the starlike counterparts of certain strong radio sources whose optical spectra exhibit red shifts much larger than those of galaxies. Before long, however, a class of quasi-stellar objects was discovered with large red shifts that have little or no emission at radio wavelengths. "Quasar" is now commonly applied to starlike objects with large red shifts regardless of their radio emissivity. *Maarten Schmidt and Francis Bello, "The Evolution of Quasars," Scientific American, May 1971, p 55*

[from *quasi-stellar*]

qua·si particle ('kwei,zai), a unit particle or quantum of sound, light, heat, etc. (a term used especially in solid-state physics).

Soviet scientists had the honor of introducing the first quasi particles, the phonons (sound quanta in a crystal lattice), and the concepts of two others: the exciton, a specially excited state of electrons in a crystal lattice; and the polaron, a conducting electron in an ionic lattice. *Mikhail D. Millionshchikov, "Physical Sciences in the Soviet Union," 1970 Britannica Yearbook of Science and the Future, 1969, p 423*

quasi-stellar object, any of a large group of astronomical bodies that are powerful sources of energy but whose exact nature has not been de-

termined. *Abbreviation:* QSO Also called QUASAR.

The extraordinary properties of quasi-stellar objects, or quasars, were not recognized until 1963, when Maarten Schmidt discovered the red shift of 3C 273. Much excitement was generated by the discovery of objects of stellar appearance which not only were strong radio sources but had large red shifts and which might therefore be the most distant observable objects in the universe. *James Terrell, "The Properties and Origins of Quasars," Science, Jan. 19, 1968, p 291*

The discovery of quasi-stellar objects, of radio galaxies and of other peculiar galactic phenomena has upset the old view that galaxies are evolving on such a long time scale that to observers on the earth they are all but unchanging. Astronomers now speak of a "violent universe" as they seek to understand the extreme physical conditions that must be present in the quasi-stellar objects and in the nuclei of radio galaxies to explain the vast fluxes of energy they emit. *E. Margaret Burbidge and C. Roger Lynds, "The Absorption Lines of Quasi-stellar Objects," Scientific American, Dec. 1970, p 22*

questionmaster, *n. British.* a person who asks questions at a quiz show; a quizmaster.

He was in at the start of many new developments of radio, and was the first questionmaster on the first full quiz show broadcast by the B.B.C. *"Obituary: Roy Rich, Former Head of B.B.C.," The Times (London), March 25, 1970, p 14*

queue·ing theory ('kju: iŋ), the mathematical study of the formation and behavior of queues or waiting lines, especially as applied to problems of traffic congestion and storage systems.

A modern society is to a large extent a system of networks for communication, transportation and the distribution of energy and goods.... queueing theory, probability theory, statistics and computer programming, are the armamentarium of network analysis. *Howard Frank and Ivan T. Frisch, "Network Analysis," Scientific American, July 1970, p 94*

quick-and-dirty, *n. U.S. Slang.* a snack bar or lunch counter.

It was after one when he finished, and we stopped for lunch at a quick-and-dirty on East Ninety-sixth and talked shop, which he said was not unusual for him. *"The Talk of the Town," The New Yorker, Jan. 17, 1970, p 23*

The office of the Massachusetts Electric Company was temporarily converted into a mock-up of a quick-and-dirty and its sign replaced with one that read AL'S BEAN POT. *Russell Lynes, "After Hours," Harper's, Jan. 1968, p 14*

quickchange, *adj.* capable of being converted quickly from passenger to cargo service.

Another useful cargo carrier is the so-called QC or quick-change aircraft or convertible passenger-freighter. *J. M. Ramsden, The Times (London), Dec. 3, 1970, p IV*

The first "quick change" (QC) jets, passenger planes that can be converted for cargo in a matter of minutes, went into service in 1966. *Kenneth E. Schaefle, "Transportation: Airlines," The 1967 World Book Year Book, p 527*

R

rack car, *U.S.* a railroad freight car with racks for carrying automobiles.

When auto rack cars were introduced in 1961, railroads carried only about 8% of the new autos between factories and new-car markets; most of these autos traveled in boxcars. With the development of three-tiered rack cars, which carry up to 18 autos, railroads were able to promise auto companies savings of up to 18% over trucks on long hauls. *Wall Street Journal, Jan. 25, 1963, p 1*

radar astronomy, a branch of astronomy that studies planets and other heavenly bodies by analyzing the echoes or reflections of radar signals sent from the earth at specific targets.

Although radar astronomy is still a very young science, it has already produced results whose scientific importance has far exceeded the most enthusiastic predictions. *Irwin I. Shapiro, "Radar Observations of the Planets," Scientific American, July 1968, p 28*

The board report also recommended learning as much as possible about the planets from the ground up and noted that radar astronomy had done particularly well with its studies of nearer planets, especially Venus. *Science News Yearbook 1969, p 83*

radial, *n.* short for RADIAL-PLY TIRE.

Advocates of radials say that they have much more stability and wear longer than bias-belted tires. *Time, April 26, 1971, p 49*

It is also pointed out that the majority of Michelin's tyres are steel-braced radials, unlike the other companies' textile radials. *Giles Smith, The Times (London), March 11, 1970, p 23*

radial-ply tire or **radial tire,** an automobile tire with parallel casing cords running at right angles to the wheel rim. Also shortened to RADIAL. Compare BIAS-BELTED TIRE.

Radial-ply tires, long known to be safer and longer wearing, will be introduced as standard equipment on one Ford Motor Company model and will be optional on other lines for 1967.... *Joseph C. Ingraham, The New York Times, Aug. 19, 1966, p 29*

But Dunlop's investment in this field is only a drop in the ocean to that which will be required of it, or for that matter any other manufacturer, if there is a call to supply radial tyres as original equipment for a mass selling car. *Clifford Webb, The Times (London), Oct. 12, 1967, p 20*

radical chic, a vogue among fashionable people of socializing with radicals.

Evenings, he [John B. Fairchild, publisher of *Women's Wear Daily*] shuns discotheques, parties and radical chic; instead, he takes the subway and bus home to his eight-room East Side apartment, dines with Jill and their four children, and listens to Shostakovich on the stereo. *"Out on a Limb with the Midi," Time, Sept. 14, 1970, p 80*

The fashionable despair, a variation on Leonard Bernstein's radical chic, seems to me nothing more than the necessary antithesis to an earlier illusion. We were brought up on the movies of the 1940s, and most of us believed in a cardboard image of the world as false as the Wyoming afternoons painted on a studio wall. *Lewis Lapham, "What Movies Try To Sell Us," Harper's, Nov. 1971, p 115*

[coined by the American journalist Tom Wolfe in his book *Radical Chic & Mau-mauing the Flak Catchers,* 1970]

radical left, another name for the NEW LEFT.

In the half of the electorate that does not care to choose between major parties and in the somewhat larger fraction that passes up the opportunity to cast primary votes are... the Wallace voters and the radical right—often ideologically distinct, though not always—and the radical left. *Richard H. Rovere, "Letter from Washington," The New Yorker, Sept. 26, 1970, p 136*

[patterned after *radical right*]

radical right, a collective name for the extreme right-wing or conservative movement in the United States, whose ideology includes militant anti-communism and anti-liberalism.

Ten years ago the liberal Establishment crashed down on the Radical Right with accusations of anti-Semitism, racism, and general kookiness. Birchers were nuts.... More often than not, they were the beneficiaries of welfare-state programs, of subsidies and social security, but none of that made them suspect government any less. *Peter Schrag, "America's Other Radicals," Harper's, Aug. 1970, p 46*

But to enact an unsatisfactory law and then try to compensate for its shortcomings by good administration is, clearly, an absurd procedure. One solution that is more logical—to abolish the income tax—is proposed chiefly by some members of the radical right, who consider any income tax Socialistic or Communistic, and who would have the federal government simply stop spending money. *John Brooks, "Profiles: The Tax," The New Yorker, April 10, 1965, p 76*

radical rightism, the ideology of the radical right.

One of the understandable themes in radical rightism is a social paranoia, a feeling that we are being manipulated by unseen inaccessible forces. *Jonathan Miller, The Sunday Times (London), March 20, 1966, p 26*

radical rightist, a member or supporter of the radical right.

Depending on the political sympathies of the accuser, blame it on the Mafia, the I.R.A., the Zionists, the Negroes, the Liberals, the Radical Rightists, or J. Edgar Hoover. *Marya Mannes, "Defense Manual for Tourists," Harper's, Jan. 1965, p 127*

ra·di·ci·da·tion (ˌrei də sə'dei ʃən), *n.* the irradiation of food to destroy disease germs.

Radicidation, or the destruction of organisms significant to public health, such as *Salmonella* species, in foods and feedstuffs, would appear to offer early promise for commercialization. *S. A. Goldblith, "Food Engineering," McGraw-Hill Yearbook of Science and Technology 1968, p 182*

[from *radiation* + *-cide* killer (as in *insecticide*) + *-ation* (noun suffix)]

rad·ic-lib ('ræd ik'lib), *n. U.S.* an epithet applied to liberals with leftist leanings; a radical liberal.

Radic-Libs [according to Vice President Spiro Agnew] resist anticrime bills, undercut the President abroad, excuse violence while they denounce the police, support fast withdrawal from Asia, pooh-pooh pornography and keep religion out of the schools. *Time, Sept. 28, 1970, p 8*

One morning last winter, a member of the White House staff shared with a visitor an analysis of the midterm elections almost as black as the coffee he sipped. The assault on the "radic-libs" had failed to divert the voters from their money worries, and the claim that the new Senate would contain a reliable "ideological majority" seemed to be wishful thinking. *Richard J. Whalen, "The Nixon-Connally Arrangement," Harper's, Aug. 1971, p 29*

radioecological, *adj.* of or relating to radioecology.

Because of their penetrating ability, radionuclides that are partially or wholly gamma emitters have great utility in radioecological studies, both as tracers and as sources of ionizing radiation in effects studies. *R. G. Wiegert, "Radioecology," McGraw-Hill Yearbook of Science and Technology 1968, p 329*

Although radioecological aspects continue to be intensively studied, particularly for marine organisms, they are not at present a limiting factor for radioactive waste management. *Pearce Wright, "Review of Metal Waste Risks," The Times (London), March 16, 1972, p 3*

radioecologist, *n.* a specialist in radioecology.

Radioecologists collect insects and leaf samples in a forest inoculated with radioactive cesium 137.... *Picture legend, "Oak Ridge National Laboratory," The World Book Science Annual 1969, p 196*

radioecology, *n.* the study of radioactivity in the environment and its effect on plants and animals, especially in a particular locality.

...radioecology concerns the interaction of radiation and radioisotopes with organisms at the population or community level of organization. *R. G. Wiegert, "Radioecology," McGraw-Hill Yearbook of Science and Technology 1968, p 328*

radio galaxy, a galaxy that emits or is a source of extensive radiation.

The first of the abnormal objects to be discovered were the *radio galaxies*. These are objects which emit intense radio signals, but look like galaxies, although sometimes their appearance is strange in comparison to that of a normal galaxy. The radio emission from the most powerful radio galaxies is equal to, and in some cases greater than, the entire output of energy from our Galaxy at all wavelengths. *Robert Jastrow and Malcolm H. Thompson, Astronomy: Fundamentals and Frontiers, 1972, p 220*

A careful search has been made for X-ray emission from the brightest radio galaxy, Cyg A, whose radio power is 10^{34} kw — a hundred billion times the heat and light radiated by the sun. *Herbert Friedman, "X-Ray Astronomy: New Window to Space," 1969 Britannica Yearbook of Science and the Future, 1968, p 207*

radioimmunoassay, *n.* a method of assaying the amount or other characteristics of a substance by labeling it with a radioactive chemical and combining it with an antibody to induce an immunological reaction. Compare IMMUNOASSAY.

The availability of pure hormone has made possible the development of a very sensitive radioimmunoassay for the hormone. *D. Harold Copp, "Calcitonin: Chemistry," McGraw-Hill Yearbook of Science and Technology 1969, p 121*

radioimmunological, *adj.* involving the use of radioimmunoassay.

Estimation of the concentration of peptide hormones in plasma can be made by radioimmunological techniques. *John Watt McLaren, "Medicine: Radiology," Britannica Book of the Year 1968, p 528*

radioisotopic, *adj.* of or relating to radioactive isotopes, as used in power-generating nuclear reactors, as tracers in medicine, etc.

In the case of quintuple payloads *Cosmos 80-84* and *Cosmos 86-90* it was stated that one satellite of each group had a radioisotopic nuclear generator. *Kenneth W. Gatland, New Scientist, Dec. 30, 1965, p 918*

radioisotopically, *adv.* with or by means of a radioactive isotope.

Dr. Cohen notes that more than a year ago one group of workers attempted to trace a radioisotopically labeled extract through the recipient's body and found that the material had a great deal of difficulty reaching the brain. *Science News, April 20, 1968, p 376*

radiolabeled, *adj.* labeled with a radioactive isotope or other radioactive substance.

Dr. Wall... will use radiolabeled THC [tetrahydrocannabinol, the active constituent of the cannabis plant] in studies of metabolism and biological distribution. *Science News, Jan. 24, 1970, p 104*

radiopharmaceutical, *n.* a radioactive drug used in medical diagnosis, therapy, and research.

In some newer systems, a physician looked at the picture of the distribution of the radiopharmaceutical within the patient's body and then, with the aid of general-purpose computers, obtained quantitative answers to questions suggested to him by the image. *Henry Nicholas Wagner, Jr., "Medicine," 1971 Britannica Yearbook of Science and the Future, 1970, p 231*

In this case, doctors used one of Union Carbide's radiopharmaceuticals, which readily concentrates in brain tumors. *Scientific American, July 1967, p 47*

radioprotection, *n.* protection against the effects of radiation.

The hypothesis predicts that this molecule will afford radioprotection only in versions in which the number of CH_2 groups is less than two.... *Jack Schubert, Scientific American, May 1966, p 48*

radioprotective, *adj.* providing radioprotection.

K. N. Prasad and M. H. Van Woert reported (*Science*, Vol. 155, pp. 470-472) that dopamine, an intermediate hormone formed by the adrenal glands in the synthesis of norepinephrine, is a good radioprotective agent. *J. Richard Thomson, "Biology: New Radioprotective Drug," 1968 Collier's Encyclopedia Year Book, p 151*

radioprotector, *n.* a radioprotective drug or other agent.

A number of radioprotectors effective only in high dosage could be similarly affected, Dr. Barnes said, adding that further investigation of radioprotectors should be made. *Science News Letter, March 6, 1965, p 149*

radiosterilization, *n.* sterilization by means of radioactive rays.

The agency's programme in this field is largely a result of Hungarian initiative and Dr. B. Toth, the Hungarian Deputy Minister of Health, when opening the conference, went so far as to describe radiosterilization as one of the most useful ways of using atomic energy for peaceful purposes. *New Scientist, June 22, 1967, p 694*

radiosterilize, *v.t.* to sterilize by subjecting to radioactive rays.

In Europe and the U.S. several new plants for radiosterilizing medical supplies were built or ordered. *John H. Stumpf, "Nuclear Energy," Britannica Book of the Year 1967, p 588*

radiotoxic, *adj.* of or relating to the toxicity of radioactive substances.

The author starts with the basic physics of radiation and rightly emphasizes the importance of using frequency (or wave-number) rather than wave-length as an independent variable. He then moves on to techniques, to radiotoxic effects, shuns photobotany (chlorophyll doesn't appear even in the index), and then speeds to photo-reception and its underlying mechanisms. *Robert Weale, "Books," Review of "An Introduction to Photobiology: The Influence of Light on Life" by Yves Le Grand, New Scientist, July 2, 1970, p 39*

radiotoxin, *n.* a radioactive poison.

Kuzin and Kryukova believe that the radiotoxins in the [irradiated] extracts penetrate the cell nucleus and combine with certain proteins such as histones and desoxyribonucleoproteins thus affecting the mechanism controlling the synthesis of nucleic acid. *Science Journal, Sept. 1968, p 9*

radiotoxologic, *adj.* of or relating to the study of radiotoxins.

Below, scientist working in the new radiotoxologic institute in Prague, Czech. Laboratory has developed safeguards for workers experimenting with radioactive substances on laboratory animals. *Picture legend, "Radiology," Britannica Book of the Year 1968, p 528*

raf·fi·né (ra fi:'nei), *French. —adj.* (feminine form **raffinée**). refined; cultivated; highbrow.

The waiter, the actor, the communist, the painter all have their says but it is through the analyst and the raffiné aristocrat (who is there by mistake) that we learn of hate-objects, projections of guilt, scapegoats, unconscious death-wishes, etc. *Jeremy Kingston, Punch, Feb. 2, 1966, p 173*

She is slightly less *raffinée* and thoroughbred than Park, but she is a heavenly dancer. . . . *Richard Buckle, The Sunday Times (London), Nov. 5, 1967, p 51*

—*n.* a fashionable dandy or rake.

He has a tendency, as "On the Stairs," to favor his vigorous vulgarians at the expense of his effete *raffinés.*

Edmund Wilson, "Books: Two Neglected American Novelists," Review of the books of Henry B. Fuller, The New Yorker, May 23, 1970, p 126

ra·ga-rock (ˌrɑː gə'rɑk), *n.* a form of rock 'n' roll using an Indian melodic form, such as the raga, and usually including a sitar or three-stringed Indian guitar among the instruments.

And Gabor Szabo, the Hungarian guitarist, has similarly attracted young audiences with his own mixture of Indian music and jazz dubbed "raga rock." *Leonard G. Feather, "The Pop Music Scene," The 1968 World Book Year Book, p 159*

Such attention as he [George Harrison] got came in oddball ways. In 1965 he created a vogue for raga-rock, by introducing the sitar in *Norwegian Wood.* It was he who interested the rest of the Beatles in transcendental meditation. *William Bender, Time, Nov. 30, 1970, p 57*

ra·gaz·za (rɑː'gɑːt tsɑː), *n.; pl.* **ra·gaz·ze** (rɑː'gɑːt tsei). *Italian.* a girl or young woman, especially of the working or middle class.

As an example, there was a sweet, plump *ragazza* called Tina Spagnolo who lived on my street, who always wore starched white dresses to set off her olive skin. . . . *Jack Richardson, Harper's, Aug. 1970, p 82*

rag trade, *Slang.* the garment industry.

Efforts are being made to get away from the "rag trade" image and draw more young people into the industry. *Ronald Kershaw, The Times (London), Feb. 19, 1970, p 26*

The rag trade's mini maxi race is hotting up. *Punch, Dec. 27, 1967, p 986*

rag trader, *Slang.* a clothes merchant; a retailer of clothing.

What his and Davidson's King's Road Developments propose instead is an "environmentally controlled" shopping mall, predominantly of high class rag traders with restaurants and a pub behind the preserved Pheasantry façade, courtyard and entrance arch. *The Times (London), Aug. 21, 1970, p 21*

rai·son·neur (re zɔ:'nœr), *n.* a character in a play, novel, etc., who rationalizes, explains, or comments upon the actions of the other characters.

Ferdyshenko (David Ryall) is brought on [in a stage production of Dostoevsky's *The Idiot*] as a guide and raisonneur, to nudge, chuckle and underline such points as have been elaborated before our eyes. "How the sweet pair of them bicker, and savour their sorrow, eh?" he smirks, or words to that effect. *Philip Hope-Wallace, "The Arts: National Disaster: National Theatre," The Manchester Guardian Weekly, July 25, 1970, p 21*

[from French, reasoner, rationalizer]

r & b or **R & B,** abbreviation of RHYTHM AND BLUES.

To keep track of and evaluate the enormous number of r.-&-b. singles on the market is a full-time job in itself. Yet reviewing black albums too often means being depressingly and misleadingly negative. *Ellen Willis, "Musical Events," The New Yorker, Nov. 23, 1968, p 135*

R & D or **R and D,** abbreviation of *Research and Development.*

"It would have been most unfortunate . . . if, for example, in 1946 we had adopted a policy that all federally supported R & D should be carried out in Federal laboratories." *Presidential Science Adviser Lee A. DuBridge, quoted in Science News, July 25, 1970, p 57*

random access, a type of access to a specific memory location of a computer in which the location may be chosen at random. *Often used attributively.*

Perhaps the most important attribute of random access to a memory is the ease with which it is possible to choose one or another command according to the process being executed, thus allowing branching into one of two or more possible programming sequences. *Jan A. Rajchman, "Integrated Computer Memories," Scientific American, July 1967, p 18*

Finally, advanced facilities for using a random-access store (magnetic disc) greatly to enlarge the effective memory size of the machine. *Donald Michie, New Scientist, Jan. 4, 1968, p 32*

R and R or **R & R,** abbreviation of *Rest and Recuperation*, a five-day vacation leave given to American servicemen (exclusive of the annual 30-day leave) during each one-year tour of duty.

One sergeant got a [punji] stake ... and when he went on a five-day R & R with his wife in Honolulu he ripped out every damn stitch. *Ward Just, "Soldiers," The Atlantic, Oct. 1970, p 81*

When I was next going to visit the Seventh Fleet, I therefore asked if another destroyer or other vessel was scheduled for an R and R visit to Hong Kong. *Joseph Alsop, Washington, D.C., in a Letter to the Editor, Harper's, Aug. 1968, p 4*

r. & r. or **r.-'n'-r.,** abbreviation of *rock 'n' roll.*

... Illustration, a Canadian consortium (eleven strong) devoted to r. & r., has just moved in. *"Goings On About Town," The New Yorker, Aug. 15, 1970, p 6*

... Tommy [Steele] turns his back on success, renounces the raucous world of r.-'n'-r., and transmutes himself into a legitimate performer, a member of the Old Vic, and, at twenty-eight, a star on Broadway. *"The Talk of the Town," The New Yorker, June 12, 1965, p 32*

rap, *U.S. Slang.* —*v.i.* **1** to have a talk; converse, especially openly and sincerely.

I went with Officers Juan Morales and Pete DiBono to the juvenile guidance center where they rap once every week with the kids in jail. *Bill Moyers, "California," Harper's, Dec. 1970, p 93*

Am I going to stay at home and get high and have a good time tonight or am I going to go out to try and rap (talk seriously) with the people, to try to organize? *Angela Davis, The Times (London), Jan. 7, 1971, p 12*

2 to get along; sympathize; maintain rapport.

[James] Buckley the candidate softly rakes "the voices of doubt and despair," claims to rap with the Silent Majority, curries the hardhat vote.... *Time, Oct. 26, 1970, p 22*

—*n.* a talk; conversation.

"Look. Around Jane Fonda you may call it a rap, but here it's still called a powwow." *Cartoon legend, The New Yorker, Aug. 8, 1970, p 36*

Delighted and amazed that these nice, all-American kids had produced and approved so "right on" a document with such overwhelming enthusiasm, I wandered out of the plenary and located the swimming pool. They rented me a suit for fifteen cents, and soon I got into a rap with a tenth grader in a bikini. She asked me, "Do you like Spañada?" *Don Mitchell, "Letter from a Cold Place," Harper's, Aug. 1971, p 26*

[perhaps from *rapport*]

rap group, *U.S. Slang.* a group that meets to discuss and work out problems together. See also RAP SESSION.

... the New York chapter of the Vietnam Veterans Against the War instituted weekly "rap groups" where men meet and talk about their experiences and feelings. *Henry L. Rosett, N.Y., "The Post-Vietnam Syndrome," in a Letter to the Editor, The New York Times, June 12, 1971, p 28*

For all the visibility of ... WITCHES [WITCH, for Women's International Terrorist Conspiracy from Hell], the heart of the [Women's Lib] movement is made up of hundreds of "rap groups," usually formed on an *ad hoc* basis. *Time, Aug. 31, 1970, p 18*

rapid eye movement, the frequent and rapid movements of the eyes which occur during the dreaming period or state known as paradoxical sleep. *Abbreviation:* REM

The drug also produces insomnia in some animals and changes the part of sleep—rapid-eye-movement (REM) sleep—that workers in this field think is associated with dreaming in both humans and animals. *Louise Campbell, Science News, Oct. 3, 1970, p 287*

rapper, *n.* *U.S. Slang.* a person who raps; talker.

French Conductor Pierre Boulez, who takes over as music director of the New York Philharmonic next season, recently journeyed to the U.S. and announced various plans for revivifying the programs of the Philharmonic .... youthful Villagers will be invited for any time between 7 and midnight to "encounter" not only the music but some strenuously avant-garde composers themselves. Boulez clearly hopes there will be as many rappers as listeners. *"Music: Unromantic Romantic," Time, Feb. 22, 1971, p 38*

rap session, *U.S. Slang.* a discussion by a group of people, usually about a specific problem.

In every major city, women, most of them young, gather for "consciousness-raising" rap sessions, the awareness rituals of The Sisterhood. *Time, Aug. 24, 1970, p 12*

... a church rap session at which a few hundred women came to talk about their abortions. ... *Jane Kramer, The New Yorker, Nov. 28, 1970, p 130*

It was not exactly an intimate rap session, as nearly 600 seamen, submariners and officers jammed a base theater at Pearl Harbor last week. But the pert WAVE spoke up boldly on behalf of two of her service friends with an unusual problem: "She works a day shift while her husband is on the night shift. Can't something be done?" *Time, Dec. 21, 1970, p 16*

rap sheet, *U.S. Slang.* a police record.

Except for so-called crimes of passion, or an occasional armed robbery, or a marijuana bust, the "Rap Sheet" of most first-termers will show from one to three pages of brushes with the law, fines, county-jail time, and probation before these men got into a California prison, or for that matter, most American prisons. *Robert M. Mailes, Sonora, Calif., in a Letter to the Editor, The Atlantic, May 1971, p 34*

rapture of the deep or **rapture of the depths,** a dazed or lightheaded feeling experienced by deep-sea divers due to nitrogen narcosis.

... deep-diving marine mammals do not suffer the nitrogen-induced "bends" and "rapture of the deep" that endanger human divers. *Scientific American, March 1970, p 64*

The nitrogen in compressed air, on the other hand,

induces a form of narcosis similar to that produced by alcoholic intoxication or the early stages of oxygen lack. The French underwater explorer Jacques Cousteau has lyrically described the condition as 'rapture of the depths'. *Peter Bennett, Science Journal, Jan. 1968, p 53*

A prolonged stay, even at 50 feet, requires the diver to decompress before returning to the surface to avoid the bends; before the diver descends 150 feet, he must beware of nitrogen narcosis, or "rapture of the deep," where every 30 feet of added depth are equivalent, in effect, to another cocktail. *John E. Bardach and Michael D. Bradley, "Oceans," 1971 Collier's Encyclopedia Year Book, p 20*

Ras Ta·far·i·an or **Ras·ta·far·i·an** (ˌræs təˈfær iːən), *n.* a member of a sect of Jamaicans devoted to the ruler of Ethiopia.

The government's failure to cope with economic problems has led to bizarre phenomena, such as the Rastafarians, a cult which deifies Haile Selassie, the Ethiopian ruler. *Jerome Fischman, "Jamaica," 1967 Collier's Encyclopedia Year Book, p 287*

— *adj.* of or designating this sect.

In Jamaica, for example, the Ras Tafarian sect believes . . . that Ethiopia's Haile Selassie is God and Ethiopia the Promised Land. . . . *Time, March 23, 1970, p 33*

[from *Ras Tafari*, the title and surname of Emperor Haile Selassie]

raster display, a type of graphic display of a computer's output. See the quotation for details.

Two broad classes of computer-display systems are now in common use: calligraphic displays and raster displays. Calligraphic displays "paint" the parts of a picture on the cathode ray tube in any sequence given by the computer. The electron beam in a calligraphic display is moved from place to place in a pattern that traces out the individual lines and characters that make up the picture. Raster displays make pictures in the same way that television sets do: the image is painted in a fixed sequence, usually from left to right and from top to bottom. *Ivan E. Sutherland, Scientific American, June 1970, p 57*

ratfink, *n. Slang.* a mean, worthless individual; an obnoxious person.

Organized education, as seen by Edgar Z. Friedenberg, becomes more than ever a mechanism for disciplining free spirits to the necessities of the industrial order; "in fitting American youth for its destiny in the free world of tomorrow, our schools may be virtually compelling them to become a bunch of ratfinks." *Arthur M. Schlesinger, Jr., "America in Transition," Review of "The State of the Nation," edited by David Boroff, Saturday Review, April 23, 1966, p 36*

. . . I should refrain from saying any more except that he seems to be one of the few writers who really enjoy words and use them properly, and that anyone who doesn't buy a copy of this book is a rat fink. *Patrick Skene Catling, Review of "The Dog It Was That Died" by Alan Coren, Punch, Nov. 24, 1965, p 777*

[from *rat* + *fink*, *n.*, slang for obnoxious person; informer; (originally) strikebreaker, of unknown origin]

rat·o·mor·phic (ˌræt əˈmɔr fik), *adj.* modeled on the behavior of experimental rats.

You say I overestimate the dangers of the Robotomorphic or Ratomorphic view, on everyday life, but with Pavlov's dogs, Lorenz's grey-legged geese, Morris's naked ape, each time an analogy of behavior was taken as a homology. *Arthur Koestler, The Times (London), Dec. 17, 1970, p 15*

He identified the stimulus-response model in psychology with the "robot model" of man, for which Arthur Koestler has coined the epithet the "ratomorphic view of man." *Philip C. Ritterbush, "Book Reviews: Interpreting the Human Species," Review of "Robots, Men and Minds" by Ludwig von Bertalanffy, Science, April 5, 1968, p 58*

ratracer, *n. U.S.* **1** an aggressive, ruthless competitor.

. . . the students of the twenties flouted rather than protested, saw their fathers as Babbitts and stick-in-the-muds, not as capitalists and ratracers, and shook their heads over the situation, not their fists. *Louis Kronenberger, "Life and Letters," Review of "The Campus Scene" by Calvin B. T. Lee, The Atlantic, Oct. 1970, p 135*

. . . in the magazine literature of the youth rebellion the father is the "rat-racer," the symbol of everything that really significant kids hate about their society. *Russell Baker, The New York Times, June 18, 1967, Sec. 4, p 14*

2 a person caught up in the confusion, rush, etc., of daily commuting or travel.

Among the reasons advanced for this two-wheeled renaissance are disillusion with the internal combustion engine, the belief among rat-racers that the physical exercise delays thrombosis, and the repeatedly proven fact that in traffic-choked cities the slender bike is the fastest means of getting from A to B. *Patrick Ryan, "And the Last Word . . . On Bicycles," New Scientist and Science Journal, July 1, 1971, p 5*

[from *rat race* aggressive activity or competition + *-er*]

rave, *n.* a bright display.

I was really interested in this remand home job. I thought it was about time I returned to teaching and this seemed to be the job. Turn the classroom into an art studio, a rave of colour, a haven for these kids. . . . *Peter Terson, "Caught in the Nets," The Manchester Guardian Weekly, Dec. 5, 1970, p 15*

rave-up, *n. British Slang.* a wild party.

She is dressed by one of the most talented (and almost certainly best looking) young designers, John Bates, whose clothes with the Jean Varon label, are stocked all over the country and who dresses debutantes for their coming out parties and dolly girls for their all-night rave-ups. *Prudence Glynn, The Times (London), Feb. 20, 1968, p 7*

Off the field the atmosphere was that of a transatlantic rave-up. *U. A. Titley, The Times (London), Feb. 23, 1970, p 6*

[from the slang verb phrase *rave up* to express in a wild, frantic manner]

Raynaud's Phenomenon, a condition in which the hand or fingers turn white or blue, due to an obstruction of blood supply.

Known as "Dead Hand" or "White Fingers" — and most recently as Vibration Syndrome — Raynaud's Phenomenon produces the same numbness and pain as a normal hand which is exposed to extreme cold for long periods but it occurs after only brief exposure to mild cold and takes much longer to overcome. *Tony Geraghty, The Sunday Times (London), March 23, 1969, p 5*

With Raynaud's phenomenon, the small arteries in the hand are constricted, disrupting the circulation. This causes the fingers to turn white, or blue if oxygen is lacking. If no primary disorder such as hypertension can explain the symptoms, then the condition is called Raynaud's disease. The condition can also affect the toes and tip of the nose. *Science News, Dec. 27, 1969, p 595*

[named after the French physician Maurice *Raynaud*, 1834-1881]

razor haircut, a haircut given with a razor instead of scissors.

Now, ours is an age where life tries to imitate art, and indeed there are a great many young guys hustling about with earnest expressions and $35 razor haircuts, and they are offering not much more than themselves as the solution to great problems. *John Corry, "Television: Watching It," Harper's, Dec. 1970, p 42*

razor's edge, a dangerously precarious position fraught with anxiety or tension.

Hussein knew that his soldiers, roughly half of them Bedouins with little use for the fedayeen, were bitterly resentful. "They are on the razor's edge," he told the French daily *Le Figaro*. *"Jordan: The King Takes on the Guerrillas," Time, Sept. 28, 1970, p 17*

[from *The Razor's Edge*, a novel, 1943, by Somerset Maugham, the title of which was probably a translation of French *le fil du rasoir*, used figuratively in the sense of a precarious situation. Maugham was born in Paris and had strong French connections.]

RBE, abbreviation of *relative biological effect* (or *efficiency*).

Mammalian cells and higher plant cells are more susceptible to damage from densely ionizing radiations, such as α-particles or fast neutrons, than from hard X-rays. In more quantitative terms, the relative biological efficiency (RBE) of these radiations compared with hard X-rays is greater than one. *Nature, March 30, 1968, p 1208*

RDA, abbreviation of *recommended dietary allowance*.

RDAs have been published by the National Research Council's Food and Nutrition Board for only a handful of trace elements. *Joan Lynn Arehart, "Trace Elements: No Longer Good vs. Bad," Science News, Aug. 14, 1971, p 113*

...between 2 and 12% of the subjects studied had intakes lower than one-half the daily recommended dietary allowance (RDA) set by the National Research Council for the various vitamins and minerals. *Margaret Markham, "Foods and Nutrition," 1971 Britannica Yearbook of Science and the Future, 1970, p 194*

read, *v.t.* **1** to decode (a genetic message).

The diagram shows how an "anticodon" (presumably I-G-C) in alanine transfer RNA may form a temporary bond with the codon for alanine (G-C-C) in the messenger RNA. While so bonded the transfer RNA also holds the polypeptide chain. Each transfer RNA is succeeded by another one, carrying its own amino acid, until the complete message in the messenger RNA has been "read." *Scientific American, Feb. 1966, p 30*

It appears that the *his*D and *his*C genes were fused as a consequence of two closely spaced mutations, one on each side of the punctuation mark separating the two genes. The first mutation was a deletion that removed a "letter" from the genetic message; the second mutation inserted an extraneous letter. Such mutations are called "frame-shift" mutations since they cause succeeding bases to be "read" in incorrect groups of three. *"Science and the Citizen," Scientific American, Jan. 1971, p 46*

2 to put (coded data) into or out of the storage of a computer.

Like some other proposed mass-memory systems, it is optical rather than purely electromagnetic as regards its method of writing-in and reading-out information. *New Scientist, Nov. 16, 1967, p 415*

—*v.i.* to put coded data into or out of a computer.

The functions of these lobes include storage and a process known as "reading-in" and "reading-out," similar to the system used in the memory storage of computers. *Science News Letter, March 27, 1965, p 194*

read·out ('ri:d,aut), *n.* the output, transmission, or display of data or information.

This machine is a simple digital computer which allows the rating of up to 20 people.... After all members have made their choices the machine gives a digital readout of the mean rating for each member of the group. *New Scientist, Aug. 8, 1963, p 292*

Most readouts of the biochemical properties of living systems come from destructive methods which usually do not preserve the proportions of the system after the cellular destruction occurs. *Tom W. Hill, Science News, Oct. 14, 1967, p 380*

—*v.i.* to transmit, record, or display data or information.

This system will readout continuously in real-time to a new second generation of still relatively simple...receivers, using a higher frequency in the 1690 to 1700 MHz band. *M. W. Kerr-Smith, "The Future of Weather Forecasting," Science Journal, April 1970, p 50*

ready-made, *n.* an ordinary object, such as a bicycle wheel or a metal rack, mounted and treated as if it were a work of art, especially in Dadaism.

Marcel Duchamp—Paintings, ready-mades, and objects done between 1912 and 1920, plus an edition of facsimile reproductions of the artist's manuscript notes during this period; through March 4. *"Goings On About Town," The New Yorker, Feb. 18, 1967, p 16*

...Lichtenstein may have started with what Duchamp called 'treated ready-mades', but he tends nowadays to invent the subjects for himself. *David Thompson, The Listener, Jan. 11, 1968, p 34*

real tennis, *British.* court tennis.

The defeat of Howard Angus, the holder and British open champion, by the Lord's professional David Cull provided the Field trophy for real tennis with its biggest surprise for years at Queen's Club yesterday. *Roy McKelvie, The Times (London), Nov. 28, 1970, p 16*

[variant of *royal tennis*. The word *real*, meaning "royal," came into English in the 1300's through French from Latin *rēgālem* but became obsolete after the 1500's except in this technical term.]

real time, time in which data or other factors on which a process or operation depends are produced almost simultaneously with the actual process or event.

The computations take place in "real time," that is, the results of the astronaut's actions happen as rapidly as they will in actual flight. *Science News, July 16, 1966, p 38*

...that thinking had to be done in what engineers call "real time"—quick decisions, made on the basis of information that becomes available almost instantaneously through the vast electronic communications network. *Evert Clark, The New York Times, June 4, 1965, p 15*

real-time, *adj.* producing data or solving problems in actual time with a process which depends on the data or solutions for its continuation or completion.

Imperial College, London, is this week the scene of the British Computer Society's "Datafair". The central theme is "real-time systems", which can be taken to mean systems that deal with problems as they appear, rather than making a separate operation of problem-solving with a consequent delay. Besides the continuous computer control of industrial and other processes, the term "real-time" in this sense also covers, for example, a system that a scientist or engineer can turn to without leaving his desk. *New Scientist, Jan. 6, 1966, p 11*

received, *adj.* commonly accepted; commonplace.

The Arts Council, the biggest organiser of Art exhibitions in the world, has appointed its first director of exhibitions. The job has gone to Norbert Lynton.... It's still heresy to say so, but Lynton has a record of turning today's heresies into tomorrow's received opinions. *"Miscellany: Exhibitionist," The Manchester Guardian Weekly, May 23, 1970, p 10*

They exchange with wary civility the well-worn coins of received ideas about the weather, politics, school, war, and Empire that they have spent a lifetime accumulating. *Brendan Gill, "The Theatre: Only Connect," Review of "Home," a play by David Storey, The New Yorker, Nov. 28, 1970, p 141*

▶ This use of *received* appears to have been taken from French through the literal translation of the stock phrase *idée reçue*, meaning a prevailing or conventional notion (literally, received idea). The phrase was already well-known in the 1800's; Gustave Flaubert wrote a satirical collection of the fashionable platitudes of his day entitled *Dictionnaire des idées reçues*.

receiving end, **to be at** (or **on**) **the receiving end,** to be the recipient (of something, originally something unpleasant but now applied as a vogue phrase to anything).

Middle aged obese housewives are the most common to be found at the receiving end, and about half of them are given the drugs because of a primary diagnosis of depression. *Oliver Gillie, Science Journal, Feb. 1970, p 7*

recessionary, *adj.* of or relating to an economic recession; characterized by a setback in sales, employment, production, etc., usually following a protracted period of inflation.

He admits himself baffled by the combination of high inflationary symptoms in prices and interest rates with recessionary symptoms in output. *Peter Jay, The Times (London), May 22, 1970, p 8*

reconfigure, *v.t.* to change the form or parts of (an aircraft, computer, etc.).

The air traffic control and navigation complex which exists today is essentially a hodgepodge of war surplus systems which have been reconfigured using modern components. *Vernon I. Weihe, Science News, June 15, 1968, p 570*

The software must be designed so that the system is self re-configuring in the event of any hardware failure. *Denys Scholes, The Times (London), April 3, 1970, p 27*

One of the 11 will now have to be reconfigured to accommodate the features that were lost on the first plane. *"The Felled Bird," Science News, Jan. 9, 1971, p 24*

recursive, *adj.* capable of being returned to or used repeatedly.

One function Professor Miller considered was the ability to deal with "recursive" programmes, that is, to interrupt a course of action to undertake another—a "subroutine"—and then to interrupt this in turn with the same subroutine, and so on. *New Scientist, Oct. 15, 1964, p 147*

recyclable, *adj.* capable of being recycled.

Considering the remarkable cost of children's books and their remarkably brief life span, publishers might do well to encase their pages and bindings in some sort of ersatz (but recyclable) horn. *Jean Stafford, "Books: Children's Books for Christmas," The New Yorker, Dec. 4, 1971, p 177*

recycle, *v.t., v.i.* to put (wastes, garbage, etc.) through a cycle of purification and conversion to useful products.

As we look toward the long-range future—to 1980, 2000 and beyond—recycling of materials will become increasingly necessary not only for waste disposal but also to conserve resources. *Richard M. Nixon, in President's Message to Congress of Feb. 10, 1970*

Officials agreed that recycling would have a chance to succeed only if separation of garbage were mandatory, scavengers were controlled by penalties, convenient collections were scheduled and there were a market for the recycled materials. *Ann McCallum, "Recycling Gains Momentum," The New York Times, June 13, 1971, Sec. 1, p 98*

red alert, an emergency state of readiness in the face of imminent danger.

Admissions to London hospitals [due to a flu epidemic] in the week ending at midnight on Monday totalled slightly over 2,000, above the figure for a similar period during the last hospital "red alert" two years ago, according to a spokesman for the city's emergency bed service. *The Manchester Guardian Weekly, Jan. 3, 1970, p 24*

He [Frank C. Erwin, Jr.] has no patience with anyone or anything he considers damaging to his beloved alma mater University of Texas—and since Erwin is chairman of the university's board of regents, his antagonists are automatically on red alert. *Time, Aug. 10, 1970, p 54*

[extended sense of the term for an air-raid alert]

redbrick, *adj.* of or relating to more modern British universities, as distinguished from Oxford and Cambridge. Compare OXBRIDGEAN.

Now an angry old man of 67, Pritchett vents some of the redbrick ferocity of early Osborne or Amis—though with more elegance—as he writes of the genteel poverty and violent lower-middle-class life that he survived. *"Books," Review of "A Cab at the Door" by V. S. Pritchett, Time, May 17, 1968, p 84*

[so called because of the buildings of red brick often characterizing the later universities, especially the civic universities founded in the 1800's]

Red Guard, 1 a member of a movement of young Maoists of China, especially those active in the Cultural Revolution.

Such developments as...the rampages of the Red Guards represent momentous changes for China. *"The Atlantic Report: The Purge in China," The Atlantic, Dec. 1966, p 26*

The Red Guards damaged a number of temples and old buildings, destroyed old books. Ancient statues were covered with red posters. The Red Guards called for the closing of churches and mosques, and for streets to be given more revolutionary names such as The East Is Red. Anything western was attacked—western dress styles, haircuts. *Anthony Lawrence, The Listener, Jan. 19, 1967, p 80*

2 a member of any of various other groups of political radicals.

Japan's Red Guards are members of the Socialist opposition—aided by Communists and the *Komeito* (Clean Government Party)—who for the past three months have charged Sato's Cabinet with everything from fraud and embezzlement to improper installation of a toilet. *Time, Nov. 4, 1966, p 35*

As in all such movements there is an extremist group, called "Red Guards" in Turin, that seeks to eliminate virtually all traditional authority, to elect professors and to confer marks based on the findings of student committees. *Robert C. Doty, The New York Times, Feb. 10, 1968, p 2*

Red Guardism, the movement of the Chinese Red Guards.

By November last year Red Guardism was in full cry, and zealous youths were swarming across China on foot and by trains, buses and boats, holding aloft little red books containing quotations from Mr. Mao.... *Tillman Durdin, The New York Times, March 5, 1967, p 2*

Red Power, a slogan used by American Indians, modeled on the term BLACK POWER. Compare BROWN POWER.

As with Black Power the burgeoning Red Power movement has two components, one cultural, the other political. The Indians want some recognition, not just that they exist but that their culture has, or at least had, worthwhile values of its own. *The Manchester Guardian Weekly, May 23, 1970, p 24*

The [Mescalero Apache] tribe's demonstration of "red power" began in 1961 when leaders drew up comprehensive development plans based on tribal priorities and consultants' reports. One concern recommended the tourist complex, another, stock raising. *Ralph Blumenthal, "Apaches in New Mexico Build A Resort and a Proud Image," The New York Times, June 10, 1971, p 26*

red-shift, *v.t.* to shift (lines of light in stars, quasars, etc.) toward the red end or longest wavelengths of the spectrum, indicating movement of the light source away from the observer.

In the spectra of quasi-stellar objects, however, these ultraviolet lines (both emission and absorption) are red-shifted into the visible region of the spectrum.... *Illustration legend, "The Absorption Lines of Quasi-stellar Objects," Scientific American, Dec. 1970, p 24*

[verb use of *red shift* the shift of stellar light toward the red end of the spectrum]

redshirt, *U.S. Sports.* —*n.* a college student of athletic ability whose normal four-year course is deliberately extended by one year, usually the sophomore year, in order that he may develop further his athletic skills.

He worked even harder in his sophomore year as a "redshirt," practicing with the varsity but not playing in any games—so that he would have an additional year of eligibility. *"Sport: Saturday's Hero" [Jim Plunkett of Stanford University, winner of the Heisman Trophy for football], Time, Dec. 7, 1970, p 78*

—*v.t.* to keep out of varsity competition for a year as a redshirt.

They [the Big Ten] also are forbidden to "red-shirt" prospects—putting them on a five-year program, keeping them out of action as sophomores in order to beef them up. *"Sport: College Football," Time, Oct. 14, 1966, p 49*

He could have been redshirted but he was an uncertain commodity last year. He came like the wind this fall. *Art Rosenbaum, San Francisco Chronicle, Dec. 3, 1963, p 44*

[so called because of the red shirts often worn by such players during practice to distinguish them from members of the varsity]

reductive, *adj.* of or relating to minimal art; minimal.

To judge by art magazines and museum programs, nothing new has been done in the past few years but Happenings, optical displays, and so-called primary structures and reductive paintings. *Harold Rosenberg, "The Art World: Defining Art," The New Yorker, Feb. 25, 1967, p 99*

reductivism, *n.* another name for MINIMAL ART.

Bernard Cohen's *White Plant* dates from the period when his earlier 'linguistic' style had degenerated into a hothouse aestheticism; the rather self-conscious reductivism of his recent exhibition was far less cloying. The odd-man-out, in that his work is figurative, is David Hockney. *Paul Overy, "Art: House Style," The Listener, Aug. 17, 1967, p 220*

reductivist, *n.* another name for MINIMALIST.

New York, architecturally closed and varied in climate, is dominated by large numbers of artists who swim in one or two schools producing closely related work—lately, the reductivists and the remainders of the Pop people. *William Wilson, "California Art: The Explosion That Never Went Boom," Saturday Review, Sept. 23, 1967, p 55*

redundancy, *n.* *Aerospace.* the ability to provide duplication or replacement of some function in case of a failure in equipment.

The Goldstone station was equipped with two completely separate systems to provide 100 percent redundancy in the reception and recording of the Ranger photographs. *Scientific American, Jan. 1966, p 61*

reference beam, the beam of laser light that is aimed at the photographic plate or film in holography.

Holography is a method of recording images on film without a lens. It requires a coherent illuminating beam, divided so that one part lights the object, while the other, called the reference beam, goes directly to the film. *Humberto Fernandez-Moran, "The World of Inner Space," The World Book Science Annual 1968, p 221*

A low-power continuous laser, bore-sighted through the high-intensity pulsed laser, provides a continuous internal reference beam for aiming the telescope in conjunction with the television camera and reticle system.... *James E. Faller and E. Joseph Wampler, Scientific American, March 1970, p 41*

The wavefront information from the object modulates the reference beam, and the resultant beam is recorded as an interference pattern on a photographic plate. *David Denby and John N. Butters, New Scientist, Feb. 26, 1970, p 394*

reg·gae ('reg,ei *or* 'rei,gei), *n.* a form of rock music of West Indian origin. See the quotation for details.

One type of music that kept within the bounds of the single [record] was "reggae," which swept Britain in the autumn of 1969. Imported by West Indian immigrants, reggae was simple, catchy, and very rhythmic; being easy to dance to, it became very popular with younger teenagers. It was also a style to which many tunes could be adapted, so that, in addition to original West Indian numbers such as Desmond Dekker's "Israelites," "Elizabethan Serenade" appeared in the charts, updated as "Elizabethan Reggae," along with a similar version of the old Everly Brothers' song "Love of the Common People." A year after its arrival reggae's popularity showed no signs of waning. *Hazel R. Morgan, "Popular Music," Britannica Book of the Year 1971, p 545*

[originally named in the British West Indies, but of unknown origin]

regional, *n. U.S.* any of a number of small stock exchanges located in various regions of the country and serving chiefly as a secondary market for shares traded on the larger exchanges.

Wall Street brokers say that a considerable amount of United States securities business is being diverted by Canadian brokers to the regionals. *The New York Times, Jan. 8, 1968, p 101*

Because of this growth—and the prospect of more to come—the cost of seats on the regionals has been rising steadily. *Time, Sept. 3, 1965, p 58*

[shortened from *regional exchange.* The British equivalent is *country exchange.*]

registered player, a tennis player of a category newly created by the International Lawn Tennis Federation, consisting of independent professionals who are eligible to play for prize money in open tournaments.

The amateurs receive only expense money; the registered players, who must be over 19 years of age, may receive cash prizes as well as expense money, as do the pros. *Bill Braddock, "Sports: Tennis," The Americana Annual 1970, p 650*

It seemed illogical, for instance, that a so-called Contract Professional, a professional who was under contract to a tennis promoter, was not eligible to represent his country in Davis Cup competition, whereas a so-called Registered Player, a professional who was affiliated with his national lawn-tennis association, was eligible. *Herbert Warren Wind, "The Sporting Scene: Tennis Troubles," The New Yorker, Oct. 2, 1971, p 98*

regs, *n.pl. Especially U.S. Slang.* regulations.

[Admiral] Zumwalt decided on Annapolis, where he starred in debate but finished 275th in conduct in his class of 615. Petty regs did not appeal to him then either. *"Humanizing the U.S. Military," Time, Dec. 21, 1970, p 21*

I know the new I.R.S. [Internal Revenue Service] regs by heart.... I even know the sections on farm income. *John Casey, "Testimony and Demeanor," The New Yorker, June 19, 1971, p 24*

▶ In British English *regs* has long been used in the Army (since about 1870 according to Partridge's *Dictionary of Slang*), chiefly in the phrase *Queen's Regs* (formerly *King's Regs*), meaning the Army's regulations governing conduct and discipline.

regulatory gene, another name for OPERATOR.

The first known class consists of structural genes, which determine the amino acid sequence and three-dimensional shape of proteins; the second is regulatory genes, which specify whether structural genes will function and there-

fore control the rate of enzyme synthesis. *Science News Yearbook 1970, p 103*

reillusion, *v.t.* to restore one's faith or illusion.

... they [the Conservatives] came to power because the electorate was disillusioned with the Labour Party rather than because they were reillusioned with the Conservatives. *The Times (London), Sept. 26, 1970, p 13*

reinforce, *v.t., v.i.* **1** to encourage or strengthen (a response to a stimulus), usually by rewarding a correct response and withholding reward for an incorrect one.

If they happen to be particularly upset by their son's stomach pains (perhaps because of their own "visceral" personalities) and tend to play down the other effects, they will "reward" or reinforce the specific symptoms whenever they occur. *John E. Pfeiffer, "Visceral Learning," Encyclopedia Science Supplement (Grolier) 1970, p 93*

With the red light on, push the manual feed switch to reward the bird every time it hits the switch. Continue to reinforce only as the bird pecks closer to the red light.... A pigeon can be trained in this way in as little as 15 minutes. *C. L. Stong, "The Amateur Scientist: The Color Vision of Pigeons," Scientific American, Oct. 1970, p 128*

2 to reward (a person or animal) for responding to a stimulus.

... we decided that this man who had been mute for 30 years had learned to be mute—or more technically had been reinforced (rewarded) by his environment for being mute. *Irene Kassorla, "Rewards and Punishments," The Listener, Aug. 29, 1968, p 266*

reinforcement therapist, a practitioner of reinforcement therapy.

This principle, the reinforcement therapists insist, applies also to mental patients previously thought to be beyond psychiatric help. *Time, July 11, 1969, p 44*

reinforcement therapy, psychiatric therapy designed to restore normal behavior by rewarding a patient whenever he responds normally to a stimulus, especially a stimulus in commonplace circumstances. The rewards are supposed to reinforce normal response until such response eventually becomes permanent. Also called OPERANT CONDITIONING.

For example, a withdrawn patient who makes an effort to talk with others receives certain rewards, such as extra food, candy, or spending money; if he withdraws into silence, these amenities are withheld. Approximately fifty institutions in the United States are using reinforcement therapy. *"Behavioral Sciences: Psychotherapy," Encyclopedia Science Supplement (Grolier) 1970, p 71*

re·jas·er (ri:'dʒei sər), *n. U.S. Slang.* one who engages in or practices rejasing.

These days, rejasers even dump junked cars neatly offshore: the hulks act like coral reefs, attracting fish—and fishermen. *Time, April 19, 1971, p 52*

re·jas·ing (ri:'dʒei siŋ), *n. U.S. Slang.* the act or practice of putting rubbish or discarded items to useful purpose.

The biggest benefit of rejasing is that virtually indestructible objects never reach the garbage heap. *Time, April 19, 1971, p 52*

" 'Rejasing'—Reusing Junk As Something Else"—is

gaining in popularity and application throughout America
... try it sometime. *Hon. Walter Flowers of Alabama, Congressional Record, Washington, D.C., April 21, 1971*

[formed as an acronym for "*re*using *j*unk *a*s *s*ome*t*hing else"]

rejectant, *n.* an insect repellent derived from a substance in plants which insects reject.

Plant-eating insects often avoid otherwise acceptable plants because the plants produce a distasteful chemical substance. Drs. J. S. Gill and C. T. Lewis of London's Imperial College believe application of such nontoxic repellents to crops might deter insects from attacking them and thus offer an alternative to toxic pesticides. To be of practical value, they say, a rejectant should be persistent and should be absorbed by the plant so that new plant growth would also be distasteful. *"A Matter of Taste," Science News, Sept. 11, 1971, p 174*

rejection, *n.* the immunological tendency of the body to attack and destroy transplanted organs and other foreign tissue.

Until the immunologists learn how to handle rejection, no transplant will be completely successful. "It's a palliative, not a cure," said Dr. Barnard, who gives transplant patients today no more than five years to live with their borrowed hearts. *"Biomedicine: Transplants: The Surgical Revolution," Science News Yearbook 1969, p 11*

rejective art, another name for MINIMAL ART.

Minimal art is Dada in which the art critic has got into the act. No mode in art has ever had more labels affixed to it by eager literary collaborators; besides being called minimal art, it is known as "ABC art," "primary structures," "systemic painting," "reductive art," "rejective art," and by half a dozen other titles. *Harold Rosenberg, "The Art World: Defining Art," The New Yorker, Feb. 25, 1967, p 108*

rejectivist, *adj.* relating to or producing rejective art.

The "no," or (as he is sometimes called) "rejectivist," painter is, as you may have guessed, Ad Reinhardt. *Robert M. Coates, "The Art Galleries: Rejections," The New Yorker, Dec. 10, 1966, p 172*

relativistic, *adj.* *Physics.* having a speed so great relative to the speed of light that the values of mass and other properties are significantly altered.

... two workers at the Tata Institute of Fundamental Research in Bombay have now shown that the cosmic radiation resulting from pulsars emitting relativistic particles can form only a very minor part of the observed background. *New Scientist, Nov. 5, 1970, p 260*

Synchrotron radiation is generated by relativistic electrons—electrons moving at speeds near that of light—spiraling about the lines of force of a magnetic field. *Herbert Friedman, "Astronautics and Space Exploration," 1971 Britannica Yearbook of Science and the Future, 1970, p 132*

relaxor, *n.* *U.S.* a substance that loosens or slackens closely curled hair.

Johnson's toughest time came two years ago, when the surge of black pride led to more natural hair styles, specifically the Afro, which severely scissored demand for straighteners and the other hair relaxors. Johnson responded by introducing Afro Sheen, a product line that includes hair spray and a "comb easy" shampoo for the natural look. *Time, Dec. 7, 1970, p 88*

releasing factor, a substance that triggers the release of hormones from a gland.

Nerve fibres coming from the hypothalamus secrete 'releasing factors'—a special type of hormone—directly into small blood vessels which carry them to the anterior pituitary. The 'releasing factors' serve in turn to regulate the production by the anterior pituitary of other hormones —such as the gonadotrophins FSH and LH which release the egg. *Illustration legend, "The Reproductive Hormones," Science Journal, June 1970, p 47*

... there appears to be a chemically distinct releasing factor for each of the six anterior pituitary hormones. *Graham Chedd, New Scientist, Jan. 29, 1970, p 200*

The neurohormones produced in the hypothalamus (a part of the bridge between the brainstem and the cerebral hemispheres) are now considered to be the agents that actually monitor the pituitary gland; they have been called "releasing factors." Although these hormones have been isolated, none was synthesized until 1970 when two teams working independently succeeded in producing thyrotropin-releasing factor (TRF). *Robert B. Greenblatt, "Medicine: Endocrinology," Britannica Book of the Year 1971, p 481*

relevance, *n.* concern with important current issues. Compare IRRELEVANCE.

The impetus came largely from student demands for "relevance," especially for the overdue admission of more minority-group students. Activism has also done much to curb the old absurdities of trivial research and needless PH.D.s. *Time, Nov. 30, 1970, p 40*

New programs offered to viewers in the fall of 1970 put a heavy premium on the word "relevance," which to the networks meant dealing with social problems that supposedly concern young people. *John M. Gunn, "Television and Radio," The Americana Annual 1971, p 663*

relevant, *adj.* concerned with important current issues. Compare IRRELEVANT.

Either we can commit ourselves to changing the institutions of our society that need to be changed, to make them —to use a term which I hate—"relevant," to make them responsive or we can sit back and try to defend them.... *Mayor Jerome Cavanagh, Detroit, quoted by Fred Pouledge, "The Flight from City Hall," Harper's, Nov. 1969, p 86*

[Adam] Walinsky is running hard against New York State Attorney General Louis Lefkowitz.... The Walinsky campaign is energetic, relevant and heavily financed. On one recent campaign day, he made half a dozen stops in the New York City area, flew into Buffalo at midnight and held a three-hour meeting before going to sleep. *"New York: Chasing a Future," Time, Oct. 19, 1970, p 20*

... museums should have a more involved or relevant public role.... *Gabriella Befani Canfield, New York, in a Letter to the Editor, The New York Times, July 1, 1970, p 44*

REM (rem), *n.* acronym for RAPID EYE MOVEMENT.

But rapid, almost flickering eye movements, now abbreviated in the trade jargon to REMs, occurred in varying stretches of five minutes to an hour, several times during a night's sleep. *Time, Feb. 14, 1964, p 46*

remote batch, a large collection of input and output data passed back and forth from one or more locations to a remote central processor or main computer.

These machines [direct input computers] are therefore converging with small industrial real-time processors in their suitability for use as remote batch terminals and in other systems. *Kenneth Owen, The Times (London), Aug. 11, 1970, p 17*

remote sensing, observation or scanning, especially of natural features, from a great distance by means of radar, aerial infrared photography, seismography, and similar techniques. *Often used attributively.*

Remote sensing involves the use of special cameras and other sophisticated instruments in orbiting earth satellites. These instruments see and record invisible as well as visible light waves given off by objects on earth. The result is a picture that is far more revealing than one obtained by regular photography. *George W. Irving, Jr., "Agriculture," 1972 Britannica Yearbook of Science and the Future, 1971, p 162*

Geologists have traditionally combined visual examination of terrestrial features and materials with less direct supplemental approaches known collectively as remote-sensing techniques. *Richard H. Jahns, "Geology: Multispectral Photography," The World Book Science Annual 1969, p 310*

A remote-sensing satellite could provide information on vegetation, soil, and water infinitely faster and often more accurately than ground observation. *Robert B. Rathbone, "Agriculture: U.S. Agricultural Research: Earth Resources Satellites," The Americana Annual 1970, p 56*

REM sleep, another name for PARADOXICAL SLEEP.

All mammals show REM sleep, but frogs and birds do not. *Philip Morrison, "Books," Review of "Sleep: Physiology and Pathology," edited by Anthony Kales, Scientific American, Aug. 1970, p 126*

Reserpine, which induces dysphoria rather than euphoria, enhances REM sleep, as does LSD. *John R. Smythies, "Drug Addiction," McGraw-Hill Yearbook of Science and Technology 1971, p 171*

Renaissance man, a man who is knowledgeable in an unusually wide variety of the arts and sciences.

Francis Plimpton is the Renaissance man; his abilities and interests run the full gamut. He is a tennis ace. He is a linguist, a poet, a wit, and a classical scholar.... *Merrell E. Clark, quoted by Geoffrey T. Hellman, "Profiles: Period-Piece Fellow," The New Yorker, Dec. 4, 1971, p 61*

"I sit here and solve mathematical problems, program electronic music, analyze architectural possibilities but somehow being a Renaissance man isn't what it used to be." *Cartoon legend, "Computers," 1971 Britannica Yearbook of Science and the Future, 1970, p 171*

▶ The term *Renaissance man*, used in its original and literal sense, refers to the so-called "universal man" or *homo universale* of the Italian Renaissance, as in the following quotation:

The two-volume manuscript finds of drawings and notes made by the epitome of the "Renaissance Man" will keep Leonardo da Vinci scholars enthralled and occupied for many years. *Fay Leviero, "Leonardo The Inventor," Encyclopedia Science Supplement (Grolier) 1967, p 404*

re·nais·sant (ri'nei sənt), *adj.* reviving; renascent.

Rapidly rising output and renaissant business confidence and investment are normally a time at which profits rise, costs are more economically spread over longer runs of production and labour has not yet begun to exploit its returning strength in the labour market. *"Anti-Inflation Defences," The Times (London), Jan. 3, 1972, p 15*

[from French]

rent strike, *U.S.* refusal by the tenants of a building to pay their rent as a protest against rent increases, poor service, etc.

The tenants of the apartments at West Madison and Albany were conducting a rent strike. *Gerald Jonas, "A Reporter At Large," The New Yorker, March 13, 1971, p 92*

The student organization also is lending moral and organizational support to the Berkeley Tenants' Union (many of whose members are students) in a widespread local rent strike. *Tom Wicker, The New York Times, Feb. 5, 1970, p 36*

re·o·vi·rus ('ri: ou,vai rəs), *n.* an echovirus associated with respiratory and intestinal infections and found also in certain animal and human tumors.

One, called reovirus, was previously known as a common virus widely distributed in animals, but it is now being found in patients with African lymphoma. *Michael Stoker, The Times (London), Sept. 19, 1967, p 8*

Reoviruses, of which there are three types, have been isolated from secretions of the respiratory tract as well as of intestines, but are relatively unimportant. *Science News Letter, Feb. 12, 1966, p 103*

[from respiratory enteric orphan *virus*; called "orphan virus" because it is not known to cause any of the diseases it is associated with]

replicase, *n.* another name for RNA POLYMERASE.

In the research, new viral RNA was produced in the test tube with the help of an enzyme, called a replicase, and strands of natural virus RNA. *Harold M. Schmeck, Jr., The New York Times, April 25, 1968, p 20*

[from *replication* + *-ase* enzyme]

replicate, *v.i.* to reproduce by cell division.

When the cell reproduces by the process of division known as mitosis, these homologous chromosomes replicate and separate, so that each of the two daughter cells has a full complement of 46 chromosomes. *R. G. Edwards and Ruth E. Fowler, "Human Embryos in the Laboratory," Scientific American, Dec. 1970, p 46*

replication, *n.* the act or process of replicating.

The RNA contains all the instructions for producing a new virus particle, including the instructions for making an enzyme, termed a replicase, that carries out the replication of the RNA itself. *Scientific American, Sept. 1967, p 103*

replicative, *adj.* causing or taking part in replication.

... current evidence favors the interpretation that DNA-polymerase functions as a repair enzyme rather than as a replicative one.... *James C. Copeland, "Molecular Genetics," 1971 Britannica Yearbook of Science and the Future, 1970, p 250*

repressor, *n.* a theoretical component of the operon whose function is to repress the action of the operator. Compare INDUCER.

The repressor determines when the gene turns on and off by functioning as an intermediate between the gene and an appropriate signal. Such a signal is often a small molecule that sticks to the repressor and alters or slightly distorts its shape. *Mark Ptashne and Walter Gilbert, "Genetic Repressors," Scientific American, June 1970, p 36*

re·pro·graph·ic (,ri: prə'græf ik), *adj.* of or relating to reprography.

The central reprographic unit is equivalent to the computer room where the main processor and general backing store are situated, while the various input devices, such as typewriters and copiers, are equivalent to the computer accessories. *Harry T. Chambers, The Times (London), Sept. 27, 1968, p 34*

re·prog·ra·phy (ri:'prɑg rə fi:), *n.* the reproduction of graphic material, especially by electronic means.

Finally, there is reprography—which runs from simple ink and spirit duplicators through photocopying equipment to off-set lithography. *F. C. Thurling, The Times (London), Oct. 6, 1967, p IV*

[from French *reprographie*, from *reproduction* + *-graphie* -graphy (recording process)]

rep·u·nit ('rep₁yu: nit), *n.* a number having one or more identical integers, such as 11, 111, 1111, etc.

"Repunits," numbers consisting entirely of 1's, produce palindromic squares when the number of units is one through nine, but 10 or more units give squares that are not palindromic. *Martin Gardner, "Mathematical Games," Scientific American, Aug. 1970, p 110*

[contraction of *repeating unit*]

reradiative, *adj.* capable of throwing off or reflecting radiation.

Thermal shielding to protect the [space] shuttle during the critical re-entry periods will probably be in the form of re-radiative sheathing of such metals as columbium, rather than ablative shielding, which would have to be replaced for each flight. *Glen Lawes, New Scientist, Dec. 11, 1969, p 548*

resegregation, *n. U.S.* renewal of racial segregation.

The government has done some resegregation—it informed private boarding schools, for instance, that an exception to the Land Apportionment Act permitting them to enroll a few African students would no longer be allowed.... *Calvin Trillin, "Letter from Salisbury," The New Yorker, Nov. 12, 1966, p 144*

And so there is a danger that sophisticated men, in trying to ease Federal enforcement in the school field, will let loose forces that would sweep away many of the gains that have been made against racial discrimination. Symbols are important in the life of politics, and weakness in the Federal Government could be taken as the signal for a general move toward the re-segregation of American life. *Anthony Lewis, The New York Times, March 2, 1970, p 36*

residency, *n. U.S.* advanced training or education in some field, analogous to medical or academic residencies.

Last winter the company instituted a series of "residencies" across the country—one- to three-week stands in Los Angeles, San Francisco, Chicago and at the University of Illinois—that combined performances with seminars and lecture-demonstrations. *Time, July 20, 1970, p 51*

residual, *n. U.S.* a fee received by a performer, writer, etc., for every repetition of a commercial or show in whose production he originally participated.

The network hopes to gross $1,000,000 from commercials for each rerun. The cut for Judy Garland and *Oz*'s other 1939 stars: nothing. It was not until 1960 that film contracts began to provide residuals for actors. *Time, Aug. 25, 1967, p 60*

re·sis·to·jet (ri'zis tou₁jet), *n.* a jet engine that uses electric resistance to heat liquid ammonia propellant, used chiefly to produce enough thrust to keep an artificial satellite steady during orbit.

Only one U.S. satellite, ATS-4 [Applications Technology Satellite-4], has ever used electric propulsion as a primary system (in ATS's case, resistojets for attitude control). *Science News, Nov. 2, 1968, p 446*

resit, *v.t. British.* to take (a written examination) a second time.

So many students resit the engineering examination each year that an eventual pass rate of 80 per cent., as suggested by Mr Alan Sim, may occur. *G. W. L. Sinclair, The Sunday Times (London), June 30, 1968, p 15*

It is not likely that many students will, in fact, resit the examinations. *The Times (London), June 25, 1970, p 4*

► This verb has also a corresponding noun, (as in "the September *resit*," a feature of many British universities), in which the stress is on the first syllable: 'ri:₁sit. Usage varies with the verb, which is pronounced either the same way as the noun or with the stress on the second syllable: ri:'sit.

resonance, *n.* an unstable elementary particle or group of particles of extremely short life.

. . . the rho meson is a particle in its own right although it is also frequently referred to as a resonance. *Thomas Groves, "Physics: Elementary Particle Physics," 1969 Britannica Yearbook of Science and the Future, 1968, p 357*

A distinctive distortion, or peak, in the spectrum was found, indicating that for a brief time (of the order of 10^{-21} second) the three neutrons were bound together as one particle by the nuclear force. Such a complex body is known as resonance. *Science Journal, Oct. 1970, p 23*

respiratory distress syndrome, another name for HYALINE MEMBRANE DISEASE.

An artificial placenta which makes it possible to supply life saving oxygen to unborn babies suffering from a dangerous disease known as respiratory distress syndrome has been developed by obstetricians at the Woolwich Hospital, London. *Science Journal, Aug. 1968, p 16*

Each year, 50,000 U.S. infants die soon after birth—at least 25,000 of them from respiratory distress syndrome (RDS). Also called hyaline membrane disease, RDS is caused by the inability of an infant's lungs to extract oxygen from the air and pass carbon dioxide out of the body. *Time, Dec. 7, 1970, p 94*

res·sen·ti·ment (rə₁sã ti:'mã), *n.* a generalized feeling of resentment or indignation harbored by a group of people against those of another group, usually of a higher economic level.

To read some of the more important and influential contemporary critics of education . . . one might think that the schools are staffed by sadists and clods who are drawn into teaching by the lure of upward mobility and the opportunity to take out their anger—Friedenberg prefers the sociological term, *ressentiment*, or "A kind of free-floating ill-temper" on the students. *Charles E. Silberman, "Murder in the Schoolroom," The Atlantic, June 1970, p 90*

[from French, literally, resentment]

re·tard ('ri:₁tɑrd), *n. U.S. Slang.* a mentally retarded person.

There are . . . heroin addicts, Air Force and CIA mental retards and Broadway Indians doing a Broadway Snake

Dance. *"The Theater: Snake Oil," Review of "Operation Sidewinder" by Sam Shepard, Time, March 23, 1970, p 49*

The younger son, self-described as "a hard-core *re*tard," dreams of escaping to the wilds of Oregon to gambol with the bears and squirrels and to drink fresh water out of running streams.... *Edith Oliver, "The Theatre: Off Broadway," Review of "The Carpenters" by Steven Tesich, The New Yorker, Jan. 16, 1971, p 76*

re·tard·ee (ri'tɑr,di:), *n.* a mentally retarded person.

All but 5% of the hospital's 4,800 patients are confined there involuntarily through civil court orders; almost half are geriatrics cases or mental retardees who receive only custodial care. *Time, April 5, 1971, p 38*

re·think ('ri:,θiŋk), *n.* the act of rethinking; reconsideration.

[Walter] McNerney [President of the Blue Cross Association of America], in a word, seems to be in the van of the rethink of social policy now going on in the U.S. And as such, his views and doubts on the financing and organisation of health services form a useful context for those suggestions now being heard in this country for moving our system in the American direction. *Peter Fiddick, "Medicine Market," The Manchester Guardian Weekly, Aug. 22, 1970, p 13*

Using the metal [titanium] to its best advantage calls for a thorough rethink of metal-working methods and of the different avenues open to the aircraft engineer, to use different types of material...in an effective combination. *Glen Lawes, "Titanium for the Aircraft Materials Prize," New Scientist, March 12, 1970, p 503*

[noun use of the verb]

ret·i·nal ('ret ə nəl), *n.* a yellow pigment in the retina.

The process [by which the visual cell converts light into an electrical signal] begins with the absorption of the incident light by the visual pigments in the disks. These pigments consist of a combination of vitamin A aldehyde, known as retinal (formerly called retinene), with a protein of the class called opsins. *Richard W. Young, "Visual Cells," Scientific American, Oct. 1970, p 81*

re·tread ('ri:,tred), *n. Slang.* a person who rehashes old material.

Last August, I suggested in these pages that Duke Ellington be given a grant of, say, a hundred thousand dollars.... The foundations, busy handing money out to retreads and the moribund, have been silent.... *Whitney Balliett,."Our Local Correspondents: A Day with the Duke," The New Yorker, June 27, 1970, p 52*

[from *retread, n.*, an old tire with a new tread]

retribalization, *n.* the act or process of retribalizing; return to tribal status or to tribal practices.

...Hausa traders from Nigeria's north have migrated to a particular quarter of Ibadan (a Nigerian city not in Hausa territory), thus reinforcing their tribal ties for purposes of maintaining an elaborate trade network. This "retribalization" is an adaptation, in a new urban setting, to the demands of their economic and political life. *Lawrence Rosen, "Behavioral Sciences," 1971 Britannica Yearbook of Science and the Future, 1970, p 146*

Provided that the Bomb or the behavioral scientists do not get us first, this last phase will see reunification and integration, a sort of global retribalization. *Time, April 26, 1971, p 64*

retribalize, *v.t.* to return to tribal status or to tribal ways and practices.

One of [Marshall] McLuhan's basic propositions is that we are crossing a technological frontier dividing the age of the collectivist from that of the individualist: We are being retribalized. *Robert Lewis Shayon, "TV and Radio: Not-So-Cool Medium," Review of "The Medium is the Message" by Marshall McLuhan, Saturday Review, April 15, 1967, p 46*

retributivism, *n.* belief in dispensing punishment to criminals as an act of retribution for the injury they have caused.

Both are influential today: "retributivism" has become at least as damaging a charge on the one side as "sentimentalism" on the other: and there is an increasing readiness to listen to experts who explain away the criminal's responsibility in psychiatric terms. *John Sparrow, The Times (London), Feb. 24, 1970, p 9*

retributivist, *adj.* characterized by retributivism.

Judicial fondness for expressionist and retributivist theories of punishment is at least partially founded on an idea that only the suffering of the criminal will appease the injured feelings of the victim. *Alan Ryan, "Views," The Listener, Dec. 30, 1971, p 894*

retro, *n.* short for *retrorocket* (rocket producing reverse thrust).

...the thrust of the retro would keep it lodged in place under the craft until it had finished burning, when it would drop away. *New Scientist, Sept. 21, 1967, p 595*

retro-engine, *n.* a rocket engine that produces thrust opposed to forward motion.

In orbit each Mariner will weigh 1200 lbs, but each carries to Mars, as well, about 1000 lbs of fuel for the 14-minute retroengine burn needed to slow it to the requisite orbital speed. *New Scientist and Science Journal, May 6, 1971, p 305*

retrofire, *n.* the ignition of a retrorocket (rocket that produces reverse thrust).

After retro-fire, a marked decrease in spacecraft velocity was noted until retro-burnout occurred at 20 feet and the verniers burned alone. *John Noble Wilford, The New York Times, May 25, 1967, p 43*

retrograde, *adj.* producing thrust opposed to forward motion. Compare POSIGRADE.

To bring a satellite to earth, scientists use devices called retrograde rockets, or, in space jargon, retro rockets. *James J. Haggerty, Jr., "Artificial Satellites: Re-entry," Encyclopedia Science Supplement (Grolier) 1965, p 307*

retroreflective, *adj.* reflecting light back to its source.

In the case of light three reflecting surfaces, all at right angles to one another, form a corner with the same retroreflective property. *James E. Faller and E. Joseph Wampler, "The Lunar Laser Reflector," Scientific American, March 1970, p 41*

retroreflector, *n.* a prismlike device that reflects a laser beam and is designed for placement on a distant object, such as a heavenly body, to calculate its distance from the earth by measuring the time elapsed to reflect a beam of light.

The *Apollo 11* crew left retroreflectors at their landing site on the Moon for a lunar ranging experiment which is being undertaken at the present time by scientists.... *Robert M. Brown, "Atmosphere," McGraw-Hill Yearbook of Science and Technology 1971, p 112*

They will also set up an improved laser-ranging retro-reflector; and another solar-wind composition collecting foil. *"Apollo 15: A Busy Weekend Ahead," New Scientist and Science Journal, July 29, 1971, p 243*

retrospective, *n.* a survey or review of one's past works.

. . . Sy Oliver, the principal arranger for Jimmy Lunceford and Tommy Dorsey between 1933 and the late forties, is holding a retrospective of his work at the Downbeat with the help of a nine-piece group that includes two trumpets, two trombones, two reeds, and three rhythm. *Whitney Balliett, "Musical Events: Jazz: New York Notes," The New Yorker, May 23, 1970, p 80*

▶ This term has been formerly applied only to an exhibition of the works of painters and sculptors.

retrospectivist, *n.* one who surveys or reviews past events.

I have a feeling that 1970 is going to be the year people in the fashion business would most like to forget. I do not somehow see retrospectivists digging it up with cries of pleasure and doing a great pastiche style job on the last year of this decade. *Prudence Glynn, The Times (London), Nov. 24, 1970, p 17*

returnable, *n. U.S.* a bottle or container that one may return to a store after its use and collect a deposit included in its purchase price.

You toss away an average of 5.5 pounds of garbage per day. Use returnables. Not disposables. An incinerator just converts plastic and wax and aluminum containers into poisonous smoke. *Advertisement by Environmental Action Coalition, The New Yorker, April 18, 1970, p 127*

[noun use of *returnable, adj.*]

Reuben sandwich. See the quotation for the meaning.

. . . the Reuben sandwich . . . has become wildly popular in most areas of the United States. . . . It is a combination of corn beef, Swiss cheese and sauerkraut served hot. *Craig Claiborne, The New York Times, Oct. 10, 1967, p 50*

[origin of the name is unknown]

rev, *v.t.* **rev up,** *U.S.* **1** to stir up.

Representative Carlton Gladder, an older man who leans into the microphone, his right hand glued inside his pocket, his left hand moving up and down as he talks: "About the time I got out of college—I worked two and a half years between high school and college—there were a bunch of idealistic youths who had been revved up by a bunch of articulate and persuasive politicians in Germany." *Bill Moyers, "Listening to America: Washington," Harper's, Dec. 1970, p 85*

2 to increase in tempo; accelerate.

The New London Faust (stereo) . . . offers lofty heights and deep lows. . . . And the symphonic postludes have been revved up rather than intensified. . . . I am thinking of the spread-eagle crescendo that spans the closing measures of Act I . . . where orchestral tone gives way to canned uproar. . . . *Robert Lawrence, "The London 'Faust'," Saturday Review, June 24, 1967, p 61*

[extended senses of *rev, v.,* to accelerate an engine, from *rev, n.,* revolution of an engine]

revascularization, *n.* the act or process of revascularizing.

The results of clinical tests were disappointing, and the medical profession dismissed the concept of surgical

revascularization of the heart as being too exotic. *Donald B. Effler, "Surgery for Coronary Disease," Scientific American, Oct. 1968, p 36*

Only four years ago this and other operations to improve the circulation of blood to overtaxed hearts were either unknown or experimental. Now revascularization, or "re-plumbing," has become the most popular item in the thoracic surgeon's repertory of heart repairs—and with good reason. *"Medicine: Old Hearts, New Plumbing," Time, May 10, 1971, p 40*

revascularize, *v.t.* to substitute new blood vessels to increase the blood supply to (the heart, etc.).

Specialists at the meeting today estimated that as many as 60 medical centers in the world might be doing operations to revascularize the hearts of gravely ill patients. *Harold M. Schmeck, Jr., The New York Times, Feb. 18, 1967, p 27*

revenue sharing, *U.S.* the distribution among local governments, especially the state governments, of a part of the revenue from Federal taxes.

At every stop except the schools, Brock's dominant theme was much the same as what President Nixon would later call "revenue sharing"—that government had to be returned to local control by way of sending the taxpayers' money back to the states, counties, cities, and towns. *Richard Harris, "Annals of Politics," The New Yorker, July 10, 1971, p 43*

. . . the opponents of revenue sharing include Mr. Nixon's two most illustrious Republican predecessors in this century: Dwight Eisenhower and Theodore Roosevelt. *William Bragg Ewald, Jr., "Ike and T. R. vs. Nixon," The New York Times, June 11, 1971, p 35*

reverse osmosis, the pumping of impure water and solvents under pressure against a semipermeable membrane which allows the passage of water molecules while acting as a barrier to the salts and other dissolved substances.

Reverse osmosis—the pressuring of solvent through a semipermeable membrane against the usual osmotic flow—has been considered for some time as a way of reclaiming water from industrial effluents. *New Scientist, Dec. 24, 1970, p 557*

A process called "reverse osmosis" may help small-volume cheese plants solve the crucial problems of how to dispose of whey. The method removes 75%-80% of whey water, and the concentrate is shipped to larger plants for drying, thus preventing the dumping of waste whey into streams, which are polluted by the waste. *Robert B. Rathbone, "Agriculture: U.S. Agricultural Research: Processing Research," The Americana Annual 1969, p 50*

reverse racism, *U.S.* discrimination directed against whites, especially unintentional discrimination resulting from extreme measures to integrate blacks.

The Detroit Public Library named Mrs. Clara Jones as its new director in mid-February 1970. Mrs. Jones became the first Negro to head a major urban public library. Because of Mrs. Jones' limited administrative experience, charges of "reverse racism" were made against the appointing body, the Detroit Library Commission. *Dan Bergen, "Libraries," The Americana Annual 1971, p 409*

reverse transcriptase, another name for TEMIN ENZYME. Also shortened to TRANSCRIPTASE.

. . . a sensitive assay for reverse transcriptase may prove

to be, at the very least, a useful tool for the diagnosis of leukemia and perhaps other forms of cancer. *Michael J. Brennan, "Medicine," 1972 Britannica Yearbook of Science and the Future, 1971, p 292*

Of the 13 milks tested only four had reverse-transcriptase activity. . . . But, it should be remembered that reverse transcriptase is as yet only on trial for its cancer-forming activity; it has yet to be proven guilty in that role. *New Scientist and Science Journal, May 20, 1971, p 436*

[from *reverse transcript* (a phrase alluding to the transcription RNA → DNA, which is the reverse of usual transcription DNA → RNA) + *-ase* enzyme]

rhab·do·vi·rus ('ræb dou,vai rəs), *n.* a virus associated with various diseases transmitted by animal or insect bites.

One of the things which is known about rabies virus is that its genetic material is ribonucleic acid (RNA). Because of this property and its morphology it has been classified with the rhabdovirus group (from the Greek *rhabdos* meaning a rod). Other members of the group are four viruses spread by the bites of arthropods.... *Colin Kaplan, "Rabies," Science Journal, April 1970, p 36*

rheumatoid factor, an antibody found especially in the blood serum of sufferers from arthritis which reacts against globulins in the individual's own serum.

. . . Dr S. Rosenblatt and colleagues in New York have found a high incidence of "rheumatoid factor" in schizophrenic patients, especially those showing depressive symptoms. *New Scientist, July 31, 1969, p 221*

rhi·no·vi·rus ('rai nou,vai rəs), *n.* a virus of the respiratory tract associated with the common cold. Compare PICORNAVIRUS.

Further, we are testing specimens from other patients with respiratory disease in order to find out how frequently hitherto unrecognized viruses can be isolated. . . . It seems likely that some of these may be fastidious rhinoviruses. *The Times (London), Sept. 3, 1965, p 14*

[from *rhino-* nose (from Greek *rhīno-*) + *virus*]

rho (rou), *n.* short for RHO MESON.

The difficulties involved in measuring the central masses and widths of short-lived particles, such as rho, stem from the fact that, in general, they are produced in strong interaction processes along with other strongly interacting particles. *Thomas Groves, "Physics: Elementary Particle Physics," 1969 Britannica Yearbook of Science and the Future, 1968, p 357*

In the heavier nuclei more and more rhos are being produced but they are also being increasingly absorbed. *Frederick V. Murphy and David E. Yount, "Photons As Hadrons," Scientific American, July 1971, p 94*

rho meson, a highly unstable and short-lived elementary particle with a mass about 1400 times that of an electron, produced in high-energy collisions between particles. Also shortened to RHO. Compare OMEGA, PHI.

The electron does not strike the proton directly but interacts with it by means of a third particle, a rho meson, which bounces back and forth between them. *"Evidence for Partons," Science News, Oct. 24, 1970, p 333*

There is a class of unstable particles, the neutral vector mesons, whose members resemble photons in many ways, with two important exceptions: they have mass and they exhibit the strong force. The most prominent is the rho

meson, which has a mass equivalent to about 750 MeV. (The mass of the proton is equivalent to 939 MeV.) Rho mesons can be created as real particles in the laboratory, and their decay products can be detected. *Henry W. Kendall and Wolfgang K. H. Panofsky, "The Structure of the Proton and the Neutron," Scientific American, June 1971, p 72*

rhubarbing, *British.* —*adj.* (of actors) muttering sounds to simulate background noise of talk or conversation.

The few attempts at pageantry generally come to grief against painted backdrops, watched by a handful of rhubarbing commoners; meanwhile, at court, Richard Burton fences for close on two hours and a half on an unchanging note of bluff ferocity with Geneviève Bujold's pertly vacuous Anne. *Tom Milne, "The Arts: The Pitying Eye," Review of "Anne of the Thousand Days" (a motion picture), The Times (London), Feb. 27, 1970, p 13*

—*n.* noisy confusion; commotion.

Prince Charles took his seat in the Lords last week like one who is already used to playing many parts. . . . Then he took his hat off again, came down the steps and warmly shook the Lord Chancellor by the hand . . . the players filed off the stage, and the silence dissolved in the rhubarbing of the multitude of spectators. *Norman Shrapnel, "Charles Joins the Club," The Manchester Guardian Weekly, Feb. 21, 1970, p 14*

[from *rhubarb*, a term used in the theater to call for background sounds of talking, based on the custom of actors, when they are depicting a mob or crowd, of saying "rhubarb" repeatedly in their own time so as to give the impression of a general hubbub. This theatrical usage is perhaps related to the U.S. slang term *rhubarb*, meaning a noisy argument or fracas, as during a baseball game.]

rhythm and blues, a blend of rock 'n' roll and blues (originally applied to a form of jazz based on blues). *Abbreviation:* r & b or R & B

. . . four young Negro men. . . . sat down to drums and electric guitars and filled the storefront with almost deafening funky rhythm-and-blues. *"The Talk of the Town," The New Yorker, Dec. 10, 1966, p 48*

The series, which has been running since 1960 with the exception of two summers, is broadening its perspectives this year to include such tangential areas of jazz as folkrock, gospel, rhythm and blues and hard rock 'n' roll. *Robert Shelton, The New York Times, June 21, 1968, p 45*

ri·bo·so·mal (,rai bə'sou məl), *adj.* of or relating to ribosomes.

Another Nobel Prize winner, Dr. James D. Watson, of Harvard University, will report on the role of ribosomal nucleic acids in protein synthesis. *The Times (London), July 25, 1964, p 5*

ribosomal RNA, a ribonucleic acid that forms part of the structure of the ribosome. *Abbreviation:* rRNA Compare MESSENGER RNA, TRANSFER RNA.

. . . when the transplant embryos are reared through the blastula and gastrula stages, they synthesize heterogeneous RNA, transfer RNA and ribosomal RNA in turn and in the same sequence as do embryos reared from fertilized eggs. *J. B. Gurdon, "Transplanted Nuclei and Cell Differentiation," Scientific American, Dec. 1968, p 33*

ri·bo·some ('rai bə,soum), *n.* any of the complex

particles in a cell that carry out the synthesis of protein and enzymes.

Protein synthesis is carried out by small particles, called ribosomes, located in the cytoplasm of the cell. Instructions for the construction of a particular protein are recorded on deoxyribonucleic acid (DNA) molecules located in the nucleus of the cell. *Judith G. Cuddihy, "Review of the Year: Biology," Encyclopedia Science Supplement (Grolier) 1967, p 69*

... ribosomes consist of two subunits, each made up of RNA and many different proteins. *Stephen Kreitzman, "Biochemistry," The Americana Annual 1969, p 124*

[from *ribo*nucleic acid + -*some* body]

Richter scale, a scale for measuring the magnitude of earthquakes, using numbers from 1 to 10, with 1 measuring seismic disturbances that can be de-detected only with sensitive seismographs and 8 to 10 measuring major earthquakes.

The record was broken when Aug. 19 passed without the recording of any tremor of magnitude eight or more on the Richter scale striking U.S. territory. *Science News, Sept. 9, 1967, p 246*

[named after Charles F. *Richter*, born 1900, an American seismologist]

rick·y-tick ('rik i:,tik), *U.S. Slang. —adj.* **1** old-fashioned or trite; rinky-dink.

Ricky-tick
Conductor jointed like a walking-stick
Insect, with silver glasses, silver punch,
And silver seat in his sere serge.
L. E. Sissman, "North" (a poem), The Atlantic, June 1970, p 104

2 Also, **ricky-ticky.** imitative of the sound of rapidly picked strings.

A big red fire engine, peanut shells on the floor, and ricky-tick banjo music summon up the plinking eighteen-nineties, or whatever. *"Goings On About Town," The New Yorker, May 18, 1968, p 6*

White music has always been very ricky-ticky, steppity-step, plunkety-plunk-banjo. *Time, Jan. 12, 1970, p 40*

—*n.* ricky-tick sound or beat, especially in jazz.

To the ricky-tick of Guy Lombardo's "I don't want to get well, I'm in love with a beautiful nurse," three maimed Army veterans fumble through a dance routine.... *Dan Sullivan, The New York Times, Feb. 5, 1968, p 29*

All the successes of the last two years were a fore-shadowing of Sgt. Pepper, which more than anything else dramatizes, note for note, word for word, the brilliance of the new Beatles. . . . it [New LP album called "Sgt. Pepper's Lonely Hearts Club Band"] sizzles with musical montage, tricky electronics and sleight-of-hand lyrics that range between 1920s ricky-tick and 1960 raga. *"Music: Pop Music," Time, Sept. 22, 1967, p 57*

rif·am·pi·cin (,rif æm'pai sən) or **rif·am·pin** (rif-'æm pin), *n.* an antibiotic drug, derived synthetically from a rifamycin, which inhibits the growth of bacterial cells and the replication of viruses by interfering with the action of RNA polymerases in the synthesis of RNA.

Rifampicin, an antibiotic developed for use against tuberculosis, was found to operate by inhibiting an enzyme. *"Cancer: Antibiotic May Inhibit Growth," Science News, April 17, 1971, p 266*

Another approach to the same question, taken by Stefan J. Surzychi of the University of Iowa, makes use of rifam-picin, the antibiotic that inactivates the variety of DNA-dependent RNA polymerase found in bacteria and blue-green algae. In the presence of rifampicin, *C. reinhardi* [*Chlamydomonas reinhardi*, a one-celled green alga] is unable to synthesize the 16 S and 23 S species of ribosomal RNA found in chloroplasts, indicating that these RNA's are synthesized from a chloroplast DNA template. *Ursula W. Goodenough and R. P. Levine, "The Genetic Activity of Mitochondria and Chloroplasts," Scientific American, Nov. 1970, p 28*

Rifampin (rifampicin), introduced as an antituberculosis remedy ... also demonstrated exciting possibilities as an antiviral agent.... Most drugs that block viral growth also damage cells. Rifampin apparently does not. *Allan D. Bass, "Drugs," The World Book Science Annual 1972 (1971), p 299*

rif·a·my·cin (,rif ə'mai sən), *n.* any of a group of substances which are the fermentation products of a fungus, *Streptomyces mediterranei*, isolated from the soil in the pine forests of southern France. Several rifamycins and their derivatives have shown antimicrobial and antiviral properties.

Another line of investigation is to take the purified enzyme and use it as a screen for agents that will inhibit the RNA-dependent DNA polymerase, but leave the normal DNA-dependent DNA polymerase alone. Already, the antibiotic rifamycin and its analogues are looking promising in this connection, and such drugs may form the basis of a possible therapy for leukaemia. *New Scientist, Nov. 12, 1970, p 313*

[from *rifa-* of unknown origin + -*mycin* a fungus product (from Greek *mýkēs* fungus)]

rift zone, *Plate Tectonics.* a zone in which a rift or fracture occurs when the large plates of the earth's crust move away from one another.

The location of the world's 529 known active volcanoes, relative to this model of mountain-building, is instructive because ... 72 occur along rift zones between separating plates. Because much of the rift zone is in deep ocean water, many active, yet hidden, volcanoes await discovery. *Robert W. Decker, "The Anatomy of a Volcano," 1971 Britannica Yearbook of Science and the Future, 1970, p 44*

In an entire separate study, the Leg 16 scientists drilled at five sites about midway between Hawaii and Central America. The discovery that metal deposits were forming in a rift zone in the Red Sea had led them to examine other rift zones, such as the East Pacific Rise, for further evidence of the nature and distribution of ore bodies. *Science News, April 24, 1971, p 279*

right, *adv.* **right on,** *U.S. Slang.* a phrase or exclamation used to show full agreement or approval and generally meaning "absolutely right," "perfectly true," "100% correct."

The phrase "Right on," which originated with the Black Panther Party, is (or was) an expression of affirmation on the revolutionary left, as in this colloquy:
Speaker: Imperialism must be smashed!
Audience: Right on!
"The Talk of the Town," The New Yorker, Feb. 7, 1970, p 21

Sir: Your "Catholic Exodus" article was right on. We especially concur with the comments you published concerning secular employment. *Michael Donahoe and Earl Blue, in a Letter to the Editor, Time, March 16, 1970, p 4*

right-on, *adj. U.S. Slang.* being right on; absolutely correct, true, or trustworthy.

William Homans Jr. was sent to Viet Nam two months ago to defend Pfc. Peterson. In Boston, Homans is known as a "right-on lawyer" — he defends blacks, war protesters and poor people. *Time, Oct. 19, 1970, p 45*

The "mass man" of sociological terminology is the "right-on man" of black slang, gliding smoothly and simplistically, and perhaps more comfortably, over questionable assumptions, and reducing himself to a cliché in the process. *Ralph Ellison and James Alan McPherson, "Invisible Man," The Atlantic, Dec. 1970, p 47*

Delighted and amazed that these nice, all-American kids had produced and approved so "right on" a document with such overwhelming enthusiasm, I wandered out of the plenary and located the swimming pool. They rented me a suit for fifteen cents, and soon I got into a rap with a tenth grader in a bikini. She asked me, "Do you like Spañada?" *Don Mitchell, "Letter from a Cold Place," Harper's, Aug. 1971, p 26*

right-to-work, *adj. U.S.* of or relating to the right of a worker to get or keep a job whether he belongs or does not belong to a labor union.

You might have then seen the virtue of the right-to-work policy.... What would have been gained... if you sanctioned a system by which this honest and qualified ex-con were compelled to join a union against his will as the price of holding his new-found job? *James J. Kilpatrick, Richmond, Va., in a Letter to the Editor, Harper's, March 1967, p 8*

The Indiana legislature repealed its "right to work" law, reducing the number of states with such legislation to 19. *Daniel Elazar, "Developments in the States in 1965: State Programs and Nationwide Concerns: Labor," Britannica Book of the Year 1966, p 8*

righty, *n. British.* a conservative or reactionary; right-winger. *Also used attributively.*

This sounds a bit like his Righty chum, Bernard Levin, but not like any Lefty I know.... Lefties don't demonstrate against the Soviet Union.... London demonstrators against the Soviet Union are commonly Lefties.... *D. A. N. Jones, "Books: Bumbling," Review of "What Became of Jane Austen?" by Kingsley Amis, The Manchester Guardian Weekly, Nov. 28, 1970, p 19*

...England's thin red line of intellectual royalists is being overrun by "progressive" reformers who deliberately sabotage old-fashioned academic virtues.... The Manchester Guardian called them a "tightly knit bunch of righties." *"Education Abroad," Time, Oct. 31, 1969, p 53*

▶ See the note under LEFTIST.

ring, *n.* **hold the ring,** to stand by a conflict without interfering (originally used in the literal sense of being part of a ring formed by onlookers at a fight).

At one point he [Sir Ian Freeland] was asked by Alan Hart: "Is there a limit to the amount of time the Army can reasonably be expected to stay here [in Ulster] holding the ring, if the humans involved here are not going to solve their own problems?" *David Wood, The Times (London), April 8, 1970, p 1*

Does the phrase "Asians helping Asians," or, as critics put it, "Asians fighting Asians," mean that the United States will provide everything but the front-line manpower, or that it will step back and help hold the ring, or that it will become a mere spectator? *Flora Lewis, "Reports: The Nixon Doctrine," The Atlantic, Nov. 1970, p 6*

The Army is there primarily to prevent communal car-

nage, secondly to defeat an armed attack upon the state by a minority of a minority, and thirdly to hold the ring while statesmen make a further attempt to find a political framework that will accommodate in peace the two historic communities in the north of Ireland. *"Why the Army is There," The Times (London), Feb. 3, 1972, p 15*

ring of fire, a belt of volcanoes surrounding the Pacific Ocean and causing violent seismic activity.

More than 80% of known active volcanoes occur on the rim of the Pacific Ocean, "the ring of fire," and in the belt from the Mediterranean Sea to Indonesia. *Robert W. Decker, "Volcano," The McGraw-Hill Yearbook of Science and Technology 1971, p 430*

ring-pull, *adj.* having a scored metal top that comes off in one piece by pulling at a small ring attached to it. Compare POP-TOP, ZIP-TOP.

Easy opening devices are undergoing considerable development — and ring-pull and zip-top cans are already available. *Digby Brindle-Wood-Williams, The Times (London), Feb. 16, 1970, p III*

ring vaccination, the vaccination of all persons connected with a case of smallpox or similar contagious disease.

The Ministry said yesterday: "Ring vaccination would be used only with the approval of Ministers and as an extreme emergency measure in a very serious disease situation." *The Times (London), March 12, 1970, p 2*

ringway, *n. British.* a circular road or highway; a beltway.

He says the G.L.C. [Greater London Council] should not have presented a plan that in law could not be approved because it included land for compulsory acquisition more than 10 years after its possible approval date. He adds that the plan omits other land which would be required for ringways. *"London Plan Costs Raised with Auditor," The Times (London), Nov. 27, 1970, p 3*

We tend to regard the fume-laden canyons of New York, ... and the engulfing concrete of flyovers and ringways as things that will inevitably come to this country. *Keith Spence, New Scientist, June 18, 1970, p 591*

rin·ky-dink ('riŋ ki:ˌdiŋk), *U.S. Slang.* —*adj.* old-fashioned or trite, often in a gaudy or cheap way.

We'd all rattle along for a mile or so in a rinky-dink parade of Pied Piper [the ice cream company] trucks, before each of us in turn, ringing his bells in salute, peeled off and headed out alone for his own territory. *Thomas Meehan, "The Pied Piper," The New Yorker, July 4, 1970, p 25*

But then came the new rocks — and the Supremes [a singing group] suddenly sounded a little rinky dink. Kind of nice, maybe, but definitely old-fashioned. *Time, Aug. 17, 1970, p 30*

—*n.* someone or something that is old-fashioned or trite, often in a cheap way.

If the Senate Majority Leader's blood brother couldn't get through, how was a rinky-dink to make connections? *Larry L. King, "Washington Report," Harper's, April 1970, p 38*

[probably originally formed in imitation of the sound of banjo music formerly played at parades. Compare RICKY-TICK.]

rip, *v.t., v.i. Usually,* **rip off,** *U.S. Slang.* to steal (from someone); rob, loot, or exploit.

A girl who was recording the proceedings with a portable television camera stood up and shouted, "We're sitting here, and Chemical Bank is gloating about how they're going to rip us off! Well, we're going to go into the streets and rip *you* off!" *"The Talk of the Town," The New Yorker, July 18, 1970, p 21*

For extra, unanticipated personal needs, he "rips off"—or steals. Some of those who take jobs in department stores or markets steal what they can.... Some who work in restaurants or drugstores let their friends in to eat or rip what they need. *"Modern Living: How Radicals Make Money," Time, June 22, 1970, p 52*

ripoff, *n. U.S. Slang.* **1** an act or result of ripping off; a theft, robbery, or exploitation.

So-Ho is an abbreviation of the city planning commission's original title for the place—"South Houston Industrial District." ... The rate of street crime is very low—because, some artists maintain, the district overlaps into Little Italy, and the Mafia does not like petty rip-offs in its own backyard. *"Art: The Last Studios," Time, July 5, 1971, p 33*

We asked him why he had chosen to work in this area instead of, say, in Greenwich Village.

"The Village is a rip-off," he said. "Nothing but junkies, perverts—it's a bad scene." *"The Talk of the Town," The New Yorker, June 12, 1971, p 28*

2 one that rips off.

"Who do you have on Haight Street today?" he [a San Francisco dope peddler] said disgustedly.... "You have burn artists (fraudulent dope peddlers), rip-offs (thieves), and snitchers (police spies)." *Adam Raphael, The Manchester Guardian Weekly, May 2, 1970, p 16*

risk, *n.* **at risk,** *British.* **1** in danger; imperiled.

Mr. Lynch declared ... "The unity we seek is not something forced but a free and genuine union of those living in Ireland based on mutual respect and tolerance." The use of force as an instrument of unification he explicitly abjured. The dismissal of two senior ministers and the resignation of a third in the small hours of yesterday morning shows that that policy is now at risk. *"A Danger to Ireland," The Times (London), May 7, 1970, p 13*

2 running the risk of becoming pregnant, especially despite the use of contraceptive measures.

There must be at least 10 million married women "at risk" in this country, and from this, I infer that however they try not to conceive, they will produce an average of two million babies a year. Since the maximum we have ever had in this country is not more than 800,000, and since many of the women will be working hard to produce in any event, I think that something must have gone sadly wrong. *Vivian Bowden, in a Letter to the Editor, New Scientist, May 25, 1967, p 492*

riveting, *adj.* stunning; spellbinding; enthralling.

Ladies disembark here and idle a few days in Ouranopolis, where the sands are endless and the sunsets are riveting.... *Geoffrey Moorhouse, "Zorba's Place," The Manchester Guardian Weekly, Nov. 7, 1970, p 15*

... am I going too fast for you? Well, *nil desperandum,* because now comes the riveting part. *S. J. Perelman, "The Pen is Mightier—and Also Pricier," The New Yorker, Dec. 26, 1970, p 21*

RNAase (ˌɑrˌen'eiˌeis), or **RNase** (ˌɑrˌen'eis), *n.* an enzyme that breaks down ribonucleic acid in cells.

The RNA-ase synthesized in 1968 is found naturally in cattle, not human beings, but knowing about it may point the way to a better understanding of human cell growth and cancer. *James S. Sweet, "Molecular Biology: Biochemistry," 1970 Britannica Yearbook of Science and the Future, 1969, p 294*

In bacterial extracts these enzymes of course readily mimic the activity of an RNA replicase and as a further hazard to this type of investigation the same extracts contain degradative enzymes (RNases) which will attack the newly synthesized RNA. *I. B. Holland, New Scientist, Oct. 7, 1965, p 14*

[from *RNA* (ribonucleic acid) + *-ase* enzyme]

RNA pol·y·me·rase (ˈpɑl i məˌreis), an enzyme that acts upon DNA to synthesize ribonucleic acid. Also called REPLICASE. Compare DNA POLYMERASE.

... only one enzyme capable of catalyzing the synthesis of RNA has been isolated. Scientists have wondered how this one enzyme, RNA polymerase, could catalyze the synthesis of such differing RNA molecules. *Earl A. Evans, "Biochemistry," The World Book Science Annual 1969, p 269*

roadcraft, *n. British.* knowledge or ability in driving a car; driving skills.

Visitors were asked to complete a 35 question form giving information about the roadcraft, temperament, habits, and safety of the car drivers with whom they most frequently travel. *Julian Mounter, The Times (London), Oct. 29, 1970, p 21*

Seeing that the car looms so large in the life of man, woman and child, it is ridiculous how little instruction in roadcraft is given at school.... *New Scientist, Jan. 18, 1968, p 147*

ro·bot·ics (rouˈbɑt iks), *n.* the science or technology that deals with robots.

Bionics is related to robotics—the design of robots, or machines that resemble men or animals or that perform some of their functions. *Morley R. Kare, "Bionics: Simulating the Functions of Living Things," Encyclopedia Science Supplement (Grolier) 1970, p 115*

Significant technological advances in the field of "robotics"—the use of robots in the field of industrial automation—were announced yesterday by Hawker Siddeley Dynamics. *Anthony Rowley, The Times (London), Nov. 1, 1968, p 23*

To me, the applied science of manufacturing robots, of designing them, of studying them, was 'robotics'.... In fact, I was sure it was an existing word. Recently, however, it was pointed out to me that 'robotics' does not appear in any edition of Webster's Unabridged Dictionary so I suppose I invented the word. *Isaac Asimov, "The Perfect Machine," Science Journal, Oct. 1968, p 115*

ro·bot·o·mor·phic (ˌrou bɑt əˈmɔr fik), *adj.* modeled on the behavior of robots.

You say I overestimate the dangers of the Robotomorphic or Ratomorphic view, on everyday life, but with Pavlov's dogs, Lorenz's grey-legged geese, Morris' naked ape, each time an analogy of behaviour was taken as a homology. *Arthur Koestler, The Times (London), Dec. 17, 1970, p 15*

The targets of discontent were to be Neo-Darwinist orthodoxy in evolution and robotomorphic views of Man. *David Newth, New Scientist, Oct. 2, 1969, p 22*

rock, *n.* short for *rock 'n' roll* (a popular form of jazz with a lively two-beat rhythm). See also ACID ROCK, COUNTRY ROCK, FOLK ROCK, JAZZ ROCK, RAGA ROCK.

Now rock has its own problems, which may well prove to be more basic than those of straight music. *Tim Souster, "Rock Music," The Listener, Dec. 9, 1971, p 781*

The film's soundtrack, brief, even denies him the support of the best argument for his generation: the distinction of its music. There is hardly any rock in it at all. *Renata Adler, The New York Times, Jan. 11, 1968, p 42*

—*adj.* of or relating to rock 'n' roll.

All over Poland, Communist Party youth clubs reverberate to the latest rock sounds. To be sure, the scene in Cracow is vastly different from the one in California.... *Time, Nov. 16, 1970, p 35*

The words by Gerome Ragni and James Rado and the music by Galt MacDermot demonstrate that a rock score can have both variety and vitality, and that racial conflicts, anti-war sentiment, and even the generation gap can be mirrored in music. *Herbert Kupferberg, "Music: Record Reviews: Hair—An American Tribal Love-Rock Musical," The Atlantic, Feb. 1968, p 133*

rock·a·bil·ly ('rak ə‚bil i:), *n.* rock 'n' roll with hill-billy music themes. *Also used attributively.*

But [Charlie] Gillett is at his frequent best talking about five basic styles that finally merged into rock: Northern Band, New Orleans dance blues, rockabilly from Memphis, Chicago rhythm and blues and vocal group rock. *Time, Sept. 28, 1970, p 47*

Rockabilly artists such as Elvis Presley (who combined country and R & B) inspired digressions in pop. *Ellen Sander, Saturday Review, Oct. 26, 1969, p 91*

Bob Dylan, seemingly unable to avoid dramatic excitement, did three songs in electric rockabilly arrangements of disarming originality with his five-man band. *Robert Shelton, The New York Times, Jan. 22, 1968, p 31*

[from *rock* (rock 'n' roll) + -*a*- (as in *rock-a-bye* or *rockaway*) + hill*billy*]

rocket astronomy, the collection of astronomical data from photographs, etc., taken at high altitude through instruments carried in a rocket.

...the emphasis is on the more modern approach which has grown up over the past 10 years as balloon and rocket astronomy have aided observations. . . . *John Gribbin, Review of "Stellar Atmospheres" by Dimitri Mihalas, New Scientist and Science Journal, March 18, 1971, p 636*

rocketdrome, *n.* an airport for rockets.

A model of a city and its rocketdrome in the year 2017 as imagined by three young Russian technicians. *The Times (London), May 27, 1970, p 7*

[from *rocket* + aero*drome*]

ro·la·mite ('rou lə‚mait), *n.* a mechanical device consisting of a thin, flexible S-shaped band looped around two or more rollers so that the rollers turn without any sliding friction.

The device, christened "Rolamite," is a product of the search for suspension systems to be used in subminiature components of nuclear weapons. Because the roller-and-spring assembly does not require precision finishing, it can be produced in miniature sizes at relatively low cost. *Scientific American, Dec. 1967, p 58*

Wide publicity was accorded a new mechanical device announced in October by the Atomic Energy Commission's (AEC) Sandia Corporation at Albuquerque, N. Mex. Called rolamite, this device virtually abolishes friction when used as a bearing in applications not involving large loading; pressures of less than 3,000 pounds per square inch. *James A. Pearre, "Invention: Rolamite," The 1968 World Book Year Book, p 377*

The major advantage of the rolamite as compared with conventional ball and roller bearings is that it is almost frictionless because the rollers are tightly locked into the S-curves, prohibiting their sliding....

Among the many applications envisioned for the rolamite are components in light switches, door hinges, pumps, pistons, and thermostats. *"Engineering," Britannica Book of the Year 1969, p 306*

[coined by its inventor, Donald F. Wilkes, an American engineer, from *rol*ler + -*amite* (arbitrary ending, perhaps as in *dynamite*)]

rollbar, *n.* a steel bar built into the roof of a car to protect the heads of passengers if the car should overturn.

Chrysler equipped its 1970 Barracuda and Challenger with hidden "rollover structures" to protect occupants from crushed car tops. It was the first time that rollbars were designed into U.S. production cars. *Jim Dunne, "Automobiles: Product Developments," The 1970 Compton Yearbook, p 139*

If the designs work out, construction of a prototype car, incorporating such safety features as a rear-view periscope to eliminate "blind spots" and built-in roll bars, could start within a year, Mr. Rockefeller said. *The New York Times, Sept. 20, 1966, p 41*

As vehicles become safer they become closer in construction to the vehicles which this system [new transportation system with a car that can be slung from a monorail] would require. Roll-bar construction will be needed to allow the vehicle to be supported from its roof. *G. W. Wells, New Scientist, Jan. 2, 1969, p 21*

roll-neck, *adj.* having a long turtleneck collar made to be rolled over.

The evening began in high spirits. Peter Maxwell Davies leapt on to the stage, this time in a turquoise roll-neck pullover.... *Desmond Shawe-Taylor, The Sunday Times (London), April 27, 1969, p 58*

But I longed to "style" the collection for 1972, to snatch off the pussycat bows and the hats and the rollneck "safe" blouses with their banal sleeves. *Prudence Glynn, "The Life and Hard Times of British Couture," The Times (London), Jan. 18, 1972, p 6*

roll-on, *adj.* **1** applied on the skin by a bottle or container fitted with a plastic roller that conveys the application without letting it spill or pour out. The principle is the same as that used to feed ink in a ball-point pen.

Among Bristol-Myers' contributions to American civilization: the first non-peroxide hair coloring (Born Blonde), the first roll-on deodorant (Ban). *Time, Feb. 12, 1965, p 60*

There is a roll-on night cream for breaking eyelashes, a regular problem for women who frequently add an extra flutter to what nature grew them. *Prudence Glynn, The Times (London), March 10, 1970, p 15*

2 that is equipped to carry cargo or freight loaded in trucks or truck trailers that are driven aboard.

. . . at the same time owners are branching out into new ship types: giant tankers and bulk carriers, chemical and liquid gas carriers, container and roll-on ships. *Michael Baily, The Times (London), April 13, 1970, p 5*

rollout, *n.* **1** *U.S. Football.* play in which a quarterback runs out of the area formed by blockers before passing.

The Cornellian had the wrong style as back-up man to Y. A. Tittle when he last was with the Giants. Old Yat was a pocket passer. Wood's preference was the roll-out. *Arthur Daley, The New York Times, Aug. 20, 1968, p 45*

Duhon . . . was a left-handed quarterback at Tulane where he set records as a scrambling roll-out runner-passer for three years. *William N. Wallace, The New York Times, Sept. 6, 1968, p 51*

2 the part of a landing after touchdown when an airplane slows down on the runway before it taxis to the unloading ramp.

If landings in Category III are adopted, however, the approach, flare decrab, touchdown and possibly rollout will be performed automatically, perhaps with the pilot monitoring the events visually on electronic devices. *Frank B. Brady, Scientific American, March 1964, p 33*

But then, two weeks following the first multiple flame-out, that same plane was loaded with 128 passengers headed for Mexico City. It landed safely. But no sooner was it on the ground—still on rollout—than all four engines quit again! *Paul Harvey, Graphic, Nov. 12, 1970, p 3*

[from the verb phrase *roll out*]

ro-ro ship ('rou,rou), a freight ship that can carry loaded trucks, trailers, or other vehicles which drive on it at one port and drive off of it at another.

. . . ro-ro ships have made possible enormous savings in distribution costs for those willing and able to profit from them. *Michael Baily, The Times (London), May 5, 1970, p I*

"Since the Channel Tunnel Study Group reported in 1964 ro-ro ships and containerization have caused sea freight rates to fall by about 40 per cent". *R. B. Wickenden, quoted by Bill Gunston, Science Journal, March 1969, p 8*

[from *roll-on roll-off ship*]

rose, *n.* **come up roses,** to come out perfect.

Circa 1964-65, those *anni mirabiles* of the Great Society, everything came up roses. An obedient Congress delivered to Lyndon Johnson Medicare, a variety of educational programs, regional health centers, Model Cities, rent supplements, and even, in the shape of the Office of Economic Opportunity, ratification of the President's "unconditional" war upon poverty. *Robert Lekachman, "Money in America," Harper's, Aug. 1970, p 32*

. . . if some real disaster hit us (eloping spouse, impotence, frigidity, bankruptcy, heart attack) we would have to soldier on, pretending that everything in the column was coming up roses. *Alan Brien, The Times (London), Dec. 12, 1969, p 24*

rotovate, *v.t. British.* to break up or till (the soil) with a rotovator.

Not until the light soil was really dry in late April was the area rotovated twice, and set with sprouted seed. *Leonard Amey, The Times (London), Dec. 7, 1970, p 6*

Would it not be better, from the point of view of soil status, to return the straw to the land, either by ploughing or rotavating it in, or (where feasible) going through the laborious business of making and applying farmyard manure? *"Science in British Industry," New Scientist, June 20, 1963, p 661*

[back formation from *rotovator*, earlier *rotavator*]

rotovator, *n. British.* a power-driven tool with rotating blades for breaking up or tilling the soil.

Mechanical rotovators and tillers will turn over the soil and applications of balanced fertilisers or composts will ensure fertility. *Lanning Roper, The Sunday Times (London), March 17, 1968, p 16*

This meant that if I worked all this into the top four inches with a rotovator I should get good results, and I did. *"Arthur Hollins Tells the Story of his Organic Farm," The Listener, Dec. 2, 1971, p 750*

[alteration of earlier *rotavator*, from *rota*ry culti*vator*]

round, *v.t., v.i.* **round down** (or **up**), to convert (currency) to the lower (or higher) value of the nearest round number.

The Decimal Currency Board have made some clear recommendations by which the new halfpenny conversion table will enable prices sometimes to be rounded down, although some may be rounded up. *The Times (London), Feb. 18, 1970, p 4*

. . . the confusions and ambiguities of the situation would give shopkeepers an irresistible chance to arrange things so that the rounding would usually be up, not down. *John Brooks, "Our Far-Flung Correspondents: By Tens," The New Yorker, Nov. 21, 1970, p 192*

rou·ti·nier (,ru: ti:'nyei), *n.* a rigidly orthodox, conventional orchestra conductor, usually considered unoriginal and, therefore, dull.

Everything was first-rate with the exception of . . . the conductor Boris Khaikin, a tired routinier. *Charles Osborne, The Manchester Guardian Weekly, Jan. 10, 1970, p 21*

Heger, an experienced man, conducts with a firm grip on the music but in the fashion of a *routinier*, making little effort to achieve the dynamic scheme of the opera, letting the orchestra (a good one) play in a competent rather than inspired manner. *"Music in the Round," Harper's, April 1970, p 117*

[from French, a very conservative person, a stick-in-the-mud]

rover, *n.* short for LUNAR ROVER.

The first rover is scheduled to take four trips of up to 32 km each with travel limited to 4.8 km radius from the landing site. *Science Journal, Jan. 1970, p 16*

rRNA, abbreviation of RIBOSOMAL RNA.

Different portions of DNA also must signal the starting and stopping points of transcriptions that produce RNA's of different types—messenger RNA (mRNA), transfer RNA (tRNA), and ribosomal RNA (rRNA)—which are used in the translation process. *Irwin H. Hershkowitz, "Genetics," The Americana Annual 1967, p 300*

Then virtually everyone still believed that the templates were the RNA molecules (rRNA) found in the small cellular particles called ribosomes. *James D. Watson, New Scientist, Nov. 24, 1966, p 425*

r-t-w, abbreviation of *ready-to-wear* (clothes).

Last week and this week Paris is showing its ready-to-wear collections. . . . A collection will be shown in February to private customers only, and thereafter in April and October . . . the two collections will be shown together. This makes sound sense, for both collections will have the same theme, neither will trail the other, and disasters like the midi which can happen if the r-t-w must anticipate couture by three months, should be avoided. *Ernestine Carter, "Fashion Plate," The Sunday Times (London), Oct. 24, 1971, p 37*

The r-t-w suits will be around 40 gns. *Antony King-Deacon, The Times (London), May 29, 1970, p 8*

ruck, *v.i. British.* to press aggressively for possession of the ball in rugby, especially as a group of forwards on a team.

In this respect their captain, Matthews, set an example with his rucking and gained them some valuable balls. *The Sunday Times (London), Oct. 2, 1966, p 20*

The forwards, as against England, took a long time to work up to anything like effective scrummaging and rucking. *The Times (London), Feb. 24, 1964, p 3*

Yet he rucks with the best, and one's memory will long cherish the sight of him defying three Harlequin forwards who were trying to wrest the ball from him. *Michael Green, The Sunday Times (London), Feb. 25, 1968, p 23*

ruff puff or **Ruff Puff,** *U.S. Military Slang.* a member of the South Vietnamese Regional Forces and Popular Forces, consisting of locally recruited militiamen responsible for defending their home districts.

"Vietnamisation;" that is the process by which American units progressively hand over combat responsibilities to the ARVN's and train the "ruff puffs" (regional and popular forces) to maintain the pacification programme. *David Fairhall, The Manchester Guardian Weekly, May 9, 1970, p 3*

[from the pronunciation of *RF, PF,* abbreviation of *Regional Forces, Popular Forces,* as words]

run-up, *n. British.* a period leading up to some event; prelude.

In the run-up to the Greater London Council elections, the capital may show few signs of urban malaise to the visitor, in town to concentrate on the tourist or business merry-go-round. *Judy Hillman, The Manchester Guardian Weekly, April 4, 1970, p 9*

The Petit Palais show offers, also, invaluable evidence in its drawing section of the ways in which Picasso manoeuvred during the crucial run-up to the "Demoiselles d'Avignon." *John Russell, The Sunday Times (London), Nov. 20, 1966, p 48*

[from the term used in the long jump (broad jump) for the preliminary run before the jump]

rurp, *n.* a type of piton shaped somewhat like a picture hook. See the quotations for details.

Scott uses a number of American rurps—their full name is "Realised Ultimate Reality Pitons"—whose blades are only 9 3/4 inches long. *Peter Gillman, The Sunday Times (London), June 15, 1969, p 22*

Bur rurps and power drills and expansion bolts are pretty much out of fashion in Llanberis these days. *Simon Winchester, "Drilling the Mountains," The Manchester Guardian Weekly, July 31, 1971, p 14*

ruth·er·ford·i·um (ˌrəð ər'fɔr di: əm), *n.* one of the proposed names for ELEMENT 104.

Russian physicists had reported... that they had succeeded in synthesizing element 104, which they named kurchatovium in honor of the physicist I. V. Kurchatov. The Berkeley group then synthesized element 104 by a different method and challenged the Russian finding, naming their discovery rutherfordium in honor of the British physicist Lord Rutherford. *Scientific American, June 1970, p 49*

RV, abbreviation of *reentry vehicle* (a spacecraft, missile, or any part of either that reenters the earth's atmosphere after completing its trajectory).

... defensive missiles with thermonuclear warheads can attack incoming reentry vehicles (RV's) in three general ways: with neutrons, X rays and blast, all products of a thermonuclear explosion. *Scientific American, Feb. 1968, p 50*

ry·a ('ri: ə), *n.* **1** a colorful handwoven rug with a deep pile, originally made by Scandinavian peasants for use chiefly as bed covers and wraps.

He sees the possibility of selling rya or Scandinavian-type rugs here.... *The New York Times, Jan. 17, 1966, p 28*

Mrs. Puotila's background in rug weaving is apparent in the linens she creates, for the colors she uses are as rich as those in a Finnish rya rug. *The New York Times, June 4, 1963, p 42*

2 the pattern or weave characteristic of rya rugs.

Now you do it. One simple stitch makes our pre-started rya hangings, rugs or cushions. Kits imported from Sweden.... *Advertisement by Skön Rug Craft in House Beautiful, March 1972, p 141*

[from Swedish, rug]

ry·o·kan (ri:'ou kɑːn), *n. sing.* or *pl.* a Japanese hotel or inn, especially one operated in a traditional style.

The Osaka area is heavily booked and even the tiny ryokan, or country inns, are doing good business. *Time, March 23, 1970, p 32*

Inexpensive hotels are in short supply in Japan, but the ryokan—the Japanese-style hotels—have recently been improved so that they are playing a far bigger part in accommodating tourists. *Arthur Reed, The Times (London), June 17, 1970, p XII*

The most charming hotel I ever stayed at was a Japanese ryokan in the mountain spa of Kinugawa north of Tokyo. Perched on the lip of a rustling gorge, fashioned from native rock, polished tree trunks and rice matting, fed by hot sulphur water that had been diverted into flower-fringed indoor pools of great beauty and cunning shape, this little inn imparted a feeling of serenity, unknown in a Western environment. *Pierre Berton, Maclean's, March 9, 1963, p 37*

[from Japanese]

S

Sa·bah·an (sə'bɑ: hən), *adj.* of or relating to Sabah, the former British North Borneo.

Some observers in west Malaysia believe that if the Sabah missions were to become fully Sabahan organizations the present campaign would come to an end. "We do not want people in Malaysia whose loyalty lies with Rome," a leading Malay said. *"Sabah Leaders Fear a Christian Coalition," The Times (London), Dec. 30, 1970, p 5*

—*n.* a native of Sabah.

Malaysia and the Philippines are squabbling over Sabah, a small state in Borneo that now belongs to Malaysia but is claimed by the Philippines.... Now, diplomatic contacts are minimal. Largely overlooked in the imbroglio are the 600,000 Sabahans themselves, who, including the Moslem minority which has considerable cultural and economic influence in Sabah, would clearly prefer to stay in Malaysia. *"The World: Southeast Asia," Time, Nov. 15, 1968, p 45*

sa·do- ('sei dou- *or* 'sæd ou-), a combining form meaning "sadistic" or "involving sadism."

sado-erotic, *adj.:* We certainly get plenty for our money: a kind of all-senses collage assembled from bits of girlie photos, tropical stills, and mock-ups of sado-erotic temple carvings.... *Norman Shrapnel, The Manchester Guardian Weekly, April 11, 1970, p 19*

sado-Fascist, *adj.:* On trial at Chester last April were Ian Brady ... and Esther Myra Hindley.... They were charged with slowly killing a ten-year-old girl and two boys.... "Their interests," she says of Brady and Hindley, "were sado-masochistic, titillatory and sado-Fascist, and in the bookshops they found practically all the pabulum they needed." *"Books," Review of "On Iniquity" by Pamela Hansford Johnson, Time, April 7, 1967, p E3*

sado-sexuality, *n.:* It was the *One Million Years B.C.* poster of a barely wolf-skinned Raquel Welch ... that led to her wider exposure. What is Hammer [Films] really promoting: Sado-sexuality? Occultism? "Pure entertainment," insists Sir James [Carreras]. *"Rise of the House of Hammer," Time, Dec. 6, 1971, p 33*

sado-snobbism, *n.:* Client prints paperbacks for all tastes from (I think) the nasty vicarious sado-snobbism of poor FLEMING to TOLSTOY, IBSEN and old FYODOR DOSTOYEVSKY now, thank God, seeping into the Supermarkets. *Observer, Aug. 30, 1964, p 28*

[abstracted from *sadomasochism*, a term used in psychoanalysis for a combination of sadism and masochism, coined in the 1920's]

sailboard, *n.* a very light sailboat with one mast, a triangular sail, and a flat hull, usually without a cockpit.

Bored with scorching up and down in outboards, people turn them in on all-purpose dinghies and the unsinkable fibre-glass sailboards that swarm like butterflies on any

lake warm enough to make dumping tolerable. *Philip Freen, "Next Best To Being a Millionaire: Live Like One —on a Boat," Maclean's, July 24, 1965, p 31*

The sailboard and other small sailboats are luring many a landlubber off the golf course and onto the water. *The New York Times, Feb. 9, 1968, p 31*

sa·lon·ist (sə'lɑn ist), *n.* another word for SALONNARD.

George Plimpton, the son of Francis T. P. and probably the best-known WASP dealer in living culture, operates like a Paris salonist among Interesting People.... *Peter Schrag, "The Decline of the Wasp," Harper's, April 1970, p 89*

sa·lon·nard (sə'lɑn ɑrd), *n.* a person who frequents salons or circles of fashionable people. *Also used attributively.* Also called SALONIST.

The author feels the need to enliven his salonnard gossip column with awful attempts at jocularity and whimsicality. *Richard Cobb, "Books: Anti-history," Review of "The Anti-Philosophers: A Study of the Philosophes in Eighteenth Century France" by R. J. White, The Manchester Guardian Weekly, Feb. 14, 1970, p 18*

[from French]

SALT (sɔːlt), *n.* acronym for *Strategic Arms Limitation Talks*, a round of talks between representatives of the Soviet Union and the United States on the subject of limiting the production of strategic nuclear weapons in both countries, begun in Helsinki, Finland, on November 17, 1969. *Often used attributively.*

He [Melvin Laird, U.S. Secretary of Defense] is now pinning his hopes for a breakthrough on an agreement at the SALT talks. But this would have to come within 12 to 18 months because the US government must then take decisions on whether or not to go ahead with a new ballistic-missile submarine programme, an advanced strategic bomber, and other, more sophisticated, weapons systems. *New Scientist, July 2, 1970, p 4*

With a new session of SALT negotiations scheduled to open this month in Vienna, the committee evidently thinks there is a chance to prevent a major new escalation of the arms race. *"Science and the Citizen," Scientific American, March 1971, p 44*

salvage archaeology, the hasty excavation of sites about to be destroyed by construction projects, flooding, etc., in order to salvage archaeological remains.

These dams, and the lakes that form behind them, are spurring the archaeologists in a continuing race with the rising waters. "Salvage archaeology" became a way of life for anthropologists in Washington after Grand Coulee Dam created Roosevelt Lake more than 20 years ago. *Gerald H. Grosso, "Cave Life on the Palouse," Encyclopedia Science Supplement (Grolier) 1967, p 30*

This is an area where the Danube narrows to run through a steep-walled canyon on its way to the Iron Gates; the site was discovered in the course of salvage archaeology in an area that will soon be flooded by a hydroelectric project. *Scientific American, April 1968, p 50*

SAM (sæm), *n.* acronym for *surface-to-air missile*, a guided missile launched from the ground or from shipboard to intercept and destroy a flying aircraft or missile.

In the case of the SAMs, Assistant Defense Secretary McNaughton thought the Russians would simply emplace the anti-aircraft missiles and not use them, as they did. *Blair Clark; "[General William C.] Westmoreland Appraised: Questions and Answers," Harper's, Nov. 1970, p 101*

sam·iz·dat (ˌsɑːm izˈdɑːt), *n.* **1** the practice of writers in the Soviet Union of secretly publishing and distributing literature banned by the government; the Soviet underground press.

By *samizdat*, Russians endlessly retype and clandestinely circulate the work of such banned writers as Alexander Solzhenitsyn. *Time, Sept. 7, 1970, p 25*

Samizdat is the hand-to-hand distribution of manuscripts, typed or photographed, of works rejected by Soviet printing houses. *John L. Hess, "Solzhenitsyn's Novel Published in Paris, Defying Soviet Censor," The New York Times, June 12, 1971, p 1*

2 the literature or writings produced by this underground press.

... the authorities may be trying to break up the system of *samizdat*—of literature published in typescript which circulates privately and gives news of the proceedings of the secret police. *Maurice Latey, "Foreign News: Soviet Scientists," The Listener, Oct. 15, 1970, p 506*

In an "Epilogue to the Russian Edition Abroad," Mr. Solzhenitsyn writes:

"This book cannot be published now in our country except in samizdat because of censorship." *John L. Hess, "Solzhenitsyn's Novel Published In Paris, Defying Soviet Censor," The New York Times, June 12, 1971, p 1*

[from Russian *samizdat*, from *sam* self + *izdat-* (el'stvo) publishing, probably coined as a pun on *Gosizdat* the State Publishing House]

S & M, abbreviation of *Sadist and Masochist.*

... we just happened to be in—um, one of those bookstores on Polk Street in San Francisco that also sell 8-mm art movies, feelthy love beads, a few leather items, and posters "as you like them," and that shelve their books according to such classifications as "Homosexual," "Lesbian," "Hetero," "S & M," etc. *Herbert Gold, "The End of Pornography," Saturday Review, Oct. 31, 1970, p 25*

sand sink, a method of removing oil spilled at sea by spraying the oil with a mixture of chemically treated sand and water which sticks to the oil and causes it to sink to the bottom.

According to all the authorities concerned with the test, the Shell "sand sink" method is eminently suitable for coping with very large oil pollution at sea. *New Scientist, June 11, 1970, p 529*

sandwich bar, a restaurant specializing in sandwiches, usually served at a counter.

With him in the dock was...John Leonard Knight, aged 33, sandwich bar proprietor, of Peaketon Avenue, Redbridge, Essex, and William John Hickson, aged 27, company director, of Petersfield Close, Upper Edmonton.... *The Times (London), Nov. 25, 1970, p 4*

sandwicheria, *n.* another name for SANDWICH BAR.

Restaurants, snack bars, cafés, cake shops and 'sandwicherias' are crowded. *Noel Clark, The Listener, April 11, 1968, p 460*

[from *sandwich* + *-eria*, as in *cafeteria*]

sand yacht, a three-wheeled vehicle with a mast and small sails, a steering wheel, and a driver's seat, used for racing with the wind on a beach or other sandy area. Also called LAND YACHT.

The first attempt to cross the Sahara by sand yacht ended in success today when eight of the fragile craft arrived at the finish line.... *The New York Times, March 16, 1967, p 62*

sand yachting, the sport of racing with a sand yacht.

Sand yachting is like gokarting—it allows the adult to fulfil his childhood dreams without him being branded as the little boy who never grew up. *Ellsworth Jones, The Sunday Times (London), Jan. 18, 1970, p 63*

sand yachtsman, a person who engages in sand yachting.

Forty sand yachtsmen from six countries had a disappointing day at St. Annes, Lancashire, yesterday when races for the international...sand yacht championships were unable to be started. *The Sunday Times (London), May 28, 1967, p 19*

sanitationman, *n. U.S.* an employee of a municipal department in charge of collecting and disposing of household refuse; a garbage and trash collector. Compare GARBOLOGIST.

The lunch was provided by the Seventh Avenue Neighbors Association as its way of thanking men who do a notoriously thankless job.... The sanitationmen left, emptying three garbage cans on their way out. *"The Talk of the Town," The New Yorker, Aug. 15, 1970, p 21*

sanitize, *v.t.* to give a wholesome appearance to; make more palatable by removing offensive aspects or elements. Compare COSMETICIZE.

Like an aging roué looking back on halcyon days, the House Un-American Activities Committee has tried to sanitize its image. It changed its name to the House Internal Security Committee in 1969 and made abortive attempts to revive its lost vigor.... *Time, Oct. 26, 1970, p 28*

[figurative sense of *sanitize* to make sanitary by disinfecting, sterilizing, etc.]

sa·pi·ent (ˈsei piː ənt), *n.* an early member of the species *Homo sapiens*; a prehistoric man.

New finds from the Omo region, and East Rudolf, North Kenya, have put the age of both large and small australopithecines back to the 2·3 million year mark, while African sapients from the Upper Middle Pleistocene are now known from the same region. *Dan Greenberg, "Books," Review of "The Evolution of Man" by David Pilbeam, Science Journal, Dec. 1970, p 80*

[from New Latin *(Homo) sapiens* (stem *sapient-*) wise or rational (man)]

▶ The form *sapient*, as an adjective, has been used

413

in English since the 1400's, but only in the original Latin sense of "wise," "sage." As a noun, meaning a wise man or sage, *sapient* was used chiefly during the 1500's and now only appears as an archaism in Sir Walter Scott's writings.

sa·ran·gi ('sɑː rəŋ gi:), *n.* a violinlike instrument of India with 29 strings.

Particularly striking on this occasion was the music of the sarangi, a bowed instrument from Northern India. It has no frets and is not stopped with the finger-tips from above but with the fingernails from the side. *Tim Souster, The Listener, May 16, 1968, p 647*

[from Sanskrit *sāraṅgī*]

▶ This term, along with a number of other musical terms of India (*veena, tabla,* etc.), have been appearing sporadically in some English contexts (travel books, books on music, etc.) since at least the 1800's. In recent years, popular interest in Indian music has made these terms very current.

sardine, *v.t.* to pack closely or into a confined area.

Coney Islanders are not going to be surprised either if, on any hot day, some new unruliness erupts among the hundreds of thousands of people who will be sardined into the famous amusement park area and on the littered beach. *Bernard. L. Collier, The New York Times, April 22, 1968, p 36*

If you are neither rich enough to voyage beyond the Continent, nor addicted to fish and chips, package deal companions sardined next to you on the beach, and the feeling that you are loved more for your bank balance than yourself, where to go for holiday becomes an increasing problem. *Angela Neustatter, The Times (London), April 18, 1970, p VII*

[verb use of *sardine, n.,* especially from the noun's appearance in such phrases as *packed like sardines*]

satcom, *n.* a satellite communications center. Compare EARTH STATION.

The difficulty of having large and small stations working through the same transponder has been circumvented by a novel technique, now adopted for the planned NATO satcom. . . . *Science Journal, Jan. 1970, p 16*

[from *sat*ellite *com*munications]

satellite, *n.* U.S. a suburban community; suburb.

In DeKalb County, Ga., a white-collar, upper-middle-class satellite of Atlanta, the residents are constantly up in arms about such things as taxes and new apartments. *John Herbers, The New York Times, June 2, 1971, p 20*

satellite DNA, a variant form of DNA (deoxyribonucleic acid, the carrier of genetic material in the cells). See the quotations for details.

Curiouser and curiouser becomes the tale of "satellite" DNA. Discovered originally in the mouse, where it constitutes some 10 per cent of the total DNA in each cell of the animal, satellite DNA can be distinguished from the rest by its different density, and by the fact that it apparently consists of repeating base sequences—i.e., multiple copies of a given sequence repeated again and again. *New Scientist, Aug. 27, 1970, p 406*

As much as 30 per cent of the DNA in the cells of many plants and animals has satellite properties, such as density

differences, that indicate it is different from the remainder of the organisms' DNA. This strange DNA, called satellite DNA, is found in species as different from one another as mice and men. *Earl A. Evans, "Biochemistry," The World Book Science Annual 1972 (1971), p 273*

satellite town or **satellite city,** another name for NEW TOWN.

Government approval has been granted for two new satellite towns in Renfrewshire, at Erskine, on the south bank of the Clyde, and at Houston, in the upland part of the county. *The Times (London), Feb. 2, 1967, p 11*

The Bulgarians have declared that their capital city, Sofia, may grow only so much and other new building has to go to satellite cities. But satellite cities or New Towns, which are once again being mentioned here, have to be properly mixed. . . . *Anthony Bailey, "Profiles: Through the Great City," The New Yorker, Aug. 5, 1967, p 34*

satellization, *n.* the act or process of becoming a satellite or subservient to another.

Not only has Fidel [Castro] resisted satellization, but he has twisted the Cuban communist party to his own purposes—using it in 1961 to set up a new Castroite political party, and then expelling the communist party organizer from the country the following year, leaving the party, in Theodore Draper's words, "dismembered, dishonored, and discarded." *Ronald Steel, "One Millionaire and Twenty Beggars," Harper's, May 1967, p 86*

They have no choice other than to align themselves with the decisions taken by others. Association is tantamount to satellization. *Pierre Uri, The Times (London), Oct. 27, 1967, p 8*

saturation dive, a dive made by saturation diving.

It is clear, however, that the "partial pressure" of oxygen should be kept between about 150 and 400 millimeters of mercury during the at-depth phase of a long saturation dive. *Joseph B. MacInnis, "Living Under the Sea," Scientific American, March 1966, p 27*

saturation diver, a diver who uses saturation diving.

. . . the *Argyronète,* a self-propelled submersible combining a house in which saturation divers can live (under sea bottom pressure) and a conventional submarine with a crew at normal atmospheric pressure. *Science Journal, Feb. 1970, p 15*

saturation diving or **saturated diving,** a method of diving used by aquanauts to shorten the time of decompression by remaining at a given depth until the body becomes saturated with the synthetic gas mixture used for breathing.

Probably the greatest single hazard of deep dives, and especially of saturation diving, is the "bends," precipitation of bubbles of dissolved gases in the blood and tissues. *"Neon for Deep Diving," Science News, Sept, 4, 1971, p 139*

Captain [George] Bond sought to overcome this unfavourable ratio of bottom time to decompression time with a new concept known as "saturated diving". . . . The important element in saturated diving is that after six days or six months of exposure to a given depth or pressure, the diver requires a single, fixed decompression period. *Norman Chase Hanson, "The Aquanauts' Next Adventure," New Scientist, Oct. 17, 1968, p 125*

saucerman, *n.* a man from outer space; someone who travels by flying saucer.

. . . Barney and Betty Hill, a Portsmouth, N.H., couple whose "abduction" by saucermen during an auto trip was described in the fast-selling book, *The Interrupted Journey* by John Fuller. *Time, Aug. 4, 1967, p 32*

Visiting saucermen from Mars might well report back to base that all our Gods must be hard of hearing. *Patrick Ryan, "And the Last Word . . . On Muezzins," New Scientist and Science Journal, Sept. 30, 1971, p 722*

S-band, *n.* a band of ultrahigh radio frequencies ranging between 1550 and 5200 megahertz. Compare L-BAND.

Investigator William L. Sjogren of the Jet Propulsion Laboratory in Pasadena' will use the S-band to study the near-surface gravitational profile of the moon and the subsurface gravity anomalies such as mascons and impact craters. *"Apollo 15: Subsatellite for Lunar Orbit," Science News, May 29, 1971, p 371*

The American Safeguard ABM system will use radars operating in the ultra-high-frequency range, at a frequency of about 400 MHz, and in the S band, at frequencies between 1.5 and 5.2 GHz. *Frank Barnaby, New Scientist and Science Journal, Feb. 11, 1971, p 293*

scag, *n. U.S. Slang.* heroin.

"I started getting high on scag at 14 or 15." *Bruce Dalton, quoted in Time, April 6, 1970, p 46*

In the film [*Scag*], two young people—a black girl from the ghetto and a white boy from a middle-class suburb—have one thing in common, scag. *Science News, Aug. 21, 1971, p 120*

[of unknown origin]

scalar-tensor theory, another name for BRANS-DICKE THEORY.

Anderson believes, though, that further measurements will merely serve to enhance his present result. If so it could be a serious set-back for newer gravitational theories such as that of Dr Charles Brans and Professor Robert Dicke. Their so-called scalar-tensor theory would produce a result at variance with Einstein's predictions by about 7 per cent. *"Active Radar Tests Support Einstein's General Theory," New Scientist, Dec. 3, 1970, p 362*

scam, *n. U.S. Slang.* a dishonest scheme; a swindle.

A gambling house is a sitting duck to every con man or outlaw who comes through; he is invariably convinced that he has a scam that you have never seen before. Once in a very great while he is right. *R. C. Padden, "Reflections Of A Gilded Cage," Harper's, Feb. 1971, p 89*

[of unknown origin]

scan, *n.* a picture of the distribution of radio-activity in the body. See also SCANNING.

A side-view brain scan, the most common of the medical diagnostic techniques that make use of radioactive tracers, reveals a brain tumor, the large dark region in the middle of the clear area. *Picture legend, "Medicine," 1971 Britannica Yearbook of Science and the Future, 1970, p 231*

An improved way of scanning the brain for tumors has been reported by two California scientists. Their technique is claimed to give a clearer image of tumors deep within the brain than has heretofore been possible and also allows multiple scans in place of one or two. *"Neurology: New Instrument Aids Spotting Brain Tumor," Science News, Sept. 3, 1966, p 166*

scanning, *n.* a diagnostic method for detecting abnormalities in the body by the use of special photographic instruments that record the movement of an administered radioactive substance as it passes through the organs, body fluids, etc. See also NUCLEAR MEDICINE, PHOTOSCANNER.

In scanning, a radioactivity compound is administered to the patient, after which the compound's distribution is mapped out by a scintillation camera that detects gamma rays coming from the child. *"Pediatrics Notes: Nuclear Medicine Expands," Science News, April 6, 1968, p 333*

. . . common studies that involved tracers were diagnoses of focal abnormalities of the brain, lung, liver, kidney, and other organs. These tests were based on a technique called "scanning," which mapped the distribution of radioactivity within the body and then displayed the data in the form of a picture of the organ or region of interest. *Henry Nicholas Wagner, Jr., "Medicine," 1971 Britannica Yearbook of Science and the Future, 1970, p 230*

scanning electron microscope, an electron microscope that uses a very fine moving beam of electrons to scan a specimen so that the image obtained, though not as sharp as that provided by the standard electron microscope, contains much more detail. *Abbreviation:* SEM Compare TRANSMISSION ELECTRON MICROSCOPE.

Since its introduction five years ago, the scanning electron microscope has established itself rapidly in a variety of fields, from microbiology to metallurgy, where the observation and understanding of surface detail is necessary. *David Kynaston, New Scientist, Feb. 5, 1970, p 256*

Two different types of electron microscope are currently in use. The transmission electron microscope is analogous to a conventional light microscope. The scanning electron microscope employs a flying spot of electrons to scan the object, producing a television-like image. *Albert V. Crewe, "A High-Resolution Scanning Electron Microscope," Scientific American, April 1971, p 26*

scatterometer, *n.* a radarlike instrument equipped with several aerials for directing a radar beam, microwaves, etc., over a wide area and recording the returned signal at all angles.

The microwave radiometer and scatterometer will use radar techniques to penetrate cloud cover. *Everly Driscoll, Science News, Oct. 10, 1970, p 305*

[from *scatter* + *-ometer*, as in *barometer, speedometer*, etc.]

scattersite housing, *U.S.* government-sponsored public housing designed to disperse low-income groups outside of the ghetto or inner city; housing provided in scattered sites throughout a city.

The issues surrounding the battle of Forest Hills in particular and the scattersite housing concept in general, are now being thrashed out in the courts rather than the streets—at least for the time being. While both sides await the decision of an appeals court on whether or not to halt construction, work continues on the project where they have almost completed placing the deep pilings and are almost ready to pour concrete. *Anthony Mancini and Roberta B. Gratz, "Scattersite Housing: The Battle of Forest Hills," New York Post, April 24, 1972, p 27*

scenario, *n.* any projected course or plan of action, especially one of several possible plans.

If either the Albanian resolution or the U.S.' dual representation resolution is adopted, the scene will shift, in time, to the Security Council chamber. There, the Council will, through a complex but securely-plotted scenario, offer Peking the China seat. *New York Post, Oct. 25, 1971, p 5*

Unfortunately there are almost no data available on fracture modes for various scenarios of mission failure. An engineering examination of this subject is urgently needed. *Carl Sagan, Elliott C. Leventhal, and Joshua Lederberg, "Contamination of Mars: Crash-Landing," Science, March 15, 1968, p 1192*

Mr Lever [Labour's Paymaster-General] makes out a splendid case for "gradual but continuous" growth as the least hopeless of our alternatives, but he spoils it by fudging the wages issue. . . . An alternative scenario (to use the jargon) might appeal to at least those Ministers who in private are sniffing eagerly for growth. They should announce that the Government will go for steady growth. . . . They should continue their policy of resisting strikes for unreasonable settlements. *The Manchester Guardian Weekly, Dec. 12, 1970, p 13*

[extended sense of the theatrical term for an outline or synopsis of a play]

scene, *n. Slang.* an area or sphere of activity, especially as a characteristic mode or manner. of living.

. . . Sue, a sophomore at the University of Washington, who now abhors the drug scene, especially "the dealers, who don't care about the poor kid on the street who gets a bum tab of acid." *Time, Aug. 17, 1970, p 39*

scentometer, *n.* an instrument that analyzes the content of breath and records the extent of dust, pollutants, etc., in it.

To enforce the [air-pollution] code, alas, the city acquired a Scentometer. The device is a plastic box that contains a sensitive mechanical sniffer through which an inspector breathes. This is a scientific means, supposedly, for calibrating stink. *Time, Oct. 19, 1970, p 14*

[from *scent* + *-ometer*, as in *barometer, speedometer*, etc.]

schlep (ʃlep), *n. U.S. Slang.* a dull, stupid, awkward fellow; a jerk.

NAT: Hello, Moe? Me. Listen, I don't know if somebody's playing a joke, or what, but Death was just here. We played a little gin. . . . No, *Death*. In person. Or somebody who claims to be Death. But, Moe, he's such a *schlep! Woody Allen, The New Yorker, July 27, 1968, p 33*

. . . Alan Arkin leans on the hood of a blue-and-orange Checker taxicab. Half Puck, half schlep, he wears black basketball-model US Keds, green fatigue pants, a $1.98 plaid shirt and a blue cotton jumper. *Thomas Buckley, The New York Times, July 10, 1966, Sec. 2, p 15*

[from Yiddish *shlep*, literally, a drag, from *shlepn* to drag]

schlock (ʃlɑk), *adj. U.S. Slang.* cheap; inferior; junky. Also spelled SHLOCK.

. . . the dealers were guilty of schlock, sleazy, bargain-basement, fast-buck advertising. *Walter Carlson, The New York Times, Feb. 4, 1965, p 50*

"Listen," he queried, "where'd you buy this here novelty — at some schlock store on the Atlantic City boardwalk?" *S. J. Perelman, "Naked in Piccadilly, W. 1," The New Yorker, Jan 27, 1968, p 30*

—*n.* something cheap or inferior; junk.

Then the director could dissolve to Miami Beach's Eden Roc Hotel and a suite decorated in Versailles schlock. *Time, Aug. 23, 1968, p 17*

". . . we can do every style of ad, depending on what fits the client. The only thing we don't do is *schlock*. If you want a lot of nasal passages or pictures of a pill gurgling through your intestines, you go to another shop." *Jack Batten, Maclean's, April 1967, p 26*

[from Yiddish *shlak* a curse]

schlock·meis·ter (ˈʃlɑkˌmaistər), *n. U.S. Slang.* a purveyor of anything shoddy, mediocre, or second-rate.

". . . real people are pretty grungy actors when you come right down to it. Like all those schlockmeisters on 'Candid Camera' [a television program]." *F. P. Tullius, "Ninety-Nine Years is Not Forever," The New Yorker, July 19, 1969, p 20*

[from *schlock* + German *Meister* master; originally applied to a dealer of cheap or second-hand merchandise, later applied in U.S. radio and television to a promoter who supplies giveaway shows with free products in exchange for publicity for the products]

schlock·y (ˈʃlɑk iː), *adj. U.S. Slang.* junky; schlock. Also spelled SHLOCKY.

Also in the cast are Arthur Kennedy, as the timid American general who refused to push the Allies' initial advantage at Anzio and, as his commanding general, Robert Ryan, whose career now seems to consist solely of playing the "special guest star" in a series of schlocky European films. *Vincent Canby, The New York Times, July 25, 1968, p 26*

schmear (ʃmir), *n. Slang.* matter; affair; business.

If there is an illiberality among us Jews, I tell Russek, it is because we never learned to sit a horse; we missed out on the whole chivalry schmear. *Gilbert Rogin, "La-Dah-Dah-Dah-Dum," The New Yorker, Dec. 18, 1971, p 33*

Seymour Krim is a hectic writer and placid talker. . . . He is taking an ideological stand against the novelist as a writer of fiction and like any other American writing nut of his generation, he took off from the American realistic novel. His own quest took him through the whole schmear and he lived to see the Holy Grail turn into a booby-trapped jerry. *Pooter, "Making Things Happen," The Times (London), Feb. 21, 1970, p I*

[from Yiddish *shmir* spread]

schoolbook, *adj. Especially U.S.* characteristic of school textbooks; oversimplified.

. . . today, because of the problems peculiar to writing the history of modern mass-art forms, and because of the jumbled circumstances in which movies survive, with knowledge of them acquired in haphazard fashion from television, and from screenings here and there, film enthusiasts find it simpler to explain movies in terms of the genius-artist-director, the schoolbook hero—the man who did it all. Those who admire "Citizen Kane," which is constructed to present different perspectives on a man's life, seem naïvely willing to accept [Orson] Welles' view of its making; namely, that it is his sole creation. *Pauline Kael, "Onward and Upward With the Arts: Raising Kane," The New Yorker, Feb. 20, 1971, p 89*

schuss·boom (ˈʃusˌbuːm), *v.i. Slang.* to ski at high speed.

He is Bucky Scudder the skier, who flashes across moguls with such control and precision. . . . as he schussbooms over a fifteen-foot dip, he hears them yell "Buuuckyyy!" as though they were yelling "Track!" in admiration of his exuberance and daring. *Thomas Williams, "The Skier's Progress," The New Yorker, Feb. 2, 1963, p 37*

[from *schuss* a fast run down a straight course + *boom*, *v.*, to sail very fast]

schuss·boom·er ('ʃus‚bu: mər), *n. Slang.* a high-speed skier.

. . . Cervenia continues to be the schussboomer's paradise. There is enough terrain hereabouts—as in most of the Alps—to make even reconstruction-minded Yankees start yodelling Dixie. *Michael Strauss, The New York Times, Jan. 20, 1967, p 33*

Schwarz·schild radius ('ʃvarts‚ʃilt), the size at which the gravitational forces of a collapsing body in space become so strong that they prevent the escape of any matter or radiation.

A black hole is the result of uninhibited gravitational collapse. . . . Eventually an object whose collapse continues reaches a limiting size that depends on its mass. The size is called the Schwarzschild radius. For the sun, it is about three kilometers. When the object shrinks to less than its Schwarzschild radius, it becomes a black hole. *Science News, Dec. 26, 1970, p 480*

[named after Martin *Schwarzschild*, born 1912, an American astrophysicist]

scientologist, *n.* an advocate or follower of scientology.

. . . Ron Hubbard's E-meter [a skin galvanometer similar to a lie detector] . . . sets you completely free from all past conditioning—presumably so you won't question the conditioning then imposed by Hubbard's scientologists. *Julian Mitchell, The Manchester Guardian Weekly, April 25, 1970, p 16*

scientology, *n.* a system combining religion and psychology which stresses spiritual and physical healing through the observance of certain tenets, founded by the American L. Ron Hubbard.

Students were hard at work in classrooms studying to pass the various stages of development in their knowledge of scientology, the proclaimed aim of which is to free people of their aberrations and to make them capable of success. *Christopher Warman, The Times (London), Sept. 2, 1968, p 3*

[from *scienti*fic + *-ology*, as in *psychology, biology,* etc.]

sci-fi ('saɪ‚faɪ), *adj. Especially U.S.* of or relating to science fiction.

In this unpersuasive sci-fi thriller directed by John Sturges . . . it is only a matter of time until someone gravely inquires: ."How worried are they in Washington?" *"Cinema," Review of "The Satan Bug," Time, April 30, 1965, p 61*

Industry is still experimenting with it [an amorphous semiconductor switch] but it seems to make feasible the sci-fi world of TV sets hung like mirrors on the wall; of an automated world that could survive a nuclear war; of button-sized computers which help control cars and run artificial environments in which a varnish-like stripe on the wall, sensitive to heat and humidity, would control furnaces, humidifiers. . . . *Alan Edmonds, Maclean's, May 1968, p 1*

[from *science f*iction, patterned after *hi-fi* (high-fidelity)]

scintillation camera, a photographic camera that detects and records the scintillations of radioactive substances, used especially to map out the distribution of radioactive substances in the body.

The scintillation camera is capable of picturing on Polaroid film two-dimensional distribution of radioisotopes and then following the rate at which these isotopes may move into and out of such organs as the liver, thyroid and kidney. *"Brain Tumors Detected by New Complex Camera," Science News Letter, May 16, 1964, p 317*

sco·line (skou'li:n), *n.* a muscular relaxant that produces a temporary condition of total paralysis.

Even more experimental than Steffy's use of electric shock is the "scoline treatment" for alcoholics first tried in Canada at Queen's University in Kingston. This treatment scares the patient almost to death. He's asked to look at, sniff and barely taste his favorite beverage and as he does so, the reclining patient is given a dose of the drug scoline, which paralyzes him almost instantly. *Barbara Frum, "They Learn to 'Cure' Themselves with SHOCK," Maclean's, Nov. 19, 1966, p 45*

[from *succinylc*holine, part of the full chemical name]

scot·o·pho·bic (‚skat ə'fou bik), *adj.* of or relating to scotophobin.

Just how so small a molecule [of scotophobin] can have so dramatic a behavioural affect is baffling. The scotophobic effect seems to be very specific for this structure. . . . Very probably some rigorous stereospecificity is involved in the scotophobic mechanism. *"Plugging In A Memory Demands A Close Fit," New Scientist and Science Journal, June 3, 1971, p 559*

scot·o·pho·bin (‚skat ə'fou bən), *n.* a chemical compound that is believed to be the basis of a specific conditioned response, fear of the dark, isolated from the brain tissue of rodents conditioned to fear darkness.

His [the neurochemist Georges Ungar's] theory: the memory message (that darkness should be avoided) is encoded by the rats' DNA-RNA mechanism into an amino-acid chain called a peptide, a small protein that Ungar managed to isolate and then synthesize. His name for it: scotophobin, from the Greek words for "darkness" and "fear." *Time, April 19, 1971, p 30*

Scouse or **scouse** (skaus), *British Slang.* —*n.* **1** the dialect of Liverpool, England.

The Governors and Staff couldn't have done more to make the little blighters feel at home; . . . introducing anoraks, jeans and bobble-caps for school wear; substituting scouse for Etonian slang. *W. F. N. Watson, Punch, Sept. 18, 1968, p 420*

2 a native of Liverpool, England. Also called SCOUSER.

Call me a Liverpudlian, or even a Scouse . . . but a "Liverpolitan"—never! There ain't no such animal. *John Tatham, The Sunday Times (London), Aug. 7, 1966, p 10*

—*adj.* of Liverpool. Also, SCOUSIAN.

. . . a man who talks in a scintillating mixture of Scouse, Irish and Welsh accents and, what with his fluent Welsh and current address in Dublin, has become a sort of Celtic scrambled egg. *David Blundy and Tom Davies, "A Little Bit of Haven . . .," The Sunday Times (London), Aug. 22, 1971, p 9*

[shortened from earlier *Scouseland*, slang name for Liverpool, because of the popularity of the sailor's stew called *lobscouse* or *scouse* in Liverpool]

Scouser or **scouser,** *n. British Slang.* another name for SCOUSE (a native of Liverpool, England).

The scousers have long been renowned for their cheeky good humour. *The Sunday Times (London), Dec. 10, 1967, p 23*

Scousian, *adj. British Slang.* another word for SCOUSE.

In their [the Beatles'] usual flat, Scousian manner, the boys sign on with old Fred, and the yellow submarine takes off. John thinks their journey is 'reminiscent in its way of the late Mr Ulysses', but you may think rather of Miss Alice when you see the wonders they are faced with: teapot fish, kinky-boot beasts, and the curious tricks that time can play. *Eric Rhode, "Films: Pepperland," Review of "Yellow Submarine," The Listener, July 25, 1968, p 125*

SCP, abbreviation of SINGLE-CELL PROTEIN.

A promising source of protein that was expected to become available in the near future is SCP (single cell protein), consisting of an edible mass of microorganisms devoid of odor or taste. *Margaret Markham, "Foods and Nutrition," 1971 Britannica Yearbook of Science and the Future, 1970, p 197*

scramble, *v.i. U.S. Football.* to run with the ball without the protection of blockers.

It was Tarkenton who engineered this monumental upheaval, mainly because he bewildered the Packers with his scrambling. *Arthur Daley, The New York Times, Aug. 13, 1968, p 31*

scrambler, *n. U.S. Football.* a quarterback who scrambles.

He [Quarterback Francis Tarkenton, New York Giants] is known in the trade as a "scrambler," who would just as soon run as throw, who can turn a potential 10-yd. loss into a 50-yd. gain. *Time, March 17, 1967, p 55*

scramjet, *n.* **1** a ramjet (jet engine in which the fuel is mixed with air compressed by the effect of high speed) which produces thrust by burning fuel in an airstream moving at supersonic speeds.

Supersonic combustion ramjets ("scramjets") theoretically could extend flight speeds to at least Mach 14. *Kenneth W. Gatland, New Scientist, May 19, 1966, p 429*

2 an aircraft powered by a scramjet.

A vehicle described by scientists as a forerunner of aircraft that will carry passengers at speeds of about 8,000 miles an hour at very high altitudes has made its first test flight.
· Called a Scramjet, the vehicle was launched Wednesday by a Scout rocket, an Air Force spokesman said. *The New York Times, Jan. 14, 1967, p 4*

[from supersonic combustion *ramjet*]

screenwash, *n. British.* the washing done by a screenwasher.

Another new feature is the "cyclic" wipers, which give not only slow and fast speeds but, if required, one wipe every 7-1/2 seconds and eight wipes in conjunction with the screenwash. . . . *The Times (London), March 5, 1970, p 16*

screenwasher, *n. British.* an automatic windshield washer.

Screenwashers are the only way of keeping the windscreen clean on the move and are slowly being standardised. *Tony Brooks, Observer, July 12, 1964, p 34*

screwup, *n. U.S. Slang.* something botched up; a bad blunder.

. . . the two men are back talking about Vietnam, about the son-of-a-bitch brigade commander who didn't give a damn about lives, only his own reputation, and some of the stupidities and screwups of the war. *Ward Just, "Soldiers," The Atlantic, Nov. 1970, p 88*

[from the slang verb phrase *screw up* to botch up]

S.D.R. or **S.D.R.s,** abbreviation of SPECIAL DRAWING RIGHTS.

. . . many economists believe that the S.D.R. represents a basic solution to the problem of providing an adequate volume of international monetary reserve to facilitate steady expansion in the volume of world trade. *Erich Heinemann, The New York Times, March 19, 1968, p 68*

Over the month, the S.D.R. holdings of the developed countries rose by $66.4m. and of the I.M.F. by $12.3m. *Anthony Thomas, The Times (London), March 3, 1970, p 24*

S.D.S., abbreviation of *Students for a Democratic Society,* any of several political organizations of radical college students, especially an American national organization formed in 1962 and split since then into various factions representing leftist, New Leftist, and anarchist views.

Chicago's Police Superintendent James Conlisk, 51, has learned a lot. . . . But Conlisk's handling of the "Days of Rage" organized last fall by the Weatherman faction of the S.D.S. was restrained enough to be cited by the National Commission on Violence as a polar opposite to the "police riot" that scarred the city during the 1968 Democratic Convention. *"What the Police Can—And Cannot—Do About Crime," Time, July 13, 1970, p 41*

Neither the American nor the German group has a clearly defined program; both are primarily protest movements against the existing order. The German student movement, the SDS, is more organized; it has headquarters and leaders. *Henry Brandon, "State of Affairs: Student Movement: German Style," Saturday Review, Sept. 9, 1967, p 10*

sea farming, another name for MARICULTURE.

Sea farming has been going on in several countries in Europe and Asia for many years. However, although the yields of food have been increased, the conclusion must be drawn that farming the sea as practiced in these countries is not fundamentally comparable with the traditional systems of agriculture, horticulture, and animal husbandry. *Pieter Korringa, "Mariculture," McGraw-Hill Yearbook of Science and Technology 1971, p 17*

Sea-lab ('si:,læb), *n.* any of several U.S. Navy underwater vessels designed to serve as habitats for aquanauts.

The goal of the Sealabs is to develop techniques whereby men can operate on the ocean floor, venturing in and out of their compartment at will with special breathing apparatus. *Walter Sullivan, The New York Times, Dec. 24, 1967, Sec. 4, p 10*

Astronaut-aquanaut Scott Carpenter, leader of the underwater teams, lived and worked in Sealab for thirty consecutive days. *Wesley Marx, Maclean's, April 2, 1966, p 28*

[from *Sea* + *lab*oratory]

search-and-destroy, *adj.* (in antiguerrilla warfare) involving the strategy of seeking out the enemy in a particular area in order to neutralize or destroy his fighting forces in that area.

After the Lunar New Year offensive, and especially in April, the allies began a number of search-and-destroy operations aimed at preventing a second enemy assault. *Joseph B. Treaster, The New York Times, May 6, 1968, p 14*

South Vietnamese troops now handle almost all search-and-destroy sweeps. One result has been a sharp curtailment in U.S. casualties. . . . *Time, Sept. 14, 1970, p 16*

second-strike, *adj.* (of a nuclear weapon) hidden or protected so that it cannot be easily destroyed, and therefore available for retaliation after an enemy attack. Compare FIRST-STRIKE.

Altogether, the U.S. "second-strike" deterrent force numbered about 4,000 warheads (1,700 missiles) against about 1,000 Soviet warheads. *Robert E. Hunter and Geoffrey Kemp, "Defense," Britannica Book of the Year 1968, p 266*

second-strike capability, the capability of a nuclear power to retaliate with second-strike weapons after a surprise enemy attack, especially on its missile silos. Compare FIRST-STRIKE CAPABILITY.

A non-aggressor nation, on the other hand, merely wants to forestall attack. This it does by aiming its missiles at a potential aggressor's cities as a retaliatory threat; then it protects these retaliatory missiles with ABMs [antiballistic missiles]. This is described as a second-strike capability. *Time, Nov. 28, 1969, p 36*

seed money, a grant of money to initiate an undertaking.

This seed money covers the legal and architectural work that must be done in order for a local group (often a church) to make application for Government-subsidized financing. Once the permanent financing is obtained, the seed money is repaid and the funds can then be re-employed in a new project. *H. Erich Heinemann, The New York Times, May 4, 1968, p 63*

see-through, *adj.* **1** transparent; permitting inspection of the inside or contents of something.

The housewife, sitting with 11 other housewives, was talking about prepackaged meat wrapped with see-through tops but with cardboard on the bottom. *Myra MacPherson, The New York Times, May 25, 1968, p 24*

Fascinating new see-through model computer actually solves problems, teaches computer fundamentals. *Advertisement by Edmund Scientific Company, Barrington, N.J., Science News, July 2, 1966, p 11*

It remained for a myriad of advanced synthetics and plastics to make see-through sculpture a burgeoning art form in the 1960s. . . . *Time, Feb. 9, 1968, p 52*

2 so thin in texture that it can be seen through; very sheer.

. . . the waitress . . . was wearing enormous false eyelashes and a black knitted see-through pants suit. . . . *Whitney Balliett, "A Reporter At Large: Charles Mingus," The New Yorker, May 29, 1971, p 49*

The playsuit is strictly see-through, but the art-nouveau crest provides opacity where it's needed most. *Picture legend, "Our Pugilistic Preview of Some Punchy Fashions," Maclean's, July 1967, p 30*

—*n.* **1** a see-through dress, blouse, or other garment.

Women's Wear Daily, which is more authoritative about see-throughs than breakthroughs, came up with the farthest-out rumor of all. *Time, Nov. 19, 1965, p 21*

2 the fashion of wearing see-through garments.

In fashion, as in every other important field, great mistakes are made. Nudity and see-through is one of them. *Drusilla Beyfus, "The Judgement of Paris," Daily Telegraph Magazine (London), Jan. 23, 1970, p 32*

seg or **seggie,** *n.* *U.S. Slang.* a person who favors racial segregation; a segregationist.

When people wore the American flag then it was to show that they were not segs, because the segs of course wore the Confederate flag. Now on behalf of a stupid and futile war the segs wear the American flag, and whether we have converted them or they have converted us is a moot point. *David Halberstam, "The End of a Populist," Harper's, Jan. 1971, p 35*

[Senator] Fulbright for the first time openly appealed for black votes, because he believed that he couldn't win without them and that the "seggies," who hated him for his stand on the war in Vietnam, would vote against him no matter what he did. *Richard Harris, "Annals of Politics: Decision," The New Yorker, Dec. 12, 1970, p 107*

sel·e·nod·e·sist (ˌsel əˈnɑd ə sist), *n.* a specialist in selenodesy.

. . . the Lunar Orbiter also carried a micrometeorite detector and enabled selenodesists to obtain more accurate data on the Moon's shape and gravitational field from precise tracking of the artificial satellite's orbit. *N. J. Trask and H. E. Holt, "Moon," McGraw-Hill Yearbook of Science and Technology 1969, p 218*

sel·e·nod·e·sy (ˌsel əˈnɑd ə si:), *n.* the study of the shape, dimensions, gravity, and other physical characteristics of the moon.

A rapidly developing field appears to be lunar geodesy, a specialty the geodesists call "selenodesy." *Waldo E. Smith, "Meetings: International Union of Geodesy and Geophysics," Science, March 1, 1968, p 1002*

[from *seleno-* moon + *-desy*, as in *geodesy*]

self-actualization, *n.* the development of a person's understanding and acceptance of himself and of his motives.

. . . Laing insists that psychotherapy must be "*an obstinate attempt of two people to recover the wholeness of being human through the relationship between them*" (Laing's emphasis). This, he insists, can be achieved only through a perception of the illusory nature of the entity individuals refer to as "I"—the ego—and a penetration to the essential humanness, to what Maslow called "self actualization." *Richard H. Gilluly, "A New Look At The Meaning of Reality," Review of "The Politics of Experience" by R. D. Laing, Science News, May 15, 1971, p 336*

San Diego's new eleven-course program will probe the status of women in comparative cultures, in literature, in sex and in "self-actualization." Key subjects for discussion will include the Women's Lib movement and U.S. education's alleged failure to spur women to pursue intellectual careers. *Time, July 6, 1970, p 54*

As a flower moves toward the florist, women move toward men who are not good for them. Self-actualization is not to be achieved in terms of another person, but you don't know that, when you begin. *Donald Barthelme, "The Rise of Capitalism," The New Yorker, Dec. 12, 1970, p 47*

self-antigen, *n.* an antibody formed in an organism in response to its own antigen.

The prediction has been made that the normal process of development of nonresponsiveness (tolerance) to self-antigens might be associated with an early maturation of lymphocytic cells and a late maturation of PAH [primary antigen-handling] cells. *W. Braun, "Antibody," McGraw-Hill Yearbook of Science and Technology 1971, p 105*

self-dealing, *n.* the use of a charitable foundation to grant loans or other financial benefits to contributors or to protect the founders' private income.

The committee's [the Ways and Means Committee of the U.S. House of Representatives] considerations were to be based on a series of written proposals ... designed (1) to prevent self-dealing between the foundation and the grantor, (2) to prevent the use of a foundation as a means of maintaining family control of a corporation or other property.... *"Foundations," The 1970 World Book Year Book, p 349*

self-destruct, *v.i.* **1** to cause one's own or its own destruction; destroy oneself.

An international team of scientists ... has designed a plastic that Guillet claims will self-destruct when exposed to sunlight, but will remain intact if it is kept indoors. *Time, May 11, 1970, p 86*

2 to disappear; evaporate.

... earning what seems to a writer easy money (i.e., money not acquired through the painful process of hunching over a recalcitrant typewriter); flinging words into the air where they instantly self-destruct and cannot hover around to haunt you as printed lines are wont to do. In short, lecturing. *Richard Schickel, "Performing Arts," Harper's, Dec. 1971, p 30*

... the women had a definition of "ego" that they all agreed was appropriate to a feminist document. Then they tackled "history." ... "our definition of 'history' is going to change as we raise our consciousness. Our definition's going to—it's going to self-destruct." *Jane Kramer, The New Yorker, Nov. 28, 1970, p 58*

self-noise, *n.* noise produced by a ship itself as it passes through water, as distinguished from the noise caused by the water's turbulence.

To reduce the quiet sub's self-noise (it roars its way through the water even when gliding on momentum alone), researchers are studying coatings to make the hull slip more easily along. *Science News, July 27, 1968, p 80*

New mountings and refitting have greatly reduced self noise in Navy ships. *New Scientist, Aug. 1, 1968, p 225*

self-replicating, *adj.* reproducing itself by itself.

Every molecular biologist believes that DNA [deoxyribonucleic acid, the carrier of genetic material in the cells] is a self-replicating molecule, and that the structure of a new piece of DNA is determined absolutely by the structure of the DNA upon which it is made. *New Scientist, Oct. 31, 1968, p 229*

self-replication, *n.* reproduction of itself by itself.

These organisms [pleuropneumonia-like organisms] which are even smaller than some viruses, are thought to possess only the minimum number of structures needed for self-replication and independent existence.... *Philip C. Hanawalt and Robert H. Haynes, "The Repair of DNA," Scientific American, Feb. 1967, p 43*

self-steering, *adj.* designed to keep a boat, etc., on a fixed course.

There was still no sign of Sir Francis [Chichester], by 8 a.m., Gipsy Moth continuing to sail on the self-steering gear which has made the single-handed voyage possible. *Ronald Faux, The Times (London), May 29, 1967, p 8*

SEM, abbreviation of SCANNING ELECTRON MICROSCOPE.

SEM's advantage over other microscopic techniques is the ability to present a three-dimensional image more realistically. *Walter Clark, "Photography," 1972 Britannica Yearbook of Science and the Future, 1971, p 311*

semiconservative, *adj. Genetics.* designating a form of replication in which the original molecular strands are conserved individually rather than together.

This mode of replication is termed semiconservative because the parental strands separate in the course of DNA synthesis; each daughter cell receives a "hybrid" DNA molecule that consists of one parental strand and one newly synthesized complementary strand. *Philip C. Hanawalt and Robert H. Haynes, "The Repair of DNA," Scientific American, Feb. 1967, p 37*

semifarming, *n.* unselective or uncontrolled farming of livestock or crops.

Because natural phenomena are controlled, the modern chicken farm is true farming, while the keeping of chickens in the farmyard is semifarming. In a similar way, sea farming is a case of semifarming. *Pieter Korringa, "Mariculture," McGraw-Hill Yearbook of Science and Technology 1971, p 17*

semiliteracy, *n.* the quality or condition of being semiliterate.

In *Extraterritorial,* he [George Steiner] warns that a more current threat, "the drift and boredom of semiliteracy"—man's marriage of convenience to his words, threatens to crush the life out of all civilized languages. *Melvin Maddocks, "Books: Babel Revisited," Review of "Extraterritorial" by George Steiner, Time, July 26, 1971, p 52*

semiliterate, *n.* a person who is semiliterate or barely able to read and write.

The BBC's Pronunciation Unit, which advises how English should be spoken, is, naturally run by a Scot. The pronunciation unit will advise anyone at the BBC who asks, but broadly speaking it is true to say that only announcers need speak BBC English.... Then there are the semiliterates who are greatly influencing the way some words are pronounced. *Terry Coleman, "As She Is Spoke," The Manchester Guardian Weekly, April 10, 1971, p 16*

[noun use of the adjective]

Sen·dai virus ('sen,dai), a paramyxovirus that induces rapid fusion of different types of cells.

New pathways were opened to the search for genetic regulators by an English group which succeeded in producing hybrid cells from human and mouse cells. The cells were hybridized with the aid of the Sendai virus, which is capable of infecting both species. *Sheldon C. Reed, "Genetics," Encyclopedia Science Supplement (Grolier) 1965, p 56*

Facilitation of this hybridization process by the Sendai virus permits fusion of the cells of man and mouse and of even more disparate species. *Victor A. McKusick, Britannica Book of the Year 1970, p 500*

The group, led by R. J. Ericsson, decided to exploit the membrane-fusing properties of Sendai virus. *"Viruses Promote Test-Tube Fertilisation," New Scientist and Science Journal, July 15, 1971, p 122*

[named after *Sendai*, a city in Japan where the virus was first detected]

send-up, *n. British.* a parody.

There too we are owlishly invited to puzzle about the death of Lermontov's hero: "His digestion was poor and his bile excessive, but otherwise he had a remarkably strong constitution." Is this a send-up of the whole business of literary scholarship and exegesis? Is Nabokov really an irascible pedant, or is this an ingenious comic *persona? Donald Davie, "Books: Nabokov's Version," Review of "Eugene Onegin: A Novel in Verse" by Aleksandr Pushkin, translated by Vladimir Nabokov, The Manchester Guardian Weekly, Dec. 17, 1964, p 11*

[from the British slang phrase *send up* to scoff at, mock, originally public-school slang meaning to send a boy to the headmaster to be punished]

sen·ghi ('seŋ gi:), *n. pl.* or *sing.* a unit of money in the Zaire Republic (the former Democratic Republic of the Congo) equal to 1/100 of a likuta.

The Congo devalued its currency by about two-thirds yesterday and introduced a new currency system of zaires, makuta and senghi. *The Times (London), June 26, 1967, p 17*

sensitivity group, another name for ENCOUNTER GROUP.

A recent development has been the spread of techniques designed to foster intensive group experience. Known by such names as T-group, encounter group, group marathon, sensitivity group, or synanon group, this rapidly spreading method has been termed by Carl Rogers "the most significant social invention of this century." *Austin E. Grigg, "Psychology: Group Therapy," The Americana Annual 1971, p 562*

sensitivity training, training in a group, usually guided by a leader or therapist, in which the members are supposed to gain deeper understanding of their own feelings and those of others in the group.

Paralleling the vogue for "sensitivity training" and other forms of group psychotherapy is the current enthusiasm for programs which apply similar strategy to addiction. Known as "therapeutic communities," they are modeled after Synanon, which was launched in Santa Monica, California, twelve years ago. *Marion K. Sanders, "Addicts and Zealots: The Chaotic War Against Drug Abuse," Harper's, June 1970, p 71*

sequential, *adj.* (of contraceptive pills) taken in a particular sequence to eliminate side effects.

...Dr. Gregory Pincus commented on the medical advertising for some newer-type sequential and low-dosage pills: "These ads are creating a false emphasis. There may be a minute lessening in side effects, but since all present side effects are insignificant, I see absolutely no advantage in sequentials." *Louis Lasagna, "Caution on the Pill," Saturday Review, Nov. 2, 1968, p 68*

—*n.* **sequentials,** *pl.* sequential pills.

Some are combinations in which both the estrogen and the progestin are taken for 21 days a month; others are "sequentials," in which the estrogen alone is taken for 14 to 16 days, and estrogen with progestin for five or six. *Time, May 2, 1969, p 36*

serotype, *v.i.* to type microorganisms by the set of antigens they have in common; classify according to serotype.

Dr Payne...said that in recent years Portsmouth has seen 331 human cases of a particular Salmonella infection: of these 271 have been traced by serotyping through the abattoir and back to the farm. *The Manchester Guardian Weekly, Aug. 29, 1968, p 9*

The different salmonella species are distinguished by a serotyping technique perfected by the Danish bacteriologist Fritz Kauffmann in 1941, and they are identified (with a few exceptions) by geographical names that indicate where they were first isolated. *Berton Roueché, "Annals of Medicine," The New Yorker, Sept. 4, 1971, p 66*

[verb use of *serotype, n.*]

service module, the unit or section of a spacecraft which contains the propulsion system and supplies most of the spacecraft's consumable elements, such as oxygen, water, and propellants. *Abbreviation:* SM Compare COMMAND MODULE and LUNAR MODULE.

The service module contains the main propulsion system that maneuvers the modules so that they can rendezvous and dock with the space station. *William G. Holder and William D. Siuru, Jr., "Skylab," Encyclopedia Science Supplement (Grolier) 1971, p 331*

servo, *v.t.* to control or assist with a servomechanism.

Another fundamental problem was to find a way of relieving and restoring the pressure in a conventional hydrostatic braking system without recourse to the alternative of fully powered braking.... As already mentioned, Ferguson solved this problem with their ingenious double-sided vacuum servo, which servos the brakes on and servos them (and the driver's foot) off. *Anthony Curtis, "Taking the Skid Out of Braking," New Scientist and Science Journal, Aug. 12, 1971, p 359*

Sev·in ('sev in), *n.* a trade name for an insecticide of the carbamate group, that acts by inhibiting the enzyme cholinesterase.

Sevin, a synthetic organic pesticide, has a low toxicity to animals and man and degrades rapidly, but it is highly toxic to bees. *"Biology," Encyclopedia Science Supplement (Grolier) 1971, p 9*

sexism, *n.* discrimination based on a person's sex; sexual prejudice; specifically, discriminatory attitudes and practices against women in business, politics, art, etc. Compare MALE CHAUVINISM.

We have heard of the extremists—ten thousand strong—called Women's Liberation, how they crop their hair short, wear baggy trousers and loose sweaters to conceal the more notable evidences of sex. "Abolish sexism!" is their slogan. *Catherine Drinker Bowen, "...We've Never Asked a Woman Before," The Atlantic, March 1970, p 82*

[patterned after *racism*]

sexist, *n.* a person who practices sexism. Compare MALE CHAUVINIST.

Just as the New York construction workers became the arch-symbols of the brutal reaction to the long-haired antiwar movement, so the *Playboy* sexist has become the target of Women's Liberation. *Clive Irving, "Views," The Listener, Oct. 22, 1970, p 538*

...the women's liberationists had decided that the Tournament of Roses parade would provide a fine opportunity for letting him know that they considered him [Billy Graham] a sexist and a false prophet. *Calvin Trillin, "U.S. Journal: Pasadena," The New Yorker, Jan. 16, 1971, p 85*

—*adj.* practicing or characterized by sexism.

Mr. Grossman would be amazed if anyone accused him of domineering or sexist behavior. Yet tacitly condoning such behavior and finding it natural are also oppressive acts. *Patricia S. Caplan, Wellesley Hills, Mass., in a Letter to the Editor, Harper's, May 1970, p 8*

Black businesswomen often contend that the toughest prejudice that they face is not racist but sexist. *"Black Capitalism," Time, Nov. 8, 1971, p 58*

[patterned after *racist*]

sexploitation, *n.* the exploitation of sex in the arts, especially in motion pictures.

But there can be no doubt that the immediate — and perhaps continuing — effects of repealing the English obscenity laws would be to admit a flood of plays, films and books whose only object was what is now called sexploitation. *Simon Courtauld, The Times (London), April 30, 1970, p 11*

Russ Meyer, the Barnum of the skinflicks, has recently been grinding out his sexploitation films under the imprimatur of major studios. *Jay Cocks, "Cinema: Valley of the Dregs," Time, Aug. 30, 1971, p 50*

[blend of *sex* and *exploitation*]

sexploiter, *n.* a motion picture produced for sexploitation. Also called ERODUCTION.

The line between the sexploiters and the ordinary Hollywood film was beginning to disappear.... The process was hastened by the Hollywood studios themselves. In 1969, Warners released *Sweet Body of Deborah* and *The Big Bounce*, each containing more nudity than any previous film from a major studio. *Arthur Knight, "Motion Pictures: End of an Era," The 1970 World Book Year Book, p 426*

sexual revolution, the overthrow of traditional sexual inhibitions and taboos, especially those that protect the institution of monogamous marriage, regarded as a major objective of the Women's Liberation movement.

Only briefly does [Kate] Millet speculate on precisely what sort of society might be produced by the successful sexual revolution for which she calls. *Time, Aug. 31, 1970, p 20*

The Sexual Revolution Conquest of the last frontier, involving the efficient management and manipulation of reproductive organs for the purpose of establishing the New Puritanism. *Bernard Rosenberg, "A Dictionary for the Disenchanted," Harper's, Nov. 1970, p 95*

Sey·fert ('sai fərt), *n.* Also called **Seyfert galaxy.** any one of a group of galaxies having very small, starlike centers which exhibit broad emission lines indicative of a high state of atomic excitation. Compare N GALAXY.

Seyfert galaxies are a class of spiral galaxies with very bright, compact nuclei. . . . Interest in Seyferts was fairly marginal until the discovery of quasars in the last decade. *Science News, June 6, 1970, p 552*

A possible link between normal galaxies and quasars may be provided by the Seyfert galaxies, which have unusually bright nuclei similar in many ways to the sharply defined quasars. *Science Journal, April 1970, p 12*

[named for Carl K. *Seyfert*, 1911-1960, an American astronomer who listed and described ten of these galaxies in the 1940's]

shades, *n.pl. Especially U.S. Slang.* sunglasses.

Kay [John Kay, a singer], who is handsome and lean and wears shades all the time because there is something wrong with his eyes, has great stage presence. *Ellen Willis, "Musical Events: Records: Rock, Etc.," The New Yorker, Aug. 10, 1968, p 88*

In the street a burly figure in dark glasses stops and stares threateningly. He comes in. Eddie snatches off the man's shades. "I haven't had them off since Buddy Holly died," giggles the stranger. *Gavin Millar, "Films," Review of "Gumshoe," The Listener, Dec. 16, 1971, p 852*

[shortened from *sunshades*]

sha·ku·ha·chi (ˌʃɑ: ku:'hɑ: tʃi:), *n.* a Japanese bamboo flute resembling a recorder.

We also have the craftsman's noblest pieces: the recurving Zen bows, the vertical *shakuhachi* flute with its five holes and its "sound of great beauty and sadness." *Philip Morrison, Scientific American, Sept. 1970, p 244*

[from Japanese]

shal·war ('ʃɑ:l wɑr), *n.* loose, billowy trousers worn by women in Pakistan.

Pakistani fashions emerge from Knobkerry, in the East Village. Joan Gregg wears a mirror embroidered kurta, $50. Renoir Daggett's . . . shalwar pants of striped cotton ($15). *Picture legend, The New York Times, Aug. 10, 1968, p 18*

Muslim children wearing their traditional baggy trousers outside Moat Girls' School, Leicester, yesterday. The shalwars will be allowed by the education authority on religious grounds, after a protest by Muslim parents. *Picture legend, The Times (London), Sept. 28, 1967, p 2*

[from Urdu]

sham·bol·ic (ʃæm'bɑl ik), *adj. British.* disorderly; in a shambles.

His office [Mr. K. Kobayashi's, a Japanese newspaper correspondent] in Printing House Square is so impeccably tidy that it is a contradiction and a standing reproach to the standard image of shambolic newspaper offices strewn with waste paper and inflated egos. *Philip Howard, "Round-up: How the World Sees It," The Times (London), June 18, 1970, p 9*

[irregular derivative of *shambles*, probably after such pairs as *symbol, symbolic*]

shape, *v.i.* **shape up,** to get into shape; ready oneself.

Gina Hawthorn, fourth in the 1968 Olympic slalom, [is] shaping up for one more attempt on a British medal at the 1972 Olympic Games in Sapporo, Japan. *John Samuel, The Manchester Guardian Weekly, Oct. 3, 1970, p 23*

. . . leaders punctuated demands for measures helpful to their communities with threats, often emphasized by the raised fist of revolution, that "the big fat Establishment," as one of them put it, had better shape up, because "New York's got a long, hot summer ahead." *Andy Logan, "Around City Hall," The New Yorker, Sept. 19, 1970, p 125*

2 *U.S.* to fall into line; behave properly; conform.

"The apparent presidential-vice-presidential view [is] that the economy can be saved or the casualty rate in Indochina lowered or civil peace restored if only Harriet Van Horne [a daily columnist] will shape up." *Washington Post editorial, quoted in Time, June 8, 1970, p 41*

shatter cone, a cone-shaped rock fragment with distinctive ridges, produced by intense shock forces.

It would be necessary to see in more detail the occurrence of tektites in relation to that of shatter cones before the two could be linked in one theory. Perhaps a search for shatter cones in areas where only tektites have so far been found would be rewarding. *H. A. Portas, Habrough, Lincolnshire, England, in a Letter to the Editor, New Scientist, Dec. 26, 1968, p 727*

shatter-coned, *adj.* characterized by many shatter cones.

The Steinheim Basin, a twin structure to the Ries Basin formed at the same time, is the prototype shatter-coned structure. *R. S. Dietz, "Astrobleme: Discoveries," McGraw-Hill Yearbook of Science and Technology 1967, p 110*

shell, *n.* a usually sleeveless and collarless over-blouse.

"But my favorite dress is one that I bought for $60 in Arizona. It has a multi-colored chiffon shell over culottes, and I haven't the faintest idea who designed it." *Judy Klemesrud, The New York Times, March 25, 1968, p 48*

sherpa, *n. British Slang.* a porter.

The next most prominent rôle [of the average husband], sherpa, involving less and lower pay, was valued at £5 a week (Euston portering rate). *The Guardian (London), May 20, 1972, p 12*

Herrligkoffer, like Dyrenfurth before him, was obliged to go international to raise the cash for basics like food and the sherpas' wages. *The Sunday Times (London), May 28, 1972, p 14*

[from *Sherpa* a member of a tribe used for portering in the Himalayas]

shift register, a computer mechanism for storing data in which it is possible to shift or manipulate the stored information in various ways.

The device in question is a single 64-bit dynamic shift register which will work at frequencies of more than 20 megahertz against the 10 megahertz or so of the fastest shift registers available today. *New Scientist, Feb. 19, 1970, p 358*

Shih Tzu ('ʃiː ˌdzuː), a toy dog of Chinese and Tibetan origin, with a long, thick black-and-white coat, a broad head, a short square snout, and large black eyes.

The 43-year-old owner-handler now has 27 Lhasa Apsos in his Kyi-Chu Kennels. There also are a boxer, two Maltese, a Prince Charles English toy spaniel and a Shih Tzu. *John Rendel, The New York Times, May 2, 1968, p 62*

[from Chinese]

ship, *n.* an orbiting or navigating spacecraft.

. . . "no decision has been made whether the crew will engage in extravehicular activity" — the official term for movement outside the ship. *Evert Clark, The New York Times, May 26, 1965, p 1*

[probably shortened from *spaceship*]

shlock (ʃlɑk), *adj.* another spelling of SCHLOCK.

Sudden sex and violent death are the two poles of most of the great art, folk art, and *shlock* art of at least (what used to be called) Western Civilization, and perhaps other civilizations too. *Edward Grossmann, "Film: Bloody Popcorn," Harper's, Dec. 1970, p 32*

shlock·y ('ʃlɑk iː), *adj.* another spelling of SCHLOCKY.

If one examines books on modern movies, the stills generally look terrible — shlocky, dated, cluttered, and artificially lighted. *Pauline Kael, "The Current Cinema: A Minority Movie," The New Yorker, April 6, 1968, p 162*

shoat (ʃout), *n.* another name for GEEP.

Their only persistent vice is letting their shoats (a cross between a sheep and a goat) wander off onto their neighbour's land. *David Blundy, "The Anguilla Story," The Sunday Times (London), June 13, 1971, p 9*

[blend of *sheep* and *goat*]

► The term *shoat* is also the name for a young weaned pig, in which sense it has been in English since the 1400's. It is probably cognate with Flemish *schote* a pig under one year old.

shock-rock, *n.* a type of rock'n'roll music designed to shock the hearer with scandalous lyrics, psychedelic sounds, etc.

Attired in the accepted uniform of Hans Brinker cap and rumpled corduroy jacket, he [the pianist Peter Serkin] goes to Greenwich Village to hear shock-rock, stays up half the night in the coffeehouses discussing philosophy and the merits of LSD. *Time, Feb. 24, 1967, p 50*

shock wave, Usually in the phrase **send shock waves through.** a violent, upsetting jolt caused by an explosive event, situation, etc.

. . . the last writer who sent shock waves through Western literature died when Louis-Ferdinand Céline completed his life's *Voyage au bou de la nuit. Friedel Ungeheuer, "France: A Struggle Against the Second-Rate," Harper's, Dec. 1969, p 125*

Because such securities [commercial paper] are usually bought by other companies that have spare cash to invest, a series of defaults could have spread financial shock waves throughout the U.S. business community. *Time, Dec. 28, 1970, p 54*

. . . the shock waves could be felt long before the opening [of the exhibition "New York Painting and Sculpture: 1940-1970" at the Metropolitan Museum of Art]. Indignation and outrage resounded in the New York reviews. *Calvin Tomkins, "Profiles: Moving With The Flow," The New Yorker, Nov. 6, 1971, p 58*

[figurative sense of the technical term for the violent effect of a blast, earthquake, atmospheric disturbance, etc.]

shoot, *v.t., v.i. Slang.* Usually, **shoot up.** to inject (a liquefied addictive drug) directly into the vein.

. . . in Toronto alone it is estimated there are 8,000 who "shoot up" (inject intravenously) amphetamines. *Sheila Gormely, The Times (London), Feb. 23, 1970, p IV*

But of course when times get hard, pushers will put anything into that white bag and sell it. Some guys have shot up rat poison and died instantly. *Pete Axthelm, "The City Game," Harper's, Oct. 1970, p 91*

Heroin addicts shoot up in a Spanish Harlem basement in New York City. *Leonide Goldstein, "Drugs and Youth," Britannica Book of the Year 1971, p 489*

Workers at The Trailer in Toronto's Yorkville Village, the first major clinic to help young people with medical and legal problems, studied amphetamine abusers for nine months and ran into not only freaks shooting every day, but "weekenders" (spasmodic drug-takers) who needed "speed" to get through school and personal crises. *Sheila Gormely, The Times (London), Feb. 23, 1970, p IV*

shoot-up, *n. Slang.* the act of shooting up a drug.

But the most dramatic technique is the "shoot-up" where the more serious addicts inject themselves or each other with a nausea-producing liquid. The shooting-up takes place in a crash pad of pulsating lights, acid-rock stereo, Day-Glo and even antiwar posters. *Time, Dec. 21, 1970, p 20*

Shope virus (ʃoup), a virus which causes papillomatosis, a disease characterized by many warts and similar growths.

Even on the clinical level, scientists moved in the direction of manipulating or changing human genes when a team of European investigators injected the Shope virus into two children in hopes of reversing an inborn metabolic error. *Science News, Dec. 12, 1970, p 444*

The Shope virus, which induces warts on the skin of rabbits, has no symptomatic effects on mice, rats, dogs, or monkeys.... *Stanfield Rogers, New Scientist, Jan. 29, 1970, p 194*

[named after Richard E. *Shope*, 1901-1966, an American physician who discovered the virus]

short fuse, *U.S.* a quick temper. See also FUSE.

Tully, a fellow notorious around Sausalito for his short fuse, nearly destroyed everything when, the morning after his defeat, he held Nixon's "last press conference" and told the reporters they wouldn't "have Nixon to kick around any more." *Russell Baker, The New York Times, Oct. 13, 1968, Sec. 4, p 10*

He [Senator Muskie] has a temper and is known to the Washington press corps variously as "testy," "peevish," and "living on the edge of resentment." But aides say he carries the short fuse in his pocket, and he can joke about it afterwards. *Joseph Kraft, "Washington," The Atlantic, June 1971, p 12*

shoulder, *n. Surfing Slang.* the calm portion of a wave breaking on the beach.

"You want a green wave with a good shoulder," says a stripling to me. He meant the kind of surf set up, not by a strong local wind, but by a ground sea running in from the Atlantic, big, regular, green rollers that, ideally, are prevented from collapsing for as long as possible by an offshore breeze. *Nicholas Evans, The Sunday Times (London), May 22, 1966, p 21*

shoulder harness or **shoulder belt,** an anchored strap inside an automobile, designed to be worn across the shoulder and chest together with a lap-belt to prevent a passenger from striking his head against the instrument panel, window, etc., especially in the event of a collision.

Padded roll bars and shoulder harnesses are standard on the Shelby Cobra, as well they might be: the $4,200 car winds up to 150 m.p.h. *Time, April 5, 1968, p 38*

A new safety seat, with built-in shoulder belts, is being developed by the General Motors Corporation and is expected to be on the company's cars in 1971. *Jerry M. Flint, The New York Times, Sept. 15, 1968, Sec. 1, p 46*

showboat, *U.S. Slang. —n.* a person who seeks or attracts public attention.

National chairmen rarely serve as showboats, and when a party controls the White House, its public image lives there. *Time, Feb. 28, 1969, p 22*

—v.t. to show off; display publicly.

The 98-year-old ballet is traditionally noted for the gaiety of its music by Léo Delibes and the opportunity it affords a ballerina to showboat her versatility as both Coppélia and Swanilda. *Time, Jan. 31, 1969, p 59*

—v.i. to make a public display.

... John Lindsay—whose skill at dramatizing his pre-

dicaments (or, as politicians call it, "showboating") is a great trial to Lindsay nonbelievers—pointed out at a press conference that because of one end-of-the-year crisis or another he had not once since his election as mayor been free to celebrate New Year's Eve in the ordinary light-hearted way. *Andy Logan, "Around City Hall," The New Yorker, Jan. 16, 1971, p 77*

"I shall not adopt a policy of showboating on this issue," he said in announcing he would not resign. *Clayton Knowles, The New York Times, July 10, 1968, p 20*

shrimp boat, one of the small plastic chips which air traffic controllers place adjacent to the blips on a radarscope to keep track of the movement of individual aircraft.

What does it take to control an estimated 9,000 aircraft taxiing, taking off, flying, and landing within the U.S. at any given moment? For the FAA [Federal Aviation Agency]—overseer of all flights operating under instrument flight rules (IFR) in the U.S.—it takes 14,000 highly trained men, extremely sophisticated electronic equipment, and ... a large supply of small plastic markers called "shrimp boats". *Scientific American, Sept. 1967, p 28*

shrink, *n. U.S. Slang.* a psychiatrist.

"What will your shrink do with you? He's dependent on you for the payments on his car." *"The Talk of the Town," The New Yorker, July 11, 1970, p 20*

... the shrink reports only to the patient, and suitable precautions have been taken to make sure the personnel department can't tap into the data. *Robert Townsend, "Up the Organization," Harper's, March 1970, p 83*

[shortened from *headshrinker*, an earlier slang term for a psychiatrist]

shrink-wrap, *n.* a protective plastic cover made by shrink wrapping.

"We can also detect pirated recordings from the shrink-wrap used to seal the record-sleeve for shop display and from the type of plastic used in the record pressing itself." *Roger St. Pierre, "Battle Joined Against the Tin Pan Alley Pirates," The Times (London), Jan. 12, 1972, p 15*

shrink wrapping, the wrapping of goods in a plastic film that shrinks over the package to conform to its shape when the package is subjected to heat.

The market for plastic packaging is seen to be saturated in some areas.... In other areas the prospects are seen to glitter. They are the areas where newer kinds of packaging, like shrink wrapping, are being exploited, and the areas where the film is not used for packaging but for other purposes well served by the peculiarities of the material. *Arthur Conway, "Books," Review of "Plastics Film Technology" edited by W. R. R. Park, New Scientist, May 14, 1970, p 345*

shtick or **shtik,** *n. U.S. Slang.* a gimmick, act, or routine, especially in a show or performance.

[Gene] Wilder has a fantastic shtick. He builds up a hysterical rage about nothing at all, upon an imaginary provocation, and it's terribly funny. *Pauline Kael, "The Current Cinema," The New Yorker, March 7, 1970, p 94*

They were taping the *Andy Williams Show* for March 27, and Joan Kennedy was doing her piano shtik, like a trouper. *Time, March 22, 1971, p 14*

[from Yiddish *shtik*, literally, a piece]

shuck, *n. U.S. Slang.* fake; bluff.

He [Bob Rafelson, a film director] and his partner, Bert Schneider, put together the Monkees and their television program. "It was a shuck, but beautiful at its own level," he said. *"The Talk of the Town," The New Yorker, Oct. 24, 1970, p 41*

It took them no time at all to see that the poverty program's big projects, like manpower training, in which you would get some job counseling and some training so you would be able to apply for a job in the bank or on the assembly line — everybody with a brain in his head knew that this was the usual bureaucratic shuck. *Irving Howe, "Books," Harper's, Feb. 1971, p 108*

shunpike, *v.i.* U.S. to travel by automobile on side roads instead of expressways, especially to enjoy the countryside.

Besides making long trips at high speed, motorists could take part in sports car rallies, chug about in antiques, "shunpike" on quiet back roads, or watch daredevil drivers skim the Utah salt flats in jet machines. *Stacy V. Jones, "The Hobbies Revolution: Car Jaunts," 1964 Collier's Encyclopedia Year Book, p 70*

[verb use of *shunpike, n.,* a U.S. term for a side road used to avoid paying a toll on a turnpike. The earliest known use of the noun, recorded in *A Dictionary of American English* (1944), was in 1853.]

shunpiker, *n.* U.S. a person who shunpikes.

Smooth roads, signposts, beautiful scenery — what more could a shunpiker want? *Advertisement by British Travel, Saturday Review, April 22, 1967, p 55*

shuttle, *n.* short for SPACE SHUTTLE.

This shuttle is nominally a two-stage vehicle consisting of a booster (first stage) and an orbiter (second stage). *Maxime A. Faget, "Spacecraft Structure," McGraw-Hill Yearbook of Science and Technology 1971, p 396*

sick-out, *n.* an organized absence of employees from their jobs on the pretext of being sick, to avoid the legal penalties that may result from a formal strike.

About 20 of Hartford's 57 black cops took part in a sick-out last year over assignment and promotion grievances. *Time, Nov. 23, 1970, p 13*

But the two most important ones in the legal context are the recent strikes involving the nation's postal workers and the "sick-out" by American air controllers. *Anthony Thomas, The Times (London), April 6, 1970, p 23*

The postal strike had barely ended when a sick-out by air traffic controllers continued the communications snarl. The controllers began a campaign of organized absence from their jobs, reporting illness, on March 25. *Paul T. Hartman, "Labor Unions," 1971 Collier's Encyclopedia Year Book, p 311*

SIDS, abbreviation of SUDDEN INFANT DEATH SYNDROME.

The higher the total infant mortality, the higher the number of SIDS cases; thus everywhere (except perhaps in Ontario) the poorer children are the more frequent target. *Philip Morrison, "Books," Review of "Sudden Infant Death Syndrome," edited by Abraham B. Bergman, J. Bruce Beckwith, and C. George Ray, Scientific American, March 1971, p 120*

sigma, *n.* **1** short for SIGMA FACTOR.

Richard Burgess and Andrew Travers of Harvard discovered a protein, known as sigma, whose sole function is to stimulate the synthesis of RNA chains. In other words, sigma is the silent partner of the enzyme RNA polymerase that catalyzes RNA synthesis. *Jacob Kastner, "Molecular Biology: Biophysics," Britannica Book of the Year 1970, p 543*

Another factor which was once thought to be like sigma now appears to be quite different, because it attaches directly to DNA, not to RNA polymerase, to turn genes on. *"A New Protein to Turn on DNA Synthesis," New Scientist and Science Journal, July 22, 1971, p 182*

2 short for SIGMA PARTICLE.

The substitute particles are all heavier than the electron. The lightest, the mu meson, is 200 times as heavy as the electron; the heaviest, the sigma, 2,400 times as heavy. *Dietrick E. Thomsen, Science News, Nov. 14, 1970, p 385*

sigma factor, a protein that stimulates the synthesis of chains of RNA (ribonucleic acid) by regulating the action of the enzyme RNA polymerase.

...the function of the sigma factor is to give the core enzyme its specificity to transcribing from a fixed point on a strand of DNA and producing RNA of defined length. *Science Journal, April 1970, p 17*

A team of biochemists... told of identifying a substance they called sigma factor, which is responsible for starting mRNA synthesis. *Jerald C. Ensign, "Microbiology," The World Book Science Annual 1972 (1971), p 338*

sigma particle, an unstable elementary particle having a mass approximately 2400 times that of the electron.

The heavy sigma particle and the antiproton are produced by allowing beams from the CERN [European Organization for Nuclear Research] 28-GeV proton accelerator to strike metal targets. *New Scientist, Sept. 17, 1970, p 566*

sigmic, *adj.* of or containing sigma particles.

Kaonic and sigmic atoms tend to go together, since experiments aimed at making kaonic atoms make sigmic ones too. *Dietrick E. Thomsen, Science News, Nov. 14, 1970, p 386*

sign-in, *n.* the collecting of people's signatures in support of a petition, demand, etc., addressed to the government or any authoritative body.

...churches organized a "sign-in" urging the Government to allocate 0.75 per cent of the gross national product as international aid. *The Times (London), May 12, 1970, p 2*

[see -IN]

Silent Majoritarian, a member of the Silent Majority.

As Mr. Goulden's article points out, Silent Majoritarians do read, although their reading patterns are different from those of intellectuals. If Eddie Rickenbacker can write a book that the Silent Majority will read, someone can do the same with the war, because the stupidity of this war transcends the boundaries between liberal and conservative. *W. D. Maurer, Berkeley, Calif., in a Letter to the Editor, Harper's, July 1970, p 12*

Silent Majority, *Especially U.S.* **1** the politically nonvocal section of the population that is believed to constitute the majority of Americans. Compare MIDDLE AMERICA.

It must be said that after hearing what the Silent Majority has to say, one can appreciate the turn to violence in America.... They say they are informed yet have never heard of, let alone read, a book on the [Vietnam] war. "I don't feel we have enough information to know whether policies are right or not. Leave it to the leader." *Bernie Koenig, London, Ontario, in a Letter to the Editor, Harper's, July 1970, p 12*

As President Richard M. Nixon and his administration began their second year in office, they appeared to be operating on one basic assumption: that there was a great silent majority in the United States which would — and should — dominate national politics in the 1970's. One political columnist saw the typical member of this silent majority as a suburbanite or small-town dweller who was deeply disturbed by high prices and taxes, crime in the streets, political demonstrations and violence, welfare "handouts," integration and black militancy, and the changing attitudes of the young toward sex, drugs, established institutions, and authority figures. *Steven V. Roberts, "United States," 1971 Collier's Encyclopedia Year Book, p 560*

2 the general American public.

To be topped in the [TV] ratings race by Hawaii Five-O was painful enough; but to be quantitatively inferior to another fraternal combination, *The Everly Brothers* (darlings of the Silent Majority), was pushing Job's fate. *Robert Lewis Shayon, "TV-Radio," Saturday Review, Oct. 3, 1970, p 48*

[from a phrase used by President Nixon in an address to the nation on November 3, 1969: "And so — to you, the great silent majority of my fellow Americans — I ask for your support."]

silent spring, the death of the spring season resulting from the wanton destruction of nature by toxic chemicals.

The Caspian Sea is probably the most dramatic battleground of Soviet Russia's looming silent spring and to date this battle is being lost to oil, petroleum products, industrial and city sewage, ballast and waste from ships. *C. L. Sulzberger, The New York Times, June 12, 1970, p 38*

If we don't develop suitable pesticides — and use them — we will really have Silent Spring because there won't be any trees left for the birds to sing in. *George Cline Smith, New York, in a Letter to the Editor, The New York Times, June 27, 1970, p 28*

[from *The Silent Spring*, a book (1962) by the American writer Rachel Carson, 1907-1964, which called public attention to the danger to ecological balance involved in the widespread use of toxic pesticides and herbicides, and which opened with a description of a spring morning with no birds left to sing]

silvichemical, *n.* any chemical substance derived from trees.

... but the research did point out two important avenues of development. One lay in the manufacture of charcoal, and the other in the development of silvichemicals. Either approach appeared to offer the possibility of a very high extraction rate for the timber.... *Aubrey Wilson, "Marketing's Contribution to Industrial Research," New Scientist, Nov. 3, 1966, p 224*

[from *silvi-* (from Latin *silva* forest) + *chemical*]

si·ma·zin ('saɪ mə zən) or **si·ma·zine** ('saɪ mə,ziːn), *n.* a moderately toxic chemical widely used as a weed killer.

Some species might even become resistant to sprays,

although the only example so far appears to be a United States groundsel reported to be undeterred by simazin and atrazin. *Leonard Amey, The Times (London), Nov. 23, 1970, p 13*

Real progress in horticultural weed control dates from the introduction of simazine, the first member of a large and versatile family of herbicidal chemicals developed in the research laboratories of J. G. Geigy of Basle, Switzerland. Simazine is only very slightly soluble in water and it breaks down quite slowly in the soil. When applied to bare soil it stays on the topmost layer, where it prevents weed germination for several months, while remaining safely out of contact with the roots of most woody plants. *New Scientist, Dec. 24, 1964, p 847*

[from *sim-* (perhaps for *simple*) + tri*azine* (chemical compound with a ring of three carbon atoms)]

simulate, *v.t.* (of a computer) to imitate or represent (a physical system or its activity); make a simulation of.

What the computer did is called *simulation*. Working from data given it, the computer calculated, or simulated, the satellite's position at various instants and produced the picture on microfilm. *The Atlantic, July 1964, p 1*

simulation, *n.* **1** the representation or imitation of a physical or social system or its activity by computers for the purpose of predicting the behavior of that system under certain conditions.

The work, started by a group of behavioural scientists and computer experts to help Kennedy in 1960, consists of building a computer model of the whole electorate. Political statements can then be tried out on it — and the computer should respond just like the voters. This idea, called simulation, originally developed for military exercises, was backed for political purposes by Edward Greenfield, a New York businessman. Simulation has come a long way since 1960. *The Sunday Times (London), Nov. 1, 1964, p 9*

Political simulation may be regarded as an experimental technique through which complex political phenomena such as a political campaign or an international relations crisis involving a series of events and a number of nation-state "actors" may be recreated or forecast under quasi-experimental conditions controlled by the simulation director. *Marshall H. Whithed, "Simulation," McGraw-Hill Yearbook of Science and Technology 1971, p 383*

2 one such representation or model.

These methods, known collectively as simulations, involve the making of numerical models of large scale systems and solving them on high-speed computers for all imaginable configurations. *Hilbert Schenck, Jr., The New York Times, Nov. 15, 1965, p 36*

sing-in, *n.* U.S. a musical act or event in which the audience serves as a chorus or joins in the singing.

Sing-in at Philharmonic Hall — Handel's "Messiah," directed (seriatim, fortunately) by nineteen directors.... *"Goings On About Town," The New Yorker, Dec. 19, 1970, p 16*

BLOOD — In this communal sing-in the myth of Orestes is confusingly applied to the Vietnam war. Much of the music (neo-folk) is agreeable, but the words cannot be understood. *"Goings On About Town," The New Yorker, March 20, 1971, p 4*

[see -IN]

single-cell protein, a protein produced from liquid or gaseous petroleum fractions that are fermented by specially treated yeast cells or other micro-organisms. *Abbreviation:* SCP

Single-cell protein is designed to be used as a food supplement in those areas of the world where protein is lacking in the diet. It can be added to bread or soft drinks or introduced into the diet in other ways. *Science News Yearbook 1970, p 278*

sink, *n.* natural disposal of particles in the atmosphere.

Once the material reaches the bottom of the pack and enters the troposphere it can be mixed vertically rather rapidly. Small particles spend about 30 days in the troposphere before being washed out by rain. Gases spend varying periods there depending on the "sinks" by which each is removed from the atmosphere: incorporation into cloud droplets, reactions with other gases, loss to finely divided liquid or solid particles or the earth's surface and so on. *Reginald E. Newell, "The Global Circulation of Atmospheric Pollutants," Scientific American, Jan. 1971, p 33*

sir·ta·ki (sir'tɑ: ki:), *n.* a Greek folk dance performed in a circle with locked arms and with sidewise, alternately crossing steps, often with improvisations by individual dancers.

He will very gently...lead you through a sirtaki and finish the dance solo with that chair held on high in his mouth. *Geoffrey Moorhouse, The Manchester Guardian Weekly, Nov. 7, 1970, p 15*

[from Greek]

sis-boom-bah, *n.* *U.S. Slang.* spectator sports, especially football.

For the next 2 1/2 years it was girls, flasks and sis-boom-bah. But the public image concealed an all-night reader who forged through Flaubert, Rimbaud, Joyce, Proust, Eliot, Pound, Cummings, Stein, Hemingway. *Time, Aug. 17, 1970, p 64*

[syllables commonly occurring in school cheers]

sit·com ('sit,kɑm), *n.* *U.S.* a type of radio or television comedy series based on contrived situations built around a character or group of characters.

...*Nancy* [is] a sappy-sounding sitcom with Celeste Holm set in the White House. *Time, March 2, 1970, p 77*

The [porno-spoofs] genre is based on the idea of inviting you to laugh at sex—as if you were watching a dirty sitcom on TV. *Pauline Kael, "The Current Cinema," The New Yorker, Nov. 6, 1971, p 190*

[from *situation* comedy]

situation ethics, a form of ethics based on the theory that absolute moral rules cannot be applied to specific situations or circumstances, each of which must be judged within the particular context of its occurrence.

Fletcher [the American theologian Joseph Fletcher] argues that situation ethics avoids the pitfalls of other approaches to morality. In both the natural-law morality of Roman Catholics and the scriptural law of Protestantism, he argues, principles become inflexible and "obedience to prefabricated 'rules of conduct' is more important than freedom to make responsible decisions." On the other hand, the antinomian, or nonprincipled, approach of the existentialists leads to anarchy and to moral decisions that are "random, unpredictable, erratic, quite anomalous." *"Theology: Situation Ethics: Between Law and Love," Time, Jan. 21, 1966, p 53*

situation room, a room, usually at a military headquarters, where reports are given on the current status of any action, operation, etc.

The intelligence "situation room" will keep the 15 permanent ambassadors of the N A T O countries and their key military commands more fully up-to-date on Russia's political and military build-up than they have ever been before. *Antony Terry, The Sunday Times (London), May 21, 1967, p 7*

When Egypt's Gamal Abdel Nasser announced that he was sealing off the Gulf of Aqaba against all Israeli vessels.... The President canceled minor appointments, put the White House Situation Room on special alert, and went before television cameras with a somber, seven-minute statement. *"The U.S.: Foreign Relations," Time, June 2, 1967, p 11*

Sitz·fleisch ('zits,flaiʃ), *n.* *German.* patience; perseverance; (literally) sitting flesh, i.e. buttocks.

The result is that it takes not only special training but a liberal endowment of *Sitzfleisch* to hear one of his [Messiaen's] pieces out from one end to the other. *Robert Evett, "A Crucifix of Sugar," The Atlantic, May 1971, p 106*

SI unit, any of the units of measurement in the international meter-kilogram-second system of measurements.

In practice it has been found that one conspicuous advantage of SI units is the simplification of calculations. *D. E. R. Lloyd, Nottingham, England, in a Letter to the Editor, The Times (London), Jan. 4, 1972, p 14*

[*SI,* abbreviation of French *Système International (d'Units)* International System (of Units)]

skateboard, *n.* See the quotation for the meaning.

...the latest candidate is skateboarding. A skateboard is a surfboard scarcely larger than a steak plate, mounted on roller-skate wheels, and a skateboarder is anyone daring enough to career over the concrete while aboard one. *Time, June 5, 1964, p 65*

skateboarder, *n.* person who rides a skateboard.

On the morning of what was probably the last truly warm, gentle Saturday of 1966, we wandered off Fifth Avenue at Seventy-second Street and into the Park, strolling among the skate-boarders, bicyclists, and English baby carriages down the slope toward Conservatory Pond. *"The Talk of the Town," The New Yorker, Nov. 26, 1966, p 52*

skateboarding, *n.* the act or sport of riding a skateboard. Also called SKURFING.

Skateboarding—or skurfing, as it's also called—was started four years ago in California by a group of surfing enthusiasts who were looking for something to do while the Pacific tides were out. *Jack Batten, Maclean's, July 24, 1965, p 26*

ski bob, a vehicle for sliding downhill on snow, consisting of a metal frame with handlebars connected to a short pivoting ski in front, and a seat attached to a longer fixed ski in the back. The rider usually wears mini-skis for balance.

The ski-bob is rather like a converted bicycle, and the rider uses small skis on each foot for steering and stopping. *Joyce Rackham, The Times (London), Oct. 21, 1967, p 28*

Although the first ski bob was apparently patented in the U.S. in 1892, the sport only recently started flourishing in the resort center of Crans-Montana in the Swiss Alps. *Time, March 17, 1967, p 36*

ski bobber, a person who engages in ski bobbing.

In addition the ski bobber wears 18-inch-long skis. Because the weight is not taken by the legs unpleasant accidents are far rarer. *The Times (London), Jan. 16, 1968, p 8*

ski bobbing, the sport of riding a ski bob.

Ehrwald is not a centre for the relatively new sport of ski bobbing, but facilities are available in a number of resorts. [Ski bobbing is] ideal for the executive whose only exercise is manoeuvring the castors of his office chair. One merely requires balance and, according to the Clarkson brochure, "the ability to ride a bicycle, a scooter, a horse, or even a fairground roundabout." . . . A number of resorts are now featuring ski bobbing. . . . *John Carter, "Travel: Skiing in Ehrwald," The Times (London), Oct. 3, 1970, p 20*

ski·doo (ski'du:), *n.* a motorized sledge moving on endless tracks in the back and movable skis in front, used for travel on snow or ice. Also called *(British)* SKI-SCOOTER.

As if 1080 poison isn't enough [to kill rodents], we have not hundreds but thousands of strychnine pills thrown from airplanes, Ski-Doos, and jeeps. *Faith McNulty, "A Reporter at Large," The New Yorker, June 13, 1970, p 56*

In the American and Canadian Arctic zones, the Eskimos are being "civilised" with central heating, drink, juke boxes, skidoos and hamburgers. *Peter Dunn, "Wally Takes Baby Kari to Live with the Eskimos," The Sunday Times (London), Aug. 1, 1971, p 6*

[from *Ski-Doo*, trade name of such a vehicle]

skiffle, *n.* a blend of country music and rock 'n' roll popular in Great Britain in the 1960's.

Skiffle was much nearer to a pop movement proper than either revivalist or modern jazz. . . . Like many of the later pop movements, skiffle too was at first unaware of its potential commercial possibilities. *George Melly, Revolt Into Style, 1970, p 25*

Saturday night at the universities was once the time for a few drinks at the local, a bus into town, a picture and a coffee. Town dance halls were not popular—too rough or too sedate—and although some unions held their own hops, where university groups tried their hand at skiffle or rock and roll, they were usually modest affairs in size at any rate. *"University Beat," The Manchester Guardian Weekly, Nov. 10, 1966, p 13*

[of unknown origin; originally applied to a form of U.S. jazz of the 1920's played with unconventional rhythm instruments such as kazoos, washboards, and saws]

skimmer, *n.* *U.S.* a simply cut dress with straight lines, often sleeveless and with a round neck. *Also used attributively.*

The shirt is represented in every shape and form, sometimes stopping where a shirt traditionally stops and sometimes growing down a few (still a very few) inches to make a skimmer dress. *Angela Taylor, The New York Times, Jan. 5, 1968, p 39*

A stylish clean-cut skimmer . . . neat, narrow, nubby. Deftly fashioned by The Sporting Tailors. *Advertisement by "The Talbots," Hingham, Mass., The New Yorker, March 18, 1967, p 194*

skimming, *n.* the practice of concealing a part of the winnings of a gambling casino to avoid paying taxes.

The Mob's technique there [Las Vegas] known as "skimming," was as simple as larceny and as easy as shaking the money tree: a part of the cash profits from six . . . casinos was simply diverted before the figures were placed in the ledger books. *Time, Aug. 22, 1969, p 18*

It was believed to be the first time indictments had been returned for so-called "skimming" of money in the casino counting rooms. *The New York Times, May 12, 1967, p 1*

skin, *adj.* *Especially U.S. Slang.* **1** showing people in the nude; nudie.

If LePeters' identity is built on a cultural fault line, the characters around him are bizarre monoliths. His boss, Bruno Glober, spends working hours slathering over skin magazines and evenings spreading around huge sums of cash raked in from an interest in an international slacks cartel. *R. Z. Sheppard, "Books," Review of "Words for a Deaf Daughter" by Paul West, Time, Sept. 7, 1970, p NY6*

2 of or relating to movies, burlesque theaters, etc., showing nudes.

The skin houses were mostly playing short subjects—a girl taking a bath in a sylvan stream, a volleyball game in a nudist camp. *Richard Schickel, "Performing Arts: Porn and Man at Yale: Dirty Movies," Harper's, July 1970, p 34*

—*v.i.* *U.S. Slang.* short for SKIN-POP.

. . . all my friends were on heroin. I snorted a couple of times, skinned a lot, and after that I mained it. *Time, March 16, 1970, p 17*

skin flick, *Slang.* a motion picture showing people in the nude, usually engaging in some sexual act; a nudie.

It started with sex educational films, and documentaries on pornography from Denmark and Sweden, and has continued with a profitable avalanche of skin flicks and stag movies, all totally explicit, and some of them, I understand, very well made. *Clive Barnes, The Times (London), Nov. 28, 1970, p 20*

'Shock films,' they called them; 'skin flicks' that dealt not with the humorous, honest, robust, Rabelaisian earthiness that *nurtures* life, but with the cologned, pretentious, effete, adulterated crud that *pollutes* life. . . . *Frank Capra, The New York Times, June 18, 1971, p 37*

skinhead, *n.* a type of young British working-class tough wearing closely cropped hair, work pants and suspenders, and hobnailed boots, who engages in street fighting. Also called AGRO-BOY.

The skinheads . . . specialize in terrorizing such menacing types as hippies and homosexuals, Pakistani immigrants and little old ladies. "Hairies," those with long hair or hippie-style clothing, are their particular enemies, but they are quite happy to break up a synagogue, a Chinese café or an Indian restaurant. *Time, June 8, 1970, p 37*

Presumably they meant the movie to observe, without either condemning or condoning, some of the oddities in our midst—Hell's Angels, greasers, skinheads, druggies etc. *Derek Malcolm, "After Chandler," The Manchester Guardian Weekly, Dec. 18, 1971, p 21*

"Why are we skinheads?" William said. He paused a moment, as though puzzled. "We got the same interests, like. See, we like tasties, we like a drop of booze, we like soft drugs. And we all belong together, like. Nobody can touch us when we're all together. Even the fuzz is a bit scared." *The New York Times Magazine, Sept. 13, 1970, p 114*

skinheadism, *n.* the practices of skinheads, especially the use of violent tactics or brutality against members of minority groups.

We are all conscious of the fact that many M.P.s on the Opposition side ... are showing great courage against a different and more menacing type of skinheadism in Northern Ireland. *Harold Wilson, speaking in the House of Commons, quoted in The Times (London), Feb. 6, 1970, p 8*

Skin·ner·i·an (ski'nir i: ən), *adj.* of or relating to the ideas and theories of the American behaviorist B. F. Skinner, born 1904, especially his concept of controlling behavior through a system of rewards and reinforcements as practiced in operant conditioning and behavior therapy.

It should be clear by now that the way a child learns to speak provides very strong evidence for a Chomskian view of language—a rationalist view—rather than a Skinnerian view—a behaviourist one. *Neil Smith, "Puggles and Lellow Lollies," The Listener, Dec. 2, 1971, p 760*

Underlying the method is the Skinnerian conviction that behavior is determined not from within but from without. *"Behavior: Skinner's Utopia: Panacea, or Path to Hell?" Time, Sept. 20, 1971, p 47*

—*n.* a supporter of B. F. Skinner or his theories.

Menninger is confident that the experts would not find it so hard to agree on courses of action, in spite of theoretical differences between them—though it's hard to see a Freudian and a Skinnerian agreeing on what should be done. *David Cohen, "The Crime of Punishment," New Scientist and Science Journal, Aug. 5, 1971, p 328*

skinny-dip, *U.S. Slang.* —*v.i.* to swim in the nude.

...one pious Mayo farmer, coming upon his Dutch summer tenants skinny-dipping in his pond, threw them off his property, because his parish priest had warned him that people who did not wear clothes were "Communist Protestants who never say their prayers." *Jane Kramer, "Letter from Dublin," The New Yorker, July 25, 1970, p 61*

—*n.* a swim in the nude.

"There's no danger. I swim farther than that every day. But I don't want to take my clothes off and march down the beach like some drunk going for a skinny-dip before an admiring throng, do you understand?" *Ralph Maloney, "Happy Ending" (a short story), The Atlantic, Sept. 1971, p 95*

skinny-dipper, *n. U.S. Slang.* a person who swims in the nude.

According to an undercover source, the skinny-dippers are a nocturnal breed and come out only at night. Of course, this is for an obvious reason: under the sun they might get well done all over. Moonlight is softer and also doesn't emphasize disfiguring (appendectomy) scars like bright sunlight. *Waylon Smithey, "Nudity Is Popular At Lake, Too," The Tuscaloosa News (Alabama), Sept. 5, 1971, p 7A*

skin-pop, *v.t., v.i. U.S. Slang.* to inject (a liquefied narcotic drug) just beneath the skin. Also shortened to SKIN.

...adolescents...inject subcutaneously (skin-pop) or into their veins (mainline) barbiturates, amphetamines, and almost anything else they can lay their hands on. *Marion K. Sanders, "Addicts and Zealots: The Chaotic War Against Drug Abuse," Harper's, June 1970, p 79*

...he had been using it [dope] for about six months, "skin-popping," or shooting it into his shoulder about two or three times a week. *John A. Hamilton, "Child Junkies*

and a Cry for Help," The New York Times, Feb. 23, 1970, p 26*

ski-scooter, *n. British.* another name for SKIDOO.

Motorized ski-scooters used by the army on manoeuvres in Lapland. *Picture legend, The Times (London), May 13, 1970, p III*

skivvy, *v.i. British Slang.* to work as a servant; do domestic or menial work.

There are now better jobs than skivvying to look for, and wages sometimes comparable with what the job-seeking housewife herself might be earning. *Angela Milne, Punch, Feb. 21, 1968, p 287*

[verb use of *skivvy, n.* a household maid]

skiwear, *n.* clothes appropriate for skiing.

Mr. Winter rid himself of some difficult lines, in a sales decline of from $30-million. "We gave up skiwear, men's wear, and teen-wear—all splinter divisions that were diluting our management effort and talent," he said. *Isadore Barmash, The New York Times, July 15, 1968, p 43*

skurfing, *n.* another name for SKATEBOARDING.

Skateboarding—or skurfing, as it's also called—was started four years ago in California by a group of surfing enthusiasts who were looking for something to do while the Pacific tides were out. *Jack Batten, Maclean's, July 24, 1965, p 26*

[blend of *skating* and *surfing*]

skydive, *v.i.* to dive from an airplane in a long free fall as a sport, often performing various soaring maneuvers before opening the parachute.

Jim Marshall [a football quarterback] is a man of considerable enterprise. He skydives and sells portable telephones; he used to peddle wigs and manage a rock group .... *"Sport: Football," Time, Oct. 17, 1969, p 46*

Mary Cushing ... snorkles, surfs, skis and sky-dives.... *Bernadine Morris, The New York Times, April 24, 1965, p 21*

skydiver, *n.* a person who skydives.

Aug. 27 Huron, O. Sky divers, leaping through an overcast from an off-course B-25, hit Lake Erie instead of their scheduled drop target at Ortners Field, Birmingham, O.... *"Disasters: Miscellaneous," Britannica Book of the Year 1968, p 287*

skyjack, *v.t.* to hijack (an aircraft) and fly it to a place other than its original destination.

Two weeks ago, any hope of reconciliation between the two sides was finally fractured when the guerrillas skyjacked three jet airliners and held as hostages 430 crewmen and passengers. *"Jordan: The King Takes on the Guerrillas," Time, Sept. 28, 1970, p 17*

Hubbard suggests that attention should also be paid to the psychology of the skyjacked passenger, who is usually passive. *"Behavior: Bringing Skyjackers Down to Earth," Time, Oct. 4, 1971, p 48*

—*n.* **1** a skyjacking. Compare HIJACK.

While world attention focused on the drama of a quadruple skyjack last week, the greater crisis of peace or war hung unresolved over the Middle East. *Time, Sept. 21, 1970, p 14*

2 a skyjacker.

Skyjack Minichiello becomes the hero of his homeland. *Alan McElwain, The Sunday Times (London), Nov. 9, 1969, p 7*

skyjacker, *n.* a person who hijacks an aircraft. Also called AIR PIRATE.

A Pan American Boeing 747 became the first jumbo jet to be hijacked when it was diverted to Cuba while flying from New York to Puerto Rico. The skyjacker, armed with a pistol and container of nitroglycerine, was greeted in Havana by Fidel Castro while the other 370 passengers were allowed to continue their journey. *"The Week," The Manchester Guardian Weekly, Aug. 8, 1970, p 3*

skyjacking, *n.* the hijacking of an aircraft. Also called AIR PIRACY.

Captured hijacker...is all smiles as he regales reporters with the tale of his 17-hour transatlantic flight to Italy in a TWA jet bound for San Francisco. The more than 50 skyjackings that occurred this year were taken a lot more seriously by the passengers and crews involved, however. *Picture legend, "Aeronautics," 1970 Collier's Encyclopedia Year Book, p 84*

Sky·lab ('skɑi,læb), *n.* **1** a United States manned space flight project following the Apollo project, designed to establish a scientific space station or orbiting laboratory near the earth.

Skylab will have the only manned space flights funded between the end of the lunar missions in the summer of 1972...and the advent of space shuttle flights scheduled for 1977-78. *Everly Driscoll, Science News, Oct. 10, 1970, p 303*

2 the earth-orbiting space station to be established by this project.

The programme includes the plans for Skylab, the orbiting scientific laboratory due for launching in 1972. *The Times (London), April 8, 1970, p 6*

Skylab will, for the first time, provide our astronauts with ample room to move about when in orbit—far different from the cramped confines of the Mercury, Gemini and Apollo capsules. *William G. Holder and William D. Siuru, Jr., "Skylab," Encyclopedia Science Supplement (Grolier) 1971, p 329*

[from *Sky* + *lab*oratory]

skylounge, *n.* See the quotation for the meaning.

...the Department experiments with a "sky-lounge." This vehicle moves on the ground to collect passengers at various downtown stations and is then lifted by a Sikorsky YCH-54A "flying crane" helicopter and flown right to the plane at the airport. *Wolf Von Eckardt, "Redesigning American Airports," Harper's, March 1967, p 75*

sky marshal, *U.S.* a federal law-enforcement officer assigned to protect aircraft and passengers from skyjacking.

An ex-Navy man was awaiting appointment by the Federal Aviation Administration as a sky marshal—a job that he characterized as "a symptom of our paranoid society." *Daniel Lang, "A Reporter At Large (Vietnam Veteran)," The New Yorker, Sept. 4, 1971, p 51*

slalom canoe, a canoe, usually with a deck, used in a canoe slalom.

As many as five modern canoes will fit on top of a car, even a bug Volkswagen—single canoes, double canoes, slalom canoes. *John McPhee, The New Yorker, March 21, 1970, p 129*

slant, *n. U.S. Army Slang.* a derogatory name for an Asian or Oriental.

Besides being called gooks, the Vitenamese are also known as slopes, slants, and dinks. *Ian Wright, The Manchester Guardian Weekly, Dec. 20, 1970, p 6*

[so called from the shape of the eyes]

slap shot, a quick shot made in ice hockey with a short, hard swing at the puck.

...his "slap shot," delivered from a full windup, has been clocked at 118.3 m.p.h., nearly 35 m.p.h. above the league average, and his "wrist shot," fired with just a flick of the stick, zings along at 100.7 m.p.h. *Time, March 1, 1968, p 46*

sleeper, *n. U.S. Slang.* a sedative or depressant.

"I've come into work bombed on sleepers a couple of times (they make you go round like you're drunk); the boss warned me." *Victoria Brittain, The Times (London), Aug. 18, 1970, p 6*

sleep-in, *n.* the occupying of a public place by a group of people to spend the night or to sleep there as a form of protest, demonstration, or indication of ownership rights.

...Six Asians who have been picketing the British High Commission building in Kampala for the past month, moved into the building today and said they would not leave until they were given permits to enter Britain.... Earlier this week, the group announced a "sleep-in" at the High Commission, but later postponed it to allow more time for the British Government to reply to their petition submitted last month. *The Times (London), March 7, 1970, p 4*

—v.i. to take part in a sleep-in.

She [Candice Bergen] has taken up the signal causes of her generation—sleeping-in with the Indians at Alcatraz, demonstrating against the ABM. *Time, Nov. 2, 1970, p 84*

[see -IN]

sleep-learning or **sleep-teaching,** *n.* instruction obtained by or given to one who is asleep, usually by means of recordings, on the theory that the sleeper's unconscious is capable of absorbing the information. Technical name, HYPNOPEDIA.

"Sleep-learning" is big business in the Soviet Union, where an increasing number of civil and military establishments are setting up dormitory facilities for pumping into trainees dull but necessary information—such as foreign language vocabularies—during the time "wasted" asleep. *New Scientist, March 5, 1970, p 446*

In Russia more than 180 educational institutes including secondary schools, polytechnicums, institutes of adult and further education, colleges for academic, industrial and military training are now fully equipped for sleepteaching. *F. Rubin, The Times (London), Sept. 19, 1970, p 13*

sleeve-note, *n. British.* a descriptive or explanatory note on the jacket of a phonograph record or album.

On this third [recording]...E. Power Briggs uses an American instrument by John Challis, and the sleeve-note gives the specification. *Roger Fiske, The Gramophone, April 1970, p 538*

slope, *n.* **·1** an economic recession.

Recession, recedence, slope, shake-out, or what have you, to the chairman of the board and the factory worker at the bench, it is something a little better than a slump and much worse than a pinch. *Alistair Cooke, "Finance: Dehiring of the Boss," The Manchester Guardian Weekly, Sept. 5, 1970, p 22*

2 *U.S. Army Slang.* a derogatory name for an Asian or Oriental (so-called from the slanted eyes).

Young GIs soon learned that there were Army names for Vietnamese too: gook, dink, and slope. *Seymour M. Hersh, "My Lai 4," Harper's, May 1970, p 55*

slot car or **slot racer,** *U.S. and Canada.* a toy car that is powered electrically to run on a slotted track while manipulated by remote control, used in slot racing.

The track on which slot cars race is a tabletop affair, somewhat similar to the familiar model-railway layout. (But devotees scorn the comparison. "You can't *race* model trains," one of them pointed out. "It's the competitive aspect that makes slot cars so popular.") *H. R. W. Morrison, Maclean's, Jan. 22, 1966, p 9A.*

Slot car lubricator increases the speed of slot racers when applied to commutator, gears, bearings and other moving parts of the car. *Science News, March 26, 1966, p 208*

slot racing, *U.S. and Canada.* the sport or hobby of racing slot cars.

. . . a rapidly growing number of Americans—adults as well as youngsters—. . . have caught the slot-racing bug. *Terrell L. Tebbetts, The Wall Street Journal, Aug. 27, 1965, p 22*

slow virus, a virus that may remain present in the body of an infected individual for most or all of his life, believed to be the cause of many chronic diseases of man.

Evidence recently came to light that implicated slow viruses in such neurological disorders of humans as multiple sclerosis and polyneuritis as well as in rheumatoid arthritis. *Robert G. Eagon, "Microbiology," 1972 Britannica Yearbook of Science and the Future, 1971, p 296*

slumdweller, *n.* an inhabitant of one of the slums of a city.

Mills Lane's Community Development Corp. has spent $1,000,000 each year since 1968 to bankroll "clean-up campaigns" in which businessmen and slumdwellers wield shovels and brooms to spruce up ghetto areas and build playgrounds. *Time, July 20, 1970, p 65*

Slumdwellers buying new homes can borrow at 4% from the National Housing Bank, which charges 10% to better-off house purchasers. . . . *The Times (London), April 4, 1971, p 59*

slumism, *n.* *U.S.* the existence or proliferation of city slums.

We must show the same unhesitating commitment to fighting slumism, poverty, ignorance, prejudice, and unemployment that we show to fighting Communism. *I. W. Abel, Pittsburgh, Penn., in a Letter to the Editor, Harper's, Feb. 1967, p 83*

slumlord, *n.* *U.S.* the landlord of a neglected or abandoned building in the slums of a city.

There are boycotts—Negro leaders prefer to call them "selective patronage movements"—against business firms that discriminate against Negroes in their personnel practices. There are rent strikes against slumlords who refuse to repair Negro tenements. *"The March in Washington," Time, Aug. 30, 1963, p 12*

Prosecution of slumlords is ineffective. *The New York Times, Jan. 27, 1965, p 31*

slumlordship, *n.* *U.S.* the condition of being a slumlord.

Within the chivalric order of slumlordship he is a very minor vassal. He owns two buildings on the Lower East Side, both nearly a hundred years old; they are separated by many blocks of slums. . . . *Richard M. Elman, "Manny Gelder: Slumlord," The Atlantic, Nov. 1966, p 128*

In fact, the charge that "Jews, predominantly" are the slumlords of Harlem is a gross libel. . . . Fortunately, the statistics on ghetto slumlordship are at hand, as contained in the first massive, detailed study of the economics of the city's housing. . . . *Richard Cohen, New York, in a Letter to the Editor, The New York Times, July 24, 1970, p 30*

slurb (slərb), *n.* *Especially U.S.* an unsightly area on the outskirts of a large city, that has been developed with cheap housing, often indiscriminately built among gas stations, used-car lots, diners, etc.

Every year, Greater Los Angeles' growth consumes 70 sq. mi. of open land. Not only is prime farm land taken out of production, but it is also developed in an inefficient way; the term "slurb" was coined in California to describe sleazy, sprawling subdivisions. By planning ahead, much land can be preserved, with houses and services concentrated between green belts. *Time, Feb. 2, 1970, p 59*

These [Japanese] are the people who are existing in air so foul, on waters so polluted, in cities so choked and "slurbs" so ugly that by comparison the New York-Washington corridor looks almost like a planned development. *John B. Oakes, The New York Times, Nov. 30, 1970, p 41*

[formed from *slum* sub*urb*]

SM, abbreviation of SERVICE MODULE.

The service module (SM) contains the main spacecraft propulsion system and supplies most of the spacecraft's consumables (oxygen, water, propellant, hydrogen). It is not manned. *Steven Moll, "The Apollo Spacecraft," Encyclopedia Science Supplement (Grolier) 1969, p 321*

smack, *n.* *U.S. Slang.* heroin.

"I started taking smack and barbiturates." *Marion K. Sanders, quoting an addict in "Addicts and Zealots," Harper's, June 1970, p 79*

Countered a bearded pusher: "Buy one tab of acid and get a free tab of smack!" Kids on bad trips were treated by volunteer physicians, and were urged over a makeshift public-address system to "bring a few joints for the doctors." *Time, Aug. 10, 1970, p 11*

smart bomb, *U.S. Military Slang.* a bomb released from an aircraft and guided to a specific target by laser and television beams.

Saigon, June 25—U.S. warplanes dropped laser-guided 2,000 pound "smart" bombs onto North Vietnam's only modern steel-producing facility, destroying that country's capacity to produce steel, U.S. headquarters announced today. *Daily News (New York), June 26, 1972, p 2*

To one who has bombed and been bombed, recent Pentagon propaganda about our new "smart" bombs is dumb and repetitious (not to say, indecent). That's the kind of sure-kill language we were using twenty-eight years ago, when I was a bombardier-navigator with the 15th Air Force in Italy. Then it was the Norden bombsight that was supposed to give us pinpoint precision bombing. *Sol Fox, "Smart Bombs and Dumb Bombs," The New York Times, June 26, 1972, p 33*

smogbound, *adj.* enveloped or surrounded by smog; covered with smog.

Other researchers had concluded that neither geological nor cultural factors seemed to affect the occurrence of hypertension. Smogbound, noise-deafened, misanthropic Londoners, who move out of the city to get more out of life, might be taking their high blood pressure with them. *Peter Stubbs and Gerald Wick, "The Grass is Always Greener on the Other Side," New Scientist, Jan. 1, 1970, p 8*

[patterned after *fogbound, snowbound*, etc.]

smogout, *n.* a condition of being completely enveloped by smog.

As these blackouts and smogouts and breakdowns continue to occur, with disastrous consequences to both the habitat and the human population, such a change may take place as was noted in London during the blitz. . . . *Lewis Mumford, "Reflections: The Megamachine," The New Yorker, Oct. 31, 1970, p 96*

smoke-in, *n.* a gathering to smoke marijuana or hashish, sometimes as a demonstration for legalizing their use.

At rock festivals like Woodstock, at demonstrations like the November moratorium or July smoke-in, you make friends. . . . *Martin Walker, The Manchester Guardian Weekly, Oct. 31, 1970, p 24*

Gone are the big smoke-ins punctuated by acid rock and strobe lights. *Gregory Wierzynski, Time, Feb. 22, 1971, p 17*

[see -IN]

smokeshade, *n.* **1** the measure of the relative amounts of black, gray, and white particle pollutants in the atmosphere.

. . . an air pollution alert is called for when carbon monoxide readings of 10 parts per million last for four hours, coupled with high four-hour readings for either sulphur dioxide or smokeshade, a measurement of particulates in the air. *Donald Janson, The New York Times, Feb. 9, 1967, p 29*

2 the pollutant particles themselves.

. . . a heavy layer of dead air—a coagulated cloud of carbon monoxide from automobile exhausts, sulphur dioxide, and smokeshade (the scientists' word for visible atmospheric dirt)—spread out over the city and hovered there for days. *Andy Logan, "Around City Hall," The New Yorker, May 15, 1971, p 117*

snarl-up, *n.* a confusion; mix-up.

Freight business is healthier, but still recovering from nightmare snarl-ups that followed the merger three years ago. *Philip Jacobson, The Times (London), Feb. 12, 1970, p 25*

"Beverly, was that an F and G in your part?" Conductor Aldo Ceccato once asked during a snarl-up in a recording session. *"Beverly Sills: The Fastest Voice Alive," Time, Nov. 22, 1971, p 58*

snatch squad, *British.* a special detachment of soldiers assigned to help quell a riot or disturbance by seizing the most conspicuous offenders.

After two hours the Army sent snatch squads into the area to bring out trouble makers and a platoon with riot shields and clubs moved in to dismantle a temporary barricade. *David Wilsworth, The Times (London), Aug. 5, 1970, p 1*

snip, *n. British Slang.* a bargain.

Just about every property man you talk to says that London County Freehold was a snip at Metropolitan Estate's offer price of about 49s. *The Sunday Times (London), Jan. 4, 1970, p 27*

Only intelligent honours graduates under 30 need apply. Snip at £4.50 a week. *Ruth Miller, "Top Women Tomorrow," The Times (London), Jan. 25, 1972, p 10*

sno·fa·ri (snou'fär i:), *n.* an expedition into a polar or other snow- or ice-covered area, usually in skidoos.

. . . the short period we have been here has brought us the experience of a new kind of mountain recreation, the snofari. Tricked out like spacemen . . . we were each equipped with a kind of bobsleigh fitted with skis fore and caterpillar tracks aft and dispatched into the mountains. *John Hennessy, "Skiing: Loveland Without Beds," The Times (London), Dec. 12, 1970, p 5*

[from *snow* + sa*fari*]

snopes (snoups), *n. U.S.* an unscrupulous type of businessman or politician, especially of the southern United States.

In the heated circumstances of the present [opposition to the nomination of Judge Harrold Carswell to the Supreme Court] Mr. Nixon would be joining the yahoos and the snopeses. *Louis Heren, The Times (London), April 10, 1970, p 10*

[named after the *Snopes* family of vicious characters in the novels of William Faulkner]

snowmobiler, *n. U.S.* a person who rides a snowmobile (a vehicle for traveling on snow), especially as a sport.

Snowmobilers have been accused of everything from terrorizing wildlife to vandalizing hunters' cabins. *Time, March 15, 1971, p 62*

"Snowmobiler's back" is a new problem for doctors and for the patients who suffer from it. The condition is produced, according to Verne L. Roberts and Robert P. Hubbard of the University of Michigan Highway Safety Research Institute, when the vertebrae of the back are rammed together upon impact as the snowmobile driver "flies" his machine through the air. *Charles F. Merbs, "Anthropology," The World Book Science Annual 1972 (1971), p 258*

snowmobiling, *n. U.S.* the act or sport of riding a snowmobile.

. . . unless you simply can't stand snow in any form, you really ought to try snowmobiling. It's a lot more thrilling than skating and less hazardous than skiing. *Hal Tennant, Maclean's, Dec. 1968, p 37*

In Michigan's Upper Peninsula, a snowmobiling club planned a fox hunt in which the winner would get to crush the panting beast under his treads (the event was squashed by public outrage). *Time, Nov. 23, 1970, p 41*

sociolinguistic, *adj.* of or relating to sociolinguistics.

According to Wolfram, 'The basic sociolinguistic method is that of correlating social with linguistic variables'. . . . The important social variables are given as Social Status, Racial Isolation, Age, Sex, and Style. *R. K. S. Macaulay, "Reviews," Review of "A Sociolinguistic Description of Detroit Negro Speech" by Walter A. Wolfram, Language, Sept. 1970, p 764*

Robbins Burling . . . in his *Man's Many Voices*, . . . compiles the sociolinguistic findings and recent ethnological work on semantic categories to show how such findings contribute to cultural theory. In effect, his message is a cultural one: the importance for individuals of maintaining distinct cultural identities at many levels, and of the constant (and patterned) innovations in all behaviour, linguistic and other, that go along with this search. *Richard Frank Salisbury, "Anthropology," Britannica Book of the Year 1971, p 96*

sociolinguistics, *n.* a branch of linguistics that deals with the social aspects of language and speech.

As it develops, the discipline has spawned such hybrids or specialties as computational linguistics, sociolinguistics, psycholinguistics, even biological linguistics. *Time, Feb. 16, 1968, p 46*

The crux of the whole problem may be that to describe literary structures in anything but a trivial way is not simply a matter of moving up to the level of socio-linguistics, but of really working at something Fowler denies the existence of. . . . *Frank Kermode, "Literature and Linguistics," The Listener, Dec. 2, 1971, p 771*

sociologese, *n.* sociological jargon.

The outcome is about 200 tables, some of them positive cadenzas of sociologese, eg: "Attitudes towards university expansion by degree of apprehension, within categories of political position per cent." *Christopher Driver, "Graduation as a Growth Industry?" The Manchester Guardian Weekly, May 22, 1971, p 13*

Brown sat down with an air of relief, and fielded the newsmen's questions in careful sociologese. *Francine du Plessix Gray, "A Reporter at Large," The New Yorker, Jan. 3, 1970, p 32*

[from *sociology* + *-ese* language, jargon]

socioreligious, *adj.* involving or combining social and religious elements.

. . . religious circles emphasize . . . the importance which should be given to socio-religious values such as . . . indissolubility of the family, conjugal love and responsible parenthood. *Paul L. Montgomery, The New York Times, Sept. 17, 1967, Sec. 1, p 27*

Why *shouldn't* they break the bread and sip the wine together? Hence the socio-religious ritual drama of black Christians knocking on white churchhouse doors crying "Honor! Honor! Unto the dying Lamb!" *Ralph Ellison, "Letters: No Apologies," Harper's, July 1967, p 18*

sociotechnological, *adj.* involving or combining social and technological elements.

The concatenation linking monocultures, pests, pesticides, and all the complex procedures to control the toxicity of pesticides constitutes another obvious example of sociotechnological failure. *René J. Dubos, Saturday Review, Dec. 2, 1967, p 70*

The forefathers of these neo-dandies erected a tremendous empire by selling kettles and knives to savages — a bold and inventive occupation expressive of great sociotechnological changes in mankind's history. The grandsons try to sell psychedelic mugs to tourists from the Midlands. *Leopold Tyrmand, "Reflections: A European from America in Europe," The New Yorker, Dec. 21, 1968, p 52*

sock, *v.t.* **sock it to someone,** *Slang.* to attack someone squarely; strike out with zest against an opponent.

I agree with Agnew all the way. I wrote a letter to him saying 'The only thing I can say to you, sir, is Sock It To Them.' *Joseph Goulden, "Voices from the Silent Majority," Harper's, April 1970, p 72*

. . . the sight of the politicians still socking it to each other was like a Punch and Judy show at a state funeral. *Dennis Johnson, The Manchester Guardian Weekly, June 20, 1970, p 13*

soft, *adj.* **1** relating to or characteristic of soft art.

By deleting from "The 1960s" all that junky stuff of Arman, Bontecou, César, Chamberlain, Latham, Gentils, Lindner, Mallary, Ortiz, Ossorio, Spoerri, Tinguely, and half a dozen "soft" (i.e., psychologically or technically tentative) paintings, those by Rivers, Copley, Kitaj, Rosenquist, Dine, Oldenburg, a much more unified — hence forceful — statement of the new taste and the values that support it could have been presented. *Harold Rosenberg, "The Art World: The Nineteen-Sixties: Time in the Museum," The New Yorker, July 29, 1967, p 81*

2 *Military.* not protected against missiles or bombs. Compare HARDENED.

Defense Secretary Laird has said repeatedly that the logical reason for Soviet development of their huge weapon is to strike first at the U.S., and to strike at our Minuteman silos below the ground. Hardened silos require a huge weight of explosives for their destruction. By contrast, our Minuteman is designed for no such first-strike function. It exists for retaliatory strikes on "soft" targets such as Soviet cities. *John L. Steele, "The Russians are Eight Feet Tall — But So Are We," Time, Aug. 3, 1970, p 11*

3 readily decomposed or oxidized in a sewage system. Compare BIODEGRADABLE.

. . . manufacturers of synthetic soap powders, pellets and liquids have been producing new "soft" detergents. *Lisa Hammel, The New York Times, Aug. 10, 1965, p 16*

soft art, art characterized by the use of pliable material, especially in works having an unfinished, tentative quality.

Under the names of antiform, process art, earthworks, concept art, soft art, and impossible art, these manifestations emphasize ideas and processes rather than finished products. They are concerned with impermanence, and their makers seem to have rejected the idea of art as a salable commodity. *Benjamin de Brie Taylor, "Art: Process Art and Antiform," 1970 Collier's Encyclopedia Year Book, p 116*

soft drug, any drug that is not considered physically addictive, such as marijuana, mescaline, and various amphetamines. Compare HARD DRUG.

. . . any recent speculation that Mr. Callaghan is minded to be tolerant about such so-called soft drugs as cannabis is misguided. *David Wood, The Times (London), March 11, 1970, p 4*

Although there was no doubt about the deleterious effects of hard drugs (heroin, morphine, etc.), there was much debate concerning the harmful effects of the softer drugs, such as marijuana. *Donn L. Smith, "Medicine," 1971 Britannica Yearbook of Science and the Future, 1970, p 233*

soft-land, *v.t.* to land (a spacecraft, instruments, etc.) slowly so as to avoid serious damage.

The four "feet" of the vehicle scheduled to soft-land two U.S. astronauts on the moon by 1970 received a patent from the U.S. Patent Office. *William McCann, Science News Letter, April 17, 1965, p 254*

—*v.i.* to make a soft landing.

On May 30 the National Aeronautics and Space Administration (NASA) launched the Surveyor I spacecraft on a mission to soft-land on the moon and photograph its surface. *"Moon," The 1967 Compton Yearbook, p 353*

—*n.* a soft landing.

If instruments are to be soft-landed on Mars using parachutes, it is important that the density of the atmosphere is sufficient to allow the parachute to act. Soft-lands

433

in bright areas—the lowlands—are therefore easier from an engineering point of view. *The Times (London), April 8, 1968, p 7*

[back formation from *soft landing*]

soft-lander, *n.* a spacecraft designed to make a soft landing. Compare LANDER.

The same method applied to the lunar soft-lander *Luna 9* enabled the Jodrell Bank observers to study its velocity changes during approach, to confirm the value of gravity at the Moon's surface, and to establish that *Luna 9's* retro rockets fired at a height of 68 km. *New Scientist, Oct. 20, 1966, p 73*

The calendar for the 1970's for unmanned flights seems set, though not all of the programs are funded. These include . . . two Mars soft landers to be launched in 1975 ($878.9 million), and the Grand Tours to the outer planets in 1977 and 1979 (up to $1 billion). *Science News, July 25, 1970, p 53*

soft landing, a slow landing of a spacecraft to avoid damaging the spacecraft or its payload.

The flight came just "at the right time for lunar launches, consistent with other Soviet lunar launches for a soft landing or orbital mission". . . . *Science News, Dec. 2, 1967, p 535*

The Soviet Union launched another unmanned spacecraft toward the moon today in an apparent attempt to achieve a soft landing of an instrument package. . . . *Theodore Shabad, The New York Times, June 9, 1965, p 1*

soft lens, a contact lens made of a porous plastic that becomes soft when it absorbs the moisture of the eyes and causes less discomfort or irritation than the harder type of lens.

"I intend using the soft lenses on every patient I possibly can," said Dr. Mary Young, who maintains a 3,000-patient-a-year optometrical practice in Braintree, Mass. *Time, May 31, 1971, p 46*

. . . a leading London eye-surgeon said to me: "Soft lenses are still experimental and at the moment you wear them at your own risk." *Mirabel Walker, "Lenses Easy On the Eye," The Times (London), Jan. 3, 1972, p 5*

soft line, a moderate, flexible attitude or policy, especially in politics. Compare HARD LINE.

The U S, Britain and the Benelux trio tend to adopt a "hard" line, favouring the removal of the Atlantic Council from Paris, even though France has not requested this. But Canada, Norway, Denmark and Italy prefer a "soft" line and want to leave the Council where it is to minimise the rupture with France. *Nicholas Carroll, The Sunday Times (London), June 5, 1966, p 4*

soft-liner, *n.* a person who adopts or follows a soft line. Compare HARD-LINER.

When a reporter asked Kissinger last week if he would characterize himself as a hard- or soft-liner, he replied: "I have tried to avoid labels like 'hard' or 'soft.'" *Time, Dec. 13, 1968, p 16*

soft rock, a low-keyed, rhythmically free, sophisticated form of rock'n'roll.

His songs delve ingeniously into hard and soft rock, blues, gospel, even country rock. . . . *Time, Jan. 11, 1971, p 40*

Some soft-rock groups—the Association, the 5th Dimension, Simon & Garfunkel—have invaded the middle-of-the-road market themselves. *Robert Christgau, "Performing Arts: Rock Critics," Harper's, Sept. 1969, p 24*

soft science, any of the social or behavioral sciences, such as political science, economics, sociology, and psychology. Compare HARD SCIENCE.

One may define technology to mean political technique as well as nuts and bolts; that is, the soft sciences along with the hard. *Ward Just, The Atlantic, Oct. 1971, p 91*

Project SIMILE Director Hall T. Sprague says these games are "to the soft sciences what a laboratory is to the hard sciences of physics, chemistry and biology." They give students, he says, "a gut-level understanding of the pressures that go with a position of power." *Time, June 3, 1966, p 43*

Although he [Brigadier General Ira A. Hunt, assistant commandant of the Engineer School at Fort Belvoir, Virginia] had been educated as an engineer, he had become increasingly interested in economics; he had taken a degree in the subject at George Washington University (on the theory that the Soviets intended to bury us with rubles rather than armies), and he liked to apply the methodology of the hard sciences to the soft sciences. *Lewis H. Lapham, "Military Theology: The Cloistered Nature of Army Life and the Habit of Mind that Makes of War a Virtuous Crusade," Harper's, July 1971, p 82*

soft sculpture, a sculpture made out of cloth, plastic, foam rubber, or other soft, pliable material.

The most noted creator of soft sculpture, Claes Oldenburg, was similarly honored [with a retrospective] at the Museum of Modern Art, New York. *Victor H. Miesel, "Art: Sculpture," The Americana Annual 1970, p 99*

software, *n.* **1** the designs, instructions, routines, etc., required for the operation of a computer or other automatic machine. Compare HARDWARE, FIRMWARE.

Software is the general term used to describe various levels of the language of computer instructions; it includes compilers and assemblers, as well as application programs in high-level languages such as FORTRAN. *Max Tochner, "Computer-Assisted Analytical Chemistry," McGraw-Hill Yearbook of Science and Technology 1971, p 58*

There are no doubt an incalculable number of scientific advances that could be brought about if scientists only knew which information to reach for in the vast sea of software (the engineer's term for printed matter—documents, plans, etc.). *Jonathan Eberhart, Science News, June 18, 1966, p 493*

2 the plans, fuel, etc., of a rocket, missile, or other space vehicle.

The US government . . . procures goods and services with sophisticated technological components (e.g. weapons, rocket boosters and analytical "software"). *Steven R. Rivkin, New Scientist, June 25, 1964, p 800*

3 anything thought of as not directly related to some operation, principal function, or objective, such as the nonmechanized elements of a mechanized system.

Generally speaking, standardization means persuading the several services to buy identical "software"—that is, the thousand and one everyday housekeeping items ranging from paint brushes to belt buckles that aren't directly related to combat efficiency. *Jerry Landauer, The Wall Street Journal, Aug. 23, 1965, p 1*

soilborne, *adj.* carried in or transmitted by the soil.

The National Agricultural Advisory Service's plant pathology department, Cambridge, who pioneered this technique in England, has been able to associate certain soilborne diseases with environmental factors such as soil type and structure, drainage, and fertilizer and spraying practices. *New Scientist, July 25, 1968, p 187*

The prevalence of soil-borne viruses in Britain has been established only within the last 10 years. *The Times (London), Dec. 23, 1968, p 12*

solar cell, a cell that converts the energy of sunlight into electrical energy.

These [thermoelectric] generators also compete with solar cells, which are widely employed for supplying electricity from sunlight in space vehicles. *Raymond Wolfe, "Magnetothermoelectricity," Scientific American, June 1964, p 70*

solar panel, a panel of solar cells.

Electrical energy was derived from sunlight by two solar panels unfolded by the astronauts from either side of the device, and the seismic package began radioing data back to earth. *Walter Sullivan, "The Rocks Yield Some of Their Secrets," The Americana Annual 1970, p 32*

solar wind, a stream of charged particles emitted into space from the corona of the sun. Compare STELLAR WIND.

The speed of the solar wind as it passes the earth has been measured at several hundred kilometers per second. *Hugh Odishaw, "A Space Age Goal: Exploring the Solar System," 1969 Britannica Yearbook of Science and the Future, 1968, p 66*

Dust in space would be expected to soak up gases from the solar wind, and also it may have gases entrapped during its formation. *David W. Parkin, "Meteoroid: Analytical Techniques," McGraw-Hill Yearbook of Science and Technology 1969, p 209*

soldier, *n. U.S. Underworld Slang.* another name for BUTTON MAN.

The Luchese family . . . was suspected of being in the narcotics traffic and because it had a large number of low-ranking members, called soldiers or button men, who might be induced to talk. *Charles Grutzner, The New York Times, Dec. 23, 1967, p 11*

solid-state, *adj.* of, relating to, or based upon solid-state physics; using the conductive and other properties of solid materials.

The availability of solid-state devices has resulted in the introduction of a new line of equipment which supersedes older vacuum-tube versions to provide improved performance, increased reliability, smaller size, and in some cases lower cost. *U. S. Berger, "Microwave Systems," McGraw-Hill Yearbook of Science and Technology 1969, p 213*

Our Trophy Line of navigation and communication equipment offers pilots and owners of business and private aircraft new savings in weight and space, as well as the increased reliability of solid state circuitry. *Advertisement by The Bendix Corporation, Detroit, Scientific American, Feb. 1966, p 7*

Epitaxy, the oriented overgrowth of one crystal upon another, is of particular interest to solid-state scientists. *New Scientist and Science Journal, April 22, 1971, p 193*

solid-state physicist, a specialist in solid-state physics.

In his studies, the solid-state physicist must have some means of knowing what compounds are likely to be semi-conducting if he makes them. *New Scientist, June 4, 1964, p 595*

solid-state physics, a branch of physics dealing with the physical properties of solid materials, such as crystals, glasses, and polymers.

From the beginning of solid-state physics, infrared, ultraviolet, and X-rays provided important methods of probing the properties in solids. *William E. Spicer, "Physics," 1972 Britannica Yearbook of Science and the Future, 1971, p 321*

A satisfactory quantitative explanation of the heat capacities of solids was one of the earliest successes of solid-state physics. *Alan Holden, "Solid-State Physics: The Scientific Study of Solids," Encyclopedia Science Supplement (Grolier) 1965, p 228*

solution set, *Mathematics.* the set which contains all the solutions to a mathematical sentence.

In current terminology the "solution set" of a false statement is not the null set but an element (member) of the null set, and since the null set has no members the statement is true of nothing. *Martin Gardner, "Mathematical Games," Scientific American, June 1971, p 123*

so·ma·to·sen·so·ry (ˌsou mə təˈsen sər iː), *adj.* of or relating to sensations involving the parts of the body that are not associated with the eyes, tongue, ears, and other primary sense organs.

Patients undergoing brain surgery, and who volunteered for the experiment, had electrodes placed directly on the surface of their somato-sensory cortex and were very lightly stimulated on their skins with small electric pulses. *New Scientist, Jan. 4, 1968, p 38*

[from Greek *sôma, -atos* body + English *sensory*]

something, *n.* **something else,** *U.S. Slang.* something special.

Buterakos beamed at me. "The sound effects are going to be something else." . . . "Wait 'til you hear that thing," Buterakos said. "It'll make the golfers jump into the next county." *George Plimpton, "The Alex Karras Golf Classic," Harper's, May 1971, p 62*

There is something about cathedral building that men like, Henry said . . . the awe is so thick you could cut it with a knife. "You are something else, Henry," Perpetua said. *Donald Barthelme, "Perpetua," The New Yorker, June 12, 1971, p 42*

son et lu·mière (ˌsɔ̃ ei lʏˈmyer), a dramatic spectacle using light effects, recorded music, and narrative, often held at a historic site. Compare SOUND-AND-LIGHT.

In this bicentennial year of Napoleon's birth . . . more than 200,000 tourists went to Corsica in 1969 to see the balls, costume pageants, and *son et lumière* (sound and light) presentations that marked the event. *"Celebrations: Napoleon Bicentennial," The 1970 World Book Year Book, p 263*

. . . we turned into Central Park south of the Metropolitan Museum, whose façade was floodlit as if for a performance of *son et lumière. The New Yorker, Aug. 17, 1968, p 21*

[from French, sound and light]

sonication, *n.* the use of high-frequency sound waves to break up matter.

Even today gross contamination is found on many product components received for clean assembly. Cleaning these parts is a major branch of ultraclean technology involving the application of special solvents, the use of 'sonication'— ultrasonic vibration—to jar the dirt loose, the testing for residual contamination and many other highly specialized procedures.... *L. B. Hall, "Ultraclean Technology," Science Journal, April 1970, p 42*

Ultrasonic treatment, or "sonication," is one of the procedures employed for disruption of the nuclei. It has proved useful, inasmuch as the nucleolar morphology and staining characteristics are unchanged. *Harris Busch, "Nucleolus," McGraw-Hill Yearbook of Science and Technology 1964, p 309*

sonochemical, *adj.* of or relating to sonochemistry.

In a new experiment performed at Stanford Research Institute, Professor Anbar has now shown that, even at the relatively low velocities at which water impinges on water in collapsing ocean waves, "sonochemical" reactions almost certainly occur.... *New Scientist, Oct. 10, 1968, p 95*

sonochemistry, *n.* the use of high-frequency sound waves to produce chemical reactions.

Research ... has shown that organic fluids can be broken down by "sonochemical" means.... The suggestion has been made that sonochemistry may be a route to novel syntheses for rocket propellants. *"Science in Industry: Israel: Sound as a Tool for the Chemist," New Scientist, Jan. 27, 1966, p 214*

soul, *n.* **1** the quality that arouses emotion or empathy, especially as exemplified in Negro music, art, and other cultural manifestations. Originally the term was used by Negro jazz musicians to describe the deeply felt quality of spiritual and gospel music when it appeared in jazz.

It is its ability to articulate this tragic-comic attitude toward life that explains much of the mysterious power and attractiveness of that quality of Negro American style known as "soul." *Ralph Ellison, "What America Would Be Like Without Blacks," Time, April 6, 1970, p 55*

2 soul music.

Soul is the pop music of the urban Negro community. It is a commercialized, stylized form of the blues, born in little bars and nightclubs on the wrong side of town. It is music to entertain, dance music; corporal, not cerebral. It relies on repetition, rhythm, vitality, and particularly bombast for its appeal. *Ellen Sander, Saturday Review, Oct. 26, 1968, p 91*

It was British groups like the Beatles and the Rolling Stones, with their heavy and acknowledged debt to American soul and blues, who revitalized rock by getting back to its roots. *Time, Sept. 28, 1970, p 51*

—*adj.* **1** arousing a feeling of kinship or a sense of mutual interest with another, especially in the distinctive spirit of black culture.

... Sonny Charles, the organist, took over, singing with a soul appeal that caught up even this predominantly white audience. *John S. Wilson, The New York Times, June 17, 1968, p 46*

Kohl shows how a sixth-grade class of wary Negro children in East Harlem learned to trust him as a teacher and trust themselves and thereby beat the system.... they listened to Bob Dylan, recorded the words of soul songs and classical blues, read poetry. *Nat Hentoff, "Books: The Most Deadly Sin," Review of "36 Children" by Herbert Kohl, The New Yorker, March 16, 1968, p 168*

With Hollywood scrambling to exploit every current trend, "soul" movies were probably inevitable. Enter *Cotton Comes to Harlem,* a meretricious thriller that should offend the sensibilities of any audience—black or white. *Time, July 6, 1970, p 70*

2 belonging to or owned by Negroes; black.

Long before "black capitalism" became a politically popular catch phrase, Negro-owned "soul banks" started sprouting in ghetto areas. *Time, Feb. 28, 1969, p 60*

soul brother, *U.S.* a fellow black man.

"Black is feeling you'll really be free when they cast a soul brother in a deodorant commercial." *Cartoon legend by Turner Brown, Jr. in "Black Is," Grove Press, 1969, quoted in Time, April 6, 1970, p 77*

Once, when there were rumors of new burnings, someone scrawled in white paint on the pavement outside my house: *Soul Brother. V. S. Naipaul, "One Out Of Many," The Atlantic, April 1971, p 82*

soul food, *U.S.* food typically eaten by blacks, especially in the South, such as chitterlings, corn bread, pig's feet, turnip greens, and fried catfish.

Soul food may be said to embrace all the food created or developed over the centuries by the Negro cooks of the South.... It embraces such obvious dishes as fried chicken, spareribs, black-eyed peas, candied yams, mustard, turnip and collard greens cooked for hours with salt pork or fat back. ... To some minds, however, the dishes that might be termed the most basic soul food are those made from the nonluxury parts of animals, particularly pork. These were the lesser cuts not generally coveted for the white man's table—pigs' feet called trotters, neck bones, pigs' ears, pigs' tails, hog maw and, the soul food to beat all, chitterlings. *Craig Claiborne, "Cooking with Soul," The New York Times Magazine, Nov. 3, 1968, p 102*

... the white girls at Barnard are demanding soul food in the college cafeteria.... *Dan Wakefield, "Daddy Strikes Back," Review of "The Conflict of Generations" by Lewis S. Feuer, The Atlantic, June 1969, p 103*

He [Father Thomas Lee Hayes, an Episcopal priest, an emissary in Sweden of Clergy and Laymen Concerned About Vietnam] also exhorted American tourists to come bearing foods that the deserters missed—soul food and peanut butter, bagels and Fig Newtons. *Daniel Lang, "A Reporter At Large: Out of It," The New Yorker, May 23, 1970, p 44*

soul music, a blend of rhythm and blues and gospel music, developed and popularized by black singers.

As the greatest living exponent of gospel music, one of the main sources of the currently fashionable soul music, she [Mahalia Jackson] should be assured of a sell-out.... *Punch, May 14, 1969, p x*

soul rock, rock'n'roll music influenced by soul music.

Because of the large audience—there are 58 percent more radios than people in the United States—programming has become more specialized. One station may play only conventional rock and roll, another only soul-rock, and a third only the most current acid-rock. *Kathryn Rose, "Television and Radio Broadcasting," 1971 Collier's Encyclopedia Year Book, p 534*

soul sister, *U.S.* a fellow black woman.

... plate glass in Negro-owned establishments remained intact and displayed the words, "Soul Brother" or "Soul Sister." *Rudy Johnson, The New York Times, June 17, 1968, p 24*

sound-and-light, *adj.* involving the combined use of light effects and recorded sound. Compare SON ET LUMIERE.

Dr. Robert E. L. Masters, 40, and Dr. Jean Houston, 31,

use a variety of non-drug stimuli—guided meditation, multisensory sound-and-light environments, electrical stimulation of the brain—to induce "altered states of consciousness...." *Time, Oct. 5, 1970, p 72*

In the midst of ... East Village [Manhattan] stands a five-story neighborhood landmark ... called Central Plaza. Other landmarks surround it: the Hebrew Actors Union, ... an ancient Ukrainian church ... antique shops, art galleries, sound-and-light discotheques.... *Robert Kotlowitz, "Performing Arts: Talent Hunt in the East Village," Harper's, March 1967, p 141*

▶ Originally this term was a translation of SON ET LUMIÈRE, as in the following quotation:

A "Sound and Light" program, using controlled light and recorded stereophonic sound, narrative and dialogue to give a dramatic presentation of history, was inaugurated at Independence National Historical Park, Philadelphia, on July 4, 1962, the first such program presented in the U.S. *Britannica Book of the Year 1963, p 589*

During the 1960's, as the *son et lumière* technique was extended to other forms of entertainment and other applications, the English term acquired a broader meaning which was not correspondingly imposed on the French phrase.

soundscape, *n.* range of sounds; musical panorama.

In this collection, he [Ataulfo Argenta, a conductor] proved his mastery of the subtle colors, treacherous rhythms, and delicate contrapuntal lines that fashioned Debussy's impressionistic soundscapes. *Time, Oct. 4, 1968, p 6*

Here, intimations of the dark progressions in the 'Munich' fugue of the Second Quartet and the icy, grinding dissonances of *A Child of Our Time* combine in a semi-palindromic wartime soundscape of a blasted and tragic grandeur.... *Bayan Northcott, "Music," The Listener, Nov. 11, 1971, p 666*

[from *sound* + *-scape* view, landscape, vista]

soup, *n.* **1** a mixture of basic chemical elements. Compare PRIMORDIAL SOUP.

By now all the vital molecular building blocks necessary for the accident of life to happen have been synthesized in the laboratory from simulated "soups". *Peter Stubbs, New Scientist, April 10, 1969, p 66*

The proposed guidelines had indicated that life probably arose from "a soup of amino-acid-like molecules" some 3,000,000,000 years ago, and that the diversity among present species is the result of evolution through natural selection. *John G. Lepp, "Zoology," 1972 Britannica Yearbook of Science and the Future, 1971, p 342*

2 the waste or residual product of a chemical process.

On cooling some plants below 0°C, supercooling occurs within the vascular system.... When ice does start to form in supercooled liquids it is a very rapid process. Ice would form in the cells as well as the vascular system and experiments show that when ice penetrates the cell membrane it destroys the cell structure. All that remains on thawing is a structureless 'soup' which rapidly decays. *D. B. Idle, Science Journal, Jan. 1968, p 60*

Nuclear reactors' uranium fuel elements ... eventually become choked, in effect, with the radioactive fragments of split atoms. When this happens the fuel must be taken to a reprocessing plant. There the fuel rods are dissolved in acid, and the reusable uranium and plutonium are separated out. What's left, in AEC jargon, is "the soup": A liquid laden with enough radioisotopes to make it one of the deadliest substances on earth. *Dennis Farney, "Atomic-Age Trash," Encyclopedia Science Supplement (Grolier) 1971, p 360*

3 *Surfing Slang.* the foam or froth formed by a wave breaking on the beach.

To the surfer each breaker has a "hook," or crest, a "shoulder," the calm portion behind the hook, and a "shore break," the final surge ending in the inevitable "soup," or foam. *Peter Bart, The New York Times, Aug. 10, 1965, p 31*

Sovietologist, *n.* another name for KREMLINOLOGIST.

The great debate among Sovietologists is whether lust for power or divergence of policy is the main cause of the perennial quarreling in the Kremlin. *Peter Wiles, The New Yorker, April 28, 1966, p 21*

Sovietology, *n.* another name for KREMLINOLOGY.

The resulting figures will thus be rather like Soviet production statistics and will presumably need a science like Sovietology for their interpretation. *Bernard Lewis, The Times (London), Dec. 24, 1965, p 7*

spaceborne, *adj.* **1** carried in or through space.

Wheat seedlings grew faster in space than on earth, and roots of the spaceborne seedlings curved upward toward the shoots and out to the side. *David E. Fairbrothers, "Botany," The Americana Annual 1968, p 117*

Loss of the eight satellites, each of which cost $1.5 million, stalled Department of Defense plans to double its spaceborne network of radio relay stations. *Science News, Sept. 10, 1966, p 176*

2 carried out in space or using spaceborne instruments.

In spite of considerable lobbying to make optical astronomy a space-borne science, many practising observers show little enthusiasm for the idea. *P. Lancaster Brown, New Scientist, March 28, 1968, p 680*

spaced-out, *adj. U.S. Slang.* stupefied by the use of narcotic drugs.

To a relieved public it seemed impossible that the police could have taken Kasabian under their wing and concocted a case against her group—the most spaced-out and helpless bunch of hippies available—but it did not seem so to me. *Frank Conroy, "Manson Wins!" Harper's, Nov. 1970, p 56*

The culture has its own in-group argot: "bummers" (bad trips) and "straights" (everyone else), "heat" (the police) and "narks" (narcotics agents) and being "spaced out" (in a drug daze). *Time, Sept. 26, 1969, p 41*

space shuttle, a space vehicle to transport men and materials to a space station. Also shortened to SHUTTLE.

Unlike the cone-shaped Apollo vehicles, which are not maneuverable in the atmosphere, the space shuttle will be capable of controlling where and how it lands. *Science News, April 4, 1970, p 343*

The space shuttle, as envisioned in 1970, was to consist of a completely reusable rocket-powered vehicle consisting of an orbiter and booster. *Richard S. Johnston, "Astronautics and Space Exploration," 1971 Britannica Yearbook of Science and the Future, 1970, p 128*

As currently conceived, the space shuttle would look more like a jumbo jet airliner than the Saturn V or Titan

IIIC rocket. *"An Integrated Space Transportation System,"* *1972 Britannica Yearbook of Science and the Future, 1971, p 30*

NASA believes it must develop the reusable rocket plane—the space shuttle—which will reduce costs of each launch. *Everly Driscoll, "Propulsion for the 1980's," Science News, Jan. 9, 1971, p 33*

spacesick, *adj.* sick from the effects of flight in space.

...Grumman engineers say that the designers of the space station will have to take the axis of the spin into consideration in planning the layout of furniture and of consoles, for if an astronaut were made to move his hand repeatedly in the wrong direction in relation to the spin, he could easily get spacesick. *"The Talk of the Town," The New Yorker, Feb. 27, 1971, p 32*

space tug, a space vehicle for servicing and linking orbiting spacecraft and space stations. See the second quotation for details.

...the so-called "space tug"...like the shuttle, would be manned but serve for transport between the space station and other objects in space, rather than between Earth and the station. *Peter Stubbs, New Scientist, July 9, 1970, p 82*

The space tug would consist of two parts: a propulsion module, which, as currently envisioned, would be approximately 22 feet in diameter and 25 feet long; and, attached to the propulsion module, a manned compartment with space for three to six people. *"An Integrated Space Transportation System," 1972 Britannica Yearbook of Science and the Future, 1971, p 31*

spacewalk, *n.* the act of moving in space outside a spacecraft.

The perspiration that shortened Astronaut Eugene Cernan's Gemini 9 spacewalk by fogging his faceplate could have been due to nerves instead of the heat of his exertions alone. *Science News, June 25, 1966, p 509*

The Gemini 8 Mission. Splashdown for the three-day Gemini 8 flight is scheduled for Friday, March 18, if all goes well, followed by color films of the space walk. *Time, March 18, 1966, p 1*

spacewalker, *n.* a person who takes a spacewalk.

Major White, who became the first American spacewalker, was protected by the regular rubberized air tight nylon suit reinforced by nine additional layers and two visors. *The New York Times, June 4, 1965, p 29*

spacewalking, *n.* the action of a spacewalker.

Spacewalking, although vitally important to orbiting space stations and any other missions that require outside repairs, will not be a part of the lunar flight. *Jonathan Eberhart, Science News, March 26, 1966, p 195*

spacewoman, *n.* a woman astronaut. Compare ASTRONAUTESS, COSMONETTE.

Valentina [Tereshkova], history's first spacewoman, is inspiring proof of the distances women have advanced in the secular world of the last hundred years....*Mary B. Hill, Maclean's, Nov. 16, 1963, p 84*

spaghetti western, *U.S. Slang.* a western (cowboy film about the American West) produced by the Italian movie industry.

As a swaggering bad guy in spaghetti westerns, Berger began to command fees that ran his annual income into six figures. *Time, April 5, 1971, p 38*

"El Topo" (it means "The Mole") was made in Mexico, and it resembles the spaghetti Westerns. It begins with a bearded stranger in black leather...riding on a sandy plain; the color looks cheap and overbright, unreal in that gaudy way that unsophisticated attempts at realism often produce—it's like Kodacolor, with aquamarine skies. But the stranger rides with his naked son sitting behind him.... And when the father and son come to a town, the town is a scene of more than usual spaghetti-Western carnage. It is a town of corpses and entrails; animals, children—everyone has been butchered, and the waters literally flow red. *Pauline Kael, "The Current Cinema," The New Yorker, Nov. 20, 1971, p 212*

Spanglish, *n.* a blend of Spanish and English spoken in parts of the western United States and Latin America. Compare FRINGLISH, HINGLISH, JAPLISH.

There were red bandanas with Texas-shaped clasps for the guests, a tour of the ranch and a historical pageant known as a "Texas Fandangle"—border-country Spanglish for fandango, the frenetic Mexican dance. *Time, April 7, 1967, p 12*

The Spanish-English potpourri is generally called Spanglish. Purists, damning "imported barbarisms," deplore the "mongrelization" of the language of Old Castile. *The New York Times, Dec. 18, 1967, p 8*

spansule, *n.* a capsule of tiny grains of medicine with varying thickness of inert coating that dissolve at different times to maintain a constant infusion of medicine into the body over the dosage period.

He swallowed a fifteen-milligram dextro-amphetamine-sulphate spansule with his coffee, looked briefly at his watch, and calculated the time span of his awareness. *Jesse Hill Ford, "The Doctor" (a story), The Atlantic, Jan. 1969, p 90*

The original "purple heart" tablet has recently undergone a change in shape to make it less recognisable to would-be-addicts, yet you print a photograph of a Drinamyl spansule for all to see. *Letter to the Editor from a General Practitioner, The Sunday Times (London), Dec. 13, 1964, p 12*

[from *span* + cap*sule*]

spare-part surgery, a branch of surgery dealing with the replacement of damaged organs, such as the heart, lungs, kidneys, and liver, either by transplantation or by the grafting of manufactured devices.

The other outstanding chapter is the final one, which deals in a refreshingly matter-of-fact way with some of the ethical, social and financial problems raised by progress in spare-part surgery. *Bernard Dixon, "Books," Review of "Spare-Part Surgery" by Donald Longmore, Science Journal, Sept. 1968, p 89*

What surgeons in all fields of spare-part surgery needed was some way of switching off the immune reaction against their grafts without at the same time lowering the body's defences against genuinely harmful foreigners. *"Science and Technology: Medicine," The Annual Register of World Events in 1967 (1968), p 387*

speakerphone, *n.* a speaker and microphone in one piece.

Emerson, a municipal court judge in Downey, Calif., finds the speakerphone invaluable for getting a brief piece of testimony from a policeman, parole officer or technical expert. *Time, April 5, 1968, p 54*

The Yellow Pages extol the advantages of the speakerphone for "hands free" telephoning, a facility much prized in kitchen and bathroom. *E. S. Turner, Punch, June 23, 1965, p 912*

Special Drawing Rights, a monetary reserve of the International Monetary Fund from which member nations may draw credit in proportion to their contribution to the Fund. *Abbreviation:* S.D.R. or S.D.R.s Also called PAPER GOLD.

There are now four assets that are counted as official monetary reserves: gold, dollars, pounds sterling and IMF credit positions. With the creation of Special Drawing Rights on the IMF, there will be five. *The New York Times, July 11, 1968, p 36*

The new special drawing rights were intended to supplement, not supplant, gold and foreign exchange. *William Davis, The Manchester Guardian Weekly, Oct. 3, 1968, p 22*

...the governors for the great powers turned more and more, as the meeting progressed, to an existing facility of the I.M.F. called Special Drawing Rights, or S.D.R.s. *John Brooks, "A Reporter At Large," The New Yorker, Oct. 23, 1971, p 128*

speed, *n. Slang.* methamphetamine, a stimulant drug. Also called METH.

Workers in The Trailer in Toronto's Yorkville Village ...studied amphetamine abusers for nine months and ran into not only freaks shooting every day, but "weekenders" (spasmodic drug-takers) who needed "speed" to get through school and personal crises. *Sheila Gormely, The Times (London), Feb. 23, 1970, p IV*

It's all over, everyone in Kansas is freaking out. It's the California kids, the California kids, they're behind it all, they're way out ahead with drugs and Speed....*David Halberstam, "The Man Who Ran Against Lyndon Johnson," Harper's, Dec. 1968, p 56*

The user tends to be nervous.... His hands tremble and he constantly scratches his nose and licks his lips. This is because the "speed" dries up the membranes of the nose and mouth, leaving an uncomfortable, itchy feeling. *Sidney Katz, "Medicine: How Can I Tell If My Child Is On Drugs?" Maclean's, Nov. 1968, p 62*

Norman was speeding, but well under the limit. "Speed" is the street name for amphetamines and amphetamine-related drugs, drugs which act as stimulants to the central nervous system. *Jonathan Black, "The 'Speed'," The New York Times Magazine, June 21, 1970, p 14*

speed-read, *v.t.* to read rapidly by taking in several words, phrases, or sentences at a glance.

I speed-read a detective novel and fall asleep by midnight. *John Casey, "Testimony and Demeanor," The New Yorker, June 19, 1971, p 24*

speed-reader, *n.* a person who speed-reads.

The Evelyn Wood Reading Dynamics Institute... teaches prospective speed-readers to see every word on the page—but to read three words at once, not one word out of three. *The New York Times, June 5, 1965, p 22*

Histoire should be read as poetry, which means it should be read aloud. Speed readers, trained to sop up information and the dull acknowledgments of psychological and sociological fiction, will have to shift into low. *"Poetry of Perception," Review of "Histoire" by Claude Simon, Time, March 29, 1968, p 62*

speed-reading, *n.* the act or practice of reading rapidly by the assimilation of several words, phrases, or sentences at a glance.

Speed reading has been adopted by many harried business executives and government officials as a cure-all for paperwork pile-ups. *The New York Times, June 5, 1965, p 22*

spider hole, *Military use.* a hole in the ground concealing a sniper.

...the Second Battalion, 35th Infantry Regiment,... had perfected a technique for finding enemy troops in the many spider holes that spot that part of the coastal plain. *The New York Times, Aug. 26, 1967, p 5*

Later I watched as Sheridan tanks crashed into the rubber trees to flush out Vietcong and North Vietnamese hiding in spider holes and bunkers. *Michael Hornsby, The Times (London), May 7, 1970, p 6*

spin·ar ('spin,ɑr), *n.* a rapidly spinning galactic body.

Current theories of explosive galaxies like NGC 1275 envision compact nuclear regions composed of millions of pulsar-like objects, or else a giant spinar containing a mass equivalent to 100 million stars and rotating with a period as short as days or months. *Science News, March 27, 1971, p 209*

[from *spin* + *-ar*, as in *pulsar, quasar*]

spinoff, *n.* a secondary product or result of some activity; by-product. Compare FALLOUT.

The vaccine is the result of a new type of ultra high-speed centrifuge that is a spinoff from atomic weapons work conducted here by the Atomic Energy Commission. *Richard D. Lyons, The New York Times, Feb. 28, 1968, p 18*

A hundred and one new technologies may have burgeoned in the laboratories and assembly plants of the Cape Kennedy subcontractors, but the spin-off in human terms—in consumer fashions and design, politics and industrial relations, entertainment and the arts—has been very nearly nil. *J. G. Ballard, The Manchester Guardian Weekly, Dec. 5, 1970, p 19*

Water pollution is among the most undesirable spin-offs of heavy industrialization and technological progress. *"Pollution," Science News Yearbook 1969, p 278*

spinout, *n.* a spin causing a car to run off the road, especially when rounding a corner at high speed.

Also popular: decorative features such as racing stripes, special identifying fender emblems and "spoilers"—vertical flaps that put pressure on the rear wheels to prevent spinouts but are largely nonfunctional at highway speeds. *Time, April 5, 1968, p 38*

spin wave, *Nuclear Physics.* a wave propagated by the deviation of a nuclear spin. Compare MAGNON.

In a mechanically ordered substance, the spins [of electrons] periodically change direction. They do this in a succession like falling dominoes, and the phenomenon has the appearance of a wave, called a spin wave, moving through the substance, turning over the spins. *Science News, Nov. 28, 1970, p 411*

splash, *v.i.* **splash down,** to land in water, especially in the ocean, after a space flight.

The mission will be over, however, when the Apollo spacecraft plunges back through the atmosphere to splash down in the Pacific Ocean north west of Hawaii. *John Noble Wilford, The New York Times, April 4, 1968, p 10*

The dramatic recovery of Gemini 9 astronauts who splashed down within two miles of the USS Wasp was witnessed as it happened by millions of television viewers both in the United States and abroad. *Science News, June 18, 1966, p 484*

splashdown, *n.* the splashing down of a spacecraft.

Gemini 11 is to end its three-day mission with a splashdown in the Atlantic tomorrow morning. *The Times (London), Sept. 15, 1966, p 1*

The spacecraft will later dive back into earth's atmosphere at a speed of 25,000 miles an hour, the same velocity it would reach on a return trip from the moon. Splashdown is expected in the Pacific Ocean northwest of Hawaii. *The New York Times, April 3, 1968, p 7*

split, *v.i. Slang.* **1** to go away; leave.

Another Pinkerton [guard]...was standing in the kitchen when we went down there...and said it was an easy night for the guards, because there were so few drunks. "I only do this part time," Chris told us.... "Hey, thanks for the cigarette. I gotta split." *"The Talk of the Town," The New Yorker, Feb. 7, 1970, p 22*

Two or three times, Mick [Jagger] is forced to stop the proceedings and plead with the audience to maintain a little order. "People!" he calls out. "People! Look, cool it! Otherwise we can't play. We *won't* play!" And then the direst threat. "We're going to *split!* Unless you cool it, we're going to *split!*" *William F. Buckley, Jr., "A Week's Journal," The New Yorker, Aug. 28, 1971, p 51*

2 to run off; desert.

They [draftees] 'split' for different reasons—anything from personal problems to political resistance—but mainly go when they get Vietnam orders. *Clancy Sigal, " 'I Am An American Military Deserter And I Ask for Political Asylum,' " The Listener, Oct. 22, 1970, p 539*

Perpetua's mother shouted. "If anyone knew how I hate, loathe, and despise turkeys. If I had known that I would cook eighty-seven separate and distinct turkeys in my life, I would have split forty-four years ago. I would have been long gone for the tall timber." *Donald Barthelme, "Perpetua," The New Yorker, June 12, 1971, p 40*

spoiler, *n.* **1** *U.S.* a third political candidate who takes away enough votes to spoil another candidate's chances of winning. See also SPOILER PARTY.

Another heated primary race pitted incumbent Senator Morse, strong opponent of President Johnson's Vietnam policy, against pro-administration Robert Duncan in a battle for the Democratic nomination for the U.S. Senate. Morse won a close victory. Conservative Democrat Phil McAlmond, who picked up 17,658 votes, was dubbed by some as a "spoiler" for Duncan. *Kenneth L. Holmes, "Oregon: State Primary Battles," The Americana Annual 1969, p 518*

It seems clear that William Buckley will poll enough votes to be a "spoiler," though it is not yet certain for whom. *Leon M. Labes, The New York Times, Nov. 1, 1965, p 40*

2 an airflow deflector on an automobile that helps reduce the danger of spinouts.

One of the Chaparrals has a high wing "spoiler," the other a more conventional spoiler rising from the rear deck. Spoilers are devices that catch the airflow over the car body and keep the rear wheels on the track. *Frank M. Blunk, The New York Times, March 31, 1967, p 41*

spoiler party, *U.S.* a third political party formed especially to split one of the two regular parties so as to spoil its chances of winning in an election.

Mr. Javits, a liberal Republican who is facing a campaign for re-election this year, described the six-year-old Conservative party as "a faction" that had been set up as "a spoiler" party. *The New York Times, Jan. 25, 1968, p 19*

...the formation of a Third, or "spoiler" party is very much on the minds of peace activists, including dissident Democrats, as a rebuke to the Johnson administration for its conduct of the Vietnam war. *Eleanor Fischer, "Martin Luther King in the White House?" Maclean's, July 1967, p 2*

spongeware, *n.* an Early American glazed earthenware with a mottled surface produced by the application of the glaze with sponges, or an imitation of this.

The dining area is weighed down by a pine cupboard filled with Staffordshire china and a Shaker dry sink filled with spongeware. *Whitney Balliett, The New Yorker, Dec. 28, 1968, p 36*

spook, *n. U.S. Slang.* a spy.

The charge may well be true, and at least one U.S. diplomat abroad affirms, "We know he is a spook," though the same accusation was equally applicable to every Chinese diplomat in Africa during the 1960s, when Peking's men were aiding insurgents everywhere. *"China: The Fall of Mao's Heir," Time, Nov. 22, 1971, p 16*

...if it is believed that the economic and political development of Thailand can be greatly shaped by the United States and that the Thais are a natural bastion against Communism...there will have to be other men in the field to watch for subversion and to frustrate it, and more men in Washington to select, guide, equip, and cover up for these spooks. *John Kenneth Galbraith, "Who Needs the Democrats?" Harper's, July 1970, p 51*

spray steel, steel made by pouring molten iron directly from the blast furnace through a ring of oxygen jets that oxidize impurities much faster than the means by which conventional steel is made.

But apart from Millom's own interests, and those of the town and the 1,200 workers who depend on the company, there is the wider question of the way spray steel is being developed as a national asset. *Peter Wilsher, The Sunday Times (London), March 12, 1967, p 24*

spread city, *U.S.* a sprawling, uncontrolled extension of a city into and beyond the suburbs.

According to Mr. Pushkarev, "spread city" is an amorphous development pattern, neither urban nor suburban nor rural, that occurs when living, working, and shopping facilities are scattered in random fashion over the landscape. *"The Talk of the Town: 1969 to 2019," The New Yorker, Feb. 22, 1969, p 30*

square one, Usually in the phrase **back to square one,** the original starting point or same conditions (in allusion to board games in which certain conditions obligate a player to return to the starting point).

Within a year price increases and wage demands will again be out of control, and within two years we shall be back once again to square one. *Fred Hoyle, The Times (London), Jan. 15, 1968, p 7*

The dilemma for the Kremlin is...thrown back to square one. *The New York Times, June 18, 1967, Sec. 4, p 1*

On balance we shall be back to square one with wages rising faster than productivity. *Bernard Hollowood, Punch, June 5, 1968, p 798*

squaresville, *Slang.* —*n.* the world or society of squares or conventional people.

Leonard Hall [former chairman of the Republican National Committee]...gave the impression of an extraordinarily intelligent man, in appearance not unlike Jack

E. Leonard [a comedian] doing a straight turn, as if all of Jack E. Leonard's hyper-acute intelligence had gone into the formidable bastions of Squaresville. *Norman Mailer, "Miami Beach and Chicago," Harper's, Nov. 1968, p 47*

If the book is intended to be the apotheosis of squaresville, I'm afraid Mr Cooper has proved to be a devil's advocate. *Montague Haltrecht, The Sunday Times (London), May 8, 1966, p 34*

— *adj.* not up-to-date or fashionable; conventional; square.

"I think the main difference [between our generation and yours] is that we were at the university to study and get a degree, and have all sorts of pleasant distractions as a bonus. We didn't question the right of the authorities to be the authorities. They set up the rules, and if you didn't like them, you could go elsewhere." ... they [the students talking to me] went away, more than ever convinced that the war between the generations was for real. And through the window there floated a querulous, puzzled voice. "A queer fish, real squaresville. You know something? I believe he really liked it that way." I did, I really did. *Alistair Cooke, "My Student Days," The Listener, July 11, 1968, p 54*

On campus, where it once was squaresville to flip for the rock scene, it now is the wiggiest of kicks. *Time, May 21, 1965, p 54*

[see -VILLE]

SRAM, abbreviation of *short-range attack missile.*

Now being flight tested, SRAM is a rocket-propelled air-to-surface bomber-launched missile. *Scientific American, Jan. 1970, p 2*

SRAM is a solid-propellant, supersonic air-to-surface missile designed to turn bomber aircraft into airborne missile launch pads. *Flint O. DuPre, "Rockets and Missiles," 1970 Collier's Encyclopedia Year Book, p 466*

SST, abbreviation of SUPERSONIC TRANSPORT.

In the U.S. the Nixon administration's request for funds for continued work on the SST was approved by the House of Representatives and rejected by the Senate. *Philip Morris Hauser, "Cities and Urban Affairs," Britannica Book of the Year 1971, p 198*

Canadian Pacific Airlines, just as eager for supersonic prestige, has already deposited $600,000 to reserve delivery positions on three Boeing SSTs. *Hal Tennant, "A Few Ifs, Ands and Buts About Supersonic Jets," Maclean's, Feb. 1968, p 3*

The industry argues that we must build SST's to retain the market which would otherwise go to the British-French Concorde. *Benjamin Esterman, The New York Times Magazine, Feb. 11, 1968, p 22*

stagflation, *n. British.* a stagnant economic condition marked by rising unemployment and spiraling inflation.

A lack of high competitiveness leads to stagflation, which tends to become a permanent feature of the economic system. *Raymond Courbis, "Inflation in France," The Manchester Guardian Weekly, Aug. 21, 1971, p 13*

Their investigation into why so much effort produced so little, and left us in the state of nearly-universal stagflation which we are enjoying today, is clever, subtle and full of fine shades of political and economic perception. *Peter Wilsher, The Sunday Times (London), Nov. 14, 1971, p 72*

[blend of *stagnation* and *inflation*]

stagflationary, *adj. British.* of or characterized by stagflation.

This was discussion of ways in which the antitrust movement could play a part in curing the stagflationary disease — the combination of rising prices and rising unemployment. ... *Peter Wilsher, The Sunday Times (London), June 27, 1971, p 54*

staging, *n.* the jettisoning of a rocket stage.

The engines of the first stage began to cut off prior to staging (separation) and to ignition of the second-stage engines. *William J. Cromie, "... One Giant Leap for Mankind," The 1970 World Book Year Book, p 66*

staging post, *British.* **1** an area where troops assemble before an action or operation.

Britain, said the Minister, already had staging posts at Gan and Mesira, and because of the Government's decision to remain east of Suez these facilities need hardly be questioned. *Hugh Noyes, The Times (London), Nov. 17, 1970, p 9*

2 a stopping place on a journey; stopover.

The position with drugs is interesting. Although France is the principal staging post between the Orient and the United States in the opium chain, and secret laboratories for transforming it into heroin exist in the south, there is, according to the police, scarcely any drug problem. *Joseph Carroll, The Manchester Guardian Weekly, Oct. 26, 1967, p 9*

3 any major or significant preparatory stage.

If the politicians can resist the temptation to use the occasion as an opportunity for another footling slanging match, we may find that the controversy sparked off by Mr. Wedgwood Benn's attack on telepolitics becomes a staging-post in the development of TV. *Bernard Hollowood, Punch, Oct. 30, 1968, p 599*

standing, *n. Law.* the legal right or qualification to institute a lawsuit because of a personal interest or stake in its outcome. See also CLASS ACTION.

A legal action requires a plaintiff, and in general, only those persons who are directly hurt by an act can sue for redress. However, more liberal rules regarding standing to sue have enabled public-spirited citizens and groups to seek aid from the courts in attempts to protect the environment. This year, in *Association of Data Processing Service Organizations* v. *Camp* (397 U.S. 150), the U.S. Supreme Court ruled that a plaintiff could be seeking to protect not only economic interests but "aesthetic, conservational, and recreational" interests as well. *Monrad G. Paulsen, "Law," 1971 Collier's Encyclopedia Year Book, p 320*

Federal District Judge William B. Jones ruled in Washington that neither group had standing to sue. *The New York Times, April 4, 1965, Sec. 4, p 9*

sta·pe·dec·to·my (ˌsteɪ pəˈdek tə miː), *n.* the surgical repair or replacement of the stapes (the sound-conducting mechanism of the middle ear).

The three little bones of hearing (called ossicles) are the malleus, or hammer; the incus, or anvil; and the stapes, or stirrup. The stapedectomy is usually successful in freeing the stapes from adhesions. *Faye Marley, Science News, Dec. 3, 1966, p 477*

[from New Latin *staped-* (stem of *stapes*) + English *-ectomy* surgery, as in *appendectomy*]

starkers, *adj. British Slang.* stark naked.

... the salesgirl had taken away all her clothes and hidden them. It was only the threat of running starkers into the street that brought them back. *Brigid Keenan, The Sunday Times (London), Sept. 6, 1964, p 40*

Most of the publicity about the third incarnation of "Hair" centered on the fact that a number of its players, both male and female, were going to strip absolutely starkers by the end of the first act. *Brendan Gill, The New Yorker, May 11, 1968, p 84*

▶ See the note under PREGGERS.

starquake, *n.* a series of rapid changes in the shape of a star or in the distribution of its matter, detected from sudden speedups in the star's pulse rate or radiation output.

...the Vela pulsar, which had been emitting sharp radio pulses almost precisely 11 times per second but which had been observed to be slowing down perceptibly, suddenly speeded up.... What could have happened? One hypothesis is that the pulsars experienced a "starquake." *Scientific American, Feb. 1970, p 44*

The favourite explanation that decreases in period, or "spin-ups", occur when starquakes take place in the deformed crust of the star seems to fall flat on its face when confronted with the discovery that the Crab pulsar, at least, also undergoes "spin-downs". *"Spinning Off Wisps can Make a Pulsar Glitchy," New Scientist and Science Journal, Aug. 26, 1971, p 452*

[from *star* + earth*quake*]

stash, *n.* *U.S. Slang.* mustache.

Sandy [a male character in the movie "Carnal Knowledge"] is a superannuated swinger, complete with stash, burns and a 17-year-old hippie on his arm. *Stefan Kanfer, "Cinema," Time, July 5, 1971, p 55*

state of the art, the level of scientific or technological development in a given field or industry at the present, or at any designated, time.

The bill recognizes these obstacles by establishing national ambient air standards. States and cities will have to meet them regardless of the state of the art of emission controls. *Science News, Jan. 9, 1971, p 23*

...these brief reports of current research are presumably intended to give an accurate idea of the 'state of the art', or of important 'breakthroughs' in particular fields. *J. M. Ziman, Science Journal, Sept. 1968, p 30*

These positions provide unusual opportunities to engineers who want to put their own ideas into practice in the overall drive to increase the state of the art. *The New York Times, Oct. 11, 1967, p 54*

state-of-the-art, *adj.* involving facilities or techniques already known or developed; not experimental or at the research-and-development stage.

Position open in several areas for design of special purpose digital equipment related to high-speed, state-of-the-art, commercial computers. *Advertisement in The New York Times, April 15, 1967, p 36*

Certainly the absence of state-of-the-art claims or gadgets implies a growing realisation that the manufacturers need to shore up their tattered images in the eyes of customers who are used to late delivery, mediocre support, and software that is at least three years behind the hardware. *New Scientist and Science Journal, Feb. 25, 1971, p 425*

STD, abbreviation of *Subscriber Trunk Dialling* (the British system enabling telephone callers to make long-distance calls directly from one region to another). Compare *U.S.* AREA CODE.

The calls came from all over Britain, often by S.T.D. *The Times (London), Nov. 21, 1966, p 1*

When you're alone in the house on a dark wet evening ...it's better than nothing to spot a crisp new STD code book, propped against the telephone by someone who hasn't thought its arrival worth mentioning. *Basil Boothroyd, Punch, Dec. 11, 1968, p 833*

steady-state, *adj.* of or relating to the theory that the universe has always existed and, though it is steadily expanding, new matter is continually being created to compensate for the destruction of matter.

An attractive possibility is to suppose that matter as originally created, whether in a single "big bang" or in a steady-state universe, is largely in the form of the hypothetical massive particles known as quarks. *Geoffrey Burbidge and Fred Hoyle, "The Problem of the Quasi-stellar Objects," Scientific American, Dec. 1966, p 52*

His [Maarten Schmidt's] study suggests that a complete survey of the sky with large telescopes would reveal as many as 14 million quasars, but since they are such short-lived objects all but 35,000 or so must have burned themselves out in the time it has taken their light to reach us. Schmidt's observations provide a strong argument against the steady-state hypothesis, which holds that the universe has always looked just as it does now. *"Science And the Citizen," Scientific American, Jan. 1971, p 47*

steady-stater, *n.* a supporter of the steady-state theory of the universe. Compare BIG BANGER.

As the galaxies move farther away from each other, steady-staters believe, new galaxies are constantly being formed out of hydrogen that is created and fill the gaps, keeping the expanding universe at a constant density. *Time, March 11, 1966, p 51*

stel·lar·a·tor ('stel ə,rei tər), *n.* a device in which plasma (highly ionized gas) is confined in an endless tube by means of an externally applied magnetic field, used to produce controlled thermonuclear power.

Medium-density plasma containers... include the stellarators, originally developed at the Princeton Plasma Physics Laboratory, and the tokamaks, originally developed at the I. V. Kurchatov Institute of Atomic Energy near Moscow. *William C. Gough and Bernard J. Eastlund, "The Prospects of Fusion Power," Scientific American, Feb. 1971, p 53*

...the Soviet plasma device called Tokamak exhibits a very low rate of diffusion even though it is likely to have the same fluctuations as similarly shaped devices such as Stellarators, which have much higher diffusion rates. *Science News, Aug. 22, 1970, p 168*

[from *stellar* generator; so called from the expectation that stellar temperatures may be generated by such a device]

stellar wind, a stream of charged particles ejected from the corona of a star into space. Compare SOLAR WIND.

Such stars [red giants] may be steadily supplying heavy metals to the interstellar medium by blowing off material in the form of "stellar winds". *Bernard Pagel, New Scientist, April 8, 1965, p 107*

stem-winding, *adj.* *U.S.* extremely good, strong, etc.; first-rate.

But Humphrey seemed temporarily to be experimenting with a different strategy. The day of Nixon's nomination, the Vice President drove from his home in Waverly, Minn., to Minneapolis, where he delivered a stem-winding, hard-line speech on the war and domestic violence. "If I'm President," he told a convention of National Catholic War Veterans, "there won't be a sellout in South Viet Nam. We can no more afford to let aggressors abroad get their way than we can let lawbreakers at home get their way." *Time, Aug. 16, 1968, p 18*

A stem-winding sermon by Reverend Cecil Todd called "Blue Print for Slavery" can be obtained by sending one dollar to *Revival Fires* in Joplin, Missouri.... *Judith Rascoe, "For Garden Country: Rally on the Right," The Atlantic, Sept. 1966, p 90*

[from *stem-winder* a first-rate person or thing, with the form influenced by *stem-winding* watch (one wound by turning the knob on the stem)]

stereology, *n.* the scientific study of the characteristics of three-dimensional objects that can be viewed only two-dimensionally.

Up to now it has not been easy to measure brain area but the rather new science of stereology, employing statistico-geometrical methods, now makes it possible to draw conclusions concerning three dimensional structures from flat images, such as cut sections. *Gordon Rattray Taylor, Science Journal, March 1968, p 32*

[from *stereo-* three-dimensional + *-logy* study of]

stereotape, *n.* a magnetic tape reproducing stereophonic sound. *Also used attributively.*

Particularly efficient was the heating and ventilation system, rapidly blasting out a stream of hot air, while the test car also boasted a Craig Pioneer stereo-tape player, which added a luxurious background of soothing music on long journeys and in London's traffic jams. *The Times (London), Jan. 17, 1967, p 9*

stereotaxic or **stereotactic,** *adj.* involving or based upon three-dimensional surveys of the brain that allow operation or research on otherwise inaccessible parts of the brain.

Utilizing three dimensional anatomical maps of the brain (stereotaxic atlases) and stereotaxic instruments which hold the head of an anesthetized animal in a predetermined plane, it is possible to insert electrodes through small holes in the skull into almost any brain structure. *Elliot S. Valenstein and Verne C. Cox, "Neurophysiology of Behavior," McGraw-Hill Yearbook of Science and Technology 1969, p 107*

Chances of successful neurosurgery are improved with the use of this stereotaxic device which, when fastened to a patient's skull, allows doctors to pinpoint the exact area of the brain where surgery is required. *Science News, Aug. 20, 1966, p 117*

First, the patient's head is clamped in a stereotactic device that enables the surgeons to take bearings in three dimensions. Then the surgeons saw through the intervening bone and insert the ultracold cannula. *Time, April 30, 1965, p 35*

[from *stereo-* three-dimensional + *-taxic* or *-tactic* arrangement, orientation]

stern drive, an inboard engine with an outboard drive unit.

When they appeared on the water about eight years ago, they looked like outboards with the power head sawed off. Closer examination revealed a drive shaft running through the transom, with an inboard engine on one end and an outboard-like lower unit on the other.

Variously called stern drives, inboard-outboards, inboard-outdrives, or just plain "I-O's," they are one of the hottest items in recreational boating. *The New York Times, Feb. 9, 1968, p 31*

Stevengraph, *n.* a picture woven in silk.

These objects which are not yet antique—being introduced in 1879—are called Stevengraphs, after their inventor, Thomas Stevens of Coventry. They were mass-produced in coloured silk on a Jacquard-type machine loom making a picture normally measuring 5-1/2 inches by 2-1/2 inches, although the cardboard mount increased the size to 8-1/4 by 5-1/4 inches. They were bound in various simple frames. The original cost was modest—a shilling apiece mounted on card, or half a crown in a "Gold Oxford Frame," securely packed in a box". *Geoffrey Godden, The Times (London), April 27, 1968, p 25*

stocking mask, a nylon stocking pulled over the head or wrapped around the face to conceal identity.

After three men in stocking masks raided Martins Bank in South Audley Street, W., the same day the £3,000 they stole was recovered from the boot of the escape car, a Jaguar, which was found abandoned in Balderton Street, not far away. *The Times (London), May 16, 1966, p 10*

STOL (stoul), *n.* acronym for *short takeoff and landing.* Compare CTOL, VTOL, V/STOL.

The STOL plane tends to be slower than a conventional plane and much slower than a jet airliner but it is faster than a helicopter. It is able to use a field much smaller than the strip that a jetliner needs. But it needs more room than a helicopter....

The true STOL plane is one that can not only fly slow enough to use relatively small fields but, once in the air, can attain a relatively high speed. France's four-engine 60-passenger Breguet can make a low-speed take-off in 1,800 feet and then cruise at 285 miles an hour. *The New York Times, Jan. 7, 1968, p 68*

STOLport, *n.* an airfield for STOL aircraft. Compare VTOLPORT.

New York City has developed plans to build a short take-off and landing airport along the Hudson River within three years.

The STOLport, designed to handle aircraft using runways only about 1,000 feet long, would be built atop a 10-story building, 300 feet wide and seven blocks long. *Science News, Feb. 22, 1969, p 190*

Immediately, New York's proposed new heliport and stolport will be used to improve connections between Manhattan and its small outlying satellite fields.... *Time, Jan. 15, 1968, p 25*

stop, *v.i.* **stop out,** *U.S.* to interrupt one's education to pursue some other activity for a brief period.

The trend of stopping out is growing, however, partly because the draft law now gives young men with high lottery numbers a new freedom. *"As College Starts, There Go the Stop-Outs," Time, Sept. 27, 1971, p 47*

stop-go, *British.* —*n.* a government fiscal policy alternating between economic expansion and contraction. Also called GO-STOP.

If Labour is returned it must speak with a clearer voice on wages. The saddest victims of inflation are pensioners and lower-paid workers, most of them Labour supporters. The victims of stop-go and unemployment are union members. *The Manchester Guardian Weekly, May 30, 1970, p 12*

—*adj.* of or characterized by stop-go.

The economic reason is that without an incomes policy

wages tend to rise faster than output, we pay ourselves more than we earn (to quote half a dozen post-war Chancellors), export prices rise, the balance of payments runs into trouble, the gnomes gather, the pound trembles, and the Government of the day deflates the economy. The "stop-go" cycle never leaves time for the development of a satisfactory rate of economic growth. *The Manchester Guardian Weekly, Aug. 22, 1970, p 12*

stop-out, *n.* *U.S.* a student who interrupts his education to pursue some other activity for a brief period.

Still, many stop-outs do better academically than their less-seasoned classmates, if only because they are a year older. *"As College Starts, There Go the Stop-Outs," Time, Sept. 27, 1971, p 47*

[from STOP OUT]

storage ring, *Nuclear Physics.* a device for storing a beam of accelerated particles in a circular track and smashing it against an opposing beam to produce the necessary energy for the creation of new particles.

. . . several storage rings for electrons have been operated with electrons of energy in the range of 500 MeV [million electron volts]. *Gerald Feinberg, "Physics," 1972 Britannica Yearbook of Science and the Future, 1971, p 314*

A storage ring is a device that takes accelerated particles from an accelerator, stores the beam in a circular track until it is built up to a proper density of protons or electrons and then collides it with a beam going in the opposite direction. This sort of collision makes a good deal more energy available for the creation of new particles than a beam of the same energy striking a stationary target. *Science News, Feb. 13, 1971, p 115*

storm surge. See the quotation for the meaning.

The gales, up to 140 miles (235 km) per hour, pile up the seawater against the land, and often a sudden onrush, or wall, of water is followed by a slow, relentless rise to levels far above normal. This is technically a *storm surge,* not a tidal wave. *A. T. A. and A. M. Learmonth, "East Pakistan: Century's Worst Disaster Takes a Staggering Toll," The Americana Annual 1971, p 64*

STP, abbreviation used as the name of a hallucinogenic drug (dimethoxy-methylamphetamine) chemically related to mescaline and amphetamine.

. . . there are chemists in laboratories in Toronto, Montreal and Vancouver who produce amphetamines and psychedelic drugs, LSD, STP, DMT and other molecular variations. *Sheila Gormely, The Times (London), Feb. 23, 1970, p IV*

In *The People Next Door,* LSD and STP users are said to require "a controlled environment indefinitely" following their initiation, a situation that develops only rarely. *Time, Feb. 15, 1971, p 34*

[from *STP* (abbreviation of *Scientifically Treated Petroleum*), a trade name for a gasoline additive]

straight, *Slang.* —*adj.* not deviating from the norm in politics, sexual habits, etc.; orthodox; conventional; normal; square.

Hiding my homosexuality from the "straight" side of my life isn't too bad; it's the unfulfilling and unsatisfactory element of my homosexuality which is uncomfortable. *Chris Lawson, Studio City, Calif., in a Letter to the Editor, Harper's, Nov. 1970, p 14*

I have never been busted for pot, my hair doesn't brush my shoulders, and you won't catch me nude in the park. I am so straight, in fact, that I actually have a job. *Henry Muller, Time, Aug. 17, 1970, p 38*

Junkies don't get cured in contemporary movies — they don't even want to be cured — so we know everyone is doomed. And the explanations never suffice: we come out still puzzled as to why people do it to themselves. Maybe the best clue to J's character is his line "I'm a very boring guy when I'm straight." *Pauline Kael, "The Current Cinema," The New Yorker, Dec. 4, 1971, p 171*

—*n.* a person who is straight; a conventional person, especially one who holds orthodox views; a square.

The silent majority, the broad group that includes blue and white collars, small businessmen, professionals, and assorted "straights" who are supposed to be susceptible to the social issue, were assiduously wooed by Nixon. *Time, Nov. 16, 1970, p 17*

. . . I do not believe the gay set is disproportionately large. An honest attempt is made by the straights, the otherwise and the police to keep the more flamboyant element under loose control. *Muriel Walcutt, Short Hills, N.J., in a Letter to the Editor, The New York Times, June 13, 1971, p 4*

straight arrow, *U.S.* a very proper, upright, straightforward person.

Smith [the tennis player Stan Smith], a wonderfully old-fashioned straight arrow, was right in character when, upon being asked if Tiriac's gamesmanship had bothered him, he said, "I don't call that gamesmanship. I call that rudeness." *Herbert Warren Wind, "The Sporting Scene," The New Yorker, Oct. 11, 1969, p 194*

straight-arrow, *adj.* *U.S.* very proper, upright, or straightforward.

The new eco-activists include groups as straight-arrow as the Girl Scouts, who last week campaigned for clean air in places ranging from Hartford, Conn., to smog-threatened Fairfax, Va. *Time, Aug. 22, 1969, p 43*

strap-on, *adj.* designed to be attached to a space vehicle or engine for additional thrust.

The vehicle seen on television appeared to have a two-stage core with four strap-on boosters, similar to those of the original *Sputnik-Voskhod* launcher. *New Scientist, Oct. 31, 1968, p 231*

The Delta's first stage is a modified Thor booster, assisted by nine strap-on solid-fuel motors. *Raymond N. Watts, Jr., "The Exploration of Venus," Encyclopedia Science Supplement (Grolier) 1971, p 351*

—*n.* a strap-on booster or engine.

Solid propellant strap-ons could be used to raise the Saturn V's orbital payload (now about 250,000 pounds) to as much as 427,000 pounds. *Jonathan Eberhart, Science News, Aug. 13, 1966, p 107*

stream, *Chiefly British.* —*v.t.* to divide (students) into separate classes according to level of intelligence or special interest.

Most of the schools streamed pupils into A, B, C, or D classes, about four out of five used some form of selection procedure, almost half were not getting a fair share of able pupils, and pupils from the working classes were over-represented. *The Times (London), Oct. 22, 1968, p 3*

—*n.* any of the classes or courses of study arranged by streaming students.

Opponents of streaming have for a long time said that

middle class children get put in the top streams because they have learnt at home to use words precisely; once there they get better verbal training and so maintain their superiority and do better still in future tests. *Tyrrell Burgess, The Manchester Guardian Weekly, Feb. 13, 1964, p 15*

streaming, *n. Chiefly British.* the division of students of a school into separate classes according to level of intelligence or special interest, as determined by examinations; homogeneous grouping. Also called TRACKING. Compare TRACK SYSTEM.

...there is far too little research evidence on the effects of streaming and other forms of in-school organization. What a school is called matters far less than what goes on inside it; and I hope that whatever government is bestowed on us next week will provide funds...to examine the internal organization of a wide variety of good State schools. *Martin Berry, New Scientist, June 11, 1970, p 521*

street Christian, *U.S.* one of the JESUS PEOPLE.

Jesus freaks. Evangelical hippies. Or, as many prefer to be called, street Christians. Under various names—and in rapidly increasing numbers—they are the latest incarnation of that oldest of Christian phenomena: footloose, passionate bearers of the Word, preaching the kingdom of heaven among the dispossessed of the earth. *"Street Christians: Jesus as the Ultimate Trip," Time, Aug. 3, 1970, p 31*

street people, a collective name for hippies or others who have rejected traditional social values, including homes, so that they are usually found congregating on streets, in parks, and in other public places.

At Berkeley an angry confrontation erupted over the university's decision to fence in a two-block, off-campus area which radical elements and "street people" had turned into a people's park. *Fred M. Hechinger, "Education," 1970 Collier's Encyclopedia Year Book, p 220*

Moreover, the existence of a student society enables street people to live virtually free. Any young person is almost guaranteed a night's shelter in any university town. You only have to ask. *Martin Walker, "Economics of Dropping Out," The Manchester Guardian Weekly, April 3, 1971, p 6*

streetscape, *n.* **1** a view or appearance of a street.

The semi-antiquarian preservation of a single isolated unit, a house here and there, or even a whole streetscape, touches only the surface of the problem. Conservation of urban identity does not imply total preservation, but the conservation of urban character and assets in the light of understanding. *Martin Biddle, New Scientist, Jan. 14, 1971, p 76*

Consider Chicago's Near West Side, now 60% nonwhite. At first glance, the five-square-mile area is dominated by the striking architecture of the University of Illinois' Circle Campus. Closer inspection reveals a streetscape of despair: low, glum buildings, boarded-up store fronts, infrequent parks, broken curbs. *Time, April 6, 1970, p 48*

2 a picture of a street.

...in his new show the Camden Town street-scape is a prime example of the way in which he can adapt the metal sinews of city-life to his purpose. *John Russell, The Sunday Times (London), Jan. 15, 1967, p 25*

[from *street* + *-scape* view, scene]

street theater, another term for GUERRILLA THEATER.

Earlier, 200 people watched an example of "street theatre", staged by the group, featuring United States marines versus Vietnamese peasants, in the main street of Newbury. *The Times (London), April 13, 1970, p 1*

streetwise, *adj. U.S.* familiar with local people and their problems; wise to the ways and needs of people on the street.

No mayor can function effectively unless he has around him competent and streetwise people who can assume much of his responsibility....*James M. Naughton, The New York Times Magazine, Feb. 25, 1968, p 58*

...a [social] worker therefore had to be wary as well as trustful, be security-minded as well as loving, and be "street-wise" as well as compassionate. This new style in social work has been evolving during the last ten years or so on the streets of New York. *Robert Rice, The New Yorker, March 27, 1965, p 78*

Take a dirt-poor Sicilian peasant kid fresh out of steerage. Make him scrappy and street-wise. *Christopher Lehmann-Haupt, "Bad-Tempered Capra-Corn," Review of "The Name Above the Title" by Frank Capra, The New York Times, June 18, 1971, p 37*

streetworker, *n. U.S. and Canada.* a social worker who befriends and tries to help troubled or delinquent youngsters of a neighborhood.

Almost all of them have quit school. The streetworker has become so friendly with them that he can sometimes return stolen goods before the police are even aware of the theft. By that time, he expects the complex problem of rehabilitating juvenile delinquents will have overwhelmed him. *David Lewis Stein, "A Harvard Man's Life Among Toronto's Young 'Have-Nots'," Maclean's, Jan. 25, 1964, p 23*

strep·to·ni·grin (ˌstrep təˈnɑi grən), *n.* an antibiotic drug related to streptomycin, used in the treatment of various cancerous tumors but too toxic for use against bacteria.

Recent studies at the National Cancer Institute have indicated the usefulness of several other drugs....Previously other investigators had shown two antibiotics, streptonigrin and actinomycin D, to be effective. *Science News, Feb. 25, 1967, p 190*

[from *Strepto*myces flocculus (the species of soil bacteria from which the drug is derived) + *nigr*-black (because the drug is obtained in the form of dark crystals) + *-in* (chemical suffix)]

Strine (strain), *Slang.* —*n.* Australian English.

Anyone who goes to Australia thinking he speaks the Queen's English is in for a shock called "Strine," meaning Australian—the cockney-like vernacular that most Aussies spout. *Time, Aug. 24, 1970, p 60*

In the language I shall now always think of as "Strine," the man who says, "Dad'll ever never sprike tan the waze goane" means that his Dad'll have a nervous breakdown, the way he's going. *Basil Boothroyd, Punch, May 5, 1965, p 656*

—*adj.* Australian.

But Keneally's normal tone is tighter, and it suggests that here is a rarity—an Australian novelist who does not use his Strine literary context as a prop or an excuse, and thus remains sensitive to his actual and historical environment. *Robert Hughes, The Times (London), Feb. 24, 1968, p 21*

strip chart

[a rendering of the Australian pronunciation of the word *Australian*]

strip chart, a graphic representation of data in the form of a long strip of paper on which the course of something, such as a patient's fever, is charted.

... the computer recorded wave variations that often are undetectable to the eye of a physician using the traditional strip chart.... *Martin Tolchin, The New York Times, Feb. 3, 1966, p 33*

Pressure transducers installed in the hydraulic braking system of each vehicle indicated fluid pressure on a two-channel stripchart recorder statically calibrated against pedal force. *New Scientist, Oct. 29, 1970, p 224*

strip city, *U.S.* a long, narrow stretch of urban development between two or more relatively distant cities. Compare SUPERCITY.

By 1980 or so, 80 per cent of us will live in cities, and the strip city—Boston to Washington, Los Angeles to San Diego, and Milwaukee to Cleveland—will have made its appearance. *J. Irwin Miller, quoted by William D. Patterson, "The Revolutionary Role of Business," Saturday Review, Jan. 13, 1968, p 68*

stro·mat·o·lite (strou'mæt ə‚lait), *n.* a calcareous rock formation containing fossil deposits of blue-green algae.

The algae, which occur associated with the sedimentary structures called stromatolites, are beautifully preserved. *Graham Chedd and Peter Stubbs, "Monitor: Cells Were Dividing a Thousand Million Years Ago," New Scientist, July 3, 1969, p 6*

Two back-to-back pages of photographs (supplied by the paleontologist Paul F. Hoffman) are memorable: on one side you see stromatolites, limy heads made by reef-forming algae, looking no different whether they are in the two-billion-year-old rock of the "east arm of the Great Slave Lake" or in the present-day tidal flats of Shark Bay in Australia. *Philip Morrison, "Books," Review of "Origin of Eukaryotic Cells" by Lynn Margulis, Scientific American, May 1971, p 129*

[from Greek *strôma, strômatos* layer + English *-lite* stone]

stro·mat·o·lit·ic (strou‚mæt ə'lit ik), *adj.* of or relating to stromatolites.

The best-preserved microorganisms occur some 90 mi east of Port Arthur, in unmetamorphosed, stromatolitic carbon-rich cherts near Schreiber, Ontario. *J. William Schopf, "Antiquity and Evolution of Precambrian Life," McGraw-Hill Yearbook of Science and Technology 1967, p 50*

strong force, the force that causes neutrons and protons to bind in the nucleus of an atom. It is stronger than any other known force and is probably interactive in meson coupling. Also called STRONG INTERACTION. Compare WEAK FORCE.

Knowledge of the internal structures of the proton and the neutron may provide the key to understanding the "strong" force that holds the atomic nucleus together and endows the universe with its stability. The strong force makes its presence known in the nuclear reactions that fuel the stars and that, on a more modest scale, provide the energy for nuclear power and nuclear explosives. *Henry W. Kendall and Wolfgang K. H. Panofsky, "The Structure of the Proton and the Neutron," Scientific American, June 1971, p 61*

The most powerful [force] is the straightforwardly named strong force, which holds together the particles making up atomic nuclei. In some way not understood, it also probably determines the nature and size of these particles themselves. *Tom Alexander, Encyclopedia Science Supplement (Grolier) 1970, p 58*

... the photon can exhibit properties once thought to be possessed exclusively by such relatively massive particles as the proton and the neutron: the heavy, durable constituents of the atomic nuclei. Such particles, which exhibit the "strong" force that binds the nucleus together, are called hadrons. *Frederick V. Murphy and David E. Yount, "Photons As Hadrons," Scientific American, July 1971, p 94*

strong interaction, another name for STRONG FORCE.

In a thermonuclear bomb...two heavy hydrogen isotopes, in this case both deuterons, fuse by the strong interaction process to form a helium-3 nucleus plus a neutron. *Freeman J. Dyson, "Energy in the Universe," Scientific American, Sept. 1971, p 56*

When physicists first began to explore atomic nuclei, they found that the force that holds nuclei together is different from either the gravitational or the electromagnetic forces they were familiar with. Because it appeared much stronger than anything else, physicists called this new force the strong interaction. *"The W Particle May Have Been Found," Science News, Aug. 21, 1971, p 121*

structural gene or **structured gene,** the part of the operon (a cluster of genes functioning as a unit) that determines the sequence of amino acids and the structure of the proteins. Compare OPERATOR.

The first known class consists of structural genes, which determine the amino acid sequence and three-dimensional shape of proteins; the second is regulatory genes, which specify whether structured genes will function and therefore control the rate of enzyme synthesis. *"Genetics," Science News Yearbook 1970, p 103*

structurism, *n.* art that emphasizes basic geometric forms or structures.

[Charles] Biederman himself, having grandly declared that both painting and sculpture were obsolete, arrived at what he has come to call "structurism"—reliefs that have the dimension of sculpture and the color of painting. *Time, Jan. 26, 1970, p 37*

structurist, *n.* an artist whose work emphasizes basic geometric forms or structures.

[Reuben] Nakian's sculpture, drawings, terra cotta statuettes and plaques are open on every level to a richly sensual interpretation, opposed to the compact, single-minded absolute sought by a younger generation of structurists. *Lucy R. Lippard, The New York Times, June 26, 1966, Sec. 2, p 21*

As book reviewer Robert E. Samples admits in that issue, he and others "in curriculum development and teacher training have been guilty for years of structuring canvases and of choosing the brushes and paints." And yet, how many structurists are willing to abandon that on which they depend? *Michael K. Lindsay, Saturday Review, Oct. 17, 1970, p 54*

—*adj.* of or characterized by structurism.

Biederman's "structurist" work developed from a study of Mondrian but differs from it in the clustered, projective nature of the relief elements and the saturated fields of colour against which they are seen. *The Times (London), March 17, 1967, p 12*

structurization, *n.* the process of arranging any complex matter into an organized structure or series of patterns.

[Pierre] Grèco asks such basic questions as what is actually meant by terms like "intelligence" or "learning".... For him,... the concept of structure and the process of structurization (an ugly but appropriate term) are essential for the understanding of human intelligence. *Marie Jahoda, Review of "Experimental Psychology: Its Scope and Method, Volume VIII Intelligence" by Pierre Oleron, Jean Piaget, Barbel Inhelder, and Pierre Grèco, New Scientist, Nov. 6, 1969, p 304*

structurize, *v.t.* to arrange in the form of an organized structure or series of patterns.

Research capacities are being structurized to the optimum in every single economic branch in order to meet the country's requirements of the scientific and technological revolution. *The Times (London), Dec. 18, 1968, p 9*

strung out, *U.S. Slang.* sick, weak, or disturbed, especially from drug addiction.

...songs are about a wild party, a girl who gets run over by a beach-cleaning truck, men hungry for women or strung out on dope and booze.... *Ellen Willis, "Records: Rock, etc.," The New Yorker, April 18, 1970, p 159*

"These are very strung-out kids with individual hangups," said Jim Fouratt ... describing the modern runaway. *Joan Cook, The New York Times, Aug. 18, 1967, p 22*

student power, the control of a school, college, or university by members of the student body.

...the place [the École des Beaux Arts in Paris] is no longer under the direction of its professors, appointed by the state, but is operating under what is called "student power." *Genêt, "Letter from Paris," The New Yorker, July 6, 1968, p 62*

Some students call for student power—others shrink from the term because they have some sense of the arduous work, the sheer tedium, the high responsibilities that are always a part of administrative power. *Richard Hofstadter, The New York Times, June 5, 1968, p 32*

Student power means absolute student control—and that means teachers as well—over everything. Our central objective is the democratization of institutions, such as factories, so that they are democratically controlled by their members. *Brian MacArthur, The Times (London), March 18, 1968, p 2*

stuff, *n.* *U.S. Slang.* **1** marijuana.

...in the U.S. it is variously called the weed, stuff, Indian hay, grass, pot, tea, maryjane and other names. *Lester Grinspoon, "Marijuana," Scientific American, Dec. 1969, p 17*

2 heroin.

Heroin itself is a nightmare almost beyond description. By any of the names its users call it—scag, smack, the big H, horse, dope, junk, stuff—it is infamous as the hardest of drugs.... *Time, March 16, 1970, p 16*

Stuff and Other Stuff, a mixture of energy-producing nuclear particles.

Stuff and Other Stuff are basically Greek alphabet soup, containing numerous pions, baryons and photons. Stuff and Other Stuff are distinguished by their quantum numbers.... Most of the pions in Stuff and Other Stuff produce high-energy photons. *"Burning Quarks to Exorcise Quasars," New Scientist, Aug. 6, 1970, p 272*

stun gas, an incapacitating gas that has the effect of causing temporary confusion and disorientation.

Police across the country have gratefully adopted Mace, a chemical stun gas in a pressurized can, as a means of coping with rioters and unruly suspects. *Time, May 17, 1968, p 75*

Just to keep the record smug, here is a run-down of anti-crowd devices which other nations, notably America, are developing:... stun gas; gas which temporarily blinds; electrified water jets; and an electronic gadget said to produce "dynamic dysentery." *Punch, Feb. 21, 1968, p 253*

stun gun, a long-barreled gun that fires a small bag containing sand, bird shot, etc. Compare BATON GUN.

Riot control in the United States is a field fast becoming strewn with gimmicks, but the stun gun has already been used effectively by the Alameda County Sheriff's Department who are called in whenever student riots at Berkeley become too much for the local police. *Ellsworth Jones and David Divine, "Stun Gun for Ulster?" The Sunday Times (London), May 30, 1971, p 5*

To maintain a constant level of effectiveness a regular stream of innovations is needed.... These include nets which can be projected over demonstrators, and a stun-gun which fires a small sand-bag. *Jonathan Rosenhead and Peter J. Smith, "Ulster Riot Control: A Warning," New Scientist and Science Journal, Aug. 12, 1971, p 375*

subcompact, *n.* Also called **subcompact car.** a small, sporty, economically priced two-door car that is slightly smaller than a compact car. Compare INTERMEDIATE.

St. Thomas, Ontario: Ford has put its new subcompact car, the Pinto, into production here. It will be on sale September 11. *The Times (London), Aug. 11, 1970, p 18*

The trend [fix-it-yourself cars] began with the introduction of two small, easily fixable models—Ford's Maverick and American Motors' Gremlin. As the automakers bring out new cars, it is continuing. On Sept. 10, General Motors will introduce its subcompact, the Vega, and executives are boasting about how easy it is to repair. *Time, Aug. 17, 1970, p 58*

The subcompacts, though, are small and cheap enough to attract many motorists who might buy bigger U.S.-made cars if they felt more flush, but whose desire for economy has been sharpened by the bite of the 1970 recession and continuing inflation. *Time, March 1, 1971, p 54*

sublanguage, *n.* a secondary or minor language differing from a standard language; the special language or speech of a group or class of people within a culture.

Jargon, the sublanguage peculiar to any trade, contributes to euphemism when its terms seep into general use. The stock market, for example, rarely "falls" in the words of Wall Street analysts. Instead it is discovered to be "easing" or found to have made a "technical correction" or "adjustment." *Time, Sept. 19, 1969, p 23*

As soon as you learn to spell and write, the language becomes educated American English, whatever one might call it, and the dialect disappears. I'm not speaking, of course, of the "hip" sub-language that rises in the city. *George Plimpton, "William Styron: A Shared Ordeal," The New York Times Book Review, Oct. 8, 1967, p 1*

subminiaturize, *v.t.* another word for MICRO-MINIATURIZE.

Moreover, the proliferation of transistorized and "subminiaturized" tape recording devices—many of them easily concealed or disguised — not only makes the activity more intriguing, but makes its proscription all but impossible to enforce. *Richard Freed, "Piracy on the High C's," Saturday Review, March 26, 1966, p 55*

subnuclear, *adj.* of or relating to the particles or phenomena within the nuclei of atoms.

Consider the vast sums conned out of the US forces for laser developments by broad hints about death-rays, or the incredible amounts of money still happily sunk in the most far-out varieties of subnuclear physics because subnuclear research once delivered the military goods. *New Scientist, May 4, 1967, p 293*

subnucleon, *n.* a hypothetical constituent of the known nuclear particles. Compare PARTON.

Like many other current theories of particle physics, Dr. Yock's begins with the assumption that the particles usually called elementary are not elementary at all. Dr. Yock postulates that all known particles are composed of six subnucleons, as he calls them, and six antisubnucleons. *Science News, Feb. 27, 1971, p 144*

Quantitative predictions, however, are notably absent from the paper, and, as in the quark case, there is as yet a lack of experimental evidence for sub-nucleons. *New Scientist, Jan. 14, 1971, p 55*

[from *subnuclear* + *-on*, as in *proton, neutron*, etc.]

subprofessional, *n.* another name for PARAPROFESSIONAL.

Dr. Gardner is training workers from the community, many of whom lack even high school diplomas, to act as therapists. The bulk of the therapeutic work is done by these subprofessionals.... *Patricia McBroom, Science News, Oct. 5, 1968, p 346*

The need is for a massive and innovative approach — from new procedures for teacher training and internship to the effective use of teachers' aides and other subprofessionals, preferably drawn from the schools' own neighborhoods. *The New York Times, March 16, 1967, p 46*

subprogram, a part of a computer program.

The input for a specific problem in Evans' program is in the form of lists of vertices, lines and curves describing the geometric figures. A subprogram analyzes this information, identifies the separate parts of the figure and reconstructs them in terms of points on a graph and the connecting lines. *Marvin L. Minsky, Scientific American, Sept. 1966, p 251*

To have a more balanced view, we have to consider how computer pictures are drawn and how subprogrammes ... work. *E. E. Zajac, New Scientist, Feb. 10, 1966, p 346*

subsatellite, *n.* an artificial satellite launched from a larger orbiting satellite.

The astronauts will seek evidence of the origin of the strange sinuous rilles; and hope that heat-flow and seismic experiments will shed light on the giant mascon forming the mare. The Command Module, piloted by Alfred Worden, will carry new equipment to map the Moon, and will eject, for the first time, a sub-satellite carrying particle detectors and a magnetometer. Tracking this craft would provide improved lunar gravity profiles. *New Scientist, Oct. 29, 1970, p 212*

subshell, *n.* any part or segment of the space occupied by the orbit of an electron.

The relation arises from the disposition of electrons around a nucleus in a series of shells and subshells, which are really a simplified physical representation of quantum-mechanical energy levels.... *Glenn T. Seaborg and Justin*

L. Bloom, "The Synthetic Elements," Scientific American, April 1969, p 57

subtext, *n.* the underlying meaning of a literary or dramatic text.

"The Lodger" demonstrates a beautiful sense of subtext — of the gap between what people say and what is on their minds — which is rather an astonishing achievement in a silent picture. *Penelope Gilliatt, "The Current Cinema," The New Yorker, Sept. 11, 1971, p 93*

Again in the kidnapping scene, when the bawdy, somehow disgraceful old Jew is confronted by strong, passionless young men ... and by a menacingly attractive young woman, you may recall *The Homecoming* [a play by Harold Pinter]. The resemblances are so strong that they suggest that the final solution lies somewhere in the subtext of Pinter's own allusive, enigmatic fantasies of persecution. *D. A. N. Jones, "Theatre," Review of "The Man in the Glass Booth," The Listener, Aug. 3, 1967, p 156*

sudden infant death syndrome, a technical name for CRIB DEATH.

This volume is the report of an international conference on the sudden infant death syndrome (SIDS in jargon) to which puzzles were brought by four groups of doctors: the epidemiologists, bearing thoughtfully tabulated numbers; the pathologists, with scalpel and lens, peering in their classic mode at the tiny dead; the physiologists, with electrocardiogram, blood-pressure record and respiratory chemistry, and the virologists, with their diagnostic tissue cultures in rapid growth. *Philip Morrison, "Books," Review of "Sudden Infant Death Syndrome," edited by Abraham B. Bergman, J. Bruce Beckwith, and C. George Ray, Scientific American, March 1971, p 118*

suedehead, *n.* a type of SKINHEAD (young British working-class tough).

The skinheads are lineal descendants of the rockers — with an added touch of mindless savagery. When their hair grows a trifle longer, they refer to themselves as suedeheads. Skins or suedes, they specialize in terrorising such menacing types as hippies and homosexuals, Pakistani immigrants and little old ladies. *Time, June 8, 1970, p 37*

sue·dette (swei'det), *n.* a suede imitation or substitute.

Swimming in suede is the new thing; swimming in cotton suedette the next best. *The Sunday Times (London), June 6, 1971, p 33*

[from *suede* + *-ette*, as in *leatherette*]

suicide seat, the seat next to the driver in an automobile, so called from the large incidence of fatality among those who occupy it in accidents.

I was in the mini-bus, in the suicide seat next to the driver. *The Guardian (London), May 24, 1972, p 10*

suicidology, *n.* the study of suicide and suicidal behavior.

Writing in the current issue of *Life-Threatening Behavior*, the new official journal of the American Association of Suicidology, Psychiatrist Blachly suggests that the suicidal person who wants to destroy his whole body may find an alternative in sacrificing just part of it. *Time, April 26, 1971, p 56*

sunseeker, *n.* a person who seeks out places of sunshine and warmth to vacation in.

Sunseekers are beginning to look farther afield than the popular Spanish mainland. *Terry Mahon, "Review of the Year," The Times (London), Dec. 31, 1970, p VII*

sunshades, *n.pl. Slang.* sunglasses. Also shortened to SHADES.

I give a lot of speeches with my sunshades on. *Frank Deford, The Sunday Times (London), May 28, 1967, p 18*

su·per·ac·ti·nide series (ˌsu: pərˈæk təˌnɑid), a predicted series of superheavy chemical elements which is to follow the transactinide series in the periodic table.

Active searches are in progress for elements 110 and 114; scientists were already talking about elements up to 121; and Dr. [Glenn T.] Seaborg, for one, has predicted elements 122 to 153. He called this grouping the super-actinide series. *Science News Yearbook 1970, p 266*

superalloy, *n.* an alloy developed to resist high temperatures, stresses, and oxidation.

Superalloys such as nickel and cobalt-base alloys, even though some of them can withstand temperatures as high as 1,800 degrees F., will not hold up under the high-temperature requirements of upcoming jets, reactors and rockets. *Edward Gross, Science News, Jan. 24, 1970, p 107*

superchurch, *n.* a large church formed by the unification of a group of separate churches.

... Episcopalians are potential participants in the proposed multichurch Protestant merger, the Church of Christ Uniting. Should the Episcopal Church join the new super-church, the questions of Episcopal belief, the Eucharist and ministerial orders could become more complicated yet. *Time, May 25, 1970, p 76*

supercity, *n.* **1** a large urban area formed by the expansion and gradual coalescence of two or more relatively distant cities. Compare STRIP CITY.

I have the recurrent nightmare of the supercities that threaten us today, the titanic conurbations—already growing before our eyes—single vast towns from Boston to Baltimore, Pittsburgh to Chicago, London to Birmingham, each with thirty million people imprisoned in asphalt forever. *James Cameron, The Manchester Guardian Weekly, Oct. 10, 1970, p 15*

2 a very large city; a megalopolis.

... daring solutions to the problems of urban design were offered by Paolo Soleri in exhibitions at the Corcoran Gallery, Washington, D.C., and the Whitney Museum in New York. He planned *arcologies,* gigantic supercities towering high in the air or floating on water, as a means of preventing man from destroying himself and his environment. *John Fowler, "Architecture," The Americana Annual 1971, p 103*

supercluster, *n.* a very large cluster of galaxies.

Present data on the sizes of clusters of galaxies, and on possible "superclusters," are too sparse to enable us to assess the validity of theories that predict the mass spectrum of condensations. *Martin J. Rees and Joseph Silk, Scientific American, June 1970, p 35*

The Local Group containing our galaxy lies at the edge of this supercluster, which is slowly rotating. *The Times (London), March 9, 1970, p 13*

They analyse the distribution, first of normal bright galaxies known to belong to a local supercluster of galaxies, and then of quasars and some peculiar galaxies. *"Statistics Put Quasars Much Nearer to Us," New Scientist and Science Journal, July 29, 1971, p 245*

supercontinent, *n.* any of several great land masses supposed to have once comprised the present continents. Also called PROTOCONTINENT.

The theory that Antarctica was once part of a super-continent of all the major land masses has been reinforced by discovery of a fossil jawbone . . . near the South Pole. *The New York Times, March 17, 1968, Sec. 4, p 11*

Dietz discounts an alternative hypothesis that all continents once were a single land mass called Pangaea. Rather he favours the notion of two supercontinents, eloquently advocated a half century ago by Wegener. Wegener's other supercontinent, called Laurasia, combined North America, Europe and Asia. *Howard Simons, New Scientist, Oct. 14, 1965, p 96*

supercountry, *n.* an extremely powerful country; a superpower.

They had turned to Bombing because the status quo no longer worked, and because bombing was the easiest thing. It was the kind of power America wielded most easily—the great technological supercountry against a very little country. *David Halberstam, "The Programming of Robert McNamara," Harper's, Feb. 1971, p 63*

supercritical wing, an aircraft wing that maintains a supersonic flow of air over the upper wing surface to reduce drag by eliminating shock-induced separation of the boundary layer.

The supercritical wing, as it is called, was developed at NASA's Langley Research Center in Virginia under the direction of Dr. Richard T. Whitcomb. *Science News, Nov. 14, 1970, p 389*

This is the first test of a new concept in aerofoil design, known as the supercritical wing. It has a shape differing greatly from conventional wings, which have a pronounced curvature from front to back so that the airflow across the wing reaches the speed of sound before the aircraft itself does. *"Aeronautics: New Wing Flies for First Time," The Times (London), Dec. 3, 1970, p 17*

supercurrent, *n.* the electric current of a super-conductor; a current that flows through a metal conductor chilled to temperatures near absolute zero without meeting resistance or requiring voltage to drive it on.

The actual behavior of a superconductor in a magnetic field depends on the strength of the field. In a weak field a superconductor acts as a perfect diamagnet and expels the magnetic field. The field falls off within a thin surface layer and is shielded from the interior of the specimen by an induced "supercurrent." *Uwe Essmann and Hermann Träuble, "The Magnetic Structure of Superconductors," Scientific American, March 1971, p 78*

superdense, *adj.* extremely dense or compact.

. . . the quasar is composed of superdense material, especially in its central core. To obtain such densities the quasars would have to be composed purely of neutrons or other neutral particles. *Science Journal, May 1968, p 7*

Soviet scientists believe that there may be similar occurrences of super-dense water in areas deep inside the Earth, where conditions, as in the atmosphere, differ from those on the surface. *New Scientist, June 13, 1968, p 590*

The idea that superdense bodies could be formed as end products of supernova explosions is not new. Hypothetical superdense stars composed almost entirely of neutrons were conceived some 40 years ago by the Russian physicist L. D. Landau and independently by J. Robert Oppenheimer. *Paul Gorenstein and Wallace Tucker, "Supernova Remnants," Scientific American, July 1971, p 81*

supergroup, *n.* a rock'n'roll group made up of members or former members of other rock groups.

A typical example was Blind Faith, consisting of Stevie Winwood (ex-Traffic), Eric Clapton and Ginger Baker (ex-Cream), and Rick Grech (ex-Family). This was a true "supergroup," since its members were excellent musicians. *Hazel R. Morgan, Britannica Book of the Year 1970, p 563*

Rock groups disintegrated rapidly, the most dramatic split finally ending the Beatles. America's most successful "supergroup," Crosby, Stills, Nash and Young, seemed to be fragmenting also. *Noel Coppage, "Recordings," The Americana Annual 1971, p 574*

superheavy, *adj.* **1** having a higher atomic number or greater atomic mass than those of the heaviest elements known.

Superheavy elements are generally created by accelerating heavy ions, such as argon, for interactions with heavier elements, such as uranium. *New Scientist, Feb. 5, 1970, p 249*

2 of or belonging to superheavy elements.

A heavy-ion accelerator is a machine especially designed to accelerate atomic nuclei that have been stripped of some or all of their attendant electrons. . . . If such nuclei are struck against other heavy nuclei, they may fuse with them and form superheavy nuclei. *"Superheavy Nuclei from Orsay's Alice," Science News, Dec. 4, 1971, p 373*

—*n.* a superheavy element.

The superheavies are designated by the prefix eka, from eka-osmium to eka-lead, and each eka-element is expected to be indentifiable in the chemical analysis along with its namesake. *Science News, Feb. 20, 1971, p 128*

This sequence is highly speculative although a group at the Rutherford Laboratory may have seen superheavies via multiple high-energy collisions. *"Man-made Cosmic Rays Go On the Air," New Scientist and Science Journal, Sept. 2, 1971, p 499*

The superheavies are particularly interesting because some of them may be relatively stable, lasting millions of years instead of fractions of a second. *"Superheavy Nuclei from Orsay's Alice," Science News, Dec. 4, 1971, p 373*

The superheavies are upon us. Last week a British research team presented their case for the creation of a superheavy element with atomic number 112. *New Scientist and Science Journal, Feb. 18, 1971, p 344*

superjet, *n.* a supersonic jet aircraft.

A $100 million order by United Air Lines for five giant 747 superjets helped bring the company a total of $961 million in new commercial business over the past month, boosted its backlog to a staggering $5.6 billion. *Time, Nov. 25, 1966, p 66*

Shall we impose the hideous noise of super-jets on communities near airports, or impose the costs of limiting them on travellers? *Gordon Rattray Taylor, New Scientist, May 2, 1968, p 250*

supermolecule, *n.* a molecule consisting of several smaller molecules.

Some scientists think this [anomalous] form of water consists of "supermolecules," each of which is composed of 4 ordinary water molecules. *"Review of the Year— Physical Sciences and Mathematics," Encyclopedia Science Supplement (Grolier) 1969, p 238*

supermultiplet, *n. Nuclear Physics.* a family or class of multiplets (related groups of nuclear particles).

. . . this led to a further grouping together of particles, in fact, to a 35-fold "supermultiplet". *The Times (London), Jan. 23, 1965, p 3*

These algebraic properties can be used to probe the problems of particle physics, especially to calculate many of the dynamical quantities. . . . For this discussion it is assumed that all the masses within a supermultiplet are degenerate. *A. Sankaranarayanan, "Current Algebra," McGraw-Hill Yearbook of Science and Technology 1968, p 141*

superovulate, *v.i.* to produce more than the normal number of eggs at one time.

Farm animals could be induced to superovulate, their fertilized eggs could be removed, and only embryos of the desired sex would then be put back into mother animals. *Robert Edwards and Richard Gardner, "Choosing Sex Before Birth," New Scientist, May 2, 1968, p 220*

superplastic, *adj.* **1** capable of plastic deformation under very small stress at high temperatures.

On a more practical level, one of the later papers at the meeting, by Professor R. B. Nicholson, of Manchester University, was concerned with the role of grain boundaries in superplastic materials. These materials are characterized by a very small grain size—of the order of a few microns—and an immense capacity for plastic deformation at elevated temperatures, without fracture occurring. *New Scientist, Oct. 8, 1970, p 65*

2 made out of a superplastic material.

Superplastic cars should be quieter, and their scrap value far higher than that of steel cars. *Geoffrey Charles, The Times (London), Dec. 18, 1968, p 17*

3 characteristic of or relating to superplastic materials.

Some alloys, when deformed at certain rates and in certain temperature ranges, can stretch out like chewing gum and be tremendously deformed without breaking. This superplastic behavior is being studied to understand superplasticity and to put it to industrial use. In one experiment, a superplastic zinc-aluminum alloy was drawn into a die to reproduce the complex shape of the IBM "Selectric" typewriter head. Accurate reproduction of the type letters was obtained. *O. Cutler Shepard, "Metallurgy," The Americana Annual 1968, p 437*

—*n.* a plastic material, especially a metal that is unusually pliable at an elevated temperature. The grain is so fine that atoms slip easily along crystal planes without cleavage.

This metal, after treatment which reduces the grain size to about a micrometre, behaves like a superplastic at room temperature—it can be stretched by a factor of about 10 in one direction without breaking. *New Scientist, Jan. 2, 1969, p 22*

While the superplastics are only starting to shed their image as laboratory curiosities, the fiber composites have almost arrived. *Gene Bylinsky, "Materials from the Test Tube," 1972 Britannica Yearbook of Science and the Future, 1971, p 406*

superplastically, *adv.* in the manner of superplastics.

At one time, it was considered that superplastic metallic alloys were amorphous-like and for this reason behaved superplastically. *O. D. Sherby, Science Journal, June 1969, p 75*

superplasticity, *n.* the property or quality of being superplastic.

Key to achieving superplasticity is in the compounding of proper metals, neither of which can have crystals more than a few millionths of an inch in diameter. *Science News, May 18, 1968, p 478*

supersonic transport, a large jet aircraft designed to fly at speeds of 1200 to 1800 miles per hour, or twice to almost three times the speed of sound. *Abbreviation:* SST See also CONCORDE.

... supersonic transports might modify the stratosphere, globally.... Present uncertainties about the engine emissions and their climatic consequences, must ... be removed before supersonic transport goes commercial. *Fred Wheeler, New Scientist, Oct. 1, 1970, p 12*

superspace, *n.* a theoretical mathematical expanse in which all three-dimensional spaces are points.

Superspace is a mathematical construction that allows physicists to order all the possible three-dimensional spaces in such a way that they can be compared with one another in the way physical theories apply to them. *Science News, June 21, 1969, p 597*

[John A.] Wheeler describes his field as "the chemistry of geometry," which takes place in *superspace* defined as "the arena within which the dynamics of space operate." In superspace there is no time. Time exists at a level less basic. *"Why Nothing Has Become Important," New Scientist and Science Journal, July 29, 1971, p 242*

superstar, *n.* **1** a person who surpasses the most outstanding figures in his field or profession; a major or principal star.

... the congress [of Catholic theologians] provided an array of superstars including The Netherlands' Edward Schillebeeckx, France's Yves Congar, Germany's Karl Rahner, Hans Küng and Johan Metz. *Time, Sept. 28, 1970, p 44*

2 a celestial body that is a powerful source of electromagnetic waves.

Throughout 1967 debate centred on ... mysterious superstars called quasars.... *The Annual Register of World Events in 1967 (1968), p 383*

supertask, *n.* any of various logical paradoxes involving the challenge to complete an infinite sequence of tasks.

The weightiest modern pieces are by Adolf Grunbaum of the University of Pittsburg. His methods go more deeply into the mathematical theory of the continuum than those of his predecessors.... By designing his imaginary mechanisms so that no infinite distances need to be traveled by any lever or cog, he demonstrates that supertasks, like the task of Achilles, can indeed be accomplished, not only in the context of the steady race but also very widely. *Philip Morrison, "Books," Review of "Zeno's Paradoxes," edited by Wesley C. Salmon, Scientific American, March 1971, p 123*

su·per·trans·u·ran·ic (ˌsuː pərˌtræns yu'ræn ik), *adj.* surpassing in mass the transuranic elements (those with atomic numbers higher than uranium); superheavy.

It appeared that supertransuranic nuclei might be made by the fusion of two fairly heavy nuclei that added up to the particular mass desired in the supertransuranic region or close to that mass. *H. E. Wegner, "Nuclear Physics," 1970 Britannica Yearbook of Science and the Future, 1969, p 378*

—*n.* a supertransuranic element.

The heavy-ion accelerator facilities at Dubna were utilized during the past year in an intensive program aimed at direct production of the supertransuranics. *D. Allan Bromley, "Physics," 1972 Britannica Yearbook of Science and the Future, 1971, p 319*

superwater, *n.* another name for ANOMALOUS WATER.

... Soviet chemist Boris V. Deryagin ... had prepared a new form of water. Called variously anomalous water, orthowater, polywater, and superwater, the material was readily prepared in milligram quantities by placing a beaker containing a large number of fine capillary tubes of silica or borosilicate glass (diameters $1\text{-}10\mu$) in a desiccator containing a second beaker of saturated aqueous potassium sulfate. The desiccator was evacuated and left undisturbed over a period of a few days to several months, whereupon anomalous water could be observed, under a microscope, to have formed in the capillaries. *James A. Kerr, "Chemistry: Physical and Inorganic," Britannica Book of the Year 1971, p 184*

suppresant, *n.* a substance used to suppress an effect, reaction, etc.

A material that is applied directly to the burning fuel to reduce the intensity or rate of burning is termed a suppressant. Chemicals known as wetting agents or surfactants may be added to water to increase its power to "wet" the surface of fuel and to penetrate fuel beds composed of duff and leaf litter. *William E. Reifsnyder, "Forest Fire Retardants," McGraw-Hill Yearbook of Science and Technology 1968, p 189*

[noun use of *suppressant, adj.* (which is usually applied to drugs or medicines)]

suprathermal ion detector, an instrument for recording the flux, quantity, density, velocity, and energy per unit charge of positive ions near the lunar surface.

[Astronaut Edgar] Mitchell struggled to loosen a dust-clogged fastener on the suprathermal ion detector that was designed to record the presence of any gases on the moon. *Time, Feb. 15, 1971, p 8*

su·pre·mo (sə'priː mou), *n. British.* a person who is highest in command or authority; the overall head or chief of one or several organizations.

For that reason Mr. Crossman becomes supremo of the social services, overlording the social security and health departments and perhaps, later, fragments broken off from the Home Office.... *David Wood, The Times (London), April 6, 1968, p 1*

The creation of a national police Supremo, with greater power over Britain's police than anyone has had before, is under consideration by the Home Secretary, Mr. Roy Jenkins. *John Barry, The Sunday Times, (London), Oct. 30, 1966, p 1*

[from Spanish, a military commander-in-chief, a generalissimo, from *supremo, adj.,* supreme]

surface-effect ship, *U.S.* an air cushion vehicle designed for travel over water. Compare GROUND EFFECT MACHINE.

The Department of Commerce and the Navy have announced a master plan for development of large, fast surface-effect ships. These are air-cushion vessels similar to the British Hovercraft. *The New York Times, Aug. 28, 1967, p 61*

... "Surface Effect Ships." ... were to be non-amphibious craft, driven by waterscrews and waterjets, respectively, and were expected to be operating by mid-1970. *John B.*

Bentley, "Water Transportation," Britannica Book of the Year 1970, p 758

surface structure, (in generative-transformational grammar) the formal structure or phonetic expression of a sentence. Compare DEEP STRUCTURE.

"John loves Mary" is the *surface structure* of the sentence. It constitutes the sort of "physical signal," or phonetic articulation, to which we can perfectly well apply the traditional syntax we have learned in school: noun, verb, object, and so on. But this surface structure tells us little and obviously differs for every language. *George Steiner, "The Tongues of Men," The New Yorker, Nov. 15, 1969, p 224*

surreal, *adj.* bizarrely fantastic or fanciful.

At present the American design for a democratic government tends to look somewhat surreal when placed in a Vietnamese context. *Frances FitzGerald, "The Struggle and the War: The Maze of Vietnamese Politics," The Atlantic, Aug. 1967, p 86*

— *n.* **the surreal,** that which is characteristic of surrealism; the bizarrely fantastic or fanciful.

[Richard] Lester's first film (in 1959) was a much-praised Sellers' short called *The Running, Jumping and Standing Still Film,* which won an Oscar nomination. Lester was then given a couple of low-budget potboilers to direct, and moved out into daylight with the two Beatles' extravaganzas, which gave the impression of being acted on flying trapezes and established Lester's image as the blithe spirit of the surreal. *Time, Nov. 17, 1967, p 60*

[back formation from *surrealism*]

surreally, *adv.* in a surreal way.

The Bleecker Street Cinema is showing a surreally funny hour of film called "No More Excuses," which is goonish, rude, and altogether relieving. *Penelope Gilliatt, "The Current Cinema: How to Mangle an Idea and Stay Radiant," The New Yorker, May 25, 1968, p 87*

surveille, *v.t.* *U.S.* to keep under close watch.

In arguing the government's case before the high court, Griswold [Solicitor General Erwin M. Griswold] said the Army's practice of surveilling civilians "from my point of view . . . went too far. It was an absence of proper civilian control." *"High Court Asked to Bar Review of Army Snooping," The Courier-Journal (Louisville, Kentucky), March 28, 1972, p A2*

If the U.S. Central Intelligence Agency is as adroit in surveilling others as it is in escaping surveillance of itself, the Republic can relax. *Clayton Fritchey, Harper's, Oct. 1966, p 37*

[back formation from *surveillance*]

SU(3) symmetry, *Nuclear Physics.* another name for EIGHTFOLD WAY.

The A2 meson is an enigma. Until it came along high-energy physicists were smug in their belief that all the strongly interacting particles fit into a classification known as "SU(3) symmetry". The A2 meson stands out as a maverick among the 100 or more other "elementary" particles, because recent data indicate that it is really two particles of the same mass, or—even more inscrutable—that it is a new type of particle—a double resonance or a dipole. Neither of these possibilities can be explained by simple theories. *New Scientist, Oct. 29, 1970, p 211*

[Special Unitary (group in 3 dimensions) symmetry]

sweat, *v.t.* *Slang.* to worry about (something).

. . . Mr. Quinn came a few days later and told him it was

quite an accomplishment that he and his father made it alone in the world, and asked him to tell how they did things—who cooked the meals, cleaned the house, took care of the laundry, and so on—told him to lay it on, that he was all ears, and not to sweat a thing because he was on their side. . . . *Theodore Weesner, "The Hearing," The New Yorker, April 10, 1971, p 38*

swing, *v.i.* *Slang.* **1** to be fashionably lively and exciting.

Joy Carroll explores the bizarre boom in everything awful enough to be good, from buggy seats to Camp statues. Now your home swings if it's decorated with JUNK. *Maclean's, May 2, 1966, p 13*

Dame Laura Knight and Mrs. J. Yeoman ("Anton" the cartoonist) are among the first 45 women who have joined this hitherto all-male club in Old Church Street, which with its new look is really beginning to swing. *The Times (London), March 10, 1967, p 12*

"This magazine has got to swing, like other magazines swing," Ackerman had once said, and he had not meant simply that it should be fashionable but that it should be aware of the way society moved. *Otto Friedrich, "The Saturday Evening Post," Harper's, Dec. 1969, p 110*

2 to swap partners for sexual purposes.

During their investigation, the Bartells met hundreds of people interested in "swinging," an activity defined as "having sexual relations as a couple with at least one other individual." . . . As Gilbert Bartell discovered, getting started in swinging is easy. All that is required is a copy of *Kindred Spirits, Ecstasy, Swingers' Life,* or any one of 50 scruffy magazines filled with ads and advice on "The Etiquette of Swinging" and "How to Organize an Enjoyable Swinging Party." *"The American Way of Swinging," Time, Feb. 8, 1971, p 36*

swing-by, *n.* a planetary trajectory in which a spacecraft uses the planet's gravitational field to achieve the orbit necessary to change course for a more distant celestial body. *Often used attributively.*

Venus swing-bys to Mercury can be accomplished in 1970 and 1973 but not again until the 1980s. *Carl Sagan and David Morrison, Science Journal, Dec. 1968, p 77*

He believes a space mission to the comet could be accomplished through a "swing-by" technique in which the spacecraft would pass near a planet, have its trajectory bent by the planet's gravity and then move on towards its goal. *The Times (London), Aug. 17, 1967, p 1*

swinger, *n.* *Slang.* **1** a person who keeps up with the latest fashions in clothes, entertainment, the arts, etc., especially those considered youthful and lively.

"I was a swinger for half my life. Anything hip in outlook and idea at once captivated me." *Leopold Tyrmand, "Reflections: Permissiveness and Rectitude," The New Yorker, Feb. 28, 1970, p 95*

I agree with Mr. Sissman that there is nothing sadder than the middle-aged swinger who has sold out to the values of his children. *Michael R. Schaefer, Chula Vista, Calif., in a Letter to the Editor, The Atlantic, June 1971, p 36*

2 a person who swaps partners for sexual purposes.

The Los Angeles *Free Press,* an underground paper, carries pages of ads for "swingers," couples or singles who want to trade bed partners. . . . *Steven V. Roberts, "Reports: Los Angeles," The Atlantic, Sept. 1969, p 35*

swing-wing, *n.* **1** an aircraft wing that can be swung backward in flight to set the craft's motion for slow, intermediate, or supersonic speeds. Also called VARIABLE-SWEEP WING and VARIABLE GEOMETRY.

The "swing-wings" and low-pressure tyres will enable the F-111 to operate from small airstrips devoid of concrete runways. *Neville Brown, New Scientist, Jan. 27, 1966, p 206*

2 an aircraft having a swing-wing.

It was the third F-111 crash since a squadron of six of the $6,000,000 swing-wings made their combat debut in Viet Nam less than a month ago. *Time, May 3, 1968, p 23*

—*adj.* of, utilizing, or relating to a swing-wing.

The F-111, a controversial swing-wing fighter designed and made by General Dynamics, saw combat duty in Vietnam for the first time but had to be withdrawn after several accidents. *John B. Bentley, "Aerospace," Britannica Book of the Year 1969, p 411*

switch, *v.i.* **switch on,** *Slang.* **1** to have a hallucinogenic experience from taking narcotics. The more common expression is TURN ON.

After rumours that you could switch on with the help of the white fibre from the inside of a banana skin it became the great mystic symbol among the Greenwich Village hippies. *The Manchester Guardian Weekly, May 9, 1968, p 6*

2 to become fashionably up-to-date; follow the latest styles in music, fashion, etc.

Nor, in this respect, would local stations financed by advertising revenue be in a more advantageous position. I only pointed to a vast audience, millions strong, which does not listen to the B.B.C.; and, I submit, will continue to remain switched off to that institution till such time as the B.B.C., stimulated by competition, gets "switched on". *Roy Boulting, The Times (London), Feb. 9, 1966, p 13*

switched-on, *adj. Slang.* keeping up with the latest and brightest ideas, fashions, etc.; highly modern and sophisticated.

Though *Sesame Street's* studio is modest—an old movie theater on Manhattan's upper Broadway—the budget is an impressive $28,000 per show. Yet because of its wide popularity, the switched-on school reaches its audience at a cost of about a penny per child; "a bargain," says Dr. Benjamin Spock, "if I ever saw one." *Time, Nov. 23, 1970, p 65*

...such young London designers as Mary Quant and John Stephen began turning out styles for their switched-on friends. *Marjorie Harris, "The Look," Maclean's, Aug. 20, 1966, p 10*

It was this factor, as much as any other, that dictated the rejection of old, cloth-cap Socialism in favour of new, switched-on technology. *The Sunday Times (London), Feb. 12, 1967, p 11*

[from SWITCH ON]

switch selling, *British.* the selling of a more expensive item to customers than the one advertised at a much lower price. The equivalent U.S. term is *bait-and-switch selling.* See also BAIT-AND-SWITCH.

...all its salesmen are, and always have been, expressly forbidden to attempt 'switch selling'. *Peter Wilsher, The Sunday Times (London), July 19, 1964, p 12*

synchronous, *adj.* **1** orbiting the earth at the same rate as the earth moves; moving in a geostationary orbit.

This week could see a new development in marine communications with the fitting of a steerable receiver/aerial to the Cunard-Brocklebank liner *Atlantic Causeway* to make possible two-way ship-to-shore communications, through the NASA ATS-3 synchronous satellite. *Joseph D. Parker, "Shipping Neglected in Space Communications," New Scientist, July 2, 1970, p 14*

2 of or relating to a synchronous satellite.

The basic idea of the communication satellite...is that an active radio repeater station high above the Earth can receive a radio transmission beamed to it and re-transmit it to an area enormously greater than any ground station could reach. There are significant advantages in using satellites at the 'synchronous' altitude of about 36,000 km. *W. T. Gunston, "Telecommunications Tomorrow," Science Journal, Dec. 1970, p 64*

synchrotron radiation, a form of electromagnetic radiation produced by the spiraling motion of high-speed electrons around a magnetic field, as in a synchrotron (a type of particle accelerator) or in some galactic nebulae.

The radiation is polarized, it shows no emission or absorption lines in its spectrum, and most peculiarly it is emitted at measurable levels over an immense wavelength range from the shortest X rays to the longest radio waves. No thermal source could have these properties. Accordingly Shklovsky suggested in 1953 that the radiation arises from electrons moving at relativistic speeds (that is, speeds near the speed of light) in a magnetic field inside the nebula; this type of radiation is called synchrotron radiation. *Jeremiah P. Ostriker, "The Nature of Pulsars," Scientific American, Jan. 1971, p 59*

Syn·com ('sin,kɑm), *n.* any of a series of U.S. communications satellites relaying radio and telephone signals from a geostationary orbit.

This synchronous orbit, which is followed by such 'geostationary' satellites as the *Syncoms* and other communications relay stations, has an approximate height of 36,000 km. *B. P. Day, Science Journal, Aug. 1968, p 63*

[from *Syn*chronous *com*munications satellite]

syndrome, *n.* a distinctive pattern of behavior.

From the way the young man talked about his machine, Nicholi easily concluded that his patient was the victim of a hitherto unrecognized emotional ailment: the motorcycle syndrome. *Time, Dec. 7, 1970, p 65*

Mr. Scribner appears to suffer from the same syndrome found in so many other public officers. On assuming office, they forthwith forget that they are occupying a public office and are not managing their private firm. *Harry H. Zucker, New York, in a Letter to the Editor, The New York Times, Nov. 6, 1970, p 40*

A student of mine explained Albuquerque's all-enveloping friendliness in terms of the Luke Short syndrome. Typically in a Luke Short novel, a cowboy, footsore and weary, comes into town carrying a saddle over his shoulders. Nobody asks any questions. Friendliness is simply his for the asking.... *David Boroff, "A New Yorker's Report on New Mexico," Harper's, Feb. 1965, p 74*

[extended sense of the medical term for a group of signs or symptoms characterizing a disease]

synectic, *adj.* of or relating to synectics.

I have come to the conclusion that there appears to be a problem-solving mechanism at work in the "mind" which can be stimulated to resolve problems adversely affecting survival, and which stimulates in a synectic fashion solutions to problems of a creative nature which enhance survival. *Rayner Garner, New Scientist, Aug. 21, 1969, p 395*

sy·nec·tics (si'nek tiks), *n.* the free and unrestrained exchange of ideas among a group of thinkers, used as a method of developing new ideas, solving problems, and making discoveries.

A new philosophy, "synectics", which is said to liberate the creative instinct and so stimulate inventiveness, is gaining a following among big corporations. *The Times (London), Aug. 11, 1965, p 11*

The idea was produced by the International Synectics Foundation, a new "think tank" at Westminster, British Columbia, of which Mr. Barry is a prominent member. *The New York Times, Sept. 19, 1968, p 48*

[probably from *syn-* together + dial*ectics*]

syn·er·ga·my (si'nər gə mi:), *n.* communal marriage.

Robert Rimmer, who wrote "The Harrad Experiment," a novel about undergraduate cohabitation, and "Proposition 21," one about group marriage, says in an interview in the current issue of Psychology Today that the time may come when two or three couples may be legally wed to each other by clergymen.

He calls this new form of marriage, in which one or both partners may be married to another person also, synergamy. But he thinks this kind of marriage won't work unless "you begin with reasonably happy monogamous marriages. You can't solve your neurotic problems in a group marriage; you just accentuate them." *Barbara Trecker, "Marriage Going Groupie?" New York Post, Jan. 3, 1972, p 7*

[from Greek *synergós* working together + English *-gamy* marriage, as in *polygamy*]

synergistic, *adj.* interacting or interdependent; mutually stimulating or responsive.

The synergistic action of these basic facets of our national economy—public information, public approval, public action—can be the difference between success and failure, survival and disintegration for the modern corporation. *William D. Patterson, Saturday Review, April 9, 1966, p 71*

We are by no means taxed for material. But we are convinced of the importance of the interdependence of science and the rest of society. This not only concerns the social implications of science, but the effects on science of decisions in Government, university councils, industry or wherever there is a synergistic or abrasive interface. This interface, we believe, has such long-range significance that we must assign a share of our limited space to it. *Ed., Science News, July 11, 1970, p 28*

[extended sense of the biomedical term descriptive of the cooperative action between different drugs, muscles, organs, etc.]

synergistically, *adv.* in a synergistic manner.

By this he meant that science and technology had come to the point where the parts fed upon each other continuously and synergistically to enlarge the whole. This was accomplished by the direct application of rational technique and mathematics, of logic and experiment, to already existent invention, leading to multiplication and cascading of our power over the environment. *Charles R. DeCarlo, The New York Times, Jan. 8, 1968, p 141*

syn·ge·ne·ic (,sin dʒə'ni: ik), *adj.* **1** of or involving an identity of genotype.

Mouse recipients of transplants are called "syngeneic" when the corresponding pair of genes in each host cell are identical with those of the homozygous tumor cells. *Faye Marley, Science News Letter, March 5, 1966, p 147*

2 of or involving similarity but not identity of genotype.

Successful transfers are more difficult with older recipients. This is consistent with Celada's report of a barrier to syngeneic transfer of immune cells which increased markedly with age. *Sanford H. Stone, Edwin M. Lerner, II, and Julius H. Goode, Science, March 1, 1968, p 995*

Our colleague, Dr Billington (see *Nature 202, 317, 1964*), found that pure-bred mouse eggs gave larger placentae when transferred to a genetically dissimilar foster mother than when transferred to the uterus of a mouse of similar (syngeneic) genotype. *D. R. S. Kirby and C. Wood, Science Journal, Feb. 1968, p 27*

[from Greek *syngéneia* kinship, relationship + English *-ic*]

system, *n.* **1 the system,** the network of established political, social, and economic institutions that control a country and suppress any attempt to change it. Compare POWER STRUCTURE and ESTABLISHMENT (def. 1).

Their [the Maoists, the radical separatists in Quebec, the Naxalites in India, the Weathermen and Panthers in the U.S.] ideologies differ, but in general their rationale is that "the system" is incapable of real change and that the official violence of the government (police, prisons, armies) can only be countered by violence. *Time, Nov. 2, 1970, p 19*

"The little guy's got his whole life and energy in the system—he thinks the system is America—and all the time the system is taking him for a ride and he don't know it." *Paul Dietsch, quoted by Bill Moyers, "Listening to America," Harper's, Dec. 1970, p 56*

2 *Cybernetics.* anything consisting of at least two interrelated parts.

Not every system is treated in cybernetics. Cybernetics is only concerned with controlled systems. To illustrate, let us consider a ship as a cybernetic system.... In an oceangoing ship a cybernetic system of servomechanisms between helm and rudder automatically corrects the course of the ship. *V. G. Drozin, "Cybernetics: A New and Fast-expanding Science," Encyclopedia Science Supplement (Grolier) 1970, p 292*

systemic painting, painting in the style of minimal art.

Minimal art is Dada in which the art critic has got into the act. No mode in art has ever had more labels affixed to it by eager literary collaborators; besides being called minimal art, it is known as "ABC art," "primary structures," "systemic painting," "reductive art," "rejective art," and by half a dozen other titles. *Harold Rosenberg, "The Art World: Defining Art," The New Yorker, Feb. 25, 1967, p 108*

systems analysis, the scientific and mathematical analysis of systems to improve their efficiency, accuracy, or general performance.

RAND systems-analyses that Secretary Robert McNamara introduced into the Department of Defense are revolutionizing administration of far-flung enterprises outside of as well as within government. *John Lear, Saturday Review, Sept. 23, 1967, p 94*

systems analyst, a specialist in systems analysis.

As a first step, the St Peter's group has employed a firm of systems analysts to analyse the flow of records in the hospitals and to suggest changes which could lead to computer handling of the data. *Dennis Hill, New Scientist, Feb. 8, 1968, p 312*

T

ta·bla ('tɑ: blə), *n.* a small drum of India played with the hand and tuned to various notes.

On *Sgt. Pepper* they used combs and paper, multiple-tracked percussion, tambouras ... a tabla, an Indian table-harp, a sitar, and a Hammond organ recorded at different speeds and then overlaid with electronic echo. *Raymond Palmer, "Mid-Month Recordings: Danger—Beatles at Work," Saturday Review, Oct. 12, 1968, p 65*

[from Hindi *tabla*, from Arabic *ṭabl* drum]

► See the note under SARANGI.

TACAN ('tæ,kæn), *n.* acronym for *tactical air navigation*, an electronic system that provides an aircraft with a continuous reading of bearing and distance from a radio-transmitting station.

This tactical air navigation system is similar in principle to the omnidirectional range and distance measuring equipment now in use. It is reputed to be slightly more accurate than the omnirange. TACAN has a higher operating frequency than VOR, and the TACAN transmitter is more compact.... *Charles F. Blair, Jr., "Air Navigation," Encyclopedia Science Supplement (Grolier) 1967, p 365*

tach·y·on ('tæk i:,ɑn), *n.* a hypothetical elementary particle with a speed greater than that of light, whose existence has been inferred mathematically from Einstein's special theory of relativity.

... tachyons, says Dr. Sudarshan, if they can exist, can go faster than light. They can go at any speed up to infinity and thus carry forces across any distance as fast as need be. *Science News, Jan. 31, 1970, p 126*

[coined by Gerald Feinberg, born 1933, an American physicist, from Greek *tachýs* swift + English *-on*, as in *electron, proton,* etc.,]

tag·me·mi·cist (tæg'mi: mə sist), *n.* a linguist who specializes in the study of tagmemes (the smallest meaningful units of grammatical form).

In practice, a transformationalist concerns himself primarily with the formulation of rules [of grammar] and of universal constraints and conventions which govern those rules; the tagmemicist deals primarily with the identification and classification of basic patterns, and the formulation of procedures which are intended to yield the correct classifications. *William Cressey, University of Michigan, Review of "A Tagmemic Analysis of Mexican Spanish Clauses" by Ruth M. Brend, Language, March 1970, p 186*

[from *tagmeme* the smallest meaningful unit of grammatical form, coined by the American linguist Leonard Bloomfield, 1887-1949, from Greek *tágma* order + English *-eme*, as in *phoneme:* "The tagmeme of exclamatory final-pitch occurs with any lexical form and gives it a grammatical meaning ... which

we may roughly describe, perhaps, as 'strong stimulus'." (Leonard Bloomfield, *Language* (1933), p 166)]

Ta·go-Sa·to-Ko·sa·ka ('tɑ: gou'sɑ: tou kou'sɑ: kə), *n.* a comet discovered in October, 1969, named for the three Japanese amateur astronomers who first sighted it. Compare BENNETT.

... the substances found in Tago-Sato-Kosaka are typical of planetary atmospheres such as are found around the outer planets of the solar system. *Science News, Feb. 7, 1970, p 241*

NASA ... claimed yet another "first"—the discovery of a big hydrogen cloud around the nucleus of the new bright comet Tago-Sato-Kosaka. *New Scientist, Feb. 5, 1970, p 247*

t'ai chi ch'uan ('tɑi dʒi: 'tʃwɑ:n) or **t'ai chi** ('tɑi 'dʒi:), a Chinese system of physical exercises similar to shadowboxing.

Rise at six and you find Chinese young people exercising in parks, on the waterfront, on rooftops. They twist and spin, jerk and wheel, doing "hard" exercises (forms of karate), "soft" (forms of *T'ai Chi-ch'uan,* the snakelike, rhythmic art), and countless improvisations of their own. *Ross Terrill, "The 800,000,000: Report From China," The Atlantic, Nov. 1971, p 92*

Embrace Tiger and Return to Mountain it is called, this being the name of one exercise in T'ai-chi, a Chinese system of callisthenics claimed to produce pliability, health and peace of mind. *John Percival, The Times (London), Nov. 22, 1968, p 9*

takeaway, *adj. British.* designating or dealing with food prepared to be eaten away from the premises. The equivalent U.S. term is TAKEOUT.

... so I said 'I'm gonna set a table under that Rembrandt.' So we did, and we got some white wine in, and we sent out to the Chinese restaurant for a Chinese takeaway curry and we brought it here. *Peter Terson, "Up You, Rembrandt!" The Manchester Guardian Weekly, April 10, 1971, p 15*

Mr Roger Masterman, general manager of a Liverpool chain of take-away chicken houses, said the local health authorities had not, so far asked him for chicken specimens. *Denis Herbstein, The Sunday Times (London), Feb. 16, 1969, p 6*

take-home sale, *British,* another term for OFF-SALE.

The cutback in mobility brought about by drinking and driving laws will mean a greater emphasis on take-home sales. *Patricia Tisdall, The Times (London), March 12, 1970, p IX*

takeout, *adj. U.S.* designating or dealing with food prepared to be eaten away from the premises. The equivalent British term is TAKEAWAY.

She *liked* canned chili and corned-beef hash, ... take-

455

out pizza pies. *Stephen Patch, "The Girl Who Sang with the Beatles," The New Yorker, Jan. 11, 1969, p 29*

The Lily-Tulip Cup Corporation introduced yesterday a packaging system designed to provide leakproof take-out containers. *The New York Times, June 29, 1965, p 45*

talk-in, *n.* **1** a protest demonstration in which the participants take turns to speak up on the issues.

Last week 180 Free University students staged a 45-hour hunger strike and talk-in at a West Berlin Protestant Student Center to demand the release of a jailed anti-Shah demonstrator. *Time, June 30, 1967, p 28*

2 an informal lecture or talk.

LeRoi Jones, poet, playwright and polemicist, sustained each aspect of his reputation Monday night, though in different degrees, at a reading at the Village Theater, an old Loew's movie house on Second Avenue near Sixth Street. It was the second in a series of talk-ins presented at that house. *The New York Times, Oct. 5, 1966, p 46*

...Studs comes up with "Hard Times—an oral history of the Depression,"...a talk-in on the psychology of remaining American, independent, and acquisitive, after laissez-fairing it to hell and back.... *John Hall, The Manchester Guardian Weekly, Oct. 3, 1970, p 22*

3 a conference or discussion.

At the end of this month the insurance industry starts its talk-in with the Monopolies Commission over fire insurance. *Gillian O'Connor, The Times (London), Sept. 7, 1970, p 18*

[see -IN]

talk show, *Especially U.S.* a television or radio show in which guest celebrities are interviewed. A British equivalent is CHAT SHOW.

What with books, magazines and talk shows, no man today is considered complete without an expressed opinion on grass. *Time, Jan. 26, 1970, p 68*

What is really lacking in all of the major TV talk shows is (dare I use the word?) commitment. *Robert Campbell Rowe, New York, "Drama: TV Mailbag," The New York Times, June 20, 1971, Sec. 2, p 19*

I do not argue that the high moments in talk shows bring out the best in either participants or watchers. They bring out the worst.... they may be judged as fully successful only when we sense someone is in danger of being emotionally gutted in public.

Talk shows have never been more popular than they are now. *Richard Schickel, "Performing Arts," Harper's, March 1970, p 116*

tam·bo·la (tæmˈbou lə), *n.* a unit of money in Malawi.

Malawi's decimal currency was to be introduced in March 1971; the new unit, the kwacha, is divided into 100 tambolas. *Elston G. Bradfield, "Coin Collecting," The 1970 Compton Yearbook, p 188*

tank top, *U.S.* an upper garment with wide shoulder straps, similar to the tops of one-piece bathing suits or men's underwear shirts.

...the staid Wall Street lawyer...turns Bloomingdale hippie in the evening, donning tie-dyed pants and tank top to weed the garden. *Time, June 29, 1970, p 39*

Miss Farrell—a tall, pretty ballerina dressed in a purple tank top and baggy rubber warm-up pants—looked inquiringly at Mr. Martins.... *The New Yorker, Jan. 27, 1968, p 25*

[named after the tank suits of the 1920's, one-piece bathing suits worn in the *tank* (swimming pool)]

tape deck, another name for a TAPE PLAYER.

The simplest playback machine is the tape deck, which has to be plugged into one's own hi-fi equipment. *Discus, Harper's, Aug. 1965, p 118*

Floodlights, sound equipment, tape-deck, and complete humourous script with blanks for personal and domestic references. *Punch, Dec. 7, 1966, p 856*

tape player, a machine for playing back sound on magnetic tapes or in cassettes. Also called TAPE DECK.

Buttons, balloons and lollipops; bull horns, projectors and tape players; car rental through Hertz, Telex through Western Union—all these things and many more are in handy catalogue.... *Philip H. Dougherty, The New York Times, June 20, 1968, p 72*

Starting this week is a £115,000 campaign for Philips car tape players. *The Times (London), May 6, 1970, p 25*

target, *n.* **on target,** on the right track.

It is always a nerve-racking business, deciding when to make the upturn, but it is going all right. We are on target. *George Brown, The Times (London), March 21, 1970, p 1*

Diddy is sure he did it; yet a blind girl near by who hears all and who proves to be on target about everything else, says he never left his seat. *"Books: Did He?" Review of "Death Kit" by Susan Sontag, Time, Aug. 18, 1967, p 88*

targetable, *adj.* that can be aimed at a target.

That huge American advantage cannot be ended in a hurry, especially since the United States will in the next few years add to its arsenal missiles capable of putting into space a number of individually targetable warheads. *The New York Times, April 8, 1968, p 46*

tax exile or **tax expatriate,** a person who leaves his country to avoid paying taxes.

Has Anthony Grey, Reuter's man lately in Peking, joined the ranks of the tax exiles? *The Manchester Guardian Weekly, Nov. 22, 1969, p 11*

The American with a numbered account is likely to have children in one of the Swiss preparatory schools, or to be a genuine tax expatriate or one of that small group who like to keep 10 percent of their portfolios outside Wall Street. Except for the tax expatriate, these people are not trying to avoid taxes; good New York law firms have already shown them how to do so profitably at home. *T. R. Fehrenbach, "Secrets of the Swiss Banks," The Atlantic, July 1965, p 36*

taxi squad, *U.S.* a group of players on a football team who participate in practice sessions but do not play in the games.

The Atlanta Falcons of the National Football League placed Bob Riggle, a defensive back, on the injured reserve list and activated a cornerback, Mike Fitzgerald, from the taxi squad. *The New York Times, Dec. 8, 1967, p 64*

Elsewhere, the Cincinnati Bengals cut Tommy Smith, the Olympic 200-meter champion in 1968 who had been on the taxi squad for two years and was trying to make the club as a tight end [the end who lines up close to the tackle]. *Alex Sachare, Tuscaloosa News (Alabama), Sept. 7, 1971, p 6*

[originally a nickname given to a group of extra players which the owner of the Cleveland Browns during the 1940's, Arthur McBride, kept on the team by putting them on the payroll of a taxi company which he owned]

tax shelter, an investment, allowance, etc., used as a means of reducing or avoiding liability to income tax.

...rapid-depreciation schedules on equipment...have hitherto made cable TV systems lucrative tax shelters. *Ralph Lee Smith, "The Battle Over Cable TV," Encyclopedia Science Supplement (Grolier) 1969, p 381*

The other portions of the tax bill curtail some common abuses of foundations as tax shelters. *Science News, Dec. 27, 1969, p 591*

Other Administration proposals chip away at a variety of much-abused tax devices. These include some debt-securities popular with conglomerates, such tax shelters as farm losses and certain trust income. *Time, May 2, 1969, p 56*

teach-in, *n.* **1** a long meeting or session held by university teachers and students for the purpose of expressing dissenting or critical views on an important political or social issue.

Before the be-ins, hippies used the sit-in to desegregate Alabama lunchcounters, and the teach-in to get the Vietnam debate going at a time when the consensus was still intact. *Douglas Hutchings, Saturday Night (Canada), Aug. 1967, p 3*

Now shifting their targets to concern for the environment, students across the country are planning a massive ecological-environmental teach-in on university campuses ....*Science News, Dec. 20, 1969, p 575*

Students held a day-long teach-in today at Belgrade University's School of Philosophy. *The New York Times, June 5, 1968, p 4*

2 any forum or seminar patterned on the university teach-in.

A series of "teach-ins" on drug addiction are to be held soon, the National Association on Drug Addiction announced on Saturday. *The Times (London), Nov. 21, 1966, p 10*

Parts are excellent, though, particularly editorial observations about the teach-in as a promising teaching device at the university level. *John Calam, "New Books," Review of "Teach-ins, U.S.A.," edited by Louis Menashe and Ronald Radosh, Saturday Review, Aug. 19, 1967, p 66*

tech·ne·tron·ic (ˌtek nə'trɑn ik), *adj.* dominated or shaped by the impact of technology and electronic computers and communications.

But in the opinion of Zbigniew Brzezinski, professor of government at Columbia University, the only revolution worth talking about these days is an American one—and it has not been run by the New Left. Brzezinski calls it the technetronic revolution. In *Between Two Ages* he discusses the repercussions of rapid change from an industrial era—with its emphasis on sheer productivity—to a period that stresses services, automation and cybernetics. *Edwin Warner, "Books: The Fragmented Soul," Review of "Between Two Ages" by Zbigniew Brzezinski, Time, Oct. 12, 1970, p 86*

The start of the second decade of jet air travel...has coincided in the final third of this century with the revolutionary emergence of communications satellites to mark the dawn of a technetronic era that will ultimately transform the Earth into a global village. *William D. Patterson, "Landmark for World Travel," Saturday Review, Oct. 24, 1970, p 27*

And as one looks back over the curve he sees that space-time has begun to contract around us: before, cultural transformations occurred over hundreds of thousands of years in the Neolithic Revolution; then, over centuries in the Industrial Revolution; and now, in the Technetronic Revolution, the transformation is occurring over mere decades. *William Irwin Thompson, "Planetary Vistas," Harper's, Dec. 1971, p 77*

[from Greek *téchnē* art, craft + English elec*tronic*]

technology assessment, the attempt to make advance assessments and predictions on the impact or effect of new technologies on society.

Technology assessment is a procedure designed to optimize the use of technology. Modern technology, which has brought social benefits and social costs, can also multiply societal options. It can do so through the enhanced capacity to perceive and predict unintended side effects by modern analytical methods reinforced by computers and through its capacity to design many alternative means to achieve a desired objective. *Milton Katz, "Decision-making in the Production of Power," Scientific American, Sept. 1971, p 192*

Particularly, may we urge that the added dimension of opinions from industry should be brought into contemplating the growing promise and popularity of "technology assessment." *Reynold Bennett, New York, in a Letter to the Editor, The New York Times, Nov. 11, 1970, p 44*

technomania, *n.* undue interest in technology or excessive use of technology without regard to its consequences, especially upon the environment.

The hostile reception of London's "Westway" shows that we are at last moving out of the age of undiluted technomania. Even if a transport system is admirably big, fast and expensive, it can yet be judged bad engineering. *Jerome R. Ravetz, Leeds, England, in a Letter to the Editor, New Scientist, Aug. 13, 1970, p 349*

The truth in this age of technomania and market sensitivity is that everyone is after information, but the Russians go about things in a way which is bound to cause offence. *Anthony Tucker, "Anything Worth Stealing?" The Manchester Guardian Weekly, Oct. 2, 1971, p 9*

technophobia, *n.* fear of the adverse effect of technology on society or the environment.

Concerned actions of dissent groups against the forthcoming nationwide census in the Netherlands are forcing government officials, politicians and sociologists to consider changing their opinions about the psychosocial effects of technophobia. *Jan Redeker, New Scientist and Science Journal, Feb. 25, 1971, p 406*

People who had, in the past, suffered from technophobia suffered even more. Others took other positions. Things were not so bad. Things could be worse....The worst was yet to come. *Donald Barthelme, "A Nation of Wheels," The New Yorker, June 13, 1970, p 38*

technopolis, *n.* a society dominated by the results of technological research and development.

"Technopolis"—the society where our lives, thoughts and happiness are determined by the applications of a science and technology which often appears to be out of control, and where blame for the dangers and unpleasant consequences that may arise is often laid on the scientists and technologists themselves, instead of on the whole community, through their chosen political representatives. *Martin Pollock, New Scientist, July 3, 1969, p 38*

Some of the changes are symbolized by Bonhoeffer's call for a "religionless Christianity," John A. T. Robinson's slogan "Our image of God must go," and Harvey Cox's celebration of technopolis and the theology of hope. *Paul K. Cuneo, Saturday Review, Jan. 6, 1968, p 35*

But there have also been several formal surveys recently showing that all is far from well inside the white coats of technopolis. *Bernard Dixon, New Scientist and Science Journal, March 11, 1971, p 527*

[from *techno-* technology + *-polis*, as in *metropolis*]

technopolitan, *adj.* of or relating to technopolis.

Even the terrifying aspects of technopolitan society—its uncontrolledness and its assumption that "can" equals "should"—are measures of the human capacity for achievement. *Alex Comfort, "The Shift In Awareness," The Manchester Guardian Weekly, June 19, 1971, p 20*

For practical-minded technopolitan man, "life is a set of problems, not an unfathomable mystery." He is too engrossed in grappling with the realities of this life to have much concern with those of the next. *Time, April 2, 1965, p 34*

[from *technopolis*, after such pairs as *metropolis, metropolitan*]

technostructure, *n.* the people in control of a technology in a society.

... management is limited by the many kinds of specialists whose views must be consulted—the experts, whether in marketing or in business-management methods, the whole class of people who occupy what Galbraith calls the "technostructure." *Charles A. Reich, "Reflections: The Greening of America," The New Yorker, Sept. 26, 1970, p 54*

To an increasing extent, decisions intended to guide operations are made by the "technostructure", that combination of technical knowledge, know-how and organizational capability which is the most valuable asset of a modern enterprise. *Kenneth Walker, "Industrial Democracy", The Times (London), March 4, 1970, p 28*

"The reason is that the first kind of conflict affronts the industrial technostructure—the establishment." *John Kenneth Galbraith, New Scientist and Science Journal, Feb. 18, 1971, p 376*

tectonic plate, another term for PLATE.

Many geologists currently believe that the lithosphere is geographically divided into 6 major slablike sections, called tectonic plates, plus a number of smaller ones. These plates contain the continents and adjoining portions of the ocean floors. *Edmund F. Grekulinski, "Plate Tectonics: New Theory Revolutionizes Geology," Encyclopedia Science Supplement (Grolier) 1970, p 130*

teeny-bopper, *n.* *U.S. Slang.* a girl (sometimes a boy) in the early teens who follows the current fashions and fads in clothing, music, etc., often adopting the styles and attitudes of hippies.

Paris is a city for adults, and the eye moves past the microskirted teeny-bopper to the thirtyish lady in a Chanel suit and high heels.... *Ward S. Just, "Americans in Paris," The Atlantic, Jan. 1970, p 20*

Later on, O'Leary plucks the flower from his pants and unzips himself to the astonished edification of the teeny-boppers milling around the stage. *Jay Cocks, "Books: Nom de Plume," Review of "Cold Iron" by Robert Stone Pryor, Time, Aug. 17, 1970, p 66*

Oh, I could replant, bulldoze the lot,
Get nursery stock, all the latest ornamentals,
Make the whole place look like a suburb,
Each limb sleek as a teenybopper's....
W. D. Snodgrass, "Old Apple Trees," The New Yorker, May 1, 1971, p 41

Teil·hard·i·an (te'yɑr di: ən), *adj.* of or relating to the French theologian Pierre Teilhard de Chardin, 1881-1955, or his theories.

Dr Doyle referred to the interest in meditation and mysticism amongst the young as one of the hopeful signs that Teilhard's optimism about the direction of social evolution was valid, but he seemed quite unaware that to most of the young in question, the whole emphasis of Teilhardian argument as displayed at the conference would be highly suspect. *John Wren-Lewis, New Scientist, Oct. 22, 1970, p 183*

His fellow romanticist Rubem Alves, a 36-year-old Brazilian Protestant, thinks man must meet the liberating event of Christ's Resurrection halfway, as "co-creator" of his own destiny (a Teilhardian notion) through the processes of political revolution. *Time, Dec. 26, 1969, p 43*

—*n.* a supporter or follower of Pierre Teilhard de Chardin or of his theories.

From the Teilhardians, the confidence that God, whoever he is, has something to do with the future and may yet meet man there. *Time, April 19, 1971, p 34*

tel·e ('tel i:), *n.* *British.* a learned spelling of the slang word *telly,* clipped from *television.*

... today's listener, sated with watching, or washing up at a time when the tele hasn't started, is supposed to use the radio like a tap. *New Scientist, Feb. 26, 1970, p 388*

... people couldn't watch their favourite programmes on the "tele".... *The Manchester Guardian Weekly, Dec. 19, 1970, p 3*

telediagnosis, *n.* a long-distance diagnosis of an illness performed by means of electronic equipment and closed-circuit television linking the physician to the patient.

Tele-diagnosis of physical ailments has been in progress for more than two years at a medical station just outside Boston which is connected by two-way television to the Massachusetts General Hospital in the city. *Michael Knipe, The Times (London), July 25, 1970, p 12*

[from *tele*vision *diagnosis*]

telefacsimile, *n.* a method of transmitting printed materials over a telephone circuit, as by an acoustic coupler.

... in 1965 a staff member of the library school of the University of New Mexico publicly advocated that libraries spend ninety per cent of their budgets on staff, telephones, copying, telefacsimiles, and the like, and only ten percent —a sort of tithe—on books and journals. *John Brooks, "Profiles: Xerox Xerox Xerox Xerox," The New Yorker, April 1, 1967, p 61*

[from *tele-* telephone + *facsimile*]

telelecture, *n.* a lecture delivered by telephone to a classroom or other place equipped with special loudspeakers and facilities for two-way communication.

Colleges today are arranging exchanges to increase their access to various competencies, providing for temporary student sojourns elsewhere, enriching their troupe of visiting scholars, or piping the specialist's voice and face in by telelecture and television. *Morris Keeton, Saturday Review, Feb. 17, 1968, p 60*

[from *tele-* telephone + *lecture*]

tel·e·on·o·my (ˌtel i:'ɑn ə mi:), *n.* the quality or characteristic of being ruled by an overall purpose.

Teleonomy denotes the characteristic "of being objects endowed with a purpose or project, which at the same time they exhibit in their structure and carry out through their performances". *Robin Monro, "Monod on Biophilosophy," New Scientist and Science Journal, Dec. 9, 1971, p 112*

If the destructive forces accelerated by science can be brought under control before they have permanently damaged the planet, it will be because the new organic model of ecological association and self-organization (teleonomy and autonomy) which was first assembled by Darwin will have at last begun to prevail. *Lewis Mumford, "Reflections: The Megamachine," The New Yorker, Oct. 31, 1970, p 88*

[from *teleo-* end, purpose + *-nomy* system of rules]

teleoperator, *n.* a robot or similar mechanical device that is operated by remote control. Compare AUGMENTOR.

... the choice of lunar exploration methods is not only between astronauts and automated spacecraft. There is a third alternative — use of remotely controlled devices with mobility, sensory and manipulative capabilities. Such devices are often referred to as "teleoperators." *William H. Allen, Washington, in a Letter to the Editor, The New York Times, Oct. 9, 1970, p 36*

[from *tele-* long-distance + *operator*]

Telex, *n.* the trade name for a communications system of teletype machines serving subscribers.

Throughout the world very long distance telephone and Telex traffic is growing faster than 25 per cent annually, and the rate of growth across the North Atlantic exceeds 40 per cent. *W. T. Gunston, Science Journal, Dec. 1970, p 63*

Telex, Western Union's direct-dial teleprinter service, had grown rapidly since its inauguration in 1958, and served more than 26,000 customers in 1968. *William H. Watts, "Telegraph," The 1969 Compton Yearbook, p 434*

The spy-story flavoring has included mention in the press of secret hotel meetings, coded Telex messages, smuggled transcripts, hidden political struggles and numbered Swiss-bank accounts. *Time, Dec. 7, 1970, p 40*

—*v.t.* Also, **telex.** to send (messages) by Telex.

They've done it by Telexing despatches (by way of Lisbon) from their own men on the spot.... *Philip Oakes, The Sunday Times (London), May 26, 1968, p 17*

The departments for which each pallet is destined are telexed ahead of the train, and the whole exercise is precisely timed so that the components are unloaded and ready at the distant production line as the shift which needs them begins work. *G. Freeman Allen, The Times (London), March 11, 1968, p V*

[from *tele*type *ex*change]

tell, *v.t.* **tell it like it is,** *U.S. Slang.* to tell the truth, no matter how unpleasant.

The [TV] series' intention, says [Andy] Griffith, is "to tell it like it is for the young people while remaining palatable to older audiences." The première involved a student who refused to pop "uppers" and "downers" like the rest of the kids. The comic relief, provided mostly by the school's bicep-brained athletic director (Jerry Van Dyke) was a downer. *Time, Sept. 28, 1970, p 66*

Tem·in enzyme ('tem ən), an enzyme that causes the formation of DNA (deoxyribonucleic acid) on a template or pattern of RNA (ribonucleic acid) in certain cancer-producing viruses, and that is re-

garded by some as essential to the ability of the virus to cause cancer. Also called REVERSE TRANSCRIPTASE.

No form of cancer in humans has yet been shown to be caused by a virus but should this be the case, the Temin enzyme may offer an unprecedented chance of attacking the disease at its roots. *The Times (London), June 26, 1970, p 6*

[named after Howard M. *Temin*, its discoverer]

Tem·in·ism ('tem ə‚niz əm), *n.* the theory that the transmission of genetic information is not an irreversible process always determined by the nucleic acid DNA, but that in certain cases RNA (ribonucleic acid) can act as a template or pattern for the formation of DNA. Teminism was based on the discovery by the biochemist Howard M. Temin, of the University of Wisconsin, that certain cancer-causing viruses whose genetic material is RNA contain an enzyme (the Temin enzyme) that causes the formation of DNA to match the viral RNA. Compare CENTRAL DOGMA.

... Dr. David Baltimore of the Massachusetts Institute of Technology reported verification of Dr. Temin's theory, now being referred to as Teminism in scientific circles, from experiments with another carcinogenic virus, the Rauscher leukemia virus, which induces tumors in mice. *Science News, July 25, 1970, p 54*

... perhaps Teminism might lead to a way of preventing the replication of RNA tumour viruses by finding a block to this extraordinary reaction. *Graham Chedd, Peter Stubbs, and Gerald Wick, New Scientist, June 25, 1970, p 614*

In the spring of 1970, scientists proved that an enzyme called RNA-directed DNA polymerase used ribonucleic acid (RNA) to make deoxyribonucleic acid (DNA). This is a reversal of what previously had been thought to be a one-way reaction — DNA to RNA. The reversal has been commonly called Teminism, after biochemist Howard M. Temin of the University of Wisconsin, who first discovered it. *Earl A. Evans, "Biochemistry," The World Book Science Annual 1972 (1971), p 273*

template, *n.* a chemical blueprint or pattern.

Howard Temin at the University of Wisconsin and others have shown that the normal processes of nucleic acid synthesis can be reversed by certain RNA tumour viruses, so that DNA is synthesized from an RNA template. *Oliver Gillie, "The Month: Cancer Research Held Back by Dogma Myth," Science Journal, Oct. 1970, p 8*

tensiometric, *adj.* of or relating to tensiometry.

... A tensiometric method utilizes a porous cup filled with water connected by a tube to a vacuum indicator. This approach measures the capillary potential or suction of soil water. *P. R. Nixon, "Soils: Soil Moisture Measurements," McGraw-Hill Yearbook of Science and Technology 1968, p 351*

tensiometry, *n.* the branch of physics dealing with tension and tensile strength.

They [researchers of the Mining Institute of the Czechoslovak Academy of Sciences] claim that these models [of proposed mines] enable reliable forecasts of what will happen to the springs if this or that method of mining is adopted. Tensiometry, stereophotography, photogrammetry, isotope and ultrasound measurements play an important role in this work. *"Mining Experiments to Save Tourist Trade," New Scientist, Nov. 18, 1965, p 497*

tera-, a prefix meaning one million millions (10^{12}) of any standard unit in the international meter-kilogram-second system of measurements (SI UNIT).

All these bodies unanimously recommend the use of the following prefixes: kilo to denote thousandfold, mega to denote millionfold, giga to denote thousand-millionfold, and tera to denote million-millionfold. They also unanimously recommend the abbreviations k, M, G and T respectively. *E. A. Guggenheim, The Times (London), Nov. 3, 1965, p 13*

[from Greek *téras* monster]

ter·a·bit ('ter ə₁bit), *n.* a unit of information equivalent to one million million bits or binary digits. Compare GIGABIT, KILOBIT, MEGABIT.

The CG-100 computer is said to have a main memory capable of holding 10 million million bits (10 terabits) of information. *"Laser Memories—Distant Pipeline or Imminent Revolution?" New Scientist and Science Journal, July 8, 1971, p 80*

[from *tera- + bit*]

ter·a·to·gen ('ter ə tə dʒən), *n.* a drug or other agent that causes malformation of an embryo or fetus.

Rubella was the first clearly defined teratogen: an agent that causes developmental abnormalities. *Louis Z. Cooper, Scientific American, July 1966, p 31*

Until German scientists reported in 1961 that 150 deformed infants—lacking developed arms and legs—had been born to women taking thalidomide during early pregnancy, the sedative was not a suspected teratogen. *Science News, July 1, 1967, p 10*

[back formation from *teratogenic* producing deformed organisms, from Greek *téras, tératos* monster + English *-genic* producing]

ter·a·to·ge·nic·i·ty (₁ter ə₁tou dʒə'nis ə ti:), *n.* the tendency to cause malformations of the embryo or fetus.

Present safety regulations vary from agency to agency and country to country, but in general they demand standard levels of freedom from toxicity, teratogenicity, carcinogenicity, etc. *Peter Beaconsfield, New Scientist and Science Journal, March 18, 1971, p 601*

The screening system is so coarse that, as a teratology panel of the Mrak Commission warned recently, in connection with thalidomide, "the teratogenicity of thalidomide might have been missed had it not produced malformations rarely encountered." *Thomas Whiteside, "A Reporter at Large: Defoliation," The New Yorker, Feb. 7, 1970, p 68*

terminal, *n.* a teletype machine or similar device for remote input or output of data, as in time-sharing.

Project MAC time-sharing system at the Massachusetts Institute of Technology has 160 terminals on the M.I.T. campus and nearby and is also available from distant terminals. As many as 30 terminals can be connected at one time, with each user carrying on a direct and in effect uninterrupted dialogue with the computer. The terminals, 30 of which are shown on the opposite page, are for the most part simple teletypewriters such as the IBM 1050 (6) and Teletype models 33 (19)....*Picture legend, "Time-Sharing on Computers," Scientific American, Sept. 1966, p 129*

One significant present trend, however, for both teaching and research simulation models, is to utilize time-share computers with a conversational mode; that is, through the use of telephone lines and remote computer terminals, simulation data can be fed to the computer in a conversational format (much like the English language) from the simulation site and the results obtained at the same remote terminal in a very short time-span. *Marshall H. Whithed, "Simulation," McGraw-Hill Yearbook of Science and Technology 1971, p 385*

territorial imperative, *Anthropology.* the supposed innate character of vertebrate animals to regard areas possessively and defend them from encroachment.

The "territorial imperative" does much to explain the causes of war, such as the Arab-Israeli dispute, which I consider almost purely territorial. *Konrad Lorenz, quoted by Edward R. F. Sheehan, "Conversations with Konrad Lorenz," Harper's, May 1968, p 74*

And he [Andrew M. Greeley] keeps talking of "primordial" human urges to differentiate between a "we" and a "they," of the "territorial imperative," and of similar speculative and ahistorical notions, as if we all agreed on what is "primordial" and as if what is "primordial" had precedence over what is civilized. *Naomi Bliven, "Books," Review of "Why Can't They Be Like Us? America's White Ethnic Groups" by Andrew M. Greeley, The New Yorker, Nov. 20, 1971, p 225*

TESL ('tes əl), *n.* acronym for *Teaching English as a Second Language.*

And though a major curriculum emphasis is developing fluency in the English language using the linguistic approach of TESL (Teaching English as a Second Language), the knowledge of Navaho is still essential to many jobs on the reservation as well as to communication with the older generation. *Estelle Fuchs, "Innovation at Rough Rock [Arizona]," Saturday Review, Sept. 16, 1967, p 83*

tes·la ('tes lə), *n.* the SI unit of measurement for magnetic flux density.

The earlier accelerator design had embodied a combined-function lattice structure—one using the same magnets for bending and focusing with a magnetic field limited to a flux density of 1.2 tesla (webers/sq.m). *Eric H. S. Burhop, New Scientist, June 18, 1970, p 574*

[named after Nikola *Tesla*, 1856-1943, Croatian-born American electrical engineer]

Te·thy·an ('ti: θi: ən), *adj.* of or relating to Tethys.

The plate that rafted India then migrated northward toward and subducted into the Tethyan trench, which ran east-west near the Equator. The plate evidently glided freely along parallel "megashears" on its eastern and western boundaries without interacting with the other crustal plates of the world. *Robert S. Dietz and John C. Holden, "The Breakup of Pangaea," Scientific American, Oct. 1970, p 33*

. . . the Tethyan system of ocean trenches—the trough into which were tipped the huge volumes of sediments later compressed into the Himalayas—formed part of the old sea floor lying to the north. *New Scientist and Science Journal, Feb. 4, 1971, p 231*

Te·thys ('ti: θis), *n.* a large triangular sea that hypothetically separated Africa and Eurasia before the drifting of continents.

Long before the existence of the present Mediterranean, perhaps a quarter of a billion years ago, a giant waterway, the Tethys, extended across southern Europe, Iran and southern China to the Pacific Ocean. The Mediterranean is generally considered to be a remnant of the Tethys. *"Probing the Mediterranean's Hidden Geological Past," Science News, July 4, 1970, p 21*

[named after *Tethys*, the wife of Oceanus in Greek mythology]

tet·ra·hy·dro·can·na·bi·nol (ˌtet rəˌhai drə'kæn ə bəˌnɔːl), *n.* the active ingredient in marijuana, first synthesized in 1966 to study the drug more precisely and found to cause LSD-type psychotic hallucinations when administered in pure form to volunteers. *Abbreviation:* THC

With the impending availability of adequate supplies of synthetic tetrahydrocannabinol we have developed and have given high priority to an intensive systematic plan of research to elucidate a number of basic facts. *Stanley F. Yolles, The New York Times, March 7, 1968, p 26*

On a weight basis, ethyl alcohol is thousands of times less potent than tetrahydrocannabinol, but in sufficient amounts it produces ill effects. *Donald W. Goodwin, St. Louis, Mo., in a Letter to the Editor, Scientific American, Feb. 1970, p 6*

[from *tetrahydro-* combined with four hydrogen atoms + *cannabinol*, a phenol derived from the resin of Indian hemp]

T-group, *n.* **1** another name for ENCOUNTER GROUP.

As a psychologist he has reservations about experimental raptures like T-groups, and a considerable sympathy with the anxieties induced in people of established habits by the suggestion that they should review them. *Innis Macbeath, The Times (London), Nov. 30, 1970, p 14*

The April 1971 issue of "The Personnel and Guidance Journal" surveys various techniques of group therapy, including the techniques that partake of new theories. Although a majority of participants in "T-groups," for instance, report favorable results, little evaluation has been done, says one article. *Richard H. Gilluly, "A New Look at the Meaning of Reality," Science News, May 15, 1971, p 337*

2 any of various group seminars conducted by trained leaders to improve relations between people employed or working in corporations, government agencies, churches, and other institutions.

The T-group, an older method [than the encounter group], uses more verbal exercises and emphasizes the "here and now"—the relationship of each group member to what is happening in the group at that particular time. It allows the participant to know what others think of him .... *Ted J. Rakstis, "Sensitivity Training: Fad, Fraud, or New Frontier?" Encyclopedia Science Supplement (Grolier) 1970, p 79*

[from Sensitivity Training *group*]

thal·as·so·chem·i·cal (ˌθæl ə sou'kem ə kəl), *adj.* of or relating to thalassochemistry.

Another useful abstraction is the "steady state" thalassochemical model. If the ocean composition does not change with time, it must be rigorously true that whatever is added by the rivers must be precipitated in marine sediments. .... *Ferren MacIntyre, "Why the Sea is Salt," Scientific American, Nov. 1970, p 106*

thal·as·so·chem·is·try (ˌθæl ə sou'kem ə stri:), *n.* the chemistry of the sea.

The task is to persuade our engineers and business companies that working with sewage and junk is just as challenging as oceanography and thalassochemistry.

Ferren MacIntyre, "Why the Sea is Salt," Scientific American, Nov. 1970, p 115

[from *thalasso-* sea (from Greek *thálassa*) + chemistry]

THC, abbreviation of TETRAHYDROCANNABINOL.

THC, a form of synthetic cannabis, has no wide circulation in Britain but control has been imposed as a precaution. *John Roper, The Times (London), July 10, 1970, p 2*

THC combined with morphine relieves pain more effectively than when THC or morphine is given separately. *"Marijuana Dependence," Science News, Sept. 11, 1971, p 175*

theater of _____. The term THEATER OF THE ABSURD inspired the formation of a number of similar terms during the 1960's, such as the ones shown below. Two of the most widely used terms, THEATER OF CRUELTY and THEATER OF FACT, are separately entered and defined.

Theater of Chance: Words must be used in an unprecedented way, if we are to hear them again, either radically out of sequence as in The Theater of Chance or as independent counters, made abstract by reiteration, as in The Brig. *Walter Kerr, "How Playwrights Lose: 'The Theater of Chance'," Harper's, Sept. 1966, p 79*

theater of despair: Madame Duras is to me a dramatist whose importance is of the order of Beckett or of Ionesco, though her work has nothing to do either with the theatre of the absurd or the theatre of despair. *Harold Hobson, The Sunday Times (London), June 12, 1966, p 25*

Theater of Involvement: At the moment, the theater is the vanguard. Its use as a revolutionary medium, deliberately intended to shock and flout the middle-class standards of order, decency, and entertainment, has a name: the Theater of Involvement. *Alistair Cooke, "Focus on the Arts," The 1969 World Book Year Book, p 52*

theater of protest: None of this was felt immediately in Britain, although the Twenties did produce a modest theatre of protest which continued to weaken accepted ideas. *The Sunday Times (London), May 28, 1967, p 25*

Theater of the Mind: The Theater of the Mind might lead to something beyond the pleasure principle, in fact, if its proponents could get past the fad of the pseudo-psychedelic, of trying to fake trips for stay-at-homes. *Donal Henahan, The New York Times, Sept. 15, 1968, Sec. 2, p 24*

Theater of the Streets: Sheffer said that the idea of getting political cabaret "out of history, out of the Berlin cafés of the twenties, and into New York City in the spring of 1968" was just as exciting, potentially, as the recent experiments in Guerrilla Theatre and the Theatre of the Streets, which lean toward direct confrontation with the Establishment through such actions as anti-Vietnam mime shows in Times Square during the rush hour. *"The Talk of the Town: DMZ," The New Yorker, April 27, 1968, p 36*

theater of violence: In the midst of one performance of the theater-of-violence satire Roda Viva, a whistle blew and men armed with clubs, pistols and boxing gloves rose on signal. .... *Time, Oct. 25, 1968, p 44*

theater of cruelty, a form of theater based on the theories of the French actor and poet Antonin Artaud, 1896-1948, in which dialogue, plot, and character are subordinated to a representation of harsh physical and sensual rituals. The audience is deliberately involved and the action is intended to provide a shocking or abrasive personal experience to all the participants.

Pierre Clementi stars as a young drama teacher in Rome whose twin aims in life are to carry the Theatre of Cruelty to its logical conclusion (revolution) and to seduce his professor's delectable daughter. *Derek Malcolm, "London Cinema: In Search of Flesh and Fortune," Review of "Tropic of Cancer" by Henry Miller, The Manchester Guardian Weekly, Oct. 10, 1970, p 21*

On the one hand, the violence doesn't bother the heads, because they don't take it for real—it's a trip, a fantasy experience, separate from day-to-day living. On the other hand, the violence is what blows their minds. Devices from the theatre of cruelty are used to set off kicky fantasies. The cruelty becomes delectable, like the gore. *Pauline Kael, "The Current Cinema," Review of "El Topo," The New Yorker, Nov. 20, 1971, p 218*

theater of fact, a form of theater that draws its subjects from events of recent history, often utilizing excerpts from actual speeches, articles, books, etc., to convey realism.

Murderous Angels is another example of The Theatre of Fact. [Conor] O'Brien has subtitled his play "A political tragedy and comedy in black and white", and the two main characters are Dag Hammarskjold and Patrice Lumumba. *Clive Barnes, The Times (London), Feb. 9, 1970, p 5*

theater of the absurd, a form of theater that stresses the absurdity of the human condition and the futility of man's attempts to cope with it. See also THE ABSURD, under ABSURD.

. . . these little tid-bits, more from the theater of the ludicrous than the theater of the absurd, have only the pretentious smell of red herring about them. *Clive Barnes, The New York Times, Jan. 11, 1968, p 41*

Like the plays of the theater of the absurd, these new movies base their form on an absence of logic. *Jane Chance, West Lafayette, Ind., in a Letter to the Editor, The Atlantic, March 1965, p 42*

therapeutic community, a mental-health group, clinic, or institution in which various techniques of group psychotherapy are used, especially to rehabilitate drug addicts.

. . . not widely known outside the mental health profession, has been the development of a method of treatment that is called the therapeutic community.

The term describes a way of operating a small psychiatric unit in a hospital. Ideally a unit will have between 20 and 40 patients; a large hospital may have more than one therapeutic community. *Richard Almond, "The Therapeutic Community," Scientific American, March 1971, p 34*

therapeutic index, an index for measuring the therapeutic value of a drug based on the ratio of the median lethal dose to the median effective dose.

The higher the therapeutic index, the better the drug, other factors being equal. If 100 grams of a drug, for example, is the dose that kills 50% of the test animals (LD[lethal dose]50 = 100), and one gram of the same drug effects a cure in 50% of the test animals of the same species (ED[effective dose]50 = 1), the therapeutic index is 100/1 = 100. *Matt Clark, "The Changing Medicine Cabinet: Laboratory Testing of New Drugs," 1969 Britannica Yearbook of Science and the Future, 1968, p 98*

thermal breeder, a breeder reactor (atomic power plant able to produce its own fuel as well as generate power with almost no loss of fissionable material) that uses relatively slow neutrons to produce fissionable material. Also called THERMAL REACTOR.

Two different breeder systems are involved, depending on which raw material is being transmuted. The thermal breeder, employing slow neutrons, operates best on the thorium 232-uranium 233 cycle (usually called the thorium cycle). The fast breeder, employing more energetic neutrons, operates best on the uranium 238-plutonium 239 cycle (the uranium cycle). *Glenn T. Seaborg and Justin L. Bloom, Scientific American, Nov. 1970, p 13*

thermal pollution, pollution by the discharge of heat into water or air, often with other waste liquids or gases, by nuclear power plants, factories, refineries, etc. Also called HEAT POLLUTION or CALEFACTION.

Hot water pollution, often called thermal pollution, may act the same way as overfertilization. . . . Warm water, even water heated by only 5 to 10 degrees F., can promote the growth of certain algae over certain others, just as sewage does, with adverse consequences for existing food chains. *"Thermal Pollution," Science News Yearbook 1970, p 300*

The release of waste heat into the environment is called thermal pollution or calefaction. *Paul Bienfang, "Taking the Pollution Out of Waste Heat," New Scientist and Science Journal, Aug. 26, 1971, p 456*

thermal reactor, another name for THERMAL BREEDER.

The fast reactor will thus be sandwiched in time between the present-day thermal reactors (the British gas-cooled type, and the water reactors developed in the US and used outside Britain) and the fusion reactors, or some other advanced, pollution-free source, to be perfected before the end of the century. *David Hamilton, "Power from the Fast Breeder," New Scientist and Science Journal, Aug. 26, 1971, p 453*

ther·mo·form ('θər mə,fɔrm), *n.* a process for shaping plastic by the application of heat.

A fairly new development, concentrated at Yate, . . . is the thermoform process whereby thin plastic film, made at Yate, is moulded into such objects as the subdivided holders in biscuit and chocolate boxes, and lightweight trays for serving meals in aircraft. *Bryan Little, The Times (London), March 20, 1970, p II*

—*v.t., v.i.* to shape (plastic substances) into desired forms by the application of heat.

To exploit the full potential of thermo-formed materials in packaging and to gain extra marketing power in a sector now being staked out by major combines. *"Debts Before Profits—A Cautionary Tale," The Sunday Times (London), Nov. 7, 1971, p 64*

thermophysical, *adj.* of or relating to the physical characteristics of substances under high temperature or increasing temperature.

More than two years in the making, this encyclopedic and unique reference work is specifically designed to give you easy access to *all* the thermophysical properties data presently available. *Advertisement for "Thermophysical Properties of High Temperature Solid Materials" by The Macmillan Company, Scientific American, Sept. 1967, p 297*

theta pinch, the rapid compression of a magnetic field surrounding plasma (highly ionized gas) to produce a controlled fusion reaction.

The high-density devices are pulsed because of the means they use to heat high-density plasma quickly. One such method is by the shock and compression of a magnetic implosion, called a theta pinch. *Dietrick E. Thomsen, Science News, Oct. 17, 1970, p 321*

The simplicity of the theta pinch as a means of achieving that sought-after goal of power from thermonuclear reactions has led to considerable studies of its real effectiveness in confining and heating up a plasma. *New Scientist, Nov. 9, 1967, p 369*

In the last two decades, plasma physicists and electrical engineers have developed variations on three basic systems, all of which meet safety criteria for controlled fusion: the theta pinch, the magnetic mirror and the torus. *Mort LaBrecque, "Power without Pollution," Encyclopedia Science Supplement (Grolier) 1971, p 367*

thick film, a relatively thick, multimolecular layer of material used in integrated circuits and in making electronic components. *Often used attributively.* Compare THIN FILM.

Thick film materials are generally deposited onto a flat substrate by a screen printing process. Materials to produce resistors, capacitors, conductors and insulating layers are supplied in the form of an ink. *Peter Kirby, New Scientist, Oct. 15, 1970, p 8*

thin film, a thin layer of electronic material used in integrated circuits. *Often used attributively.* Compare THICK FILM.

Optical interference in a thin film can be explained in terms of the wave theory of light. *Philip Baumeister and Gerald Pincus, "Optical Interference Coatings," Scientific American, Dec. 1970, p 59*

Assignment—Develop advance thin-film processes and materials, improve photoetching techniques, and process thin-film components. *The New York Times, July 12, 1967, p 54*

thing, n. *Slang.* that which one likes best or does best (used especially in the phrases **do one's thing** or **do one's own thing).**

[What] I admire about Robbins is that he's making a lot of money. That's just his thing. He's doing his own thing. *"The Talk of the Town," The New Yorker, Nov. 29, 1969, p 48*

"My life-style revolves around my work—photography. I [Chet Morrison] don't advocate anybody else's doing what I've done or thinking what I'm thinking. Everybody ought to do his own thing." *"The Latest American Exodus," Time, Nov. 30, 1970, p 14*

He [a colonel] told her a little sheepishly that it's *his thing,* using the vernacular with a smile because doing your thing reminded him of hippies; flower children, and here he was a colonel of infantry. I'm doing my thing, killing gooks. *Ward Just, "Soldiers," The Atlantic, Nov. 1970, p 87*

Quite a few people prefer to do their own thing on holiday, of course. *Richard Milner, The Sunday Times (London), April 11, 1971, p 41*

There can be no doubt that Emerson once wrote "do your thing."

The phrase appears in "Essays," 1841, page 45, which was the first edition: "But do your thing, and I shall know you. Do your work, and you shall reinforce yourself." *William H. Gilman, The New York Times, Oct. 20, 1968, Sec. 4, p 15*

thingism, n. emphasis on or concern with physical objects and details in literature and art.

The aim is not solely to mock materialism: Godard is also influenced, reportedly, by the poetry of Francis Ponge, which is concerned with "Thingism," the seeming life and effect of "things." But the film mainly explores the Americanization (read "modernization") of French life and the pressures of artificially stimulated consumerism which, Godard implies, makes prostitutes of us all to some extent. *Stanley Kaufman, "Films," The New Republic, May 9, 1970, p 24*

[translation of French *chosisme,* from *chose* thing + *-isme* -ism]

think tank, a center or institute for theoretical studies, especially of the problems of culture and society, and research in science and technology.

But even the contemplation of such scientific gallantry cannot wholly stifle niggling doubts as to whether the brilliant lads in the ivory think-tank at Lathom, Lancs, may have overlooked the most urgent need of the fenestrated commonalty. What we want in the glazing line, before the windscreens for aerial white elephants, crystalline griddles or vari-tintable fanlights, is the window that never needs cleaning. *New Scientist, Dec. 10, 1970, p 424*

The 'think tanks', the oldest and most important being the RAND Corporation, have had much influence on developments. *Ian Priban, Science Journal, March 1969, p 90*

The Urban Institute was set up by the Johnson Administration as a private, nonprofit corporation to serve as the Government's "think tank" for research into city problems. *David R. Jones, The New York Times, Sept. 11, 1968, p 24*

think-tanker, n. a member of a think tank.

Throughout this century think-tankers have been confidently predicting the imminent exploitation (an appropriate term) of the seas. *Colin Moorcraft, Review of "Living Underwater" by Farooq Hussein, New Scientist and Science Journal, Sept. 2, 1971, p 536*

thin-layer chromatography, a method of analyzing the chemical substances of a mixture by passing it through a thin layer of filtering material. Compare GAS-LIQUID CHROMATOGRAPHY.

Sperling analyzed a series of hallucinogenic tryptamines by gas and thin-layer chromatography. *Albert R. Sperling, "Psychopharmacological Drugs," McGraw-Hill Yearbook of Science and Technology 1971, p 360*

thi·o·rid·a·zine (,θαi ə'rid ə,zi:n), n. a drug used as a tranquilizer in the treatment of schizophrenia and senility, and in the study of learning capacity.

Tranquilizers such as thioridazine forestall behavioral disorganization in schizophrenics and make them less excitable. But recent findings by Dr. Michael J. Goldstein of the University of California at Los Angeles indicate that some schizophrenics may do better without tranquilizers. *"Schizophrenia: Tranquilizer Treatment," Science News, June 26, 1971, p 430*

[from *thio-* sulfur + piper*idi*ne a blood vessel dilator + *-az* nitrogen + *-ine* (chemical suffix)]

third market, *U.S.* the market in listed stocks not traded on a stock exchange; over-the-counter trading in listed stocks, as distinguished from trading on a national exchange or in unlisted stocks. Compare FOURTH MARKET.

Unable to get discounts on the Big Board, mutual funds, pension funds and other institutional investors are channeling a growing share of their business to regional exchanges and the so-called third market, where brokers arrange private trades of listed stocks. *Time, Nov. 30, 1970, p 73*

Mutual funds, for example, trade in large amounts and severely strain an exchange market accustomed to handling smaller transactions. One consequence has been fragmentation of the central market through the growth of off-board trading in listed stocks—the so-called "third market." *William L. Carey, The New York Times, Dec. 21, 1970, p 35*

Third World, a collective name for the group of underdeveloped countries, especially of Africa and Asia, that receive aid from both the Communist world and the non-Communist world and therefore cannot be aligned with either.

The students, following the gospel of Marcuse, look to the Third World, to Fidel Castro and Ho Chi Minh, for salvation. *Philip Shabecoff, The New York Times Magazine, April 28, 1968, p 116*

Europeans are quite as anxious as Canadians about American policing of nationalist revolutions throughout the emerging "third world". *Kenneth McNaught, Saturday Night (Canada), Nov. 1966, p 15*

. . . western techniques, unadapted, cannot be grafted on to Third World economies without some transitional period in which the new skills and attitudes needed can be learnt. *Alistair Hill, New Scientist, Oct. 29, 1970, p 227*

[translation of French *tiers monde*, in which *tiers* is an archaic form instead of the normal *troisième* because the French expression, in use since the late 1940's, was based on the eighteenth-century *tiers état*, the Third Estate, i.e. the commoners as against the other two estates of nobles and clergy]

Third Worlder, one belonging to the Third World, especially an African or Asian.

Third Worlders preferred skinheads, violent but human, to the polished pseudo-sophistication of non-artist critics . . . . *The Times (London), Aug. 15, 1970, p 6*

It seems that, in the rapid switch from a mainly agrarian economy to a semi-industrialized one, there is a technological hiatus. Skills which the average 16-year-old western youth would have little difficulty in mastering apparently pose almost insoluble problems for the average Third Worlder. *Alistair Hill, New Scientist, Oct. 29, 1970, p 227*

Third Worldism, a movement supporting the Third World; sympathy and support for the aspirations of Third Worlders.

By a feat of political wizardry, the Swedish ability to leave the international dirty work to other nations, which might have been simply admired as shrewd or clever, has been elevated in the local mythology to the status of a high moral stand. This allows a comfortable slide from the pragmatic what's-in-it-for-me attitude toward neutrality that dominates the adult population to the revolutionary Third Worldism of large sections of Sweden's politically active youth and intellectuals. *Steven Kelman, "Letter from Stockholm," The New Yorker, Dec. 26, 1970, p 46*

tho·lei·ite ('θou li:ˌαit), *n.* a form of basalt, usually containing quartz and alkalic feldspar.

The tholeiites represent the primary magma generated in the upper mantle beneath the oceans. *Lawrence Ogden, "Geology: The Zoned Earth," Britannica Book of the Year 1966, p 340*

Lava and feeder dikes from the mantle form the volcanic layer; its rocks are oceanic tholeiite (or a metamorphosed equivalent), which is rich in aluminum and poor in potassium. *H. W. Menard, "The Deep Ocean Floor," Scientific American, Sept. 1969, p 130*

[probably irregularly from Greek *thóloi* (plural of *thólos* dome) + English *-ite*]

tho·lei·it·ic (ˌθou li:'it ik), *adj.* of or containing tholeiite.

. . . most terrestrial tholeiites occur in flat-lying masses resulting from rock flow, which may be similar to the lunar maria where the rocks sampled by Surveyors V and VI are located. They concluded that the lunar rocks are most likely tholeiitic in composition. *George R. Tilton, "Geochemistry," The World Book Science Annual 1969, p 306*

threads, *n.pl. U.S. Slang.* clothes.

A down-to-earth club, whose youthful patrons seem more interested in music and dancing than in ogling other people's threads. *"Goings On About Town," The New Yorker, Nov. 22, 1969, p 6*

Nixon—who himself wears somber grays and blues—had his staff order some kitschily elaborate threads for 150 of his White House police from a Washington military tailor. *Time, Feb. 9, 1970, p 7*

throughput, *n.* the amount of data put through a computer; a computer's input and output collectively.

. . . time sharing (or milti-programming) is already well established as a means of increasing the throughput and utilization of a computer. *A. E. Brock, New Scientist, June 24, 1965, p 883*

throwaway, *adj.* **1** designed to be thrown away after use; disposable.

An instant teetotaler? No, Mrs. Helms is a founder of a Washington, D.C., antipollution group dedicated to (among other things) stamping out throwaway containers that do not decompose. *Time, Sept. 7, 1970, p 26*

Throwaway umbrellas made of paper have just been marketed on an experimental basis by a Tokyo paper goods firm. The umbrellas, which collapse to fit in pocket or handbag, are made from a water-repellent paper developed by the Oji Paper Co. and have no metal parts at all. *New Scientist, Oct. 15, 1970, p 126*

2 casual; offhand.

His [Georges Brassens, a French singer's] songs give a better idea of the man than the few throwaway remarks he will volunteer about himself. *Peter Lennon, "The Arts: Keeping His Distance," The Manchester Guardian Weekly, Dec. 13, 1969, p 20*

. . . here is an author who is refreshingly gentle and sympathetic; a comic leg-pull or shrewd aside is his most lethal weapon; he has a beguiling throw-away humour. *Venetia Pollock, "Other New Novels," Review of "The Late Breakfasters" by Robert Aickman, Punch, June 10, 1964, p 873*

[from *throwaway, n.*, any disposable item, from the verb phrase *throw away*]

thrust chamber, the chamber of a rocket in which the expansion of gases produces enough thrust for takeoff.

Bacchus [a rocket] would have an enlarged first stage —Octavie—with four long tanks and eight thrust chambers, supporting two further liquid propellant stages, Diane and Mirible. *New Scientist, May 9, 1968, p 270*

thruster or **thrustor,** *n.* any of various small engines for producing thrust, as for maneuvering a spacecraft.

The *Glomar Challenger* is placed in position over the drilling pipe by extra side propulsion propellers called thrusters, which are controlled by computers. *Walter B. Charm, "Working the 'Glomar Challenger': Drilling Holes in the Ocean Floor," Encyclopedia Science Supplement (Grolier) 1970, p 153*

At 6:00 a.m. on the second day in orbit, Conrad reported to ground control in Houston that No. 8 thrustor (out of 16) was "not up to snuff." *Jonathan Eberhart, Science News, Sept. 24, 1966, p 223*

thrust stage, a stage extending into the auditorium, with seats on three sides of the stage.

"Hedda Gabler" was not meant for anything but a proscenium stage. Putting it on the thrust-stage was like entering a vintage Rolls for the Mille Miglia. *Gareth Lloyd Evans, "The Arts: The Achievements of Stratford, Ontario: Theatre," The Manchester Guardian Weekly, Dec. 19, 1970, p 17*

The Fine Arts Theatre, in which this program was performed, is a compact, multipurpose amphitheater seating 600, which can be utilized for conventional theatricals, as a thrust stage, or even—with the built-in pit—for musicals and intimate opera. *Irving Kolodin, "Music to My Ears," Saturday Review, June 1, 1968, p 22*

thumper, *n.* a device for producing a shallow seismic wave to test structural properties of the lunar surface.

This time, they [astronauts] will also have brought along a variety of ordnance to make different types of explosions for the benefit of the seismometer—a sort of walking stick called a "thumper," which sets off a small charge whenever it is tapped against the ground, and a mortar, which will fire charges to varying distances. *Henry S. F. Cooper, Jr., "Letter From The Space Center," The New Yorker, Jan. 9, 1971, p 70*

thy·ris·tor (θai'ris tər), *n.* a transistor or semiconductor that forms an open circuit until signaled to switch to the conducting state by a controlling electrode.

If thyristors are used to control the motor of an electric car, the vehicle moves smoothly but with poor efficiency at low speeds. *New Scientist, March 12, 1970, p 510*

[from Greek *thýra* door + English trans*istor*]

thy·ro·cal·ci·to·nin (ˌθai rouˌkæl sə'tou nən), *n.* another name for CALCITONIN.

. . . three hormones, calciferol, thyrocalcitonin and the parathyroid hormone are linked together in the delicate control of the level of calcium in the blood. *W. F. Loomis, "Rickets," Scientific American, Dec. 1970, p 89*

tie-break, *n. British.* a system for breaking a tie in tennis in which the player winning five points out of nine takes the set.

In principle, the tie-break is an undesirable expedient, but there is a case for it in indoor tournaments confined to one court. *Rex Bellamy, The Times (London), March 5, 1970, p 13*

It was the first time that a tie-break system had been used, and though confusing at first it eventually served its purpose of getting matches finished in reasonable order. *Alan Dunn, "Sport," The Manchester Guardian Weekly, Nov. 21, 1970, p 23*

After a poor start Metreveli chased every ball Anderson hit at him and, with a little more luck on the Russian's side in the tic-break, the result could have been different. *"Anderson to Face Rosewall in Final," The Times (London), Jan. 3, 1972, p 7*

tie-dye ('tai,dai), *v.t., v.i.* to dye (clothes or fabrics) by tying them tightly into knots before immersing them into the dye, so as to produce unusual designs in the tied portions not penetrated by the dye. See also BANDHNU.

Simple bias-cut skirts are made of panne velvet tie-dyed by hand to rare shades. *"On and Off the Avenue: Gifts for Women," The New Yorker, Nov. 21, 1970, p 155*

Old and young believe in the efficacy of the handmade as a kind of talisman against the evils of technology. Making a thing from beginning to end, however badly, is felt to be better and more "human" than being part of an operation involving others and/or mechanical aids. But what the boys who tie-dye and the grandmothers who rug-hook are doing is, in effect, as mechanical as anything done by a machine. *Janet Malcolm, "On and Off the Avenue," The New Yorker, Sept. 4, 1971, p 61*

—*n.* a tie-dyed garment.

. . . the stars fussed with their see-through dresses, tie-dyes and black ties and then paraded up a red-carpeted walkway. *"Show Business: Mocking the Mockery," Time, April 20, 1970, p 72*

time dilation, a slowing down or stretching out of time for a speeding object as its velocity increases relative to another object traveling at a different velocity.

One consequence of the special theory of relativity is that rate of time flow is not the same in two coordinate systems moving relative to one another. This phenomenon, known as time dilation, accounts for the slowing down of high-velocity natural clocks as recorded by a stationary observer. *"Special Relativity Survives the Test of Time," New Scientist, Dec. 4, 1969, p 497*

After two years of acceleration at that rate [a steady acceleration of one "g"] the spacecraft's velocity would be such for "time dilation" to have an effect. In other words time would be slowing down on board the craft and, to those on board, a single lifetime would be longer than for those on earth. *Anthony Tucker, "To the Moon—and Then to the Stars?" The Manchester Guardian Weekly, Jan. 2, 1969, p 7*

time reversal, a principle in physics which postulates that if the time in which a sequence of operations occurs is reversed, the same sequence will occur again but in the reverse order. *Often used attributively.*

Another symmetry consideration is that of "time reversal." This notion says in effect that a motion-picture film of any process should show the system appearing to obey the same laws of physics whether the film is run forward or backward. *Gilbert Shapiro, Scientific American, July 1966, p 75*

Time-reversal invariance refers to the principle that the direction of the flow of time should have no effect on the validity of physical laws. *Gary Mitchell, "Physics: Elementary Particle Physics," The Americana Annual 1970, p 546*

Another aspect of symmetry is called time-reversal symmetry and postulates that there is no way to tell the difference between a particle going forward in time and an antiparticle going backward in time. In practice this means that particle happenings should be reversible. That is, if a neutron and proton come together to form a deuterium nucleus and a gamma ray (and they do), then with equal facility a gamma ray and a deuterium nucleus should come together and yield a neutron and proton. *Dietrick E. Thomsen, Science News, March 28, 1970, p 327*

time-shared or **time-share,** *adj.* of or relating to time-sharing.

Display unit designed by John Ward and Robert Stotz has access to the large time-shared central computer at the Massachusetts Institute of Technology. *Cyrus Levinthal, Scientific American, June 1966, p 52*

Although this concept was not new, it was not until 1969 that time-shared systems began to flourish. *Arthur G. Anderson and Richard E. Matick, "Computers," 1971 Britannica Yearbook of Science and the Future, 1970, p 170*

Because the high cost of computer installation forces many organizations to operate on a time-share basis, the nonfederal centers pose a special danger to privacy. *Arthur R. Miller, "The National Data Center and Personal Privacy," The Atlantic, Nov. 1967, p 57*

time-sharing, *n.* the use by many persons at remote locations of a single central computer whose speed in processing data is greater than the combined speed of all the users.

Time sharing allows the user access to a much more powerful computer than he could afford to buy. This is because he is one of a large group of users who share the computer's time, and hence its cost, from individual terminals. *R. Elliot Green, Science Journal, Oct. 1970, p 69*

Time-sharing is generally described as simultaneous access by multiple users to a single large computer. In reality, the machine moves swiftly from user to user, processing programs both sequentially and independently. *William D. Smith, The New York Times, Jan. 9, 1967, p 137*

timetable, *v.t., v.i. British.* to set a timetable (for any activity).

Apart from the music wing (and the 26 pianos in the building) next year the school will admit 15 musically talented children who will be separately timetabled to give full scope for their abilities. *Stephen Jessel, The Times (London), Oct. 20, 1970, p 4*

. . . students are not allowed to attend all four quarters in one year; they are expected to do two, they may do three, but never four. This system poses tremendously complicated problems of time-tabling. . . . *Lord Bowden, The Listener, April 11, 1968, p 468*

[verb use of the noun]

tissue typing, a procedure for determining the compatibility of tissues. This technique is used especially before an organ transplant by having a computer match the tissue of a donor with those of several potential recipients to select the recipient most compatible with the donor's tissue.

Tissue-typing, we now know, is essential in the transplantation of any organ in contact with the bloodstream. *Murray Sayle and Alfred Byrne, The Sunday Times (London), Dec. 10, 1967, p 46*

. . . the improvement in tissue typing (to match the tissue of donor and recipient) and a better understanding of how to control rejection had resulted in a success rate in most centers of 80% for kidney transplants between living relatives and of 50% for cadaver kidney transplants. *Jack W. Cole, "Medicine," 1971 Britannica Yearbook of Science and the Future, 1970, p 236*

TLP, abbreviation of *transient lunar phenomena.*

Sudden local increases in brightness in certain regions of the Moon have been puzzling astronomers for centuries. Herschel reported events of this kind, known as Transient Lunar Phenomena (TLPs), in 1787. *"Selenology: Changes In Brightness," The Times (London), Jan. 8, 1972, p 16*

. . . they are most common at the time of lunar perigee, and there is an association, too, with the so-called TLPs, elusive reddish glows which have been recorded in certain areas (notably that of the brilliant crater Aristarchus and the huge walled plain Alphonsus). *Patrick Moore, New Scientist and Science Journal, Jan. 28, 1971, p 186*

together, *adj. U.S. Slang.* free of confusion, anxiety, etc.; mentally and emotionally stable.

Crockett is "just about the most together brother on the bench," says Ken Cockrell, a black activist lawyer in Detroit. *Time, April 6, 1970, p 60*

"People don't realize that a young lady of twenty-two who's been through what Twiggy has been through has got to be a very together person to survive," Justin said. *"The Talk of the Town," The New Yorker, Dec. 18, 1971, p 31*

—*adv.* **get it all together,** *U.S. Slang.* to get free of confusion, anxiety, etc.; get a sound, positive, stable attitude or outlook on life.

For him, Deborah had thrown out all her posters, and with him she had moved from Hesse and Alan Watts to Mann and Kierkegaard. "Let's face it, babe, they've got more to say. I mean, they've really got it all together." *Alice Adams, "Ripped Off" (a story), The New Yorker, May 22, 1971, p 41*

to·ka·mak ('tou kə,mæk), *n.* a device for producing controlled thermonuclear power, in which plasma (highly ionized gas) is confined in an endless tube by magnetic fields produced by currents outside the tube and inside the plasma itself.

Stellarators and tokamaks are two varieties of toroidal or doughnut-shaped chambers in which physicists are trying to achieve controlled thermonuclear fusion. Recently the tokamaks have produced plasmas nearer to fusion conditions than any other devices have been able to do. . . . *Science News, Feb. 20, 1971, p 129*

Medium-density plasma containers with a toroidal geometry include the stellarators, originally developed at the Princeton Plasma Physics Laboratory, and the tokamaks, originally developed at the I. V. Kurchatov Institute of Atomic Energy near Moscow. The only essential difference between these two machines is that in a stellarator a secondary, plasma-stabilizing magnetic field is set up by external helical coils, whereas in a tokamak this field is generated by an electric current flowing through the plasma itself. *William C. Gough and Bernard J. Eastlund, "The Prospects of Fusion Power," Scientific American, Feb. 1971, p 53*

[from Russian *tokamak*, an acronym for a phrase roughly equivalent in English to "*to*roidal *ca*mera *mag*net"]

toke (touk), *n. U.S. Slang.* a puff on a cigarette, especially a marijuana cigarette.

. . . yes, Mailer was bitter about drugs. If he still took a toke of marijuana from time to time . . . still! Mailer was not in approval of any drug, he was virtually conservative about it. . . . *Norman Mailer, "The Steps of the Pentagon," Harper's, March 1968, p 48*

. . . he [a pothead] sits down on the steps in front of the sheriff's place, lights up, and takes a few tokes. *F. P.*

Tullius, "Ninety-Nine Years Is Not Forever," The New Yorker, July 19, 1969, p 20

[shortened from *token* (i.e. a small portion of a smoke, a mere taste)]

tokenism, *n.* a policy or practice of attempting to fulfull one's obligations with token efforts or gestures.

On the drive to the campus, Powell asked how many blacks attended the school, and the student said there were about fifteen. "Fifteen!" Powell fumed in mock-anger. "Why, that's tokenism, sheer tokenism!" "No, sir," the student replied politely, "that's the basketball team." *Richard M. Levine, "The End of the Politics of Pleasure," Harper's, April 1971, p 53*

Norman Walton, a history professor at predominantly black Alabama State University in Montgomery, said most references to Negroes in that state's history books were examples of tokenism. *Paul Delaney, The New York Times, June 7, 1971, p 20*

When I subsequently said some critical things about the planning of the programme I was told, "Oh well, it was a good piece of *tokenism.*" Watch out. "Tokenism" is a new vogue word of the communicators. *Harold Webb, London, in a Letter to the Editor, The Times (London), Dec. 10, 1971, p 13*

tol·ley ('tɑl i:), *n.* a marble used to shoot at marbles; a taw or shooter.

Playing marbles requires a player to bend double to flick the tolley and we feel that ladies in this position are open to ridicule at the very least. *The Times (London), Feb. 18, 1970, p 2*

[of unknown origin]

Tom, *U.S. Slang.* —*n.* an Uncle Tom (a Negro servile to white society).

The late William Dawson was the only other Negro in Congress when Powell arrived, and together they represented the two available alternatives, the Tom and the Bad Nigger, the one meekly accepting the system on its own terms, the other staging fake confrontations with it which produced a measure of vicarious revenge for black people but few real gains. *Richard M. Levine, "The End of the Politics of Pleasure," Harper's, April 1971, p 59*

. . . "This building is not integrated. No Whites, Black ONLY. Police not pass this door. Black, white or toms." *Adam Raphael, "Black Hole, Fully Integrated," The Manchester Guardian Weekly, Dec. 12, 1970, p 5*

—*v.i.* Often in the phrase **Tom it,** to be or act like an Uncle Tom. Also, UNCLE TOM.

"She [the singer Bessie Smith] was an absolutely direct black woman. No Tomming, not a shade of the phony to her." *John Hammond, quoted by Whitney Balliett, "Jazz Records," The New Yorker, Nov. 6, 1971, p 172*

In Mr. Wright's view, the whole gamut of Negro behavior . . . involves one form or another of "Tomming it:" being like Uncle Tom. *Conrad Knickerbocker, The New York Times, March 5, 1966, p 25*

Tomism, *n.* *U.S.* short for UNCLE TOMISM.

. . . the extremist group that captured control of Wayne State University's student newspaper last year and turned it into a black separatist organ. . . . Recently, on vague grounds, it condemned one Hamtramck labor-relations aide for "Tomism and treason to his black brothers." *"Business: Labor: Black Rage on the Auto Lines," Time, April 11, 1969, p 58*

Was there a black identity beyond the limited roles that the official world allowed? One could always hustle the world, could con it, or adopt some form of Tomism, but was there a way of really making it without pretending that one was white? *Peter Schrag, "The New Black Myths," Harper's, May 1969, p 38*

ton-up ('tən,əp), *adj. British Slang.* that rides a motorcycle at high speeds; that does "a ton" (a speed of 100 miles an hour).

Sunning themselves by the warm walls were all varieties of layabouts and modern youth beatniks, mods, and ton-up boys; promenading gently, the tourists and coloured families in their Sunday, holiday best. *The Manchester Guardian Weekly, April 22, 1965, p 6*

. . . pretty headscarves fluttering, they [girls and young women] flash past in sports cars and on the pillions of scooters. But all this, *and* leather-jacketed ton-up motorcyclists, would have been inconcievable when Charlotte and Emily Brontë, somewhat older by now, walked four tough miles from Keighley after changing their books at a private circulating library. *Thomas Armstrong, "Writers' Regions: The Pennines," Punch, Feb. 3, 1965, p 169*

topless, *adj.* **1** without a top or upper garment to cover the breasts.

It was the silly season. And the 'topless' dress (for wearing which three young women appeared briefly at Bow Street on 21 August) was much in the news. *The Annual Register of World Events in 1964 (1965), p 29*

. . . we did demand a few brief deletions of visual material, including the topless bathing suit, a strip-tease scene, and a magazine cover with the title "Jazz Me, Baby!" *Robert E. Kintner, "Television and the World of Politics," Harper's, May 1965, p 128*

2 wearing a topless garment; exposing the breasts.

. . . the State Supreme Court of California . . . decreed that bare breasts do not a brothel make, and that "topless" waitresses do not necessarily incite to violence or public disorder. *Alistair Cooke, The Manchester Guardian Weekly, March 7, 1970, p 5*

One evening a couple of weeks ago the CBC's National News . . . flashed a picture of a topless dancer across the nation's TV screens. *Gerald Taaffe, Maclean's, Sept. 17, 1966, p 4*

3 employing or featuring waitresses, dancers, or others wearing topless garments.

. . . the evidence mounted that a topless bar no more incites to lust and criminality than a swimming pool or a bust of the Venus de Milo. *Alistair Cooke, The Manchester Guardian Weekly, March 7, 1970, p 5*

. . . the sexual acculturation of the rest of the world sags furthest behind Los Angeles in the free exposure of the American former-male's mammary fixations. And by this I mean not only the topless restaurant, but the ice cream parlor as well. . . . *"On Manners, Music, and Mortality," an Interview with Igor Stravinsky, Harper's, Feb. 1968, p 43*

—*n.* **1** a topless waitress, dancer, etc.

He advertised for "College Topless Queens," "Put Yourself Through College by Becoming a Topless!" he shouted, intimating that a high IQ was no hindrance if other vital statistics were in evidence. . . . *Ninette de Vries in Punch, Saturday Review, April 22, 1967, p 80*

2 a topless dress, bathing suit, etc.

. . . even his critics grant that Rudi's topless was only an incident in his rapid rise to leadership as the most way-out, far-ahead designer in the U.S. *Time, Dec. 1, 1967, p 34*

3 a bar, restaurant, nightclub, etc., featuring topless waitresses or performers.

"I hope you don't have toplesses in Toronto. We stopped it here. Soon as one has it, then the other guy across the street has to have it. . . ." *Barbara Frum, Saturday Night (Canada), Sept. 1967, p 24*

to·pos ('tou,pas), *n.* a commonplace notion or stereotyped expression.

Furthermore, why does Dr [George] Steiner have such a Romantic hostility to annotation? He speaks as though a man is born with an innate knowledge of the identity of Orpheus and of the *topos* of modesty and is insulted when the purity of his mind is violated by an immodest footnote. Surely the ignorance of the student is our very *raison d'être*, not our cue for despair. *Edward Greenwood, "English-teaching in Our Universities," The Listener, April 14, 1966. p 533*

[from Greek *tópos* place; (in rhetoric) a commonplace]

TOPS (taps), *n.* acronym for *thermoelectric outer planet spacecraft*.

As early as 1968, NASA began working on TOPS (Thermoelectric Outer Planet Spacecraft), a craft that could undertake a journey of 3 billion miles through the asteroid belt to the farthest planet, Pluto, 30 to 40 times farther away from the sun than the earth. The spacecraft could continue transmitting information out to possibly 100 astronomical units—perhaps beyond the solar system. As it passes each planet, it would transmit data from sensors about the planet's atmosphere, temperatures, radio emission and various other characteristics. *Science News, Jan. 30, 1971, p 77*

torque, *v.t., v.i.* to give a turning or twisting force to an axle, bolt, wheel, etc.; apply torque.

During high altitude chamber experiments on man's ability to work in a near vacuum, Lockheed's Lou Testaguzza performed simple tasks of threading nuts, torquing bolts and connecting electrical cables on an adjustable panel. *Science News, Sept. 24, 1966, p 222*

"Better make sure it's running before you get on the road," another of them said.

"Gun it!"

"Torque out!" *Perdita Buchan, "It's Cold Out There" (a story), The New Yorker, Sept. 14, 1968, p 48*

Electronic circuitry translates the displacement of the accelerometer's pendulum into an electrical signal, which is amplified and sent to a torquing device on the pivot axis of the pendulum. *Cornelius T. Leondes, Scientific American, March 1970, p 82*

[verb use of the noun]

total, *U.S. Slang.* —*v.t.* to wreck beyond repair; destroy totally.

An accident serious enough to "total" a car generally "totals" the occupants as well. *Advertisement by Leyland Motor Corporation of North America, Scientific American, April 1968, p 90*

. . . she said, "What happened to the car?"

"Totalled," he said.

"Oh. . . . Exactly how did it happen?"

"We'd gone to a dance at the high school," he told her. "I was in the driveway, coming out, and these kids were going to turn in. I was standing still. They didn't make the turn and ran into me." *Katinka Loeser, "The Houses of Heaven" (a story), The New Yorker, April 3, 1971, p 38*

And, oh, yes: Townshend did total his instrument during his last song. *Ellen Willis, "Musical Events," The New Yorker, Aug. 28, 1971, p 81*

—*v.i.* to be totalled.

. . . yes, there it is, the beautiful movie, wandering off among far-away drive-ins at the intersections of numbered highways. Glimpsing a frame or two, motorists will total and die. *Jean Goldschmidt, "Pursuits," The Atlantic, June 1971, p 64*

total theater, a stage play or other production that makes use of a maximum of theatrical effects.

Boldly, he [Flemming Flindt, director of the Royal Danish Ballet] choreographed "total theater," in which a work was not "evaluated solely on the intricacy of its movements but on its overall theatrical impact." *Time, Feb. 24, 1967, p 51*

He sees in them total theater in which music, words, book, movement, decor blend into a seamless whole. *Thomas Lask, The New York Times, Jan. 23, 1968, p 37*

touch-tone, *adj.* involving the use of push buttons to transmit electronically coded signals.

This will tie the computer even more to the telecommunications systems, allowing the computer to 'remote' its power to where it is needed. Indeed, the telephone will probably become the most widely used 'terminal' of the 1970s—incorporating voice output and touch-tone input. *Earl Joseph, Science Journal, Oct. 1970, p 103*

The touch-tone telephone allows the user to put numeric data into a system via telephone lines without introducing the problem of voice recognition. *New Scientist, May 28, 1970, p 430*

The Touch-Tone dial meets the needs of most motion-handicapped individuals. Those unable to operate it with a finger or a prosthesis can usually dial with a mouth stick. *Gale M. Smith, "Telephone Equipment, Customer," McGraw-Hill Yearbook of Science and Technology 1971, p 412*

The central processor is equipped to answer the phone, as a switchboard does. Computer output is translated into signals that are then transmitted back to the instrument in voice form. Thus one can dial the computer directly, send messages from the Touch-Tone panel, and receive an audible voice output. *R. Clay Sprowls, "Computers," Encyclopedia Science Supplement (Grolier) 1971, p 146*

towaway, *U.S.* —*n.* the towing away and impounding of an illegally parked car.

On a weekday basis—despite the published warnings about illegal parking—towaways averaged close to 200 cars daily during February. *The New York Times, March 5, 1967, p 75*

—*adj.* of or involving the towing away and impounding of an illegally parked car.

Mr. O'Donnell was asked why the Mayor, whose own official car was found double parked two weeks ago in the towaway zone of mid-Manhattan, had not disciplined himself at that time. *Seth S. King, The New York Times, Feb. 12, 1967, p 38*

If a man living in the New York area decides to take his wife out to dinner and a Broadway play he had better be ready to shell-out at least $35. Fifteen dollars for dinner and $20 for two tickets to the theater. And you can add to that the $25 towaway charge for illegal parking. *Goodman Ace, Saturday Review, June 3, 1967, p·8*

tower block, *British.* a tall residential or office building.

Modern "industrialized" methods of building tall tower blocks increase productivity, but present the designer with new stability problems. *W. W. Frischmann and P. W. Copp, New Scientist, May 23, 1968, p 388*

Tower blocks can be accused of leading to eardrum degeneration, owing to constant use of high-speed elevators, without any risk of a return to lots of little low-built homes in gardens. *R. G. G. Price, "Silver Lining," The Atlantic, Oct. 1966, p 127*

Office tower blocks provide new opportunities for fresh-air providers. *Patrick O'Leary, The Times (London), April 20, 1970, p III*

town house, *U.S.* an attached one-family house; row house. The equivalent British term is *terrace house.*

In some metropolitan areas, or in parts of them, land may indeed be too scarce and thus too expensive to permit another round of old-style suburbanization. There, people will move into "townhouses" and semidetached houses, which have less privacy than single family houses, but still provide private yards and a feeling of separateness from the next-door neighbors. *Herbert J. Gans, The New York Times Magazine, Jan. 7, 1968, p 85*

The younger Mr. Plumer had got wind of a developer who was looking around the neighborhood for a site on which to build small town houses for rent and was thought to be considering an abandoned school nearby and a certain parking lot. *Anthony Bailey, The New Yorker, Aug. 5, 1967, p 38*

tracker dog, a bloodhound or other trained dog used to track fugitives.

Police with tracker dogs search the area in Epping Forest where the body of a murdered woman was found. *The Times (London), March 31, 1966, p 5*

A relatively new bleeding disease that affected several hundred dogs used by the armed forces in Vietnam . . . had been called canine hemorrhagic fever and tracker dog disease, among other designations, and its cause had not been determined after more than a year of intensive study. *J. F. Smithcors, "Veterinary Medicine," 1971 Britannica Yearbook of Science and the Future, 1970, p 285*

tracking, *n. U.S.* another name for STREAMING. See also TRACK SYSTEM.

Tracking can be a useful educational device if tests are frequently administered and if movement from one track to another is made easy. *The New York Times, June 23, 1967, p 36*

. . . on the secondary level, till very recently, most teachers resisted community demands for an end to tracking. *Ray Halpern, "Tactics for Integration," Saturday Review, Dec. 21, 1968, p 49*

[from *track* a class or course of study arranged by homogeneous grouping of students + *-ing*]

track record, the record of performance made by a person, business, etc., in a particular field or endeavor.

In sum, your endorsement of four Democrats—in one by ignoring the issues and in two others by placing rhetoric over commendable track records—gives credence to the belief that you have ceased your role as an independent newspaper to take up one as spokesman for the Democratic National Committee. *Herbert V. Camp, Jr., Hartford, Conn., in a Letter to the Editor, The New York Times, Oct. 29, 1970, p 42*

A modern university president is expected to have practical vision, a good track record in administration, and

national prominence as a scholar. *Warren G. Bennis, "Searching For The 'Perfect' University President," The Atlantic, April 1971, p 40*

[transferred sense from the racing term for the record of speed set by a contestant at a particular distance and track]

track suit, a suit used by athletes (originally track athletes) to keep warm.

At which point, the one remaining member of the British Olympics Team (all the rest having fainted from the altitude) took off his tracksuit, walked to the solitary starting block, and, clutching his magic pebble, set off at a comfortable jog-trot to win the hundred metres. *Alan Coren, Punch, Feb. 28, 1968, p 294*

One morning, in the vestibule of the hotel in Peking, I met a group of astonishingly tall men and women in track suits. Their eyes radiated Olympic health. *Olof Lagercrantz, "The Playing Fields of Peking," The New York Times, June 18, 1971, p 39*

track system, *U.S.* an educational system in which students are grouped according to ability or aptitude as shown in standardized tests. Compare STREAMING.

Among the most publicized recommendations were proposals that widespread busing be adopted, moving city students to the suburbs; that school parks be built, in which all levels of education would be at one site; that compensatory education, such as the Head Start programs, be widened, and that track systems setting levels of the curriculum for slow students and gifted students be eliminated. *Martin Gansberg, The New York Times, Jan. 12, 1968, p 57*

[Carl F.] Hansen's track system, which became a focal point for criticism of the schools, was the prime example of a well meant idea that the former superintendent [of schools in the District of Columbia] was not flexible enough to adapt to changing educational needs. *Susan L. Jacoby, Saturday Review, Nov. 18, 1967, p 73*

trade-off, *n.* an exchange; arrangement; bargain.

But now that the U.S. industrial and social system is delivering such "disproducts" as pollution and racial tension and no longer seems to be supplying the compensating efficiency, many Americans feel they have been swindled in the trade-off. *Time, March 23, 1970, p 75*

. . . the interlinking of agreements about different classes of commercial products or different types of financial transaction are characteristic of all trade negotiations and international monetary conferences. Trade-offs between apparently unrelated topics are a classic feature of international diplomacy. *Keith Kyle, The Listener, Oct. 15, 1970, p 506*

Canaris's view of all City Hall hearings as cynical charades is shared by many students of municipal politics, who argue that in nearly every case political trade-offs have been made and decisions reached earlier, at executive sessions. *Andy Logan, "Around City Hall," The New Yorker, Oct. 30, 1971, p 109*

tra·hi·son des clercs (tra hi:'s5̄ dei 'klerk), *French.* intellectual treason; the abandonment of intellectual principles by intellectuals.

. . . nonliterary people . . . may from time to time choose to use literature as a term of reference. This seems to me one of the most serious trahisons des clercs of our time. *Angus Wilson, The Manchester Guardian Weekly, May 9, 1970, p 18*

More *trahison des clercs:* in the *New Scientist* out today readers will learn of something called nAch, short for "need-to-achieve", invented by David McClelland, American professor of psychology. *"Business Diary: Coining It," The Times (London), Jan. 27, 1972, p 21*

There was *trahison des clercs* to the precise extent that literary thought and political action had lost contact with each other. *Paul de Man, The New York Review of Books, June 23, 1966, p 17*

trail bike, a lightweight, rugged motorcycle for use on rough terrain.

Anyone hoping to escape the filth and din of cities for the quiet beauty of our woods, mountains or deserts is in for a rude shock. He is greeted by the rattling snarl of trail bikes, dune buggies and the like. *Timothy W. Brown, Los Angeles, Calif., in a Letter to the Editor, Time, Sept. 12, 1969, p 17*

Tranquilite, *n.* See the quotation for the meaning.

'Tranquilite' is the name Professors Paul Ramdohr and Josef Z. eringer, of the Max Planck Institute for Nuclear Physics at Heidelberg, West Germany, have given a new mineral they discovered in Moon rock samples collected by *Apollo 11* astronauts. Tranquilite is a compound of titanium, iron and magnesium, and is related to the Earth mineral titaniferous magnetite, a type of iron ore. The German researchers decided to name the new mineral after the Sea of Tranquility where it was found. That will be reviewed, however, by the International Nomenclature Commission before Tranquilite becomes the mineral's permanent name. *Science Journal, May 1970, p 23*

trans·ac·ti·nide series (træns'æk təˌnaid), a predicted series of heavy chemical elements which is to follow the actinide series (ending with element 103 or lawrencium) in the periodic table. Compare SUPERACTINIDE SERIES.

The element 104 begins a new series. Dr. Glenn T. Seaborg, head of the Atomic Energy Commission and Nobelist in chemistry for discovery of transuranian elements, called the new element the first of the transactinide series. This series should extend from 104 to 112. *Science News Yearbook 1970, p 265*

transcribe or **transcript,** *v.t. Genetics.* to form or synthesize (a molecule of messenger RNA) from the genetic information imparted by DNA. Compare TRANSLATE.

The latest research . . . suggests that, in its action against viruses, rifampicin blocks protein synthesis late in the virus growth cycle and that it does not interfere with the synthesis of the enzyme essential for transcribing RNA from DNA. *Science Journal, Feb. 1970, p 16*

DNA unwinds and either duplicates or is transcribed into messenger RNA (m-RNA). . . . *Science Journal, April 1970, p 17*

transcriptase, *n.* short for REVERSE TRANSCRIPTASE.

The transcription processes, and the replication of DNA and of viral RNA, could be understood in terms of three distinctive enzymes: DNA-replicase, transcriptase, and RNA-replicase. *Joshua Lederberg, "Molecular Biology," 1972 Britannica Yearbook of Science and the Future, 1971, p 306*

transcription, *n.* the process by which messenger RNA is formed from DNA. Compare TRANSLATION.

Gene transcription, whereby enzyme reactions mediate the synthesis of RNA molecules from DNA templates, has been investigated mostly in microbial organisms. . . . *P. Dennis Smith, Pamela B. Koenig, and John C. Lucchesi, "Cytology: Inhibition of Development in 'Drosophila' by Cortisone," Nature, March 30, 1968, p 1286*

The discovery in 1970 that RNA tumor viruses contain certain enzyme (polymerase) activities capable of reversing the familiar direction of genetic transcription—that is, using RNA as a template (model) for the formation of DNA, the genetic coding material—promised an extraordinarily rich harvest for cancer researchers. *Michael J. Brennan, "Medicine," 1972 Britannica Yearbook of Science and the Future, 1971, p 292*

transearth, *adj.* in or toward the direction of the earth, especially of a spacecraft returning to earth.

Then, at 12:10 A.M. Christmas Day, came the crucial moment—ignition of the SPS [Service Propulsion System] to boost Apollo VIII out of lunar orbit on the transearth trajectory. *John H. Glenn, Jr., "Focus on Space," The 1969 World Book Year Book, p 48*

transfer cell, a specialized plant cell which exchanges dissolved substances with its surroundings and transfers them across the plant membranes.

In flowering plants, transfer cells are found where the embryo sac (a gametophyte) comes into contact with its host (a sporophyte) or, later, where the embryo absorbs from nutritive tissues such as the endosperm. *Brian E. S. Gunning and John S. Pate, "Transfer Cell," McGraw-Hill Yearbook of Science and Technology 1971, p 420*

transfer factor, a substance that may transfer cellular immunity from one person to another. It has been isolated from white blood cells and is smaller than an antibody or protein cell.

It appears that the normal body produces a different specific transfer factor against each foreign substance to which its cellular immunity system reacts. . . . The possibility that the transfer factor might be useful in treating some forms of cancer is still largely conjectural. *Harold M. Schmeck, Jr., "New Factor Used to Fight Disease," The New York Times, April 19, 1972, p 11*

Another possible way around the problem [of organ rejection] is not to transplant cells at all, but instead to use a very mysterious molecule known as transfer factor. Transfer factor . . . can apparently, when given to people suffering from immune deficiency diseases, transfer to them the immunological status of the donor. *Graham Chedd, New Scientist and Science Journal, May 13, 1971, p 396*

transfer RNA, a special form of RNA (ribonucleic acid) which attaches itself to specific amino acids and transports them to their proper site in the protein chain. *Abbreviation:* tRNA Compare MESSENGER RNA, RIBOSOMAL RNA.

Each transfer RNA is a relatively small molecule with less than 100 nucleotides in its chain, and all of the transfer RNA's have a similar sequence of nucleotides at the two ends of the chain. They are unique in that they contain certain unusual purines and pyrimidines—that is, ones other than adenine, guanine, cytosine, and uridine. *Claude A. Villee, Jr., "Biochemistry," 1969 Collier's Encyclopedia Year Book, p 136*

In the cytoplasm a number of ribosomes attach to the messenger RNA, each ribosome making a protein chain of its own. Adaptor molecules of RNA (also known as transfer RNA) assist in this process; they translate the nucleotide sequence of messenger RNA into an amino acid sequence. *Robert Cox, "The Ribosome—Decoder of Genetic Information," Science Journal, Nov. 1970, p 57*

transformation, *n.* **1** any of various rules for deriving different types of grammatical sentences from more basic underlying ones. See also DEEP STRUCTURE, SURFACE STRUCTURE.

We have a considerable knowledge about universal (that is, expected) features of language: which segments are probable in any phonological system, which unusual and therefore possibly valuable for determining genetic relationship; which kinds of transformations (like those that delete identical noun phrases in constructions such as relative clauses) have close to universal status, making them a weak source of support for genetic relationship. *Robert D. King, Review of "A Comparative Quantitative Phonology of Russian, Czech, and German" by Henry Kučera and George K. Monroe, Language, June 1970, p 488*

2 a form of genetic transmission in which DNA (deoxyribonucleic acid) passes out of a cell into the chromosome of another.

In bacterial transformation a bit of DNA penetrates the boundary of a bacterial cell and becomes incorporated into the cell's genetic apparatus. *Alexander Tomasz, Scientific American, Jan. 1969, p 38*

transformational grammar, a grammatical system in which sentence structures are derived by transformation. Compare GENERATIVE-TRANSFORMATIONAL GRAMMAR, PHRASE-STRUCTURE GRAMMAR.

"Now, the fundamental idea of transformational grammar is that the bracketed and labelled representation of a sentence is its surface structure, and associated with each sentence is a long sequence of more and more abstract representations of the sentence—we transformationalists call them phrase markers—of which surface structure is only the first"....*Noam Chomsky, quoted by Ved Mehta, "Onward and Upward With the Arts: Linguistics," The New Yorker, May 8, 1971, p 53*

Generative, or transformational, grammar grew in part from M.I.T. computer experiments to produce mechanical translations of foreign languages. In its simplest form it starts with a sentence like "I see the cat." Then it is "transformed" into "I see the cat clearly running." *Austin C. Wehrwein, The New York Times, Dec. 29, 1965, p 32*

transformationalism, *n.* the linguistic theory or study concerned with transformations and transformational grammar.

He frequently contrasts his position with that of proliferating Bloomfieldians busily at work on linguistic theory, with no mention of some schools of thought which were very evident in 1968—though there are three or four brief mentions of transformationalism (which the reader is told is recent, p.1). *Charles-James N. Bailey, Review of "Sets and Relations in Phonology" by J. W. F. Mulder, Language, Sept. 1970, p 672*

transformationalist, *n.* a follower or advocate of transformationalism. Compare GENERATIVIST.

...the school of transformationalists contends that language is an innate, instinctively acquired facility; the study of it should start with sentences, then try to discern the rules by which a sentence conveys its meaning. *Time, Feb. 16, 1968, p 46*

The second example is from phrase-structure grammar (which some of the more condescending transformationalists are already calling "classical linguistics"). The interconnected boxes are a graphic device to show how the sentence, "What do you advise me to give my wife for

Christmas?" is analyzed. To do this, you peel the grammatical construction apart by orderly stages, much as a mechanic disassembles an automobile...on to the ultimate constituents. *Andrew Schiller, "The Coming Revolution in Teaching English," Harper's, Oct. 1964, p 83*

I have also operated with transformations, but the paper does not aim to be a transformational syntax. Some of my notational practices deviate from those of strict transformationalists; thus, I sometimes alter more than one element in a single transformation. *Charles E. Bidwell, Language, April/June 1965, p 238*

transform fault, *Geology.* a deep fault forming a steplike pattern on the edge of a plate and indicating the path of the plate.

Global analysis has established that the big shears called transform faults are the zones along which crustal plates glide as they separate. *"When Greenland and North America Parted Company," New Scientist and Science Journal, Aug. 26, 1971, p 450*

translate, *v.t.* *Genetics.* to form or synthesize (an amino-acid molecule) from the genetic information imparted by messenger RNA. Compare TRANSCRIBE.

In this way, the transfer-RNA molecules act as "translating devices," translating a codon at one end into an amino acid at the other. *Isaac Asimov, "Unraveling the Code of Life," The World Book Science Annual 1965, p 150*

translation, *n.* *Genetics.* the formation of amino acids based on the messenger RNA template. Compare TRANSCRIPTION.

Translation is the process whereby the genetic information contained in m-RNA determines the linear sequence of amino acids in the course of protein synthesis. Translation occurs on ribosomes, complex particles in the cytoplasm. *Robert G. Eagon, "Microbiology," 1971 Britannica Yearbook of Science and the Future, 1970, p 241*

translunar, *adj.* in or toward the direction of the moon, used especially of a spacecraft traveling to the moon.

The U.S.S.R. on April 7 launched Luna 14 into a parking orbit and then into a trans-lunar trajectory. It went into orbit around the moon on April 10. *Mitchell R. Sharpe, "Astronautics: Space Probes," Britannica Book of the Year 1969, p 125*

Once satisfied with the tests, the craft will set off towards the Moon—the translunar coast [coasting toward the moon]. *Tony Osman, New Scientist, Oct. 26, 1967, p 235*

transmission electron microscope, an electron microscope that transmits electrons through a specimen so that all the illuminated points of the image are produced at the same time.

Two different types of electron microscope are currently in use. The transmission electron microscope is analogous to a conventional light microscope. The scanning electron microscope employs a flying spot of electrons to scan the object, producing a television-like image. *Albert V. Crewe, "A High-Resolution Scanning Electron Microscope," Scientific American, April 1971, p 26*

transplantate, *n.* an organ or section of tissue that has been transplanted, especially from one person to another.

He [Dr Walter Jacoby] obtained his first transplantates from the Humboldt University in East Berlin, and used them mainly for treating damage to the meninges resulting from accidents or tumour operations. *New Scientist, Feb. 19, 1970, p 366*

The success of this treatment rests on the suppression of rejection reactions by the conservation process. The same procedure cannot, however, be used for heart or kidney transplants since in these cases far more than the mere physical structure of the transplantate is required. *"First Nerve Transplant Successfully Bridges Gap," Science Journal, April 1970, p 14*

transracial, *adj.* across racial boundaries.

The Merediths' decision is part of a growing phenomenon known in sociologists' jargon as transracial adoption. *"White Parents, Black Children: Transracial Adoption," Time, Aug. 16, 1971, p 46*

trans·sex·u·al (træn'sek ∫u əl), *n.* a person whose sex is anatomically uncertain or who is anatomically normal but considers himself or herself as belonging to the opposite sex; someone who lacks sexual identity.

The Gender Identity Clinic of the Johns Hopkins Hospital has performed sexual adjustment operations on 14 male transsexuals as part of a pilot study to determine the effects of such surgical changes. The results so far do not show any major psychological changes following the operations.... *Science News, May 23, 1970, p 506*

—*adj.* of or relating to transsexuals or transsexualism.

As probably everyone in the world but a few Tibetan monks knows by now, the story [of "Myra Breckinridge"] concerns a Myron who becomes a Myra after a transsexual operation. He-she determines to conquer Hollywood and devastate mankind. *"Cinema: Some Sort of Nadir," Time, July 6, 1970, p 70*

transsexualism, *n.* the condition of being a transsexual.

One of the specialists, who has been working in the area of transsexualism for more than 20 years, said yesterday: "Those who have the operations are seriously disturbed people." *The Times (London), Dec. 21, 1970, p 2*

trans·ves·tist (træns'ves tist), *n.* a person who dresses in the clothing of the opposite sex.

In any case, as a broad generalisation, provided that there is no "early" conditioning which makes homosexuality or heterosexuality the accepted norm, either or, indeed, both states can well be regarded as normal. End-product transvestists or ambivalents would continue to be the exception. In a word such people may be and often are homosexuals but homosexuals are rarely the transvestists or ambivalents. *Rowland Bowen, Mullion, Cornwall, England, in a Letter to the Editor, New Scientist, Dec. 17, 1970, p 522*

...or the special separate significance of the transvestist's 'little retreat', almost fetishistic in itself. *Wallace Hildick, The Listener, Nov. 2, 1967, p 578*

[variant of *transvestite*]

trash, *U.S. Slang.* —*v.i., v.t.* to destroy willfully and at random, especially as a symbol of rebellion.

A Harvard senior argued that "one just should be here, not to trash or fight but to be on the right side." *Time, May 11, 1970, p 24*

The *Times,* too, has likened the American left to the Nazi movement, saying in a recent editorial that "it is not surprising that the new breed of campus revolutionaries intent on destroying all freedom except their own are now

turning to what they call 'trashing'—the setting of fires, hurling of rocks, smashing of windows—ominously reminiscent of the shattered storefronts with which the Nazis sought to intimidate their political opponents of a generation ago." *"The Talk of the Town," The New Yorker, June 27, 1970, p 25*

Backstage at *Comes a Day* he got drunk and trashed his dressing room.... *Time, March 22, 1971, p 26*

—*n.* an act of trashing.

In Baltimore last week an American Weatherman told Martin Walker how the system is supposed to work: "Look, even when we lose we win. We know how the Man is. The Man is repressive. The Man is Fascist.... Every trash we do, every bomb we plant, is forcing the Man to repress that much more and that much more visibly." *"The Politics of Gelignite," The Manchester Guardian Weekly, Nov. 7, 1970, p 1*

trasher, *n.* *U.S. Slang.* a person who trashes.

...current revisionist efforts...give cachet to today's radical anarchists and mindless "trashers" by comparing them favorably with our Colonial rebels. *Rev. William S. Reisman, Garrison, N.Y., in a Letter to the Editor, The New York Times, Oct. 13, 1970, p 44*

trav·el·a·tor or **trav·el·la·tor** (træv'ə,lei tər), *n.* *British.* a moving platform or sidewalk operating like a conveyor belt to carry pedestrians between certain points.

...the suburban traffic of the two lines should be concentrated on either a rebuilt King's Cross or a new station on the site of Somers Town goods depot, linked, perhaps, by a travelator.... *W. Fawcett, Bletchley, Bucks, England, in a Letter to the Editor, "London's Stations," The Manchester Guardian Weekly, Sept. 15, 1966, p 16*

The scheme, linked by travellator to Sheperds Bush Underground station, also includes four 20-storey blocks of flats.... *The Times (London), Aug. 10, 1970, p 12*

[patterned on *escalator*]

tree diagram, (in generative-transformational grammar) a diagram of a sentence or phrase in which the components are shown as subdividing branches of the main structure.

If we want to show deep structure with a tree diagram, it will often be necessary to reorder the morphemes of a sentence so that those elements that are closely connected in meaning are grouped together. Just as *leave a light on* has a deep structure that groups its morphemes in a fashion not suggested by the linear sequence, namely (*leave . . . on*) plus (*a light*), so do other expressions.... *Thomas Pyles and John Algeo, English: An Introduction to Language, 1972, p 139*

tremblant, *adj.* set on springs to make a trembling or vibrating motion.

...a very fine diamond tremblant brooch in the shape of a five petalled flower brought the same price. *Geraldine Keen, The Times (London), March 26, 1970, p 12*

trendily, *adv.* *British.* fashionably.

...Hans Christiansen, director of the Royal Greenland Trading Company...plans to sell what he trendily calls "pre-pollution" ice to clink in the glasses of comfort-loving stay-at-homes. *New Scientist, April 30, 1970, p 253*

trendiness, *n.* *British.* fashionableness; up-to-dateness.

They start up in a blaze of glory as a "hot shop" and attract advertising directors anxious to show their trendiness. *Nicholas Faith, The Sunday Times (London), Sept. 14, 1969, p 26*

trendsetter, *n.* a person or thing that helps establish a new fashion or trend.

Model girls are accepted trendsetters in the fashionable world. *Prudence Glynn, The Times (London), Feb. 27, 1968, p 7*

Last week . . . the 19-year-old Jacob Riis public-housing project on Manhattan's Lower East Side . . . dedicated a new three-acre open space that is likely to be a trend setter for cities across the nation. *Time, June 3, 1966, p 44*

trendsetting, *adj.* capable of setting a trend or fashion.

This collection is not trendsetting nor is it haute couture in the traditional sense; the sole consistency is in skirt length. *Prudence Glynn, The Times (London), July 21, 1970, p 7*

The two parks, models of excellent design, are like a small electric charge of new ideas that could change New York's park and playground program from moribund to trend-setting. *Ada Louise Huxtable, The New York Times, Feb. 2, 1966, p 29*

trendy, *British. — adj.* fashionable; stylish.

Why in all the thousands of years that hairdressers have been hacking away at the male nape have they never devised a really efficient method of stopping itchy snippets going down the collar? Could static be brought into preventive play or is an invertible chair and reliance on gravity the better answer? Must we be draped for the ritual in that winding sheet which inevitably sets the thoughts on first and last things: Would not a trendy karate jacket encourage more clients? *New Scientist, Oct. 8, 1970, p 61*

Like any topical issue, eco-theology has yielded its share of trendy superficiality. *Time, June 8, 1970, p 49*

The country must return to nationalism and decency, which the "trendy intellectuals" had been trying very hard to rub out. *Daily Telegraph (London), June 6, 1972, p 30*

— *n.* a person who keeps up with the latest trends and fashions; a fashion plate.

These are stock characters going through familiar contortions — doing their thing, as we middle-aged trendies are only too inclined to say, tapping away so remuneratively in our pad. *Norman Shrapnel, The Manchester Guardian Weekly, May 22, 1971, p 19*

Up here among us trendies, it's Christmas red in tooth and claw, friends, and don't you forget it. . . . *Alan Coren, "Oh Come, All Ye Trendy!" Punch, Dec. 17, 1969, p 989*

But at least the revenue men won't be poking about Cork, interfering with decent trendies and tourists downing their modestly alcoholic pot-and-lemon. *Richard Milner, "Genuine Moonshine," The Sunday Times (London), June 20, 1971, p 45*

tri (trɑi), *n.* short for TRIMARAN.

Since a tri needs only one float in the water at a time — the windward one rides up in the air, slowing the boat down by its weight and wind resistance — Kelsall took the logical step of abolishing one. *Peter Laurie, The Sunday Times (London), April 11, 1971, p 23*

tri·bo·log·i·cal (ˌtrɑi bəˈlɑdʒ ə kəl), *adj.* of or relating to tribology.

. . . although a spot of oil can work wonders on a squeaking hinge, a relatively smaller spot of catalyst will liven up a chemical reaction. To an extent the effect of catalyst is proportional to its quantity, which is not true of lubricant. And lubricants will work the tribological oracle for many

sorts of rubbing surface: a substance which is a catalyst for reaction A may leave reactions B to Z unmoved. *New Scientist, Sept. 10, 1970, p 545*

tri·bol·o·gy (trɑiˈbɑl ə dʒi:), *n.* the study of interacting surfaces, dealing especially with the problems of friction, wear, etc., in technology.

Leeds University and the University College of Swansea, for example, have centres concentrating·on tribology — the science of lubrication and wear. *Nigel Hawkes, "Innovation and the Universities," Science Journal, March 1970, p 75*

The fact that it was recently thought necessary to introduce a new word into the English language, tribology, is a sign of both the previous unsatisfactory state of lubrication awareness and the rapid progress now being made. *G. F. Bowen, The Times (London), April 3, 1968, p I*

[coined in 1965 by a group of British scientists in consultation with the editors of the *Oxford English Dictionary* from Greek *tríbos* rubbing (from *tríbein* to rub) + English *-logy* study of]

tri·chlor·o·phe·nol (ˌtrɑi klɔr əˈfi: nɔːl), *n.* a highly toxic fungicide and bactericide which serves as the basic material for hexachlorophene (an antibacterial substance in certain soaps).

The substances known as the trichlorophenols and compounds of pentachlorophenol, which officials of the F.D.A. [Food and Drug Administration] believe may be chemical precursors of dioxin under certain thermal and other conditions, are used widely in the manufacture of a large variety of consumer products, ranging from paper to laundry starch and hair shampoo. *Thomas Whiteside, "Department of Amplification," The New Yorker, March 14, 1970, p 129*

trickle-down, *adj. U.S.* of or based on the economic theory that money flowing into the economy, especially from the government, will stimulate growth by distribution through big business rather than stimulating growth by direct benefits, such as welfare or public works.

At the Harvard Law School Forum in September, for example, he [Senator Edward M. Kennedy] said, "Richard Nixon was elected in 1968 because people like you sat on their hands. . . . And so Richard Nixon won with fewer votes than he had when he lost in 1960 . . . while five and a half million potential voters under twenty-five stayed home. . . . And we have a return to trickle-down economics. . . ." *"The Talk of the Town: Kennedy on Fifth Avenue," The New Yorker, Dec. 4, 1971, p 47*

Though any such new apartments would almost certainly be in the luxury category, proponents of the "trickle-down" theory argue that trading up will open enough older, cheaper units along the line to keep the middle class in the city, and perhaps, in time, even provide better housing for much poorer New Yorkers. *Andy Logan, "Around City Hall," The New Yorker, June 26, 1971, p 82*

trickle-irrigate, *v.t.* to irrigate by slow application of water at designated intervals, usually with small-diameter hoses.

Vast areas in the Negev Desert of Israel are now trickle-irrigated. *Sylvan Wittwer, "Agriculture," The World Book Science Annual 1972 (1971), p 255*

tri·jet (ˈtrɑiˌjet), *n.* an aircraft with three jet engines.

Originally designed for shorter-range routes than the 747, the trijets are now being offered in stretched intercontinental versions as the two manufacturers compete for orders. *Time, Jan. 19, 1970, p 44*

Their estimate for the number of trijets needed by the airlines of the free world by 1980, has dropped only marginally in the last year or two, despite the recent slump in airline growth, and now stands at 775. *Tony Dawe, "Why TriStar Changed Its Stripes," The Sunday Times (London), Aug. 8, 1971, p 35*

—*adj.* having three jet engines.

The Soviets have developed ... the Tu-154 trijet airbus with a 250-passenger capacity.... *Robert B. Hotz, 1970 Collier's Encyclopedia Year Book, p 83*

tri·ma·ran ('traɪ mə,ræn), *n.* a sailboat with three hulls set side by side and a common deck. Also shortened to TRI.

The fastest craft under sail are the new multihulled, water-skimming catamarans and trimarans, which make good family boats because they don't roll and heel in rough weather. *Philip Freen, Maclean's, July 24, 1965, p 31*

At the Pen Duick stand, a model represented the competition they may have from Tabatly: a 61-foot light-alloy tri-maran slated for the race if it passes its tests. *Denis Powel, The New York Times, Feb. 9, 1968, p 30*

[from *tri-* three + cata*maran*]

trip, *Slang.* —*n.* **1** the hallucinatory experience produced by taking LSD or another psychedelic drug. See also ACID TRIP, BAD TRIP.

Charley, the thirty-six-year-old man cuddling the toy, has taken LSD. He is acting strangely, but his trip will end in a few hours and with luck he will be back to normal. *Richard Todd, "Turned-On and Super-Sincere in California," Harper's, Jan. 1967, p 42*

One girl was taking LSD for the first time and during the midst of the trip suddenly—it was like a flash of insight came over her—she started almost screaming ecstatically: "I found the secret." *A. Y. Cohen, "Out of the Air: Eschatological Escalope," The Listener, Dec. 19, 1968, p 825*

He [the Rev. James E. Smith, of the United Church of Canada] has returned more than a few teeny-boppers to their distraught parents. He's seen youngsters suffer through bad drug "trips." He's had Yorkville's self-help Diggers organization call a boycott against his church-basement drop-in centre. *Harvey L. Shepherd, "A Centre Where Hippies Can Drop In, Turn Off, and Think About Going Home," Maclean's, Aug. 1968, p 2*

2 any stimulating experience.

The psychiatrist looked at him and said, "You're high, aren't you?" The guy said yes, he sure was, and the psychiatrist signed something and then looked up at the fellow and said, "You'll like the army. It's a good trip." *Dan Wakefield, "Supernation at Peace and War," The Atlantic, March 1968, p 48*

Part of the message is in the drug argot that he [Southern Baptist Arthur Blessitt] raps out to his street audiences: "You don't need no pills. Jes' drop a little Matthew, Mark, Luke, and John. Christ is the ultimate, eternal trip." *Time, Aug. 3, 1970, p 32*

3 any obsessive course of action, state of mind, etc., on which one embarks or in which one is involved for a time.

"We think John Lennon is a fink pacifist on a super ego trip," she said. *"The Talk of the Town," The New Yorker, Feb. 21, 1970, p 29*

—*v.i.* Often, **trip out.** to experience the hallucinatory effects of LSD or other psychedelic drug.

They went to the seedy suburb of Haight Ashbury, the capital of the hippies, to smoke a little (pot), to love a little (sex), to trip a little (LSD).... *Adam Raphael, The Manchester Guardian Weekly, May 2, 1970, p 16*

Somebody slipped some acid [LSD] into the potato and corn chips at a swinging singles party in the Marina del Rey section of Los Angeles, and nearly 40 of the 200 guests tripped out. *Time, April 20, 1970, p 8*

The worst bummer of all times was recorded by Robert Louis Stevenson. It seems that the good Dr. Jekyll tripped out on a mysterious powder and ended up as the nefarious Mr. Hyde. *"The Drug Scene, Dr. Jekyll and Mr. Cocaine," Science News, April 17, 1971, p 264*

triumphalism, *n.* the doctrine or belief that the teachings of a particular faith are eternal and indestructible.

Wayne H. Cowan, managing editor of the liberal Protestant journal, Christianity and Crisis, said the pastoral "mutes the triumphalism of the past, but still places great emphasis on the mystery and infallibility of the church." *John Leo, The New York Times, Jan. 12, 1968, p 25*

Without the nostalgia for the pre-Conciliar years of exclusivity and triumphalism, the Teilhard approach makes a perfect sense of the present and even a sense of joy at the prospect of the future. *Catholic Herald, June 9, 1972, p 4*

triumphalist, *n.* a follower of triumphalism.

The favourite sport of the triumphalist was heretic hunting. *Rev. Peter Hebblethwaite, SJ, The Times (London), April 22, 1967, p 12*

—*adj.* of or relating to triumphalism.

The Mexican hierarchy's triumphalist view that the Church had never erred, and had nothing to learn or be sorry for, epitomized the traditionalists' resistance to ecumenism.... *Francine du Plessix Gray, "Profiles: The Rules of the Game (Ivan Illich)," The New Yorker, April 25, 1970, p 56*

tRNA, abbreviation of TRANSFER RNA.

Busby and Hele have managed to show that the tRNA of the livers of laying hens is 25 per cent more active in the formation of lysyl-tRNA than in those of immature controls. *New Scientist and Science Journal, March 18, 1971, p 598*

troi·ka ('trɔɪ kə), *n.* a group of three administrators or rulers; a triumvirate. *Also used attributively.*

Dynamic as the innovate Government-university-industry troika is, it has raised some questions about the role of the university as an academic institution and of the professor as a teacher of students. *Henry R. Lieberman, The New York Times, Jan. 8, 1968, p 139*

... he [President Lyndon B. Johnson] reorganized the District government, replacing the old troika Commission with a single Commissioner—Walter E. Washington.... *Richard H. Rovere, The New Yorker, Sept. 23, 1967, p 168*

Columbia University will set up a "troika" system, with two executive vice presidents as key assistants to the president. *Murray Schumach, The New York Times, June 3, 1971, p 44*

[from Russian *troika* a three-horse team or sled; any group of three; popularized in this sense by the Soviet proposal in 1961, after the death of the U.N. Secretary General Dag Hammarskjold, to replace the vacant office with a *troika* of three Secretaries General, one from each side of the Iron Curtain and one from the neutral countries]

tro·po·e·las·tin (‚trou pou i'læs tən), *n.* a substance from which elastin, the basic unit of elastic tissue, is formed.

. . . Dr. Sandberg reports isolation of the precursor molecules, subunits of elastic tissue. Called tropoelastin, each subunit is built of 800 amino acid molecules that may constitute a spherical protein. *Barbara J. Culliton, Science News, April 25, 1970, p 416*

Tropoelastin has an amino acid composition much like that of elastin, with two significant exceptions: it contains no desmosine and has a much higher content of lysine than elastin does. *Russell Ross and Paul Bornstein, "Elastic Fibers in the Body," Scientific American, June 1971, p 51*

[from *tropo-* tendency toward + *elastin*]

Trots, *n.sing.* or *pl.* **1** a Trotskyite.

Non-violence needs civil disobedience, and any Communist or Trots sees red at the mention of civil disobedience. *Stewart Meacham, quoted by Francine du Plessix Gray, "A Reporter At Large: The Moratorium and the New Mobe" [New Mobilization Committee to End the War in Vietnam], The New Yorker, Jan. 3, 1970, p 38*

2 Trotskyites.

The Alliance sent over a delegation. But having resisted a Communist Party takeover in its early days, it is now definite on the fact that it has no "Trots" on the Council. *Jean Stead, "Student Power Struggle in Britain," The Manchester Guardian Weekly, May 30, 1968, p 5*

trouser suit, a British term for PANTSUIT.

"I do not expect the law to be very broadminded but trouser suits are quite normal these days." *Edith Merchant, quoted in "Trouser Suit Upsets Judge," The Times (London), Feb. 24, 1970, p 2*

tube, *n.* Usually, **the tube.** *U.S. Slang.* television. Compare BOOB TUBE, BOX.

Viewers were inundated by an avalanche of campaign commercials this year. Probably more money was spent in 1970 to reach voters through the tube than in any other off-year election. *Kathryn Rose, "Television and Radio Broadcasting," 1971 Collier's Encyclopedia Year Book, p 534*

As the reader may recall, my last column nattered at some length on the perennially reliable theme that the arts are in a dire way; and it gave warning that in future I might be obliged to turn for material to the tube. *Igor Stravinsky, "Performing Arts: A Maker of Libretti," Harper's, April 1970, p 112*

[from the picture *tube* (cathode ray tube) which reproduces the images on the television screen]

Tu·dor·be·than (‚tu: dər'bi: θən), *adj.* of or relating to a style of furniture and interior architecture prevalent in England between 1500 and 1700, characterized by massive, sturdy forms and elaborate carving in wood.

. . . a fine Tudorbethan home in the country for weekends and holidays. *Kirsten Cubitt, The Times (London), Oct. 5, 1970, p 7*

. . . the regulars in their accustomed trilbies sit slightly perplexed on uncomfortable Tudorbethan high-backed settles. *Derek Cooper, The Manchester Guardian Weekly, Oct. 31, 1970, p 14*

[contraction of *Tudor-Elizabethan*]

tumorigenic or **tumorgenic,** *adj.* producing tumors.

Once normal plant cells have been subjected to that triggering irritation they can be transformed into tumor cells not only by the tumor-inducing principle of bacteria but also by various other tumorigenic agents. *Armin C. Braun, Scientific American, Nov. 1965, p 79*

In animal model systems the loss of contact inhibition induced by SV40 is clearly associated with the development of tumorgenic potential by the cells. *Stuart A. Aaronson, "Transformation, Cell," McGraw-Hill Yearbook of Science and Technology 1971, p 421*

tumorigenicity or **tumorgenicity,** *n.* tumor-producing tendency or capacity.

By refined methods of collection and extraction, the TRC [Tobacco Research Council] workers were able to show that rather more than 50 per cent of the tumorigenicity of 24-hour condensate (an extract made and applied to the mice within 24 hours of smoking the cigarettes), was due to stable, non-volatile carcinogens. *Donald Gould, New Scientist, May 25, 1967, p 478*

To his delight he found the new cells to have a dramatically reduced malignancy — only one in 10^6 produced a tumour in mice compared with almost 100 per cent tumourgenicity shown by Ehrlich cells. *"Hybrids Show Up Gaps In Malignant Cells," New Scientist and Science Journal, June 24, 1971, p 732*

tune-out, *n. U.S.* the turning off of a particular broadcast; refusal to watch a certain television or radio program.

None of the nation's 690 TV channels is black-owned. Though blacks are virtually disfranchised by TV and get, at best, an hour a week of programming by and for them on a few local channels, there is no indication of a black tune-out. A recent Harris survey found that blacks watch an average 18.5 hours of TV a week compared to 14.7 hours for whites. *Time, April 6, 1970, p 59*

[patterned after *blackout* (as in a *news blackout*)]

Tu·pa·ma·ro (‚tu: pə'ma: rou), *n.* a member of an extreme left-wing guerrilla organization in Uruguay, known for their acts of terrorism.

Tupamaros have been jailed in Uruguay for crimes, not for their political beliefs, despite this propaganda claim of the urban guerrillas. *Marvin Alisky, Tempe, Ariz., in a Letter to the Editor, The New York Times, Aug. 18, 1970, p 34*

The killing of Dan Mitrione by the Tupamaros in Uruguay represents the wanton murder of a defenseless man and can do no more to bring about social change than the torture of political prisoners can assure the maintenance of free society. *Edward M. Kennedy, "Beginning Anew in Latin America," Saturday Review, Oct. 17, 1970, p 19*

Uruguay's Tupamaros take their name from Tupac Amaru, a Peruvian Indian who led a revolt against the Spanish in Peru in the 18th century. *Norman Lewis, "Planet Earth: Latin America," The Sunday Times Magazine (London), Sept. 26, 1971, p 11*

turboelectric, *adj.* of or relating to the generation of electricity by a turbine.

Turboelectric or diesel-electric installations are employed where great flexibility of control is desired. *"Ship Power Plants," The 1967 Compton Yearbook, p 570*

turbopump, *n.* a turbine-driven pump, especially that component of a rocket engine which regulates thrust.

The basic idea of a nuclear rocket engine is very simple. Such an engine consists of a nuclear reactor whose purpose is to heat hydrogen to as high a temperature as possible; a nozzle through which the hot hydrogen expands; and a turbopump to force the hydrogen through the system. *Roderick W. Spence, Science, May 31, 1968, p 953*

The TVA began construction of a pumped storage station at Racoon Mountain, 6 mi. W of Chattanooga, with a capacity of 1,350 Mw. in four groups of reversible turbopumps. It was scheduled to go into service in 1974-75. *Lucien Chalmey, "Fuel and Power: Electricity," Britannica Book of the Year 1971, p 346*

turbotrain, *n.* a train powered by turbine engines, capable of speeds up to 170 mph.

We already have the technology to build fast, comfortable passenger trains. Such trains are, in fact, already in operation in Japan, Italy, and a few other countries. Experimental samples—the Metroliners and Turbotrains—also are running with spectacular success between Washington and Boston. *John Fischer, "The Easy Chair," Harper's, April 1970, p 28*

The Turbotrain is less of a threat to Hovertrains than Britain's Advance Passenger Train. *Peter Rodgers, "French Hovertrain in the Lead?" The Manchester Guardian Weekly, Feb. 21, 1970, p 22*

. . . it [Canadian National Railways] has now ordered five of the turbotrains developed by the U.S.'s United Aircraft Corp. Even without roadbed improvements, these lightweight, low-slung, turbojet-powered whiz-bangs should be able to clip nearly an hour off the present five-hour Montreal-Toronto run. *Time, May 27, 1966, p 52*

The French Railways are interested only in their "turbotrain" and are openly hostile to the privately owned "aerotrain." *New Scientist, July 23, 1970, p 187*

Tur·ing machine ('tur ɪŋ), an ideal automatic computer that is capable of performing an infinite number of any type of calculation. See the first quotation for details.

A Turing machine is a "black box" (a machine with unspecified mechanisms) capable of scanning an infinite tape of square cells. The box can have any finite number of states. A finite portion of the tape consists of nonblank cells, each bearing one of a finite number of symbols. When the box views a cell, it can leave a symbol unaltered, erase it, erase it and print another symbol or print a symbol in a blank cell. *Martin Gardner, "Mathematical Games," Scientific American, June 1971, p 120*

While modern digital computers are not Turing machines and have limitations which the idealised Turing machine, with its infinite memory, does not have, they are much more flexible and capable in a practical way than the machines Turing envisaged. *J. R. Pierce, "Computers and Music," New Scientist, Feb. 18, 1965, p 423*

[named after Alan M. *Turing*, 1912-1954, a British mathematician who first described such a machine in 1936]

turn, *v.i., v.t. Slang.* In the phrases:

turn off, to lose or cause to lose interest, liking, or enthusiasm; the opposite of *turn on.*

. . . long after they had stopped making simple, happy dance music; when the kids finally turned off, it was less because the Beatles were esoteric than because they were old hat. *Ellen Willis, "Musical Events: Records: Rock, etc.," The New Yorker, July 6, 1968, p 58*

"We were sympathetic to the problems of the young and found ourselves increasingly turned off by friends who kept mouthing the same old clichés." *Irving Harrison (a former N.Y. architect), quoted in Time, Nov. 30, 1970, p 13*

This gratuitous, incestuous plugging of its own mini-personalities which Radio-1 is for ever indulging in is what really turns one off. *Wilfred De'Ath, The Listener, March 28, 1968, p 419*

turn on, 1 to be or cause to be stimulated by drugs; to get high on narcotics. Also, SWITCH ON.

. . . he regularly turned on with marijuana or blew his mind with LSD. *John Corry, The New York Times, March 21, 1966, p 1*

People at pot parties "turn on" together; an LSD guru "turns on" his congregation. *Saturday Night (Canada), June 1967, p 24*

. . . six per cent of the students support the war, a quarter have indicated they will go into exile or prison rather than submit to the draft, and fewer than half have never turned on. *Jacob Brackman, "Onward and Upward with the Arts: The Graduate," The New Yorker, July 27, 1968, p 56*

2 to cause to become interested, aroused, or enthusiastic; to stimulate or excite.

A few of the jailed Americans are professional smugglers, supplying the Mob in the U.S. "But most of them," says [John T.] Cusack, "are not pros in the true sense. They have no records. They are users, and many of them are 'missionaries.' They want to turn others on—and if there's a profit in it, so much the better." *Time, April 13, 1970, p 36*

"Sometimes hundreds of people walk out of our performances but we will reach *some* people. If we turn on one or two people each night, that's enough for us." *Charles Marowitz, The New York Times, Sept. 8, 1968, Sec. 2, p 5*

Terry Scott is another funny man who is still looking for the writers who can turn him on. *Peter Black, "Television: Nay, Nay, Nay," The Listener, Jan. 4, 1968, p 27*

turnkey, *adj.* supplying a complete product or service by contract.

The company unwisely signed some "turnkey" contracts to supply complete plants at a fixed fee. *Time, Jan. 31, 1969, p 52*

There is tremendous scope here for developing—and exporting—complete fishing "turnkey systems", with fishing vessels, refrigeration plant, factory and mother ships as parts of an integrated package. *Michael Shanks, The Times (London), April 22, 1968, p 25*

Enable the city to use the "turnkey" program under which the Housing Authority would buy a completed building from a private builder rather than build it itself. *Steven V. Roberts, The New York Times, March 1, 1968, p 26*

[originally used in the building trades to indicate the day the contractor will complete the job and the owner merely need turn the key of the door]

turn of the screw, an act or instance of using pressure or force to gain an end.

. . . President Nixon first asked that expenses be kept to a minimum, then emphasized the demand more strongly, and at last, only a week before the budget was submitted to Congress, added a "final turn of the screw." *Science News, Feb. 7, 1970, p 149*

In the years after 1960 British traditions of the rule of law that had deep roots in South Africa were steadily compromised by a series of arbitrary police-state measures, especially when it came to habeas corpus and free speech. The final turn of the screw was given to the racial legislation of apartheid: all blacks in so-called "white areas," covering 86 per cent of the land, were declared temporary sojourners with no permanent rights. *The New York Times, Sept. 11, 1966, Sec. 4, p 2*

It would be easy in such cases to see merely another turn of the screw in the Soviet government's effort to contain the effects of de-Stalinisation. *Encounter, May 1972, p 28*

► There are two possible explanations of the origin of this term. The obvious first thought is to connect it with Henry James's novel, *The Turn of the Screw*, but the meaning of the phrase there is an increasing pain or torment. Perhaps the phrase is more clearly related to the idiom "putting the screws on" (i.e. exerting pressure or force on someone). Brewer's *Dictionary of Phrase and Fable*, under the heading *to put on the screw*, also gives *"to give the screw another turn*, to take steps (or additional steps) to enforce one's demands."

turn-on, *n. Slang.* excitement; stimulation.

He also offers a large number of lubricious case studies, thus providing shopgirls too shy to read Harold Robbins in public with the kind of mild turn-ons they seem to crave.... *Richard Schickel, "Books in Brief," Review of "The Affair" by Morton Hunt, Harper's, Feb. 1970, p 122*

two cultures, Usually, **the two cultures.** the arts and humanities, or social sciences, on one hand, and the physical sciences and engineering technology on the other, viewed as two distinct and often conflicting cultures dominating the thinking of modern society.

The conference called on UNESCO to convene a worldwide conference that might be instrumental in narrowing the gap between the two cultures. Expressing belief in, "the usefulness of a sincere comparison of points of view between scientists — and particularly physicists and biologists — and representatives of the social sciences, political sciences and mass communication media" the science ministers requested UNESCO to plan such a conference.... *New Scientist, July 2, 1970, p 3*

To the scientists who gathered in Chicago this week for the annual jamboree of the American Association for the Advancement of Science, it must have seemed that Snow's model of the two cultures had some deep validity. *"A Time of Torment for Science," Science News, Jan. 2, 1971, p 5*

[from *The Two Cultures and the Scientific Revolution*, title of a celebrated lecture delivered by the English writer C. P. Snow in 1959 at Cambridge University, in which Snow expressed his concern over the lack of communication between the scientific and the literary-scholarly community]

ty·lo·sin ('taɪ lə sən), *n.* an antibiotic derived from a species of streptomyces, used in the treatment of animal diseases.

Tylosin is not used in human medicine, and to that extent its use in animals could be reasonable. *Bernard Dixon, "Antibiotics on the Farm—Major Threat to Human Health," New Scientist, Oct. 5, 1967, p 35*

Antibiotics (including synthetic antibacterial agents) which have been used as feed additives, and which are now classified as 'therapeutic', are penicillin, tetracyclines, tylosin, sulphonamides and nitrofurans. *Karl Hammond, "Therapeutic Antibiotics Unwise in Feedstuffs," Science Journal, March 1970, p 4*

[perhaps from *tylosis*, the name of several diseases (from Greek *týlōsis* formation of a callus) + *-in* (chemical suffix)]

U

Ü·ber·frem·dung (‚Y bər'frem duŋ), *n. German.* See the quotations for the meaning.

Nowhere in Europe have relations between guest and host become more acrimonious than in Switzerland. *Uberfremdung* (over-foreignization) has been a battle cry of the far right for the past five years. *Time, June 8, 1970, p 39*

The issue of *Überfremdung* ("over-alienation"; i.e., the high percentage of foreign workers in Switzerland) continued to make news. *Melanie F. Staerk, "Switzerland," Britannica Book of the Year 1969, p 709*

► The diacritical mark over the *U* is omitted in the first quotation.

UDI, abbreviation of *Unilateral Declaration of Independence* (originally referring to the declaration of independence from Great Britain issued by the premier of Southern Rhodesia, Ian Smith, on November 11, 1965).

For, let's face it, UDI means much more than Rhodesia's headstrong, headlong and premature attempt to go it alone. We have to remember that roughly half the people of Britain — supporters of both Conservatism and Socialism — feel deeply wounded by our sudden decline and fall of the heart of a great Empire. "We won the war," they say, "and we have lost the peace." *Bernard Hollowood, Punch, Feb. 2, 1966, p 148*

Support for a U D I is growing after the continued refusal of the T G W U's [Transport and General Workers' Union's] No. 1 Docks Groups to allow work to start on the terminal until a wage agreement is made for all London's enclosed docks. *Stephen Fay, The Sunday Times (London), Nov. 23, 1969, p 25*

u·fo·log·i·cal (‚yu: fə'lɒdʒ ə kəl), *adj.* of or relating to the tracking of unidentified flying objects.

As for 1966, it has got off to a very promising start with the U.F.O. flap in Michigan. The ufological definition of a flap is a concentration of sightings in a small area within a short period. The Michigan flap is either a remarkable case of mass hysteria or a U.F.O. classic. *"The Talk of the Town: Saucer Flap," The New Yorker, April 9, 1966, p 32*

u·fol·o·gist (yu:'fɑl ə dʒist), *n.* a person who studies or keeps track of unidentified flying objects, usually called flying saucers.

Saucer buffs, or "ufologists," point out that the Air Force's Project Blue Book, the best source of saucer statistics, has recently published a list of eight hundred and eighty-six sightings for 1965. *"The Talk of the Town: Saucer Flap," The New Yorker, April 9, 1966, p 32*

. . . these civilizations [supposedly advanced civilizations in the Milky Way] are probably separated from one another by anywhere from 300 to 1,000 light-years, Sagan estimates (a light-year is the equivalent of 6 trillion miles). This deflates the argument of UFOlogists that saucers have begun observing the earth because of man's recent technological strides. *Time, Aug. 4, 1967, p 33*

[from *UFO*, abbreviation of Unidentified Flying Object + *-logist*, as in *geologist, zoologist*, etc.]

ugly American, an American living abroad who presents an unflattering image of Americans, especially by his insensitivity to the natives and their culture.

. . . he can spring before us a host of odd and funny foreigners: bogus Russian counts, semi-aristocratic Slavic ladies, German officers, and an early type of the ugly American abroad. *William Barrett, The Atlantic, May 1965, p 152*

I don't think we were Ugly Americans; perhaps just Unaware, or Unlettered. *David Butwin, "To Reach the Untaxable Ports," Saturday Review, March 9, 1968, p 76*

[from *The Ugly American*, a book of stories about Americans in southeastern Asia, written by Eugene Burdick and William Lederer and published in 1965]

ultimatism, *n.* an uncompromising attitude or tendency; extremism in opinion or belief.

To persuade a woman to like herself and to accept herself sexually, which was one of Freud's aims, isn't necessarily to persuade her to stay in the kitchen—though it may well be to tell her, Miss Millett's arrogant ultimatism notwithstanding, that if she does prefer to stay at home, this doesn't stamp her as inferior or brainwashed or a "chattel" of the "master group." *Irving Howe, "Books: The Middle-Class Mind of Kate Millett," Review of "Sexual Politics" by Kate Millett, Harper's, Dec. 1970, p 122*

ultimatistic, *adj.* characterized by ultimatism; extremist.

What this style of argument (*not "really" democratic*) betrays, apart from contempt for precision of language, is a quite American kind of ultimatistic moralism—the feeling that a valued phenomenon must maintain a state of near-perfection if it is to be worth preserving. *Irving Howe, "Books: The Decline in Democratic Sentiment," Review of "Four Essays on Liberty" by Isaiah Berlin, Harper's, Aug. 1970, p 97*

ultraclean, *adj.* maintaining a high level of cleanliness, especially under germ-free conditions, as by the use of sterilized laboratories and instruments, isolation techniques, and the like.

Ultraclean technology can reduce rejection rates, increase reliability and make possible new products and procedures that otherwise would be unachievable. *L. B. Hall, Science Journal, April 1970, p 41*

ultrahigh, *adj.* of the highest degree; extremely high.

Under ultrahigh pressure, matter could achieve a fifth state, becoming a supermetal. *Science News, April 20, 1968, p 378*

Where applicable, Dr Pyke describes first the traditional methods and then goes on to show the latest developments in the technology of a particular process, whether this is a fully automated bakery with continuous dough-making, or the ultra-high-temperature treatment of milk. *Ella M. Barnes, Review of "Food Science and Technology" by Magnus Pyke, New Scientist, Oct. 17, 1968, p 152*

ultraleft, *adj.* extremely radical.

. . . the violent campaign of land seizures was . . . spearheaded first by the Naxalites, a small ultra-Left Maoist splinter group from the Communist Party of India (Marxist), itself the product of a split from the pro-Moscow Communist Party. *The Manchester Guardian Weekly, Aug. 15, 1970, p 12*

The ultraleft adventurism practiced by Kim Il Sung is very dangerous to the peace of Korea, for no one can say with certainty that he will not unleash another war against the Republic of Korea, especially if his dream of achieving unification by force in his lifetime is taken into consideration. *President Park Chung Hee, "Korea: Building a Nation," Britannica Book of the Year 1971, p 796*

—*n.* **the ultraleft,** extreme radicals as a body or movement.

The ultraleft found its voice by protesting against the new Tokyo international airport in Chiba Prefecture and by joining cause with irate farmers fighting eviction from their farmlands. *Stuart Griffin, "Reason to Riot?" New Scientist and Science Journal, Sept. 30, 1971, p 740*

ultraleftist, *n.* an extreme radical.

As an ultraleftist, of course, Wu would hardly expect a warm welcome from as revisionist a country as the Soviet Union. *"The World: More Pieces in the Chinese Puzzle," Time, Oct. 11, 1971, p 13*

ul·tra·mi·cro·tome (ˌʌl trə'mɑi krəˌtoum), *n.* an instrument used to cut extremely thin sections of tissues for examination by an electron microscope.

A new cryogenic ultramicrotome is used to section frozen biological specimens. *Picture legend, The World Book Science Annual 1968, p 222*

. . . £20,704 for the purchase and installation of an electron microscope and ultra-microtome for research in the Bland-Sutton Institute of Pathology. *The Times (London), Jan. 18, 1968, p 10*

ultramilitant, *adj.* militant to an extreme.

The Justice Department had reports that shotguns and rifles purchased by Panthers were transported to New Haven. Panthers and members of the ultramilitant white Weathermen brought dynamite into the city. . . . *"The Panthers on Trial," Time, May 11, 1970, p 25*

M. Nicoud first gained attention last spring as one of the leaders of a new, ultra-militant shopkeepers' organization, known as the "Tour du Pin Movement" after the small town in the Grenoble area where it began. *Edward Mortimer, The Times (London), March 11, 1970, p 6*

ultraminiature, *adj.* extremely small.

Monitoring the composition of an astronaut's breath during a mission is the job of a tiny analyzer now being built for the space agency. Key elements in the device, an ultraminiature vacuum pump and a mass spectrometer, will be worn directly under the astronaut's chin, in a unit about one inch in diameter and four inches long. *Science News, Dec. 7, 1968, p 573*

ultraminiaturized, *adj.* reduced to an extremely small size.

Zimmerman, like most scientists, doubts that man will soon reproduce his brain in electronic hardware. But, using a multitude of ICs [integrated circuits], ultraminiaturized, working in parallel, together with functional circuits, he may build electronic devices tomorrow that seem like impossible dreams even today. *George A. W. Boehm, "The Microelectronics Revolution: The Functional Vanguard," The World Book Science Annual 1968, p 215*

ultrasonogram, *n.* a recording or tracing made by an ultrasonograph.

During 1970, the use of these "ultrasonograms" in the diagnosis of brain tumors and eye disorders remained largely experimental and was nowhere in routine clinical use, but the technique was attracting increasing interest and was being successfully extended to such fields as cardiology, abdominal exploration (kidney stones show up particularly clearly), and obstetrics and gynecology. . . . *Charles Süsskind, "Electronics," 1972 Britannica Yearbook of Science and the Future, 1971, p 242*

ultrasonograph, *n.* an instrument using ultrasonic waves (those of a frequency of 15 to 20 megahertz) to penetrate tissue and make recordings of abnormalities.

Clearly, then, obstetric diagnosis has benefited enormously from the application of ultrasonics. Where to from here? Donald's group at Glasgow have recently been experimenting with a newly developed, more powerful ultrasonograph. He hopes that this will mark the beginning of really sophisticated foetal medicine. *Roger Lewin, "A Penetrating Gaze Into the Womb," New Scientist and Science Journal, Sept. 2, 1971, p 523*

ultrasonography, *n.* the use of ultrasonic devices in detecting abnormalities in the body.

. . . a research team at Bristol General Hospital . . . hope that they will soon be using ultrasonography for routine diagnosis of disease affecting the mitral valve of the heart. *New Scientist, Nov. 16, 1967, p 404*

ultrasonologist, *n.* a specialist in the use of ultrasonic devices in medical research and diagnosis.

Another reason ultrasonics is gaining acceptance in obstetrics is that it is offering ever greater accuracy in recording events in the womb. Four kinds of diagnoses made on 521 pregnant women gave an accurate reading 96 to 100 percent of the time, Ross Brown, ultrasonologist at the University of Oklahoma Medical Center, reported . . . . *Joan Lynn Arehart, "Sounding Out the Womb," Science News, Dec. 25, 1971, p 424*

umbilical, *n.* **1** short for UMBILICAL CORD.

Bacchus [an underwater habitat] will receive its breathing mixture either by means of an umbilical from the surface or from high pressure storage bottles situated in the capsule itself. *New Scientist, Feb. 27, 1969, p 458*

2 a connection; link.

Hamlets living on beer and thatch would have been abandoned centuries ago—and perhaps never existed at all—if there had been no twisting lanes to give them perspective and act as an umbilical to the outside world. *Dennis Johnson, The Manchester Guardian Weekly, Feb. 14, 1970, p 11*

umbilical cable, another term for UMBILICAL CORD.

The operators, working under normal atmospheric pressure, will travel in the capsule to a compartment fitted permanently over the well-head on the ocean floor. The mobile capsule is powered and serviced by an umbilical cable, running from a support ship. *New Scientist, July 16, 1970, p 133*

umbilical cord, any long cord or cable by which a person or thing remains connected to a ship, spacecraft, the ground, etc. Also called UMBILICAL CABLE or UMBILICAL.

. . . more than 100 miles above the surface of the earth, Edward H. White II, attached to Gemini IV by a 25-foot "umbilical cord," spent 20 minutes maneuvering in space and testing his 20-layer space suit. *John H. Glenn, Jr., ". . . Before This Decade Is Out . . .," The World Book Science Annual 1969, p 14*

With a good wind the kites will soar to a height of 2,000 feet or more, towing in their wake perhaps half a mile of umbilical cord which pays out so rapidly that it singes the gloved hands of the flyers. *Geoffrey Sheridan, The Manchester Guardian Weekly, May 23, 1970, p 16*

umbrella, *adj.* covering many or a variety of things; comprehensive; general.

The scientists, convinced of the errors of Freud, maintain that therapies based on conditioning and learning theory—grouped under the umbrella term "behaviour therapy"—are much more effective and practical than in-depth, "arty" therapy which lays bare the patient's soul. *New Scientist, Dec. 24, 1970, p 541*

The executive board is headed by Paul Hall, president of the Seafarers International Union of North America. But the Board is composed of representatives of many different organizations, from sheet metal workers, to barbers to office employes, all under the umbrella title of maritime trades. *Peter Millones, The New York Times, Feb. 15, 1968, p 23*

In 1911, the Swiss psychiatrist, Eugen Bleuler, coined for the same conditions the name schizophrenia, meaning "split mind." The umbrella word has stuck, though modern methods of diagnosis have created new sub-divisions in the disease. *Alfred Byrne and Lewis Chester, The Sunday Times (London), May 15, 1966, p 13*

umpty-umpth, *adj.* *U.S.* last in a series of greater numbers than that suggested by *umptieth.*

[Daniel] Barenboim is preparing plenty for the pairing. Currently on a three-month U.S. tour, he is now two-thirds through his umpty-umpth cycle of the 32 Beethoven sonatas at Manhattan's Tully Hall. He is also well into a guest-conducting series with the Philadelphia Orchestra. *Time, Dec. 7, 1970, p 74*

unbundle, *v.t.,* *v.i.* to separate (the costs of different products, services, etc.) into separate transactions.

The industry giant, International Business Machines Corp. (IBM), faced with several antitrust suits . . ., decided in response to "unbundle" or separate the costs of computer software and hardware, previously offered as a package deal. *Marcelino Eleccion, Britannica Book of the Year 1970, p 321*

uncap, *v.t.* to disclose or reveal.

. . . G. Harrold Carswell . . . last week uncapped the surprise of the political season: quitting the Fifth Circuit Court of Appeals, he declared his candidacy for Florida's Republican senatorial nomination. *Time, May 4, 1970, p 19*

Uncle-Tom, *v.i.* to act as an "Uncle Tom"; cater to others in a slavish, fawning manner. Also, TOM.

Married or not, for sexual reasons or social ones, most women still find it second nature to Uncle-Tom. *Gloria Steinem, "What It Would Be Like if Women Win," Time, Aug. 31, 1970, p 22*

. . . "Sun Ra, and his Men, from Outer Space, are here to entertain you now," Uncle-Tomming with a snarl and a hidden barb, converting a contemptuous self-parody into camp, the classic put-on. *Eric Larrabee, "Performing Arts: The State of Jazz," Harper's, Dec. 1968, p 134*

. . . an obligation . . . applies constantly to all underdog groups, constantly tempted by rewards to uncle-tom, to pull the forelock. . . . *Marghanita Laski, "Women in a Man's World: The Secondary Sex," Punch, Aug. 9, 1967, p 210*

Uncle Tomish, characteristic of an "Uncle Tom"; servile, slavish, or fawning.

. . . Negro comedians of past years were limited to playing Uncle Tom-ish, lazy, smiling, shuffling menials. *Steve Allen, "What Are We Laughing At?" The 1970 Compton Yearbook, p 81*

The [black] students are "suffering from the shock of integration and are looking for an easy way out of their problems. The easy way out is to let them have black courses . . . and give them degrees. But what in hell are soul courses worth in the real world? No one gives a damn if you've taken soul courses. They want to know if you can do mathematics and write a correct sentence." . . . The trouble was that the radical young reject this kind of argument as bourgeois and Uncle Tomish. *Time, May 9, 1969, p 13*

Uncle Tomism, Uncle Tomish behavior. Also called TOMISM.

Negro leaders have access to the School Board and the superintendent, they serve on the school administration's advisory committees, and they are frequently consulted (if not heeded) on policy decisions. What Pittsburgh considers to be Negro militancy would be regarded as Uncle Tomism in New York. . . . *Peter Schrag, "Pittsburgh: The Virtues of Candor," Saturday Review, Nov. 19, 1966, p 83*

uncool, *adj. Slang.* unpleasant, troublesome, or disturbing; lacking self-control or sophistication; not cool.

On occasion, the subject turned to drugs. It was uncool in a state whose government likes to see its grass mowed, not smoked. *Time, Feb. 16, 1970, p 62*

"There are some very uncool people here—cats who come because they like a fight, and when I suspected this I really thought about packing up." *Mary Finnigan, The Sunday Times (London), Sept. 21, 1969, p 3*

We didn't talk politics—that would have been uncool. *Calvin Tomkins, "Profiles: Moving With the Flow," The New Yorker, Nov. 6, 1971, p 72*

uncorrectable, *adj.* irremediable; irreparable.

. . . a regularly scheduled airliner bound for Boston radioed the Logan tower to report a sudden failure of all navigational and directional instruments, as well as an undiagnosed and uncorrectable loss of power. *Roger Angell, "Turtletaub and the Foul Distemper," The New Yorker, May 30, 1970, p 26*

For many years, facial paralysis has been uncorrectable. Lately, however, surgeons have been experiencing success with several new operations. *Time, Sept. 21, 1970, p 57*

uncorrectably, *adv.* irredeemably; hopelessly.

In outline, Skelton's life there in the caravan on the edge of the high meadow over the lake, in a place that must be uncorrectably gloomy during the wet rains of winter, seemed cagelike and hopeless to me—unacceptably lonely. *John McPhee, "Pieces of the Frame," The Atlantic, Jan. 1970, p 45*

undercharacterization, *n.* too little development of the characters in a novel, short story, drama, etc., or the themes in a piece of music.

Couples [a novel] is flawed by overwriting and undercharacterization, but the charge of irrelevance will no longer stand up. *"Books: Authors," Review of "Couples" by John Updike, Time, April 26, 1968, p 50*

undercharacterize, *v.t.* to fail to develop the characters enough in a novel, short story, drama, etc., or the themes in a piece of music.

But in the wry second movement (taken fast) the players needed more detailed help with phrasing, and the work as a whole was undercharacterized. *Joan Chissell, The Times (London), Dec. 16, 1970, p 11*

underclass, *n.* the class of people who remain on the lowest economic level.

But he [Martin Luther King] could not, states Williams, relate to the black underclass or understand its impatience with a system that refused to recognize its legitimate demands. *Time, Aug. 17, 1970, p 12*

"Social scientists have a great deal to tell us about the life styles of various class groupings . . . but the larger societal mechanisms that produce the underclass have been largely ignored." *Lee Rainwater, quoted by Jonathan Steele, The Manchester Guardian Weekly, April 24, 1971, p 18*

"Third, the 'underclass', especially its black elements, but also the Spanish speakers and the Appalachians, has begun to turn its desperation from a burden into a weapon." *Joseph G. Herzberg, The New York Times, April 7, 1968, p 29*

underdevelop, *v.i.* to become less developed and fail to remain economically self-sufficient by losing or wasting capital, resources, etc.

But on closer inspection, there is something very radically wrong with Uruguay. Its GNP regularly declines from year to year. It is a developed country that is underdeveloping at speed. *Richard Gott, The Manchester Guardian Weekly, Aug. 15, 1970, p 4*

—*v.t.* to cause to underdevelop.

"For 20 years we have been underdeveloping ourselves. We have missed our last chance. The country [Czechoslovakia] is ruined." *The Times (London), Dec. 31, 1968, p 9*

[back formation from *underdeveloped, adj.*]

underdrawing, *n.* an outline drawing put on a canvas, mural, etc., prior to the application of paint.

Metropolitan Museum, Fifth Ave. at 82nd St.—An impressive exhibition of seventy Italian frescoes detached from the walls of Tuscan churches and monasteries of the Middle Ages; in many cases, the original underdrawings accompany them. *"Goings On About Town," The New Yorker, Oct. 12, 1968, p 12*

The other new application of an old technique is the use of infra-red radiation to examine the "underdrawings" of mediaeval European paintings. *New Scientist, Oct. 3, 1968, p 37*

underground, *n.* any group, organization, or movement whose activities are outside the established society or culture.

Investigators will infiltrate the "underground" of the drug world, seeking to break the links between smuggler, pedlars, and addicts. *Peter Harvey, The Manchester Guardian Weekly, April 4, 1970, p 10*

. . . so-called undergrounds—the hippie communes, the drug subcultures, the anti-Establishment press—actually are about as clandestine as a circus parade. . . . *John Fischer, "The Easy Chair: Notes from the Underground," Harper's, Feb. 1970, p 12*

What these film makers, who proudly identify themselves as the "underground," profess to want is the freedom to create motion pictures in accordance with their own, intensely personal artistic visions, untrammeled by anything that has gone before. *Arthur Knight, "Look What's Happening to the Movies," The 1969 World Book Year Book, p 120*

The Catholic "underground" has removed worship from the sanctuary entirely and transferred it to private homes. *Edward B. Fiske, The New York Times, May 26, 1968, Sec. 4, p 4*

The Underground is comprised of artists whose concepts reflect highly specialized, distilled styles. *Saturday Review, Oct. 26, 1968, p 88*

In America, the word "underground" is now being applied to persons involved in producing and selling erotic literature, photographs, and movies. *Leopold Tyrmand, "Reflections: Permissiveness and Rectitude: The Underground," The New Yorker, Feb. 28, 1970, p 96*

—*adj.* of or belonging to an underground.

The lot of underground newspapers anywhere in the U.S. is a hard one, inasmuch as the papers often reflect a zest for rebellion and four-letter words. *Time, March 23, 1970, p 38*

Many Soviet intellectuals continued to criticize government policy through underground publications, which the police were unable to suppress. *Ellsworth Raymond, "USSR," The Americana Annual 1970, p 699*

. . . "There were underground filmmakers coming out of the wall all over the neighborhood. I saw some of their work and thought I could do as well." *"The Talk of the Town: Film Club," The New Yorker, Jan. 13, 1968, p 20*

The Paris café theatres, an underground movement for 18 months now, providing valuable experience for writers and performers, are just now beginning to bear fruit. *The Times (London), March 11, 1968, p 6*

In the last half-year, serious-pop music has attained a beachhead on radio with stations that program "progressive rock" or "underground" music. *Robert Shelton, The New York Times, April 5, 1968, p 54*

From some of these occasional users Dr. Ludwig and Dr. Levine were able to compile some interesting insights into the "underground" use of hallucinogenic drugs. *Harold M. Schmeck, Jr., "LSD," 1967 Collier's Encyclopedia Year Book, p 36*

underground church, a church that functions outside of an established or organized religious denomination.

Divine Disobedience is divided into three long sections. The first, and sketchiest, is an account of the communal lifestyle of East Harlem's Emmaus House, a prototype for countless so-called "underground churches." When Francine [Francine du Plessix Gray] began her project, Emmaus House was a hotbed of zealous ecumaniacs, bent on building a new kind of parish with home rule and spontaneous liturgies. *Time, July 27, 1970, p 73*

Among the best-known of these are the so-called "underground churches" among American Catholics. While the bishops debate technical questions such as when laymen can receive the wine as well as the host during Holy Communion, thousands of Catholics are going ahead on their own to see what sort of meaningful worship is possible in small groups where the emphasis is on discussion, the use of ordinary bread and wine, and lay participation in all aspects of the service. *Edward B. Fiske, The New York Times, July 14, 1968, Sec. 4, p 9*

underground press, the unconventional newspapers and periodicals published by those who consider themselves to be outside the established society or culture.

A wave of parajournalistic publications, the so-called underground press, was mounting a serious challenge to established dailies. *Richard T. Baker, "Newspapers," The Americana Annual 1970, p 503*

The "underground press" continued to grow, numbering approximately 150 papers at year-end. The papers, originally created to reflect the life-style of hippies and drop-outs, were changing their editorial focus from drugs and rock music to radical politics. *M. Dallas Burnett, "Newspapers," The 1969 Compton Yearbook, p 346*

underkill, *n.* **1** an inability to defeat an enemy.

As for the nation's nuclear forces, Mr McNamara cited a 200 per cent increase "in the number of nuclear warheads and total megatonnage in the strategic alert forces" . . . . Obviously, Goldwater's fears of America lapsing into a state of "underkill" were groundless. *Howard Simons, "Keeping Ahead of Mao," New Scientist, March 10, 1966, p 618*

2 something that causes far less harm than one could reasonably inflict.

. . . says the University of Chicago's Philip B. Kurland, "it seems clear enough that those who indiscriminately stamp documents as 'confidential,' 'secret' or 'top secret' cannot be the judges of their own judgments." Noting that "our legal tradition has special repugnance toward prior restraint," Harvard's Paul A. Freund maintained that "risk for risk, the law has opted for underkill in duels over publication." *"Toward the Legal Showdown," Time, July 5, 1971, p 13*

[patterned after *overkill*]

underoccupied, *adj.* **1** having fewer occupants than there is room for.

To find room in this way for the elderly and others needing small homes would release seriously underoccupied large houses for bigger families. *The Times (London), March 23, 1970, p 5*

. . . many large apartments . . . have been under-occupied simply because their rents are low. *Yvonne R. Freund, New York, in a Letter to the Editor, The New York Times, May 23, 1970, p 22*

2 having little to do; not sufficiently employed.

Its [Mexico City's] street scenes off the massive dual carriageways have an impressive shabbiness—that stained and damaged identity of overoccupied housing and underoccupied people. *Arthur Hopcraft, The Manchester Guardian Weekly, June 6, 1970, p 5*

underproduce, *v.t.* to produce less than the usual amount.

In the Russian Republic, according to the State Planning Commission, meat will be underproduced by 40% in 1970, eggs by 44%. *Time, May 4, 1970, p 35*

[patterned after *overproduce*]

underproductivity, *n.* insufficient or inadequate productivity.

The university [the University of the West Indies] is having a strongly positive effect upon the realization of a national system of education. In raising the volume and quality of the manpower and by encouraging studies of the factors, notably teacher efficiency, that lie at the root of educational underproductivity, it can decisively affect this serious problem. *Reginald Murray, "Changes in Education," The Times (London), Sept. 14, 1970, p III*

underreact, *v.i.* to react with less force or intensity than the circumstances require.

The police, taken unawares and unprepared, took their response from a page of the riot manual of the early '60's. First they underreacted, allowing the march to become a mob and the mob to become milling looters. *"The South: Death in Two Cities," Time, May 25, 1970, p 25*

[patterned after *overreact*]

under-reaction, *n.* an act or instance of under-reacting.

The difference is in the creases of your suit, in the way tension is replaced by boredom and over-reaction with the danger of under-reaction. *Julian Mounter, "Drivers Need to Take Greater Care," The Times (London), Jan. 13, 1972, p I*

undertax, *v.t., v.i.* to tax insufficiently or inadequately.

Ralph Nader has added the reform of property taxes to his roster of causes, charging that so much business and industrial real estate is undertaxed as to constitute "a national scandal of corruption, illegalities and incompetence." *Time, May 3, 1971, p 49*

"The root causes of our trouble are not mysterious," Mr. Rockefeller said in his text. "We are overspending. And we are undertaxing." *Richard L. Madden, The New York Times, May 23, 1968, p 23*

[patterned after *overtax*]

undertaxation, *n.* insufficient or inadequate taxation.

Overtaxation of buildings gives slum landlords an incentive to not improve their property, because that would only bring higher assessments and taxes. Meanwhile, the undertaxation of land helps speculators hold property out of use while they wait for a city's growth to raise its price. *Time, April 4, 1969, p 56*

underwhelm, *v.t.* to create a feeling of indifference in; fail to excite or arouse enthusiasm.

On Tuesday Mr. Barber made me a present of something approaching £200 a year—before allowing for the higher prices and charges which I shall now have to pay for Government services. It was very nice of him and I suppose I should be duly grateful. But I am bound to say, churlish though it may seem, that I am distinctly underwhelmed by his generosity. *Peter Jay, "The Effects of the Cuts on Growth," The Times (London), Oct. 30, 1970, p 11*

Rockefeller's long, prepared speeches in more formal settings often underwhelm his audiences, but his peppy little talks followed by question periods show a perky platform style. *Time, May 17, 1968, p 15*

[from *under* + *overwhelm*]

undock, *v.i., v.t.* to disconnect (orbiting spacecraft).

Cosmos 212 and 213 docked, coasted and undocked in orbit automatically. . . . *Science News, May 18, 1968, p 473*

On the third day of the flight, Conrad undocked Gemini and used his thrusters to back slowly away from the Agena until the 100-ft. rope was taut between them. *Time, Sept. 23, 1966, p 67*

UNDP, abbreviation of *United Nations Development Program,* an organ of the UN that oversees funds for aiding needy or developing countries.

This project [reporting of locust migration between countries] which lasted six years and involved 30 or so countries . . . was the biggest single scheme ever financed by the UNDP. *P. T. Haskell, Science Journal, Jan. 1970, p 66*

unflappability, *n.* calmness; composure; self-possession.

All the young Americans seem to respond to Mark Satin. His enthusiasm for the job and general air of unflappability seem catching. *Anastasia Erland, "Mark Satin, Draft Dodger," Saturday Night (Canada), Sept. 1967, p 22*

unflappable, *adj.* not disturbed or agitated; unruffled; calm. Compare FLAPPABLE.

The United States Government, in the words of Chairman Arthur M. Okun of the Council of Economic Advisers, remained "unflappable," even though the rush cost it more of its dwindling supply of gold. *Edwin J. Dale, Jr., The New York Times, March 10, 1968, Sec. 4, p 6*

[from *un-* not + *flap* confusion, excitement (especially in the phrase *in a flap*) + *-able*; originally applied to Harold Macmillan, born 1894, British Prime Minister from 1957 to 1963]

unflappably, *adv.* calmly.

Particularly if the City unflappably sticks to its bowlers in astrakhan weather. *Brian Moynahan, The Sunday Times (London), April 20, 1969, p 25*

. . . Clark remains unflappably unimpressed with the importance of putting great numbers of people in jail. *Fred P. Graham, The New York Times, Oct. 20, 1968, Sec. 4, p 13*

u·ni·sex ('yu: nə₁seks), *adj.* designed or suitable for both sexes; not distinguishing or discriminating between males and females.

"Unisex" clothes were advertised from the walls of London's subway, and the psychological implications of unisex were eagerly discussed. *Phyllis W. Heathcote, "Fashion and Dress," Britannica Book of the Year 1970, p 341*

Garbed in loose-fitting tunics and trousers, the Chinese have a unisex look. *Seymour Topping, "China: Great Feats Accomplished by Mass Efforts," The New York Times, June 26, 1971, p 8*

Greenwich Village, always the firstest with the weirdest, has just spawned the world's "first unisex boutique for men and women from 16 to 25." *The Manchester Guardian Weekly, Nov. 21, 1968, p 4*

Twenty-six angry women, representing 120,000 female workers, were urged that the time had come for "unisex" jobs to be accepted. *The Times (London), March 19, 1970, p 22*

—*n.* integration or equalization of the sexes in work, sports, fashions, etc.

To Charles Winick, professor of anthropology and sociology at the City University of New York, the rise of "unisex" in the U.S. has ominous connotations for the future of the nation. In a survey of 2,000 different cultures, Winick found that some 55 were characterized by sexual ambiguity. Not one of those cultures has survived. *Time, Oct. 12, 1970, p 57*

Drug addiction, drag and unisex are now much more fashionable subjects for the popular press. *Nicholas Swingler, "Call Girls: Business Still Booming," The Manchester Guardian Weekly, Aug. 21, 1969, p 9*

[from *uni-* one + *sex*]

unisexed, *adj.* not distinguishable by sex.

In the background busy young men and women, sartorially unisexed, were laying out the ground plans. . . . *Charlotte and Denis Plimmer, "Alice Through the Cathode Ray Tube," Punch, Sept. 3, 1969, p 381*

unisexual, *adj.* of or relating to unisex or unisexuality.

"It astounds me that we have progressed so far in sexuality that ultimately [fashion designer] Rudi Gernreich's unisexual concept should be as asexual as the Virgin birth. . . . It's ending up to be the same bag." *Malcolm Boyd (an Episcopal priest), quoted in "People," Time, Feb. 23, 1970, p 36*

unisexuality, *n.* unisex look or appearance.

In ballet, adults adore the unisexuality of Nureyev; in books, children prefer easy-to-read real-life adventures to fairy tales with their "idealized, romantic role-models of the masculine and feminine." *Time, Oct. 12, 1970, p 57*

If it works in the Village, it won't be long before unisexuality starts creeping uptown—and over the Atlantic? *The Manchester Guardian Weekly, Nov. 21, 1968, p 4*

unitholder, *n. British.* a stockholder in a unit trust.

One great advantage of unit trusts is that unit-holders can buy or sell at any time, and get the 'true' value of their investment. *Margot Naylor, Your Money, 1965, p 87*

The recent unit trust management mergers raise the interesting question: what are a unitholder's rights when a management company changes hands? *Margaret Stone, The Times (London), March 28, 1970, p 21*

unit pricing, the pricing of commodities by the pound, ounce, or other standard unit together with the overall price.

. . . unit pricing of grocery items . . . permits instant comparison of relative costs of different brands and sizes. *Thomas T. Semon, New York, in a Letter to the Editor, The New York Times, July 8, 1970, p 42*

Essentially, unit pricing means that shoppers will find two prices on the food items they select—the total price and the price per standard unit of measurement. Thus, a 7 1/2-ounce box of detergent might be labeled 65 cents, or 8 2/3 cents an ounce. *Robert B. Melton, "Food," 1971 Collier's Encyclopedia Year Book, p 239*

unit train, a freight train which operates as a permanent unit, without uncoupling and reassembly of cars, in transporting goods from one fixed point to another.

. . . the most important innovation came in 1962 with the introduction of the "unit train," that is, a train that shuttles constantly back and forth between the mine and the power station, thereby achieving optimum equipment utilization. *John F. Hogerton, Scientific American, Feb. 1968, p 27*

. . . the competition of river barges has spurred the railroads to introduce massive, low-cost "unit" trains and to cut rates to the bone on everything from steel to fertilizer for river valley deliveries. *Marvin J. Barloon, "The Coming of the Super-Railroad," Harper's, April 1967, p 67*

unit trust, *British.* a mutual investment company; a mutual fund.

There are now so many unit trusts that it is hard to make a choice. *Margot Naylor, Your Money, 1965, p 89*

Small unit trusts are often difficult to promote, uneconomic to run and remain static—to the detriment of both managers and unitholders. *Richard Milner, The Sunday Times (London), May 26, 1968, p 26*

unk-unks, *n.pl. U.S. Slang.* a series of unknowns, especially of inexplicable calamities.

Lately the industry has suffered a succession of blows: a slow-down in space exploration, a $6.9 billion cutback in Washington's defense budget, and a fall-off in orders for commercial aircraft. As a result, aerospacemen have come down with a severe case of what they call the "unk-unks" —the "unknown unknowns." *Time, March 9, 1970, p 63*

"Unk Unks"—aerospace jargon for "unknowns"—are the villains favoured by Lockheed to explain the extraordinary series of financial disasters that has led it to the verge of bankruptcy. *Adam Raphael, The Manchester Guardian Weekly, Aug. 1, 1970, p 24*

unleaded, *adj.* another word for NONLEADED.

Performance is improved when cars burn gas without lead, which tends to clog pollution control gadgets. In February, Henry Ford sent an open letter to the presidents of 19 oil companies, demanding that they speed their marketing of unleaded gas. *Time, July 20, 1970, p 65*

unpeople, *n.* people lacking the semblance of humanity or individuality.

People on foot on a hot road in the country walking from nowhere to nowhere, a suitcase on their head. Tired people. Unpeople. *Jonathan Steele, The Manchester Guardian Weekly, March 21, 1970, p 6*

They are so devoid of romance or passion they're like the un-people at the end of "1984." *Pauline Kael, "The Current Cinema: Somebody Else's Success," The New Yorker, Oct. 25, 1969, p 177*

unperson, *n.* a political or other public figure who has lost his importance or influence and has been relegated to an inferior or inconsequential status.

. . . Molotov, too, is an unperson, dead politically if not corporally. *Harry Schwartz, The New York Times, Nov. 6, 1967, p 46*

—*v.t.* to cause to become an unperson.

What is of greatest value is not only the account of the indictment of Khrushchev and his "unpersoning," but the sketch of the careers and personalities of Brezhnev and Kosygin, which is fuller and more convincing than I have seen elsewhere. *Richard Symont, Review of "Unpersoned" by Martin Page and David Burg, The Manchester Guardian Weekly, March 31, 1966, p 11*

. . . *The Fierce and Beautiful World*, by Andrei Platonov, unpersoned under Stalin. *W. L. Webb, The Manchester Guardian Weekly, Jan. 16, 1971, p 19*

[originally used in George Orwell's novel *1984* to describe people eliminated from official existence by the eradication of their names from all documents, newspapers, etc.]

unquantifiable, *adj.* of a character or quality that is not measurable or easily caculable.

And what would Britain gain in return? A spurt in growth of British trade and industry from the "dynamic effects" of the European market, but a spurt that is "unquantifiable"...."*Common Market: Will Harold Rat?*" *Time, March 9, 1970, p 29*

William James's studies of human consciousness and Sigmund Freud's investigations into the subconscious were fruitful but relatively subjective. For them and their followers psychology was the study of the inner processes of the mind, and since these processes were, and still are, invisible and unquantifiable, speculation on them is necessarily subjective and, in this sense, unscientific. *Berkeley Rice, The New York Times Magazine, March 17, 1968, p 85*

unstrikable, *adj.* that cannot be legally subjected to a strike by workers.

In Antigua itself, the entire military reserve force (30 men) was called up because of strikes which the government thought might develop into disorder. Civil servants stopped work because of the suspension of two customs clerks and were joined by employees of shops and supermarkets. The government speedily passed legislation declaring certain services such as the courts and the cable office to be essential and therefore unstrikable. *C. G. Lindo, "Caribbean Colonies and Associated States," 1971 Collier's Encyclopedia Year Book, p 157*

Un·ter·mensch ('un tər,menʃ), *n.; pl.* **Un·ter·men·schen** ('un tər,men ʃən). *German.* a person regarded as less than human; a subhuman.

In Britain, only a century ago, the workers were widely regarded as Untermenschen, sub-species fortunate to live in their hovels, to eat bread and enjoy long hours in foul mines, mills and factories. *Bernard Hollowood, Punch, April 24, 1968, p 587*

To the Germans, Lithuanians were *Untermenschen*, a second-class people to be exploited and, when politically expedient, enslaved. *Edward M. Potoker, Saturday Review, March 26, 1966, p 34*

up, *n. U.S. Slang.* another word for UPPER.

In Hollywood, a boy of eleven . . . has been pushing "ups" (amphetamine and methedrine pills) and "downs" (barbiturates, tranquilizers) since he was nine....*Time, Feb. 16, 1970, p 36*

upconvert, *v.t.* to change by means of an upconverter.

. . . a laser beam can be used to upconvert infrared light to visible light....*"The Talk of the Town," The New Yorker, April 11, 1970, p 34*

upconverter, *n.* a converter from one form of radiant energy to another.

A new system called an upconverter . . . can produce a three-dimensional color image from infrared waves. Basically, the system is composed of a crystalline material, such as potassium dihydrogen phosphate, into which are beamed and mixed the infrared waves and laser light, explains Dr. Arthur H. Firester. The laser beam pumps the infrared photons into visible light. The system, successful in the laboratory stage, has worked as far as 10 microns into the far infrared region. *Science News, April 4, 1970, p 345*

update, *n.* the most recent or up-to-date information available.

. . . I'm going to pass you the general· procedures for the re-entry, you'll get the 63-1 updates and the general details on your next pass....*The New York Times, June 8, 1965, p 22*

Update Pad: information on spacecraft attitudes, and other data, transmitted to the crew in standard format; e.g. manoeuvre update, navigation check, landmark tracking,

entry update, etc. *Adam Hopkins, The Sunday Times (London), July 13, 1969, p 13*

[noun use of *update, v.,* to bring up to date]

upmanship, *n.* the art or practice of scoring an advantage or being one-up on someone.

Nifty for cocktail parties and upmanship: While everyone discusses plot and character, you talk of plasticity of space, electricity of motion, and the director as creator. *Rollene W. Saal, "Pick of the Paperbacks," Review of "Cinema and Art" by Ralph Stephenson, Saturday Review, Dec. 17, 1966, p 37*

"Well, what's your price?" Morgan asked....John D. Jr. said, "I did not come here to sell. I understood you wished to buy." Honors evened in upmanship. *Charles Poore, The New York Times, May 25, 1965, p 39*

[short for *one-upmanship*. See the etymology under ONE-UP.]

upper, *n. U.S. Slang.* a stimulant drug. Also called UP. Compare DOWNER.

It was a glorious cruise, save for . . . one major misunderstanding in 1962 when Atlanta police charged him with being in the company of an excessive number of amphetamine tablets and assorted other "uppers"—a condition inspiring Jack Paar to fresh public tears and Brother Dave Gardner to the successful investment of $5,000 in attorney's fees. *Larry L. King, "Whatever Happened to Brother Dave?" Harper's, Sept. 1970, p 54*

uprate, *v.t.* to increase in rating, especially rating of power; upgrade; improve.

Missing power machines, in which only part of the power supplies and accelerating equipment are built at the first stage,...can be uprated comparatively cheaply. *Illustration legend, "Rethinking the 300 GeV Machine," Science Journal, Sept. 1970, p 60*

uptight, *adj. Slang.* **1** very uneasy or apprehensive; anxious.

I don't think that I'm in the position to discuss the pain of other writers. Individuals deal with it as they can. But I *do* say that sometimes you can get so *uptight* about your *disadvantages* that you ignore your advantages. *Ralph Ellison, quoted by James Alan McPherson, "Indivisible Man," The Atlantic, Dec. 1970, p 60*

2 nervous; tense; irritable.

I'm getting a little uptight, just about washing my hands, because I can't find the soap, which somebody has used and not put back in the soap dish, all of which is extremely irritating if you have a beautiful patient sitting in the examining room, naked inside her gown....*Donald Barthelme, "Sentence" (a story), The New Yorker, March 7, 1970, p 35*

When Mia Farrow left New York for India she was hassled and really uptight. *Paul Saltzman, Maclean's, June 1968, p 47*

3 strait-laced or conventional; stiff; formal.

"Nobody gives you a ride or takes you in for a night. I tell you the French people are—" "Uptight?" I offered. She nodded. *David Butwin, "Booked for Travel: The Gauloises Men," Saturday Review, Oct. 10, 1970, p 42*

In black with a white collar, he [the British actor Nicol Williamson] could be impersonating an uptight Calvinist parson. *Melvin Maddocks, "Theater: A Mod Hamlet," The Atlantic, Oct. 1969, p 132*

Who would have thought that an uptight institution like the august Oxford University Press would have done a thing like this? Here is a . . . spirited and spiritous piece of autobiography and served up as a book, a book by a genuine Oxford mandarin, an historical Fellow of Balliol. *Peter Laslett, "Oxonian Extraordinary," The Manchester Guardian Weekly, Aug. 28, 1969, p 18*

upward-mobile, *adj.* characterized by upward mobility.

Mrs. Johnson divides all Christmas cards into three groups: (1) reciprocals, (2) sent but not received and (3) received but not sent. . . . For a typical upward-mobile professional couple in their thirties or forties (such as the Johnsons) the three groups of cards may be about equal. *"Science and the Citizen," Scientific American, March 1971, p 48*

upward mobility, the ability or tendency to rise from a lower to a higher economic or social class.

His Jewish wedding supper was disastrous. . . . Surely people who have been hungry in their youth might be treated with a little more humanity, and even some affection, when they proudly put on a spread for their children. Peerce simply joined the ranks of the middle-class moviemakers who love peasants but consider it repulsive when middle-class people show the gusto of peasants. Upward mobility is an unfortunate drive in one who hopes to be an artist. *Pauline Kael, "The Current Cinema," Review of "Goodbye, Columbus," directed by Larry Peerce, The New Yorker, March 13, 1971, p 89*

upwelling, *n.* the rising of nutrient-laden waters from the ocean depths to the surface.

Once they [the rising ocean currents] reach the upper level of the ocean, where sunlight penetrates, they turn it into a garden of phytoplankton—the tiny floating plants that are the bottom link in the sea's food chain. Actually the "upwelling" occurs only in a few areas like the extremely rich fishery off Peru. *Time, Aug. 31, 1970, p 46*

It would obviously be worthwhile to stimulate upwelling artificially, not only because of the probability of high fish yields but also because the stable ecological communities that inhabit the natural areas of ocean upwelling are models of efficient food production for man, with none of the drawbacks—such as herbicides, pesticides, pollution and excessive human intervention—that such highly productive systems usually entail ashore. *Gifford B. Pinchot, "Marine Farming," Scientific American, Dec. 1970, p 19*

Thus the creation of an artificial upwelling has particular biological and economic attractions, in areas where the deep water is found close to the shore. *Paul Bienfang, "Taking the Pollution Out of Waste Heat," New Scientist and Science Journal, Aug. 26, 1971, p 456*

ur- (ur-), a prefix taken from German, meaning "original" or "earliest," used especially in music and the arts.

ur-instrument, *n.:* . . . the Purcell-Bach-Handel age is "in," and with it an exaggerated interest in the historical instruments of the period. Purists insist not only on the ur-text but on the ur-instruments as well . . . those amateur and misguided musicologists who insist upon the ur-performance of music and who proceed to "ur" the recorder into every historical period possible. *J. G. Mitchell, "They Shall Have Music: 'Drop Thy Pipe . . .'," The Atlantic, March 1964, p 176*

ur-performance, *n.:* The BBC . . . are offering the symphonies in urtext and (as far as may be) in ur-performance —that is, with original mistakes uncorrected (or original strokes of inspiration restored?), and with an orchestra of the size and proportions that might have been used in

original performances. *Hugo Cole, "The Arts: The Sound of Beethoven," The Manchester Guardian Weekly, April 18, 1970, p 20*

ur-racialism, *n.:* The Border Ballads trace the development of border separatism. If you will turn to page 314 of your *Oxford Book of Ballads,* you will fall upon a nugget of ur-racialism which, in its social, sexual and political implications might have wept from the pen of J. Baldwin. *Alan Coren, Punch, Aug. 18, 1965, p 227*

ur-tank, *n.:* Above is Leonardo da Vinci's design for an ur-tank, and left, a model made from his plans, illustration in *Leonardo da Vinci by Jay Williams. Picture legend, Punch, Nov. 9, 1966, p 718*

urtext, *n.:* This is the last word on Feuerfest, unless someone produces an urtext containing Strauss's own marginalia on the subject. *Saturday Review, Aug. 26, 1967, p 92*

urb (ərb), *n.* *U.S.* an urban or metropolitan area.

" . . . The City is obsolete. Ask the computer. It is to the urb what LSD is to the electronic yokel; that is, it ends all goals and objectives and points of view." *Marshall McLuhan, quoted by Mordecai Richler, "Books: Madison Avenue Guru," Review of "Counterblast" by Marshall McLuhan, The Manchester Guardian Weekly, June 20, 1970, p 18*

What is all this space, space, space? How do I get out of here? The urb has been Renewed by an Expert. *John Thompson, Harper's, May 1969, p 48*

The growth of American suburbia, fed by the yearning for a home of one's own, raises problems for urb and suburb alike. . . . *Herbert J. Gans, The New York Times Magazine, Jan. 7, 1968, p 25*

[abstracted from *urban* and *suburb*]

urban guerrilla, **1** a revolutionary who uses guerrilla tactics in the cities to spread terror and undermine the government.

The terrorist activity is worldwide, and most of it is carried out by a new type in the history of political warfare: the urban guerrilla. *Time, Nov. 2, 1970, p 19*

2 an organized band of urban guerrillas.

In Guatemala the peasant-based groups of Cesar Montes and Yon Sosa were bombed and cajoled out of the countryside in 1967 and have been operating ever since as an urban guerrilla, effective at kidnaping diplomats. . . . *Richard Gott, "Latin American Guerrillas," The Listener, Oct. 1, 1970, p 438*

urbanoid, *adj.* having the characteristics of a large city.

I use "kakotopia" [*kakos* = bad] as the opposite of "utopia," to describe a misplanned and ugly urbanoid place. *Lewis Mumford, "Reflections: The Megamachine," The New Yorker, Oct. 10, 1970, p 100*

urbanologist, *n.* a social scientist who specializes in the study of cities and their problems.

. . . they are the "Establishment" and "silk-stocking" suburban types who make their livings as "research directors, associate professors, social workers, educational consultants, urbanologists. . . ." *Fred H. Harris, "The Making of a Majority," Harper's, May 1970, p 49*

In another essay urbanologist Daniel Moynihan restates his now well-known conclusion that "the streets of the Negro slums contain the wreckage of a generation of good intentions on the part of the American liberals." *Donald Young, "The Problems That Beset Us," Review of "Republican Papers," edited by Melvin R. Laird, Saturday Review, Aug. 10, 1968, p 32*

urbanology, *n.* the study of cities and their problems.

The "urbanologist" aspires to be a student of the entire city, an ecumenist of the metropolis, whose concerns go beyond brick and mortar to budgets and laws, souls and sensibilities. Just as the word urbanology is a cross between Latin and Greek, the science—or is it an art?—is a mélange of many disciplines. *Time, July 28, 1967, p 11*

Levine believes the Center will play a crucial and dynamic role as an internal-change agent in the University itself, helping to bring together many existing talents within the University to provide an interdisciplinary approach to solving the problems of the nation's cities. "Urbanology," as some have called the field, has far more questions than answers today. *"Johns Hopkins Launches Urban Center," Johns Hopkins Journal, Dec. 1968, p 1*

urban renewal, a program for replacing slums and inadequate housing in a city, by either renovation or rebuilding.

The heart of downtown Denver has been torn out in the name of urban renewal, with one old-fashioned block of Larimer Street left to preserve its memory....*James Reston, The New York Times, Aug. 28, 1970, p 30*

Angry black teen-agers then led a charge across the Penn Central tracks into the fringe of the white business district. The litany of their grievances was reproachfully familiar: too little urban renewal, too few jobs, inadequate play areas, inadequate communication between black and white leaders. *Time, July 20, 1970, p 13*

Urban renewal amounted to slum clearance without concern for the interests of the residents, usually indigent, who originally lived in these areas. *Steven H. Leleiko, New York, in a Letter to the Editor, The New York Times, June 6, 1971, Sec. 8, p 13*

urban sprawl, the uncontrolled growth of a city over the countryside.

We see nineteenth-century urban sprawl as the trams reach out to Highgate....*"Books," Review of "Victorian and Edwardian London From Old Photographs," The New Yorker, May 23, 1970, p 140*

The automobile has brought another consequence that tends to be overlooked but is no less serious: by fostering "urban sprawl" it has in effect isolated much of the population. *William F. Hamilton II and Dana K. Nance, "Systems Analysis of Urban Transportation," Scientific American, July 1969, p 19*

As presently applied, property taxes promote urban decay and penalize improvements while simultaneously encouraging land speculation and the wasteful disorder known as urban sprawl. *Time, April 4, 1969, p 52*

ur·o·ki·nase (ˌyur ou'kɑiˌneis), *n.* a protein enzyme that dissolves blood clots.

...a new class of drugs is emerging with the ability to dissolve clots already formed—something the anticoagulants will not do. One of the most promising of these drugs is a substance called urokinase, found as a trace in human urine. *Harold M. Schmeck, Jr., The New York Times, Dec. 3, 1967, Sec. 4, p 7*

From this research has come a wealth of fundamental data and substances such as streptokinase and urokinase, with which the clot, once formed, may be dissolved, have recently been discovered. *Colin Roberts, "Thrombosis and How to Prevent It," New Scientist and Science Journal, Sept. 16, 1971, p 620*

[from *uro-* urine + *kinase* an enzyme that catalyzes inactive enzymes]

Utah effect, the increase in the number and energy of mu mesons within successively deeper levels of the earth's surface.

The record of more than 200,000 mu mesons in the last three years shows an anomaly, the so-called Utah effect. The proportion of mu mesons arriving from vertical directions is higher than it should be and rises as the depth below the earth's surface (and therefore the energy of the mu mesons) increases. *"The W Particle May Have Been Found," Science News, Aug. 21, 1971, p 121*

[so called from the discovery of this effect in underground experiments performed in a silver mine at Park City, Utah]

V

vac·ci·nee (ˌvæk sə'ni:), *n.* a person who has been vaccinated.

> ...it was of cardinal importance to show that the [rubella] virus does not spread from vaccinees to pregnant women.... *Donald N. Medearis, Jr., "Medicine: Pediatrics," 1970 Britannica Yearbook of Science and the Future, 1969, p 276*

V-agent, *n.* any of a class of extremely toxic nerve gases, including GB and VX.

> Today, as the world knows well, the V-agents that resulted from this British research and development programme, lie stockpiled in the US, partially in ready-to-fire munitions in quantities estimated at tens, if not hundreds, of thousands of tonnes. Thus are the grisly technical frontiers of chemical warfare pushed back.... *Robin Clarke, Science Journal, Dec. 1970, p 9*

> The Americans call the latest nerve gases V-agents. *Ian Low, New Scientist, Feb. 29, 1968, p 465*

val·i·no·my·cin (ˌvæl ə nou'mai sən), *n.* an antibiotic derived from soil bacteria that activates the movement of ions in cells.

> ...a Russian group...have used a battery of physical chemical techniques to discover the structure of the antibiotic valinomycin. *New Scientist, July 31, 1969, p 225*

> These antibiotics (the cyclic polypeptide valinomycin and the gramicidins are more familiar examples) act by allowing potassium ions, protons and other cations but generally not sodium ions, to move across cell membranes and, in particular, across the mitochondrial membrane.... *Nature, March 30, 1968, p 1209*

> There is no significant difference in permeability between the alkali metal ions, but by incorporating certain cyclic polypeptides (for example, Valinomycin) into the liposomes, they can be made permeable to K^+ and Rb^+ but not to Na^+ or Li^+. *Alec Bangham, New Scientist, Jan. 14, 1971, p 64*

[from *valine* an amino acid + *-mycin* a soil bacteria derivative, as in *actinomycin*]

Va·li·um ('vei li: əm), *n.* Also popularly spelled **valium.** the trade name of DIAZEPAM.

> His dose of Valium, to contain his agitation, was reduced. *Michael Crichton, "The High Cost of Cure," The Atlantic, March 1970, p 53*

> "There was some bad stuff on the news." I swallowed two yellow Valium and got into bed. "Sharon Tate and a lot of people in her house were killed. Weird stuff with ropes and hoods." *Frank Conroy, "Manson Wins!" Harper's, Nov. 1970, p 53*

> Federal officials said that vials of dexedrine, valium and compazine were found in her luggage when she arrived at Cleveland Hopkins International airport on a flight from Toronto. *The Times (London), Nov. 4, 1970, p 8*

value-added tax, a sales tax levied on a product in such a way that a manufacturer, wholesaler, retailer, etc., is taxed only for that part of the sales price which represents the value added at his particular stage of the production and distribution process. *Abbreviation:* VAT Also called ADDED-VALUE TAX.

> Nations that use indirect taxes, such as turnover or value-added taxes, can remit them on exports and impose them on imports.... *The New York Times, May 24, 1967, p 67*

> ...the point was made that the adoption of a form of value-added tax could provide a Tory Government with a useful export incentive. *David Wood, The Times (London), Feb. 2, 1970, p 1*

> In Belgium introduction of the value-added tax (VAT), due in January 1970, was deferred for 12 months, partly on the ground that such an increase in indirect taxation would aggravate inflation in an already overheated economy. *James G. Morrell, "Consumer Expenditures," Britannica Book of the Year 1971, p 225*

vanity surgery, plastic surgery to improve the appearance, as by face lifting, reshaping the nose, or removing fat from the abdomen.

> The deft use of vanity surgery, as the Brazilians call it, has provided women who flock in from all over the world with new faces, larger (or smaller) bosoms, slimmer hips and even bottoms sculpted into svelte contours more suitable for slacks. Vanity surgery is now as acceptable in Rio as bleach-blonde hair. One local television personality, Dercy Gonçalves, who has been thoroughly reshaped, is not in the least reluctant to discuss it. *Time, March 23, 1970, p 71*

va·rac·tor (və'ræk tər), *n.* a diode semiconductor in which the capacitance can be varied with the voltage. *Often used attributively.*

> The varactor—a special type of semiconductor diode that has a voltage-variable capacitance—serves the same purpose as the conventional mechanically variable capacitor in the tuning circuit. The use of a varactor eliminates complex mechanical linkages inside the tuner and makes remote control much simpler. *William Wollheim, "Recordings: Audio Equipment," The Americana Annual 1969, p 575*

> It has been possible in the past to make radar sets using transistor oscillators and varactor multiplier chains as the source of microwaves, but these systems are complex and expensive. *New Scientist, March 31, 1966, p 835*

[probably from *variable* cap*acitor*]

variable geometry, another name for SWING-WING. *Often used attributively.*

The Boeing Company, competing with Lockheed to build the American plane, uses a radically different approach—a "variable geometry" or "swing-wing" that can be set at three positions for slow, intermediate or supersonic speeds. *The New York Times, Nov. 20, 1966, Sec. 12, p 13*

The French variable geometry aircraft, the Mirage G, made its first flight today at the Melun-Villaroche military airfield near Paris. *The Times (London), Oct. 19, 1967, p 1*

variable-sweep wing, another name for SWING-WING.

The X-5 was the first aircraft to incorporate variable-sweep wings, a feature now part of the F-111 fighter and Boeing's supersonic transport. *Science News, Feb. 24, 1968, p 188*

va·room (və'ru:m), *v.i.* U.S. to travel or take off with a roar, as that made by the motor of a racing car. See also VROOM.

The way the show tells it, there are these four really neat-looking southern-California guys whose job it is to raise the very Ned with boring old Rommel's boring supply lines and how they do it is to go varooming all over the desert in a couple of jeeps in search of the thousands of comical Germans.... *Michael J. Arlen, "The Air: Perspectives," The New Yorker, Jan. 21, 1967, p 76*

In the première, Parks laconically brought an autistic child to his senses in a scenic Wyoming camp for disturbed children and then varoomed off, presumably toward a less tearjerking episode. *"Television," Review of "Then Came Bronson," Time, Sept. 26, 1969, p 38*

[imitative of the roaring sound]

vas·o·ac·tive (,væs ou'æk tiv), *adj.* acting on the blood vessels, as by constricting or dilating them.

Complement seems to have three functions: it makes bacterial cells adhere to phagocytes; it releases vaso-active substances, which may help to localize antigen/antibody complexes; and, thirdly, it kills cells directly by making lesions in cell membranes. *Bernard Dixon, "Pooling Theories on Blood," Science Journal, May 1968, p 40*

A vasoactive peptide, perhaps responsible for the local swellings, has been isolated from plasma from [angioneurotic edema] patients during attacks.... *Chester A. Alper, "Complement, Serum," McGraw-Hill Yearbook of Science and Technology 1971, p 156*

[from *vaso-* vessel, blood vessel + *active*]

VAT, abbreviation of VALUE-ADDED TAX.

The Shadow Cabinet was ... unable to decide whether a VAT (excluding food) would be more satisfactory than a combination of purchase tax and excise duties on goods which might come under the new tax. *Francis Boyd, The Manchester Guardian Weekly, Feb. 7, 1970, p 9*

The remaining 700m will come from vat, which the state will not be retaining at all this year. *Patrick Brogan; "M. Giscard's £166m Boost to Economy," The Times (London), Jan. 13, 1972, p 15*

The Belgian government may well have noted the experience of the Netherlands, where introduction of the VAT in 1969 so accentuated inflationary pressure that the retail price index rose by 7%, necessitating imposition of a price freeze by the government that had very limited success in curbing wage demands. *James G. Morrell, "Consumer Expenditures," Britannica Book of the Year 1971, p 225*

VC, abbreviation of *Vietcong* (the pro-Communist guerrilla force in South Vietnam).

The VC had recently captured two Americans, a captain and a sergeant, and had committed appalling atrocities against them, which was unusual because in the past atrocities had been used regularly against the South Vietnamese, but not against the Americans. *David Halberstam, "The Programming of Robert McNamara," Harper's, Feb. 1971, p 64*

...a helicopter equipped with loudspeakers began broadcasting this message:

"Attention people of Bensuc! You are surrounded by Republic of South Vietnam and allied forces. Do not run away or you will be shot as V.C. Stay in your homes and wait for further instructions from the air and on the ground. You will not be hurt if you follow instructions." *The New York Times, Jan. 11, 1967, p 3*

vector, *v.t.* to carry or direct toward a particular point or on a particular course.

Decades ago Wegener proposed that the drift of the continents was vectored by forces he termed *Westwanderung* (westward drift) and *Polarfluchtkraft* (flight from the poles). Although real, these forces are minuscule and not likely to be the underlying cause of drift. *Robert S. Dietz and John C. Holden, "The Breakup of Pangaea," Scientific American, Oct. 1970, p 41*

[from Latin *vector* carrier, but influenced in meaning by various modern technical uses of the noun]

vector meson, any of a class of elementary particles with masses greater than 1200 million electron volts, including the omega, phi, and rho mesons.

There is a class of unstable particles, the neutral vector mesons, whose members resemble photons in many ways, with two important exceptions: they have mass and they exhibit the strong force. The most prominent is the rho meson, which has a mass equivalent to about 750 MeV. (The mass of the proton is equivalent to 939 MeV.) Rho mesons can be created as real particles in the laboratory, and their decay products can be detected. *Henry W. Kendall and Wolfgang K. H. Panofsky, "The Structure of the Proton and the Neutron," Scientific American, June 1971, p 72*

Photons are carriers of the electromagnetic force, yet when they strike nuclei, they behave like vector mesons, carriers of the strong nuclear force. *Science News, Feb. 7, 1970, p 151*

The discovery of vector mesons (ρ-mesons, ω-mesons) has been essential for understanding nuclear forces and for interpreting nuclear spectra. *Science, July 5, 1968, p 12*

ve·du·tis·ta (,ve du:'tis tə), *n.; pl.* **ve·du·tis·ti** (,ve du:'tis ti:). an artist who paints or draws panoramic views of places, usually towns and cities.

Another school which has risen dramatically in popular esteem in recent years is that of the Venetian vedutisti of the eighteenth century. *Geraldine Keen, The Times (London), May 9, 1970, p 19*

...an exhibition of drawings by an eighteenth-century Florentine named Giuseppe Zocchi, who rendered the world around him exactly as he saw it. Zocchi was a *vedutista*, or depicter of views, and the eighteenth century was a time of viewmaking. *"The Talk of the Town: Views," The New Yorker, May 18, 1968, p 32*

[from Italian, from *veduta* a painting or drawing of a place, (literally) a view + *-ista* -ist]

vee·na ('vi: nə), *n.* an ancient stringed instrument of India. See the first quotation for details.

"The veena is associated with the Goddess Saraswati,"

he said. "It's the oldest of the Indian instruments — a fretted stringed instrument made of rosewood or ebony and like that, with a hemispheric resonator at the bottom and another, smaller one, a seasoned gourd, near the top of a long neck." *"The Talk of the Town," The New Yorker, March 2, 1968, p 30*

Ravi Shankar, master of the sitar (a more elaborate successor of the veena) has already played there. *The Times (London), June 9, 1970, p 12*

[from Sanskrit *vīnā*]

▶ *Veena* appears to be the only current spelling of this word. The spelling *vina* is shown in the *OED* as having been used in the 1800's. See also the note under SARANGI.

vegetable, *n.* a person who is like a vegetable; a lifeless, inert creature.

Shall we cure all the common and known diseases and thereby condemn each and every citizen to senescence and a living death as vegetables? *Eugene Garfield, New Scientist, June 18, 1970, p 590*

Details of the torture inflicted on Basque nationalists imprisoned in Spain ... have reached Britain in a letter smuggled from a prison in Cadiz ... it describes, particularly the mental deprivations intended to turn intelligent men into vegetables.... *Patrick Keatley, "'Mental Torture' for Basques," The Manchester Guardian Weekly, Dec. 26, 1970, p 4*

Then you had a motorcycle accident.... There were the usual morbid rumors that you were permanently disfigured or that you had become a vegetable. *Richard R. Lingeman, "Bob Dylan, I'm Writing to You," The New York Times, June 25, 1971, p 32*

vegetablize, *v.i.* to be or live like a vegetable; lead a monotonous existence; vegetate.

She doesn't want children: "I think I'm a bit frightened by the whole childbearing thing and the effect I've seen it have on my friends — sort of vegetablizing while it's going on." *Ruth Brandon, The Times (London), July 20, 1970, p 5*

▶ This verb was used in the 1800's in the transitive form as a technical term meaning to convert to a vegetable substance.

veiling luminance, the dissipation of light by water.

When one is driving in a fog at night, the headlights seem unable to penetrate the fog because so much of their light is scattered back to the eye by tiny droplets of water. The same phenomenon, known as veiling luminance, makes it difficult to use artificial light to see under water. One can now overcome veiling luminance to a remarkable extent with a stratagem that electronically manipulates pulses of laser light. *"Science and the Citizen: Chopped Pulses," Scientific American, Dec. 1970, p 41*

Vel·cro ('vel krou), *n.* Also popularly spelled **velcro**. a trade name for a nylon fabric with a tiny hook on each fiber that adheres easily to other cloth surfaces, especially with deep or loose pile.

The important foul-weather outfit has a new advantage this year. Velcro has been added. All openings (pockets and zippers) are doubly protected with this peelable, secure closing. *Helen Nichols, The New York Times, Feb. 9, 1968, p 31*

They also considered covering both the floor and the soles of the shoes with Velcro, the material that clings to

itself by microscopic hooks in its fibres, but since Velcro, which holds very well against any vertical pull, gives way when it is peeled sidewise, they found that an astronaut in Velcro shoes would come unhooked if he leaned over. *"The Talk of the Town," The New Yorker, Feb. 27, 1971, p 33*

The proofed poplin coat has a zip-up front for cold weather wear; a quick-fasten velcro strip for brief sorties to feed the meter or dive into a restaurant. *Suzy Menkies, The Times (London), Feb. 23, 1968, p 12*

ven·dange (vã'dãʒ), *n. French.* the harvesting of grapes; vintage.

France was preparing that weekend for the most sacred rite of autumn, the *vendange* or grape harvest. By the train station in Nîmes, crowds of arriving Spaniards lounged and dozed, waiting to be fetched to vineyards in the region to take up the fortnight's labors. *David Butwin, Saturday Review, Oct. 10, 1970, p 43*

"The grapes are bursting on the vines ... a fantastic year for the Rhône Valley wines, you must come for the *vendange*," Monsieur Verdeau wrote with unaccustomed verve.... *Mary Roblee Henry, "6000 Bottles of Wine," The Atlantic, May 1969, p 69*

verbal, *n.* a verbal confession introduced as evidence at a trial.

... in criminal cases, upwards of three quarters of convictions secured at trial are the result of confessions or "verbals," alleged admissions by the defendant at time of arrest, put in evidence by the police. Many barristers believe that verbals are all too often invented by the police. *Horace Judson, "The British Constitution," The Atlantic, Feb. 1970, p 22*

Unkind policemen, accused for the umpteenth time of "planting" vital evidence or inventing "verbals" — false oral confessions put into an accused man's mouth — have been known to call defence lawyers' benches: "Cowards' castle." *Fenton Bresler, "Do You Solemnly Swear?" Punch, Nov. 5, 1969, p 765*

ver·kramp·te (fər'kra:mp tə), *n.* the name given in South Africa to a member of the extreme right-wing faction of the National Party, which favors rigid policies toward black Africans. *Often used attributively.*

... Vorster defended his 'outward-looking' foreign policy, which was unpopular among the *verkramptes*, saying that establishing diplomatic relations with neighbouring African-led States made no difference to the policy of separate development. *The Annual Register of World Events in 1968 (1969), p 318*

After Vorster dropped him from the Cabinet in 1968, Hertzog became leader of South Africa's *verkramptes* (narrow-minded ones), in opposition to Vorster's *verligtes* (enlightened ones). *Time, Oct. 24, 1969, p 38*

[from Afrikaans, literally, cramped (one)]

ver·lig·te (fər'lix tə), *n.* the name given in South Africa to a member of the liberal faction of the National Party, which favors moderate policies toward black Africans. *Often used attributively.*

If the *verkramptes* of Louis Stoffberg and Dr Herzog win the day, against Mr Vorster's *verligtes* and their good neighbour policy towards black Africa, it will be a useful gain for Peking. *Patrick Keatley, The Manchester Guardian Weekly, July 24, 1969, p 14*

The campaign is being fought largely in the press and, apparently, behind the scenes in Afrikaner political circles as a further manifestation of the "verkrampte" (reactionary) versus "verligte" (enlightened) factions in the ruling Nationalist Party. *The Times (London), Aug. 5, 1968, p 4*

[from Afrikaans, literally, enlightened (one)]

vernier rocket, a small auxiliary rocket engine used for minute adjustments in velocity or trajectory, as before a spacecraft soft-lands or docks.

On Jan. 9, 1968, following a 66-hour flight, a large retrorocket and three smaller vernier rockets slowed Surveyor VII from 6,000 to 3 mph. *William J. Cromie, "Exploring the Moon by Proxy," The World Book Science Annual 1968, p 42*

[from *vernier* a scale or device used for making fine adjustments in a mechanism or equipment (named after French mathematician *Vernier*, 1580-1637)]

ver·ti·port ('vər tə,pɔrt), *n.* a landing and takeoff area for VTOL aircraft. Also called VTOLPORT.

The major part of the Southampton team's survey... has been concerned with possible sites for 'vertiports' in or near the city centres of these candidate towns. *Angela Croome, Science Journal, March 1970, p 6*

Research and development costs, of which the Government would find half, would be in excess of £200m., while a "vertiport" in the capital could cost a further £50m. *Arthur Reed, The Times (London), Feb. 9, 1970, p 18*

[from *verti*cal takeoff and landing + air*port*]

vex·il·lol·o·gy (,vek sə'lal ə dʒi:), *n.* the study of flags.

Vexillology is not normally a very vexed subject. It concerns the design, making and history of flags. *Daily Telegraph (London), Nov. 19, 1971, p 13*

[from Latin *vexillum* a flag or banner + English *-ology* study of]

vibes, *n.pl. Slang.* short for VIBRATIONS.

"The vibes were bad," he said affably. "On Friday night, they were beautiful. You couldn't walk twenty-five feet up on the hill without someone smiling at you. But things began going bad yesterday afternoon." *Whitney Balliett, "Newport Notes," The New Yorker, July 17, 1971, p 80*

"We're not getting the right vibes," I said. *Patrick Campbell, The Sunday Times (London), Oct. 1, 1967, p 10*

► *Vibes* is also the short form of *vibraphone,* a percussion instrument.

vibrations, *n.pl. Slang.* a feeling or sense of what others are thinking (supposedly from vibrations emanating from their minds).

There is also the thought that Lindsay or Gardner might run as a Democrat, leading the moderate wing of the Republican Party into the Democratic camp. The vibrations out of New York are that Lindsay is quite interested in these possibilities. *Elizabeth B. Drew, "The White House Hard Hats," The Atlantic, Oct. 1970, p 56*

Vibration Syndrome, another name for RAYNAUD'S PHENOMENON.

Known as "Dead Hand" or "White Fingers" — and most recently as Vibration Syndrome — Raynaud's Phenomenon produces the same numbness and pain as a normal hand which is exposed to extreme cold for long periods but it occurs after only brief exposure to mild cold and takes much longer to overcome. *Tony Geraghty, The Sunday Times (London), March 23, 1969, p 5*

vi·bron·ic (vai'bran ik), *adj.* of or involving electronic vibrations.

One interesting suggestion for phonon-terminated lasers is the possibility of continuously tuning the laser frequency over the broad vibronic sideband. *Leo F. Johnson, "Laser: Crystal Lasers," McGraw-Hill Yearbook of Science and Technology 1967, p 210*

victimologist, *n.* a specialist in victimology.

There is less consensus about the role of the victim in rape cases. Some victimologists contend that rape victims invite attack. But Amir believes that fewer than 20% of rapes are precipitated by the woman's being "negligent or reckless or seductive." *"Behavior: Is the Victim Guilty?" Time, July 5, 1971, p 46*

victimology, *n.* the study of victims and their roles in the crimes committed against them.

For the first time in the U.S., three courses in victimology are being offered, one at the University of California, the others at Northeastern University and at Boston University Law School. *"Behavior: Is the Victim Guilty?" Time, July 5, 1971, p 46*

"All this stuff about motivation and victimology, I don't follow it," he said. *The Sunday Times (London), Sept. 11, 1966, p 7*

Victor Charlie, *U.S. Military Slang.* **1** a Vietcong guerrilla.

Nobody can hear Westmoreland talk about Vietnam with the military cliché of "real estate," or hear his men say they have to get them one "Victor Charlie," without being aware that the American killer-boy scout is one of the more brutal dangers to be unleashed on this sad, sad world. *Jack Ludwig, Saturday Night (Canada), Aug. 1968, p 15*

2 the Vietcong.

He asked the young man where he had acquired all this erudition, and was told about being shot out of a helicopter by Victor Charlie and about relieving eight months of hospital tedium by reading science. *Richard H. Rovere, "Letter from Washington," The New Yorker, June 18, 1966, p 135*

Also shortened to CHARLIE.

[from *Victor Charlie,* the communications code name for *VC,* abbreviation of *Vietcong*]

video cartridge or **video cassette,** a cartridge or cassette of videotape used in cassette television.

If you want live television you press one button; if you want a fresh daily newspaper printed right in your home, you will press another. The video cartridge, or cassette, will transform television by the mid-1970's, and for that matter phonographs and records, as we know them, may disappear because in this home electronic center anybody can bring to heel virtually anything he wants at any hour of the night or day in the line of amusement or information, by sight, sound, or both — and in color, at that. *Richard L. Tobin, Saturday Review, Oct. 10, 1970, p 61*

Nineteen seventy one is to be the first year of the video-cassette industry. *Timothy Johnson, New Scientist and Science Journal, May 6, 1971, p 328*

If all the promises and forecasts made for the video-cassette, as it is generally known, were to be fulfilled it could revolutionize public habits in the entertainment field. *Chris Dunkley, The Times (London), Sept. 26, 1970, p 12*

videodisc, *n.* Also spelled **video disc.** a disc for recording sounds and images for use in television sets in the same way video cartridges are used.

Thin flexible video discs which can be played through an ordinary domestic TV set have been developed.... The necessary reproduction equipment is far cheaper than that required for the various cassette systems more generally favoured at present. *Science Journal, Oct. 1970, p 16*

videoize, *v.t.* to convert for use on television.

Young copywriters who had been yanked away from the preparation of cigarette ads for the magazines rushed around talking about... techniques for "videoizing" the usual advertising forms. *Thomas Whiteside, "Annals of Advertising," The New Yorker, Dec. 19, 1970, p 88*

videophone, *n.* a telephone combined with a television camera and screen so people talking on the telephone can see each other. Also called PICTURE-PHONE, VIDEOTELEPHONE, and VIEWPHONE.

On the personal communication side, apart from videophones and radiotelephones small enough to be carried in the pocket, he sees the main trend as being towards far greater communication between the ordinary person and computers of all kinds. *Bryan Silcock, The Sunday Times (London), Sept. 24, 1967, p 2*

One of the most talked-about of these gadgets is the video-phone,... but experts in the industry are cool to the video-phone. "It costs a lot and doesn't add much to communications," says Gordon Thompson, a researcher and sort of one-man think-tank at the Northern Electric Company of Canada. *Walter Stewart, Maclean's, Dec. 1968, p 19*

videoplayer, *n.* a television set that will replay programs recorded on videotape and inserted into it.

In October 1969, Sony Corporation announced it would market a videoplayer that uses cassettes similar to those used in tape recorders. An adapter will permit home recording in black and white or color on the cassettes. *"Review of the Year: Transportation and Communication," Encyclopedia Science Supplement (Grolier) 1970, p 358*

videotelephone, *n.* another name for VIDEOPHONE.

You need not leave home from one day to another, and you will have your wife for company because she can browse through the shops on her screen, order the goods on her keyboard, and see Mother on videotelephone. *R. Ian Hart, "Future Developments in Telecommunications," New Scientist and Science Journal, Dec. 23, 1971, p 232*

We'll communicate by video-telephones without having to go and see people. *Hunter Davies, The Sunday Times (London), Aug. 13, 1967, p 17*

Viet (vyet), *U.S.* —*n.* a Vietnamese.

'No-one' said the GI 'sees the Viets as real people'. *Henry Brandon, The Sunday Times (London), Nov. 23, 1969, p 13*

They were Viets, all 15 of them ... asking me the question I feared most: "My? My? My?" (American? American? American?). *Robert Anson, Time, Sept. 7, 1970, p 18*

—*adj.* Vietnamese.

Neither the leaders nor the public expressed any illusions about freedom in North Viet Nam, and both agreed that the Hanoi government commands more loyalty from its citizens than the Saigon regime. Said Ralph Comfortes of Los Angeles: "We are supporting a government that has no support from the Buddhists. We don't have the support of the Viet peasant." *"No Illusions About Saigon," Time, Oct. 31, 1969, p 21*

Vietnamization, *n.* **1** the act or process of Vietnamizing.

South Vietnamese combat deaths rose as those of the U.S. forces dropped, the consequence of the Vietnamization of the war. *Richard Butwell, "Vietnam War," The Americana Annual 1970, p 739*

Last week, in a further Vietnamization of the war, the last of the bases that made up the McNamara line were turned over to the South Vietnamese army (ARVN). *"Border Recessional: The Return of Con Thien," Time, July 19, 1971, p 19*

2 the policy of a gradual withdrawal of American combat forces from Vietnam and their replacement by Vietnamese troops, as a means of ending American military involvement in Vietnam.

Saigon no more believes in Vietnamization than Moscow believes in socialism. Therefore Ni K'e-hsun is locked in. Vietnamization will not take place. *General Chu of the People's Liberation Army, quoted by Ross Terrill, "The Inscrutable West," The Atlantic, Aug. 1970, p 69*

The first adjustment involved the gradual passage of the military burden from American troops to the forces of the Saigon government—Vietnamization. *Joseph Kraft, "In Search of Kissinger," Harper's, Jan. 1971, p 56*

Vietnamize, *v.t.* to place under Vietnamese control or authority; specifically, to transfer gradually the conduct of (the Vietnam war) to the Vietnamese by a phased withdrawal of American combat forces and their replacement by Vietnamese troops.

Nixon chose to assume the operational responsibility for at least a limited de-escalation... of the war, in which he seems to have lost faith and which he is in the process of "Vietnamizing" or "de-Americanizing." *Richard H. Rovere, "Letter from Washington," The New Yorker, Jan. 17, 1970, p 61*

The war is being Vietnamized, which means that American troops are leaving gradually and the local people will carry out our commitments in Vietnam, Laos, Cambodia, Thailand.... *Anthony Lewis, The New York Times, Oct. 24, 1970, p 31*

Vietnik, *n. Slang.* a person who opposes or demonstrates against U.S. involvement in the war in Vietnam. Compare PEACENIK.

I would rather trust the decisions of the elected rulers of 200 million Americans and 10 million Australians than the noisy utterances of irresponsible Vietniks, one-track intelligentsia and even well-intentioned editors. *Mike Janzen, Maclean's, Oct. 15, 1966, p 64*

To get the cold shoulder, hard baton, or padded cell treatment meted out to Vietniks in the US or underground writers in the Soviet Union, an English liberal now has to do something pretty outrageous, like sacking an embassy. *Christopher Driver, The Manchester Guardian Weekly, Jan. 25, 1968, p 5*

[from *Vietnam* + *-nik*]

viewphone, *n.* another name for VIDEOPHONE.

In association with the "viewphone", access could be gained, on demand, to a wide range of information sources for local visual display on the customer's screen. *Albert Hare, New Scientist, July 16, 1970, p 22*

villagization, *n.* (in parts of Africa and Asia) the placement of land under the control of villages.

But the nomadic use of the remaining area needs study; "villagization" in the Kenya sense is unlikely to be the answer. *Roy Lewis, The Times (London), March 31, 1967, p 13*

...the majority of land-owners in more than 140,000 Indian villages have declared themselves in favour of Gramadan (gift of village), a more radical concept which involves the principle of villagisation (as distinct from nationalisation) of land. *Geoffrey Ostergaard, Birmingham, England, in a Letter to the Editor, The Manchester Guardian Weekly, Aug. 22, 1970, p 2*

-ville (-vil), a chiefly U.S. slang suffix used to form nouns (and sometimes adjectives) denoting a state or condition characterizing a place, person, or thing. Typically an *-s* is added to the root form together with *-ville*. The suffix often carries with it the suggestion of smallness, backwardness, dullness, etc. The place name suffix is not entirely unknown in Great Britain (e.g. Perkinsville in County Durham, England), but it is rare. The following is a selection of recent uses of *-ville*:

doomsville, *n.*: The only sure-fire attractions? "Country-and-western music. If you brought Barbra Streisand here, it would be doomsville." *Hal Tennant, Maclean's, March 1968, p 19*

for keepsville: Or, as London sales chief Roy Kirkdorfer puts it, "When you sign on with Bernie, it's for keepsville." *The Sunday Times (London), June 5, 1966, p 7*

freaksville, *adj.*...the film ["Portrait of Jason"] is a good deal more than an unusually frank interview with a homosexual who, at one point, exults: "I'm bona fide freaksville!" *Vincent Canby, The New York Times, Sept. 30, 1967, p 26*

Nowheresville, *n.*: Sitting contentedly on the banks of the Illinois River in the very heartland of America, Peoria has for years been the butt of jokes, the gagman's tag for Nowheresville. *Time, Oct. 21, 1966, p 26*

weirdsville, *n.*: Yorkville Village does measure up to the East Village in New York or Haight Ashbury in San Francisco. It's an area that reads hippie weirdsville to the old folks, refuge to runaway teenyboppers and a place to play for rock musicians. *Jack Batten, Maclean's, Feb. 1968, p 39*

See also the main entries DRAGSVILLE, DULLSVILLE, ENDSVILLE, and SQUARESVILLE.

vin·blas·tine (vin'blæs,ti:n), *n.* an alkaloid derivative of the red periwinkle of Madagascar, used in the treatment of leukemia and lymphoma.

Plant derivatives, such as vincristine and vinblastine, kill cells at or near mitosis. *Barbara J. Culliton, Science News, Dec. 21, 1968, p 627*

...actinomycin D and vinblastine...induce temporary remissions in certain types of cancer.... *William Spector, "Medicine," 1971 Britannica Yearbook of Science and the Future, 1970, p 224*

[from *Vinca rosea* (the Latin name of the red periwinkle) + leuko*blast* a budding white blood cell + *-ine* (chemical suffix)]

vin·ca·leu·ko·blas·tine (,viŋ kə,lu: kou'blæs,ti:n), *n.* another name for VINBLASTINE.

Of the alkaloids isolated some eight years ago from the periwinkle plant (*Vinca*), experience has shown that two, vincristine and vincaleukoblastine, have therapeutic value. Vincristine, combined with steroids, is proving useful in treating acute leukemia of children.... Vincaleukoblastine is most useful in the treatment of conditions like Hodgkin's disease. *Martin C. G. Israëls, "Medicine: Hematology," Britannica Book of the Year 1969, p 498*

vin·i·fy ('vin ə,fai), *v.t.* to make wine from; to convert the juice of (grapes, etc.) into wine by fermentation.

They [Californians] like to drink wine, and despise New York State winemakers for trying to vinify table grapes.... *Christopher Driver, "Sea Food and Wine from the West Coast," The Manchester Guardian Weekly, July 10, 1969, p 19*

[from Latin *vīnum* wine + English *-ify*, as in *fructify, acidify*, etc.]

vi·rid·i·an (və'rid i: ən), *adj.* green; verdant.

...I was uneasy, oppressed by the viridian hills flecked with black, unmoving cattle. *Ted Walker, "Estrangement," The New Yorker, June 13, 1970, p 30*

...a geometrical forest scene drawn in vigorous triangular forms of yellow ochre, Venetian red and black, and it is inhabited by three viridian nudes who are clearly related to Cézanne's 'Bathers'. *Quentin Bell, "The Omega Revisited," The Listener, Jan. 30, 1964, p 200*

[from Latin *viridis* green + English *-ian*]

vi·ri·on ('vai ri:,ɑn), *n.* a virus particle consisting of RNA enclosed in a protein shell and capable of controlling the form of a virus in replication.

The central dogma of molecular biology, that DNA makes RNA which, in turn makes protein, has been severely shaken by the results of some experiments.... These indicate that in certain tumour-producing viruses the first two steps may be reversed and it is RNA from the virus chromosome or virion which makes DNA. *Science Journal, Sept. 1970, p 19*

We decided...to fractionate a number of virions, or virus particles, and to try to find a component or components responsible for inducing interferon. *Maurice R. Hilleman and Alfred A. Tytell, "The Induction of Interferon," Scientific American, July 1971, p 28*

vi·sa·giste (vi: za'ʒi:st), *n.* an expert in applying facial cosmetics; a makeup artist.

The crop-eared look is a natural for a new hair style and just imagine what the visagistes will be able to do recreating a historical Cromwell makeup, warts and all. *Prudence Glynn, The Times (London), May 5, 1970, p 9*

[from French, from *visage* face, visage + *-iste* -ist]

vision-mix, *v.i.* to combine film shots in motion pictures or camera views in television.

He [Mike Leckebusch, a television director in Germany] also vision mixes himself. In England and elsewhere it is the practice to employ vision mixers, the director shouting the appropriate shot numbers to him. *Michael Wale, The Times (London), Aug. 19, 1970, p 11*

As a director, I [Rollo Gamble, a BBC television director] prefer light entertainment. I believe it really can be an art form, as *television*. It's great fun, vision-mixing. You have cameramen roaming around the studio, ad libbing shots within an overall plan, and you see something you like on the monitors and cut from one to another. *Patrick Skene Catling, "Television," Punch, Oct. 6, 1965, p 508*

visual instrument, an electronic keyboard instrument for producing patterns of different colors on a screen, played by itself or as an accompaniment to music.

Mr. [Bob] Siegel was giving the first public performance of the Mosaicon, which is a visual instrument he recently invented. Now, a visual instrument is just like a musical instrument except that it emits colors instead of sounds. *"The Talk of the Town: The Mosaicon," The New Yorker, Sept. 12, 1970, p 32*

visual pollution, defacement, such as of natural surroundings by billboards, high buildings, urban blight, etc., or of posters by graffiti.

The chief weapon in the arsenal of those fighting visual pollution here is a law that restricts the type, size, number and placement of roadside advertising signs. *Bayard Webster, "Lake George Winning Fight on Visual Pollution," The New York Times, June 30, 1971, p 43*

vital statistics, a woman's bust, waist, and hip measurements.

His wife's vital statistics [in the metric system] will turn out to be 92-61-92 instead of 36-24-36. *David Hamilton, New Scientist, April 30, 1970, p 247*

We may be freed from concern with cleavages, bras, "falsies," vital statistics. Our children will not have our society's unhealthy pre-occupation with breasts forced on their attention.... *Michael J. G. Stanford, The Manchester Guardian Weekly, July 2, 1964, p 16*

► This is a facetious application of the term for birth, death, marriage, and similar statistics.

voice-over, *n.* the voice of a narrator, commentator, or announcer speaking off screen in a motion-picture film, television commercial, etc. *Often used attributively.*

The voiceover during the 60-second spot has been saying right along: "Cigarette smoke contains some interesting elements: carbon monoxide, formaldehyde, benzopyrene, hydrogen cyanide." *Time, Nov. 15, 1968, p 58*

One hears [Henry] Miller's prose as one reads him.... But when that same prose is used in the film as a voice-over narration, it doesn't have the drive of common speech, it has the static fake poetry of cultivated literary language. *Pauline Kael, "The Current Cinema," Review of Henry Miller's "Tropic of Cancer," The New Yorker, March 7, 1970, p 97*

—*adv.* in a voice-over; speaking without being seen.

More cheers. A band started playing. Mr. Nixon stepped away from the ramp. "And now Mr. Nixon is plunging into the crowd," Mike Wallace said, voice-over. *"The Talk of the Town," The New Yorker, Nov. 16, 1968, p 51*

...it's all done voice-over, except for the flashbacks before the war. *Penelope Gilliatt, "The Current Cinema: Tell Me When I Can Look," The New Yorker, Aug. 7, 1971, p 65*

voiceprint, *n.* a graph of the patterns of pitch, juncture, etc., in a person's speech, produced on a sound spectrograph and regarded by some as sufficiently distinctive to be used for the purpose of individual identification.

...the assumed analogy between fingerprints and voiceprints is false: finding a similarity between fingerprints involves the objective study of anatomical evidence but finding a similarity between voiceprints is a matter of subjective judgment on the observer's part. *"Science and the Citizen: Trial by Voiceprint," Scientific American, Dec. 1969, p 54*

...unless the protagonists of voiceprints can come up with a far more rigorous proof of the technique's validity than they have provided hitherto, its use in courts of law is more likely to hinder the course of justice than aid it. *New Scientist, April 30, 1970, p 216*

voiceprinter, *n.* an instrument for producing voice-prints.

Another major protagonist [of *The First Circle*, a novel by Aleksandr Solzhenitsyn] is Lev Rubin, the philologist who develops the voiceprinter. *Time, Sept. 27, 1968, p 26*

voiceprinting, *n.* the method of identification based on voiceprints.

One of the most interesting examples involved the identification of Nasser and Hussein as the speakers in a radio conversation conspiring to blame the United States and Great Britain for the Arab failure in the Middle East war, a use of voiceprinting which was widely publicized. *Cecil R. Frost, "Voiceprints and Speaker Identification in Police Applications," Encyclopedia Science Supplement (Grolier) 1968, p 352*

Voiceprinting, a technique developed by Dr. Lawrence G. Kersta, helped to convict Edward King (right) of arson. *Illustration legend, "Electronics," 1968 Collier's Encyclopedia Year Book, p 236*

For Lev Rubin [a central character of *The First Circle*, a novel by Aleksandr Solzhenitsyn], a linguist, the fascination of the job, as well as his continuing belief in communism, disposes of any scruples he might have in a similar situation. He is offered the chance of trying out his "voice printing" technique to identify an unknown caller, and he seizes this opportunity with enthusiasm. *Sara White, New Scientist, Dec. 10, 1970, p 450*

volunteer army, an army of volunteer military personnel.

...there remains a serious question as to whether a volunteer Army would attract enough manpower to back up the U.S.'s worldwide commitments. *Time, Oct. 26, 1970, p 26*

vo·lup·té (vɔ: lYp'tei), *n. French.* voluptuousness.

The evils of *volupté*, vice, debauchery, prurience, and excess stood always with the enemy of revolution, no matter what his circumstances—were he a boorish villager or a depraved aristocrat. *Leopold Tyrmand, "Reflections: Notebook of a Dilettante," The New Yorker, Nov. 9, 1968, p 68*

She had this flesh, these sex attractions and talents—*volupté*, she had. *Saul Bellow, "Mr. Sammler's Planet," The Atlantic, Nov. 1969, p 143*

vox pop, *British Slang.* an opinion on some current topic given by a person who is stopped in the street and questioned by a television or radio reporter.

A few days ago, a BBC camera crew went round Washington collecting vox pops—close-ups of men in the street saying pithily what they think of things. *Gerald Priestland, The Listener, Feb. 8, 1968, p 164*

"You find a different class of people in England", we are assured by one vox pop. *Julian Critchley, The Times (London), Nov. 20, 1968, p 9*

[shortened from Latin *vōx populi* the voice of the people, the expressed general opinion (attested in the *OED* since about 1550). "The Latin maxim *Vox Populi vox Dei* 'the voice of the people is the voice of God', is frequently cited or alluded to in English works from the 15th cent. onwards" *(OED)*.]

vroom (və'ru:m), *n. U.S.* the roaring sound of a racing-car or motorcycle engine. See also VAROOM.

The trooper lies on his back, drinking a Pepsi-Cola and reading *Hot Rod* magazine, hearing the vroom-vroom of engines, seeing the open highway in the mind's eye. *Ward Just, "Soldiers," The Atlantic, Oct. 1970, p 75*

They ["Nam's Angels"] are not satisfied, however, with their Hondas, which are underpowered for the workout they get on a patrol through the boondocks.... The foursome would prefer tough scramblers, "with big drive sprockets, knobby wheels—and more vroom." *Time, May 2, 1969, p 33*

What will an electric car cost? How far will it go? Will it be inexpensive to operate? Will it have a touch of vrrroooom? *Clifford B. Hicks, "Here Comes the Electric Car," The World Book Science Annual 1967, p 197*

[imitative of the sound]

V/STOL ('vi:ˌstoul), *n.* acronym for *vertical or short takeoff and landing*, a cover-all term for VTOL and STOL.

Technical and operating problems have hampered the growth of V/STOL (vertical or short takeoff and landing) aircraft, light airplanes, and helicopters in serving the market for transporting travelers to major airports from home or office. *Bernard K. Thomas, Jr., "Aerospace Industry: Civil Aviation in 1966: Short-Haul Transports," The Americana Annual 1967, p 29*

VTOL ('vi:ˌtoul), *n.* acronym for *vertical take-off and landing*, used to describe an aircraft other than a helicopter that can take off and land vertically. Compare CTOL, STOL, QTOL.

In another two or three years these new crossbreeds between a small plane and a helicopter, the VTOL fans believe, will take us from tiny landing fields or even rooftops anywhere in our metropolitan areas to airports or nearby cities. Perhaps. Those VTOLs will be hellishly noisy and

sound no more pleasant than their name. *Wolf Von Eckardt, "Redesigning American Airports," Harper's, March 1967, p 75*

... the ... "soft landing module" ... is half way between a helicopter and a VTOL aircraft.... *Raymond Baxter, Punch, July 5, 1967, p 23*

VTOLport, *n.* another name for VERTIPORT. Compare STOLport.

The reason, it said, was the need for less land area for VTOLports and for fewer planes because VTOL planes spend less time on the ground. *Edward Hudson, The New York Times, March 26, 1967, p 54*

vulcanist, *n.* another name for HOT MOONER.

The moon remains a puzzle, and there is still no solution to the question about crater origin. At the moment, vulcanists remain vulcanists and impact supporters remain impact supporters. *Patrick Moore, "The Moon Reconnoitred," New Scientist and Science Journal, Jan. 28, 1971, p 185*

VX, symbol for a very lethal nerve gas. Compare BZ, CS, GB.

The chemical formula of VX is still a secret, although the WHO [World Health Organization] report suggests that the agent is ethyl S-dimethylaminoethyl methylphosphonothiolate.... Also a liquid but several times more toxic than Sarin and much less volatile, VX is lethal either when inhaled or deposited on the skin. *Matthew S. Meselson, Scientific American, May 1970, p 18*

The U.S. variation of the gas—VX—accidentally killed more than 6,000 sheep near the Army's Dugway Proving Grounds in western Utah last March. *Time, Sept. 6, 1968, p 40*

W

wafer, *n.* a very small, thin disk of silicon, orthoferrite, etc., containing one or more integrated circuits. Compare CHIP.

By suitable masking and "doping" techniques, which selectively altered the electrical behavior of small regions, several score transistors could be created on each wafer. *F. G. Heath, "Large-Scale Integration in Electronics," Scientific American, Feb. 1970, p 22*

Millions of silicon semiconductors grown on to a silicon wafer can act as a target for a vidicon TV-camera tube. In a vidicon tube light falls on a target forming a charge pattern which is scanned by an electron beam. *New Scientist, Oct. 15, 1970, p 126*

waffling, *adj.* vague; indecisive.

What is most likely is that there will be few abstentions and a large majority for a waffling resolution . . . calling for Israel to withdraw from the conquered territories but not passing judgment on the original conquests. *Richard H. Rovere, "Letter From the United Nations," The New Yorker, July 8, 1967, p 67*

If it is succeeded by a weak, waffling Phase II, warns Arthur Okun, a member of TIME's Board of Economists, the nation will be "no better off on the inflation front than if nothing had been done—perhaps worse off because of disappointed expectations." *"The Economy: What to Do in Phase II," Time, Oct. 11, 1971, p 41*

[from *waffle*, a chiefly British slang verb meaning to talk vaguely or foolishly, say nothing at length]

wage drift, an upward movement of wages resulting in an increase in average earnings over the official average wage rates of a country.

What the report revealed was this—"wage drift," or the addition to workers' earnings that local bargaining adds to national wage agreements, has been running at a rate of 4 per cent. a year, and not the 2 per cent. that has been officially estimated. *The Sunday Times (London), May 19, 1968, p 34*

We have experienced "wage drift" in industry for many years. *Bernard Hollowood, Punch, July 10, 1968, p 37*

wage-push inflation, the cost-push resulting from inflationary wage increases.

Wage-push inflation got its strongest nudge in construction; union craftsmen wrung out raises averaging 17 1/2%. *Time, Dec. 28, 1970, p 53*

What is wrong in Britain has been over-emphasised during the past three years. It has become fashionable to say that the British don't work hard enough, that they rely too much on the Welfare State, that they manage to keep a wage-push inflation in times of crippling deflation, and what with the dockers' strike and the consumer boom. *Bernard Beguin, The Manchester Guardian Weekly, March 14, 1968, p 13*

wage stop, *British.* the principle or policy of not allowing an unemployed person to receive more money from public funds than he would earn while working.

The wage stop is the device used to stop families receiving more in social security payments than their normal income from full-time work. *Pat Healy, The Times (London), Dec. 1, 1970, p 10*

wage-stop, *v.t. British.* to apply the wage stop to (an unemployed person).

Ninety per cent of the people wage-stopped under the NJC [National Joint Council] ruling would be lifted back to full benefit, and the total number of wage-stop cases would be halved. *"Insight on the Hidden Power of Bureaucracy," The Sunday Times (London), Aug. 8, 1971, p 9*

wait, *v.i.* **wait for it,** *British.* wait till you hear this (used to prefigure a surprise).

But—wait for it—an unimpeachable scientific source maintains that Loch Ness is probably one of the most unpolluted stretches of water in Britain. *John Kerr, The Manchester Guardian Weekly, Aug. 1, 1970, p 9*

Since then, a (wait for it) Joint Study has been in preparation—the study to end all studies, old Whitehall soldiers are calling it. . . . *Nicholas Taylor, The Sunday Times (London), Dec. 7, 1969, p 12*

When I opened my paper today, there was a whole page of gaudy advertisements by, wait for it, local churches. *William Davis, Punch, Oct. 15, 1969, p 628*

▶ In the sense of "take it easy, don't be in such a hurry," the expression *wait for it* has long been used in Great Britain, originally as an echo of the military interjection addressed to nervous recruits who tend to perform a drill movement before actually hearing the command. So a sergeant will say, "Slope—wait for it—arms!"

walking catfish, a species of catfish that can crawl over ground by means of its spiny fins and live on land for extended periods by taking in air through its auxiliary breathing apparatus.

An example of an imported species that became a dangerous threat to the freshwater ecology of the subtropical United States in less than two years is *Clarias batrachus*, the "walking catfish." It was imported by tropical-fish dealers from Southeast Asia; a few specimens escaped from aquariums into Florida waters. *D. A. Brown, "Animals and Wildlife," The 1970 Compton Yearbook, p 119*

The walking catfish, which moves much like an infantryman wriggling under barbed wire, was soon classified as belonging to the *Clariidae* family and the *Clarias* genus, but the species was unknown. *Al Volker, Science News, Oct. 26, 1968, p 423*

walk-off, *n.* **1** the act of walking off.

The walk-off is the bittersweet image by which, undoubtedly, Chaplin wishes to be remembered. *"Quixote With a Bowler," Time, Jan. 5, 1970, p 51*

2 an abrupt departure from a meeting, etc.; a walkout.

Prince Bernhard of the Netherlands had opened the five-day conference, being attended by 3,000 delegates from more than 100 countries, but he had left just before Mr. Haitink's walk-off. *The Times (London), Nov. 3, 1970, p 6*

The 22 Springbok cricketers who held a two-minute walk-off at Newlands Ground here yesterday in protest against apartheid in cricket are being congratulated by sportsmen all over the world. *Stanley Uys, The Manchester Guardian Weekly, April 10, 1971, p 6*

3 something that marks a departure or withdrawal; a farewell.

Mr. Ellington's part consisted of his signature theme, "Take the 'A' Train," a medley of his familiar tunes and, as a walkoff, another Ellington signature, "Things Ain't What They Used to Be." *John S. Wilson, The New York Times, March 4, 1968, p 30*

walk-on, *n.* a minor part in a play or movie; an unimportant role.

Irony is not sarcasm, drama is not pageantry, and the new sociology cannot be propelled backward into time. The very title betrays the facile irony: *The Great White Hope* is a walk-on; the film, based on Howard Sackler's Pulitzer-prizewinning play, concerns the Doomed Black Hope. *Time, Oct. 19, 1970, p 87*

—*adj.* appearing or performing on stage.

The name summons up fond and durable memories: the gum-chewing philosopher of humor, the man of homely common sense that somehow added up to uncommon wisdom. Out of it he [Will Rogers] fashioned not one, but a half-dozen careers—rodeo bronco rider, walk-on humorist (before the phrase had even been invented), Ziegfeld Follies headliner, movie star, radio commentator, newspaper columnist—a one-man galaxy of talent. *Time, Sept. 28, 1970, p 19*

► A *walk-on* in the original sense is a small, nonspeaking role or the actor playing it.

wall, *n.* **1 the Wall, a** the 26-miles long wall dividing East and West Berlin.

. . . he is a photographer in a small town near Hamburg, she is a nurse in East Berlin. They meet casually and arrange to see each other again. Then the Wall separates them. *Oscar Handlin, "The Atlantic Bookshelf: Reader's Choice," Review of "Two Views" by Uwe Johnson, The Atlantic, Jan. 1967, p 117*

b the remains of the western wall of Solomon's Temple in Jerusalem, known as the Wailing Wall.

The Army had strictly forbidden anyone without special authorization to cross from Jewish Jerusalem. Otherwise, all of Israel would have tried to crush into the stricken Old City on the day the Wall was taken. *Flora Lewis, "A Reporter at Large," The New Yorker, July 1, 1967, p 48*

For the first time in nearly 2,000 years the Wailing Wall, the remains of Solomon's temple compound, was in Jewish hands. Israel has vowed never to give back the Wall. *Time, Aug. 3, 1970, p 19*

2 jump (or **leap**) **over the wall,** to leave the church or a religious order.

No one knows exactly how many religious have jumped over the wall—partly because it is so easy today for a priest, nun or brother simply to take a leave of absence and never return. *Time, Feb. 23, 1970, p 51*

Mr. Vizzard was a Jesuit seminarian who yearned for the world, leapt over the wall, and found what he was looking for in Hollywood. *Richard Schickel, "Books in Brief: Non-Fiction," Review of "See No Evil" by Jack A. Vizzard, Harper's, April 1970, p 110*

► The expression *leap over the wall* may have been popularized by the book *I Leap Over the Wall*, 1949, by Monica Baldwin (the niece of former British Prime Minister Stanley Baldwin), written after she left an enclosed religious order to which she had belonged from 1914 to 1941.

Wallaceism, *n.* **1** the policies associated with George C. Wallace, born 1919, governor of Alabama, especially opposition to racial integration and championship of states' rights in the South.

. . . he [President Nixon] was talking about: expanding the Republican base against Wallaceism in the South. *Robert D. Novak, "Reports: Washington," The Atlantic, April 1970, p 10*

2 a word, phrase, or statement typical of Governor George C. Wallace.

Denouncing the "overeducated, ivory-tower folks with pointed heads looking down their noses at us"—a Wallaceism denoting anybody who is in favor of civil rights, plus all three branches of the U.S. Government. . . . *Time, Sept. 13, 1968, p 18*

wall-attachment effect, another name for COANDA EFFECT.

. . . the "wall-attachment" effect (a preference for moving along a wall rather than through an open space—one of the fundamentals of fluidics component design). *Fred Wheeler, New Scientist, May 16, 1968, p 350*

wall cloud, another name for EYEWALL.

The eye [of a hurricane] is bounded by so-called "wall clouds," which are towering thunderstorm clouds that extend to great altitudes. *Louis Battan, "Killer Storms," 1972 Britannica Yearbook of Science and the Future, 1971, p 122*

wallcovering, *n.* a covering of plastic, fabric, etc., usually with ornamental designs, for pasting on interior walls.

The wallcovering on three walls is glossy yellow p.v.c. [polyvinyl chloride] by Nairn of Lancaster and the remaining wall surface is finished in plain white emulsion paint. *The Times (London), Dec. 11, 1970, p 16*

wallpaper music, *British.* recorded music piped in to an office, restaurant, etc., through a public-address system; background music.

"It's the 'wallpaper music' I'm against—the plastic, bland pop stuff that churns out as a comfy background you don't really have to notice," says John Peel. . . . *Michael Moynihan, The Sunday Times (London), Sept. 22, 1968, p 3*

. . . BBC radio was transmitting 'wallpaper' music almost round the clock. *The Annual Register of World Events in 1968 (1969), p 440*

wall-to-wall, *adj. Chiefly U.S.* extending from one end or extreme to the other.

The only way you could counter their Mediterranean

ships is with enough ships that there wouldn't be room for theirs — wall-to-wall ships. *Paul Warnke, "Reports: Washington: Wall-to-Wall Ships," The Atlantic, May 1970, p 20*

The slow-selling Imperial (competitive with Cadillac and Lincoln) has been stretched 5 in. in length, to a total 229.7 in., and now comes with a wall-to-wall front grille that conceals the headlights. *Time, Aug. 30, 1968, p 47*

It will never be easy to found an all-Europe university, just as it is not easy to foresee an all-Europe computer manufacturer or a Continental wall-to-wall version of General Electric. *John Fischer, "The Editor's Easy Chair: Field Notes on the Europeans," Harper's, May 1967, p 24*

... he [Bobby Hackett] made a highly successful series of wall-to-wall mood-music recordings with Jackie Gleason — "Music for Lovers Only," "Music, Martinis, and Memories," "Music to Remember Her." *Whitney Balliett, "Musical Events: Jazz Records," The New Yorker, Nov. 25, 1967, p 222*

[originally applied to carpeting covering an entire floor]

waltz, *n. Slang.* a thing accomplished with ease; something simple; a breeze.

... his [Tony Jacklin's] bold putt from twenty-five feet hit the back of the cup, jumped up in the air, landed outside the cup, and toppled in. After that, it was a waltz. *Herbert Warren Wind, "The Sporting Scene," The New Yorker, Aug. 1, 1970, p 62*

Though Dancer eased him up at the end, Nevele Pride won in a waltz. *Time, July 5, 1968, p 38*

[from the slang verb phrase *to waltz through* something, meaning to do easily, breeze through it]

Wan·kel engine (ˈwɑːŋ kəl *or* ˈvɑːŋ kəl), Often shortened to **Wankel,** *n.* an internal-combustion engine that is smaller and lighter and has fewer components than conventional engines because of its nearly triangular rotating pistons, which spin in one direction without the reciprocating movement of a conventional engine.

... the top names in the [motor] industry — with a few exceptions — will either be developing Wankel engines or be in a position to get hold of one quickly. *Peter Rodgers, The Manchester Guardian Weekly, Nov. 14, 1970, p 16*

Compared to like-rated conventional engines, the Wankel is 30-50% lighter and smaller, has 40% fewer parts, operates on non-leaded fuel, and is very responsive to antipollution devices. *Frank A. Smith, "Transportation," 1972 Britannica Yearbook of Science and the Future, 1971, p 332*

[named for Felix *Wankel,* born 1902, the German engineer who invented it]

wantable, *adj.* desirable; attractive.

This collection is not trendsetting nor is it haute couture in the traditional sense; the sole consistency is in skirt length. But it is extremely pretty, wantable and smart in a personal private way. *Prudence Glynn, The Times (London), July 21, 1970, p 7*

warden, *v.i.* to guard or protect as a game warden.

The flight of one young bird represented the culmination of many weeks' continuous wardening by the Nature Conservancy and the Royal Society for the Protection of Birds. . . . The adult birds were first seen in a remote valley in March and wardening continued until the eaglet hatched. *The Times (London), Aug. 1, 1970, p 3*

The wardening of Exmoor, for example, with its wide acres of moorland under rising pressure of visitors, is described as rudimentary. *Christopher Hall, "Penny-Pinching in the Park," The Manchester Guardian Weekly, July 3, 1971, p 15*

[verb use of *warden, n.*]

war-game, *v.t.* to examine or test (a plan, strategy, etc.) by means of a war game (simulated military confrontation).

At one point Nixon told Kissinger: "Let's you and me war-game this," and they worked the plans over to see, as Nixon put it, "where the weak points might be." *Time, Oct. 5, 1970, p 13*

— *v.i.* to engage in or play a war game.

War-gaming is the preoccupation of tens of thousands of mini-generals round the world. *Time, Jan. 4, 1971, p 48*

War gaming has been practised for many years, and computerised war gaming is now common. *Joseph Hanlon, "The Implications of Project Cambridge," New Scientist and Science Journal, Feb. 25, 1971, p 422*

war-gamer, *n.* one who engages in war games.

The collector of lead toy soldiers is not the same as the war-gamer. And the collector of miniature military models will mount a one-man cavalry charge if the ignorant call his pieces "toys." *Donald Wintersgill, "Soldiers for Sale," The Manchester Guardian Weekly, Jan. 9, 1971, p 17*

War gaming has been practised for many years, and computerised war gaming is now common. But the tools to be developed by Project Cambridge would have two important benefits for war gamers. . . . *Joseph Hanlon, "The Implications of Project Cambridge," New Scientist and Science Journal, Feb. 25, 1971, p 422*

war·gasm (ˈwɔrˌgæz əm), *n. U.S.* **1** the sudden outbreak of total war.

But if an all-out exchange — "wargasm," in the jargon — were to take place, it would end, in Mr. Rusk's words, "with a handful of miserable survivors contemplating the folly of man." *Daniel Lang, "A Reporter At Large (Atomic Bombs)," The New Yorker, Jan. 9, 1971, p 54*

2 a crisis that could lead to the outbreak of total war.

Goodman had found much to displease him then, and kept referring to the "wargasms" of the Kennedy Administration, which wargasms he attached with no excessive intellectual jugglery to the existential and Reichian notions of the orgasm which Mailer had promulgated in his piece *The White Negro. Norman Mailer, "The Steps of the Pentagon," Harper's, March 1968, p 55*

[blend of *war* and *orgasm*]

wart, *n.* blemish; imperfection. Especially in the phrase **warts and all,** with none of the imperfections concealed.

. . . Jeremy Seabrook's series on Blackburn seemingly polarised two attitudes: either the place has no warts at all or, if it has, we must parade them to show how jolly honest we're all being. *Kathryn Davies, Wilpshire, near Blackburn, England, in a Letter to the Editor, The Listener, Oct. 8, 1970, p 488*

They are impatient with the old standard of factual, objective, measurable, and verifiable truth, which, though necessarily imperfect, is at least a crude portrait of the world as it is — warts, halos, significance, and all. *Herbert Bruckner, "Can Printed News Save a Free Society?" Saturday Review, Oct. 10, 1970, p 55*

But he gives an honest picture, private warts and all,

of what it was like for a self-searching young man to cut his milk teeth on a seething India and the jungle. *Christopher Wordsworth, "Books: With the Gurkhas," Review of "A Child at Arms" by Patrick Davis, The Manchester Guardian Weekly, Aug. 15, 1970, p 18*

The people who had worked for educational reform sent a rebuttal letter that said, in part, "We believe it is crucial to the future life and progress of our community to have a newspaper unafraid to comment and to show us up, warts and all." *Calvin Trillin, "U.S. Journal: Nampa, Idaho," The New Yorker, Oct. 31, 1970, p 107*

[apparently the expression originated from an apocryphal story about Oliver Cromwell, who was supposed to have asked his portrait painter to paint him "warts and all"]

washeteria, *n. British.* **1** a self-service laundry.

Maybe he agrees with the school of thought that holds that the expansion of washeterias and the contraction of the average British kitchen will eventually make all but the family with small children unwilling to pay even £56 for a washing machine. *Gwen Nuttall, The Sunday Times (London), Jan. 26, 1969, p 29*

Now that we have grown accustomed to the blandishments of all-night coinops, express dry cleaning, of television while you wash, and something called Washeterias, the next step may be drive-in laundries. *Elizabeth Good, The Sunday Times (London), July 17, 1966, p 30*

2 a self-service car wash.

... I have long grown accustomed to a cafeteria but I now clean my car at a car washeteria. *Arnold Wilson, Bath, England, in a Letter to the Editor, The Times (London), Dec. 24, 1970, p 9*

[patterned after *cafeteria*]

Wasp (wɒsp), *n.* a white Anglo-Saxon Protestant, especially one belonging to the group of middle- and upper-class Americans descended from British and northern European settlers who espouse and represent the cultural and religious traditions of their ancestors. *Often used attributively.* Compare ASP.

"Mr. Plimpton is the quintessential Wasp," Johnston has said. "He's the most intense embodiment of the Wasp I can imagine. I have an immense respect for him." *Geoffrey T. Hellman, "Profiles: Period-Piece Fellow (Francis T. P. Plimpton)," The New Yorker, Dec. 4, 1971, p 74*

"If we could find 3,000 well-qualified teachers we would not hesitate to make French an obligatory course," an official said. But he admitted that such a move might run into resistance. "Let's face it," he said. "We've got an enormous Wasp community." *Edward Cowan, The New York Times, June 2, 1968, Sec. 1, p 20*

[On the Cairo television] I watch something new to me called "Jet Jackson—World Commando." It consists of the hero, a straight, clean-limbed young WASP with a private jet fighter, punching coloured villains in the face. *David Wheeler, "A Tootle for Cleopatra," The Manchester Guardian Weekly, March 17, 1966, p 14*

[originally *WASP*, an acronym (used especially in statistical and sociological studies of American ethnic groups) formed from the initials of *White, Anglo-Saxon, Protestant*]

Waspdom, *n.* the characteristics, beliefs, attitudes, etc., of Wasps.

Thus Roman Catholics like William Buckley, Sargent Shriver and Ted Kennedy are pushed toward Waspdom by their associations, professions and life styles. *Time, Jan. 17, 1969, p 21*

The foundation of WASP dominance in national politics and culture rested on the supposition that WASPdom was the true America.... *Peter Schrag, "The Decline of the Wasp," Harper's, April 1970, p 86*

Waspish, *adj.* belonging to or typical of Wasps.

Hannah stayed in Philadelphia for three years, photographing... her college classmates. She says that she hated the Waspish ambience of the school, but she had got a scholarship at the end of her freshman year, and she wanted to keep it. *Jane Kramer, "Profiles: Founding Cadre (of Women's Liberationists)," The New Yorker, Nov. 28, 1970, p 129*

I cannot recall Booz, Allen's Cleveland man by name. He reminded me of many youngish management consultants I have known who worked for any of the Big Three: Booz, Allen and Hamilton; McKinsey and Co., Cresap, McCormick and Paget. He was a Harvard Business School graduate, WASPish, attractive, crisp, alert, and formidably informed. *Warren G. Bennis, "Searching For the 'Perfect' University President," The Atlantic, April 1971, p 41*

waste, *v.t. U.S. Military Slang.* to destroy; kill.

Then somebody said "What do we do with them?" A GI answered "Waste them." Suddenly there was a burst of automatic fire from many guns. *Seymour M. Hersh, "My Lai 4: A Report on its Massacre and its Aftermath," Harper's, May 1970, p 69*

[probably from the idiom *to lay waste*]

wastemaker, *n.* a person, company, industry, etc., that produces an excessive amount of waste by the prodigal use of products and resources.

New York generates three times as much waste per capita as London; Americans are "the wastemakers." *J. Wreford Watson, "America the Waste-Maker," The New York Times, Dec. 23, 1970, p 27*

And as we succeed in raising the standard of living so we shall become increasingly preoccupied with man's activities as a waste-maker. *The Manchester Guardian Weekly, Feb. 27, 1971, p 13*

[from *The Wastemakers*, a book, 1960, by Vance Packard, critical of the product-design field]

water bed, a bed with a mattress consisting of a water-filled vinyl bag and usually equipped with a temperature-control device.

But his efforts to improve it led him [designer Charles Prior Hall] to a much splashier creation, which is now making an appearance—and creating a sensation—in department stores across the nation. It is the water bed, the bounciest bedroom invention since the innerspring mattress. *"The Waves of Morpheus," Time, Sept. 7, 1970, p 42*

And the waterbed ("ideal for pregnant women"), a kind of gigantic hot water bottle, must surely be the ultimate in nocturnal comfort. *David Clutterbuck, New Scientist and Science Journal, March 4, 1971, p 515*

water cannon, a large nozzle usually mounted on a truck to shoot water at high pressure.

At one point police used water cannons to stop the demonstrators when they tried to storm the center court. *The New York Times, May 4, 1968, p 50*

Water-cannon, which misleadingly sound like large water-pistols, seem to be shared between firemen and police, as far as I can make out from reports concerned more with brutality than technology. *R. G. G. Price, Punch, April 24, 1968, p 600*

In the fighting which followed several people were batoned by police and a number of marchers and by-standers were hosed down by water-cannon. *Simon Hoggart, "Unhappy Anniversary," The Manchester Guardian Weekly, Oct. 9, 1971, p 9*

water pulse, water applied to the teeth in a spurt with a water-spray device to remove particles of food.

Fairly refined switch gear and valves ... let the user control the intensity of the water pulses. The first days with the pulsed water cleaner can cause bleeding gums, as can a new toothbrush. A hand-held probe directs the fluid on to the teeth. *New Scientist, Oct. 15, 1970, p 130*

water II, another name for ANOMALOUS WATER.

... our investigations led to the truly astonishing discovery in 1962 of a new, stable form of water with a density almost one and a half times that of ordinary water and a molecular structure that can only be described as polymeric. We named this new form of water water II, to distinguish it from ordinary water, or water I; some workers in the U.S. call it polywater. *Boris V. Derjaguin, Scientific American, Nov. 1970, p 52*

Watson-Crick, *adj.* of or relating to various genetic concepts and hypotheses, such as the double helix and the central dogma, postulated by the American biologist James D. Watson, born 1928, and the English biologist Francis H. C. Crick, born 1916.

Dr. Commoner disputed the so-called Watson-Crick Theory, which holds that all genetic traits are basically derived from the structure of a kind of master molecule in the chromosomes called deoxyribonucleic acid, or DNA. *The New York Times, April 2, 1968, p 52*

The implication here is that most of this particular fragment of messenger RNA associates with itself to form a double-helical structure like the Watson-Crick spiral of DNA. *Graham Chedd and Peter Stubbs, New Scientist, May 8, 1969, p 278*

wave, *n.* *U.S.* **make waves,** to cause disturbance; upset a normal course or routine.

Perhaps people marked McManus as a simple creature of his environment, not so much to be listened to as led. Something of a hard-nose with an Irish talent for hotheadedness, but never one to make waves, to rock the boat. *Paul Good, Harper's, Sept. 1971, p 72*

This is the kind of broker you love to have working for you. He [Jim Curran] makes no decisions himself, merely accepts orders directed to him. He makes no waves, runs up no extensive phone bills, keeps his major account supplied with gifts of wine, dinners, and tickets. *Brutus, "Confessions of a Stockbroker," The Atlantic, June 1971, p 48*

... Red Garland, Philly Joe Jones, and Wilbur Ware are a combination that makes waves in this little bar. *"Goings On About Town," The New Yorker, July 10, 1971, p 3*

wave cloud, a lens-shaped cloud held stationary by a high point of the wave motion of air, used as an indicator of air waves by glider pilots.

Wave clouds from the Alleghenies often appear over Washington, D.C., and over the New Jersey coast. Seen from Black Forest, wave clouds over the Rockies appear and disappear, very small fish in the vast sky; but the effect is electric: there she blows, the wave! Let's go. *Wolfgang Langewiesche, "The Upward Miracle: The Arts and Joys of Gliding," Harper's, Nov. 1971, p 125*

way, *n.* *U.S. Dialect.* **no way,** under no circumstances.

... none of these conditions will ever get any better. ("No way," as they keep saying ....) *Andy Logan, "Around City Hall," The New Yorker, Dec. 25, 1971, p 50*

way-out, *Slang.* —*adj.* far removed from the conventional or the ordinary; far-out.

This could be followed up by other practical steps such as a pooling of research in the "way out" field of nuclear fusion.... *Christopher Layton, The Times (London), April 13, 1967, p 23*

Ernst W. Nay—Knoedler, 14 East 57th. This way-out West German virtuoso puts on a razzle-dazzle performance of expressionistic stunts. Bright, chromatic circles cavort and tumble, dynamic space pulses in a polyphony of color and line. High ocular entertainment, mainly for the pure in art. *"Art in New York," Time, Jan. 31, 1964, p NY8*

—*n.* a person who holds very unconventional or radical views.

The end of the sixties marked a turning point in the public's attitude toward its environment. The change was well expressed by a participant in a 1969 conference sponsored by the conservationist Sierra Club: "Two years ago we were considered way-outs. Nobody knew what conservation meant." *"Review of the Year: Environmental Sciences," Encyclopedia Science Supplement (Grolier) 1970, p 158*

Either way, the tribes who first gathered for that gigantic be-in at Golden Gate Park on January 14, 1967, have been scattered. The philosophy, such as it was, is in shreds, the drop-outs have copped out, the redskins have bitten the dust, the way-outs have faced the nitty-gritty (truth). *Edward Thorpe, The Manchester Guardian Weekly, Oct. 17, 1968, p 19*

weak force, the force that governs the interaction of neutrinos. It is probably interactive in fermion coupling and causes radioactive decay. Its hypothetical quantum is the W particle. Also called WEAK INTERACTION. Compare STRONG FORCE.

... the weak force ... appears to play a role at both the nuclear and atomic levels, modifying the behavior of the first 2 forces [gravity and electromagnetism] and causing radioactive decay. The weak force is only a trillionth as strong as electromagnetism. But feeble as it is, the weak force is still a trillion trillion trillion times stronger than gravity. *Tom Alexander, "Science Rediscovers Gravity," Encyclopedia Science Supplement (Grolier) 1970, p 59*

... compared with any other particles, such neutrinos are virtually aloof from interactions with matter.... It is not surprising then that the force that governs the interactions of neutrinos is known as the 'weak' force. *Colin Ramm, "High Energy Neutrinos," Science Journal, April 1968, p 56*

Physicists distinguish four different kinds of force by which objects in the universe act upon each other: the strong nuclear force, the weak force, electromagnetism and gravity. *"The W Particle May Have Been Found," Science News, Aug. 21, 1971, p 121*

The intermediate boson was originally postulated by theoretical physicists as the quantum of the weak force, in analogy to the pion (the quantum of the nuclear force), the photon (the quantum of the electromagnetic force) and the graviton (the proposed quantum of gravity). *"Science and the Citizen: Gold in a Silver Mine," Scientific American, Oct. 1971, p 42*

weak interaction, another name for WEAK FORCE.

This weak interaction, as its name implies, is very much

weaker than the strong interaction. Its main effect is to govern certain long-lived modes of radioactive decay for certain particles. Historically it first showed up in nuclear beta decay. *"Physics and Chemistry: Particle Physics," Science News Yearbook 1969, p 154*

Sunlight is sustained by the thermonuclear, the weak-interaction and the opacity hangups. *Freeman J. Dyson, "Energy in the Universe," Scientific American, Sept. 1971, p 58*

wealth tax, an annual tax on all of an individual's assets above a specified minimum, whether they produce income or not.

A Wealth Tax...has the disadvantage of being extremely difficult to collect, as it is administratively equivalent to the imposition of Estate Duty on all wealthy people once a year. *The Times (London), June 11, 1970, p 11*

Weatherman, *n.* a member of a militant revolutionary youth organization in the United States that split off from the politically radical but less extreme SDS (Students for a Democratic Society).

The Federal Government reaffirmed last week that the bellicose Weathermen deserve to be taken at their word when they vow to make war on American Society. *Time, Aug. 3, 1970, p 10*

...the alleged bias for "activists" typically meant that delegates were presidents of youth organizations or youth members of town councils, not Weathermen or Panthers as the word suggests. *Don Mitchell, "Letter from a Cold Place: Heavy Snow and Cheerless Rhetoric in the Mountains of Colorado," Harper's, Aug. 1971, p 26*

[the name was taken from a line in the song *Subterranean Homesick Blues*, by the American folk singer and composer Bob Dylan, born 1941:

"You don't need a weatherman
To know which way the wind blows."]

we·del ('vei dəl), *v.i.* to ski by performing Wedeln.

They wedeled down the 1,200-ft. slope or slammed through the slalom course. *Time, Nov. 15, 1968, p 49*

[back formation from *Wedeln*]

We·deln ('vei dəln), *n. sing. or pl.* a skiing maneuver consisting of quick, short swiveling movements down a sloping course.

On the subject of language, it is better, in the ski world, to talk English resolutely, although technical terms should be always in German, French or Italian.

"Like *Wedeln*," I said.

"What's that?" said a great-niece.

"Useful word," I said. "It's a series, really, of short rhythmic parallel turns in the fall line, characterised by fluid continuity minimal upper body movement." *Stephen Potter, "The Abominable Ski-Man," Punch, Feb. 19, 1969, p 256*

Down he goes, anyway, his Wedeln so crisp he never seems to care at all for the configuration of the snow.... *Thomas Williams, The New Yorker, Feb. 2, 1963, p 37*

[from German, from *wedeln, v.*, to wag the tail, from *Wedel* tail]

weepie or **weepy,** *n. British Slang.* an overly emotional or sentimental book, film, play, etc.; a tear-jerker.

And *Sunrise at Campobello* [a motion picture], a strange throwback to the Forties, was a weepie about the last days of F.D.R. *Paul Mayersberg, "The Fantasy of Power," The Listener, Jan. 25, 1968, p 105*

Never mind whether it is neo-realism (or any sort of realism), it could be a pleasant evening in the cinema if it worked simply as a glossy weepy. *John Russell Taylor, The Times (London), Aug. 14, 1970, p 10*

Each of these is handled by no means artlessly, but each suffers from a fatal desire not to cause offence which ultimately turns the whole thing into a superior kind of weepie. *Derek Malcolm, The Manchester Guardian Weekly, Jan. 30, 1971, p 21*

weight-watcher, *n.* a person who tries to control his weight by dieting; a dieter.

Weight-watchers and manufacturers of diet foods in the United States may perhaps be excused if they have had the feeling this past year of being treated like yoyos. *Peter Gwynne, Science Journal, Nov. 1970, p 6*

Italians are not exactly the keenest weight-watchers in the world and hardly let a day go by without forking into the pasta. *Roger Lewis, The Sunday Times (London), Nov. 10, 1968, p 35*

[from *Weight Watchers, Inc.,* an organization of dieters]

weirdo, *U.S. Slang. —n.* an odd or eccentric person.

Not that this lunatic commotion ["Cul-de-Sac"] in which an American thug confines a pair of married weirdoes for about 24 hours in an 11th-century castle on the coast of northern England is without certain recommendations. It compares as black comedy to John Huston's "Beat the Devil," so it's something you'll probably want to see. *Bosley Crowther, The New York Times, Nov. 8, 1966, p 44*

—adj. odd; eccentric; queer.

He is being blackmailed by a weirdo youth who carries out the pretense of being his son.... *Time, Feb. 16, 1968, p 36*

welfare mother, *U.S.* a woman who is on relief because she has small children and no husband to support them.

The needs of the working man denied marginal security, the jobless veteran, the pressured pensioner, the welfare mother, and the harried commuter in our cities involve the whole range of vital urban services—police, fire, sanitation, health, education, jobs, and recreation. *John V. Lindsay, "For New 'National Cities'," The New York Times, June 9, 1971, p 43*

welfarist, *n.* an advocate of welfare programs such as public relief for the poor, unemployment insurance, social security, etc.; one who believes in the principles of the welfare state.

...the welfare state...is not incompatible with the police state. George Wallace is a welfarist, and so is Mayor Daley. *Richard H. Rovere, "Letter from Washington," The New Yorker, Oct. 12, 1968, p 201*

"Much of the black militant talk these days is actually in terms far closer to the doctrines of free enterprise than to those of the welfarist of the 30's...." *Ward S. Just, "Reports: Campaigning, Nixon: Wyoming," The Atlantic, July 1968, p 7*

Wendy house, *British.* a playhouse for a child.

Business in the garden furniture section at Chelsea show was brisk by all accounts, and this does not surprise me because there is a strong move towards making the garden an extension of the home....So no wonder there is a market for children's seesaws, swings, paddling pools, Wendy houses and the like. *Roy Hay, "Garden As Part of the Home," The Times (London), May 30, 1970, p 25*

A loud din arising from one Wendy house attracted the attention of the teacher. *Elspeth Huxley, Punch, March 1, 1967, p 291*

[so called from the little house built around Wendy by Peter Pan in J. M. Barrie's play *Peter Pan*]

West·po·li·tik ('vest pou li:,ti:k), *n.* a policy, especially of a Communist country, of establishing normal diplomatic and trade relations with Western countries. Compare OSTPOLITIK.

Dubček...has spoken excitedly in private of West German Chancellor Willy Brandt's *Ostpolitik*, and urged that Eastern Europe respond with a creative *Westpolitik*. *Time, May 18, 1970, p 29*

Once his *Westpolitik* was launched, Brandt began a complex series of diplomatic maneuvers with the East. *Time, Jan. 4, 1971, p 14*

[from German, Western policy]

wet lab, a compartment in an undersea habitat where aquanauts prepare for and return from missions.

Their [the aquanauts'] oxygen-nitrogen breathing mixture was maintained at the outside (water) pressure of over two atmospheres.... Because internal and external pressures were identical, a floor hatch in the habitat's wet lab could be kept open permanently for ready access to the water. *Myril Hendershott, "Oceanography," The Americana Annual 1970, p 517*

whee, *v.t.* **whee up,** *U.S. Slang.* to fill with excitement or exuberance.

...I got so patriotically wheed up that I ended by calling for three cheers for General Douglas MacArthur and getting, of course, dead silence. *L. E. Sissman, "Innocent Bystander: Confessions of An Ex-Quiz Kid, A Vote for Children's Lib," The Atlantic, March 1971, p 36*

"... my first start against the White Sox meant so much to me.... I was all wheed up, feeling great. I knew I would win, but I wanted to do something real spectacular." *Denny McLain, quoted by Arthur Daley, The New York Times, April 17, 1966, Sec. 5, p 2*

[from *whee*, interjection used to show great joy or delight]

wheeler[1], *n. U.S.* a shrewd dealer or operator.

Herbert Itkin, the 41-year-old lawyer who has been mentioned as a murder target in the kickback case involving former city Water Commissioner James L. Marcus, is described by a friend as a "superb story teller, fast mover and wheeler." *The New York Times, Jan. 13, 1968, p 17*

[probably shortened from *wheeler-dealer, n.* See the etymology of WHEELER-DEALER, *v.*]

wheeler-dealer, *v.i. U.S. Slang.* to wheel and deal; trade or scheme shrewdly.

While LBJ wheeler-dealered in his ornate Capitol suite of crystal chandeliers and gold-embossed doorknobs ... Sam [Sam Houston Johnson], a solitary and rather shadowy figure, accomplished grub work.... *Larry L. King, "Washington Report: LBJ's Secret Brother Meditates on History," Harper's, April 1970, p 38*

[verb use of the U.S. slang term *wheeler-dealer, n.* one who trades or schemes shrewdly, from the verb phrase *wheel and deal*, in which *wheel* literally means to act as a "wheel" or "big wheel" (slang for an important or influential person, a leader)]

wheeler-dealing, *n. Slang.* shrewd scheming or trading.

The men in New York kept the lines open into the night, repeating the selections into the phone as they were announced in Manhattan, playing dummy hands and wondering what wheeler-dealing was going on over telephone lines among the various managements. *Robert Lipsyte, The New York Times, Feb. 1, 1968, p 42*

In the event, all the arm-squeezing and whispered wheeler-dealing along the corridors had its intended effect. *Brian MacArthur, The Times (London), April 8, 1968, p 2*

wheelie, *n.* a stunt in which a lightweight vehicle is made to stand for a moment on one or two of its wheels.

A popular sport for young bicycle riders is "doing a wheelie." This means lifting the front wheel off the ground and balancing on the rear wheel alone. *Stacy V. Jones, The New York Times, Nov. 12, 1966, p 45*

Then he discovered a way to turn his motorcycling skill into real money, by becoming a stunt rider. "I started out with simple things—wheelies, crashing through fire walls, jumping a box of rattlesnakes. Once I had two mountain lions tied to the end of the ramp as I rode down it." *Evel Knievel, quoted by Dick Adler, "A Touch of Evel," The Sunday Times Magazine (London), June 27, 1971, p 41*

where, *adv.* **where it's at,** *U.S. Slang.* the place where the most important activity, development, etc., is; central place of greatest activity.

"Since you instinctively rap with those who are Now, you will always be more or less where it's at and should readily find your bag." *Cartoon legend, The New Yorker, Oct. 25, 1969, p 61*

"This crazy Katz knows where it's at, if it's anywhere," he said poetically. "To say any more is to say too much." *Jonathan Baumbach, Review of "Creamy and Delicious" by Steve Katz, Saturday Review, Oct. 10, 1970, p 34*

I...see in this the final proof that Eliot [the central character in C. P. Snow's novels] is the ultimate square. As they said only yesterday, *he just doesn't know where it's at.* He tries to make some connection between today's slaphappy sexual customs and George Passant's ambidextrous pioneer work in the English provinces but never makes the connection a vital part of the book's structure. *Richard Jones, "The End of the C. P. Snow Affair," Review of "Last Things" by C. P. Snow, The Atlantic, Sept. 1970, p 114*

whiffleball, *n.* a lightweight, hollow, plastic ball with openings or holes to catch the air and reduce its speed and distance of travel. Originally developed for golf practice in a confined area, whiffleballs are made like a softball and are used by children to play baseball or some variation of it. Also spelled WIFFLE BALL.

...they were mingling with the other occupants of the Sheep Meadow—picnickers, folk singers, kids playing with whiffleballs and baseballs.... *"Talk of the Town: Parade," The New Yorker, July 11, 1970, p 20*

whipcord, *adj.* taut, tough, or sinewy.

He [René Belbenoit] was deeply tanned, middle-aged, and he had the whipcord conditioning of an athlete. *Edwin Fadiman, Jr., Review of "Papillon" by Henri Charrière, Saturday Review, Oct. 24, 1970, p 70*

Many experts believed that [Ferdinand Lewis] Alcindor, with his size, reach, long legs with whipcord muscles, and ability on offense and defense, might become basketball's greatest attraction. *Robert Cahn, "Biography," Britannica Book of the Year 1969, p 140*

[figurative sense of *whipcord*, *n.*, a thin, tightly twisted cord used for whips]

whiskers, *n. pl.* a composite of monocrystals, used as a reinforcing material.

Scientists were also exploring the possibility of incorporating monocrystalline fiber composites, called whiskers, into filling materials, such as silver amalgam, silicate cement, and acrylic resin. *Clifford H. Miller, "Medicine: Dentistry," The World Book Science Annual 1967, p 315*

"Whiskers" are single crystals, an inch or more long. Ordinary crystalline substances, such as salt and sugar, are aggregates of many crystals; pure single crystals rarely occur in nature. *Anthony Standen, "Chemical Research," 1969 Collier's Encyclopedia Year Book, p 164*

whistle-blower, *n. Chiefly U.S. Slang.* a person who exposes, denounces, or informs against another.

"They didn't send baskets of fruit," volunteered an aide. If they didn't, an impartial observer might suggest that they should have. And when they reflect more fully on how well the majority leader handled a whistle-blower and protected their interests perhaps they will. *John A. Hamilton, "Blowing the Whistle on 'The Bosses'," The New York Times, March 23, 1970, p 40*

[from the idiom *blow the whistle* (on someone)]

whistle-blowing, *n. Chiefly U.S. Slang.* the act or practice of a whistle-blower.

Further, the Code [of Good Conduct of The British Computer Society] contains secrecy clauses that effectively prohibit Nader style whistle-blowing to call public attention to harmful practices. *Joseph Hanlon, "Single Minded Service," New Scientist and Science Journal, Dec. 9, 1971, p 69*

white backlash, another term for BACKLASH (def. 1).

The so-called "white backlash," fearful resentment among white property-owners over the economic and territorial advance of Negroes, has raised serious concern in Republican circles over the possibility of Mr. Brooke's retaining for Republicans the seat held by retiring Senator Leverett Saltonstall. *The New York Times, Oct. 23, 1966, Sec. 4, p 3*

white finger or **white fingers,** other names for RAYNAUD'S PHENOMENON.

A few weeks ago the Transport & General Workers' Union and the Federation of Civil Engineering Contractors both decided to back a three-year research project by Liverpool University into Raynaud's Phenomenon—known as white finger—costing £500 a year. *Alan Dawson, The Times (London), July 6, 1970, p 18*

white knight, a political reformer or champion of a cause.

The Italian Communist Party . . . will take its members into the regional election campaign next month as white knights dealing with the joint evils of corruption and reaction. *Peter Nichols, The Times (London), April 23, 1970, p 7*

. . . unlike other political white knights, Lindsay [Mayor John Lindsay of New York] has curiously escaped a major journalistic unhorsing. *Time, June 29, 1970, p 60*

white noise, an overlay of nondescript sound to cover up distracting or annoying noises. Also called ACOUSTIC PERFUME.

The most widely used of the noisemakers produce a mild form of radio static called "white noise" by engineers. Turned down to a discreet volume, the static masks distracting outside noises and disturbing interior echoes. *Time, May 4, 1970, p 92*

[extended sense of the technical term for a sound covering the range of audible frequencies, such as the sound of a jet engine]

whitey, *n. U.S. Slang.* **1** (used as a proper noun) white men collectively; white society.

. . . the Black Power movement sees concern for the environment as another of whitey's ways to avoid tackling urban ghettos. *Jon Tinker, New Scientist, June 11, 1970, p 525*

Senator Jordan warned the convention of "the gap between the Negro middle-class politician and the Negro citizen. That citizen is beginning to hate us as much as he hates Whitey." *Dan Wakefield, "Supernation at Peace and War," The Atlantic, March 1968, p 73*

Some Negroes, she says, feel as Billy does: that Durward has "sold out to Whitey" by marrying a white girl. *Bonnie Buxton, "Can George Hees's Beautiful Daughter Roslyn Find Happiness With a Handsome Washington Lawyer Who Happens to be a Negro? Yes!" Maclean's, March 1968, p 39*

2 (used as a common noun) a white man.

The confrontation began after six youths from the camp taunted six park policemen chanting: "Going to get me a whitey!" and "Going to get me a honky!" *The New York Times, June 21, 1968, p 24*

who·sit ('hu: zit), *n. Slang.* contraction of *who's it*, used in the sense of "so-and-so."

When De Gaulle was out of power, he liked to describe the continual shifts of Ministers in the Fourth Republic's Cabinets by saying, "*Chose, machin, chouette* [thingamabob, thingamajig, whosit] are being replaced by *chouette, machin, chose.*" *Time, Nov. 23, 1970, p 25*

Wiffle ball, another form of WHIFFLEBALL.

He [David Eisenhower] had to settle for passing the afternoon playing Wiffle ball on the south lawn of his father-in-law's White House. *Time, May 25, 1970, p 43*

wig, *v.i. U.S. Slang.* **wig out, 1** to get high or lightheaded on or as if on narcotic drugs.

Astonishing supermarket full of senior citizens who all look stoned out of their minds. Wigging out on the gherkins. *Paul Tyner, The Atlantic, Feb. 1968, p 123*

2 to get very excited or enthusiastic.

"A teeny-bop," translates as a "teen-age R & R nut who wears $3.98 boots, a transistor at the ear and who wigs out over the Stones, the Turtles, the Beatles, and anything else with a concussive 4/4 beat." *Angela Taylor, The New York Times, Dec. 27, 1965, p 20*

[ultimately from *wig*, *n.*, U.S. slang (especially jazz) term for the head or mind, and initially (1930's) a person's hair]

wiglet, *n.* a small hairpiece added to a woman's hair to make it longer or higher, to frame the face, etc.

Wiglets set in long loopy curls were attached to the crown of the head, while separate curls were used to cascade down the back in more elaborate evening styles. *Kenneth E. Battelle, "Hair Styles," 1968 Collier's Encyclopedia Year Book, p 250*

In her salon she has a very wide selection of wigs, "almost" wigs, braids, wiglets, chignons and postiches. *The New York Times, Feb. 24, 1965, p 44*

wildlifer, *n.* a person who advocates the protection of wildlife.

It none the less ill becomes the Wildlifers to aid and abet so aggressive and systematic a piece of pollution promotion. *The Times (London), Nov. 18, 1970, p 12*

There will of course be carping critics of a Grand Canyon Dam . . . do-gooders, conservationists, starry-eyed liberals and wild-lifers. *Bruce Stewart, "Think Big: An Open Letter to the Secretary of the Interior," Harper's, Aug. 1965, p 63*

wild-track, *adj.* that is recorded with sound or voicing separate or different from the action shown on film; off-screen.

Another humanising technique is to explain the idea in a 'wild-track' (that is, off-screen) commentary while showing film of people going about their business in easily recognisable and vaguely apposite ways. For instance, the commentary discusses the impact of the Common Market on food prices while the viewer watches a perfectly ordinary film sequence of housewives shopping in the supermarket. *Keith Kyle, The Listener, Oct. 15, 1970, p 506*

A simple, straightforward commentary and some "wild track" recording of music and dialogue (one wonders if the dialogue actually relates to the scenes one is witnessing) add to the realism of the visuals. *New Scientist, Feb. 2, 1967, p 284*

wildwater, *n.* water with strong currents; the turbulent part of a stream. *Often used attributively.*

Evans had beaten the man who was acknowledged to be the best wild-water boater in southern California. . . . *John McPhee, "The Sporting Scene: Reading the River," The New Yorker, March 21, 1970, p 133*

East Germany's supremacy was broken on the third day of the world wildwater canoe championships on the Lieser river here today when their representatives won only two of the seven events. *The Times (London), Aug. 14, 1963, p 4*

wind (waind), *v.t., v.i.* **wind down,** to reduce gradually so as to bring or come to an end; de-escalate; phase down.

. . . Nixon may be able finally to wind the war down. *Ronald Dworkin, The Listener, Oct. 29, 1970, p 601*

With the headquarters offices empty, the war—in that theater, anyhow—would soon wind down, and we could all go home, *John Fischer, "The Easy Chair: War As Theater of the Absurd," Harper's, March 1970, p 28*

But now, when the war is supposed to be "winding down," . . . there is no reason to believe that the consequences of an invasion now would be any different from what the consequences would have been then. *"The Talk of the Town," The New Yorker, March 13, 1971, p 30*

wind-chill factor ('wind,tʃil), wind velocity as a factor in determining the cooling effect of moving air on the body.

During the past few days the temperatures in the Fort Greely area have ranged from about 15° to 45°F below zero, including a windchill factor that has driven the temperature down to −50° and even lower. *The Times (London), Feb. 12, 1965, p 11*

wind-down ('waind,daun), *n.* a winding down; a gradual suspension.

Kwangtung province alone has mobilized 50,000 industrial workers and 280,000 peasants for the heroic propaganda and purification push, or, as Peking labels it, the "purification of class ranks in the countryside." In effect, the campaign heralds the official wind-down of the Cultural Revolution, a finale that is to climax in "all-round victory." *China: Errant Army, Stubborn Peasants," Time, Feb. 21, 1969, p 29*

The dispirited ones say that the US lead in technology has now gone for ever and, as proof, point to the reduction in the number of students enrolling for engineering courses, the cutback in government research and development spending, the cancellation of the SST, the wind-down of space exploration, and the technological emergence of Japan and Europe. *"Electronics Men in the Slump," New Scientist and Science Journal, July 8, 1971, p 95*

Even now, with the virtual completion of the wind-down begun in 1970, the military break with Indochina is not final. *Geoffrey Tebbutt, "Australia Pulls Out of Vietnam," The Manchester Guardian Weekly, Dec. 25, 1971, p 3*

wind loading, the stress exerted on a structure by the force of the wind.

The statistical approach treats wind loading as a problem of probability and the emphasis is laid on designing within the constraints of what is calculated to be "acceptable risk". *The Times (London), March 23, 1970, p 23*

When the computer program was written it was decided not to restrict wind loading calculations merely to British local conditions but to extend them to different climates, with particular reference to various areas in the developing world. *New Scientist and Science Journal, May 13, 1971, p 388*

window, *n.* **1** a region of the electromagnetic spectrum, such as the radio region, whose radiation is not absorbed by the earth's atmosphere and is able to reach the earth.

One window is that portion called the visible spectrum through which the optical telescopes receive their information either by eye, photographic plate or photocell. The other window is that through which the aerials of the radio telescopes can operate. *P. Lancaster Brown, New Scientist, March 28, 1968, p 680*

Earth's atmosphere acts as a strong absorber of the electromagnetic radiation of most wavelengths. Radiation reaches the ground only through a series of 'windows', the widest of which is in the radio region of the spectrum. *K. A. Pounds, Science Journal, April 1970, p 62*

2 short for LAUNCH WINDOW.

The Soviet and American vehicles flew to Venus close together because both were fired during one of the periodic "windows" for such shots. These are brief periods of time when Venus is overtaking the earth and relative positions of the two planets are propitious. *Walter Sullivan, The New York Times, Oct. 18, 1967, p 30*

Between February and April next year the 'window' will be open for launchings to Mars and there is the chance of sending craft on fly-by, orbital or lander missions. *Science Journal, Dec. 1968, p 17*

wing, *v.t.* **wing it,** *U.S. Slang.* to improvise.

Cox: The resistance put up against us dictates [our] strategy.

Bernstein (lounging in an armchair in tartan slacks): You mean you've got to wing it. . . . I dig absolutely. *Time, Jan. 26, 1970, p 12*

wipe-out, *n.* **1** *U.S. Slang.* a fall from an upright position on a surfboard, motorcycle, skis, etc.

Like a practiced surfer, he was balanced carefully in the curl, in control of his board and in no apparent danger of a wipe-out. *Time, Aug. 15, 1969, p 11*

Even when elated beginners go too fast and hit a bump, the worst that usually happens is a harmless wipe-out in soft snow. *Time, March 17, 1967, p 36*

Knievel [motorcyclist Evel Knievel] still limps because of a severe wipeout in Las Vegas three years ago, when he jumped the fountains at Caesars Palace. *"The Talk of the Town," The New Yorker, July 24, 1971, p 23*

2 total defeat or annihilation.

...Danny's was closed for unknown reasons, its liquor license revoked. Elvin didn't bat an eye. He was accustomed to wipe-outs. *Albert Goldman, "Jazz Meets Rock," The Atlantic, Feb. 1971, p 104*

The idea that the United States, capable of the final human wipe-out, could possibly lose to the Republic of North Korea, even supported by the Chinese Communist infantry, was too patently nonsensical. *Russell Baker, The New York Times, May 12, 1970, p 38*

with-it, *adj. Slang.* fashionably up-to-date.

...his [Pierre Trudeau's] managers created a new image of him as the youthful, debonaire, "with-it" man of the jet-set age. *John S. Moir, "Trudeau, Pierre Elliott," The Americana Annual 1970, p 694*

...Meyer Davis led his orchestra in such purportedly with-it numbers as "I'm Going Out of My Head" and "Love Is Blue." *Charlotte Curtis, The New York Times, June 19, 1968, p 50*

The papier-mâché toe rings are very simple and very with-it. *Marjorie Harris, Maclean's, Oct. 1, 1966, p 15*

Hooper Bolton must have one of the most "with-it" collections of jewelry in London. *The Times (London), July 22, 1965, p 12*

[from the slang phrases *be with it, get with it*, to be or get smart, alert, etc., originally a carnival and circus phrase]

with-it-ness, *n. Slang.* the quality or character of keeping up with the latest trends; up-to-dateness.

Late Night Line-Up's quality stems, I suppose, from its creative freedom—its freedom from press criticism (it goes out too late for a mention in the dailies), from the attention of the rating statisticians....It is extremely well served by its staff of editors...who radiate a youthful enthusiasm and with-it-ness. *Bernard Hollowood, "On the Box," Punch, Sept. 10, 1969, p 434*

...modernity...can now just as often be caution in the cinema, with film after film chasing with-itness and looking more and more conventional. *Penelope Gilliatt, "The Current Cinema: Then As Now," The New Yorker, July 18, 1970, p 45*

Bond told us it could be fun and it could be won. So we allowed ourselves to enjoy those exploits, that with-it-ness and all those easy ladies. *H. R. F. Keating, "Crime," Review of "Zoom!" by Peter Townend, The Times (London), Jan. 27, 1972, p 10*

witster, *n.* a person who is adept in uttering witticisms; a wit.

...I'm fresh from the feet of S. J. Perelman....The quiet, talkative steel-rimmed, urbane, lumpen doyen of Hollywood and "New Yorker" witsters....*John Hall, The Manchester Guardian Weekly, Dec. 12, 1970, p 15*

[from *wit* + *-ster* (as in *punster, jokester*)]

wok (wak), *n.* a traditional Chinese cooking utensil shaped somewhat like a bowl.

...it is no longer necessary to trek down to Chinatown for woks. Macy's has them, made of stainless steel and with black hard-plastic handles. *"On and Off the Avenue: And All Through the House," The New Yorker, Nov. 28, 1970, p 163*

[from Cantonese]

Women's Lib, a militant movement of women calling for liberation from sexism and all other forms of male domination. Also called WOMEN'S LIBERATION, FEM LIB.

While some fear that Women's Lib is a threat to the family, many experts believe that its more sensible goals could strengthen it. As women become increasingly emancipated—by child-care centers and equal-employment practices—they could have more time for intellectual and emotional fulfillment. *Time, Dec. 28, 1970, p 38*

I personally don't believe in Women's Lib for black women, as we have always been liberated to work—many times at menial jobs. *Gladys Lesley Davis, Peekskill, N.Y., in a Letter to the Editor, The New York Times, June 27, 1971, p 31*

Women's-Libber, *n.* another name for WOMEN'S LIBERATIONIST.

Women's-Libbers, both of them (it was too bad that the linesman in question was a woman), they said that they didn't care what happened to the prize money....*Time, Oct. 11, 1971, p 44*

A batch of Pain Parlors and guillotines that had already been delivered to the stores (and reportedly all bought up by camp-minded adults), however, provoked an angry delegation of women's-libbers to picket Nabisco's embarrassed Park Avenue headquarters last month with signs blaming the rise in juvenile crime on their monster kits. *"On And Off The Avenue," The New Yorker, Dec. 11, 1971, p 109*

Women's Liberation, another name for WOMEN'S LIB.

...the editors of *Harper's* wish to reassert our belief that Women's Liberation is a development of possibly very great significance to the future of American Society—certainly this movement is showing itself to be a major force in the social and cultural atmosphere currently surrounding us. *Harper's, March 1971, p 4*

Women's Liberationist, a member, follower, or supporter of Women's Lib; a militant feminist. Also called WOMEN'S-LIBBER.

Construction workers waving their flags, Women's Liberationists waving their bras—these threaten to become the unsmiling faces of the '70s. *Melvin Maddocks, Time, July 20, 1970, p 30*

Good causes attract poor advocates. The demands of the women's movements, at least those demands that can be brought to socioeconomic focus, are transparently just..So much so that to some people, including the more fanatical Women's Liberationists, they also seem a little dull. *Irving Howe, "Books: The Middle-Class Mind of Kate Millett," Review of "Sexual Politics" by Kate Millett, Harper's, Dec. 1970, p 110*

woodhenge, *n.* a prehistoric circular structure of wood, found in various places in England; a wooden henge.

The four largest henge monuments in England, each surrounded by earthworks measuring more than 1,000 feet in diameter, are Avebury and three woodhenges: Mount Pleasant (near Dorchester), Durrington Walls and Marden (both on the River Avon). *Scientific American, May 1970, p 58*

work, *v.t. Slang.* to beat up; work over.

One older student told me:... "If I see a black man getting worked I'm going in with bottle and fist and I'm going in to kill...." *Martin Woollacott, The Manchester Guardian Weekly, Aug. 22, 1970, p 10*

workaholic, *n.* a person having an uncontrollable need to work incessantly.

The workaholic "drops out of the human community," Oates says, and "eats, drinks and sleeps his job."... How does a workaholic know that he is one? Sometimes he finds out only when he suffers a heart attack — or when, as in Oates' case, his five-year-old son asks for an appointment to see him. *"Behavior: Hooked on Work," Time, July 5, 1971, p 46*

Abingdon Press will publish "Confessions of a Workaholic" by pastoral counselor Wayne Oates on September 11, in paperback, $1.45. The author coined the word "workaholic" to describe those people so involved in their work that it interferes with their health, personal happiness, social functioning and interpersonal relationships. Mr. Oates contends that addiction to work is favored by society and fostered by industry. He tells of his own "addiction" and how he has reformed. *Publishers· Weekly, Sept. 11, 1972, p 44*

[coined from *work* + *alcoholic*]

workfare, *n.* a welfare program in which recipients of public welfare payments are required to work at assigned jobs or to enlist in job training.

One of Evers' programs is what he calls workfare; he has said that everybody ought to work for what he gets, that welfare ought to exist only for those who can't work or for whom no jobs can be made available. *Robert Canzoneri, "Charles Evers: Mississippi's Representative Man?" Harper's, July 1968, p 71*

The new law will take 18 months to set up and, at that, is expected to increase the number of recipients registered for workfare by no more than 30,000. *"Small Step, Big Symbol," Time, Dec. 27, 1971, p 26*

Just as in the domestic welfare reform programme, Nixon calls for work-fare instead of welfare, so in foreign policy the "do-it-yourself" principle will be applied. *Henry Brandon, The Sunday Times (London), Jan. 25, 1970, p 8*

[from *work* + *welfare*]

work-in, *n.* a form of protest demonstration in which a group of people report to work or study but disregard the rules and procedures they normally follow.

Last summer more than 3,000 city welfare employees staged a "work-in," during which they showed up at the office but refused to process cases, *Time, Aug. 23, 1968, p 50*

Several hundred students decided yesterday to hold an all-night "work-in" in their library after the principal had refused to call an emergency meeting of the university court. *The Times (London), March 6, 1970, p 2*

Mr Davies did not visit the John Brown yard, where stewards claim to have taken over control for a work-in by the 2,500 employees. *Geoffrey Whiteley, "Cold Comfort for the Clyde," The Manchester Guardian Weekly, Aug. 7, 1971, p 7*

[see -IN]

world-class, *adj.* of international note or quality.

...Granados was in glorious voice and in total sympathy with Ashkenazy, who showed himself a world-class accompanist. *Mary Stott, The Manchester Guardian Weekly, July 18, 1970, p 21*

It is now widely known that Fisons claims to have pulled a potentially world-class drug, Intal, out of its rag-bag of health food and proprietary pharmaceuticals interests. *James Poole, The Sunday Times (London), Nov. 23, 1969, p 26*

world line, the path of an elementary particle through space and time.

The strong gravitational field of the collapsing star bends the "world lines," or space-time paths, of photons emitted by the star. *Scientific American, Nov. 1967, p 89*

Minkowski's 4-dimensional device time is no more than a mathematical device allowing one to represent the history of a particle by a world-line, the direction of which at any instant gives the velocity of the particle. *G. K. Goiffin, New Scientist, Sept. 19, 1968, p 618*

worry beads, a string of beads played with for relaxation or distraction, originally chiefly in countries of the Middle East.

Worry beads and clunky ball-bearings are two traditional office diversions for nervy captains of industry.... *The Times (London), Nov. 7, 1970, p 12*

Top brass relaxation rooms should also be provided, plentifully equipped with worry beads.... *"The Last Word on Counselling," New Scientist and Science Journal, Dec. 9, 1971, p 105*

He [Marshall Frady, author of "An American Innocent in the Middle East"] calls the "worry beads" used by many Arabs, Greeks, and for that matter, Israelis, "Islamic prayer beads." *Herbert F. Morris, Washington, D.C., in a Letter to the Editor, Harper's, Jan. 1971, p 8*

worrying, *adj.* causing worry; distressing.

The continuous decline in the percentage of students achieving the necessary 'A' levels to enter university physics courses since the early 60s is worrying. *New Scientist, Jan. 1, 1970, p 4*

W particle, a hypothetical elementary particle that is the carrier, or quantum, of the weak force.

Evidence of the existence of a hitherto hypothetical subatomic particle — the intermediate boson, or *W* particle — has been found in an abandoned silver mine in Utah. The finding, made by a group of physicists from the University of Utah led by Jack W. Keuffel and Haven E. Bergeson, was reported recently at the 12th International Conference on Cosmic-Ray Physics, held in Tasmania. *"Science and the Citizen: Gold in a Silver Mine," Scientific American, Oct. 1971, p 42*

For the weak nuclear interactions, the exchange particle, although as yet undetected experimentally, has been labelled the intermediate vector boson, or W-particle.... *New Scientist and Science Journal, Feb. 4, 1971, p 230*

wraparound, *adj.* **1** completely encircling or surrounding.

The Volkswagen is the German's ideal image of space: it's a wraparound, secure little thing.... *Marshall McLuhan, Maclean's, Sept. 1967, p 14*

2 all-inclusive; all-embracing.

The social issue, the wraparound inphrase of the year, covering dissatisfaction with protest, fear of crime, and disgust with drugs, promiscuity and pornography, had less universal impact than initially assumed. *Time, Nov. 16, 1970, p 17*

3 of or designating letterpress printing adapted to a flexible plate for a rotary press, as opposed to a flat-bed press, thus gaining the advantage of speedy reproduction.

Wraparound letterpress printing is the direct transfer of ink to paper from a thin, flexible relief plate which is wrapped around the cylinder of a rotary press. *Donald J. Byers, "Wraparound Printing," McGraw-Hill Yearbook of Science and Technology 1969, p 284*

wrist, *v.t.* to move, send, throw, etc., by a movement of the wrist.

Evans rounded off a hectic but disappointing few seconds by wristing the second rebound high over the bar. *Tom German, The Times (London), Sept. 16, 1970, p 14*

[verb use of the noun]

write, *v.t.* to release or print out (data) from the memory of a computer.

A core whose dimensions are measured in thousandths of an inch, is a tiny doughnut-shaped object pressed from a mixture of ferric oxide powder and other materials and then baked in an oven. Millions of cores are used for very large computer memories. They are strung, or "sewn," into a wire mesh. Then other wires are passed through them in three planes so that appropriate pulses can cause each core to absorb ("read") or release ("write") information bits. *Henry R. Lieberman and Louis Robinson, The New York Times, Jan. 9, 1967, p 136*

wrongo, *n. Slang.* a wrongdoer; badman.

It has taken Peter [Fonda] the longest to establish priorities, to coincide his intelligence and his energy.... But the career has gone from bullying waste to something measurable. His scenario for *Easy Rider* was sometimes self-indulgent. Its villains were as exaggerated and snarling as the overdrawn wrongos of his Dad's old oaters ["horse operas" or westerns].... *"The Flying Fondas and How They Grew," Time, Feb. 16, 1970, p 63*

Deploring the good-guys-and-wrongos syndrome of US foreign policy, he [John Kenneth Galbraith] remarks that "money serves as a substitute for intelligence." *Kenneth Allsop, Punch, Nov. 12, 1969, p 801*

WWW, abbreviation of *World Weather Watch.*

At the time of its inception in 1967 the WWW plan relied entirely on improving and extending existing systems. *M. W. Kerr-Smith, Science Journal, April 1970, p 48*

WWW is in effect a complete new global weather service sponsored by the World Meteorological Organisation and now accepted by all its 130 member States. *Peter Collins, The Sunday Times (London), April 30, 1967, p 28*

X

xen·o·graft ('zen ou,græft), *n.* a graft of tissue taken from an individual of another species.

A xenograft, formerly heterograft, is one in which there is interspecific difference between donor and recipient, as between a man and a monkey. *John Bergan, "New Parts for Old: The Latest Medical Adventure," 1969 Britannica Yearbook of Science and the Future, 1968, p 177*

If the donor and recipient are non-identical members of the same species, the graft is called an allograft or homograft; if they belong to different species, the graft is called a xenograft or heterograft. *Keith James, New Scientist, Nov. 9, 1967, p 364*

[from *xeno-* foreign (from Greek *xénos*) + *graft*]

xer·o·gram ('zir ə,græm), *n.* a xerographic copy.

The general editor in sending back a delaying or rejection notice often sends comments from his "expert." In recent years xerography has been of the greatest assistance.... But not everybody sends xerograms of the original report. *R. Douglas Wright, "Truth and its Keepers," New Scientist, Feb. 26, 1970, p 404*

xer·ox ('zir,aks), *v.t., v.i.* to make copies of graphic material by a xerographic or dry photocopying process.

In view of the sentiments expressed at the meeting, I thought that the affluent group would be more likely to spend their money on xeroxing Foxe's Book of Martyrs, but I was wrong. *John Transom, New Scientist, Dec. 31, 1970, p 604*

Morning coffee, in-box, out-box, Xeroxing, and other matters were handled by staff services. *Robert Townsend, "Up the Organization," Harper's, March 1970, p 87*

[from *Xerox,* trade name for a xerographic process and machine]

X-ray astronomer, a specialist in X-ray astronomy.

The group of X-ray astronomers at Massachusetts Institute of Technology have made a speciality of studying X-rays emanating from the centre of our Galaxy. *New Scientist and Science Journal, March 11, 1971, p 534*

X-ray astronomy, the astronomical study of X-ray stars.

...the accidental discovery of the X-ray source Sco[rpius] X-1 ushered in the new field of X-ray astronomy.... *Science Journal, May 1970, p 17*

The young field of X-ray astronomy has found another mystery: a second pulsating X-ray star quite different from the only other one known. *"Astronomy: A New X-ray Pulsating Star," Science News, April 3, 1971, p 239*

X-ray nova, a nova (type of star that suddenly becomes very bright and then fades) that emits X rays.

Meanwhile, the second example of an 'X-ray nova' was reported during the summer of 1969, based on observations from two US Vela satellites built to monitor man-made nuclear explosions in space. *K. A. Pounds, Science Journal, April 1970, p 64*

X-ray pulsar, a pulsar that is the source of powerful X-ray emissions.

One of the most remarkable developments of X-ray astronomy was the Mar. 13, 1969, discovery of an X-ray pulsar in the Crab Nebula. Pulsars, celestial objects which emit vast amounts of power in brief intense bursts with extremely precise periodicity, were first observed in the radio region. *Richard B. Hoover, "X-ray Astronomy," McGraw-Hill Yearbook of Science and Technology 1971, p 441*

X-ray scanning, a method of testing for flaws in solid objects by using an X-ray machine.

Recently developed techniques of nondestructive testing consist of holography, the light-scattering properties of liquid crystals, infrared scanning, microwave scanning, x-ray scanning, neutron radiography, and acoustic emission. *John R. Zurbrick, "Nondestructive Testing," McGraw-Hill Yearbook of Science and Technology 1971, p 36*

X-ray star or **X-ray source,** an astronomical source of X rays concentrated at a point; a celestial body that emits X rays.

New discoveries would shed light on the relationship between pulsars and other kinds of X-ray stars.... *New Scientist, Dec. 3, 1970, p 364*

Most of the known discrete X-ray sources lie close to the Milky Way and therefore very probably belong to the local galaxy. *K. A. Pounds, Science Journal, April 1970, p 61*

X-ray telescope, a telescope used in X-ray astronomy, consisting of mirrors focused on a gas-filled X-ray scintillation counter, which is attached to a rocket and telemeters X-ray emissions to earth.

X-ray telescopes using confocal paraboloidal-hyperboloidal mirrors have been fabricated and flown on Aerobee rockets to obtain photographs of the Sun in the soft x-ray region. *Richard B. Hoover, "X-ray Astronomy," McGraw-Hill Yearbook of Science and Technology 1971, p 439*

XYY syndrome, a congenital disorder of males resulting from the presence of an extra male chromosome (XYY instead of XY) in the cells, and thought to be characterized by aggressive behavior, low intelligence, and social inadequacy. Compare KLINEFELTER'S SYNDROME.

The XYY syndrome, a defect in sexual chromosomes, has, for instance, been linked to criminal behavior in some men. *Science News, Oct. 19, 1968, p 388*

The judge, however, ruled that there was insufficient evidence to prove that there was any relationship between the XYY syndrome and human behaviour.... Hall Williams argues that an extra chromosome might be used as additional evidence in establishing a defence of insanity or of diminished responsibility, but by itself the extra chromosome complement *does not* establish diminished responsibility or disease of the mind. *Oliver Gillie, "Criminals Are Made, Not Born — XYY Chromosome Theory Exploded," Science Journal, Dec. 1970, p 8*

Y

YAG (yæg), *n.* acronym for *yttrium aluminum garnet,* a synthetic crystal of aluminum oxide used to generate laser beams. Compare YIG.

Mr. Hill said that, at the moment, the neodymium doped YAG laser operating in the second harmonic mode provides hundreds of kilowatts at a wavelength of 0.53 microns. It can be operated at pulse rates of up to 10 Hz. *New Scientist, April 17, 1969, p 123*

For the time being the new team will concentrate on producing calcium tungstate and Yttrium Aluminium Garnet (YAG) crystals. *The Times (London), Sept. 18, 1968, p 25*

ya·ki·to·ri (ˌyɑ: ki'tɔr iː), *n.* a Japanese dish of grilled or skewered chicken, usually boneless and served with soy sauce.

The victory feast was elaborate in the best Japanese manner: wild boar soup, egg roll, raw fish, grilled eel and steaming platters of *yakitori....Time, Dec. 9, 1966, p 35*

To stop him [the cook] from frying, simply hold up your hand. A similar technique, both of cooking and eating, applies in the hundreds of *yakitori* (chicken) restaurants scattered round Tokyo.... *"Mapping Way to Menus," The Times (London), June 17, 1970, p VII*

[from Japanese, from *yaki* grilled + *tori* chicken]

Yard (yɑrd), *n.* another name for MONTAGNARD.

From the beginning, the Americans, unlike the Vietnamese, got along well with the "Yards." *Time, July 19, 1968, p 31*

Once trained and equipped, the "yards" (short for Montagnards) displayed an unhappy tendency to join FULRO [Front Unifié de Lutte des Races Opprimées, or United Front for the Struggle of Oppressed Races] when their enlistment was up, feeling that the Saigon government posed more problems for them than the Viet Cong. *Time, Feb. 14, 1969, p 37*

[from the pronunciation of the final syllable of *Montagnard*]

yawn, *n.* a tiresome thing or person; a bore.

He [Théophile Gautier] thought the cathedral [of Valencia] a big yawn after the marvels of Burgos and Seville and, like Swinburne, he was sickened by the ornamentation of the other churches. *Kenneth Tynan, The New Yorker, July 25, 1970, p 34*

"Then in January we felt the full blast of their campaign," Mr Wilson paused and derisive laughter greeted his next sentence. "The Prime Minister took to the road." But by mid-March Sir Alec had become a yawn. "Tedious repetition alternated with repetitive tedium, depending on which of two speechwriters was writing his speeches." *Peter Jenkins, "Mr. Wilson's Searing Indictment," The Manchester Guardian Weekly, April 9, 1964, p 4*

yenbond, *n.* a Japanese government or corporation bond. *Often used attributively.*

There was some future possibility of a yenbond market for the financing of international direct investment, said Mr. Iwasa. *The Times (London), Oct. 5, 1970, p 19*

[from *yen* the Japanese monetary unit + *bond*]

yen·ta ('yen tə), *n. U.S. Slang.* a female gossip or busybody.

... Miss Rivers, a card-carrying yenta, displays gravelly authority in "Just Like a Man," a song from "Two's Company" for which Ogden Nash has furnished an extra pair of closing lines.... *Douglas Watt, "Popular Records," The New Yorker, Oct. 24, 1970, p 169*

To the less friendly, she [Congresswoman Bella Abzug] comes on as a sumo liberal, a lady wrestler, Joan of Arc resurrected as an elemental *yenta. Time, Aug. 16, 1971, p 27*

[from Yiddish *yente* a plain woman or housewife, originally a woman's name]

yé·yé ('yei,yei), *adj.* of or relating to the mod style of music, clothes, etc., in France, especially during the 1960's.

The jet screechings, like a thousand pieces of chalk rubbed on a thousand blackboards and then amplified like yé-yé music, will blow out the frontal lobes of those waiting at the gate.... *Horace Sutton, Saturday Review, March 4, 1967, p 49*

The first day of the fashion shows was a limping, half-hearted one that started with Réal. That's the name of a high-priced haute couture boutique here, run by Arlette Nastat, a forever yé-yé designer.

Réal's customers include Brigitte Bardot, her sister Mijanou and 35 other women whose names are all listed on the program. *Gloria Emerson, The New York Times, July 23, 1968, p 42*

—*n.* the yé-yé style of music, clothes, etc.

Turning back to business, Régine disclosed that the orchestra Chez Régine will play anything "from yé-yé to regular music, which is coming back." *Marylin Bender, The New York Times, July 3, 1968, p 30*

[from French slang *yé-yé*, from English *yeah, yeah*, interjection used in the songs of some rock groups, especially the Beatles]

YIG (yig), *n.* acronym for *yttrium iron garnet*, a synthetic crystal of iron oxide with versatile magnetic properties, used especially in laser modulation. Compare YAG.

The ferrimagnetic nature of YIG offers three interesting possibilities for modulation. *Leo F. Johnson, "Crystal Lasers," McGraw-Hill Yearbook of Science and Technology 1967, p 210*

Gas lasers offer some advantages in infrared gas analysis as selective sources, and their potential is now being helped by the development of yttrium-iron-garnet (YIG) modulators capable of working out to 3.5 micrometres. *D. W. Hill, The Times (London), May 13, 1968, p IV*

yip, *n. U.S.* short for YIPPIE.

After swallowing and, at times, choking on an unending diet of ... the gappy generation, with-it, hung-up, love-in,

way-out, freak-out, out of sight, uptight, trips, hips, yips, drugs, thugs, dig, groove, swing and all the power the LOVE can bring, I wish to protest.... *Mrs. Anthony J. Keeley, Jr., Red Bank, N.J., in a Letter to the Editor, Time, Feb. 16, 1970, p 4*

yip·pie ('yip i:), *n.* Also frequently spelled **Yippie.** *U.S.* any of a group of politically active, radical hippies. Also shortened to YIP.

In Anaheim, Calif., about 300 garishly garbed Yippies "liberated" Disneyland. Before the cops arrived, the raiders hoisted a Viet Cong flag atop a fort on Tom Sawyer's Island and yowled slogans like "Free Mickey Mouse!" *Time, Aug. 17, 1970, p 35*

The idea is to relate city revolt to the arty underground. Or, as R. G. Davis, king of the San Francisco yippies, poses it in Owen's advance: "Can guerrilla theatre actually be similar to armed revolution?" *The Manchester Guardian Weekly, Jan. 16, 1969, p 4*

[supposedly formed from *YIP* (abbreviation of *Youth International Party*, the professed name of the yippie group) + hip*pie*]

Young Lord, *U.S.* a member of the *Young Lords*, a radical organization of young Spanish-speaking Americans, chiefly of Puerto Rican descent, seeking to gain political and economic power for Latin-Americans in the United States.

Then there were the Young Lords ... who seized the First Spanish Methodist Church in East Harlem. Religion, you understand, is the oppressor, unresponsive to the needs of the community, an arm of the Establishment, and so on, and the Young Lords went about the work of the Revolution by sitting in, and seizing, the First Spanish Methodist Church. *John Corry, "The Politics of Style," Harper's, Nov. 1970, p 62*

We had camera crews that were coming, but the Young Lords were having a sit-in, and they had to cover that first. *"The Talk of the Town," The New Yorker, Feb. 13, 1971, p 31*

youth culture, the values and mores of the generation under thirty viewed as a distinctive culture.

Kaplan [John Kaplan, author of *Marijuana—The New Prohibition*] cites a recent historical study, which found that the Volstead Act "resulted largely from pressure by white rural Protestants to have made illegal a practice that they associated primarily with urban Roman Catholics." It was a way of censuring not only drinking behavior but an "entire life-style, including Catholicism." In the same way, Kaplan charges, marijuana bans are vain expressions of opposition to the youth culture, and they do more harm than good. *"The Law: If Pot Were Legal," Time, July 20, 1970, p 41*

A great many people, especially the better educated, take it for granted that today's "youth culture" is the wave of the future. They assume that as the present generation of college students become the young adults of tomorrow, their new life-styles will come to dominate American society and our economy. *Peter F. Drucker, "The Surprising Seventies," Harper's, July 1971, p 35*

youthquake, *n.* the world-wide agitation caused by student uprisings and other expressions of rebellion and radicalism among the youth during the 1960's and 1970's.

Play Power, his [Richard Neville's] exploration of the ... youthquake, is at once spirited, informative, and clearly the work of an engaging and concerned man. *Mordecai*

Richler, *The Manchester Guardian Weekly, Feb. 28, 1970, p 18*

He was an Aquarian, yet not of this Aquarian Age of psychedelic blast-offs and amplified youthquakes. *Time, Jan. 11, 1971, p 54*

[from *youth* + earth*quake*]

yo-yo ('you,you), *adj.* going up and down; fluctuating.

Dr. Sacks spoke of a "Yo-Yo effect" in which some patients [treated with L-Dopa] alternate between sudden restless excitements and a reversion to their original immobility. *Israel Shenker, "The Remarkable Effects of L-Dopa," Encyclopedia Science Supplement (Grolier) 1970, p 213*

Certainly it is not a quickie device which destabilizes the tax system. Congress has come to object to "yo-yo" tax devices. *Henry C. Wallich, Yale University, in a Letter to the Editor, The New York Times, Dec. 16, 1970, p 47*

−*v.i.* to waver or fluctuate.

The hard facts underlying our economic health−as op-posed to the headlines and Treasury press releases−just don't yo-yo about like this. *Punch, April 12, 1967, p 514*

There is plenty of room for debate on this point, because the Supreme Court has yoyoed on the issue of the right to travel. *Fred P. Graham, The New York Times, Dec. 17, 1967, Sec. 4, p 12*

But its profits have yo-yoed up from £28,200 to £97,100 through 1958/67, which must leave the Berger Jenson parent wondering what might have been if the accent had been on "service." *Richard Milner, The Sunday Times (London), March 9, 1969, p 29*

−*n. U.S. Slang.* a stupid person, probably so called from the comparison of a yo-yo's motion to a "jerk" (a fool).

Upon catching their attention, he would leer, and cate-gorize them in a loud, mocking voice. ("Weirdo" was one of his favorite appellations; also "Freak," "Yo-Yo," and "Creep.") *James Stevenson, "The Pianoforte Factory Revisited," The New Yorker, Nov. 28, 1970, p 40*

[from *yo-yo*, a toy spun up and down on a string]

Z

za·ire (zɑːˈir), *n.; pl.* **za·ires** or **za·ire.** the basic unit of money in the Zaire Republic (the former Demo-cratic Republic of the Congo), equal to 100 makuta. 0.50 zaire = $1. 1.20 zaire = £1.

A little over a year ago, the Government, with Inter-national Monetary Fund advice, performed a drastic 3-for-1 currency devaluation, replacing the inflation-riddled franc with a new currency, the zaire, worth about $2. *Alfred Friendly, Jr., The New York Times, July 9, 1968, p 2*

"They tried to recruit former Katangese gendarmes while they were in Mutshatsha. They offered seven zaires (£5) to every man who enlisted. In Mutshatsha two former gendarmes fell to the temptation." *The Times (London), Nov. 9, 1967, p 6*

Za·ir·e·an (zɑːˈir iː ən), *n.* a native or inhabitant of the Zaire Republic, the name since November 1971 of the former Democratic Republic of the Congo (capital, Kinshasa).

All Zaireans may keep their present first names or opt for local ones until the party congress next May decides whether people should be identified by their surnames or their first names. *"Zaire President Changes Name," The Times (London), Jan. 13, 1972, p 6*

zap, *Slang, chiefly U.S.* −*v.t.* **1** to shoot; hit.

". . . I worry about my own son getting hit by a sniper because of that damn long hair. It's dangerous to walk around looking hairy, man. You could get zapped." *Dave Gardner, quoted by Larry L. King, "Whatever Happened to Brother Dave?" Harper's, Sept. 1970, p 61*

2 to beat; defeat.

"No police force can stop a riot," a captain said. "They'll need the Army to zap those hoodlums, just like in Detroit." *Thomas A. Johnson, The New York Times, May 1, 1968, p 14*

3 to engage in a confrontation or attack verbally.

They [homosexuals] have also made it a practice to "trash" (wreck) restaurants, publishing houses, and other businesses that discriminate against the third world of sex; "dump on" (heckle) religious leaders, such as Billy Graham, who don't like them; and "zap" (confront) politicians until they express themselves one way or the other on equal housing and employment rights for homo-sexuals. *Faubion Bowers: "Homosex: Living The Life," Saturday Review, Feb. 12, 1972, p 24*

4 to move or make quickly.

For quick acceleration . . . the nickel-cadmium batteries would cut in briefly, could zap the car from a standstill to 50 m.p.h. in 20 seconds. *Time, Dec. 22, 1967, p 56*

Nobody except his grandmother thought he'd live over-night, for he [the jockey Willie Shoemaker] weighed only two and a half pounds, but she zapped up an incubator for him−a cardboard box lined with cotton wool, which she put in the oven of the kitchen stove. And it did the trick. *Audax Minor, The New Yorker, Sept. 19, 1970, p 131*

−*v.i.* to go quickly; move fast.

Nothing is quite as sad as watching Lynn watching Lightfoot zap off out of a parking lot. I wondered how she'd get back. "By bus, or hooking a ride with someone," Light-foot said. *Marjorie Harris, Maclean's, Sept. 1968, p 55*

−*n.* **1** vitality; force; zip.

. . . when the heat's too much and the gin's lost its zap (gin rummy, of course), tranquilize your jangled nerves with the Swinging Wonder. *The New York Times, Aug. 2, 1968, p 3*

2 a confrontation or attack by opponents.

... her [Congresswoman Bella Abzug's] constituency included a large, politicized gay minority. Her platform called for an end to discrimination based on sexual orientation and for fairer taxes for unmarried men and women. Despite six zaps, New York's Mayor Lindsay has consistently refused to meet with any homosexual delegation. However, last May he did declare: "Antihomosexual policies are arbitrary victimization." *Faubion Bowers, "Homosex: Living The Life," Saturday Review, Feb. 12, 1972, p 26*

—*interj.* imitative of the sound, speed, suddenness, etc., of a hard blow.

Bang! Zap! Pow! With flashing laser beams and cracking doomsday machines, the deadly-serious superheroes swarmed out. ... *Douglas Marshall, Maclean's, March 1968, p 77*

I'm extremely curious about a drug called dilantin they give to epileptics but someone has shown it has remarkable effects on non-eps as well. Something like eliminating excessive randomness, electrical discharges in the brain like sunspots. Zap! There went one. *Paul Tyner, "Author to Editor: Extracts from the Letters of A Young Writer," The Atlantic, Feb. 1968, p 125*

[originally *zap!*, interjection used in the comic-strip balloons of Buck Rogers and Flash Gordon comics to render graphically the blast of space guns]

Za·pa·tis·mo (ˌsɑ: pɑ:'ti:z mou), *n. Spanish.* adherence to the revolutionary ideals, especially in agrarian reform, of the Mexican revolutionist Emiliano Zapata, 1880?-1919.

Mr. Womack describes the military and political evolution of Zapàtismo well enough, but this inevitably leads him out of Morelos, and there, like Zapata, he is not as at home. *Malcolm Deas, "Grey Guerrillas," Review of "Zapata and the Mexican Revolution" by John Womack, The Listener, Oct. 29, 1970, p 596*

Za·pa·tis·ta (ˌsɑ: pɑ:'ti:s tɑ:), *n. Spanish.* an advocate of Zapatismo; an adherent of Zapata.

Méndez Arceo's diocese, which is in the state of Morelos, south of Mexico City, was the terrain of Zapata's revolution, from 1911 to 1916, and the Bishop has always declared himself to be a staunch Zapatista. *Francine du Plessix Gray, "Profiles: The Rules of the Game (Ivan Illich)," The New Yorker, April 25, 1970, p 50*

zeit·ge·ber or **Zeit·ge·ber** ('tsait,gei bər), *n. sing. or pl.* any of various time indicators, such as light, dark, or temperature, that influence the workings of the biological clock.

Still, the circannual clock itself is not an adequate regulator. As we have seen, it is never set at exactly 365 days. If the natural environment played no part, the clock and the animal's rhythm would become increasingly out of phase with the natural seasons. Hence the animal still must depend on *Zeitgeber*, or cues from the environment, to correct the clock and thus entrain its rhythm each year. *Eric T. Pengelley and Sally J. Asmundson, "Annual Biological Clocks," Scientific American, April 1971, p 79*

The rhythms are clearly driven by an internal clock, since they continued for several days in constant light or constant darkness, and moonlight could act as a phase-setting factor (or *zeitgeber*) for both rhythms. *Graham Chedd and Peter Stubbs, New Scientist, Aug. 21, 1969, p 369*

The question of biological clock master key aside, most scientists of either school concur that external or geophysical factors can reset the clock or throw it out of phase. Light is considered by many researchers to be the most critical external timer or *zeitgeber*. *Joan Lynn Arehart, "The Search for Clues To the Rhythms of Life," Science News, Sept. 11, 1971, p 179*

[from German *Zeitgeber*, literally, time giver]

ze·ner diode ('zi: nər), a silicon semiconductor used as a voltage stabilizer.

... certain devices showed continuing growth. ... These included color television picture and power tubes, integrated circuits, field-effects silicon transistors, rectifiers, and zener diodes. *Allan Y. Brooks, "Electronics," 1970 Collier's Encyclopedia Year Book, p 223*

The Zener diode is in effect a variable resistor that automatically maintains fixed voltage in a circuit. *J. Barry Shackleford, "The Amateur Scientist," Scientific American, May 1970, p 132*

[named after Clarence *Zener*, an American physicist of the 1900's]

zero norm, *British.* another name for NIL NORM.

In principle at least, this type of operation does not need to use a zero norm—as the 1966 freeze did. It would be possible for wages to be semifrozen, with maximum increases of 2%, or 4%, or whatever. *The Sunday Times (London), June 18, 1972, p 62*

zero population growth, the condition in which a population ceases to grow and a balance is reached in the average number of births and deaths. *Abbreviation:* ZPG

If winter [in Alaska] is unusually long, a whole species [of migratory birds] may achieve zero population growth because it lacks time to hatch and rear its young before the ice begins to return in late August. *"The Vanishing World of Trapper Joe Delia," Time, July 27, 1970, p 49*

How attainable is zero population growth in the U.S.? That is, what would have to happen to bring the net reproduction rate to 1.0? *"Science and the Citizen," Scientific American, April 1971, p 50*

But there is more behind the current drive than law or militant women's groups. Transition from a time in which babies were the thing to an era of zero population growth must have profound consequences on the relations between men and women and on the structure of society. We have only begun to see some of the effects. *Philip H. Abelson, "Women in Academia," Science, Jan. 14, 1972, p 127*

Zhda·no·vi·an (ʒdɑ:'nou vi: ən), **Zhda·nov·ite** ('ʒdɑ: nə,vait), or **Zhda·nov·ist** ('ʒdɑ: nə vist), *adj.* of or relating to the Soviet policy or practice of Zhdanovism.

It is, indeed, a Leninist principle to make what is usable in non-socialist culture contribute to socialist culture, though this has been forgotten because of the indiscriminateness with which Zhdanovian aesthetics were applied. *Ronald Stevenson, The Listener, Oct. 22, 1970, p 557*

Four times last year, before the Central Committee suppressed it altogether in a fit of Zhdanovite rage, the union's weekly, *Literarni Noviny*, was forced to accept a different editor. *Claire Sterling, "Foreign Report: Prague," Harper's, Aug. 1968, p 68*

Then in 1948, along with other political events, all Czechoslovak cultural life fell under the powerful influence of Zhdanovist esthetics and Stalinist practices. *Milos Forman, Saturday Review, Dec. 23, 1967, p 11*

Zhda·nov·ism ('ʒdɑ: nə,viz əm), *n.* the strict political control of writers and other intellectuals in the Soviet Union fostered under Stalin by the Communist leader and general Andrei Z. Zhdanov, 1896-1948.

Ehrenburg at last ventured on criticism of Zhdanovism and made an open plea for greater artistic freedom in Russia. *"Obituary: Ilya Grigorevich Ehrenburg," The Annual Register of World Events in 1967 (1968), p 520*

Lukacs's ideological dependence on Stalinism is deeper than even such declarations suggest. He has been one of the very few theoretically educated adherents of 'socialist realism', perhaps the only important expounder of the so-called 'aesthetic ideal' of Zhdanovism. *Isaac Deutscher, "George Lukacs and 'Critical Realism'," The Listener, Nov. 3, 1966, p 659*

zilch, *n. U.S. Slang.* nil; nothing; zero.

"Seventy-five percent of our alcoholics eventually return to work, but our record of drug rehabilitation is zilch." *Donald Mahoney, quoted in Time, June 29, 1970, p 70*

Finishing second in the division or losing the league playoff is worth virtually zilch. *Jim Bouton, The New York Times, Oct. 10, 1970, p 25*

zing, *v.t.* **zing up,** *Slang.* to give life or zest to.

. . . Charles Revson is the philosopher-king of the cosmetic world. . . . He claims to know by instinct how to "zing up" a face. . . . *Kennedy Fraser, "On and Off the Avenue: Feminine Fashions," The New Yorker, Nov. 14, 1970, p 154*

[verb use of the slang noun *zing* liveliness, zest]

zing·er ('zɪŋ ər), *n. Slang.* **1** one who has spirit or vitality; a peppy person.

The only Republican thing about Barbara Howar is her famed friendship with Henry Kissinger, Washington's most sought-after bachelor. A stunning blonde zinger from North Carolina, Mrs. Howar, 36, got her social start as a Johnson campaign volunteer in 1964 and as the wife of a rich Washington builder. . . . *Time, Nov. 30, 1970, p 32*

2 something that hits the mark, such as a witty retort, or the like.

. . . you had to get right in there with Williams, stand eyeball to eyeball, and plant the zinger on him, bang . . . . *John Corry, "The Return of Ted Williams," Harper's, June 1969, p 74*

No sooner did Cavett sit down than he tossed a zinger . . . . *"Television—It Isn't As Easy As It Looks," Time, June 7, 1971, p 32*

Ann-Margret is giving him a hard time on the home front, too, cooking lousy dinners, casting aspersions on his sexual prowess, and tossing out little zingers about his advancing age like "Flab is reality." *Time, Oct. 12, 1970, p 7*

3 something very much out of the ordinary.

"I think every actress needs one zinger of a part early in her career." *The Times (London), May 30, 1968, p 10*

Zi·no·viev·ite (zi:'nɔ: vye,vaɪt), *n.* a follower of Grigori E. Zinoviev, 1883-1936, one of the Bolsheviks who advocated worldwide revolution.

When the failure of the collectivization became widely known, we were all taught to blame scheming kulaks, rightists, Trotskyites and Zinovievites for what was happening. *Nikita Khrushchev, "Khrushchev Remembers," The Times (London), Nov. 24, 1970, p 10*

▶ Zinoviev is chiefly associated with the famous "Zinoviev letter," which outlined a plan for a Communist revolution in Great Britain. The letter was identified in 1970 as being in the handwriting of Captain Sydney Reilly, who was involved in various intrigues to cause a rupture in Soviet-British relations. Though Zinoviev was long ago cleared of any connection with the notorious letter, his name is still associated with it as symbolic of the policy of exporting revolution.

zip code, *U.S.* a five-digit number used to identify a mail-delivery zone in the United States. The corresponding system in Great Britain is called POSTCODE.

Five number zip codes now permit electronic sorting of mail, eliminate many handlings, . . . can speed the mail. Every postoffice has a special zip code number. Ask your letter carrier for the zip code of your delivery office—and start using it now after the state name in your address. *Advertisement by the U.S. Postal Service, The Atlantic, Feb. 1964, p 30*

The first three digits of the familiar five-digit zip code system identify sectional centers, and the last two indicate the particular post office. *Edward C. Burks, The New York Times, Jan. 2, 1968, p 23*

[from *ZIP*, acronym for *Zone Improvement Plan*, the U.S. Postal Service system of coding by zones for faster mail sorting and delivery, introduced on July 1, 1963, + *code*]

zip-code, *v.t. U.S.* to provide with the zip code.

Third-class bulk mailers earn their lower postage rates by zip-coding every address, sorting the mail in numerical sequence, facing it and tieing it in bundles, placing it in properly tagged sacks and delivering it to the Post Office . . . . *Fred Woolf, the Bronx, in a Letter to the Editor, The New York Times, April 27, 1970, p 32*

zip-top, *adj.* having a top that may be removed by pulling a strip around its rim. Compare POP-TOP.

Easy opening devices are undergoing considerable development—and ring-pull and zip-top cans are already available. *Digby Brindle-Wood-Williams, The Times (London), Feb. 16, 1970, p III*

zir·cal·loy or **zir·ca·loy** ('zər kə,lɔɪ), *n.* an alloy of zirconium and other metals, widely used for its heat-resistant and corrosion-resistant properties, especially in reactors to separate the fuel from the coolant.

It will have a capacity of 125 tons per year of uranium oxide, and 50 tons of zircalloy products from Indian zircon, to be used for containing uranium oxide in fuel elements and structural elements in reactor assemblies. *S. K. Ghaswala, Science News, Aug. 10, 1968, p 146*

This [clad metal] may be aluminum, stainless steel or zirconium (usually a zirconium alloy called zircaloy). *John Kenton, "Atomic Energy," Encyclopedia Science Supplement (Grolier) 1968, p 218*

[from *zirconium alloy*]

zizz, *n. British Slang.* a short sleep; a nap or snooze.

As the lights begin to fade leaving Laurie alone while the others retire to have a "zizz" or unpack their luggage a desperate sense of emptiness and loneliness hangs in the air of the stuffy winter apartment [The Hotel in Amsterdam]. *Philip Hope-Wallace, The Manchester Guardian Weekly, July 11, 1968, p 14*

The comatose Alaska Way made turf history by snatching a few minutes zizz in her starting stall before the 1,000 Guineas, thereby missing the break. *Roger Mortimer, The Sunday Times (London), May 12, 1968, p 22*

[imitative of the hissing sounds made by sleepers, often represented in cartoon balloons as zzz . . .]

zof·tig, zof·tic, or **zof·tick** ('zaf tik), *adj. U.S. Slang.* pleasantly plump; having a full, curvaceous figure; luscious.

As he was being led to his first display case of the day, a seminar in the postwar American novel, a *zoftig* woman in a purple catsuit accosted him by the chapel. *John Updike, Bech: A Book, 1970, p 121*

A demonstration record the year before had won her an appearance on NBC's *Dean Martin Show.* "From hearing your record," the star told her, "I expected some tall, zoftic girl. Are you a midget?" The 5-ft. 1-in. Karen [Karen Wyman], having steeled herself to be blasé over meeting "this 52-year old man," found that "he was gorgeous, and I broke out in hives." *Time, July 27, 1970, p 41*

Some of those Chinese heads are pretty zoftick, and when they wink at a person you can't help but smile back. *S. J. Perelman, "Missing: Two Lollapaloozas—No Reward," The New Yorker, Oct. 17, 1970, p 39*

[from Yiddish *zaftig,* literally, juicy]

zone melting, another name for ZONE REFINING.

. . . William G. Pfann . . . invented zone melting, a purification process for metals, semiconductors, and other materials. This technique led to the large-scale manufacture of transistors, diodes, and integrated circuits. *"Chemistry," 1969 Britannica Yearbook of Science and the Future, 1968, p 258*

zone refining, a method of purifying metal in which a high-temperature heat source is passed along the metal, carrying off impurities and concentrating them at one or both ends of the treated metal. Also called ZONE MELTING.

Germanium was produced that contained less than one atom of impurity per trillion atoms of germanium. This is comparable to one grain of salt in a carload of sugar. The material was prepared by zone refining where a heat source is moved along an ingot of metal, and a seed crystal, added to the melt, triggers crystallization. A typical crystal thus formed is from 1 to 1.5 inches thick and 6 inches long. *Eugenia Keller, "Chemistry," The Americana Annual 1971, p 199*

First the aluminum was refined in Europe by a hazardous process involving electrolytic reduction of aluminum triethylene, a very explosive material. Then it was further purified in the United States by zone refining. *Science News, March 29, 1969, p 308*

zonked, *adj. Slang.* stupefied, especially from narcotics or alcohol.

. . . "Guys are always stoned. Either they're high from pills to keep them awake or they're zonked on a joint they had on a break." *Time, June 29, 1970, p 70*

"I was at the be-in, though. It was beautiful." "Naw, it didn't make it," one of the other boys announced. . . . "Too many kids wandering around zonked out." *Jane Kramer, "Profiles: Paterfamilias (Allen Ginsberg)," The New Yorker, Aug. 24, 1968, p 39*

It seems to me that most of the drivers one meets should not be allowed to take charge of a car when sober—let alone when three-parts zonked. *New Scientist, Nov. 19, 1967, p 185*

[probably from *zonk!,* an interjection imitative of the sound of a stunning blow on the head]

zooman, *n.* a person concerned with animals in a zoo.

. . . the studies of dedicated field biologists have produced information, particularly on social and breeding behaviour, which is useful to the zooman. *Clive Roots, New Scientist, May 28, 1970, p 423*

zoomer, *n.* a camera lens that can zoom in or out for wide-angle or close-up shoots; a zoom lens.

So he edges close to the television crew and waits for their whoop of delight as the zoomer sweeps the horizon and zeros in on the parachutes. *Alistair Cooke, The Manchester Guardian Weekly, April 25, 1970, p 5*

zoomy, *adj.* by means of a zoom lens; using a zoomer.

. . . what Angus Wilson has called "the mysterious bond that ties gentleness to brutality, a bond that has made our times at once so shocking and so hopeful." Instead, we've been getting glib "statements" and cheap sex jokes, the zoomy shooting and shock cutting of TV commercials . . . . *Pauline Kael, "The Current Cinema: Numbing the Audience," The New Yorker, Oct. 3, 1970, p 78*

ZPG, abbreviation of ZERO POPULATION GROWTH.

Reaching this situation, defined by demographers as NRR (Net Reproductive Rate) = 1.0, would not lead to zero population growth (ZPG) at once, because of persons still living who were born when the NRR exceeded 1.0. *Paul R. Ehrlich and John P. Holdren, Saturday Review, Oct. 3, 1970, p 58*

"The mother of the year should be a sterilized woman with two adopted children." This shocker comes from Paul Ehrlich, a dark, intense young man who is one of the founders of ZPG—Zero Population Growth, Inc. A politically oriented action group, the new organization has as its main goal a maximum of two children in every family. *I. A. Sandoz, "People in the News," 1971 Collier's Encyclopedia Year Book, p 412*

zve·no (zve'nou), *n.* an experimental type of collective or state farm in the Soviet Union. See the quotation for details.

I strongly suspect that one reason for inefficiency is the very large size of the farms. . . . This is a matter of serious concern to Soviet specialists. Some of them advocate the use of small groups of peasants (the zveno system); five or six peasants, members of a collective or state farm, are allocated land, animals, and machines and left free to work at their own pace, their income depending on what they produce. *Alec Nove, "Life Down on the Russian Farm," The Manchester Guardian Weekly, Nov. 28, 1970, p 6*

[from Russian, literally, link (of a chain)]